Information Technology and Organizations:

Trends, Issues, Challenges and Solutions

VOLUME 2

**2003 Information Resources Management Association
International Conference
Philadelphia, Pennsylvania, USA**

May 18-21, 2003

**Mehdi Khosrow-Pour
Information Resources Management Association, USA**

D1127914

IGP

IDEA GROUP PUBLISHING

Hershey • London • Melbourne • Singapore • Beijing
http://www.idea-group.com

E-Business: A Value Chain Perspective

Mohammed H. A. Tafti and Khalid Soliman
Frank G. Zarb School of Business, Hofstra University
Hempstead, NY 11549, USA
(516) 463-5720, (516) 463-1549
Mohammed.H.Tafti@hofstra.edu, Khalid.Soliman@hofstra.edu

ABSTRACT

Many organizations have successfully developed effective strategies for utilization of the e-commerce technology. Their success to gain competitive advantage is due to sound business strategies to create more value by proper deployment of e-commerce technology in various areas of their business processes. What are the major areas in which deployment of e-commerce technology has effectively added value, and what factors are responsible for its success? Many of these areas/factors, as discussed in the following sections, are effectively explained with a framework derived from corporate value-chain model.

INTRODUCTION

The growth of e-commerce has been astounding in various stages during the past several years. This has resulted in the development of a new generation of business, where millions of people and organizations are exchanging massive amounts of information each day directly and quickly (Evans and Wurster, 1999; Keough, 2001). Although many organizations have successfully transpired their business to gain competitive edge in this new era, some others were either left behind or have failed to successfully utilize the Internet to create an e-business environment. What are the underlying reasons why some companies are more successful in using e-commerce than others? What are the main factors that may lead to successful implementation of e-commerce? One effective approach to shed some light on these questions is to study the impact of this technology on the corporate value chain. The purpose of this paper is to explore areas in the value chain where application of this technology can add value most.

E-COMMERCE AND VALUE CHAIN MODEL

The value chain model, as originally demonstrated by Porter (1985), identifies nine strategically relevant activities that create value and reduce cost in a specific business. These nine value-creating activities consist of five primary activities and four support activities. The primary activities represent the sequence of bringing materials into the business (inbound logistics), converting them into final products (operations), shipping out final products (outbound logistics), marketing, and service. The support activities include procurement, technology development, human resource management, and firm infrastructure. This model is very helpful for identifying specific activities in business where competitive strategies can be applied and where information systems are most likely to have a strategic impact. Successful implementation of e-commerce in an organization should be based on a thorough understanding of the areas in the value chain where e-commerce can add value most. More importantly, to succeed in gaining competitive advantage, e-commerce is to be based on the overall corporate strategy (Slywotzky and Morrison 2000; Porter, 2001). Among a host of critical areas/factors in the value chain that major organizations have taken into consideration for establishing a sound e-commerce strategy include role of intermediaries, value pricing, logistics/purchasing, fulfillment, and value nets among others. Following sections present an analysis of these areas.

Role of Intermediaries

Intermediaries may be more important now than ever before because most of the rapidly growing Internet businesses are essentially middlemen (Gaullagher, 1999). For example, companies such as Ama-zon, CD-Now, Egghead.com, Cisco, and E*Trade can all be thought of as middlemen-resellers of products provided by some other source. Intermediaries will continue to be important because they provide consumers with selection, specialized distribution, and expertise (El Sawy et al., 1999). Some internal disintermediation may take place, in which employees will be removed if they add little value or even negative value to the distribution channel. For example, Dell, Cisco, and some online brokerages have eliminated staff in an attempt to realize cost savings in certain areas. Exhibit 1 illustrates an example of the role of intermediaries in the process of purchasing a book online from Amazon.com.

Value Pricing

In addition to employing e-commerce technology to enhance distribution channels, this technology is also used to redefine pricing strategies. Most companies pursuing a premium pricing strategy, for example, can use the Internet to better understand their customers. The Internet allows companies to price with far more precision than they can off-line and to create enormous value in the process. Value pricing involves several approaches. One approach to pricing involves businesses offering heavily discounted prices in an attempt to attract customers to their web sites. Another approach involves businesses transferring their "off-line" prices to the Internet. Neither of these approaches is very efficient because they do not maximize value. An attractive alternative approach is to utilize the Internet to track customers buying habits and adjust prices accordingly, thereby uncovering new market segments. The Internet allows companies to test prices continually in real time and measure customer responses. For example, in one study an electronics company reduced four products' prices by 7%, which increased sales from 5% to 20% (Baker et al 2001).

Brand Differentiation/Loyalty

Pricing is just one of several ways for a company to differentiate itself from the competition. Another way in which a company can differentiate itself is by promoting brand loyalty. Brand loyalty encourages repeat customers and helps to create long-term profitability.

A study performed by Bain & Company showed that in many industries, the high cost of acquiring customers made customer relationships unprofitable in the early years. In later years, however, companies could earn big returns because customer purchases would exceed the cost of servicing them. According to the study, increasing customer retention rates by 5% increased profits by 25% to 95% (Reichheld and Schefter, 2000). A major benefit of customer loyalty is that loyal customers often refer new customers to a supplier.

E-Procurement

E-commerce technology has provided organizations with the capabilities to improve the effectiveness and efficiency of the logistics and purchasing functions. Firms such as Wal-Mart and Amazon.com are currently outsourcing delivery, relying on logistics companies to deliver the product to the customer. Wal-Mart has even set up arrangements with smaller distributors such as Fingerhut and Books-A-Million to satisfy all facets of smaller orders (Kopczak, 2001).

E-procurement is the term currently used to denote the process of using the Internet to integrate supply chain partners through collaboration on key initiatives and to improve the purchasing process within organizations. A major benefit of e-procurement is the cost savings aspect. In fact, organizational costs of placing orders can be reduced by as much as 75% through utilization of the Internet. It also offers organizations the ability to use the Internet to search for the best pricing available. The overall advantage of practicing e-procurement is the fact the more automation allows partners quicker access to information. E-procurement also results in better communication among supply chain partners and consequently better supplier-customer relationships. Organizations are able to maintain tighter control over the purchasing process. Only those suppliers that organizations deem to be "preferred suppliers" will be able to transact business with the organization. Currently, e-procurement is being utilized primarily for the purchase of office supplies and items which are used for repair and maintenance of the organization's facilities (Smock, 2001).

E-Fulfillment

Today's marketplace offers new challenges to organizations. A key initiative organizations have undertaken to better compete is that of "E-fulfillment". It can alter the way customers purchase as well as the manner in which manufacturers deliver the product to consumers. Technology has also allowed distributors and suppliers to focus on providing value-added services to complement their product offering. E-Fulfillment contrasts with traditional fulfillment. Suppliers are now capable of accepting order online via the Internet and having the information sent directly into their order processing systems, something not possible via traditional fulfillment. Orders placed via e-fulfillment tend to be smaller than those placed via traditional fulfillment channels. The expected and actual lead times are shorter than those witnessed via traditional fulfillment (Kopczak, 2001).

Value Nets

Firms are continually seeking out new ways to attract and maintain customers. A development that has proven to be effective in attracting and servicing customers is that of the *Value Net* (Bovel & Martha, 2000). A value net is a network consisting of partnerships, which assists in the transfer of information among supply chain partners on a regular basis. The main benefit of a value net is the competitive advantage it offers to all participating organizations. The primary concept behind a value net is its ability to allow firms to address and solve customer problems, rather than just selling a product. A popular trend in the marketplace to address niche markets is that of the online-service company. This form of business interacts directly with the customers primarily via the Internet. The advantage of this form of business is that it provides enhanced service to the customer in the form of direct door-to-door delivery for customers. This is a distinct competitive advantage that firms are looking to exploit.

A FRAMEWORK FOR ANALYSIS

A sound e-commerce implementation requires top management commitment to clearly define corporate strategy in order to integrate Internet technologies into value-added activities. Exhibit 2 presents a framework for analysis of factors relevant to e-commerce implementation. This model consists of five major dimensions: 1) business opportunity, 2) corporate strategy, 3) Internet technologies, 4) value chain impact, and 5) areas of e-commerce implementation.

Business Opportunity

Various business opportunities may be created by changing the internal operating processes in order to improve services. The Internet technology facilitates implementation of the necessary changes in order to increase efficiency, cut costs, and improve channels of communication. At the same time, external forces are pressuring businesses to offer more service, 24 hours a day, 7 days a week. For example, in the distribution industry, customers expect more value-added services from its distributors which require changes in business processes through the Internet technology (El Sawy et al., 1999).

Corporate Strategy

Corporate strategy varies widely by company and type of business. However, Internet technology can provide universal benefits to both the business-to-consumer and business-to-business segments, including product/service differentiation, system integration, cost reduction, and expansion of market share. For example, Dell uses technology to differentiate its products by offering custom-built PCs over the Internet. Corporate strategy provides the framework for employing technology throughout an organization.

Internet Technologies

For the purpose of this study, Internet technologies refer to the Internet, Intranet, Extranet, and any other technology (e.g., customization technology) used in combination with Internet technology. The company web page usually contains links to the organization's Intranet and Extranet. The Intranet may be connected to a database that manages the storage of company data. The Extranet is way for companies to communicate with its external partners, while offering customization and privacy. Customization technologies enable businesses to provide specialized services.

Value Chain Impact

The integration of corporate strategy with Internet technologies often affects many relationships in the value chain. Technology may help to expand the role of a distributor, while reducing the role of other middlemen, such as wholesalers and suppliers. In addition, Internet technologies can change relationships in the value chain. For example, web sites provide customers with more information to compare services of different businesses. However, it can also be argued that Internet technology shifts bargaining power to suppliers and other intermediaries. Suppliers can "lock in" customers by using customer information to provide value-added services, such as automatic inventory replenishment.

E-Commerce Implementation Areas

Six major areas, among others, indicated in the literature to have bearing on successful implementation of e-commerce. These areas as discussed in a previous section are Intermediaries, value pricing, brand differentiation, e-procurement, e-fulfillment, and value nets. The degree of significance of each area may depend on specific organizational culture, technology structure and experience, and industry. One approach to examine validity of each area (a subject for future studies) is a systematic case study of major organizations that have gained considerable experience in e-commerce implementation.

NOTE: Full paper including exhibits, and references available from the authors upon request.

A Prosed Model for Tacit Knowledge Capture Between Consultancies and Freelance Subcontractors

W A Taylor
School of Management, University of Bradford
Emm Lane, Bradford
BD9 4JL, West Yorkshire, U.K.
Telephone: +44 (0)1274 234325
Fax: +44 (0)1274 234355
E-mail: w.a.taylor@bradford.ac.uk

N A Boraie
House of Egypt Management Consultants (Egypt)/
Triple Line Consulting (UK), The Oxford Centre for Innovation
Mill Street, Oxford, OX2 0JX, U.K.
Telephone: +44 (0)1865 811144
Fax: +44 (0)1865 793165
E-mail: nevert_b@hotmail.com or nevert@tripleline.com

ABSTRACT

There is a perceived knowledge gap where consultancy organizations sub-contract work to freelance consultants in the field, who often gain valuable tacit knowledge that is not subsequently captured by their sponsors. At the macro level, this could impact the design, approach and monitoring of technical assistance programs.

The research surveyed 138 European consultancies active in developing countries (in Egypt in particular), addressing three questions:
* *Are they aware of potential loss of tacit knowledge from sub-contractors?*
* *Do they perceive any value in capturing this knowledge?*
* *To what extent and how is localized knowledge captured?*

Few respondents had formal systems and to this end we propose a 'Revolving Door' procedural model, a practical tool suitable for smaller consultancies with limited resources.

INTRODUCTION

European consulting organizations act as knowledge brokers, members or leaders of projects in developing countries, and sub-contract assignments to freelance consultants. While there are project reviews, final reports, monitoring and evaluation activities and audits, what is often missed is the capture of tacit knowledge gained 'on the ground', which could affect their capability to undertake future assignments. Indeed, there are low levels of awareness of knowledge management or even of the European Commission's "Knowledge Management Made in Europe" initiative.

When operating in developing countries where business cultures depend heavily upon trust and personal relationships, local tacit knowledge can be valuable to avoid loss of credibility and even ridicule.

LITERATURE

Knowledge is the lifeblood of consulting firms, but studies focus on how large consulting firms capture and share knowledge (Hansen et al, 1999; Sarvary, 1999; Weiss, 1999) with little exploration of smaller organizations, who rely on personal networks to assemble project teams (Reimus, 1997; Raz, 2001). This highlights the importance of psychological contracts (Argyris, 1960; Rousseau, 1995; Ghoshal and Moran, 1997), with consequent implications for trust, loyalty and security of employment, as well as the knowledge transfer process.

Freelance consultants have little incentive to share their knowledge with the main contractor, who needs it to enhance future capability. The role of a consultant is changing to one of coach and mentor within client organizations, but more significantly within the consulting network (Ingleson, 2001), sharing knowledge twice – once to the client and once to the company.

The trade-offs between codified and personalized knowledge management approaches is echoed in Nonaka and Takeuchi's (1995) distinctions between the socialized transfer of tacit knowledge and system-based transfer of explicit knowledge. Equally, the many classifications of knowledge (Tsoukas and Vladimirou, 2001) include phrases such as know-how, know-why, care-why (Garud, 1996; Quinn et al, 1996) etc. However, we emphasise the importance of situated knowledge (Billett, 1996).

SUMMARY OF RESEARCH

The questionnaire was sent to 138 European consultants operating in Egypt (a large recipient of aid/technical assistance, close to Europe yet culturally distinct), and ten were interviewed. We chose not to persist with reminders to boost the response rate (34%), as the response level was an indicator of the topics' importance, a finding in its own right.

The sample size is statistically small but significant as the research elicits tacit knowledge and first-hand experience from practitioners.

Local Experience

Some 75% considered localized regional experience very important for business development, commercial prospecting and for proposal writing (88%), whereas local language capability was not.

There was little perceived motivation to capture local tacit experience as business was won without it, and thus the focus was on forging local alliances – "attempting to "act" local can often be offensive". Local partners executed 30% of an assignment.

Table 1: Respondent profile

Country	Questionnaires Sent	Responses			%
		Questionnaire /Interview	General responses	Declined	
Belgium	11 (8%)	1	0	1	1 (1%)
Denmark	13 (9%)	2	2	1	5 (4%)
France	10 (7%)	2	2	0	4 (3%)
Germany	23 (17%)	0	1	2	3 (2%)
Greece	8 (6%)	1	1	0	2 (1%)
Ireland	6 (3%)	3	0	0	3 (2%)
Italy	8 (6%)	0	3	0	3 (2%)
Luxembourg	1 (1%)	0	1	0	1 (1%)
Netherlands	9 (7%)	3	0	3	6 (4%)
UK	40 (29%)	14	3	1	18 (13%)
Others**	9 (7%)	0	0	1	1 (1%)
TOTAL	**138 (100%)**	**26 (19%)**	**13 (9%)**	**9 (6%)**	**34%**
		48 responses or 34%			

Table 2: Criteria to implement KM

Ranking	Criterion	Importance
1	Capturing valuable knowledge to win new business	86%
2	Resources constraints	64%
3	Costs constraints	64%
4	To access new ideas and boost intellectual capital	50%
5	Time constraints and to shorten the learning curve	43%
6	To secure repeat assignments	36%
7	To raise corporate profile	7%

One observation was "the importance of intuition, knowledge, perception of body language and voice intonation and mannerisms is underrated, as is the manner and delivery of questions".

Knowledge Capture Systems

Only 38% of respondents had formal systems, and only half were computer-based, relying instead on networking and face-to-face meetings. One comment was "like most consultancies of our size, knowledge management relies on 'water-cooler' exchange, based on case stories and experiences". Knowing *where* to find knowledge was key, not capturing and storing it. Mentoring, coaching and debriefing were highlighted as essential.

Only 63% distinguished between tacit and explicit knowledge: "Personally I have never thought of it as knowledge management, but more as a common sense approach to developing one's consultancy skills". The majority (90%) stressed maintaining good personal relationships with subcontractors based on mutual trust and respect.

Criteria

Table 2 highlights the business prerequisites to implement a knowledge management system. Successful project teams easily get repeat assignments, and there is no concern to capture local tacit knowledge from freelancers as "you can always hire them again".

Perceptions

Many felt that knowledge capture should be a natural process, based on personal chemistry, not a system. Conversely some thought "all consulting companies should make it a specific contractual requirement that all output or knowledge gained is provided electronically to the main contractor". Others were less positive, e.g. "not in my company - management time is scarce. It's the usual excuse - too busy looking for work or else doing it". Another respondent added "I doubt it for consultancies, but maybe for multinationals with large projects. This is something for academics like Peters, Handy and Hofstede to do case material for MBA students to chew over".

DISCUSSION

Consulting firms are often portrayed as leading-edge knowledge practitioners, yet our study suggested otherwise (Reimus, 1997; Raz, 2001). Consultants still perceive 'knowledge is power' versus 'sharing knowledge is power'.

There is a heavy reliance on local expertise, and capturing valuable local tacit knowledge remains informal and unstructured, driven by the complacency that sub-contractors can be re-hired. This belief may be fundamentally flawed as it would be ignoring the changing nature of the psychological contract. Freelance consultants possess valuable knowledge that can be purchased by the highest bidder. Unless the nature of sub-contracting is based upon reciprocity and consultant loyalty, re-hiring may not be a viable option.

Secondly, if knowledge is not shared widely within the firm, it cannot be leveraged to generate further innovation or amplify the firm's thinking power.

Since all respondents intend to remain in the region, the behavior towards the management of knowledge is at considerable variance with their criteria of winning new business. Beyond all the rhetoric, knowledge is still something 'nice to have' rather than a business imperative.

Figure 1: Revolving Door Model

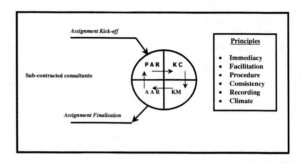

Clearly this is only an exploratory study of a small number of European consultancies, but highlights the issues and challenges for many consulting firms. We therefore propose the 'Revolving Door Procedure' as a simple tool to capture tacit knowledge in operational settings.

The Revolving Door Procedure

The approach is simple and as Andrew McMahon, a Lotus veteran and senior product marketing director at Groove Networks, observed "To really make knowledge sharing work, you have to find a way to connect people with each other that doesn't require unnecessarily technical overhead", (Roberts-Witt, 2002). The model was inspired by the US Army's After Action Review (Meliza, 1995) and essentially assesses what was intended to be achieved, what actually was achieved, and why there was a difference.

The four phases are:
- *Pre-action review (PAR)* – performance standard established based on expectations of the team before the assignment, using a standardized questionnaire.
- *Knowledge Capture (KC)* – on-going process capturing knowledge on an immediate basis, rather than at the formal end of the project
- *Knowledge Management (KM)* – documentation, analysis and updating of knowledge captured. At the project level to ensure speedy identification of difficulties and problems to enable corrective action. At the corporate level to impact broader policy issues to address underlying causes.
- *After action review (AAR)* – adopting the principles advocated by Garvin (1996), i.e.

    Immediacy - while knowledge is fresh and there is still a team mindset.

    Facilitation - using trained facilitators with good understanding and intuition. The value of the knowledge captured depends on asking the right questions.

    Procedure - simple and direct with a minimum of bureaucracy, so paperwork does not impede free interchange of views and ideas.

    Consistency - applied across all project components and become a standardized framework embedded and internalized into working practice.

    Recording - simple, so it can be communicated upwards and between organizations.

    Climate - open and frank dialogue so participants feel able to discuss mistakes without fear of negative consequences, or implications for future assignments.

To overcome the perception that consultants may be giving away their priceless knowledge, the Revolving Door model should be 'sold' as a benefit that will accelerate and enhance their personal worth, and be a selection factor for future assignments.

CONCLUSIONS

Consultancies are aware of potential loss of tacit knowledge from sub-contractors, but are passive as they still win new business. Our interviews and open-question responses highlighted the need for capturing sub-contractor knowledge more systematically and formally, and to better understand the nature of psychological contracts.

The literature has yet to address this dimension of knowledge management, which is significant for many smaller consulting organizations. Our proposed model may provide one practical way of turning unreflective practice into a reflective one (Tsoukas and Vladimirou, 2001).

At the policy level, tacit knowledge capture could affect the design, monitoring and implementation of large-scale technical assistance programs, and ensure better use and impact of resources directed at sustainable development. Therefore, knowledge management should be part of any corporate social responsibility exercise.

REFERENCES

Argyris, C. (1960) Understanding Organizational Behavior. Homewood, Ilinois. Dorsey Press.

Billett, S. (1996) Situated learning: Bridging sociocultural and cognitive theorising. Learning and Instruction, 6(3), pp263-280.

Garud, R. (1996) On the Distinction between Know-How, Know-What and Know-Why Proceedings of the American Academy of Management, 1996.

Garvin, D. A. (1996) Putting the Learning Organization to Work. HBS Video Series. Harvard Business School Publishing. Video.

Ghoshal, S and Moran, P. (1997) Employment security, employability and sustainable competitive advantage. Fontainbleau, INSEAD. Working Papers 97/20SM.

Hansen, M., Nohria, N. and Tierney, T. (1999) What's your strategy for managing knowledge? Harvard Business Review, March-April, pp106-116.

Ingleson M. (2000) Background to Knowledge Management as a Business Issue. Cambridge Market Intelligence Limited, Inside Careers.

Meliza, L.L. (1995) ATAFS: A first generation 'smart' AAR system. U.S. Army Research Institute for the behavioral and social sciences. http://www-ari.army.mil/atafs.htm

Nonaka, I. and Takeuchi, H. (1995) The Knowledge Creating Company: How Japanese companies create the dynamics of innovation, Oxford University Press.

Quinn, J.B., Anderson, P and Finkelstein, S. (1996) Managing professional intellect: Making the most of the best. Harvard Business Review, 74(2), pp71-80.

Raz, T. (2001) Wishing Up on Knowledge Management. www.myprimetime.com

Reimus, B. (1997) Knowledge Sharing within Management Consulting Firms, Kennedy Information Inc.

Roberts-Witt, S. (2002) Know Thyself. PC Magazine. March 2002, Vol.21 Issue 6, p. 87.

Rousseau, D.M. (1995) Psychological contracts in Organizations. Thousand Oaks, California, Sage.

Sarvary, M. (1999) Knowledge management and competition in the consulting industry. California Management Review, 41(2), pp95-107.

Tsoukas, H. and Vladimirou, E. (2001) What is organizational knowledge? Journal of Management Studies, 38(7), pp973-993.

Weiss, L. (1999) Collection and connection: The anatomy of knowledge sharing in professional service firms. Organizational Development Journal, 17(4), pp61-77.

Improving Innovation Performance through IS Enabled Knowledge Scanning

Qiang Tu
College of Business, Rochester Institute of Technology
Rochester, NY 14623
Phone: (585) 475-2314, Fax: (585) 475- 5975
Email: tuq@mail.rit.edu

INTRODUCTION

To remain competitive or even survive in today's highly uncertain environment, many firms are searching for a panacea that can solve all the problems. Some firms opted for business process reengineering (BPR), and even more chose the technology route by investing heavily in enterprise resource planning (ERP) systems, hoping for a quick fix. But the reality is that there are no magic pills to cure everything. Studies show that majority of BPR and ERP projects didn't achieve their original goals (Hammer and Champy, 1993; Sheer and Habermann, 2000). In the long run, the best guarantee for sustained competitiveness in today's unpredictable market is continuous innovation in products and processes to quickly adapt to the changing environment (Tushman and O'Reilly, 1997; McGrath, 2001).

Firm's capability for continuous innovation cannot be achieved by simply acquiring new technologies. It must involve constant accumulation of knowledge and information, and complex interaction among people, processes and technology (Sage, 2000). Given the importance of manufacturing innovation to the firm's long-term competitiveness (Cusumano, 1988), it will be interesting to identify the primary factors that affects a firm's innovation performance.

Previous studies have looked at the impact of some important content and process factors on innovation performance, such as types of innovation (Knight, 1967; Zaltman etc., 1973; Daft and Becker, 1978), attributes of innovation (Rogers, 1983), leadership styles (Van de Ven, 1986), champions of innovation (Howell and Higins, 1990), organizational culture and organizational structure (Nord and Tucker, 1987), absorptive capacity (Cohen and Levinthal, 1990), and organizational learning (McKee, 1992).

This is a large scale survey study focuses on innovation performance in manufacturing setting. Two new organizational level variables are introduced, i.e., information systems (IS) usage and knowledge scanning mechanism. The roles of information technology and knowledge have been discussed in innovation literature (Damanpour, 1991; Ettlie, 2000), but empirical studies concerning these important variables are scarce, especially at the organizational level (Berry and Taggart, 1994). This paper also made an effort to develop valid and reliable measurement instruments for organizational level IS usage, knowledge scanning and manufacturing innovation, which could be a valuable tool for future related studies.

THEORETICAL FRAMEWORK AND HYPOTHESES DEVELOPMENT

The theoretical model in Figure 1 suggests that a firm's innovation performance is directly affected by the firm's level of knowledge scanning and exploration activities, while the level of knowledge scanning activities is facilitated by effective organization- wide use of information systems. The three constructs in the model are described.

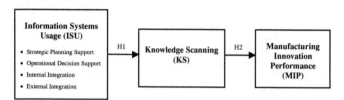

Figure 1:Theoretical Framework

Information Systems Usage (ISU)

While previous studies on IS usage are extensive (Szajna, 1996), their definition of IS usage are mostly at the individual or task level. Few studies look into the organizational level and inter-organizational IS usage effectiveness issues. Meanwhile, the measures for IS usage in many existing studies are either actual usage time logs or single item instrument with limited reliability and validity. Comprehensive and reliable measurement scales for IS usage at both individual and organizational level are necessary to facilitate research in this field.

Doll and Torkzadeh (1995) are the first to develop an instrument for IT usage patterns at the task level. They conceptualize the IT usage pattern into five dimensions: 1) problem solving: the extent that an application is used to analyze cause and effect relationships; 2) customer service: the extent that an applications is used to service customers; 3) decision rationalization: the extent that an application is used to improve the decision making processes or explain/justify the reasons for decisions; 4) vertical integration: the extent that an application is used to coordinate one's work vertically with superiors and subordinates; and 5) horizontal integration: the extent that an application is used to coordinate work activities with others in one's work group. Although this instrument focused primarily on individual and work group mechanisms, it did offer some useful directions for conceptualizing the organizational level IS usage construct. Using Doll and Torkzadeh (1995) instrument as starting point, along with comprehensive literature review, the organizational level IS usage construct in this study is re-conceptualized as the extent to which IS is used by the firm to promote integration, support decision making and assist in strategic planning.

In summary, four major dimensions of organizational-level IS usage were proposed and their definitions are listed below:

Operational Decision Support. The extent that IS is used by the firm to help monitoring, justifying and improving daily operational decision processes (Doll and Torkzadeh - Decision Rationalization; Boynton and Zmud - Management Support).

Strategic Planning Support. The extent that IS is used by the firm to help formulating, justifying, improving long-term business planning processes and establishing competitive advantage (Boynton and Zmud – Strategic Planning & Competitive Thrust).

Internal Integration. The extent that IS is used by the firm to facilitate information sharing and coordinate work activities within the organization (Doll and Torkzadeh – Vertical Integration & Horizontal Integration).

External Integration. The extent that IS is used by the firm to service and communicate with external constituencies, such as customers, suppliers, government agencies, research institutions, etc. (Doll and Torkzadeh – Customer Service).

Knowledge Scanning (KS)

Knowledge Scanning is defined as the organizational mechanisms that enable the firm to effectively identify and exploit relevant external and internal knowledge and technology. There are many activities that signify the existence of such a mechanism in an organization. An important dimension of Boynton and Zmud's (1994) conceptualization of firm's capability to absorb new knowledge is the IT-management-process, i.e., various routines and procedures that embody the pragmatic knowledge to foster appropriate IT use. Cohen and Levinthal (1990) suggest that absorptive capacity for new knowledge and technology is likely to be developed as a byproduct of routine R&D activities.

Employee training such as sending employees for advanced technical training, or encouraging them to monitor and read the technical literature in their areas of expertise, could be another important knowledge scanning activity (Cohen and Levinthal, 1994). Finally, inter-organizational learning activities, such as benchmarking of best practices, strategic alliances, and customer and supplier surveys may also serve as effective knowledge scanning activities (Levinson and Asahi, 1995).

Manufacturing Innovation Performance (MIP)

In their article describing the evolution of large scale manufacturing firms, Bolwjin and Kumpe (1990) noted that many large multinational firms have passed the efficiency, quality and flexibility phase. The ideal firm in the 1990s is the innovative firm that emphasizes uniqueness. Since the concept of innovation has both a content component and a process component (Wolfe, 1994), the conceptualization of manufacturing innovation in this paper will not only involve developing new products, but also creating new ways for customer service, shop floor management, and supply chain management (Cusumano, 1988).

Research Hypotheses

Swanson (1994) modified the dual core model of organizational innovation (Daft, 1978) by adding a third IS core as strategic linkage between the firm's technical core and administrative core, but the paper did not further elaborate how this IS core will actually function to improve organizational innovation. This paper proposes that use of IS can greatly facilitate the firm's knowledge scanning and exploration activities, which in turn impacts innovation performance (Corso and Paolucci, 2001).

In today's fast changing competitive environment, there's a strong need for easier and better knowledge sharing (Marshall, 1997). However, for many firms, a significant amount of organizational knowledge remains unmanaged, undiscovered, and unorganized, thus invisible to the firm when needed (Van den Hoven, 2001). Use of IS should greatly help the firm's knowledge management processes. Studies show that implementation of information technology can significantly enhance the knowledge workers and workforce learning (Gaimon, 1997). In fact, when the IS is fully integrated with the entire enterprise system, it becomes an organizational memory IS (Wang, 1999) that serves as a cumulative knowledge repository for the firm (Hackbarth and Grover, 1999). Therefore, it is hypothesized that:

Hypothesis 1: Firms with higher levels of IS usage will have higher levels of knowledge scanning.

Manufacturing innovations do not happen overnight. It requires years of learning and knowledge accumulation. There is consensus among researchers and practitioners that organizational learning is a key vari-able that drives innovation (Stata, 1989; McKee, 1992). Knowledge scanning and exploration are critical components of organizational learning. Empirical studies have shown that firms with higher levels of absorptive capacity, i.e., the capability to exploit and assimilate external knowledge and information, are typically more effective in new product development (Cohen and Levinthal, 1990). A survey study by Tsai (2001) also found that an organization unit's absorptive capacity has significant positive impact on its innovation performance. McGrath (2001) study of 56 new business development projects again confirmed that higher level of knowledge exploration is positively related to higher adaptation and innovation capacity. It is therefore hypothesized that:

Hypothesis 2: Firms with higher levels of knowledge scanning will have higher levels of manufacturing innovation performance.

RESEARCH METHODOLOGY

In this section, research methods are described for survey instrument development and hypothesis testing. The instrument development process for IS Usage (ISU), Knowledge Scanning (KS) and Manufacturing Innovation Performance (MIP) included several phases: item generation, pre-pilot study, pilot study, and large-scale data collection and analysis.

A comprehensive literature review was completed to define the constructs and identify an initial list of items. To improve content validity, a pre-pilot study was completed that involved structured interview with four manufacturing managers and six academic experts. The interview results were carefully analyzed and a common pattern of thinking was recognized, which formed the basis for further revision of the research constructs and measurement items. A pilot study was then completed by surveying senior manufacturing managers. The study provided valuable preliminary information about the reliability and validity of the measurement scales. It also gave a final opportunity to purify the scales. The final version of the questionnaire was administered through large-scale mailing to 2831 manufacturing managers who were randomly selected from SME's U.S. membership database. There were a total of 320 responses from the mailings, of which 303 were complete and usable.

Assessment of Measurement Properties

Tests of unidimensionality, discriminant validity, and reliability are important for establishing construct validity (Sethi and King, 1994). The assessment of these measurement properties will be discussed for ISU, KS and MIP.

Information Systems Usage (ISU)

The Information Systems Usage (ISU) construct was initially represented by four dimensions comprising 25 items in the large-scale survey, including Operational Decision Support (ODS) (4 items), Strategic Planning Support (SPS) (5 items), External Integration (EXI) (9 items), and Internal Integration (INI) (7 items).

Initial reliability analysis for each of the four ISU dimensions showed that the Corrected Item-Total Correlation (CITC) scores for all items were above 0.50. However, the "Alpha if deleted" score indicated that removing EXI1 would improve reliability of EXI dimension. Thus item EXI1 was dropped at this stage. Factor analysis of the INI dimension revealed two factors (Factor 1: INI1, INI2, INI3, INI6, INI7 and Factor 2: INI4, INI5). Referring to the contents of each item, Factor 2 does not make too much theoretical sense. It was thus decided that items INI4 and INI5 be removed.

The remaining 22 ISU items were submitted to construct-level exploratory factor analysis to check for discriminant validity of the measurement instrument. Four factors emerged from the factor analysis with all factor loadings above 0.50 and most above 0.60. Serious cross-loading occurred on item INI7. Hence item INI7 was dropped. Finally, construct-level exploratory factor analysis was done again. This time four clear factors emerged with all items loaded correctly on the expected dimensions. Most factor loadings were above 0.60. No cross-loading was observed.

Knowledge Scanning (KS)

KS was conceptualized as have a single dimension and 7 items. Reliability analysis showed satisfactory Alpha score of 0.80. CITC scores for all items were above 0.50 except KS7 (We seek to learn from conducting R&D activities) with a CITC score of 0.48, slightly below 0.50. Considering the importance of item KS7 to this construct, KS7 was retained. To ensure unidimensionality of the 7 items, exploratory factor analysis was performed and one single factor emerged with all factor loadings close to or over 0.70.

Manufacturing Innovation Performance (MIP)

The MP construct was conceptualized as having one dimension and 5 items. Reliability was good with an Alpha score of 0.78. CITC scores are all above 0.50. To ensure the discriminant validity of the five items, an exploratory factor analysis was performed using all 5 items that measure MIP. One clear factor emerged with all factor loadings above 0.70.

Hypotheses Testing Results

To check for the preliminary statistical validity of the two hypotheses, the Pearson correlation coefficients of the two hypothesized relationships were calculated using a composite score for ISU, KS and MIP. The composite scores were computed by taking the average score of all items in a specific construct. The results are presented in Table 1. More rigorous hypotheses testing using LISREL structural modeling can be done at a later stage.

Hypothesis 1, which claims that organizations with high-levels of ISU have high-levels of KS, is supported by the correlation analysis. The Pearson correlation coefficient is 0.561, which is statistically significant at the 0.01 level. Hypothesis 2, which states that KS will have a direct positive impact on MIP, is also supported. The Pearson correlation coefficient is 0.473, which is also statistically significant at the 0.01 level.

DISCUSSION AND CONCLUSION

As Swanson (1994) pointed out, the existing literature regarding the role of IS in innovation is both fragmented and limited. Dodgson (1993) also noted that the impact of recent technology on the processes and outcomes of organizational learning provide fertile ground for future research. This study is possibly one of the first large-scale empirical efforts to investigate and measure ISU and to examine its impact on the firm's knowledge exploration capacity and manufacturing innovation performance. Measures for ISU, KS and MIP were developed through very carefully designed large-scale data collection process and rigorous instrument validation methods. The content domain of the constructs has been covered adequately because care was taken during item generation. The instruments exceed generally accepted validity and reliability standards for basic research. The resulting instrument can be widely used in future research, and they should facilitate interdisciplinary studies in IS management and manufacturing management. The instruments can also be used as a valuable tool for practitioners to evaluate their firm's level of ISU, KS and MIP.

The results of this study show that ISU has a positive and statistically significant effect on KS. It indicates that extensive use of IS at various levels and functional areas of a firm is indeed a valid way to facilitate knowledge exploration and organizational learning. Advanced

information systems, especially web-base systems, offer extremely powerful and flexible tools for storing, organizing, processing and retrieving complex knowledge and information. The results also confirmed the positive relationship between KS and MIP. The ability to scan the environment for new knowledge and ideas enhances the individual and organizational knowledge base and thus increases the opportunity for innovation success.

Downs and Mohr (1976) criticized innovation research for instability in empirical findings. Damanpour (1991) challenged the "instability" argument and suggested a contingency approach by evaluating the moderating power of various moderators. Future research can examine the proposed relationships in a contingent manner by incorporating some contextual variables such as environmental uncertainty level, industry type and size of the firm. It will also be interesting to further examine the differing impact of the four sub-dimensions of IS usage on knowledge scanning and manufacturing innovation.

REFERENCES

Berry, M. M. J. and Taggart, J. H., (1994). Managing technology and innovation: A review. R & D Management, 24(4), pp. 341-353 (13 pages).

Bolwijn, P. T. and Kumpe, T., (1990). Manufacturing in the 1990s - Productivity, Flexibility and Innovation. Long Range Planning, 23(4), pp. 44-57 (14 pages).

Boynton, A. C., Zmud, R. W., and Jacobs, G. C. (1994). The Influence of IT Management Practice on IT Use in Large Organizations. MIS Quarterly, Vol. 18, No. 3, pp. 299-318.

Cohen, W. M. and Levinthal, D. A., (1990). Absorptive Capacity: A New Perspective on Learning and Innovation. Administrative Science Quarterly, 35(1), pp. 128-152 (25 pages).

Corso, M. and Paolucci, E. (2001). Fostering innovation and knowledge transfer in product development through information technology. International Journal of Technology Management, 22, pp. 126-148.

Cusumano, M. A., (1988). Manufacturing Innovation: Lessons from the Japanese Auto Industry. Sloan Management Review, 30(1), pp. 29-39 (11 pages).

Daft, R. L. (1978). A Dual-Core Model of Organizational Innovation. Academy of Management Journal, 21(2), pp. 193-210.

Daft, R. L. and Becker, S. W. (1978). The innovative organization. Elsevier, New York, NY.

Damanpour, F., (1991). Organizational Innovation: A Meta-Analysis of Effects of Determinants and Moderators. Academy of Management Journal, 34(3), pp. 555-590 (36 pages).

Dodgson, M., (1993). Organizational learning: A review of some literatures. Organization Studies, 14(3), pp. 375-394 (20 pages).

Doll, W. J. and Torkzadeh, G. (1995). The Development of a Tool for Measuring the Effective Use of Information Technology in An Organizational Context. Working Paper, The University of Toledo.

Downs, G. W. and Mohr, L. B., (1976). Conceptual Issues in the Study of Innovation. Administrative Science Quarterly, 21(4), pp. 700-714.

Ettlie, J. E. (2000). Managing Technological Innovation. John Wiley & Sons, Inc. New York, NY.

Gaimon, C., (1997). Planning information technology-knowledge worker systems. Management Science, 43(9), pp. 1308-1328.

Hackbarth, G. and Grover, V., (1999). The knowledge repository: Organizational memory information systems. Information Systems Management, 16(3), pp. 21-30.

Hammer, M. and Champy, J. (1993). Reengineering the Corporation, Harper Collins Books, New York.

Howell, J. M. and Higgins, C. A., (1990). Champions of Technological Innovation. Administrative Science Quarterly, 35(2), pp. 317-341 (25 pages).

Knight, K. E. (1967). A descriptive model of the intra-firm innovation process. Journal of Business, 40, pp.478-496.

Levinson, N. S. and Asahi, M., (1995). Cross-national alliances and interorganizational learning. Organizational Dynamics, 24(2), pp. 50-63 (14 pages).

Table 1: Construct Level Correlation Analysis Results

Hypothesis	Independent Variable	Dependent Variable	Pearson Correlatio
H1	Information Systems Usage (ISU)	Knowledge Scanning (KS)	0.561**
H2	Knowledge Scanning (KS)	Manufacturing Innovation Performance (MIP)	0.473**

** Correlation is significant at the 0.01 level

Marshall, L., (1997). Facilitating knowledge management and knowledge sharing: New opportunities for information professionals. Online, 21(5), pp. 92-98.

McGrath, R. G. (2001). Exploratory learning, innovative capacity, and managerial oversight. Academy of Management Journal, 44(1), pp. 118-131.

McKee, D., (1992). An Organizational Learning Approach to Product Innovation. Journal of Product Innovation Management, 9(3), pp. 232-245 (14 pages).

Nord, W. R. and Tucker, S. (1987). Implementing routine and radical innovation. Lexington Books, Lexington, MA.

Rogers, E. M. (1983). Diffusion of innovations. Free Press, New York, NY.

Sage, L. (2000). Winning the Innovation Race: Lessons from the Automotive Industry's Best Companies. John Wiley & Sons Inc. New York, NY.

Sethi, V. & King, W. R. 1994. Development of measures to assess the extent to which an information technology application provides competitive advantage. Management Science, 40(12): 1601-1627 (1627 pages).

Scheer, A. and Habermann, F. (2000). Making ERP a Success. Communications of the ACM, 43(4), pp. 57-61.

Stata, R. (1989). Organizational Learning – The Key to Management Innovation. Sloan Management Review, Spring, pp. 63-74.

Swanson, E. B., (1994). Information systems innovation among organizations. Management Science, 40(9), pp. 1069-1092 (24 pages).

Szajna, B. 1993. Research: Determining information system usage - Some issues and examples. Information & Management, 25(3): 147.

Tornatzky, L. G. and Klein, K. J., (1982). Innovation Characteristics and Innovation Adoption-Implementation: A Meta-Analysis of Findings. IEEE Transactions on Engineering Management, 29(1), pp. 28-45 (18 pages).

Tsai, W. (2001). Knowledge transfer in intraorganizational networks: Effects of network position and absorptive capacity on business unit innovation and performance. Academy of Management Journal, 44(5), pp. 996-1004.

Tushman, M. L. and O'Reilly, C. A. III. (1997). Winning through innovation: Leading organizational change and renewal. Harvard Business Press, Boston, MA.

Van de Ven, A. H., (1986). Central Problems in the Management of Innovation. Management Science, 32(5), pp. 590-607 (18 pages).

Van den Hoven, J. (2001). Information resource management: Foundation for knowledge management. Information Systems Management, 18(2), pp. 80-87.

Wang, S (1999). Organizational memory information systems: A domain analysis in the object-oriented paradigm. Information Resources Management Journal, 12(2), pp. 26-35.

Wolfe, R. A., (1994). Organizational innovation: Review, critique and suggested research directions. Journal of Management Studies, 31(3), pp. 405-431 (27 pages).

Zaltman, G., Duncan, R. and Holbek, J. (1973). Innovations and organizations. John Wiley & Sons, New York, NY.

A Context-Based Organization Modeling for E-Learning Initiatives

Kam Hou Vat
Faculty of Science & Technology
University of Macau, Macau
fstkhv@umac.mo

ABSTRACT

This paper investigates the design of an architectural model suitable for the development of a specific electronic learning (e-learning) paradigm. This model is derived from a series of organization modeling activities capitalizing on knowledge development and transfer among organizational members. Specifically, we describe our architectural initiatives in terms of the organizational components designed to support knowledge processes evolving over selected domains. To realize the e-learning services in an organization, whose activities are being virtualized over the Internet, we emphasize the importance of developing e-learning services not from the limitations of current technologies, but from the reality of organizational goals. Thereby, the paper presents our interpretation of the essential contexts in applying information technology (IT) to support the argument that it is important to involve organizational concerns to develop e-learning initiatives.

1 INTRODUCTION

In the emerging knowledge economy [OECD 1996], there have been many terms to describe the use of technology for learning. E-learning [Rosenberg 2001] has been interpreted as the use of Internet technologies to deliver a broad array of solutions that enhance learning and knowledge sharing, which go beyond the traditional paradigms of training to include the delivery of information and tools that improve performance. In fact, the 'e' in e-learning should render additional connotations other than the usual electronic context. First, 'e' is for experience in the sense that e-learning should change the character of the experience of learning through offering the options of time-shifting, place-shifting, granularization, simulation and community support. Second, 'e' is for extension in the sense that e-learning should emphasize the ongoing process of learning instead of an event-based activity, which could hardly linger with the learners throughout their later careers. Moreover, 'e' is for expansion in the sense that e-learning should offer access to an unlimited number of topics, beyond the limitations of the classroom, for audience-in-the-large who are interested to participate. It has been our experience that the easy part of implementing e-learning is the technology. The tough part is to invent and innovate the organizational context to create new models of experiences for knowledge sharing with the technology. The interesting part is how to blend the well-known classroom learning and e-learning in appropriate and supercharged ways. On conceiving the strategic foundation to accommodate the development of e-learning among organization members, we find the notion of learning organization [Garvin 1993; Levine 2001; Senge 1990], quite compatible for our purpose. According to Senge [1990], a learning organization is "where people continually expand their capacity to create the results they truly desire, where new and expansive patterns of thinking are nurtured, where collective aspiration is set free, and where people are continually learning how to learn together." Thereby, with e-learning, we are not just introducing new technology for learning; instead, we are introducing a new way to think about learning. People learn in many ways – through access to well-designed information, by using performance-enhancing tools, through peculiar experience, and from one another. In order to leverage the potential of e-learning technology for sustained, beneficial change for an organization, we need a sound architectural model to develop the organizational environment that encourages learning as a valuable activity.

2 MODELING ORGANIZATION FOR E-LEARNING

The primary purpose of organization modeling is to propose a suitable organizational architecture, which fits the targeted e-learning context, and thereby makes organizational design disciplined [Morabito, Sack and Bhate 1999; De Hoog, et al 1994]. The central idea behind our approach is that an organization can be sufficiently understood and integrated as a set of behavioral specifications. Each specification represents a view designed to characterize the organization premised on some set of core concepts known generally as the organizational constructs, such as people, structure, process and technology. The proposed architecture typically incorporates an overall schema produced by applying information modeling ideas to an organization's various constructs, each of which should have its own meta-model typically represented in the form of an object constrained by its specific contextual business rules stipulating its behavioral properties. In an organizational context, each instance of a behavior is usually specified in a contract, providing a dynamic aspect to modeling objects of interest. Basically, we maintain that organizations can be described in a relatively stable fashion with a constant set of core organizational constructs. Still many other management notions are advanced every day, such as e-learning, which represent variations of existing constructs. So, we call these variations the *derived* constructs. Together, the core and the derived constructs comprise the individual domains of an organization, and such an *organizational domain* is a distinct but integral part of an organization's overall architecture.

3 INNOVATING ARCHITECTURAL COMPONENTS FOR E-LEARNING

We believe the creation of an organizational model for e-learning is an important ongoing process of architecting a learning organization. Particularly, we are interested in expressing the inter-relationship among the relevant architectural components. Put it simply, we conceive the architecture of an e-learning organization to be composed of the following components: the Information System (IS), the Individual Learning (IL), the Organizational Learning (OL), the Intellectual Property Management (IPM), and the Knowledge Management (KM).

- *The IS-component.* This component operates on the information system (IS) paradigm [King 1996] of identifying relevant data, acquiring it, and incorporating it into storage devices designed to make it readily available to users in the form of explicit knowledge (routine reports and responses to inquiries). Principally, IS directly relates to managing data and information rather than knowledge and learning. But the IS infrastructure, including the application programs which transform data into more valuable information relating to particular decisions, or activities in the organization, is of fundamental importance to implementing any of the other architectural components in a learning organization. It is also considered as part of the *structural capital* of the organization.

- *The IL-component.* The individual learning (IL) [Kim 1993] component focuses on cultivating *human capital* [Becker 1993] of the organization. It serves to provide training and education for individuals through the institution of workshops, apprenticeship programs and the establishment of informal mentoring programs. Typically, an IL component provides free use of the IS infrastructure to access both structured and unstructured material in order to pursue an explicit educational path for online self-learning.

- *The OL-component.* The organizational learning (OL) component focuses on cultivating the *social capital* [Probst and Buchel 1997] of the organization. It is characterized by the use of communities of practice approaches, leading to the formation of collaborative groups composed of professionals who share experiences, knowledge and best practices for the purpose of collective growth. The conceptual basis is that social capital, in the form of various group and organizational competencies and capacities, can be developed, refined, and enhanced to enable the organization to adapt to changing circumstances, through such processes as teamwork, empowerment, case management or development-centered career paths.

- *The IPM-component.* This component deals with the issue of intellectual property management (IPM) [Stewart 1997; Sveiby 1997] underlying the activities that are involved in leveraging existing codified knowledge assets in the form of patents, brands, copyrights, research reports and other explicit intellectual property of the organization. The conceptual basis for this component is that such codified knowledge assets may be thought of as the realized human and social capital in the form of *intellectual capital.*

- *The KM-component.* The knowledge management (KM) component focuses on the acquisition, explication, and communication of mission-specific professional expertise that is largely tacit in nature to organizational participants in a manner that is focused, relevant and timely [King 1996; van der Spek and De Hoog 1995]. The conceptual basis is that an organization's *knowledge capital* in the form of tacit knowledge can, in part, be made explicit, and leveraged through the operation of KM-related processes and systems developed for knowledge sharing.

More precisely, we could express the inter-relationships of the various components within an e-learning organization as follows:
<Organizational Architecture> ::= <Structural Capital> +
        <Human Capital> +
        <Social Capital> + <Intellectual Capital > +
        <Knowledge Capital>

In any organization, the specification of a domain is often done through an information-modeling construct. In our discussion, we call this construct a *molecule*, a term borrowed from elementary chemistry. The process of building a molecule for a given organizational domain involves taking the knowledge areas from the specific domain and connecting them together in a particular manner. Using the idea of an organizational molecule, we might further refine the individual architectural components as:

<Structure Capital>	**::= Molecule <IS-component>**
<Human Capital>	:= Molecules {<IL-component>, <IS-component>}
<Social Capital>	::= Molecules {<OL-component>, <IS-component>}
<Intellectual Capital>	::= Molecules {<IPM-component>, <IS-component>}
<Knowledge Capital>	**::= Molecules {<KM-component>, <IS-component>}**

4 CONCLUSION – CONTEXTUAL CHALLENGES IN E-LEARNING

For each of the architectural components in the overall organizational model, we have to conceive the appropriate e-learning services to support its mission. There are generally three important contexts:

automating, informating, and knowledging, worthy of our attention. In the past decade, we have witnessed the organization's continuous move from a principle of automation to one of integrative processes. While automation involves the removal of the individual from a process, the principle of *informating* [Zuboff 1988] suggests a form of process abstraction and integration between the individual and the computer system. Basically, informating makes people more productive through their use of, and process integration with IT. It serves to increase the capacity of people to understand the entire value-adding learning process. On the other hand, the idea of *knowledging* [Savage 1990], refers to individual and organizational learning, and is characterized by the active involvement of the individual with his or her work. Knowledging includes a dynamic interaction between the explicit and the tacit forms of knowledge. Each successive organizational progression from automating to informating to knowledging, as required in today's knowledge organization, requires higher levels of process abstraction and a broad range of process integration and alignment. Therefore, the creation of a specific e-learning model must be situated in a context of adaptability. This organizational concern is always a big challenge for today's information systems architects. We need the cooperation of the organizational architect, a new figure responsible for designing structures across organizational boundaries, engineering processes into strategic capabilities, developing individual competencies into a learning organization, aligning information technology with organizational imperatives, and integrating the disparate pieces that constitute the organization.

5 REFERENCES

Becker, G.S. (1993). *Human Capital: A Theoretical and Empirical Analysis with Special Reference to Education* (3rd Edition). University of Chicago Press: Chicago.

De Hoog, R., et al. (1994), "Organization Model: Model Definition Document," Technical Report. Univ. Amsterdam and Cap Programmator. Deliverable DM6.2c of ESPRIT Project P5248 (KADS-II).

Garvin, D.A. (1993), "Building a Learning Organization," *Harvard Business Review*, 71 (4), pp. 78-91.

Kim, D.H. (1993), "The Link between Individual and Organizational Learning," Sloan Management Review, Fall 1993, pp. 37-50.

King, W.R. (1996), "IS and the Learning Organization," Information Systems Management, 13 (3), Fall 1996, pp. 78-80.

Levine, L. (2001), "Integrating Knowledge and Processes in a Learning Organization," *Information Systems Management*, Winter 2001, pp. 21-32.

Morabito, J., Sack, I., and Bhate, A. (1999). *Organization Modeling: Innovative Architectures for the 21st Century*. Prentice Hall PTR.

OECD (1996), *The Knowledge-Based Economy*. Organization for Economic Cooperation and Development, OCDE/GD(96)102, Paris, 1996.

Probst, G. and B. Buchel (1997), *Organizational Learning: The Competitive Advantage of the Future*, Prentice-Hall (Europe), Herdsfordshire, UK.

Rosenberg, M.J. (2001). *E-Learning: Strategies for Delivering Knowledge in the Digital Age*. McGraw Hill.

Savage, C.M. (1990). *Fifth Generation Management: Integrating Enterprises through Human Networking*. Digital Press.

Senge, P. (1990). *The Fifth Discipline: The Art and Practice of the Learning Organization*. Currency Doubleday, London, U.K.

Stewart, T.A (1997), "Intellectual Capital: The New Wealth of Organizations," Doubleday, New York, 1997.

Sveiby, K.E (1997). *The New Organizational Wealth*. Berrett-Koehler Publishers, Inc.

Van der Spek, R., and De Hoog, R. (1995), "A Framework for a Knowledge Management Methodology," In: Wiig, K.M. (ed.), Knowledge Management Methods. Arlington, TX, USA: Schema Press, 1995, pp. 379-393.

Zuboff, S. (1988). *In the Age of the Smart Machine: The Future of Work and Power.* New York. Basic Books.

Coming to Terms with the New Economics of Information

Stijn Viaene and Guido Dedene
K.U.Leuven, Department of Applied Economics
Management Information Systems Group
Naamsestraat 69, B-3000 Leuven, Belgium
Phone +32 16 32.68.91, Fax +32 16 32.67.32
{Stijn.Viaene;Guido.Dedene}@econ.kuleuven.ac.be

ABSTRACT

This mini-paper elaborates on the new economics of information and the nature and management of the modern firm.

INTRODUCTION

Information used to be inextricably intertwined with the physical flow of elements through the value chain. Nowadays, we have attained a level of technological sophistication, supported by adherence to standards, low-cost information and communication technology (ICT) accessibility and critical mass, that allows us to separate the physical flow from the informational glue that holds it together. This offers new and exciting opportunities for broadening the scale and scope of the firm and the richness and reach of its offerings. Under the reign of what Evans and Wurster [4] term "the new economics of information" the alternative to the stove-pipe, vertically integrated value chains has become feasible: value networks of outsourced, decentralized, self-standing businesses that cooperate as a virtual enterprise on the basis of well-defined (strategic) service-level agreements. Yet, coming to terms with the new network-centric business environment proves to be difficult. In a naturally progressing discussion we elaborate on closely intertwined management themes pertaining to the firm's realignment with these new economics of information.

CONTEXT VS IDENTITY

Besides deregulation and globalisation, technological progress stands out as the key transformational factor shaping the modern context of the firm. Coming to terms with this context in the first place means appropriating oneself a clear strategy. Strategy is about what firm one wants to be to which group of customers, and about making distinguishing, defendable and, ultimately, profitable choices. Technological advancement has opened up avenues for commerce and business that could previously only be dreamed of.

The problem is that the emergence of new, exciting and promising technological possibilities has a tendency of starting waves of (rational) herd behaviour toward its adoption. This makes firms into slaves of their context. Simplistic defensive tactics, initiated by fear of missing out on an opportunity, can hardly be perceived as a source of lasting competitive advantage or profitability. Blending into the context by rushing into best practice or standardized technology is by no means a guarantee for survival. This can only be attained by setting oneself apart from the herd, the context, by creating oneself an identity, and, most importantly, by moulding the new technology to serve a chosen, proprietary strategy of sustainable competitive advantage. This requires a great deal of creative thinking and discipline [15]. First know who you are and who you want to be before you start changing your identity in response to a changing context or newly emerging technology, however exciting.

IDEA VS IMPLEMENTATION

Strategy formulation and strategy implementation are very distinct activities. During implementation constraints initially external to the inception of the idea, constraints related to finite resources, and elements of inertia, constraints related to legacy, become apparent. Implementation rests on problem solving ability and on the careful preparation and execution of a migration path for transforming the *as is* into the *would be*.

Legacy tends to play a major part in the effective instantiation of strategy set out over time. Note that, what is now considered legacy has once helped the firm create its identity. It can be an asset, as well as a liability. This all depends on how one envisages the future of its context (industry) and strategy (value proposition) and whether, and to what extent, it still embodies the required agility. Also, making *tabula rasa* in the face of continuous change, where one would try to replace the *as is* in one big bang operation with the *would be*, in most cases is not practically realistic due to the finite nature of resources, lack of experience and elements of inertia typically resisting the process of change. The main idea is to focus on the opportunity cost of not choosing for the alternatives offered in a continuously changing environment. The right strategic attitude here is one of "conservative radicalism" [11].

EFFECTIVENESS VS EFFICIENCY

Effectiveness is about getting the right things. Efficiency is about getting things right. Effectiveness comes first: First choose the right configuration of business components, then get the value network up and running efficiently. This is one of the most pervasive themes in management literature since Mintzberg's [13] "strategy precedes structure"-mantra.

"Don't Automate, Obliterate," [9]. That is, generating high-quality implementations is useless if the business configuration is wrong. This old adage was reiterated by business process reengineering adepts. Sadly enough, it was all too often learned the hard way (e.g. in the postlude of the total quality management era [8]). The distinction between effectiveness and efficiency closely parallels that between idea and implementation. The former essentially requires vision, the latter rests on problem solving–that is, implementation of ideas in a real-life context characterized by several forms of inertia, uncontrolled complexity and constraints exogenous to the initial ideas. The tricky thing here is to avoid settling for compromises that may make one forego its identity, its brand.

PROCESS VS WORKFLOW

The distinction between process and workflow is central to the work of Keen [10-12]. Process is nothing like "the over-narrow view of processes as workflow"–that is, the mechanical (re)engineering definition of process as a sequence of activities. The former is about recognizing what opportunities and threats are out there, about deciding what one wants to be and can be, about who to team up with to deliver, and, most importantly, about how to organize for it. The creation of a combative value network is the central theme. Taking on a process perspective at rethinking one's business means focusing on the separation of concerns in terms of roles and corresponding business components, but also, and especially, on the coordination of promises and commitments, rather than just to look at the mechanical flow of activities embedded within the individual networked components.

Keen's process is more commonly referred to as the virtual organization. This type of organizing emphasizes a tight, but not sticky, cooperation of a complex network of interacting components, in which boundaries between the actors seemingly dissolve; seemingly, because there is a clear alignment of objectives. The virtual organization challenges the rigidity and inflexibility at the boundaries of contemporary firms, which prevents them from swiftly teaming up with new, value-adding business partners. The big paradox of virtual organizing, however, is that the boundaries—that is, the interfaces—of the components in such a network should be more clearly delineated (separation of roles) and transparently described (specification of interfaces) than ever before. The intended enterprise is an extended enterprise, or rather, an extensible enterprise, inclusive, rather than exclusive: inclusive along the supply chain, and inclusive of the markets [7,16].

DECONSTRUCTION VS RECOMBINATION

The very success in deconstructing the traditional value chain will eventually be judged by the success of the complementary activity of creatively recombining the necessary pieces into a new, value-creating, open, yet proprietary, unique value network. The crucial insight is that the identities, and thus the strategies, of the parts in a value network and the identity of the whole value network cannot be conceived independently, at least to some degree. That is, we only come to understand the true synergy and meaning of this complex whole from the preconception of the identities and meanings of its parts and their interrelationships. There is a hermeneutic circle involved that is fundamental to any act of creative destruction: "The movement of understanding is constantly from the whole to the part and back to the whole. Our task is to extend in concentric circles the unity of the understood meaning. The harmony of all the details with the whole is the criterion of correct understanding. The failure to achieve this harmony means that understanding has failed," [5].

In his position paper on strategy and the internet Porter [15] therefore, quite controversially at first sight, asserts that this quest for strategic fit among parts may prompt businesses to "once again focus on building close, proprietary relationships with fewer suppliers, using the internet technologies to gain efficiency improvements in various aspects of those relationships." However, the fact alone of envisioning the enterprise as a synergistic network of openly interoperating, self-constituting components (bonded by a common mission) is likely to be capable of creating an agility far beyond that of a ponderous, monolithic whole.

CHANGE MANAGEMENT

Change management [14] emanates from all the above. It starts out from the paradigm of constant change and builds on the premise that change can be managed—that is, systems can be designed to swiftly adapt to changing circumstances, even those that cannot possibly be foreseen. Design for change requires dealing with change in a consistent, systematized and institutionalized way—that is, faithful to a strategic identity, even though this too is subject to change. The ultimate goal: a learning organization, organized to be (self-)reflective and

(self-)corrective [2-3]. Reflection and correction are a continuous (human) activity and are performed at all the different levels throughout the enterprise value network. This is what makes the enterprise a synergistic, reflective "community-of-practice" [1-2], whose identity is both recognized and legitimized by its semi-autonomous parts or sub-

communities, that all have a clear value-adding function of their own. The instrumentarium of organizational change management is vast and the skills involved are numerous (see e.g. [17]). Evidently, good political, people and business skills are at least as important as good analytical, technological and systems skills.

The above discussion on strategy, process, technology and people allows us to grasp the true scope and meaning of change management, organizational learning and knowledge management. The latter can broadly be defined as the multidisciplinary art and science that is continuously in search of synergistic combinations of technology and the creative and innovative capacity of human beings to increase the profitability of the enterprise. It is fostered by managing the enterprise-wide access to and membership of the corporate mind and memory of the enterprise, the home of shared business (meta)knowledge, given lifeblood by developing skills "at creating, acquiring, and transferring knowledge, and at modifying its behavior to reflect new knowledge and insights," [6]. In a context shaped by the new economics of information the true mission of information resources management is to enable communities-of-practice to evolve as freely as possible.

REFERENCES

[1] Bourdieu, P., 1977. Outline of a theory of practice. Cambridge University Press.

[2] Brown, J., Duguid, P., 1991. Organizational learning and communities-of-practice: Toward a unified view of working, learning, and innovation. Organization Science 2 (1), 40–57.

[3] Dixon, N., 1999. The organizational learning cycle: How we can learn collectively. Gower.

[4] Evans, P., Wurster, T., 1999. Blown to bits: How the new economics of information transforms strategy. Harvard Business School Press.

[5] Gardamer, H.-G., 1976. The historicity of understanding. In: Connerton, P. (Ed.), Critical sociology, selected readings. Penguin Books Ltd.

[6] Garvin, D., 1993. Building a learning organization. Harvard Business Review 71 (4), 78–91.

[7] Gummesson, E., 1998. Implementation requires a relationship marketing paradigm. Journal of the Academy of Marketing Sciences 26 (3), 242–249.

[8] Hamel, G., Prahalad, C., 1994. Competing for the future: Breakthrough strategies for seizing control of your industry and creating the markets of tomorrow. Harvard Business School Press.

[9] Hammer, M., 1990. Reengineering work: Don't automate, obliterate. Harvard Business Review 68 (4), 104–112.

[10] Keen, P., 1997. The process edge: Creating value where it counts. Harvard Business School Press.

[11] Keen, P., 1999. Designing new organizational structures - Problems and prospects. http://www.peterkeen.com/fripres.htm

[12] Keen, P., McDonald, M., 2000. The e-process edge: Creating customer value and business wealth in the Internet era. McGraw-Hill.

[13] Mintzberg, H., 1979. The structuring of organizations. Prentice Hall.

[14] Nickols, F., 2000. Change management 101: A primer. http://home.att.net/~nickols/change.htm

[15] Porter, M., 2001. Strategy and the internet. Harvard Business Review 79 (3), 62–78.

[16] Prahalad, C., Ramaswamy, V., 2000. Co-opting customer competence. Harvard Business Review 78 (1), 79–87.

[17] Senge, P., 1994. The fifth discipline: The art and practice of the learning organisation. Currency/Doubleday.

A Framework for Knowledge Management Adoption in a Steel Company

Nahed A. Azab, MSc.
Regional IT Institute11A
Hassan Sabri Street, ZamalekCairo, Egypt
Tel. : +202 737-5206 / 737-5207
Fax : +202 739-1380
E-mail : nahed@tedata.net.eg

Khaled Wahba, PhD, Assistant Professor
Cairo University, Faculty of Engineering
11A Hassan Sabry Street, Zamalek, Cairo, Egypt
Tel. : +202 737-5206 / 737-5207
Fax : +202 739-1380
E-mail : khaled.wahba@riti.org

ABSTRACT

Knowledge management is emerging as a key management tool for the new century. To achieve a sustained competitive advantage, management needs to understand, implement and support a new competence throughout the organization: the ability to manage knowledge effectively. Knowledge management is the process of making creative, effective and efficient use of all the knowledge and information available to an organization for the benefit of its customers, staff, and thus the company. Knowledge is therefore an intellectual asset, which in the new global economy will become more important than the traditional capital assets.

This paper aims to investigate the value of intellectual capital at EZDK (Steel Products Sales & Marketing Arm of Ezz-Dekheila Alliance - the largest steel products marketing and sales company in the Middle East, located in Egypt). It will help develop a clear understanding of knowledge and culture within EZDK. The research will also highlight the procedures necessary to establish a framework for knowledge management within the company. Finally, The research will try to depict the techniques to be used in order to generate, capture, distribute and measure knowledge in the company.

BACKGROUND

Knowledge and individual expertise are now seen as vital to the success of a business; "*the company that is not managing knowledge is not paying attention to business*", observed Thomas Stewart, author of *Intellectual Capital*, in his keynote presentation at Training 2000.

Knowledge management is a combination of management awareness, attitudes and practices, systems, tools and techniques designed to release the power of knowledge.

In fact, knowledge management presents a significant business opportunity. According to industry pundits Ovum (cited on the website, www.supportindustry.com), the worldwide knowledge management market will be worth $US 12.3 billion by the year 2004. More specifically, Ovum forecasts that the worldwide market for knowledge management-related software will increase from $US 515 million in 1999 to $US 3.5 billion by 2004. Knowledge management-related services are expected to grow from $US 2.6 billion in 1999 to $US 3.5 billion by 2004.

What's really driving knowledge management is something bigger: a desire by many organizations to harness the brainpower within them. More than merely trying to "work smarter, not harder", organizations see knowledge management as a means of cultivating their intellectual assets and realizing a harvest of efficiencies in operations, and innovations in products and business practices. (These assets range from documents, patents, and copyrights to the ideas and suggestions of employees). As significant, this harvest yields competitive advantages, which lead to tangible (and ideally, sizeable) profits.

This paper provides some guidelines useful to apply knowledge management concept within EZDK. It helps identifying knowledge within the organization, as well as transforming this knowledge from an abstract concept to an increasingly tangible and manageable asset. The paper demonstrates also the challenges facing knowledge management in the company, and the policies to be shaped. Finally, the research will reveal the approach that could be followed to measure the return on knowledge management, and the potential advantages of harnessing the skills and knowledge of EZDK employees.

KNOWLEDGE MANAGEMENT: STATE-OF-THE-ART

In seeking a definition of knowledge, Badenoch et al. (1994) consulted key sources in the field and found what could be the simplest definition of all: that knowledge is "organized information in people's heads." (Stonier, 1990).

Brooking (1999) differentiated between data, information and knowledge by explaining each one separately as follows:

While Data are facts, pictures, and numbers – presented without a context, Information is organized data that has value to someone in the context of their work or life. Knowledge is information in context, together with an understanding of how to use it.

Wilson (1996) presents a useful illustration of this issue with the notion of the processing hierarchy see figure 1.

Theory and experience have demonstrated that, from a management perspective, there are clear distinctions between two types of knowledge. Common practice now refers to them as *explicit* and *tacit* knowledge. Macdonald (1999) described both types of knowledge as follows:

- ***Explicit knowledge*** is precisely and clearly expressed, with nothing left to implication. Generally in the business situation it is fully stated and openly expressed without reservation. Companies hold substantial documented knowledge in patents, technical specifications and procedures. Additionally, information is routinely collected, stored and distributed as management information. Financial, marketing, production and service information is usually codified and is ready for different distribution channels.

Figure 1: The processing hierarchy (Wilson 1996)

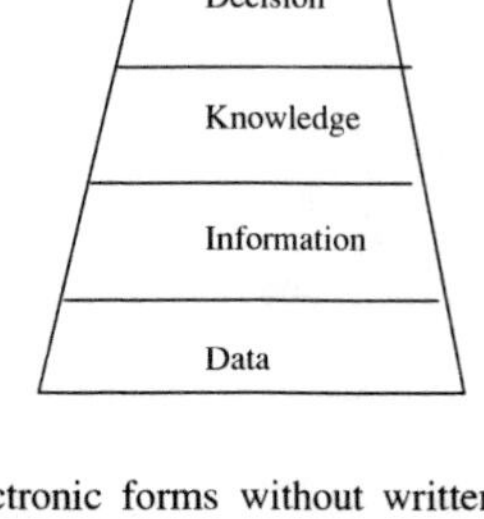

- ***Tacit knowledge*** is understood but not clearly expressed. It is often personal knowledge embedded in individual experience and involves intangible factors, such as personal belief, perspective and values. The most valuable asset of every organization is the hidden or tacit knowledge buried in the memories of employees and other people in regular contact with the organization. This experience includes learning from doing as well as study, observation and informal information or even gossip. By definition, this is more difficult to recognize and collect let alone codify, store and distribute. So, Knowledge management is an effort by organizations to manage some or all of the knowledge within them as a resource, much as they manage real estate, inventory, and human resources.

Managing knowledge as a resource spans a continuum from generating efficiency to fostering innovation. At the efficiency end of the continuum, knowledge management is seen as an effort to build a repository of data and information that workers need, and provide them with efficient access to it. As Microsoft founder Bill Gates noted in his presentation at COMDEX Fall 1999: "Corporate information today is so hard to find. It is kept in folders, or anecdotally understood by people in the company." He added, "Knowledge workers need to share things, and need access to the right information at the right time. This is so hard today." Corporate Yellow Pages – an effort to create a Yellow Pages-like listing of expertise in an organization, represent a popular method of providing efficient access to knowledge within an organization.

At the innovation end of the continuum, knowledge management is seen as an effort to spark new products, processes, and business opportunities that help an organization thrive. For example, Tom Davenport, a professor of information technology at the University of Texas and one of the key authors in this field describes efforts by Dow to "harvest value" from little-used patents and licenses.

Core Processes of Knowledge Management

There are a number of activities which can be regarded as the core processes of knowledge management, and which are all fairly closely related. Among the various knowledge management processes proposed, we found that the most appropriate to be applied in our case study are the following: (see **figure 2**)

For details about each process, interested reader can consult the work of Probst, 1999 and Liebowitz 1999.

Intellectual Capital

Many people confuse knowledge management with intellectual capital. Carliner (2001) explained that intellectual capital is an effort by organizations to place a financial value on its tacit and explicit knowledge or in other words, it is the term given to the combined intangible assets that enable the company to function. Although many parts become involved in knowledge management projects, determining methods for measuring the value of intellectual assets is almost exclusively an effort of the financial community. Brooking (1999) demonstrated that the intellectual capital of an enterprise could be split into four categories; **Market assets, Intellectual property assets, Infrastructure assets, Human centered assets.** Webb (1998) stated that various techniques have been put forward for measuring the efficiency of information services, such as performance measures, but concrete measures of the actual value of the information provided have not been as readily available.

Hamel (1995) noted that in a world where knowledge is central, a company's value in terms of its intellectual assets is not shown on the balance sheet. As he says "there is no funds flow statement for knowledge". However, Robinson & Kleiner (1996) writing were discussing measurement and valuation techniques to be applied to intellectual capital, which they saw as not only to intellectual property concepts such as patents and licenses, but also to less tangible assets like know-how, skills and information systems.

Figure 2: Core processes of knowledge management (after Probst, 1999, Liebowitz, 1999)

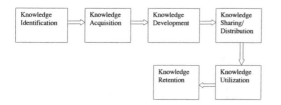

Main Challenges of Knowledge Management

There are many challenges facing knowledge management, which are summarized by Santosus (2001) into the following points:
- **Getting employees on board:** the major problems that occur in knowledge management usually result because companies ignore the people and cultural issues.
- **Allowing technology to dictate knowledge management:** Knowledge management is not a technology-based concept. While technology can support knowledge management, it is not the starting point of a knowledge management program.
- **Not having a specific business goal:** a knowledge management program should be aligned with the business goal. While sharing best practices is a commendable idea, there must be an underlying business reason to do so.

Knowledge Management in Practice

Many organizations worldwide took wide steps in incorporating knowledge management on their business; these organizations adopted this concept differently choosing the ways that could best sustain their competitive advantage to attain the most benefits they can get.

Many organizations had to change their management style from a centralized to a decentralized one to speed up the decision making process, because a rigid company cannot manage knowledge effectively especially when the company is operating in many countries worldwide like Buckman laboratories, which are serving customers in 90 countries (Buckman, 1997).

Sometimes, however, decentralization could hinder knowledge sharing due to the fact that business units could be isolated the one from the other. Hewlett Packard (HP) managers however were able to overcome this problem; although business units that perform well have a high degree of autonomy which does not encourage these business units to invest time or money in leveraged efforts that do not have an obvious and immediate payback for the unit, the fact that employees move from one business unit to another allows a great degree of informal knowledge transfer within HP (Davenport, 1998).

In EZDK, the management style is centralized, which will not constitute an obstacle for applying knowledge management in the organization due to the small number of the employees (50 employees) and the fact that most of them work in the head office. Moreover, the nature of the business itself dictates that all decisions should be taken in the head office, which leaves limited responsibilities for EZDK's employees working in the plants.

To oversee and better manage knowledge in many organizations, new positions were created; companies like Coca Cola, Sequent, Hewlett Packard, and PriceWaterhouse Coopers have established positions like Chief Knowledge Officer (CKO). Another position, which is Knowledge Analyst, exists at FedEx; knowledge analysts assist the CKO in analyzing the knowledge process within the firm in order to improve human performance (Liebowitz, 1999).

Case Study Site

EZDK (Steel Products Sales & Marketing Arm of Ezz-Dekheila Alliance) is Egypt's largest steel marketing company. EZDK was founded by Mr. Ahmed Ezz in 1999. EZDK's product range includes steels used for construction (long products) – such as rebars, wire rod and wire mesh – and flat steel that is demanded by the expanding industrial sector, both in Egypt and in many countries worldwide. EZDK was created as a result of the strategic alliance of both Ezz industries and ANSDK (Alexandria National Steel – Dekheila) companies, and is responsible for the sales, marketing, and coordination of the products of both companies. Ezz industries comprises two plants: ESR (Ezz Steel Rebars, established in 1995) and ESM (Ezz Steel Mills, established in 1994). ANSDK - established in 1982 (in Alexandria) as a joint stock company - was the main competitor to Ezz before the alliance took place.

Ezz-Dekheila Alliance was created in 1998 to satisfy the growing demand for steel products. Nowadays, this alliance has a full control over the market as their local market share reached more than 60%. Ezz Industries tends to use its technical and marketing skills to unlock unused potentials in ANSDK. The production capacity of the company is 5 million tons per year; 2 million tons of flat steel (used in the manufacturing of many products such as cars, machines, home appliances, etc.) and 3 million tons of rebars used for construction. Most of the rebars production is targeted to the local market (75%), and the rest is allocated for exports; whereas the flat steel is the other way around.

PROBLEM DEFINITION

EZDK is growing fast, and so its accumulated knowledge. There is no formal system that can capture and exploit the company's dispersed knowledge. Knowledge acquired through experience doesn't get fully reused because it is not represented in an appropriate form to the employees who might call for it.

OBJECTIVE OF THE STUDY

The research objective is to propose a framework for adopting knowledge management in EZDK.

This objective would be realized over two phases. In the first phase, we will try to identify the knowledge in the company as well as to assess the current culture. While in the second phase, we will set a knowledge strategy to support EZDK's business strategy.

RESEARCH METHODOLOGY

In the beginning, it must be clear that developing a knowledge creating organization is not a short-term project. The process takes time, resources and eventually involves everyone in the organization. Before developing a strategy to adopt knowledge management within EZDK, we need first some important information to help us prepare and plan for this strategy.

We used two means to realize these assessments, which are interviews with key people in the company, and a survey conducted on the employees:

Interviews

Three interviews were carried out, with EZDK's Marketing Director (structured interview), a Sales Analyst (unstructured interview), and the third interview was held with the IT Specialist (structured interview). The main questions in these interviews were:

- What are the various products and their markets?
- What are the structure and the main activities of the employees in EZDK?
- What is the knowledge that exists in the company and where can it be found?
- What is EZDK's competitive advantage and the knowledge required to sustain it?
- What is the IT situation in EZDK?

Questionnaire

A questionnaire was distributed to 40 employees (including 15 middle and senior managers) in EZDK, due to the relatively small number of staff in the company. The questions of this questionnaire were adapted from previous research on knowledge management conducted by Jordan and Jones (1997), Anderson (1998), and Wolf (1999). The result of this questionnaire will contain quantitative and qualitative data types, that need to be analyzed through descriptive statistics (frequency distribution) in order to assess the culture of people in the company.

Research Conceptual Framework

Determining the culture in EZDK depends on two independent variables and a moderating one. The independents variables are the methods used by staff to acquire information and the knowledge management environment. The moderating variable is demographic.

The questionnaire is divided into three parts. The following lines state the main questions in the questionnaire. For a complete listing of the questionnaire, the reader could refer to the (Azab, 2002).

Part I: Personal information
- Do you want to mention your name?
- Please indicate your sex.

- Please tick the group of age you are belonging to.
- Which function do you have in EZDK?

Part II: Questions concerning the methods used by staff to acquire information in EZDK
- Do you have an overview of the knowledge available in EZDK?
- What kind of media do you use predominantly to obtain information?
- What occasions do exist for an exchange of information in EZDK?
- How does information exchange take place between older experienced employees and younger ones in EZDK?
- What does the EZDK management do to improve the information acquisition of the employees?

Part III: Questions testing the knowledge management environment in EZDK
- Do you have a general overview of knowledge management?
- Please rank barriers facing you to share knowledge in EZDK?
- The availability of the knowledge base makes you less creative?
- Do you feel that privacy of employees is an issue concerning the sharing of knowledge?
- The knowledge gathering process may require reviewing your personal work documents/or emails so as to add information to the knowledge repository. Do you feel this invades your privacy?
- Does sharing of knowledge in your job situation decrease your competitiveness with other colleagues for promotions?

DATA COLLECTION, AND ANALYSIS

Interviews' Analysis

The main information obtained from the interviews is presented in the following lines. For a complete interviews' analysis, the reader could refer to (Azab, 2002).

Analysis of the knowledge in EZDK:

The actual knowledge that exists in EZDK, i.e. its competitive knowledge position, could be classified into four types:
- Documented explicit knowledge.
- Undocumented explicit knowledge.
- Observable tacit knowledge, which can be obtained by watching a professional's behavior.
- Embedded tacit knowledge, which is almost impossible to identify and acquire.

We will focus in our research on the first two types; the following lines will explain these two knowledge types within the organization.

Documented explicit knowledge:

This knowledge is easy to acquire; it could be found in patents, files and on simple computer applications like word processors and spread sheets. Documented explicit knowledge includes the following:
- ISO certifications. EZDK trademarks, its position in the steel market as a steel producer, its market share and its customer base.
- Market advantages (local market): low production costs, stable prices, high quality products, fast orders deliveries, and reliable services to customers.
- Market advantages (international market): low prices.
- Key assets: flat steel products, which are considered a new industry line (production started in 2000). There exist few competitors in these products.
- Policies and procedures set in ANSDK.
- High standards in technical knowledge in all production lines.
- Local and international competitors.
- Products' prices of local and international competitors.
- Local market share.
- Local market consumption.
- Excess capacities in EZDK and competitors.
- Discounts and incentives offered by competitors.
- Monthly price differentials between EZDK and other producers in the

local market.
- International export prices versus EZDK export prices.
- Local sales and average selling prices by sector for flat steel products.
- International development for flat steel prices.

Undocumented explicit knowledge
    This knowledge is uncontrollable and not easy to be documented, it resides only in people's heads. Acquiring it requires costs and efforts to get it from professionals. Undocumented knowledge can be summarized as follows:
- Products specifications of the competitors, their qualities and their defects.
- Market advantages of the competitors locally and internationally.
- Prime competencies of competitors.
- Business strategies and production plans of competitors.
- Competitors' positions with regard to knowledge.
- Customers' behaviors.
- Customers' relationships and treatments.
- Customers' business and the projects they are involved in.
- Business strategies of customers.
- Product optimization between the products of the different plants.
- Market forecasts.
- Characteristics of successful and bad transactions.

Questionnaire Analysis
    The response rate was 100%, and the average response time was from 10 to 15 minutes. Time spent on the questionnaire was satisfying allowing respondents to give fair answers.
    We will explore some of the questionnaire analysis. For a complete analysis, the reader could refer to (Azab, 2002).

Analysis of part I:

Name	70% (28 employees) of the respondents mentioned their names.
Sex	77% (31 employees) of the respondents were male.
Age group	67% (27 employees) of the respondents are from 21 to 30, 28% (11 employees) are from 31 to 45, 5% (2 employees) are from 46 to 65.
Job title	12% (5 employees) of the respondents are officials in charge, 25% (10 employees) are team leaders, 15% (6 employees) are heads of departments, 38% (15 employees) have other job titles.

Analysis of part II:
    Questions in part II investigate the methods used by employees to acquire information in EZDK.
- Do you have an overview on the knowledge available in EZDK?

    The more employees are aware of what knowledge exists in EZDK, the higher the chance of sharing knowledge and using knowledge base in the company. 50% (20 employees) of the respondents have a good general overview on the knowledge available in EZDK; they are mainly head of departments and team leaders. The other 50% (20 employees) have good overview in their field of activities (see **figure 2**).

- What kind of media do you use predominantly to obtain information?

Telephone	53% (21 employees)
Facsimile	18% (7 employees)
Email	48% (19 employees)
Internet	75% (30 employees)
Magazines/Catalogues	43% (17 employees)
Professional literature	30% (12 employees)

- How does information exchange take place between older experienced employees and younger ones in EZDK?

    This question was developed to investigate whether knowledge is transferred from experienced employees to fresh ones and how it is transferred.

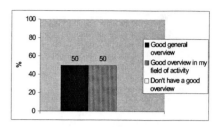

Figure 2: Staff overview on the knowledge available in EZDK

    40% (16 employees) of the respondents revealed that there is no regular exchange; whereas 40% (16 employees) of the respondents declared that knowledge transfer is accomplished through mixed project teams.
    23% (9 employees) of the respondents stated that individual trainings are carried out before older employees leave the company. Few respondents (mainly managers) proclaimed that there exists regular instruction sessions for younger employees (8% - 3 employees) (see figure 3).

Analysis of part III:
- Do you have a general overview of knowledge management?
    53% (21 employees) of respondents have a general idea about knowledge management; whereas 47% (19 employees) of them don't (see **figure 4**). This reflects that almost half of the employees are aware of this concept, which means that adopting it in EZDK would be easier for them than for others.

- Please mark barriers facing you to share knowledge in EZDK?
    Employees were asked to indicate the barriers or obstacles to knowledge sharing in their organization. **Table 1** displays the respondents' opinion regarding the barriers they encounter to knowledge sharing. As we can see one of these main barriers is that most of the employees retain knowledge they possess because it consolidates their position in the company. Another important obstacle to sharing knowledge is that there exists a lack of trust among employees that makes them think that their ideas could be taken over or that others data could be incorrect.

Questions concerning privacy:
    The next three questions investigate privacy issues concerning the employees at EZDK (see **table 2**).
    As a result of the questionnaire analysis, we deduced that an adequate number of employees (50%) has good overview of the knowledge available in the company. There is no regular information exchange from older to younger employees. Employees are interested in gathering information from various sources, depending mainly on the Internet, which means that they are computer literates and makes using a knowledge base a natural act for them.
    More than half of the staff (53%) is aware of the knowledge management concept, which will facilitate adopting it in the company. We also realized that there is not enough policies and procedures set and implemented from the part of the management to support knowledge sharing; this process should be considered when developing a knowledge strategy to adopt knowledge management in EZDK.

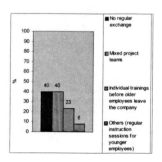

Figure 3: Information transfer from older employees to younger ones in EZDK

Figure 4: Staff awareness about knowledge management and their perception of its purpose

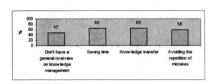

When it comes to the employees' privacy, most of them don't find that sharing knowledge will be intruding their privacy, except when it is related to viewing their personal work and emails.

Table 1: Barriers to knowledge sharing

"Turf protection" knowledge is power.	60% (24 employees)
People scare that ideas will get hijacked.	60% (24 employees)
Distrust in other colleagues data.	58% (23 employees)
Organizational rigidity and specialization (lack of multi-skills)	55% (22 employees)
Culture of working alone in small offices.	48% (19 employees)
Strong departmental barriers.	48% (19 employees)
Lack of communication	48% (19 employees)
Expert knowledge in the heads of individuals.	48% (19 employees)
Personal data stores are common.	45% (18 employees)
Management doesn't encourage knowledge sharing between employees.	43% (17 employees)
Rapidly changing technology makes keeping up difficult.	8% (13 employees)

This cultural assessment indicate that there exists a promising knowledge sharing culture among a high percentage of the staff, but it is done occasionally on individual basis, and not through EZDK policies. This is not a good foundation for knowledge sharing because employees may change their behavior toward transferring knowledge depending on different situations or perhaps on different colleagues relations.

The questionnaire don't only help in providing a cultural assessment on EZDK, but it also helps to increase understanding of the need for change and individual ownership of the process. As a result, this questionnaire not only gathers the information for planning, but it actually starts the process of change.

DISCUSSION AND FINDINGS

Knowledge has to be seen as a strategic resource that must support business strategy; knowledge architecture then is constructed at a strategic level forcing us to link knowledge strategy to the business strategy of the organization (see **figure 5**).

We should start by performing a SWOT (Strengths, Weaknesses, Opportunities, Threats) analysis on EZDK from which we will derive the company's business strategy. Once stating EZDK's business strategy, we could then recognize the knowledge required to execute it. By comparing the knowledge that the company should acquire to its actual knowledge, we could then indicate the knowledge gap in the company. After accomplishing these processes, we should able to develop a knowledge strategy that supports the company's business strategy.

Knowledge Strategy

Having identified the knowledge required to execute the EZDK's business strategy, the actual knowledge that EZDK's possesses, and the strategic knowledge gap accordingly, we are then ready to set the firm's knowledge strategy. Ultimately, this knowledge strategy must be translated into an "*intellectual capital* strategy" and a "*knowledge manage-*

Table 2: Employees privacy issues

	Yes	No
- Do you feel that privacy of employees is an issue concerning transferring of knowledge?	35% (14 emp.)	65% (26 emp.)
- Does sharing of knowledge in your job situation decrease your competitiveness with other colleagues for promotions?	13% (5 emp.)	87% (35 emp.)
- The knowledge gathering process may require reviewing your personal work documents/or emails so as to add information to the knowledge repository. Do you feel this invades your privacy?	70% (18 emp.)	30% (12 emp.)

There are many barriers that hinder knowledge exchange between employees that should be overcome in order to build a learning organization, which creates the environment for knowledge management.

Figure 5: Linking knowledge strategy with business strategy.

ment strategy" to support its implementation (see **figure 6**).

We conclude then that a strategic view of knowledge comprises in fact three strategies: the knowledge strategy, the intellectual capital strategy, and the knowledge management strategy.

These strategies are related to each other and each one represents knowledge from a relevant perspective. In order to clarify the difference between these three strategies, we can consider knowledge strategy as the ends or what we need to achieve, intellectual capital strategy as the means or how, and knowledge management strategy as the management aspect or wherefore concerned with defining the roles, structures, controls and policies, etc.

Time constraints impose an order to addressing the issues identified while setting a knowledge strategy; because of the time required to develop and manage knowledge, knowledge strategy will be devised into 2 parts: a short-term knowledge strategy and a long-term one.

The short-term strategy is directed first toward exploiting the existing documented and controllable explicit knowledge within the company in order to make better use of it, and second by combining the external knowledge identified in the knowledge gap and adding it to the company's knowledge base. The long-term strategy tackles first the current non-documented and uncontrollable knowledge present in the company, then the knowledge that should be acquired internally in the company and demonstrated in the knowledge gap.

All three strategies are explained thoroughly in (Azab, 2002).

FINDINGS

- Knowledge in EZDK is scattered and not harnessed to its maximum efficiency, which constitutes a loss in such valuable organization resource.
- Knowledge in EZDK is not reused in a transparent and neutral way.
- The main impediments towards applying knowledge management within EZDK are the lack of motivating employees from the part of the management in the company, and the culture that tends toward knowledge hoarding as a result of the staff worries about loosing individuals' credibility of ideas.
- There exists two types of explicit knowledge within EZDK, the first is documented and controllable; and the second is undocumented, uncontrollable and documenting it necessitates cost, time and effort.
- A high percentage of employees use the Internet efficiently.
- There is a potential sharing culture among employees but needs to be better organized.

CONCLUSION

The research started by highlighting some of the important knowledge management topics that was used throughout the research, then by assessing the company from various perspectives. The next in the research was working toward setting a knowledge strategy for EZDK, which should definitely be aligned with the company's business strategy.

To be capable of realizing the suggested knowledge strategy, this strategy should be interpreted into two other strategies: "*the intellectual capital strategy*" and "*the knowledge management strategy*". The intellectual capital strategy deals with the ways to leverage the in-

Figure 6: Components of knowledge strategy

tellectual capital of the organization, whereas the knowledge management strategy is concerned with the means to manage the intellectual resources and capabilities in the firm including choosing the right people for each job, determining the schedules and policies to be put, and the decisions to be made in order to execute the knowledge strategy proposed before.

Applying the recommendations of this research to the company would allow the reuse of knowledge to become a part of the corporate culture. This would leverage the skills of the employees, which predominantly would allow the company to sustain its competitive advantage.

The research succeeded in presenting a practical and clear depiction regarding applying knowledge management on the case study chosen. It went smoothly from one idea to another following the pre-determined logic.

A future work could be to try to capture the tacit knowledge within EZDK, since it is the most valuable knowledge in the company. Managing such knowledge remains a major challenge because it cannot be codified.

REFERENCES

Annie Brooking (1999), *"Corporate memory: strategies for knowledge management"*, International Thomson Business Press.

Azab, Nahed A (2002) *"A Framework for Knowledge Management Adoption in a Steel Company"*, MSC Thesis, (supervisor: Khaled Wahba), School for Computing Science, Middlesex University, London, UK.

Gary Abramson (1998), *"Intellectual capitalism measuring up"*, http://www.cio.com/archive/enterprise/051598_intellectual_content.html?printversion=yes

Charles Despres, Daniele Chauvel (2000), *"Knowledge horizons: the present and the future of knowledge management"*, Butterworth – Heinemann.

Gilbert Probst, Steffen Raub and Kai Romhardt (1999), *"Managing knowledge: building blocks for success"*, John Wiley & Sons Limited.

Goodwin, Eric *"The journey toward knowledge management"*, http://www.kmworld.com

Jay Liebowitz (1999), *"Building organizational intelligence: a knowledge management primer"*, CRC Press.

Jeff Angus, Jeetu Patel & Jennifer Harty (1998), *"knowledge management: great concept...but what is it?"*, TechWeb, http://content.techweb.com/se/directlink.cgi?lwk19980316s0045

Karl-Erik Sveiby (2001), *"What is knowledge management"*, http://www.sveiby.com.au/knowledgemanagement.html

Mark W. McElroy (2000), *"The new knowledge management"*, Knowledge Management Consortium International (KMCI), Inc.

Megan Santosus & John Surmacz (2001), *"The ABCs of knowledge management"*, http://www.cio.com/research/knowledge/edit/kmabcs.html

Michael H. Zack (1999), *"Managing codified knowledge"*, http://web.cba.neu.edu/~mzack/articles/kmarch/kmarch.htm

Michael H. Zack (1999a), *"Developing a knowledge strategy"*, http://web.cba.neu.edu/~mzack/articles/kstrat/kstrat.htm

Sylvia P. Webb (1998), *"Knowledge management: linchpin of change"*, Aslib, the Association for Information Management.

Thomas H. Davenport (1998), *"Knowledge management at Hewlett-Packard, early 1996"*, http://www.bus.utexas.edu/kman/hpcase.htm

VNU Business Media (2001), *"Eight things that training and performance improvement professionals must know about knowledge"*, http://www.lakewoodconferences.com/kmwp/main.html

William E. Fulmer (1999), *"Buckman Laboratories"*, Harvard Business School.

XSEL Group, Inc. (2001), *"Building & proposing customer value"*, http://www.xsel.com

Design of an Instrument for Improving Project Management Efficiency through Projects' Knowledge-Based Evaluation

Sameh Ahmed Hemeid, MBA
Building Sector Manager, Project Management Department
Schneider Electric Egypt
68 Tayran Street, Cairo, Egypt
Tel.: +202 40 10 119, Fax.: +2015 412 441
Sameh_hemeid@eg.schneider-electric.com

Khaled Wahba, PhD
Assistance Professor, Cairo University
Faculty of Engineering
11A Hassan Sabry Street, Zamalek, Cairo, Egypt
Tel.: +202 737 5206, Fax.: +202 739 1380
Khaled.wahba@riti.org

ABSTRACT

Making knowledge and experience available to entry-level project managers is not a dream anymore. The knowledge (experience) transfer in the project management can contribute severely to improving its efficiency. Multinationals are not exceptions themselves, even if they had nurtured the learning organization and created the necessary flexible type of organization.

In this research, an instrument was designed for project management's based on knowledge management which includes four components: the project management's knowledge areas process diagrams, the knowledge base, the knowledge threshold matrix and the knowledge look up map. *This instrument serves as a tool for entry-level project managers to know; the project management processes; the project management's knowledge areas; the desired level of knowledge in each knowledge area; and to define basis for evaluating project management. The evaluation output is the input to the knowledge base. They can capitalize on the previous experiences existing in this knowledge base to: support decision-making; improve risk management; improve the organizational performance and the efficiency of the project management, hence, enhancing the quality of service leading to better customer relation management. This evaluation can complement the financial evaluation currently used in the company to evaluate projects. In addition, of giving input to the knowledge base, the evaluation methodology, if supported by management commitment, can also be the mechanism that insures the sustainability of our knowledge initiative.*

1 OVERVIEW

"Business firms are organizations that know how to do things", Economist Sidney Winter. *"Knowledge is the new basis for competition in post-capitalist society"*, Peter Drucker. *"An investment in knowledge pays the best interest"*, Benjamin Franklin. *"Knowledge is power"*, Anonymous.

Those phrases can be interpreted as; knowledge should not be dispersed and should only be kept for personal use to take better decisions than others. However, the prominent authors never intended to convey that meaning, actually they meant the opposite. Information gives power to both the individual and the organization only when it is solid and tangible, only when it can be shared, and only when it can be processed.

Knowledge is power, but what is knowledge, do we mean the implicit or explicit knowledge. Do we mix it with data or with information? How we define the knowledge in organization? Many organizations have adopted different knowledge management initiatives and invested considerable costs, time and efforts for that purpose. The outcomes of these initiatives were doubtful in terms of its effectiveness. We believe that the failure of knowledge management initiatives was not

always the case. There were success stories here and there. To improve the success rate, the initiatives have to be narrowed to specific business application/function areas. The project management is the application area to focus on to guarantee: customer satisfaction, profitability and reasonable return on the investment. It is the kitchen of the organization where it cooks its work to produce a product according to a customer need. The organization knowledge and experience lays their dispersed in forms, processes, routines and personnel. The usage of this knowledge and experience is jeopardized by the diversity and hidden characteristics of knowledge.

The project management institute (2000) defines the project as a temporary endeavor undertaken to create a unique product or service. The project manager competes demands for: scope, time, cost, risk, and quality. Projects are usually divided into several phases to improve management control and provide for links to the ongoing operations of the performing organizations. The most important characteristic of projects is progressive elaboration. The project management institute literally defined Progressive elaboration characteristic as follows: progressive means 'proceeding in steps; continuing steadily by increments,' Elaboration means' worked out with care and detail; developed thoroughly (Project management institute, 2000). It is that characteristic that provided us with the backbone of the system to track down the project through it's road map. We conclude a project phase generally be reviewing of both key deliverables and project performance to date. We can also divide each project or project phase into many processes. A project processes is a series of actions bringing about a result. Process groups are Initiating, Planning, Executing, Controlling and Closing (Project management institute, 2000). The same analogy can be applied aiming at enriching the logic of the entry-level project managers (and even other project managers) and helping them to improve their decision-making. The project management body of knowledge represented the desired skills and knowledge within the project management context (Project management Institute, 2000).

2 PROBLEM DEFINITION AND RESEARCH OBJECTIVES

The most annoying issue was watching businesses going from one project to another, the knowledge and experience of these projects were kept with the project managers who executed the projects and was not transferred to other project managers. This simply led the company to repeat the same mistakes, pursue the same bad project while they should have learned that they should not. The transfer of such experience was limited only to verbal and weak communication. The documented knowledge (explicit) only represented a tiny amount of the available knowledge, even that documented part could not be benefited from, as it was not part of a comprehensive system. We define the research problem as the loss of project management experts' knowledge due to not documenting the executed projects' experiences.

So, the purpose of this study was to develop a knowledge-based instrument to be used in the project management department in a manufacturing company in Egypt (SEE), resulting in: an efficient and effective project management through providing knowledge based decision support system and creating the methodology to evaluate (scale) the projects based on knowledge.

3 STATE-OF-THE-ART

Senge, et al. (1994) Explored the learning organization, and sat the basics and rules of the game. Thanks to them, now, the disciplines that need to be mastered in order to put into practice the learning organization are understood. They are; personal mastery, mental models, shared vision, team learning and system thinking. Senge and his colleagues showed us the embedded essence of what we were trying to describe while we talked about different facets of it: to marry the individual development of every person in the organization with superior economic performance. This is the simplest, and most complicated in the same time, way to tell organization how to do it.

Organizations wants to establish its own learning organization: for superior performance, to improve quality, for customers, for competitive advantage, for an energized committed workforce, to manage change, for the truth, because time demands it, because we recognize our interdependence and because we want it (Senge, et al. 1994). The learning organization most importantly provides the environment that encourages synergy between the different outputs, applying the multiplier effect to boast organization economic performance. Figure 1, illustrates the generic organizational analysis model they reached. They designed the model to unfolding the implicate order by human beings (experts) into the explicate order. Going through the domain of enduring change, or deep learning cycles: where individuals who have capabilities to capture the knowledge and experience exist. Transferring to the domain of actions, or organizational architecture: which is responsible for bringing about results. We need to know which, when and how we should measure results. The evolution of the given model is; logical, represents the methodology that should be adopted when pursuing knowledge initiatives. Implicitly, the model tells what we need to have (do not have) to create the learning organization: the experts, the knowledge workers, the competent resources, the infrastructure, innovation, and the culture. We made use of that model in designing the instrument.

Michael H. Zack (1999) article on developing a knowledge strategy focuses on knowledge and learning. They tell how business organizations are coming to view knowledge as their most valuable and strategic resource, and bringing that knowledge to bear on problems and opportunities as their most important capability. Zack (1999) article was self-explanatory when he said that a knowledge-based competitive advantage is also sustainable because the more a firm already knows, the more it can learn. It can combine its learning experiences into a "critical learning mass" around particular strategic areas of knowledge. They can use this map to strategically guide their knowledge management efforts, bolstering their knowledge advantages and reducing their knowledge weaknesses.

Assessing an organization's knowledge position requires cataloguing its existing intellectual resources by creating the knowledge map. Zack (1999) classifies knowledge according to whether it is core, advanced or innovative. Knowledge generated within the firm is especially valuable because it tends to be unique, specific, and tacitly held. It is therefore more difficult for competitors to imitate, making it potentially strategically valuable.

Davenport & Prusak (1999) defined knowledge as a fluid mix of framed experience, values, contextual information, and expert insight that provides a framework for evaluating and incorporating new experiences and information. They drew a scale as follows: data, information, knowledge, experience, ground truth, complexity, judgment, and beliefs. Davenport & Prusak (1999) quoted Sidney Winters knowledge codification as: tacit, not teachable, not articulated, not observable in use, rich, complex, and end up with undocumented. Though this codification is

Figure 1: Generic Organizational Analysis (Peter Senge, 1994)

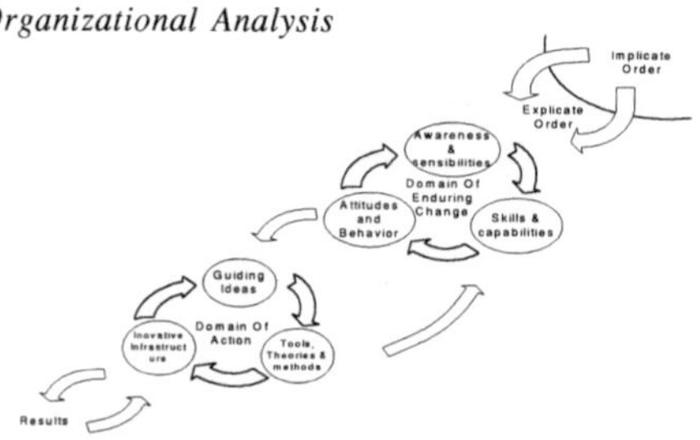

not complete, but it has inspired me to where to focus my research area. What is the knowledge we target to capture and make use of it? We need to understand that explicit knowledge captured in documents and databases is different from implicit knowledge, which lays in minds of people. The second is the most valuable to organizations while it is very expensive and difficult to manage.

Capitalizing on their scale and codification, we chose to focus into managing the knowledge and experience. They identified one of the prime benefits of experience is that it provides a historical perspective from which to view and understand new situations and events. In addition, they provided dozens of business examples that lighted our way.

Davenport & Prusak (1999) said: ''The perception and the reality of a new global competitiveness, rapid change, increasing competition for the dollars of increasingly sophisticated consumers have led companies to seek sustainable advantage that distinguish them in their business environment''. Among diminishing physical assets, knowledge is a sustainable and an everlasting asset. Ford never recorded the reason of success of Taurus experience. International harvester, No one was there after 20 years of building the truck factory in Russia to benefit from the first experience.

Davenport & Prusak (1999) quoted Arthur Hugh Clough saying: ' Grace is given of God, but knowledge is bought in the market." They also presented the knowledge market theory that taught us new vocabulary and terminology of the market as: buyers, sellers, brokers, and price system mechanism. The theory drew our attention to observe the organization from a different cross-sectional view, the knowledge cross-sectional view. The awareness of the existence of such cross-sectional view derives people to think differently. They are pushed to find themselves a suitable positioning in the organization structure according to that view.

Many critics reroute the failure of knowledge projects to the huge size of knowledge that were flooding from the information systems and knowledge management initiatives. We believe that there are many reasons why we need to reconsider knowledge initiatives as: The escalating rate in the growth and the diversity of knowledge and information, The fractionation of the disciplines into narrow specialty fields, augmenting a trend toward depth rather than breadth, An increase in professional mobility, leading to a discontinuity of focus and experience within an individual's career, and ultimately fewer real experts, Increasing demand for the secularization of knowledge to enable democratic processes, and presumably, more appropriate application of knowledge, The lack of any formal framework which explicitly represents the collective knowledge base and problem solving processes, in order to enable meaningful dialogue and action, irrespective of expertise.

Somehow, if it was possible to map out the collective knowledge base, then it may be possible to manage Trans-disciplinary problems (projects) without being overwhelmed by complexity. Human experts do this implicitly, much to the consternation of their protégées. This ability to synthesize and apply essential knowledge is what makes experts valuable. Experts report that the ability to handle knowledge increases significantly once this plateau of essential knowledge is reached, but there is something which lay people find highly undemocratic about expertise, namely that the means by which the expert draws conclusions is not explicit and universally accessible. Knowledge mapping therefore represents an opportunity not only to solve wicked problems, but also to democratize the understanding of Trans-disciplinary processes.

What would induce individuals to volunteer the recording of personal knowledge mapping processes for storage and access in a public domain environment, or even within their particular private enterprise? Some form of tagging, analogous to genetic coding, is needed allowing for the tracing of knowledge to its source(s).

Knowledge is the sixth dimension in the company balance scorecards system along with the other five dimensions: financial; customer; employee; growth; and internal business processes. Knowledge management is the dream of every promising organization. Many books and studies have been trying through the last decade to tell organizations how to do it. Unfortunately, most of the efforts were theoretical frameworks or discrete examples from different types of organizations. The way we see, we can help people and organizations to apply it and get the benefits is to narrow the talk to certain application areas.

Project management is the application of knowledge, skills, tools and techniques to project activities to meet project requirements (Project management institute, 2000). The project management institute has identified nine modules that together combine the project management activity. These modules are project integration management, project scope management, project time management, project cost management, project quality management, project human resources management, project communication management, project risk management and project procurement management (Project management institute, 2000). Furthermore, for each of these modules they recognized certain knowledge areas. They defined those knowledge areas and demonstrated them by the tools and techniques applied in them. We capitalized on that model, but we adopted it to match the company's (under study) project management activity and processes. Following the breakdown and the given subsets of the project management's knowledge areas done by the project management institute we found it detailed to the right level where we could still catch and feel the knowledge areas. Allowing us to study each area and measure our performance and our evolution in these areas. Our feedback was crossed checked with other industry visionaries inside the company who agreed that the knowledge and practices are applicable to company projects; and that there is great consensus on their value and usefulness.

4 THEORETICAL FRAMEWORK AND RESEARCH DESIGN

The virtual border shown in figure 2 is splitting the explicit knowledge space from the implicit knowledge space. We divided the implicit knowledge space into: the skills & talents and the illusion. Again we divided the skills and talent space into: The shadow space that represents the experts experience which mates with them as long as they stay in the organization; The trace space that represents the experience kept in the organization after they leave. Knowledge is the universal space to a normal person. That person (organization) claims that he knows his solar system (explicit knowledge space), what he knows really is his earth (documented knowledge), he can understand that there are other planets (not documented explicit knowledge spaces) exists inside his solar system but he can not see. If the sky is clear (learning organization), they can find ways to see those other planets (either easily document that knowledge or hardly document it with some efforts). What he can hear writers (scientist) talk about is the rest of his galaxy (implicit knowledge space) but he can never see it with his bare eyes. We will focus our study to try to help that person (organization) to see and benefit from the other plants (not documented explicit knowledge spaces) in that person

Figure 2: Knowledge Space Map (Authors)

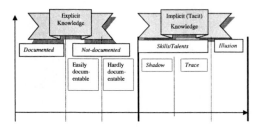

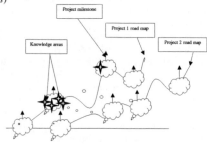

Figure 3: The project road map showing milestones and knowledge areas (Authors)

solar system. The scope has enlarged to cross the virtual boundary to deal with part of the universal space (implicit knowledge space).

If we can imagine the projects' road maps given in Figure 3, each project has a specific rod map. We can divide the project management activity into several phases or milestones all of them are located on the road map. Each milestone has its own knowledge areas (knowledge cloud). If we can understand and declare the knowledge areas inside each cloud then we can capture, store and make use of the knowledge concentrated in these areas. By declaring these knowledge areas we can light the way for the entry level project managers to insure that they; do not loose the way go on their own most of the way. By completing the map: we were able to; evaluate our knowledge position in each knowledge area, guide the entry-level project managers where they can find the knowledge and experience related to each knowledge area.

We illustrated in figure 4 the main relationship among the study variables and the components of the project management's knowledge management instrument. We believe that targeting efficient project management would lead to many positive results for the individual/ organization as: better usage of company resources; improving customer relation management; minimizing risks; increasing profitability. In addition, the learning organization climate that surrounds the organization under study encouraged us to pursue that knowledge initiative. The management commitment, cultural / behavioral issues, organization type / structure and availability of knowledge officers represented the moderating variables of the relation understudy. The research provided answers to questions as: How can we evaluate projects based on knowledge? What are the specific knowledge areas in project management for SEE? What is project specific level of knowledge comparing to the minimum level of knowledge required in specific knowledge area? What is the project management's knowledge look up map? What is the effect of organization type on knowledge sharing (dissemination)? What is the role of management commitment on knowledge (willingness of experts) leveraging? What is the role of availability of knowledge workers in the success of implementing the instrument?

The instrument were designed to achieve the objective of four components: the project management's knowledge areas processes diagrams, the knowledge base, the knowledge threshold matrix and the knowledge look up map.

The first component is the project management's process flow diagrams. The process diagram of the project management's activity

Figure 4: the Relationship between the variables under study

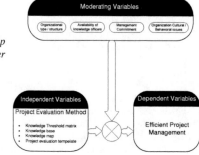

knowledge areas were defined through the different process groups comprising the project management activity. That component guided the entry-level project managers; through identifying the project management related knowledge modules (integration, scope, time, cost, quality, human resources, communication, risk, and procurement) and the knowledge areas existing in each module. In addition, it elaborated the progressive elaboration of the project through the knowledge modules, their interrelation and how to follow it in executing projects.

The second component is the knowledge base. The knowledge-based evaluation provided input to the knowledge base. To carry out the evaluation, we had a committee to evaluate the company projects in the closing meeting, which takes place at closing the project. The knowledge base provided the project managers with: projects database that can be searched according to scope, market sector, complexity and others; knowledge areas minimum desired level of knowledge; projects good/bad experience; and projects risk management good/bad experience. The knowledge-based evaluation acts as the mechanism to sustain the enrichment of the knowledge base with new projects' experience.

The third component is the knowledge threshold matrix. For each of these nine knowledge modules combining the project management activity, the related knowledge areas were defined. Reviewing the design suggested by the project management institute and mapping it to the company understudy reached the matrix design. Discussing them with industry visionaries with project management experience refined the design and the scale. The matrix provided a method to classify the knowledge position; whether it is basic, likely favorable or differentiating position; required in each knowledge area. Such classification unveiled the strengths and weaknesses in each knowledge position for each knowledge area. The organization, knowing its weaknesses and strengths made use of such analysis. The entry-level project managers compared their knowledge to the required one. The result of the comparison tells them where they need to consult the knowledge map to find out where about they can find the required knowledge.

The fourth component is the knowledge map. The knowledge look up map guides the person looking for knowledge, information and data to where he can find what he is looking for through multi-medias as documents, reports, company forms, databases and human beings (experts). The map tells that person the name of the source of knowledge and the location of the source of the knowledge.

The instrument was designed to be a multimedia tool with two interfaces. The first interface will be through the process diagrams screens. The second interface will be through selecting a project from the project database according to different criteria's as scope, duration, market sector, client, consultant and others mentioned in the project evaluation template. Through the multimedia tool, the users will be able to move interactively between the two interfaces.

The research followed the triangulation (Hybrid) classification. The classification of the research is qualitative in the knowledge management area and quantitative in the business application area (project management). This is mainly due to two dimensions of the research topic: knowledge management and project management.

The questionnaire was designed for identifying the desired level of knowledge in each knowledge area in each module. The selected sample evaluated the minimum desired level of knowledge in each of the project management's knowledge areas. The collected data were analyzed statistically to determine the knowledge threshold required in each knowledge area.

The population of this research is of two categories: the project managers and industry visionaries in the company under study (or in the industry). The expert project managers, as the users of the instrument, could understand and gave valuable opinion on it. The industry visionaries with previous experience in project management have insight and strategic contribution that added value to the research.

The sample was selected so it can provide valuable input (data) in both parts of the research, the static and dynamic part, from the overall two-dimensional population. By valuable input, we meant that the sample can understand professionally the nature and the importance of the knowledge project, they can decode the terminology of the questionnaire they can relate their answers to match the research requirement,

and they can contribute and add value to the project. For identifying the desired level of knowledge in each knowledge area, we used the questionnaire to collect the necessary primary data. The sample for the questionnaire was composed of two categories: seven experts project managers out of twenty-one-project manager in the company; and six industry visionaries from the company with good experience in project management.

Table 1: the Raw Data Table

We will collect the data for the research through two types of sources: primary, where we collected it through running a questionnaire to two categories of people working inside the organization; and secondary, where we gathered data through the books, specialized magazines, articles and internet papers together with the researcher practical experience. In addition, ran unstructured interviews with the industry visionaries to review the adequacy of the instrument. The interviewers complemented and enriched the instrument by their insights and contributions. we adopt their comments into the instrument to make it more solid and comprehensive.

5 ANALYSIS AND DISCUSSION

Each person on each category of the sample selected one of the three levels of knowledge as the minimum required level of knowledge in each knowledge area. We define the three levels of knowledge as follows: Basic knowledge: the essential knowledge required in performing the task; it is what we call the must be knowledge. Likely favorable knowledge: the knowledge that if not acquired it is likely that the person will not perform the task; it is what we call the-should-be knowledge. Differentiating Knowledge: the innovative knowledge that if existing can help people to perform tasks differently: it is what we call the could be knowledge.

In the first stage of the data analysis, the data collected of each of the two categories was analyzed separately. The result for each category was the scale with the highest number of persons. At that stage, a desired minimum level of knowledge for each knowledge area for each category was reached. When the two categories desired level of knowledge was the same, the result was considered as the minimum desired level of knowledge for that knowledge area. In case the two categories desired level of knowledge was different; the result was considered as the one of the first category as the minimum desired level of knowledge.

According to the qualitative nature of the data collected and analyzed in our research, most of our findings were of qualitative nature. As a byproduct, we deducted quantitative analysis for the research data.

Table 2: the Semi-analyzed Data Table

The multi-media tool has two interfaces. Through these screens, the users could identify: The name of the knowledge area, the interrelation between the knowledge areas inside the process group, the interrelation between the different process groups combining the project. The desired minimum level of knowledge in each knowledge area (refer to table 3 for the final results of the research), the source of knowledge name and its location, the good/bad experience history in the specific knowledge area.

The second interface will be through selecting a project from the project database according to different criteria's as scope, duration, market sector, client, consultant and others mentioned in the project evaluation template. For the selected projects, the user can find out the evaluation given to the project in each knowledge area and the most important good/bad experience in the project.

We limited the evaluation to give only two good/bad experiences only for the whole project to avoid gathering repeated knowledge and to avoid a famous pitfall of the knowledge/information projects that they gather huge amounts of knowledge that makes it difficult for users to find the required information. The users could move interactively between the two interfaces looking for knowledge.

In addition, as a byproduct to the findings mentioned in this section, we can deducted some quantitative analysis. (See table 4 below)

Table 4 gives us a comparison about the relation between both categories' answers. The difference between the two categories indicates that we have one of the following cases: First, the first category, the industry visionaries, is away from the present project managers and they do not understand exactly the requirement of the position at least nowadays. Second, the second category, the expert project managers, is missing some basics of the position requirement and they need to have adequate training.

Authentication and confidentiality issues of the designed system are not different from any other information system and knowledge systems. A special attention would be given to our system, as it contains the know how of the company. The system includes the good experience that can invite the competition to a short way to catch up with the company. The system includes the bad experience that can give a lead to the competition to the pitfalls of the company to make the necessary propaganda. In addition, the instrument can point clearly to the knowledge sources of the company and soon making them vulnerable. The paradox of the knowledge system as usual, we need to make knowledge accessible and available but in the same time, we need to design tough security system. We need to solve that dilemma, do we share knowledge or we keep it confidential. A trade off has to take place here, meaning, we should seek to reach that critical balance. The royalties and credit rights are very important issues that need to be looked after to guarantee the success of the system.

Table 3: The Results Table

Scope	Initiation	D	E	? (D)
	Scope Planning	D	D	D
	Scope Definition	B	B	B
	Scope Verification	B	B	B
	Scope Change Control	E	E	E
Time	Activity Definition	E	E	E
	Activity Sequencing	D	D	D
	Activity Duration Estimation	E	E	E
	Schedule Development	E	E	E
	Schedule Control	E	E	E
Cost	Resource Planning	D	E	? (D)
	Cost Estimation	E	E	E
	Cost Budgeting	E	B	? (E)
	Cost Control	E	E	E
Quality	Quality Planning	B	E	? (B)
	Quality Assurance	E	B	? (E)
	Quality Control	D	B	? (D)
Human Resour	Organizational Planning	D	B	? (D)
	Staff Acquisition	E	E	E
	Team Development	E	D	? (E)
Communic ation	Communication Planning	D	D	D
	Information Distribution	D	D	D
	Performance Reporting	D	E	? (D)
	Administrative Closure	E	B	? (E)
Risk	Risk Management Planning	B	E	? (B)
	Risk Identification	D	E	? (D)
	Qualitative Risk analysis	E	E	E
	Quantitative Risk Analysis	E	E	E
	Risk Response Planning	D	D	D
	Risk Monitoring And Control	D	E	? (D)
Procurement	Procurement Planning	E	E	E
	Solicitation Planning	E	E	? (B)
	Solicitation	B	B	B
	Source Selection	E	E	E
	Contract Administration	E	E	E
	Contract Close Out	B	D	? (B)

Table 4: Category A & B comparison

First Category / Second Category	Basic Knowledge		Likely favorable knowledge		Differentiating knowledge	
	Number	%	Number	%	Number	%
Basic Knowledge	3	12.5%	2	8%	2	8%
Likely favorable knowledge	3	12.5%	16	67%	5	20%
Differentiating knowledge	1	4%	1	4%	5	20%

6 CONCLUSION

Project management is not only one of the departments of an electrical distribution equipment manufacturing (tailored product) company. Project management is: the connecting ring between the upstream sales activity and the final production activity; the pot where sales and marketing, procurement, planning, production, quality and after sales services departments' work is melted; the key administrator of the customer relation management; and the responsible for the project/company profitability. We designed the project management's knowledge management instrument to serve as the pool that entry level (sometimes even expert project managers as well) can seek support through navigating into the project management knowledge areas and experiences. It will prevent or at least minimize the loss of the project management experts knowledge and keeps it stored in the knowledge base.

The project managers can capitalize on the previous experiences existing in this knowledge base to: support decision-making; improve the organizational performance and the efficiency of the project management, hence, enhancing the quality of service leading to better customer relation management. Creating the knowledge base was not the only product of the research; the more important output was establishing the mechanism, which guarantees the continuity of our knowledge project. The mechanism established here is the knowledge-based project management's evaluation methodology. The knowledge-based evaluation methodology can complement the financial evaluation currently used in the company to evaluate projects. In addition, of giving input to the knowledge base, the evaluation methodology, if supported by management commitment, can also be the mechanism that insures the sustainability of our knowledge project. In addition, while the company is moving to a new management through process ISO procedure, the research provides a framework that will support implementing the new procedure.

The success of such instrument will depend mainly on the management commitment. The management commitment can have a positive/negative impact on even other factors that affects the success. This commitment must be tangible through seen solid actions as: encouraging the knowledge workers, establishing incentive and crediting systems, inspiring the people to change their culture and behavior and basically creating the learning organization climate.

The knowledge map helps the company and company's management to trace the knowledge to its generating source and allow giving credits and royalty rights to those who shared their knowledge.

The system has the essence of its continuity embedded in it; as the evaluation methodology (the mechanism), the knowledge map (the royalty), the management commitment (incentives and reward systems), and the return. However, a special care should be given to the authentication issue of the knowledge system as the system incorporates the company know how, the most precious competitive advantage. The paradox should be solved via trade off between knowledge sharing and confidentiality.

REFERENCES

Senge, P., Kleiner, A., Roberts, C., Ross, R., & Smith, B. (1994) the fifth discipline field book: strategies and tools for building a learning organization 1st ed. U.S.A.: Currency doubleday.

Davenport, T., & Prusak, L. (2000) working knowledge: how organizations manage what they knew 2nd ed. U.S.A.: Harvard business school press.

Project management institute (2000) a guide to the project management body of knowledge 2nd ed. U.S.A.: Project management institute, Inc.

Pfeffer, J., & Sutton, R. (2000) the knowing doing gap: how smart companies turn knowledge into action 2nd ed. U.S.A.: Harvard business school press.

Cohen, D., & Prusak, L. (2001) in good company: how social capital makes organizations work 1st ed. U.S.A.: Harvard business school press.

Zack, M. (1999) 'developing a knowledge strategy'. California management review, Vol. 41, No. 3, spring, 1999, pp. 125-145.

Intentional Communication Breakdowns in Virtual Communities of Interest: A Hindrance to End-User Knowledge Management

Christian Wagner, Fion Lee, Rachael Ip, and Karen Cheung
Department of Information Systems, City University of Hong Kong
Tel: (852) 2788-7546, Fax: (852) 2788-8694
E-mail: iscw@cityu.edu.hk

ABSTRACT

Virtual communities of interest offer their participants the opportunity to exchange knowledge and information as well as to engage in social exchange. Yet not all these exchanges are helpful to the community. In fact, some are intentionally manipulated by their originators to result in a communication breakdown. This study explores the existence of such communication breakdowns, their underlying pattern, and their effect on knowledge and information sharing, using transactional analysis.

1. INTRODUCTION

Shortly after the September 11 terrorist attack, communication on the ISWorld e-mail list went out-of-control. Some participants had used the forum for statements in sympathy of the victims, which resulted in a political debate, personal accusations, and the actual shutdown of the discussion forum on September 14, 2001. While there had been previous, albeit less severe, events of a similar nature, this was the first time a complete, mandated shutdown occurred on ISWorld. And yet, ISWorld is by no means the only community where such events occur. In fact, communication breakdowns of this nature seem to be a normal occurrence in communication groups, even though their outcome is counterproductive to the information exchange, and to the enhancement of community within the discussion groups.

The very negative nature of the dialogue in the ISWorld following 9/11 even led to a change in ISWorld policies (i.e., moderation) to avoid future reoccurrences. Clearly, there is recognition that communication breakdowns are highly counterproductive. But despite the policies, there seems to be no stop to such occurrences, leading us to ask the question of how these communication breakdowns occur, and how they can be avoided. It is a conjecture of this article, that communication breakdowns of this sort are in fact intentional and follow a "script", which allows their identification and avoidance (by enlightened discussion members or community managers). Purpose of this article is the study of this phenomenon.

We investigate four questions related to communication breakdowns. First, are these breakdowns accidental, or are they intentional manipulations of discussions? Second, what would be the pattern of such manipulations? Third, what would be the impact of such manipulations on knowledge creation and knowledge sharing, and fourth, what countermeasures could be applied to avoid communication breakdowns?

As part of the argument, we present *Transactional Analysis* (Berne, 1972) and show its applicability to communication in virtual communities. The community we will choose for this analysis is the Leica Users Group (LUG), although some of our examples are motivated by comments made in the ISWorld community.

2. VIRTUAL COMMUNITY

2.1. Overview

Virtual communities have emerged as sources of knowledge and information in recent years. For example, as illustrated in the Cluetrain Manifesto (Locke, et al., 2001), communities frequently know more about a company's product than the company itself, and half of the Fortune 500 companies are expected to develop virtual communities as a source of knowledge and information by 2005.

Formally, virtual communities are best described as communities that exist in a computer mediated space, which have built up relationships between community members, and whose activities are supported by information and communication technology, see for instance (Rheingold, 1993), (Hagel and Armstrong, 1997), (Carver, 1999), (Jones and Rafaeli, 2000), (Romm and Clarke, 1995), (Craig and Zimring, 2000), (Hesse, 1995), (Erickson, 1997), and (Ho, et al., 2000). Howard (1993) calls virtual communities "*social aggregations* that emerge from the Net when enough people carry on public discussions long enough, with sufficient human feeling, to form webs of *personal relationships* in cyberspace" ((Rheingold, 1993). Hagel and Armstrong (1997) highlight the issue of *member-generated content*. Another definition by Carver (1999) states that virtual communities are "about aggregating people. People are drawn to virtual communities because they provide an engaging environment in which to connect with other people – sometimes only once, but more often in an ongoing series of interactions that create an atmosphere of trust and real insight".

With some research focusing on the development of communities, seemingly no attention has been given to the opposite, namely *communication breakdowns* which occur in such communities from time to time. These breakdowns result in a partial or complete stop of information exchange, and possibly lead to the destruction of "social capital" that would otherwise foster future discussions and knowledge sharing. Because of this potential significant impact, and the lack of current research, we chose to target communication breakdowns in this study. Following our interest in knowledge management, we chose to target communities designed to exchange knowledge and information, in other words, communities of interest. Hence from now on, when we refer to virtual communities, we will imply a reference to communities of interest, not necessarily virtual communities in general.

2.2. Structuring Mechanisms of Virtual Communities

The structural mechanisms by which virtual communities are set up are usually quite simple and directed towards the exchange of information and knowledge. A community is formed around a special need, interest, or practice, such as a shared interest in travel, photography, or a shared professional interest such as research and teaching in information systems. Community members communicate through message exchange, via e-mail to a central site (e-mail broadcasting), or posting on a shared bulleting board, or similar message sharing/proliferation mechanism.

Contributions are clearly identified by sender, date, topic, and such, thus enabling simple forms of categorization, search, threading, and sorting. A major purpose of the sites is information sharing and broadcasting, such as the announcement of upcoming events.

Virtual communities are however not just knowledge exchange mechanisms, they are also communities, and thus can have a social agenda. Members exchange personal information, recognize each other, and may even transcend from virtual into real communities. Nevertheless, focus on the mission of the community (i.e., the shared interest) is important, and therefore such communities frequently have a code of conduct, formalized moderation, or a person who can grant and revoke access rights. Nevertheless, they are highly self-managed and frequently organized and managed by "end-users" rather than IT professionals. As a consequence, they can neither rely on technical skills of their organizers, nor on information management skills. Essentially, the technology used determines the organization of the knowledge body, while contributions, together with self-management and some forms of monitoring and moderation determine the content.

2.3. Information, Knowledge and "Off-Topic" Contributions

Virtual communities have a topical focus. Nevertheless, their members have the choice to either communicate "on-topic" or "off-topic". On-topic issues are clearly desirable to enhance the community's knowledge and information base. Off-topic comments do not directly relate to the discussion issue, but can nevertheless be useful. It can be information and knowledge rich, but not entirely topical. The other, less informational, form of off-topic comments can help to build up relationships in the virtual community, by allowing members to share feelings and satisfy some of their emotional needs in addition to their informational needs. In fact, the social capital created through personal, off-topic interactions can help the community to grow closer and become more effective in generating and disseminating knowledge and information. Unfortunately, off-topic discussions are frequently less rational than the on-topic discussions, so it is easier to drift off into highly emotional and irrational debates. As a result, off-topic comments are a likely source of communication breakdowns.

Whether on- or off-topic, comments can contain information and knowledge. While these two categories are sometimes difficult to differentiate from each other, we refer to information as factual data about the topic. Examples of information would include a list of different printer models for a particular brand, or the maximum pixel resolution of a digital camera model. Knowledge, by comparison, encompasses principles, rules, heuristics, plans and other generally applicable relationships. For example, if a discussant explains the relationship (formula) between digital resolution and digital photo print size, or a discussant explains how to choose a printer, then we will consider this knowledge. Compare for instance Wagner (2000) on differences between information and knowledge.

3. COMMUNICATION BREAKDOWN

3.1. Overview

A communication breakdown is a sudden stop in information flow on a thread, a topic, or the entire virtual community information exchange. It is usually identified by participants explicitly stating that they are discontinuing their participation, a successful appeal by others to discontinue a thread, or the explicit call for stoppage of a dialog by the community manager. Typically participants make comments such as "let's not argue about this anymore", "let's take this argument offline", "please refrain from commenting on this subject," or such. The community manager may make stronger statements such as "you are asked to immediately cease to comment or you will be removed from

this site," or "no more comments are allowed on this thread", or "the board will be closed for discussion until further notice".

With groups of highly accomplished individuals and a history of communication it is difficult to understand why such problems should occur at all. Transactional analysis (Berne, 1972) sheds some light on the phenomenon in regular (non-virtual) communication.

3.2. Analysis of Transactions in Inter-Person Communication

Transactional analysis is a theory of personality and social action based on the analysis of transactions between two or more people, on the basis of specific defined ego states, demonstrated during communication (Berne, 1972). Transaction analysis seeks to interpret the transactions carried out during inter-person communication and to discover which role each person assumes in each stimulus-response exchange. Its underlying assumption is that communicators can assume three roles: parent, adult, or child. Information and knowledge exchange typically takes place at the adult-adult level, while other communications, such as parent-parent, or child-child, are designed to promote *well-being* among communicators (Berne, 1964).

Adult-adult communication is the driver of information and knowledge exchange in virtual communities. Communication at other levels leads to emotional satisfaction, if it is complementary, that is at a level desired by all communicators. For example, if one communicator wants to assume the child role, and another the parent role, then the resulting communication is complementary, thus providing emotional benefit to the communicators. Problems occur when communicator roles are mismatched, or communications are "crossed". For example, A wants to communicate at the adult level (information exchange), but B responds at the parent level (parent-to-child). A asks "where can I find the author guidelines for the *XYZ Journal*?" B replies "you aren't ready yet to publish in the XYZ journal". At such a point in time, a mismatch occurs which leads to frustration in at least one of the communication partners, so that the communication likely terminates (Harris, 1969).

Crossed communications often happen accidentally, as one of the discussion partners accidentally adopts a role that forces the other communicator into a role he or she does not want to adopt. However, communication breakdowns might also be deliberately created, when at least one of the communicators purposely manipulates the communication. The motive for this activity is the individual's goal to prove to the other person(s) in the argument, and possibly the entire community "I'm OK and you are not", which might translate into forms of "mine is better than yours", such as "my research is better than your research", "my beliefs are better than your beliefs", or simply "I'm a better person than you are." The manipulator would do this by engaging other participants into an agitated discussion leading to the adoption of increasingly extreme positions, followed by a sudden "switch" that would leave the other participants exposed in their extreme positions. The operational aspects of this behavior will be discussed in more detail in the following section.

Transaction analysis identifies several types of such behavior, most of them leading the instigator in a "winning" position, while other participants are made to look evil, incompetent, or helpless. Transaction analysis uses the term "game" which originates from game theory, and identifies a multi-party situation where each party has objectives, a set of "moves" it can make, where moves result in outcomes, and outcomes have pay-offs. The intentional discussion manipulator creates a zero-sum game, with him or her intended to "win the argument", and other participants losing. Games are defined as sets of ulterior transactions, repetitive in nature, with a well-defined psychological pay-off (Berne, 1972). An ulterior transaction means that the agent pretends to be doing one thing while really doing something else. Specifically, the game player (instigator of the breakdown) will pretend to carry on an adult communication, while at the same time sending out covert signals leading to crossed communication.

3.3. Operational Aspects of Game Playing

Operationally, a game player (instigator) sets up a situation that leads to communication breakdown by using phrases that can be inter-

Figure 1: Gaming Behavior Flowchart

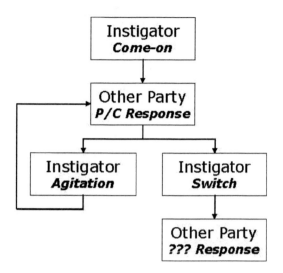

Figure 2: Communication Breakdown

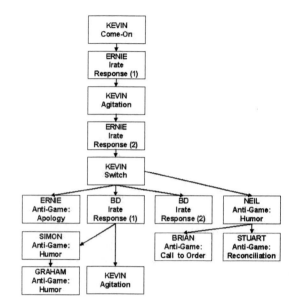

preted at more than one level. The game starts with a "come-on" (a usually thinly disguised message that says "I'm ok and you are not"), followed by the other party's angered, non-adult response, possibly several rounds of further discussion agitation, and then the "switch" in which the gaming communicator frustrates the other side. The prototypical pattern of gaming behavior is shown in the flowchart in Figure 1.

A communication following this pattern might unfold as follows.

Come-on "Our journals have to be more rigorous than those elsewhere, because otherwise they don't count for tenure decisions."
Response "You are so arrogant."
Agitation "Maybe your response is the result of an underlying inferiority complex? I am just reporting the facts."
alternatively
Switch "I am sorry you feel like this, I was just trying to explain our publish-or-perish challenge."

The instigator explains that he is facing more rigor (implying he is better), and consequently drawing an angry response. The instigator may then either continue to anger the other party, or pretend he wanted to neutrally report the situation, thus suggesting the other side overreacted.

4. STUDY AND FINDINGS

4.1. Research Questions

In this study we are interested in examining the four questions. First, do intentional communication breakdowns occur in virtual communities? Second, how would intentional communication breakdowns occur? Third, what would be the impact of such communication breakdowns? Fourth, what avoidance or recovery techniques could be used to counteract intentional communication breakdowns?

4.2. Methodology

We chose protocol analysis to analyze the phenomenon in an exploratory fashion. Two main coders evaluated two message digests against an *a priori* created coding scheme. One digest contained communications from August 8, 2002, with a number of hostile arguments, while the other digest, dated January 7, 2002, contained few hostilities. After completion of their coding process, the coders compared results. In case of any discrepancies, they consulted an auxiliary coder, discussed their different interpretations, and then settled for a mutually agreeable interpretation.

4.3. Mis-Communication Pattern

Figure 2 depicts part of the communications of the communication where the breakdown occurred (August 8). For brevity, we show only the 14 messages directly related to the breakdown, rather than all 35 messages in the message digest. No communication breakdown occurred on January 7, and there was only one potential attempt (one message) that day to instigate a breakdown.

Figure 2 shows a communication pattern similar to the template depicted in Figure 1. In this situation, Kevin, the instigator uses a come-on and one further agitation against Ernie, who becomes the angry (parental) responder. An interesting variation in this communication is the fact that another participant joins in ("BD") who also responds to the come-on. In the end, Kevin tries once more to agitate BD (since Ernie has stopped "playing"), but Kevin does not succeed.

4.4. Effect on Knowledge and Information Sharing

An analysis of the communications by type of contribution offers further insights, as exhibited in Table 1.

On the "game day" when the communication breakdown occurred, less than half of the 35 messages were on-topic, thus less than half of the comments contributed to the growth of knowledge or information within the community. Furthermore, 31.4% of all messages were on-topic information, with 8.6% each being questions and knowledge answers. By comparison, on the random day, 57.4% of the messages were on-topic, and the overall information, knowledge or question contributions accounted for 96.3% of all messages. Overall, the contributions for the game and random day were significantly different from each other ($C^2 = 16.06$, dF = 4, p < 0.001).

Table 1: Messages by Contribution Type

| | Game Day | | | | | Random Day | | | | |
| | On Topic | | Off Topic | | Total | On Topic | | Off Topic | | Total |
	No.	%	No.	%	%	No.	%	No.	%	%
Knowledge	3	8.6	0	0.0	8.6	5	9.3	0	0.0	9.3
Information	11	31.4	6	17.1	48.6	21	38.9	19	35.2	74.1
Question	3	8.6	0	0.0	8.6	5	9.3	2	3.7	13.0
Game	0	0	6	17.1	17.1	0	0.0	2	3.7	3.7
Anti-Game	0	0	6	17.1	17.1	0	0.0	0	0.0	0.0
Cumulative	17	48.6	18	51.3	100.0	31	57.4	23	42.6	100.0

4.5. Recovery Techniques

The communication breakdown pattern in Figure 2 also identifies several communication recovery techniques. Ernie used an adult apology to return to adult communication. Neil, Stuart, Graham, and Simon used lighthearted replies (humor) to welcome Kevin into the community. Brian commented in a role we might characterize as "meta-parent", calling discussants to order. Brian is the list owner and thus has the authority to enforce rules. His comment in fact also contained an element of humor. Hence, even in this short communication exchange, we can observe humor, adult apology, and call-to-order as three recovery techniques, with humor being the most popular.

5. INTERPRETATION AND CONCLUSIONS

Game playing and the resulting destructive communication is a widespread behavior in many virtual communities, especially if they are end-user managed and therefore without internal power relationships.

Game playing is a behavior independent from the mission of the community, but is driven by individuals' desire to receive emotional satisfaction from "winning" the argument. Game playing appears to result in a reduction of knowledge and information exchange, as much effort is spent on the argument and recovery from it, instead of on valuable exchanges.

Given that the communication is highly patterned, it can be recognized and can be avoided by the participants who are the end-users of the information and communication system. If left alone, game playing can quickly deteriorate the communication to the point of breakdown, can turn active into passive participants, and can lead to defections among former participants.

Much work needs to be done to study this phenomenon in detail. We will need to analyze larger numbers of communications to develop a more comprehensive set of game playing behaviors. We also need to determine the impact of game playing on communication more formally, for example with respect to the loss of knowledge content, or the bandwidth wasted for nonproductive communication. This will allow us to offer more formal conclusions concerning the phenomenon.

6. REFERENCES

Berne, E. *What Do You Say After You Say Hello?*, Grove Press, New York, 1972.

Carver, C. "Building a Virtual Community for a Tele-Learning Environment," *IEEE Communication Magazine*, (37:3), March 1999, pp. 114-118.

Craig, D.L. and Zimring, C. "Supporting collaborative design groups as design communities," *Design Studies* (21:2), 2000, pp. 187-204.

Erickson, T. "Social interaction on the net: Virtual community as participatory genre," *Proceedings of the HICSS-30*, 1997, pp. 13-21.

Hagel, J. and Armstrong, A.G. *Net Gain: Expanding Markets through Virtual Communities*, Harvard Business School Press, Boston, Massachusetts, 1997.

Harris, T.A. *I'm OK - You're OK*, Avon, New York, 1969.

Hesse, B.W. "Curb cuts in the virtual community: Telework and Persons with Disabilities," *Proceedings of the 28th Annual Hawaii International Conference on System Sciences*, 1995, pp. 418-425.

Ho, J., Schraefel, M.C. and Chignell, M. "Towards an Evaluation Methodology for the Development of Research-Oriented Virtual Communities," *Proceedings of the 9th International Workshops on Enabling Technologies: Infrastructure for Collaborative Enterprises*, 2000, pp. 112-117.

Jones, Q. and Rafaeli, S. "Time to Split, Virtually: 'Discourse Architecture' and 'Community Building' as means to Creating Vibrant Virtual Metropolises," *Electronic Markets: International Journal of Electronic Commerce & Business Media* (10:4), 2000, pp. 214-223.

Locke, C., Weinberger, D., Searls, D. and Levine, R. *The Cluetrain Manifesto: The End of Business as Usual*, Persus Publishing, 2001.

Rheingold, H. *The Virtual Community: Homesteading on the Electronic Frontier*, Addison Wesley, London, England, 1993.

Romm, C. and Clarke, R.J. "Virtual Community Research Themes: A Preliminary Draft for A Comprehensive Model," *Proceedings of the 6th Australasian Conference On Information Systems*, Curtin University, Perth, Australia, 1995, pp. 57-70.

Smith, K.C. "How not to get involved in an Internet 'flame' war," *Dermatology Times*, April (23:4), 2002, pp. 58-59.

Organizational Knowledge Management: Enabling a Knowledge Culture

Steven Walczak
University of Colorado at Denver, The Business School
Campus Box 165, PO Box 173364, Denver, CO 80217-3364 USA
swalczak@carbon.cudenver.edu

Dale Zwart
Generation 21 Learning Systems
1536 Cole Boulevard, Suite 250, Golden, CO 80401
dale.zwart@gen21.com

ABSTRACT

Many organizations are realizing the requirement for management of intellectual capital in today's global and information intensive economy. Knowledge management initiatives that are not supported by management or that do not have a knowledge sharing business culture will produce sub-optimal results and may fail altogether. A knowledge sharing culture is created through both management practices and organizational structure. In this article, a "knowledge culture" structure is presented that promotes the sharing, utilization, and creation of knowledge for gaining organizational competitive advantage.

INTRODUCTION

The worldwide economy has shifted from an industrial manufacturing/product oriented economy to one based on knowledge and services, where the principle commodity is information or knowledge. Effective management of intellectual capital is a critical issue facing organizations in today's global and information-driven economy. Knowledge management is not really about managing knowledge, but rather managing and creating a corporate culture that facilitates and encourages the sharing, appropriate utilization, and creation of knowledge that enables a corporate strategic competitive advantage.

The need for developing a "knowledge culture" is obvious for most service organizations (e.g., the product of a consulting firm, such as Accenture, is knowledge). Many service organizations are already performing knowledge management under the name of CRM (Customer Relationship Management), with large customer and product or service databases centered on content management (sharing, distribution, and utilization of knowledge). The need for increased efficiency and productivity produced by the downsizing trends in organizations during the downward trend in the recent economy is emphasizing the need for knowledge management, or a "knowledge culture", in manufacturing and retail industries as well.

Another motivation for examining the knowledge management methodology at an organization is the effect of corporate culture on new strategic initiatives. With the continuing globalization of the economy, organizations are facing increasing pressure to effectively manage their intellectual capital. Organizations that attempt to introduce a knowledge management initiative without having a managerial support structure will soon find that the investment in knowledge management does not produce any perceived benefits (Swan et al., 2000; Zammuto et al., 2000; Zammuto and O'Connor, 1992). Gold et al. (2001) state that organizational structure is an important factor in leveraging technology and more specifically that organizational structures must be flexible to encourage sharing of knowledge and collaboration across traditional organizational boundaries to promote knowledge creation.

Achieving a "knowledge culture" requires managerial focus in three areas: preparing the organization, managing knowledge assets, and leveraging knowledge for competitive advantage (Abell and Oxbrow, 1997). Preparing the organization is the first step in developing a "knowledge culture" and often involves changing the culture of the organization, changing the way employees work and interact. Organizational culture shifts are difficult to accomplish. Smaller organizations, 200 or fewer employees, and newer entrepreneurial organizations will have an advantage in making the prescribed culture shift over larger and older organizations that have a long history of corporate culture and a more rigid managerial structure.

BACKGROUND

Various taxonomies of knowledge and knowledge management exist (see Alavi and Leidner, 2001). For purposes of this article, knowledge is defined as any data, skill, context, or information that enables high quality decision making and problem solving to occur. Knowledge management then is any process (either formal policy or informal personal methods) that facilitates the capture, distribution, creation and application of knowledge for decision making. This decision making may be at the tactical level of day to day operations performed by an employee or at a more strategic level of developing organizational strategy by upper level management and every level of decision making in between. In other words, effective knowledge management makes sure that every employee (at all levels) has access to appropriate and the highest quality of information available at the time when a decision needs to be made. The "knowledge culture" is critical to the success of knowledge management within an organization as it signals a managerial commitment to knowledge management initiatives and promotes sharing of tacit knowledge for higher quality decision making.

Nonaka (1994) defines types of knowledge as tacit or explicit. Tacit knowledge is knowledge that is internal to a person, including cognitive learning, mental models, and technical skills. Explicit knowledge is knowledge that has been encoded into some media external to a person including paper documents, electronic databases and files, and the operating procedures of an enterprise.

Four tacit and explicit knowledge transfer mechanisms are found in organizations: socialization, externalization, internalization, and combination (Nonaka, 1994; Nonaka and Konno, 1998). Socialization is the process of transferring tacit knowledge to another individual who encodes the new knowledge in tacit form. Socialization may be performed informally, such as casual conversations around the coffee machine or lunch table, or more formally as in a mentoring program. Because of the personal nature of tacit to tacit knowledge transfer, traditional hierarchical management schemas do not promote this type of knowledge sharing.

Externalization is the process of encoding tacit knowledge into some explicit format, such as email messages or company correspondences. Internalization is the process of accessing explicit knowledge and then this knowledge is "learned" by the individual and becomes part of their tacit knowledge resources. Internalization necessarily adds context to knowledge as explicit sources such as a large organizational database are accessed and interpreted by an individual. Finally, combination is the translation of explicit knowledge into a new explicit format and may include the addition of new contexts or simply changing the encoding format of the explicit knowledge. All three of externalization, internalization, and combination are facilitated by information technology research, such as wireless computing for distribution of information to facilitate internalization and voice recognition systems that would facilitate externalization of knowledge.

The "knowledge culture", described in the next section, enables flexible management of corporate knowledge assets that will facilitate both explicit and tacit knowledge sharing and utilization and consequently knowledge creation.

A KNOWLEDGE CULTURE MANAGEMENT STRUCTURE

Traditional hierarchical management structures, as displayed in Figure 1, allow vertical knowledge transfer through typical chain-of-command, but inhibit horizontal knowledge transfer that must cross the organization's functional boundaries. The development of knowledge teams composed of knowledge workers from cross-functional areas of the organization is a first step towards developing a fully distributed knowledge transfer system (both vertical and horizontal) within the organization. Cross-functional team members provide knowledge sharing, intended or indirect, from their knowledge team back to their original functional areas.

However, the scope of teams is limited to the organizational problem assigned to the team and results in limited knowledge sharing throughout the organization. The idea of teams and knowledge sharing must be extended to include all aspects of the organization. A knowledge team-based organizational structure is displayed in Figure 2. The knowledge organization of Figure 2 is composed of knowledge groups that are composed of knowledge teams, which are built from knowledge workers selected for participation on a knowledge team due to their tacit knowledge and skills. Ideally, the knowledge workers on any knowledge team come from different organizational (and educational) backgrounds and will bring a diversity of tacit knowledge and skills to the team.

Adoption of a new organizational structure (the "knowledge organization") or managerial methodology ("knowledge culture") faces resistance within the organization. Resistance to change may be minimized by reducing the perception of change for the stakeholders. The knowledge team management structure may be aligned to an existing hierarchical management structure by initially aligning the knowledge groups with the existing functional areas of the organization including: accounting, marketing, production, research. Knowledge teams or intermediate groups of knowledge communities are then aligned with the subdivisions within each functional area.

The recognition of individual personnel as knowledge workers will promote the development of new knowledge teams to address an organization's opportunities and consequently will facilitate the development of knowledge team communities that are diverse and more focused on a knowledge-oriented problem solving. Knowledge workers are expected to share and utilize knowledge with other team members to produce the highest quality decisions. New knowledge teams and groups will develop around product lines or other core competencies of the

Figure 1. Traditional Organization Management Hierarchy (partial).

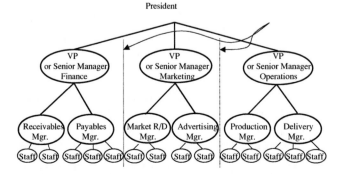

Figure 2. Elements of the Knowledge Organization Hierarchy.

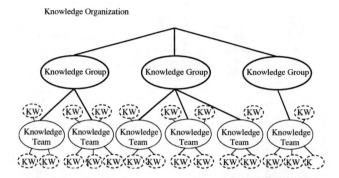

enterprise. Knowledge teams should be created dynamically to take advantage of an organization's business opportunities or new business strategies.

Over time, the idea of an accounting (or other functional) branch of the organization will be replaced by communities of knowledge workers that have knowledge/expertise in accounting and may thus utilize other tacit knowledge to specialize in functional capabilities within a knowledge group. Knowledge teams that identify the need for specific knowledge (e.g., accounting or marketing) would then recruit knowledge workers that had the desired tacit knowledge to join the team (from a dissolving team that has already accomplished it's primary purpose or from a team that did not have a current need for the requested knowledge worker's tacit knowledge).

Knowledge gaps on a knowledge team are identified by performing a knowledge mapping process during team formation and whenever a new knowledge worker is added to the team. Since the knowledge organization is a community of knowledge teams and knowledge groups, the aggregation of knowledge maps for all teams serves as a knowledge map of the organization. The dynamic nature of knowledge teams and the strategic knowledge goal of knowledge creation imply that knowledge maps should continue to be performed every time a new knowledge team is developed to acquire newly created knowledge assets in the aggregated organizational knowledge map.

Motivating Employees To Adopt The "New" Knowledge Culture

Because the role of a knowledge worker may be a new role within the organization's culture, the development of a knowledge culture for sharing, dissemination, and utilization of knowledge will take some time. Motivating the desired knowledge culture and corresponding knowledge sharing behavior is facilitated through evaluating entire knowledge teams as a unit without reverting to individual praise or blame. Those teams that achieve a knowledge community approach to problem solving must be rewarded and acknowledged throughout the new "knowledge organization".

Another motivational strategy for the new knowledge culture may be based on rewarding the development of knowledge that is subsequently utilized by other knowledge workers or knowledge teams. Any knowledge that is externalized into explicit form or combined from one explicit encoding into a more useful format becomes eligible for a knowledge-use award (either monetary or other intangible benefits), but the awards are based on subsequent use of the new explicit knowledge by other knowledge workers. A similar approach can be used to encourage the internalization transfer of new knowledge by rewarding knowledge teams for incorporating explicit and tacit knowledge from other knowledge teams and groups (or even other knowledge workers) into their knowledge team solutions. Wiig (1995) discusses other standard management practices for motivating employees to become knowledge workers. The critical aspect of any motivation strategy with respect to the "knowledge culture" is that knowledge sharing within knowledge teams and across knowledge teams and groups is rewarded, not individual performance (which would lead to knowledge hoarding).

Knowledge Creation And Assessment Within The "Knowledge Culture"

The knowledge organization management structure promotes the development of intellectual capital or knowledge creation in several ways. The "knowledge culture" community of knowledge workers will provide a diverse background of tacit knowledge and the combination of these various knowledge sources into a knowledge team enables the creation of new views, behaviors, ideas, etc. As stated above, knowledge teams are dynamic and should be formed to address specific business opportunities or challenges. Whenever a knowledge worker leaves one knowledge team and joins another, the knowledge worker takes all of the acquired tacit knowledge from the previous team, such as best practices or lessons learned. Consequently, the rotation of knowledge workers into new knowledge teams also serves to propagate the application of appropriate (best) knowledge into new business areas.

A key element of any knowledge management process model is assessment to evaluate the appropriateness or utility of knowledge owned and created (or acquired) by the knowledge organization. The knowledge culture method assumes that all knowledge workers are involved in the assessment process, since each worker utilizes different explicit and tacit knowledge assets. Knowledge workers within a knowledge team or group will provide consensus support for knowledge actions taken by the team and thus provide peer evaluation of all knowledge-based behaviors.

EVALUATING THE "KNOWLEDGE CULTURE"

The best evaluation of the knowledge culture and the knowledge organization management structure is empirical evidence by organizations that have implemented the knowledge organization structure. AES (Applied Energy Services) Corporation founded in 1981 with eight people, became the largest independent power producer in the United States in 1988, currently owns or has investments in 173 facilities in 27 countries worldwide and now employs over 10,000 people. The culture at AES Corporation enables and requires individuals to make decisions and the organizational culture adopts and supports those decisions. Individuals closest to the action make decisions for the corporation (AES, 2000).

A large percentage of AES people are active in new business development (AES, 1997). Decision making by AES's knowledge workers is supported through a team-based approach were team members advise and help educate decision makers with current knowledge (AES, 2000). Through the initial development of a knowledge culture and empowering knowledge workers within a knowledge team framework, AES has achieved continued growth in the power services industry.

Another example, but of a partial knowledge culture, is PRI Automation which produces advanced automation systems and software for the semiconductor industry. One of the core competencies of PRI is customer service. Field service representatives at PRI are the knowledge workers serving on various customer specific or product specific knowledge teams that form the customer support knowledge group. Field service knowledge workers use Palm VII palm PCs and wireless connectivity to access explicitly encoded performance support knowledge. The source of the performance support knowledge is encoded tacit knowledge from other field service knowledge workers and teams.

One of the ROIs that PRI Automation is interested in obtaining from its knowledge management initiatives is improved data accessibility. PRI estimates that malfunctions of its products may cost customers up to $1,000 of lost profit per minute and up to $100,000 per incident. Previously, PRI had relied on service manuals, which were out of date almost as soon as they were printed. By empowering their field service knowledge workers to access critical knowledge when and where it is needed (PRI uses Generation 21's TKM™ system), PRI has reduced typical data access times from 30 minutes to 5 minutes and increased the quality of the knowledge-based problem solving for a potential net ROI of $25,000 per incident (Mabe, 2001).

The PRI Automation case above shows that organizations can achieve competitive advantage through implementation of part of the "knowledge organization" structure. However, the gains from a partial

implementation are still dependent on developing a knowledge culture that is organization wide so that knowledge workers are compelled to utilize appropriate knowledge for decision making. Larger organizations may select to implement knowledge teams within a single functional division or in multiple divisions, but temporarily not aggregate the knowledge teams into knowledge groups. These partial strategies will still result in performance gains if accompanied by the necessary cultural shift that encourages knowledge workers to share and utilize knowledge to improve the quality of their decision making process.

Various metrics may be used to evaluate the impact of the knowledge culture on the organization. Various authors (Edvinsson and Malone, 1997; Sveiby, 1997) discuss the problems of developing metrics for an abstract concept like knowledge, and tying it to organizational performance and suggest the development of intermediate metrics.

Some metrics would depend on the purpose for a knowledge team and the business domain and may include reduced customer service time or product manufacturing/assembly time, and increased customer satisfaction ratings. These metrics are concerned with the knowledge team productivity and the leveraging of knowledge. Metrics that focus on the "knowledge organization" management process will measure the overall effect on the organization through traditional metrics, but should also evaluate the development of tacit intellectual capital in the knowledge workers. Metrics that directly measure potential tacit knowledge increase would include increasing formal training and mentoring program completion, the number of times a knowledge worker can serve as a mentor, and number of successful knowledge teams in which the knowledge worker has participated as a member. Other metrics should seek to gauge knowledge worker satisfaction and would include a knowledge worker turnover metric.

The successes of various metrics in determining the impact of KM on organizational performance are still being evaluated. The metrics described above provide an initial means for measuring the effect of defining and implementing a knowledge culture for the organization, with supporting management structure and motivational strategies.

CONCLUSIONS

A critical issue in adoption of knowledge management initiatives is the preliminary preparation of the organization to accept, adopt, and utilize the new knowledge management process. Preparing an organization for knowledge management initiatives means changing or adapting the organizational culture to facilitate, support, and encourage the sharing, appropriate utilization, and creation of new knowledge. The resulting "knowledge culture" will maximize the competitive advantage realized from any knowledge management process.

The "knowledge organization" management structure, presented in this article, facilitates the development of a "knowledge culture" within an organization by first supporting the decision making of knowledge workers. Secondly by facilitating the exchange of tacit knowledge through interaction in knowledge teams with other knowledge workers (Nonaka and Konno's (1998) socialization process). Horizontal knowledge transfer is also facilitated as knowledge workers migrate to new knowledge teams working on new business opportunities or needs.

Two cases, AES Corporation that has a complete "knowledge culture" and PRI Automation that has implemented knowledge workers and knowledge teams, demonstrate the competitive advantages enabled through a supporting "knowledge culture." Additional recommendations for metrics are given that target the cultural aspects of a knowledge organization by measuring knowledge worker satisfaction and knowledge creation in addition to traditional financial metrics commonly used by organizations to measure organizational performance. Future research is needed to further investigate the relationship between degrees of "knowledge culture" within an organization and organizational performance.

REFERENCES

Abell, A. and Oxbrow, N. (1997), "People Who Make Knowledge Management Work: CKO, CKT, or KT?", in Liebowitz, J. (Ed.), *Knowledge Management Handbook*, CRC Press, Boca Raton, FL, Chapter 4.

AES Corporation. (1997), "Founders Corner", available on-line as of 20 September 2002 at: http://www.aesc.com/culture/founders/fcjuly1997.html.

AES Corporation. (2000), "Potholes in the Road, Part 2", available on-line as of 20 September 2002 at: http://www.aesc.com/culture/founders/fcpotholes02.html.

Alavi, M. and Leidner, D. E. (2001), "Review: Knowledge Management and Knowledge Management Systems: Conceptual Foundations and Research Issues", *MIS Quarterly*, Vol. 25 No. 1, pp. 107-36.

Edvinsson, L. and Malone, M. S. (1997), *Intellectual Capital*, HarperCollins, New York.

Gold, A. H., Malhotra, A. and Segars, A. H. (2001), "Knowledge Management: An Organizational Capabilities Perspective", *Journal of Management Information Systems*, Vol. 18 No. 1, pp. 185-214.

Mabe, C. (2001), "Improved Profitability Through Total Knowledge Management™(TKM™", White paper available from Generation 21 Learning Systems, Golden, CO (www.gen21.com).

Nonaka, I. (1994), "A Dynamic Theory of Organizational Knowledge Creation", *Organization Science*, Vol. 5 No. 1, pp. 14-37.

Nonaka, I. and Konno, N. (1998), "The Concept of "Ba": Building a Foundation for Knowledge Creation", *California Management Review*, Vol. 40 No. 3, pp. 40-54.

Sveiby, K. E. (1997), *The New Organizational Wealth*, Berrett Koehler, San Francisco, CA.

Swan, J., Newell, S. and Robertson, M. (2000), "The diffusions, design, and social shaping of production management information systems in Europe", *Information Technology and People*, Vol. 13 No. 1, pp. 27-45.

Wiig, K. M. (1995), *Knowledge Management Methods*. Schema Press, Arlington, TX.

Zammuto, R. F., Gifford, B. and Goodman, E. A. (2000), "Managerial ideologies, organization culture and the outcomes of innovation: A competing values perspective", in Ashkanasy, N., Wilderom, C. and Peterson, M. (Eds.), *The Handbook of Organizational Culture and Climate*, Sage, Thousand Oaks, CA, pp. 263-80.

Zammuto, R. F. and O'Connor, E. J. (1992), "Gaining advanced manufacturing technology's benefits: The roles of organization design and culture", *Academy of Management Review*, Vol. 17, pp. 701-28.

An XML-based Security Protocol for Semi-Autonomous Agents

Allen Johnston and Merrill Warkentin
Computer Systems Administrator, Management & Information Systems
Engineering Research Center, College of Business & Industry
Mississippi State University, Box 9627, P.O. Box 9581
MS STATE, MS 39762-9627, MS STATE, MS 39762-9581
Phone: (662) 325-4900, Phone: (662) 325-1955
Fax: (662) 325-7692, Fax: (662) 325-8651

ABSTRACT

Future inter-networking environments will be characterized by extensive interactions between multiple servers and their agents. This hyper-interactive environment will expose all parties to significant new risks and liabilities. It will be imperative that intelligent agent behavior be guided by the prescribed intentions of the agent owners who develop and introduce them. The XML-based protocol presented in this paper, if widely adopted by agent developers, provides a practical method for ensuring such compliance. Agents embedded with these protocols will exhibit behavior consistent with the predetermined security position of the owner along several key continua, while still enabling independent autonomous control. A proposal for this XML protocol is presented, along with suggestions for future research.

AGENTS AND MULTI-AGENT SYSTEMS

Modern systems architectures are highly interconnected – the TCP/IP protocol enables nearly all network systems to be inter-operable. In this environment, many organizations are deploying intelligent software agents, which can act on behalf of the agents' owners in various ways (Chan et al., 1999; Gannon, 1998; Grimes, 1998). Agents can automate various activities and act on behalf of their owner in problem solving and decision making activities, repetitive tasks, finding and filtering information, and intelligently summarizing complex data. Just like their human counterparts, intelligent agents have the capability to identify patterns in their environment, to learn from their owners, and even to make recommendations to their owners regarding a particular course of action.

Consideration of the dynamics of an agent-based system requires the recognition of three basic components: external environment, internal environment, and information structure among autonomous agents (Szczerbicki, 1996b). An information structure is formed by the exchange of messages between external and internal agents and facilitates various forms of collaboration among agents (Lashkari et al., 1994). However, communicating agents must share a common syntax and protocol regardless of the origin of the agents.

Multi-agent systems (MAS), and agent communications in particular, lack explicit design regulations. Inherent in the design goals of the Extensible Markup Language (XML) is its extensibility, flexibility and ease of use. Because it is extensible, XML can be applied to a variety of applications for which data do not have a standardized structure. Therefore, XML provides a useful method for creating meaningful semantics that can easily be expressed and understood by software agents (Shiau et al., 2000) during agent communications.

SECURITY CONSIDERATIONS

Early research into security considerations theorized two methods for agent development and trust measurement (Maes, 1994). Applying a semi-autonomous approach to software agent development provides an increased level of trust. However, this method requires a high skill level on behalf of the programmer, as well as a high level of insight of the domain in which the agent will exist. A "knowledge-based approach" would allow the agent to use programmed knowledge to adapt and contribute to an objective. However, this approach provides a lesser degree of trust to the user due to its higher degree of autonomy. Although the intelligent agent can perceive its domain and respond proactively, the manner in which it responds may not be consistent with the security posture desired by the agent deployer.

To facilitate the process of secure agent development, the characteristics of agent information exchange must be identified. The characteristics must be considered in a broad sense because of the dynamic nature of risk identification. Consider the risk associated with an electronic commerce (e-commerce) transaction. Personal information is often required by business entities prior to a sale, service, or license activation. When dealing with the dissemination of personal identity information, a certain amount of risk of identity manipulation can be expected. Additionally, the risk associated with the knowledge of an agent's history is significant. An agent's deployer may not want to provide a history of previous agent destinations or communications. If considered from a "brick and mortar" perspective, a potential customer of an establishment might not want to provide the details of where he or she had shopped prior to this visit. Finally, agent task information provides the details of the operating goals of the agent. This information consists of domain search goals, price strategies, and other product search criteria. This type of information, if intercepted unbeknownst to the deployer, can be used in a manner that negatively impacts the ability of the agent to perform its tasks.

Based upon these risks, three categories of information involved in agent communications are proposed. The categories are Personal Information, Agent and Host Information, and Agent Task Information (see Table 1).

Within each broad category, there are subcategories that contain the actual information objects, or risk objects, such as name, address, and telephone number. Within any particular agent, each instance of such objects may have a current value. This approach is intended to provide flexibility for the addition or deletion of risk objects depending

Table 1. Categorized Agent Information

Personal Information
- Identification data such as name, address, social security number
- Financial data such as credit history, income, account balances
- Medical data such as insurance coverage, medical history
- Legal data such as legal history, parole status

Agent and Host Information
- Agent source address
- Agent destination address history
- Agent communication history with hosts or agents
- Host address
- Host communication history with agents

Agent Task Information
- Agent task goals
- Task data such as host domain goals (.com, .edu, etc.), price considerations

upon their applicability to various domains. The value assigned to a particular risk object represents an agent's desire for relative openness in information exchange. The proposed logic that drives the agent's intelligence will assume a risk object that does not contain a value to be private and not available for disclosure.

SECURITY SOLUTION

One primary goal of any security system implementation is to increase the level of user confidence in the system. XML statements within multi-agent systems can be used as a method for providing a secure structure within which to define security protocols. The protocols, or rule structures developed to dictate the actions of the agents, will derive from insight into the security aspects of agent-to-agent, agent-to-host, and host-to-host communications.

The information exchange that occurs in agent communications can be defined or limited by an established set of protocols that promote the security posture desired by the deploying host. This posture is unique to the mission of the agent and may vary depending on a multitude of circumstances and influences. Examples of agent delimitations based on deployer preference include restricting the range of hosts and agents with which it can interact and limiting the types of information it can retrieve and provide in agent-to-agent or agent-to-host communications. A rule-based system (RBS) approach can be employed to generate a risk assessment conclusion based on tacit knowledge of the risks involved in information exchange. The conclusion can be any action or stance such as to close communications or to proceed with a financial data exchange.

A rule set can be established for risk assessment prior to, and separate from, any knowledge of the specific risk objects defined for an agent. The RBS approach also allows layers of rules to be established, whereby each layer is specific to a particular type of knowledge. This layered approach allows knowledge to be applied in a modular fashion, pseudo-independent from additional layers (Dhar et al., 1997). Following an RBS model, a series of "if-then" statements can be constructed that will comprise the lowest layer. These rules will form the logic necessary to meet a conclusion that accurately reflects the desired security posture of the agent owner based on the risk parameters and values provided by the agent. When an agent, populated with a desired set of risk object-value pairs, encounters another agent or host, the unknown agent or host must be able to provide an adequate set of object-value pairs for rule instantiation. If the communicating party cannot supply the required data for first level rule instantiation, the communication must be aborted.

The required object-value pairs will be determined by either agent or host involved in the communication. This process of evaluating minimum trust requirements is referred to as intent evaluation. An agent must be able to assess the communicating device's intent for information sharing; therefore, rules must be formed to guarantee a break in communications if the situation warrants. Therefore, agents must also be equipped with the necessary logic for negotiating a restricted message exchange, and the message format must be flexible enough to provide agents the ability to vary the amount of information obtained or gathered. Assuming the intent evaluation was successful, an agent must be able to assess the security posture of another agent or host, even if some object-value pairs are unavailable.

In order to implement a rule-based agent messaging architecture, a flexible format for representing risk object-value pairs must be established. The format must allow an interfaced user the opportunity to relate a risk tolerance posture that can be interpreted consistently and correctly. The language of the message must also be flexible enough to allow a user to add or remove risk parameters without disrupting the ability of the agent to communicate with other agents or hosts; therefore, risk object-value pairs will be expressed in XML format. Consider the following example of an XML structured agent design.

```
<?xml version='1.0' encoding='utf=8'?>
<AgentData>
    <Personal>
        <Identification>
```

```
            <Name>John Doe</Name>
            <Address>1 Home Rd.</Address>
            <Email>doe@hostname.org</Email>
            <SSN/>
        </Identification>
        <Financial>
            <Credit>Citibank</Credit>
            <CardNum/>
        </Financial>
    </Personal>
    <Agent>
        <HostIP>192.168.1.1</HostIP>
        <HostName>homepc.domain.net</HostName>
        <History>130.10.1.20</History>
    </Agent>
    <Task>
        <Quantity>2</Quantity>
        <ItemNum>3874490</ItemNum>
<HighPrice>$120.00</HighPrice>
    </Task>
</AgentData>
```

The XML element names are descriptive of their respective contents, and some of the elements are empty. In this case, the logic states that the missing information is withheld intentionally. This knowledge, in conjunction with other element contents, forms a picture of the security posture of the agent deployer.

DISCUSSION AND SUMMARY

In order to ensure that agents can be used by their owners effectively without exposing the owners to undesired risk, it is imperative that agent developers adopt XML-based standards for representing various security attributes and attribute values (Warkentin et al., 2001). Interorganizational systems cannot have a significant impact unless a standard data representation scheme is used for data of mutual value. The true potential of intelligent agents to efficiently exchange information will not be unlocked unless and until there is a common standard for the representation of all product and service attributes which can be easily transferred and interpreted by all economic players across the Internet. An international standardized data representation scheme for product and service attributes would extend the capabilities of agent-based data mining processes, thus further improving the efficiency of all marketspaces throughout the World Wide Web.

REFERENCES

CHAN PK FAN W PRODROMIDIS AL and STOLFO SJ (1999) Distributed Data Mining in Credit Card Fraud Detection. *IEEE Intelligent Systems and their Applications* **14**(6), pp. 67-74.

DHAR V and STEIN R (1997) Seven Methods for Transforming Corporate Data into Business Intelligence.

GANNON T and BRAGGER D (1998) Data Warehousing with Intelligent Agents. *Intelligent Enterprise* **1**(1), pp. 28-37.

GRIMES S (1998) Agents Come in From the Cold. *Database Programming and Design* **11**(4), pp. 48-53.

LASHKARI Y METRAL M and MAES P (1994) Collaborative Interface Agents. *Proceedings of the National Conference on Artificial Intelligence.*

MAES P (1994) Agents that Reduce Work and Information Overload. *Communications of the ACM* **37**, pp 31-40.

MAES P GUTTMAN RH and MOUKAS AG (1999) Agents that Buy and Sell. *Communications of ACM* **42**(3), pp 81-87, 90-91.

SHIAU J RATCHEV M and VALTCHANOV G (2000) Distributed Collaborative Design and Manufacturability Assessment for Extended Enterprise in XML-Based Agent System. *Proceedings of the 9th IEEE International Workshop*, pp 260-265.

SZCZERBICKI E (1996) Signed Directed Graphs and Reasoning for Agents and Multi-Agent Systems. *International Journal of Systems Science* **27**, pp 1009-1015.

WARKENTIN M SUGUMARAN V and BAPNA R (2001) Intelligent Agents for Electronic Commerce: Trends and Future Impact on Business Models and Markets. *Internet Commerce and Software Agents: Cases Technologies and Opportunities*, pp 101-120.

Strategies of Organizational Informatization and the Diffusion of IT

Ruediger Weissbach
Lecturer at the University of Applied Sciences Hamburg
IuK GmbH, Dortmund, Riesenweg 19, D-22119 Hamburg, Germany
fon: +49 – 40 – 715 65 91, fax: + 49 – 40 – 2021 19 775
r.weissbach@sh-home.de

INTRODUCTION

The demand for a *strategic use of IT* is an often heard, but a rarely checked demand. Therefore some aspects should be discussed to get a more realistic view upon the 'strategic use' of IT:
- Which factors do influence the diffusion of IT in number and regarding to the real patterns of usage?
- Does the introduction of new information technology happen in accordance to strategic approaches?

This paper founds on the author's dissertation (Weissbach 2000), which analyzed the diffusion of ISDN (Integrated Services Digital Network) telephony in Germany. The results of the dissertation have been reviewed and refined regarding to some other actual trends.

THEORETICAL BACKGROUND

"Informatization"

A key term in the analysis of the strategic use of IT is the term of *"informatisation"* (Nora & Minc 1979). (The English translation, *The Computerization of Society*, differs a little from the meaning of the original term.) Informatization can be regarded as a new quality of technical rationality (Marwehe 1996) and differs from classical rationalization in overcoming the restraint upon single functions. So the organizational rationalization joins the technical rationalization.

While at first the term was used in a more general context, later it was extended to the level of the individual organization. In this research context, informatization can be defined as the process of the planned and systematical usage of IT penetrating organizational functions.

The Diffusion of IT

Technology *diffusion* means the diffusion of technology in the market. The early discussion about the diffusion of capital goods was dominated by structural aspects like the companies' size or the grade of centralization (Fantapie Altobelli 1990). Later theories focus more upon the actors: In the approach of Kotzbauer (1992), the individually perceived grade of an innovation influences the diffusion of a technology. A medium grade of innovation will be advantageous to get adopted. Rogers (1995) argues for a more dynamical approach and defines diffusion as a process by which an innovation is communicated through certain channels over the time among the members of a social system. As a network technology, the benefits of communication technologies are depending on the quantity of other (linked) users.

The aspect of communication is emphasized in the concept of the so-called *Leitbildern* (leading visions) (Marz / Dierkes 1992). These are paradigms which perform as well an agenda setting function (the leading function) as an imaging function which is establishing a community.

Evidentially, the individual adoption of a new technology influences the adoption by other actors. Professional journals and the direct communication in professional groups are the channels, in which concepts and experiences are discussed and in which the *Leitbilder* are distributed.

Management Strategies and IT

In the first decades of IT development, IT was assessed as a 'simple' technology for rationalization. But since around 1.5 decades management strategies like *Business Process Reengineering* (Hammer & Champy 1994), *Virtual Organizations* (Davidow & Malone 1993) or the paradigms of *electronic / mobile commerce* are basing on the possibilities of IT for organizational and business changes. The paradigms of electronic commerce need by definition completely IT based, integrated business process chains from the suppliers to the customers. According to the new possibilities and the new technological paradigms, the new approaches and strategies have changed the focus towards the categories of *communication* and *knowledge* beside the category of *labor*. So a direct relation between management strategies and the usage of new information technologies could be expected.

DESIGN OF THE STUDY

The study bases on the analysis of 92 case studies. 80 of them are published, 12 case studies base on own interviews. Most of the published case studies were found in management publications, congress proceedings and in marketing brochures of the carrier, the former *Deutsche Bundespost* (now: *Deutsche Telekom*). As a basic assumption, the published case studies were assessed as innovative examples for the usage of the technology. The case studies were analyzed regarding
- the ideas of the usage of ISDN (*Leitbilder*),
- the introduction of the new technology,
- the patterns of the technology's usage,
- the relation between the technological attributes and the organizational structures,
- the relation between the different groups of actors,
- the changes over the time.

The analysis of the hard facts was completed with a qualitative interpretation of the motives with a raw structure, but without a detailed scheme.

The results of the dissertation have been reviewed and refined regarding to actual technological and management trends (hardware: UMTS / WLAN, storage systems; software: CRM, general strategies: electronic commerce / mobile commerce).

INFLUENCING FACTORS ON THE IT INTRODUCTION

Strategy Or Accident?

The analysis of the case studies shows that the concrete process of IT introduction is a more complex process than discussed in the past. The management strategy is the background for the interpretation of the technology, but the strategy does not explain the process sufficiently. Strategic aspects will influence the attitude against a new technology, but the attitude will not take a direct effect on the buying decision.

The concrete process of IT introduction is influenced by
- technological attributes,
- external factors (laws, standards, the diffusion of complementary goods, ...),
- internal factors (organizational culture, economical situation, ...).

The technological quality is important, but not sufficient for the decision for a new IT product. Important supplementary factors are

- the substitution of an old product, which is influenced by the conditions of depreciation,
- breaks in the organization's development, such like acquisitions or new co-operations, and
- the concrete requirement for special technical features (in the case of ISDN: rapid file transfer, especially of image files).

In the buying act, the importance of technological attributes falls back behind the individual situation, like existing technologies, depreciation, leasing contracts, the concurrence of other projects, the compatibility to existing business processes and the personnel situation.

Also we have to consider, that an organization's strategy is not homogenous. The different (groups of) actors in an organization may have different aims, and the strategy of the technical management might differ from the strategy of the financial management or the production management. Therefore the process of informatization is reflecting the divergent strategies of the different groups in the management. These strategies can change over the process of technology introduction. "The strategy" as a single, unified strategy is a myth!

The Relationship Between Management Strategies And Technology Strategies

A direct dependence of technology strategies from business strategies should be expected, but this is an exception. An (abstract) management paradigm doesn't determine concrete decisions about IT. Even the paradigm of e-commerce is not coupled with obligatory products, only with standards. On the other side, concrete IT products can be related to various management strategies. An infrastructure technology can be set in relation to several management strategies.

The strategies of informatization are oscillating between actual business strategies on the one side and technical and economical constraints on the other side.

This weak relation between technology strategies and business strategies must be seen in a correlation with the life-cycles of IT and of management strategies. The introduction of new technologies and the substitution of old technologies in the market lasts over a longer period, often longer than a decade. So the longer the life-cycle of an (information) technology, the higher is the probability that management strategies will change over the time. Early concepts like the usage of ISDN as a LAN technology were superseded over the technology's life cycle. The possibility of a variable interpretation regarding to different management strategies allows a long-lasting modernity.

Technology Driven Implementation Versus Organizational Driven Implementation

The phrase 'organization before technology' is a 'tradition' in change management. But a technology driven implementation of information systems can catalyze new experiences and can enable innovative processes, if the implementation phase will be used for learning. So a multi-step implementation of a new technology is a common practice: In the first step, a new product will be introduced to solve a concrete problem. This problem could be for example a removal, a replacement purchase (after the end of a maintenance contract or because of higher maintenance costs for the older product) or a special new requirement. The usage patterns are often conventional. In later steps, more innovative features can be introduced.

In the case of ISDN, this technology was used at first as a replacement for older PBX (with lower maintenance costs) and for data transfer between the headquarter and branch offices respectively between suppliers and customers. Innovative applications like telephone conferencing or integrated multi media applications like the simultaneous transfer of speech and images have been the trigger for the implementation of ISDN only in a few cases.

In some business branches companies in a central function forces the diffusion of ISDN in this sector. Sometimes these companies offer special services, just like technology support or consulting.

Originality, Prototypes And Templates

In the ISDN introduction process, we see some specific qualities of the several business branches, according to specific business processes. Technology suppliers publish and offer approved solutions for specific use cases. These technical and organizational solutions will be templates for implementation processes. So a certain standardization of solutions will progress.

CONCLUSION

The results of this study show, that the processes of the ISDN implementation are complex processes which are strongly influenced by organizations' individual aspects. General management strategies have only little influence on concrete decisions and implementation processes. They will set up an interpretation and restraint frame, which has to be filled individually for each organization, but supported by common visions.

Normative approaches are not adequate to describe the real processes of informatization and technology diffusion, neither on a macro level nor on the level of individual organizations. In reality, these processes are more complex and must be analyzed with a background which reflects technological, economical and organizational factors over the life cycle of the technology.

As a consequence for the actors, the IT suppliers have to offer strategies for a 'smooth' transformation into new 'IT landscapes'. Technological compatibility in combination with migration checklists, experienced consultants and system experts are an efficient way to increase the acceptance of a new product or a new technology. Approved solutions could be published and will influence the further discussion and deciding processes.

The customers' management has to solve the problem of deciding on long-range investments without transparency about the future management strategies. So there exist two effective strategies for the customers' IT management:

(1) Introducing information systems requiring a short-range amortization. This strategy doesn't reflect potential developments, but sometimes it will be economically necessary. Typically the usage of the systems is conventional, but the technology can be the base for later developments.

(2) Introducing information systems with a special view on a flexible usage as a 'service' for different management strategies and for an innovative use of the technology. This strategy requires a high level of business skills in the information systems management and needs a close integration of business and technology management strategies.

REFERENCES

(The following list contains only the most important references.)

Davidow, W. & Malone, M. (1993). Das virtuelle Unternehmen. Frankfurt (M.) / NYC: Campus

Davidson, E. (2000). The Metaphorical Implications of Data Warehousing. In: S. Clarke & B. Lehaney (Eds.), Human Centered Methods in Information Systems: Current Research and Practice (pp. 159-174)

Fantapié Altobelli, C. (1990). Die Diffusion neuer Kommunikationstechniken in der Bundesrepublik Deutschland. Heidelberg: Physica

Hammer, M. & Champy, J. (1994). Business Reengineering. Frankfurt (M.) / NYC: Campus

Kotzbauer, N. (1992). Erfolgsfaktoren neuer Produkte. Frankfurt (M.): Peter Lang

Marwehe, F. (1996). Informatisierung von Organisationen. Dortmund: BWV

Marz, L. & Dierkes, M. (1992). Leitbildprägung und Leitbildgestaltung. Berlin: WZB

Nora, S. & Minc, A. (1979). Die Informatisierung der Gesellschaft. Frankfurt (M.) / NYC: Campus

Rogers, E. (1995). Diffusion of Innovations. NYC

Weissbach, R. (2000). Strategien betrieblicher Informatisierung und die Diffusion von ISDN. Dortmund: IuK

Business Website Design: Some Emerging Standards for Developers

Carmine Sellitto and Andrew Wenn
School of Information Systems
Victoria University of Technology
PO Box 14428 MCMC, Melbourne, Victoria, 8001, Australia
carmine.sellitto @vu.edu.au, andrew.wenn@vu.edu.au

Design is done for a reason, and if you do it well your business will prosper. If you do it poorly, people will leave your website.

Jakob Nielsen, *internet.au*, October 2002

INTRODUCTION

There can be little doubt that an increasing amount of business is being done on the internet. The websites that are at the center of this new way of thinking and working are a constantly growing and evolving entity. It is also clear that a website must evolve with time to reflect the changing needs of the organisation it represents and the organisation's user community. Websites that have been designed appropriately will have a definitive edge in attracting users in the emergent trend of electronic commerce (Fisher, 1999). Forresters Research has found that simplicity in website design is of paramount importance in that it contributes to successful website use (Cavanagh, 1999) and simple web design has been advocated as the differentiator between a successful and unsuccessful website (internet.au, 2002; Nielsen, 2000).

Website design is also an evolving practice (Sellitto & Wenn, 2000). Whilst Brody (1996) suggests that good design should aim at making information visible and manageable – good design needs constant redesign. Appropriate web design should utilise information as its currency with interface design being a vehicle for conveying that information.

In an earlier paper, we proposed some standards that encompassed issues associated with accessibility, proper encoding and metadata inclusion (Wenn & Sellitto, 2001). This paper examines some of the less technical features of website development focusing on issues associated with the visual and information design aspects of websites. These issues generally have a higher degree of subjectivity – they include the areas of information quality, effective information visualisation and presentation design.

EVALUATING AND PROMOTING INFORMATION QUALITY

The Web is a valuable resource for people seeking information, however because information on the Web is subject to change, up-grade and alteration it is difficult to assess for quality and accuracy (Sellitto, 2001a). Traditionally, many information publications such as books, journals, manuscripts have been required to meet an editorial review process before being printed which has assisted in implementing a quality control mechanism. However, with the proliferation of the World Wide Web, this review process can be circumvented allowing individuals to easily publish on-line (Sellitto, 2002). Consequently, issues associated with information quality become important for all web developers.

Not all web information is created equally and some web information is more valuable than others. Web information quality can be gauged by factors such as value, reliability, currency, content and source (Davenport, 1997; Sellitto, 2002). The quality of on-line information is thus integral to web design. Poor quality of information can be considered to be a reflection on web design.

The library community has historically evaluated information quality in the traditional print media using criteria such as content, purpose, scope, currency and cost (Gordon-Murnane, 1999). When it comes to evaluating web information, the library community has provided numerous suggestions for establishing criteria for determining on-line information quality. In addition to this list, Phillips from UC Berkeley suggests that there if there are links to external sites then an evaluation of these links should be provided (Phillips, 1998). A *critical thinking* approach to web information evaluation has been suggested by Grassian (1998), where sources of the information form the primary criteria for information validity.

The Grassian list of assessment criteria includes:
- Content and Evaluation— Who does the site represent? Is the information based on research or scholarly undertakings? Are references available?
- Source and Date— Who is the author and what expertise do they have? When was the web page produced, updated, revised and authorised?
- Structure— Is the structure and presentation style of the information consistent with the discipline that it represents?

Another methodology for evaluating on-line information is based on applying a series of questions to an informational web page (Alexander & Tate, 1999). Each affirmative response to a question posed about the information would suggest the information is of a high quality (high scores equate with high quality information).

Alexander and Tate identify five criteria on which to evaluate and score for information quality:
- Authority— Can the author of the information be identified? Is there a telephone number or postal address stated? Is there copyright or disclaimer?
- Accuracy— Can the information be collaborated in other sources? Are there referees listed for further investigation?
- Currency— Are there dates indicating when the web page was first created, updated and/or revised? Is the information current?
- Objectivity— Is the information provided as a public source (.gov or .org URL inclusion)? Is the information free of advertising? If advertising exists is it related to the information content?
- Coverage— Is the information complete? Is the information part of a larger piece of work?

Berkman (1998) provides a business perspective to on-line information evaluation. The assessment criteria he suggests addresses business requirements for using information to gain market advantage and strategic position. Berkman's checklist for assessing the quality of business resources includes measures such as how searchable the information is, timeliness, how frequently updated and information storage. The assumption is that such assessment is applied to sources after they have been found to be credible. Davenport (1997), on the other hand, identifies information and knowledge as being integral to an organisation and suggests some six categories for assessing information— accuracy, timeliness, accessibility, engagement, applicability and rarity.

The following set of good practice guidelines for evaluating and promoting information quality can be proposed:

Achieving information authority and currency
- Display the company or an author's name on all web pages
- A date of the last web page modification or revision should be always displayed
- A contact email AND either a telephone number and/or postal address needs to be provided

Meeting Information Accuracy
- References and sources should be provided when factual or corporate information is listed
- If linking to other sites the provide a brief assessment of each link

Addressing information structure
- The information should be presented in the style that the websites visitor community would be accustomed

INFORMATION PRESENTATION ASPECTS OF WEB DESIGN

Standards that relate to the visual and presentation aspects of web design are not clearly defined. Numerous authors (Nielsen, 2000; Norman, 1998; Schneidermann, 1999) advocate the practice of simplicity and elegance in web page design to convey the greatest amount of information to the user. The success of a website is not solely reliant on the implementation of technical standards considering that a site with numerous encoding errors and/or poor accessibility adaptation can be very successful (Sellitto & Wenn, 2000).

Good design for human interface interaction can be achieved by using an uncluttered screen layout, this in turn encourages the fluid delivery of information (Brody, 1996). Fuccella and Pizzolato (1999) suggest that a well designed website needs to incorporate a successful fusion of important web entities and elements including— navigation, graphics, content and interface layout. Lynch and Horton (1999) further indicate that important characteristics of website and web page design needs to address aspects of navigation, interface design, graphics and multimedia. Small and Amone (1999) argue that motivational aspects of a website are important design features which encourages users to be 'sticky' and keep coming back. Thus it appears that some of the important issues that good web design practice should address and encompass are website navigation, graphics and images and information presentation and display. These are discussed in the following section.

Website Navigation

On-line navigation is not easy. Users can arrive at a web page from numerous points ranging from links that are internal to a site, a source external to the site or a search engine listing. Consequently, some key questions that users find themselves asking (Powell, 2000) are:
- Where am I?
- Where can I go to next?
- Have I been there before?
- Can I get home from here?
- How did I get here?

Users do not see some web page links because they are not evident, thus links must be clearly designated to remove uncertainty on the part of users. To instil a sense of control when moving about a site, navigation cues should be provided on each page of a website (Nielsen, 2000). Research has shown that when users were given visual cues to locate links, as opposed to using the pointer to search for links, they were able to find the information seven times faster (Bailey, Koyani, & Nall, 2000).

Appropriate navigation cues can be easily achieved by simple and elegant menu bars located at the top or bottom of a page. It has been found that important links and information needs to be positioned higher

on a web page (Bailey et al., 2000). This will allow users to move *through* a website with some sense of control and not have the feeling of being lost. Websites that have deeply nested pages should provide a means of letting a user know where they are located which can easily be achieved by using a visual trail (for example a breadcrumb trail) or a hierarchical map (Nielsen, 2000).

Unvisited links need to be blue and underlined and users should not be required to move the mouse to determine where links are on a page (Lynch & Horton, 1999; Nielsen, 2000). It has become a standard to show visited links as purple, allowing website visitor to see where they have been, and it is good practice to distinguish between internally directed links and links that point to a different website (Spool, Scanlon, Schroeder, Snyder, & DeAngelo, 1997). Spool and colleagues further suggest that because users can be slowed down when they are confronted with similar looking links that it is appropriate that links be descriptively labelled so that users can discriminate between them. A text link is more favourable to a graphic link considering that graphics take longer to download and do not change colour after being selected (Bailey et al., 2000).

A corporate logo is a form of identity (branding) and may also serve as a sub-conscience navigational aid for users (O'Brien, 2000). Users have a sense of location which allows them to confirm where they are— have I left the site? The logo also serves as a reinforcement of the quality of information that may be found on the page— this is a reputable organisation, the information is likely to be truthful. A logo can also be used as a navigational aid which allows a user return to the HOME page— I can go back to the corporate HOME if I get lost. Links that lead to dead ends (the dreaded "error 404. The page cannot be displayed") are a consequence of poor web page maintenance a concept that Nielsen (2000) refers to as *linkrot*.

Links should always be active or be removed to reduce user frustration and the back button should not be relied upon as the primary source of assistance in returning to previous pages.

Information Architecture

Information architecture refers to the way that information is effectively and successfully presented on a web page (Davenport, 1997; Wurman, 1996). Aspects of displaying information online include the positioning and presentation of text on the screen, page scrolling, text size, font variation, margins and white space (Schriver, 1997).

Positioning dark text on a white background appears to increase the legibility of text when compared to other combinations of background colour and text (Spencer, 1969). Schriver (1997) indicates that keeping within the same font family enhances on-line legibility and that no more than two different font types should be used for on-line presentation.

Reading practices in the Western world are orchestrated around a left to right and up-down prospective. Web page design should attempt to mimic the vertical prospective that the human eye is accustomed to when reading text (Lynch & Horton, 1999). Thus, horizontal scrolling of a page is counter to normal visual reading behaviour and is not a good design practice. This also highlights another important issue, the role of culture in information presentation and the need to consider the prospective audience.

Sentence length is also important and can be a significant factor in influencing reading rate, however it appears that comprehension is unaffected by line length (Dyson & Kipping, 1999). It has been shown that users find it difficult to read edge to edge on a screen and that readers experience eye strain, and have difficulty discerning the start of new lines – more often loosing their point of reference (Schriver, 1997). Thus, text on web pages should occupy a central location and should be sufficiently indented to prevent text running edge to edge. Horton (1994) advocates that the optimum length of screen line length should be no more than 40 characters and line lengths of less than 20 characters have been found to affect the visual and spatial association between words leading to a reduction in legibility. Dyson and Kipping's (1999) research suggests that line lengths of about 100 characters are read faster than shorter lines, however the longer line length is more difficult to read. These authors advocate 55 characters per line as optimum web page line length.

Because reading from an electronic screen is slower and more tiring than reading text on paper, sentence length and reduced word counts on a web page have led to people scanning for key words in order to find relevant information (Nielsen, 2000). Morkes and Nielsen (1997) observed that people scan text on the screen moving to deeper levels of the information content as they require. A consequence of this *scanning and drill-down* behaviour is that many users do not like long pages. For instance Black (1997, p. 53) states that 75% of people only ever read the top of a web page and never scroll. Web page content should be such so as to increase in volume as one navigates *into* the website. Hierarchical navigation should be utilised with each tier encountered containing more information as users seek out further resources about a particular area of interest (Nielsen, 2000). Users should be able to move from page to page by selecting links (paging) without always scrolling to important information. This is particularly true for home pages and menu pages where users fail to scroll past the first page when they reach a site unless the information is relevant and useful— thus, page scroll should be kept to a minimum (Dyson & Kipping, 1999).

Web Page Download

Excessive download times is problem that has been encountered by web users for many years and shows little sign of diminishing (Nah, 2000). Several studies indicate that fast web page download is the definitive feature that determines the success of a website and that users will not wait more than 10 seconds for a page to download using a 28.8kbps modem (Nielsen, 2000; Pockley, 1998; Spool et al., 1997). Others suggest that it is not unreasonable to expect a page to load in less than 8 seconds with a 56kbps modem (O'Brien, 2000). Graphics, artwork and images constitute the web page components that determine the relative speed of page delivery. A web page that includes a large number of graphic files will take a relatively long time to download to reach a user. In a restrictive bandwidth environment, where many users operate with modem speeds of no greater than 28kbps even though they have a 56kb modem— file size becomes critical for fast download. Consequently good web design should aim at building web pages that will download sufficiently fast enough to meet the expectations of the majority of users of that website.

Good Practice Recommendations for Presenting Web Information

Navigation
- All links must be coloured blue and underlined; visited links should be purple
- All links need to be active (avoid *linkrot*)
- It is preferable to use text rather than image links
- All web pages must have some form of navigation cue
- Position important links higher up on web pages
- Deeply nested hierarchical sites should let users know their location by using, for example, a bread crumb trail
- Each page should allow the visitor to return to the Home page

Information Architecture
- Use a dark text on a white or lighter background
- No more than two different font types should be used.
- In pages aimed at a Western culture audience use a left to right and vertical perspective in page layout
- Text on web pages should occupy a central location
- Line length should be between 40-60 characters
- Keep page scroll to a minimum (1-2 pages)
- Horizontal scrolling of pages should be avoided

Web Page Download
- Balance download time against the value of information content.
- Aim at download times of no more than 10 seconds with a 28kbps modem and 8 seconds with a 56kbps connection.

CONCLUSION

This paper has discussed and proposed some good practice guidelines for website design and development that need to be part of the skill set that e-commerce builders need to acquire or at least have awareness. The web design features discusses are the more subjective features associated with web design and hence are more prone to being inadvertently misunderstood and misused by developers. This paper is a starting point for discussion of an important and critical area of website development that is often ignored or poorly explained. Good web design practices are constantly evolving and are by no means complete. Future website interface design will need to address issues associated with the next generation of e-commerce applications – for example the use of the PDA, mobile telephones, Web TV and other Internet devices for delivering e-commerce services (See for example Holzschlag, 2000).

BIBLIOGRAPHY

Alexander, J., & Tate, M. A. (1999). *Checklist for an Informational Web Page, Wolfgram Memorial Library Information Gateway.* Retrieved 30/3/2002, from Available: http://www2.widener.edu/Wolfgram-Memorial-Library/webevaluation/inform.htm

Bailey, R. W., Koyani, S., & Nall, J. (2000). *Usability Testing of Several Health Information Web Sites: Technical Report*: US National Cancer Institute.

Berkman, R. I. (1998). *Finding Business Research on the Internet: A Guide to the Web's Most Valuable Resources.* New York: Find/SVP.

Black, R. (1997). *Web Sites that Work.* San Jose, CA.: Adobe Press.

Brody, F. (1996). Interactive Design: State of the Art and Future Developments: An Argument for Information Design. In N. Brody (Ed.), *Multimedia Graphics* (pp. pp. 16-19). London: Thames & Hudson.

Cavanagh, L. (1999). Web Secrets: Learning From Past Successes: Seybold Report on Internet Publishing. *Desktop, 138,* p. 64-66.

Davenport, T. H. (1997). *Information Ecology: Mastering the Information and Knowledge Environment.* New York: Oxford University Press.

Dyson, M. C., & Kipping, G. J. (1999). *An Experimental Investigation on the Effect of Line Length and Number of Columns on Reading Performance.* Retrieved 31/3/2002, from Available: http://www.rdg.ac.uk/AcaDepts/lt/main/resea/fund/proj/line.html

Fisher, J. (1999). Trading Electronically: it really does matter who designs your website. In S. Lee (Ed.), *Preparing for the Global Economy of the New Millennium: Proceedings of the Pan Pacific Conference XVI, May 31-June 2* (pp. 202-214). Suva, Fiji: Pan Pacific Business Association.

Fuccella, J., & Pizzolato, J. (1999). *Internetworking: Separating Content from Visuals in Web Site Design*: Internet Technical Group: Sandia Corporation.

Gordon-Murnane, L. (1999). Evaluating Net Evaluators. *Searcher, 7*(2), p. 57.

Grassian, E. (1998). *Thinking Critically About World Wide Web Resources.* Retrieved 30/3/2002, from Available: http://www.library.ucla.edu/libraries/college/instruct/web/critical.htm

Holzschlag, M. E. (2000). I Want My WebTV. *Web Techniques, 5*(3), 34-37.

Horton, W. (1994). *Designing and Writing On-line Documentation: Hypermedia for Self Supporting Products.* New York: Wiley.

internet.au. (2002). Interview: Jakob Nielsen. *internet.au*(84), 26-28.

Lynch, P. J., & Horton, S. (1999). *Web Style Guide.* Boston: Yale University Press.

Morkes, J., & Nielson, J. (1997). *Concise, Scannable and Objective: How to Write for the Web.* Retrieved 31/3/2002, 2002, from [Available] http://www.useit.com/papers/webwriting/writing.html

Nah, F. H. (2000, 21-25 May 2000). *A Study of Web Users' Waiting Time.* Paper presented at the Proceedings of the 11th Information Resources Management Association (IRMA) International Conference, Alaska, USA.

Nielsen, J. (2000). *Designing Web Usability: The Practice of Simplicity.* New York: New Riders Publishing.

Norman, D. A. (1998). *The Invisible Computer*. Boston: MIT Press.

O'Brien, T. (2000). *E-commerce Handbook: A Practical Guide to Successful e-business Strategy*. Melbourne: Tri-Obi Productions.

Phillips, M. (1998, March 2001). *Critical Evaluation of Resources*. Retrieved 27 September 2002, 2002, from http://www.lib.berkeley.edu/TeachingLib/Guides/Evaluation.html

Pockley, S. (1998). *RMIT Web Site Review*. Melbourne: RMIT.

Powell, T. A. (2000). *Web Design: the complete reference*. Berkeley: Osborne/McGraw-Hill.

Schneidermann, B. (1999). *Readings in Information Visualisation: Using Vision to Think*. New York: Morgan Kaufmann.

Schriver, K. A. (1997). *Dynamics in Document Design: Creating Text for Readers*. New York: John Wiley & Sons.

Sellitto, C. (2001a, 20-24 May 2001). *Evaluation of the Quality of Medical Information on the Web: An Overview of the Current Assessment Frameworks*. Paper presented at the Proceedings of the 12th Information Resources Management Association (IRMA) International Conference, Toronto, Canada.

Sellitto, C. (2002). The Quality of Medical Information on the Internet: Some Current Evaluation Frameworks. In A. Armoni (Ed.), *Effective Healthcare Information Systems* (pp. p. 1091-1095). Hershey, PA: IRM press.

Sellitto, C., & Wenn, A. (2000, 30 November - 1 December 2000). *Web Site Design: Emerging Standards for Business*. Paper presented at the Proceedings of the 1st Working for e-Business Conference: Challenge for the New Economy, Perth, Western Australia.

Small, R. V., & Arnone, M. P. (1999). Evaluating Web Resources With Young Children: Information Literacy New Instructional Models. *Library Talk, 12*(3), p. 14.

Spencer, H. (1969). *The Visible Word* (2nd ed.). New York: Hosting House.

Spool, J. M., Scanlon, T., Schroeder, W., Snyder, C., & DeAngelo, T. (1997). *Web Site Usability: A Designer's Guide*. North Andover, MA: User Interface Engineering.

Wenn, A., & Sellitto, C. (2001). Emerging Technical Standards: towards an identification of the skills sets needed by website developers. In A. Wenn (Ed.), *Skill Sets for the E-commerce Professional: Proceedings of SSECP 2001* (pp. 101-110). Melbourne: Victoria University of Technology.

Wurman, R. S. (1996). *Information Architects*. New York: Graphics Press.

Do IT Professionals Think Differently?

Hongjiang Xu
Business Information Systems Department
Central Michigan University
Mt. Pleasant MI 48858, USA
Hongjiang.Xu@cmich.edu

Latif Al-Hakim
Faculty of Business
University of Southern Queensland
Toowoomba 4350, Australia
Hakim@usq.edu.au

INTRODUCTION

Data and information are among an organization's most valuable assets (Klein 1998, Shanks & Darke 1998). Quality comprises not only the safety and availability of the organization's data, but also the reliability and the accuracy of the information (Huang, Lee & Wang 1999, Madnick, Wang & Zhang 2002). There is much evidence to show that information quality problems are common in real world practice (Huang et al 1999, Redman 1998). There are research focus on what skills are important in making sure data quality (Chung, Fisher &Wang 2002) and how to assess the quality of data (Pipino, Lee & Wang 2002). The aim of this paper is to examine whether the IT professional in various organizations have different focus in data quality.

The paper considers three Australian case large organizations. The cases are a federal government department, a government funded research institution that have many divisions across Australia, and a higher educational institution. Table 1 provides an overview of the three case organisations. It includes a description for each organisation which includes the number of employees, the annual revenue, total assets, and the number of accounting information systems staff.

THE INTERVIEWS

Representatives from five stakeholder groups were interviewed from each organization two groups from IT professionals and three groups from various management levels. Table 2 summarises the case study respondents who were the different stakeholder groups interviewed in the three cases. The table gives details of participants, their posi-

tions/ work roles, their organisations, and the stakeholder group they belong to. It shows also the number of officers interviewed.

A set of twenty success important factors (Xu & Al-Hakim, 2002) was derived. Systematic analysis was then employed to determine the categories to which those factors belong. The study derives these factors from three sets of sources: data characteristics factors; industry factors and organizational factors. The first includes the nature of information system and data quality policies and standards. The second set comprises stakeholder related factors. The third set covers organization culture, performance evaluation and team work as shown in Table 3.

CASE A

Both IT and business professionals consider the commitment of top management is extremely important while the nature of the accounting information system is considered unimportant factor for the data quality. However, it was found that IT professionals were more concerned about systems and technical issues. They seemed to have confidence about the newer technology, and have greater trust in the systems' abilities to produce high quality information. Even when they were considering organisational issues, they still related those issues to the systems. IT professionals seemed to be more systems-orientated.

On the other hand, business professionals were more concerned about the human related factors' impact on information quality, such as communications and staff turnover. Even when they were talking about systems issues, their focus was still from the human perspective, rather than the technological perspective. They believed that people's understanding of systems would impact on the quality of the information which systems produced.

IT Professionals believe that the usage and the usefulness of the information have an impact on the information quality. The IT manager noted:

> One of the problems is it isn't fully used, and hopefully it should improve the quality of your data after you re-use its code. But on the other hand, you have a system that is being used by a lot of people, and therefore, all the bugs should have been found in it.

The IT manager emphasised that *human errors* had much more impact on accounting information quality than *system failure*.

Table 1. Overview of Case Organisations

	Description	Number of employees	Annual revenue ($'000)	Total assets ($'000)	Number of AIS staff
A	Federal Government department	2,500	16,000	300,000	100
B	Government funded research institution	6,400	800,000	1,300,000	300
C	Higher educational institution	1,200	98,000	139,000	50

Table 2. Summary of Case Study Interviews.

Profession	Stakeholder	Organizations		
		A	B	D
IT Professionals	Information custodians	IT manager	IT manager	IT manager
	Data / database managers	Data manager and Data Administrator (DA)	Database Administrator (DBA)	DA
Business Professionals	Information producers	Financial system manager	System accountant manager	Accountant and Payroll Officer
	Information consumers	Business Senior manager	Senior manager	Two Section Managers
	Internal auditors	Internal auditor	Internal auditor	Internal auditor
Number of Interviewees		6	5	7

Table 3. Classification of the Success Factors

Category	IS / DQ Characteristics	Stakeholders' Related Factors	Organisational Factors
Factors	Nature of the IS	Top management's commitment	Training
	DQ policies & standards	User focus	Org structure & culture
	DQ controls & approaches	Employee relations	Performance evaluation & rewards
	Role of DQ and DQ manager	Information supplier quality management	Manage change
	Internal control	Audit and reviews	Evaluate cost/benefit tradeoffs
	Input control		Teamwork (communication)
	Understanding of the systems and DQ		
	Continuous improvement		

From one area, a lot of data quality is affected by how accurately the information is entered into the system by business users of system. Well, the systems get more complex. However, a well designed system, old or new, should be able to accommodate.

Communication within the organisation was perceived by business professionals to be an issue that might cause data quality problems. The Senior Manager of the organisation stated:

I think when you find things aren't going well in an organisation; it always comes back to the same problem. It is communication. Everybody complains of not knowing what is going on, not being told the right things.

However, it appears that the nature of some people, as they were reluctant to disclose information that they had. As the information producer stated:

Well, that is the case. If you know something that someone else doesn't, then you are in a stronger position.

CASE B

While IT people thought systems controls were more important, accounting professionals thought differently. Accountants tended to believe that human process controls were more important than system controls. They believed that human related factors had much more influence on accounting information quality. They argued that although IT people could build in many controls into systems, at the end of the day it still relied on people to enforce those rules and controls. Furthermore, there were some human related factors that the computer could not control.

From the viewpoint of business professionals, Case B had issues of under-reasoning for education and training because, as stated by the System Accountant Manager; *"it is not just how to use the system, but you need to incorporate policies and procedures and best practices"*.

However, the IT manager believed that organisations have to implement new systems because technology had changed and so had business needs. He stated:

At the moment we are actually doing a review, talking to all of our finance people in our divisions. It is a business needs review to see if the system we have now is meeting our requirements. So we will either decide whether to stay with it or to change to something else.

The answer of Case B Internal Editor was that:

If there is change, I guess everyone has to be on board with the change, or at least know what their responsibilities are and what they need to do. So things need to be well-planned and well-documented, so that if we just suddenly change everything and there hasn't been enough thought about what procedures need to change, it will cause serous problems.

CASE C

The analysis of Case C reveals that there is consistency in the viewpoints of IT professionals. Unlike other cases, IT professionals tended to have the same viewpoints of the business professionals in regard to internal control and continuous improvement and team work and communications. Top management was regarded as one of most important critical factor by both IT and business professional. This is consistent with the findings of cases A and B.

CONCLUSION

The two main conclusions regarding the IT professional perceptions are:
1. There is a great emphasis on the 'input control' and the 'nature of the

Table 4. *Stakeholders Rating of the Importance of the Factors (Case C)*

Category	Factors	Stakeholders Info producer	Info custodian	Info user	DBA	Auditor	Mean
AIS characteristics	Nature of the AIS	7	9	5	7	5	6.6
DQ characteristics	DQ policies & standards	9	9	9.5	2	8	7.5
	DQ controls & approaches	7	9	8	9	8	8.2
	DQ vision	10	8	5	6	6	7
	Internal control	9	10	10	3	9	8.2
	Input control	9	9	9	9	8	8.8
	Understanding of the systems and DQ	8	9	9	9	8	8.6
	Continuous improvement	6	9	9	7	7	7.6
Stakeholders' related factors	Top management's commitment	8	9	9	8	9	8.6
	DQ manager	3	?	?	7	?	5
	User focus	7	8.5	8	8	1	6.5
	Employee relations	7	10	9	8	7	8.2
	Information supplier quality management	10	7	9.5	8	5	7.9
	Audit and reviews	6	9.5	9	3	6	6.7
Organisational factors	Training	9	10	9.5	9	9	9.3
	Org structure	5	7	8	4	6	6
	Org culture				8		8
	Performance evaluation & rewards	10	7	8	5	5	7
	Manage change	10	10	9	8	7	8.8
	Evaluate cost/benefit tradeoffs	10	6	9	7	6	7.6
	Teamwork (communication)	10	10	9	8	6	8.6
Overall		8	8.55	8.33	6.63	6.55	7.54

Legend: 1, 2, 3 ... = Rating of the importance {1 as not important at all, 10 as extremely important}
? = The stakeholder wasn't sure / clear about the factor
Blank = the stakeholder did not rate the factor or the factor wasn't included

IS' by the IT professional. IT professional's perception about the importance of 'internal control' is relatively low. Business professionals tended to believe that human related factors have much more influence on the quality of IS.
2. 'Team work' and 'personnel competency' are other factors that did not rated very high by the IT professionals. However, the respondents' perception in regard to the effect of 'measurement and reporting' and 'continuous improvement' for insuring the data quality of "IS" is comparatively low.

REFERENCES

Chung, W. Y., Fisher, C. & Wang, R. Y. 2002, 'What skills matter in data quality?', *Proceeding of the Seventh International Conference on Information Quality*, November, pp. 331-342.

Huang, Huan-Tsae, Lee, Y. W. & Wang, R. Y. 1999, *Quality information and knowledge*, Prentice Hall PTR.

Klein, B. D. 1998, 'Data quality in the practice of consumer product management: Evidence from the Field', *Data Quality*, Vol. 4, no. 1, September.

Madnick, S., Wang, R. & Zhang W. 2002, 'A framework for corporate Hoseholding', *Proceedings of the Seventh International Conference on Information Quality*, November, pp. 36-46.

Pipino, L., Lee, Y. & Wang, R. Y. 2002, 'Data quality assessment', *Communications of the ACM*, April, pp. 221-218.

Redman, T. C. 1998, 'The impact of poor data quality on the typical enterprise', *Communications of the ACM*, February vol. 41, no. 2.

Shanks, G. & Darke, P. 1998,' Understanding data quality in data warehousing *A semiotic approach*', *Proceeding of the 1998 Conference on Information Quality*, Boston, Massachusetts, October.

Xu, H., & Al-Hakim, L. 2002, 'Accounting information systems data quality: A critical success factors approach', *In Issues & Trends of Information Technology Management in Contemporary Organisations*, Khosrow-Pour, (ed.), Idea Group Publishing, Hershey, PA. pp1144-1146.

Knowledge Discovery Process from Sales Data

Katsutoshi Yada
Faculty of Commerce, Kansai University
Yamatecho, Suita, Osaka, 564-8680 Japan,
Email: yada@ipcku.kansai-u.ac.jp
Tel&Fax: +81-6-6368-1121

ABSTRACT

This paper describes the framework of knowledge discovery process in sales data and how the active mining system is applied to the data in the real business world by using the domain knowledge. First the framework of the knowledge discovery process in database is reviewed. It is not clear how users construct actual data mining process and use the domain knowledge in the existing model. We propose two-dimensional matrix of knowledge for sales data analysis to understand knowledge discovery process from purchase history. We distinguish data mining process from creation of business action. We point out that efficient knowledge discovery can be achieved by intensively introducing domain knowledge of experts to the creation of business action.

1. INTRODUCTION

With the propagation of information technology typically represented by Internet, enormous amount of data can be accumulated, and there are now strong interests among researchers and businessmen on the study of data mining (Hamuro, 1998). Despite of the efforts of the analyzers, the knowledge cannot be effectively discovered very often. In Japan, many companies have also been studying the introduction of data mining system, and effective management of business process by data mining is considered to be very important in future.

In cooperative research and study with many firms, we have successfully discovered useful knowledge by data mining (Hamuro, 2001; Ip, 2000; Ip, 2002). In the present article, we try to elucidate the process of knowledge discovery from sales data and to construct a process model for efficient data mining based on these experiences. In the conventional process model, steps of typical data processing are expressed, and it gives no clear explanation as to which kind of knowledge it is converted in the analyzing process or how the domain knowledge should be introduced. By the use of "two-dimensional matrix for type of knowledge", we clearly identify the type of knowledge to be converted in the data mining process and the route of the conversion. We also assert that business action is created from interaction between tacit knowledge and explicit knowledge of the data analyzers and the marketing staffs and that domain knowledge should be efficiently introduced to discovery process.

2. REVIEW OF THE EXISTING STUDIES

Here, we will review the existing studies on knowledge discovery process. The problems in the framework of conventional knowledge discovery process are pointed out, and we will clearly define the primary aim of the present article.

2.1 Framework of Knowledge Discovery Process

Matheus et al. (1993) explained a model of the entire system and its elements along the knowledge discovery process. As major domains, they cited acquisition of data, processing, extraction of pattern, expression of knowledge, and evaluation.

In a narrow sense, data mining is a process to extract patterns between data. In this case, important elements are expression of knowledge, criteria for evaluation, and development of algorithm. The exist-

ing study on knowledge discovery process (Valdes-Perez, 1999) puts emphasis on the interaction between the analyzer and the system. The analyzer utilizes knowledge base currently existing in and out of the system such as the analysis in the past or opinions of experts and extracts useful and beneficial rules. In the knowledge discovery in reality, it is important how human action can intervene into the knowledge discovery process (Langrey, 1998), and it is asserted that we must be definitely conscious about the utilization of the introduction of domain knowledge.

Here, we will review the study of Fayyad et al. (1996) on the knowledge discovery process (Fig. 1). According to their study, the starting point of the knowledge discovery is to define the ultimate purpose and to understand the application area and related domain knowledge. Then the data sets necessary for the discovery are accurately defined, and various attribute groups are prepared (preparation of target data). Normally, such data include a plenty of noises, abnormal values, and defective values, and it is a pre-process of these data under a certain rule. Important attributes are estimated and selected from the advance analysis, and the adjusted data set is prepared. By collating these data with the purpose of analysis, the most adequate data mining algorithm is selected. Or, is it a regression model? These problems must be clearly recognized and due consideration must be given on the characteristics of the data set used, and the most appropriate method is selected. And a pattern really interesting is extracted.

The pattern discovered from the above steps is offered to the person concerned in charge of evaluation. Up to the time when useful meaning will be found, the procedure is turned back to the preceding step, and try-and-error attempt is repeated.

2.2 Problems in the Existing Studies

The framework of conventional knowledge discovery process does not give useful suggestion almost at all for the data mining of the business field (Yada, 2002). Basically, the above model is a general model relating to knowledge discovery, and it is difficult to give sufficient suggestion to a specific problem such as purchase data analysis for the customer.

The following two points are the most important: First, what is really converted in the knowledge discovery process is the part of data with the meaning called "information" or "knowledge". In the process model as given above, it is the part where only data processing is handled.

Figure 1: The existing framework of knowledge discovery process

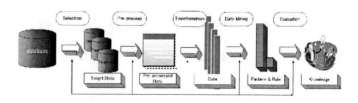

The knowledge discovery processing is a process where a wide variety of information and knowledge are integrated and are converted to new knowledge (Cowan and Foray, 1997; Tell, 1997). Nevertheless, it is not elucidated what kind of knowledge it is or how it is converted. In the course of knowledge discovery process, we must indicate the route of concrete knowledge conversion and efficiently carry out the discovery process.

The second problem can be summarized as follows: In all of the existing models, it is suggested that the introduction of domain knowledge is indispensable for the discovery of useful knowledge, but none of these models clearly indicate how the domain knowledge should be introduced in reality. Typically, there are many models, which advocate the introduction of domain knowledge to all processes. However, this is practically impossible. It is difficult to obtain suggestion as to at which stage the introduction of domain knowledge leads to more efficient knowledge discovery. For the purpose of efficiently discovering useful knowledge, we must present accurate definite strategy on how the introduction of domain knowledge is to be utilized in the knowledge discovery process.

In the present article, a framework is presented, by which the type of knowledge to be discovered can be classified, and the positioning of analysis to be carried out in the knowledge discovery process is defined. By the use of this framework, it is possible to understand how the discovery process is advanced and also to offer the directivity (principle) of the analysis. Then, a strategy is presented as to how the data of domain knowledge can be used in the knowledge discovery process for the purpose of efficiently utilizing valuable domain knowledge inside and outside of the company.

3. KNOWLEDGE DISCOVERY PROCESS FROM SALES DATA

The purpose of this paper is to develop a framework for giving guidelines for knowledge discovery process useful in the analysis of purchase history of the customers such as POS data with ID. In order to increase the effectiveness of the knowledge discovery process, discussion will be made on how the domain knowledge is introduced.

3.1 Two-dimensional Matrix of Knowledge Type Extracted from Purchase History

To evaluate the knowledge discovery process, we focused the attention, not on data processing, but on the meaning of data to be processed and converted, i.e. on information and knowledge.

The data to be processed in the knowledge discovery process from purchase history and the type of knowledge to be discovered can be easily understood if these are expressed in two-dimensional matrix as shown in Fig. 2. The first dimension is the dimension of analysis level. The analysis level ranges from macro-level such as the entire market to micro-level at the position of customers. In actual analysis, the data can be classified according to these levels.

The analysis of the extreme macro-level is the analysis relating to the entire market such as market share, transition of sale, etc. In the

Figure 2: Two-dimensional matrix of knowledge type

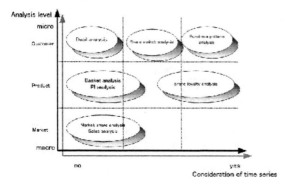

more detailed level, basket analysis, brand switch analysis (Berry and Linoff, 1997), etc. are included as the analysis of commodity level. Further, in the analysis of customer level, detailed analysis is conducted such as transition analysis (decil analysis) on the amount of sales proceeds for each customer and purchase pattern analysis (Woolf, 1993; Hawkins, 1999).

The second dimension relates to how to handle the time series data in the contents of analysis. In typical POS data with ID, lines of receipts of the customer are accumulated in time series, and purchase behavior of the customer can be identified for a considerably long period. The second viewpoint is how far the changes of situation over the course of time should be considered by the use of these time series data in the analysis.

In a typical POS analysis, the accumulated time series data are converged together and sales proceeds (e.g. sales proceeds for each commodity) are calculated. In such type of analysis, time series data are not effectively utilized almost at all. On the other hand, as the analysis for effectively utilizing the detailed time series data, there are analyses with more emphasis on the changes over time: the analysis of the changes before and after business action, i.e. verification of sales promotion effects such as coupon sale, or an analysis of purchase pattern for long period (Hamuro, 2001).

3.2 Knowledge Discovery Process and Creation of Business Action

1) Knowledge Discovery Process

In any of the cases, the analysis of purchase history is started from left lower portion of the matrix. That is, to acquire basic knowledge of the entire market, it is carried out from basic analysis such as analysis of brand share, total sales amount, etc. In these analyses, the analyzer gives no consideration on the changes over time. The time series data are put together and the tendency in the market is identified. Then, it is turned to the analysis with the time taken into account such as expansion of the entire market, transition of sale of each individual commodity, etc.

Next, as the analyses of commodity level, more detailed analysis of PI (purchase index) value per number of commodities sold or basket analysis is conducted. The former is the calculation of sales proceeds per 1,000 customers who visited the store, and this is also used for the comparison of selling powers of commodities between the stores with different scale. Basket analysis is an analysis to define the characteristics of the commodities purchased at the same time. Many of these analyses are analyses for each commodity in a certain fixed period, and much consideration is not given on time base in most cases. Also, brand loyalty analysis is an analysis to elucidate loyalty and commitment of a consumer to commodity for long period. The change of situations due to time is taken into account in this analysis.

The analysis on the extreme micro-level and complicated analysis based on sales data is an analysis with attention focused on behavior of the customers. For instance, decil analysis is an analysis for customer management. In this analysis, the customers are divided to 10 groups depending on sales amount for each customer in a certain fixed period, and the results are utilized for identification and management of excellent customers for the store. In addition, there are brand switch analysis or purchase pattern analysis for the customers in long period using time series data.

As described above, typical knowledge discovery process is started from the simplest basic analysis on left lower portion of the matrix, and it is advanced to the analysis of customer level by taking more detailed and complicated time base into consideration. Naturally, it is needless to say that the more it is advanced toward time series analysis of the customer level on right upper portion, the higher technical ability and analyzing ability are required. However, it depends on the purpose of project, budget, duration of the project and strategy of the firm as to up to which step the analyses should be performed in the process. Useful knowledge for execution of business action is acquired from a part or all of these processes. Useful knowledge is not necessarily discovered from the detailed analysis. However, in a typical analytical process, the most detailed analysis is performed, and the results of all analyses are evaluated one after another, and the usefulness of the knowledge is evaluated from the viewpoint of the execution of the business action. If the knowledge is not acquired from these processes, the viewpoint must be changed, and it should be started again from new basic analysis.

2) Knowledge Discovery and Creation of Business Action

Next, we will discuss the knowledge in business and the knowledge creating process. In Western Epistemology, knowledge is considered as "a justified true belief", and attention is focused on explicit knowledge (Nonaka and Takeuchi, 1995). The knowledge handled in existing and our researches relates only to the explicit knowledge. Is it really possible to explain knowledge discovery only from the explicit knowledge?

We believe that it is difficult to explain all of the processes to discover new knowledge using only the explicit knowledge. In the knowledge, there is also tacit knowledge (Polanyi, 1995), which cannot be expressed by words and is difficult to transfer to the other person. New knowledge is born not only from the integration of the explicit knowledge but also from interaction between tacit knowledge and explicit knowledge (Nonaka, 1994; Yada, 1998). In organizational knowledge creating process, Nonaka (1995) defined the process of "socialization", by which two or more people have tacit knowledge in common, and the process of "externalization", by which an individual converts the tacit knowledge shared in common to explicit knowledge and demonstrated that new innovation is developed from the interaction process between explicit knowledge and tacit knowledge in individuals and organizations. In the conventional process model, due consideration is not given to such interaction of knowledge.

We consider that the knowledge expressed by two-dimensional matrix as given above is entirely different from the new business action. The knowledge expressed by 2-dimensional matrix is produced by the existing analytical method or it is born through integration of these knowledge. However, business action is not automatically born from these knowledge. An expert of marketing, who interprets the meaning from these knowledge and who has sufficient tacit knowledge on the market, gives birth to the business action as a new idea. Therefore, we propose a model shown in Fig. 3 as the knowledge discovery process including the new business action.

We do not believe that useful patterns and rules obtained from the data are automatically converted to business action. First, in a field where a data analyzer and an expert (on marketing) commonly share the context of analysis results, tacit knowledge acquired in the data mining process is shared in common. This is what Nonaka (1995) called a process of socialization. Next, a person in charge of marketing integrates this with the accumulated experiences, and it is transferred to the process of externalization where new business action is developed. Business action is not automatically given by the data mining system. The patterns and the rules obtained are fused with the existing knowledge, i.e. it is born from interaction of explicit knowledge and tacit knowledge.

3) Introduction of Domain Knowledge

As pointed out in many studies, the introduction of domain knowledge is indispensable for the discovery of the knowledge useful for business. Many of the existing studies recommend that the domain knowledge should be introduced in all steps of the knowledge discovery process, but this is not very efficient and not very practical. Therefore, for the purpose of efficiently introducing domain knowledge of the person in charge of marketing in the knowledge discovery process, it appears to be essential to concentrate the efforts from the scene of internalization to the step of externalization for the creation of business action. We have been making it possible to achieve efficient knowledge discovery by limiting the introduction of domain knowledge to the interpretation of rules, to common sharing of the context of analysis, and to creation of business action.

In order to efficiently introduce domain knowledge, the expert must use the expression easily understandable – in other words, the rules, which can create "a clue" for the new business. In some cases, even when the accuracy of model may be low, suggestion valuable for the marketer may be offered. Osawa (2001) expressed this phenomenon by a concept of "chance discovery" and performed a study from multilateral approaches. In order to introduce domain knowledge more efficiently, a study of "chance discovery" based not only on the extraction of rules but also on the development of business action has important meaning. In future, the application of this type of study to the field of business may offer big business chance.

4. CONCLUSION

In the past, there has been only a framework as general theory for the model of knowledge discovery process, and it has been difficult to give important suggestion to the knowledge discovery in reality. In this paper, we presented a framework with focus on the change of knowledge type in the knowledge discovery process in the data mining from purchase history data. The knowledge discovery process in reality can be understood as the conversion of knowledge on 2-dimensional matrix expressed by analysis level and time base. It is important to distinguish the knowledge obtained from analysis from business action. We pointed out that it is effective to evaluate the patterns and the rules thus obtained and to introduce domain knowledge in the step to create business action.

However, we did not discuss fully on the analysis of the process to create the business action to be actually constructed. In particular, the externalized business action must be integrated well with the existing explicit knowledge. In the present study, we did not deal with the process of combination to full extent. This remains to be the subject of our study in future.

REFERENCES

Berry, M.J.A, and Linoff, G., Data Mining Techniques: For Marketing, Sales, and Customer Support, John Wiley & Sons, 1997.

Cowan, R. and Foray, D., "The Economics of Codification and the Diffusion of Knowledge," Industrial and Corporate Change, Vol. 6 No. 3, pp.595-622, 1997.

Fayyad, U., Piatetsky-Shapiro, G., and Smyth, P. "From Data Mining to Knowledge Discovery in Databases," AI Magazine 17, pp.1-34, 1996.

Hamuro, Y., Katoh, N., Matsuda, N., and Yada, K., "Mining Pharmacy Data Helps to Make Profits," Data Mining and Knowledge Discovery, Vol. 2 Issue 4, pp.391-398, December 1998.

Hamuro, Y., Katoh, N. and Yada, K., "Discovering association strength among brand loyalties from purchase history," Proc. 2001 IEEE International Symp. on Industrial Electronics, pp.114-117, Pusan June 2001.

Hawkins, G. E.. Building the Customer Specific Retail Enterprise, Breezy Heights Publishing, 1999.

Ip, E., Yada, K., Hamuro, Y., and Katoh, N., "A Data Mining System for Managing Customer Relationship," Proceedings of the 2000 Americas Conference on Information Systems, pp.101-105, August 2000.

Ip, E., Johnson, J., Yada, K., Hamuro, Y., Katoh, N. and Cheung, S., "A Neural Network Application to Identify High-Value Customer for a Large Retail Store in Japan," Neural Networks in Business: Techniques and Applications, Idea Group Publishing, 2002, pp.55-69.

Figure 3: Knowledge discovery and creation of business action

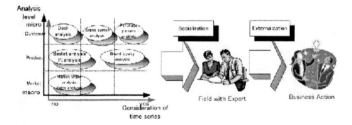

Langley, P. "The Computer-aided Discovery of Scientific Knowledge, Proc. 1st International Conference on Discovery Science (Lecture Notes in Artificial Intelligence 1532), Springer-Verlag, pp.25-39, 1998.

Matheus, C. J., Chan, P. K., and Piatetsky-Shapiro, G. "Systems for Knowledge Discovery in Databases," IEEE Transaction on Knowledge and Data Engineering, Vol.5, pp.903-913, 1993.

Nonaka, I., "Dynamic Theory of Organizational Knowledge Creation," Organization Science, Vol. 5 No. 1, pp. 14-37, 1994.

Nonaka, I. and Takeuchi, H., The Knowledge-Creating Company, Oxford University Press, 1995.

Osawa, Y., "The Scope of Chance Discovery," New Frontiers in Artificial Intelligence, LNAI 2253, pp.413, 2001.

Polanyi, M., Personal Knowledge –Towards a Post-Critical Philosophy, Routledge and Kegan Paul, 1962.

Tell, F., Knowledge and Justification –Exploring the Knowledge Based Firm, Linkoping University, 1997.

Valdes-Perez, R. E. "Principles of Human Computer Collaboration for Knowledge Discovery," Artificial Intelligence 107, pp.335-346, 1999.

Woolf, B. P., Customer Specific Marketing, Teal Books, 1993.

Yada, K., Katoh, N., Hamuro, Y., and Matsuda, Y., "Customer Profiling Makes Profits: How did a Japanese firm achieve competitive advantage through the knowledge creation?" Proceedings of The Practical Application of Knowledge Management 98, The Practical Application Company, pp.57-66, March 1998.

Yada, K., "The Future Direction of Active Mining in the Business World," Frontiers in Artificial Intelligence and Applications, Vol.79, IOS Press, pp.239-245, 2002.

Incremental Indexing and Its Evaluation for Full Text Search

Hiroshi Yamamoto, Seishiro Ohmi, Hiroshi Tsuji
Hitachi, Ltd.
3-8,Kitakyuhozi-cho 3-chome, Chuo-ku, Osaka, 541-0057 Japan
Tel: 81-6-6281-8331(Direct), Fax: 81-6-6281-8390
yamamohi@itg.hitachi.co.jp

1. INTRODUCTION

N-gram indexing method is the most popular algorithm for the Japanese full text search system where each index consists of serial N characters [1][2]. N-gram based indices can be made in the system. For the English full text search system, indices are based on a word that consists of N-gram (N characters). For the Japanese full text search system, indices are not based on a word but a gram (a character) [3][4][6][7]. In general, the system has 2-gram index in order to save the volumes of index file while there are many words that consists of more than three serial characters and some serial two characters are meaningless from the view of search terms[3][8]. In short, 2-gram can be uniformly used on indices are extracted from the target document for full text search. The advantage of N-gram indexing method is to avoid false drops in the full text search system because indices are uniformly based on 2-grams that are extracted from target documents. On the other hand, the disadvantage is less efficient of searching because the index that can be often used in searching is created with the same method as the index that cannot be often used. In short, the index that can be often used in searching equally based on 2-grams the same as the index that cannot be often used in searching.

In order to improve the performance of 2-gram based test search system, this paper presents supplemental indexing algorithm, called **incremental word indexing method**. Basic idea under this research is that words used frequently in search terms should be indexed.

With incremental word indexing method, indices that are based on words used frequently in search terms should be added to uniformly 2-gram based indices. So this method can maintain the advantage to avoid false drops. This method can improve the performance searching with using supplemental indices that consist of **words**, without using uniformly 2-gram based indices. Consequently if we can specify the word used in search terms, the performance of searching can be improved efficiently.

The summery of the **incremental word indexing method** is following. About the word that is frequently used in search terms, indices should be based on a word or n-gram (n is more than two). The word that is frequently used in search terms means 'the word that is frequently used in search condition'. With using the above-mentioned supplemental indices those length are shorter than 2-gram based indices, we can improve the performance for searching.

Fig.1 shows the outline **incremental word indexing method**. When we search with the Japanese word "Sei-Butsu-Gaku" in case of N-gram indexing method, the both of the 2-gram "Sei-Butsu" based index and the 2-gram "Butsu-Gaku" based index must be referred. On the other hand, in case of **incremental word indexing method**, the only word "Sei-Butsu-Gaku" based index must be used, if the word "Sei-Butsu-Gaku" is defined to be frequently used in search terms. The length of the word "Sei-Butsu-Gaku" based index is much shorter than the amount both of the length of the 2-gram "Sei-Butsu" based index and the 2-gram "Butsu-Gaku" based index. So the searching performance with incremental word indexing method is better than N-gram indexing method based on 2-gram. But generally the total capacity of the indices with incremental word indexing method is larger than with N-gram indexing method based on 2-gram, because the indices based on the word that is frequently used in the search terms should be added to 2-gram based indices with incremental word indexing method.

Then there is a problem: what kinds of words should be indexed and how does it improve the performance? This paper shows the experimental simulation for the variety of retrieval patterns and the guideline for system optimization.

2. TARGET OF INCREMENTAL INDEXING EVALUATION

The searching method is one of the most important factors of the document management system and the knowledge management system. Moreover the searching methods for the above-mentioned system need to be efficient. Under these circumstances, it is important to obtain how to use the incremental indexing system appropriately.

First of all we know there is tradeoff: if the many words are incrementally indexed, the performance becomes better but the index file becomes larger. Second we know Zipf's law: if the distinct words in some sample texts are arranged in decreasing frequency order and rank orders are assigned, then the frequency of occurrence of the r-th words in frequency order multiplied by rank r is approximately constant.

These imply that there are an appropriate number of words for the incremental word indexing. Our target is to clarify the guideline to optimize followings for the Japanese full text search with incremental word indices.

(a) The relationship between the pattern for the frequency of occurrence in search terms and the pattern for the incremental word index
(b) The performance (searching time) and system resources (memory and capacity of indices) on each condition of (a)

Let us estimate the time (T) for searching and the capacity (C) of indices with the following two values as parameters for our evaluation:

(i) The number (M) of words for incremental index those are added to the basic 2-gram index

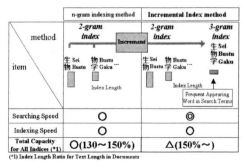

■Supplemental indexing for the frequent appearing word in search terms

item \ method	n-gram indexing method		Incremental Index method		
	2-gram index	Increment	2-gram index	→	3-gram index
Searching Speed	○			◎	
Indexing Speed	○			○	
Total Capacity for All Indices (*1)	○(130～150%)			△(150%～)	

(*1) Index Length Ratio for Text Length in Documents

Fig.1 Incremental Indexing Method

(ii) The appearing ratio of the word in the search terms in the search transaction with incremental word indices

Our experimental simulation uses the newspaper articles for one year. It is expected that the analysis for the simulation result shows the number and the kind of the word used with incremental indexing in a suitable direction. It is also expected that the sensitive analysis for the parameters suggest the suitable guideline to estimate the search execution time and the index capacity.

For example, with using results of this analysis, it can be expected to take the following approach.

- In case that the appearing ratio of the word in the search terms is XX in the searching system, and if the average time for searching is YY as the needed condition, it is clarified that the total capacity of indices need to be AA and the pattern for the incremental word index need to be BB.
- In case that the appearing ratio of the word in the search terms is XX in the searching system, and if the pattern for the incremental word index is WW and the total capacity of indices is ZZ, it is clarified that the average time for searching must be CC.

3. EVALUATION FOR INCREMENTAL WORDS INDEXING METHOD

Our simulation for above-mentioned our target are followings.
(1) The environmental conditions for our simulation are followings.
   (a) Search Engine: Windows2000 platform Bibliotheca21 (made by Hitachi),
   (b) Database: One hundred thousands articles (About 200MB),
   (c) Machine Environment:
      OS: Windows2000 Professional /CPU: 250MHz/ Real Memory: 256MB,
   (d) Search Execution: ten thousands executions per index pattern per search pattern as follows with searching trace log for the analysis,
   (e) Indices: Not incremental word index; incremental 3-gram based index; about the word used frequently in search terms, incremental index is based on 3-gram; for example, when we search with the Japanese word "Kei-Zai-Haku-Syo", incremental indices for searching are based on 3-gram "Kei-Zai-Haku" and "Zai-Haku-Syo",

(2) Words for incremental indexing are extracted as follows:
   (a) Extract all words that consist of more than three serial characters from database,
   (b) Select M words from all N words extracted. (M=0, 100, 500, 1000).
   (c) On this simulation, we select M (M=1000) words about an "economy" as frequent appeared in search terms. Incremental 3-gram based indices correspond to M (M=0,100,500,1000) words can be added to basic 2-gram indices. Table 1 shows all the pattern of indices on this simulation. (Each index consists of incremental 3-gram based indices and basic 2-gram indices.

Table.1 All the pattern of indices

Index Pattern	Structure for Full-text Search Indices	
	Basic Index (2gram)	Incremental Index (3gram)
Index Pattern 0	2gram Index for 100,000 paper articles	None
Index Pattern 1	2gram Index for 100,000 paper articles	3gram index for frequency of top 100
Index Pattern 2	2gram Index for 100,000 paper articles	3gram index for frequency of top 500
Index Pattern 3	2gram Index for 100,000 paper articles	3gram index for frequency of top 1000

Table.2 Search patterns

Case (Search Patterns)	Frequency of top 1000 words (%)			
	Top 100	101~500	501~1000	Others
Case 1	100	0	0	0
Case 2	50	50	0	0
Case 3	34	33	33	0
Case 4	70	20	10	0

(3) Simulation cases are shown in Table 2.

On each case in Table 2, with the index pattern shown in Table 1, the total capacity of all indices and the average, maximum and dispersion of execution time with search execution for 100,000 paper articles can be obtained.

(4) We will analyze the tendency for the search execution time on following conditions.

This simulation shows the guideline and condition for the high performance searching depends on the value for indices capacity and the searching execution time for each search pattern.

(i) On condition that each pattern of indices in Table.1 are used for searching;
   If the number (M) of words that is defined to be frequently appeared in search terms can be 0,100,500 or 1000 (M=0,100,500or1000), incremental 3-gram based indices are added to be created depend upon the number (M) of words appeared frequently in search terms.
(ii) On condition that each search pattern in Table 2,
   On condition that the appearing ratio of the word in the search terms can be changed, the average searching execution time is depend on each condition.

The above-mentioned simulation is on going, the result of analysis can be obtained until the middle of February 2003.

4. EXTENDED ANALYSIS FOR INCREMENTAL INDEXING
The followings are complemented experimentation plan:
(1) Extension for search patterns and indices patterns,
(2) Depend upon the tendency of the result of this simulation, We increase the number of the frequent appearing word, and refine the kind of the word in search terms,
(3) Document database in other domain such as patents and technical documents,
(4) Relationship between term frequency and document frequency,
(5) The number of the target document for searching.

5. CONCLUSION
On search performance, the incremental word indexing supplements simple n-gram indexing for Japanese full text search system. As side effect, the supplemental algorithm adds the volume of index file. Trend analysis in our research will show the guideline for full text search system design.

REFERENCES
[1] Shannon, Claude E., "Prediction and Entropy of Printed English", Bell Systems Technical Journal, 30, 50-64. (1950)
[2] Marc Damashek. Gauging Similarity with N-Grams: Language-

Independent Categorization of Text. Science, Vol.267, pp.843-848, 10 February 1995.

[3] Sugaya, N et al., A full-text search system for large Japanese text basis using n-gram indexing method, *proc. 53rd Annual Convention IPS Japan*, 5T-2, 3(1996)

[4] Hosono, K., Current State of Research and Development on Digital Libraries in Japan, 2nd IFLA General Conference - Conference Proceedings - August 25-31, 1996

[5] Sato, T., *et al.*, NTCIR-2 Experiments Using Long Gram Based Indices, Osaka Kyoiku University

[6] Matsui, K., Namba, I., Igata, N., Hi-speed Fulltext Search Engine, IPSJ SIGNotes Contents Digital Document No.007,1997

[7] Ogawa, Y. and Iwasaki, M., A new character-based indexing method using frequency data for Japanese documents, In Proc. 18th ACM SIGIR Conf., pp. 121—129 (1995).

[8] Kawashimo, S., et al. Development of full text search system Bibliotheca/TS (in japanese). In Proc. of 45th JIPS Conf. (3), pp. 241-242, 1992.

Indexing by Conditional Association Semantics

Xiaowei Yan, Chengqi Zhang, Shichao Zhang, and Zhenxing Qin
Faculty of Information Technology
University of Technology, Sydney
PO Box 123, Broadway, Sydney NSW 2007, Australia
Tel: +61-2-9514 4534, Fax: +61-2-9514 4535
{xyan,chengqi,zhangsc}@it.uts.edu.au

ABSTRACT

Prevailing information retrieval methods are based on either term similarity or latent semantics. Terms are considered independently. This paper presents a new strategy for information retrieval, i.e., indexing by conditional association semantics. *In our approach, the conditional association semantics of terms will be considered during semantics indexing.*

1. INTRODUCTION

Data on the WWW are usually structureless, dynamical, undisciplined, uncertain, and enormous. A large number of information sources, with their different levels of accessibility, reliability and associated costs, present us with a complex problem of information gathering. On the other hand, search engines often return many thousands, even millions of results in response to a user query. It would be difficult for a user to browse so much information searched. In particular, it is an important challenge to identify which pieces of the information are really useful to the user. Therefore, there have been many intelligence-based methods for information gathering (or information filtering) from the WWW proposed in recent literature [3-6].

To reduce irrelevant information searched, this paper presents a new strategy for information retrieval, named as indexing by conditional association semantics. Conditional association semantics is a relationship among terms of a document and a query. We begin with giving the problem statement and some related work in Section 2. Then a synthesizing model by weighting is presented in Section 3. In Section 4, a relative synthesizing model for association rules from unknown data sources is described. In Section 5, we conclude this paper.

2. PROBLEM STATEMENT

Generally, a user query can be described by using natural language, keywords, or a database query language [5]. The simplest form of a user's query is a list of one or more keywords. Experienced users may state their queries in an appropriate form to get what they want. However, there are still many inexperienced users. A typical user does not have the aptitude of using Boolean logic statements. The user is not often an expert in the area that is being searched. He may lack the domain-specific vocabulary, and usually start searching with a general concept of the information required.

A limited knowledge of both the specific vocabulary in a particular area and what is exactly needed leads to the uses of inaccurate and misleading search terms. Even when the user is an expert in the area, the ability to select the proper search terms is constrained by lack of knowledge of the author's vocabulary. Each writer has his own vocabulary formed by his life experiences, environment where he grew up, and ability to express himself. Thus, an information retrieval system should provide tools to overcome the search specification problems discussed above, and automatically assist a user for developing a search specification that represents both the need of the user and the writing style of the

authors. The searched information should be relevant to the user's query. However, there is often too much information related to a user query, for a user to browse.

Because information gathering plays a very important role, many researchers are delving into this area. A typical approach is to design a search engine. In the current market, search engines mainly fall into three types, keyword-based search engines, meta-search engines, and FAQ-based search engines. Most of current search engines are keyword-based, such as Yahoo and MSN. These engines accept a keyword-based query from a user and search in one or more index databases. They usually have huge databases of web sites that can be searched by inputting some text. Search engines index their information by sending out spiders or robots, which follow links from web sites and index all pages they come across. Each search engine has its own formula for indexing pages. Some index the whole site, while others index only the main page. Despite its simplicity, these engines typically return many thousands, even millions of sites in response to a simple keyword query, which often makes it impossible for a user to find the required information. For example, when we searched for "how to write a grant proposal", Google returned 366,000 sites, Yahoo returned 581,000 pages, and AltaVista returned 64,165 pages. The overloading is certainly a key problem for these search engines. Also, if you look at the first 50 pages from each search engine, the ranking is quite different due to the different ranking formulae. What we observe is that different search engines are good at different queries.

Based on the above analysis, the problem for our research can be formulated as follows. For a set of data sources from the Web, we are interested in *reducing irrelevant information by conditional association semantics*.

3. SIMILARITY MEASURES BY ASSOCIATION SEMANTICS

Let D be the set of terms in a given document, and Q be the set of terms in a query. There are two prevailing methods. One is based on terms of similarity, and another is based on latent semantics. Terms are considered independently in these models. In fact, all terms in D (or Q) have association semantics. In general, for any S the subset of D (or Q), and x in S, there is a semantics set of x, given S. This association semantics of terms should be considered in semantic indexing. We now present an approach for measuring similarity between two documents by latent semantics.

For a term t of D, the association semantics of t is a set of all possible semantics of t, denoted by $AS(t \mid D)$. That is,

$$AS(t \mid D) = \{ s \mid s \text{ is a possible semantics of } t \text{ given } D \}$$

We define the distance between terms t_1 and t_2 of D below based on association semantics.

$$m_{AS}(t_1, t_2) = \frac{|AS(t_1 \mid D) \cap AS(t_2 \mid D)|}{|AS(t_1 \mid D) \cup AS(t_2 \mid D)|}$$

Example 1. Let t_1, t_2 and t_3 be three terms, and $AS(t_1 \mid D) = \{a_1, a_2, b_2, c_1\}$, $AS(t_2 \mid D) = \{a_2, b_1, b_2, c_1\}$, and $AS(t_3 \mid D) = \{a_1, a_2, b_2, c_1, c_2\}$. Then

$$m_{AS}(t_1, t_2) = \frac{|AS(t_1 \mid D) \cap AS(t_2 \mid D)|}{|AS(t_1 \mid D) \cup AS(t_2 \mid D)|} = \frac{3}{5} = 0.6$$

$$m_{AS}(t_1, t_3) = \frac{|AS(t_1 \mid D) \cap AS(t_3 \mid D)|}{|AS(t_1 \mid D) \cup AS(t_3 \mid D)|} = \frac{4}{5} = 0.8$$

$$m_{AS}(t_2, t_3) = \frac{|AS(t_2 \mid D) \cap AS(t_3 \mid D)|}{|AS(t_2 \mid D) \cup AS(t_3 \mid D)|} = \frac{3}{6} = 0.5$$

The distance between a document D and a query Q can be then defined as follows, where $D = \{d_1, d_2, ..., d_n\}$ and $Q = \{q_1, q_2, ..., q_k\}$.

(1) The simplest similarity measurement is

$$M_{AS}(D,Q) = \frac{|(AS(d_1 \mid D) \cup \cdots \cup AS(d_n \mid D)) \cap (AS(q_1 \mid Q) \cup \cdots \cup AS(q_k \mid Q))|}{|AS(d_1 \mid D) \cup \cdots \cup AS(d_n \mid D) \cup AS(q_1 \mid Q) \cup \cdots \cup AS(q_k \mid Q)|}$$

(2) For a rigorous similarity measurement, and without losing generality, we assume $n \, {}^3 \, k$. We construct the following distance table between terms.

In Table 1, $a_{ij} = m_{AS}(d_i, q_j)$ when $i = 1, 2, ..., n$ and $j = 1, 2, ..., k$; $a_{ij} = 0$, when $i = 1, 2, ..., n$ and $j = k+1, ..., n$.

We take the greatest value in the above as the distance between D and Q. That is,

$$M_{AS}(D,Q) = Max\{m_i\}_{i=1}^{N}$$

(3) The Boolean OR-Query, can be described in a standard format as a Boolean expression. The common Boolean expression is

$$Q = (q_1 \wedge ... \wedge q_i) \vee (q_{i+1} \wedge ... \wedge q_j) \vee ... \vee (q_{k+1} \wedge ... \wedge q_n)$$

Assume that $Q_1 = \{q_1, ..., q_i\}$, $Q_2 = \{q_{i+1}, ..., q_j\}$, ..., and $Q_m = \{q_{k+1}, ..., q_n\}$. Then the query can be expressed as

$$Q = Q_1 \vee Q_2 \vee ... \vee Q_m$$

The similarity measurement between D and Q is defined as

$$M_{AS}(D, Q) = Max\{M_{AS}(D, Q_1), M_{AS}(D, Q_2), \tfrac{1}{4}, M_{AS}(D, Q_m)\}$$

***Table 1**: Mutual distances among terms given* D *and* Q

	q_1	q_2	...	q_k	$\varnothing$	...	$\varnothing$
d_1	a_{11}	a_{12}	...	a_{1k}	$a_{1(k+1)}$	...	a_{1n}
d_2	a_{21}	a_{22}	...	a_{2k}	$a_{2(k+1)}$	...	a_{2n}
...	...	...	...	...	...	...	...
d_n	a_{n1}	a_{n2}	...	a_{nk}	$a_{n(k+1)}$	...	a_{nn}

4. PROCEDURES FOR SIMILARITY CALCULATION

Because the similarity using latent semantics is similar to that of association semantics, we only present algorithms to compute the similarity of association semantics. Let D be a given document and Q be a query. We have,

Procedure 1. *SimpleSimMeasure*
begin
Input: D: a document, Q: a query;

Output: $M_{AS}^{sim}(D,Q)$: the similarity;

(1) **for** $d \in D$ **do**
   begin
      generate $AS(d \mid D)$;
      let $AS_D \leftarrow AS_D \cup AS(d \mid D)$;
   end
   for $q \in Q$ **do**
   begin
      generate $AS(q \mid Q)$;
      let $AS_Q \leftarrow AS_Q \cup AS(q \mid Q)$;
   end

(2) **let** $M_{AS}^{sim}(D,Q) \leftarrow |AS_D \cap AS_Q| / |AS_D \cup AS_Q|$;

(3) **output** the similarity between D and Q is $M_{AS}^{sim}(D,Q)$;

endall.

The procedure *SimpleSimMeasure* estimates the similarity between two documents, D and Q, by using latent semantics.

An algorithm for calculation of the rigorous similarity of association semantics is given below, where, for simplicity, $D = \{d_1, d_2, ..., d_n\}$, $Q = \{q_1, q_2, ..., q_k\}$, and $n = k$.

Procedure 2. *RigSimMeasure*
begin
Input: D: a document, Q: a query;

Output: $M_{AS}^{rig}(D,Q)$: the similarity;

(1) **input** the weight set $\{w_1, w_2, ..., w_n\}$;
      for $d \in D$ **do**
         generate $AS(d_1 \mid D), AS(d_2 \mid D), ..., AS(d_n \mid D)$;
      for $q \in Q$ **do**
         generate $AS(q_1 \mid Q), AS(q_2 \mid Q), ..., AS(q_n \mid Q)$;
(2) **for** $d \in D$ **do**
      for $q \in Q$ **do**
         let $a_{ij} \leftarrow m_{AS}(d_i, q_j)$;
(3) **let** $I \leftarrow$ the set of all possible reorders of $(1, 2, ..., n)$;
      let $M_{AS}^{rig}(D,Q) \leftarrow 0$;
      for $i = 1$ **to** n **do**
         for any $(l_1, l_2, ..., l_n) \in I$ **do**
         begin
            let $tem \leftarrow w_1 * a_{i l_1} + w_2 * a_{i l_2} + ... + w_n * a_{i l_n}$;
            if $tem > M_{AS}^{rig}(D,Q)$ **then**
               let $M_{AS}^{rig}(D,Q) \leftarrow tem$;
         end

(4) **output** the similarity between D and Q is $M_{AS}^{rig}(D,Q)$;

endall.

The procedure *RigSimMeasure* estimates the similarity between two documents, D and Q, by using association semantics.

5. COMPARISON AND SUMMARY

For convenience, our comparison is only focused on the simplest formulae of conventional similarity measurement $M_{pre}(D, Q)$, the similarity measurement by latent semantics $M_{LS}(D, Q)$, and the similarity measurement by association semantics $M_{AS}(D, Q)$. We have

$$M_{pre}(D,Q) = \frac{|D \cap Q|}{|D \cup Q|}$$

$$M_{LS}(D,Q) = \frac{|(LS(d_1) \cup \cdots \cup LS(d_n)) \cap (LS(q_1) \cup \cdots \cup LS(q_k))|}{|LS(d_1) \cup \cdots \cup LS(d_n) \cup LS(q_1) \cup \cdots \cup LS(q_k)|}$$

$$M_{AS}(D,Q) = \frac{|(AS(d_1 \mid D) \cup \cdots \cup AS(d_n \mid D)) \cap (AS(q_1 \mid Q) \cup \cdots \cup AS(q_k \mid Q))|}{|AS(d_1 \mid D) \cup \cdots \cup AS(d_n \mid D) \cup AS(q_1 \mid Q) \cup \cdots \cup AS(q_k \mid Q)|}$$

Suppose $D = \{d_1, d_2, d_3\} = \{discovery, data\ set, knowledge\}$, and $Q = \{q_1, q_2\} = \{mine, rule\}$. Certainly, we have

$$M_{pre}(D,Q) = \frac{|D \cap Q|}{|D \cup Q|} = 0$$

In order to apply $M_{LS}(D, Q)$ and $M_{AS}(D, Q)$, assume $LS(d_1) = \{discovery\}$, $LS(d_2) = \{data\ set, database\}$, $LS(d_3) = \{knowledge\}$, $LS(q_1) = \{mine, belonging\ to\ me\}$, $LS(q_2) = \{rule\}$ and $AS(d_1|D) = \{discovery\}$, $AS(d_2|D) = \{dataset, database, document\ set\}$, $AS(d_3|D) = \{knowledge, rule, law, data\}$, $AS(q_1|Q) = \{mine, discovery, extraction, learning\}$, $AS(q_2|D) = \{rule, knowledge, law\}$. Then, we have

$$M_{LS}(D,Q) = \frac{|(LS(d_1) \cup \cdots \cup LS(d_n)) \cap (LS(q_1) \cup \cdots \cup LS(q_k))|}{|LS(d_1) \cup \cdots \cup LS(d_n) \cup LS(q_1) \cup \cdots \cup LS(q_k)|} = 0$$

$$M_{AS}(D,Q) = \frac{|(AS(d_1 \mid D) \cup \cdots \cup AS(d_n \mid D)) \cap (AS(q_1 \mid Q) \cup \cdots \cup AS(q_k \mid Q))|}{|AS(d_1 \mid D) \cup \cdots \cup AS(d_n \mid D) \cup AS(q_1 \mid Q) \cup \cdots \cup AS(q_k \mid Q)|} = \frac{4}{10} = 0.4.$$

As we have seen, with the explosive growth of information on the WWW, there is a great need for efficient information searching relevant to user queries. By using search engines, such as Yahoo, MSN, and Google, many thousands, even millions of results are usually returned in response to a user query. It would be difficult for a user to browse so much searched information. In particular, it is an important challenge to identify which pieces of the information are really useful to the user. In this paper, we designed a new strategy for information indexing by conditional association semantics. The proposed approach can efficiently reduce irrelevant information searched.

6. REFERENCES

[1] C. H. Chang and C. C. Hsu. Enabling concept-based relevance feedback for information retrieval on the WWW. *IEEE Transactions on Knowledge and Data Engineering*, 1999, 11(4): 595-609.

[2] N. R. Jennings, K. Sycara, and M. Wooldridge. A roadmap of agent research and development. *Autonomous Agents and Multi-Agent Systems*, 1998, 1(1): 7-38.

[3] V. Lesser, B. Horling, F. Klassner, A. Raja, T. Wagner, and S. Zhang. A next generation information gathering agent. *Proceedings of the 4th International Conference on Information Systems, Analysis, and Synthesis*, Orlando, FL, July 1998.

[4] V. Lesser, B. Horling, F. Klassner, A. Raja, T. Wagner, and S. Zhang. BIG: An agent for resource-bounded information gathering and decision making. *Artificial Intelligence Journal, Special Issue on Internet Information Agents*, Vol. 118, 1-2(2000): 197-244.

[5] S. Li and P. Danzig. Boolean similarity measures for resource discovery. *IEEE Trans. Knowledge and Data Eng.*, vol. 9, 6(1997): 863-876.

[6] X. Wang, Shichao Zhang, P. K. Khosla, H. Kiliccote and Chengqi Zhang. Anytime algorithm for agent-mediated merchant information gathering. *Proceedings of the Fourth International Conference on Autonomous Agents*, Catalonia, Spain, ACM Press, June, 2000: 333-340.

K-NN Search in Non-Clustered Case Using K-P-tree

Yang Zhi-rong and Li Lei
Software Institute, Sun Yat-Sen University, Guangzhou, 510275, China
Tel: 8620-83836474, or 8620-84110658-100, Fax: 8620-84037785
roz@163.net

ABSTRACT

Although it has been shown that all current indexing techniques degrade to linear search for sufficiently high dimensions, exact answers are still essential for many applications. A concept of "non-clustered" case is proposed in this paper. And aiming at the characteristics of such case, a new index structure named K-P-tree and a K-NN searching algorithm based on it is presented. By starting with the Self-Organized Mapping method, the partition procedure of K-P-tree does not depend on the dimensionality. Furthermore, the partition locating and pruning also benefit from the fact that only the inner borders between the partitions are recorded merely via some hyper planes. The query experiments indicate that K-P-tree outperforms many current k-NN searching approaches.

1. INTRODUCTION

In many multimedia applications, the multimedia objects are usually mapped to feature vectors in high-dimensional spaces and queries are made on those features vectors. In these cases, one of the most frequently used yet expensive operations is to find k-nearest neighbors to a given query object.

Two surveys in [WSB98, GG98] provide background and analysis on the index structures. These index structures are divided into two major groups. One group is the space-partitioning methods like k-d tree [Ben75, FBF77], K-D-B tree [Bob81] or hB-tree [LS90] dividing the data space along predefined hyper planes in different dimensions on respective levels. The major problem of space-partitioning methods is that their consumption in memory is exponential to the dimensionality and many of the sub partitions are empty and gratuitous. The other group is the data-partitioning methods such as R*-tree [BKS90], X-tree [BKK96], M-tree [PMP97], SR-tree [KS97], A-tree [SYU00] and iDistance [CBK01] using some simple shapes like hyper rectangles or hyper spheres to bound the pattern clusters. Unfortunately such methods have to confront the complicated problem of handling overlaps and indexing the edges.

Some data clustering approaches, such as LVQ [Koh01], CURE [GRS98], and MACT/SACT [QQZ01] have been introduced into this area. But they mainly aim at solving the data mining problem and identify the clusters, while the retrieval acceleration is usually under minor consideration.

In [WSB98], with several observations and analyses, it shows that all current indexing techniques degrade to linear search for sufficiently high dimensions. Hence in [WSB98] and [GIM99], they resort to the solution without exact answers, and some techniques are employed for approximated k-NN search.

However, since index is solely an auxiliary structure to accelerate the information retrieval, it is somewhat irrational to confine the host applications to the error-tolerant. Although the optimizing problem of similarity search is invincible in theoretically high dimensionality, exact answers are still essential for many applications.

The research in this paper is to advance the solution of k-NN searching problem in a distribution case where the patterns cannot be grouped by distinct borders.

2. NON-CLUSTERED CASE

Most current approaches attempt to develop a universally applicable system and they overlook the peculiarity of the pattern distribution. Actually, to differentiate the density level is very important in this process.

A critical concept to describe distribution density is *cluster* which usually refers to a subset of the patterns, where the distances between its members are far less than those between its members and other patterns.

If the patterns are distributed densely in some "natural" clusters with distinct borders, the similarity searching problem is well solved.

(1) If the distances between clusters are far larger than the cluster sizes. The patterns are densely distributed in some clusters, and the sizes and the shapes of those clusters are neglectable during the search process. It is enough to represent the clusters only with their centers.

There are many approaches to find the centers, e.g. Self-Organized Map [Koh01] proposed by Kohonen. And after fast centers finding, one can locate any of these clusters only by their centers. Such simple representation and locating method are enough and efficient for this case.

Even this assumption does not hold if in some local area, the strategies in [PMP97, YL02] have been propsed to stipulate that the clusters locating is still strictly accurate.

(2) If the distances between clusters are close to the cluster sizes, the cluster sizes and shapes are not neglectable. The data clustering techniques in [GRS98, QQZ01, Koh01] must be employed to recognize the clusters and to delineate the cluster borders. And the problem of indexing each cluster recursively reduces to original one at a smaller scale.

Nevertheless, if the distances between clusters are far less than the cluster sizes, it is probable that there are no "distinct" borders between the "clusters". This case is very prevalent, e.g. the uniform distribution data. What is more, even if the original data can be grouped into clusters, it is still probable that there is no distinct border within individual groups. In fact, under the premise of uniform distribution, it has been shown that most of the current index structures and similarity search algorithms, including the latest ones like A-tree and iDistance, deteriorate dramatically when dimensionality increases.

Hence it leads us to focus on the last case of distribution. Before presenting the definition of "non-clustered", we shall introduce some related notations.

Given a set of patterns denoted $Patterns$ and a division of denoted π. π is a class of pattern sub sets and each member of π is called a :

Definition 2.1 , $\pi = \{C_i, i = 1,2,..., k\}$ where $Patterns = \bigcup_{i=1}^{k} C_i$ and $C_i \cap C_j = \varnothing$. Suppose the center of a class is denoted by $\tilde{C}_i$, then we use the cluster radius to describe the size of C_i, which is defined as

$$r_i = \max\{d(c_i, x) \mid x \in C_i\}.$$

And the minimum distance between the respective members from two classes and ($i \neq j$) is used to describe their cluster distance:

Definition 2.2 $d(C_i, C_j) = \min\{d(x, y) \mid x \in C_i, y \in C_j\}$

Definition 2.3 Given a threshold δ (e.g. δ=10 or δ=100), two classes C_i and C_j ($i \neq j$) are δ-*mergable iff* $d(C_i, C_j) > \delta \times \max\{r_i, r_j\}$.

For convenience, we will use the term *mergable* short for δ-mergable unless otherwise stated.

When the *mergable* predicative holds for C_i and C_j, it means C_i and C_j are so close in some direction(s) that they can be merged into one cluster.

For convenient expression, we define the following boolean function for the *mergable* predicative: $CM(C_i, C_j)$ =1 if C_i and C_j are mergable; Otherwise $CM(C_i, C_j)$ =0. It is obvious that $CM(C_i, C_j) = CM(C_j, C_i)$

Definition 2.4 $Degree(C_i) = \sum_{\substack{j=1 \\ j \neq i}}^{k} CM(C_i, C_j)$

The *degree* function of a class returns the connectivity between other classes.

Definition 2.5 A division $\pi = \{C_i, i = 1, 2, ..., k\}$ is $\theta - non - clustered$ *iff* $E(\pi)/k > \theta$.

Here $E(.)$ is the mathematical expectation and θ is a given threshold, say, θ=0.5 or θ=0.9. Likewise, in contexts without confusion, we use the term *non-clustered* short for $\theta - non - clustered$.

Definition 2.6 A pattern set *Patterns* is *non-clustered iff* all divisions of *Patterns* are *non-clustered*.

When the *non-clustered* predicative holds for a pattern set *Patterns*, it means by any way we divide *Patterns*, each class can always be merged with most of the other classes. The whole pattern set behaves in integrity and there is no way to find some "natural" borders to separate its members. The problem can be simplified as dividing a high-dimensional sub space with a special shape, as well as locating and pruning the partitions.

In this paper, a new approach is proposed to solve the problem in the last case. By starting with the SOM method, our partitioning method does not depend on the dimensionality. Furthermore, the partition locating and pruning also benefit from that only the inner borders between the partitions are recorded merely via some hyper planes.

3. DATA STRUCTURE

In order to construct a balanced index structure, before dividing the pattern set, we should get its compact form.

Definition 3.1 Suppose $X \in R^n$ is the distribution of a stochastic variable x, and $C_X \in R^n$ is the distribution of another stochastic variable c_x. C_X is the set of reference vectors of X *iff* $p(x) = p(c_x)$. Here $p(\cdot)$ is the probability density function.

There are many methods to get the reference vectors, one of which is the Self-Organizing Map (SOM) [Koh01]. With proper configuration, the output of SOM approximates the original distribution with a much smaller set of reference vectors. And each reference vector is the centroid (mean value) of its corresponding pattern set.

In our approach, some sub spaces are defined to enclose each pattern sub set and the inner borders between these sub sets.

Definition 3.2 The partition defined on a given set of hyper planes B is a subspace of R^n, denoted $P(B)$, where

$$P(B) = \{ x \mid x \in R^n \wedge x \cdot q - \alpha > 0, \text{ for all } b = H(q, \alpha) \in B \}.$$

Here B is called the border of P, each $b \in B$ is called a border segment of $P(B)$.

Definition 3.3 $P(B)$ is the enclosed partition of vector set . (In the pseudo code listed below, without confusion, the term "enclosed" will be omitted.)

Definition 3.4 $P(B_1)$ is called child partition of $P(B_0)$ and $P(B_0)$ is called parent partition of $P(B_1)$. It is easy to see that

$$P(B_1) \subseteq P(B_0).$$

A child partition inherits all border segments from its parent. And usually with some additional ones, the child partition represents a smaller region.

For neighborhood preservation, it is advantageous to designate each pattern to its nearest reference vector. Under such premise, we can easily compute the enclosed partitions with the reference vectors. Because it is not difficult to prove that the border segments between two pattern sub sets are a pair of hyper planes with negative directions to each other, which locate in the middle of the respective reference vectors. And the pair of hyper planes is orthogonal to the line through the two reference vectors.

Given two pattern sub sets X_i and X_j ($i \neq j$), whose reference vectors are c_i and c_j, and whose enclosed partitions are $P(B_i)$ and $P(B_j)$, respectively. The border segments between X_i and X_j are $b = H(q, \alpha)$ and $b' = H(q', \alpha')$, $l = 1, ..., k$, where

$$-q = q' = \frac{c_j - c_i}{\|c_j - c_i\|}, \text{ and } -\alpha = \alpha' = \frac{c_i + c_j}{2} \cdot q' = \frac{\|c_j\|^2 - \|c_i\|^2}{2\|c_j - c_i\|}.$$

Obviously it is profitable to compute only one border segment in each pair and to store them together in the upper level. In each node of K-P-tree, a bitwise mask indicates the valid border segments for the corresponding partition. Likewise, another bitwise string indicates the directions for those valid border segments.

As shown in Figure 4.1, a node of the K-P-tree has the following structure:

TPartition : (*border_mask, border_directions, segments, patterns, children*), where

border_mask and *border_directions* are BITWISE elements mentioned above.

segments refers to the border segments in the next level, which is an array of hyper planes with size of NUM_SEGMENTS, where

$$\text{NUM\_SEGMENTS} := \frac{k*(k-1)}{2}; \quad //k \text{ is the partition count in each level}$$

As we know, if $q \in R^n - \{0\}$, $\alpha \in R^1$, then the (n-1)-dimension set $H(q, \alpha) = \{x \in R^n \mid x \cdot q = \alpha\}$ defines a hyper plane in R_n. Hence we use the pair (q, α) to represent a hyper plane.

patterns is the entry for the set of vectors within the enclosed partition defined by *segments*. It is a null pointer for intermediate nodes, *children* are the entries to the child nodes.

The index construction for K-P-tree is simple: (1) Get the reference vectors by means like SOM; (2) Divide the pattern set by designating each pattern to it nearest reference vector; (3) Compute the border segments, afterwards log the indicator of validity and directions (border_mask and border_directions); (4) Recursively apply the procedure in steps (1)-(3) on each sub pattern set until the size of which is less than a given leaf threshold.

4. SEARCH ALGORITHM

The search algorithm comprises a main procedure and two subroutines to locate a leaf partition and to judge the intersection.

Figure 4.1 The K-P-tree structure

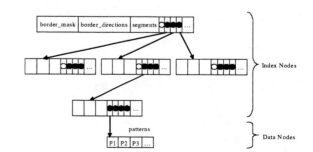

The first subroutine follows the definition of half-space: First compute the location of input pattern, which is stored in the bits of location_code. Afterwards, by masking the invalid bits and comparing with the border segment directions indicator, only one child partition is located. Then by recursively applying LocatePartition procedure, we get the process in pseudo C codes to locate the leaf partition which the input pattern belongs to.

```
#define Positive( x , h ) ( x · h.q − h.α > 0 ) ? 1 : 0;
function LocatePartition(VECTOR input , TPartition parent ) : TPartition
{
    BITWISE location_code;
    for(i=0;i<NUM_SEGMENTS;i++)
        location_code[i] = Positive( input , parent .segments[i]);
    for each child of parent do
        if (location_code & child.border_mask == child.border_directions)
            return child;
}

function LocateLeaf(VECTOR input , TPartition root ) : TPartition
{
    TPartition child := root ;
    while( child  is not a leaf)
        child := LocatePartition( input , child );
    return child ;
}
```

The second subroutine, *Intersectant*, and the main procedure are list below.

```
function Intersectant (VECTOR input , REAL r̂_min k max , TPartition child ) : BOOL
{
    for j:=1 to NUM_ SEGMENTS do
        if child .border_mask[j] then
        {
```
$$y := x - \frac{(x \cdot q - \alpha) \cdot q}{\| q \|^2};$$
```
            if d(input, y) < r̂_min k max then
                return true;
        }
    return false;
}

function k_NN_Search(VECTOR input , int k , TPartition root ) : Pattern_Set
{
```
$leaf$:= LocateLeaf($input$, $root$);

$result0$:= k_NN_Search0($input$, k , $leaf.patterns$);

$\hat{r}_{\min k \max}$:= max{ $d(input, y)$ }, where $y \in result0$;

$Queue$:= { $root$ }; $Possible$:= $\varnothing$;

while($Queue \neq \varnothing$)
```
    {
```
$node$:=pop($Queue$);

if $node$ is not a leaf then

    for each $child$ of $node$ do

      if Intersectant($input$, $\hat{r}_{\min k \max}$, $child$) then

        Append $child$ to $Queue$;

else

      $Possible$:= $Possible \cup node.patterns$;
```
    }
```
return k_NN_Search0($input$, k , $Possible$);
```
}
```

The main function, k_NN_Search, consists of three steps: (1) an exhaustive search procedure, k_NN_Search0, is employed on the leaf partition which the input pattern belongs to; (2) a pruning process is employed to find all possible partitions partitions with $\hat{r}_{\min k \max}$; (3) the exhaustive search will employed again on the possible pattern set.

The partition locating in (1) has been presented in the preceding section and the exhaustive search in (1) and (3) is simple. To determine whether a given partition contains one or more k-nearest neighbors in step (2), we make use of the property of intersection.

Consider $r_{\min k \max} = \max\{d(input, y) \mid y \in KNN\}$, where KNN is the set of k-nearest neighbors. We denote $S(input, r_{\min k \max}) = \{x \mid d(input, x) < r_{\min k \max}\}$. It is easy to see that $S(input, r_{\min k \max})$ is a hyper sphere and $KNN \subseteq S(input, r_{\min k \max})$. Hence it is easy to see that given an enclosed partition $P(B) \neq leaf$ and its pattern set $PS \subseteq P(B)$, there will be $PS \cap KNN \neq \varnothing$ iff $\exists b \in B$, b intersects the hyper sphere $S(input, r_{\min k \max})$.

During the pruning process, since $\hat{r}_{\min k \max} \geq r_{\min k \max}$, if b does not intersect the hyper sphere $S(input, \hat{r}_{\min k \max})$ for any $b \in B$, then the partition $P(B)$ and its pattern set PS can be safely pruned.

A static pruning is applied in the main procedure as presented above, where $S(input, \hat{r}_{\min k \max})$ is invariable during the pruning process. Some dynamic strategies can be employed. For example, when a leaf *node* is popped from *Queue*, the exhaustive search, k_NN_Search0, is applied to $Possible \cup node.patterns$ to get more accurate $\hat{r}_{\min k \max}$ for further pruning. Moreover, some heuristic information, say $d(input, c_i)$, can be used as the key to sort the *Queue* in addition to dynamic adjusting $\hat{r}_{\min k \max}$. With these dynamic strategies, the pruning effect can be enhanced so that step (3) benefits, though the step (2) suffers from the cost of additional operations.

5. QUERY EXPERIMENTS

The purpose of the experiments is to test the query performance of our method and several current multi-dimensional index structures with varying dimensionality. The selected approaches in comparison were iDistance [CBK01] on behalf of data partitioning with hyper spheres, A-tree [SYU00] on behalf of data partitioning with rectangles and hB-tree [LS90] on behalf of space partitioning.

Figure 5.1 Performance of query on synthetic data with varying dimensionality

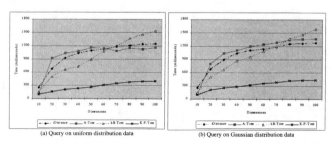

Figure 5.2 Performance of query on real data with varying dimensionality

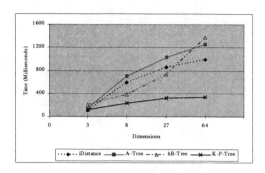

All the experiments were performed on a PC with AMD Athlon 850 CPU, 512MB RAM and several GB hard disk space. To avoid the interference of I/O cost, we configured all the index structures and all vector data stored in the main memory.

We evaluated the structures on synthetic databases of two typical kinds of non-clustered data sets by searching the nearest neighbor of a randomly generated vector. The first was uniform distribution and the second was Gaussian distribution with some randomly chosen peaks. The size for all data sets was 10,000, and the dimensionality ranged from 5 to 100 with step size of 5. For K-P-tree, we used k=6 for each level. For convenient observation, the query process was repeated by 1,000 times and the query time consumed is shown in Figure 5.1(a) and 5.1(b).

In our experiment, we also used real data, which are color histogram vectors extracted from a clipart database with size of 7,600. Since there was no predefined relationship between these selected pictures, they can be deemed as non-clustered data. The dimensions selected in this experiment are 3, 8, 27, and 64. The input vector was also extracted from a picture which is randomly selected from a picture set SS. We configured half pictures were contained in DB while the other half was not. Likewise, the query was also repeated by 1,000 times and the query time consumed is shown in Figure 5.2.

6. CONCLUSION

In this paper we have pointed out the importance of discriminating the distribution density, based on which we proposed the concept of "non-clustered case". Aiming at the characteristics of such distribution we have presented a hierarchical index structure named K-P-tree and a k-NN searching algorithm based on it. By partitioning the patterns based on SOM and only storing the inner borders via the simplest shape, hyper planes, our method achieve very good searching efficiency. The query experiments indicate that K-P-tree outperforms many current k-NN searching approaches such as iDistance, A-tree and hB-tree. Furthermore, the structure of K-P-tree is so flexible that it can be applied to various applications.

REFERENCE

[Ben75]　　Jon Louis Bentley: 'Multidimensional Binary Search Trees Used for Associative Searching', ACM Vol.18, No.9, 1975, pp.509-517.

[BKK96]　　Berchtold, S., Keim, D., Keriegel, H.-P: 'The X-tree: An index structure for high-dimensional data', Proceedings of the 22nd International Conference on Very Large Data Bases, (Bombay), 1996, pp.28-39.

[BKS90]　　Beckmann N., Kriegel H.-P, Schneider R., Seeger B.: 'The R*-tree: An Efficient and Robust Access Method for Points and Rectangles', Proc. ACM SIGMOD Int. Conf. on Management of Data, Atlantic City, NJ, 1990, pp. 322-331.

[CBK01]　　Cui Yu, Beng Chin Ooi, Kian-Lee Tan, H. V. Jagadish: 'Indexing the Distance: An Efficient Method to KNN Processing', Proceedings of the 27th VLDB Conference, Roma, Italy, 2001.

[FBF77]　　Jerome H. Friedman, Jon Louis Bentley, Raphael Ari Finkel: 'An Algorithm for Finding Best Matches in Logarithmic Expected Time', ACM Transactions on Mathematical Software, Vol.3, No. 3, September 1977, pp.209-226.

[GG98]　　Volker Gaede, Oliver Günther: 'Multidimensional Access Methods', ACM Computing Surveys, Vol.30, No.2, 1998, pp.170-231

[GIM99]　　Aristides Gionis, Piotr Indyk, Rajeev Motwani: 'Similarity Search in High Dimensions via Hashing', Proceedings of the 25th VLDB Conference, Edinburgh, Scotland, 1999.

[GRS98]　　Sudipto Guha, Rajeev Rastogi, Kyuseok Shim: 'CURE: An Efficient Clustering Algorithm for Large Databases', Proceedings of ACM SIGMOD'98 Conference, 1998.

[Gut84]　　Guttman, A: 'R-trees: A dynamic index structure for spatial searching', Proceedings of the ACM SIGMOD International Conference on Management of Data, 1984, pp.47-54.

[Koh01]　　Kohonen T.: 'Self-Organizing Maps', Third Edition, Springer, 2001

[KS97]　　N. Katayama and S. Satoh: 'The SR-tree: an Index Structure for High-Dimensional Nearest Neighbor Queries', Proceedings of the 1997 ACM SIGMOD Int. Conf. on Management of Data, 1997, pp. 369-380.

[LJF94]　　Lin, K.-I., Jagadish, H., Faloutsos, C.: 'The TV-tree: An index structure for high-dimensional data'. VLDB J. Vol.3, No.4, 1994, pp.517-543.

[LS90]　　David 9. Lomet, Betty Salzberg: 'The hB-Tree: A Multiattribute Indexing Method with Good Guaranteed Performance', ACM Transactions on Database Systems, Vol.15, No.4, 1990, pp.625-658.

[PMP97]　　Paolo Ciaccia, Marco Patella, Pavel Zezula: 'M-tree: An Efficient Access Method for Similarity Search in Metric Spaces', Proceedings of the 23rd VLDB Conference, Athens, Greece, 1997.

[QQZ01]　　Qian Wei Ning, Qian Hai Lei, Zhou Ao Ying: 'Merging Cluster-Trees: Clustering Very Large Databases', Proceedings of The 18th National Conference on Data Bases, China, 2001, pp.128-133.

[Rob81]　　Robinson, J. T.: 'The K-D-B-tree: A search structure for large multidimensional dynamic indexes', Proceedings of the ACM SIGMOD International Conference on Management of Data, 1981, pp.10-18.

[SYU00]　　Y. Sakurai, M. Yoshikawa, S. Uemura, and H. Kojima. 'A-tree: An Index Structure for High-Dimensional Spaces Using Relative Approximation', Proceedings of the 26th VLDB Conference, 2000, pp.516-526.

[WSB98]　　Roger Weber, Hans -J. Schek, Stephen Blott: 'A Quantitative Analysis and Performance Study for Similarity-Search Methods in High-Dimensional Spaces', Proceedings of the 24th VLDB Conference, New York, USA, 1998.

[YL02]　　Yang Zhi Rong, Li Lei: 'Hierarchical Index of High-Dimension Point Data Using Self-Organizing Map', Computer Research and Development, Vol. 39, 2002

Rates of Change in Ad-hoc Networks

Alec Yasinsac[1]
Florida State University
Tallahassee, Florida 32306-4530 USA
Tel: 850.644.6407 ~ Email:yasinsac@cs.fsu.edu

ABSTRACT

Ad hoc networking techniques allow low power devices to communicate among themselves utilizing one another as communications relays. Often the resulting networks are highly dynamic, with nodes entering and leaving the network, often for short duration membership.

In this paper, we systematically address issues associated with changes that occur in ad hoc networks. We consider the functionality impact of change and address bounds on optimization that exist when change rates are high.

1. DYNAMICS OF AD HOC NETWORKS

Networks come in all shapes and sizes, with a wide variety of characteristics. We are concerned with networks that have no permanent structure, essentially, all nodes are not only mobile, but they characteristically regularly move about. These networks are comprised of nodes with limited transmission ranges and depend on other nodes to relay traffic in order to expand their broadcast domain. We commonly term these *ad hoc networks* because networks form, change, and dissolve in an ad hoc way, often and quickly, and as a matter of routine. The networks that they form are often highly dynamic.

This paper addresses questions about functional limitations that high and fluctuating rates of change cause in ad hoc networks. In the rest of this section, we systematically set up the discussion by defining key terms and follow with an argument about the important metrics and the bounds that apply given assumptions about these metrics.

1.1. Nodes, Links, Networks and Notation

Ad hoc networks are collections of nodes that intercommunicate by relaying messages across peer to peer links. We label our nodes in capital letters, while links are pairs using the lower case letters that correspond to the nodes that the link connects. Thus, a link between nodes A and C is represented as (a, c), or equivalently as (c, a).

A network consists of a collection, or set, of interconnected nodes. If we label networks with upper case letters from the end of the alphabet, we can say that nodes A and B are elements of network X:

$$\{A, B\} \subseteq X$$

and that if link (a, b) exists, it is also an element of X.

$$(a, b) \in X$$

We define a path as a set of interconnected links that connect two nodes. Paths are represented as ordered tuples, with the number of entries dependent on the number of links that must be crossed. Thus, a

path from A to B that must go through C and D (in that order) would be labeled (a, c, d, b), or equivalently (b, d, c, a). These relationships are casually illustrated in Figure 1.

1.2. Network Structure Rate of Change

The *ad hocness* that is a primary characteristic of the networks we consider, results in dynamic networks. As the rate of change increases, the nature of these networks becomes progressively more complex. For example, when a link forms, it may join a node to a network, establish a cycle in an existing network, or merge two networks. Conversely, dissolving a single link can have the opposite three effects.

We consider the specific types of network structure change in order to better understand the nature of networks with high rates of change. We note that there is presently no existing set of measures to reflect these notions.

1.3. Discrete Structures in High Rate of Change Networks

One way to think about network changes is to consider the network structure during static periods, as addressed in [1]. If we define change to occur instantaneously, then we can theoretically identify the network structure at any instant. Practically, network structure change does not occur instantaneously, but rather injects a "change interval" where the system neither has the previous structure, nor the next structure. Still, if the change interval is sufficiently small, we can act as though changes are instantaneous with little impact on our results.

Most attempts to manage ad hoc networks are based on two assumptions regarding the rate of change:
(1) The change interval is insignificant and
(2) There are long network structure static intervals that have a computationally significant interval between relevant changes in the network structure.

The impact of the former depends on the accuracy of the latter. Functions on ad hoc networks assume that the network is static for relevant changes for a period longer than is required to complete the function. For example, a node count function may not succeed if it cannot expect that the connected nodes will not change before the start function completes.

In networks with low rates of change and long static intervals, the change interval is less significant, since network changes occur regularly, and quickly, in ad hoc networks. Adding or deleting a link in a network routinely takes a few seconds at the most. If the network structure is routinely static for hours at a time, the few seconds it takes to make a structural change is insignificant relative to the network structure static intervals. However, if the network structure intervals are short, the few seconds that it takes to make changes have a larger impact.

1.4. Sparsely Populated Ad hoc Networks

Considering the rate of change in network structure necessarily requires scope. We now consider some subtleties of how changes effect sparse versus dense networks. We suggest that large networks will have more changes than will smaller networks. Thus, larger networks are more difficult to manage because of the larger number of changes that occur, and correspondingly, the static intervals are shorter. Conversely, each link in a smaller network tends to be more important to the traffic

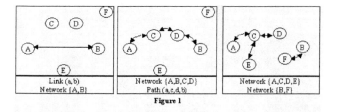

Link (a,b)
Network {A,B}

Network {A,B,C,D}
Path (a,c,d,b)

Network {A,C,D,E}
Network {B,F}

Figure 1

in that network, so a larger percentage of changes are significant relative to more network functions.

Some networks will have few nodes and few links, while others will have numerous nodes, but are sparsely connected, while still others will have few nodes that are highly connected. We posit that the rate that changes take place has different impacts in each situation. In a sparsely populated network, dissolution of a node is more likely to split the network into two disconnected networks than loss of a single node in a densely populated network. Similarly, loss of a single link is more likely to separate a node from the network if the network is sparsely connected (few links per node) than a more densely connected network.

For the rest of this paper, we employ the somewhat uncomfortable use of the phrase "more dynamic" to address this rate of change. A network that is more dynamic than another has a higher rate of network structural change and a longer static interval on average. We now offer a series of metrics that categorize the dynamic nature of ad hoc networks in the next section.

2. RATE OF CHANGE METRICS

We now define measures of the dynamic nature of ad hoc networks. We introduce building blocks that we use later to make our argument about bounds on routing efficiency. We partition our metrics into architectural and application oriented metrics.

2.1. Architectural Rate of Change Metrics

2.1.1. Link Lifetime

The first metric that we introduce is the network average link lifetime. Intuitively, a network with shorter average link lifetime is more dynamic than a network with longer average link lifetime. This metric is easy to compute: simply sum the duration of the existence of each link that has existed in the network, and divide that by the number of links that have existed. We give the Link Lifetime Average for network X with n total links as:

$$\text{Avg\_LLt(X)} = \frac{\sum_{i=1}^{n} LL_i}{n}$$

Practically, it is more difficult to compute the average link lifetime of an ad hoc network, since acquiring complete information is unlikely. Rather than computing the average link lifetime of a network, we begin our arguments by assuming a value for this metric and reason about the resulting impact on network functionality. It is strait forward to model link lifetime using statistical methods. By fixing link lifetime and varying the distributions and impacts of differing assumptions, we can observe the results as the link lifetime increases and decreases.

2.1.2. Node Lifetime

A second metric is node lifetime. Each time a node enters or leaves the network, there is a connectivity impact that may be greater than having a single link change. The computation for the average node lifetime is similar to the average link lifetime, where m is the number of nodes that have existed in X:

$$\text{Avg\_NLt(X)} = \frac{\sum_{i=1}^{m} NL_i}{n}$$

2.1.3. Number of Links per Node

We introduce a metric that connects links and nodes: the average number of links per node. This metric characterizes the redundancy and connectivity of the target network. When considered as a factor of change, it also allows reasoning about how functionality changes as connectivity changes. Simply stated , the number of links per node is represented as the number of links (n) divided by the number of nodes n in the network.

$$\text{Avg\_LpN(X)} = \frac{n}{m}$$

2.1.4. Percentage of change per unit time

We now return to our earlier example of the total and percent of network changes and use this metric as the springboard into talking about application metrics. We define this metric as the number of changes divided by the desired number of intervals of the selected time units. If we elect hours as our time of choice, we sum the number of changes to links and nodes and divide by the number of hours that elapsed in the desired measurement interval.

$$\text{Change(X)} = \frac{\Delta m + \Delta n}{\# hrs}$$

We generate our recommended enhancement to this metric by including the total number of nodes in the computation.

$$\text{Percent\_Change(X)} = \frac{\Delta m + \Delta n}{\# hrs * (m + n)}$$

All of the metrics that we have defined so far are related. If the link and node lifetimes for network X are longer than those for network Y, the percent change of X will necessarily be larger than the percent change of Y. We can also observe limits between these metrics. For example, the number of links can change without the number of nodes changing, since a node may have several links in the network. Conversely, if there are changes in the number of nodes, there must also be changes in the links, since a node is only a member of the network if it has a link in the network.

2.2. Application-Oriented Rate of Change Metrics

We now move on to application-oriented metrics. These metrics reveal the properties that allow us to recognize boundaries on ad hoc network functionality.

2.2.1. Path Length

Nodes communicate through a network over a series of links that together constitute a path. Consider an ad hoc network of n nodes where we desire to identify a path between nodes A and B. Notationally, a path is an ordered set of nodes (represented in lower case) that begins at the source and terminates at the destination. For example, if node C lies between A and B and if A can send messages to B, but they must be relayed by C, we represent the path between A and B as {a, c, b}, or equivalently {b, c, a}, and we term C an intermediate node between A and B.

2.2.2. Path Lifetime

As with links, paths come and go in ad hoc networks. There must be at least one path between any two nodes in a network, however, as links dissolve, paths may also dissolve. We now consider the average path length within a network. In order to facilitate discussion, we assume that we can enumerate the total number of paths in a network, call it q. We then define the average path length as the sum of the number of links in each path divided by the sum of the number of paths in each link.

$$\text{Avg\_PL(X)} = \frac{\sum_{i=1}^{q} PL_i}{q}$$

Another metric for functions that are concerned with paths is path lifetime. This metric can be convenient to perform functions between nodes, e.g. forming a circuit or authenticated route. The path lifetime provides a guideline on how much time the function can take and yet expect not to run out of time, as we described earlier.

We can generate a metric for average network path lifetime similar to that for link lifetime. Path lifetimes will be significantly shorter than link lifetimes in ad hoc networks, since dissolution of any link in the path also dissolves the path.

$$Avg\_PLt(X) = Avg\_LLt(X) / Avg\_PL(X)$$

Similarly, we can compute the path lifetime based on the node lifetime, by recognizing that any path between A and B that traverses i links, must also traverse i-1 intermediate nodes. Then the definition of the average path lifetime for network X may be stated, relative to nodes rather than links, as:

$$Avg\_PLt2(X) = Avg\_NLt(X) / (Avg\_PL(X) - 1)$$

2.3. A Few Illustrations

We argue that the metrics above are practical, that is, that ad hoc networks where these metrics are meaningful exist. To illustrate their utility, we identify four potential ad hoc network categories that correspond to different rates of change.

1. Low Rate of Change Ad hoc Network. The least dynamic (or most stable) category includes ad hoc networks where links exist on the average some number of hours, up to several days. Changes at this rate are relatively easy to handle and do not consume a significant percentage of network resources. An example of such a network is an office environment where employees carry their laptop computers, connected by roaming wireless communications, home and to work with them. While the change rates may peak in the morning and again in the afternoon, the average link lifetimes will likely be hours.
2. Medium Rate of Change Ad hoc Network. We consider networks with average link lifetime of ten minutes to a few hours as a medium rate of change network. The changes at these intervals do not consume even a local majority of the network resources, but the resources consumed are statistically significant. An example of such a network is a delivery service network, where communication between carriers is via short wave radio. Each vehicle may operate primarily within its own area with links to adjoining areas that are interrupted intermittently.
3. High Rate of Change Ad hoc Network. High rate of change networks are characterized by link lifetimes between a few seconds and a few minutes. Managing change in these networks can take a majority of the available resources. An example of such a network is a wireless network between hand held devices in a crowd where individuals move about independently and communicate via low-power, broadcast medium.
4. Very High Rate of Change Ad hoc Network. These networks are characterized by average link lifetimes of just a few seconds. The primary concern for any function on these networks is resource allocation, and their utility is suspect with current technology. An example of such an ad hoc network environment is that of airplanes in a combat or other high-speed environment.

3. IMPACT AREAS

Thus far, we have presented the foundation for reasoning about the nature of rate of change limitations. We now address the impact that rate of change has on applications.

There has been a significant amount of work done on ad hoc routing [2, 3, 4, 5, 6] most geared toward optimizing either the number of messages or time required to acquire an effective route, where a route is available (we do not consider "wait and see" routing protocols where route requests are held and re-forwarded when new links appear). Flood routing provides a ceiling in both areas.

More formally, for any ad hoc network comprised of n nodes, the largest number of messages that are required to derive a route is 2n. If we choose to optimize the number of messages in a new routing protocol, any routing protocol that systematically produces a route with fewer

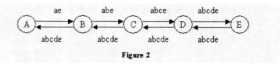

Figure 2

than 2n messages is superior to flooding. In a given environment, if there is no protocol that can systematically produce an effective route with fewer than 2n messages, then flooding is the optimal routing algorithm.

The metrics described above help us to reason about this problem. In this section, we argue that optimization is not possible for some functions in Highly Dynamic networks and use of predetermined routes or circuits may not be possible in networks that are Very Highly Dynamic.

3.1. Bounds on Routing Protocols in Ad hoc Networks

As we described earlier, applications that require circuits are particularly vulnerable to the network dynamic nature. On demand routing protocols generally produce such a circuit. We use the Secure Routing Protocol (SRP) [6] to illustrate how rate of network change can limit network functionality.

SRP is a leapfrog protocol that begins with a route request. Each node that receives the route request appends their address and retransmits if the request is new, and discards otherwise. The route request protocol continues until all nodes in the network receive the route request. If the destination node receives the route request, it prepares a route reply packet directed to the reverse path of the first received route reply. When the originating node receives the route reply, it utilizes the established circuit to communicate with the destination node. Figure 2 illustrates the messages in SRP.

The goal of SRP is to establish a secure route, (circuit) between two hosts on an ad hoc network. SRP establishes a route with only n + l messages, where n is the number of nodes in the network and l is the path length, a substantial reduction in the number of messages over flooding.

The time required to complete SRP is twice the sum of the times required to move between nodes on the resulting path. Our first observation regarding the impact of the dynamic network nature is that SRP cannot be effective unless the average path lifetime is at least twice as long as the average time required to complete SRP. Otherwise, we should expect that the path identified in SRP would be invalid by the time the protocol completes.

While SRP offers an improvement in the number of messages over flooding, in terms of time, SRP is no better than flooding. Flooding can establish a circuit in the time that it takes to traverse the path from the source to the destination and back; the same amount of time as SRP.

This leads to our first rule regarding bounds on functionality of highly dynamic ad hoc networks, where T(f) is the time required to complete function f.

Rule 1.   For any function f that must access a circuit on network X will not be effective unless T(f) < avg_PLt(X)/2, or equivalently if

$$T(f) < Avg\_LLt(X) / 2*(Avg\_PL(X)).$$

Consider some subtleties of this observation. First, we do not claim that functions that violate this rule will never work. Certainly, for shorter circuits or with low probability on longer circuits, functions that violate this rule may occasionally work. However, we cannot *expect* the function to complete its task if Rule 1 is not met.

Secondly, the average link lifetime is a critical element of this computation. In networks in category 4 (very high rate of change), where link lifetimes are only a few seconds, it is likely impractical to expect to be able to utilize circuits at all. Even category 3 networks may be constrained if reliability is essential, or if transmission times are long because of high traffic load or other reasons. Intuition has sensed these observations in the past, but Rule 1 formulates a mechanism to systematically reason about these limiting factors.

3.1. Tuning Factors for Effective Functions in Ad hoc Networks

Another important question is "Can we use Rule 1 to derive a rule that guarantees that such a function will complete"? Since our approach is loosely probabilistic, we prefer to deal with terms such as "likely" and "expected" rather than "guarantee". However, if we accept a slightly loosened form of guarantee, "statistically insignificant" and set that threshold arbitrarily to be less than one percent, we can derive some helpful results.

Rule 2.   Any function f that must access a circuit on network X will not be time constrained if

$$T(f) < avg\_PLt(X)/200, \text{ or equivalently if}$$
$$T(f) < (Avg\_LLt(X)) / 200*(Avg\_PL(X)).$$

Our arbitrary selection of one percent as our statistically insignificant threshold is fine for illustration, but likely not practical. Although the exact figure will be highly context driven, most network functions cannot endure a one percent failure rate. Fortunately, we can easily tune this threshold and restate Rule 2 as:

Rule 2': Any function f that must access a circuit on network X will not be time constrained relative to the threshold factor (tf) if:

$$T(f) < avg\_PLt(X)/(2* tf), \text{ or equivalently if}$$
$$T(f) < (Avg\_LLt(X)) / 2*(tf*(Avg\_PL(X))).$$

4. CONCLUSION

In this paper we have shown how the varying rates of change in ad hoc networks affect the their functionality. We categorized these rates and established metrics to allow systematic analysis of their impact. We went on to address specific functional bounds that may occur for highly dynamic ad hoc networks, showing how one secure routing algorithm cannot be effective in very highly dynamic networks. Using our threshold factor, we show how to use our metrics to gauge functionality in any ad hoc network.

Our work and examples in this paper are limited by space to focus on applications that employ circuits in ad hoc networks. However, these metrics and techniques are applicable to a wide variety of functions and environments and can be a productive mechanism for designing and analyzing applications in ad hoc networks.

ENDNOTE

[1]   This material is based upon work supported in part by the U.S. Army Research Laboratory and the U.S. Army Research Office under grant number DAAD19-02-1-0235.

5. BIBLIOGRAPHY

[1] Prosenjit Bose, Pat Morin, Ivan Stojmenovic and Jorge Urrutia, "Routing with Guaranteed Delivery in Ad Hoc Wireless Networks", Wireless Networks, Vol. 7, pp. 609-16, 2001, Kluwer.

[2] Stephen Carter and Alec Yasinsac, "Secure Position Aided Ad hoc Routing", to appear in Proceedings of the Third International Conference on Computer and Communication Networks, IEEE Computer Society Press, November, 2002

[3] C. Perkins and E. Royer, "Ad hoc On-Demand Distance Vector Routing," Proceedings of the 2nd IEEE Workshop on Mobile Computing Systems and Applications, February 1999, pp. 90-100.

[4] Y. Ko, and N. Vaidya, "Location Aided Routing in Mobile Ad Hoc Networks," The Fourth Annual ACM/IEEE International Conference on Mobile Computing and Networking, October 1998.

[5] S. Yi, P. Naldurg and R. Kravets, "Security-Aware Ad-Hoc Routing for Wireless Networks," UIUCDCS-R-2001-2241 Technical Report, August 2001.

[6] Papadimitratos and Z.J. Haas, "Secure Routing for Mobile Ad hoc Networks," SCS Communication Networks and Distributed Systems Modeling and Simulation Conference, January 2002.

The Negotiation of Privacy Policies in Distance Education[1]

George Yee and Larry Korba
Institute for Information Technology, National Research Council Canada
Montreal Road, Building M-50, Ottawa, Ontario, Canada K1A 0R6
Email: George.Yee@nrc-cnrc.gc.ca   Larry.Korba@nrc-cnrc.gc.ca

ABSTRACT

This paper presents an approach for the negotiation of privacy policies for an e-learning service. Both negotiating under certainty and uncertainty are treated. The type of uncertainty discussed is uncertainty of what offers and counter-offers to make during the negotiation. The approach makes use of common interest and reputation to arrive at a list of candidates who have negotiated the same issues in the past, from whom the negotiator can learn the possible offers and counter-offers that could be made. Negotiation in this work is done through human-mediated computer-assisted interaction rather than through autonomous agents.

1 INTRODUCTION

Most distance education innovations have focused on course development and delivery, with little or no consideration to privacy and security as required elements. However, it is clear that there will be a growing need for high levels of confidentiality and privacy in e-learning applications, and that security technologies must be put in place to meet these needs. The savvy of consumers regarding their rights to privacy is increasing; new privacy legislations have recently been introduced by diverse jurisdictions [17,18]. In addition, the move to corporate outsourcing of distance learning will lead to requirements of confidentiality of student information, to protect company sensitive information that might be disclosed if training records were obtained by competitors.

A promising solution to the lack of privacy and security for e-learning systems is to put in place a policy-based management system, i.e. formulate privacy and security policies for the e-learning system and back them up with security mechanisms which ensure that the policies are respected. Policy-based management approaches have been used effectively to manage and control large distributed systems. As in any distributed system, e-learning may also use a policy-based framework to manage the security and privacy aspects of operations. However, policies must reflect the wishes of the e-learning consumer as well as the e-learning provider. In this paper, we describe an approach for the negotiation of privacy policies between an e-learning consumer and an e-learning provider. We examine negotiation under certainty and uncertainty (where the offers and counter-offers are known or unknown, respectively) and propose a scheme for resolving the uncertainty using the experience of others who have undergone similar negotiation. The choice of whom to call upon for negotiation experience is resolved through the identification of common interest and reputation.

The negotiation approach presented in this paper does not employ autonomous agent negotiation (AAN). We find that: a) AAN is not necessary for our application area, b) current AAN technology would be unable to capture all the nuances and sensitivities involved with privacy policy negotiation, including cultural impacts [13], and c) the level of trust that consumers would have in autonomous agents negotiating privacy policy would be low.

In the literature, most negotiation research is on negotiation via autonomous software agents. This research focuses on methods or models for agent negotiation [1,2,3] and can incorporate techniques from other scientific areas such as game theory [4], fuzzy logic [5,6] and genetic algorithms [7]. The research also extends to autonomous agent negotiation for specific application areas, such as e-commerce [8,9] and service level agreements for the Internet [10]. Apart from negotiation by autonomous software agents, research has also been carried out on support tools for negotiation [11,12], which typically provide support in position communication, voting, documentation communication, and big picture negotiation visualization and navigation.

Regarding privacy negotiation, there are related works such as P3P [14], APPEL [15], and PSP [16], which provide ways of expressing privacy policy and preferences. Service providers use P3P to divulge their privacy policies to consumers. APPEL is a specification language used to describe a consumer's privacy preferences for comparison with the privacy policy of a provider. PSP is a protocol in the research stage that provides a basis for policy negotiation. These works are not necessary for the purposes of this paper. They only serve as illustrations of what has been done in the related area of capturing privacy preferences in a form amenable to machine processing.

The remainder of this paper is divided as follows. Section 2 considers the mathematical structure of negotiation. Section 3 examines negotiation under certainty and uncertainty. For the latter case, we explore using the experience of others in making decisions. Section 4 gives a scheme for negotiating privacy policy under uncertainty. Section 5 presents our conclusions.

2 NEGOTIATION – STRUCTURE AND REPRESENTATION

Negotiation Example

This example illustrates negotiation to produce a privacy policy for a person (consumer) taking a course from an e-learning provider. Suppose the item for negotiation is the privacy of examination results. The employer would like to know how well the person performed on the course in order to assign the person appropriate tasks at work. Moreover, management (Bob, David and Suzanne) would like to share the results with management of other divisions, in case they could use the person's newly acquired skills. The negotiation dialogue can be expressed in terms of offers, counter-offers, and choices, as follows (read from left to right and down, as shown below).

As seen in this example, negotiation is a process between two parties, wherein each party presents the other with offers and counter-offers until either an agreement is reached or no agreement is possible. Each party chooses to make a particular offer based on the value that the choice represents to that party. Each party chooses a particular offer because that offer represents the maximum value among the alternatives.

PROVIDER	CONSUMER
OK for your exam results to be seen by your management?	*Yes, but only David and Suzanne can see them.*
OK if only David and Bob see them?	*No, only David and Suzanne can see them.*
OK. Can management from Divisions B and C also see your exam results?	*OK for management from Division C but not Division B.*
How about letting Divisions C and D see your results?	*That is acceptable.*

Each party in a negotiation shares a list of items to be negotiated. For each party and each item to be negotiated, there is a set of alternative positions with corresponding values. This set of alternatives is explored as new alternatives are considered at each step of the negotiation. Similarly, the values can change (or become apparent), based upon these new alternatives and the other party's last offer.

Let R be the set of items r_i to be negotiated, $R = \{r_1, r_2,...,r_n\}$. Let $A_{1,r,k}$ be the set of alternatives for party 1 and negotiation item r at step k, $k=0,1,2,...$, in the negotiation. $A_{1,r,0}$ is party 1's possible opening positions. Let $O_{1,r,k}$ be the alternative $a \in A_{1,r,k}$ that party 1 chooses to offer party 2 at step k. $O_{1,r,0}$ is party 1's chosen opening position. For example, for the first negotiation above, the provider's opening position is "exam results can be seen by management". Then for each alternative $a \in A_{1,r,k}$, $V_k(a)$ is the value function of alternative a for party 1 at step k, $k>0$, and

$$V_k(a) = f(I, O_{1,r,k-1}, O_{2,r,k-1}, \cdots)$$

where I is the common interest or purpose of the negotiation (e.g. negotiating privacy policy for "Psychology 101"), $O_{1,r,k-1}$ is the offer of party 1 at step $k-1$, $O_{2,r,k-1}$ is the offer of party 2 at step $k-1$, plus other factors which could include available alternatives, culture, sex, age, income level, and so on. These other factors are not required here, but their existence is without doubt since how an individual derives value can be very complex. Let $a_m \in A_{1,r,k}$ such that $V_k(a_m) = max \{V_k(a), a \in A_{1,r,k}\}$. Then at step k, $k>0$ in the negotiation process, party 1 makes party 2 an offer $O_{1,r,k}$ where

$$O_{1,r,k} = a_m \qquad if \quad V_k(a_m) > V_k(O_{2,r,k-1}), \qquad (1)$$
$$= O_{2,r,k-1} \quad if \quad V_k(a_m) \leq V_k(O_{2,r,k-1}). \qquad (2)$$

Equation 1 represents the case where party 1 makes a counter-offer to party 2's offer. Equation 2 represents the case where party 1 accepts party 2's offer and agreement is reached! A similar development can be done for party 2. Thus, there is a negotiation tree $\vec{r}$ corresponding to each item r to be negotiated, with 2 main branches extending from r at the root (Figure 1). The 2 main branches correspond to the 2 negotiating parties. Each main branch has leaves representing the alternatives at each step. At each step, including the opening positions at step 0, each party's offer is visible to the other for comparison. As negotiation proceeds, each party does a traversal of its corresponding main branch. If the negotiation is successful, the traversals converge at the successful alternative (one of the parties adopts the other's offer as his own, equation 2 above) and the negotiation tree is said to be *complete*. Each party may choose to terminate the negotiation if the party feels no progress is being made; the negotiation tree is then said to be *incomplete*.

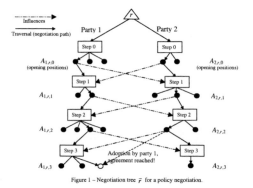

Figure 1 – Negotiation tree $\vec{r}$ for a policy negotiation.

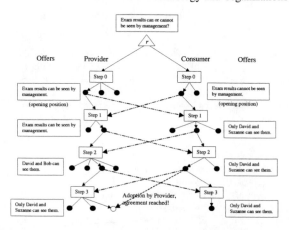

Figure 2 – Negotiation tree for the first part of the above negotiation.

In Figure 1, the influences arrows show that a particular alternative offered by the other party at step k will influence the alternatives of the first party at step $k+1$. Figure 2 illustrates the negotiation tree using the first negotiation above.

3 NEGOTIATION IN CERTAINTY AND UNCERTAINTY

The following definition defines the meaning of negotiating in certainty and uncertainty.

Definition: Party i *negotiates in certainty* if for every negotiation step k, party i knows both $A_{i,r,k}$ and $O_{i,r,k}$. Otherwise, party i *negotiates in uncertainty*.

Negotiation in certainty is therefore the type of negotiation illustrated in the example of section 2. At each negotiation step, each party knows the alternatives and knows what offer he is going to make. What is more interesting, however, is negotiating in uncertainty. What if a negotiating party does not know what the alternatives are or what offer or counter offer would be appropriate, at any particular step? This party may arrive at such a state as follows:
a) The other party's last offer may be a surprise (e.g. it is not understood).
b) He does not fully appreciate the value of the item under negotiation.
c) He may not be able to discern the values of his alternatives (not be able to compute $V_k(a)$).

In this case, the negotiating party may make use of the experience or decisions of others who have already negotiated the same item.

Negotiation in Uncertainty Example
Suppose you have been offered new employment and it is time to negotiate your benefits, including your salary. You know what you want in terms of vacation, sick leave, and training. However, when it comes to salary, you find it difficult to know what would be a fair salary, since both the job and the company are new to you. You have to negotiate in uncertainty. In this case, and what you may do naturally, is seek out others who you trust and who have negotiated salaries with this company in the past, for similar types of jobs. You would like to know how they negotiated their salaries, what alternatives they considered, and what counter-offers they made based on offers made by management. You may not use their figures exactly but you may use their alternatives with different figures.

3.1 Reputation
As the previous example shows, negotiating an item in uncertainty may be facilitated through the use of knowledge from other parties who have negotiated the same item in the past. The question now is "Which

other parties' negotiations knowledge should be used?" This is where reputation is employed.

Definition: The *reputation* of a provider or consumer is a quality that represents the degree to which he has fulfilled the commitments that he has made, either explicitly or implicitly. The commitments could be in everyday life (e.g. commitment to be faithful to a spouse) or in commerce (e.g. commitment to deliver work on time, commitment to respect a privacy policy, or commitment to pay for goods received).

The idea is to use the relevant knowledge of those having sufficiently high reputations. These parties would need to have a sufficiently high reputation and share your interest or purpose for the negotiation (I above). There may be other factors too, such as whether or not you know the party personally or have dealt with the party in the past. For manageability, we do not consider these other factors here.

A party's reputation is built-up over time from transactions with other parties. A particular transaction t occurs between 2 parties and has associated reputation factors that contribute to determining the reputation of either party from the point of view of the other party. So for example, if party 1 purchases a book from party 2, factors contributing to party 2's reputation (from party 1's point of view) include whether or not the book received was the one ordered, whether or not the book was delivered on time, and party 2's performance history with other buyers. Factors contributing to party 1's reputation (from party 2's point of view) include party 1's credit history, the nature of past dealings with party 1, and party 1's performance history with other sellers.

One way to compute reputation is simply to rate the performance of a provider or a consumer on the associated reputation factors for a given transaction t. Let $t_{i,j}$ represent a transaction that party i has with party j. Let $q_1(t_{i,j}), ..., q_n(t_{i,j})$ be the associated n reputation factors for transaction $t_{i,j}$ assigned by party i to party j, where each reputation factor (rating) is ≥ 0 and ≤ 1 (each factor is an assigned score such as 3/5 or 6/7). Then party i assigns party j a reputation component $p(t_{i,j})$ corresponding to transaction $t_{i,j}$, where

$$p(t_{i,j}) = \frac{1}{n} \sum_{k=1}^{n} q_k(t_{i,j}) \quad .$$

Over the course of m transactions $t_{i,j}$, party i assigns party j a reputation $P_{i,j}$, where

$$P_{i,j} = \frac{1}{m} \sum_{t_{i,j}} p(t_{i,j}) \quad .$$

Notice that $0 \leq p(t_{i,j}), P_{i,j} \leq 1$. Suppose now that there are h parties that have had transactions with party j. Then party j has reputation P_j, $0 \leq P_j \leq 1$ where

$$P_j = \frac{1}{h} \sum_{i} P_{i,j} \quad .$$

In calculating the P_j by averaging over the $P_{i,j}$, we are in effect building consensus, so that any bias by a particular party is mitigated to some extent. Of course, the degree of mitigation is greater the greater the number of parties averaged.

In the literature, there has been much research done on reputation [19]. Our formulas are consistent with what other researchers have done. In particular, Zacharia and Maes [20] have claimed that reputation in an online community can be described in terms of ratings that an agent receives from others. As a well-studied example, eBay client transaction ratings [21] are not too unlike our proposal above. As another

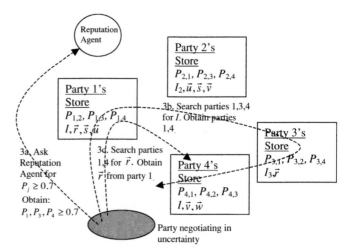

Figure 3 – Using the negotiating experience of others.

example, Cornelli et al [22] used a rating system to allow servents (a servent is an entity that is both a server and a client) to accumulate reliability reputations for other servents from which they download in a P2P network. These reputations are then use by resource requesters to assess the reliability of a potential provider before initiating a download.

4 SCHEME FOR NEGOTIATING PRIVACY POLICY UNDER UNCERTAINTY

We now describe an overall scheme on using the experience of others for negotiating privacy policy under uncertainty, as follows:

1. Every e-learning participant (both providers and consumers) accumulates negotiation experience in the form of negotiation trees (section 2).
2. Every e-learning participant calculates and stores the reputations $P_{i,j}$. A *reputation agent* can access these $P_{i,j}$ to calculate and store the P_j. This can be done periodically to keep the P_j fresh.
3. A participant who is negotiating in uncertainty would obtain assistance, in the form of negotiation alternatives and offers made, from other reputable participants who have negotiated the same issue. The participant would:
   a. Identify which parties are reputable by asking the reputation agent for reputations P_j which exceed a reputation threshold H. Call this set of reputable parties J. That is, $J = \left\{ j : P_j \geq H \right\}$ The value of H can be set according to the level of reputation desired.
   b. Among the parties in J, search for parties that have the same interests I as the participant. This produces a subset J_s.
   c. Among the participants in J_s, search for negotiated items r that match the item the participant is currently negotiating. This produces a subset $J_r \subseteq J_s$.
   d. Retrieve the matched negotiation trees $\vec{r}$ of participants in J_r.
      Use the alternatives and offers in these retrieved negotiation trees to formulate alternatives and offers. This is a manual step, supported by an effective user interface for displaying (or summarizing) the information to the participant for a decision on the alternatives. Note that the retrieved trees may be complete or incomplete (section 2).
   e. Update his current negotiation tree.

Step 3 may be done in real time if reputations and past negotiation trees are all in place. Hence a negotiator can receive help in this manner at any negotiation step, if desired. Figure 3 illustrates the above scheme, using $H = 0.7$.

Copyright © 2003, Idea Group Inc. Copying or distributing in print or electronic forms without written permission of Idea Group Inc. is prohibited.

5 CONCLUSIONS

This paper has presented an approach for negotiating privacy policy in distance education using negotiation trees and reputations. The paper categorized two types of negotiations: negotiating in certainty and uncertainty. The problem of negotiating in uncertainty was discussed and a solution given – that of using the negotiation experiences of reputable people with matching interests as aids in deciding which negotiating alternatives and offers should be employed. A scheme on how this could be done was presented. Our application of negotiation trees in tandem with a reputation approach to policy negotiation is unique. It should facilitate the implementation of privacy mechanisms, which are key to the wide spread adoption of distance education.

A prototype of a reputation-based negotiation mechanism for privacy policy in an agent-based e-learning application is currently under development. A separate paper will report on the results of this project.

6 REFERENCES

[1] P. Huang and K. Sycara; "A Computational Model for Online Agent Negotiation"; Proceedings of the 35th Annual Hawaii International Conference on System Sciences, 2002.

[2] F. Lopes et al; "Negotiation Tactics for Autonomous Agents"; Proceedings, 12th International Workshop on Database and Expert Systems Applications, 2001.

[3] M. Benyoucef et al; "An Infrastructure for Rule-Driven Negotiating Software Agents"; Proceedings, 12th International Workshop on Database and Expert Systems Applications, 2001.

[4] Y. Murakami et al; "Co-evolution in Negotiation Games"; Proceedings, Fourth International Conference on Computational Intelligence and Multimedia Applications, 2001.

[5] R. Lai and M. Lin; "Agent Negotiation as Fuzzy Constraint Processing"; Proceedings of the 2002 IEEE International Conference on Fuzzy Systems, Volume 2, 2002. FUZZ-IEEE'02.

[6] R. Kowalczyk and V. Bui; "On Fuzzy E-Negotiation Agents: Autonomous Negotiation with Incomplete and Imprecise Information"; Proceedings, 11th International Workshop on Database and Expert Systems Applications, 2000.

[7] M. Tu et al; "Genetic Algorithms for Automated Negotiations: A FSM-Based Application Approach"; Proceedings, 11th International Workshop on Database and Expert Systems Applications, 2000.

[8] M. Chung and V. Honavar; "A Negotiation Model in Agent-mediated Electronic Commerce"; Proceedings, International Symposium on Multimedia Software Engineering, 2000.

[9] B. Limthanmaphon et al; "An Agent-based Negotiation Model Supporting Transactions in Electronic Commerce"; Proceedings, 11th International Workshop on Database and Expert Systems Applications, 2000.

[10] T. Nguyen et al; "COPS-SLS: A Service Level Negotiation Protocol for the Internet"; IEEE Communications Magazine , Volume 40, Issue 5, May 2002.

[11] B. Boehm et al; "Developing Groupware for Requirements Negotiation: Lessons Learned"; IEEE Software, May/June 2001.

[12] D. Druckman et al; "Artificial Computer-Assisted International Negotiation: A Tool for Research and Practice"; Proceedings of the 35th Annual Hawaii International Conference on System Sciences, 2002.

[13] G. Kersten et al; "The Effects of Culture in Anonymous Negotiations: Experiments in Four Countries"; Proceedings of the 35th Annual Hawaii International Conference on System Sciences, 2002.

[14] W3C; "The Platform for Privacy Preferences"; http://www.w3.org/P3P/

[15] W3C; "A P3P Preference Exchange Language 1.0 (APPEL1.0)"; W3C Working Draft 15 April 2002, http://www.w3.org/TR/P3P-preferences/

[16] Carnegie Mellon University; "Privacy Server Protocol Project"; Internet Systems Laboratory, Robotics Institute and eCommerce Institute, School of Computer Science, http://yuan.ecom.cmu.edu/psp/

[17] Canadian Standards Association Privacy Principles on the web at: http://www.csa.ca/standards/privacy/code/Default.asp?language=English

[18] Department of Justice; Privacy provisions highlights, http://canada.justice.gc.ca/en/news/nr/1998/attback2.html

[19] L. Mui et al; "Notions of Reputation in Multi-Agents Systems: A Review"; AAMAS'02, Bologna, Italy, July 2002.

[20] G. Zacharia and P. Maes; "Collaborative Reputation Mechanisms in Electronic Marketplaces"; Proc. 32nd Hawaii International Conf. on System Sciences, 1999.

[21] C. Dellarocas; "Analyzing the Economic Efficiency of eBay-like Online Reputation Reporting Mechanisms"; Paper 102, Center for eBusiness@MIT, July 2001. Available at http://ebusiness.mit.edu/research/papers/102%20Dellarocas,%20eBay.pdf

[22] F. Cornelli et al; "Choosing Reputable Servents in a P2P Network"; WWW2002, Honolulu, Hawaii, May 2002.

ENDNOTE
[1] NRC Paper Number: NRC 44985

Towards Powerful, User-Friendly Authentication: The Check-Off Password System ("COPS")

Ernst Bekkering, Merrill Warkentin, and Kimberly Davis
Department of Management & Information Systems
College of Business and Industry, P.O Box 9581
Mississippi State University, MS STATE, MS 39762-9581
(662) 325-8475, (662) 325-1955, (662) 325-8066–Fax: (662) 325-8651
tjb6@msstate.edu, mwarkentin@acm.org, kdavis@cobilan.msstate.edu

ABSTRACT

Passwords have always been the dominant method of information system user authentication. The level of security provided by passwords has been an ongoing concern. Strong security requirements mandate that users are issued passwords of sufficient length and with sufficient variability in characters, but these passwords tend to be difficult to remember. Conversely, when users select their own, more easily-remembered passwords, the passwords may also be easier to violate or "crack." The proposed study presents a new approach to entering passwords, which combines a high level of security with easy recall for the user. The Check-Off Password System (COPS) is more secure than user-selected password systems, as well as high-protection, assigned password systems. However, we hypothesize that users will prefer this system to traditional assigned-password systems despite the more cognitively involved input mechanism, because it is easier to recall the COPS "password." Our findings will establish COPS as a valid alternative to current user authentication systems.

BACKGROUND

Despite continuing improvements in computer and network technology, computer security continues to be a concern. At the recent 2002 PC Expo, 74% of respondents stated that they would be working on computer security in 2003, and 80% consider security products a "hot" technology (Ames, 2002). A recent study found that the average cost of security breaches is currently $193,000 (Yager, 2002). That survey also reported that 24% of IT leaders are delaying deployment of Web services and 18% are delaying the implementation of wireless networks due to security concerns (Yager, 2002). In a different study, 90% of respondents detected computer security breaches within the last twelve months, but only 34% of intrusions were reported to law enforcement (Computer Security Institute, 2002).

One of the causes of these security breaches is the lack of effective user authentication, primarily due to poor password system management. Poor password practices occupy the number 2 spot on the Top 20 list of General Vulnerabilities (The SANS Institute, 2002). Yet even with today's high-speed computers, an eight-character password can be very secure indeed. If a Pentium 4 processor can test 8 million combinations per second, breaking an eight-character password would take more than 13 years on average (Lemos, 2002). Clearly, the potential for password security is not fully utilized.

PASSWORD STRATEGIES

The Federal Information Processing Standards (FIPS) publication 112 (National Institute of Standards and Technology, 1985) includes requirements for different levels of password security. At the highest level, these criteria include passwords with 6 to 8 characters composed from the full 95 printable character ASCII set. Furthermore, the guidelines specify using an automated password generator, individual ownership of passwords, use of non-printing keyboards, encrypted password

storage, and encrypted communications with message numbering. The theoretical number of passwords is approximately 6.7×10^{15} ($= 95^8 + 95^7 + 95^6$). However, to utilize the full set of characters, all non-alphanumeric characters must have an equal chance of selection as the alphanumeric characters. But passwords with non-alphanumeric characters can be hard to remember. Consider, for example, passwords such as " ,swFol=; " or " >_F<"Yjz ". To avoid having to use such awkward passwords, we have devised a new password interface for user authentication, described below.

When allowed to select their own password, users tend to select passwords which may be easy to remember, but may also be easy to crack. On the other hand, when they are assigned a cryptographically strong password, users will generally find them difficult to remember, and will frequently record them in writing. To remedy these potential security problems, various strategies are currently used. Some organizations attempt to reduce the number of passwords needed by using a single system sign on (SSO) (Boroditsky & Pleat, 2001). Others are researching the possibility of using graphical mechanisms (Real User Corporation, 2002) (Bolande, 2000) (Jermyn, Mayer, Monrose, Reiter, & Rubin, no date) or combining passwords with keystroke dynamics (Monrose, Reiter, & Wetzel, 1999). Organizations can instruct their members in the proper selection of passwords to varying degrees, from simple instructions regarding the minimum number of positions and the minimum variability of characters, to extensive instructions and even feedback mechanisms where weak passwords are rejected immediately (Bergadano, Crispo, & Ruffo, 1998) (Jianxin, 2001). Weirich and Sasse (2001) advocate proper instruction and motivation of users, as well as a flexible approach depending on the organization and type of work for which the security is needed.

In a study of password usage, Adams and Sasse (1999) identified the following four factors that negatively influence the use of passwords:

- the need to remember multiple passwords due to the use of different passwords for different systems and the requirement to change passwords at intervals;
- lack of user awareness regarding the requirements for secure password content;
- perceived lack of compatibility of passwords with work practices; and
- incorrect user perception of organizational security and information sensitivity.

Though the latter three factors can be remedied with organizational measures such as review of password policies and user education, the first factor remains grounded in the limitations of human memory. Since the number of secure systems used by each individual is bound to increase rather than decrease, memory limitations must be accommodated.

HUMAN MEMORY

A heuristic for the capacity of the human short-term memory system states that an individual can recall seven plus or minus two (7 ± 2) chunks of information (Miller, 1956). This rule of thumb applies only to information to be recalled for relatively brief periods without rehearsal. Information can be maintained for longer periods of time, but elaborate rehearsal is required for transfer to long-term memory (Hewett, 1999) (Newell & Simon, 1972). A recent model describes a *working memory*, which is part of the larger memory system and not distinct from long-term memory (Anderson, 1994). In this model, memory limitations also depend on the ability to retrieve information from long-term storage to working memory. Regardless of the cognitive model, a capacity limitation exists. The proposed password system addresses this memory capacity limitation by offering a process that is easier than FIPS-compliant password systems, yet is more secure.

THE CHECK-OFF PASSWORD SYSTEM (COPS)

Traditional password systems either assign an ordered series (sequence) of characters which may or may not spell something meaningful to the user, or users are allowed to select their own ordered sequence of characters. In either case, the order of the characters is significant and must be maintained. A strength of the Check-Off Password System (COPS) is that the order of characters within the password is irrelevant, and therefore the user can choose to remember them in many ways. COPS balances the security of system-selected passwords with the memorability of meaningful character combinations. It assigns each user a set of 8 different characters (the "COPS password") selected from the sixteen most commonly used lower case characters (AskOxford.com, 2002) (the "COPS Superset"), including all five major vowels (e a r i o t n s l c u d p m h g). The user is able to form any word or words from these 8 characters, and may use any of the characters more than once in doing so. For example, suppose a user were issued the characters, "ulatsreg" (in no particular order), which we will refer to as the "Example Password." Using the characters in the Example Password, one user might form the compound word "starglue" in order to remember the eight characters, whereas another user may select "gluerats", "slugtears", or "restgulag". In other words, while the Example Password (and every COPS password) consists of a random selection of 8 alphabetic characters without repetition, users may reorder those characters (and use characters more than once) to form their own "password" (similar to an anagram) to facilitate recall. The user may even use characters not found in the COPS Superset (b f y w k v x z j q) to form a memorizable password, since those characters will not be included on the input interface (the COPS selection grid, as described below). For example, by using the "b" character, a music aficionado could form the password "greatblues" from the Example Password. Finally, an automated password generator might include a facility for suggesting words from a dictionary.

To authenticate the user, COPS presents an 8-by-7 grid of checkboxes, each with a character randomly selected from the COPS Superset. The user checks off only the boxes showing the assigned characters in the COPS password. With 56 grid cells (boxes) and only 16 characters to choose from, characters will appear more than once, requiring an average of 3.5 check-offs.

Consider the Example Password again ("ulatsreg"). To enter the password, the user would be presented with a grid such as the one shown in Figure 1 below, which demonstrates a failed attempt to enter the Example Password. To successfully enter the Example Password, the user would need to check the box for every "u" appearing in the grid (i.e., three checkboxes with a "u" would need to be checked), and the user would need to check the box for every "l" appearing in the grid (i.e., four checkboxes with an "l"), etc. If the user fails to successfully check all of the necessary boxes, she will be presented with a new grid in a randomized layout (which will almost certainly be different than the preceding layout). In Figure 1, the user has neglected to check off the "s" box in the fourth row of the second column. The login attempt will fail, and on the next attempt, a completely new grid layout will be presented.

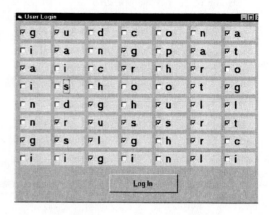

Without the ever-changing grid interface, the number of possible combinations would be no higher than C(16,8) or 12,870, because the presence of one instance of a character would determine the result for all other instances of the same character. In other words, if one "t" is selected, all other boxes with a "t" on the same interface should also be selected. Even with a new layout on each login attempt, a human cracker can manually try to enter all 12,870 combinations, because he can see the characters in the checkboxes. Of course, time considerations would make this impractical. A computer can run through combinations much faster, but if the characters are blended into a background graphic for each new login interface, the computer could only "see" them with Optical Character Recognition (OCR). This is much more processor-intensive than entering a simple string. As long as the layouts are randomly generated and OCR cannot be used effectively, the number of possible combinations with 56 check-off boxes either selected or not selected will remain 2^{56} or 7.2 x 10^{16}.

Although the semi-self-selected passwords using COPS are easy to remember, the system also requires user input which is more cognitively challenging than traditional password systems. If only one check-off box is erroneously missed or selected, an entirely new check-off grid must be generated and completed, thereby increasing the cognitive load of the activity. This may generate resistance to adoption on the part of the system user. In new technology implementations, the Technology Acceptance Model (TAM) indicates that perceived ease of use (PEOU) and perceived usefulness (PU) are considered antecedents of intention to use, which in turn is an antecedent to actual use (Davis, 1989). Therefore, it is imperative that we test the PEOU and PU of COPS in order to evaluate its actual potential as a preferable alternative to current user authentication methods.

PROPOSAL AND DISCUSSION

In order to evaluate the efficacy of COPS, we will conduct a controlled empirical study of COPS and existing alternatives, comparing user perceptions and measures of efficiency. Users will be experienced system users who have previously used multiple password systems. Treatment groups include those with (1) self-selected passwords without restrictions, (2) system-assigned passwords from the list of common passwords found in Spafford (1988), (3) system-assigned passwords following the FIPS standard for high protection (National Institute of Standards and Technology, 1985), and (4) system-assigned "passwords" in the Check-Off Password System (COPS). Standard pre-test and post-test research instruments for the Technology Acceptance Model (TAM), modified as appropriate, will be applied to the various treatment groups, and short-term and medium-term recall performance will be measured. Results will be evaluated with standard tests of variance and covariance to determine the effectiveness of each password strategy in terms of both performance and user acceptance. Whereas COPS may be mathematically more secure than the alternatives, the research questions are: (1) to what extent will users accept this system, and (2) will users be able to successfully remember their COPS password and be able to log into the system? We will also employ software routines to attempt to crack the COPS password-protected systems and compare those results to the results from similar tests performed on the alternative password systems.

When completed, this study will expand our knowledge of password system acceptance by users by comparing users' perceptions of various alternatives along with the effectiveness of each system as a strong user authentication protocol. Only when viewed in their entirety can the alternative techniques be reasonably compared. The results of this study will be reported at the conference.

REFERENCES

Adams, A., & Sasse, M. A. (1999). Users are not the enemy. *Communications of the ACM, 42*(12), 40—46.

Ames, B. B. (2002). PC developers worry about security. *Design News, 57*(16), 29.

Anderson, J. R. (1994). *Cognitive Psychology and Its Implications* (4th ed.). New York, NY: W. H. Freeman.

AskOxford.com. (2002). *What is the frequency of the letters of the alphabet in English.* Available: http://www.askoxford.com/asktheexperts/faq/aboutwords/frequency [2002, 9/29/2002].

Bergadano, F., Crispo, B., & Ruffo, G. (1998). High dictionary compression for proactive password checking. *ACM Transactions on Information and System Security (TISSEC), 1*(1), 3—25.

Bolande, H. (2000, November 26, 2000). *Forget passwords, what about pictures?* Available: http://zdnet.com.com/2102-11-525841.html [2002, 9-18-2002].

Boroditsky, M., & Pleat, B. (2001). *Security @ The Edge - Making Security and Usability a Reality with SSO.* Available: http://www.passlogix.com/media/pdfs/security_at_the_edge.pdf [2002, 9-18-2002].

Computer Security Institute. (2002). *Cyber crime bleeds U.S. corporations, survey shows; financial losses from attacks climb for third year in a row.* Available: http://www.gocsi.com/press/20020407.htmlApril 7, 2002].

Davis, F. D. (1989). Perceived Usefulness, Perceived Ease of Use, and User Acceptance of Information Technology. *MIS Quarterly, 13*(Issue 3), 318.

Hewett, T. T. (1999). *Cognitive factors in design (tutorial session): basic phenomena in human memory and problem solving.* Paper presented at the Proceedings of the third conference on Creativity & cognition, Loughborough, United Kingdom.

Jermyn, I., Mayer, A., Monrose, F., Reiter, M. K., & Rubin, A. D. (no date). *The Design and Analysis of Graphical Passwords.* Available: http://www.usenix.org/publications/library/proceedings/sec99/full_papers/jermyn/jermyn_html/camera3.html9/18/2002].

Jianxin, J. Y. (2001, 2001). *A note on proactive password checking.* Paper presented at the Proceedings of the 2001 workshop on New security paradigms, Cloudcroft, New Mexico.

Lemos, R. (2002). *Passwords: the Weakest Link?* Available: http://news.com.com/2009-1001-916719.html [2002, 9-18-2002].

Miller, G. A. (1956). The magical number seven, plus or minus two: some limits on our capacity for processing information. *Psychological Review, 63,* 81-97.

Monrose, F., Reiter, M. K., & Wetzel, S. (1999, 1999). *Password hardening based on keystroke dynamics.* Paper presented at the Proceedings of the 6th ACM conference on Computer and communications security, Kent Ridge Digital Labs, Singapore.

National Institute of Standards and Technology. (1985). *Federal Information Processing Standards Publication 112.* Available: http://www.itl.nist.gov/fipspubs/fip112.htm9-18-2002].

Newell, A., & Simon, H. A. (1972). *Human Problem Solving.* Englewood Cliffs, NJ: Prentice-Hall.

Real User Corporation. (2002). *The Passface™User Authentication System.* Available: http://www.realuser.com/cgi-bin/ru.exe/_/homepages/users/passface.htm [9/18/2002.

Spafford, E. H. (1988). *The Internet Worm Program: An Analysis* (Technical Report Purdue Technical Report CSD-TR-823). West Lafayette, IN 47907-2004: Purdue University.

The SANS Institute. (2002). *The Twenty Most Critical Internet Security Vulnerabilities (Updated).* Available: http://www.sans.org/top20.htmMay 2, 2002].

Weirich, D., & Sasse, M. A. (2001, 2001). *Pretty good persuasion: a first step towards effective password security in the real world.* Paper presented at the Proceedings of the 2001 workshop on New security paradigms, Cloudcroft, New Mexico.

Yager, T. (2002). Security Part 1: Strategies. *InfoWorld, 24*(Issue 33), 1.

Web Services and Workflow Modeling

Vincent C. Yen
Department of Management Science and Information Systems
Wright State University
Dayton, Ohio 45435
Vince.Yen@wright.edu

ABSTRACT

"Web services" is an emerging field on the Internet. Recent surveys indicate that majority of large companies have started experimenting the technology. The paper aims to explore the role of workflow modeling in the world of Web services. What are the features of workflow modeling in the Web services environment? What are the differences of the workflow concept used in Web services and in workflow modeling management systems? What are the implications of this new paradigm to the professionals of management information systems? These are some of the questions to be discussed in this paper.

INTRODUCTION

Recently there is a proliferation of activities on the subject of "Web services". Once may find all the Information about such activities from a few Web sites, e.g., http://www.w3.org/, www.WebServices.org, and the Web sites of all major software companies. "Web services" is not an abstract concept; it actually could be build with proper tool available now. Some companies are providing such services now, see www.xmethods.net. A report from the FactPoint Research and Consulting Group (2002) indicates how well received of the idea of Web services by Fortune 1000 companies. The report says:

"Almost half of the respondents to our survey this spring are already piloting or deploying live applications based on Web services. In fact, Fortune 1000 companies are the most aggressive adopters of Web services applications. They are clearly   convinced that Web services are a strategic technology."

So the present state of technology does allow companies and individuals creating Web services. Microsoft Visual Studio .Net - a popular development tool for creating Web services has been on the market for almost a year. Java 2 Enterprise Edition (J2EE) is also a development tool. Some small scale demonstration projects could be found at many Web sites, including Microsoft. For example, BasicOptionPricing by WebserviceX.NET for European call and put options, the Black Scholes analysis, adjusting for payouts of the underlying American options. However, business use of Web services technology and implementation is still in its early infancy, the realization of its full impact to the business world remains many years away.

Our focus is to explore the role of workflow modeling in the business application development with Web services. We begin with an explanation "Web service" and "workflow modeling".

WHAT IS "WEB SERVICES"?

The phrase "Web Service" has been defined in many different ways. For example,

Web services encompass a vision of a fully integrated computing network that include PCs, servers, handheld devices, programs, applications and network equipment, all working together. This network can perform distributed computation with the best-matched device for the task and deliver the information on a timely basis in the form needed by the user.
(Castro-Leon, 2002)

Castro-Leon extrapolates that "under Web services, almost any program can be viewed as a building block to build more complex functions. In a recursive fashion: the new system could, in turn, become a

building block for an even more complex system." This statement is most intriguing because it points out the possibility of building any applications using any programs on the Internet.

Stated in another way (Ambrosio, 2002), "Web services" has a goal of making different software-based systems work together over the Web on Internet. From the business point of view, the services allow software and data to communicate with each other, internally or externally, via the internet without manual intervention." Under this paradigm, the existing infrastructure of information technology could be re-used, and the cost of system integration would be drastically cut.

Another useful definition is found from W3C (2002) on a working draft of Web Services Architecture. They define

"A Web service is a software system identified by a URI, whose public interfaces and bindings are defined and described using XML. Its definition can be discovered by other software systems. These systems may then interact with the Web service in a manner prescribed by its definition, using XML based messages conveyed by internet protocols."

WORKFLOW MODELING AND WORKFLOW MANAGEMENT SYSTEM

The Website of the Workflow Management Coalition (WfMC): www.wfmc.org is a definitive source of information for the concept of workflow and its management systems. The coalition attempts to define a unified concept of workflow and how it should be managed within and across the boundaries of organizations. The concept of workflow as defined by WfMC is:

The automation of a business process, in whole or part, during which documents, information or tasks are passed from one participant to another for action, according to a set of procedural rules.

A WfMC white paper (1998) defines a business process as "a set of one or more linked procedures or activities which collectively realize a business objective or policy goal, normally with the context of an organizational structure defining functional roles and relationships." For example, "getting a loan" and "making a course registration" both are business processes involving procedures and activities. A business process may have *sub-processes*. Each process/sub-process consists of *activities*, and that in turn, consists of *work items*. An activity may be manual or machine dependent and is considered as a logical step in the process, (e.g., filling out an application,) and normally is handled by workflow participants. After completion (may be partial completion) of an activity, work items are passed to another participant or a process. Workflow specifies the order of activities that may be performed, according to a set of procedural rules, in a business process.

Casati et al (1997) developed a workflow description language in which a business process is viewed as a set of tasks and relationships among tasks. Tasks are elementary work units to be done by a person, by a software system or by both of them. Therefore, the two terms 'task' and 'activity' are equivalent. A workflow specifies which tasks should be executed, in which order, who may be in charge of them, which operations should be performed by external systems or databases. In the example of 'getting a business loan' process, check client's credit, review client's employment status, calculate the loan's limit, are tasks that may be required.

WHAT IS A WORKFLOW MANAGEMENT SYSTEM?

Now we look at the notion of the workflow management system (WfMS) because it helps to explain the difference from a business application system. The defining concept of a workflow management system as found in Allen (2001) is:

A system that defines, creates and manages the execution of workflow through the use of software, running on one or more workflow engines, which is able to interpret the process definition, interact with workflow participants and, where required, invoke the use of IT tools and applications.

In essence, WfMSs should be implemented as software that is capable of 1) interpreting the process definition, 2) interacting with workflow participants, and 3) invoking IT tools and applications. A rigorous process definition language has been proposed by Casati et al (1997). A WfMS basically consists of a business process enactment component and a task-processing component. The task- processing component checks, executes, and reports task's status to the workflow engine. The business process (a set of tasks) enactment component reacts to events by activating tasks, assigning them to agents, and work with other systems of databases. This component works as a workflow control center with scheduling and assignment capabilities and is usually called the workflow engine.

THE DIFFERENCES BETWEEN WEB SERVICES AND WORKFLOW MANAGEMENT SYSTEMS

"Web services" has a goal of creating a new piece of business application system by composing from existing system components within and across organization boundaries on the Internet. So, the first characteristic is that the new application has to be built on the Internet. Second, it has to interact with the existing system components on the Internet regardless of the language used by system components. Developing Web services under these two fundamental conditions requires establishing a workable infrastructure in which software components are described at a semantic level and invoked by application programs or other Web services. The infrastructure consists of Internet standards such as HTTP, XML, SOAP, WSDL, and UDDI. (Curbera et al 2002). A brief explanation of each standard and their relationships is shown in Figure 1.

Although the basic workflow concept used in Web services and WfMSs are the same but the implementation circumstances are different. In composing a Web service from other Web services there is a need for conceptual workflow analysis before it could begin with orderly construction. Because Web services are built upon the special infrastructure, new languages are developed for workflow modeling purposes, for example, the recently announced Business Process Execution Language for Web Services (BPEL4WS) by IBM and Microsoft.

The goal of WfMC is to support the users of workflow technology for all purposes. Under the influence of new Internet technologies,

WfMS is also evolving into distribution of work among organizations from its earlier role of managing the distribution of work between people. The Workflow Management Coalition (WfMC) has announced the release of its Workflow Standard *XML Process Definition Language - XPDL 1.0* (Marin, et al, 2002). Together with other WfMC standards, XPDL (also based on XML specification) provides a framework for implementing business process management and workflow engines, and for designing, analyzing, and exchanging business processes.

The standards developed by BPEL4WS and by XPDL are different. BPEL4WS centers on issues of importance in defining Web services; however, XPDL has emphasis on the issues of distribution of work. A detailed comparison may be found in (Shapiro, 2002). Interestingly, according to Fischer (2002) WfMC has not only developed XPDL specification that essentially contains all features of BPEL4WS, and also a Wf-XML, the process execution standard. In addition, XPDL is only one of five functional interfaces to a workflow service as identified by WfMC (1998). The WfMC's standards form a superset of all workflow standards.

So far we only mentioned two workflow modeling languages, there are other languages developed or under development by software companies, e.g., BPML – the Business Process Markup language is developed by the Business Process Management Initiative. Clearly for the benefit of end users, all existing workflow language standards should unify into one.

AN EXAMPLE OF WORKFLOW FOR WEB SERVICES

Workflow modeling languages for Web services such as BPEL4WS is a product of collaborative effort between IBM and Microsoft. BPEL4WS actually inherits the languages of IBM's WSFL (Web Services Flow Language, and Microsoft's XLANG (Web Services for Business Process Design). Therefore BPEL4WS has features from its predecessors. WSFL consists of flow models and global models. Flow models use acyclic graph to describe sequence of functionalities provided by a set of Web services in order to achieve a new business process. Global models describe how a set of Web services interact with each other. XLANG on the other hand uses a block structured language format. These two models provide a high-level platform for defining workflow between system components and the related traffic management, and they are generic features in workflow modeling languages. To give a hypothetical example of a loan application Web services and how an acyclic graph may be applied to describe the composite service, we first assume that a credit check web service at CreditCheck.com, an internal developed customer asset estimation service named CustomerAE.service, and a loan decision and recommendation service at LoanDecision.com are available. A composite Web service expressed graphically is shown in Figure 2.

IMPLICATIONS IN THE PRESENCE OF WEB SERVICES

In an October 2002 survey conducted by Evans Data Corp (2002), the most important reasons to adopt web services are:
1. 24% opted for "Common fabric for systems and application integration"
2. 24% - Mechanism for integrating processes with partners & customers

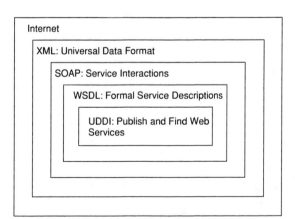

Figure 1. Fundamental Infrastructure of Web Services

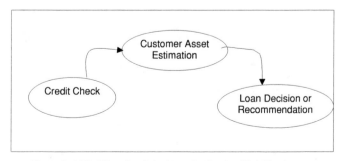

Figure 2. A Workflow Graph for Loan Application Web Services

3. 19% - Modular code components that can be reused
4. 16% - Reduced development and maintenance time
5. 10% - Ability to extend the life and value of legacy systems
6. 7% - High-profile vendor promotion and evangelism

The survey result provides some basis for our inference in the presence of Web services.

MIS Professionals

From item 1, MIS professionals need to expand their business problem analysis beyond their organization boundaries. This is because the new Web Services standards at the higher level are built upon the notion of business rules, business processes, and workflow concepts. A business application system is a system of components of business processes. A business process defines a procedure for conducting a business activity. A well prepared business procedure is defined by a set of clearly stated business rules. The ability to effectively use services/processes within or external to an organization requires a good understanding of all business processes involved. This is an area where MIS professionals can play an important role.

Patterns of Web Services

Although Web services is designed to be able to integrate various services based on the Internet, but in business applications the interest is to solve business problems. Due to significant differences in business operations among business organizations, it is not surprising that there will be patterns of Web services developed for each type of business. Like WfMSs, Allen (2001) classifies WfMS by production, autonomous workflow engines, embedded workflow, administrative, collaborative, and ad-hoc categories. The need to study Web service by type of business or industry is further supported by the fact that there are about 400 standards consortia working on XML definitions for the business processes (Castro-Leon, 2002). Similar situation is expected to occur in Web services applications (item 2 above).

Fast Development for Complex Systems

Complex business application systems, e.g., the supply chain management system, involving multi-process, and multi-workflow are also being developed. It is easy to imaging that complex projects come with high degree of difficulty and cost. Web service technology allows the work to be decentralized and distributed among intra/inter-organizational systems and then integrated. Since critical business components may be available on Internet, thus the use of such components (items 3 and 4 above) with Web services would accelerate the speed of system development.

Increased Reusability and Decreased Cost

Services on the Internet could be potentially reused (item 4) by any other services though the Web services framework. This includes currently inaccessible services due to lack of the infrastructure for delivering such services on the Internet. With Web services fully established, all services on the Web become reusable resources. Since services are available on the Internet, they would be widely used. The fact that

services could be made available on demand without reinventing the wheels, the cost of developing a business application would go down necessarily.

Legacy Applications Modernization

Item 5 indicates that Web services may be the most promising way to tap and support huge database of end users that are on mainframes and midrange-class server systems across enterprises. Another application of Web services on enterprise legacy systems is to achieve standardization across all their platforms, software, and hardware. These applications of Web services are internal integration activities to an enterprise and therefore they are expected to be most active in the next few years.

CONCLUSION

This paper examines some aspects of Web services at a high level view. We briefly discussed the technology of Web services and its implications. Web services is being developed at a very rapid pace by the software industry. This technology will influence the way we work and interact in the near future. For MIS professionals this is a new area for work and research.

REFERENCES
Allen, R. (2000), Workflow: An Introduction, in The Workflow Handbook 2001, edited by Fisher, L., Workflow Management Coalition.

Ambrosio, J. (2002). Web Services: Report from the Field. Application Development Trends, Vol. 9, No. 6, June, 2002.

Casati, F., Ceri, S., Pernici, B., and Pozzi, G., (1997), Advances in Object-Oriented Data Modeling, edited by Papaxoglou, M., Spaccapietra, S., and Tari, Z., The MIT Press.

Castro-Leon, Enrique (2002). A perspective on Web Services, http://webservices.org/article/articleprint/113/-1/24/ of IntelPublishing.

Evans Data Corp. (2002). Enterprise Development Management Issues 2002: Vol. 2. http://www.EvansData.com.

Hollingsworth, D., (1995). Workflow Management Coalition - The Workflow Reference Model, Doc. # TC00-1003. The Workflow Management Coalition.

Marin, M., Norin, R., and Shapiro, R. Edited. (2002); Workflow Process Definition Interface — XML Process Definition Language. Document Number: WFMC-TC-1025. Document Status: 1.0 Final Draft.

Fischer, L. (2002). The WfMC Heralds BPEL4WS Standards for Business Process Management Industry. URL: http://xml.coverpages.org/WfMC-Heralds-BPEL4WS.html.

Plummer, D. et al. (2001). Requirements for Web Services: Terms and Technology, Gartner Research Note COM-12-7087.

Shapiro, R. (2002). "A Comparison of XPDL, BPML, and BPEL4WS." Published by ebPML.org. 'Rough Draft' version 1.4.

WfMC , (1998), Workflow and Internet: Catalysts for Radical Change, A white paper by Workflow Management Coalition, www.wfmc.org.

W3C (2002), Web Services Architecture, W3C Working Draft. http://www.w3.org/TR/2002/WD-ws-arch-20021114/.

Component Context Specification and Representation in System Analysis and Design

Zheying Zhang and Janne Kaipala
Department of Computer Science and Information Systems
University of Jyväskylä, PL 35, FIN-40351 Jyväskylä, Finland
zhezhan@cc.jyu.fi, jka@it.jyu.fi

ABSTRACT

The apparent lack of design information is one of the most significant barriers that system developers face to reuse or change component-based information systems. This paper tackles the problem by presenting and exemplifying the frameworks of component context and its hypertext data model. It addresses the possible linking of contextual knowledge to components, including the conceptual dependencies of component construction, reuse, and implementation, as well as the rationale behind design and reuse processes. Furthermore, it illustrates the hypertext approach to contextual knowledge representation, which provides ways for users to express, explore, recognize, and negotiate their shared context.

1 INTRODUCTION

In order to succeed in collaboration, a component based development (CBD) environment should provide ways for users to express, explore, recognize, and negotiate their shared context. The context is elaborated in terms of the specific application domains and specific intentions, which increase richness of interactions among stakeholders while avoiding repetition, and thereby enhancing reusability.

As Jones [1] indicates only 15% of the requirements for a new system are unique to the system while the remaining 85% comes from requirements of existing systems. Information systems development (ISD) is hereby a process to retrieve and adapt reusable components. The component retrieval process is contextual: a system designer is faced with specific application domains which he looks with some design decisions in mind. The support of the retrieval process requires that knowledge should be provided about contexts in which component can be used. Generally, a component repository does not carry information about the possible use situations, and little semantic support can be provided in the search task. Our view is that knowledge about the use context of components needs to be formalized, stored, and presented with components.

Context exists at various layers of understanding and can be defined and used from many perspectives due to different situations. In a CBD environment, a context forms specific relationship types among components and its development environment [2], such as the conceptual or semantic relationships between components, the domain specific relationships between components and its development environment, and the rationale of component design and reuse [3]. The contextual knowledge will benefit system development activities by increasing available knowledge and richness of interactions between components and users; capitalizing on existing knowledge and previous experience of stakeholders involved in the system development project and decreasing difficulties resulting from individual differences in understanding in a specific application domain.

However, current modeling techniques do not document the reasoning and the rationale behind the suggested solution. The design models are often not communicative, and descriptions cannot be fully understood by users and stakeholders [4]. This makes it difficult to understand models and reuse older ones or parts of them. The purpose of this paper is to present the taxonomy of contextual knowledge for components generated during system analysis and design, and to build a hypertext data model for further implementation. The specification of component context recapitulates our preceding research in component definition [2], at the same time the data model represents solutions to component context definition and utilization.

2 COMPONENT CONTEXT IN SYSTEM ANALYSIS AND DESIGN

Understandability and readability of a component is crucial for its reuse and evolution. While component interface provides essential information, in order to select and reuse a component various forms of contextual knowledge is needed, including the domain description, the conceptual structure and dependency, and the rationale that records predictable and unpredictable ways and environments to facilitate reuse. An extensive context framework has to be developed in order to provide enhanced services in the reuse and the system development processes. The framework must include both the static information derived from component concept and content and the ongoing arguments and decisions which reveal CBD processes. Accordingly, we incorporate the conceptual dependency and the rationale in the component context framework.

2.1 Conceptual Dependency

With the growing number of concepts and the increasing interdependency of ISD methodologies, the components generated from design models become increasingly complex. They are often designed with extremely subtle dependencies on other components that are not explicitly described [5]. However, the construction and maintenance of component-based system analysis and design models require clear understanding of the dependencies between components. Conceptual dependencies between components exist thereafter. The conceptual dependency, as determined by conceptual semantics, forms a way of representing the relationships between components based on a particular meaning of the concepts [6]. It implies the information about how components may and should be used or have been reused in conjunction with other components. There are varied conceptual dependencies with wide variations in the format and content across different contexts, e.g. the definition dependency, the reuse dependency, and the implementation dependency. Clearly, the dependencies between components are necessary and desirable. They need to be clearly expressed by component designers and well understood by users.

Definition Dependency. A definition dependency from a concept CP_x to a concept CP_y is created if CP_x is used in the definition of CP_y [7]. In short, it represents part-of relationships among components. The part-of relationships always exist in component-based systems. They are closely interrelated, but difficult to track in a complex system design if the tool does not facilitate the representation of the definition dependency. For example, a small granularity level component, like the class *PhoneNumber*, is always involved in one (or more) relatively large granularity level component(s), like a class diagram specifying the structure of phone book. Moreover, components can be used as a part of a "larger" component on the same granularity level for a wider or more complete definition, like the relationship between a state transition diagram and the decomposed diagrams therein.

Reuse Dependency. The introduction of component technology into system analysis and design is likely to require a major paradigm shift in design practices in order to better incorporate reuse. Some components are closely related by means of reuse. The reuse dependency identifies the conceptual adaptation between a reusable component and the target ones. In general, it can be divided into "reuse-by-copy" and "reuse-by-reference". Reuse-by-copy occurs when the component user copies (parts of) a component and changes it to meet local needs. Reuse-by-reference on the other hand requires that the same component is used and shared by all users. The reuse dependency indicates the ways to replace or update a component. For example, any modifications on a component will reflect the components having "reuse by reference" dependencies on it, and component users thereby should inspect all reuse related components thoroughly before making any modification.

Implementation Dependency. An implementation dependency describes how a component depends on other components for its implementation [8]. It connects the components that specify the same problem domain or solution but are generated at different development stages. The implementation dependency presents a traceable relationship between components from the high level requirements down to the final implementation, and it thus helps users to trace components' implementation in both forward and backward directions [9, 10]. It enhances reuse by enabling the use of high-level requirement components as the basis to select lower level design or code components [9-11]. Moreover, it enables to analyze the impact of changes in requirements to the rest of the design [10, 11].

The different types of dependencies help designers easily keep track of components at different system development stages, and their interrelationships. Through the definition dependency and reuse dependency component users can see the impacts of possible component update and replacement: "Which other components use this component?" or "Which components are (re)used by this one?". Furthermore, when different types of dependencies have been calculated, it is possible to create a component dependency graph for the design project, by which system designers have the possibility of marking selected components as critical, to indicate that they must not be affected by a component update or replacement, which provides support for component configuration management and change management.

2.2 Rationale

Successful ISD stories address that knowledge from the past and from various stakeholders is used in its processes. Rationale captured in system analysis and design, is one way to keep such knowledge. It includes decisions, alternatives, arguments, and assumptions [11-15]. Generally, the rationale varies widely in quality, formality and in the level of detail across different components and the discussion issues [10]. In a component-based system analysis and design, the rationale records the understanding of why a component has been developed and reused the way it has. More specifically, it records distinct purposes and concerns from component designers and users. On one hand, component design involves decisions and assumptions that drive component reuse, on the other hand, the component reuse process produces feedback that supports component maintenance and system evolution [16, 17]. While considering the different purposes of component context, we distinguish between the design rationale and the use rationale.

Design Rationale. In practice, the design rationale recorded by component designers serves as an externalization of a design for both component users and designers, while it communicates design information to them. Consequently, design rationales provide domain information and answer specific questions of component definition and maintenance. A well-designed component can be easily reused in different design scenarios within the same domain. Therein, design rationale is an ideal way for component designers to record the assumptions of diverse design scenarios and to supervise the component reuse process by suggesting component users that where and how the component should be modified to meet a new set of requirements.

Use Rationale. In general, component users capture use rationale in the sequential stages of a component reuse process: search, selection, adaptation and integration [3]. Accordingly, use rationales can be categorized according to these stages. The rationale under this context has two major functions. On one hand, it reflects the scenarios of using a component, on the other hand, it evaluates the component complexity and reusability and provides feedback for component maintenance.

The loss of design information becomes a problem when systems have to change to meet unanticipated requirements. The engineers responsible for system evolution must analyze the design and infer the reasons for particular design choices. As a reference to the system engineers, the rationale identifies the justification for the evolution of systems by recording component design and reuse activities as the arguments for and against the alternatives and the final decisions, which will significantly decrease the cost of system evolution [16, 17]. Moreover, a chronological display of the rationales provides clear understanding of the component evolution process, facilitating maintenance and reuse.

3 LINK TYPES FOR CONTEXTUAL INFORMATION REPRESENTATION

Hypertext is a feasible approach to model integration and context representation [11, 18-24] especially for the rationale that can be captured any time at the analysis and design stage. It represents and integrates contextual information by means of nodes and links. Nodes represent components and their contextual information while links represent their relationships. These links can carry different types of information, such as the conceptual dependencies and the rationale. Accordingly, we distinguish between three types of traceability links: association, annotation and debate links, as shown in Table 1. These links are applied according to the link types presented by Oinas-Kukkonen [23], and we further consider the reuse subtype links.

Association Links are defined mainly to represent the conceptual dependencies between components. In practice, they represent relationships between related artifacts such as components, documents, a part of a component, and a part of a document. They are generated to let users perform several tasks during design: track the composition of components, track the modification and refinement history of a component, manage the repercussions of changes in one on other components that reuse and depend on it [10], identify the requirements related to components, and ensure consistency between the components in the successive stages of the life cycle. Due to the diverse roles which association links take in different contexts, further link semantics can be expressed by the subtypes, like the definition dependency (e.g. is-part-

Table 1. Types of links for component context representation

Traceability Link Type	Subtypes	Contextual knowledge
Association	Definition dependency: is-part-of Reuse dependency: is-reused-by-{copy, reference} Implementation dependency: is-implemented-by	Conceptual dependency
Annotation	Design rationale: design rationale Use rationale: rationale-for-component-{search, selection, adaptation, integration}	Rationale
Debate		

of), the reuse dependency (e.g. reuse-by-copy) and implementation dependency (e.g. implements).

Annotation Links provide a way to connect information, namely an annotation node, to a (part of the) component or a (part of the) document. In essence, they support reuse processes by capturing information related to a particular design situation, and component reuse and maintenance process. Annotation links lead to annotation nodes that allow free text representation, thereby enabling the recording of any information that demands text representation, including textual design rationale. The more structured approach to capturing arguments over design decisions is provided by debate links.

Debate Links represent the argument-based rationale behind components including reasons for evolutionary steps and contextual information in the design and reuse phases. They integrate the stakeholders' arguments to the design components. In order to provide a clear overview of the captured rationale, we can further categorize rationale in line with phases of the life cycle and the aspects of the issues to be argued.

4 HYPERTEXT DATA MODEL FOR CONTEXTUAL INFORMATION REPRESENTATION

In terms of component-based reuse, the hypertext data model has two kinds of nodes: component nodes (or design elements inside a component) and contextual information nodes (e.g. Questions, Answers, Arguments and Annotations). As shown in Fig. 1, both types of nodes can be sources or targets of links. Moreover, the link source can be specified as a piece of text inside a node. As stated in section 3 we propose traceability links to connect the component nodes and contextual information nodes. Different types of traceability links are used under different contexts.

Arrows in Fig. 1 demonstrate the information flows that are traceable between two types of nodes. In detail, the source of an annotation link can be any node and the target is an annotation node. Similarly, a debate link can start anywhere and the link target is a debate node. The source and target of an association link can be any node.

Links have attributes such as subtype, keywords, creator, creation time, which can be used to define further link semantics for reuse purposes. The contextual information nodes can be organized into named collections: Questions belong to "debate spaces" and Annotations belong to "annotation spaces". Furthermore, debate nodes are linked by using specific link types: Questions are linked to Answers by "answers-to-question", and Arguments are linked to Answers by "supports" or "objects-to" links.

In order to demonstrate the representation of component context, we discuss a mobile phone user interface design scenario within the phone product family. Suppose that the company has created a mobile phone user interface design architecture, domain models, and a set of reusable components to quickly deliver mobile phones in various versions. In this scenario, the company plans to deliver a user interface design of mobile phone version 4.4 by reusing components from the prior 4.2 version. Compared with version 4.2, a new feature in version 4.4 is an improved calendar that provides a "structured date editor". Accordingly, the requirements list of version 4.4 is created by reusing the requirements list version 4.2. Meanwhile, new requirements are added, including the requirement "The Calendar shall support structured date input". As shown in Fig. 2, in the process of creating the new require-

Fig. 1. The hypertext data model

Fig. 2. Examples of different traceability links in a mobile phone user interface design scenario

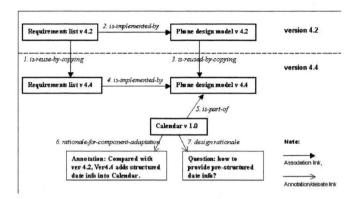

ments list, traceability links such as reuse dependency (arrow 1) have been created, and the implementation dependency (arrow 2) was traced to get the corresponding design model components of version 4.2. Hereby, the design models are reused by copy (arrow 3), and a new implementation dependency is created between the requirements list and the design model components (arrow 4). At the same time, structured date input function is added into the *Calendar* component, and the rationale about the different implementation alternatives and decision related to the structured date input function are recorded by the annotation link (arrow 6) and the debate link (arrow 7).

In this brief scenario, information is captured by creating different types of contextual links during the analysis and design processes. The links represent various conceptual dependencies and rationales. Although the presented scenario is simple and uncompleted, as compared with the phone development life cycle, masses of contextual information and 14 contextual links have been created. Without the context specification and its hypertext representation, the substantial knowledge about the component logic and semantic structure and about the design rationale is buried in the development process and is difficult to remember, retrieve, and reuse after the project.

5 CONCLUSIONS

Component context drives reuse activities from the requirements analysis towards the final implementation in a CBD environment. However, the benefits of component context will not come to full fruition unless they are elaborately defined and directly integrated into the basic development activities of ISD [25]. In this paper we have tried to increase the understanding of component context in perspectives of conceptual dependencies and rationales that supports CBD. The different types of dependencies and rationales assemble the different aspects of component context, which constitutes the conceptual foundation of component reuse. They are provided as an adjunct part of a component and embedded in the CBD processes. Furthermore, the mechanisms of component context representation and the approach to facilitating the contextual knowledge are proposed and demonstrated by showing the hypertext data model which consists of two types of nodes (component and contextual information) and three types of traceability links (the association link, the annotation link, and the debate link). The hypertext data model represents concepts and mechanisms to facilitate the representation of syntax and semantics of components and the contextual information between components and its design environment. We believe that once it is integrated to a CASE tool, the hypertext supported CASE tool can better support information tracing and the interaction between components and stakeholders. We expect this to alleviate the difficulties resulting from individual differences in understanding the system architecture and its components in a specific application domain and to make CBD more practical and effective.

REFERENCES

1. Jones, T.C., Reusability in Programming: A Survey of the State of the Art. IEEE Transactions on Software Engineering, 1984. 10(1).

2. Zhang, Z. Defining Components in a MetaCASE Environment. Proceedings of the 12th Conference on Advanced Information Systems Engineering (CAiSE*00). 2000. Stockholm, Sweden: Springer.

3. Zhang, Z. and K. Lyytinen, A Framework for Component Reuse in a Metamodelling based Software Development. Requirements Engineering Journal, 2001. 6(2): p. 116 - 131.

4. Bubenko, J.A. Challenges in Requirements Engineering. Invited talk at the Second IEEE International Symposium on Requirements Engineering. 1995.

5. Edwards, A., et al. Software Component Relationships. Proceedings of the eighth Annual Workshops on Institutionalizing Software Reuse (WISR8). 1997. Columbus, OH.

6. Schank, R.C., Conceptual Dependency: A Theory of Natural Language Understanding. Cognitive Psychology, 1972. 3(4): p. 532 - 631.

7. Castellani, X. Overviews of Models Defined with Charts of Concepts. IFIP WG8.1 International Conference on Information System Concepts: An Integrated Discipline Emerging. 1999. Leiden, the Netherlands.

8. Whittle, B., Models and Languages for Component Description and Reuse. ACM SIGSOFT, 1995. 20(2): p. 76 - 87.

9. Jarke, M., Requirements Tracing. Communications of the ACM, 1998. 41(12): p. 32 - 36.

10. Ramesh, B. and M. Jarke, Towards Reference Models for Requirements Traceability. IEEE Transactions on Software Engineering, 2001. 27(1): p. 58 - 93.

11. Barber, K.S., et al., Requirements Evolution and Reuse Using the Systems Engineering Process Activities (SEPA). Australian Journal of Information Systems, 2000. 7(1): p. 75 - 97.

12. Lee, J. and K. Lai, What's in Design Rationale. Human Computer Interaction, 1991. 6(3-4): p. 251 - 280.

13. Perry, D.E. and A.L. Wolf., Foundations for the Study of Software Architecture. ACM SIGSOFT Software Engineering Notes, 1992. 17(4): p. 40 - 52.

14. Tracz, W., L. Coglianese, and P. Young, A Domain-Specific Software Architecture Engineering Process Outline. ACM SIGSOFT Software Engineering Notes, 1993. 18(2): p. 40 - 49.

15. Sommerville, I. and P. Sawyer, Requirements Engineering: A Good Practice Guide. 1997: John Wiley & Sons. 391.

16. Monk, S., et al. Supporting Design Rationale for System Evolution. Proceedings of the Fifth European Software Engineering Conference. 1995.

17. Bratthall, L., E. Johansson, and B. Regnell. Is a Design Rationale Vital When Predicting Change Impact? - A Controlled Experiment on Software Architecture Evolution. Proc. Conference on Product Focused Software Process Improvement (PROFES'2000). 2000. Berlin: Springer-Verlag.

18. Bailin, S.C., et al. KAPTUR: Knowledge Acquisition for Preservation of Tradeoffs and Underlying Rationale. Proceedings of the 5th Annual Knowledge-Based Software Assistant Conference. 1990.

19. Creech, M.L., D.F. Freeze, and M.L. Griss. Using Hypertext in Selecting Reusable Software Components. Hypertext 1991. 1991.

20. Sutcliffe, A. Requirements Rationales: Integrating Approaches to Requirements Analysis, Designing Interactive Systems: Processes, Practices, Methods, & Techniques. Proceedings of DIS'95. 1995: ACM Press.

21. Robbins, J.E., D.M. Hilbert, and D.F. Redmiles. Software Architecture Critics in Argo. 1998 International Conference on Intelligent User Interfaces. 1998. San Francisco, CA, USA.

22. Mannion, M., et al. Reusing Single Requirements From Application Family Requirements. 21st IEEE International Conference on Software Engineering (ICSE'99). 1999.

23. Oinas-Kukkonen, H., Improving the Functionality of Software Design Environments by Using Hypertext, Department of Information Processing Science. 1997, University of Oulu: Finland. p. 130.

24. Kaipala, J., Integrating MetaCASE Environments by Using Hypertext - Conceptual, Functional and User Interface Considerations in MetaEdit+, Department of Computer Science and Information Systems. 1999, University of Jyväskylä: Finland. p. 114.

25. Keller, R.K. and R. Schauer. Design Components: Towards Software Composition at the Design Level. International Conference on Software Engineering. 1998: IEEE Computer Society.

Individual Behavioral Consistency in Virtual Communities

Zheng Xin
Department of Information Management & Information Systems
Fudan University, Shanghai, 200433, China
xin_zx@21cn.com

Zhang Cheng and Chan Hock Chuan
Department of Information Systems
National University of Singapore, 117543, Singapore
zhangche@comp.nus.edu.sg, chanhc@comp.nus.edu.sg

ABSTRACT

Compared to a traditional community, relational contact via computer-mediated communication (CMC) becomes the main behavior in a virtual community (VC). Consequently individual behaviors are different from that in real life. Previous studies on VC claimed contradictory impacts on individual behavior: some believed interpersonal relation became hokey in the community while others thought it became genuine. Therefore a question on individual behavior in VC arises: as the physical world changes to the virtual one, will individuals still keep their behaviors probabilistically consistent? Using individuals in online alumni associations as samples, we study consistency of individual behavior, i.e. whether individuals behave consistently across time in a VC; and the impact of the environmental stimuli on individual behavior, i.e. whether individuals behave differently in different VCs across time. Posted messages in the forum, including the posting frequency and message length, are chosen as the objective measurement of individual behavior in this study. The result shows that individuals still keep their consistency in VC activities, as in the physical community. However it is not so clear about consistency across VCs. This behavioral study provides a fresh approach to analyze individual behavior in CMC: firstly behavioral information is mined objectively, to avoid any psychological bias from subjective data; secondly it emphasizes on discovery of common behavioral characteristics from regular life, rather than seeking their internal causes.

1. INTRODUCTION

Research shows that people spend a large part, about 75%, of their lives in communication (Tubbs and Moss, 2000), which means individuals develop and maintain their inter-personal relationships during most of their life. As people communicate with one another, a community is developed simultaneously as the social relationships draw people together (Heller, 1989).

In CMC, communicators' main behaviors are moved from physical contact to the relational one via network, which consequently changes community characters. Some researchers believe that inter-personal relationships via CMC may be impersonal, hokey and illusionary (Heim, 1993; Stoll, 1995) while others assert that genuine communities are commonly developed via CMC (Parks, 1996; Rheingold, 2000). As psychological studies have claimed that communities influence individuals in them (Seidman, 1990), the above conflicting visions raise psychological questions on individual behaviors in VC: do individual behaviors become fluctuating in these VCs which consequently causes those conflicting conclusions?

Although the common consistency of individual behaviors in the physical society has been proved (e.g. Burger, 1990; Hjelle and Ziegler, 1992), such consistency has not ever been tested in a virtual environment. If it cannot be held in the computer world, CMC studies may face some doubt on the generality of their results, i.e., whether individual behavior in one particular experiment can be representative. Furthermore, from behaviorism's perspective, proving and understanding individual behavioral consistency in VC provides a theoretic foundation for predicting, and even controlling, behavior in it. Today, more and more people immerse in CMC as a main communication method and more businesses, especially those related to electronic commerce, are devel-

oping their B2C (business to customer) relationships online. Some companies build online forums to facilitate customer discussion about their product/service quality as part of their CRM (customer relation management) strategy. This study may help them understand more about customer behavioral regularity and adopt suitable online communication scheme to provide more customer satisfaction.

This paper aims to analyze individual behavioral consistency via CMC and is a research on psychological issues in VC. In the following sections, we introduce the research hypotheses and method after literature review. Then sample data is collected to examine such consistency, followed by the discussion and conclusion.

2. LITERATURE REVIEW

CMC studies put much attention on analyzing the different effects of computer-based media. A major theory is the media richness theory, Daft and Lengel (1984), which claims that media richness is an objective and fixed property of any communication media. However, researchers are also drawn to the psychological reasons for users to choose a medium for communication (Huang et al., 1998). Such psychological perspectives can integrate rational and social view of media choice and consequently affect user behavior and communication efficiency (e.g. Fu et al., 1998).

In community psychology (e.g. Orford, 1992; Duffy and Wong, 1995) and personality psychology (e.g. Burger, 1990, Hjelle and Ziegler, 1992), researchers focus on considering people within the contexts of social settings and systems, i.e., the community to which they belong. Lewin (1997) developed a widely-accepted equation to represent individual behaviors in context: $B=f(P,E)$. Behavior is a function of the person, the environment and the interaction between the two. Such claim of the interaction impact between the individual and the situation provides a theoretic motivation to consider the consistency of human behaviors in virtual communities: as the physical world changes to the virtual one, can individuals keep their behaviors consistent enough, which reflect their personalities?

Before going further, terms of personality and behavior should be further defined and clarified. Personality is a complex pattern of an individual as a result of the continual interactions among himself, his behavior and the external environment around him (Bandura, 1982). Most personality theory researchers believe that personality shows consistency across time and across situations (Hjelle and Ziegler, 1992). In other words, an individual's behavior patterns display probabilistic consistency across time and situation (Burger, 1990).

Behavior is what an individual is doing, which is observable by another person (Skinner, 1938). Behaviorism views behavior as the physiological reaction to external stimuli, such as Hull (1934), or immanent cognition, such as Tolman (1948). Since individual learning, or adapting, process occurred as a result of responding to or operating on their environments, behaviorists believe that individual behaviors are predictable and controllable as consistency leads to predictability. The assumption of the probabilistic consistency (Hergenhahn and Olson, 1998) of behavior is common in psychology studies.

3. RESEARCH HYPOTHESES AND METHOD

3.1. Research Hypotheses

We focus on the text-based online-forum to study individual textual behavior in VCs while ignoring other factors, such as video, audio and so on. Therefore, an individual's activity in a VC can be described as follow: one logins to a forum, browses and posts messages to share ideas with others, and then quits. As a result, posting messages is individual behavior in a VC. There is valuable information hidden behind it: the frequency of posting and the length of posted message represent an individual's immersion in that VC and in its topics; the time of a posting a message marks when the individual enters the community. Since unwelcome and outliers' messages can be deleted by the forum master, existing messages represent poster's membership and his influence in that VC. In summary, we consider the frequency and the length of messages as the characteristics of posting behavior to measure. The different forums an individual attends are treated as the different VCs: an individual faces different people and discusses topics that are usually different across forums.

We choose a large online alumni-association service provider in China, http://www.5460.net, which was founded in 1998 and had over 5-million members at the end of 2001. It mainly provides text-based forum, chat-room and album for classmates to communicate online. Each association is viewed as an independent VC. Since alumni association has many important and basic elements common to other types of VCs, such as web-page interface, posting mechanism, community leader, membership system, email information for asynchronous contact, and so on, choosing them as the subject will not affect the generality of the result.

Based on previous CMC and psychological studies on individual behavior in the community, we summarize two propositions. Concerning the consistency of individual behavior, we get proposition 1: individuals would behave consistently across time in a VC. Most personality studies agree that an individual's behavior patterns display some consistency (Burger, 1990). Although an individual does not always behave exactly the same in similar situations across time, such consistency still exists which describes what the individual will usually do in such a situation. Although not every one behaves the same way, what we expect is the consistent behavior patterns that may exist in the majority of the population. Furthermore, based on this consistency, the regularity of some individuals' behavior pattern, i.e. the time correlation of individual's behavior, can be predicted. Therefore, we make the following hypotheses:

H1a. A majority of individuals' posting frequency would be consistent across time in a virtual community.

H1b. A majority of individuals' posting length would be consistent across time in a virtual community.

H1c. Some individuals' posting frequency would have significant correlation with time periods.

H1d. Some individuals' posting length would have significant correlation with time periods.

Concerning the impact of the environmental stimuli on individual behavior (e.g. Skinner, 1938), we get proposition 2: individuals would behave differently in different virtual communities across time. Studies in personality psychology argue that there is some consistency in individual behavior across different situations. However in our studies, the alumni associations of college class, high-school class and primary-school class, mostly of different sizes, are also the chronological and distinguishing experience to the individual, which reflects his different growth stages. As personality is a life long development, individual behavior may be influenced greatly by age and consequently a person may behave differently across different alumni association across time. In this setting, the environment may play an important role on individual behavior. Therefore, the following behavior patterns are hypothesized:

H2a. A majority of individuals' posting frequency should not be consistent across different virtual communities.

H2b. A majority of individuals' posting length should not be consistent across different virtual communities.

3.2. Method

To gather objective data, we gathered individual activity information in VCs without questionnaires or prior announcements. Therefore psychological bias occurring in subjective responses to surveys and controlled experiments can be greatly avoided and individual behaviors in VCs are natural. The data, including the message content, length, date and so on, are gathered from the web pages for future analysis. This behavioralc study focused on discovering common behavioral characteristics from individual observable activities, not on seeking their internal causes.

We determine some basic criteria of choosing communities. First, to study active communities, a lower-bound requirement of its size is necessary. Here we choose forty, which is usually the minimum size of classes in China colleges. Second, the VC should have at least one master. Based on our pre-sample test of 50 associations, one of the distinguishing signs of inactive communities is that these do not have a master. Third, the community should be open to the public (the website allows the community itself to determine whether to open to public visitors). From a total of 214,504 registered associations, 1931 satisfy the criteria. Out of these, 324, i.e. one-sixth of them, are randomly chosen. In each chosen community, we randomly pick one individual to study, so altogether 324 individual samples are chosen. After tracing their postings, we find that only 225 of them are active in the community, i.e. posting more then one message. Out of these, 88 join more then one community simultaneously. As a result, 369 record sets of individual behavior in VCs over time are gathered finally. In these data, the average number of posted messages is 59.1, with a standard deviation of 80.8. The average word count of what each individual posts is 3607.0 words, with a standard deviation of 7855.0. The average membership duration of these individuals is 72.8 weeks, with a standard deviation of 39.9.

4. ANALYSIS

We compare the mean of each sample's posting frequency and posting length in the former half of his community life to the latter, using his / her posting frequency / length for each week. This is repeated using frequency and length for each month. Analysis is done with SPSS. Where a result shows there is a significant difference, it means that the individual's posting behavior cannot be viewed as consistent in a VC, and vice versa. Our analysis is based on 95% confidence, which is the traditional significance level used by psychologist (Burger, 1990). The results show that 68.8% (74.0%) of individuals do not show significant difference in posting frequency, measured weekly (monthly). 81.0% of individuals do not show significant difference in posting length either measured weekly or monthly. In summary, H1a and H1b are supported, i.e. a majority of individuals' posting frequency and posting length has no significant difference across time in a VC.

Based on this consistency, behavioral regularity, i.e. the time rule behind behaviors, can be predicted. Consistency does not necessarily lead to regularity, but is a precondition of it. Therefore, we cannot expect to find as much regular behavior as that of consistent one. But a higher percentage of regularity supports stronger behavioral consistency in a VC.

Here we consider two levels of regularity: daily and weekly. Daily regularity refers to whether an individual has behavioral patterns based on the hours of a day, as in our physical life where we commonly work in the daytime and rest at night. To check for daily regularity, we divide 24 hours of a day into eight segments from one am to twelve pm, each containing a 3-hour period. Data of individual posting frequency and posting length are summarized based on these segments to study the correlation between behavior and time segments. Weekly regularity refers to whether an individual has behavioral patterns based on the days of a week, as in our physical life where we work on weekdays and rest in the weekend. Similarly, data of posting frequency and posting length are summarized based on diurnal segments, from Monday to Sunday, to study the correlation between behaviors and these segments. Result shows that a large, though smaller, portion of the individual behavior show correlation with time periods. Based on 5% significance test, 32.0% (8.1%) of the individuals show significant daily (weekly) regularity of posting frequency, while 32.2% (7.9%) of them show significant daily (weekly) regularity of posting length. It also indicates that individuals may be more regular in daily life in a VC. Like in physical world, people usually have a relatively fixed timetable for work, dining and rest in daily life, but they will face different events in a week so their activities in diurnal segments may be less regular. This similarity between the virtual and the physical community encourage us to consider the influence of physical world to the virtual one and the consistency of individual personality in both worlds.

To get insight on individual regularity in a VC, the correlations of their online behaviors with time are summarized: the average absolute value of Pearson correlation is 0.50 (0.38) on daily (weekly) regularity of posting frequency, and 0.49 (0.38) on posting length. As correlations ranging between the absolute value of 0.30 and 0.60 obtain enough practical and theoretical value in making predictions in personality research (Hjelle and Ziegler, 1992), this result shows a significant trend of behavior regularity in a VC. Also, 66.4% (58.0%) have greater than 0.30 absolute Pearson correlation on daily (weekly) regularity of posting frequency, with 65.3% (57.5%) on daily (weekly) regularity of posting length. In summary, H1c and H1d are supported.

Multiple VC participation occurred for 88 samples. They belong to more then one community simultaneously, varying from two to seven. They participate in a total of 223 virtual societies. Among them, 60.2% attend two communities simultaneously, which covers 48.0% of 223 communities, while the rest are even more active.

We compare the means of each sample's posting frequency and posting length, measured over weeks and months, across different communities. The result indicates that 51.1% (42.0%) of samples show significant difference in their posting frequency, measured weekly (monthly), in different communities, while 43.2% (33.0%) of them have significant difference in posting length, measured weekly (monthly). In summary, H2a and H2b are not supported as only some individuals, and not the majority of samples, behave differently across VCs. It is hard to claim whether individual behavior is inconsistent over virtual communities based on current data. From behaviorism's perspective, this result may be caused by insufficiently strong environmental stimuli, i.e. different online alumni associations in this study may not offer significantly different experiences to the individual. From personality theory's point of view, this result is natural: an individual's internal factors cause him to express same traits and to behave consistently over a range of situations. For example, diffidence may cause the person to be wordless in most cases. Study also showed that people would behave more consistently in low-constraint or weak-pressure situations rather than high-constraint ones (Monson et al., 1982). Since alumni association is such a free place for individuals to communicate, it is not surprising to find many samples behave consistently across various communities although these associations represent different chronological and distinguishing experiences to them.

5. CONCLUSION

This behavioral study provides a fresh approach on analyzing individual observable activities in CMC: firstly it mines individual behavioral information objectively and avoids any psychological bias usually occurring in surveys or controlled experiments; secondly it does not emphasize on seeking the internal causes of behaviors but rather on discovering common behavioral characteristics from individual's regular life.

By using individuals in an online alumni association as samples and collecting their activity information objectively from the website, we study the consistency of individual behavior and the impact of the environmental stimuli on it. Results show that individuals show consistency in VCs, as in the physical communities. However there is less evidence that such consistency exists across different VCs.

Behavioral consistency in VC is the precondition of further research on human behaviors and psychological issues in online behaviors. Without such consistency foundation, studies on VC may face some doubt whether individual behavior in one survey or experiment can represent his usual behavior, and lead to the problem of repeating studies to validate individual responses. This work provides a way to answer this question in CMC. Based on this observed consistency in a virtual community, individual online behavior is predictable and controllable. Therefore, online business may explore further into customer behavioral regularity and adopt suitable online communication/ negotiation scheme to provide more customer satisfaction.

Because of the generality of our study, the result could apply to other forms of virtual communities, such as B2C electronic commerce, customer community and many other online CRM forms. As more companies are developing their online support forums as a part of their CRM strategy, to facilitate customers sharing comments and ideas about products and services, studying individual behaviors in VCs may help organizations understand, predict and satisfy members' sense of belonging to their communities.

REFERENCES

Bandura, A., "Self-efficacy Mechanism in Human Agency," *American Psychologist* (37), 1982, pp.122-147.

Burger, J.M, *Personality*, Wadsworth, 1990, 2nd Edition.

Daft, R.L. and Legnel, R.H., "Information Richness: a New Approach to Managerial Behavior and Organization Design," *Research in Organizational Behavior* (6), 1984, pp.191-233.

Duffy, K.G. and Wong, F.Y., *Community Psychology*, Allyn and Bacon, 1995.

Fernback, J., and Thompson, B., "Virtual Communities: abort, retry, failure?" *Computer mediated communication and the American collectivity*, May, 1995.

Fu, X., Shi, M., Wu, S., Sun, X., Yang, M. and Yan, G., "The Interactions Among Media and Psychological Functions on Video-mediated Communication," *Proceedings of 3rd Asia-Pacific Computer Human Interaction*, 1998, pp.232-236.

Heim, M., "The Erotic Ontology of Cyberspace," *The Metaphysics of Virtual Reality*. Oxford University Press, 1993.

Heller, K., "Return to Community," *American Journal of Community Psychology* (17), 1989, pp.1-15.

Hergenhahn, B.R., and Olson, M.H., *An Introduction to Theories of Personality*, Prentice Hall, 1998, 5th Edition.

Hjelle, L.A. and Ziegler, D.J., *Personality Theories: Basic Assumptions, Research, and Applications*, McGraw-Hill International, 1992, 3rd Edition.

Huang, W., Watson, R.T. and Wei, K.K., "Can a Lean E-mail Medium Be Used for Rich Communication? A Psychological Perspective," *European Journal of Information Systems* 7(4), pp.269-274.

Hull, C.L., *Principles of Behavior*, Appleton-Century-crofts, 1934.

Lewin, K., *Resolving Social Conflicts & Field Theory in Social Science*, American Psychological Association, Washington DC, 1997.

Monson, T.C., Hesley, J.W., and Chernick, L., "Specifying When Personality Traits Can and Cannot Predict Behavior: an Alternative to Abandoning the Attempt to Predict Single-act Criteria," *Journal of Personality and Social Psychology* (43), pp.385-399, 1982.

Orford, J., *Community Psychology: Theory and Practice*, New York: J. Wiley, 1992.

Parks, M. R., "Making Friends in Cyberspace," *Journal of Computer-Mediated Communication*, 1(4), 1996.

Rheingold, H., *The Virtual Community: Homesteading on the Electronic Frontier*, MIT Press, 2000.

Seidman, E., "Pursuing the meaning and utility of social regularities for community psychology," *Researching community psychology: Issues of theory and methods*, American Psychological Association, 1990, 1st edition.

Skinner, B.F., *The Behavior of Organisms: An Experimental Analysis*, Appleton-Century company, 1938.

SPSS, Statistical Package for the Social Sciences, SPSS Inc. http://www.spss.com.

Stoll, C., *Silicon Snake Oil: Second Thoughts on the Information Highway*, 1st edition, Doubleday, 1995.

Tolman, E.C., "Cognitive maps in rats and men," *Psychological review*, 55(4), pp.189-208, 1948.

Tubbs, S. L. and Moss, S., *Human Communication*, 8th edition, McGraw-Hill, 2000.

Heterogeneous Data Mediation Using Meta-models
– An Architectural View

Luyin Zhao
School of Management, Rutgers University
luyin@pegasus.rutgers.edu

Keng Siau
College of Business Management, University of Nebraska-Lincoln
ksiau@unl.edu

ABSTRACT

This research-in-progress paper introduces the concept of data mediation and a typical mediation architecture used by previous solutions, points out limitations of this architecture and states why meta-model can be adopted for better interoperability. Based on the latest meta-model standard from Object Management Group - CWM, a new mediation architecture is proposed. Final discussion is on future research in terms of prototyping, toolkit and formalizing meta-model standard for data mediation.

INTRODUCTION

Data mediation is a research area that deals with integrating information from different, usually heterogeneous, data sources, including regular databases, XML source, record files, email systems, etc. The software that handles or masks data heterogeneity from end users is called a *mediator*.

Mediation based interoperability provides users with (probably converted) data view and query language for querying heterogeneous data sources. This type of interoperability is considered at the *data* level in contrast to the *service* level interoperability (CORBA, DCOM). More specifically, mediation solutions provide users a way to send on-demand queries to heterogeneous data sources. In other words, in users' eyes, there is a homogeneous (common) view despite the heterogeneous data sources. User queries issued on this view are intercepted by the mediation system and converted to query formats that can be accepted by heterogeneous data sources[1].

EXISTING DATA MEDIATION ARCHITECTURE

In information mediation research community, there are several research projects that have been completed. Two of the most important ones are TSIMMIS (by Stanford University [3][4]) and MIX (by University of California at San Diego [1][2]). Both of them use a typical mediation architecture with major components shown in Figure 1.

– Common data schema (model) definition

The purpose of defining a common data schema is because heterogeneous data sources have different data schemas (e.g., relational database has relational schema, XML database has tree-like schema, etc.) Common data schema provides users with a common view so that queries can be issued on this view.

– Common query language definition

Common query language provides a single query language for querying different data sources.

– Wrappers

Wrappers sit on top of heterogeneous sources to export data in a uniform format to the mediator. Wrappers provide access to heterogeneous data sources by converting application queries into source specific queries or commands. Wrappers also accept user queries, decide whether they are allowed, translate them into queries that underlying data sources can recognize, and return query results to mediator by converting results into formats as defined by the data schema.

The above mediation architecture has many limitations in the aspects of:

– Handling the diversity of data schemas

Although there might be multiple mediators in a mediation system that handles a set of data sources, the variety of data sources can be significant in terms of different data schemas. Therefore choosing of common mediation data schema is preferably dynamic (depend upon actual data sources) instead of static in order to avoid losing too much information during the conversion to common data schema.

– Meeting different query preferences

Information users usually have different query language preferences. Therefore forcing them to use a query language that is specific to the common data schema may be very time consuming and error-prone.

– Providing a true independent middleware that is comparable to CORBA/DCOM

This mediation architecture does not:
(1) Allow data sources to publish their schema precisely in a neutral way for communication purpose, which is similar to publishing CORBA services using IDL.
(2) Allow data users to choose their preferred data schemas and query languages, which is similar to the flexibility possessed by CORBA clients.

META-MODEL BASED DATA MEDIATION

Simply speaking, meta-data is data that describes data. Correspondingly, meta-model is the meta-data for defining meta-data. Common Warehouse Meta-model (CWM), a new standard adopted and maintained

Figure 1 – A typical mediation architecture

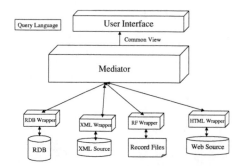

by Object Management Group (OMG) recently, is a typical and relatively complete meta-model standard for defining meta-data for all aspects of data warehousing [5][6].

Database or data warehousing domains can have many meta-models for exchanging meta-data. Similarly, for the purpose of data mediation, we only need meta-models that can be used for exchanging:

(1) Different data schemas. For example, relational data schema, XML schema, record file schema, etc. For this purpose, we may borrow some meta-models from the "Resource" level meta-model from CWM standard.

(2) Different query languages. For example, SQL, XQL, etc. Currently there is no standardized meta-model for this purpose. Although this part may need extensive work, we believe it is viable as long as meta-model for data schemas can be standardized.

Being meta-model enabled, data sources become capable of providing interchangeable data schemas and data queries to other entities using a precise, neutral, standard, and metadata way. The consequence is that a "tighter" common data schema and an appropriate query language could be chosen by end users for querying heterogeneous data sources.

Based on the above discussion, we propose a meta-model based mediation architecture as shown in Figure 2. This architecture assumes underlying data sources are all meta-model aware. Being meta-model aware can eliminate the use of wrappers. In this architecture, the way data sources present themselves to the mediator and receive queries is implementation-independent encoded as mediation meta-model compatible meta-data. The mediator has a meta-model parser for converting between original meta-data (data schemas, queries) and meta-model compatible meta-data. In addition, if necessary, the schema integrator can do semi-automatic schema integration with the help of end users by rendering the integration process using UML. Customized data schema view indicates that end users are able to select their preferred view of integrated schema. For example, when 90% underlying data sources are XML, a user may want to use XML view as the common data schema. Because the mediator receives meta-model encoded data schemas from underlying data sources, it is easy for it to integrate these schemas into different views.

Meta-model based data mediation inherits the data encoding approach of CWM. That is, meta-data is represented at two layers: At the level that needs to interact with end users (we call it presentation layer), for example, data providers and data users, meta-data is represented using UML to take advantage of its visual description and user interaction capability. While at the data transmission layer, XML is used to encode meta-data because XML is Web friendly and self-described.

Instead of using one specific data schema (meta-data) as adopted by previous mediation solutions, a mediation meta-model (meta-meta-data) is used as the communication language between mediator layer and data source layer. That is, all meta-data (encoded data schemas) transferred over the network must conform to the mediation meta-model specification. This mediation architecture provides a more independent data schema encoding and exchanging approach while leaving the flexibility of selecting integrated data schema and query language to users.

A sample scenario is that, first, data sources provide mediation meta-model encoded data schema to the mediator. In this way, the mediator can gather data schema information from various data sources. Second, the mediator user chooses what common data schema he (she) would like to use. Because the mediator has model information from all data sources, it is able to transform those data schemas to an available common model chosen by the user. The conversion is based on predefined mapping rules. As an example, [7] proposes a MOF based metadata solution for database schema integration. Finally, the user issues appropriate queries based on the common data schema. The queries will be encoded again using mediation meta-model and transferred back corresponding data sources.

CONCLUSIONS AND FUTURE RESEARCH

The advent of XML and meta-model standard (CWM) provides new approach to meet Web information interoperability requirements. Different from previous information mediation solutions that used a

Figure 2 – Meta-model based mediation architecture

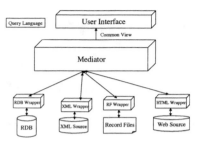

common mediation model with a single data view and query language, this paper proposes a meta-model based mediation model that connects data source side and mediator side by meta-data rather than specific common data schemas, therefore allowing users to choose their preferred data schemas and query languages. Initial architectural investigation shows positive potentials for further research in this area. Apparently the next step is to build a prototype to validate the architecture and discover hidden problems. Some of the most important issues we envision to work on include:

–Design a set of mediation meta-models for the scope of prototyping

Although CWM provides a good startup in terms of offering many standardized meta-models for resources (data sources) such as XML, RDB and Record, there is no standardized meta-model for queries. However, technically this should not be a big issue since the standardization of meta-models for data schema indicates the feasibility of designing meta-models for queries.

–Evaluate and find a toolkit

Because of the huge complexity of handling problems like meta-model processing, certain toolkits are absolutely necessary for prototyping purpose. CWM standard contributors like Oracle, IBM, and Meta Integration Technology Inc. are in the process of developing such toolkits. We will evaluate these toolkits and use them for the prototype.

FOOTNOTES

[1]   Please note that semantic interoperability is not the focus of this paper

REFERENCES

[1] Baru, C., (1999). Xviews: XML Views of Relational Schemas. Proceedings of the 10th International Workshop on Database and Expert Systems Application. 700-705.

[2] Baru, C., Gupta A., Ludäscher, B., Marciano, R., Papakonstantinou, Y., Velikhov, P., & Chu, V., (1999). XML-Based Information Mediation with MIX. Proceedings of the 1999 ACM SIGMOD international conference on Management of data. 28 (2), 597-599.

[3] Molina, H.G., Hammer, J., Ireland, K., Papakonstantinou, Y., Ullman, J., & Widom, J., (1995). Integrating and Accessing Heterogeneous Information Sources in TSIMMIS. Proceedings of the AAAI Symposium on Information Gathering, 61-64.

[4] Molina, H.G., Papakonstantinou, G., Quass, D., Rajaraman, A, Sagiv, Y., Ullman, J., Vassalos, V., & Widom, J., (1997). The TSIMMIS approach to mediation: Data models and Languages. Journal of Intelligent Information Systems. 2, 117-132

[5] OMG, (2001). Common Warehouse Meta-model standard, http://www.omg.org/technology/cwm

[6] Poole, J., Chang, D., Tolbert, D., & Mellor, D., (2002). Common Warehouse Meta-model - An Introduction to the Standard for Data Warehouse Integration. Wiley Computer Publishing.

[7] Tan, J., Zaslavsky, A., & Bond, A., (2000). Meta Object Approach to Database Schema Integration. Proceedings of International Symposium on Distributed Objects and Applications. 145-154.

Tip of the Iceberg Simplicity in E-Commerce: Issues for Educators

Laura Lally
BCIS/QM Department, Hofstra University
Hempstead, NY 11549-134
516- 463-5351
acslhl@hofstra.edu

ABSTRACT

Educators must address issues of hidden complexity in E-commerce, to prepare students for the realities of designing and managing full scale web sites. This paper addresses the problem from the theoretical perspective of Charles Perrow's Normal Accident Theory, as extended by Lally. Three key areas of E-commerce are examined where the complexity, tight coupling, control and change, suggested by the extended theory, can impact E-commerce success: 1) the World Wide Webs infrastructure, 2) the growing size and sophistication of Web sites, and 3) the increasing interactivity and personalization of Interface design.

INTRODUCTION

As E-commerce matures as a discipline, educators must address why so many Dot.Com businesses have been failures. They need to provide students with an enhanced theoretical foundation, as well as practical suggestions, for building successful E-commerce applications. This paper will argue: 1) the ease of Internet use masked the complexity of the Internet's underlying infrastructure, and 2) the ease of designing simple sites masked the complexity of full E-commerce sites. During the 1990s, this "Tip of the Iceberg Simplicity" lured many entrepreneurs and investors into many short lived Dot.Com ventures.

NORMAL ACCIDENT THEORY AND INFORMATION TECHNOLOGY

This paper will draw on Lally's (2002) extension of Perrow's Normal Accident Theory (1984, 1999). Perrow developed his theory studying complex systems such as nuclear power plants. He distinguished characteristics of systems that would permit single failures, called "incidents" such as an operator error, to propagate into major accidents such as meltdowns. Systems that had these characteristics were likely to be subject to accidents in the normal course of their operation. Perrow concluded that accident prone systems are more:

1) **Complex**--with multiple versus linear interactions, and invisible interactions with only the "Tip of the Iceberg" visible, leading to the problem of **"unknowability,"**
2) **Tightly couples**--with no slack time to allow incidents to be intercepted,
3) **Poorly controlled**--with less opportunity for human intervention before problems spread.

Lally argued that Normal Accident Theory is a sound theoretical perspective for understanding the risks of Information Technology, because IT is:

1) **Complex**--The hardware that makes up IT infrastructures of most organizations is complex, containing a wide range of technologies. Software often contains thousands of lines of code written by dozens of programmers. Incidents such as bugs can, therefor, propagate in unexpected ways.
2) **Tightly coupled**--Both hardware and software are designed to increase the speed and efficiency of operations. Incidents such as operator errors can quickly have real world impacts.
3) **Changes in software**--Security features are often not built into systems. Testing of software is often inadequate in the rush to meet release deadlines.

Lally applied this theory to various aspects of Information Technology including reengineering (Lally, 1996, 1997), the Y2K problem (Lally 1999), hiring (Lally, 2000), (Lally and Garbushian, 2001). Lally concluded (Lally 2002) that the rapid pace of **change** in Information Technology is further exacerbating factor increasing the likelihood of disasters.

1) **Changes in Hardware**--According to Moore's Law, hardware doubles in power every 18 months. As a result, hardware continues to evolve rapidly. Furthermore, entirely new kinds of hardware appear and must be integrated into existing systems.

2) **Changes in Software**--New software released fuel revenue streams in the software industry, resulting in mandatory "upgrades" every two years. The changes create an additional learning burden on users. Programmers are again under time pressure that can result in poor testing and de-bugging (Halfgill, 1998), (Westland, 2000), (Austin, 2001).

In addition to these first order effect, changes in IT also create second order effects by enabling changes in organizational processes. These processes can also become more complex, tightly coupled, and poorly controlled, further increasing the problem of serious accidents. As a result, IT users are faced with complex, tightly coupled, poorly controlled systems that undergo radical changes on a regular basis, making these systems more prone to "Normal Accidents".

This paper will apply Lally's extension of Perrow's theory to E-commerce, specifically to the issues of complexity, coupling, control and change in E-commerce infrastructures and interfaces. Recommendations for E-commerce educators for providing a more complete theoretical and practical foundation for the field will conclude the paper.

THE SIREN CALL OF FALSE SIMPLICITY

Although electronic commerce has existed for over twenty years in the form of EDI, before the Internet and its World Wide Web interface appeared, the costs associated with EDI implementations excluded all but large organizations such as Proctor and Gamble and Wall-Mart from enjoying its benefits (Schneider and Perry, 2000).

The infrastructure of the Internet and brought the benefits of EDI within the reach of small to medium sized businesses. The Internet was public and had much lower start up costs. It had an open architecture, not proprietary standards, making connections easier. As a result many smaller organizations began using the Web to exchange information with suppliers and customers. New organizational structures, including "pure play" businesses like Amazon.com and Ebay appeared without any physical retail outlet, beyond their Web site and underlying infrastructure. Small businesses targeting limited market niches (ostrich feathers, hand carved chess sets) were able to use the Internet to create a global retail presence.

The user friendly interface of the World Wide Web also fueled the enthusiasm. The Web was simple to use and the basic features of HTML generators like Frontpage and Dreamweaver straightforward to master. Simple sites involving text, links, graphics, and an email generator could be designed in a few hours. Hosting costs for simple sites, such as the text based sites used by news columnists, were only a few thousand dollars a year.

This tip of the iceberg simplicity attracted thousands of small and medium sized businesses to the Web and thousands of potential Web designers into E-Commerce classes. However, the realities of designing, creating, and maintaining many of the Web based businesses envisioned resulted in much disillusionment.

INFRASTRUCTURE ISSUES

"The information technology and communication systems that support E-commerce are so incredibly complex that few (if any) people understand all the components in depth" (Davis & Benamati, 2002. P, 8).

The World Wide Web is built on a telecommunications infrastructure that is **highly complex**. Transmission media can include local phone lines, satellites, DSL lines, cable connections, leased lines, and fiber optic cables. The topology of systems connecting to the Web can range from stand alone PCs, to LANs and WANs. The TCP/IP protocol on which the Web runs is a complex four layer packet switching protocol. Although the Web allows for local failures to be circumvented, identifying, isolating and fixing a failure is a time consuming task requiring high levels of expertise. Web site designers need to be aware of the underlying infrastructure issues that can affect a site's performance.

Information posted on the World Wide Web is disseminated globally within seconds making the Web **tightly coupled**. This tight coupling allows for the inexpensive dissemination of important information such as breaking news. However, false information and rumors can spread just as quickly having real world implications. When Dell Computer's mainframe failed to send the proper data to its web page server, monitors were listed as selling for $0. Over a hundred orders came in before the problem was realized and fixed (Gates, 1999). In the post 9/11 environment, research and government sites also became aware that the information on their sites might be used by potential terrorists and removed information. Web designers need to be made aware of the importance of the accuracy of their site's information content, and also realize that information posted on a publicly accessible site can be accessed by malicious individuals as well as its intended audience.

Individuals can create Web sites and businesses easily that span international jurisdictions, making the Web **difficult to control**. Laws regarding what constitutes a legitimate business vary from one nation to the next. Web sites can provide products such as drugs without prescriptions, or services such as gambling that circumvent local legislation. Nations also differ regarding intellectual property rights and Web oriented legislation is still catching up with the ability of Web technology to disseminate copyrighted information with ease. Wrongdoers can be hard to isolate and prosecute. Web designers need to be aware of potential legal issues regarding the products and services offered by their site.

The Web's open architecture allow for new users and sites to be added, removed, and replaced continually, making the Web subject to continual **change**. The topology of the Web changes on a daily basis as does the range of technologies that make of the Web's infrastructure. Web based businesses can appear and disappear overnight. Finally, the TCP/IP protocol of the Net makes the Web a "stateless system"--it does not remember the transactions that occurred in the past, raising the problem of **unknowability**. Web designers need to be aware of emerging Web technologies, such as mobile devices with limited bandwidth, and how these technologies will impact the design of their sites.

HACKERS AND HIDDEN COMPLEXITY

Everyday users of the World Wide Web may be able to treat the Web as a black box, but for designers of Web based businesses, it is a recipe for disaster. Malicious users such as hackers can exploit their understanding of the Web's complexity to their own advantage.

Instances of hacker attacks that steal sensitive information such as customer credit card numbers are common. Denial of service attacks on "Pure Play" sites such as E-Trade and Amazon have resulted in millions of dollars of lost revenue. Infrastructure problems have shut down day-trading sites during peak hours (Lemos, 2001), (Vijayan, 2002).

THE GROWING COMPLEXITY OF WEB SITES

Web sites, themselves, have grown in complexity. Early sites were primarily two-tiered architecture, "transactional" client-server sites, providing simple navigation and email links. Many early successes, however, scaled up into three-tiered architecture "interactional" sites. These sites could include: 1) interactions with databases involving knowledge of SQL or other query languages, 2) CGI forms and Java applets that required sophisticated programming far beyond the knowledge required to use HTML generators, and 3) links to organizational mainframe based systems such as ERP systems requiring knowledge of SAP.

E-business sites also required shopping carts, and the ability to process payments. Although "off the shelf" versions of these features are available they often must be tailored for a particular business. For example, a book or CD store can allow customers to leave products in their shopping carts for two weeks, but sites selling one of a kind collectibles cannot. The ability to tailor content to users involves artificial intelligence technology that is another major challenge. Jeff Bezos has commented that it is the complex back-end software that gives Amazon.com its competitive edge (Bezos, 2001).

As sites grew in complexity, their interfaces also became more complex. As features such as high resolution graphics, sound, and video became available, Web designers began adding them to their sites. Each of these tools required more learning on the part of Web designers. Throughout the 1990's these tools evolved quickly resulting in new releases every year or two, making the task of keeping current even more daunting. Although multimedia features provided the potential for creating more entertaining and attractive sites, these features also greatly increased the site's load times, a major problem for users with low bandwidth connections. New site features such as frames often made sites more difficult to navigate and print. Excess use of features like Flash animations wasted users time and made sites difficult to navigate (Flanders, 2002). Usability theory and theories of human computer interaction exist (Nielsen, 1999) but are still not practiced by many Web designers.

CONCLUSION

This paper has presented Lally's Extension of Normal Accident Theory as a starting point for identifying potential problems in E-Commerce resulting from complexity, tight coupling, and change. Designers of E-Commerce courses should address these issues and incorporate methodologies for dealing with these problems.

REFERENCES AVAILABLE UPON REQUEST

Measuring the Readiness of Globalisation:
A Metrics Based Approach

Yi-chen Lan and Khaled Md. Khan
University of Western Sydney, Locked Bag 1797, Penrith South DC, 1719, NSW, Australia,
Tel: +61-2-9685-9283, Tel: +61-2-9685-9558
Fax: +61-2-9685-9245, Fax: +61-2-9685-9245
yichen@cit.uws.edu.au, k.khan@uws.edu.au

ABSTRACT

The aim of this paper is to propose a metrics based conceptual framework for the assessment of enterprise globalisation readiness. The increasing adoption of information technology (IT) has become an imperative enabler for enterprises pursuing globalisation. However, a major concern —how the preparedness of globalisation would be measured —has received little attention from the research community. In order to identify and resolve this missing puzzle in enterprise globalisation, this study is initiated by reviewing the important globalisation issues, followed by the application of a metrics based measurement model. This would provide enterprises an assessment framework for evaluating their global readiness. Our model is based on a hierarchy of globalisation issues with their associated weighting factors. The factors and sub-factors are used to define their strengths weaknesses as in a particular context. The final output of the measurement framework will conclude with a degree of readiness of the globalisation process.

INTRODUCTION

Globalisation has increasingly been recognised as the crucial business strategy for enterprises to remain in the digital competitive era. Without a doubt, the information technology serves an imperative role in the enterprise's global transition process. Enterprises engaged in globalisation have been insinuated to deliberate a number of issues that are essential in the evolution. These fundamental issues are identified in the areas embracing business information systems management, people management, technology management, end user management, and culture. Nevertheless, most globalisation studies are principally spotlighted on the identification of issues, recommendation of resolutions, and construction of transition frameworks. However, there is virtually no indication of the measurement of the enterprise's globalisation attainment. This study combines the fundamental issues together with the measurement attributes, and attempts to construct a global readiness model that will provide an evaluation instrument to enterprises in assessing their global transition achievement. To measure the readiness of a globalisation goal, we use the classical factor criteria and metrics model (Cavano and McCall 1978). The readiness of a globalisation goal can be measured in terms of a set of criteria. Each criterion can then be quantitatively measured against a set of metrics. We will discuss the further in the subsequent section.

LITERATURE REVIEW

Speedy evolution of information technology enables the vision of enterprise globalisation becoming reality. However, many firms have misjudged the level of sophistication and complexity, and derived an incorrect interpretation of how information technology will assist the process of global transition. For example, firms are eager to develop corporate websites and implement e-commerce functions because it is believed that this is the only way of becoming competitive in the global market. Due to this incorrect belief, senior executives are often have the impression that building an e-commerce website is the only path towards globalisation, thus making inappropriate decisions. Enterprise globalisation is not merely constructing an online-transaction enabled website. It involves understanding organisational structure, recognising and resolving global transition issues in relation to information technology, culture, human resources, business strategic planning, and a national and regional perspective. These issues have been carefully classified into five categories by one of the authors' recent work (Lan, 2002). The principal concept of categorisation of globalisation issues is to provide organisations with an abstract view of concerns with the global transition. Each of the five categories is outlined and briefly discussed as follows.

Information Technology Management

The implementation of global information systems is based on the coordination and inter-communication of software applications, hardware components, telecommunications, networks infrastructure, and network management in a cross-border business environment (Sankar & Prabhakar, 1992). Rapid evolution of technologies causes efficient and effective performance of global information systems as a result of real-time and accurate transborder data flows. Organisations need to realise and understand the technological issues involved in order to adopt the most suitable technologies for global information systems. The essential technological issues and implication of global transition that need to be considered are telecommunication availability, network infrastructure, security, systems equipment, data resources utilisation, systems standards, software applications availability, systems integration, and systems recovery.

Business Information Systems Management

In the process of globalisation, business and information system strategies are often the senior executives' major concern. The alignments of global information strategy and the new business visions are crucial to the success of global business operations. Areas in this category and the transition implication contain information systems planning, information systems organisation alignment, information systems effectiveness, productivity measurement, business reengineering, competitive advantage, information quality, office automation, identification of global business opportunities, systems reliability, availability, and transferability.

People Management

People are major players in designing, implementing and utilising information systems. When investigating the human resources management in the global business environment, a number of areas need to be considered as crucial to the success of globalisation. These areas are recruiting, training, organisational learning, cross-cultural skills development, and global team development.

End User Management

End users are the ultimate group of people using the global information systems on a regular basis. The task of managing and supporting end user groups is not only in maintaining business information operations but is the

Table 1. GISM issues: category and associated subcategories

GISM issues main category	Subcategories
Business information systems management	Strategic planning, Reengineering and change, Managing IT quality, Productivity, Systems development and implementation
People management	Role of senior management, Staff recruitment and training, Benefits and compensation
Information technology management	IT infrastructure, Business applications, Telecommunications network, Data and information systems improvement
End user management	Organisation learning, Operation and support
Culture	Education, Demographics, Individual and interpersonal perspectives, Geography and economy

key to evaluating and improving the global information systems. The fundamental concerns of the end user management category in globalisation context include managing end user computing facilities, end user computing education, introducing and learning new global information systems, help desk support, and end user involvement in global information systems development.

Culture

When addressing information systems and technology globally, culture is an important aspect to be considered as it influences the success or failure of global transformation. In the new challenge of globalisation the reality of cultural diversity is not avoidable. Instead, organisations should be encouraged to embraces diversity and turn the multicultural characteristics into strategic advantages. Understanding this diversity is crucial to conducting any global business. As Kincaid correctly points out (Kincaide, 1999) doing business "requires a deep respect of the country's culture, religions and institutions".

In order to group global transition issues more precisely each of these categories are further grouped into a number of subcategories. Table 1 summarises these subcategories under their associated main categories.

GLOBAL READINESS METRICS DEVELOPMENT

Developing and implementing an appropriate global transition measurement will provide benefits to companies in various aspects. Firstly, the measurement is to help the company understanding basic behaviours of the business system, exploring and discovering the relationships between business and information systems; secondly, it is to evaluate the status of projects and their relationships to business plans. This evaluation is used to judge progress toward corporate or business unit strategic goals or specific initiatives; and thirdly, it is to identify opportunities for future improvement.

In order to construct such appropriate and precise measurement for evaluating company's global achievement, it is crucial to develop the measurement model in a systematic manner. We have used the classical factor criteria metrics (FCM) model (Cavano and McCall, 1978) as a tool for our purpose. We believe that globalisation readiness is also a quality issue that is measurable. FCM has been widely used to measure software quality attributes. It is based on a simple structure, which contains a globalisation readiness goal, a set of criteria for the goal, and a set of metrics.

Enterprises first need to set a globalisation goal. The measurement of the goal could be based on a set of criteria. Each of these criteria could be quantified in terms of a set of metrics. This hierarchical structure goes from a high level issue to more specific measurable issues. A goal could equate a main category or a subcategory as defined in Table 1.

Generally, the measurement model development starts with determining what to measure. In the context of globalisation, the objects to be measured are the five categories of global transition issues mentioned earlier. However, due to the broad coverage of individual category, each of these is further classified into various subcategories. There are 18 subcategories and they are referred as the measuring factors (see Measurement factors and criteria section below).

The second step of the model development deals with defining measurement criteria. Based on the definition of each factor (subcategory), numerous issues can be identified and transformed into the measurement criteria, which the organisations have to accommodate during the process of global transition. Consequently, a measurement technique should be designed to assess these criteria. In this study, the measurement technique is designed in a 100 percent scale, which is partitioned in ten measurement blocks (0 – 9), thus block 0 embraces 0 % – 10%; block 1 for 11% – 20% and so forth.

MEASUREMENT FACTORS AND CRITERIA

Once the measurement objects, criteria and measuring techniques are defined, the measurement model is ready in its implementation position. The reset of this section outlines measuring factors and the associated measuring criteria of each GISM issue category.

1. Category: Business information systems management
  1.1 Factor: Strategic planning
      Measuring criteria:
      1.1.1 Applying information systems for global business opportunities and competitive advantage
      1.1.2 Alignment of information systems and business objectives
      1.1.3 Understanding of information systems roles, contribution and justification of information systems investments
  1.2 Factor: Reengineering and change
      Measuring criteria:
      1.2.1 Business processes are reengineered through the adoption of IT
      1.2.2 Developing necessary procedures and programmes for managing business reengineering changes
      1.2.3 Applying quality assurance scheme for organisational management
      1.2.4 IT professionals possess business-oriented competence when developing global information systems
  1.3 Factor: Managing IT quality
      Measuring criteria:
      1.3.1 The global information system is reliable, available and transferable within the organisation
      1.3.2 Applying appropriate quality control mechanisms for inputs and outputs of information systems
      1.3.3 Applying software quality assurance standards in the development and maintenance of global information systems
  1.4 Factor: Productivity
      Measuring criteria:
      1.4.1 Developing an appropriate measurement and improvement of information system productivity and effectiveness
      1.4.2 Full utilisation of data resources
  1.5 Factor: Systems development and implementation
      Measuring criteria:
      1.5.1 The new global information system has been constructed, implemented and managed
      1.5.2 Implementing office automation

2. Category: People management
  1.1 Factor: Role of senior management
      Measuring criteria:
      1.1.1 Possessing quality skills in people management
      1.1.2 Developing training programmes for senior management in IS and cross cultural skills
  1.2 Factor: Staff recruitment and training
      Measuring criteria:
      1.1.1 Retaining, recruiting, and training IT personnel
      1.1.2 Sufficient and availability of IT staff
      1.1.3 Organising and managing expatriated employee and assignments
  1.3 Factor: Benefits and compensation
      Measuring criteria:
      1.1.1 Incorporating multinational compensation schemes into the company's policy
      1.1.2 Company's travel activities are minimised to reduce unnecessary costs

3. Category: Information technology management
 1.1 Factor: IT infrastructure
  Measuring criteria:
  1.1.1 Appropriate computer hardware and operating systems have been selected and the management and support procedures are clearly outlined
 1.2 Factor: Business applications
  Measuring criteria:
  1.2.1 Appropriate software applications have been identified, constructed, implemented, and managed
  1.2.2 Information systems are integrated across all business functions
 1.3 Factor: Telecommunications network
  Measuring criteria:
  1.3.1 Appropriate management, planning, support, and availability of telecommunication infrastructure and technology
 1.4 Factor: Data and information systems improvement
  Measuring criteria:
  1.4.1 Procedures for continuous Improvement of data, information and knowledge quality
  1.4.2 Developing security, control, and disaster recovery capabilities
  1.4.3 Integration of databases for data mining ability

4. Category: End user management
 1.1 Factor: Organisation learning
  Measuring criteria:
  1.1.1 Procedures for facilitation and management of organisational learning
  1.1.2 Enhancing staff absorption of the new information systems
  1.1.3 Procedures and facilities for end user computing
 1.2 Factor: Operation and support
  Measuring criteria:
  1.2.1 Procedures for managing IT operations
  1.2.2 Developing help desk support

5. Category: Culture
 1.1 Factor: Education
  Measuring criteria:
  1.1.1 Investigation of the level of general education of people at the region or nation
  1.1.2 Investigation of the level of computer knowledge of people at the region or nation
 1.2 Factor: Demographics
  Measuring criteria:
  1.2.1 Investigation of regional or national gender perspective
  1.2.2 Investigation of age distribution of the region or nation
  1.2.3 Investigation of regional or national religion
 1.3 Factor: Individual and interpersonal perspectives
  Measuring criteria:
  1.3.1 Investigation of leadership style of the region or nation
  1.3.2 Investigation of values and goals of individuals and groups of the region or nation
  1.3.3 Investigation of interpersonal communications of the region or nation
 1.4 Factor: Geography and economy
  Measuring criteria:
  1.4.1 Investigation of currency stability
  1.4.2 Coping with time-zone difference

MECHANISM FOR CALCULATING GLOBALISATION ACHIEVEMENT

After the evaluation, a calculation mechanism should be applied to conclude the globalisation achievement. This calculation mechanism is described as follows. The first calculation item is the achievement of each measurement factor. It is derived from the average of the associated measuring criteria. For example, the "strategic planning" measurement factor consists of three measuring criteria (1-3), and their measuring results are 9, 8, and 8 respectively. Thus the achievement level of "strategic planning" is 8.3 (or equivalent to

Table 2. Sample numeric weightings of GISM issue categories

	Multinational	International	Global	Transnational
Information Technology Management	0.22	0.22	0.21	0.20
Business Information Systems Management	0.22	0.21	0.22	0.24
End User Management	0.20	0.19	0.19	0.20
People Management	0.19	0.20	0.20	0.20
Culture	0.17	0.18	0.18	0.16

83% according to the 100% scale defined earlier). After the achievement levels of all measurement factors are determined, each GISM issue category can be evaluated. Once again, this is calculated from the average of associated measurement factors.

The final step of calculating the achievement level of the entire global IT transition is determined by amalgamating all calculated achievement levels of GISM categories and the GISM issues priority model. Depending upon the type of MNC organisational structure, each GISM issue category is assigned a numeric weighting, which is decided in accordance with the level of importance in GISM issues priority model identified by Lan (2002). Table 2 illustrates sample numeric weightings of GISM issue categories of four multinational organisational structures. For instance, if a company's organisational structure is "global" type, thus the numeric weightings of the GISM issue categories are 0.21 for "information technology management", 0.22 for "business information systems management", 0.19 for "end user management", 0.20 for "people management", and 0.18 for "culture".

The measured results indicate not merely the company's achievement level in globalisation; they also specify the less emphasised aspects, which the company has to pay more attention for future improvement. A detailed conceptual model of measuring global IT transition achievement is illustrated in Figure 1.

CONCLUSION

Global transition is a long-term and costly project. Organisations involved in this transformation activity should have a mechanism to measure the entire globalisation process. In order to indicate the level of global transition achievement in any stage of transformation process, it is essential to develop a precise metrics that allows organisations to adopt and maintain the evaluation protocol.

In this study, a factor criteria metrics model or FCM model defined by Cavano and McCall is applied for the development of achievement model for measuring the readiness of globalisation. According to the structure of the FCM model, the components related to the measurement of global transition achievement are identified. The measurement factors are based on the categories and subcategories of global information systems management issues; and the criteria are defined in accordance with the fundamental issues of each

Figure 1. Conceptual model of globalisation achievement measurement

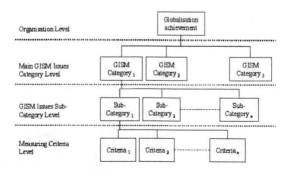

factor. To determine the level of achievement, a calculation mechanism is designed in conjunction with the weightings of GISM issue categories.

Although this model represents the conceptual framework of measuring global transition achievement, it is expected in future that the model would be applied to the industrial methodological exercise. Further, this can be achieved by a more conclusive study for generalising the model in mathematical or logical orientations.

REFERENCES

Cavano, J. and McCall, J. (1978) A Framework for the Measurement of Software Quality. Proc. ACM Software Quality Assurance Workshop, November 1978, pp. 133-139.

Kincaide, J. (1999). A CT passage to India, Computer Telephony, Feb, 100-114.

Lan, Y. (2002). GISM issues for successful management of the globalisation process. Proceedings of the Third Annual Global Information Technology Management World Conference, June, 224-227.

Sankar C. S. and Prabhakar P. K. (1992). The Global Issues of Information Technology Management. Chapter 11: Palvia Shailendra, Palvia Prashant and Zigli Ronald M. (Eds.) Key Technological Components and Issues of Global Information Systems, Idea Group Publishing, PA U.S.A., pp.249-250.

JMX-Based Network Service Management

Guilan Kong, Boyi Xu, and Lan Fang
Beijing Institute of System Engineering
Mailbox 9702-19, Beijing, 100101, China
Tel: 86-10-66356598   Fax: 86-10-64836117
glkong2002@yahoo.com.cn

ABSTRACT

Service Level Management is an important concept and implementation on network emerging as the times require. But the state-of-the-science SLM in nature is Network Service Management. JMX is a type of dynamic management technology. CIM is a set of standards-based resource and instrumentation models under the auspices of the DMTF. JMX and CIM have been widely used in the area of Network Service Management. This paper deals with our project of integrating JMX, CIM technologies into Network Service Management framework.

1. INTRODUCTION

1.1. Motivation for Network Service Management

As network is growing larger and the services it provides are growing more comprehensive, rapid and flexible providing of services, coupled with ensuring that these services are highly available is the most important guarantee to network users. It is absolutely vital to keep services highly available and accessible, as downtime in e-commerce will be translated into the loss of productivity, opportunities, revenues and profits. These requirements have been accelerating the evolution of Network Service Management.

1.2. Definition of Network Service Management

Traditional network management systems are focused on network elements such as switches and routers, but nowadays, network management, system management and application management trend toward being integrated together. Because service consumers today are mostly Internet surfers, service management is considered as a branch of network infrastructure management.

Network Service Management is focused on the management of the services that network provides, such as database access, DNS, DHCP, etc., although information on network elements is also available. In general, NSM includes data collection, status polling, event processing and status report.

1.3. Technical Background

To face new challenges to manage service-driven network environment, some new management technologies and standards come forth. There are several candidates for becoming the new management protocol or technology of choice: SNMPv3, CMIP, JMX, WBM, WBEM. As a type of open, standard, portable and scalable technology, Java Management Extension (JMX) has been regarded as the most suitable technology in the area of Network Service Management. Web-based Enterprise Management (WBEM) is an initiative by DMTF trying to integrate all these standards. WBEM consists of four components: Web client, Common Information Model Object Manager (CIMOM), CIM repository and CIM data provider. Combining JMX with CIM is a good choice to implement Network Service Management.

2. FRAMEWORK OF NETWORK SERVICE MANAGEMENT

The goal of Network Service Management is to monitor and maintain network services. The manageable resources of network services include the status and the environment of services. The status of one service comprises the accessibility, the response delay and the exact downtime of the service. The environment of one service comprises IP address of the host, running port and the manager of the service, etc. Network Service Management involves an activity of monitoring network services, auto-polling of network services and the data collection of services. For Internet users, the majority of services are provided on IP network, so NSM in our project is IP-centric.

In our project, we design the framework of NSM to have four multi-level components: the top level is master (management application); the middle-level is distributed manager (MBean server) and database; the bottom level is service agent (data collector) on the managed host. Master is for administrator to control and configure the whole management system, and it provides management information browsing to both administrator and general users. Distributed manager provides core services management functions, such as status polling, data collection, interaction of service agent and distributed manager, etc. In our design, we split core functions on distributed manager into five parts: discovery, capabilities checker, data collector, status polling and service reporter. Service agent aims at the data collection of the managed service. Database services for the storage of collected data.

In the following, we'll discuss more about the functions developed on the distributed manager. Firstly, discovery in NSM consists of two parts: one is to discover an IP address, the other is to discover the services supported by that IP address. In fact, what the discovery process does is to generate an event implying a new IP address has been discovered. Secondly, capabilities checker is responsible for discovering all the services that can be monitored, such as http, DNS, etc. Thirdly, there are two major ways that NSM collects data about the network services. The first is through polling. Polling process connects to one network service and performs a simple test to see if the service is responding correctly. If not, events are generated. The second is through service agent. The polling process will only operate on services that have been previously discovered by capabilities checker. Lastly, the final process is service reporter. By analyzing data stored in the database, this process can show users the current status of services through web browser.

The framework of NSM is shown as Figure 1.

We plan to use JMX architecture to implement the NSM framework discussed above. And as CIM is adopted widely in the area of system management, we plan to use CIM to model manageable services, and to develop service agents communicating with CIMOM to get or set data about managed services. Wrapped by Java, CIM-based service agent can be a component of JMX architecture.

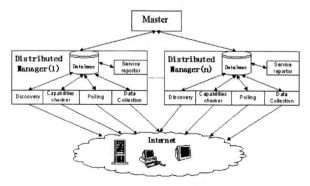

Figure 1 Network Service Management Framework

ment Beans (MBeans) are employed to instrument resources being managed. Simply put, an MBean provides a programmatic interface for managing one network resource. MBeans come in two flavors: Static and dynamic. Dynamic MBeans can change their behavior at run time.

3.2. Agent level

The JMX Agent level provides management agent. The main component of an agent is the MBean server. The MBean server is used to register and interact with MBeans. At this time, there is no direct access to an MBean, the MBean server hides their implementation behind a standardized management interface and mediates between all different interactions. The MBean server can be dynamically extended by adding MBeans. There is one MBean server per JVM. Also defined at the agent Level are protocol adaptors that enable external applications to interact with the MBean server through various protocols. Protocol adaptors must be implemented as MBeans in order to register with the MBean server.

3.3. Manager level

The JMX Manager level is the domain of custom management applications that can operate as a manager for distribution and consolidation of management services. Another JMX manager interfaces with agent via the connector, and support for different management application protocols is achieved at the agent Level using protocol adaptors. JMX manager interfaces with external database using JDBC.

JMX defines additional APIs in supplementary specifications for some common management protocols. Using these APIs, we can build capabilities at the JMX Manager level and Agent level to bridge to existing management system.

Figure 2 depicts the JMX management model.

In addition, JMX provides a number of Java APIs for existing standard management protocols. These APIs are independent of the three-level model, yet they are essential because they enable JMX applications in the Java programming language to link with existing management technologies.

The JMX architecture is as Figure 2.

4. INTEGRATING JMX INTO NSM

4.1. Necessity of JMX and CIM in NSM

The growth of the Internet has given rise to many new technologies to serve the increasing demands of the current generation of applications. JMX is emerging as the preferred way to build Network Service Management system. Chief among the reasons for this growing trend is the ease of this new technology. JMX provides a flexible, distributed, and dynamic management infrastructure to be implemented. The key features JMX provides are: Platform independence, Protocol independence, Information model independence and Management application independence.

In NSM framework described above, there are two crucial sides. One is the core functions developed on the distributed manager. They need a message or event mechanism to coordinate them and they must be developed to interact with manager easily (MBean server can manage MBeans well). The other is the data collection of managed services. As we all know, polling process is just for the accessibility and response delay of services, so CIM-based service agent is the key process for the data collection of the environment of one service.

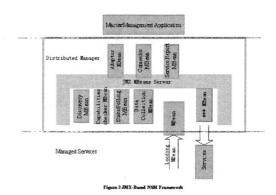

Figure 3 JMX-Based NSM Framework

Considering the advantage of JMX technology, we integrate JMX architecture into NSM framework.

4.2. Integrate JMX Architecture into NSM Framework

In JMX architecture, the instrumentation level instruments the manageable resources by standard or dynamic MBean, then register to the agent (MBean server), and agent plays the role to coordinate MBeans and lets management applications connect and interact with all MBeans, then communicates with the manager through connector or protocol adaptor.

By integrating JMX architecture into NSM, we instrument the core functions on distributed manager such as discovery, capabilities checker, status polling, data collector and service reporter through MBeans, and register these MBeans to an MBean server, and through the message mechanism of MBean server they can communicate with each other.

Figure 3 shows this framework.

4.3. Integrating CIM-based service agent with JMX

In our research, we call those applications that reside on service host to get or set data of managed services service agent. It's an important way to implement data collection through service agent. Since JMX provides SNMP API for developer in network management field, when a service host supports SNMP, we can develop a SNMP adaptor to communicate with SNMP agent on remote host to get or set MIB information. But what should we do if the service host does not support SNMP? In this instance, the principal problem is how to model manageable services and instrument the application that collects data of managed service. In our project, we use CIM standard to model managed services, and develop CIM data provider of each managed service, then we develop CIM-based application as a service agent to communicate with CIMOM to get or set data of each managed service. The next work is to use Java to wrap CIM-based application (if CIM data provider and CIMOM not implemented in Java, it will be a big problem, such as WMI). JMX provides WBEM API for CIM/WBEM developers. We can use this API to develop CIM adaptor MBean on the distributed manager to communicate with the CIM-based service agent. Currently, we have implemented data collector on distributed manager for SNMP service.

Figure 4 shows the structure of JMX and CIM working together.

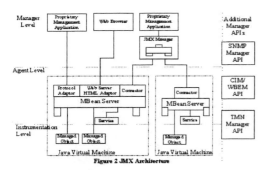

Figure 2 JMX Architecture

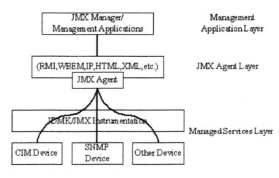

Figure 4 JMX and CIM working together

5. CONCLUSION

Network Service Management is the fundamental implementation of the SLM. JMX, as a 3rd generation management technology, brings deployment flexibility through protocol independence and dynamic extensibility and scalability.

CIM is a most comprehensive Information Model to define services data. To use CIM to instrument network, system, application, service, etc. is the future trend of network management.

Combining JMX with CIM can trigger a great advancement in network management. Development of telecommunication network services management is in progress.

6. REFERENCES

1. Java Dynamic Management Kit (JDMK) 2.0 White Paper, *Dynamic Management for the Service Age.*
2. http://www.openwings.org/openwings-0.9/tutorial, Openwings Management Service Specification Alpha Ver 0.72.
3. *Java Management Extensions (JMX),* Christophe Ebro
4. *JMX Specification Lead*, Sun Microsystems, Inc.
5. http://www.opennms.net/users/docs/docs/html/part2.html
6. http://www.opennms.net/users/docs/docs/html/part3.html
7. http://www.opennms.net/users/docs/docs/html/part4.html
8. http://ca.com/products/descriptions/tng_slm.pdf
9. http://www.iseeman.com/docs/wmi.html

Exploring the Frontier of E-Innovation

Dr Ping Lan
School of Management, University of Alaska Fairbanks
PO Box 775-6080, Fairbanks, AK, 99775, USA
ffpl@uaf.edu

ABSTRACT

This article aims to examine the changes to innovation brought about by the Internet. Based on a systematic survey on the current efforts made by industry and academia in expanding the frontier of innovation, it found that E-innovation—innovations closely tied to a digital platform— is expanding traditional innovation in three aspects: having an obvious tendency to software development, requiring a dual-effort delivery, and deploying different managing/operating toolkits. These expansions are leading E-innovation to become a new paradigm for carrying out creative activities.

INTRODUCTION

Innovation is playing an increasing role in our society. Yet, an asymmetry exists at the current stage. We have a quite clear idea about how innovation has been playing an important role in forging the New Economy. However, we do not have a satisfactory picture of how innovation itself has been or is being transformed in the Digital-business environment, although some efforts on the part of both industry and academia have been made during the last several years to deal with the Open Source Software Movement and to promote Online Innovation or E-innovation or Distributed Innovation or Connected Innovation (Lan 2002). Given the fact that role of the new innovation is expanding rapidly, this article aims to check the changes to innovation brought about by the Internet through analyzing the current efforts made by industry and academia in expanding the frontier of innovation

Following the above design, this paper is divided into the following sections. Section one focuses on examining the changes of innovation in its underlying media. It finds that differing from traditional innovation which uses diversified media to change the combinations of production factors, E-innovation shows a convergence and is bias towards software innovation.

Section two concentrates on checking the changes of innovation in its delivery. It argues that one distinguishable feature of E-innovation is its dual-effort delivering, which means that an innovation is conducted or completed through both internal and external efforts.

Section three mainly deals with the changes of innovation managing/supporting tools. It displays that different rules and new tools such as "groupware" are bundling E-innovation to mainstream business closely with both internal and external environments.

CHANGES OF INNOVATION IN ITS UNDERLYING MEDIA

Although Schumpeter defines innovation as a change of a production function, or a new combination of production factors; highlights the importance of entrepreneurs in this process, and points out the trigger effect created by the increasing purchasing power of innovators, he does not get into the black box to discuss the innovation mechanism. Many studies have been trying to expand Schumpeter's study in this area. However, before the wide spread of IT and Internet technology, there is not a common underlying media for changing a production function or creating a new factor combination. It means that in the traditional innovation paradigm, each innovation uses different medium to carrying out its tasks.

Differing from traditional innovation in which innovators use diversified media to change the combinations of production factors, current innovation shows a convergence in its underlying media and is bias towards software innovation. As pointed out by Quinn et al (1996) that most innovation occurs first in software, and software is the primary element in all aspects of innovation from basic research through product introduction.

This digital form tendency means that E-innovation could greatly share coded knowledge and deal with mainly digital objects. The task, the process and the delivery of the creation activities in E-innovation are related or transformed to information flows, which can be finally converted to the flows of digital signals. The digital form of E-innovation does not mean that E-innovation cannot be involved in physical jobs such as having physical experiment, or introducing physical products/functionalities. However, it does suggest that E-innovation focuses on the information and its flows companied with these physical works.

The software-based innovation also brings changes to innovation in its usage. In this area, E-innovation shows a feature of bi-focus instead of the single focus possessed by traditional innovation. Single-focus innovation means that the purpose of innovation is to provide or introduce a new product or service with a new functionality. Bi-focus innovation means that while it provides or introduces a new product or service with a new functionality, it also creates a new channel or environment for delivering or upgrading a traditional or a new functionality. In pursuing the bi-focus innovation, "solutions" oriented innovators lie at the customer-supplier interface. They are working with related stakeholders to uncover, or better define problems for which a total solution can be developed. In this manner, E-innovation realizes freedom-generation opportunities based on the Network Intelligence, since combining product and channel innovation could greatly facilitate process-automation, operation-simplification, input/output-realization, and system-synchronization. The bi-focus feature of E-innovation results from and also results in the following phenomena: digitization of traditional physical activities/processes, the convergence of different activities, and creation of new value chains or threads.

CHANGES OF INNOVATION IN ITS DELIVERY

In terms of the delivery of innovation, Schumpeter's model shows a linear routine. Innovation starts at exogenous science and invention; then followed by entrepreneurial activities and innovation investment, which leads to new production pattern and changing market structure; after that it enters the period of reaping profits or diffusing innovation.

Unsatisfying with this closed linear model, many research and business application are trying different models. The departure of innovation from Schumpeter's closed linear model is a continuous process. Although different people use different terms to describe the changes of innovation, one aspect is common that all they agree that current innovation shows distributed nature. Distributed nature means that E-innovation is open and decentralized in a much higher degree. This nature is inherited from the basic nature of the Internet, which enables E-innovation to act in two distinguishable ways as mentioned in some academic research. Firstly, it allows E-innovation to accommodate creative efforts in a larger scale, no matter these efforts reside inside an organization or outside the boundary of the organization. Secondly, it allows E-innovation to progress in a non-linear way, which offers more interface opportunities. Due to the distributed nature, E-innovation is horizontal oriented instead of vertical oriented

The distributed nature is reflected in innovations' delivery. Current E-innovation shows a feature of dual-effort instead of uni-effort as traditional innovation does. Uni-effort means an innovation is conducted or completed within a firm. The assets used to deliver the innovation usually are limited to what the firm owns. As suggested by Sawhney and Prandelli (2000) that uni-effort innovation has difficulty to renew itself in a knowledge economy although it is effective in minimizing disturbances, perturbations, and change. Clearly, in a highly complex environment, it will be unlikely that any single organization will possess, or wish to possess, all the necessary skills and technological collateral to meet the broad, enterprise-wide needs of its customers.

Dual-effort means that an innovation is conducted or completed through both internal and external efforts of an enterprise. The assets used to deliver an innovation can come somewhere out of its control. This expansion of E-innovation with regard delivery makes E-innovation a new catalyst and a new channel for organizing innovation activities. In pursuing a dual-effort innovation, a synergy is required to build not only a strong knowledge base, and a solutions-based portfolio, but also a mechanism for coordinating co-creation. By doing so, the horizon of an innovation is enlarged from within the boundary of a firm to the boundary of a reachable or manageable network. At the same time, the delivery channel of an innovation is increased from a linear path to a non-linear net. The dual-effort feature of E-innovation results from both distributed networking and the E-business culture. The former enables the synergy of both internal and external creation through the Internet. The latter is accelerating or driving the transform of firms.

Linux, the pioneer of open source movement, started from the operating system. In its development, Linux resembles a free "knowledge market," completely open and unstructured. It does not limit participation of any interested individual. In fact, it benefits from the creativity and collaborative efforts of a large number of developers. Individual developer can freely download Linux for further development. As a condition, all the developers should clearly specify every change they made in a file. In this process, intellectual property rights are not controlled by any single entity.

CHANGES OF INNOVATION IN ITS MANAGING/ SUPPORTING TOOLKITS

As mentioned earlier, one missing component in Schumpeter's framework is how to conduct innovation in a targeted environment. The development of IT and Internet technology is greatly enriching innovation in this area. It has only been less than a decade since companies started using the Web to share information and streamline purchasing. Now, enterprises have begun using new Web software tools to help employees and business partners work together to make products faster and more cheaply.

Collaboration software lets dispersed engineers send, view, and mark up drawings, and even share the controls of a solid modeler while they simultaneously design a product. The upshot is that tasks that took days in past workflows now shrink, in some cases, to minutes. (Dvorak 2001). The software's key capabilities—chat, discussion forums and resource-allocation features— overcome the problems that arise when teams consist of people in different physical locations and when workers simultaneously juggle several projects. Once, software tools for programming teams meant a code repository and a bug-tracking database. But as companies find themselves hiring distributed project teams and juggling multiple simultaneous projects, they are turning to tools that provide the communication and resource-allocation features that traditional programming utilities lack. All of them rely on the Internet and intranets to provide a foundation for collaboration. People are just starting to realize the benefits of the Web as an interactive medium (Johnson 1999).

The burgeoning of innovation tools and the changes of innovation delivery, are undoubtedly changing the organization or management of innovation. The major changes can be observed from the following aspects. Firstly, E-innovation is decoupling innovation activities, which means that E-innovation has smaller basic building block for carrying out creative activities. The combination of digital form of objects and powerful computing and networking technologies make individuals to become free agents in certain degree. They can undertake different activities without much limitations of time-and-space. This freedom in fact "chops" a typical innovation-activities-chain into many pieces spatially and temporally.

Secondly, e-innovation is deploying new rules, which means that E-innovation is changing the practices of organization structure, incentive mechanism, and intellectual rights protection in innovation governess. Differing from traditional innovation management, in which inward-oriented innovation process was surrounded by an absolute monopoly firewall and suffers an asynchronous technology transfer, E-innovation aims to balance "copyright" and "copyleft" by sharing creative fruits, to make "inward-oriented-process outward" (Fingar et al. 2000) by absorbing or leveraging external innovation efforts, and to synchronize technology development and adaptation by dismantling barriers of knowledge flows.

Summarizing the above analysis on E-innovation, it is apparent that much attention has been paid to identify and take the advantages of new innovation, or changes to innovation. By using the Internet to plan, initiate, conduct, run, facilitate, and/or promote innovation for operating on a digital platform, innovators and related stakeholders have to aware the difference between E-innovation and traditional innovation, so that they are maximize their efforts.

REFERENCES

Dvorak, Paul (2001). Getting ready to collaborate. *Computer-Aided Engineering,* Vol. 20, Issue 10, pS1-3.

Fingar, Peter Kumar, Harsha and Sharma, Tarun (2000). *Enterprise E-Commerce.* Tampa, Florida: Meghan-Kiffer Press.

Johnson, Amy Helen (1999). Teamwork Made Simple, *CIO Magazine.* November 1.

Lan, Ping (2002). E-innovation: An Emerging Platform For a Networked Economy, *International Journal of E-business* (Forthcoming).

Quinn, James Brian, Baruch, Jordan J. and Zien, Karen Anne (1996). Software-Based Innovation, *McKinsey Quarterly,* Issue 4, pp.94-119.

Roberts, Edward B. (2002). Introduction, in Roberts, Edward B. (ed.) Innovation: Driving Product, Process and Market Change, Jossey-Bass: San Francisco, pp.1-6.

Sawhney, Mohanbir and Prandelli, Emanuela (2000). Communities of Creation: Managing distributed innovation in turbulent markets, *California Management Review*, Vol. 4.2 Issue 4, pp.24-54.

Implementing ERP Systems using SAP

Linda K. Lau
College of Business and Economics, Longwood University
Farmville, VA 23909
Phone: 434-395-2778, Fax: 434-395-2203
E-mail: llau@longwood.edu

ABSTRACT

This paper commences with a brief description of Enterprise Resource Planning (ERP), followed by a description of SAP, the largest ERP enterprise software provider in the world. SAP's flagship software program, the R/3 system, is portrayed in more detail. The capabilities of the R/3 system, the three-tier client/server technology it employs, its hardware and software, and several problems associated with its implementation and use are discussed. The two R/3 implementation tools – namely, the Accelerated SAP and the Ready to Run systems – are also described. Finally, the paper concludes with several important issues that managers must consider before implementing any ERP system.

INTRODUCTION

Since first envisioned in the 1960s, integrated information systems have expanded tremendously in scope, evolving from inventory tracking systems, to Materials Requirements Planning (MRP), and finally to Enterprise Resource Planning (ERP) (Brady, Monk, and Wagner, 2001). Today, almost every organization integrates part or all of its business functions to achieve higher efficiency and productivity. Since its conception in 1972, SAP has become the largest developer of enterprise software applications in the world.

The purpose of this article is to provide readers with a general understanding of ERP and a more detailed description of SAP and its flagship product, the R/3 system. The bulk of the article is devoted to describing SAP R/3's capabilities, its three-tier client/server technology, the hardware and software needed, and some problems with the R/3 system. Two implementation tools – namely, the Accelerated SAP and the Ready to Run systems – have been developed by SAP to expedite the lengthy system implementation process, and both are described in the next section of the article. The last section discusses several critical issues that managers must consider before making the final decision to integrate all the business functions in the organization.

ENTERPRISE RESOURCE PLANNING (ERP)

Enterprise Resource Planning (ERP) is the process of integrating all the business functions and processes in an organization. It achieves numerous benefits. First, a single point of data entry helps to reduce data redundancy while saving employees' time in entering data, thereby reducing labor and overhead costs as well (Jacobs and Whybark, 2000). Second, the centralization of information, decision-making, and control leads to increases in efficiencies of operations and productivity, as well as coordination between departments, divisions, regions, and even overseas operations. This is especially true for multinational corporations, for which global integration could result in better communications and coordination around the world and the global sourcing and distribution of parts and services could provide appropriate benchmarks for worldwide operations. Third, the sharing of a centralized database provides business managers with accurate and up-to-date information with which to make well-informed business decisions. Further, it reduces data redundancy while improving data integrity. Fourth, functional integration consolidates all sorts of data, such as financial, manufacturing, and sales, to take advantage of bulk discounts. ERP is especially important for companies that are "intimately connected" to their vendors and customers, and that use electronic data interchange to process sales transactions electronically. Therefore, the implementation of ERP is exceptionally beneficial to businesses such as manufacturing plants that mass-produce products with few changes (Brady, Monk, and Wagner, 2001). ERP provides companies with a competitive advantage.

With the rapid growth of e-commerce and e-business in recent years, coupled with the growing popularity of concepts such as supply-chain management, customer relationship management, e-procurement, and e-marketplace, more and more organizations are integrating their ERP systems with the latest Business-to-Business applications. This new challenge is often referred to as Enterprise Commerce Management (ECM). The major enterprise software providers are Oracle, PeopleSoft, J.D. Edwards, and SAP.

SAP AG

Systemanalyse und Programmentwicklung (SAP) was founded in 1972 in Mannheim, Germany, by five former IBM systems engineers. In 1977, the company was renamed Systems, Applications, and Productions in Data Processing (SAP), and the corporate headquarters was moved to Walldorf, Germany. The primary goal of SAP is to integrate all the business functions in an organization, so that changes in one business process will be immediately and spontaneously reflected by updates in other related business processes. Designing revolutionary and innovative software packages implemented on a multilingual (in more than 20 languages by 2000), multi-currency, and multinational platform, SAP is the world's largest enterprise software provider of collaborative e-business solutions (Buck-Emden, 2000).

Initially, the R/1 system (abbreviated for "runtime system one", indicating real-time operations) was developed in 1973 to solve manufacturing and logistics problems. Over time, it expanded into other contemporary markets such as services, finances, and banking, and added more business functions; for instance, the Asset Accounting module was added in 1977. The more integrated, mainframe-based R/2 system was launched in 1979. The first version of the R/3 system was released in 1992, while the Internet-enabled Release 3.1 was completed in 1996. By 2001, SAP had annual sales of $6.4 billion, making it the third largest software vendor in the world (behind Microsoft and Oracle). Currently, SAP employs over 27,800 people in more than 50 countries, has 1,000 partners around the world who have installed 50,000 systems, serves 10 million users at 18,000 organizations in over 120 countries, and specializes in 21 industries. SAP has established seven "bleeding edge technology" research centers around the world. The latest, at Queensland University in Australia, conducts research on voice recognition and mobile computing. The other corporate research centers are located in Palo Alto, CA; Karlsruhe, Germany; Brisbane, Australia; Sophia Antipolis, France; and Johannesburg, South Africa (SAP Corporate Research, 2002). These centers conduct research on E-Learning, mobile computing, intelligent devices, e-collaboration, advanced customer interfaces, and technology for application integration.

THE R/3 SYSTEM

The R/3 system is a powerful enterprise software package with several significant updates over the mainframe-based R/2 version. The R/3 system has three major function modules: SAP Financials, SAP Human Resources, and SAP Logistics (Larocca, 1999). The financials module is an integrated suite of financial applications containing submodules such as financial accounting, controlling, investment management, treasury cash management, enterprise controlling, and real estate. All issues regarding recruitment and training are managed using the human resources module, which contains personnel administration and personnel planning and development submodules. The logistics module manages issues related to sales and distribution, production planning, materials management, quality management, plant maintenance, logistics information systems, project systems, and product data management.

The R/3 Reference Model is equipped with more than 8,000 configuration options (Jacobs and Whybark, 2000). The newest version of R/3 is the SAP R/3® Enterprise, which has new and continuously improved functions, provides flexibility and optimization, and utilizes innovative technology to manage collaborative e-business processes.

Capabilities of the R/3 System

While designing the R/3 system, SAP developers choose the best, most efficient ways in which business processes *should* be handled, and incorporate these "best practices" into the system (Brady, Monk, and Wagner, 2001). Therefore, clients of the R/3 system may need to redesign their ways of conducting business to follow the practices dictated by the R/3 developers. In some situations, organizations may need to reengineer their business processes in fundamental ways, revamping old ways of conducting business, redefining job responsibilities, and restructuring the organization. R/3 systems can, however, be customized to address global issues where different countries have different ways of doing business; country-specific business practices pertaining to accounting, tax requirements, environmental regulations, human resources, manufacturing, and currency conversion rules can be built into R/3 systems.

Unlike the R/2 system, the R/3 system requires only a single data entry, and it provides users with immediate access to and common usage of the data. This new system was designed around business processes and applications such as sales orders, material requirements planning, and recruitment. An important advantage of the R/3 system is its ability to run on any platform, including Unix and Windows NT. R/3 also utilizes an open architecture approach, so that third-party software companies are allowed to develop add-on software packages and integrate hardware equipment such as bar code scanners, PDAs, cell phones, and Global Information Systems with the R/3 system (Buck-Emden, 2000). Sophisticated and more advanced users can design customized graphical user interfaces (GUI) screens and menus and/or create ad hoc query reporting trees and customized reports using the ABAP Workbench tools (Larocca, 1999). The object linking and embedding (OLE) technology allows files from other applications such as Microsoft Office and Corel Office to be easily integrated with the R/3 system. The SAP On-line Help Documentation, available in both standard and compressed HTML, is contained on a separate CD-ROM.

In 1996, in order to better streamline the R/3 system, it was broken down into the following five categories of components as part of the SAP Business Framework: industry-neutral, industry-specific, Internet, complementary, and custom. SAP continues to develop software components such as the SAP Advanced Planner & Optimizer (SAP APO), SAP Customer Relationship Management (SAP CRM), and SAP Business Information Warehouse (SAP BW), to form the technical foundation for the http://www.mysap.com/ e-business platform.

The Three-Tier Client/Server Technology

It was the advent of inexpensive hardware and the improvement of client/server technology in the 1990s that propelled SAP to develop the SAP R/3 system, which was designed for the client-server environment. The client/server distributed computing architecture allows users to access the system via any computer that is connected to the network, even working from home. The R/3 system utilizes the same three-tier hierarchy configuration as the Relational Database Management System (RDBMS). The user interface layer refers to the GUI of the client computer, which serves as a means for the end user to communicate with the applications and database servers. The business logic layer consists of the application server, which performs all the administrative functions of the system, including background processing, printing, and process request management. The innermost layer consists of a central computer that contains the database server, the data dictionary, and the Repository Information System, which is used to retrieve information on the objects in the data dictionary. An improved version of the three-tier architecture is the four-layer client/server configuration, with an additional layer for Internet service (Buck-Emden, 2000).

Hardware and Software

The hardware components of an SAP R/3 installation include the servers that house the databases and software programs, the client workstations for user interfaces, and the network communications system that connects servers and workstations. The software components of an SAP R/3 installation consist of the network infrastructure, the operating systems, the database engine, and the client desktop. Several application programs are installed onto the servers: the main function modules, the customized as well as the interface programs, and the ABAP/4 (Advanced Business Application Program) developer's workbench programming tools. ABAP programmers use ABAP/4 to develop regular application programs that are included with the R/3 system as well as customized software programs for their clients (Buck-Emden, 2000). Some commonly used ABAP/4 tools are: the ABAP List Processing, used to list reports; the ABAP Query, used to develop queries; the Screen Painter, used to design screens; and the Menu Painter, used to create menus. Third-party vendors are permitted to develop customized add-on software programs to be linked with the R/3 system. The data repository for the RDBMS and the basis module (as a prerequisite for all application modules) are also installed onto the servers.

Problems With SAP R/3

Although SAP touts its R/3 system as a revolutionary, efficient, and innovative software program, the system does have a few drawbacks. Because of the complexity of the R/3 system, many assumptions must be made in order to confine the number of configuration options available. However, once the system is configured, all the options are fixed and cannot be changed. Further, users must enter all the fields before they are allowed to proceed to the next screen or activity (Jacobs and Whybark, 2000). Consequently, many people find the R/3 system to be relatively rigid. Nevertheless, the flexibility of the SAP system can be improved by installing specially designed customized applications developed by ABAP programmers.

A second potential problem with R/3 has been mentioned above. In order to increase the efficiency of doing business, SAP developers incorporated "best practices" into the R/3 system. Basically, they decided how clients *should* conduct their businesses. However, not all businesses agree with this philosophy, and this approach may not be acceptable or applicable to some organizations. In such instances, it may be extremely important for organizations to continue with their usual ways of doing business and hence for the system administrator to configure the system according to these established practices (Jacobs and Whybark, 2000). These simply may be incompatible with the R/3 system.

SAP attempts to incorporate all business practices, including environmental and other regulations into the R/3 system. However, three types of misfits (relating to data, process, and output) can occur due to incompatibilities between software functionality and organizational requirements (Soh et al., 2000). Major multinational corporations that installed similar R/3 systems in several different countries could experience any of these mismatches in the systems due to differences in cultural and regulatory environments. The unique context of each country in which an organization operates must be carefully enmeshed into the traditionally Western-biased business practices inherent in the R/3 systems. Further, there is the problem of migration between software versions, in which the newer version is sometimes not backward-compatible with the older version.

When using the SAP On-line Help Documentation, the version number listed on the Help CD-ROM must correspond with the version of the SAP GUI (Larocca, 1999). However, even when the two versions correspond, incompatibilities may be present, because changes and upgrades in a higher version of the software are not updated in the Help CD-ROM of the same version number. Further, the Help CD-ROM has limited searching capabilities on some concepts, rendering the help feature an inefficient support tool. In addition, not all materials are properly translated from the original German version, and not all the help documentation has been translated.

TWO R/3 IMPLEMENTATION TOOLS

R/3 system implementation is both expensive and time-consuming; a complete implementation can cost between one and several million dollars and can take more than 3 years. Only Fortune 500 corporations can afford such extensive deployment of ERP as R/3 systems represent. In an attempt to target small and medium-sized companies as well as large organizations that are interested in only partial ERP integration, SAP developed two implementation alternatives: the Accelerated SAP and Ready to Run R/3 programs.

The Accelerated SAP (ASAP) program is a rapid implementation tool designed to install the full R/3 system quickly and efficiently by focusing on tools and training and utilizing a five-phase, process-oriented strategy for guiding successful implementation (Larocca, 1999). The five phases are project preparation, business blueprint, realization, final preparation, and go live and support.

Designed for small to medium-sized companies, the SAP Ready to Run R/3 (RRR) program complements the ASAP system by bundling the server and network hardware systems with a pre-installed, pre-configured base R/3 system, an operating system, and a database management system (Larocca, 1999). This approach yields significant cost and time savings by reducing the implementation schedule by as much as 30 days. The RRR solution includes a specially developed online tool called the System Administration Assistant, which allows a minimally trained system administrator to manage the system effectively. A RRR system can be purchased through any SAP hardware vendor partner such as Hewlett-Packard, Compaq, IBM, NCR, Siemens, or Sun Microsystems. It can be supported by operating systems such as Microsoft Windows NT, IBM AS/400, and Unix. The databases supported by the R/3 systems include Microsoft SQL server, DB2, Informix, Oracle, and Dynamic Server. All the options in the SAP system are configured using the SAP Implementation Guide (IMG).

IMPORTANT ISSUES TO CONSIDER BEFORE IMPLEMENTATION

Before integrating business functions, managers must consider several important issues that will help them decide whether an ERP integration using the SAP R/3 system is the right choice for their organization. First, managers must consider the fundamental issues of system integration by analyzing the organization's vision and corporate objectives (Jacobs and Whybark, 2000). For instance, does management fully understand its current business processes, and can it make implementation decisions in a timely manner? Is management ready to undertake drastic business process reengineering efforts to yield dramatic outcomes? Is management ready to make any changes in the structure, operations, and cultural environment to accommodate the options configured in the R/3 system? As in any type of system implementation, active top management support and commitment are essential to the success of the project. Next, management needs to decide on the key related implementation and business issues and how to proceed. Certainly, ERP is not suitable for companies that are experiencing rapid growth and change in an unstable environment that are undergoing change in the corporate management and philosophy, or that will be experiencing merger or liquidation in the near future.

Another important question for managers to consider is how much to implement. For instance, is the organization embarking on an ambitious journey of revamping the whole enterprise using a complete integration, or is the organization employing a franchising strategy of implementing a partial integration across a few divisions with uncommon processes (Koch, 2002)? The bigger the organization, the more complex the business processes are and the greater the difficulties in implementing the SAP system (Brady, Monk, and Wagner, 2001). On the other hand, organizations considering a partial implementation must deal with the problems associated with using multiple vendors. They also need to consider simultaneous versus piecemeal implementation because of the ripple effect caused by decisions made in one module (Brady, Monk, and Wagner, 2001). In general, in order to maintain a smooth transition of the business processes and operations, simultaneous integration of the whole system, instead of functional or departmental integration, is highly recommended.

People-related issues such as corporate philosophy and leadership style can play an important role in the implementation process. Employees can be quite wary of any kind of change in the business processes, particularly during periods of economic downturn. In order to reduce users' resistance to change, employees must be educated about the ERP installation. Such educational endeavor should include a concise introduction to the basic concepts and architecture of ERP systems, including actual screen shots of the function modules. During these training sessions, it is important to discuss the managerial issues involved and to build a basic understanding of the integration concepts prior to the actual installation of the ERP system.

Several activities must be performed before and after an ERP implementation. For instance, managers must conduct a feasibility study of the current situation to assess the organization's needs by analyzing availability of hardware, software, databases, and in-house computer expertise, and make the decision to implement ERP where integration is essential (Buck-Emden, 2000). Further, organizations need to exploit future communication and computing technology to integrate the ERP system with e-business applications. Oftentimes, additional new hardware and specialized professionals are needed to run the powerful software system. Depending on the size of the company and the modules installed, the cost of implementation can range from one million to five hundred million dollars, and will take as long as two years for a mid-size company and seven years for a large, multinational corporation to complete.

SUMMARY

This paper provides readers with a general understanding of Enterprise Resource Planning (ERP); of SAP, the third largest software vendor in the world; and of SAP's R/3 system. The capabilities of the R/3 system include complete system integration, global accessibility, scalability, and open architecture. The three-tier client/server technology refers to the user interface layer, the business logic layer, and the database server layer. The hardware elements for an R/3 installation include the usual servers and client workstations, but the software requirements are more elaborate. Some of the problems associated with the R/3 system include the adopting organization's need to reengineer business processes, the misfits and mismatches between system functionality and organizational requirements, and inadequacies in the SAP On-line Help Documentation. The Accelerated SAP and Ready to Run systems are two implementation tools designed to expedite the implementation process. Several critical issues that managers must consider before making any SAP implementation decision are discussed. Some of these issues are: the organization's readiness and ability to accept and implement major installation; the size of the implementation; and users' resistance to change.

REFERENCES

Brady, Joseph, Ellen Monk, and Bret Wagner. Concepts in Enterprise Resource Planning. Boston, MA: Course Technology, 2001.

Buck-Emden, Rudiger. The SAP R/3 System: An Introduction to ERP and Business Software Technology. Reading, MA: Addison-Wesley, 2000.

Jacobs, Robert, and Clay Whybark. Why ERP? A Primer on SAP Implementation. New York, NY: Irwin McGraw-Hill, 2000.

Koch, Christopher. "The ABCs of ERP." http://www.cio.com/research/erp/edit/erpbasics.html. February 7, 2002.

Larocca, Danielle. SAMS Teach Yourself SAP R/3 in 24 Hours. Indianapolis, IN: SAMS, 1999.

"SAP Corporate Research: The Innovative Force Behind Tomorrow's Technology." http://sap.com/company/research/. Retrieved on October 4, 2002.

Soh, Christina, Siew Kien Sia, and Joanne Tay-Yap. "Cultural Fits and Misfits: Is ERP a Universal Solution?" Communications of the ACM 43.4 (April 2000): 47.

From Ontology to Service Discovery in Bluetooth

Maria Ruey-Yuan Lee
Shih Chien University
70, Ta-Chi Street, Taipei, Taiwan
E-mail: Maria.Lee@mail.usc.edu.tw

Ching Lee
Hyper Taiwan Technology Inc.
7F, No 92, Sec 1, Na-Hu Road, Taipei, Taiwan
E-mail: Ching.Lee@hyperinterop.com.tw

ABSTRACT

Discovery services in a dynamic environment, such as Bluetooth, can be a challenge because Bluetooth is unlike any wired network, as there is no need to physically attach cables to the devices you are communicating with. Regular Bluetooth service discovery protocol may be inadequate to match different service naming attributes. To support the matching mechanism and allow more organized service discovery, service relation ontology is proposed to extend and enhance the hierarchical structure introduced in the Bluetooth specification. A frame-based approach is used to codify the service relation ontology, which represents the relations of service concepts. A semantic matching process is introduced to facilitate inexact matching, which leads to a situation in which a simple positive or negative response can be meaningful. The semantic matching process improves the quality of service discovery.

INTRODUCTION

Bluetooth™ is set to be the fastest growing technology since the Internet or the cellular phone [Bray and Stuman 2002]. Bluetooth has created the notion of a Personal Are Network (PAN), a close range wireless network to set to revolutionize the way people interact with the information and technology around them. Bluetooth is unlike any wired network, as there is no need to physically attach a cable to the devices you are communicating with. In other words, you may not know exactly what devices you are talking to and what their capabilities are. To cope with this, Bluetooth provides inquiry and paging mechanisms and a Service Discovery Protocol (SDP). Service discovery, normally, involves a client, service provider, and seek out or directory server. Bluetooth does not define a man machine interface for service discovery; it only defines the protocol to exchange data between a server offering services and a client wishing to use them. The SDP in Bluetooth provides a means for applications to discover which services are available and to determine the characteristics of those available services [Bluetooth Specification 2001]. However, service discovery in the Bluetooth environment is different from service discovery protocol in traditional network environments. In the Bluetooth environment, the set of services that are available changes dynamically based on the RF proximity of the device in motion.

The Bluetooth SDP uses 128-bit university unique identifiers (UUIDs) which are associated with every service and attributes of that service. However, UUID-based description and matching of services are often inadequate [Avancha, Joshi and Finin 2002]. For example, consider a wireless hotspot such as airport terminal or shopping mall where clients use handheld devices to discover information about available services such as "rail". Using regular Bluetooth SDP, the request may fail if a series of UUIDs stores its service as "metro" or "train" or "bart" etc. In addition, the current version of Bluetooth SDP does not support service registration; the airport information would likely not be able to register its services to facilitate users' needs. Most hotspots services, such as mall, airport terminal etc, are associated with a great amount of more sophisticated attributes than a simple portable device and peripherals service. Using UUIDs to specify requests would lead to a meaningless response.

To tackle this problem and enhance the quality of service discovery, we provide the Bluetooth SDP matching and browsing mechanism to use ontology modeling concepts associated with UUIDs to service in hotspot environments. After introduction, the body of this paper is organized into four sections. The first section provides a brief explanation of Bluetooth service dis-

covery application profile and shows its objectives and supports. The second section focuses on service browsing. A Service Relation Ontology (SRO) is introduced to model the service ontology. A frame-based representation is used to present the service concepts. The third section examines service searching, which describes semantic searching processes. It provides a service records example and also introduces the concepts of service search patterns. The final section discusses the different ontological approaches and shows its advantages and disadvantages.

BLUETOOTH SERVICE DISCOVERY APPLICATION PROFILE

Service discovery is a process by which devices and services in networks can locate, gather information about and ultimately make use of other services in the network. Service discovery is fundamental to all Bluetooth profiles and is expected to be a key component of most Bluetooth applications [Miller and Bisdikian 2001].

The identified objectives for Bluetooth SDP are:

- Simplicity: Because service discovery is a part of nearly every Bluetooth usage case, it is desirable that the service discovery process be as simple as possible to execute.
- Compactness: Since service discovery is a typical operation to perform soon after links are established, the SDP air-interface traffic should be as minimal as feasible so that service discovery does not unnecessarily prolong the communication initialization process.
- Versatility: It is important for SDP to be easily extensible and versatile enough to accommodate the many new services that will be deployed in Bluetooth environments over time.

SDP supports the following service inquires:

- Search by service class
- Search by service attributes
- Service browsing

SERVICE BROWSING

Service browsing in Bluetooth is used for a general service search and provides the user with answers to such questions as: "What services are available?" or "What services of type X are available?" In the Bluetooth specification, a service browsing hierarchy is suggested. The hierarchy includes browse group descriptor services records (G) and other service records with (S) [Bluetooth Specification 2001].

Service Relation Ontology

We propose Service Relation Ontology to extend and enhance the hierarchical structure introduced in the Bluetooth specification. The ontological relation model has been applied to e-Commerce [Lee, Sim, Kwok 2002]. Ontology represents an explicit specification of a domain conceptualization [Gruber 1993]. The classes and relations of the service relation ontology are shown in figure 1, which support *gradation*, *dependence* and *association* classes among concepts. The hierarchical graph illustrates inheritance, where each class on the lower level inherits properties from the preceding level.

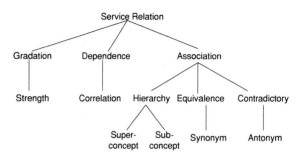

Figure 1. Service Relation Ontology

The three classes identified in figure 1 are:

- Class gradation – to order strength of a concept, which represents a semantic relation for organizing lexical memory of adjectives [Fellbaum 1998].
- Class dependence – to model the semantic dependence relations between concepts, that is correlation.
- Class association – consists of three sub-classes:
  - ➢ Equivalence – represents the same concept meaning between or among concepts.
  - ➢ Hierarchy – represents the broader or narrower concept relations.
  - ➢ Contradictory – represents opposing values of an attribute.

The six ontological relations identified in figure 1 facilitate the effective application of electronic lexicons for Bluetooth service discovery. The operations of the relations are given as follows:

- Super-concept: If a concept has a broader meaning than another concept, then the concept is called super-concept. For example, "audio" is a super-concept of "cellular" and "intercom".
- Sub-concept: If a concept has a narrower meaning than another, then the concept is called sub-concept. For example, "cordless phone" and "mobile phone" are sub-concepts of "phone" whereas "phone" is a super-concept.
- Synonym: If two concepts share similar properties, then they are synonyms. For example, "cell phone" and "cellular phone" are synonyms.
- Antonym: Of two concepts have opposite properties, and then they are antonyms. For example, "wire" and "wireless" are antonym or "symmetric" and "asymmetric" are antonyms.
- Strength: If a concept is associated with a scale (such as short, square and long) representing degree and grades, then the concept has strength. For example, "decline", "plummet" and "nosedive" are concepts that are similar in meaning but differ in their strengths.
- Correlation: If a concept is dependent on another concept, then they have correlation. For example, the relationship between bandwidth of a transmission system and the maximum number of bits per second that can be transferred over that system.

Concept Representation

A frame-based approach is used to codify the service relation ontology, which represents the gradation, dependence and association of service con-

```
<concept>
    Service Name: Mobile phone
    Property:{ }
    Super-concept: {Phone }
    Sub-concept: { }
    Synonym: { Cellular phone}
    Antonym: { Wire phone}
    Correlation: { }
    Strength: { }
<end_concept>
```

Figure 2. An example of the service concept representation.

cepts [Lee, Sim and Kwok 2002]. Figure 2 shows an example of a frame and various slots to represent a concept.

The above service name slot is self-explanatory, both sub-concept and super-concept facilitate categorization, sub-assumption and inheritance. The property slot captures the features, attributes, and characteristics of service concepts. It has the same interpretation as the notion of property of objects in an object-oriented paradigm (OOP). In an OOP, a class of objects inherits prosperities from an ancestor class; in the above formalism, a concept inherits the features (attributes and properties) from concepts that subsume it. The synonym and antonym slots define the (inter-) relations between (and among) concepts with similar or opposite meanings respectively. The correlation slot models depend on concepts. Correlation differs from property because it models the reliance of some attributes of a concept C_1 on the corresponding attributes of another concept C_2. However, correction does not necessarily imply that C_1 is a sub-class of C_2, hence C_1 does not necessarily inherit every attribute from C_2. The strength slot enables service discovery adjectives of different degrees to be compared.

SERVICE SEARCHING

Service searching in Bluetooth is used to inquire search service by service class and attributes. In particular, when searching for specific service and provide the user with the answers to such questions as: "Is service X available, or is service X with characteristics 1 and 2 available?" [Muller 2001]. However the class of the service defines the meanings of the attributes, so an attribute might mean something different in different service records.

Semantic Searching Process

Based on the proposed service ontology, we provide a semantic matching process to allow matching different naming attributes. Figure 3 shows the semantic matching process. The key of the searching engine process is a knowledge base, the service ontology, with information about service instances. The searching process first listens to query and extracts service name. It then matches to the service records to determine whether it can answer the query. Upon failure, it responds with no matching message. Otherwise, the engine extracts the relationships that the service ontology describes and uses them to arrive at a service searching pattern solution to a given service discovery query.

Service Records

A service record holds all the information a server provides to describe a service. Table 1 shows an example of the Bluetooth headset service record [Bray and Sturman 2001].

The example table illustrates how a service record is made up. For example, when a client acquires a "headset" service, the semantic searching engine reaches the service name in the service record. It then goes to the service ontology to get its related concepts, such as its "synonym" concept, earphone. The process continues until the ontology concept frame ends.

Service Search Patterns

A service search pattern is used to support a list of UUIDs to locate matching service records. A service search pattern matches a service record if

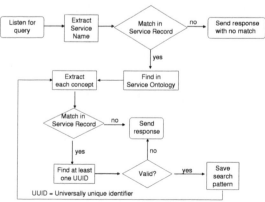

Figure 3. Semantic Matching Process

Item	Type	Value	Attribute
ServiceRecordHandle	Unit 32	Assigned by Server	0x000
ServiceClassDList			0x001
ServiceClass0	UUID	Headset	0x1108
ServiceClass1	UUID	Generic Audio	0x1203
ProtocolDescriptorList			0x0004
Protocol0	UUID	L2CAP	0x0100
Protocol1	UUID	RFCOMM	0x0003
ProtocolSpecificParamater()	Unit8	Server Channel #	
BluetoothProfileDescriptorList			0x0009
Profile()	UUID	Headset	0x1108
Parameter()	Unit 16	Version 1.0	0x0100
ServiceName	String	"Headset"	0x0000+language offset
Remote Audio Volume Control	Boolean	False	0x0302

Table 1. Bluetooth headset service record example (source from: [Bray and Sturman 2001])

each and every UUID in the service search pattern is contained within any of the service record's attribute values. A valid service search pattern must contain at least one UUID. The UUIDs need not be contained within any specific attributes or in any particular order within the service record.

DISCUSSION

[Avancha, Joshi and Finin 2002] has discussed that using ontology to describe services can facilitate inexact matching because it provides a structure for reasoning about the deriving knowledge from the given descriptions. They have commented that describing service ontologically is superior to UUID-based descriptions. They use the DAML+OIL (Darpa Agent Markup Language and Ontology Inference Layer) to describe their ontology and a Prolog-based reasoning engine to use the ontology. Although DAML+OIL is becoming a standard for use in the semantic Web, the ontology developers may have difficulty understanding implemented ontology or even building new ontologies because they focus too much on implementation issues. Moreover, direct coding of the resulting concepts is too abrupt a step, especially for complex ontologies. In this paper, we provide a language-independent concept model for representing the "context-dependent" classification knowledge. The classification knowledge is to organize words into groups that share many properties. The context is dependent on Bluetooth service discovery concepts.

CONCLUSION

We have introduced a service ontology concept modeling to enhance the Bluetooth service discovery. We have shown a frame-based presentation to support gradation, dependence and association classes among concepts. The semantic searching process allows matching different naming attributes to increase the quality of service discovery.

We envision the semantic service discovery solution can also be applied to wireless LAN, IEEE 802.11b and wide-area wireless networks. By looking at the rapid deployment of wireless technologies in hotspots such as cafes, shopping malls and restaurants around the world, the semantic service discovery will play an important role in future mobile-commerce applications.

Our future work includes evaluating semantic matching performance both in response time and processing time. We will need to compare the response and processing times for service discovery queries in the enhanced Bluetooth SDP with those in the regular system. We will also investigate the possibilities of developing m-commerce applications using semantic service discovery.

ACKNOWLEDGMENT

This work reported in this paper has been funded in part by the Department of Information Management, Shih Chien University and Hyper Taiwan Technology Inc. The authors would like to thank Scott Lai of Hyper Taiwan Technology for insightful discussions.

REFERENCES

[AVancha, Joshi and Finin 2002] Avancha, S., Joshi, A., and Finin, T. Enhanced Service Discovery in Bluetooth, Communications of the ACM, June 2002, 96-99.

[Bluetooth Specification 2001] Bluetooth Specification Version 1.1, February 2001.

[Bray and Sturman 2001] Bray, J., Sturman, C. Bluetooth Connect without Cables, Prentice-Hall, 2001.

[Fellbaum 1998] Fellbaum, C. WordNet: An Electronic Lexical Database, the MIT Press, 1998.

[Gruber 1993] Gruber, T, Translation Approach to Portable Ontology Specifications, Knowledge Acquisition, 5(9) 199-220.

[Lee, Sim, and Kwok 2002] Lee, M., Sim., K., and Kwok, P. Concept Acquisition Modeling for E-commerce Ontology, in Sollten, K. (ed)., Optimal Information Modeling Techniques, IRM Press, 2002, 30 -40.

[Miller and Bisdikian 2001] Miller, B., and Bisdikian, C. Bluetooth Revealed, Prentice Hall, 2001.

An Empirical Study on the Influencing Factors of Website Development in the Public Sector

Jae-Kwan Lee
Soongsil University, Dongjak-Gu, Seoul, 156-743, Korea
jklee@ssu.ac.kr 82-2-820-0561

ABSTRACT

A new framework for managing the Website development in the public sector is proposed and tested empirically with a sample of 65 city Websites. The framework consists of basic dimensions and a 2x2 matrix that is a simplified revision of the Mohammed et al. (2002)'s Marketspace Matrix. The 2x2 matrix includes development stages and design modes of public Websites. The four factors in the matrix, Publicity, Local Service, Differentiation and Participation, together with two basic dimensions of Attracting and Delivering in Simeon (2001), were proved to be important elements in a workable research framework. The effects of dimensions/factors and the role of the Attracting are discussed in depth.

1. INTRODUCTION

Public institutions as well as business organizations use the Internet to deliver a wide range of information and services at an increasing level of sophistication. "Governments will be leading users of e-business opportunities" (Jutla et al., 2002). E-government projects, the BEGIX of Bertelsmann Foundation(begix.de) and the Internet Resources Guide(govtech.net) are those examples with great attention.

However, Websites are so complex that it is difficult for governments to select proper tools from the Internet tool-kits, invest in more effective dimensions, and achieve innovative goals strategically. This paper proposes that we need a simpler method for developing the Website strategy for public institutions. The research objectives are twofold:

(1) A simple framework for managing the Website development process is proposed and tested empirically with a sample of 65 city Websites. The framework consists of basic dimensions and a simplified version of the Mohammed et al.(2002)'s Marketspace Matrix.

(2) The effect of dimensions/factors is tested by use of regression analysis. A special attention is paid to a basic dimension of online 'Attracting' that is important for public institutions which usually do not use offline advertising aggressively.

If we identify basic dimensions or factors and their causal relationships, we can construct a workable Balanced Scorecard(BSC) system for monitoring the Website development process. A famous example of BSC in the e-government sector is Bertelsmann Foundation's BEGIX, which was designed to evaluate overall e-government performance. We need some knowledge about the relationship among dimensions/factors to apply the BSC to the Website development in the public sector. This paper is organized as follows: theoretical review, designing the instrument, data collection and analysis, discussions and conclusions.

2. THEORETICAL REVIEW

Many researchers on e-Business address the stages of Website development process. Green (1998) suggests three stages: Attracting, Transforming, and Utilization of Media Technology. Simeon(2001) suggests the AIPD - Attracting(A) refers to online and offline strategies employed to get the Internet users to visit a Website; Informing(I) relates to the exchange of fundamental information about company and products; Positioning(P) refers to activities which show the service differentiation strategies of a Website; and Delivering(D)

highlights the technical infrastructure for the presentation and delivery of information and service.

Since Simeon's components are too much software-oriented and the Positioning may be an inappropriate concept for the public sector that lacks market competition, it is necessary to revise the components to find proper concepts for the public sector. Positioning can be replaced by the term 'Community' which means a network enabling its members to interact and providing services based on the differentiation strategies on a Website. Therefore, the AIPD will be replaced by AICD(Attracting, Informing, Community, and Delivering) in this paper.

Mohammed et al. (2002, p.556-580) developed a 5x4 matrix framework called 'Marketspace Matrix' by dividing marketing levers into five elements(Product, Price, Place, Communication, and Community) and by dividing the relationship phase into four stages(Awareness, Exploration, Commitment, Dissolution). "As the matrix is a newly developed tool, its use will continue to evolve" (Mohammed et al., 2002, p.563).

We select five from the nine dimensions of 5x4 matrix to construct a core of the framework in this paper as follows: The Exploration and Dissolution that are not salient in public institutions are eliminated; Three marketing mix elements in the original Marketspace Matrix, Product, Price and Place, are combined into a term 'Informing'; Awareness and Commitment are replaced by similar terms, Attracting and Empowerment. Hence, the core of the framework consists of a 2x2 matrix with two development stages(Informing and Community), two design modes(Communication and Empowerment) and a separate dimension, Attracting.

The Communication in this paper is a new term corresponding to the traditional concept of 'promotion', as defined in Mohammed et al.(2002, p.12). Marketing is still peripheral to the management of public services. It is important not to overemphasize the extent to which the marketing orientation has influenced the public sector(Walsh, 1994). Empowerment is one of the most frequently cited key words in the public sector. Drummond et al.(2000) discuss the market orientation in police services and explain the factors as including communication and empowerment. Bertelsmann Foundation(2001, 2002) emphasizes online participation supported by Internet tools such as online meeting place and online debate/voting. But we need a clear operational definition of the term of empowerment that seems somewhat vague.

Davis(1999) defines the community empowerment model as a model that has a mechanism to provide the community issues and decision-making information to its members, along with interactive support. Fourie(1999) suggests effective empowerment programs with directing by clear goals, providing tools, preparing relevant contents, user involvement and supportive climate. Marketplaces create community programs in a number of ways: message boards, forum, collaborative work tools and links(Kim, 2000; Lee, 2001).

Jutla et al.(2002) present a list of metrics for innovation and a model of government support for e-business readiness. Two items, the online transformation of services and the frequency of innovative new services, are selected from the list and their mean value is used as a dependent variable called 'Innovation(or INNOV)' in this paper.

Simeon(2001) shows that a regression of Informing, Positioning and Delivering on Branding Potential as a dependent variable is significant. However, the validity and significance of a four-factor model with AIPD were not examined because he believed that Attracting often involved a wide range of non-Internet strategies. But it is important to study the role of online Attracting. Some would argue that awareness or attracting is the key of success in today's online business. Mohammed et al.(2002, p.208) argue that focusing on customer experience is "the single most profitable thing". The customer experience relates to Community and Empowerment rather than Attracting.

3. DESIGNING THE INSTRUMENT

In general, there are so many criteria that studying on the Website evaluation model seems to be complex. For instance, a table of the criteria presented on WorldBest.com(worldbestweb sites.com/criteria.htm) includes more than one hundred items relating to design, functionality, contents, and many others. But a systematic study based on a simpler list becomes possible if we focus on a few strategic factors and modify Simeon(2001)'s components as following:

Attracting consists of the following five items to measure the utilization level of tools on a homepage used to get Internet users to have a good impression on the Website:

- Design of Logo and Tagline(quick summary of what a Website is all about)
- Graphics(e.g., layout, color and figures of a homepage)
- Institution's Self-advertising(e.g., banner, button, interstitials)
- Services for Attracting(e.g., quiz, lottery, e-card, maps, weather, channels, download service)
- Contents for Attracting(e.g., entertainments, culture, tourism, game, kids, health, gallery)

Informing consists of eight items developed by modifying Simeon(2001)'s components: Local Links, Contents for Publicity, Reports, Descriptions on the Institution, Descriptions on Online Administrative Services, Projects, Contact Information and Counseling.

Community consists of 11 items: Online Forum, Events, Partner Links(or Ads.), e-Magazine(or Newsletter or Webcast), Message Boards, Users' Participation(e.g., articles, photos, personal links), Focus of News, Vision(or values), Domain Identity, Community Services(or online support for community meeting or networking), and Contents for Learning. We can use a good example for rating each item, for instance, 'Citizen Discussion Room' of Ulsan City(eulsan.go.kr) as a benchmark example for Online Forum System.

Delivering is measured on dichotomy (1 or 0) depending on the presence or absence of features for each item. A simple list of nine tools that are fundamental and easy to check is: Search Engine, Mailing List, Framework, Multimedia, Password System, FAQ, Chat, Downloadable Publications and Update Indication.

Innovation: Public institutions have to utilize the Internet for actual service innovation. Hence, two variables indicating the innovation results are selected: the e-transformation level of existing services and the frequency of new innovative services. They are rated on a five-point scale: "Never(1), Only Descriptions(2), Online Request(3), Partial(4), Full Processing(5)" for the first item and "Never(1), …, Many New Systems(5)" for the second item. Such quantification is possible because the introductions of new innovative systems on the public Website are prevailing, to name a few, Docket Access, View Property Assessments, and Request for Proposals of Philadelphia(phila.gov) and Citizen Assessment Systems, Citizen Satisfaction Monitor, OPEN(Online Procedures Enhancement) System of Seoul(metro.seoul.kr).

Every item except Delivering is graded on a five-point scale. The components in Informing can be summarized by two sub-dimensions: basic information about institution, products and local services and extended information for contacting and counseling. On the other hand, Community includes more diverse sub-dimensions representing online meeting-place, tools for relationship-building and differentiated promotion. The Communication or Empowerment items are not shown on the above lists, since the lists were developed according to the four stages of AICD. But it is expected that they will be identified explicitly at the following factor analysis.

4. DATA COLLECTION AND ANALYSIS

This paper focuses on the test of models through inspecting small number of well-developed Websites in detail, not on the comparative study by a large-scale survey. Therefore, we confine the sample units to cities, counties or states that usually have close relationships with locals/ citizens. We also con-

fine the scope to the Websites written in English or Korean, considering the language ability of inspectors. Hence, a sample of 65 official Websites is selected: 28 winners/finalists of the Best of the Web 2000 and 2001(centerdigitalgov.com), 26 Korean best city sites(100hot.co.kr), and 11 worldwide cities(officialcitysites.org).

Six teams of 23 graduate students who are enrolled on e-Business and Internet Marketing classes worked together to inspect the Websites during August-November 2002 by using the inspection method explained in Cunliffe(2000). SPSS 9.0 for Windows was used to analyze the data. Cronbach's ± values indicating the scale reliability for the dimensions in Section 3 are 0.780 for Attracting, 0.653 for Informing, and 0.748 for Community. Moderately low value of ± for Informing is due to Contact Information and Counseling. But because ± is greater than 0.6 and it is expected that the roles of the two items may be important, all the 24 items in A, I, C are used together to extract factors.

Table1 shows a result of the factor analysis. After all, Contact Information, Counseling, and Message board are deleted in Table1 due to their low reliability (±<0.6). The Message Board is generally considered as an important tool for allowing people to meet on a Website(Kim, 2000, p.33). However, it was inevitable to delete it because it is so singular that the difference between countries is significantly large; Korean Websites use Message Boards very much and actively whereas foreign Websites hardly use it.

The five factors in Table1 are named Differentiation(DI), Attracting(A), Participation(PA), Pub-licity(PR), and Local Service(LS), respectively, to represent the meaning of items loaded high on each factor. For the development stage, Informing is divided into two factors PR and LS, and Community is divided into two factors DI and PA. We can also interpret the factor structure in a view of Website design mode for public institutions. PR and DI correspond to the concept of 'Communication' and LS and PA correspond to the concept of 'Empowerment'.

As explained in Section 2, Communication refers to promotion or differentiation in traditional Marketing while the Empowerment refers to participative problem solving. Therefore, the 2x2 matrix shown in Table 2 is proved to be workable framework for the study. The reliabilities for five factors in Table1 and four dimensions in Table 2 are larger than 0.6, which is a generally acceptable level for an exploratory study. To develop a measure for each factor/dimension, we define the degree of closeness of x_i^k (= the level of attribute i attained by Website k) to ideal value x_i^* as a membership function d_i^k. If x_i^* is a maximum, $d_i^k = x_i^k / x_i^*$ (Zeleny, 1982, p.159). Hence, the following measures are formulated: $d_A = X_A/25$, $d_I = X_I/30$, $d_C = X_C/50$, $d_D = X_D/9$, $d_{PR} = X_{PR}/15$, $d_{LS} = X_{LS}/15$, $d_{DI} = X_{DI}/30$, $d_{PA} = X_{PA}/20$, $d_{CC} = X_{CC}/45$, $d_{EM} = X_{EM}/35$. Table 2 summarizes the results of the regression analyses to answer the research questions. A discussion based on the results will be followed in Section 5.

5. DISCUSSIONS

Many public Websites show active utilizations of the tools for attracting. Good examples are Button Licensing, My California, Web Winner, Contest and Lottery of California State(ca.gov) and e-Card, Quiz, Awards, Channel and Lottery of Washington State(access.wa.gov). But the mean value of 59% for Attracting is very low and its variation is very large. Although there are some cities like New York(home.nyc.gov), Taegu(daegu.go.kr) and Pohang(ipohang.org) showing excellence in all dimensions, many cities are

Table1. Factors in the Dimensions A, I, C for Public Institutions (n=65)

Component Items	Factor 1 DI	Factor 2 Attracting	Factor 3 PA	Factor 4 PR	Factor 5 LS	Cronbach's α
Focus of News	.742					
Domain Identity	.738					
Community Services	.717					.796
Events	.640					
Contents for Learning	.526					
Vision(or Values)	.446					
Institution's Self-advertising		.793				
Logo and Tagline		.730				
Services for Attracting		.692				.780
Graphics		.677				
Contents for Attracting		.650				
Online Forum			.723			
Users' Participation			.701			
e-Magazine			.584			.647
Partner Links(or Ads.)			.529			
Projects				.835		
Contents for Publicity				.761		.677
Descriptions on Institution				.551		
Descriptions on Admin. Service					.730	
Reports					.598	.637
Local Links					.455	

Table2. 2×2 Matrix by Development Stages and by Design Modes

Design Modes / Stages	COMMUNICATION (CC) 9 items, α = 0.799	EMPOWERMENT (EM) 7 items, α = 0.647
INFORMING (I) 6 items, α = 0.700	PUBLICITY(PR): Descriptions on Institution Contents for Publicity Projects	LOCAL SERVICE(LS): Descriptions on Admin. Services Local Links Reports
COMMUNITY (C) 10 items, α = 0.779	DIFFERENTIATION(DI): Events Focus of News Domain Identity Vision or Values Community Services Contents for Learning	PARTICIPATION(PA): e-Magazine Partner Links Online Forum Users' Participation

unbalanced between Attracting and other factors. For example, the Attracting is poor compared with other excellent dimensions in Boston City(cityofboston.gov), Virginia State(vipnet.org) and Montgomery County(montgomerycounty md.gov), and the cities vice versa can be easily found.

The first four models, Model 1~Model 2' in Table 2 show whether each input variable is influential or not on the innovation level. Both main dimensions(Communication and Empowerment) in Model 1' and four factors(PR, LS, DI, and PA) in Model 2' are all significantly influential. But the p-value of Attracting is 0.09 in model 1 and 0.114 in model 2.

It means that colorful designs and attracting features of a homepage have not necessarily anything to do with innovation. This message can offer a good piece of advice for managers of Websites. Considering the arguments in the literature, this result has an important meaning. Some emphasize the maximization of the loads in a home or opening page(Lapham, 1995). Others emphasize the importance of simplicity of the homepage repeatedly(Easton, 1999). This study can give an answer to these arguments. Attracting and Delivering are strongly emphasized in many cases, but the fact that those have not necessarily an influence on innovation should be acknowledged.

However, Attracting cannot be entirely ignored due to a skeptical result. There are notable opinions like "The Web is still a developing medium, with no firmly established standards for either presenting advertising or measuring its effectiveness"(Black, 2001) and "The choice of tools must be consistent with positioning choice or learning trends" (Mohammed et al., 2002, p.578). The possibility that Attracting has a significant influence on major dimensions depending on the phases of Website development(starting phase or maturity phase) and the types of organizations(businesses or nonprofit organizations) should be considered. So at the next step, we can study on the question what the effects of Attracting and Delivering on other factors than innovation, are.

The results of a regression of A and D on each I, C, CC, or EM are summarized as the following: Delivering has influences on all the four dimensions; Attracting has an effect on C and EM. As shown in Table 3, although R^2 values are moderately low, both Attracting and Delivering have a positive impact on C in model 3 and on EM in model 4, respectively. Because Delivering

refers to the technical infrastructure for the presentation and delivery of information and service, it can be easily inferred that it has an effect on the main dimensions, Informing, Community, Communication and Empowerment. Unlike Delivering, Attracting does not show wide effects and has influences on Community and Empowerment. Since Attracting represents users' look-and-feel about a Website, it would have strong connection with Community and Empowerment, which encourage users to stay and participate.

6. CONCLUSIONS

Main dimensions/factors for the public Website development are found theoretically and empirically. Two new perspectives augment the existing AIPD framework(Simeon, 2001) to study the Website development process in depth: (1) The design modes of Communication and Empowerment and (2) A 2x2 matrix including two development stages and two design modes of public Websites, which is a simplified revision from Mohammed et al. (2002)'s Marketspace Matrix. Four factors in the 2x2 matrix, Publicity, Local Service, Differentiation, and Participation, together with two basic dimensions of Attracting and Delivering, are proved to be important elements in a workable research framework. And subtle subjects like the effects of dimensions/ factors and the role of Attracting were discussed.

Because the cyber space has not shown any determined shape through the short periods of the introduction and the spread, it is hard to set up a universal model or to deduce a general rule. Therefore, proper case studies or modifications of the model need to be continuously tried. This exploratory study has its limits in instrumentation, sampling, and the narrow range of selected category. If the approach presented here is applied to other categories or fields, the component items and scales need to be modified appropriately.

REFERENCES

Bertelsmann Foundation(2001), *E-Democracy Around the World*, Phil Noble & Associates, Inc.

Bertelsmann Foundation(2002), *Balanced E-Government*, www.begix.de/

Black, J.(2001), "Online Advertising: It's Just the Beginning", *Business Week*, July 12, 2001.

Cunliffe, D.(2000), "Developing Usable Websites: A Review and Model", *Internet Research*, 10(4), pp.295-307.

Davis, C.M.(1999), "A Survey of Web-based Community Information Systems", Doctoral Dissertation, University of Michigan.

Drummond, G., J. Ensor, A. Laing & N. Richardson(2000), "Market Orientation Applied to Police Service Strategies", *International Journal of Public Service Management*, 13(7), pp.571-587.

Easton, J.(1999), *StrikingItRich.com*, Korean Version translated by K.M. Lee, Book Club, Seoul.

Fourie, I.(1999), "Empowering Users -Current Awareness on the Internet", *Electronic Library*, 17(6), pp.379-388.

Green, S.H.B.(1998), "Cyberspace Winners: How They Did It", *Business Week*, June 22, pp.154-160.

Jutla, D., P. Bodorik, & J. Dhaliwal(2002), "Supporting the E-Business Readiness of SMEs:
   Approaches and Metrics", *Internet Research*, 12(2), pp.139-164.

Kim, A.J.(2000), *Community Building on the Web*, Peachpit Press, Berkeley, CA.

Lapham, C.(1995), "The Vision of an Accomplished Webmaster", *CMC Magazine*,
   December 1, 1995, p.3.

Lee, J.(2001), "A Study on the Evaluation Factors for Cyber Community Websites"(Korean), *Journal of Customer Satisfaction Management*, 3(2), pp.91-110.

Mohammed, R.A., R.J. Fisher, B.J. Jaworski, & A.M. Cahill(2002), *Internet Marketing: Building
   Advantage in a Networked Economy*, McGraw-Hill Companies, Inc.

Simeon, R.(2001), "Evaluating the Branding Potential of Websites Across Borders", *Marketing
   Intelligence & Planning*, 19(6), pp.418-424.

Walsh, K.(1994), "Marketing and Public Sector Management", *European Journal of
   Marketing*, 28(3), pp.63-71.

Zeleny, M.(1982), *Multiple Criteria Decision Making*, McGraw-Hill, Inc.

Table3. A Summary of Regression Analyses

Model	Dependent Variable	Independent Variables	Unstandardized B	Std. Error	Standardized β	p	Adjust R^2	p
1': Modes & A, D	INNOV	constant	-.771	.346		.030		
		dcc communication	2.202	.439	.391	.000		
		dEM empowerment	3.280	.591	.493	.000	.757	.000
		dA attracting	.570	.331	.126	.090		
		dD delivering	.329	.383	.061	.394		
1': Modes	INNOV	constant	-.597	.329		.075		
		dcc communication	2.147	.434	.381	.000	.747	.000
		dEM empowerment	3.927	.513	.591	.000		
2': Factors & D	INNOV	dPR publicity	1.038	.378	.196	.008		
		dLS local service	1.098	.554	.164	.052		
		dDI differentiation	1.420	.405	.306	.001	.753	.000
		dPA participation	1.976	.358	.445	.000		
		dA attracting	.540	.337	.120	.114		
		dD delivering	.244	.395	.045	.539		
2': Factors	INNOV	dPR publicity	1.096	.368	.207	.004		
		dLS local service	1.200	.557	.180	.035	.747	.000
		dDI differentiation	1.388	.408	.299	.001		
		dPA participation	2.336	.303	.526	.000		
3: A, D on C	Community	constant	.294	.089		.002		
		dA attracting	.223	.096	.273	.023	.225	.000
		dD delivering	.325	.114	.334	.006		
4: A, D on EM	Empowerment	constant	.357	.069		.000		
		dA attracting	.269	.074	.396	.001	.323	.000
		dD delivering	.257	.088	.318	.005		

Assurance Through Control Objectives, A Governance Basis for Managing Corporate Information Assets

Dan Shoemaker and Antonio Drommi
College of Business Administration, University of Detroit Mercy
Detroit, Michigan 48219
(313) 993-3337 voice (313) 993-1052 fax
Shoemadp@udmercy.edu and drommia@udmercy.edu

INTRODUCTION

Information security systems have to meet two logical criteria to be effective. First the protection must be *complete*, in the sense that the response should address the entire problem (e.g., everything that requires assurance is secured). And second the safeguards have to be *uniform*. That is, there should be an organization-wide commitment to security. The first principle is established through a systematic implementation strategy. The second requires the organization to define substantive policies, roles and responsibilities, educate employees and describe and enforce accountability. The problem is that this effort takes time and precious resources.

Nevertheless there are very real and substantive consequences if the security protection scheme is inconsistent. For example, a secure network without policies to control the people who operate it can be breached no matter how sophisticated the technology employed. One recent illustration of how that exact scenario played out is the national database, which was raided by four inside employees for the credit information of 30,000 individuals. That information was sold to an identity theft ring, which subsequently used it to commit massive credit card fraud.

As a matter of fact there are actually very few breaches of corporate information security that directly involve the technology. Specifically, seventy two percent of the serious losses recorded by the FBI in 2001 originated from the actions of inside people rather than hackers (CSI 2002). Which underscores the principle that, no matter how robust the encryption scheme, there are no practical safeguards unless everybody involved understands what constitutes a violation and what the consequences are for committing one. So, the correct response in nearly three-quarters of the cases last year should have been a systematic set of organizational control procedures, not a more sophisticated firewall.

THE THREE BUILDING BLOCKS OF A SYSTEMATIC SOLUTION

Which conveniently leads us to the theme of this paper. Control objective based security frameworks are constructed around three high-level principles. Figure One itemizes these and illustrates their relationship to each other.

The first principle is standard best practice. This term just denotes the fact that the collective body of knowledge of the profession can be tapped for expert advice about the best way to respond to a practical concern. When best practices are formally recorded and conveyed as a set of recommendations this is called a "standard". Standards are disseminated by acknowledged and authoritative entities.

The second principle is governance. This is the generic organizing and control function that underwrites any form of proper management. Where that governance applies directly to the supervision of the organization's information assets it is specifically termed "information governance". The information governance function seamlessly integrates every aspect of information and technical assurance into a single coherent and continuously evolving response. In that respect substantive information governance is attained through a tangible, organization-wide system of rational policies, and their attendant control objectives. Figure Two outlines that.

The process focuses specifically on establishing an integrated and documented set of policies, which are aimed at ensuring that the complete set of information assets is fully secured. These must be sufficiently detailed to allow employees in the entire organization to understand how to establish tangible control over their applicable operational activities.

Since that implies a comprehensive set of components that have to be related, there is an implicit requirement for some sort of infrastructure. Which brings us to the final principle, organizational infrastructure. The role of infrastructure is to make two intangible concepts real. Figure Three portrays that.

An infrastructure is nothing more than the particular embodiment of the concepts of best practice and information governance in a given organization. It is always documented in an explicit and traceable way. Tangibility is the key attribute. Accordingly, security infrastructures are implemented by the deliberate deployment of a set of rationally derived relationships and processes, embodied as a specific framework of control objectives. Operationally, a security infrastructure forges a specific link between the overall business strategy and information security requirements. This is illustrated in Figure Four.

Figure Two: Levels of Information Management

Figure One: Fundamental Components of Information Assurance

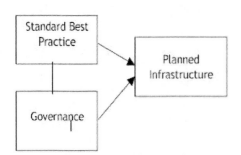

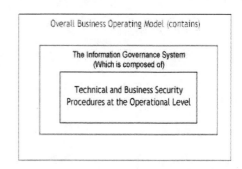

A formal strategic planning and development process such as this represents the ideal means to transform intangible concepts into a working day-to-day security operation. However in order to do this, the generic best practices specified in the expert model have to be adapted to the specific environment. The practical approach to this is hierarchical. Or in essence an optimum solution is engineered top-down. In practice this is called "tailoring" (or sometimes "customization"). Tailoring creates a tangible, complete and rational document set, which em-

Figure Three: Relationship of the Concepts of Best Practice and Governance to Infrastructure

Figure Four: The Relationship between Strategic Planning and Security Infrastructure

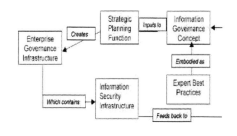

bodies all necessary security activities down to the level of utilitarian tasks. The end product is a set of explicit procedures that convey the exact substance (e.g., assigned activities) of the assurance tasks to every employee sufficient to ensure effective coordination of the work.

The Three Standard Models

There are three globally accepted frameworks that embody these three principles in a security infrastructure. These are COBIT (ISACA, 2002) ISO/IEC 15408: (ISO, 1997) and BS 7799 (BSI, 2000). Each has a slightly different orientation but they all convey a complete conceptual model, with the necessary actions spelled out through a distinctive set of control objectives. These control objectives are nothing more than the explicit definition of the desired result or purpose to be achieved by the security element they are attached to. Accordingly, the aggregate set of control objectives provides a concrete and detailed picture of the security solution that each of these standards represents.

COBIT

COBIT supports the development of clear policies and procedures that enforce operational control over IT. It was developed out of 41 primary sources, which is important since legitimacy is an essential requirement of any best practice standard. COBIT assumes that effective security control is based on four domains labeled: *1) planning and organization, 2) acquisition and implementation 3) delivery and support* and *4) monitoring*. Each of these domains is further defined by a set of 34 high-level control objectives, which embody 318 itemized control objectives. Figure Five outlines that structure:

Figure Five: The COBIT Hierarchy of Control Statements

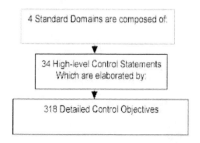

We are going to employ the first of these domains (planning and organization) to illustrate this model. The planning and organization domain (PO) contains eleven of the 34 high-level control objectives, which essentially represent the topics that must be specifically addressed as part of the security assurance for that domain. These eleven are:

PO1	Define a strategic IT plan
PO2	Define the information architecture
PO3	Determine the technological direction
PO4	Define the IT organization and relationships
PO5	Manage the IT investment
PO6	Communicate management aims and direction
PO7	Manage human resources
PO8	Ensure compliance with external requirements
PO9	Assess risks
PO10	Manage projects
PO11	Manage quality

Since these are topics rather than explicit procedure specifications their precise implementation is essentially unclear at this level. Therefore each is further elaborated by 95 explicit control objectives. A number of these are aligned to every high level objective but there is never any less than one for each. Overall there are 318 control objectives in the COBIT model. These provide the real value since they specify in very precise terms what must be done to satisfy its general purposes. We are going to use the first control objective PO 1.1 (*IT as part of short and long range planning*) to demonstrate the level of specificity that this offers. That objective elaborates, the high-level control objective PO1 (*define a strategic IT plan*) which is part of the Planning and Organization (PO) Domain. This objective simply specifies that IT must be included as part of the long- and short-range business planning process. The steps that are required to satisfy this objective are itemized within the body of the description (from COBIT, 3rd Edition):

PO 1.1 IT as part of long- and short-range planning

Senior management is responsible for developing and implementing long- and short-range plans that fulfill the organization's mission and goals. In this respect, senior management should ensure that IT issues as well as opportunities are adequately assessed and reflected in the organization's long- and short-range plans. IT long- and short-range plans should be developed to help ensure that the use of IT is aligned with the mission and business strategies of the organization.

It cannot be stressed enough that the COBIT framework embodies 317 other statements of this type. As such, it should be clear that it offers very detailed guidance about the actions that must be taken to secure an IT function. The next model at is similar in its focus but it allows the organization to integrate security requirements into any information technology product or process.

Example: Establishing Information Security through ISO/IEC 15408

The goal of ISO/IEC 15408:1997 is to embed detailed information security requirements into the functional specifications of any IT product, system, or process. There are three parts to this standard. Each describes the implementation process for security controls that can be used to describe the behavior of a given Target of Evaluation (TOE). These control objectives are captured in a generic reusable Protection Profile (PP), which is then specifically tailored for a given product as a Security Target (ST). Figure Six illustrates this:

Figure Six: Implementation of a 15408 Protection Profile

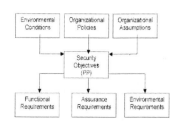

Implementation revolves around the formulation of a reusable Protection Profile (PP), which in essence is the general set of selected security objectives for the organization. The PP allows an organization to create a global set of security requirements (Note: consumers can also employ a PP to specify IT security features to prospective suppliers). Operationally this profile is specified top-down, through the involvement of stakeholders. However, as the drawing illustrates the actual implementation of the security function is bottom-up because the explicit form of the security for any given instance is tailored to each security target.

These security objectives are then tailored into the specific functional, assurance and environmental requirements for any given security target. The security target (ST) expresses the particular security requirements of a given product as well as the security functions to be evaluated. Where the STs are represented as a definition of outcomes for assessment it is called a target of evaluation (TOE). Targets of Evaluation (TOEs) are composed of security objectives and assessment criteria specified in the standard.

The final model adds the policy dimension to the control objective concept. Because of that, it is the only one that builds a formal and permanent organization-wide information security management system (ISMS).

Example: Establishing Information Assurance through ISO/IEC 17799

The International Organization for Standardization (ISO) created ISO/IEC 17799:2000 as the means to implement a comprehensive and persistent information security management system (ISMS). It touches on every aspect of IT security. It forces companies through a step-by-step assessment of their business needs and appropriate responsibilities with respect to security. It centers on developing a set of rational policies, which are designed to ensure that every aspect of the company's information resources will be secured.

The information security management system is formulated based on ten security domains containing 127 high-level Control Objectives. The complete set of these control objectives is assumed to describe and embody all aspects of security for information and IT. By developing concrete responses to each of the high level objectives, the manager can ensure that a capable IT control system is in place for any type of organization at any level of security desired.

This originates from a risk assessment. Management uses this approach to map where the organization is in relation to the best-practice ideal defined by the Standard. Figure Seven describes that process.

ISO/IEC 17799 bases the security solution on comprehensive definition of policies, roles and responsibilities. This approach creates a complete and systematic enterprise governance response rather than a specifically IT oriented one. As we said earlier, the primary criterion for judging the effectiveness of a security solution is whether it is complete. This model provides assurance that the entire enterprise will be completely, correctly (with respect to best practice) and effectively secured, which might make it the most attractive of the three popular control objective based approaches discussed here.

Figure Seven: Sample Process for Implementing 17799

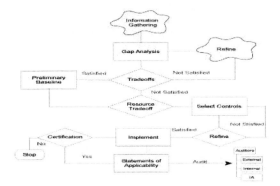

SUMMARY AND A SHORT CONCLUSION

Information assets are more difficult to account for and control than conventional physical assets. That is, because IT work involves the production of virtual, highly dynamic products, which makes it hard to know WHAT to secure let alone how to do it properly. This has been such a universal and pervasive problem that the logical response was appropriately best practice models that can provide the comprehensive basis for information security assurance.

The International Standards Organization (ISO) has developed two formal reference models (ISO/IEC 15408 and ISO/IEC 17799) and the Information Systems Audit and Control Association/Foundation (ISACA/F) has provided another (COBIT). These frameworks serve both as a fundamental checklist for itemizing the elements involved in assuring a virtual asset as well as a foundation for building common understanding of the mechanisms required for security assurance.

This is highly advantageous because, notwithstanding the issue of whether technology can ever fully confront all of the issues associated with information security, a governance solution is more easily understood and accepted by the non-technical managers who oversee the bulk of the company's work. Furthermore security governance can be implemented without involving expensive technology, which means that it is less likely to involve capital investment. Finally it creates a comprehensive and consistent policy and procedure framework, which communicates and coordinates security assurance procedures corporation-wide. And since all of these are built through a definition process they can be altered in a rational and systematic fashion to meet changes in the original situation. Given the challenges of an uncertain age, a detailed governance based audit and control infrastructure built from expert advice and capable of serving as the basis for reliable and comprehensive information security protection, is an invaluable asset.

REFERENCES AND ADDITIONAL READING

1. *7799 Standards Can Enhance Your Organization's Information Security Program* Business/Technology Editors, InfoWorld, 10, 2001

2. Ashton, Gerry, *Cleaning up your Security Act for Inspection*, Computer Weekly Jan 18, 2001

3. British Standards Institution, *BSI 7799:2, 1999*

4. *Internet Business News*, CSI survey, *FBI/Computer Security Institute, April 8, 2002*

5. Dorofee A.J., JA Walker, RC Williams, Risk Management in Practice, Crosstalk, Volume 10 #4, April 1997

6. European Accreditation (EA), EA 7/03, EA Guidelines for the Accreditation of Information Systems

7. Favell, Andrew, *Don't Leave it to Luck*, Computer Weekly, Oct 11, 2001

8. Goodwin, William UK's security code of practice becomes worldwide standard Computer Weekly, Jan 25, 2001

9. Information Systems Audit and Control Association (ISACA), *Framework*, COBIT (third edition)

10. Mcclure, Stuart, SECURITY WATCH: Mass manipulation isn't reserved just for presidential elections: IT world be warned, InfoWorld, Nov 20, 2000

1. Simons, Mike, *NHS takes unpopular BS 7799*, Computer Weekly, Jan 18, 2001

2. Swanson, Marianne, *Security Self Assessment Guide for Information Technology Systems,* National Institute of Standards and Technology NIST 800-26, November 2001

3. United Kingdom Accreditation Service (UKAS), Assessment of Approved and Notified Bodies

4. United Kingdom Accreditation Service (UKAS), UKAS Directory of Accredited Inspection Bodies

5. United Kingdom Accreditation Service (UKAS), UKAS Application for Approval.

Design of Lowpass Narrowband FIR Filters Using IFIR and Modified RRS Filter

Gordana Jovanovic-Dolecek
INAOE, Puebla, Pue., Apartado 51 y 216, Z.P. 7200, Mexico
phone & fax:+ 2222-47-0517
gordana@inaoep.mx

Vlatko Dolecek
University of Sarajevo
Bosnia and Herzegovina
vdolecek@hotmail.com

Isak Karabegovic
University of Bihac
Bosnia and Herzegovina
isak@bih.net.ba

ABSTRACT

This paper presents a new efficient method for the design of narrowband lowpass (LP) finite impulse response (FIR) filters using a modified interpolated finite impulse response (IFIR) filter and an improved recursive running sum (RRS) filter. Since the number of parameters of the RRS filter is increased the adjustment of the frequency characteristic of the interpolator filter using fewer stages of the RRS filter is possible.

INTRODUCTION

The main disadvantage of FIR filters is that they involve a higher degree of computational complexity comparing to IIR filters with equivalent magnitude response. Many design methods have been proposed to reduce the complexity of FIR filters in the past few years for example (J. W. Adams and A.N.Willson, 1984), (Y.Lian and Y.C.Lim, 1998), (M.E.Nordberg, 1996), (A.Bartolo, B.D.Clymer, 1996) etc. One of the most difficult problems in digital filtering is the design of narrowband filters, (Mitra 2001). The difficulty lies in the fact that such filters require high-order designs in order to meet the desired specification. In turn, high order filters require a large amount of computation so are difficult to implement.

We consider the design of lowpass narrowband FIR filters with cutoff frequencies considerably lower than the sampling rate. One efficient technique for the design of FIR filters is called the interpolation FIR (IFIR) technique (Saramaki at al, 1988). The basic idea is to implement a FIR filter as a cascade of two FIR sections, where one section generates a sparse set of impulse response values and the other section performs the interpolation. Therefore, the IFIR filter is a cascade of two filters

$$H(z) = G(z^M)I(z) \tag{1}$$

where $G(z^M)$ is an expanded shaping or model filter, $I(z)$ is an interpolator or image suppressor and M is the interpolation factor. The advantage of this structure is based on the design of the prototype FIR filter $H(z)$ by using smaller order filters $G(z)$ and $I(z)$. Further simplification can be obtained using a running sum (RRS) filter as an interpolator, (Dolecek and Reyes, 1999). The system function of the RRS filter is given as

$$H(z) = \left(\frac{1}{M} \frac{1-z^{-M}}{1-z^{-1}} \right)^K = \left(\frac{1}{M} \sum_{n=0}^{M-1} z^{-n} \right)^K \tag{2}$$

where K is called the stage. As seen in equation (2), all coefficients are equal to 1 and therefore it is not necessary to apply any multiplication.

The frequency response of the RRS filter can be expressed as:

$$H(e^{j\omega}) = \left\{ \frac{\sin\frac{\omega M}{2}}{M\sin\frac{\omega}{2}} e^{-j\omega[(M-1)/2]} \right\}^K \tag{3}$$

This is a linear-phase lowpass filter with a very wide transition band, and whose passband is only a small portion of the resulting bandwidth. The frequency response has nulls at integer multiples of $2p/M$. This makes it a natural candidate for elimination of images introduced by $G(z^M)$, provided that the baseband of the filter $G(z^M)$ is narrowband. The RRS filter has only two parameters : M and K, which must be chosen so that the RRS filter eliminates images of the expanded model filter, and, so that the resulting filter satisfies the given specification. In order to improve the frequency characteristic of the RRS interpolator for a given M and K, we propose a modification, as described in the next section.

2. MODIFICATION OF RRS FILTER

The parameters of an RRS filter are M and K. If the specification is not satisfied for a given M we must increase K to the next integer value. To avoid doing this, we modify the structure of the RRS filter by introducing additional parameters.

We can generate the triangular stepped sequence by multiplying the RRS sequence with the corresponding sparse RRS sequence, as shown in the next equation

$$X(z) = [\sum_{i=0}^{2N-1} z^{-i}] [\sum_{k=0}^{N-1} z^{-2k}] \tag{4}$$

* Note that N is an integer.

Using $M=2N$ according to the equations (2) and (4) we can write the system function of the modified RRS filter

$$H_m(z) = [\frac{1}{M} \sum_{i=0}^{2N-1} z^{-i}]^{k1} [\frac{1}{N} \sum_{k=0}^{N-1} z^{-2k}]^{k2} = H(z)X_1(z) \tag{5}$$

where k_1 and k_2 are the stages. We now have 3 parameters, M, k_1, and k_2 which can be used to adjust the frequency characteristic of the interpolator filter in the IFIR structure. Note that the modified RRS filter is a cascade of the original RRS filter and the corresponding sparse RRS filter with the halved order.

Example 1:

We consider $N=4$, $k_1=0$ and $k_2=0$. From (5), we have

$$H_m(z) = [\frac{1}{8} \sum_{i=0}^{2\cdot4-1} z^{-i}] [\frac{1}{4} \sum_{k=0}^{4-1} z^{-2k}] = H(z)X_1(z). \tag{6}$$

Figure 1: Magnitude responses

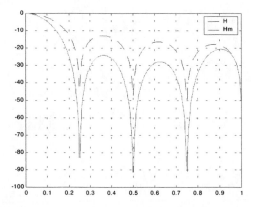

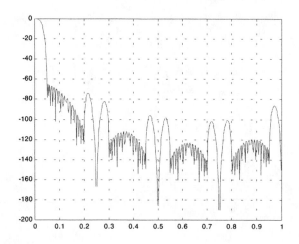

The corresponding magnitude responses are shown in Figure 1. We see that the magnitude response of the RRS filter is improved.

3. PROPOSED STRUCTURE

We propose the modified RRS filter as the interpolator in the IFIR structure. The resulting structure is shown in Figure 2. Adjusting all three parameters of the modified RRS filter we can satisfy the given specification using the lower order interpolator filter.

The method is illustrated in the next example.

Example 2:

We design the filter having these specifications: Passband and the stopband frequencies are w_p=.01 and w_s=.05, respectively. Passband ripple is Rp=0.1 dB and the stopband attenuation is As = 60dB.

The direct design using the Parks McClellan algorithm results in a filter of the order 172. If we use the IFIR structure with the RRS filter and the interpolation factor M=8 we obtain the order of the model filter of only N_G=22. The resulting magnitude response does not satisfy the stopband specification if we use the number of stages k_1=3.

In order to improve the stopband characteristic we use the modified RRS filter with k_1=3, k_2=1 and M=8. The corresponding magnitude response is shown in Figure 3. Observe that the stopband specification is satisfied. Note that the specification is also satisfied using K=4 in the RRS filter, but this filter is more complex than the modified RRS filter with k_1=3 and k_2=1.

Figure 2: Proposed structure

4. CONCLUSIONS

The method for the design of narrowband FIR filters is proposed. It is based on the use of the IFIR structure and the modified RRS filter which is used as an interpolator. The modification of the RRS filter enables decrease in the number of stages of the RRS filter. As a result the given specification is satisfied using less complex interpolator filter making the overall complexity of the design lower. The only restriction is that the interpolation factor in the IFIR structure must be even.

REFERENCES

J.   W. Adams and A.N.Willson, Jr., (1984), Some efficient digital prefilter structures, *Trans. Circuits & Sysems*, CAS-31, 260-266.

Y.   Lian and Y.C.Lim, (1998), Structure for narrow and moderate transition band FIR filter design, *Electronics Letters*, 34, No.1, 49-51.

M.   E.Nordberg, (1996), A fast algorithm for FIR digital filtering with a sum of triangls weighting functions, *Circuits, Syst. Signal Processing*, 15, No.2, 145-164.

A.   Bartolo, B. D. Clymer, (1996), An efficient method of FIR filtering based on impulse response rounding, *IEEE Trans. Signal Processing*, 46, No.8, 2243-2248.

G.   Jovanovic-Dolecek and A. Sarmiento Reyes, (1999), An efficient method narrowband FIR filter design, *Computacion y Sistemas*, 2, 78-86.

S.   K. Mitra, (2001), *Digital Signal processing: A Computer-Based Approach*, Second edition: McGraw-Hill, New York.

T.   Saramaki, Y., Nuevo, and S. K. Mitra, (1998), Design of computational efficient interpolated FIR filters, *IEEE Transaction on Circuit and Systems*, 35, 70-78.

A Comparison of Different Solution Approaches to Simultaneous Manufacturing Kanban Design and Scheduling

In Lee, Ph.D.
Assistant Professor in Information Systems
Department of Information Management and Decision Sciences
College of Business and Technology, Western Illinois University
Macomb, IL 61455
(E-mail) I-Lee@wiu.edu

ABSTRACT

This paper evaluates several artificial intelligence heuristics for the simultaneous Kanban system design and scheduling on flexible manufacturing systems. The objective of the problem is to minimize the total production cost that includes due date penalty, inventory, and machining costs. We show that the simultaneous Kanban design and scheduling decisions are critical in minimizing the total production cost (approximately 40% cost reduction over scheduling without Kanban design decision). To identify the most effective search method for the simultaneous Kanban design and scheduling, we evaluated widely known artificial intelligence heuristics: genetic algorithm, simulated annealing, tabu search, and neighborhood search. Computational results show that the tabu search performs best in terms of solution quality. The tabu search also requires much less computational time than the genetic algorithm and simulated annealing.

1. INTRODUCTION

This paper investigates the use of artificial intelligence heuristics as a means of concurrently determining Kanban design and production schedule of customers' orders. The decision problem is defined as follows. A manufacturing system employs a Kanban-based pull system with a flexible manufacturing system. The flexible manufacturing system consists of a series of work centers. Each order consists of multiple units of finished products. The machines in the system are dedicated to processing at most one unit of each order, and the unit can be processed on at most one machine at any time. The customers' orders must be processed in the same sequence by each of the serial machines, given the processing times of the unit of each order on each machine. Kanban is used to control the work-in process (WIP) inventory. There are a limited number of Kanban containers between work centers. Each Kanban container can contain a certain amount of WIP inventory. Kanban containers move WIP parts between work centers. The objective of the above decision problem is to make Kanban design and scheduling decisions to minimize the total production costs.

Traditionally, process design and scheduling have been considered two separate manufacturing decisions. Decision flows sequentially from an upstream design and engineering function to a downstream manufacturing function. Engineering function determines plant layout and process design based on the product design and products' sales estimates. Subsequently, manufacturing function determines production schedules based on the actual demand or demand forecast of products. Due to the sequential nature of the decision-making, the feedback from the manufacturing to engineering is long and costly. In make-to-order production system, production schedules change dynamically based on the market needs with a fixed manufacturing process. Recently, computer integrated manufacturing has opened an opportunity for a rapid integration of process design and scheduling.

The objectives of our research are three-fold: (1) to design a solution representation for artificial intelligence heuristics that incorporates both Kanban design and scheduling decisions; (2) to perform a sensitivity analysis on the number of Kanban containers, due date penalty cost, and inventory cost; and (3) to compare and improve the performance of artificial intelligence heuristics. The rest of the paper is organized as follows: In section two we discuss the Kanban-based manufacturing facility and decision problems. In section three we compared sequencing with Kanban design and sequencing without Kanban design on some sample problems. In section four we compare four artificial intelligence heuristics and present the improved two-phase tabu search for the Kanban design and sequencing problems.

2. KANBAN DESIGN AND DECISION PROBLEM

The motivation of this study comes from integrating Kanban design and scheduling decisions for customer orders to minimize the total production cost. Kanban design is typically concerned about deciding the number of Kanban containers and the capacity of each Kanban container. Scheduling is concerned about determining production sequence of customers' orders. While these two decisions are typically made independently of each other, they can have a tradeoff effect on the total production cost. For example, the primary objective of Kanban design is to minimize inventory cost and improve product quality. On the other hand, the objective of the sequencing is to minimize the makespan or due date penalty cost. Since these two objectives usually conflict with each other, the decisions should be made simultaneously to minimize the total production cost. In the following, we discuss the problem in the context of a metal part manufacturing system followed by the discussion of the objective function.

The system consist of the sequence of a saw machine, a drill, an inspection machine, a plasma burn, a harden furnace, a temper furnace, a paint booth, and a banding and palletizing machine. A certain number of Kanban containers are located between machines. The system uses these containers between the workstations to regulate inventory and production. When a container reaches its maximum capacity, the upstream workstation stops producing that part type. A simple pull system is used to trigger the upstream production of metal parts. Customer orders trigger production of metal parts at the banding and palletizing machine. As soon as a Kanban container is empty at the banding and palletizing machine, the container moves to a paint booth and joins a queue waiting for part painting. Within this system, machines located along the production line only produce desired amount of work-in-process metal parts when they receive an empty Kanban container. At the top, raw bar stock is fed into at the saw machine from the inventory site. All metal parts require identical process routings but different processing times. The time required to set up a machine for processing a specific metal part usually depends on the kind of metal part processed previously on the machine. In other words, the setup times on the machines are sequence-dependent.

Recently, more and more manufacturing companies are using an electronic Kanban system instead of a paper-based Kanban system. They have deployed advanced manufacturing technologies such as computerized process control, automatic guided vehicles (AGV), and computerized short setups for change of jobs. Large manufacturing companies such as GM and Ford have used Electronic Data Interchange (EDI) technology to achieve an effective Just-In-Time inventory control and supply chain management.

In this paper, the objective function measures the total production cost with three decision variables: the number of Kanban containers between work centers, the capacity of each Kanban container, and the sequencing of customer orders. Each order is an indivisible production element that needs to be delivered to customers on the due date. Each order triggers successive production events from downstream to upstream according to the production process. If a Kanban-triggered production is completed, there is no delay in moving the Kanban container to its downstream work center. A final assembly for a specific order starts after all required parts arrive at the assembly stage. In the scheduling of metal fabrication and assembly tasks, due dates play a significant role in minimizing the overall production costs. Substantial due date penalty cost may occur when products are delivered late, and unnecessary inventory carrying costs can occur when component or assembly tasks finish early (Faaland and Schmitt 1987). It is also important to minimize machining cost in order to reduce the total production cost. The total production cost function assumes an implicit tradeoff since minimizing due date penalty cost may increase inventory carrying costs and machining costs.

3. A PRELIMINARY STUDY OF KANBAN DESIGN AND SCHEDULING

In order to study the impact of the simultaneous Kanban design and sequencing decisions on the production cost, we compared the performance of (1) sequencing with Kanban design and (2) sequencing without Kanban design on sample problems. The objective function determines the production sequence, the number of Kanban containers, and the capacity of each Kanban container to minimize the total cost.

The scheduling task involves determining the production sequence of customers' orders. We assume that there are five work centers and four spaces between two workcenters where Kanban containers are located. The work centers have to be set up when the type of job changes and the time for setting up the work centers depends on the type of job that was processed last. The number of Kanban containers and the capacity of the Kanban containers are also represented in an integer form.

In our preliminary experiments, we assume that a manufacturing system processes 8 to 25 different orders, each order requiring order units of 20 to 60. The maximum number of Kanban containers is set to 20 and the maximum capacity of each Kanban container is set to 20 units. The manufacturing system consists of five serial work centers, each processing a single operation. The sequence-dependent setup times of the order types were generated randomly from the range [25, 125]. The processing times for each unit product within an order were generated randomly from the range of [2, 6]. Due date for each order was randomly generated with a formula of the due date tightness factor* {uniform distribution of [1, 0.5 * (average setup time + total processing time for all orders)]}. Note that a smaller number of due date tightness factor results in shorter due dates for orders.

To understand the effect of simultaneous Kanban and scheduling decisions on the production cost, a tabu search method was used to develop an optimal/near-optimal solution to the problem where sequencing with a Kanban design and sequencing without a Kanban design were considered, respectively. Due date tightness factor was set at 0.5. The experiments replicated 10 problems for each problem size. Sequencing with a Kanban design decision has a significant performance improvement over sequencing without a Kanban design decision (24.24% to 42.90% performance advantage). This result strongly suggests that the scheduling decision without considering a Kanban design may be suboptimal at best under a dynamic market environment.

4. A COMPARISON OF HEURISTICS FOR KANBAB DESIGN AND SCHEDULING

Several well-known artificial intelligence heuristics such as genetic al-

gorithm, simulated annealing, and tabu search have been used to solve complex optimization problems such as sequencing and traveling salesman problems. Since it is known that in solving certain problems, certain heuristics are more suitable than other heuristics, a question arises what kind of heuristics are most suitable for the problem we discussed. We compare four heuristics described in section three: tabu search (TS), simulated annealing (SA), genetic algorithm (GA), and neighborhood search (NS).

Results were evaluated using the consistency of solution quality and computational time. In all comparisons, the pair-wise t-tests were performed at a significance level of 0.05. We evaluated the consistency of the solution quality using an average relative percentage deviation (ARPD) from the best-known solution returned in all the runs.

We examined 24 problem sets of varying sizes. Each problem set had 10 replications. The 24 problem sets were obtained by varying the number of orders (8, 10, 13, 15, 20, and 25) and the number of work centers (3, 4, 5, and 6). The results of 10 runs for each problem set have been averaged.

The solution quality of the tabu search was better (significance level of 0.05), with less computational time, than that of the simulated annealing and genetic algorithm across all problem sizes. As expected, the neighborhood search performed worst, but needed the smallest computational time. When the number of orders was small, the overall solution quality of the genetic algorithm was comparable to that of the simulated annealing but the genetic algorithm took more than two times longer than the simulated annealing. We also observed that the solution quality of the genetic algorithm deteriorated rapidly as the number of orders increased from thirteen to twenty five.

As the number of work centers increased, the overall solution quality deteriorates in all heuristics except for the tabu search. All heuristics needed more computational times. This result may be attributable to the fact that as the number of work centers increases, the problem complexity increases. While the previous heuristics have shown to be effective in escaping local optima, it is well known that when the solution space is extensive, premature convergence may occur. Based on the experimental results, the tabu search was selected to further improve the solution quality and computational time. We name the previous tabu search as one-phase tabu search.

To further improve the solution quality and computational time, we present a two-phase tabu search. To enhance a tabu search capability, a domain-specific knowledge is used to ramp-start the solution search process. The two-phase tabu search incorporates the order-based sequencing. The order-based sequencing for customers' orders focuses on minimizing due date penalty costs. Starting from the order-based sequencing which minimizes the due date penalty, the subsequent search focuses on minimizing the total production cost.

The solution quality of the two-phase tabu search was better (significance level of 0.05), with less computational time, than that of the one-phase tabu search, except for seven problem sets out of twenty four problem sets. On average, the two-phase tabu search was 0.72% better in solution quality with 3.24% less computational time. The difference in the solution quality was especially pronounced at the early stage of the search. The results can be attributable to the synergy between the order-based sequencing and tabu search: the order-based sequencing minimizes the due-date penalty more effectively, and the second-phase tabu search minimizes the total production cost.

REFERENCES

Askin, R. G., M. G. Mitwasi, and J. D. Goldberg, "Determining the Number of Kanbans in Multi-item Just-in-Time Systems," *IIE Transactions*, 25, No. 1, 1993, pp. 89-98.

Bowden, R.O., J.D. Hall, and J.M. Usher, "Integration of Evolutionary Programming and Simulation to Optimize a Pull Production System." *Computers & Industrial Engineering*, 31, no. 1-2, 1996, pp. 217-220.

Cleveland, G. A. and S. F. Smith, "Using Genetic Algorithms to Schedule Flow Shop Releases," In *Proceedings of the Third International Conference on Genetic Algorithms and Their Applications*, Arlington, VA, 1989, pp. 160-169.

Co, H.C., and M. Sharafali, "Overplanning Factor in Toyota's Formula for Computing the Number of Kanban," *IIE Transactions*, 29, No. 5, 1997, pp. 409-415.

Faaland, B. and Schmitt, T., "Scheduling tasks with due dates in a fabrication/assembly process," *Operations Research*, Vol. 35, No. 3, 1987, May-June, pp. 378-388.

Gabbert, P. S., D. E. Brown, C. L. Huntley, B. P. Markowicz, and D. F. Sappington, " A System for Learning Routes and Schedules with Genetic Algorithms," In *Proceedings of the Fourth International Conference on Genetic Algorithms and Their Applications*, San Diego, CA, 1991, pp. 430-436.

Hall, J.D., R.O. Bowden, R.S. Grant Jr., and W.H. Hadley, "An Optimizer for the Kanban Sizing Problem: A Spreadsheet Application for Whirlpool Corporation," *Production & Inventory Management Journal*, 39, No. 1, 1998, pp. 17-23.

Hum, S.-H., and C.-K. Lee, "JIT scheduling Rules: A Simulation Evaluation," *Omega*, 26, No. 3, 1998, pp. 381-395.

Lummus, R.R., "A Simulation Analysis of Sequencing Alternatives for JIT Lines Using Kanbans," *Journal of Operations Management*, 13, No. 3, October, 1995, pp. 183-191.

Malek, M., M. Guruswamy, and M. Pandya, "Serial and Parallel Simulated Annealing and Tabu Search Algorithms for the Traveling Salesman Problem," *Annals of Operations Research*, 21, 1989, pp. 59-84.

Sidney, J. B., "Optimal Single-Machine Scheduling with Earliness and Tardiness Penalties," *Operations Research*, 25, 1977, pp. 62-69.

Yan, H., "The Optimal Number of Kanbans in a Manufacturing System with General Machine Breakdowns and Stochastic Demands," *International Journal of Operations & Production Management*, 15, No. 9, 1995, pp. 89-103.

A Methodology for Developing Complex Information System Based Multiple Intelligent Agents

Yao Li, Feng Xiaosheng, and Zhang Weiming
Department of Management Science and Engineering, School of Humanities and Management
National University of Defense Technology, Changsha, 410073, Hunan, China, PRC
Tel: 860(731)4225384
{Liyao, Xshfeng, Wmzhang}@nudt.edu.cn

ABSTRACT

This article presents a methodology for developing a complex information system by integrating Organization Theory with Multiply Intelligent Agents technology. The main idea of this method: the complex information system is regarded as a multi-agent organization, analyzed the organization characteristic of multi-agent systems according as computing organization theory, and built the organization model, accordingly formed the strict specification. Secondly all types of organizational roles taken on by multiple intelligent agents are fixed on according as techniques in existence and available resources, and the responsibility and granularity are also made sure from this. Then, conceptual models of all kinds of agents are designed by adopting Belief-Desire-Intention (BDI) architecture in according with the organization model, and a clear and operable development pattern (i.e. interaction model and BOS model) is built for realizing the system on computer. Finally, according to the conceptual models, the prototypal complex information system is got quickly by programming on a cooperative working platform (MBOS).

1. INTRODUCTION

Now agent technologies are being applied to the development of large-scale and complex commercial, industrial, military, educational and medical treatment information systems. Such systems are so complex, involving hundreds, perhaps thousands of agents, that we can design and implement them vary hard. Therefore there is a pressing need for Software Engineering techniques to support the analysis, design and implement processes of such complex information systems [1].

Software development methodologies have evolved from the class waterfall model, to a spiral model, to prototyping, to object-oriented and, recently, to scenario-based design [2]. However, all these existing methodologies are not suitable to develop an agent-based complex information system. Some techniques are difficult to adequately capture the autonomous problem-solving behavior, or the smart decision making of an agent, and some techniques fail to describe the richness of interactions between agents and the complexity of organizational structures in an agent-based complex information system, and so on. For these reasons, developing an agent-based complex information system requires a new conceptual framework and a new methodology for the analysis and design.

In this paper, we present a methodology for developing a complex information system by integrating Organization Theory with Multiply Intelligent Agents technology. We divide a development lifecycle of an agent-based complex information system into three phases: 1) Multi-Agent Organizational Design (MAOD) for building system organizational model at the macro level; 2) Agent-oriented Design (AD) for building agent conceptual models based on Belief-Desire-Intention (BDI) architecture[5], interaction model between agents, and BOS model at the micro level; 3) Multi-Agent Systems Realization (MASR) for implementing the multi-agent systems on a cooperative working platform (MBOS)[9]. A development lifecycle is shown in Figure 1.

In the phrase of MAOD, the complex information system is regarded as a multi-agent organization, analyzed the computing organizational characteristic of multi-agent systems according as organization theory, and built the organizational model, accordingly formed the strict specification. Then, all types of organizational roles taken on by multiple intelligent agents are fixed on according as techniques in existence and available resources, and the responsibility and granularity of each agent are also made sure from this.

In the phrase of AD, conceptual models of all types of agents are designed by adopting Belief-Desire-Intention (BDI) architecture in according with the organization model, and a clear and operable development pattern is built for realizing the system on computer.

In the phrase of MASR, the prototypal complex information system is programmed on a cooperative work platform, called MBOS, which includes agents building toolkit specifically tailored to the conceptual models of BDI agents.

The methodology we propose is appropriate for the large-scale and complex information system, especially for hiberarchy, with the following main characteristics:

(1) It is assumed that the goal obtained by a system that maximizes some global quality measure is consistent with the one of the system components.

(2) Agents are coarse-grained computational systems, each making use of significant computational resources.

(3) The overall system contains a comparatively large number of agents, perhaps hundreds of agents, which are distributed over the different geographic locations.

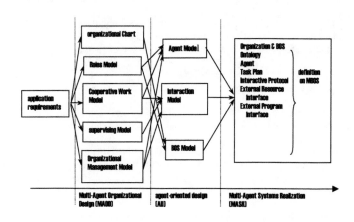

Figure 1. A development lifecycle of an agent-based complex information system.

The remainder of this paper is structured as follows. Multi-Agent Organizational Design is discussed in section 2, Agent-oriented Design in section 3 and Multi-Agent Systems Realization, related work and some conclusions are presented in section 4.

2. BUILDING AN ORGANIZATIONAL MODEL FOR MULTI-AGENT SYSTEMS

Our methodology is intended to allow a developer to analyze systematically requirements by building a multi-agent systems organizational model. The methodology borrows some terminology and notation from Organization Theory [4][5]. It provides an agent-specific set of concepts and models through which the developer view building an agent-based complex system as a process of organizational design. By this methodology, a software developer can understand and model an agent-based complex system precisely step by step.

In the methodology, a set of concepts of a multi-agent organization includes: organization, organizational benefit, organizational structure, organizational process, role, responsibility, authority, cooperation, control, and so on. Modeling a multi-agent organization can divide into modeling organizational structure and modeling organizational process, and the result of modeling includes five items: Organizational Chart, Roles Model, Cooperative Work Model, Supervising Model, and Organizational Management Model.

By this methodology, we will gain an artificial computational organization, which consists of multiply intelligent agents. And the intelligent agent is a computing entity, which is semi-autonomy and constrained by organizational principia [6][7].

2.1 Organizational Model

Organizational Model is composed of five constituents (see figure 1): Organizational Chart, Roles Model, Cooperative Work Model, Supervising Model, and Organizational Management Model.

Organizational Chart is used to render the main roles and the authority relationships in a computing organization. For example, Figure 2 is a part of organizational Chart of Multi-agent Intelligence processing Cooperatively Systems (MICS)[8]. In the vertical, it shows the authority and accountability relations, and in the lateral, it shows the divided work and cooperation relations.

Roles Model specifies each role in an organizational Chart. Here a role is viewed as an abstract description of a computing entity's expected function. We can characterize each role by two types of attribute: responsibility and authority. Template for a role schema is as follows:

Role Name : <define the name of the role>
Role Description : <describe the role shortly>
Responsibility : <define the functionality of the role>
Basic Skill Set : <define all the basic skills which the role must has
            for undertaking its responsibility>
Function Set : <define all the functions which the role must perform by
            its basic skills or cooperating with other agents>
Service Set : <define all the services which the role provides to the
            public>
Safety Condition Set : <list all the limit conditions about the role>
Authority : <define the rights associated with the role>
Resource Permission : <define all the resources about knowledge or
                information that can legitimately be used to
                carry out the role >
Monitor Permission : < define all the underlings and monitor contents >

Cooperative Work Model describes dependencies and relationships among the various roles in a multi-agent organization, which is central to the way in which the system functions. Cooperative Work Model defines the operational flow computationally, specifies all kinds of information needed for performing an operation, e.g. the flow initiator, the flow finish, each step in an operation process, information passing rules between steps, cooperative relations between roles, interactive protocols, etc.

Modeling cooperative work process is based on three kinds of analysis:
(1) Operation activity analysis: analyzing which activities the organization should has in order to achieve its goal. Only through analyzing operation

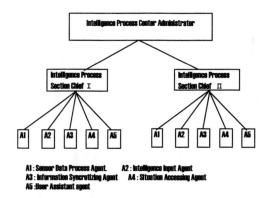

Figure 2. A Part of Organizational Chart

activity strictly, you can make certain which tasks each role must perform, which tasks belongs to the same type, logic relations between the tasks, which task is important or imminent.
(2) Decision-making analysis: analyzing which kind of decision-making in each operation activity, which department or role to make the decision, which way to realize the decision-making, etc.
(3) Relation analysis: analyzing all the relationship about authority, responsibility, communication, and coordination in an operation flow.

Supervising Model builds a control mechanism according as the Cooperative Work Model. In Supervising Model, formal controls are designed to ensure that members of an organization act in ways that lead to the attainment of organizational goals. Control mechanism can be considered as either a part of organization structure or as a process. The basic elements of control mechanism are standard setting, measurement, and action. Control mechanisms consist of these three activities designed to ensure that tasks are carried out and completed in a desired manner. Standards specify desired states for all three steps in the task sequence. Control mechanisms then measure the actual state of operation and output. Through a comparison between standard and actual, the control process is designed to correct work that is not proceeding well by showing where adjustments need to be made.

In theory, we also can view the lifecycle of multi-agent organization as four stages consisting of initial birth, aggregation, regulation, and maturity. In our methodology, we attempt to divide the organizational change into two parts: large and complex change is made by system administrator; small adjust or adapt is made by intelligent agent which plays manager's role. By this ways, the organization is kept to be stability, persistency, and adaptability, from birth to maturity gradually.

Organizational Management Model is used to analyze and design organization process. It models the changes of activities going on within a organizational structure, by analyzing task uncertainty and resource, and constituting relevant organizational management strategies.

Five basic organizational management strategies, we think, are as follows:
(1) Responsibility Assignment strategies: defining all the roles distributing within agents.
(2) Agent Realizing strategies: defining each agent's granularity, skills, resources, relative location, main realizing techniques, etc.
(3) Optimizing Work Process strategies: defining optimal cooperative work strategies according to the changes of goal, task, environment, etc.
(4) Coordination Control strategies: defining some control strategies to improve system coherence and coordination
(5) Reliability strategies: defining some strategies to keep problem-solving reliable and secure.

2.2 The Analysis Process

We have designed a multi-agent organization modeling method [9][7]. A multi-agent organization can be modeled according to following steps.
1.   Define the multi-agent organization goal and identify the goals of all administrative levels in this organization by a goal hierarchy diagram.

First, identify the collective goal, and then decompose it into goals of all administrative levels.

2. Identify all operation activities or tasks to realize goals, and classify them.

Developer should analyze all kinds of operation activities and available resources associated with them carefully. For example, all the tasks that Intelligence Process Section II in Figure 2 should accomplish are 1) Syncretizing multiply information sources; 2) Accessing situation cooperatively; 3) Providing information sharing service.

3. Design problem-solving and managing flow chart.

In our methodology, we have a diagram, called Problem-solving and Managing Flow Chart [9], to describe the problem solving activities recurrently flowing in a relatively stable program.

First, all operation activities are divided into long-term tasks and short-term tasks. For each long-term task, draw the problem-solving flow chart. Then, incorporate the same function in all problem-solving flow chart to form a department's problem-solving flow chart. Finally, for each short-term task, design associated work team, elaborate the full problem-solving flow chart.

Based the full problem-solving flow chart, design the control mechanism for the main task, gain the full elaborate Problem-solving and Managing Flow Chart.

4. Define managing roles and problem-solving roles.

According to the Problem-solving and Managing Flow Chart, study out each role's input object, output object, needed skills, functions, and services, and make out all the limit conditions about the role. At the same time, stipulate authority associated with the role's responsibility.

5. Build cooperative work model and supervising model.

Specify the details of Cooperative Work Model and Supervising Model according as the Problem-solving and Managing Flow Chart and Role model.

6. Set up full organization structure, and form Organizational Chart.

From now on, we have got a full organization structure, and we can draw the Organizational Chart.

7. Make certain agents taking on the roles.

We need to analyze the environment and techniques to realize an agent, and identify each agent taking on the roles. There is not necessarily a one-to-one mapping between roles and agents. If you identify each agent taking on the roles, you also make certain each agent's granularity.

8. Build organizational management model.

By analyzing task uncertainty and resource, and constituting relevant organizational management strategies, e.g. Responsibility Assignment strategies, Agent Realizing strategies, Optimizing Work Process strategies, Coordination Control strategies, Reliability strategies, and etc.

3. DESIGNING MULTI-AGENT SYSTEMS BASED ON BELIEF-DESIRE-INTENTION ARCHITECTURE

The aim of our design process is to transform the abstract organizational model into lower abstract models about what is required of each individual agent in order to take on its roles and how to interact with other agents in an organization. The design process involves three models for each type of agent. The *Agent Model* identifies one type of agent that takes on some roles, and is created from Roles Model, Cooperative Work Model, and Organizational Management Model. The *Interaction Model* specifies the details of interactions between agents, such as interactive protocols, interactive languages, and constrains in an interaction, which is created from Cooperative Work Model, Supervising Model, and Organizational Management Model. The *BOS model* documents a set of BOS (section 3.3), which a multi-agent organization consists of, and each agent must belong to one of a BOS.

3.1 Agent Model

In our methodology, we design and implement the agent with Belief-Desire-Intention structure (BDI), which is called CSA (Constrained-by-organization Semi-autonomic Agent, CSA), where the Semi-autonomic primarily refers to being capable of autonomous and flexible action under abiding by the organizational rules. The architecture of CSA is presented in Figure 3.

Each type of Agent Model is specified by Belief-Base, Goal-Set, and Plan-Library, specific to belief-desire-intention architecture. Belief-Base describes the information about the environment and internal state that an agent taking on some roles may hold. Goal-Set describes the goals that an agent may

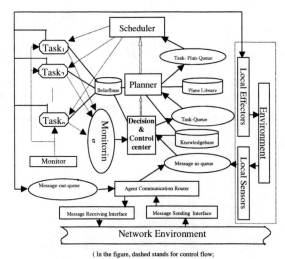

(In the figure, dashed stands for control flow;
real line stands for information flow)
Figure 3. CSA Architecture.

adopt, and the events to which it can respond. Plan-Library describes the plans that an agent may employ to achieve its goals or respond to events it perceives.

Belief-Base consists of abstract entities and concrete entities. Abstract entities are self or acquaintance information, such as, basic skills, functions, services, authorities, acquaintance, and so on. Concrete entities are state information about a particular application domain. Some entities are defined from the Ontology of the application domain. All the entities are from the Roles Model, and these roles are that the agent is taking on. We use a Framework for representing the knowledge about each entity and its properties.

Goal-set is a set of goal and event formula signatures. Each formula in Goal-set is an operation on some elements in Basic skill set, or Function set, or Service Set, but Goal-Set must includes the operation on each element in Function Set. If not, the agent can't take the responsibility of the role. The agent performs a goal by finding the set of plans in plan-Library whose solving-goal matches the goal formula, and executing the plans to determine the success or failure. Apparently, the goals in Goal-set are compatible with the beliefs in belief-Base [14].

Plan-Library is a set of plan. Each element in Goal-Set at least matches the solving-goal of one plan in Goal-Set. That is to say, there are several plans that have the same solving-goal in Plan-Library. Each plan is specified by plan name, solving-goal, precondition, and a state transition diagram. A state transition diagram is interpreted as a recursive finite-state machine. A state transition diagram describes a plan how to achieve its solving goal. A state transition diagram has three types of node: start states, internal states, and end states, and one type of directed edge: behavior rules. Each behavior rule consists of two parts: conditions →action. It means if the agent's belief satisfies the conditions then agent to take that action. All the actions belong to the agent's basic skills in its Belief-Base, or cooperative actions with the other agents, or executing a plan in Plan-Library.

3.2 Interaction Model

Interaction Model specifies interactive relationships between cooperation agents in MAS. In analysis stage, we have described coordination relationships and control relationships between roles by Cooperative Work Model, Supervising Model, and Organizational Management Model. Now we use these analysis results to design interaction details between agents taking on specific roles.

Interaction Model consists of interactive protocols, which is a structured pattern of interaction between agents. Each interactive protocol is defined by a finite automata and stipulations. The finite automata describe the specific executing steps to perform an interaction. The stipulations describe the interactive languages, ontology, and constrains about the interaction.

3.3 BOS Model

A social organization is generally composed of several smaller basic organizations. So, the cooperation exists both among these basic organizations and within each of them. For example, a university consists of many departments, and a department is divided into several teaching and researching sections or administrative sections. If a section is regarded as a basic organization, the organization is then composed of chief of the section, several staff members, and the public facilities.

In our methodology, we present a Basic Organization Structure (BOS) concept [12]. The basic organization cells, called BOS, are used to model the smallest groups of agents in a LAN. By this way, the interrelations among several agents and among groups of agents can be controlled more effectively; thus the system will run effectively and cooperatively as a whole and implement the corresponding global and local goals. BOS is mainly used to support the cooperative problem solving among the coarse-grained, loosely coupled, and groups of semiautonomous agents.

BOS model are simply used to model a multi-agent organization, and it is created from organizational Chart and Roles Model. For example, Figure 2 showing a part of organizational Chart of MICS can be modeled by three BOS as follows:

Intelligence-Process-Center=(Administrator; Section Chief , Section Chief)

Intelligence-Process-Section- = (Section Chief ; Sensor Data Process Agent, Intelligence Input Agent, Information Syncretizing Agent, Situation Accessing Agent, User Assistant agent).

Intelligence-Process-Section- = (Section Chief ; Sensor Data Process Agent, Intelligence Input Agent, Information Syncretizing Agent, Situation Accessing Agent, User Assistant agent).

4. CONCLUSIONS AND FURTHER WORK

Building large and complex information systems needs the support of integrative software developing environment. MBOS (Multiply Basic Organization Structure)[8] is a software platform for creating and deploying organizationally intelligent agents that can cooperate with other agents. MBOS means multiply Basic Organization Structure (BOS), which are the basic organization cells composing of complex organization. MBOS can be used to build the large and complex dynamic control systems as a multi-agent organization by BOS, which is combining fast and nested and consists of multiply agents. MBOS provides with some tools for ontology creation, agent creation, BOS creation, organization creation, Integrating preexisting software, etc., and it can support cooperating effectively between agents and between organizations. MBOS also have coordination control tools and visualization monitor tools, and can support the reengineering of organizational structure and the optimization of operation flow of complex information system. So that it makes a complex information system be developed gradually and incrementally. In our methodology, after the phrase of Agent-oriented Design, we have obtained all agent conceptual models, interaction models between agents, and BOS models at the micro level. So we can implement the multi-agent systems on the MBOS immediately.

Now, more and more research work is about agent-oriented software engineering. Much of them are associated with object-oriented analysis and design [1]. But we think the philosophy of agent-oriented approach clashes with the philosophy of agent-oriented approach, and agent-oriented software developing needs new methods. The methodology we presented is not the same as the Gaia [10] and MaSE [11] also. In the analysis stage of Gaia, the roles in the system are identified from individuals, departments within an organization, or organizations themselves. In the analysis phase of MaSE, the roles are defined

from accomplishing some system level goals. In our methodology, you should design roles by Problem-solving and Managing Flow Chart. Our methodology is more suitable to develop the large and complex information systems with hierarchy organization in a complex and static environment.

The methodology we presented here is summarized from the development of MICS, and is especially for Multiply Intelligent Agent Developing Environment MBOS. So in the future, we should research this methodology thoroughly and practice it more and more.

ACKNOWLEDGMENTS

This research was partly supported by a project from NSFC, which Grant No. is 79800007.

REFERENCES

[1] M. Wooldridge and P. Ciancarini. Agent-Oriented Software Engineering: The State of the Art. In P. Ciancarini and M. Wooldridge, editors, *Agent-Oriented Software Engineering*. Springer-Verlag Lecture Notes in AI Volume 1957, January 2001.

[2] Tung Bui, Jintae Lee. An agent-based framework for building decision support systems. Decision Support Systems, 25(1999): 225-237

[3] Yao Li. MICS Technology Report. School of Humanities and Management, National University of Defense Technology. 2000.10

[4] Robey D. Designing Organizations. Richard D Irwin,INC,1986

[5] Yang Honglan, Zhang Xiaorong. Modern Organization Theory (in Chinese) . Shanghai: Fudan University Press. 1996

[6] Yao Li. Building the Organizational Model of DAI System. In Computer Engineering (in Chinese), 1997, 23(3), 15-19

[7] Yao Li, Zhang Weiming, Chen Wenwei, Wang Hao. Research on the Building Technology of Multi-Agent Systems. In Journal of Computer Research & Development (in Chinese), 1999(July), 36(Suppl): 50-53

[8] Yao Li, Zhang Weiming, et al. Multiply Intelligent Agent Developing Environment MBOS. In Computer World (in Chinese), 2001,7,23(28)

[9] Yao Li, Zhang Weiming. Intelligent and Cooperative Information Technology (in Chinese). Beijing: Publishing House of Electronics Industry, 2002: 168-181

[10] M. Wooldridge, N. R. Jennings, and D. Kinny. The Gaia Methodology for Agent-Oriented Analysis and Design. Journal of Autonomous Agents and Multi-Agent Systems. 2001, 3(1): 45-67

[11] Clint H. Sparkman, Scott A. Deloach and Athie L. Self. Automated Derivation of Complex Agent Architectures from Analysis Specifications. Proceedings of the Second International Workshop On Agent-Oriented Software Engineering (AOSE-2001), Montreal, Canada, May 29th 2001.

[12] Yao L., Zhang W., et al. (2002). Basic Organization Structure Model for Cooperative Information Processing. In: Mehdi Khosrow-Pour. Eds. Issues and Trends of IT management in Contemporary Organizations. Idea Group Publishing. 836-839.

[13] Wooldridge M., Jennings N.R.& Kinny D. (2000). The Gaia Methodology for Agent-oriented Analysis and Design. Journal of Autonomous Agents and Multi-Agent Systems. 3(3), 285-312.

[14] Michael Wooldridge. Intelligence Agent. In Gerhard Weiss, eds. Multiagent System: A Modern Approach to Distributed Artificial Intelligence. the MIT Press,1999,27-78

[15] M. Wooldridge, N. R. Jennings, and D. Kinny. The Gaia Methodology for Agent-Oriented Analysis and Design. In Journal of Autonomous Agents and Multi-Agent Systems. 3(3):285-312. 2000.

Virtual Reality, Telemedicine and Beyond

Franco Orsucci
Institute for Complexity Studies, Rome, Italy
Email: franco.orsucci@ixtu.org
Tel:+39 0642011683 Fax: +39 0642013952

Nicoletta Sala
University of Italian Switzerland, Mendrisio, Switzerland
E-mail: nsala@arch.unisi.ch
Tel: + 41 91 640 48 77 Fax: + 41 91 640 48 48

ABSTRACT

Virtual Reality (VR) is the technology that allows its users to become immersed in a computer generated virtual world. Virtual reality includes the technology for three dimensional (3-D) displays, methods for generating virtual images including 3-D modeling and techniques for orienting the user in the virtual world. Medicine is one of the major application areas for virtual reality, along with games and scientific visualisation. The medical application of VR was stimulated initially by the need of medical staff to visualise complex medical data, particularly during surgery and for surgery planning, and for medical education and training. These applications have naturally extended to include telemedicine and collaboration, involving sharing information across individual medical staff and across geographical locations. Surgery-related applications of VR fall mainly into three classes: open surgery, endoscopy, and radiosurgery. The aim of this paper is to describe some examples in these research fields.

1. INTRODUCTION

Virtual Reality (VR) has different field of applications. For example, in education (Winn, 1993, Youngblut, 1998, Sala, 2002), and in medicine. Medical education was the first area in which VR made a significant contribution. There are probably two main reasons for this. One is that education is less critical, in terms of patient survival, than is actual surgery or surgery planning. These latter two areas of application remain less developed commercially and more experimental in nature. The other reason is the established technology for applying VR to education in other fields, especially aviation. Approaches to learning to navigate within a human body have benefitted from techniques developed to train pilots to fly advanced commercial and military aircraft. There are quite strong similarities between the two application fields since both combine the need for great manual dexterity in a 3D environment with life-critical information access and decision making. Although medical "flight simulators" - based on datasets from actual bodies, both dead and alive - do not yet have the same status as those used in aviation training, it seems likely that such a time is not long off. Increased realism, especially in the simulation of body behaviours, combined with enhanced feedback and the difficulties of training these skills in other ways, seem to make this inevitable.

Another area of medical education to which VR is being applied is that of dealing with catastrophic emergencies threatening or damaging the health of large numbers of people: earthquakes, plane crashes, major fires, and so on. Here, rather general VR techniques are used to simulate a disaster scene. Trainee medical and paramedical staff use such environments to learn how to allocate resources, prioritise cases for treatment, and so on. The disaster scene can be walked through, situations are encountered and decisions made. More recently, the scope of VR applications in medicine has broadened to include physical and psychiatric rehabilitation and, to a lesser extent, diagnosis. VR is proving surprisingly powerful as a therapeutic tool for both mental and physical disabilities. The scope of this survey reflects the range of medical applications to which VR is being applied, and which is briefly outlined above.

Excluded from consideration in this survey are applications in health education for the general public (largely covered by on-line or CD-ROM-based multimedia presentations and not addressed by VR), visualisation of large-scale medical databases (i.e. medical records from large numbers of patients - although VR is being applied in this area), and the application of VR to the architectural design of medical centres. The implementation and integration of new communication technologies within organizations creates complex changes in communicative practices.

Advances in telecommunications and digital technology allow organizations to extend their boundaries beyond physical and geographic barriers. Within healthcare settings, telemedicine applications allow physicians to examine patients at remote locations via various types of telecommunications technologies. These telecommunications connections allow psychiatrists and patients to be present in a new way. This paper explores implications of this presence in the context of a psychiatric exchange. We have organized the paper as follow: section 2 introduces the concept of presence, section 3

focuses upon the Doctor and Patient Dyad, section 4 describe the Virtual Reality and its medical applications, section 5 introduces an examples for better health and therapy: the Angelo Project.

2. THE CONCEPT OF PRESENCE

The concept of presence is defined as: "...the fact or condition of being at the specified or understood place" (Kim & Biocca, 1997). Kim and Biocca (1997) suggest that the experience of presence oscillates around three senses of place: the physical environment, the virtual environment, and the imaginal environment (for example, daydreaming). In a traditional, face-to-face environment, the physical environment is relatively transparent to the interaction. Many information cues present in the physical environment can be incorporated into a communication exchange without the conscious awareness of the individuals involved. For example, a physician may notice that a patient seems to walk into an examining room in a reticent way. These nonverbal cues may aid the physician in formulating a diagnosis. When videoconferencing technology is used to bridge remote locations, a virtual environment is created. Many information cues present in the physical environment are not available in the virtual environment. This virtual environment can create a sense of telepresence. Telepresence describes the subjective sensation of being in a remote or artificial environment, but not the surrounding physical environment (Kim & Biocca, 1997). Lombard and Ditton (1997) suggest that telepresence creates an "illusion of nonmediation" where a person: "...fails to perceive or acknowledge the existence of a medium in his/her communication environment and responds as he/she would if the medium were not there." This illusion of the absence of mediation may suggest to the participants they are receiving all information cues relevant to interaction, when in fact they are not.

3. FOCUS UPON THE DOCTOR AND PATIENT DYAD

Telepsychiatry has been explored for over 40 years through a wide range of technologies. Research has compared the telepsychiatry interview to the traditional face-to-face interview across various diagnoses and conditions. Though technology has evolved dramatically, many conclusions regarding the viability of telepsychiatry over the years have remained very similar.

The first implementation of telepsychiatry was conducted by Wittson in the early 1950s at the Nebraska Psychiatric Institute (NPI), where he investigated the potential of closed-circuit television as a teaching aid (Wheeler, 1994; Wittson & Benschoter, 1972). Ten years later, the first telepsychiatry consultations were performed at NPI. The researchers involved in the trial determined that "...the isolation of the therapist from the patients had almost no effect on group sessions" (Wheeler, 1994, p. 2). Additionally, researchers found patients and relatives were very receptive to this form of communication (Wittson & Benschoter, 1972).

Similar results were found in New Hampshire where researchers explored the use of two-way-video consultations between community family physicians and psychiatrists located at Dartmouth Medical School. Dartmouth researchers argued: "...television has presented almost no difficulties as a medium for psychiatric consultation. It has not proved to be a significant barrier in establishing rapport with the patient or in perceiving emotional nuances" (Solow, Weiss, Bergen, & Sanborn, 1971, p. 1686). Telepsychiatry presented an additional benefit in that local physicians became educated in the treatment of their patients through observations of the interviews with remote psychiatrists. Local physicians reported notable changes in their use and knowledge of psychotropic drugs.

A telepsychiatry program for children that linked a medical school and an inner-city, child-health station received similar support from users, while also providing the additional benefits of improved access and decreased travel time (Straker, Mostyn, & Marshall, 1976). Findings from programs developed in the 1960s and 1970s suggest that both patients and therapists "...do not feel that televised sessions interfere with the quality of therapeutic relationships" (Maxmen, 1978, p. 452).

Another study, conducted in the 1980s, directly examined telepsychiatry, in comparison to traditional, face-to-face interviews and found no significant difference in patient and physician perceptions of the two (Dongier, Tempier, Lalinec-Michaud, & Meunier, 1986). These initial explorations suggest the technology may be adequate for diagnosis of some conditions.

A pilot study of telemedicine used for patients with obsessive-compulsive disorder showed that telemedicine resulted in near-perfect inter-rater agreement on scores on semi-structured rating scales for obsessive-compulsive, depressive, and anxiety disorders (Baer, Jenike, Leahy, O'Laughlen, & Coyle, 1995).

4. VIRTUAL REALITY AND ITS MEDICAL APPLICATIONS

What is Virtual Reality? VR is a set of computer technologies which, when combined, provide an interface to a computer-generated world, and in particular, provide such a convincing interface that the user believes he is actually in a three dimensional computer-generated world. This computer generated world may be a model of a real-world object, such as a house; it might be an abstract world that does not exist in a real sense but is understood by humans, such as a chemical molecule or a representation of a set of data; or it might be in a completely imaginary science fiction world. A key feature is that the user believes that he is actually in this different world. A second key feature of Virtual Reality is that if the human moves his head, arms or legs, the shift of visual cues must be those he would expect in a real world. In other words, besides immersion, there must be navigation and interaction. According to an assessment on current diffusion of VR in the medical sector, gathered by the Gartner Group, forecast of VR future in this area are quite promising. Within the medical application its strategic relevance will increase and gain importance. It is envisaged that by year 2000 despite possible technological barriers, virtual reality techniques will be integrated in endoscopic surgical procedures. VR will affect also the medical educational strategy for students as well as experienced practitioners, who will increasingly be involved in immersive simulated techniques. It is expected that these educational routines can become of routine by year 2005. VR has been until now widely underused, probably because of prohibitive hardware costs, nevertheless this technology is pushing forward new challenges and advances that will materialise by year 2000.

The medical use of VR will take place mainly in four domains:
- teaching: VR will reproduce environments or special conditions that will enable to educate medical personnel.
- simulation: VR will mix video and scanner images to represent and plan surgical intervention, effects of therapy.
- diagnostics: it will be possible to forecast the effects of complex combinations of healing treatments.
- therapy: A valuable exploitation of VR in the medical sector is seen with interest in the therapy of psychiatric/psychological disorders such as acrophobia, claustrophobia, nyctophobia, agoraphobia, eating disorders, etc. Therapeutic techniques will include practices that will allow the patients to reproduce and master problem environments.

5. AN EXAMPLE FOR BETTER HEALTH: THE ANGELO PROJECT

The aim of the Angelo Project is to provide a new approach to what is becoming an important social and business issue, namely quality of work for call centre employees. Market research shows that it costs roughly ten times more to acquire a new customer than to maintain an existing one. Levels of customer satisfaction depend partly on technology but largely on the operator's behaviour. It follows that happy call centre operators are likely to translate into better business performance. Angelo is based on the assumption that operators' quality of work depends on the quality of the working environment.

A high quality working environment will take into account differing individual needs, strategies and preferences thus allowing operators a significant degree of control over key environmental parameters. At the same time, it will provide operators with rapid access to quality information and an ergonomic human-machine interface. Angelo creates such an environment by integrating research results and technologies from a number of different disciplines. In particular the project will use advanced techniques in knowledge engineering and linguistic analysis to analyse customer-operator interactions and provide operators with immediate access to relevant information resources. The project will apply advanced sensor technology for measuring environmental and physiological variables, adaptive computing techniques to model and anticipate operator needs and requests as well as augmented reality tools to enhance the human-machine interface. This way, Angelo will introduce important innovations in workplace design, allowing an unprecedented degree of individual control over the working environment.

The project evaluates industry requirements and functional specifications; develop appropriate measurement system, communication equipment and human interface components; develop information management and network components; integrate, network and put in operation through volunteers taken from a user group. At the same time, disseminate the results in a user-friendly form.

Figure 1 shows the Angelo Project scheme.

6. CONCLUSIONS

In this paper we have introduced some applications of Virtual Reality in different medical fields. There are other medical applications, for example:
- Mental and physical diagnosis and skills rehabilitation
- Complex medical data visualisation for diagnosis and surgery planning, including telemedical (remote diagnostics) applications.
- Integrated simulators for medical training

For mental and physical rehabilitation, the virtual worlds created must be believable and realistic, combining detail and fast response times. For visualising complex anatomical data, for diagnosis and surgery planning, as well as training in such operations, the needs are the same. There should also be a strong focus on user involvement and trials, from the earliest stages of needs analysis and research project planning. No department can succeed alone

Figure 1. Angelo Project scheme.

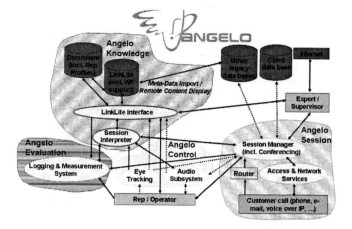

in these areas, which are by their nature multidisciplinary. Perhaps the two main weaknesses of existing applications of VR to Medicine are the relatively poor realism, and weak usability. Both of these issues could be addressed using local skills. The main research issue in Medical VR is to convey sufficiently finely-detailed 3D structures with very fast interactivity. The combination of these two factors, which tend to trade off each other, is the key to using VR in medicine for more than fairly crude simulations of relatively simple and routine activities.

REFERENCES

Winn W., A Conceptual Basis for Educational Applications of Virtual Reality. In University of Washington, Human Interface Technology Laboratory of the Washington Technology Center, Seattle, WA, 1993, Technical Publication R-93-9.

Youngblut C., Educational Uses of Virtual Reality Technology, Institute for Defense Analyses, IDA Document D-2128, (1998, January (Available http://www.hitl.washington.edu/scivw/youngblut-edvr/D2128.pdf)

Sala N., Virtual Reality as an Educational Tool, *Proceedings International Conference on Computers and Advanced Technology Education (CATE)*, Cancun, Messico, 2002 pp. 415 – 420.

Kim, T., & Biocca, F. (1997). Telepresence via television: Two dimensions of telepresence may have different connections to memory and persuasion. *Journal of Computer Mediated Communication*, 3(2)

Lombard, M., & Ditton, T. (1997). At the heart of it all: The concept of presence. *Journal of Computer Mediated Communication*, 3(2)

Wheeler, T. (1994). In the beginning...telemedicine and telepsychiatry. *Telemedicine Today*, 2(2), 2-4.

Wittson, C., & Benschoter, R. (1972). Two-way television: Helping the medical center reach out. *American Journal of Psychiatry*, 129(5), 624-627.

Solow, C., Weiss, R., Bergen, B. & Sanborn, C. (1971). 24-Hour psychiatric consultation via TV. *American Journal of Psychiatry*, 127(12), 1684-1686.

Straker, N., Mostyn, P., & Marshall, C. (1976). The use of two-way TV in bringing mental health services to the inner city. *American Journal of Psychiatry*, 133(10), 1202-1205.

Maxmen, J. (1978). Telecommunications in psychiatry. *American Journal of Psychotherapy*, 32, 450-456.

Dongier, M., Tempier, R., Lalinec-Michaud, M., & Meunier, D. (1986). Telepsychiatry: Psycyhiatric consultation through two-way television. A controlled study. *Canadian Journal of Psychiatry*, 31, 32-34.

Baer, L., Elford, R., & Cukor, P. (1997). Telepsychiatry at forty: What have we learned? *Harvard Review of Psychiatry*, 5(1), 7-17.

Warisse Turner, J. (2001) Telepsychiatry as a Case Study of Presence: Do You Know What You Are Missing?, *JCMC* 6 (4)

Riva G. (Ed.) (1997, 1998) *Virtual Reality in Neuro-Psycho-Physiology*, Ios Press: Amsterdam, Netherlands.

Orsucci, F. (2002) *Changing Mind. Transitions in natural and artificial environments*. World Scientific Pub. Singapore

The Angelo Project is a research funded by the European Union (EU IST 11696).

XML Storage in Relational Databases: An Approach Combining Description Logic and Statistics

Mourad Ouziri, Christine Verdier

Laboratoire d'Ingénierie des Systèmes d'Information (LISI)

7,av Jean Capelle, 69621 Villeurbanne Cedex, France

{mouziri, cverdier}@lisi.insa-lyon.fr

ABSTRACT

We propose in this paper to jointly use the description logic (DL) and probabilistic approaches to store documents in relational databases. The description logic is used to generate a first database schema by reasoning capabilities over the conceptual part of the documents. The resulting schema is normalized. Indeed, we add to the DL knowledge base, which represents the documents, some ontological assertions specified in the DL formalism. Then probabilistic calculus is used to optimise the generated database schema by computing some statistical measurements over the extensional part of the documents.

1. INTRODUCTION

Document is the main information support in most organizations. It is used as data source to store, visualize and exchange data. It represents the most useful information support for the human beings and particularly the end-users. Data in documents are semi-structured. This means that document structure is not given, the data types are not defined and the data structure may be absent, irregular, implicit or partial. These features make the description and the manipulation of data easy. Databases are based on models which store typed and well structured data (see Kappell, 2001) for a comparison of the relational data model and the semi-structured data). Thus, it is difficult to store semi-structured data in a conventional database management system.

In this paper we propose to create a correct database schema for semi-structured data. We use the relational model which is the most efficient and mature system in database technology to store and query large amount of data. A normalized schema is produced from the conceptual level of the document. To obtain this schema, we use two tools: the description logics (Borgida 1995) to compute the database schema and some statistical measurements to optimize this generated schema.

The combination of the description logic reasoning and probability allows us to create a semantically correct database schema.

We consider two main groups of related works: the schema modeling from the XML tree structure and from the DTD (Document Type Definition) structure. The second paragraph presents our theory: the construction of the schema and its optimization. A running example is given at the end of this paper.

2. RELATED WORKS

2.1. Modeling the XML Tree Structure

In this approach, a XML document is considered as an oriented and labeled tree (Buneman, 1997 and Abiteboul, 1997) in which the internal nodes represent the elements of the document, the leaves represent the data or the attributes and the edges formalize the relations of element-sub-element inclusion or element-attribute and are labeled by the name of the sub-element. A tree is represented by several relational schemas. In the MONET data model (Schmidt 2000), for a XML document, the tree represents all the binary relations between all the nodes of the tree and the relations associating the nodes and their values or their attributes. A method of hybrid so-called storage has been developed in the NATIX system (Kanne, 1999). In this approach, a XML document is seen as a tree structure. An object storage model is used for the physical level in which the sizes of the nodes and pages disks are considered to optimize the storage of the document nodes. In (Florescu 1999), the authors presented six schemas to represent the document graph into relational tables: three for the edges and two for the leaves .

This approach is relatively well adapted for the design of wrappers for federating heterogeneous data sources. Moreover, the rebuilding of the original document is highly reliable and is very simple for exchanging the contents of the database. It is done in a reduced time. We think that this model provides a good medium to establish an algebra, especially for the operations on the structure such as the navigation in the documents, the union, the intersection, the subtraction between documents, etc. This model considers a XML document as a tree structure. The syntactic aspects are obviously treated but the semantic ones aren't.

2.2. Modeling the XML DTD

A DTD (Document Type Definition) is a XML structure description format. In some applications, the lack of DTD makes difficult to extract similarities between the structures of different XML documents and to find an optimal common schema. The generation of the database schema from a DTD is a simple and direct process: the content of the DTD represents a set of instructions defining the structure of the documents. The database schema design from a DTD (Schmidt 2000, Shanmugasundaram 1999) can be made differently according to the data model to generate, namely relational model (Bourret 1999, Klettke 1999), object-relational model (Klettke 2000) or pure object model (Christophides 1994).

The DTD modeling approach requires the existence of a DTD and produces a database schema dedicated to store XML documents. It validates the DTD used to generate the database. This database is restricted to a dedicated application and cannot be used with documents containing various structures.

2.3. Description Logic Approach

The description logic (DL) is a reasoning formalism at the conceptual level. It provides users with various inference capabilities that allow them to deduce implicit knowledge. Extending of database systems with logics capabilities has been studied by different authors (Brodie 1989, Hacid 2000, Gõni 1995). In (Calvanese 1999), a XML DTD is represented in the DL formalism as a tree structure using the *f* and *r* fillers to respectively specify the first and the rest of an element. The *TBOX* is generated from the rules definitions by creating the assertions from the DTD elements and rules. The reasoning functionalities (instance validation, DTD inclusion, disjunction, equivalence, etc.) are then performed on the knowledge base. In (Hacid 2000), an algorithm of DL-based knowledge base generation is presented. It is generated from a XML document and a database schema inference. This algorithm creates a concept for each node and its definition assertion is a concatenation of all sub-elements assertions until the leafs. The database schema is generated by calculating the *lcs* (Least Common Subsumer) of *k* objects, where *k* is a threshold.

3. NORMALIZED SCHEMA GENERATION AND OPTIMISATION

The system proposed is at the junction of the DL and the XML tree structure approaches. The DL approach offers a good tool to formalize the knowledge, a well-known structure to extract semantic constraints. So, the system is based on DL and probability to generate a normalized and optimized relational schema to store and to query the XML documents collection. To generate a normalized schema, semantic relations between the documents concepts are necessary since the documents give only information on the structural relations between the concepts (entities). However, normalization is a semantic level task that can't be carried out only starting from the information extracted from the XML documents. Semantics is represented by a domain ontology that is merged as assertions in the DL-based knowledge base (KB) which is created from the XML documents. The semantics is here extracted from the total conceptual diagram implying all the terms of the domain.

The system is working as the following. For each document, the only intentional part of a KB is created. The KB is developed in the DL formalism. The *lcs* (least common subsumer) of each equivalent concept [Cohen, 1992] are computed over the KB. These concepts are deduced from the ontology and DL reasoning. The ontological assertions are taken into account because they are useful to generate a normalized schema. Then, the schema generated is optimized by reducing the number of generated tables. This is done by computing the Bayes probability on the documents instances. The figure 1 presents the general architecture of the system.

3.1. Normalized Schema Generation

To generate the relational schema, the procedure presented in (Hacid 2000) is extended with the addition of the semantic relations between the concepts of the documents. Indeed, the use of information concerning the semantic nature is necessary because documents give only information on the structural relations between the concepts. Semantics is represented by a domain ontology. Thus, the assertions generated from the XML documents representing the intentional definitions of their concepts are merged with those extracted from the ontology representing the semantic relationships between the documents concepts.

The DL-based knowledge base is created following these steps (see [Baader 1991] for the syntax and the semantic of the terminological constructors used):

Step 1: Create a knowledge base from the XML documents collection.

For a document leaf l, we add to the KB the assertion : $l \subseteq$ Type where $Type \in [String, Number, Date]$ is the concept representing the type of the concept l extracted from the ontology.

Starting with the leafs and for a concept node C, we insert to the KB the assertion $C \subseteq \forall C_1 \Pi ... \forall k. C_k$ for each outgoing arc labeled $l,..., k$ of the node C such that $l \subseteq C_1$ and $k \subseteq C_k$ are in the KB (see the paragraph 4).

Step 2: Using the synonym relationships given by a domain ontology, we insert to the KB the assertions $A \equiv C_A$ for each concept A, where C_A is the canonical term of all synonym terms. For example, if *Patient* and *Human* are two terms in the documents concepts and if we suppose that in the domain ontology, the canonical term of all terms designing a person is *Person*, thus, we add to the knowledge base the assertions:

Human $\equiv$ Person   Patient $\equiv$ Person

Step 3: for the *(N, N)* entity relationships, we add to the KB the assertions relating the concepts and specifying the common attributes. For example, *Patient* and *Doctor* are two entities linked by the *(N, N)* association *Exam* which has an attribute *result*. Our reasoning algorithm creates a third relational table which links the two tables corresponding to *Patient* and *Doctor* and contains the common attribute *result*. With this end, we add to the KB this ontological assertion:

Exam $\subseteq \forall$ examined. Patient $\Pi \forall$ examiner. Doctor $\Pi \forall$ result. String Π (=1 examined) Π (=1 examiner) Π (=1 result)

and we modify the descriptions of *Patient* and *Doctor* by respectively adding, the inverse of the roles *examined* and *examiner* (noticed *examined^{-1}* and *examiner^{-1}*) as follows:

Patient $\subseteq ... \Pi \forall$ examined^{-1}. Exam   Doctor $\subseteq ... \Pi \forall$ examiner^{-1}. Exam

Step 4: now, the KB contains all the needed assertions representing the documents concepts and their semantic relationships. So we can compute the first relational schema from the KB. Its optimization will be presented in the next paragraph. The relational schema corresponds to the most specific structure for each equivalent concepts. To get the equivalent concepts, we build a graph $G (V, A)$ where each node (n) represents a concept (C) and for each equivalence $(\equiv)$ relationship between two concepts C_i and C_j, an edge is created from n_i to n_j, corresponding to concepts C_i and C_j respectively. The equivalent concepts are obtained by computing connected sub-graphs of G. For each connected graph, we compute the *lcs* concept of the concepts represented by its nodes. A relational table is created for each *lcs* concept (*Patient* and *Exam*); we call this table *primary table*. Its attributes correspond to *lcs* concept roles (without inverse roles). We create tables also for the roles which do not participate in the *lcs* such as the roles *address* (of *Patient*) and *doctor* (of *Exam*). We call these tables *secondary tables*.

3.2. Schema Optimization

A schema optimization is used to reduce the number of the tables generated at the previous steps. The normalized relational schema is generated from the intentional part of the KB (*TBOX*) and the optimization operation is based on the statistical calculus performed over the extensional part (*ABOX*). This process is based on the data distribution (from the documents collection). The roles of the secondary tables are put back in the primary tables and the secondary tables are deleted from the DB schema. The process is performed as follows. For each role, we compute two statistical values: the conditional probability and repetition frequency of a generated table attribute. A conditional probability is calculated for each attribute of the secondary tables. If this attribute probability tends towards 1 then the attribute is put in the primary table and deleted from the secondary table. The second measure calculated is used in the inverse sense of the first one. If the repetition frequency of an attribute in a primary table is greater than a threshold, then this attribute is deleted from its primary table and we create a secondary table for it. The two tables are linked by a foreign key.

3.2.1. *Conditional Probability*

This measure is computed for each attribute of secondary tables. This measure is aimed to reduce the number of tables that are generated during the attributes transfer between the primary and secondary tables. The primary table attributes can contain some null-value tuples when the attribute is not an attribute of the *lcs*. If the number of null-value of an attribute is not large compared to the size of its primary table then its is transferred from the secondary table to the primary one. Therefore, there will be less joints when evaluating queries. The conditional probability, $P(<child> / <parent>)$, to have an element *child* as sub-element (child element) of another element *parent* (parent element) expresses the percentage of the element *parent* having the element *child* as sub-element, over the documents collection. This probability is computed using the Bayes theorem. Thus,

$$P(<child> / <parent>) = \frac{P(<child>.<parent>)}{P(<parent>)}$$

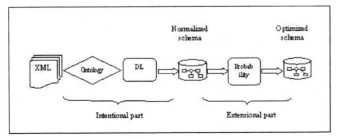

Figure 1. Schema generation process

The element probability is calculated as:

$$P(<element>) = \frac{occurrence\ number\ of\ <element>}{number\ of\ documents}$$

by simplification we write,

$$P(<child>/<parent>) = \frac{occurrence\ number\ of\ <child>\ as\ sub\text{-}element\ of\ <parent>}{appearance\ number\ of\ <parent>\ in\ the\ collection}$$

we formulate it as:

$$P(<child>/<parent>) = \frac{\sum S(<child>, <parent_i>), \forall i \in [1, n]}{n}$$

where n is the occurrence number of the element $<parent>$ over the documents collection, $<parent_i>$ is the ith occurrence of the element and S is a function defined as:

$$S(<child>, <parent_i>) = \begin{cases} 1 & if\ <child>\ appears\ at \\ & least\ once\ in\ <parent_i> \\ 0 & else \end{cases}$$

This probability is a correlation measure of an element $<child>$ with its parent $<parent>$. For example, if $P(<address>/<Patient>)$ is greater than a threshold (near to 1), then the attribute which corresponds to $<address>$ is put back from the secondary table (*Patient1*) to the primary table (*Patient*).

3.2.2. Repetition Frequency

This statistical measurement is used jointly with the conditional probability for the attributes of the primary tables. Some elements can appear more than once in their parent elements. This corresponds to the *(*, N)* cardinality between the elements. To avoid redundancy storage of the relational database tuples, these elements are stored in separated tables from their parents tables. For example, if the element *doctor* of *Exam* appears more than once, this statistical measurement is computed for this element to decide if we create or not a separated table for the attribute *doctor*. The computation of this measurement is performed for a child attribute over all the XML documents collection. For an element $<child>$ associated to an element $<parent>$, the repetition frequency (*FR*) of $<child>$ represents the average of repetition number of the child element in its parent element over all the collection. It is computed as follows:

$$FR(<child>, <parent>) = \frac{\sum Nb(<child>, <parent_i>), \forall i \in [1, n]}{n}$$

where n is the occurrence number of the element $<parent>$ over the documents collection, $<parent_i>$ is the ith element instance and $Nb(<child>,<parent_i>)$ designs the number of elements $<child>$ in the element $<parent>$. If $FR(<child>, <parent>) > threshold$ then we create a separate table to store the attribute corresponding to $<child>$.

The thresholds values depends on the database size and mainly on the attributes access frequency. In the figure 2, we present a complete algorithm for generating a normalized relational schema for XML documents collection.

The thresholds values depends on the database size and mainly on the attributes access frequency. In the figure 2, we present a complete algorithm for generating a normalized relational schema for XML documents collection.

```
Input: Semi-structured graph G = (V, A, r)
Output: Normalized relational schema
KB = GenKB (G);                    // generate the knowledge base of G
Ge = equivalenceGraph(KB);         // construct the concepts equivalence graph
Cs = connected (Ge);               // compute the connected sub-graphs of Ge
for each cs_i ∈ Cs                 // compute the lcs of the equivalent concepts
     lcs = lcs ∪ computelcs(cs_i);
     construct the non lcs concepts : nonlcs
end for
for each concept c_i ∈ lcs    create a table t_ c_i_lcs;
for each concept c_i ∈ nonlcs    create a table t_ c_i_nonlcs;
// Schema optimization
for each t_c_i_nonlcs
     for each attribute a_i of t_ c_i_nonlcs
          p_i = P(a_i / c_i)    // conditional probability
          if (p_i > threshold)
               delete a_i from t_ c_i_nonlcs;
               add a_i to t_ c_i_lcs ;
          end if
     end for
end for
for each t_ c_i_lcs
     for each attribute a_i of t_ c_i_lcs
          f_i = FR(a_i / c_i)    // repetition frequency
          if (f_i >> threshold)
               delete a_i from t_ c_i_lcs;
               add a_i to t_ c_i_nonlcs ;
          end if
     end for
end for
```

Figure 2. A normalized relational schema generation

4. RUNNING EXAMPLE

In this section, we apply the algorithm presented in the previous section to a XML documents collection represented by the two structures of the opposite documents structures.

The knowledge base generated for these XML documents (extended with the ontological assertion *Exam*) is :

```
<Patient n°>              <Patient n°>
   <name> <\>               <name> <\>
   <name> <\>               <Doctor id>
   <address> <\>               <name></>
   <Doctor id>              <speciality></>
      <name></>             <result></>
      <result></>         <\Doctor>
   <\Doctor>             <\Patient>
<\Patient>
```

Patient1⊆ ∀ name.String ∏ ∀ address. String ∏ ∀ doctor. Doctor1 ∏ ∀ examined⁻¹. Exam ∏ (≥ 1 name) ∏ (=1 address) ∏ (≥ 1 doctor)
Patient2 ⊆ ∀ name. String ∏ ∀ doctor. Doctor2 ∏ ∀ examined⁻¹. Exam ∏ (=1 name) ∏ (≥ 1 doctor)
Doctor1 ⊆ ∀ name. String ∏ ∀ result. String ∏ ∀ examiner⁻¹. Exam ∏ (=1 name) ∏ (=1 result)
Doctor2 ⊆ ∀ name. String ∏ ∀ specialty. String ∏ ∀ result. String ∏ ∀ examiner⁻¹. Exam ∏ (=1 name) ∏ (=1 result) ∏ (=1 specialty)
Exam ⊆ ∀ examined. Patient ∏ ∀ examiner. Doctor ∏ ∀ result. String ∏ (=1 examined) ∏ (=1 examiner) ∏ (=1 result)
We compute now the lcs of equivalent concepts (manually created):
Patient = lcs (Patient1, Patient2) ⊆ ∀ name. String ∏ ∀ doctor. Doctor ∏ ∀ examined⁻¹. Exam ∏ (= 1 name) ∏ (≥ 1 doctor)
Doctor = lcs (Doctor1, Doctor2) ⊆ ∀ name. String ∏ ∀ result. String ∏ ∀ examiner⁻¹. Exam ∏ (=1 name) ∏ (=1 result)

The primary tables are Patient (n°, name), Doctor (id, name) and Exam (n°, id, result). The secondary tables are Patient1(n°, address) and Doctor2 (id, speciality). To optimize this schema, we have calculated these probabilities over numerous XML documents:
P(<address>/<Patient>) = 0.98, then we bring back the address attribute to the table Patient and thus we delete the secondary table Patient1 form the schema.
P(<speciality>/<Doctor>) = 0.8, the domain experts says that the attribute specialty is essential, thus, it may be queried frequently. To avoid many joints, we bring back it to its primary table, Doctor.
Fr(<name>/<Patient>) = 1.05, then the name attribute is kept in its primary table. The final schema is given as: *Patient (n°_pat, name, address), Doctor (id_dct, speciality), Exam (n°_pat, id_dct, result).*

5. CONCLUSION

We think that the handling of the information can be made in an effective way only if it is managed in a DBMS which offers a better effectiveness in terms of storage quality, speed and queries processing. For our application domain, this led us to study the storage of the medical files, represented in XML documents, in relational databases. The lack of schema in XML documents led us to study the techniques of automatic relational schemas generation starting from XML documents. We show that only the document couldn't be used to generate a normalized schema. We add a semantic knowledge to the system, represented by a domain ontology. This knowledge enables us to generate a normalized schema in the third normal form. We have used some artificial intelligence techniques namely, description logic, which allows us to use many reasoning services at the conceptual level. A knowledge base in the description logic formalism is created from the XML documents and is merged with the ontological assertions to express all the semantic information about the documents. We use some probability measurements over the documents to reduce the relational tables number. Consequently, we optimize the queries evaluations.

6. BIBLIOGRAPHY

Abiteboul S. Querying semi-structured data. *In Proceedings of ICD*, 1997.

Baader F., Hanschke, P. A Scheme for Integrating Concrete Domains into Concept Languages. *IJCAI 1991: 452-457, 1991*

Borgida A. Description Logics in Data Management. *IEEE Transactions on Knowledge and Data Engineering, 1995.*

Bos B. "The XML Data Model". *http://www.w3.org/XML/Datamodel.html, 1999.*

Bourret R., Bornhövd C., Buchmann A. A Generic Load/Extract Utility for Data Transfer Between XML Documents and Relational Databases. *Technical report DVS99-1 Dept of CS, Darmstadt univ, Germany 1999.*

Brodie M.L. Future intelligent information systems: AI and database technologies working together. *In J. Mylopoulos and M.L. Brodie, editors, Readings in Artificial Intelligence and Databases, p 623-640. Morgan Kaufmann, 1989.*

Buneman P. Semi-structured data. *In Proceedings of the Sixteenth ACM SIGACT-SIGMOD-SIGART Symposium on Principles of Database Systems, 1997.*

Calvanese D., De Giacomo G., Lenzerini M. Representing and reasoning on XML documents: A description logic approach. *Journal of Logic and Computation, 9(3): 295-318, 1999.*

Christophides V., Abiteboul S., Cluet S., Scholl M. From Structured Documents to Novel Query Facilities. *In Proc. Of ACM SIGMOD Conf. On Management of Data, Minnesota, 1994.*

Cohen W., Borgida A., Hirsh H. Computing least common subsumers in description logics. *In Proc of AAAI-1992, p 754-760.*

Florescu D., Kossmann D. A Performance Evaluation of Alternative Mapping Schemes for Storing XML Data in a Relational Database. *Technical Report, INRIA, France, 1999.*

Gõni A., Blanco J.M., Illarramendi A. Connecting knowledge bases with databases: a complete mapping relation. *In Proc. of the 8th ERCIM Workshop. Trondheim, Norway, 1995.*

Hacid M-S, Soualmia F., Toumani F. Schema Extraction for Semistructured Data. *Proc. of the 2000 Int Workshop on DL, Aachen, Germany, p 133-142, 2000.*

Kanne C., Moerkotte G. Efficient Storage of XML Data. *Technical Report, University of Manheim, Germany, 1999.*

Kappell G., Kapsammer E., Retschitzegger W. ML and Relational Database Systems – A Comparison of Concepts. *In Int Conf on Internet Computing (IC'2001) Las Vegas, USA.*

Klettke M., Meyer H. XML and Object-Relational Databases Systems: Enhancing Structural Mappings Based On Statistics. *WebDB (Informal Proceedings) 2000.*

Schmidt A., Kersten M., Windhouxer M., Waas F. Efficient Relational Storage and Retrieval of XML Documents. *In International Workshop on the Web and Databases, Dallas TX, USA, 2000.*

Shanmugasundaram J., Tufte K., He G., Zhang C., DeWitt D., Naughton J. Relational Databases for Querying XML Documents: Limitations and Opportunities. *In Proc of the 25th VLDB 1999 Conference, p. 302-314, Edinburg, Scotland.*

Stakeholder Involvement in Electronic Commerce Projects: Examples from the Public Sector

Anastasia Papazafeiropoulou
Department of Information Systems and Computing,
Brunel University Uxbridge UB8 3PH, United Kingdom
Phone: 0044 1895 203375 Fax: 0044 1895 251686
e-mail: anastasia.papazafeiropoulou@brunel.ac.uk

ABSTRACT

The public sector is becoming gradually an important player in the electronic commerce market, as it engages in the development of applications that offer better services to companies and citizens. At the same time, the uptake of electronic commerce practices by public sector bodies is viewed as very important for the development of global electronic commerce user communities. In this paper we examine four electronic commerce implementation cases in the public sector from a variety of national contexts. Similar to previous information systems research we note that technology alone is not sufficient for the successful implementation of complex electronic commerce applications and illustrate the influence of social interaction among entities effecting the system. We support that the managers of such applications have to consider the widest array of stakeholders in order to control the evolution of the project in the best way. The paper argues that a holistic consideration of these issues that encourages broad stakeholder involvement can support the development of electronic commerce in the public sector.

1. INTRODUCTION

The rapid expansion of network technologies enables easier communication among business partners, companies and citizens making electronic commerce a common practice for day-today transactions. The public sector is also increasingly embracing new information technologies and uses electronic networks in order to offer electronic services to citizens and companies. Such initiatives may give governments the opportunity to streamline the delivery of their services to the public, serving the citizens through diverse channels. The public sector can benefit from the use of the new technologies in terms of improvement of productivity and international competitiveness (Evans, 1998), saving of transaction-costs and improvement in the quality of service offered to the citizens (Ytterstad *et al.*, 1996).

In this paper we examine four cases of electronic commerce applications for the public sector, which have been implemented with mixed results. We observe that the interaction between the stakeholders related to the system have positively or negatively influenced the evolution of the four systems. We use stakeholder analysis to study the role of different stakeholder groups related to the system and investigate the impact of their views and interests on its evolution.

The paper is structured as follows. In the next section we present selected case studies of electronic commerce applications in the public sector. These projects have been developed in various countries and therefore their implementation reflects the interaction of different cultural and technological environments. In section 3 we classify the four cases as successes or failures according to the level of user acceptance. The various stakeholders involved in the four selected case studies are described in section 4, focusing on groups of stakeholders who were not directly involved with the development of the systems but proved to be extremely important for their evolution. The paper concludes with the observation that the managers of electronic commerce applications for the public sector have to consider the widest array of stakeholders in their effort to move towards successful implementations.

2. ELECTRONIC COMMERCE IN THE PUBLIC SECTOR. FOUR CASE STUDIES

In the current section we describe four cases of electronic commerce applications in the public sector; the VAT submission management and reimbursement system in Greece, the NHSnet in United Kingdom, the TradeNet in Singapore and the Minitel system in France. The selection of these cases is based on the observation that they represent examples of different cultural and technological contexts, they are characterized by the participation of a large number of stakeholders, but also they represent a mixture of success and failure. Specifically, the Minitel and TradeNet systems have been reported as successful implementations of interorganisational information systems, while the VAT submission and NHSnet systems have not. The authors were directly involved in research in the two latter cases, where they were in direct contact with key stakeholders, thus gaining an in depth understanding of the different perceptions about the systems as explained further in section 5. The examination of the other two cases (the TradeNet and the Minitel) is based on the literature and official government reports. The following paragraphs provide a brief overview of the four cases that will be used to guide the analysis in this paper.

The VAT Submission Management and Reimbursement System in Greece

The Greek government, following the example of other European countries, has initiated a project to introduce electronic commerce in the public sector in order to provide high quality services to Greek citizens. Part of this initiative is a project for electronic Value Added Tax (VAT) submission, management and reimbursement system. This has been the first engagement of the Greek Ministry of Finance with the electronic commerce technology. The ministry is one of the most technologically advanced in Greece and one of the main 'players' in the design of the national electronic commerce strategy and was therefore keen on acting as an exemplar of new information technology user.

The implementation of the system stared with an agreement among the interested parties to create initially an 'experimental system' with the participation of a small number of pilot users such as the Greek Telecommunication Organization (OTE), the information center of the ministry of finance (KEPYO) and a bank association (DIAS). The Athens University of Economics and Business was responsible for the development of the experimental system, which was delivered to the end users in 1997. As we will explain in the next section the use of the system was problematic; consequently, the Ministry of Finance has decided to extend the experimental system to a pilot one, forming four expert committees: the technical, the incorporation and re-engineering, the awareness and the legacy formulation. The basic task of these committees was the proposal of solutions that will lead to the achievement of the original's project aims. The initial results of this effort were formulated and published in 1998 (Greek Ministry of Finance, 1998). The experimental system is ready and has been tested in a laboratory environment. At the moment the system has been fully implemented. However, its adoption is only partial and limited to non-financial transactions.

The NHSnet in United Kingdom

The NHSnet is the product of the NHS-wide networking project, launched by the Information Management Group of the NHS Executive in 1993 in Britain. Its purpose was the improvement of the communication in the British health sector. The NHS-wide network infrastructure was expected to cover communication for a variety of information flows across different levels. The business areas covered by the network included patient related service delivery, patient related administration, commissioning and contracting, information services, management related flows and supplies of NHS organizations. The development of the network was progressed rapidly and was widely available three years after its launch, in 1996. The fast establishment of the system was due to the NHS Executive's initiative in the development of the network, the establishment of the standards and the effort to include all the interested parties in the implementation of the system.

However, the implementation of the system has been problematic. The network was met with mixed feelings particularly by some of its prospective users. Doctors, in particular, recognized on the one hand the need for the network but, on the other hand, were reluctant to use a system that, in their view, did not cater adequately for the confidentiality of the exchanged personal medical data (Pouloudi, 1997). The NHS Executive decided to make a thorough study of the security issues involved in the implementation of the system and the resulting report (NHS Executive, 1996) has been recognized by the doctors as a first step towards addressing the security problem. The debate about the suitability of the security measures has gone on as more governmental bodies became indirectly involved in the choice of acceptable security policies (see Pouloudi, 1998). As a consequence of this debate and uneasiness of the key stakeholders about its security, the network is still not being used as intended for the facilitation of electronic information exchange between healthcare professionals. The British government has announced a plan for the successful implementention of the NHS net and with the aim to solve the security problems and achieve the full operation of the system until 2005 (NHS Executive, 1998)

The TradeNet in Singapore

The Singapore government developed and implemented TradeNet, its first nation-wide EDI system, in 1989. TradeNet links the private trading community to government agencies to process trade documents for cargo clearance. TradeNet has been characterized as one of the most successful interorganizational systems (Tan, 1998) primarily due to its contribution to 'a larger vision' of building Singapore's information infrastructure: "TradeNet helped Singapore acquire the capacity to build value-added networks, develop a national EDI infrastructure and move a step closer to becoming a fully networked society" (ibid., p. 149). It has been argued that the participation of several key participants in meetings during all the development and implementation stages of the system ensured user satisfaction and participation leading to the successful implementation of the pilot system.

The Minitel system in France

The Minitel system in France started in the 1970s as a way towards the digitalization and modernization of the French society. The system was one of the most successful in comparison with other videotext systems developed in United Kingdom, Germany and USA (Cats-Baril et al., 1994). The success factors were the design of the terminal, the architecture of the network, the billing system and the regulatory environment. Apart from its financial success for the government, the system has shown a positive social impact, becoming an integral part of the French life style. The system started as a technological innovation but its developers realized the necessity of the consideration of the interest of the obvious (e.g. France Telecom, consumers) and nonobvious stakeholders (e.g., newspaper publishers) and their expectations in order to ensure wide acceptance.

3. ASSESSMENT OF THE FOUR CASES

The notion of information systems failure had been extensively investigated (Lucas, 1975, Lyytinen, & Hirschheim, 1987, Cavaye, 1996; Cavaye &

Cragg, 1995). Electronic commerce applications are not immune to failure with reports on many abandoned electronic commerce implementations and dot.com failures (Damsgaard & Lyytinen, 1998, Doukidis & Smithson, 1995, (Kuo, 2001)).

There are multiple approaches to the definition and study of IS failures, that can form the basis for our understanding of interorganisational information systems failure. In this paper we adopt Lyytinen and Hirschheim's (1987) taxonomy of information systems failure phenomena, which distinguishes between four failure notions, namely:

- *Correspondence failure*, the information system doesn't match its goals
- *Process failure*, the information system has not been designed within the budgeted time and cost
- *Interaction failure*, the information system is not used
- *Expectation failure*, the information system does not fulfil its stakeholders' expectations

The last notion of failure has a broad meaning so that the three other failure notions may be interpreted as special instances of expectation failure, reflecting the gap between stakeholders' expectations expressed in some ideal or standard and the actual information systems performance (Lyytinen 1988).

According to this definition of failure we can assess the four cases under investigation as success or failures (see table 1). Specifically, with respect to the electronic VAT submission system, there is not evidence for correspondence failure or process failure. Although the system was ready-to-use at the end of 1997 *none* of the pilot users actually used it, fact that forced the developers to make a 'laboratory' test of the system in order to examine its functionality. The absence of system's users leads to conclusion of interaction failure and subsequently expectation failure.

Similarly, in the case of the NHSnet the development of the network was progressed rapidly and was widely available three years after its launch within the budgeted time and cost. However, although there was no evidence of corespondent or process failure the system wasn't used by one of the major user groups: the doctors. This case is also a typical example of interaction failure and expectation failure.

The other two cases (Minitel, TradeNet) present examples of systems delivered on time within budget while they had wide acceptance form their users.

It is important to note the four systems are in different development stages. The two failures (NHSnet and VAT declaration system) are still in an interim phase while the successful examples (Minitel, TradeNet) have been finalised.

In many cases, failures result from social and political factors, which are often ignored. In the next section we identify the stakeholders related to the four systems in order to get a better understanding of their expectations and reasons for success or failure of the corresponding systems.

4. STAKEHOLDERS IN THE CONTEXT OF THE PUBLIC SECTOR ELECTRONIC COMMERCE PROJECTS

We argue that one of the key elements of interorganisational co-ordination is the interaction between those who directly or indirectly affect or are affected by the interorganisational systems. The variable and often conflicting perspectives of these *stakeholders* are given secondary importance in most approaches. We believe that the identification of an interorganisational system's stakeholders is critical for our understanding of the system, its use and its implications. Indeed, this process is critical for discovering the complexity of the system, especially in terms of the conflicting effects that it may have for resulting in expectation failure.

Table 1: Assessment of the four cases as success or failures

	Corresponde nce failure	Process failure	Interaction failure	Expectation failure	Overall assessment	Project stage
VAT system	no	no	yes	yes	Failure	Interim
NHSnet	yes	yes	yes	yes	Failure	Interim
Minitel	yes	yes	Yes	Yes	Success	Final
TradeNet	yes	yes	yes	yes	Success	Final

Table 2: Stakeholder groups in the four case studies

VAT submission system Greece	Minitel system France	TradeNet Singapore	NHSnet United Kingdom
• The information Center of the Ministry of Finance • Independent tax technicians • Bank association • Athens University of Economics and Business • The Greek Telecommunication Organization	• France Telecom (Intelmatique) • Subscribers-citizens • Users-business • Information providers • Advertising organizations • Regulatory authorities • National policy consultants	• Government agencies • Trade intermediaries • Trade firms • Financial institutions • Port authorities	• Doctors in primary care (GPs) • Hospital doctors • Health authorities (purchasers) • Healthcare organizations (providers) • The department of health and the NHS executive

All cases examined in this paper are characterized by the participation of a large number of stakeholders. In table 2 we present the stakeholders (i.e., those people or groups of people that were directly or indirectly involved or affected in the development, implementation or usage of the system) as they have been identified in the four cases under investigation (Papazafeiropoulou et al., 2002).

The TradeNet is one case where the early involvement of the key stakeholder groups ensured the acceptance and successful adoption of the system. However, it should be noted that this is a perception that is created by our reading of the literature. Whilst it might be an appropriate reflection of the key stakeholders' perceptions of the system, it still reflects the perspective of the researchers reporting on the case. These researchers are also stakeholders, operating in a particular context; their perspectives are shaped by their cultural assumptions and their perception of the context and may thus be biased and limited.

The research in the other cases has shown that less obvious stakeholders may often influence substantially the evolution of the systems. In the information systems research the main groups of stakeholders reported as interested parties are the developers, users and managers of the system (Ruohonen, 1991). In the case of interorganisational information systems (such those investigated in this paper), the number of individuals and groups of stakeholders that can affect or be affected by the project is much broader. Additionally, less obvious, 'external' stakeholders such as the press, the academic community or the non-governmental political parties may play in important role to the successful implementation of a project. The examination of the four case studies has shown that failure to consider such stakeholders may have important implications for the project management.

For example in the VAT submission system case, although the users and developers of the system had been identified and included in the project, other groups of stakeholders have been excluded during the initial phase (Themistocleous, Poulymenakou, Laopidis, 1998). According to the ministry of economics these groups were legacy advisors; professional associations such as chambers of commerce; software and hardware vendors and business consultants who later formed the "expect consultant groups".

In the case of the Minitel system in France, newspaper owners and politicians originally had strong objections against the system. The newspaper owners felt that the new videotext system was a serious threat to their business, while some politicians thought that the system could be abused by the state. Those conflicting views posed difficulties in the implementation of the system and forced the government to seriously consider those two groups of stakeholders.

The experience of the NHSnet is similar. It was only after the British Medical Association was represented by security consultants that the issue of confidentiality became center-stage and the NHS Executive committed to a detailed study of security issues. Interestingly, as security became a primary concern, more stakeholders (e.g., the Data Protection Registrar or security consultants) actively sought their involvement in the NHSnet implementation debate.

The investigation of the above cases leads to the conclusion that a thorough stakeholder analysis of the domain under investigation is very important for the managers of electronic commerce projects for the public sector. This analysis could help to an in-depth understanding of the variety of stakeholders involved and their viewpoints. The case studies presented in this paper demonstrate that unless such analysis is undertaken, stakeholders who may be critical for the acceptance and 'success' of a system become obvious only with hindsight.

5. CONCLUSIONS

Electronic commerce applications are increasingly introduced to the business community but their development had been until now rather spontaneous in nature. The applications for the public sector need special attention due to the impact their implementation may have on society. Using four case studies from different national contexts, the paper considered how the adoption of the system is typically contingent on the involvement of a great range of stakeholders.

Thus, the investigation of the four cases lead to some conclusions that may have important implications for the managers of such systems. The main argument in our analysis is that these managers should have in mind that stakeholders that might initially seen as unimportant can turn out to play a vital role in a successful or a problematic implementation. Thus, the consideration of the widest range of stakeholders is crucial for the effective system management.

Further research in the area would include the examination of other factors, apart from the stakeholders involvement, that influence the evolution of a project, that may be related to more technical aspects. The importance that managers should give to social or technical aspects in different stages during the life span of the project will also be interesting. This analysis could lead to the definition of a multidimensional framework that will guide in a more detailed way both technical system development and social processes of awareness and negotiation regarding electronic commerce in the public sector.

REFERENCES

Axelsson, B., & Easton, G. (Ed.). (1992). *Industrial Networks: A New View of Reality*. London: Routledge.

Cats-Baril, W., Jelassi, T., Teboul, J., (1994) Establishing a National Information Technology Infrastructure: The case of the French videotext system, Minitel, In C. Ciborra and T. Jelassi (Ed.) *Strategic Information systems: A European perspective* (pp. 73-98) John Wiley & Sons

Cavaye, A. (1996). The implementation of Customer Oriented Inter-Organizational Systems: an investigation from the sponsor's perspective. *European Journal of Information Systems*, 5 (2), 103-119.

Cavaye, A. L. M., & Cragg, P. B. (1995). Factors contributing to the success of customer oriented interorganizational systems. *Journal of Strategic Information Systems*, 4 (1), 13-30.

Damsgaard, J., & Lyytinen, K. (1998). Governmental intervention in the Diffusion of EDI: Goals an conflicts. In K.V. Andersen (Ed.) *EDI and Data Networking in the Public Sector* (pp. 13-41). Kluwer Academic Publishers

Doukidis, G., Smithson, S., (1995), Information systems in the national context: The case of Greece (pp. 190-191), Avebury

Evans, D.S. (1998). The cultural challenge of the information superhighway. *European Business Review*. 98(1), 51-55.

Greek Ministry of Finance (1998), Technical expert group. Final Technical Report, Greek Ministry of Finance.

Håkansson, H. (Ed.). (1985). Industrial Technological Development: A Network Approach. London: Croom Helm

Kalakota R. & Whinston A. (1996). *Frontiers of Electronic Commerce*, Addison-Wesley Inc.

Kling, R. (1978). Value-conflicts and social choice in Electronic Funds transfer developments. *Communications of the ACM* 21 (8), 642-657.

Kuo, J. D. (2001). *Dot.bomb, Inside an Internet Goliath - from Lunatic Optimism to Panic and Crash*, Little, Brown, London.

Lucas, H. C. (1975). *Why Information Systems Fail*. Columbia University Press, New York

Lyytinen K., (1988). Stakeholders, Information System failures and Soft Systems Methodology: An assessment. *Journal of Applied Systems Analysis*, 15, 61-81

Lyytinen, K., & Hirschheim, R. (1987). Information Systems failures – a Survey and classification of the Empirical Literature. In *Oxford Surveys in Information Technology* (pp. 257-309). Oxford: Oxford University Press

NHS Executive (1996). The use of encryption and related services with the NHSnet: A report for the NHS Executive by Zergo Limited, Information Management Group.

NHS Executive. (1998). INFORMATION FOR HEALTH: an Information Strategy for the modern NHS 1998-2005. A national strategy for local implementation. NHS Executive.

Papazafeiropoulou, A., Pouloudi, A. & Poulymenakou, A. (2002). Electronic Commerce Competitiveness in the Public Sector: The Importance of Stakeholder Involvement. *International Journal of Services Technology Management* 3, 82-95.

Pouloudi, A. (1997). Conflicting concerns over the Privacy of Electronic Medical Records in the NHSnet. *Business Ethics: A European Review*, 6 (2), 94-101.

Pouloudi. A., (1998). Stakeholder Analysis in Health Interorganizational Systems: The case of NHSnet. In K.V. Andersen (Ed.) *EDI and Data Networking in the Public Sector* (pp. 83-107). Kluwer Academic Publishers.

Pouloudi, A., & Whitley, E. A. (1997). Stakeholder identification in interorganizational systems: gaining insights for drug use management systems. *European Journal of Information Systems*, 6 (1), 1-14.

Poulymenakou A., Holmes A., (1996). A contingency framework for the investigation of information systems failure. *European Journal of Information Systems*, 5, 34-46.

Ruohonen, M. (1991). Stakeholders of strategic information systems planning: theoretical concepts and empirical examples. *Journal of Strategic Information Systems*, 1 (1), 15-28

Tan, M., (1998) Government and private sector perspective of EDI: The case of TradeNet. In K.V. Andersen (Ed.) *EDI and Data Networking in the Public Sector* (pp. 131-153) Kluwer Academic Publishers.

TEDIS. (1991), *Survey report of EDI in the EC & EFTA member states: 1990*. Brussels: The European Communities, The Commission of the European Communities

Themistocleous M., Poulymenakou. A., Laopodis V. Electronic Commerce in the public sector: Towards a framework for consideration. In G.Doukidis, H. Gricar, J.Novak (Ed.), 11th International Bled Electronic Commerce Conference Volume 1 (Research)

Ytterstad, P., Akselsen, S., Svendsen G., & Watson, R.T. (1996) Teledemocracy: Using Information Technology to Enhance Political Work. *MISQ Discovery* (http://www.misq.org/discovery/ articles96/article1/ index.html) *(See also Ytterstad, P., & Watson, R.T. (1996) *MIS Quarterly* 20(3), 347).

Analysis of Current Data Mining Standards

Janusz Swierzowicz
Rzeszów University of Technology
2 W.Pola, 35-959 Rzeszow, Poland
tel:+4817-8651424, fax: +4817-856-2519
jswierz@prz.rzeszow.pl

ABSTRACT

This paper examines the objective assumptions for Data Mining Process standardization, which simplifies integration of Information Systems with Data Mining models. In doing so it provides an overview of the more important characteristics of Cross Industry Standard Process Model for Data Mining (CRISP-DM), Application Programming Interface OLE DB for Data Mining (API OLE DB DM), and Predictive Model Markup Language (PMML).

INTRODUCTION

Information Technology development has strong effects on data resources. In this fast rising volumes of data environment, human abilities in memory capacities and low data complexity or dimensionality analysis cause data overload problem. It is impossible to solve this issue in a human manner – it takes strong effort to use intelligent and automatic software tools for turning rough data into valuable information [2-7,9-10]. One of the central activities associated with understanding, navigating and exploring the world of digital data is Data Mining. It is an intelligent and automatic process of identifying and discovering useful structures in data such as patterns, models and relations. We can consider Data Mining as a part of the overall Knowledge Discovery in Data process, which is defined as "the nontrivial process of identifying valid, novel, potentially useful, and ultimately understandable patterns in data" [4], it should support us as we struggle to solve data overload and complexity issues.

Data mining applications have to process data of diverse nature, drawn from different storage architectures, then use multiple data-specific exploration algorithms, and present results in a variety of forms. Data mining processes and models are used as a part of commercial Information Systems including those in enterprise resource planing, customer relationship management and in processing engineering and scientific data as well. With the fastest acceleration of online data resources in the Internet, the World Wide Web is a natural domain for using data mining techniques to automatically discover and extract actionable information from Web documents and services, especially in e-business. We have named those techniques as Web Mining. We also consider text mining as a data-mining task that helps us summarize, cluster, classify and find similar text documents.

Technological standards play an important role in Information Technology development [7]. Now, many organizations are developing technological standards for various aspects of data mining. Several standardization efforts [6] are undertaken on models, attributes, application programming interfaces, processing of remote and distributed data as depicted in Figure 1.

This issue is discussed in following chapters
Cross Industry Standard Process Model for Data Mining – CRISP DM

CRISP DM was developed in the year 2000 by a consortium of data mining vendors and advanced users (e.g. SPSS, NCR Daimler-Benz, Mercedes-Benz and OHRA) [3]. The CRISP-DM applies across different industry sectors (e.g. automotive, aerospace, insurance) was designed to make data mining projects easily adopted as a key part of business processes. The main assumption in this model preparation was its neutrality with respect to industry, method, tool and application. It consists of task described at four levels of abstraction: *phases, generic tasks, specialized tasks and process instances.*

Figure 1. Data mining standards in various aspects

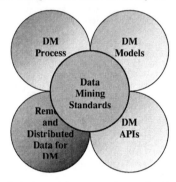

At the top level, the data mining process is organized into the following phases:
- *Business understanding* that focuses on understanding the project objectives and requirements from business perspective,
- *Data understanding* that includes initial data collection, identification of data quality problems and detection interesting data subset to form hypotheses for hidden valuable information,
- *Data preparation* that covers construction of the data set for modeling tools. This phase focuses on tables, records and attributes selection as well as transformation and cleaning of data.
- *Modeling* that focuses on selection of various modeling techniques and on tuning for values of optimal parameters,
- *Evaluation* of the model quality with respect to achieving the business objectives,
- *Deployment* that involves applying models within decision making process in organization. It takes simple forms as reports generation as well as repeatable mining process.

The second level is the level of *generic tasks*. It was introduced to cover whole data mining process, all possible data mining applications and new modeling techniques e.g. [1].

The third level is the *specialized tasks*. It describes how the general task differed in various situations.

The last but not least is the *process instance* level. It is a record of the actions, decision and results of an actual data mining engagement.

CRISP-DM distinguishes between following dimensions of data mining context:
- The *application domain* (e.g. banking, education, customer relationship management [2, 6, 13, 14]) is the area in which project take place,
- The *data mining problem type* (e.g. data description and summarization, segmentation, concept descriptions, classification, prediction, dependency analysis, etc.) describes the specific classes of objectives that the mining process deals with,
- The *technical aspect* (e.g. missing values) describes technical challenges that usually occur during data mining,
- The *tool and technique* that specifies which DM tools and/or techniques (e.g. Clementine, Poly Analyst, Weka [14]) are applied during the DM project.

APPLICATION PROGRAMMING INTERFACE OLE DB FOR DATA MINING

The API OLE DB DM is an example of a new protocol that simplifies communication and provides better integration of data mining tools with data based management applications. A virtual object that is similar to a table (the Data Mining Model DMM) can be created with CREATE statement, browsed with SELECT, populated with INSERT INTO, refined or used to derive prediction. A fundamental operation is the training of DMM, follow by use of the model to derive prediction [11,12]. The operation is executed in the following steps:

- Create an OLEDB data source and obtain an OLE DB session object
- CREATE MINING MODEL ...
- INSERT INTO   //training data into the model
- SELECT ...
        FROM .....
        PREDICTION JOIN

PREDICTIVE MODEL MARKUP LANGUAGE (PMML)

Predictive Model Markup Language (PMML), managed by the Data Mining Group [6,15] is the most widely deployed data mining standard. It is based on an XML mark up language to describe statistical and data mining models. It describes the inputs to data mining models, the transformations used prior to prepare data for data mining, and the parameters that define the models themselves. It is used for a wide variety of applications, including applications in e-business, direct marketing, finance, manufacturing, and defense in products released by such vendors as Angoss, IBM, Magnify, Microsoft, MINEIT, NCDM, NCR, Oracle, Salford Systems, SPSS, SAS and Xchange. The current standard - PMML 2.0 - supports several predictive model types: Tree Model, Neural Network, Clustering Model, Regression Model, General Regression Model, Naïve Bayes Models, Association Rules Model, and Sequence Model. These categories cover the most popular data mining methods that are likely to find in contemporary data mining tools.

CONCLUSION

User participation in the standardization process is becoming more important. This issue should be also considered in the process of selection of data mining methods and tools.

REFERENCES

1.   Abbass H.A., Sarker R.A., Newton C.S.: Data Mining. A Heuristic Approach, Idea Group Publishing, Hershey, London, 2002,

2.   Berry M., Linoff G.: Data Mining Techniques, John Wiley & Sons, Inc, New York, 1997

3.   Chapman P., Clinton J., Kerber R., Khabaza T., Reinartz T., Shaerer C., Wirth R. : CRISP-DM 1.0. Step -by - step data mining guide, CRISP-DM Consortium, 2000

4.   Fayyad, U., M., Piatetsky-Shapiro, G., Smyth, P., and Uthurusamy R.: From data mining to knowledge discovery: An overview. Fayyad, U., M. et al. (ed): Advances in Knowledge Discovery and Data Mining, AAAI Press/The MIT Press, Menlo Park, CA, pp.1-34, 1996

5.   Fayyad, U.: The Digital Physics of Data Mining, Communication of the ACM, March, 2001/Vol.44, No.3 pp.62-65

6.   Grossman R.,L., Hornick M.F., Meyer G.: Data Mining Standards Initiatives, Communication of the ACM, August, 2002/Vol.45, No.8 pp.59-61

7.   Jacobs K.: Global Aspect of Information Technology Standards and Standardization, Information Management, Vol. 15. No.1/2, 2002, pp.8-35

8.   Landauer T. K.; "How much do people remember? Some estimates of the quantity of learned information in long-term memory," Cognitive Science, 10 (4) pp. 477-493 (Oct-Dec 1986).

9.   Leavitt N: Data Mining for the Corporate Masses?, Computer, May, 2002/Vol.35, No.5 pp. 22-24

10.   Liautaud B.: e-Business Intelligence: Turning Information into Knowledge into Profit, McGraw-Hill, New York, 2001

11.   OLE DB for Data Mining Specification, Version 1.0, Microsoft Corporation, July 2000

12.   Seidman C. : Data Mining with Microsoft® SQL Server 2000 Technical Reference, Microsoft Press, 2000

13.   Swierzowicz J.: A Management Information System for Classification of Scientific Achievements, Evolution and Challenges in System Development, Zupancic et al (ed), Kluwer Academic/Plenum Publishers, New York, pp.735-740, 1999.

14.   Swierzowicz J.: Decision Support System for Data and Web Mining Tools Selection, Issues and Trends of Information Technology Management in Contemporary Organizations, Khosrow-Pour M. (ed), Idea Group Publishing, Hershey, London, 2002, pp.1118-1120

15.   www.dmg/org

The Modeling of the History of Information

Andrew S. Targowski
Department of Computer Information Systems, Western Michigan University
Kalamazoo, MI 49008
(269) 387-5406   fax (269) 387-5710
targowski@wmich.edu

ABSTRACT

In this paper, we will analyze the architectural relationships between intellect, politics, and labor in an historical context to understand the relationships, rules, and eventually laws that govern social development. Through such a structural understanding of the past, it may be possible to better predict the future. A by-product of this analysis should be understanding the historical background for the emerging new sciences of information management and communication in business.

INTRODUCTION

The aim of analyzing the role of information throughout history is to define the convergence between the cumulative evolution and revolution of labor, intellect (knowledge), and politics.

The architectural approach to history is a new layer over the quantitative history based on statistical data. In architectural history, we seek a "big picture" of "ages" and "revolutions" to develop some criteria-oriented views of the world and its future predictability.

PERIODIZATION OF MODERN TIMES

In this paper, we address the task of establishing some information-oriented relationships between the Intellectual Revolution, the Political Revolution, and the Labor Revolution of modern time, depicted in Figure 1.

This modern period of history begins with the Renaissance for a rebirth of learning following the darkness of the medieval period. The modern times started in 1453 when Constantinople fell to the Ottoman Turks. Many scholars who fled from the Byzantine Empire were fleeing westward for safety - (some are still fleeing). Their learning spread rapidly with the development of printing. This boosted the questioning of established ideas regarding religion, art, and science.

The challenge of fresh ideas also gave impetus to explorers, who began to open up new lands and trade routes, and to the religious leaders who set in motion the Reformation.

The Age of Reason and The Era of Modernity. The first heroes of the *Age of Reason* were the printer-publishers who fed the inky stream where knowledge flowed from mind to mind, from generation to generation. The sciences advanced in logical progression through modern history: mathematics and physics in the seventeenth century, chemistry in the eighteenth century, biology in the nineteenth century, and psychology in the twentieth century.

The Age of Discoveries. Since 1500 A.D., the map of the civilized world has been transformed beyond all recognition. Prior to this time, it was composed of a belt of civilizations girdling the Old World from the Japanese Isles on the northeast to the British Isles on the northwest. The main line of communication was provided by the chain of steppes and deserts that cut across the belt of civilizations from the Sahara to Mongolia.

The Age of Technology and The Modern Era. In the 19th century, technology advanced not empirically, but through the application of science in business. The Industrial Revolution mechanized manufacturing and created factories that utilized water and steam power. Railroads eliminated wilderness and electricity lit homes and minds. The first computer *calculating engine*," was developed by Charles Babbage in 1822 and improved in 1832,

although it was premature and only useful in simplistic calculations. The telegraph was designed and facilitated long distance communication. Communication through publications was also a tool for the dissemination of knowledge.

The Modern Era of the 19th century glorified rationality. Western communities became modern just as soon as they had succeeded in producing a bourgeoisie that was both numerous and competent enough to become the predominant element in society (Toynbee 1954). In this era, an industrial urban working class arose. A split between rich and poor began to play a significant role in the development of social dynamics. Later on, this split in the *Information Age* would include the information-rich and the information-poor.

The Eras of Modernization and Post-Modernism
The Scientific Revolution

In the 20th century, atomic physics, modern medicine with secrets of heredity, transportation technology, military technology, microelectronics (transistors, integrated circuits), computers, telecommunications, information systems, high technology (smart devices and processes), marked the present level of science.

The Control Revolution began in the United States in the late 19th century, the basic communication technologies are still in use a century later: photography and telegraphy (1830s), rotary power printing (1840s), the typewriter (1860s), transatlantic cable (1866), telephone (1876), motion pictures (1894), wireless telegraphy (1895), radio (1906), and television (1926). This control technology emerged as a means of controlling the influence of the Industrial Revolution, which was experiencing capacity shortage and delays in production and transportation. The following developments in electronics, computers, information systems, and communications are part of the control revolution.

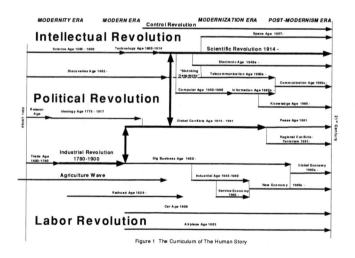

Figure 1 The Curriculum of The Human Story

The Modernization Era occurred when businesses and institutions invested in capital equipment to effectively compete in productivity, innovations, profitability, and market share. This trend gave the birth to Big Business, Service Economy and Global Economy.

Further analysis of civilization and culture will be limited to information technology.

The Age of Electronics and Microelectronics. Two major developments occurred independently during the late 1940s which triggered an enormous impetus to the modernization of civilization. One was the development of the programmable electronic computer (ENIAC 1946). The second was the invention of the transistor (1947). Subsequent improvements in solid physics led to the present-day silicon chip with its large-scale integrated circuits.

The Computer Age. In the year 2002, we celebrated 1000 years of using ZERO in Europe (transferred by Pope Sylvester II from the Arabic University in Spain). Thus, throughout the last millennium, man has long been developing computing technology. However, only in the last 50 years has the computer become available for practical applications. In the 1950s, computers automated scientific calculations. In the 1960s, computers were used in simple commercial and governmental applications (data processing). In the 1970s, computers were applied to large-scale systems of businesses (airline reservation systems), administration, and defense. In the 1980s, the quiet revolution of microcomputers led to the installation of 80 million units and 50 million terminals. Almost every professional or hobbyist became preoccupied with learning "IBM DOS" or a way to print a "file." The jargon of computer hardware and software entered the language of the average citizen. Today, we could not operate without computers.

The Information Age. In the 1980s and 1990s, information technology created an appetite for user-friendly computers and a need for customized relevant information and information services. At the corporate level, MIS is expanding into the Executive Information System (EIS) and other systems such as CIM (Computer Integrated Manufacturing), electronic mail, electronic publishing, and so forth. These systems increase the quality of targeted information and competition in time through inter-business horizontal telecommunication. In the home, entertainment is brought in through more TV channels, satellite receivers, and cable. Teleshopping, telebanking, and telecommuting have increasingly become more practical and effective. The list of information systems and services is almost endless. The Information Age has transformed and developed the industrial economy into an informed economy. This is evident because employment in the information sector now exceeds employment in traditional sectors.

The Knowledge Age. In the classic economy, the sources of wealth include land, labor, and capital. For 200 years, manufacturing facilities have brought prosperity to firms and their shareholders. Now, another engine of wealth is at work. It is science, technology, creativity, innovation, skills, and information, and it can be summarized in one word: knowledge. Knowledge creates awareness based on scientific facts, rules, laws, coherent inferences, and well-defined methods. Knowledge provides a point of reference, a standard for our way of analyzing data, information, and concepts.

There is a great lagoon of knowledge within our globe that can be commercialized. The following data illustrates this premise: there are growing numbers of research centers (about 2000 world class), 3.5 million scientists and engineers worldwide, universities (about 1000 world class), university teachers (about four million worldwide) (Kurian 1984), and 1000 multinational corporations, including about 50 stateless consortia.

The Telecommunications Age. Telecommunications is a rapidly growing and changing field. The most significant milestone in advanced telecommunications was the launch of Telstar in 1962. The launch was preceded by the invention of the telegraph by Samuel F. B. Morse in 1837, the telephone by Alexander Graham Bell in 1876, and later radio and television. Telstar began as a very small and simple communications satellite in a low Earth orbit, designed to relay television signals between the United States and Europe. The global satellite system INTELSTAL (Early Bird) was put into operation in 1965 with a maximum capacity of 240 two-way telephone circuits. Today's system capacity is 200 times larger with cost reductions of 90 percent. Over 100 nations take advantage of TELSTAL services. Other types of telecommunications systems are developing in areas such as mobile satellite communications (business and personal), global information systems, teleconferencing, business TV broadcasting, distance learning, home health care services, and

the Global Positioning System (GPS). The geostationary orbit now houses more than 200 communications satellites, with the potential of telecommunications just being identified.

The Interactive Age. Multimedia machines, which combine video, images, sound, and data, are expected to create a new generation of electronics, combining the functions of personal computers, televisions, video cassette recorders, and game machines. Computer and consumer electronics companies have long hailed "multimedia" as an all-purpose product for work, play, and education.

The Communications Age. The value of communication for humankind has moved from the psychological cognition (Sigmund Freud, 19th century) to a sociological process of conflict resolution. The Knowledge Age and human understanding are rooted in the act of communication or, more precisely, in communicated data, information, concepts, knowledge, wisdom, and volition. When communicated choices define social action, successful business organization and lives result.

Communism was defeated in 1989-91 not by military force, but by life, the human spirit, conscience, and the resistance of man to manipulation. It was defeated by revolt against censorship and by better global communication. A generation ago, social theorist Marshall McLuhan (1968) proclaimed the advent of a "global village," a sort of borderless world in which communication media would transcend the boundaries of nations. "Time" has ceased, "space" has vanished.

The Communication Age is also driven by technology, which foresees the death of distance. The "death of distance," according to Cairncross (1997) will be the single most important economic force shaping all of society over the next half century.

TOWARDS THE ELECTRONIC GLOBAL VILLAGE

Figure 2 illustrates the birth architecture of the Electronic Global Village and the future utopia. The result of EGV, EGC, and telecities can be the Healthy World Human Family Utopia. This utopia can be perceived as a technique to manage the growing, educated, and aware population of conflict-less nations. Paradigms of revolutions and ages are provided in Table 1. The ultimate target of the Control Revolution is the development of the Electronic Global Village.

The consequence of EGV is the emergence of the Electronic Global Citizen (EGC), who can take advantage of the Global Information Infrastructure (GII). These citizens, who live in a telecity where local municipal area networks telecommunicate through a teleport will be able to use information services and participate in the Interactive Age.

As Fukuyama (1992) brilliantly argues, the economic logic of modern science together with the "struggle for recognition" leads to the eventual collapse of tyrannies, witnessed in both the West and the East.

THE PARADIGMS OF REVOLUTIONS AND AGES

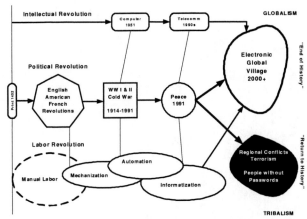

Figure 2 The Birth of the Electronic Global Village and the Future Utopia

Table 1 The Paradigms of the Revolutions and Ages

Revolution/Age	Paradigm	Shift From	Shift To
Reason Age 1452-1775	Rationality	Superstition	Objectivity
Science Age 1500-1800	Method	Belief	Theory
Technology Age 1800-1914	Model	Idea	Solution
Scientific Revolution 1914--	Truth	Views	Laws
Electronic Age 1940s--	Control	Mechanization	Automation
Computer Age 1950-1980	Processing	Facts	Data
Information Age 1980s--	Pro-acting	Measurement	Concept
Knowledge Age 1980s--	Awareness	Intuition	Rules
Telecommunications Age 1980s--	Reach-Out	Local	Global
Communications Age 1990s	Opportunities	Isolation	Connection
Interactive Age 1990s--	Involvement	Top-Down	Feed-Back
New Economy 1990s--	Maximizing opportunities	Capital	Networked knowledge
Global Economy Age 1990s--	Marketplace	Many	One
Electronic Global Village 2000--	Movement	Things	Thinking

REFERENCES

Beninger, James, R. (1986). *The Control Revolution.* Cambridge, MA.: Harvard University Press.

Cairncross, Frances. (1997). *The Death of Distance.* Cambridge, MA.: Harvard Business School Press.

Clarke, Arthur C. (1945). "Extra-Terrestrial Relays: Can Rocket Stations Give Worldwide Radio Coverage?" *Wireless World.* pp. 305-308.

Fukuyama, F. (1992). *The End of History and the Last Man.* New York: The Free Press.

Kuhn, Thomas. (1970). *The Structure of Scientific Revolution.* Chicago: The University of Chicago Press.

Kurian, T. (1984). *The New Book of World Rankings.* New York: Facts On File Publications.

McLuhan, Marshall. (1962). *The Gutenberg Galaxy.* Toronto, Ont.: University of Toronto Press.

Targowski, Andrew (1990). "Strategy and Architecture of the Electronic Global Village." *The Information Society,* vol. 7, pp. 187-202.

Toynbee, Arnold. (1954). *A Study of History,* vol. 8. London: Oxford University Press.

Information Infrastructure in Developing Countries: Bridging the Urban - Rural Divide

Venkatesh X. Subramanian
American Express Financial Advisors
2639 AXP Financial Center
Minneapolis, MN 55474
Phone: 612-678-5511, Fax: 612-671-7863
Venkatesh.x.subramanian@aexp.com

Subhash Wadhwa
Department of Mechanical Engineering
Indian Institute of Technology– New Delhi
New Delhi - 110019, India
Phone: 91-11-6591057
swadhwa@mech.iitd.ernet.in

William A. Estrem, Ph.D. and Monideepa Tarafdar, Ph.D
College of Business, Graduate Programs in Software, University of Saint Thomas
1000 LaSalle Street, Mail TMH343 Minneapolis, MN 55403-2005, 2115 Summit Avenue, Mail OSS 30 St. Paul, MN 55105
Phone: (651) 962-4415, Phone: 651-962-5433
Fax: (651) 962-4210, Fax: 651-962-5543
waestrem@stthomas.edu, mtarafdar@stthomas.edu

ABSTRACT

Developing countries need to stimulate economic and social development in their rural areas to minimize the gap some call the "Digital Divide." However, they are often unable to deliver basic telecommunications infrastructure services to remote communities due to the high costs and other barriers. In this paper, we examine approaches that could be used to deploy simple and practical information infrastructure leveraging technologies such as portable computers, wireless telecommunications, and alternative energy sources like solar power as a means of delivering basic Internet access to remote areas at comparatively low cost. We examine some of the key challenges likely to be encountered in implementing such an initiative and possible solutions to meet those challenges.

1. INTRODUCTION

Developing countries have long faced profound and systemic problems caused by inadequate information and telecommunications infrastructures that have constrained their ability to deliver services that would promote equitable social and economic growth to the residents of their rural areas. These infrastructure gaps, often referred to as the "Digital Divide", have emerged over the years in developing countries between urban and rural areas, exacerbating problems caused by the migration of rural populations to urban areas in search of better education, health care and economic opportunities.

In this paper we identify and examine key infrastructure barriers to rural social and economic progress in developing countries and describe how current technologies can be deployed to provide a simple, practical and affordable solution to overcome these barriers.

We consider the following questions:
- What are the challenges that governments of developing countries are likely to encounter as they implement large-scale deployment of information and communication infrastructure services to their rural populations?
- How can current technologies be deployed to help developing countries overcome their infrastructure barriers and thus deliver basic information and communication infrastructure and services to their rural populations?
- What currently available technology solutions could be employed to address and overcome these challenges in a practical and affordable manner?
- What technical and social challenges will be associated with the implementation of the proposed solution?

How can converging technologies could be deployed to help developing countries overcome their infrastructure barriers and thus deliver basic their information and communication infrastructure and basic services to their rural populations? What challenges are governments likely to face as they seek to engage in large scale deployment of converging technologies, and what solutions might be available to overcome the same?

The rest of the paper consists of a survey of academic and practitioner literature. Based on the literature, some conclusions and suggestions have been put forward, regarding the possibility of use of converging technologies in developing countries. Finally, the technical and social challenges associated with such efforts have also been highlighted.

We examine technology applications in India and other countries in Asia, Latin America and Africa in order to gain a better understanding of how converging technologies can be used to overcome infrastructure barriers and the challenges of implementing these technologies.

2. LITERATURE REVIEW

To better understand these questions, we examined academic and practitioner literature related to the applications of information technology applications in India and other developing countries in Asia, Latin America, and Africa to gain a better understanding of how these technologies can be used to overcome existing infrastructure barriers. We also studied some of the challenges related to the implementation these technologies.

Various studies have addressed the need for addressing the information and infrastructural needs of developing countries. Fakeeh (2001) observes that even though in developed countries there are significant trends that are bringing together computing and communications technologies, the economic and social benefits of information technology for developing countries have been lacking [1]. Fleming (2001) suggests that factors such as low literacy and technical skills, and inadequate transportation infrastructure are partly the cause of this inequity [2]. However, there is general agreement (Fleming 2001, Cavanaugh 1998, Hudson 1995), that information and telecommunications infrastructure is one of the most crucial links in the development process [3], [4]. In this context, the large-scale deployment of information technologies in developing countries could provide significant benefits by promoting economic opportunities and enabling the delivery of basic services in the areas of health, education, and commercial services into remote and rural areas.

According to Rischard (1996), these technologies have also been used to provide distance learning, surveillance and control of epidemics and contagious diseases, and the dissemination of information on best healthcare practices to doctors, nurses, health agents, and community leaders (5).

One of the key challenges and opportunities faced in progressive developing countries such as India is the re-engineering of the several existing government processes towards effectively supporting the rural sector. There are multiple agencies involved with multiple decision-makers and often conflicting priorities and objectives. Simply providing greater information availability through information technology may not be enough. Architectures for supporting the re-engineering of group decision processes should be explored.

We conduced a study of the academic and practitioner literature in this area and examined such technology applications in India and other countries in Asia, Latin America and Africa in order to gain a better understanding of how converging technologies can be used to overcome infrastructure barriers. We also studied some of the challenges of implementing these technologies.

2.1. Trends

Communication and information technology have always been important enablers for creating prosperity for countries. The degree of a country's prosperity can also be related to its willingness and capability to adopt new technologies.

India's 1991 economic liberalization radically transformed the urban landscape in terms of productivity, efficiency. It promoted the development of a communication and educational infrastructure that was radically different from the past. However, India's rural areas lag far behind, and still lack many of the most fundamental infrastructure services. With 70% of the countries population residing in these rural areas and an equal percentage of its gross domestic product being derived from those areas, it is critical that India include the rural areas in its efforts to create a more prosperous future.

To a large degree, most developing countries face similar disparities in growth and demographics of their rural and urban areas. Rural to urban migration in developing countries has forced governments to focus their scarce resources on developing the infrastructure within cities. Hence, it is common within developing nations to find highly developed and well-connected urban centers existing in the midst of rural communities that possess little or no information infrastructure. Consequently, the urban areas have become over-crowded and rural areas have been decimated as their most productive citizens migrate to the urban areas. This phenomenon has caused a host of social and economic problems besides imposing many indirect costs in terms of grinding poverty, lost productivity, and squandered opportunities. This "Digital Divide" also offers a stark contrast in developing countries between urban and rural centers in terms of education, healthcare, sanitation, communications power, and transportation services. Developing robust and sustainable rural networks in each of these areas is crucial for the success of any long-term development plans.

Radio and television have played increasingly important roles throughout the twentieth century. These broadcast technologies have been used by both governments and Non Government Organizations (NGO) to bring about much needed development in rural parts of the world by using them to disseminate agriculture and health-related information.

The greatest stimulant to India's economy during the 1960's was the Green Revolution that transformed rural activity and productivity. Renowned agricultural scientist, Dr. M S Swaminathan, and his colleagues had achieved a breakthrough in creating a hybrid variety of rice and wheat that produced much higher yields. To generate awareness and acceptance among the agricultural community, the institute he headed setup 2,000 model farms in and around New Delhi that promoted the use of hybrid grains. Radio offered all that an under-developed country required to implement this farming technology. It could cover a large area at a very low cost, maintaining the infrastructure was relatively inexpensive, it could integrate well with the governments communication and information structure, and the unit cost per radio was inexpensive when converted to a cost per person.

Likewise, NGO's have employed radio as a tool to deliver much needed information to rural parts of the world. "Developing Countries Farm Radio Network", an NGO based in Canada has, since 1979, used the radio to achieve their goal "to promote practices, in food production and processing, in health, in small-scale rural enterprises and in natural resource management, that lead to sustainable rural livelihoods in developing countries." Their approach has

been to "link almost 500 rural radio stations so that they can share expertise and experience. Working together, they can greatly enhance their capacity to provide relevant development programming for millions of people who depend on agriculture for their livelihood."

The advent of television further strengthened this fabric of communication. However, broadcast television is still a one-way medium and while it provides a powerful visual medium, the benefits of interactivity are not possible.

Limitations on access and the ability of people to interact with credible sources of information resulted in new inefficiencies. If the flow of information to a remote area can be controlled or restricted, that control can be used to artificially manipulate local economic conditions. In one case, for example, a local trader provided villagers with price quotes for their produce that were roughly half the actual prevailing market prices. In another case, farmers needing to acquire legal records in order to arrange bank loans, needed to pay bribes and kickbacks to local officials (9) Over the years, such examples of corruption and inefficiency have become institutionalized in developing countries and has severely inhibited rural development efforts.

2.2. Wireless Internet as the Next Medium

Freling (2001) describes the Internet, as the next medium in communications and its potential benefits for rural communities, "Using a combination of solar energy and wireless communications technology, rural and remote parts of the world have the opportunity to leapfrog sustainably into the 21st century. Once compelled to migrate to over-crowded towns and cities in search of economic opportunity, rural villagers may now choose to stay close to home ... where they are more closely connected to each other and to nature." (10)

Some of the limitations to development of such large scale and hybrid sequences are imposed by:
    lack of faster and reliable communication
    need for real time information
    lack of proper educational facilities and educational related information
    lack of information on employment and entrepreneurial opportunities
    lack of proper health related information

These are obstacles that can be overcome by the introduction of the Internet to rural areas. Internet expands the scope of the existing communication systems as a more effective means of development as shown in Figure 1.

It is evident that the large-scale deployment of Internet access into rural areas of developing countries such as India could provide significant socio-economic benefits. By providing more equitable access to increasingly important infrastructure services such as the Internet, governments can allow a higher proportion of their populations to remain residents of rural areas while still enabling them to participate in the benefits that are now only available by emigration to urban centers.

Infrastructure: Implementing this initiative will require, every village to be provided with a computer, phone line/wireless connection, a location to house the two in proper conditions, person to operate and train the villagers, so they become self sufficient over time, and a connection to the Internet. Though

Figure 1 : Expanding Applications of Internet

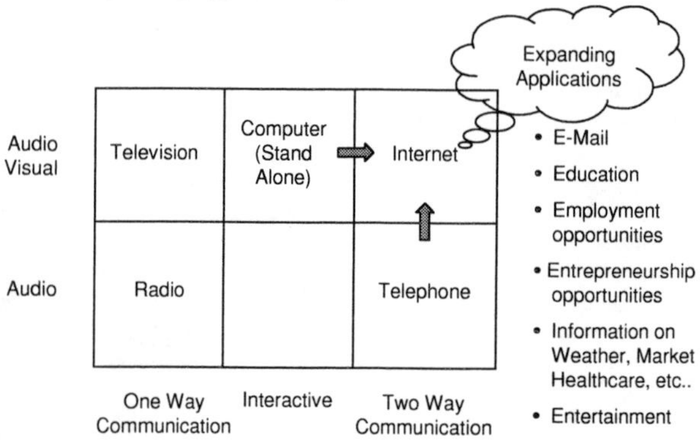

this might sound ambitious, the costs when considered are in fact quite realistic if done in a phased manner. A rough arithmetic as follows puts the total cost of implementation at around $ 1.2 Billion in India's case without the telecom infrastructure costs.

On a 3 year implementation plan this translates to roughly $ 400 million per year but the challenge however is going to be in estimating the ongoing costs of communication and in establishing the costs of getting Internet access to these areas.

Not withstanding the financial implications, central to the eventual consideration and implementation of such a proposal rests is on the ability to deliver at least three supportive resources, viz. telecommunications, power, and a skilled workforce to implement the initiative.

2.3. Telecommunications Infrastructure

An key factor for future economic development is the establishment of a sustainable and scalable telecommunication infrastructure. Frank Tipton state in the ASEAN Economic Bulletin that "in the developed world, on average, there are nearly 50 phone lines per 100 people whereas in low income countries, there are only 1.4 phone lines per 100 people" (11). India, which has over 600,000 villages, still has 225,000 villages to be covered by some form of communication . As of 1998, China had covered less than 300,000 villages of the 740,000 villages that span its vast region with a telecommunication link. The same pattern is repeated in other developing countries, hampering growth prospects of these economies. Compounding these coverage issues are complex technology-related challenges that governments often face. Rapid changes in technology has made it difficult for governments and companies to deploy systems without fear of building in obsolescence. The telecommunications industry is strewn with technologies that once looked promising only to be discarded within a relatively short period of time. This poses immense risks on governments as they consider adopting new technologies.

India has, over the past 50 years, been able to install only 26.8 million lines. In the next 3 years the country's Telecommunications Department plans to invest $10 billion to lay an additional 13 million phone wires (13). Comforting as it may seem to grow coverage by 50%, it still falls far short of real demand. Furthermore, inadequate infrastructure in most developing countries exacts a high cost for maintaining these antiquated "landlines", quite disproportionate to the services they offer. This requires governments to heavily subsidize these facilities, given their inability to extract sufficient revenues from the population being served.

Rural areas present other issues as well. Villages are usually isolated clusters and are located in remote and sometimes inaccessible areas due to terrain effects. Mountains and jungles create significant barriers to deploying landlines to reach these remote areas. This demands highly innovative solutions in not just establishing the communication system, but in also integrating them with existing systems and ensuring compatibility with broad-based infrastructure upgrades that will occur in the future.

The economic challenges of reaching rural communities can thus be summarized into the following core issues:
- Low telephone demand
- Low utilization
- Dispersed subscribers
- Difficult terrain
- Isolation from the national network
- Lower levels of potential short-term revenues (14)

The biggest need in any rural infrastructure project is the staying power of the project through a length of time needed to achieve economies of scale. Given the sparse and dispersed population in these areas, there is a need for several forces to interplay. To be profitable, low installation and operating costs coupled are critical. Initial subscribers, typically people in business or government who have a real need for telecommunication services, will look for other ways to serve their needs, if the service is too expensive or of poor quality (14). On the other hand, if an adequate service is provided at a high cost, the necessary revenues are difficult to generate, and due to a consequent lack of demand, services cannot be provided in a profitable manner. Therefore, either initial installation costs and subsequent maintenance cost for any communication system has to be low enough so that it can be sustained within a low population base, or funding should be sufficient to cover a period of time that is required to achieve profitability through economies of scale.

2.4. Closing the Gap: Wireless Solutions

Considering the economic constraints imposed by remote, low density communities and the socioeconomic benefits that could be realized, a practical, low cost solution should be considered as a starting point. A wireless infrastructure may be the only viable solution that can deliver the required coverage in a cost-effective manner.

The installation costs of a basic wireless infrastructure for delivering basic telecommunications services are becoming increasingly affordable. Operation and maintenance costs of wireless infrastructure can also be significantly lower than conventional landlines because the physical assets are concentrated within manageable areas, unlike land lines, where a fault in the line can occur anywhere along their paths.

The benefits of wireless solutions are evident in their ability to deliver coverage at comparably lower costs compared to running landlines to individual subscribers. Moreover, given that wireless allows the user to be mobile, it offers an ideal solution for the poor regions of the world. Here, villages could share their resources and bring accessibility to a wider area unlike permanently installed landlines. For example, mobile phones are being promoted in rural Bangladesh with Grameen Telecom, offering cellular phones to Bangladeshi village women as part of its micro credit program, which makes small loans to entrepreneurs. The women sell minutes to locals who speak to their relatives in other villages or towns, and the women get much-needed financial independence (13).

Current mobile telecommunications systems such as the GSM are gradually incorporating data communications technologies such as General Packet Radio Service (GPRS) or Cellular Data Packet Data (CDPD). If these services are available, voice and data telecommunications can easily be provided to the rural communities. Handset manufacturers such as Nokia and Ericsson are introducing handheld mobile devices which can make use of solar power and remain in operation for several hours.

2.5 Alternative Energy Sources

Providing a reliable source of energy is a crucial requirement for the deployment of any telecommunications infrastructure. Sixty percent of rural India is not connected to the central power grid; a situation not uncommon in most developing countries (15). Today, the power requirements for provisioning basic wireless Internet services in a rural community can be achieved by using a variety of alternative energy sources such as solar energy, wind power, hydroelectric, biomass conversion, and a variety of other techniques.

Solar photovoltaic systems provide the simplest and most direct technique for creating the electrical power needed to meet the relatively low energy requirements of a personal computer and a wireless access device.

Companies such as Solardyne Corporation offer low-cost, portable solar photovoltaic systems capable of powering a computer for the same length of time. These systems are easy to transport and install. They are stand-alone devices that require little or no maintenance and have proven their ability to enable untethered computing capabilities. Because of their relatively low cost, ability to operate independently, and rugged design, these systems are ideal for applications that require a computer to be operated in a remote location.

They can also be linked to a solar powered wireless device that in turn gets connected to the Internet and delivers instant two way communication capability. Testimony to such a design lies in Provenir, a remote village in the Amazon forest with a population of 600. Today, due to a joint initiative of Solarquest, the US Department of Energy and American Electric Power, this village is connected to the Internet. There is a "The 2,500-watt solar power system and 16 storage batteries that provides electricity for lighting for adult and children's classes, three computers, a satellite receiver/sender for broadband Internet access, a refrigerator/freezer for medicine and vaccines and AEP's Datapult energy monitor which will show how the solar panels are performing and the electricity is being used on AEP's web site". (17)

2.6. Skilled Resources

Low cost labor continues to be the resource in greatest abundance in most developing countries and it is readily available to assist in the deployment and maintenance of the proposed communication solution. While each economic landscape will require a creative approach in terms of how it taps into its labor pool, labor availability offers countries an opportunity to use the deployment initiative as an economic stimulus.

An example of how a creative solution can be found is available by studying the labor pool in India. To channel the deployment initiative the government could use its force of 300,000 to facilitate the setting up of Internet and e-mail facilities at village communication centers. This would bring some of the benefits of information technology to the rural areas. This could be a feasible solution specially because as courier services and e-mail have mushroomed, especially in urban areas, the quantity of mail passing through post offices has been almost halved (16).

2.7. The Role of the Government

The role of the government cannot be minimized in supporting and laying down the foundations for such an endeavor. This role can extend from laying out the broad national framework for rural access of the Internet, to identifying areas of services of the government that can be brought directly to the villagers. It is government that will need to support the initial investment required to assure implementation of such an initiative.

Needless to say, the role of the government cannot be minimized in laying down the foundations for such an endeavor. This role can extend from laying out the broad national framework for rural access of the Internet, to identifying areas of services of the government that can be brought directly to the villagers. Bypassing intermediaries in the system, the issue of graft and corruption to provide basic services can be overcome. Middlemen, who use their availability of commodity prices, or lack thereof at the farmers end, will be forced to provide fair prices to avoid being relegated to the margins of the market.

3. EXAMPLES

The following examples provide illustrations of some of the initiatives that are currently underway in India and other developing countries, for using converging technologies to set up the information and communication infrastructure, confirming that some of the opportunities and challenges are currently being reflected in the corridors of these countries. We're presently going through a period of experimentation and it might be safe to assume that like most experiments, we might stumble upon success and not realize it till later when the luxuries of today have become necessities of tomorrow.

Freling (2001) reports that with the introduction of wireless telephony, many rural villages are further empowered economically. Up-to-date knowledge of farming techniques and market prices helps farmers to obtain higher value for their produce. By taking digital photographs of locally made arts and crafts, and uploading these images onto a website, village artisans can make their goods directly available to a worldwide audience. Cultural products such as music are especially well-suited to village-based ecommerce since they can be transmitted electronically without having to deal with the cost, logistics, and delay of physical transportation. Solar-powered connectivity provides a conduit through which information as well as trade and commerce may flow to and from rural parts of the world previously isolated and cut off (10).

Another example of the power of the Internet can be seen in Warana, where the cooperative movement and information technology has come together. The project involves a cluster of 70 villages in Warana in the western Indian state of Maharashtra. There are 25 cooperatives with a total turnover of Rs. 600 Crores (US$ 127 Million). The main hub of the Rs. 2.5 Crore (US$ 500,000) project set up by the National Informatics Center and the Maharashtra government is at the Warana Engineering College and the second hub is at the sugar cooperatives administrative building. Both have VSAT's. Information kiosks have been set up at six or seven business centers in the villages. Here and elsewhere, farmers check rates at different Mandis (markets) and choose the days when they can get a better price. They have learned to access veterinarian advice on e-mail. With computerization of land records, farmers have been set free from the clutches of the local village landlord (17).

In a joint initiative between Solarquest, American Electric Power, and the U.S. Department of Energy, a remote village known as Provinir was connected to the Internet. Provinir, located in the Amazon forest has a population of 600 people. The system used a 2,500-watt solar photovoltaic power system to provide the electricity needed to power lighting for two classrooms, three computers, a satellite receiver/sender, and a refrigerator/freezer used for medicine and vaccines (18).

These examples demonstrate the feasibility of employing these systems in India and other developing countries. Such technologies can be used very

Table 1 : Estimated installation costs per site

Basic Personal Computer with peripherals	$ 600.00
Solar Photovoltaic Power system	$ 600.00 (19)
Mobile phone or wireless transceiver	$ 100.00
Furnishing and accessories	$ 200.00
Transportation, installation, and training	$ 500.00
Cost per site	$2,000.00

fruitfully, for progress and development in the information infrastructure for many of the rural lands in developing countries.

4.0 A PROPOSED SOLUTION

We propose a basic solution for reaching remote rural villages using a personal computer, wireless telecommunications services, powered by an alternative energy source. The initial configuration would require each site to be provided with at least one computer, a wireless connection to an Internet service provider, and a solar photovoltaic energy system. The wireless connection could be provided using mobile data communications such as GPRS or CDPD, or using a Wireless Local Loop connection to a regional central office. The village would need to provide a proper location to house the system. It is essential that resources be provided to operate and administer the system and to educate and train the local residents so that they become self-sufficient over time.

While the typical costs per site are modest, the aggregate costs are significant. The estimated fixed costs of implementing wireless Internet capabilities in remote villages are shown in Table 1. This figure does not include the associated telecommunications infrastructure costs that may be incurred by the Internet Service Provider.

In a country like India with an estimated 600,000 potential sites in remote villages, the initial investment could cost nearly US$1.2 Billion. In addition to these fixed costs, there would be additional variable costs of providing Internet access and maintaining the system over its useful life. To ensure that the investment is well utilized, it is essential to ensure that adequate effort is devoted to educating the residents on proper maintenance, administration, and utilization of the system.

5. CONCLUSIONS

As suggested by Rischard (1996), "New low-cost and converging technologies offer developing countries unprecedented opportunities for rapid development…. Yet these technologies also raise the threshold of competitiveness" (5). The digital divide between developed countries and developing countries is a serious one and is constantly increasing. This requires developing countries to receive a significant lift in their pace of development which cannot be achieved without developing their rural landscape.

This significant lift can be provided only by using appropriate converging technologies which have at their heart the Internet as the delivery vehicle of health, education and socio-economic services to rural areas.

The concepts and examples discussed in this paper, point to certain ways in which these technologies can be used in a generic manner. It would be worthwhile to conduct case studies in specific countries in order to explore solutions appropriate and specific to the social and cultural framework of individual countries and societies.

We recommend that further research be conducted with a specific developing country as a case study, in order to understand the true cost of such a large-scale deployment of converging technologies and challenges that might exist not uncovered in this paper.

REFERENCES

1)   Fakeeh, K. A., "Recent Developments in Information technology and its Impact on Global Economy", Issues and Trends of IT Management in Contemporary organizations, Proceedings of the IRMA International Conference, 2001, pp. 212-215.

2)   Fleming, S. T., "Information Needs for a developing Country", Issues and Trends of IT Management in Contemporary organizations, Proceedings of the IRMA International Conference, 2001, pp. 223-225.

3)   Cavanaugh, K., "Bandwidth's New Bargainers", Technology Review, November-December 1998, pp. 62-65.

Fleming, S. T., "Information Needs for a developing Country", Issues and Trends.

4)   Hudson, H., "World Bank Report on Economic and Social Benefits of Rural Telecommunications."

5)   Rischard, Jean-Francois, "Connecting Developing Countries to the Information Technology Revolution", SAIS Review 16.1 (1996) 93-107, Copyright © 1996 The Johns Hopkins University Press.

6)   Wadhwa, S., Bhattacharya, S., "Re-engineering the Group Decision Process", Vision, MDI, Journal, December 2000.

7)   Ganguly, Meenakshi, "Dr. Swaminathan – A Profile", TIME Magazine, TIME 100: August 23-30, 1999 VOL. 154 NO. 7/8

8)   Developing Countries Farm Radio Network, "Local Radio for Sustainable Rural Livelihood, Programs Goals and Objectives", http://www.farmradio.org/english/program.html#goals

9)   "Village Voices"; The Times of India dated 01/31/2000

10)   Freling, Robert .A, "Solar Vision", , International Journal of Humanities and Peace, Annual 2001 v17 il p67(2)

11)   Tipton . F, "Bridging the digital divide in Southeast Asia", ASEAN Economic Bulletin, April 2002 v19 il p83(17)

12)   "USO Funds for rural telephony" ; Business Line Internet Edition dt. 11/08/2000. Copyright The Hindu Business Line & Trebica Internet Initiatives Inc.

13)   Kriplani, Manjeet, "Taking the isolation out of poverty India, Bangladesh and Sri Lanka go cellular" , Business Week dt. 05/03/1999

14)   "Rural Telephony Market Analysis", White Paper by STMI.com http://www.stmi.com/whitepaper.html

15)   Mehta, V. S., "Solar Energy: Imperative for Rural India", The Economic Times, 7) India, March 25, 2000.

16)   "Please Mr. Postman"; The Times of India dt. 12/07/20003

17)   "India at grassrootlevel.com" ; The Economic Times dt. 04/09/2000

18)   "Solar Powered Internet Connection for Remote Bolivian Village"; © 1997-2001Xantrex Technology, Inc.@ www.traceoffgrid.com/readingrooms/stories/6.html

19)   Morgan Babetter, "Solar Power to Light SW Bell Pay Phones" St. Louis Post-Dispatch dt. 12/15/92

BIBLIOGRAPHY

Cavanaugh, K., "Bandwidth's New Bargainers", Technology Review, November-December 1998, pp. 62-65.

Developing Countries Farm Radio Network, "Local Radio for Sustainable Rural Livelihood, Programs Goals and Objectives", http://www.farmradio.org/english/program.html#goals

Fakeeh, K. A., "Recent Developments in Information technology and its Impact on Global Economy", Issues and Trends of IT Management in Contemporary organizations, Proceedings of the IRMA International Conference, 2001, pp. 212-215.

Fleming, S. T., "Information Needs for a developing Country", Issues and Trends of IT Management in Contemporary organizations, Proceedings of the IRMA International Conference, 2001, pp. 223-225.

Freling, Robert .A, "Solar Vision", , International Journal of Humanities and Peace, Annual 2001 v17 il p67(2)

Ganguly, Meenakshi, "Dr. Swaminathan – A Profile", TIME Magazine, TIME 100: August 23-30, 1999 VOL. 154 NO. 7/8

Hudson, H., "World Bank Report on Economic and Social Benefits of Rural Telecommunications."

"India at grassrootlevel.com" ; The Economic Times dt. 04/09/2000

Kriplani, Manjeet, "Taking the isolation out of poverty India, Bangladesh and Sri Lanka go cellular" , Business Week dt. 05/03/1999

Mehta, V. S., "Solar Energy: Imperative for Rural India", The Economic Times, India, March 25, 2000.

Morgan Babetter, "Solar Power to Light SW Bell Pay Phones" St. Louis Post-Dispatch dt. 12/15/92

"Please Mr. Postman"; The Times of India dt. 12/07/20003

Rischard, Jean-Francois, "Connecting Developing Countries to the Information Technology Revolution", SAIS Review 16.1 (1996) 93-107, Copyright © 1996 The Johns Hopkins University Press.

"Rural Telephony Market Analysis", White Paper by STMI.com. http://www.stmi.com/whitepaper.html

"Solar Powered Internet Connection for Remote Bolivian Village"; Ó 1997-2001Xantrex Technology, Inc. @ www.traceoffgrid.com/readingrooms/stories/6.html

Tipton . F, "Bridging the digital divide in Southeast Asia", ASEAN Economic Bulletin, April 2002 v19 il p83(17)

"Village Voices"; The Times of India dated 01/31/2000

"USO Funds for rural telephony" ; Business Line Internet Edition dt. 11/08/2000. Copyright The Hindu Business Line & Trebica Internet Initiatives Inc.

Wadhwa, S., Bhattacharya, S., "Re-engineering the Group Decision Process", Vision, MDI, Journal, December 2000.

Analysis Pattern Definition in the UML

Ernest Teniente
Universitat Politècnica de Catalunya
Dept. Llenguatges i Sistemes Informàtics
Jordi Girona 1-3, 08034 Barcelona (Catalonia)
teniente@lsi.upc.es

ABSTRACT

We identify the UML diagrams and elements that must be used to define an analysis pattern and we explain how analysis patterns defined in this way can be used in the context of the Unified Process. Our proposal is illustrated by means of an example aimed at modelling a generic sports competition.

1. INTRODUCTION

A pattern identifies a problem and provides the specification of a generic solution to that problem. The use of patterns in software development increases reusability of software components and reduces errors of the software delivered. Patterns can be used at each stage of the software development process. Thus, we distinguish among analysis, architectural, design and language patterns.

A *design pattern* [GHVJ95] describes the structure of the solution to a problem that appears repeatedly during software design and the interaction between the different components involved in the solution. Therefore, a design pattern is domain-independent since it is applicable to any software system, provided that the problem addressed by the pattern is encountered during the design of that system.

The analysis model constitutes a permanent model of the reality in itself and, as such, it is independent of a particular implementation technology [Pre00, Mac01]. Therefore, an *analysis pattern* must describe both the structural and dynamical properties of a basic, generic, application domain as perceived by the system user. In this sense, an analysis pattern is application dependent since its semantics describes specific aspects of some domain or software system [Fer98].

The general structure provided by an analysis pattern can be used to define several software systems sharing the features described by the pattern. Developing a particular system applicable to a specific application domain corresponds to adapt the pattern to take the specific aspects of the domain into account.

Analysis patterns provide several advantages to software development. First, they reduce the costs of information systems development because of the reuse of existing solutions. Second, they speed up the development of concrete analysis models that capture the main requirements of a generic application domain. Third, they improve the quality of analysis models by favouring reusability and reducing software errors.

Although some authors like [Fer98, Fow99, FY00] have used the UML to show examples of analysis patterns, it does not exist yet, as far as we know, a precise statement of the UML diagrams that must conform an UML analysis pattern. This is the main goal of this paper: to determine the UML diagrams that must be specified to define an UML analysis pattern.

Moreover, we identify some UML elements that may not be present in these diagrams to ensure we develop an analysis model and we explain how our analysis patterns can be used according to the Unified Process [JBR99, Lar02]. Our proposal is illustrated by means of an analysis pattern that models a generic sports competition.

2. ANALYSIS PATTERNS AND THE UML

Unfortunately, we do not find a clear agreement regarding the kind of patterns that can be defined at the analysis level of information systems development. For instance, [Fow97] proposes analysis patterns that define appro-

priate solutions to model specific constructs that may be found during the specification of different information systems. On the other hand, [FY00] proposes patterns that define a conceptual model for a single information system domain.

In fact, we may distinguish two different approaches regarding the definition of patterns at the analysis stage of the software development process: conceptual modelling patterns and analysis patterns. A *conceptual modelling pattern* is aimed to represent a specific structure of knowledge (for instance a Part-Of relationship) that we encounter in different domains. An *analysis pattern* specifies a generic, domain-dependent, knowledge required to develop an application for specific users.

Our notion of analysis patterns coincides with that of [FY00]. [Fow97] patterns correspond more to conceptual modelling patterns, according to our terminology.

Unfortunately, previous work does not provide, to our knowledge, a sufficient proposal to define analysis patterns in the UML. For instance, [Fer98, p. 37] states that "an analysis pattern is a set of classes and associations that have some meaning in the context of the application" but their examples are illustrated not only by means of class diagrams, as we could expect from the previous definition, but also with state and sequence diagrams.

Later on, [Fow99] develops UML versions of analysis patterns that appear in some chapters of [Fow97]. However, only class diagrams are translated into the UML and, unfortunately, no discussion is given about which of the several UML diagrams should be used to define analysis patterns in this language.

More recently, [FY00, p. 184] states that "a semantic analysis pattern is a pattern that describes a small set of coherent use cases that together describe a basic generic application". It provides some examples of analysis patterns described with analysis class diagrams, state diagrams, sequence diagrams, etc. However, their sequence diagrams specify object interaction and this can only be done if responsibilities are assigned to objects during the analysis stage. Taking this decision involves design and technological issues and, in this way, it is not possible to define an analysis model which is technologically independent.

3. DEFINITION OF ANALYSIS PATTERNS IN THE UML

According to our previous definition, we view an analysis pattern just as a conceptual schema (an analysis model) of a generic application. The UML includes nine types of diagrams to represent different parts of the system [BRJ99]. However, some of them are not useful to define an UML analysis model since they address technological issues. For instance, a deployment diagram shows the configuration of run-time processing nodes and, thus, it is not independent of a particular implementation environment. For similar reasons, object, activity and component diagrams can be discarded to define analysis patterns in the UML.

Therefore, an analysis pattern should be defined in terms of use case diagrams, class diagrams, interaction diagrams and statechart diagrams. However, each of these diagrams may be defined at different stages of the development process and the way they are defined (and also the UML constructions used to define them) depends on the particular stage we are involved in. For this reason, the definition of analysis patterns in the UML requires a clear statement of the boundary between analysis and design.

Craig Larman [Lar98] provides a good criteria that can be used to define this boundary. His main idea, also sketched in [Boo96, FS97], is to define the system behaviour as a 'black box' at the analysis level, before proceeding to a logical design of how a software application will work. According to this criteria, operations responding to external events are not assigned to classes during analysis and they are recorded in an artificial type named *system*.

We also assume that the UML diagrams that define an analysis pattern are non-redundant [CST02]. A UML specification is redundant when a certain aspect of the system is defined in more than one diagram. As shown in [CST02], non-redundant conceptual schemas contribute to desirable properties of the specifications and facilitate software design.

3.1 The Use Case Diagram

Use cases define possible ways users may use a system to meet their goals. They are documented by means of the *Use Case Diagram*, which identifies the main ways a user may interact with the system, and the *Use Case Definition*, which describes the typical course of events that occurs as a result of actor actions required to perform a particular execution of a use case and the system responses to them.

Use cases are mainly used to model the context and the requirements of the software system. However, we believe that it is useful to define, at least, the use case diagram in an UML analysis pattern since it gives a clear idea of all functionalities provided by the software system and the relationships among them. On the contrary, we do not see a clear contribution of use case definitions to UML analysis patterns since the information they provide is also stated by means of system interaction diagrams and operation contracts as we will see in Section 3.3. In this sense, we regard use case definitions as a mean to define those diagrams more than as a permanent model in itself.

The use case diagram of Figure 3.1 defines the most important functionalities of a generic sports competition.

We hope the name of the use cases is clear enough to describe intuitively its intended functionality. Note that some of the use cases require the execution of other use cases to perform satisfactorily. Thus, for instance, to add a new player and to add a new referee requires to add them also as a new person. Moreover, removing a team requires to remove all its players. We provide a more precise definition of the behaviour of some of these use cases in Section 3.3.

3.2 The Analysis Class Diagram

The Analysis Class Diagram specifies the structural properties of the classes that model concepts of the problem domain. It is described by means of *class diagram* in which no operations are defined and it is complemented with *textual constraints*, that define conditions that the information must satisfy but that can not be graphically specified in the UML, and with *derived attributes*, that specify information that can be computed from other elements of the class diagram.

Figure 3.2 shows an analysis class diagram of a generic sports competition. For the sake of simplicity we assume that we model a single league and

Figure 3.1 – Main use cases for a generic sports competition

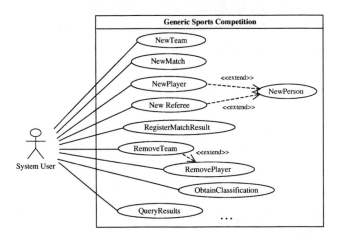

Figure 3.2 – Analysis class diagram for a generic sports competition

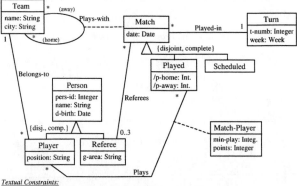

Textual Constraints:
- Class identifiers: (Team, name); (Turn, t-numb); (Person, pers-id)
- A player may not play a match if his team is not one of the teams involved in the match
- The two teams that play a match are different teams
- A team plays exactly 1 match in a certain turn

Derived Attributes:
- p-home of Played = sum of points scored by the players of the home team of the match
- p-away of Played = sum of points scored by the players of the away team of the match

that a team plays exactly two times (home and away) with any other team. A match is defined by two teams and it is played in a certain turn. A match can be scheduled or played. If it is played, we also know the points of both teams that played the match.

Several people are involved in the sports competition. They can be classified into either players or referees. A player belongs to a team and may play several matches. Clearly, a player may not play a match if his team is not involved in the match. Moreover, a player may not be also a referee of the competition.

The formalization in the OCL of some textual constraints and derived attributes of the previous example would be:

context Team **inv:** — two different teams may not have the same name
Team.allInstances -> forAll(t1, t2 | t1 <> t2 **implies** t1.name <> t2.name)
context Match-Player **inv:**
— A player may not play a match if his team is not involved in the match (self.Player.Team = self.Match.home) **or** (self.Player.Team = self.Match.away)
context Match **inv:** — the two teams that play a match are different teams
self.home <> self.away
context Played **inv:** — derivation rule for p-home
p-home = self.match-Player -> select (mp | mp.Player.Team = self.home) -> sum( )

As we said, operations are not specified in the analysis class diagram since we regard the system as a black box during the definition of analysis patterns. Moreover, there are several other elements that can be used in the definition of UML class diagrams in general but that do not make sense for analysis class diagrams. For each of such elements [OMG01], we briefly justify why this is the case:
- **Attribute visibility**: it specifies whether an attribute can be used by other classifiers. This concept does not model the problem domain but the solution domain and, thus, it does not make sense at the analysis level.
- **Navigability**: it states whether an association may be traversed towards other instances in that connection. However, at the analysis level, associations represent existing relationships among real-world concepts. Therefore, all associations can be traversed in all possible directions and so we do not have to specify its navigability.
- **Association**-end visibility: it specifies the visibility of the association end from the viewpoint of the classifier on the other end. Visibility is required to be able to navigate from one end of an association to another. As we have just seen, navigability is a design issue which is not relevant at the analysis level.

3.3 System Interaction Diagrams and Operation Contracts

When the system behaviour is specified as a "black-box", it does not make sense to specify the interaction among objects to fulfil a given functionality but just to specify the interaction among the external actors and the system regarded as such "black-box". This is why we talk about *system interaction diagrams*.

A system interaction diagram shows the external actors that interact with the system, the system as a 'black box', system events that actors generate, their order and the system response. Interaction diagrams may be illustrated either by means of collaboration or sequence diagrams. The following sequence diagram defines the interaction required by the use case NewTeam:

Remove Player

removePlayer (pers-id: Integer)

This interaction required to execute newTeam is very simple. In fact, it is enough to specify the name and the city of the team to register a new team.

System interaction diagrams are complemented with operation contracts to precisely specify the system response to the external events. There is a one to one correspondence between events and operations and, therefore, we have to specify an operation contract for each event occurring in a system interaction diagram.

In the UML, an operation contract includes the *signature of the operation*; its *precondition*, i.e., a set of conditions that are guaranteed to be true when the operation is executed; and its *postcondition*, i.e., a set of conditions that hold after the operation execution. The following contract specifies the semantics of the operation *newTeam*:

context System :: newTeam (name: String, city: String)
post: t.oclIsNew ( ) and t.oclIsTypeOf (Team) and t.name = name and t.city = city

As a consequence of the execution of this operation it happens that an object t of the class Team is created, with attribute values corresponding to the operation parameters name and city. Note that, since we consider that our UML analysis pattern is non-redundant, the previous operation contract must not check that any other team identified by name exists because this is guaranteed already by the textual constraints of the analysis class diagram.

There are several elements that can be used to define operations on the UML but that do not make sense at the analysis level. For each of such elements [OMG01], we briefly justify why this is the case:

- **Assigning operations to classes**: it can only be done if responsibilities are assigned to objects during analysis. However, this decision involves design issues and, therefore, it makes difficult to define an analysis model which is technologically independent. Moreover, it does not make much sense to specify the internal behaviour of an information system when it is regarded as a "black-box".
- **Operation visibility**: it specifies whether an operation may be invoked by other operations. It involves modelling the internal behaviour of the system and, thus, it does not make sense for analysis patterns. In fact, at this level we assume that all operations are public since all of them can be executed by external actors.
- **Abstract operation**: an operation is abstract if it is not implemented in the class where the operation is defined, i.e. no method for it is provided on that class. Clearly, this issue involves technological considerations and, thus, it does not make sense at the analysis level.
- **Completeness of postconditions**: [Lar02, p. 181] suggests that it is not necessary to specify completely the postcondition of the operation contracts. However, we disagree with this opinion since we think that the behaviour of the system can only be precisely specified if we define a complete set of non-redundant postconditions. Therefore, we believe that an analysis pattern should contain a complete and non-redundant operation contract for each event appearing in a system interaction diagram.

Another important aspect that must be considered during the definition of system interaction diagrams of analysis patterns is the way presentation details are taken into account. In fact, a system interaction diagram describes the basic interaction that an actor must perform to execute a given use case, without going into particular details on how it will be actually performed for a given interface.

As an example, in the following system sequence diagram we do not care about whether the user selects the player to be removed from a list of players or whether he just writes the pers-id of the player on a certain form.

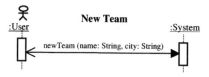

New Team

newTeam (name: String, city: String)

Clearly, presentation details have nothing to do with the concrete semantics of the application. Moreover, different implementations of a particular application semantics may require different presentation details according to the specific preferences of the users of each application. Nevertheless, considering different presentations does not imply any change on the application semantics.

Another example of a more complex system sequence diagram to specify the interaction required by the use case RegisterMatchResult, with the corresponding operation contracts, is:

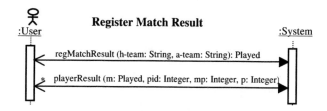

Register Match Result

regMatchResult (h-team: String, a-team: String): Played

playerResult (m: Played, pid: Integer, mp: Integer, p: Integer)

context System :: regMatchResult (h-team: String, a-team: String): Played
post: let m = Match.allInstances -> select (m | m.home = a-team and m.away = a-team) **in**
m.oclIsTypeOf (Played) and result = m
context System :: playerResult (m: Played, p-id: Integer, min: Integer, p: Integer)
post: mp.oclIsNew ( ) and mp.oclIsTypeOf (Match-Player) and
mp.min-play = min and mp.points = p and
mp.Played = m and mp.Player = (Player.allInstances-> select (p | p.pers-id = p-id))

3.4 Statechart Diagrams

Statechart Diagrams illustrate the states of objects and the behaviour of these objects in reaction to an event. An analysis pattern must include a statechart diagram for each object class with an important dynamic behaviour. As an example, the dynamic behaviour of *Match* may be specified by means of the following statechart diagram:

newMatch Scheduled regMatchResult Played

At the analysis level, statechart diagrams are defined by means of *protocol state machines* [OMG01, 2-170]. Each event appearing in a protocol state machine requires a corresponding operation of the class for which the statechart diagram is defined. Its behaviour is defined by an operation contract instead of the specification of action expressions on transitions.

4. ANALYSIS PATTERNS AND THE UNIFIED PROCESS

The use of our UML analysis patterns does not enter in contradiction with the incremental and iterative nature of the Unified Process [JBR99, Lar02].

The inception phase of the Unified Process involves the identification of relevant use cases, which are specified by means of the use case diagram and the use case definition. Our analysis patterns cover the inception phase since they provide the corresponding use case diagram, while the behaviour stated by the use case definition is provided by means of system sequence diagrams and operation contracts.

During the first iteration of the elaboration phase, system sequence diagrams, the analysis class diagram and operation contracts are developed in the Unified Process. Clearly, this phase is also covered by our patterns since they include the corresponding diagrams.

Statechart diagrams and some concepts of use case diagrams (like relating use cases) or the analysis class diagram (like modelling generalization) of our analysis patterns are usually delayed until the third iteration of the elaboration phase in the unified process (at least in Larman's interpretation of this process [Lar02]).

We can conclude, therefore, that our UML analysis patterns cover the diagrams developed during the inception phase and the first part of the elaboration phase of the unified process. For this reason, given an analysis pattern, we can apply the unified process as usual by assuming that those steps have been performed already. In fact, it would be enough to adapt the pattern to take the specific aspects of the domain where the system is to be developed into account and, then, proceed with the other phases of the unified process.

5. CONCLUSIONS

We have shown that analysis patterns must be defined in the UML by means of a use case diagram, an analysis class diagram, system interaction diagrams with their corresponding operation contracts and statechart diagrams. We have also identified some UML elements that these diagrams may not contain to ensure that an analysis pattern corresponds to an analysis model and we have shown that analysis patterns defined in this way can be used in the context of the Unified Process.

Our proposal has been illustrated by means of a (partial) example aimed at modelling a generic sports competition. Since the general structure provided by an analysis pattern is valid to define several software systems sharing the features described by the pattern, it is enough to adapt this pattern to develop a software system applicable to any specific sports competition.

ACKNOWLEDGMENTS

This work has been partially supported by the Ministerio de Ciencia y Tecnología and the FEDER funds, under the project TIC2002-00744.

REFERENCES

[Boo96]   G.Booch. "Object Solutions: Managing the Object-Oriented Project", Addison-Wesley, 1996.

[BRJ99]   G.Booch; J.Rumbaugh; I.Jacobson. "The Unified Modeling Language User Guide", Addison-Wesley, 1999.

[CST02]   D.Costal; M.R.Sancho; E.Teniente. "Understanding Redundancy in UML Analysis Models", 14th Int. CAiSE Conference, LNCS 2348, Springer, 2002, pp. 659-674.

[Fer98]   E.B.Fernandez. "Building Systems Using Analysis Patterns", 3rd Int. Software Architecture Workshop (ISAW3), ACM, 1998, pp. 37-40.

[Fow97]   M.Fowler. "Analysis Patterns – Reusable Object Models", Addison-Wesley, 1997.

[Fow99]   M.Fowler. "Analysis Patterns", http://www.martinfowler.com/apsupp/, 1999.

[FS97]   M.Fowler and K.Scott. "UML Distilled", Addison-Wesley, 1997.

[FY00]   E.B.Fernandez; X.Yuan. "Semantic Analysis Patterns", 19th Int. Conf on Conceptual Modeling (ER'00), LNCS 1920, Springer, 2000, pp. 183-195.

[GHJV95] E.Gamma; R.Helm; R.Johnson; J.Vlissides. "Design Patterns – Elements of Reusable Object-Oriented Software", Addison-Wesley, 1995.

[JBR99]   I.Jacobson; G.Booch; J.Rumbaugh. "The Unified Software Development Process", Addison-Wesley, 1999.

[Lar98]   C.Larman. "Applying UML and Patterns", Prentice Hall, 1998.

[Lar02]   C.Larman. "Applying UML and Patterns: An Introduction to Object-Oriented Analysis and Design and the Unified Process", 2nd Ed., Prentice Hall, 2002.

[Mac01]   L.A.Maciaszek. "Requirements Analysis and System Design – Developing Information Systems with UML", Addison-Wesley, 2001.

[OMG01] OMG. "Unified Modeling Language Specification", Version 1.4, September 2001.

[Pre00]   R.Pressman. "Software Engineering: A Practitioner's Approach", Fifth Edition. McGraw-Hill, 2000.

E-Colonialism - The New Challenge of the 21ˢᵗ Century

V. S. Venkatesan and Neetha Nambiar
Graduate School of Management, University of Western Australia
35 Stirling Highway, Crawley WA 6009 Australia
Tel: 61 8 9380 3980; Fax: 61 8 9380 1072
vvenkate@ecel.uwa.edu.au

BACKGROUND

The concept of colonialism entails the exploitation of a weaker country by a stronger one and dates back from the Greek period (Ferro 1997). Colonizers sought resources unavailable at home and, in return, sent colonial administrators, immigrants, and a language, educational system, religion, culture, laws and lifestyle that were not traditional in the colonized country (McPhail 1987). Throughout history colonialism has assumed different forms and was imposed over a range of civilizations, most of which, eventually gained their freedom. But if colonialism, in its narrow definition, came to an end with the defeat of the French in Vietnam or Algeria, of the British in India, or the Dutch in Indonesia, colonial domination has nonetheless survived in one form or another (Fieldhouse 1999). One such manifestation of colonialism is 'electronic colonialism' or 'e-colonialism'.

The history of several Asian and African nations attests to the effects of industrial colonialism and highlights the potential for information to become a tool in spawning a new breed of colonialism. Many nations, despite having a high level of education and culture, did not recognise the growth of industrial colonialism. Likewise, the emergence of e-colonialism may not be initially perceivable thus making researchers in this area complacent (Shaw 2000).

Previous research on e-colonialism dealt with television and newspapers as media with potential to generate colonialism of the information age (McPhail 1987). The advent of computer-mediated communication technologies: Internet, World Wide Web etc., has added a new twist to past debates on e-colonialism.

E-colonialism goes beyond the existing debates on digital divide which concerns the socioeconomic issues emerging from uneven access to technology on a narrowly defined micro level. Extensive media coverage on digital divide may have caused the greater effects of the information revolution to be largely overlooked (Gruenwald 2001). The all-encompassing issue of e-colonialism brings such large-scale concerns to the forefront and throws light on the various implications of the technological revolution – implications that have so far been side stepped in the interest of 'development'.

INFORMATION REVOLUTION

With the onslaught of the information revolution, the influence of the Internet has grown far beyond the expectations of its originators (Rosenberg 1997). From its humble beginnings as a research oriented computer network, the Internet has become a worldwide phenomenon. The rapid growth of the Internet has brought with it a growing disparity between the technology haves and the technology have nots, and this forms the basic tenet of the concept of e-colonialism.

Such disparity has always existed but now, more than ever before; unequal adoption of technology excludes many from experiencing the benefits of the information revolution. The world has never before faced such a glaring contrast in the human condition – extravagant wealth and tremendous advances in science and technology alongside harsh poverty and suffering faced by a full third of humanity (Chanda 2000). Thus, although the Internet offers a wide range of options for communication and exchange of information, there may be a need to consider the impact of these technological developments on society (Salpini 1998).

Currently, developed countries appear to dominate the Internet with the developing world left in the sidelines (Norris 2001). This is revealed by a perfunctory search of the Internet – most websites are in English and usually sourced from the United States. If measures are not taken to locate sites in the developing world and establish them as information providers, most developing countries may become 'electronic colonies' that are force-fed information generated by the developed world.

IMPLICATIONS OF E-COLONIALISM

Macro Level

The large-scale effects of the information revolution are starkly obvious in the great divide between the developed and developing world. On one hand, there are many third world countries concerned about basic amenities such as access to radio and television. Conversely, there are other nations some of which have been industrialized for over a century and are, accordingly, in a much better position to reap the rewards of the information revolution. The disparity is visible in the different levels of Internet access available to countries in the developed and developing world (Table 1).

In India, where the population numbers over one billion, 7.6 million use the Internet. In comparison, among the 275 million inhabitants of the United States, 130 million use the Internet. Similar disparities are observed by comparing the figures for Australia to that of South Africa and other parts of Africa (Kowalczykowski 2002).

In India, where the population numbers over one billion, 7.6 million use the Internet. In comparison, among the 275 million inhabitants of the United States, 130 million use the Internet. Similar disparities are observed by comparing the figures for Australia to that of South Africa and other parts of Africa (Kowalczykowski 2002).

As revealed in Table 2, in the United States, Canada and parts of Europe Internet access is available to larger segments of the population in comparison to nations in Africa and Asia. Such figures are glaring representations of the wide chasm that separates the developed and developing world.

The issue of Internet access naturally relates to the issue of Internet sourcing. Many third-world countries do not have the resources or the expertise to provide access to the Internet for their citizens, let alone relay information by way of the Internet. Therefore, information that is published on the Internet about most developing countries is likely to be generated by third party groups purporting to be the authority on that country. This may result in such groups dominating the information about a country's cultural, economic and political status and placing an interpretation on the information that suits their own needs.

Table 1: Comparison of Telecommunication statistics for USA, South Africa, Australia and India

Country	Total Population Estimate ('000)	Internet Usership in 2001	Number of internet hosts (2001)
USA	275,306.41	130,114,957.00	104,482,787.59
South Africa	43,949.10	4,019,968.00	295,830.12
Australia	19,182.75	7,630,484.00	1,699,995.54
India	1,026,877.60	7,638,233.00	49,732.77

Source: (Euromonitor 2002)

Table 2: Number of Internet users worldwide as of September 2002

	Users in millions	Users as percent of total world users	Users as percent of population
World total	605.60	100.0	9.7
Africa	6.31	1.0	0.7
Asia/Pacific	187.24	30.9	5.3
Europe	190.91	31.5	26.2
Middle East	5.12	0.8	2.9
Canada & USA	182.67	30.2	57.2
Latin America	33.35	5.5	6.2

On a macro level, the power of the Internet to bring down borders is irrefutable. This can, however, cause a blurring of national identities and enable large economies to dominate smaller cultures and define the 'global culture' (1999). Research in various developed and developing countries reveal the price of a globally shared media perspective (White 2001). That price is homogenization. There is undoubtedly evidence to suggest such a trend with children from developing countries idolizing American celebrities and discarding their local beverages for Coca Cola and Coffee.

The nationality of the major providers of news and information globally is another reflection of the domination of the Internet by developed countries. Presently, there are four main news agencies, and each one represents the main colonial forces in our history. The 'Associated Press' and 'United Press International' are American agencies, 'Reuters' is English and the 'Agence-France Presse' is French. The end result is a possibly unbalanced, biased flow of information that ignores the rights of the developing world to be heard.

Implications on a Micro Level

On a micro level, cost factors in the provision of hardware and software may exclude many from the possibility of even possessing and using many information technologies (Lamb 2000; Sittenfeld 2002). Those without access to the Internet may face the prospect of being further isolated politically, economically and culturally from the rest of the world (Jordan 1999). Within most developing countries, the political parties and other corporate/government bodies that control the network and the media content could significantly influence the message to the masses. Given the poor level of education and the religious and sociopolitical scenario in many such countries, this could have a significant impact on the population (Robinson and Kaye 2000).

Rapid technological developments can potentially disadvantage developing countries, where average household income levels do not allow for the purchase of a computer. Since external communications networks are owned by multinational companies, communication charges can also contribute to the foreign debt of the nations, thus impeding the development of government-funded networks hooked up to the Web (Spennemann, Birckhead et al. 1996).

On a corporate level, some companies gain an upper hand over smaller commercial concerns through technological resources that enable them to advertise over the Internet. Such a divide is known to exist in developed economies, even in the absence of monetary constraints (Lieberman 2000; Venkatesan and Robinson 2002). The recent antitrust suit against Microsoft provided an opportunity to view the great potential for power that lies within the Internet (Lohr 2002). With its lucrative hold on the software market Microsoft is one of many such large corporate concerns that wield enormous influence over the computer industry and, in turn, the Information Technology industry worldwide.

CONCLUSION

The twenty first century promises to be one in which the full significance of global automation of information will be felt and with this will come the various effects of e-colonialism. While the Internet facilitates the sharing of information globally, it also threatens cultural diversity, the loss of local culture and the manipulation of the less developed. The impact of e-colonialism can potentially be just as devastating as that of mercantile colonialism in the nineteenth century.

The solution does not lie in restricting the spread of information technology. The information revolution has brought numerous benefits to society and any attempts to eradicate the Internet would be counterproductive. What is required are strategies to confront the issues presented by e-colonialism by bridging the technological divide created by the information revolution through improved technological access to the developing world. The 'colonization' of the technologically poor must be impeded by improving the accessibility of the Internet across and between nations to ensure that no one is left behind in the global movement towards technological advancement.

REFERENCES

Anonymous (1999). Americanization: Electronic colonialism, Rotman School of Management.

Chanda, N. (2000). "The digital divide." Far Eastern Economic Review.

Euromonitor (2002). Country Data, Euromonitor's Global Market Information Database.

Ferro, M. (1997). Colonization: a global history. London, Routledge.

Fieldhouse, D. K. (1999). The West and the third world: trade, colonialism, dependence and development. Oxford, Blackwell Publishers.

Gruenwald, J. (2001). "Seeking answers to the global digital divide." Interactive Week.

Jordan, T. (1999). Cyberpower: The culture and politics of cyberspace and the Internet. London, Routledge.

Kowalczykowski, M. (2002). "Disconnected continent." Harvard International Review 24(2): 40-43.

Lamb, P. (2000). "Poor forgotten as "digital divide" still gapes." Pacific News Service.

Lieberman, D. (2000). "America's digital divide: on the wrong side of the wires." USA Today.

Lohr, S. (2002). "For Microsoft ruling will sting but not really hurt." New York Times: 1.

McPhail, T. L. (1987). Electronic colonialism: the future of international broadcasting and communication. Newbury Park, Sage Publications.

Norris, P. (2001). Digital divide: Civic engagement, information poverty and the Internet worldwide. New York, Cambridge University Press.

NUA Internet (2002). NUA Internet How Many Online, NUA Internet Surveys.

Robinson, T., J. and B. K. Kaye (2000). "Using is believing: the influence of reliance on the credibility of online political information among politically interested Internet users." Journalism and Mass Communication Quarterly 77(4): 865-879.

Rosenberg, R. S. (1997). The social impact of computers. San Diego, Academic Press.

Salpini, D. (1998). World Conference on Information Technology, Federal Communicators Network.

Shaw, J. M. (2000). "The view from "down under": ARLIS/ANZ and the world of art librarianship." INSPEL 34(1): 22-30.

Sittenfeld, C. (2002). "From the digital divide to one economy." Fast Company(65): 50.

Spennemann, D. H. R., J. Birckhead, et al. (1996). "The electronic colonization of the Pacific." Computer-Mediated Communication Magazine 3(2).

US Census Bureau (2002). International Data Base, US Census Bureau.

Venkatesan, V. S. and K. Robinson (2002). E-divide issues in regional Australia. IRMA Conference, Seattle, USA.

White, L., A. (2001). "Reconsidering cultural imperialism theory." Transnational Broadcasting Studies Journal Spring/Summer(6).

Renovation of an IT Infrastructure and its POC Analysis

Masaru Furukawa
19-31, Gofuku, Toyama City, Japan (930-8555)
Phone and Fax: +81-76-445-6477
E-mail: frukawa@eco.toyama-u.ac.jp

ABSTRACT

In recent years the evolution of highly developed and complicated computerization has boosted the importance to business of IT infrastructure. Enhancement of business agility is not possible unless greater flexibility is built into IT infrastructure. More often than not, MIS's today are not flexible enough in this sense to agilely accommodate demands for system change incessantly confronting them.

We have been concentrating our research on MIS flexibility, its evaluation and the development of methodology for its enhancement. This paper aims to present a comparative evaluation via POC (penalty of change) analysis of system alternatives involving a case of renovation of IT infrastructure. To start with, we will define the concept of MIS flexibility. We will then describe an actual case of renovation of IT infrastructure and define the problem it involved and go on to illustrate the evaluation of MIS flexibility via POC analysis.

INTRODUCTION

In recent years the evolution of highly developed and complicated computerization has boosted the importance to business of IT infrastructure. Enhancement of business agility is not possible unless greater flexibility is built into IT infrastructure. More often than not, MIS's today are not flexible enough in this sense to agilely accommodate demands for system change incessantly confronting them.

We have been concentrating our research on MIS flexibility, its evaluation and the development of methodology for its enhancement. This paper aims to present a comparative evaluation via *POC* (penalty of change) analysis of system alternatives involving a case of renovation of IT infrastructure. To start with, we will define the concept of MIS flexibility. We will then describe an actual technology implementation and define the problem it involved and go on to illustrate the evaluation of MIS flexibility via *POC* analysis, enumerating project risks accompanying the technology implementation.

OVERVIEW OF THE POC ANALYSIS

POC as a Substitute Index of MIS Flexibility

For the present purpose, let us draw on the definition of MIS flexibility and the scheme for its evaluation that we proposed in Furukawa (2001a, 2001b) as the following.

Agile management cannot be realized unless well-renovated IT infrastructure guarantees maximally efficient implementation of MIS change at a minimal cost and in a minimal time. The business value of an MIS (hereafter to be referred to as MIS value for short) is generated by the use process of an application function working on IT infrastructure (Hamillton, 1981). Then MIS value (V) might be represented by the following formula:

$$V = \frac{f(F,U)}{g(C,T)} \%_o \qquad (1)$$

where *C, T, F* and *U* stand for cost, time, function and use, respectively. Incidentally, Johanson et al (1993) defines MIS value in terms of quality, service, cost and cycle- time.

As regards the evaluation of MIS effectiveness, methods traditionally utilized have been, in the classification of cost/benefit methodology, "Total Quantification with Qualitative analysis (JIPDC, 1981)", "Information Economics" and "Contribution to Corporate Performance" (Utunomiya, 1993; Myer, 1989). But perception and use of a particular information system can be heavily conditioned by personal and situational variables (Lucas, 1974). This fact in particular makes it difficult to evaluate MIS effectiveness quantitatively. Deemed relatively reliable for this purpose, however, are the following five measures: "High levels of system use", "User satisfaction with the system", "Favorable attitudes about MIS function", "Achievement of objectives", "Financial payoff" (Laudon, 2000). In fact, many MIS researchers have shifted their focus to the human and organizational measures of system success such as information quality, system quality, and the impact of systems on organizational performance (DeLone, 1992).

These evaluation methods or criteria focus on the numerator of formula (1), which in effect represents the MIS use process, *i.e.* how easily adaptable an MIS is for the user. Quick use of an adapted MIS enables a) quick recognition of an environment change, and b) quick decision-making on countermeasures against the change. However, for all the research efforts on this adaptability, we know of no established methods that an organization could use to maximize above-mentioned six kinds of MIS value.

On the other hand, c) quick implementation of countermeasures chosen to cope with environmental changes involves change of an MIS itself. These days MISs are growing increasingly large in scale, as are the demands for modification of existing ones to cope with incessant changes inside and outside organizations. Unfortunately, however, we have no systematized methods we can turn to for minimizing the cost and time required to meet change demands, *i.e.* the denominator of formula (1). We hear of many cases of MIS implementation that have met with troubles such as failure to deliver by the due date, excess over an estimate, productivity deterioration (increases in backlogs), malfunctioning (activity inability, operational inability, increases in bugs), system failure (failure of a system to be used as intended). All this shows that no reliable methods have been established to estimate or predict the denominator of formula (1), *i.e.* the cost and time required for MIS implementation and in the use process.

Therefore, let us postulate MIS flexibility as an ability to absorb future change demands on an MIS, and let us express it formulaically with (1):

$$Flex = \frac{Const}{g(C,T)} = \frac{1}{POC} \qquad (2)$$

where C and T stand for cost and time, respectively.

Formula (1) suggests that *POC* can serve as a substitute index for quantitative evaluation of the flexibility of an MIS. It also obviously shows the following relationship between MIS flexibility and *POC*:
- If *POC* is high, MIS flexibility is low.
- If *POC* is low, MIS flexibility is high.

POC can serve as an index for measurement of the ability to absorb future demands for MIS change and can be accounted for in terms of cost and time.

Structure of MIS Flexibility

As detailed in a relevant section in Furukawa 2001b, a moderate renova-

Figure 1: Structure of MIS Flexibility

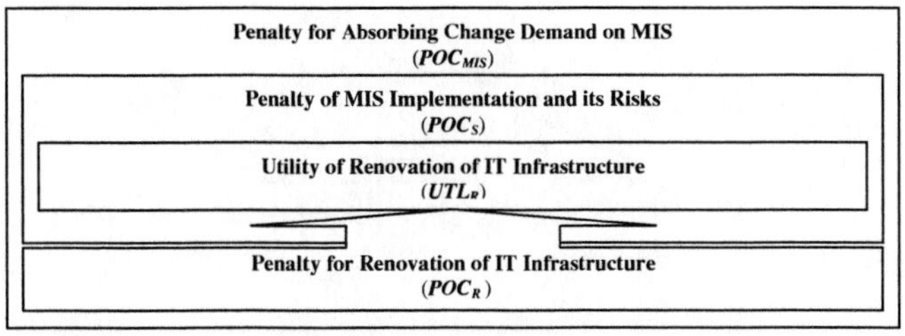

Table 1: Factors for POC Calculation

Change Demand k ($l=3$)				Set of Risk Evasion Strategies	Occurrence Probability of Change X
p ($q=8$)	Combination of Alternatives (Al_{ip})			St_{ip} $i=n(p)$	$\Pr(X_{ip})$
	$k=1,$ $j=2$	$k=2,$ $j=2$	$k=3,$ $j=2$		
1	Al_{11}	Al_{12}	Al_{13}	St_{11}	$\Pr_{11}$
				St_{21}	$\Pr_{21}$
				St_{31}	$\Pr_{31}$
				St_{41}	$\Pr_{41}$
				St_{51}	$\Pr_{51}$
2	Al_{11}	Al_{12}	Al_{23}	St_{12}	$\Pr_{12}$
				St_{22}	$\Pr_{22}$
3	Al_{11}	Al_{22}	Al_{13}	St_{13}	$\Pr_{13}$
				St_{23}	$\Pr_{23}$
4	Al_{11}	Al_{22}	Al_{23}	St_{14}	$\Pr_{14}$
				St_{24}	$\Pr_{24}$
				St_{34}	$\Pr_{34}$
5	Al_{21}	Al_{12}	Al_{13}	St_{15}	$\Pr_{15}$
				St_{25}	$\Pr_{25}$
6	Al_{21}	Al_{12}	Al_{23}	St_{16}	$\Pr_{16}$
				St_{26}	$\Pr_{26}$
7	Al_{21}	Al_{22}	Al_{13}	St_{17}	$\Pr_{17}$
				St_{27}	$\Pr_{27}$
				St_{37}	$\Pr_{37}$
8	Al_{21}	Al_{22}	Al_{23}	St_{18}	$\Pr_{18}$
				St_{28}	$\Pr_{28}$
				St_{38}	$\Pr_{38}$

tion of IT infrastructure can contribute to greater ease and efficiency of MIS modification [**utility of renovation**].

We know from experience that modification of an MIS is liable to expose it to system risks of some sorts or other, and that these risks are most to blame for impairment of MIS efficiency. However, if we moderately renovate IT infrastructure by building into it some preemptive risk-evasion strategies by anticipation, these strategies can be expected to reduce system risks that future MIS modification would almost inevitably entail. But implementation of such a renovation incurs a *POC* of its own [***POC* of renovation**]. Therefore let us represent MIS flexibility in terms of the substitute index of *POC* as in Figure 1. This figure suggests that the *POC* [POC_R] paid for a moderate renovation of IT infrastructure can generate the benefit [UTL_R] [**utility of renovation**] of reducing the *POC* (POC_S) that processing of demands for system change would incur in future (Hereafter let us use the term "*renovation of IT infrastructure*" to refer to the application of IT to an existing MIS for enhancement of its flexibility).

The above observation allows us to represent the *POC* of a whole MIS change (POC_{MIS}) with formula (2):

$$POC_{MIS} = POC_S + (POC_R - UTL_R) \qquad (3)$$

Future-Oriented POC Analysis

The *POC* analysis we proposed in Furukawa (2001a) has been expanded and generalized as summarized below (Furukawa, 2002):

Enhancement of MIS flexibility cannot be realized unless the possibility of system risks is reduced by means of moderate strategic renovation of IT infrastructure. This infrastructure renovation actually means providing preemptive risk-evasion strategies in anticipation of future MIS modification. What we should consider in this connection is how to evaluate what combination of system alternatives would incur the least *POC* (cost and time). For this purpose, it is necessary to enumerate a possible set of risk-evasion strategies we should provide for application to the combination of system alternatives, and evaluate both the penalty of change the very provision of these strategies would incur and the utility that their application would also generate (*i.e.* their utility in reducing penalty that we would otherwise have to pay when addressing change demands in future).

Since anticipatory provision of evasion strategies for possible future system changes, by its very nature, involves predictive uncertainty, it should be dealt with as a probabilistic event. Therefore, before going on into our detailed discussion, let us refer to a related idea involving a probabilistic event in the form of formula (3), an idea proposed by Chryssolouris, G. et al (1996) in the context of the evaluation of flexibility of manufacturing systems:

$$POC = \sum_{s=1}^{n} Pe(X_s)\Pr(X_s) \qquad (4)$$

where

X_s = the state after change s (1, 2,..., S)
$Pe(X_s)$ = the penalty for change s,
$\Pr(X_s)$ = the occurrence probability of change s.

The calculation of *POC* can be viewed as an application of single-attribute decision-making under conditions of uncertainty (*i.e.*, the decision problem of selecting a combination of system alternatives for the enhancement of

MIS flexibility); X_s is a possible future scenario (*i.e.*, the state brought about by the implementation of the sth system change); $Pe(X_s)$ is the attribute value for the future scenario (*i.e.*, required management resources for the sth change); and $\Pr(X_s)$ is the probability of the possible occurrence of the future scenario; the numerical value of *POC* is the expected value of the penalty payable for the system change leading to the possible future scenario.

Here, let us represent a change demand as $k(1 \leq k \leq l)$, a system alternative for a change demand k as $j(1 \leq j \leq m(k))$ and a combination of system alternatives for a change demand as $p(1 \leq p \leq q)$. Where the number of change demands is l, the number (represented as q) of combinations of system alternatives for processing all change demands can be represented as $q = n(1) \times n(2) \times ... \times n(l)$ ($q=8$ in Table 1). On the other hand, let us represent a set of risk-evasion strategies for p as $i(1 \leq i \leq n(p))$ and enumerate a set of risk-evasion strategies(i) to be provided for each p of q combinations of system alternatives and let us give the notation of $\Pr(X_{ip})$ to the probability of the occurrence of the state of affairs where a set of risk-evasion strategies (i) will be applied. Then, the expected value of POC_p (*POC* payable for execution of each p of the q combinations of system alternatives) can be represented with formula (4) after the fashion of Chryssolouris, G. et al (1996).

$$POC_p = \sum_{i=1}^{n(p)} Pe(X_{ip})\Pr(X_{ip}) \qquad (4)$$

In order to process all ($=l$) change demands, we need to implement q combinations of system alternatives for them. And each of these combinations of system alternatives is supposed to have been provided with a set of risk-evasion strategies in advance. An aim of this paper is to establish the methodology for selecting a system plan comprised of combinations of system alternatives and sets of risk-evasion strategies, which will best serve the purpose of MIS flexibility enhancement. A combination of system alternatives that will show the lowest value of *POC* (POC_{min}) can be represented with formula (5) (Furukawa, 2002):

$$POC_{min} = \sum_{p=1}^{q} \min POC_p \qquad (5)$$

As the structure of MIS flexibility in Figure 1 visually shows, enhancement of MIS flexibility can only be realized by reduction of system risks via renovation of IT infrastructure. In order to evaluate a system plan, therefore, we must enumerate all sets of risk-evasion strategies to be applied to combinations of system alternatives, and then we must estimate both the penalty for the provision of the strategies (POC_R), and the penalty for the implementation of the system alternatives (POC_S) and the utility (UTL_R) that the application of the strategies will generate in the enhancement of MIS flexibility.

The following formula (6) represents the effect of the application of a set of risk-evasion strategies to a combination of system alternatives in future. This formula means that a combination of system alternatives that will incur the lowest penalty (POC_{min}) can be identified through close scrutiny of what set of risk-evasion strategies will be the best one to be applied to a combination of system alternatives to be implemented to process all change demands. There can be no doubt about the validity of this idea, insofar as it closely reflects the fact that one and the same IT infrastructure is shared by all possible application systems.

$$Pe(X_{ip}) = POC_S(p) + POC_R(ip) - UTL_R(ip) \qquad (6)$$

where

$POC_S(p)$ = the penalty for applying a combination of system alternatives p to all change demands (without a set of risk-evasion strategies provided),

$POC_R(ip)$ = the penalty for providing a set of risk-evasion strategies i for a combination of system alternatives p,

$UTL_R(ip)$ = the utility of applying a set of risk-evasion strategies i to a combination of system alternatives p.

CASE STUDY OF AN IT INFRASTRUCTURE RENOVATION

A Case of Preparation for the New Millennium

System designers ought to have been able to foresee the occurrence of the year 2000(Y2K) problem at the stage when the data were being designed. This even implies that they virtually programmed the Y2K problem, which they could have averted, as was the case with Company X.

Company X was one of the first corporations in Japan that have introduced computers. In the late 1960s, they also undertook a change in their application system from batch to on-line real time processing. The change was executed by adding DAM files (direct access method) and programs written in Assembler for real-time processing to the existing batch processing system. The new system was only used during the daytime. The old batch system took over data from the new system after regular office hours for processing during the night. A scrap-and-build approach to the system development had been dismissed in order to meet the demand of the executives, who were anxious to start using the new system as soon as possible.

In the late 1980s, with rapid business and environmental changes pressing upon them and with an increasingly large-scale and complicated system to attend to, the MIS Division of the firm had inevitably been swamped with a huge backlog and they had been incessantly making desperate efforts for sheer maintenance of the system they had built 20 years before. After racking their brains about how to overcome their predicament, they decided to adopt a scrap-and-build approach after all and replace old DAM files and others with a relational database (RDB). The procedure that they worked out for the change consisted of:

- building a new RDB normalized with a data dictionary (DD), with all data from the existing MIS integrated into it,
- creating an interface between the existing MIS and the new RDB,
- and finally switching over from the existing MIS to the new system, which would access the new RDB directly.

This renovation cost far more than expected and required serious efforts of the engineers. But both the running cost and the backlog decreased as the changeover progressed. In the fall of 1999, most IT personnel in the world were in great fear of the arrival of the Y2K. At this time, the changeover of the

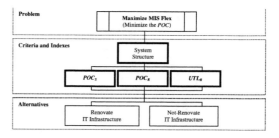

Figure 2: Description of the Problem via AHP

firm's MIS had already been completed. Because of the superior flexibility of the IT infrastructure (system structure), the expansion of the date-fields to accommodate the change of millennia was completed by the next day by a mere modification of the definition of the date-fields in the DD.

To build a DB with a DD, it is indispensable to carry out the definition of key fields and their relationship, which incurs a POC of its own. But properly created, a DD will bring us utilities such as the ease of data use, which enhances the agility of decision-making on selection of strategy alternatives for coping with environment changes and the ease of MIS renovation, which enhances the agility of the execution of the selected action.

DEFINITION AND ANALYSIS OF THE PROBLEM VIA AHP

Let us imagine Company X being currently involved in a predicament described above, and in order to define the problem it is faced with, let us represent it by means of Analytic Hierarchy Process (AHP) as in Figure 2. The decision Company X is required to make is whether to execute a renovation of IT infrastructure or not. Since the decision, needless to say, is going to be made in the expectation that a renovation will generate utility, the goal of the problem is "maximization of MIS flexibility (*i.e.* minimization of the POC)". The criteria and indexes for flexibility evaluation are described in Table 2 with regard to general categories of factors underlying MIS flexibility. In this case, however, estimations of POC_S, POC_R and UTL_R need to be conducted with a particular focus on the flexibility factor of "System Structure."

Table 3 and Table 4 show the result of the evaluation of a renovation after the fact, and the Total Score of Table 4 indicates that "Renovate IT infrastructure" had an advantage after all. But as we proposed in the formulation of formula (6), a renovation of IT infrastructure (*i.e.* provision of risk-evasion strategies) needs to be executed in advance against the possibility of system changes that may be demanded in future. Then, unless we predict all change demands that may be made on the existing MIS in future, we cannot estimate POC_S, POC_R and UTL_R before the fact.

Table 2: MIS Flexibility and Indexes for its Evaluation

Category	Meaning	Risk-prone change	Risk	Evasion Strategy	Index for Evaluation			
					Viewpoint	Cost	Time	Utility
Hardware / Exchangeability	Eminess of exchange and change of hardware	Machine replacement	System unusable	Enhancement of Connection interchangeability, Enhancement of Upper compatibility (open protocol, open system)	Enhancement of Connection interchangeability, Enhancement of Upper compatibility (open protocol, open system)	Human resources (Man-month)	Time distance (exchange speed)	Shortening of exchange time, reduction of cost
		Upgrading base software	System unusable	Enhancement of Connection interchangeability, Enhancement of Upper compatibility Multiplexing, back up & recovery, insurance & maintenance contract, out-sourcing (external equipment)				
Hardware / Fault tolerance	Ability to continue to provide service on given application functions	Trouble outbreak from bugs in basic software	System uncontrollable, System breakdown	Back up & recovery, preventive maintenance	Availability	Opportunity loss, Recovery cost	MTBT, MTTR	Reduction of opportunity loss and recovery cost
		Trouble outbreak from bugs in application programs	System unusable, System failure	Thoroughness of testing, standardization, educational training, back up & recovery				
		Trouble outbreak from operational error	System failure	Educational training, job enrichment, out-sourcing (skilled engineer)				
Application system / System structure	Ability to add new application functions easily (degree of structuring)	External environmental changes, Enterprise-oriented changes in managerial function and /or in business process	Delay in due date delivery, excess over the estimates, productivity deterioration, malfunction, system failure	Technological strategies Standardization of protocol (open systems) / Structured analysis / design / programming, and Data-Oriented Approach (Structuring, Normalization)	Structuring of System and program	Cost for change structuring, Cost for structuring	Time for change demands, Time for structuring	Reduction of POC for design
				Organizational strategies Accumulation of engineers' experience and enhancement of skills, educational training of users, Workload (reduction of engineers' overload), Job enrichment, Practical use of external consultants	Quality of database (Number of scores paths from application program to data, Number of programs and data requiring change, ratio of management-target entities included in database), Tendency of backlog volume on the time axis	Cost for change demands, Cost for database development	Time for change demands, Time for database development	Reduction of POC for design
Application system / Service area	Ability to provide unexpected-request service to customer for the first time	Request for unexpected business field	Delay in due date delivery, excess over the estimates, productivity deterioration, malfunction, system failure	Rearranging management-target entities and Building database	Ratio of BPs and management-target entities given a service	Cost for change demands, Cost for new service	Cost for change demands, Time for new service	Reduction of POC for design
Application system / IT adoption	Ability to provide a service with unexpected new technology and/or method	IT innovation, Implementation of new technology	Delay in due date delivery, excess over the estimates, productivity deterioration, malfunction, system failure	Accumulation of engineers' experience, R&D, Standardization of system development, Educational training (dissolution of skill deficiency)	Technological continuity and degree of experience	Cost for change demands, Cost for expertise enhancement depending on proficiency levels	Time for expertise enhancement depending on proficiency levels	Reduction of POC by learning

Table 3: Evaluation of the Problem

View Point for Evaluation			Accomplished Modification	
Ratio of Programs Structured			Standardized database accessing statements for all programs	
Ratio of Subsystems Structured			Secured the mutual independency of subsystems in existing MIS via database	
Ratio of Data compiled into Database			Built up Data Dictionary by normalizing whole data in existing MIS	
Criteria		Method for Evaluation		Result of Evaluation
POC	Cost	Cost for renovation of existing MIS infrastructure		$1 million? 120 man-month
	Time	Time for renovation of existing MIS infrastructure		12months
Utility	Indexes	The number of programs required to access necessary data		Reduced to 30 percent
		The number of programs requiring modification to accommodate future change demands		Reduced to 65 percent
		The number of data-items that need to be added and/or changed to accommodate future change demands		Reduced to 35 percent
		Ratio of management-target entities included in Database		65% of all the management-target entities of the Enterprise
	Cost	Reduction of cost required to accommodate future change demands in comparison with the alternative of Not-Renovate		Reduced to 70 percent
	Time	Reduction of time required to accommodate future change demands in comparison with the alternative of Not-Renovate		Reduced to 60 percent

Table 4: AHP Calculation

Weight via Paired Comparison

	Cost	Time	Utility	Weight
Cost	1	3	1/5	0.188
Time	1/3	1	1/7	0.081
Utility	5	7	1	0.731

Calculated via Paired-Comparison

Total Score of Each Alternative via AHP

Alternatives	Cost	Time	Utility	Total Score
Renovate	1/3	1/5	9	0.718
Not -renovate	3	5	1/9	0.228

CONCLUSION

In this paper, we have defined the concept of MIS flexibility in terms of *POC* and in relation to IT infrastructure renovation and proposed a Future-Oriented *POC* analysis. We have also given an account of an actual case of renovation of IT infrastructure and defined the problem it involved. We have then wound up our discussion by illustrating the evaluation of MIS flexibility via our proposed *POC* analysis. The Future-Oriented *POC* Analysis, which we have presented in this paper, has revealed that the *POC* analysis can serve as an effective and useful tool for the evaluation of IT infrastructure, and ultimately for the development of methodology for enhancement of MIS flexibility.

REFERENCES

Chryssolouris, G.., (1996). Flexibility and Its Measurement, *Annals of the CIRP*, 45(2). 581-587.

DeLone, William H., & Ephraim R. McLean, (1992). Information System Success: The Quest for the Dependent Variable. Information Systems Research. 3(1), 60-95.

Furukawa, M. (2001a). Conceptual Model for MIS Flexibility Evaluation. Information Systems Evaluation Management. Ed. Grembergen, W.V. Idea Group Publishing. 146-166.

Furukawa, M. (2001b). Database Agile Management Dependent on MIS Infrastructure. Conference Proceedings of Informing Science 2001. Krakow, Poland. 198-213.

Furukawa, M. (2002). Evaluation of New Technology Implementation via POC Analysis. The Proceedings of the 2002 Informing Science + IT Education Conference in Cork, Ireland. 523-531.

Johanson, H.J., McHugh, P., Pendlebury, A.J., & Wheeler, W.A. (1993). Business Process reengineering: break point strategies for market dominance. Wiley. p.4.

Hamilton, S., & Chervany, N.C. (1981). Evaluating Information System Effectiveness - Part l: Comparing Evaluation Approaches. MIS Quarterly. 5(3), 55-69.

Laudon, K.C., & Laudon, J.P. (2000). Management Information Systems: Organization and Technology in the Networked Enterprise (6th Ed). Prentice Hall, Inc.

Lucas, H.C. Jr. (1974). Toward Creative Systems Design. Columbia University Press.

Myer, N.D., & Boone, M.E. (1989). The Information Edge. The Carswell Company.

Japan Information Processing Development Center (JIPDC). (1981). Users Guide for Information System (I). (in Japanese).

Utunomiya H., Ohashi H.,Takahashi I., & Miyagawa Y. (1993). The Evaluation of Information Systems. Journal of Information Processing Society of Japan. 96(90), 1-40. (in Japanese).

Strategic Use of Virtual Organization

Jinyoul Lee and Mike (Tae-In) Eom
Assistant Professor of MIS, Doctoral Student in MIS
School of Management
State University of New York at Binghamton
Binghamton, NY 13902-6015
Phone: 607-777-2440   Phone: 607-777-6734
Fax: 607-777-4422   Fax: 607-777-4422
jylee@binghamton.edu   bd25694@binghamton.edu

Bonn-Oh Kim
Associate Professor
Albers School of Business and Economics
Seattle University
Pigott Building, 900 Broadway
Seattle WA 98122
Phone: 206-296-2806
bkim@seattleu.edu

INTRODUCTION

In the modern business world, it is very common to use Internet technology to create e-businesses, implement e-commerce, etc. However, what is completely missing is the rethinking of the concepts of time and space in virtuality. What we are shaping in the Internet is essentially different from the conventional concepts of time and space after removing the constraints of time and space in business activities in the network. Without knowing this fact, all activities in virtual space will be redundant to what we have done in the real world, resulting in the Internet bubble economy.

This paper introduces 'desocialization', a new premise of timelessness and spacelessness in virtual organization. Our efforts now focus on imposing the strategic use and adoption of virtual organization. We must clearly state that the foundation of this study is to emphasize the roles of human players in business organizations. Therefore, virtual organization in this study is best described as a socio-technical product of the social activities of human players. With this newly defined virtual organization, it is fairly simple to re-construct strategies to manage virtual organization.

Most studies in strategy posit that the goal of strategy is to gain and sustain competitive advantages for a long haul (Ginsberg and Venkatraman, 1985). Accordingly, organizations with rare, valuable, and costly-to-imitate resources may enjoy a period of sustained competitive advantage in choosing and implementing their strategies and subsequently achieve extraordinary economic performance (c.f., Barney, 1997). Note that sustained competitive advantages denote something that cannot be displaced by strategic imitation by others or by substitutes. In this study, we introduce resource-based views to gain insight into the sustained competitive advantages in virtual organization. Thus, the purpose of this paper is to find the strategic use of virtual organizations in the context of the new premise, desocialization.

RESOURCE-BASED VIEW AND IT

Resources were formerly represented only by the organization's physical assets and capital (Barney, 1997). However, the term 'resources' has been broadened to an extent that encompasses all of the organization's assets (e.g., capabilities, competencies, organizational processes, organization attributes, information, and knowledge) that enable the organization to conceive and implement strategies that improve its efficiency and effectiveness (Daft, 1983). Hence, this study employs the latter perspective of resources, because virtual organization's resources are mainly focused on organizational processes with human players and formal and informal structures of organizations.

The resource-based view of organizational strategy has two key assertions: resource heterogeneity and resource immobility (Mata, et al., 1995). The organization is said to have sustained competitive advantages if it possesses unique resources (resource heterogeneity), and places a significant cost disadvantage to competitors when they attempt to obtain, develop, and use the resources (resource immobility). In other words, the organization has sustained competitive advantages, when it executes a unique (set of) strategy that requires resources and capabilities, which adds values and enforces competitors to face significant disadvantages in acquiring them (Mata, et al., 1995). Essentially, a strategy is based on the internal analysis of the organization in terms of resources and capabilities, and value, rareness, imitability, and organization of resources (VRIO) determine resource heterogeneity and immobility. Hence, the organization should be able to answer a series of questions to ensure a sustained competitive advantage: is a resource valuable?; is it heterogeneously distributed across competitors?; and is it imperfectly mobile? Then, a good understanding of the use of internal resources and capabilities may provide organizations direction in terms of implementing (a set of) strategy (e.g., Teng, Cheon, and Grover, 1995; Andreu and Ciborra, 1996; Duhan, Levy, and Powell, 2000).

What is the role of Information Technology (IT) in the process of implementing strategy? Many studies found that while implementing their strategy, organizations exploit IT as a valuable resource that captures sustained competitive advantages (e.g., Brown and Magill, 1994; Das, Zahra, and Warkentin, 1991; Karimi, Gupta, and Somers, 1996; Teng, Cheon, and Grover, 1995). For instance, among IT-related/generated resources, proprietary technology and technical/managerial IT skills are found to be potential sources of sustained competitive advantage for organizations (c.f., Mata, et al., 1995). This is in line with three strategic roles of IT proposed by Johnston and Carrico (1988). According to them, IT can be deployed strategically in three different roles: traditional, evolving, or integrated, which will be elaborated later.

In sum, resource-based views imply that IT is a potential source of sustained competitive advantages and creates idiosyncratic capabilities and definitive core competencies. We apply the resource-based view to virtual organizations in an attempt to seek more effective and strategic ways to operate the virtual organization. Specifically, the resource-based view of strategy is applied to the life cycle and dynamic view model of virtual organization proposed by Lee and Jayatilaka (2002).

DESOCIALIZATION - THE NEW PREMISE OF VIRTUAL ORGANIZATION

Many studies attempt to explain virtualization, but none of them gives us a complete explanation. Here, we discuss virtualization as *desocialization* due to its unique characteristics of timelessness and spacelessness. Since virtual organization started from the interconnected computer networks with high-speed data transmission, it removes distance boundaries and time constraints (c.f., Mowshowitz, 1997). Desocialization, in this context, means it becomes less frequent to interact with other human players in traditional settings. Thus desocialization does not mean individualism. Rather, it implies the alternative way of socialization, virtualization, in virtual space.

The most important fact of desocialization is the rapport between members of the organization. Unlike in traditional organization settings, members of virtual organizations build pure essence and trust. Biased impressions and thoughts are hardly exchanged due to the characteristics of open environment. Another aspect of desocialization is "emptying of organization" where emptying of information and knowledge has already occurred (Giddens 1984, 1990). Every effort is made to convert business data into information systems (IS). Thus IS generates information that helps in the emptying of information in organizations. IT made this phenomenon possible that leads to the separation of information from its organizations. Recently, knowledge, a supposedly higher format of information, is managed by knowledge management systems (KMS), another evidence of the separation of knowledge from its organizations. Because data, information and knowledge of organizations are emptying from their organizations, the separation of the organization from its four dimensional entity is implemented in the form of virtual organization (Giddens 1984,

1990). Desocialization will explain the life cycle of virtual organizations and the dynamic view of virtual organizations in terms of social norms, cultures, and values (Lee & Jayatilaka, 2002).

Life Cycle of Virtual Organization

Lee and Jayatilaka (2002) proposed that the three stages of virtual organizations emerged from metaphorical analysis in virtual organization literature. The first stage is the *formation* of the virtual organization (conceptualization). This is a stage where the organization comes into existence as a formal organization. After the initial formation, the organization goes through a process of *virtualization* where social mechanisms develop. Finally, the virtual organization goes through *expansion*. This theory imposes the meanings of ontology and epistemology of virtual organization. The metaphors of science and technology become the foundations for virtual organization and they set its properties – formation, ontological establishment. The virtual organization becomes a possibility due to technology. After the virtual organization is formed, the next step is to embellish it as a meaningful organization with the metaphors of culture and relationship – virtualization and epistemological establishment. Finally, it becomes a balanced virtual organization. Then conflicts occur within the organization to compete and survive among members that leads to the metaphor of war, expansion.

Dynamic View of Virtual Organization

We, as a society, possess enough IT capabilities to convert our imagination into a possible form – virtual organization – as we discussed in the previous section. The IT capabilities make the formation of virtual organizations feasible in practical use. Although IT plays a crucial role in the formation of today's virtual organization, there are other factors (which are conceptualized as virtualization and expansion) that interact with the concept of formation through IT. Therefore, we can take an alternative view of virtual organization. Lee and Jayatilaka (2002) proposed Figure 1 to show the dynamic view of virtual organization. It is a dynamic view because it proposes the relationship between each component of the virtual organization.

In Figure 1, there are two types of lines: continuous lines and discontinuous lines. Continuous lines represent structuration (Giddens, 1984) between each component. Structuration is divided into institutionalization interaction and engineering interaction (Barley and Tolbert, 1997). Line a is an engineering interaction because there is no human player (members of virtual organization) involved. Instead, designers or developers of virtual organization mainly participate in this process. Line b, c, d, and e are institutionalization interactions since these are structured by the interaction between human players and institutions (Giddens 1984). Line f, g, and h are neither institutionalization interactions nor engineering interactions. These are the special forms of human interests exchange (human interfering interaction) that explain why members of virtual organizations compete (line g and h) or cooperate (line f).

A virtual organization is not a mere technical foundation to substitute the real world counter part, but is an organization that exists in our ontological and epistemological recognitions. Its ontological meaning enforces membership of associated organizations and its epistemology enhances the social realization of being a member of virtual organizations. For instance, trust among members explains the new phenomenon of virtual organizations. Members of

virtual organizations build trust based on impersonal information/communications such as person's background, exchanges of emails, fax, postings, etc. This is not the lack of a socialization process but is an alternative way of compensating the lack of a traditional communication channel of trust building - virtualization. It is believed that not every virtual organization has similar ways of replacing traditional communication channels with desocialization. Virtualization implies that each virtual organization is expected to determine the most appropriate way of facilitating a desocialization process of its own. In addition, dissemination and sharing of information and knowledge (e.g., knowledge management) within virtual organizations can be another example. Virtual organization which is used to leverage the expertise of each diversely-located member can be a good example of desocialization. The above examples are good sources of sustainable competitive advantages explained in the next section.

In the next section, we emphasize on how effectively and efficiently virtual organizations can be operated in terms of utilizing or deploying resources to create a sustainable competitive advantage.

STRATEGIC USE OF VIRTUAL ORGANIZATION

Strategy and Life Cycle of Virtual Organization

As mentioned earlier, IT can be deployed strategically in three different roles: traditional, evolving, or integrated (Johnston & Carrico, 1988). In a traditional role, IT performs mere back office functions in a way that automates, maintains, and supports office routines, inventory control, and cost-saving administrative operations. IT has evolved to support organizational strategy. However, its competitive potential is not explicitly incorporated. That is, once a strategy is established, IT is deployed to champion that strategy so that the organization can achieve its intended goal. In an integrated role, IT is indispensable to organizational strategy. IT enables the organization to seek opportunities by creating new products and services, and to alter linkage with suppliers and customers. That is, organizational strategy is driven by IT and IT should be capable of changing the structure, processes, and scope of organizations in a way that facilitates the competitive use of IT. Figure 1 shows the relationship between strategic deployment of IT and the virtual organization life cycle.

A *formation* is a stage in which a virtual organization comes into existence as a formal organization. That is, a virtual organization is formulated and structured to accomplish the shared goal of participants (science). Organizations on virtual space become possible due to advanced information and communication technologies (technology). At the stage of formation, Virtual organizations deploy IT in a traditional role such as supporting and improving administration of member activities/tasks and decision-making. IT is deployed focusing on establishing linkages and operations between functions and members/participants (c.f., Johnston and Carrico, 1988). Hence, goals and technologies cannot be the source of sustained competitive advantage because they are not heterogeneous and immobile. At best, a virtual organization can achieve (temporary) competitive parity being the first to use technology (first-mover advantage). Eventually, competitors can catch up by accessing the necessary resources such as capital and technology.

Virtualization is a stage and process in which social mechanisms develop. Virtual organizations flourish by establishing their own culture (shared

Figure 1: Dynamic View of Virtual Organization

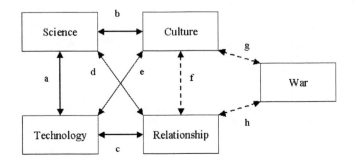

Figure 2: Strategic IT deployment and VO life cycle

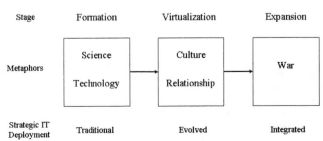

belief and value system), norms, and standard operating procedures (SOP), etc. Culture, norms, and SOPs are institutionalized within virtual organization through relationships. In other words, virtual organization at this stage defines and develops strategies at the corporate and business levels so that IT is evolved to facilitate, support, and/or capitalize on the strategies (c.f., Johnston and Carrico, 1988). This can be interpreted as an establishment of guidelines/directions that ensure building relationships among members, which is socially complex and ambiguous to figure out. That, in turn, leads to sustainable competitive advantages. A collaborative and cooperative working environment that results from uniquely embedded cultures in virtual organization can be another source of sustained competitive advantage.

Expansion is a stage in which a virtual organization is expected to develop and grow for the next level. Virtual organizations become organizations in which conflict and cooperation among members/participants become a part of organizational norms in an attempt to be a complete organization. In doing so, virtual organizations deploy IT in more proactive and integrated ways to better manage conflict and encourage cooperation. Integrated IT can provide a better communication channel and linkages among members/participants and ultimately establish new relationships and SOP in its newly defined boundary. In this regard, a virtual organization may continue to ensure the competitive use of IT to achieve benefits in managing conflict and cooperation (c.f., Johnston and Carrico, 1988). For instance, conflict has two opposite effects, depending on how it is managed. If managed better, it creates productive discussion and stimulates creative thinking (i.e., cognitive c-type conflict; Amason, et al., 1995). Otherwise, it becomes detrimental to the virtual organization by fostering cynicism and distrust among involved members (i.e., affective a-type conflict; Amason, et al., 1995). Well-managed c-type conflict (while minimizing the effect of a-type conflict) would be a key to the successful expansion of virtual organization. This c-type conflict could be achieved by facilitating frank communication and open consideration of different alternatives and opinions. The way of resolving/managing conflict (c-type conflict) can be a unique know-how that is heterogeneous and hard to imitate (immobile) tacit asset (c.f., Amason, et al., 1995).

Strategy and Dynamic View of Virtual Organization

As mentioned, resources and capabilities include an organization's financial, physical, individual, and capital attributes that enable the organization to coordinate and exploit its other resources to generate competitive advantages (c.f., Hitt and Jones, 1992; Stalk, Evans, and Shulman, 1992; Prahalad and Hamel, 1990). We investigate the dynamic view of virtual organization in terms of VRIO analysis.

Value of resources means the ability of the organization's resources and its capabilities to respond to external competition. In order for resources to be of value, they must enable the organization to seize opportunities or neutralize external threats. Engineering interaction, which happens between the goal of virtual organization and the instrument (technology), can be valuable, but not necessarily the source of sustained competitive advantages because it can be imitated and is easily obtainable (homogeneous and mobile). It is a pure interaction between the goal and the instrument that excludes members of the virtual organization. This interaction can either be technology-driven (by advanced communication technology) or goal-driven (by organizations in need of formulating the organization) in virtual space. For example, an organization can find a communication platform suitable for the concept of work-at-home in the virtual setting, or a network platform suitable for virtual organizations, which aims at leveraging expertise from each member/participant through the exchange and sharing of information and knowledge. However, institutionalization interaction increases the value of resources through structuration in terms of the use of systems and ease of use. As members of virtual organizations use the systems, they extend the knowledge of systems. As members use the system thoroughly, they build new communication channels between members, accept the new organizational structure, and trust each other, thereby making systems valuable.

Rareness measures the discrepancy between the organization and the others with regard to the possession of valuable resources and capabilities. As desocialization indicates, implementing Knowledge Management Systems (KMS) is necessary for virtual organizations. Without proper KMS, virtualization is meaningless because there is no way of sustaining core competencies. As members use systems, their expertise and knowledge is accumu-

Table 1: VRIO Analysis of Virtual Organization

Strategic IT Deployment	Interaction Type	VRIO Analysis	Activities	Heterogeneity	Immobility	Competitive Advantages
Traditional	Engineering	Value	Technology-imperative VO; Goal-driven VO	no	no	No sustained competitive advantages; temporary competitive parity at best
		Rareness	Knowledge Management	yes	yes	
		Imitability	Core competencies; SOPs	yes	no	
		Organization	Systems analysis & design	no	no	
Evolved	Institutionalization	Value	Use of systems; ease of use; trust	no	yes	Sustained competitive advantages on resource heterogeneity
		Rareness	Expertise; Upgraded systems; SOPs	yes	no	
		Imitability	Abstraction; Security	yes	no	
		Organization	KMS; DSS	yes	no	
Integrated	Human Interfering	Value	Communication channel; Organization boundaries; Trust	no	yes	Sustained competitive advantages on resource immobility
		Rareness	Culture; Interpersonal relationship; SOPs	no	yes	
		Imitability	Conflict management	yes	no	
		Organization	Autonomy; Empowerment	no	yes	

lated. In this stage, it is common to upgrade the systems to tune their business processes and this is a proof of structuration. With this system configuration, SOPs are built and internalized. The culture and working environment of virtual organizations are formed in this open, innovative, decentralized, or relationship/person-oriented manner. Simultaneously, interpersonal relationships commonly resulting from a large number of small decisions and actions among members/participants are constructed and can be hard to imitate.

Imitability assesses if other organizations without a particular resource face significant cost disadvantages in obtaining it compared to organizations that already possess it. Core competencies and SOPs initially provide hard-to-imitate business processes. Because core competencies and SOPs are embedded in the systems, members eventually acknowledge and attach symbolic meanings to the systems. Human interfering interactions manage conflicts and facilitate cooperation, institutionalized as norms and their consequences.

Organization measures if the organization is "organized" to fully exploit the competitive potential of its resources. From the initial systems analysis and design processes, a virtual organization is built. However, key success factors of systems lie in the use of KMS and decision support systems (DSS). Numerous components of the organization are relevant to this aspect, including organizational structure and policies such as a reporting system, a management control system, and bonus/compensation policies. When combined, these components[1] enable the organization to realize its full potential for competitive advantages (Amit and Schoemaker, 1993). Human interfering interaction is the special form of member exchange that explains why members of virtual organizations compete or cooperate to resolve the balance of power between them.

CONCLUSION

IT can be a critical resource to attain competitive advantages by providing information for better decision-making and implementing innovative new processes to create products and services (Teng, Cheon, and Grover, 1995). IT can also be deployed in a way that transforms internal resources and capabilities into an organizations' core competency. For instance, IT can improve work practices. The improvement can be shared, and embedded across the organization via communication, which in turn develops into core competencies. (i.e., organizations can be leveraged by making capabilities rare, valuable, difficult to imitate and with no strategically equivalent substitutes). In so doing, IT evolves from being a key resource to an enabler to achieve competitive advantage stemmed from core capabilities (Prahalad and Hamel, 1990; Andreu and Ciborra, 1996; Bharadwaj, 2000; Duhan, Levy, and Powell, 2000). Table 1 summarizes the strategic use of virtual organization. In the stage of engineering interaction, virtual organization barely creates competitive advantages, however, resource heterogeneity is added in institutionalization interaction and resource immobility is equipped during human interfering interaction.

This study explored how competitive advantages are gained in virtual organizations. Several benefits have been identified. Firstly, the new meaning of desocialization in this study re-illuminates the meaning of ontological and epistemological existence of virtual organization. Thus it resets the benefits, values, strategies, cultures, etc. to operate virtual organizations with their full potential, giving better positions than other competitors. Secondly, with the introduction of the framework of virtual organizations (Lee & Jayatilaka, 2002), it gives the sense of current positioning of virtual organizations. Figure 1 (life cycle) helps top managers recognize their current positions and the desirable positions. The dynamic view of virtual organization (Figure 2) shows the progress of its institutionalization processes. With its three different types of interactions – engineering, institutionalization, and human interfering interactions, top managers can organize its structure very efficiently and effectively to achieve its goals. Finally, top management can strategically deploy IT to focus heavily on the stages and dynamics of the virtual organization in ways that fully exploit its potential to create sustained competitive advantage. This in turn leads to organizational economic performance.

FOOTNOTES

[1] They are often called complementary resources (Barney, 1997)

REFERENCES

Amason, A., Thomson, K., Hochwarter, W., and Harrrison, A. (1995). Conflict: an important dimension in successful management teams. Organizational Dynamics. 24 (2). 20-35.

Amit, R. and Shoemaker, P. (1993). Strategic assets and organizational rent. Strategic Management Journal. 14 (1), 33-45.

Andreu, R. and Ciborra, C. (1996). Organisational learning and core capabilities development: the role of IT. Journal of Strategic Information Systems, 5 (2), 111-127.

Barley, Stephen R. and Tolbert, Pamela S. (1997). Institutionalization and Structuration: Studying the links between Action and Institution. Organization Studies, 18 (1). 93-117.

Barney, J. (1997). Gaining and sustaining competitive advantage, Boston, MA: Addison-Wesley Publishing Company, Inc.

Bharadwaj, A. (2000). A resource-based perspective on information technology capability and firm performance: an empirical investigation. MIS Quarterly. 24 (1). 169-196.

Daft, R. (1983). Organization Theory and Design, New York: West.

Duhan, S., Levy, M., and Powell, P. (2000). Information systems strategies in knowledge-based SMEs: the role of core competencies, European Journal of Information Systems. 10. 25-40.

Giddens, A. (1984). The constitution of society. Berkeley, CA: University of California Press.

Giddens, A. (1990). The Consequences of Modernity. Stanford, CA: Stanford University Press.

Hitt, C. and Jones, G. (1992). Strategic management theory: an integrated approach. Boston: Houghton Mifflin.

Johnston, H. and Carrico, S. (1988). Developing capabilities to use information strategically. MIS Quarterly. 12 (1), 37-48.

Lee, J. and Jayatilaka, B. (2002). The Discovery of Virtual Organization: Metaphorical Analysis. Working Paper.

Lee, J., Jayatilaka, B., and Kwok, R. (2002). Virtual Organization: Duality of Human Identities in Consciousness and Entity. Proceedings of Information Resources Management Association International Conference (IRMA). Seattle, WA.

Mata, F., Fuerst, W., and Barney, J. (1995). Information technology and sustained competitive advantage: a resource-based analysis. MIS Quarterly. 19 (4). 487-505.

Mowshowitz, A. (1994). Virtual Organization: A Vision of Management in the Information Age. The Information Society. 10. 267-288.

Mowshowitz, A. (1997). Virtual Organization. Communications of the ACM. 40 (9). 30-37.

Prahalad, C, and Hamel, G. (1990). The core competence of the organization. Harvard Business Review, May-June, 79-93.

Teng, J., Cheon, M., & Grover, V. (1991). Decisions to outsource information systems functions: testing a strategy-theoretic discrepancy model. Decision Sciences, 26 (1), 75-103.

Small Businesses and CRM: An Application Framework for a Light Approach

Leonardo Mangia
SET-Lab, University of Lecce,
via per Arnesano, 73100 Lecce, Italy, tel/fax +390832320229
leonardo.mangia@unile.it

ABSTRACT

For a long time the big companies have spoken about tools for CRM (Customer Relationship Management). Many projects in this theme have failed, maybe, because the technological aspect has taken over in comparison to the marketing one. The necessity to create good relation that gives satisfaction for the customer and income for the company is a strong need also in the small business. Besides, in relation to the big companies, the small companies can not even think about big investments in IT.

The main purpose of this paper is that to give an overview about an application framework for a CRM innovative tool, of simple implementation and maintenance for the small businesses. This paper describes the requirements, the functionalities and the important aspects that characterize this framework and the design approach to follow for its implementation. Other papers will illustrate, instead, in details the components of this framework, their design and implementation, the results that derive from the adoption of this framework in the existing reality.

1. INTRODUCTION AND BACKGROUND

All managers agree that the knowledge of the customer is one of the most important element of business success for a company that should work to obtain the loyalty of the actual customer and to make new ones [1]. This is true in the big companies, where it's always spoken about the attention for the customer, and also in the small business where the reduced dimensions can however work well, on a competitive market, with many customers with different needs.

In the small business, unlike of the large companies, the IT systems are many times bought from third parts, or in outsourcing, or in ASP mode and so it's not thought to create CRM project which, in IT side, try to change, in same part or completely, these systems [2]. So it's necessary for the small business to design and realize systems that collect the customer's information coming from different channels and by the various components of the IT system to obtain an integrate tool for the knowledgement and the completed management of the customer or prospect without changing the systems that already exist.

The CRM systems can give enormous advantages in the correct use of modern network technologies and in particular of Internet technology [3]. In fact with this technology, and with the consequently standardization of the communication protocols and interfaces, it's possible to offer the services of the CRM systems on the Internet channel to anyone who have a web-browser and is able to connect himself on Internet. So it's easy to understand that the CRM tool, by different operation and information viewing, is released directly to the customers and to the various operators that are interested in the customers relationship (for example call and contact center operator, financial promoters, and sales director).

Also the new release of the leader products has demonstrated that the CRM tool obtains a big advantage to incorporate the Internet tech-nology standard. In fact Siebel, for example, has distributed in '99 a CRM package completed based on Web and also Kana Corporation with its Kana e-service.

The tool is an essential component of a large strategy that transforms the management of the relation with the customer from a single component of the company, in most cases that are limited to a call center, to a really business process that also include new channels (web in all of them) and that always aim to develop constant and long term relation with the most important customers. Large investments in big IT architecture that promise an integrate CRM without the right attention to the marketing strategy and to a new organization are the principle aspects of big failure.

Thinking about light tools that easily and continually adapt themselves to the marketing strategies linking itself, without changes, the already existing IT modules can be the key to understand the CRM project management in IT aspects.

This is still true in the SB that, like the big company, feel the need of the CRM tool but hasn't economic capabilities to confront the large investments, neither the possibility to modify the existing IT.

So in the small business IT the design of a CRM tool can be referable to a design of a Web Application which, respectfully with the marketing strategy, allows a complete customer knowledge to all the operators involved in direct and indirect relation. For the design and the development of such Web Application it's useful to use an methodology and tools like HDM with its last development (W2000) [5], OOHDM and WebML [6].

2. THE CHARACTERISTICS OF THE FRAMEWORK

The actual and complex configuration of the CRM system is, like in ERP system, the synthesis of various evolutions. Understanding these evolutions, without thinking about the CRM system as a new revolution in IT, means to understand the effective function, its limits with other applications and the requirements of such system.

Already the traditional system of management of the interaction with the customers (for example, order management in a commercial company or the traditional desk system in the credit companies) have the customer entity, but the interaction with the customer is very low and so the customer's centric characteristic became less.

The first step toward the CRM, as interaction with the customer supported by the computer, are the sales force automation system (SFA).

Following the increase diffusion of the free telephone call numbers has multiplied the interaction by phone between customer and company creating a vast support center (known as call center or contact center) that offer operation and information services, help desk and complaint desk. This support centers sometimes substitute the traditional channel (for example a bank branch).

At the end, the web at the beginning of 1995 became the standard information channel for the public and for the customer and evolves in an interactive channel for the self service sale according to the Amazon case for the mass public (B2C commerce) and CISCO case for the business customers (B2B commerce).

The effect of Internet on the CRM world is very profound. Schematically, Internet has influenced the CRM world in two ways.

- Internet has transformed the interaction between the companies and the customer, in terms of quantity and quality of contacts forcing the CRM system to collect all these information to create a large view to the customer.
- Internet has raised the contractual power of the customer. The customers have now an easy access to a large quantity of information and transaction. This has develop the self service aspects of the customer forcing the companies to open a part of the IT system toward the outside.

These four application areas - Order Management, SFA, Call Center, Web – born as separated and independent automatization, have standardized themselves in applicative package, and, already at the end of 90's are CRM suites, following a similar evolution to the ERP. So in this way we have a global management architecture of the customers that became an essential competitive tool for all the typologies of the companies [7].

2.1. Operational CRM and Analytical CRM

With the preceding considerations in mind we can understand as an CRM architecture can be divide in two different parts:

Analytical CRM (or Customer Insight functionality):
- business event monitoring (ex. birthday day, nameday, loan maturity or stock maturity);
- Design, creation and monitor for marketing campaign;
- Tableau de Bord: summary of customer situation by a set of KPI (Key Performance Indicator) also in comparison to the budget;
- Business Intelligence: customer behaviour analysis to extract target that answer to a set of appropriate business requirements;
- Data Mining e Customer Scoring;

Operational CRM (or Customer Interaction functionality):
- Channel and campaign management
- management and development of the customer relation;
- product sales;
- Help desk and Customer Care;
- expert evidence and Contact Center;
- maintenance and enrichment of the customer information.

The inheritance of the Customer Care systems has made to concentrate, in some projects, the attention on the Customer Interaction functionalities. The companies, instead, feel the need to integrate the commercial functions inside the CRM to improve the ability to design and to plan new marketing actions and new products, to plan and to control the results of the marketing investments also in comparison to the budget. All of this because on the markets has became strong the need to push to increase the proper share and the customer loyalty especially in the moments of crisis when the attention to the aspects of commercial strategic planning is still greater: the good knowledge of the customer base and their correct demands represents not a negligible competitive advantage.

More and more therefore to the CRM systems it's not only in demand a support in the activities of interaction, through the various channels, with the customer (operational CRM /Customer Interaction) but also a support to explore well the customer base and their demands (analytical CRM /Customer Insight) [8].

This type of support is not only destined to the central marketing but also to the outskirts. In a credit company, for example, a sales division manager, or a bank branch director, or a simple advisor can have the necessity to extract a target of clients that answer to determined business requirements (possession or not possession of products, particular values on the behavioural indexes, etc.) to create a mini marketing campaign on a new product for his customers.

2.2. The requirements

According with the preceding considerations the requirements for an application framework destined to the design of a CRM system in a Small Business are the followings:

Adaptability

Easily the framework has to suit himself for the various and dynamics demands of the marketing strategies with low production costs and times. Nothing has to be tied up to hardly maintainable architectures.

Operational CRM and Analytical CRM

The framework has to integrate both the functionalities of operational CRM (direct customer interaction) and those of analytical CRM (functionalities that allows to plan and to control commercial activity on a set of customer).

Separation between CRM tools and legacy system

The framework has to foresee a separation between the functionalities of the CRM and the modules of the legacy system.
This separation is submitted:
- to a middleware layer when the purpose is to integrate real-time functionality in the CRM system (for example products trading on-line)
- to a CRM system local database, populated through ETL tools (Extraction, Transformation and Loading); this database memorizes the information ready for the analysis in the Analytical CRM functionalities.

This separation allows different times and ways to develop CRM system and legacy system.

Multi channel

The support to the multi channel is one of the most important characteristic for a innovative CRM system and it must be analysed under two different aspects:
- the CRM system use a multi channel architecture to contact in the best way the customer;
- a CRM system integrates all information coming from the different channels

Multi level

All the actors of the commercial hierarchy have to be able to use the CRM system; from operational marketing operators (for example advisors and financial promoters for a credit company) to strategic marketing operators (bank branch director, sales division director, marketing director). Different informative and operational view are able for every role.

Custom designed for every role

In the framework every logical resource (menu items, data, functionality, web links, ...) must be defined and connected to the user's role and/or to the customer's service model. This will allow to dynamically customize the application according to the role of the user login to the system or according to the type of the customer on which the user is operating (ex. retail customer or corporate customer).

Flexibility through Standards

The possibility for a CRM system to receive information from, or to provide information to, other tools (such as Data Mining tools, Campaign Management), should be based upon well-accepted technical standards (ex. XML).

3. THE FRAMEWORK

The architecture, in agreement to the preceding requisite, is represented in the Figure 1. Such architecture is composed from two main elements:
- a customer database;
- a web and palm-based front-end with the Operational CRM and the Analytical CRM functionalities.

Figure 1: The architecture of the application framework

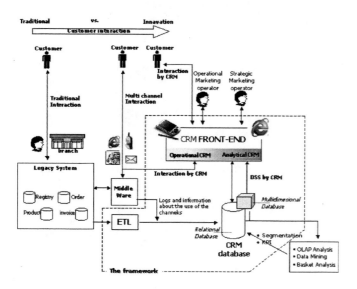

The framework doesn't include as main component the real-time connection to the legacy system: the purpose for CRM architecture is to support the complete knowledge of the customer with the scope to increase the company value proposition and not to support, with any cost, the direct interaction with the customer. Such connection can be inheritance of that is already realized for a direct customer interaction (ex. Internet banking or call center).

3.1. The Database.

The direct access from the CRM tools to the departmental database is sufficient in the Operational CRM functionalities

but not in Analytical CRM ones. So it is necessary that the suites of the CRM has its own database that collects all the information of the customers in a centric customer logic. It can be called Customer Database, or Data Mart Marketing, or other, but one thing is sure, it contains all the information that are needed for the functional side of the analytical CRM in a different logic of that of the legacy system or of the company data warehouse. It is, in fact, a database characterized from all the information that are needed to individualize the profile and the behaviour of the customer, either linked directly to the business (ex. possession and use on different channels of products of the company), or that linked indirectly to the business (ex. participation to commercial in-bound or out-bound campaigns with a relative outcome).

This database is supplied through ETL procedures registered at established frequency. The main area for the CRM database are: Users, Customer and Products.

Even though the logic of construction of the database remains the same, the data model diagram can change with regards to the specific company (ex. credit banks, multi utilities, training center).

As one part of the database is a relational database it is also characterized by a multidimensional part (OLAP cubes) that consents to have a tableau de bord (DSS that support the marketing decisions) on every level of hierarchy of operators that use CRM.

3.2. The front-end

The front-end is a Web portal application and an Palm Based application (to support as best possible the mobility of the sales agents) that gives availability to the operators the functionalities of the Operational CRM and that of the Analytical CRM.

This Web Application is designed and realized following the W2000 methodology. This methodology models the viewed and operated information differentiated by the users type but also the multi device delivering. This approach guarantees the usability, coherence in the presentation and in the navigation of the information, easy maintenance and

accuracy in the execution of operations/transactions on Internet technology.

This Web application is customisable according to the needs of the company.

Similar to the CRM database the front-end is characterized by three fundamental sections:
* user desktop,
* customer dashboard,
* product form.

At the moment of the users login the front-end presents the user's desktop. Such desktop visualises all the commercial information that interests the user (ex. news, to do list, appointments of the day, business alert). With the user's desktop it is possible to enter, according to his profile, to all the functions of the CRM.

These functions (ex. customer search, extraction of personalised targets, management targets of campaigns) help to reach to the selection of a customer.

After the selection of the customer there will appear the customer's dashboard. This form refers all the synthesis information (ex. KPI) and operational information (ex. anagrafic and owned products). From this form it is possible to recall all the operations on the customers (fix and carry out an appointment, the purchase of a new product, etc.). This dashboard opens automatically (through the use of the CTI technology – Computer Telephone Integration) to the call center operator, for example, when the customer telephones. This same customer form can be used with informative and operational views clearly distinct, even by the customer itself when the company wants to give the repeated functions to the customer by Internet for example.

The selection of a product gives way to the opening of the product form that has all the information on the product, and also on the same products that are in competition and, eventually, the use of the product on a customers. Figure 2 shows an example of a navigation between the three main parts of one possible front-end.

4. THE APPROACH

To collect, keep and run the information on an only one database, is the first step for the realisation of a CRM project; this is in perfect agreement with the centralization of the CRM database in the framework previously described. In this stage it is fundamental to be able to focus the informative requirements of the customer in this way to be able to value and decide for the best data model diagram to keep this informative property.

Figure 2: An example of a navigation between the three front-end parts

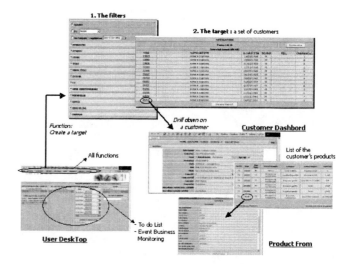

Once it's known the set of information that wants to be managed you need to understand which forms of informative systems are able to give us this information and with what frequency. For the aggregated information (heritage segment, risk index of the customer, etc.) you must provide to (in case they are not present in the legacy system or in the company data warehouse) local algorithms to the database (ex. store procedure) for their calculation.

Completed the information stage you must pass to the development of the front-end. The strategy to use is certainly an increasing development strategy. Once the general structure that wants to be given to the CRM portal is given you must insert slowly the functions of the Operational CRM and those of the Analytical CRM. These functions must respond perfectly to the marketing strategies of the company and in no way obstruct or modify the way of operating, re-define by any eventual and suitable projects of own change management orientated to the customer of the company. It is important to consider the possibility that at new releases of the functions on the CRM Web portal must correspond informative notes, days of formation in classes or tools of CBT (Computer Based Training) so to spread the learning between the operators of the CRM on instruments that they have in their disposition to reach the budget targets putting in practise commercial and marketing strategies of the company.

5. CONCLUSION

The application framework and the relative approach presented in this article has already been used in a middle sized bank (about 80 bank branch and 400 CRM operators). At the moment it is in a experimentation stage in a smaller bank (45 bank branch and 250 operators). These two experiences have put to evidence many good points in the approach presented and they have given a way to test a database model, a set of parametric procedures for its filling and a personalized front-end completing in this way, even in the technological details, the solution that has just been proposed.

More than adjusting the approach with experience, the present attentions are also turned to test possible database and front-end models for the multi-utility and commerce retail companies.

The approach, that has just been proposed, is addressed to SB but presents some aspects that can be followed also in CRM projects in large companies when the management want to follow a step by step development not letting the technological aspect prevail, with large investments in big architectures, on the marketing one.

6. REFERENCES.

[1] Thompson, B. (2001): "What is CRM", retrieved from the web at http://www.CRMguru.com, January 2001

[2] Gupta, B. (2002) "Success of Outsourcing Customer Relationship Management Functions: An Empirical Study", IRMA2002, Seattle, Washington, USA

[3] Dunn, J. and Varano, M. :"Leveraging Web-based Information System", Information System Management, Fall 99, 60 - 69

[4] Kos, A. J., Sockel, H. H. and Louis K. Falk (2001). Customer Relationship Management Opportunities. *Ohio CPA Journal, 60 (1)*

[5] V.Perrone, M. Maritati, P. Paolini, L. Baresi, F. Garzotto, L. Mainetti: "Hypermedia and Operation Design: Model, Notation and Tool Architecture". Official Deliverable D7 of the Europen Project UWA IST2000-25131.

[6] S. Ceri, P. Fraternali, A. Bongio: "Web Modeling Language (WebML): a modeling language for designing Web sites", to appear on Proc. Int. Conf. WWW9, Amsterdam, May 5 2000

[7] Thomas, P. and Rainer, A.: "Customer Relationship Management in the Pharmaceutical Industry" 34th Hawaii International Conference on System Sciences – 2001

[8] Jutla, D., Craig, J. and Bodorik, P. : "Enabling and Measuring Electronic Customer Relationship Management Readiness" 34th Hawaii International Conference on System Sciences – 2001.

Collaborative Engineering Communities - Architecture and Integration Approaches

Norbert Gronau
University of Oldenburg, Department of Computer Science
Chair of Business Information Systems
Escherweg 2, 26121 Oldenburg, Germany
Tel. +49 441 97 22 150, Fax +49 441 97 22 202
E-Mail gronau@wi-ol.de

ABSTRACT

Regarding the growing task distribution in the area of design and product development (engineering) the idea of communities gets more importance next to the creation of classical development partnerships in engineering. Communities are known as a new organizational kind for users of electronic communication media. The main aim of this paper is to transfer the idea of communities to engineering networks. Therefore an overview on creation, requirements and profit of collaborative engineering communities is provided. Also a possible integration is shown between collaborative engineering environments and enterprise resource planning systems.

Keywords: engineering, community, portal, collaboration, life cycle management, virtualization, ERP system, integration

1. THE CONCEPT OF A COLLABORATIVE ENGINEERING COMMUNITY

A collaborative engineering community will be understood as an organizational kind of collaboration between firms in the area of product development, which integrates all users and organizational units joining in the product life cycle and which provides all data, information and knowledge elements necessary for telecooperation.

Specially because participants of the late phases in the product life cycle like customers and consumers should be integrated (Richter and Krause 2001) common approaches for engineering networks (Puffaldt 2001) have to be widened.

The community approach presented here is different from commercial off-the-shelf product life cycle management (PLM) solutions, because these do not integrate consumers and vendor independent distributors. Available PLM systems like SAP R/3 or PTC's Windchill allow an access to data and functionality only for users directly participating on design, engineering, development, prototyping, manufacturing, assembly and quality assurance. Although it is possible to grant access to other participants in the process of product development, this is limited to users with the same role properties. Such role properties can be for instance abilities to work with engineering applications or a common understanding for the structure of the product. This is one reason that in the vendor independent truck market there is no direct access to engineering information although trucks are long living investment goods.

Also with the available PLM solutions it is not possible that consumers directly or through their distributors judge quality, lifetime and ergonomic properties of products or parts. This information has a strong influence on decisions concerning the further development of the product, but is actually only available in a derived matter (e.g. through spare part orders) or many times filtered and converted (e.g. through statistic census).

Main aim of the development of collaborative engineering communities is to integrate the groups of consumers and independent distributors in the design phase of product life cycle. The available PLM solutions are only partially appropriate to reach this goal.

Additionally representatives of the consumers are integrated in the process of engineering. The integration can be done using communities described in the following section.

2. COMMUNITIES AS A NEW FORM OF GROUP ORGANIZATION

Communities are one kind of loosely organized groups discussed in the field of internet economy. Lechner and Schmid (1999) define communities as an association of singles (agents) which share a common language, values and interests and which communicate with each other in roles using electronic media. The members of a community can share the same or complementary interests. Frequently the equality or complementarity of interests is only a question of the degree of abstraction or of the wording of the interests. In a society which produces a good all members have the same interest to produce the good and to maximize their individual profit. On the other hand the interest of agents which belong to exchange relations is complementary. In this case supplier and buyers of parts or customers and vendors can be distinguished. These groups define themselves nearly completely by a common interest in a special topic. Members of communities identify themselves with a nickname, but provide much more information about them, depending on the kind of community. Earlier communities are used only to communicate or to exchange information. Therefore only a few rules exist how to behave in a community. If a moderator exists who supervises the posting of articles of community members and who purges unallowed articles from the discussion area of the community, it can be supposed principally that a heterarchical coordination of topics discussed in the community exists (cf. Corsten and Goessinger 2001).

2.1 Typology of communities

Precursors of communities are newsgroups widely used in the internet and extranets in the area of business to business communications. Another kind of group creation different from communities are groups of persons which are summarized belonging to a common work context. Here groups are not individually generated but ordered by management or pretended by business processes. Frequently these groups are working together using internet technologies, too.

Communities and the other mentioned groups can be put in order into a grid which differentiates between the anonymity of the users and the mechanisms of interaction (fig. 1). The differentiation using mechanisms of interaction is described in the following section.

Fig. 1: Differentiation of groups using interaction and identity

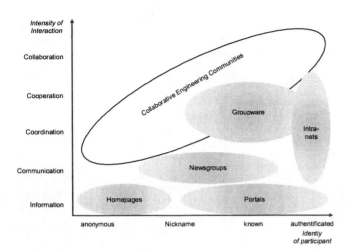

2.2 Mechanisms of interaction

A descriptive property of distributed systems is the concerted fulfillment of the task. Formal mechanisms of interaction with different degrees of intensity are communication, coordination, cooperation and collaboration. All mechanisms of interaction base on information exchange.

Communication

Communication is defined as the exchange of information. Information are defined as purpose or target oriented data in the field of business information systems. An equation of information and knowledge which can be found in literature sometimes is however wrong because knowledge needs human beings as knowledge bearers. Of course it is possible to change knowledge into information during explication (Gronau and Kalisch 2002).

Specially in engineering it can be seen that the task fulfillment does not become more efficient with access to information only. Orientation knowledge is rather necessary to be able to put the information in order, to value them and to determine their profit. Information does not contribute more to the design of task fulfillment in an distributed context than the exchange of data. Specially information does not structure or priorize task sequences.

Coordination

Mechanisms are needed to handle complex economic systems and to fulfill the system's purpose which provide a guiding influence on the system's elements and the processes running in the system. The main task of these mechanisms is named coordination. The aim of coordination is to integrate the actions of elements and subsystems to reach the goals of the whole system (Fischer 1994). Coordination has therefore an integrating and tuning function during task fulfillment in distributed systems. It does not describe the distribution of actions between elements of the system while working together on a common task.

Cooperation

Cooperation can be defined as the shared production of goods or services between distributed agents, organizational units or organizations (Schmidt 1997). If the cooperation is supported by appropriate media it is called telecooperation (Reichwald et.al. 2000). The degree of spatial or temporal distribution can be pictured using the so called „Anytime-Anyplace-Matrix" (OHara-Devereaux and Johansen 1994).

Collaboration

Communication, coordination and cooperation describe tasks which are fulfilled by single elements of distributed systems. A special case of

cooperation is the common execution of an action or a set of actions at the same object by distributed task agents. This shall be named as collaboration. Examples for collaboration in the field of engineering are the common distributed edition of a document or the common definition of product properties. The cooperation mechanism has to be supplemented with features securing a consistent, unified and reusable work result. With coordination the work tasks are fulfilled uniquely by task members 1,2 or 3 (persons or groups) which exchange start and end dates, task descriptions and take over conditions to assure a common work result. With collaboration an integration of work fulfillment takes place. The task members work together to fulfill the task to that a dissolution of partial actions is no longer possible. Therefore the information on tasks must be shared and supplemented by a version management, field and data set locks and different access rights..

3. ENGINEERING AND LIFECYCLE MANAGEMENT

The term engineering combines all actions in the process of product development, which are design, work planning, NC programming and the handing over of results to manufacturing and assembly. The life cycle management approach covers also the collection, processing and archiving of all product relevant data in the whole life cycle of a product. This life cycle begins at development and goes from manufacturing, productive use, collection of quality data during usage till the scrapping of the product concerning recycling aspects.

In this paper specially the integration of vendor independent distributors and consumers in the cycle of product life time is described. Main questions in this approach are the integration between separately working information systems and the generation of a feedback loop to the early stages of product life cycle. The business aim is to collect data only once and then use often to minimize change efforts. With a content oriented viewpoint it is the aim to use knowledge from the usage of a product during the development of its successor. This could not be done systematically in the past because a complete set of usage data was only available in special cases (e.g. with documentation obliged assets) and no suitable interface between the different systems collecting life cycle data existed.

4. REQUIREMENTS FOR COLLABORATIVE ENGINEERUNG COMMUNITIES

The further development from working groups in the field of engineering to communities is supported by the following trends:
- The rapidly growing bandwidth of the internet, specially of the WWW, now allows next to communication, information and cooperation a spatial distributed collaboration.
- Because of the increasing importance of life cycle management the communication with (possible) product users in all stages of the product life cycle becomes more important.
- Communities, actually used for exchange of opinions mostly are enriched with collaborative elements like the judgment of articles written by other community members or the signing of shares which are recommended in the community. It can be expected that new impacts for electronic business processes can be generated by the idea of communities (Truscheit 2000).
- The stronger systematization and segmentation of sourcing instead of manufacturing (establishing of system suppliers with far-reaching responsibility for product development) produce a heavy need for cooperation between firms.
- Because the market claims for shorter development times, customer requirements and consumer reactions are to be integrated more efficiently into the engineering process.

Collaborative engineering communities need a lot of organizational and technical flexibility to reach fast and efficient changes in the configuration of partners participating in the development phase and in the process models of product development with a low effort of hierarchical interventions, if possible.

Fig. 2: Proposal of an architecture for collaborative engineering communities

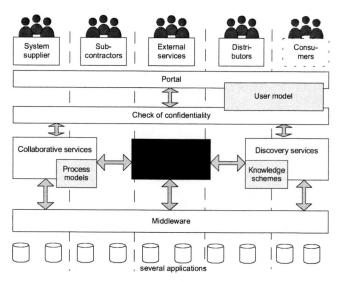

Their information systems architecture, which is defined as a planned cooperation of technical, organizational, cost-related and social aspects during development and usage of business information systems, needs a high ability of self-organizing and partial decision autonomy to be able to integrate new cooperative partners into the engineering community very fast. For that appropriate coordination mechanisms are to be delivered to differentiate between certain levels of confidentiality on the one hand and to develop a common understanding (contents and semantics) for facts on the other hand.

5. PROPOSAL FOR AN ARCHITECTURE

Basing on the considerations in the past sections an architectural model for collaborative engineering communities was developed (fig. 2).

Different groups of users and other participants in the engineering process form the collaborative engineering community. As a rough classification of the different roles and perspectives the following scheme can be used:

- *System supplier*, which are responsible also for development and cost against a contract awarder. A system supplier typically is responsible for the delivery of complete modules. He manufactures these modules in cooperation with his contract awarder and other supplier (Luczak and Eversheim 1999)
- *Subcontractors*, which deliver material and parts defined by the contract awarder, but are not system supplier.
- *External services*, which supervise the project course (in the area of construction known as project steerer). They are less interested in technical parameters of material and parts but more interested in parameters of the process model (dates, budgets, capacities).
- *Distributors*, which sell the product to the final customers and which are first contact for product properties (during purchasing and if quality defects are occurring)
- *Consumers*, which play a part in some stages of the process or are related to some components and which are not covered by one of the other roles.

5.1 Description of the architectural building blocks

It was detected as useful to grant access for all types of users by a common portal. A portal not only indicates the unified access but at the collaborative engineering community it also delivers the personalization after an appropriate authentication.

The results of personalization and authentication determine the possibilities for the members to move inside of the collaborative engineering community. The results are represented by the view models in the user model. Here it is defined, which information is accessible by a certain group member in a certain role. The accessibility is defined for objects, process steps and competitive relevance. A user in the role of a system supplier sees these parts in the object area, which are delivered by himself and surrounding parts to be able to check assemblies.

In the process area the accessibility of certain process information is defined. The role external service perhaps does not need information from the usage stage of product life cycle. On the other hand user groups as cooperation partner should only be able to see product properties from the stage of product definition and then be integrated highly into the results of field surveys.

Crosswise to these aspect definitions basing on objects or process stages the degree of confidentiality is defined for sets of information. The resulting view of users on the collaborative engineering community is determined by the totality of restrictions and releases.

A block layer between portal and system functionality supervises during all activities of the users, that the maximum valid view is not exceeded. To log accesses and access trials and to canal accesses the block layer is formed as a separate software module. This makes the protection easier against security holes.

On the next layer of the architectural model of the collaborative engineering community services are provided. It is stated that the most users need the discovery services, which allow a supply with information or reports about process steps or objects. In the discovery services a realization is possible of

- search engines
- information warehouse technologies
- life time tracing systems (Anderl 2000)

and other on digital past data basing information procurement tasks. As a supporting element the discovery services use a meta model of the information sources available in the community, which is named as a collection of knowledge schemes. This kind of meta modeling can be compared with the representation of repositories in data warehouses (Mertens and Wieczorrek 2000) and contains:

- descriptions of knowledge sources
- time data (dates of creation and of input into the system)
- source descriptions
- classifications
- key words
- format information and
- links between the knowledge sources

The collaborative services provide tools for the joint distributed design and engineering. Today available systems allow joint viewing, digital mockup and joint editing. These functions will be enlarged with rising bandwidth on the internet. Process models are used here in the same function as the knowledge schemes of the discovery services.

A central element to assure a common understanding between different groups of users is the usage of a common world of terminology. Independent term contexts are defined in the different user groups at first, because special and local networks of terms and meanings are used. In the process of communication with other user groups terms are interpreted in a different manner, which impairs the efficiency of communication and any collaboration based on that communication. A solution for this problem is the usage of ontologies (Maedche 2001). This task is fulfilled from a component called ontology service. A proposed task of the ontology service is the standardization of different term usage and the generation of hints if not solvable conflicts occur. Then a manual solution of the problem is necessary to extend the taxonomic knowledge.

The access to the applications reachable via the collaborative engineering community is delivered by a middleware building block. The middleware provides appropriate functions or applications for every user according to the user model with the permitted set of data and information. Possible applications are

- business administration and information systems (Gronau 1999)
- production engineering tools
- product data management systems and

Tab. 1: Collaborative functions of common CAD systems (Ibelings 2001)

System	Manufacturer/ Distributor	collaborative functions
CATIA V4 R. 2.4	Systemes Dassault	File-Sharing and Locking, Web Conferences
One Space Version 5a	CoCreate	Virtual real time conference room
SwissPrecision Manager	Precisionsoft	Accesses during release process
DIG-CAD 4.0	LLH Software	Joint Viewing
Windchill	Parametric Technology	Visualization in the Internet
SolidWorks 2001	SolidTeam	Concurrent Environment
CADRA 11.5	SofTech	Project management, right management for groups and users
Xbrioso	Tecoplan	Virtual project room
Unigraphics V 17	Unigraphics Solutions	Viewing and Application Sharing
Solid Edge	Unigraphics Solutions	Automatic messaging mechanism

- CAD systems

CAD systems are a possible class of applications because they support collaborative work at least a little (tab. 1).

5.2 Presentation of a process example

A process example for the use of a collaborative engineering community is described as following:

The consumer, a customer of a truck rental company, wants to criticize the operating lever of the windshield wiper. Using the portal he gets access with the role „occasional user of the product". From the provided truck models he chooses that one he rented. Three-dimensional views and other product defining properties are gathered from the product data management or ERP system of the truck manufacturer, as far as the information is released for his role. In this process it is possible to state that the user's critic does not only concern one truck model but a whole family of trucks.

The consumer chooses one from a list of released aspects and is also able to describe the part he wants to criticize. The ontology service now tries to create a corresponding link between the description of the user and the part name in the manufacturer's ERP system. This can be done interactively if no clear identification is possible.

Now the consumer enters his text about the insufficient usability of the part and stores his article. If he is a registered user of the platform he can see and judge entries of other users. If the manufacturer has defined and stored design targets and if they are released for his role the user can read these targets, too.

This process example shows how life cycle management can be enriched by information from the consumers view, while permanently the product model of the manufacturer is used. Additionally it is possible to gain relevant information for the customer relationship management.

6. CONCLUSIONS

One of the critical success factors for the integration of collaborative engineering communities into life cycle management is the availability and accessibility not only of data but also of related knowledge. One possible solution path could be the integration of specialized knowledge management systems, which link knowledge bases with product data management systems. Another key task will be the integration of the heterogeneous data stocks. Middleware solutions seem to be able to realize this in the framework of a collaborative engineering community.

REFERENCES

Anderl, R., Daum, B., John, H.: From product data management to the management of product life cycle (in German) ProduktDatenManagement 1 (2000) 2, S. 10-15

Borghoff, U., Schlichter, J.: Computer Supported Cooperative Work. An introduction in distributed applications (in German). 2nd edition Berlin Heidelberg New York 1998

Corsten, H., Gössinger, R.: Order decomposition and allocation in company networks (in German). PPS Management 6 (2001) 1, pp. 35-41

Fischer, T.: Coordination of business control tasks in a framework of integrated enterprise information systems (in German). Renningen 1994

Gronau, N.: Management of manufacturing and logistics with SAP R/3. 3rd edition München Wien 1999

Gronau, N., Kalisch, A. (2002). Knowledge Content Management System - A Framework integrating Content Management and Knowledge Management. Arabnia. H. et. al. (Eds.): Proc. of the International Conference on Information and Knowledge Engineering (IKE'02), Las Vegas 2002, pp. 150 - 153

Ibelings, I.: Collaborative CAD Systems (in German). Industrie Management 17 (2001) 3, pp. 53-61

Kersten, W., Kern, E.-M.: Collaborative Engineering – Fiction or reality (in German)? In: Dangelmaier, W. u.a. (Eds.): Models in E-business. Paderborn 2002, pp. 289-299

Lechner, U., Schmid, B. et al: A reference model for communities and media (in German) - Case Study Amazon.com. In: Englien, M.; Homann, J. (Eds.): Communities in New Media (GeNeMe99),. Lohmar 1999, pp. 125-150

Lindemann, U., Glander, M., Grundwald, S., Reicheneder, J., Stetter, R., Zanner, S.: Flexible integration of product development and assembly planning (in German). Industrie Management 16 (2000) 1, pp. 23-27

Luczak, H., Eversheim, W. (Eds.): Telecooperation. Industrial applications in product development (in German). Berlin Heidelberg u.a. 1999

Mertens, P., Wieczorrek, H.W.: Data X Strategies. Data Warehouse, Data Mining and operational systems in practice (in German). Berlin Heidelberg New York 2000

Maedche, A., Staab, S., Studer, R.: Ontologies (in German). Wirtschaftsinformatik 43 (2001) 4, S. 393 – 395

OHara-Devereaux, M., Johansen, R.: Global Work. Bridging Distance, Culture and Time. San Francisco 1994

Puffaldt, J.: Cooperative product development (in German). Industrie Management 17 (2001) 3, S. 25-28

Reichwald, R., Moeslein, K., Sachebacher, H., Englberger, H.: Telecooperation. Distributed types of work and organization (in German). 2nd edition Berlin Heidelberg New York 2000

Richter, K., Krause, L.: Usage of product data management as key technology for E-business (in German). Industrie Management 17 (2001) 3, S. 81-85

Schmidt, D.O.: Company cooperations in Germany. Prerequisites and distribution (in German). Wiesbaden 1997

Truscheit, A.: Virtual social Networks: Communities in Cyberspace (in German). In: Schneidewind, U. u.a. (Eds.): Sustainable Information society. Analysis and recommendations for design from management and organizational viewpoint. Marburg 2000

Benefit Realisation and ERP Systems

Paul Hawking

School of Information Systems, Victoria University

MMC 14428, Victoria University of Technology, Melbourne, 8001

Victoria, Australia , Tel: 61 03 96884332, Fax: 61 03 96885024, Paul.hawking@vu.edu.au

ABSTRACT

The global ERP industry blossomed in the 1990's automating back office operations and in the new century moves have been made to introduce a "second and third wave" of functionality in ERP systems to facilitate benefit realisation. Research up to date has been limited in respect to these "second wave" implementations. The benefits and barriers to attaining benefits are presented with analysis of the extent that financial metrics are used to measure benefit attainment in core SAP systems. The main findings of the paper indicate that many ERP implementations do not attain expected benefits and the main reason for this lack of attainment are people related issues namely change management.

INTRODUCTION

ERP sales now represent a significant proportion of total outlays by business on information technology infrastructure. A recent survey of 800 U.S. companies showed that almost half of these companies had installed an ERP system and that these systems were commanding 43% of the company's application budgets (Carlino, 1999a). The global market for ERP software, which was $16.6 billion in 1998, is expected to have a compound annual growth rate of 32%, reaching more than $66 billion in sales by 2003 (Carlino, 1999b) and is estimated to have had 300 billion spent over the last decade (Carlino, 2000). More recent estimates show a slowing in demand for core ERP systems with an increasing emphasis on upgrades and extended functionality "bolted on" to existing systems especially with a move towards e-business. Companies are focussing on benefit realisation. This research focuses on the expected benefits how, they are measured and the barriers preventing this realisation.

ERP Market Penetration

Market penetration of ERP systems varies considerably from industry to industry. A recent report by Computer Economics Inc. stated that 76% of manufacturers, 35% of insurance and health care companies, and 24% of Federal Government agencies already have an ERP system or are in the process of installing one (Stedman, 1999). Over 60% of the U.S. Fortune 1000 companies are using ERP systems and this has resulted in the major ERP vendors targeting small to medium enterprises (SME's, also known as SMB's) to generate new sales (Stein, 1999; Piturro, 1999). This has seen the development of new implementation methodologies and modifications of ERP systems to reduce implementation complexity and the associated costs. Vendors are also extending beyond their core ERP systems to support web-based applications, e-commerce, and customer-relationship management.

The 5 leading ERP vendors (SAP, Oracle, Peoplesoft, JD Edwards, and Baan), account for 62% percent of the total ERP market revenue (Carlino, 1999b). SAP is the largest ERP software vendor with approximately 39% market share. The company has approximately 27,800 employees and 17,500 customers in 110 countries representing 44,500 installations (SAP, 2002)

SAP Australasia

In the Australasian region there are 387 SAP customers. Of these, 329 were based in Australia and 58 in New Zealand. Business Review Weekly (2000) annually produces the *BRW1000*, which is a ranking by revenue of the largest listed, private, government and foreign enterprises operating in Australia. Using the BRW1000 it was ascertained that SAP had the following market penetration:
- The largest 5 employers use SAP
- 3 out of top 5 private companies
- 4 out of top 5 public companies
- 2 out of top 3 building materials companies
- 2 of top 3 diversified resources companies
- 2 of top 3 diversified industrials companies
- 2 out of top 3 energy companies
- 3 out of top 5 mining companies

The managing director (Bennett, 2002) of SAP Australia was quoted recently:

> "What we're seeing here now is that Australian ... businesses are gradually and steadily rolling out IT systems that will enable them to take advantage of and grab opportunities when the global economy bounces back."

He was reporting on the expansion of mySAP.com licenses in the Asia-Pacific region and the move to "second wave" products. MySAP.com is a new term used to describe SAP's range of products. Many companies initially implemented their ERP systems to cope with the Y2K issues and replace poor exiting and disparate systems (Deliotte 1999, Krumwiede et al, 2000). Once companies had stabilized their ERP implementation they then started looking for avenues whereby they leverage their investment to gain a competitive advantage. This was usually achieved by business process optimization, implementing added core ERP functionality, and or by implementing add on products such as data warehousing, customer relationship management, advanced planner and optimizer, and e-business functionality. This expansion of the existing core R/3 system with either third party "bolt-on" products or SAP new products is referred to as "second wave" (Deliotte 1999). Along with the move to added functionality, SAP Australia moved to restructure their internal business units to move the focus from the product to the customer, which seems to take account of the need to build the business through customer retention and value adding rather than plumbing new markets (Bennett, 2001). One additional market being explored is the small to medium enterprise (SME) market, with SAP launching two new solutions to cater for this (Bennett, 2001).. In Australia, there are 10,000 small-medium enterprises with the subsidiaries of multi-nationals constituting 40% of the SME's

SAP Australasia Implementations

From 1989 to July 2000, 387 customers implemented or were in the process of implementing SAP software. This does not include update or upgrade implementations. Nolan and Norton (2000) grouped implementations into levels of maturity. The data indicates that approximately 65% of companies have had their ERP systems for at least two years. They argued that when evaluating costs of an ERP implementation, the company's previous experience with ERP systems should be considered. Their maturity classifications were:
- Beginning – implemented SAP in the past 12 months,
- Consolidating – implemented SAP between 1 and 3 years,
- Mature – implemented SAP for more than 3 years.

Applying the maturity classification to the above data indicates that the majority of Australasian companies are in the Consolidating stage (58.4%) then followed by the Mature phase (37.2%) and the

Beginning phase (11.6%). It could be argued that companies in the consolidating and Mature phases are those most likely to be involved in second wave implementations. Therefore it would be expected to see an increase in "second wave" products post 2001 as the majority of ERP implementations occurred pre 2000.

SAP's "second wave" products include Business Information Warehouse (BW), Knowledge Warehouse (KW), Strategic Enterprise Management (SEM), Customer Relationship Management (CRM) and Advanced Planner and Optimisation (APO). SAP recently has grouped these "second wave" products and its ERP system (R/3) with added e-Commerce functionality (Workplace/Portal and Marketplace) and referred to it as mySAP.com. Table 1 reinforces the premise that a significant increase in the implementation of "second wave" products as companies move into the consolidating and mature phases.

Table 1. Second wave Implementations by Year (Bennett, 2001)

Software	Pre 2001 Implementations	Live 2001 Implementations	% Increase	KeyMarket
R/3	506	na		All
CRM	19	69	363%	AU/NZ
eProc	25	56	224%	AU/JP/SG
BW	168	263	156%	AU/JP
APO	32	73	228%	AU/NZ
Workplace	44	122	277%	AU/Korea

ERP Benefits & Barriers

In order to study the benefits and barriers of ERP implementations a previous Australian study by Deloitte's Consulting (1999) was used to set the benchmark categories of benefits and barriers. Deloittes also categorised the barriers as being People (P), Business Process (Pr) or Technology (T) focussed (See Table 2). These categories formed the basis for the survey sent to respondents.

Table 2. ERP Benefits & Barriers (Deloitte, 1999)

R/3 Benefits	R/3 Barrier	Focus
Financial Cycle Close Reduction	Lack of Discipline	P
Productivity Improvements	Lack of Change Management	P
Procurement Cost Reduction	Inadequate Training	P
Order Management Improvements	Poor Reporting Procedures	T
On Time Delivery Improvements	Inadequate Process Engineering	PR
Personnel Reductions	Misplaced Benefit Ownership	P
IT Cost Reduction	Inadequate Internal Staff	P
Cash Management Improvement	Poor Prioritisation of Resources	T
Inventory Reductions	Poor Software Functionality	T
Maintenance Reduction	Inadequate Ongoing Support	T
Transportation/Logistics Reduction	Poor Business Performance	PR
Revenue/Profit Increase	Under Performed Project Team	P
	Poor Application Management	T
	Upgrades Performed poorly	T

RESEARCH QUESTIONS

The primary objective of the study was to survey a range of information system professionals and seek responses to issues including the current & historical SAP implementation details and to further ascertain the penetration of "second wave" products together with the degree by which organisations use metrics for their core and "second wave" systems. The first part of the study as presented in this paper provides an analysis of the views of 48 IS professionals. More specifically the research questions of the paper are:

RQ1.   What are the expected versus actual benefits of ERP systems?
RQ2.   What are barriers to attainment of ERP benefits?
RQ3.   What performance metrics are used to analyse ERP products?

METHODOLOGY

The research questions were studied by gathering data in a survey of those information system professionals listed as working within a cross-

section of the Australian marketplace. The SAP Australian User Group(SAUG) commissioned this research to provide added value to their members and to contribute to the ERP research base in Australia. The user group lists many of Australia's leading companies as its members and represents approximately 50% of the SAP customers. The key contact details for each member company (166) were provided to the researchers for the purpose of this study. The initial survey instrument was developed based on the fields that were identified in the literature and used email and Web based survey as the delivery platform. Several studies (Stanton & Rogelberg, 2001; Dillman, 1998; Comley, 1996; Mehta & Sivadas, 1995) have compared email and Web based survey methods versus mail information collection methods and have proposed that email surveys compared favourably with the postal methods in the areas of cost, speed, quality and response rate. The use of an email directing the respondent to a web site was used with the initial web direction being sent to 166 user group members. It was necessary to preen the email address book to remove and amend email that had bounced back.

RESULTS

Survey Instrument

The survey instrument had 30 questions covering four areas; demographics, expected versus actual benefits, barriers to benefit attainment and financial metrics used to measure benefits. Closed questions were used with Yes/No and seven point Likert scale responses. Open-ended questions sought responses from the cohort allowing for qualitative data to be collected. The original email listing contained 166 potential respondents. A number of emails were undeliverable due to members of the cohort moving positions, having incorrect email addresses, having changed email addresses or automatic out-of-office responses. There were 2 unusable replies leaving a total of 48 usable responses out of 151 possible respondents. The overall response rate once removing the undeliverable addresses was 31%.

Demographics

Responses were received from 48 IS professionals and the data was analysed to present position, organisation type, organisation size, revenue and number of SAP users. Responses for the whole cohort are presented in Table 3. Respondents were predominantly high in the organisational structure being either an IS or business manager. They were mainly from a spread of organisations that spanned most sectors of the Australian marketplace. Respondents came from all spectrums of business as determined by organisation spend.

Table 3. Demographic Breakdown Of Respondents (N=48)

Position	No	Organisation type	No	Organisation	No
Revenue($AUDmillion)		No			
CIO	6	Public Service	11	Large(>1000)	21
IT Manager	10	Manufacturing	8	Large-Med(750-1000)	8
Support &					
Services Manager	8	Utility	7	Med-Large(500-749)	3
SAP Manager	8	Mining Oil & Gas	6	Medium(250-499)	10
Business Manager	14	Services	4	Small(<250)	6
IT Development	2	Education	2		
		Chemicals	1		
		Other	9		
		Number FTEs	**No.**	**Number SAP Users**	**No.**
		>1001	33	>501	25
		502-1000	3	251-500	8
		101-500	8	101-250	8
		<100	1	<100	7
Total	48	Total	48	Total	48

R/3 Profile

The R/3 profile was sought from the sample. As would be expected many organisations had a 3.x version as their initial implementation but

Graph 1. Core R/3 System Profile (N=48)

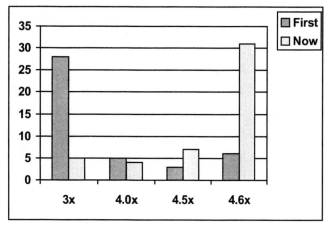

have upgraded to the later 4.6 version. The 4.6 version has the increased functionality to introduce second wave "e" functionality and these organisations are well positioned to move to these new applications. Graph 1. shows the implementation histories.

Expected versus Actual Benefits

Respondents were asked to rate on a seven point likert scale the expected benefits of their R/3 systems. They were further asked to rate the actual benefits obtained. The results are displayed in Table 4. Financial Cycle was rated highest (5.2) with Revenue Increase rated lowest (3.2). Several time based (On Time Delivery 4.4) or productivity based (Order Management 4.4) benefits were rated highly. Comparing the expected versus actual benefits fell into two distinct groups; differences of less than 1 likert point and difference of greater than one likert point (Table 4). IT Costs seem to be the most under-performed benefits with a difference of 1.5.

Table 4. Expected Vs Actual Benefits (N=48)

R/3 Benefits	Expected	Actual	Difference
Financial Cycle Close Reduction	5.2	4.6	0.6
Productivity Improvements	4.9	3.8	1.1
Procurement Cost Reduction	4.8	3.8	1.0
Order Management Improvements	4.4	3.8	0.6
On Time Delivery Improvements	4.4	3.1	1.3
Personnel Reductions	4.0	2.7	1.3
IT Cost Reduction	4.1	2.6	1.5
Cash Management Improvement	3.9	3.2	0.7
Inventory Reductions	3.9	3.1	0.8
Maintenance Reduction	3.9	2.8	1.1
Transportation/Logistics Reduction	3.5	2.8	0.7
Revenue/Profit Increase	3.2	2.5	0.7

Core R/3 Barriers

Respondents were asked to rate on a seven point likert scale the expected barriers of their R/3 systems. AS mentioned previously the Deloitte categories were used to specify the nature of the barriers and these are shown in Table 6. People based barriers seem to dominate; Discipline (4.4), Change management (4.3), Training (4.2) and Internal Staff (3.3) all show that the implementation are firstly people projects. Technical based barriers were rated lower; Software (2.9), Upgrades (1.6) and Application (2.2). This would show that technical issues are not insurmountable and are really well supported.

Table 6. Current R/3 Obstacles/Barriers (N=48)

Current R/3 Barrier/Obstacle	Mean	Deloitte Category
Lack of Discipline	4.4	P
Lack of Change Management	4.3	P
Inadequate Training	4.2	P
Poor Reporting Procedures	4.2	PR
Inadequate Process Engineering	3.9	PR
Misplaced Benefit Ownership	3.8	P
Inadequate Internal Staff	3.3	P
Poor Prioritisation of Resources	3.0	T
Poor Software Functionality	2.9	T
Inadequate Ongoing Support	2.7	T
Poor Business Performance	2.4	PR
Under Performed Project Team	2.3	P
Poor Application Management	2.2	T
Upgrades Performed poorly	1.6	T

P = People, PR = Process, T = Technology

Financial Performance Measures

It was considered important that for companies need to move towards benefits realisation then there should be some form of assessment of the current level of benefits from their ERP system. The respondents were asked to indicate if their organisation had formal financial measures for their core R/3 systems. The majority (72%) of the organisational had no formal ROI in place. Further, the majority of organisations had no ROI (52%) or break-even (64%) planned or estimated. The financial responses are in Table 7.

Table 7. Financial Performance Data (N=48)

Formal ROI In-Place	%	Time-Frame	ROI Planned %	Break-Even Estimated %
No	72	Less 2 Years	5	10
Yes	28	2-5 Years	32	16
		Greater 5 Years	10	10
		None Planned	53	64

DISCUSSION

What are the expected versus actual benefits of core R/3 systems?

The SAP ERP system provides a range of tangible and intangible benefits to companies as identified by the sample. A respondent commented on the ability of SAP to provide a platform for future business operations,
"SAP benefits - consolidation of IT systems, a common view (or "a single truth") as data is common to all".

Additionally another respondent commented,
"SAP provides the framework to add required additional functionality and expand its user base with future business expansion".

The benefit companies most expected to achieve with their current implementation was reduction in the financial cycle close. This may have been reflective of the time of year the survey was conducted in relation to the end of the financial year. Previous research (Deliotte, 1999) indicated that there is a discrepancy between what companies expect to achieve and what they actually achieve with their ERP implementations. Companies usually realise a number of unexpected benefits associated with improvements in performance. These maybe negated due to the maturity of Australian companies and the associated experience of using their ERP system and the availability of industry benchmarks. A respondent commented that benefit analysis was difficult when strategic benefits are difficult to categorise and calculate. The respondent indicated that his organisation had won contracts based "partly" upon the fact that the IT core systems was SAP. The trouble was that the "partly" was difficult to calculate. This difficulty with strategic benefits has an impact on the ROI type cost benefit analysis. Another respondent to the survey also commented on this strategic benefit,

The largest gap between expected and realised benefits was that of a reduction in IT costs. Research (Deloitte, 1999) has shown that this failure of ERP systems to live up to this expectation is not limited to any one ERP vendor.

What are barriers to attainment of ERP benefits?

The respondents indicated that obstacles that limited benefit attainment for their ERP implementation had little to do with lack of software functionality or major technical issues, but were related to people issues. Five of the top seven obstacles could be classified as people issues. It interesting to note that two of the top three issues are related to change management. A respondent touched upon this point,

"... *additionally the culture was not geared for the solution when it was rolled out. Change Management was poorly handled and this showed in user acceptance of the system*".

A number of the respondents commented on the lack of management support and understanding,

"....*Insufficient management awareness of SAP capability, leading to sub-optimal use of SAP in the business*".

"*A big part of our issue was lack of management support for implementation due to changes in mgmt team and direction mid-stream*".

Another respondent commented on the inability of the organisation to properly integrate the ERP with current business operations,

"Like many public sector organisations we have implemented SAP and only use a fraction of the functionality without attempting to integrate with operational systems. This has resulted in the cost and effort required for an ERP when we only have an accounting system".

What performance metrics are used to analyse core SAP and second wave products?

The study indicated that the majority (73%) of the sampled companies had no formal measures in place to measure return on investment from their ERP implementation. However when companies were asked to estimate the time frame for ROI twenty-one companies responded. Of these 81% expected a ROI in less than five years. Respondents indicated that the lack of formal ROI in place in organisations can have several explanations. Older implementations may have had ROIs done initially but once the implementation consultants/team moved on the ROI was not a priority task. There was also some comment how an upcoming upgrade or the adoption of added functionality means that the R/3 system never stands still long enough to be measured.

CONCLUSION

Many companies implemented an ERP system to address a number of immediate problems such as Y2K and disparate or poor systems. These same companies have now moved beyond this initial implementation and are looking for ways to optimise their investment. This includes extending the implemented functionality of their ERP system and or implementing new components such as data warehousing, customer relationship management or advanced planning and optimisation. The purpose of this research was to present the findings of a research project investigating the nature of ERP implementations in Australia, the benefits and barriers in implementation, the measures for measuring the investment in the ERP system and the push into "second wave" applications. Australian SAP customers have reached a level of maturity in their use of ERP systems. First implementations have been in-place between 2-4 year with the majority of the sample undertaken at least one major upgrade. Further, a significant number have implemented "second wave" functionality with at least one of the mySAP component. The results show that when considering a range of benefits implementations do not live up to their expectations. People-related issues dominated the barriers to attaining expected benefits with change management ranked very highly. Software, hardware or integration issues were not ranked highly. There was a lack of metrics used to measure the financial "success" of the core implementations. The main reasons for the lack of financial metrics seemed to be constantly moving imple-

mentations that are difficult to measure, difficulty in quantifying and measuring benefits and the fluid nature of organisations in stressed commercial environments.

In the Australasian region many companies are now looking at how to get added benefits from their initial investment in their ERP system. They are increasing the level of functionality offered by their ERP system or implementing some of the "bolt on" solutions such as data warehousing and customer relationship management. It appears that many companies were pushed down the ERP path by year 2000 compliancy and or poor disparate systems. These implementations have matured to a certain extent enabling companies to investigate how they can further leverage their investment in the ERP system. The second-wave of implementations are proactive compared to the reactive nature of initial implementations and are strategic in nature forming the basis for future initiatives.

REFERENCES

Bennett, C. (2001) SAP Update, delivered to SAUG Plenary, December 2001.

Bennett, C. (2002) SAP expands mySAP.com user base with new contracts and additional licenses, Located at http://www.sap.com/australia/company/press/2002/0508.asp Accessed May 2002.

BRW, (2000) Business Review Weekly, The BRW1000 Located at http://www.brw.com.au/stories/19991113/intro.htm Accessed May 2002.

Carlino, J. (1999a) AMR Research Predicts ERP Market will Reach $66.6 Billion by 2003, Located at www.amrresearch.com/press/files/99518.asp Accessed July 2000.

Carlino, J. (1999b) AMR Research Unveils Report on Enterprise Application Spending and Penetration, Located at www.amrresearch.com/press/files/99823.asp Accessed July 2000.

Carlino, J. (2000) AMR Research Predicts Enterprise Application Market will Reach $78 Billion by 2004, Located at www.amrresearch.com/press/files/ Accessed August 2002.

Comley, P. (1996) "The Use of the Internet as a Data Collection Method", *Media Futures Report*, Henley Centre, London

Deloitte, (1999) "ERPs second wave", Deloitte Consulting.

Dillman, D. (1998) "Mail and Other Self-Administered Surveys in the 21st Century: The Beginning of a new Era", *Discussion paper of the Social and Economic Sciences Research Centre*, Washington State University, Pullman.

Iggulden, T. Ed. (1999) Looking for Payback, *MIS*, June 1999, pp. 75-80

Krumwiede, Kip R. et al (2000) Reaping the Promise of Enterprise Resource Systems, *Institute of Management Accountants*, October 31, 2000 Located at http://www.erpsupersite.com/scream/nov/1/sm-20001101a.htm Accessed Sept 2001.

Mehta, R. and Sivadas, E. (1995) "Comparing response rates and response content in mail versus electronic mail surveys", *Journal of the Market Research society*, 37, pp. 429-439.

Nolan And Norton Institute, (2000) *SAP Benchmarking Report 2000*, KPMG Melbourne.

Piturro, M. (1999) How Midsize Companies Are Buying ERP, *Journal of Accountancy*, September 1999, 188(3) pp. 41-47.

SAP, (2002) SAP Corporate Profile, Located at http://www.sap.com/company/profile_long.htm Accessed May 2002.

Stanton, J. and Rogelberg, S. (2000) "*Using Internet/Intranet Web Pages to Collect Organizational Research Data*", Bowling Green State University

Stedman, C. (1999) What's next for ERP? *Computerworld*, *33*(33) August 16, pp. 48-49.

Stein, T. (1999) Big strides for ERP, *InformationWeek*, (715) January 4, pp. 67-69.

Network Security Course Model

Mariana Hentea, Ph.D.

Assistant Professor, Information Systems and Computer Programming, Purdue University Calumet

2200 Wicker Avenue, Hammond, IN 46323, Telephone: 219-989-3225, Email: henteam@calumet.purdue.edu, Fax: 219-989-3187

Susan E. Conners, Ph.D.

Associate Professor, Information Systems and Computer Programming, Purdue University Calumet

2200 Wicker Avenue, Hammond, IN 46323, Telephone: 219-987-2605, Email: conners@calumet.purdue.edu, Fax: 219-987-2858

ABSTRACT

The objective of this paper is to present a model for an undergraduate Network Security Course. The components in the model are designed to be core concepts and do not necessarily represent any particular vendor's system. It is a generic course model with emphasis on security issues and technologies. The primary components of the course and the importance of the topic being added to core curricula are discussed in the paper.

INTRODUCTION

The growth of computer networks has been phenomenal over the last several years and they are a major communication link for people around the world. Computer networks and their related technologies have evolved at a rapid pace with the hardware and software constantly changing and challenging networking professionals to keep pace.

These networks are used by government, public and private entities to communicate with the world. Securing the networks has become of paramount importance. "The terrorist attacks of last September permanently changed the terms of debate for subsequent discussions of IT security and the technical response to potential terrorist threats", (Coffee, p. 25,2002). There is currently a national discussion on how best to secure government networks.

The security of corporate networks is of equal concern. "CIOs are most worried about internal and external security breaches and cyber terrorism", (Kirkpatrick, p.67, 2002). The nation's economy relies on business networks being operational and secure. The failure or compromising of large-scale corporate networks will severely hamper business operations.

In addition to the larger issues of government and corporate network security, the networks accessed for personal reasons should be equally secure. The old conventional wisdom of find the best hackers and hire them to secure your network is not a wise path to follow. Clearly, this topic is an educational priority for IT programs. These courses must be offered in higher education programs with trained educators and researchers working in this field.

This paper discusses a model for a network security course in a curriculum, the course model, the specific components of the model, and the technologies used to teach the course at the undergraduate senior 400 level. This course supports scholarly education and does not focus on topics for certification exams.

OVERVIEW OF NETWORKING CURRICULUM

The current program that utilizes this course is a four-year baccalaureate degree in computer technology with a specialization in systems and networking. The overall program includes core technical courses, general education courses, and a specialization sequence in networking courses. The core technical courses include programming, systems analysis, web development, and database. The general education courses consist of math, English, physics, economics, communications, humanities and social science. The networking courses are comprised of operating systems classes, data communications, local area networks, wide area networks, hardware and software evaluation, and network security.

The issue of security covers multiple areas and there are security components in applications, network software, the operating system, hardware, and others. All of these forms of security are important to the overall security of information, which is what is protected [Maiwald, p. XXVI, 2001). Throughout the curriculum, security is discussed as a component of each of the various courses on operating systems, local area networks, wide area networks, and system administration. Students are continually taught the importance of security at all levels of the courses and the programs.

The significance of the topic of network security requires a separate course to integrate the components of the previous courses and build upon that knowledge. This is not an introductory level course. The course model is presented with the understanding that the prerequisite courses have been completed and the students have studied various aspects of security in their other courses. These prerequisite courses discuss the details of security as it applies to the specific topic taught in the course. The network security course is taught in the senior year of the program and requires students to integrate and synthesize the prior knowledge. Placing the course in the senior year prepares students to enter the workforce with the most recent issues on security. The course model is constructed to provide information for other programs wishing to develop a similar course.

OVERVIEW OF COURSE MODEL

The objective of the class is to allow students to obtain the skills required to pursue a job in all areas of the Security Industry: Consulting (Professional) Services, Developers for Security Products, and Managed Security Service Providers. The course provides an integrated, comprehensive, up-to-date coverage of the techniques, security tools, and applications vital to Internet applications and networking. The classroom instruction provides a practical approach of both the principles and practice of network security. Topics include system-level security issues, types of attacks, information security services, information security process, and information security best practices such as use of firewalls, routers, and trusted systems, monitoring and detection techniques, virtual private networks, E-commerce security needs, encryption, intrusion detection, and configuration recommendations for common operating systems (Windows NT, Unix, Linux, and Windows 2000) as well as security trends and new technologies (see Appendix A).

Students are taught ethics and professionalism as required of the work force in the information security industry. The ethics imply integrity, trust, correctness, assurance and confidence that no intentional attacks are made against any system. They also learn key architecture issues for securing the network and Internet connection. In addition, students learn how to set up and work with firewalls, authentication and encryption techniques, access controls, discovering and handling an actual attack, recovery from security breaches, and prevention of hacker attacks. Students acquire skills on planning, writing and implementing security policies, developing and maintaining security products. The class stresses issues on security architecture for the enterprise as well as requirements and design of the security products.

At the end of the course, students should be able to support the tasks required of the network managers and administrators responsible for the set up and maintenance of enterprise network security to protect information and systems from attack.

COMPONENTS OF COURSE MODEL

Although security topics for Microsoft Windows and Linux were covered in prior courses such as Network Administration, Operating Systems, or Data Communications, there is a need to cover extensively topics regarding security model, authentication mechanism, and encryption, security interface for Microsoft Windows 2000, UNIX and Linux systems. Students were provided with published information and hints on how to overcome the security flaws in these systems to avoid exploitation of vulnerabilities.

Teaching the most current developments in the Information Security is crucial to the success in the academic level, specifically when teaching emerging technologies. The basic concepts and terms are taught by the instructor using Power Point slides based on the material covered in the book (Maiwald, 2001), handouts with additional notes and material from professional magazines and other books (Stallings, Jamsa, Klevinski, etc.). The focus is to teach the material covering information security as well as the technologies supporting it. The amount spent on each topic is correlated with the importance of the topic. In addition, the emphasis is on problem solving skills. Students are required to execute assignments at home (not more than five), lab assignments, research paper, and paper presentation. Both lab and home assignments are based on the most relevant topics and greater importance is given to long-term retention of concepts and techniques taught and discussed in class. Lab assignments are built progressively starting with isolated systems and simple security architecture to moderately and complex security architecture models recommended by Computer Emergency Response Team (CERT) and SANS Institute.

Since information security processes, interaction, communication, and leadership skills are encouraged, lab assignments are executed in teams. Students are organized to work in team groups, each team made of three to four members. Students are encouraged to discuss, exchange ideas, and plan for accomplishing the lab assignments. The lab assignments are designed to gradually build a security program for the network lab within the campus. When performing the lab assignments, students are required to follow the phases of the information security process as it was defined in the class. Information security process is comprised of five key phases: 1) assessment, 2) policy writing, 3) implementation, 4) training, and 5) auditing.

By emulating the business processes in the lab, students are better prepared for the real business activities required in any organization when performing information security tasks. For each lab assignment, students have to write a lab report that includes all phases of the information security process, testing tools, decisions, observations, difficulties, constraints, plans for evolution of the security policy. Students have to write a security policy for each lab assignment. Besides technical skills, students' writing skills are reinforced.

The schedule for most of the lab assignments is based on rotation. Due to the limited hardware and software product licenses (see Appendix D); only one team can work on a topic at a time. The time allocated for a lab assignment varies from 2 to 6 hours. The allocated time is a function of the assignment difficulty, importance of the objectives, availability of the hardware and software in the lab. However, a few assignments can be performed at the same time with all the teams because Microsoft Windows 2000 is available to all students.

In addition, students are required to write a research paper. The paper has to be presented in class within a 15-minute time allocated to each student. The student may choose a topic from a list suggested by the instructor (see Appendix B), or a special topic proposed by the student and approved by the instructor. The instructor sets the quality standards for the paper such as the following: 1) the information included in the paper should reflect current thinking and opinions on the topic gathered from journals and weekly magazines and newspapers, 2) the paper should be a minimum of 10 pages and should be provided with a list of references (at least three additional references other than the text book), and 3) the paper is due before the scheduled presentation. At the end of semester, students provide a 15-minute presentation for the research paper to the class. The presentation allows a student not only to demonstrate their research results, but also to improve their communication skills by talking and answering questions to an audience.

TECHNOLOGIES REQUIRED

Students are taught Information Security on broad topics and best practices. Best practices concept refers to a set of recommendations that generally provide an appropriate level of security. Information Security is taught as a continuous and proactive process to manage risk. Students are taught how to react in critical situations as well as the importance of Contingency Plans such as Incident Response, Backup and Archiving, and Disaster Recovery. These are the basis of the actions that can be used when an incident causes the loss of data or service, device, or network failures.

There is an emphasis on the use of automated tools for testing the lab configurations for finding exposures to vulnerabilities instead of manual methods. For example, students were encouraged to perform penetration testing using tools provided in the lab or public tools from trusted sources such the ones suggested in Appendix C.

The Internet changes not only the way the technology is created or deployed, but also the way we use it in our jobs and daily life including how we learn to use it. Teaching network security concepts and terms is also based on the information distributed via the Internet. The most current security incidents, attacks, or vulnerabilities are made known via Internet. Dedicated and recognized organizations (see Appendix C) provide continuously up to date information about security incidents and vulnerabilities to enterprises, businesses, organizations, government, and security professionals.

The class uses information published via Web to support the teaching of the most current trends or standards. Students use the public information distributed via the Web when planning for the home or lab assignments. This allows students to be exposed to real problems that they have to consider in accomplishing their assignments. By exposing students with the news distributed by dedicated organizations that support computer and network security, students learn that the Internet can be used in their daily task when performing security administration tasks.

For example, one home assignment required students to provide a report with at least five security incidents reported via the Web. The students had to search for security incidents that were made known to the public, needed to identify specific information about each incident, and had to write a report. The specific information was a defined set of basic concepts and terms that were taught in the class. The results of the home assignments are evaluated not only using the written report, but also the additional information that students provided including their expressed satisfaction of being empowered with more knowledge.

The e-learning environments are more conducive and lead to a better understanding of the concepts taught in the traditional framework of the class. The end result is a more informed student with more confidence in his thinking and problem solving skills. However, the effectiveness of the e-learning is not magical; it is also related to the individual who wants to search for more sources of information.

Besides using the Web for findings and research of information, students use the Web as mechanism to download the most recent software updates for the software and hardware products installed in the university network lab. Given the nature of the dynamics of the telecommunications and information technologies, the products have to be continuously updated.

For one assignment that required use of Windows 2000 software, students first assessed the software version provided in the lab, then planned for downloading the software updates from the Microsoft Web site, installation in the designated machines, and verification of the updating process as well as testing the new features supplied with the most current version of the software. When implementing a security policy for a lab assignment that used Microsoft Windows 2000, students assessed the security flaws published by various sources (see Appendix C) before planning and writing the security policy. This is the basis of the future security professional awareness for checking the most recent published vulnerabilities.

In addition, the Web is used by students for getting informed about the quality ratings of the products used in the information security industry including the products used for the lab assignments and demonstration of the technologies. These all concur to advantages for students such as easy and quick access to information, familiarity with the real business problems to be solved, etc.

The web based system Blackboard (www.blackboard.com) is used as a mechanism of delivering the course material, instructor's notes, homework and lab assignments, and delivery of messages.

SUMMARY AND CONCLUSIONS

The course model discussed provides an example for a network security course. The importance of these types of courses must be emphasized in Information Technology programs to provide government and business the trained professionals required to secure their networks. In light of recent events, this topic has gained national prominence in government and corporate circles. Academic programs and departments should work with government and industry to educate IT students and professional on network security. This model is presented to assist other institutions that wish to incorporate a network security course into their curriculum.

This course model integrates specific skills from lower level courses and integrates them to form a knowledge base for further study of network security. The course covers techniques, security tools and applications that are essential to every business and computer system. In addition to technical skills, the topics of ethics and professionalism are addressed. The components of the course include also aspects of the security model, authentication mechanism, encryption, and interfaces for MS Windows 2000, Unix, and Linux operating systems. The technologies utilized in the class are hardware (firewalls and routers with firewall capabilities) as well as software products for network security. In addition, automated tools for penetration testing are used for the verification of the implemented security policy.

In conclusion, the importance of the network security course and other courses described in the paper are aligned with the national, regional, and local security concerns. Models for security courses and programs of study must be developed to meet this challenge. Consequently, all Information Technology and related programs need to include the network security training in their curricula. This is an opportunity for academic programs to provide government and industry with trained IT professionals ready to meet the security challenge.

APPENDIX A: TOPICS TAUGHT IN CLASS

1. Information Security Basics
2. Types of Attacks
3. Information Security Services
4. Legal Issues in Information Security
5. Policy
6. Managing Risk
7. Information Security Process
8. Information Security Best Practices
9. Internet Architecture
10. Virtual Private Networks
11. E-Commerce Security Needs
12. Encryption
13. Hacker Techniques
14. Intrusion Detection
15. UNIX Security Issues
16. Linux Security Issues
17. Windows NT Security Issues
18. Windows 2000 Security Issues
19. SNMP v3
20. Biometric Systems
21. Information Security Products Evaluation
22. Current and Future Information Security Industry Trends

APPENDIX B: SUGGESTED TOPICS FOR PRESENTATION

1. Data Encryption Standards
2. General Authentication Techniques
3. Network Backups
4. Types of Attacks
5. Security Issues for Wireless Networks
6. Security Devices and Measures
7. Firewalls and Building Internet Firewalls
8. Recent Advances in Intrusion Detection
9. Biometric Systems
10. Security Architecture for Enterprise
11. Writing a Security Policy
12. Security Requirements for Systems
13. Virtual Private Networks (VPNs)
14. Router Attacks and Reconfiguration
15. Security Issues for Microsoft Windows 2000
16. Security Issues for Microsoft Windows NT
17. Security Issues for Linux and UNIX Systems
18. Security for Internet and Standards
19. Applied Cryptography
20. Recovery from Security Attacks
21. Prevention versus Detection
22. Web Security
23. SNMP Security Issues
24. Security Management
25. Electronic Mail Security
26. IPSec Standard Implementation
27. Passwords Vulnerabilities
28. Testing Network for Vulnerabilities
29. Auditing Techniques
30. Security Awareness Training
31. Server Security
32. Security Maintenance

APPENDIX C: SUGGESTED WEB SITES

1. www.cerias.purdue.edu
2. www.cert.org
3. www.ietf.org/rfc
4. www.gocsi.com
5. www.securityfocus.com
6. www.snmp.org
7. http://csrc.nist.gov/icat
8. www.sans.org
9. www.nipc.gov
10. www.fedcirc.gov
11. www.sei.org
12. www.isalliance.org
13. www.antionline.com
14. www.loph2.com
15. www.infowar.com

APPENDIX D: LIST OF HARDWARE AND SOFTWARE TO BE USED FOR THE LAB ASSIGNMENTS

1. 4 Cisco 2621 routers
2. 3 Firewall appliances (different technologies and manufacturers: Nokia, Global Technology Associates, SonicWall)
3. 6 3COM LAN switches
4. Hubs, cables, connectors, adapters
5. 25 Personal Computers
6. CheckPoint FireWall-1 Next Generation
7. Microsoft Windows 2000 Server Software
8. Microsoft Windows 2000 PC Software

9. Linux Red Hat Software
10. Penetration testing tools (free download)
11. Intrusion Detection (free download)
12. Anti-virus software (free download).

REFERENCES

Assaf, N., Luo, J., Dillinger, M. and Menendez, L., Interworking between IP   Security and Performance Enhancing Proxies for Mobile Networks, IEEE   Communications Magazine, May 2002, Vol. 40, No. 5, pp. 138-144.

Chang, R.K.C., Defending against Flooding-Based Distributed Denial-of-Service   Attacks: A Tutorial, IEEE Communications Magazine, October 2002, Vol. 40, No. 10, pp. 42-51.

Coffee, P., 2002, Focus on Identity, Vigilance. EWeek v19 n36, p.25. Ziff Davis Publications.

Cybenko, G., Giani, Annarita, Thompson, P., Cognitive Hacking: A Battle for the Mind, 2002, COMPUTER, Vol. 35, No. 8, pp. 50-56.

Frischholz, R. W., Dieckmann, U., BioID: A Multimodal Biometric Identification System, 2000,   COMPUTER, Vol. 33, No. 2, pp. 64-68.

Jamsa, J., 2002, Hacker Proof, The Ultimate Guide to Network Security, Second Edition, Thomson Delmar Learning, United States.

Kara, A., Secure Remote Access from Office to Home, IEEE Communications Magazine, October 2001, Vol. 39, No. 10, pp. 68-72.

Kenneally, E., Who's Liable for Insecure Networks?, Computer, June 2002, Vol.   35, No.   6, pp. 93-95.

Kirkpatrick, T. A., 2002, Rethinking Risk, CIO Insight. September 2002, n18 Ziff Davis   Publications.

Klevinski, T. J., Laliberte, S., Gupta, A., 2002, Hack I.T. – Security Through Penetration Testing, Addisson-Wesley, New York, New York.

Maiwald, E., 2001, Network Security: A Beginner's Guide, Osborne/ McGraw-Hill, New York, New York.   Manikopoulos,   C.   and Papavassiliou, S., Network Intrusion and Fault Detection: A Statistical Anomaly Approach, IEEE Communications Magazine, October   2002,   Vol. 40, No. 10, pp. 76-82.

Miller, S.K., Facing the Challenge of Wireless Security, 2001, COMPUTER, Vol. 34, No. 7, pp. 16-18.

Oppliger, R., Security at the Internet Layer, 1998, COMPUTER, Vol. 31, No. 9, pp. 43-47.

Pankanti, S., Bolle, R. M., Jain, A., Biometrics: The Future of Identification, COMPUTER, 2000, Vol. 33,   No. 2, pp. 46-47.

Papadimitratos, P. and Haas, Z.J., Securing the Internet Routing Infrastructure, IEEE   Communications Magazine, October 2002, Vol. 40, No. 10, pp. 60-68.

Phillips, P. J., Martin, A., Przybocki, M., An Introduction to Evaluating Biometric Systems, 2000,   COMPUTER, Vol. 33, No. 2, pp. 56-63.

Stallings, W., 2000, Network Security Essentials: Applications and Standards, Prentice Hall, Upper Saddle River, New Jersey.

Identifying IT/IS Strategy Profiles in Manufacturing SMEs

Chris E Hillam and Helen M Edwards

School of Computing and Technology, University of Sunderland, Edinburgh Building, Chester Road, Sunderland, SR1 3SD, UK

Tel: +44 (0)191 515 2855, Fax: +44 (0)191 515 2703, e-mail: {chris.hillam, helen.edwards }@sunderland.ac.uk

INTRODUCTION

The problem of alignment of business strategy to IT/IS strategy has been widely reported as one of the key concerns currently facing organisations. This alignment or linkage has been defined by (Reich and Benbasat 1999) Reich and Benbasat as "the degree to which the IT mission, objectives and plans support and are supported by the business mission, objectives and plans." A number of studies focusing on this subject have reported on a range of issues such as the measurement of this linkage (Reich and Benbasat 1999), and the critical success factors involved (Teo and Ang 1999) and (King, Cragg et al. 2000). King et al (2000) (King, Cragg et al. 2000) and Gupta et al (2000) (Gupta, Karimi et al. 1997) report that where business strategy and IT/IS strategy are well aligned, organisational performance is enhanced. Much of this work tends to concentrates on larger organisations, with relatively little work undertaken in the SME community. Notable exceptions include Levy et al's work (1999, 2001) (Levy, Powell et al. 1999) (Levy and Powell 2000) (Levy, Powell et al. 2001) assessing IT/IS strategy development frameworks within SMEs, and Bergeron's application of a strategic matrix aiming to identify opportunities for implementing IT/IS for competitive advantage in SMEs (Bergeron and Raymond 1992).

This paper presents some case study research undertaken within five manufacturing SMEs in the north east of England, and describes part of a longer term study examining how SMEs plan IT/IS strategy, and what SME expectations are in terms of business benefits from their IT/IS investments. The empirical results from these case studies when compared with existing literature and strategies reveal the existence of a range of IT/IS strategy approaches in manufacturing SMEs. This is explored and presented via a proposed IT/IS strategy profile framework which is discussed and described using some of the case study examples.

METHODOLOGY

The broad research aim was an in-depth investigation of the issues associated with SME planning of business strategy and IT/IS investment. To achieve this, a qualitative, constructivist methodology was adopted, in line with a grounded theory approach (Strauss and Corbin 1990) (Strauss and Corbin 1998). Semi-structured interviews were conducted with key managers within each organisation to provide a rich organisational picture, and "produce rounded understandings" on the basis of this contextual data (Mason 1996). The interviews were conducted initially in the first three companies over a period of three to four months, with each interview being taped and transcribed for detailed analysis. The focus of the interviews was the company management of IT/IS planning and investment. In particular what the triggers were for IT/IS investments, and how company management identified proposed business benefits resulting from these investments. Each interview lasted for approximately an hour, and the interview data therefore provided as in-depth empirical data, including individual manager's perceptions of these issues. The resulting transcribed data sets were coded and analysed, using a supporting software, to reveal a number of themes and factors influencing and affecting SME investment in IT/IS (Hillam and Edwards 2000). This coding process was lengthy and was based upon the iterative process of constant comparison where emergent themes, properties and dimensions of the data were constantly identified and refined (Strauss and Corbin 1998) (Miles, 1994). The discussions outlined below are based largely upon the first three cases, with some reference to cases four and five where data collection and analysis is still ongoing, and based upon the developed theory from the earlier cases.

In addition to this grounded theory approach, the interviews were supported by the use of a questionnaire (adopted from the work done by Conant et al 1990) (Conant, Mokwa et al. 1990) to identify a strategy typology for each organisation according to the Miles and Snow typology (1978) (Miles and Snow 1978). Their work resulted in the identification of the following four strategy types:

- *Defenders* – organisations which have narrow product market domains, and by concentrating on this narrow focus seek to improve the efficiency of their existing operations.
- *Prospectors* – organisations with a strong interest in product or market innovation, who continually search for market opportunities. Such companies are often identified as instigators of change or uncertainty, and as such are not always deemed to be efficient operators.
- *Analysers* – organisations which may be operating in a variety of environments, but who monitor, analyse and respond to new ideas.
- *Reactors* – organisations in which managers observe and react to change and uncertainty, but do not always respond effectively to such change.

Subsequent studies (Parnell and Wright 1993) (Thomas, 1996) (Henderson 1998) have built upon and further validated the Miles and Snow strategy typology concept. The inclusion of the strategy typology tool in this current study was deliberate, in order to provide a baseline for the senior management perspective of each organisation's strategy typology. Such data could then be appraised against existent literature and case studies according to the strategy types described above. Despite the limitation of selecting only five case studies, it is interesting to note that traits of each of the four strategic types were detected. However the only overall strategy type not to emerge as dominant was reactor.

DISCUSSION

Background information and detail on the case study analysis has been reported in a previous paper (Hillam, Edwards et al. 2002). Table One identifies the individual case study companies, in terms of basic organisational information, a summary of the company IT/IS and the strategy typology determined from the questionnaire.

The following discussion outlines the difficulties facing SMEs in planning and formalising their IT/IS strategies, and justifying IT/IS investments. The IT/IS strategy profile framework that has been developed during the data analysis phase of the work is also illustrated and described. The overview of this strategy profile is illustrated in Table Two, and the following discussion will briefly clarify each of the profile headers as well as providing an overview of some of the company data leading to the identification of these themes. As such some insight is provided to the development of the coding and analysis of the overall study.

Table 1: Overview of case study companies

Co.	Product	Customers	Turnover and no of employees	Management / Ownership	Overview of IT/IS	Strategy Typology
1.	Steel coils and steel blanks	50% supplied to one key automotive customer, 50% to non-automotive sector	£27 million pa 90 empl	Joint financial venture between Japanese company and UK company	Finance and stock system purchased by sister company 8 years ago – most recent IT/IS investments relate to specific, individual PC-based applications: QA system System links to customers EDI links with automotive customer	Analyser with some Prospector and Reactor traits
2.	Industrial fuses	Large customer base of OEMs and wholesalers	£4 million pa 70 empl	Family owned	Recently implemented (Oct 2001) ERP system covering accounts, stock control, MRP and Works Order Processing. Facility for developing web-based marketing. PC based applications (spreadsheets) developed by users	Strong defender traits
3.	Industrial filters	Range of large European OEMs, mostly in the automotive sector	£4 million pa 85 empl	Family owned	Finance, stock control, MRP system purchased and implemented over 8 years ago. PC based applications using Access and Excel Have developed interactive product database for potential customer use – not as yet implemented	Analyser with some defender and prospector traits
4.	Interior automotive components (door panels)	One key automotive customer	£24 million pa 250 empl	Joint financial venture between Japanese company and UK company	Main IT/IS implemented ten years ago. Still in place but currently being reviewed for upgrade or replacement. Number of additional applications covering Quality, production control, customer EDI links – PC based. Additional spreadsheet developments by individual users	Strong defender traits
5.	Soft furnishings, cushions.	Range of 6-8 key UK based retail outlets	£2.4 million pa 45 empl	Family owned	Accounting, stock and MRP system – in place for last five years, not used to full potential, with much of the data input done retrospectively to support the financial, accounting needs. Limited user base, some use of Excel applications. EDI links with major customers.	Strong prospector traits

A FRAMEWORK FOR IDENTIFYING IT/IS STRATEGY PROFILES IN SMES

Strategy Focus

The first four headers illustrated in the profile can be discussed together and are grouped under the broader heading of strategy focus. The Miles and Snow strategy typology results in the identification of one of four types. Whilst these are not linked explicitly to IT/IS strategy, the results of the five cases are interesting when compared with the strategic focus of each organisation's IT/IS investment. The strategic focus of the IT/IS investment in this instance is defined according to Levy (Levy, Powell et al. 2001) as being orientated predominantly towards cost reduction or value added business activities. Detailed analysis of company data revealed that specific IT/IS investments within the same company could have either a value added or cost reducing focus. However in there was evidence to support some linkages between these

two headers. One example of this is Company Two which exhibited strong defender characteristics, largely based upon recent market and customer influences. IT/IS investments within this organisation were mostly based around controlling and improving internal business processes. This contrasted with Companies One and Five which both demonstrated prospector strategy traits, and therefore would be expected to concentrate on developing new market opportunities. Interestingly both organisations have used planned and recent IT/IS investments as part of their sales strategy to develop new and existing business. Both cases cited and reported achieved increased sales figures as justification for the investment.

Ballantine (Ballantine, Levy et al. 1998) observed that SMEs were under increased pressure from customers to adopt IT/IS. Whilst the observed number of cases in this study is too small to make general statements that would support this view or otherwise, there were several interesting examples cited by interviewees. These included examples that suggested that much of the initiative of these investments came from the SMEs themselves rather than the customers. Companies One and Five in particular showed evidence of some innovative business and IT/IS developments, geared towards either further developing a customer partnership, or supporting and developing customer communication links. These included system links for sales forecasting, provision of scheduling information related to customer orders, as well as systems with a rather more speculative objective of targeting new customer business. In both cases, the 'smaller supplier' company took the development and investment initiative.

Customer Dominance

Linked with the strategic focus and typology is the degree of customer dominance. Here this is defined simply in terms of the level of influence that customers exert upon the SME. Again contrasting examples are provided by two of the case study companies. Company Four works exclusively with one customer. In this instance customer dominance is clearly high, resulting in company strategy being focussed upon this one customer's needs and requirements. Company Three however had a wide and varied customer base, with no one customer dominating the overall customer profile. Customer dominance was therefore defined as low for this organisation, it being unlikely that any one customer would be in a strong position to "pressure" the supplier into IT/IS development or investment. Consequently in Company Three, beyond general efficiency issues in managing the customer base, there was little evidence of specific IT/IS development or investment geared towards improving and developing customer partnerships.

INTEGRATION OF IT/IS APPLICATIONS.

Using a similar case study approach, Levy mapped the IT/IS applications found within the case study companies according to two factors(Levy, Powell et al. 2001). Firstly whether the application is seen predominantly to have an internal (based around internal business processes) or external focus (supporting external business processes with customers or suppliers). The second dimension to Levy's model is the degree of integration. Here the degree of integration would be identified as low where stand alone spreadsheets formed a significant part of the IT/IS in the organisation, and high if the organisation was working with a well integrated ERP system. As in Levy's study, the degree of IT/IS integration also emerged from this investigation as being a significant factor. All five organisations had integrated manufacturing control packages, all used in very varying degrees. Company Two had recently

Table 2: Outline for SME IT/IS Strategy Profile.

Miles and Snow Business Strategy Typology			
Defender	Analyser	Prospector	Reactor
Strategic Focus of IT/IS			
Value-added		Cost reduction	
Customer Dominance			
High		Low	
Focus of IT/IS investment			
External with customer focus		Internal with operational focus	
Control of IT/IS investment costs			
High		Low	
Identification of proposed business benefits from IT/IS investment			
Detailed and formal		Little detail/informal	
IT/IS applications integrated			
Well integrated and centralised		Not well integrated – isolated IT/IS applications	
IT/IS responsibility			
IT/IS manager's position stable		IT/IS manager/department personnel frequently changes	
IT/IS expertise (IT/IS Manager)			
High		Low	
IT/IS expertise (Users generally)			
High		Low	

(Note that IT/IS expertise here is understood to include both technical and well as application understanding).

implemented an ERP system and this system supported the main business activities, with very little evidence of other applications being used or developed. Companies One, Three and Four all ran integrated systems that had been in place for a long time. Although each company experience was clearly different, the common themes amongst them were that the basic financial and stock modules were used and that the systems in all three companies do support the basic business functions. User and manager perceptions in Companies Three and Four indicated a broad dissatisfaction with the system, and a perceived need to replace the system to improve basic management information such as stock holding accuracy. This was also true of Company One except that recent IT/IS investments geared around stand alone applications, led managers to state that they were reasonably happy with the current IT/IS support and developments, and saw no urgent need to review the company-wide integrated stock system. Company Five owned a little-used integrated manufacturing package inherited from a previous management regime, and was embarking upon a major review and investment in an integrated package to support current needs.

SME MANAGEMENT DECISION MAKING AND INVESTMENT JUSTIFICATION

The problems of justifying investments in IT/IS are well documented (Ballantine, Levy et al. 1998) (Ballantine and Stray 1998) (Hochstrasser 1992) (Hogbin and Thomas 1994) (Farbey, Land et al. 1993) (Symons 1994). This justification process is clearly a huge problem and needs to be analysed and considered using a systematic approach that takes account of the complexity of IT/IS spend.

Cost was identified by most interviewed as one of the most (if not the most) dominant factors influencing their decision making process when investing in IT/IS. However despite the level of agreement on the need to keep costs down, the interview data analysis showed a number of conflicting patterns of behaviour regarding cost control and level of spend. The following summaries provide examples of these:

- A clear rigorous process for costing IT/IS spend, followed by an informal doubling of this precise costing for budgetary purposes.
- Conflicting evidence of the level of spend for a recent IT/IS, quoted by managers (sometimes the same manager but at different times in the interview schedule) at completely different spending levels. The order of magnitude difference being in the region of over eight times the cost originally quoted.
- Evidence of considerable effort and investment made in an IT/IS development with no proven use or benefit – this perceived by the researcher as a "political development".

Such patterns of behaviour may seem to fall in line with claims that the resource poverty (Thong and Yap 1995) (Yap, Soh et al. 1992) existing within many SMEs often results in an environment characterised by lack of conscious, strategic planning (Cragg and King 1993). As a result IT/IS investment in SMEs has often been considered to be impulsive and lacking in systematic planning. The research findings from this work indicate that there is a strong need to control costs and spend, but that the resource limitations facing most SMEs may often result in the lack of a formal IT/IS strategy.

As a consequence, it is believed that the further development and application of such a framework will help to formalise within an organisation the strategic focus and may also assist SMEs with the review or identification of potential IT/IS opportunities and their associated business benefits. This led to the inclusion of two further factors in the framework described above – namely company approach to cost control of IT/IS investments, and degree to which proposed business benefits are formalised and recorded.

IT/IS RESPONSIBILITY AND EXPERTISE IN SMES.

Past work by Fink (Fink 1998) in SMEs summarised a number of factors as being significant in facilitating the adoption of IT/IS in SMEs. These include the Managing Director's attitude to IT/IS and knowledge of IT/IS capability. (King and Teo 1994) (Cragg and King 1993) also suggest that strong technical support and expertise are significant factors in facilitating successful introduction of IT/IS in SMEs. It was therefore interesting to note that all five case study organisations had recently (within the previous two years) taken the decision to establish a level of IT/IS expertise in-house. At its lowest level this provided technical support to deal with the increased level of PC usage, and to provide some basic hardware and networking support. At this level alone the implication of this decision is important because of the associated cost implications to the average SME, essentially raising the level of company investment in IT/IS quite significantly.

Other issues of note were how stable the IT/IS management role had been within each organisation. In Companies One and Two the responsibility for IT/IS had remained with the same manager/department for a lengthy period, with differing results. On one hand a rather more autocratic approach to IT/IS strategy formulation appeared to have been taken, whilst on the other a more consultative approach was employed. With the latter consultative approach it was also evident that communication and understanding of the resulting IT/IS plans was good.

Conversely in Companies Three and Four, responsibility for IT/IS had changed several times in recent years. In both examples the respective management teams claimed that this had not affected IT/IS developments. However the interview data revealed a number of conflicting statements that indicated that these recent changes did have an impact upon IT/IS strategy, and there were a number of "political" issues that emerged from these discussions. This corresponds with the need to balance power between the user and the IT/IS department (McFarlan and McKenney 1983). Although McFarlan's comments are clearly based around larger organisations and data processing departments, the essential points remain relevant – that the balance of power between management and users needs careful management in order to avoid any conflict between innovative IT/IS developments and the need for control. These observations lead to the inclusion of IT/IS responsibility and the stability of this position in the company, and the level of IT/IS expertise in the company, to be identified as an importance element in the IT/IS strategy profile. Company Five at the outset stated that they wished to establish and develop IT/IS expertise on-site to support a major planned investment is IT/IS.

CONCLUSION

The IT/IS strategy profile presented here has been developed from a study undertaken within a small sample of manufacturing SMEs in the north east of England. The framework is intended to support SMEs in formalising their approach to IT/IS planning and investment. Ongoing data collection and analysis is currently being conducted in the final two case study companies to further develop and validate this framework, and the findings from the first stage of the study.

REFERENCES

Ballantine, J., M. Levy, et al. (1998). "Evaluating information systems in small and medium-sized enterprises: issues and evidence." European Journal of Information systems 7: 241-251.

Ballantine, J. and S. Stray (1998). "Financial appraisal and the IS/IT investment decision making process." Journal of Information Technology 13: 3-14.

Bergeron, F. and L. Raymond (1992). "Planning of information systems to gain a competitive edge." Journal of Small Business Management 30(January): 21-26.

Conant, J. S., M. P. Mokwa, et al. (1990). "Strategic Types, distinctive marketing competancies and organisational performance: a multiple measures-based study." Strategic Management Journal 11: 365-383.

Cragg, P. B. and M. King (1993). "Small firm computing:motivators and inhibitors." MIS Quarterly March: 47-60.

Farbey, B., F. Land, et al. (1993). How to assess your IT investment, Butterworth-Heinemann.

Fink, D. (1998). "Guidelines for the succesful adoption of Information Technology in Small and Medium Enterprises." International Journal of Information Management 18(4): 243-253.

Gupta, Y. P., J. Karimi, et al. (1997). "Alignment of a firm's competitive strategy and Information Technology sophistication: the missing link." IEEE Transactions on Engineering Management 44(4): 399-413.

Henderson, I. (1998). An analysis of the Latent Typology of Miles and Snow. British Academy of Management Annual Conference, University of Nottingham.

Hillam, C. and H. M. Edwards (2000). Company Approaches to IT/IS Investment and the Resulting Evaluation. 7th European Conference in Information Technology Evaluation, Trinity College Dublin, Ireland, MCIL.

Hillam, C., H. M. Edwards, et al. (2002). The Link Between Company Typology and IT/IS Investment in SMEs: A View from the Trenches. Ninth European Conference on Information Technology Evaluation, Universite Paris-Dauphine, France, MCIL.

Hochstrasser, B. (1992). Justifying IT Investments. Advanced Information Systems: The new Technology in today's business environment, UK.

Hogbin, G. and D. V. Thomas (1994). Investing in Information Technology: managing the decision-making process, McGraw-Hill.

King, M., P. Cragg, et al. (2000). IT alignment and organisational performance in small firms. 8th European Conference on Information Systems.

King, W. R. and T. S. H. Teo (1994). "Facilitators and inhibitors for the strategic use of information technology." Information and Management 27: 71-87.

Levy, M. and P. Powell (2000). "Information systems strategy for small and medium sized enterprises: an organisational perspective." Journal of Strategic Information Systems 9: 63-84.

Levy, M., P. Powell, et al. (1999). "Assessing Information systems strategy development frameworks in SMEs." Information and Management 36: 247-261.

Levy, M., P. Powell, et al. (2001). "SMEs: aligning IS and the strategic context." Journal of Information Technology 16: 133-144.

Mason, J. (1996). Qualitative Research. London, Sage Publications Ltd.

McFarlan, F. W. and J. L. McKenney (1983). "The information archipelago - governing the new world." Harvard Business Review(July - August): 91-99.

Miles, M. and A. M. Huberman (1994), Qualitative data analysis, Sage Publications.

Miles, R. E. and C. C. Snow (1978). Organisational strategy, structure and process, McGraw-Hill.

Parnell, J. A. and P. Wright (1993). "Generic Strategy and Performance: an Empirical Test of the Miles and Snow Typology." British Journal of Management 4: 29-36.

Reich, B. H. and I. Benbasat (1999). Measuring the Information Systems-Business Strategy relationship. Strategic Information Systems Management. R. D. Galliers, D. E. Leidner and B. S. Baker, Butterworth Heinemann: 329-366.

Strauss, A. and J. Corbin (1990). Basics of qualitative research: Grounded theory procedures and techniques, Sage Publications Ltd.

Strauss, A. L. and J. Corbin (1998). Basics of Qualitative Research: Techniques and Procedures for Developing Grounded Theory. London, Sage Publications Ltd.

Symons, V. J. (1994). Evaluation of Information Systems investment: towards multiple perspectives. Information Management: the evaluation of information systems investments. L. Willcocks, Chapman & Hall: 253-268.

Teo, T. S. and J. S. Ang (1999). "Critical success factors in the alignment of IS plans with business plans." International Journal of Information Management 19: 173-185.

Thomas, A. S. and K. Ramasawamy (1996), "Matching managers to strategy: further tests of the Miles and Snow typology." British Journal of Management 7: 247-261.

Thong, J. Y. L. and C. S. Yap (1995). "CEO characteristics, Organisational Characteristics and Information Technology Adoption in Small Businesses." Omega International Journal of Management Science 23(4): 429-442.

Yap, C. S., C. C. P. Soh, et al. (1992). "Information systems success factors in small businesses." International Journal of Management Science 20(5/6): 597-609.

NETWORK RISK ASSESSMENT FOR SYSTEMS CHANGE

Philip J Irving, Principal Lecturer. philip.irving@sunderland.ac.uk
Helen M Edwards, Professor (Software Engineering). helen.edwards@sunderland.ac.uk
University of Sunderland, School of Computing and Technology, David Goldman Informatics Centre
St. Peter's Campus, SUNDERLAND, SR6 0DD. UK., Tel: +44 (0)191 5152408, Fax: +44 (0)191 5152781

ABSTRACT

Risk assessment for systems implementation (or change) normally focuses on the software development aspects of the process or user interactions with a system. However, there is an important connection between the software system and the network upon which it runs. Changes to one can have significant impact on the other. The need to consider this interaction is presented and the lack of available literature to support this activity is outlined. Examples are given to illustrate the effect of failing to evaluate networks within the risk assessment of systems change.

INTRODUCTION

Many risk assessment methods consider computer systems to be complex socio-technical systems: and thus they provide mechanisms for assessing the interaction between, for instance, the users and the software. However, the fact that such systems are frequently composed of sub-systems often seems to be overlooked. Whereas, changes to a sub-system needs to analysed not only in isolation, but also in terms if the impact on the whole. One sub-system that we believe is frequently overlooked in terms of its importance in terms of complexity of systems change is the network. However, corporate networks are, perhaps, the single most important subsystem of all: for data (often mission critical) flows through the network like blood flows through the human body. Moreover, just as the body suffers if blood ceases to flow, so the organisation may cease to function if the data doesn't reach its destination. Two examples seek to illustrate this point: consider a bank where the cash machines take half an hour per transaction, or a company trading on-line that takes 40 minutes for a customer to pass through the checkout. In either case, the software systems may function correctly, but the outcome "falls short of what was expected" (Kontio, 1997). The failure may, in such cases, be a result of ineffective networks (rather than faulty software) and issues outside the boundary set by the software project manager.

In this paper we seek to draw attention to the need for effective research into relevant risk assessment and mitigation practices for coping with systems changes in networked environments. To present our argument we outline the lack of existing literature, provide a summary of the consequences of network failures, discuss the impact of systems change on networks and network changes on systems before drawing the conclusion that further work is required in the area.

LITERATURE REVIEW

Network Risks in Systems Change

For any researcher investigating a problem area an initial task is the review of relevant literature. In this case the required literature would be both general risk literature and specific work on risk assessment for networks. Such literature was indeed acquired. However, the search for "network risk assessment" returned papers focusing simply on the aspect of security risks. This is undoubtedly an important concern, for example vulnerabilities in the area of security can lead to theft, fraud, data loss or even a Denial of Service (DoS) attack (Brooke, 2000; Myerson 1999). However, this is not the only area of risk in the networked environment: for example, preventing effective use of a network will also deny the users the services which they require. Thus a software project which causes a network to under perform will also lead to the serious situation of a DoS, yet no evidence of such research has been uncovered in literature surveys conducted by the authors. It was considered that a literature search of network design would also be useful in identifying risk assessment strategies for networks: but again, in practice, that also produced little of relevance to software development and change. The authors and a masters project student have carried out extensive searches using the digital library of the IEEE and ACM, ScienceDirect, Web of Science, Google and other search engines and have only been able to retrieve network risk assessment research covering security, results of these searches are reported in Velde (2002) and Irving (2002).

This absence of a literature review perhaps indicates a large gap in current risk thinking. Risk doesn't just apply to the development/change process, it applies to implementation of that process. Most authors in computing will recognise that failure to correctly specify the design will cause many problems in implementation; yet none seem to be considering risks arising from, for example, failure to review the network.

Consequences of Network Failures

It can be argued that failure to consider network failure is as damaging as failure to consider design problems: if the design of the project is flawed then the product may be totally unusable or require extensive re-working. Whereas, where the underlying network is incapable of supporting the project then project implementation may well bring down the entire network and all the mission and safety critical systems, which operate upon it. Indeed surveys in 1994 (Disaster Recovery Planning, 1994) in the US highlighted the following effects of computer outage:

1. The average company will lose 2-3% of gross sales within 8 days of a sustained computer outage.
2. The average company that experiences a computer outage lasting 10 days will never fully recover. 50% will be out of business within 5 years.
3. The chances of surviving a disaster affecting the corporate data processing centre are less that 7 in 100. The chances of experiencing such a disaster are 1 in 100.

This survey shows the effects of a sustained computer outage across a sample of 100 companies in the US. The companies in the survey ranged from sole traders to multi-national organisations. Whilst the authors recognise that in terms of a 2002 paper this information is dated, few would argue that the stakes (and the risks), given the prevalence of the internet, are now much higher.

Network failure can also lead to data loss, Cipriano (1994) reported that "Among companies that experience severe data loss, 43% never reopen and 90% go out of business within 2 years". Indeed the authors have personal experience of companies that would be unlikely to survive more than a week if they lost their network.

NETWORK RISK ASSESSMENT DISCUSSION

Given the impact of network failure it might be expected that project managers would take this into account in their risk assessment. However, the limited evidence accrued thus far, from the literature and in discussion with practitioners, suggests that this factor is rarely considered. Perhaps this confirms Keil et al's assertion that "project managers believe they can control these risks" (Keil et al,1998). It is a fact that networks, although rapidly developing still lag behind computing power in terms of speed (Irving 2003); thus the effects of failure to give appropriate consideration to the network are irreversible. There may be no mitigation path available: a network cannot be simply "upgraded", this needs to be a planned change. Change here is another long project in which a careful analysis must be undertaken to determine the effects of the change to all systems. Obviously this can seriously delay the implementation of the project.

The problem is further compounded in many organisations where network management staff are often completely divorced from systems developers~~ment staff~~: and are ~~quite often~~ ~~under~~ ~~or completely~~ different management. But, rationally we can see that- most applications developed are dependent upon the network. Moreover, changes made to the network will affect what the software development team are producing. Therefore, to make progress we need to assess risk within a network context from two perspectives:
i. System changes that affect networks
ii. Network changes that affect systems

The latter perspective should be the domain of the networking team, the former the domain of the development team. However, just as Kontio (1997) advocates a close working relationship with the users, the authors would advocate a close working relationship between the teams.

Systems Change: Impact on Networks

There are many situations in which a change to the software or the system will affect the operation of the network. Whilst in some cases, the network may be able to be upgraded and cope with the change, there are other instances where the network cannot be upgraded. As a means of demonstrating such points, there follows an example of a project in which risk assessment of systems change/implementation failed to recognise the impact of the changes to the network. A simple illustrative bandwidth example is given below (Figure 1). This illustrates the failure of the software developers to take into account the abilities of the company's current network, which in turn leads to the system being unusable. More details and further examples can be found at (Irving,

Figure 1: Bandwidth example

Company 1 is a medium sized highly profitable organisation based in a listed Victorian building. Four years ago, they spent a large amount of money having a network installed and a networked sales order system developed. Whilst this software helped them to be successful, it is now found to be constraining their growth and they contracted a software consultancy to develop new software. As they are due to move to purpose built premises in one year they wish to spend very little money on the current building. The new system was much improved resulting in an increase in the amount of data to be shipped on the network. Thorough testing was undertaken on the consultant's premises and the software approved. Upon implementation at company premises, the performance of the software was so poor that it immediately had to be withdrawn. The first analysis of the problem showed that the PCs were less powerful however, a suggested upgrade failed to improve performance. The root cause of the problem was that the network bandwidth could not support the requirements of the new software.

2002).

For this example changing the network architecture was out of the question because of the huge costs imposed by constraints of the building. Therefore, the new software could not be used. Risk assessment for the network had not been undertaken resulting in catastrophic consequences for the project.

Network Change: Impact on Systems

Just as the software project manager should consider how the software changes will affect the network, so the network team should consider the problems that a network change can make to software and its users. This illustrates that the network and development teams need to maintain regular contact. An example case study can be found at (Irving, 2002).

CONCLUSIONS

Most risk assessment methods define a boundary for the system being changed: however, computer systems almost always comprise of sub-systems which need to integrate successfully with the other systems. Unfortunately the risk assessment methods that have been analysed by the authors fail to adequately recognise the impact that the network and software components of a systems can have on one another. This paper has highlighted the need to investigate this aspect of systems change further. The authors are in the early stages of a research project which will both gather empirical data from practitioners and evaluate existing risk assessment and mitigation approaches in order to develop an approach that reflects the interconnection that exists between systems and networks.

REFERENCES

Brooke, P. (2000). *Network Computing.* October 30th 2000.

Cipriano, M:.(1994). Marketing director for Mountain Network Solutions.

Disaster Recovery Planning (, 1994). Disaster Recovery Planning: Managing Risk & Catastrophe in Information Systems", 1994. ExertExtract published in *On-track Ltd Data Protection Guide* 1994.

Irving, P. (20022). *Examples of Network Risks.* o osiris.sunderland.ac.uk/~cs0pir/irma2003.

Irving, Philip .J. (2003). Computer Networks. Learning Matters, London. ISBN: 1903337062.

Irving, Philip .J. (2003). Local Area Networks. Crucial Publishing, London.

Keil M, Cule, P.E., Lyytinen, K. and Schmidt, R. (1998) "Against all odds: A new framework for identifying and managing software project risks". *Communications of the ACM*, Vol. No. 41, no. 11 pages 77-83.

Kontio, J. (1997) *The Riskit Method for Software Risk Management, Version 1.00.* CS-TR-3782 University of Maryland (can be downloaded from http://mordor.cs.hut.fi/~jkontio/riskittr.pdf)

Myerson, Judith (11999). Risk Management . *International Journal of Network Management* Vol 9, Pages 305-308.

Velde, N-H. (2002). *Risk Assessment of Network and Systems Changes.* MSc IT Management Project, University of Sunderland, UK.

Development of a Framework for Secure Patch Management

Lech J. Janczewski and Andrew M. Colarik
The University of Auckland, Department of MSIS, Private Bag 92019, Auckland, New Zealand,
Tel: 64 9 373 7599, ext 87538/83048, Email: lech@auckland.ac.nz or colarik@auckland.ac.nz

ABSTRACT

With the growing expansion of Internet connectivity and usage by consumers and merchants, financial institutions and governmental entities, the requirement for stable and secure software is being elevated to the legislative and judicial levels. No longer can software manufacturers disregard this growing requirement in fulfilling their commercial obligations. The issuance of a patch is the beginning and not the end of a software developer's obligations to its customers and all subsequent parties impacted by its product.

In this paper, the authors provide a framework detailing the components of a secure patch management system, a discussion on the necessity of managing and securing each phase/component, and some basic patch issuance concerns with regards to the supporting legal environment.

INTRODUCTION

Books, journals and mass media are full of stories about people trying, intentionally or unintentionally, to cause damage to information systems. Every year, several internationally renowned organizations (like CSI/FBI or CERT) produce detailed reports indicating the nature of these activities [CSI/FBI, 2001]. An elaborate taxonomy of attacks [Denning, 1999] as well as many methods of handling threats has been created and developed by security organizations.

Generally, attacks prevention and handling could be accomplished in two major ways: implementation of the full risk analysis, like that promoted by Common Criteria [2000] or following the baseline approach [von Solms, 1996]. The first is very costly and detailed, while the second allows for a quick increase of system security, not necessarily tailored for a particular application. What is important, however, is the fact that both approaches consider development of a security policy as a fundamental requirement.

Security policy is usually divided into three distinctive parts [Forch, 1994]: prevention activities, handling of security alerts, and disaster recovery (security in time). These parts address detailed issues related to handling threats against hardware, software, personnel and organizational matters (security across domains).

One particular issue spans both (time and domains) dimensions of the security policy: introduction of new software components into a system. These new parts are generally prepared by the primary developers as a result of:

- Discovering some errors in the existing software,
- Enhancing the system with options previously nonexistent,
- Changes in the client requirements or environment.

In the past, contacts between a software developer and a user were very intimate as they usually were members of the same business organization. They may have even shared the same room. In contrary, more and more users are implementing products "off-the-shelf" and the contact between the developer and the end user is quite loose. They are usually far away, both in real distance as well as in the organizational space. Hence, the user must have detailed information about his/her system and communicate this to the software developer. On the other hand, the developer must provide good information to the user. Both

sides must be aware of the way in which the proper selection and transport of the upgrades, method of their installations, payments for said upgrades, and any applicable warranties. Any fault in this process could have disastrous effects on the IT system. Thus, creating a dramatic situation for the whole business organization.

This paper proposes a framework for conducting secure patch management, examines some of the technical and legal management issues in the distribution and installation of patches, and suggests several ways of improvement.

SECURE PATCH MANAGEMENT SYSTEM COMPONENTS

For the purposes of this paper we define secure patch management as a system incorporating the following components (refer to Figure 1): A patch event notification, an integrity and authentication check of the patch event notification, a patch version applicability verification, patch transport and delivery, a patch file integrity verification, a trial installation of the patch, patch deployment, and recipient audit component.

Apart from the technical procedures, listed above, there are other, equally important issues related to the distribution and installation of software patches. These procedures result from the fact that in the majority of cases the producer of the patches and their receivers are separate business entities. Therefore, there is a need to set up their mutual obligations under the law, such as the forms of payment for the patches, installations, liabilities, etc.

This paper will concentrate mostly on the technical issues listed above, but a brief summary of the business problems will be presented at the end.

DISCUSSION OF THE MAJOR ELEMENTS OF THE FRAMEWORK

Patch Event Notification

The first and perhaps the most important component is the patch event notification. This component performs the function of making the user aware that a patch has been developed and is available for deployment in a timely manner. Without such timely notification of the issuance of a patch, a patch becomes functionally useless.

To facilitate the notification process, a set of procedures or the establishment of a notification system is required to ensure timely notice of the existence of a newly issued patch. This system may be procedural, semi-automated, or fully automated. This system may come in the form of a push, a pull, or a combination of the two processes. The evening news broadcasts the availability of the latest patch to correct of security flaw is an example of a push process. Where the user visits the respective software manufacturer to determine the latest news of software updates is an example of a pull process. An e-mail service that an individual subscribes to and may post to notify its entire subscription list of the availability of a new patch is an example of a combination process.

The level of detailed information contained within the event noti-

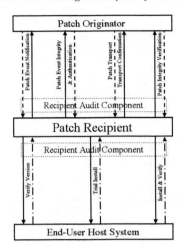

Figure 1: Secure Patch Management System framework

fication should facilitate an informed and corrective response from the end user or system administrator. Upon receipt of a patch issuance, the responsible party wishing to apply the patch should be able to make an assessment as to the significance of the patch if applied to the existing system. Details such as software name and version, any operating system distinctions that the patch was intended to service, the location of the patch, the date of issue, any acquisition or download requirements, and perhaps any additional information required for the decision that the patch is required and necessary to the continued use of the software product.

The patch event notification should be made available to all responsible parties whose functions are maintaining the smooth operation of the host system where the software product resides, i.e. system administrators or end-users.

Patch Event Integrity and Authentication

Once a patch event notification has been received, its integrity and authentication should be seriously considered. This commonly overlooked step is to confirm that the patch event notification actually came from the software manufacturer and has not been modified either intentionally or through error. Data origin authentication allows sources of received data to be verified as claimed and data integrity is used to detect unauthorized changes in data during transmission [Tripunitara, 1998].

When the availability of a patch has been communicated through the public and/or private media networks such as television, it is not uncommon to hear of hoaxes or statements made with bad information. Traditionally, upon becoming aware of a new patch, users visit the manufacturers web site and provide their own verification of the patch's existence. Newsgroups provided a more focused topical dissemination of patch availability but rely upon interested third party contributions. Industry standards of authentication are rarely found in use with newsgroup postings. Another alternative are numerous management services that provide timely notification of issued patches and updates. Companies such as Net Infrastructure [2002], PatchLink [2002], and Mission Critical Linux [2002] are a few examples of the type of management services available. These services are generally provided by e-mail notification but may include remote operational updates.

To prevent unscrupulous individuals from misinforming users, cryptographic methods may be utilized to provide patch event authentication [Stallings, 1999]. Mechanisms such as private and public key exchange, and digital certificates that are processed through professional trusted third parties [VeriSign 2002], have been utilized in this capacity. Hinde [1999] states that "an 'electronic signature' is any substitute for a handwritten signature on and electronically generated document". A handwritten signature does not necessarily have the same capacity to

ensure the origin and integrity of data as a digital signature but can serve to authenticate data in some way.

Patch Version Verification

At this point, a user has received a patch event notification through some dissemination vehicle and has verified the integrity and authenticity of the patch event notification. The user must determine that the information contained in the patch notification is applicable with regards to the software and its current revision level. It may be stated that the version level of any given installed software shall dictate which patch file or files are required.

When a patch event notification occurs, the patch version must be compared to the existing installation software version. This is generally done through the use of manuals, installation diskettes and CD-ROMs, version references listed within the menus of the software, and stored within the operating system registry. In addition to manually referencing the software version, third party applications and diagnostic utilities can provide an accurate version level such as Norton System Works [2002].

In a secure and automated approach to version verification, it would be appropriate and practical to verify that the patch and software versions match at the notification, acquisition, and installation phase of an update. Customized software must also be considered when deciding the applicability of any given patch. Assuming that the patch is indeed required for the continued operation of the intended software product, successful patch transport becomes the next issue.

Patch Transport and Delivery

Historically, a CD-ROM or floppy diskette would be delivered via the postal authority. The medium may be delivered via certified mail or by special courier. In the age of the Internet, electronic delivery occurs by downloading the patch file(s) via the manufacturer's web site using file transfer protocol (FTP). Acquiring the patch may also be completed via newsgroups and e-mail distribution as an attachment file to the communication. But all of these methods bring into question the integrity of the patch file(s). The least likely method for receiving corrupted or tampered patch files is by receiving a CD-ROM or floppy diskette by mail. While it is unlikely that a subversive individual would be able to intercept and modify the files, corruption at the time of disk replication has been a diminishing yet reoccurring problem. In addition, what is to stop some enterprising individual or firm from creating official looking diskettes and mailing them in some professional manner to a system administrator? An uninformed employee may simply perform the update and unwillingly become an accomplice to creating a backdoor pipeline that may be used to exploit a company's computer resources.

Electronic delivery via the Internet provides less assurance of integrity. Web sites and FTP servers can be spoofed, session requests may be diverted, files may be modified prior to download and during download, or have additional files bound to the patch file(s). What is needed to improve total system security is some form of patch integrity verification. In the case of receiving an update patch via mail service, additional customer information may be provided or integrated into the shipping invoice or incorporated into the original software install. For example, the installation software and updates issued by Great Plains Dynamics [2002] integrates the customer name into the authorization code. For electronic delivery of patches, use of a generated hash function or message digest that is based on the original patch file may provide a means for patch integrity verification. Essentially, a hash function or message digest is a mathematical function that takes a variable-length input string and converts it into a fixed-length binary sequence. It is a uniquely, identifiable digital fingerprint designed in such a way that it is hard to reverse the process by making it difficult to find two strings that would produce the same hash value [Schmidt, 1990].

The manufacturer of the patch could provide access to a pre-generated hash function based on the original patch. This would permit the user to validate that the patch file has not been modified by anyone since its original creation. A user would be able to generate a hash function from the downloaded file and compare it with the original provided by the manufacturer. A match would verify the integrity of the patch.

Patch Trial Installation

The smooth and consistent operation of the software system is one of the primary objectives of the system administrator and the end user. It is very easy to assume that a patch that is provided by the manufacturer will only improve the software's performance. However, experience teaches that no software system operates in a vacuum. Hardware, other software, operating systems, and other available utilities impact the total information processing system environment. Manufacturers of software can only attempt to provide stable products in a continuously evolving, diverse, and customized system environment. As a result, an aspect of securing the integrity of the system in which the software operates is to provide a test bed for the trial installation of a patch. SAP software has a system test area known as the sandbox or test system. SAP recommends that updates and modifications to the system are to be implemented in the sandbox before full deployment [SAP, 2001]. In addition, products such as GoBack 3 by Roxio [2002] provide users the ability to uninstall updates when system integrity needs to be restored.

Patch Deployment

Once the patch installation has been tested and deemed appropriate for the system, patch deployment should be prompt and complete. Regardless of whether the patch is deployed manually, through semiautomated, or fully automated means, access control and authorization must be a considered component of this phase. A distributed system of checks and balances may wish to be employed that allows the responsibilities of patch acquisition and installation to be divided between individuals to ensure that all procedures have been followed prior to installation.

Recipient Auditing of the Components

The last component in a secure patch management system is one that should be fully integrated into all aspects of secure patch management. This component is the audit function. "System audit logs provide information about usage characteristics on a computer system" [Schultz et al, 2001] and are a key component in transmission controls [Aggarwal et al, 1998]. When an event notification occurs a log entry should document the receipt and details of the notification. The resulting authentication of the event notification should also be documented. This will provide a comprehensive list of valid and in valid sources for notification. The version verification that the patch file is applicable or non-applicable should be included in the audit log. Whether a software patch is received by mail or electronic means, the source information and acknowledgment of delivery should also be included in the log. All patch integrity checks should be fully documented and recorded. All trial installations of the patch and the resulting consequences should be recorded along with a system snapshot of available hardware and software components. Once the patch has been deployed, all appropriate documents and manuals should be updated to reflect the current version. Lastly, a distributed storage and access of all audit logs should be implemented to ensure that the documentation trail is not altered or deleted without the highest level of access.

DISCUSSION OF THE SEMI-TECHNICAL COMPONENTS OF THE FRAMEWORK

An important issue, which so far has not been well researched, is the problem of where to store all the available patches. In the case of such companies like Microsoft or IBM, producing and announcing new patches to the existing systems is relatively simple. Large companies such as these may produce patches that even the most unexperienced user would be able to direct their search efforts for upgrades to the well-known software manufacturer.

In our opinion, there is not a straightforward solution to this problem unless big companies control and coordinate all points of entry.

Another issue surfaces and becomes more complicated when dealing with open source systems like Unix or Linux. It is generally left to the user to determine which of the available patches developed to resolve a given issue is the best selection. The question that lies at the core for this type of approach is how does a user know that a patch produced by company A has or has not incorporated new changes that may have been incorporated by a patch developed by company B?

A good secure patch management system must be scalable and accommodate diverse access to patches regardless of the size of manufacturer or the size of the recipient. In the case of a small installation, patch introduction would be relatively simple: usually an owner/user installs basic software components from one source manufacturer, such as Microsoft or Apple Computer. But in the case of company-wide installations, there may be hundreds of different components, sources, and locations. Servicing updates could become an extremely challenging task for even a large organization. This concept suggests the introduction of automation into the process, including the receiving of information about the availability of a patch, its download, and its testing, and installation.

Another open research question is that of organizing libraries containing information about the available patches and the patches themselves. At present we are vigorously researching this particular issue.

The possibility of automating the process of delivery and installation of software patches raises an interesting technical as well as legal issue: to what extent would a user allow the supplier to penetrate their installation? This type of legal issue emerged with the introduction of Windows 95 and continues with Windows XP. Microsoft has included a clause in its accept/decline portion of its licensure agreement stating that it may remotely examine and update the configuration of a user's system. In addition, this issue extends to push technologies such as Java applets and ActiveX modules that promote the acquisition and delivery of a user's system information.

A discussion of the legal aspects will take place in the next section (non-technical components), but there are some additional technical issues hat need to be considered. The first is how to set up the smooth exchange of information between the user of a system and a developer, and to do so such that unauthorised reads by a third party would be prevented. This also needs to be conducted such that confidential information of the accessed party is not disclosed. One possible solution could be to produce a sort of a system passport or system ID that would contain a listing of all components and versions, and be located separately from the real system, i.e. getting access to this file would not compromise the security of the rest of the system. One may expect that such a solution would be eagerly promoted by the software developers but would be strongly opposed by software users, especially those who are using non-registered software.

DISCUSSION OF THE NON TECHNICAL COMPONENTS OF THE FRAMEWORK

Most of the non-technical issues concentrate on the problem of validating electronic documents, i.e. delivery and deployment. In the case of more advanced users or bigger installations, successful deployment of a patch management system would require the automation of the process. The deployment of automating the entirety of the patch management system implies that the parties involved in the process would trust the electronic-only-data for the clearing of their financial and business obligations.

When electronic-only transaction systems are deployed, it is in domestic markets that business obligations may mainly be executed and enforced. Problems begin when there is a need to cross international borders. This can be illustrated in the best way by comparing the transaction policies of dot-com companies. Amazon.com is readily accepts orders coming from outside the USA [Amazon.com 2002], but is reluctant to ship goods outside the USA territories (books excluded).

Another issue, which is not yet solved, is the validity of digital signatures, necessary in electronic commerce for such things as contracts, integrity validation of files, and others. While many countries have introduced related legislation, like USA [Digital Signature, 2000],

Ireland or Poland [Zalewski, 2001], others have not. These laws are also not entirely clear as to international jurisdiction.

Yet another quite interesting issue, which has not yet been solved, is of setting the date and location of an electronic transaction. A document signed between two parties, one located in New Zealand and the other in United Kingdom could bear a date/time stamp of 6th of April at 6:00 pm in New Zealand or 5th of April, 6:00 am in UK. Which date/time stamp is valid? This question is not as insignificant as one may suggest. 12 hours difference means that having $1M for 12 hours may produce a gain or losses of around $68 (with 5% interest per annum). The functional aspects of transaction agreements create a series of time constraints that may not so easily be resolved when they transcend international borders.

As a software manufacturer, consider all of these non-technical issues in the context of supplying a software fix, patch or update. If such a firm conducts business in a manner that exposes its customer to additional risks resulting in damages, hasn't the firm failed to fulfil its fiduciary responsibility? If the technology is available to secure the communication transactions and the firm does not utilize these, is it not in some way responsible for subsequent damages? If a patch is installed and it causes the system integrity to fail, isn't the firm culpable in the resulting crash?

We believe that the very nature of the software industry and electronic transactions across international borders renders many of these issues moot while licensure agreements shield the manufacturer, and practical jurisdiction is rare. It may very well take several hall-mark legal cases to void/modify the licensure agreement and an international treaty on jurisdiction to remedy this situation.

CONCLUSIONS

In this paper we have presented a framework for securing patch management, a collection of important issues in patch management, a discussion and series of research questions that are being pursued. These issues and questions can be divided into three, quite separate, domains:
- Technical problems related to identifying the patch and transporting it safely to the destination, and its deployment,
- Confidentiality issues resulting from the need to exchange important information between the supplier of the patches and their end user,
- Inadequacy of the law to handle the exchange of information in the electronic form only, especially in the case of international contacts.

We signalled the important issues within each of these domains. We believe that the future of the efficient utilization of patch management systems lies in the automation of the process. However to be successful, it requires finding solutions to all of the problems mentioned in this paper. At the University of Auckland, we are currently researching these issues, with special emphasis on the technical aspects of secure notification, transporting, and deploying patches, resulting in the development of a refined architecture encompassing all the functions mentioned in this paper.

REFERENCES

[Aggarwal et al], Aggarwal, R., Rezaee, Z., Soni, R., *Internal control considerations for global electronic data interchange*, **International Journal of Commerce & Management**, Volume 8, No. ¾, 1998.

[Amazon.com, 2002], http://www.amazon.com/help/Payment Methods - We Accept *and* Shipping restrictions

[Common Criteria, 2000], httm:// www.csrc.nist.gov/cc/ccv20/ccv2list.htm.

[CSI/FBI, 2001], *2002 Computer Crime and Security Survey*, http://www.gocsi.com/press/20020407.html.

[Digital signature, 2000] http://www.mbc.com/db30/cgi-bin/pubs/LMZ-E-SIGN.pdf

[Denning, 1999], Denning, D., *Information Warfare and Security*, Addison Wesley, 1999.

[Forch, 1994], Forch, K., *Computer Security Management*, Boyd & Fraser, 1994.

[Great Plains Dynamics, 2002], http://www.greatplains.com/

[Hinde, 1999], Hinde, S., *Step into a secure New World - Compsec '99 Report*, Computers and security, Volume 18, No. 8, 1999.

[Mission Critical Linux, 2002], http://www.missioncriticallinux.com

[Net Infrastructure, 2002], http://www.netinfra.com/patching.htm

[Northon System Works, 2002], http://www.symantec.com/sabu/sysworks/basic/

[Patch Link, 2002], http://www.patchlink.com

[Roxio, 2002], http://www.roxio.com/en/products/datarecoverypc.jhtml

[SAP, 200] SAP R/3 Upgrade Guide. SAP Labs, Inc. 2001. http://wwwtech.saplabs.com/docs/sysadmin/upgrades.pdf

[Schultz et al, 2001], Schultz, E., Proctor, R., Mei-Ching Lien, Gavriel Salvendy, G., *Usability and Security An Appraisal of Usability Issues in Information Security Methods*, Computers & Security, Volume 20, No. 7, 2001.

[Schmidt, 1990], Schmidt, D., *GPERF: A Perfect Hash Function Generator*, Second USENIX C++ Conference Proceedings, April, 1990.

[Stallings], Stallings, W., *Network Security Essentials*, Prentice Hall, 1999

[Tripuntara, 1998], Tripunitara, Spafford, E., *Issues in the incorporation of securities services into a protocol reference model*, Fifth ACM Conference on Computer and Communications Security, 1998.

[Verisign, 2002], http://www.verisign.com

[von Solms, 2996], von Solms, R., *Information Security Management: the Second Generation*, Notes on Information Security Management, IFIP, 1996.

[Zalewski, 2001], Zalewski, T., 2001, *Front wewnetrzny (Internal front)*, Polityka, No 41, 2001

Operators Not Needed? The Impact of Query Structure on Web Searching Results

Bernard J. Jansen

School of Information Sciences and Technology , The Pennsylvania State University , 001 Thomas Bldg , University Park, PA, 16801, USA
Phone: 814-856-6459 Fax: 814-865-6426, Email: jjansen@acm.org

ABSTRACT

Most Web searchers use extremely simple queries. There is an assumption that the correct use of query operators will improve the quality of results. We test his assumption by examining the impact of query operators on the documents retrieved from Web searching. We compare the results from queries without operators to results from the same queries using a variety of operators on several major web search engines. There were 1900 queries submitted, which returned 18,332 documents. In general, there was an average 66% similarity between results from the queries with and without operators. Implications on the effectiveness of current searching techniques, for future search engine design and of future research are discussed.

INTRODUCTION

The vast majority of Web queries contain no query operators (Hoelscher, 1998; Jansen, Spink, & Saracevic, 2000; Spink, Jansen, Wolfram, & Saracevic, 2002). The use of Boolean operators is typically about 8% in these Web searching studies. It has been assumed that correct usage of query operators would increase the effectiveness of Web searches. However, it appears that the majority of Web searchers continue to use very simple queries, with little to no use of query operators, even though many of these techniques (e.g., phrase searching and must appear operators) are easy to employ (Korfhage, 1997) and well known (Sullivan, 2000a). Web searchers seem to be employing an ineffective and inefficient strategy for finding information.

Studies and data suggest that Web users may be finding the information they want using simple queries, however. A survey of users on the Excite Web search engine reports that nearly 70% of the searchers reported locating relevant information on the search engine (Spink, Bateman, & Jansen, 1999). Web searchers are not utilizing advanced searching operators, but they appear to be finding information using a technique that should be ineffective or at least inefficient.

The objective of this study is to determine the effect of query operators on the results retrieved by Web search engines. This knowledge is essential to understanding how users search the web, for the development of instructional material for web searching, and for design of search interfaces the support the information seeking process. In this paper, we present an overview of related literature, research methodology, and research results from various perspectives. We end with a discussion of results and directions for future research.

RELATED STUDIES

Search engines are the major information retrieval (IR) systems for users of the Web, with 71% of Web users accessing search engines to locate other Web sites (CommerceNet/NielsenMedia, 1997). There are approximately 3,200 search engines on the Web (Sullivan, 2000b). Those utilized in this research are Alta Vista, Excite, FAST Search, GoTo, and Northern Light.

There have been relatively few studies comparing the retrieval results of different search engines using different approaches to query formulation (Eastman, 2002; Jansen, 2000). Eastman (2002) explored the precision of search engines using a variety of topics and query formulations. The researcher notes that precision did not necessarily improve with the use of the advanced query operators. We could locate no study focusing the on the change in results from a large number of queries across multiple search engines. Jansen (2000) examines the changes in results using a small sample, fifteen queries, and five search engines utilizing different searching operators. The researcher reports a 70% similarity in results between queries with no operators and the queries with operators.

There has been some research examining Web searching in general. Research shows that Web queries generally have two terms (Jansen, Spink, Bateman, & Saracevic, 1998; Silverstein, Henzinger, Marais, & Moricz, 1999), cover a variety of topics (Wolfram, 1999), and are primarily noun phrases (Jansen & Pooch, 2001; Kirsch, 1998). Other studies show that most Web searchers, usually about 80%, never view more than ten results (Hoelscher, 1998; Jansen et al., 2000; Silverstein et al., 1999). Examining Web information systems, the ability of Web search engines to successfully retrieve relevant documents has been investigated several times (Leighton & Srivastava, 1999; Zumalt & Pasicznyuk, 1998).

RESEARCH DESIGN AND METHODOLGY

We investigate the effect of complex queries (i.e., those using advanced syntax, such as Boolean operators) on the results retrieved by Web search engines relative to the results retrieved by simple queries (i.e., those with no advanced syntax).

Selection of Queries and Results

We randomly selected a stratified sample of 100 queries from an Excite search service transaction log. Queries of the following lengths were selected for this study: 10 queries of 4 terms, 31 queries of 3 terms, and 59 queries of two terms.

Along with selecting the queries, there is the issue of results Based on "typical" Web searcher behavior, only the first ten results in the results list were selected for comparison. We examined these results only for changes in the first ten results. We did not evaluate the results for relevance.

Searching Rules

These five search engines offer a variety of advanced searching options. Some searching options are available from each search engine's main search page, others on a 'power' searching page. For this research, only those advanced searching options available from the search engine's main page were utilized. Of the five search engines, two offer four advanced search options (+, ", AND, and OR) from the main page, and three search engines offer two advanced searching options (+, and "). All of the search engines offer dropdown boxes (e.g., language of results, document collections to search) for refining the search. When dropdown boxes were present on the main search page, the default options were utilized.

Research Structure

Each of the 100 original queries was submitted to the five search engines for a total of 500 queries. The query was then modified with the advanced searching operators supported by the respective search engines. The entire process of submitting the simple and advance queries took 5 minutes or less. For example, the simple query *digital library* could be modified using the must appear operator *(+digital + library)*, phrase searching operator *("digital library")*, the AND operator *(digital AND library)*, and the OR operator *(digital OR library)*. These modified queries are the complex queries.

RESULTS

Of the 500 simple queries, 498 returned at least 10 results. One query returned 3 results, and one query returned no results. Therefore, there were 4983 results to use as the baseline (i.e., 498 x 10 + 3). As stated, results that appeared greater than position 10 in the results list were not utilized. Of the 1400 complex queries, 1325 returned ten or more results. There were 31 queries that returned fewer than ten results but more than zero results. There were 44 queries that returned no results. Altogether, there were 13,349 results returned by the complex queries. Combined with the 4,983 results from the simple queries, a total of 18,332 results were used in the analysis.

The match had to be exact when comparing the results between the simple and complex queries. The documents listed had to be the identical page at the same site. Different pages from the same site were not counted as matches. The identical pages at different sites were not counted as matches. Furthermore, if results appeared in both lists but in a different order, they were counted as matches as long as both were listed in the first ten results.

Simple Versus Complex Query Comparison

The aggregate results of the analysis of the 18,332 results are displayed in Table 1.

The baseline mean for the simple queries was 9.99, and the mean for the complex queries was 6.55. This means that, on average, 6.55 of the ten results retrieved by the complex queries also appeared in the baseline results for the corresponding simple query on that search engine. The results were analyzed using a paired sample t test, as reported in Table 1. The analysis revealed a significant difference between the two groups (t=40.287; p<0.01).*Results by Query*

The number of matching results by queries length is graphically displayed in Figure 1.

Table 1: Comparison of Simple versus Complex Queries on Major Web Search Engines.

Category	Average Number of Matching Results	Standard Deviation	Mode	Paired sample t
Simple Queries	9.99	0.03	10	-
Complex Queries	6.55	3.77	10	40.287

In terms of the number of matching results, the range for three and two term queries was similar (see Figure 1). The range for four-term queries was lower. However, there was a great deal of disparity among all three query lengths. One of the lowest, a two- term query, *internet capitalist,* had an average of only 3.6 matching results. One of the queries with the greatest number of matching results was a three- term query, *grape seed extract.* As a synopsis, the top 15 queries with the greatest overlap of results are displayed in Table 2.

Figure 1: Number of Matching Results between Simple and Complex Queries

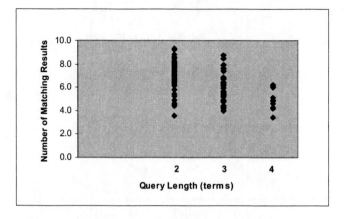

Table 2: Comparison of Results by Query for Top 15 Queries.

Query	Average Number of Results that Appear in Baseline	Standard Deviation	Mode
bonsai trees	9.3	1.3	10
fuzzy logic	9.2	1.4	10
ear cleaning	8.8	2.0	10
grape seed extract	8.7	2.1	10
bread machines	8.6	1.9	10
self esteem	8.6	2.9	10
car insurance	8.5	2.8	10
bull riding	8.5	2.2	10
adult friend finders	8.4	2.5	10
morgan horse	8.4	2.2	10
nudist colonies	8.3	2.4	10
scream queens	8.2	2.5	10
neck pain	8.1	2.4	10
talk shows	8.1	3.2	10
poetry contest	8.1	2.7	10

Results by Search Engine

The analysis was conducted for query operators by search engine, with the results displayed in Table 3.

The first column in Table 3 is the heading for the number of matching results. The top row lists the searching engine; the second row displays the corresponding advanced query operator. From each row in column 1, one can move right across the table to the occurrences for each in the *No.* column, which is the number of times that the results from the complex queries contained that number of exact matches. For example, there were 651 complex queries that return ten results identical to the corresponding simple queries. Moving further to the right, each column shows the number of occurrences for each search engine and operator for a given number of matching results. The average number of matching results and the standard deviation is also given.

As Table 3 illustrates, the effect of the specific operators varied depending on the search engine involved. With Alta Vista, the average for the must appear operator was half of what it was for phrase searching. With Excite, the average for phrase searching was about half of the other three operators. With FAST Search, there was a marked drop using phrase searching. The matching results of the GoTo operators were both greater than seven matches. The default algorithms for Excite, FAST Search, and Northern Light are illustrated with 100% matches between the simple and complex queries.

Table 3 shows that there were 651 (47%) complex queries that retrieved identical results as the simple queries. All ten results from these 651 complex queries were identical to the results from the simple queries. This occurrence is by far the most frequent; the next highest occurrence was 163 (12%) complex queries that retrieve no matching results.

Table 3: Comparison of Results by Search Engine and Operator

Matching Results	No.	AV	EX	FS	GT	NL	AV	Ex	FS	GT	NL	EX	NL	Ex	NL
		+	+	+	+	+	"	"	"	"	"	AND	AND	OR	OR
Average		3.0	7.9	10	9.4	10	6.0	5.0	3.8	7.2	6.0	7.9	3.1	10	2.57
SD		3.2	3.5	0.0	1.5	0.0	4.5	3.8	2.9	3.4	2.8	3.5	2.9	0.0	2.9
Paired sample t*		21.11	6.00	-	3.74	-	8.54	12.63	19.69	7.46	23.36	6.04	23.36	-	25.53
10	651	9	67	100	77	100	48	21	1	44	7	67	5	100	5
9	45	4	2	0	12	0	0	3	2	3	14	1	3	0	1
8	49	1	4	0	3	0	1	6	8	4	13	5	3	0	1
7	54	0	3	0	0	0	1	7	8	4	15	3	5	0	8
6	45	4	1	0	3	0	1	3	11	7	8	1	4	0	2
5	54	5	3	0	1	0	1	8	11	2	10	3	5	0	5
4	55	10	2	0	1	0	3	4	6	1	7	2	13	0	6
3	59	4	3	0	1	0	1	7	5	6	7	3	11	0	11
2	91	18	4	0	0	0	6	9	8	6	4	4	17	0	15
1	79	15	4	0	1	0	9	5	8	8	7	4	8	0	10
0	163	25	7	0	0	0	20	18	20	1	3	7	26	0	36
NR	55	5	0	0	1	0	9	9	12	14	5	0	0	0	0
Total	1400	100	100	100	100	100	100	100	100	100	100	100	100	100	100

Vista, EX – Excite, FS – FAST Search, GT – GoTo, NL – Northern Light, NR – No Results returned by query. (2) Missin
: to a zero standard deviation.   * p<0.01

The results were analyzed using a paired sample t test, as reported in Table 3, fifth row. The analysis revealed a significant difference between the results of each search engine operators relative to the results retrieved by the simple queries on the respective search engines, with the except of when there was no difference (i.e., noted as -).

We conducted a regression analysis to determine any significant relationship among the variables, query length, search engine, and query operator on the results retrieved. The overall model was significant (F= 21.99, p<0.01) with an R-squared of 0.05. Query length was a significant predictor of results (t=-6.156, p<=0.01), with a beta weight of -0.164. As query length increased, the number of matching results decreased. Query operator was also a significant predictor (t=6.156, p<0.01), with a beta weight of 0.145. Although significant, as the beta weights show, neither query length nor query operator had a substantial impact on the number of matching results. Search engine was an insignificant predictor of matching results.

DISCUSSION OF RESULTS

Approximately 66% of the results were identical regardless of how the searcher entered the query. Referring to the data displayed in Table 1, a paired sample t-test (t= 40.287, p<0.01) shows that the results from the simple queries are significantly different from the results for complex queries. However, the betas show that the impact of operators is relative low indicting that there are other factors that influence results. For example, terms have been show to impact query results (Spink & Saracevic, 1997). Additionally, as with all tests of statistical significance, one must ask "what different does this make in the 'real world'?".

Is it practical to learn and utilize the query operators if on average they are only going to present about three or four results that are different from those retrieved by just entering the query terms? Are the three or four different results worth the increased probability of entering a complex query incorrectly? As the complexity of queries increases, so does the probability of error.

The findings of this research suggest that the use of queries operators is generally not worth the trouble for the typical Web searcher (i.e., one who uses two terms and is interested only in the first ten results).

Based on their conduct, it appears that most Web searchers do not think it is worth the trouble either. The relative precision of simple Web queries meets the information needs of most Web searchers.

In reviewing the analysis by search engine, outlined in Table 3, there was a great deal of overlap between query results for most search engines. The mode for all five search engines, regardless of search operator was ten. With Excite, 78% of the results are identical, regardless of the present or absence of advanced searching operators. Based on the rather random results retrieved, Alta Vista appears to adhere to the theoretical model of no ranking feature when Boolean-like operators are used in a query.

CONCLUSIONS AND FUTURE RESEARCH

This research indicates that use of complex queries appears to have a moderate impact on the results retrieved. Approximately 66% of the top ten results on average will be the same regardless of how the query is entered. Based on the actions of most web searchers, the approximately three or four different results may not be worth the increased effort required to learn the advanced searching rules or the increased risk of making a mistake.

Given that the typical web searcher seldom uses advanced operators, web search engines appear to be compensating for the searching characteristics of their users. Based on the results of this research, it appears that the ranking algorithms of these search engines generally adhere to the following rule: *Place those documents that contain all the query terms and that have all the query terms near each other at the top of the results list*. Although an over simplification of what can be complex algorithms, a ranking rule like this would negate the impact of most query operators for the topmost ranked documents.

This study measured the change in the results list of complex versus simple queries. The natural next step is to measure the change in precision. One might expect that the complex queries would improve precision (i.e., the ratio of retrieved relevant documents to the total retrieved documents); however, this assumption would have to be tested. Given the observed changes in ranking by some search engines, the introduction of Boolean operators may result in a precision decrease.

REFERENCES

CommerceNet/NielsenMedia. (1997). *Search Engines Most Popular Method of Surfing the Web* [web site]. Commerce Net/Nielsen Media. Retrieved 30 August, 2000, from the World Wide Web: http://www.commerce.net/news/press/0416.html

Eastman, C. M. (2002). 30,000 Hits May be Better than 300: Precision Anomalies in Internet Searches. *Journal of the American Society for Information Science and Technology, 53*(11), 879-882.

Hoelscher, C. (1998, July 1998). How Internet Experts search for Information on the Web. In *Proceedings of the World Conference of the World Wide Web, Internet, and Intranet*, Orlando, FL.

Jansen, B. J. (2000). An Investigation into the Use of Simple Queries on Web IR Systems. *Information Research: An Electronic Journal, 6*(1), 1-10.

Jansen, B. J., & Pooch, U. (2001). Web User Studies: A Review and Framework for Future Work. *Journal of the American Society of Information Science and Technology, 52*(3), 235-246.

Jansen, B. J., Spink, A., Bateman, J., & Saracevic, T. (1998). Real Life Information Retrieval: A Study of User Queries on the Web. *SIGIR Forum, 32*(1), 5-17.

Jansen, B. J., Spink, A., & Saracevic, T. (2000). Real Life, Real Users, and Real Needs: A Study and Analysis of User Queries on the Web. *Information Processing and Management, 36*(2), 207-227.

Kirsch, S. (1998). *The future of Internet search (keynote address)* [website]. Keynote address presented at the 21st Annual International ACM SIGIR Conference on Research and Development in Information Retrieval, Melbourne, Australia. Retrieved 16 August, 1999, from the World Wide Web: http://www.skirsch.com/stk.html/presentations/sigir.ppt

Korfhage, R. (1997). *Information Storage and Retrieval*. New York, NY: Wiley.

Leighton, H., & Srivastava, J. (1999). First 20 Precision among World Wide Web Search Services (Search Engines). *Journal of the American Society for Information Science, 50*(1), 870-881.

Silverstein, C., Henzinger, M., Marais, H., & Moricz, M. (1999). Analysis of a Very Large Web Search Engine Query Log. *SIGIR Forum, 33*(1), 6-12.

Spink, A., Bateman, J., & Jansen, B. J. (1999). Searching the Web: A Survey of Excite Users. *Journal of Internet Research: Electronic Networking Applications and Policy, 9*(2), 117-128.

Spink, A., Jansen, B. J., Wolfram, D., & Saracevic, T. (2002). From E-sex to E-commerce: Web Search Changes. *IEEE Computer, 35*(3), 107-111.

Spink, A., & Saracevic, T. (1997). Interaction in Information Retrieval: Selection and Effectiveness of Search Terms. *Journal of the American Society for Information Science, 48*(5), 382-394.

Sullivan, D. (2000a). *Search Engine Sizes*. Retrieved 30 August, 2000, from the World Wide Web: http://searchenginewatch.com/reports/sizes.html

Sullivan, D. (2000b). *Search Watch*. Search Engine Watch. Retrieved 1 June, 2000, from the World Wide Web: http://searchenginewatch.com/

Wolfram, D. (1999). Term Co-occurrence in Internet Search Engine Queries: An Analysis of the Excite Data Set. *Canadian Journal of Information and Library Science, 24*(2/3), 12-33.

Zumalt, J., & Pasicznyuk, R. (1998). The Internet and Reference Services: A Real-world Test of Internet Utility. *Reference and User Services Quarterly, 38*(2), 165-172.

MANAGING END-USER SYSTEM DEVELOPMENT: LESSONS FROM A CASE STUDY

Murray E. Jennex, Ph.D., P.E.

San Diego State University, murphjen@aol.com, 603 Seagaze Dr. #608, Oceanside, CA 92054, 760-722-2668 (fax)

ABSTRACT

How much end-user computing is too much? Should end users develop systems? This paper reports on a study of the engineering organizations within an electric utility undergoing deregulation. The study was initiated when management perceived that too much engineering time was spent doing IS functions. The study found that there was significant effort being expended on system development, support, and ad hoc use. Several issues were identified affecting system development, use of programming standards, documentation, infrastructure integration, and system support.

INTRODUCTION

Due to deregulation the subject utility organization assessed its engineering staffing. They determined their staffing needed to be lowered by approximately 25%. A change management team was formed for identifying where work effort could be reduced. During this process it was noticed that the engineering organizations were spending significant amounts of time and effort on information technology (IT) related tasks. To assess this IT usage a team was formed consisting of engineering and information systems (IS) representatives and led by the author, a former member of the engineering organization and at the time of the study, a member of IS. The team collected an inventory of IT products and resources used by engineering organizations but not supplied, supported, or controlled by IS. The team also assessed how IT usage could be better managed by engineering.

The team found a significant amount of effort expended by engineering on IT including system development and significant system support and ad hoc reporting efforts. Analysis of these efforts found several problems that caused additional wasted efforts and significant expenditure of additional funds. This analysis provides insight into how an organization can better manage end user computing (EUC).

BACKGROUND

The subject organization's Year 2000 (Y2K) effort documented 151 applications supported by Engineering where the support consists of personnel and/or annual renewal/licensing costs. Additionally, IS supports another 11 applications used by engineering. Finally, discussions with various managers and supervisors indicated that there was a number of 'local' databases and programs developed and/or supported within engineering. Also, there was a perception that significant engineering resources were being used to support IT needs due to a lack of support by IS for engineer IT needs.

EUC is the adoption and use of IT by personnel outside of the IS organization to develop applications to support organizational tasks (Powell and Moore, 2002). Reviewing the literature found few sources related to end user system development. Dodson (1995) and KPMG (1999) warned of the dangers of unmanaged end user system/application development but provided little guidance into how to manage this development. Munkvold (2002) found that high computer skill self-efficacy within end users coupled with a low regard for IS leads to end user system/application development. Wagner (2000) investigated the use of end users as expert system developers and found that end users have significant domain knowledge. However, it was also found that end users had difficulty knowing and expressing what they know, making their contribution limited in content, quality, size, and scalability. Taylor, et. al. (1998) agrees that end users do not produce good systems and identified duplication of effort, low quality, and lack of training in system development methodology as issues. However, McBride (2002) found that imposing system development methodology on end users might be regarded as an attempt to impose IT culture. Finally, Adelekun and Jennex (2002) found that EUC development issues could be caused by end users not identifying appropriate stakeholders for assessing success of end user developed systems/applications.

METHODOLOGY

The team consisted of engineers serving as computer representatives/liaisons, considered to be subject matter experts (SMEs) and IS personnel serving in the engineering support systems group. The author served as project manager. Data was collected using informal surveys and interviews, and forty structured interviews. The process was to first generate an inventory of IT applications used by the engineering organizations but not maintained by the IS group. The scope of the inventory was any specialized software/hardware for data collection, testing, and analysis, specialized databases, any software used for system development, any generic software that was being customized through the generation of macros, scripts, or programs, and any other software/hardware assessed to be important to engineering and worthy of inclusion. A first cut inventory was generated using the Y2K inventory. This was validated using surveys/interviews to validate the Y2K inventory and to expand the inventory as necessary.

The second step was to generate a list of IT resources existing within each engineering organization. IT resources were considered to be engineers with IT skills in demand by their coworkers such that they spent significant amounts of time assisting management or their group with IT support. The initial list of resources was developed by the SMEs. After conducting 40 interviews of selected individuals, the list was finalized by the project manager. A set script was used for determining what amount of IT support was being provided by engineers to engineers, any additional inventory items, general levels of automation and needed IT, and what issues were involved in using IT in engineering. Interview subjects were selected based on input from the SME's and known expertise and/or participation in IT development.

The final step was to take the gathered data, analyze it with respect to dollars and time invested as well as issues identified, and generate a set of recommendations for improving management of the IT effort in the engineering organizations. This was documented in a final report by

Jennex, et. al. (2000) that was presented to IS and engineering management and is used as the data source for this paper.

FINDINGS

The assessment found a significant but poorly managed investment in IT in terms of money, time, and expertise. With respect to the management of IT, it was observed that IS is tasked with managing the infrastructure, networks, and enterprise level applications. This provides an overall organizational perspective and strategy for managing these assets. Engineering IT is managed at the division level and was found to lack an overall engineering strategy for the use, adaptation, and implementation of IT. Additionally, IT was unevenly applied throughout the engineering divisions. Some groups were fully automated; others with process steps automated but not the overall process; and still others were not automated at all. The net effect was that IT assets were not performing as effectively as they could and many engineers were expending more time and resources than they should to obtain the information and data they needed. Specifics on these findings are provided in the following paragraphs.

Investment

The inventory recorded 267 applications with supporting hardware. This number excludes enterprise work process systems, basic personal productivity applications (MSOffice, WordPerfect, Access, etc.), and plant control applications. Included are the analysis tools, graphics packages, scheduling tools, equipment databases, image and web editing and authoring tools, and data collection tools used by engineers. The team was confident this number reflected at least 90% of what was in use. The investment in terms of dollars and effort was not totally determined, not all numbers were known and not all groups were willing or able to report all costs. However, with about 30% of the inventoried applications reporting this data it was found that approximately $1,650,000.00 had been spent to purchase these applications with an additional 5 person years (during the last 2 years) expended on development. Additionally, $290,000.00 was spent annually on license or maintenance fees and 10 full time equivalent engineers (FTEs) were expended maintaining these applications. Finally, an additional approximate 10 FTEs were expended assisting other engineers in the use of these tools. For political reasons there were significant exclusions from these figures including 45 FTEs and $335,000.00 in annual licensing cost supporting plant control IT. The team was confident that purchase and support costs and efforts would at least double if all the information was available. For perspective, these numbers were not expected and were considered by management to be extremely excessive although Panko (1988) found in the 1980s that 25-40% of IT expenditures were in EUC and not under IS control.

Engineer Involvement in IT

It was observed that engineers supported IT three ways; supporting other engineers' use/acquisition of IT, learning to use the IT, and maintaining applications; building queries, macros, and reports for special/ad hoc information requests; and developing IT solutions for supporting engineering processes. It was reported previously that approximately 20 FTEs were expended for the first item and approximately 5 person/years were expended (over the last 2 years) for the third item. Doubling these values (per the team's estimate) gives 45 FTEs/year for items one and three. The second item was found to take approximately 5% of each engineers' time. Taken as a whole this is a fairly extensive activity, approximately 21 FTEs yearly. Combining these efforts and excluding assets dedicated to plant IT support, approximately 66 FTEs/year (14%) are spent on IT functions. This was considered excessive.

The need for engineering to provide their own IT support was attributed to several reasons but is due primarily to three issues. The first is that engineering applications are generally not supported by IS so expertise to assist engineers with these applications only exists in engineering. The second is that due to lack of standardization there are multiple products supporting the same function, this makes having central support prohibitively expensive, experts would be needed for over 200 applications and devices that in many cases are only used by a few people. The third is a suffering relationship between engineers and IS.

The ability to do ad hoc reporting was considered a tremendous strength. The team did not see the need for ad hoc reporting decreasing. However, there were several issues that caused the time needed for this activity to be greater than it needed to be. Chief among these are a lack of standard query/reporting tools, a lack of advanced training in the use of the available tools, and a lack of integration of the site databases resulting in more complex and time consuming query/report generation.

The ability to develop new systems for addressing specific engineering problems was considered a strength and a need by the engineering organizations. The team agreed that this function would continue to require engineering involvement. However, this is the function least understood by engineering with respect to cost and process. Engineers followed minimal processes and considered the Capability Maturity Model, CMM, processes followed by IS to be a waste of time and money (IS is a CMM Level 2 shop). The processes followed by engineering need to be formalized so that resources applied to project development are accounted for, the highest priority projects are performed first, projects are performed cost effectively, and the resulting systems are documented and designed to IS standards (this reduces maintenance and conversion to enterprise application costs).

Other Issues Affecting Engineer Involvement in IT

There are many plant digital systems that are approaching their end of life and need to be updated. Systems were found running on Windows 3.1 and DOS as well as using 8" and 5 1/4 " floppy drive technology. Expertise and hardware for maintaining these systems is disappearing. Problems arise as replacements are investigated for these systems and as new equipment/software is purchased for resolving new problems. Infrastructure is standardized on proven technology and is not leading edge. Engineers tend to buy leading or even bleeding edge products. This results in some new products not being able to function within the IS environment and requiring engineers to purchase equipment of an older standard. However, it is not good practice to develop replacement systems for the older infrastructure in place, instead, developers need to anticipate where the infrastructure is going and design for that. The issue is how to incorporate leading edge solutions needed by engineering into the IS infrastructure while maintaining the reliability and coherence of the infrastructure.

There is a great deal of memory stored in systems no longer supported by IS. Also, there is a great deal of knowledge as to why things are done a certain way built into macros, programs, reports, databases, and models that is not captured in a retrievable manner. As engineering undergoes change there is a potential for a great deal of this knowledge to be lost. Additionally, engineering's current knowledge management practices assume a static work force and will not work well with a changing work force.

Digital cameras and the use of digital images are rapidly growing. Their use has had a very positive impact on productivity. However, due to a lack of standards on types of equipment, software, and formats there exists the potential for the benefits of the productivity improvement to be lost to slower network speeds, dealing with different formats, and incorporating images into processes not designed to handle them.

Use of the external Internet has had significant productivity benefits with respect to research and document and contact information retrieval. However, use of the internal Intranet has had lesser results. This is attributed to a lack of a web strategy, resources, and standard tools/design practices.

It was observed that the distinction between the business systems maintained by IS and plant systems maintained by engineering is blurring. Plant information flows across the business network on a routine basis. Plant processes have been developed that rely on email to transmit data. Plant support productivity has improved by using the business networks to access and maintain plant systems. The key issue is to recognize that the boundary for protecting plant information now extends to the Intranet firewalls.

ANALYSIS

What these findings show is that left unmanaged, EUC can cause organizations to shift significant resources away from their central focus or function. They also show that an IS group that focuses on providing enterprise level systems can fail to support specific user needs. While this is predominantly an IS management issue, there are two issues specific to IS development. The first is the issue of end user IS development that does not follow IS standards. This case found end-user applications that did not have documentation, were low in quality, or that were designed such that they could not interface with the organizational infrastructure. These findings result in much higher maintenance costs. To illustrate these problems, two applications were found that the team was told "unofficially" cost a total of approximately $1,000,000.00 with neither able to perform the function it was purchased for due in total or in part to incompatibility with the infrastructure. The engineering group paid IS approximately $40,000.00 in labor costs to make one application work. The other application was abandoned after IS spent approximately one-person week working with the vendor to see if it could be made to work and determining that it could not. Both applications were built without consideration of IS standards for the operating environment and consulting the appropriate stakeholders with the result that neither worked. Additionally, neither utilized IS standard interfaces or programming guidelines causing low quality and making both difficult to understand and work with from the IS developer viewpoint. While these two examples are the extreme, they were not isolated cases. Numerous examples were found where engineering groups bought or developed hardware and/or software without regard for IS development standards with the result that additional effort was required to get the hardware and/or software to initially work or to maintain it over its useful life.

There is also a potentially large problem with those applications and systems developed without documentation. An example was an application developed to model the fire protection system. The application is used to evaluate potential work activities to determine impact on the fire protection system and to determine what compensatory measures need to be taken to ensure the fire protection system will still function when portions of it are taken out of service for maintenance. The application was designed, built, maintained, and supported by the fire protection engineer. No documentation was found. The concern is what happens if this engineer leaves, as a replacement has nothing to learn from. The organization has grown to rely on this application and its loss would severely impact the organization. Again, this was not an isolated case. Numerous examples were found of special reports, databases, spreadsheets, and applications that were built to satisfy specific needs but which are not documented. All rely on the engineer using them to maintain and enhance them and would be lost should the engineer leave and the report, database, spreadsheet, or application have a failure or need to be modified.

What makes these issues significant to this and all organizations is that it has the potential to lead to inaccurate data and incorrect decision-making. Research into spreadsheet errors by KPMG (1999) and Panko (2000) found very high incidence of errors. KPMG (1999) suggests implementing standards in design. Dodson (1995) expects up to 80% of system development will be by end users and that if done without standards and standard methodologies will result in high maintenance costs. It is suggested by this study that doing end user development according to IS development standards is important.

The second issue is the large amount of ad hoc reporting. This can be reflective of several problems. It can be due to simply having lots of unstructured questions requiring ad hoc searches and queries. It can also be due to enterprise database systems not addressing requirements of sub-organizations and being poorly organized and documented. Interviews recorded numerous complaints of end users not knowing where data was. Engineers that spent significant time assisting in ad hoc reports and queries stated that their time was taken in assisting with SQL and finding out where data was kept. To address this the organization is considering publishing a data road map. Another problem are standard reports. There is no process for tracking end user reports to determine

if they are used in sufficient quantity to warrant inclusion in the enterprise system. The team did not consider this very important but from the interviews it appeared that there were several organizations doing the same or similar reports. Discussions with IS and end user managers found no awareness of what reports and queries were being run although both groups expressed interest in making repeatedly run reports and queries part of the formal system. This leads to the key issue of IS focusing on the enterprise level and allowing end users to go their own way. This case is an example of more effort than necessary being expended on ad hoc reporting because the enterprise database structure was not available to the end users and no effort is being made to monitor end user usage for common reports and queries. Dodson (1995) found that these are common problems when IS focuses solely on the organizational systems. What makes this issue more significant is the ability to generalize the average of 5% time spent on ad hoc reports to other organizations. This was considered excessive by the engineering organizations' management and would probably be considered excessive in most organizations. One of the more interesting questions for further research is what level of ad hoc reports and queries is acceptable. Perhaps the most interesting observation during the study was the generally held opinion that the ability to do ad hoc reports was a great strength. While this is an indication of system flexibility and end user ability, it did not occur to anyone that large amounts of ad hoc reports and queries could also be a negative indicator.

CONCLUSION

The major conclusion is that EUC left on its own is costly. This is especially true for end user system development and leads to the proposition that end user system development should be performed just like IS system development. The earlier examples of the two systems purchased for approximately $1,000,000.00 that did not work are even more striking when it is realized that the IS department estimated they could have designed and built both systems for approximately $250,000.00. This estimate was based on using in house knowledge and expertise, standard objects from the IS object library, and existing infrastructure. That the IS department was not considered for this work is indicative of the low level of trust between the organizations. The primary recommendation for getting end user system development to implement IS design standards is to create end user led development teams that use IS developers as resources. Another possibility is training and qualifying end user system developer as IS developers and including training on IS design standards. Ultimately the findings of Wagner (2000) and Taylor, et. al. (1988) are reflected in this case.

A secondary conclusion is that EUC should be monitored and expectations as to what are acceptable levels of activity established. The purpose of this monitoring is to ensure that productivity improvements due to incorporating common end user activities into the organizational systems are realized.

In conclusion, this case illustrates that EUC problems identified in the 1980's have not changed. This leads to the conclusion that while it appears interest in EUC has waned (based on the author's perception from doing the background research for the paper and serving as EUC track chair for the 2003 Information Resource Management Association conference) the need for continued research in EUC is still great.

REFERENCES

Available Upon Request

Enhancing E-Learning with a Document Control Environment

Ajin Jirachiefpattana, Ph.D.
Department of Computer and Statistics, Faculty of Arts and Sciences, Dhurakijpundit University
Laksi, Bangkok 10210 Thailand., Tel: (66 2) 9547300-29 Ext. 257, Fax: (66 2) 5899605-6
Email: ajin@dpu.ac.th

Waraporn Jirachiefpattana, Ph.D.
School of Applied Statistics, National Institute for Development and Administration
Bangkapi, Bangkok 10240 Thailand, Tel: (66 2) 3777400-99 Ext. 2458, Email: waraporn@as.nida.ac.th

ABSTRACT

E-learning allows us to learn anywhere and usually at anytime convenient to the students. Modern technologies such as computers and the Internet are main infrastructures that enable teachers and students to exchange electronic documentation. To make e-learning successful, however, it is necessary to have the ability not only to exchange electronic documents but also to control such documents after delivery. That is, after a document leaves the teacher's desktop, control is necessary to ensure that the document is only disseminated to his/her intended students. Therefore, this paper presents an environment that is able to track and control all delivered documents, and how to integrate such an environment into e-learning.

Keywords: E-learning, Document control, Document tracking.

INTRODUCTION

E-learning is the electronic or digital delivery of knowledge, information, education and training. It can be CD-ROM-based, network-based, Intranet-based, or Internet-based. It includes text, video, audio, animation, and virtual environments. E-learning allows you to learn anywhere and usually at anytime, as long as you have a properly configured network and computer. It can suffer from many of the same pitfalls as classroom learning, such as boring slides, monotonous speech, and little opportunity for interaction. As in every form of learning, the quality of e-learning is in its content and its delivery [4, 6, 7, 8].

In a typical learning environment, it can be either active or passive, or both. Active learning is the goal-keep learners awake, keep them engaged in their learning, and make them energized participants. That is, one of the requirements of e-learning is the ability to exchange electronic/digital information and documents between a teacher and students. Whenever information or documents leave the teacher or student, control is necessary to ensure that the information or documents are only disseminated to their intended audience. People who write, create, and send information should have the ability to control whatever they send. In lieu of document security, the user loses control of data when he pushes the send button on his email GUI or posts a valuable document on a human resource server.

Thus, this paper presents an environment, which provides access control that stays with documents and data after they are delivered, and how such an environment is incorporated into e-learning.

MODERN DOCUMENT EXCHANGE

Electronic document exchange is quickly becoming the main way that organizations disseminate information. Email, Word, spreadsheets, and the Web are part of our everyday lives. In this electronic world, nobody thinks twice about zipping up important files with confidential data and sending them from a desktop in the teacher's office to students in the campus.

There is no arguing that the Internet and other technology has made our lives easier, business processes faster, and data more available. But it has also created some new challenges.

In today's work environment a person must be able to send a file with confidence that it won't be intercepted, tampered with, or viewed by someone other than the intended recipient. We all know this is easier to say than to have done. Script kiddies, electronic vandals, and even corporate spies are ubiquitous. Passwords and other confidential information are passed over networks in the clear, and the everyday computer user doesn't think much about security.

There are five different things a systems administrator should consider when trying to create an environment in which a user community can exchange information securely [1, 2, 5, 9].

Authentication guarantees that computers, users, or companies accessing documents are who they claim to be

Access Control requires users to have the appropriate permission for viewing sensitive data

Message Integrity guarantees a document has not been altered

Accountability provides an audit trail for tracking electronic transactions

Revocation provides a means to dynamically deny access to data at any time without having to recover copies

Without all five of these elements considered, document exchange can be a company's worst liability.

Whether blackhat, whitehat, or greyhat, hackers are a legitimate concern when talking about document control and privacy. They find ways to put themselves in the middle of a transmission being conducted by two other parties, who believe their connection, is secure. They find ways to steal passwords and bring down websites. Hackers also do some good. They find vulnerabilities in software, report weaknesses to the technology community in general, and post information about how to fix the vulnerabilities they expose.

In large part, information transmitted across networks, including the Internet, is transmitted "in the clear." For example, Internet e-mail flows in plain text from the teacher, through one or more Internet gateways, to the student.

Sending e-mail over the Internet can be likened to sending a postcard in the snail mail system. Neither the electronic nor the paper version is in an envelope and many employees and contractors will handle it as it travels to its destination. Any of the handlers can read the email or postcard and it may even get lost.

On the Internet, people who make it their business to hack networks and computers have tools readily available to help them. Network sniffers can be used both for good (network administration functions) and evil (stealing information). Unauthorized sniffers can be extremely dangerous to a network's security because they are virtually impossible to detect and can be inserted al-

Figure 1: A Simple Example of the Man-In-The-Middle Attack

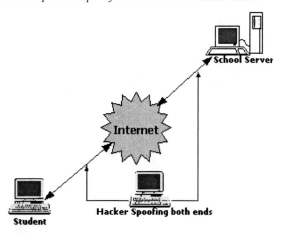

Figure 2: Major Software Components in a Document Control Environment

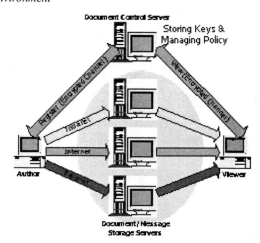

most anywhere on a network.

In addition to readily available tools, hackers have figured out how to shim themselves between the route of a two-way communication. In a Man in the Middle Attack, as shown in Figure 1, a hacker places his system between that of a sender and receiver. By spoofing both ends of the communication, a hacker can monitor all the traffic between the endpoints. Admittedly, this is a complex task. But once a hacker successfully executes the attack, he can put the exploit on the Internet for all kinds of script kiddies to download and deploy.

This becomes a scary scenario when we talk about the world of on-line confidential document exchange. What if a hacker successfully planted himself between a home-computer-user doing on-line document exchange? The user sends passwords, account numbers, and confidential information across a wire assuming that he is talking to the school, when his confidential information might be making an intermediary stop at the Dark Lord's computer.

The Man-in-the-Middle attack exploits two problems that must be solved when implementing a good all around security program:

File Interception . Interception and alteration of transmitted data by people other than the data's intended recipient

Authentication. Ensuring a person or computer system is, in fact, whom you intended or want to communicate with

PERSISTENT DOCUMENT CONTROL

As now discussed ad-nauseum, file level protection is as important as network level security. After a file leaves the teacher's desktop, control is necessary to ensure that the information is only disseminated to its intended students.

People who write, create, and send all that data inside those zip files, emails, marketing.html, and exam.docs should have the ability to control whatever they send. In lieu of document security, the user loses control of data when he pushes the send button on his email GUI or posts a valuable document on a human resource server.

Maybe an organization sells information like lead sheets that they do not want freely distributed. Or maybe another organization inside the same company needs to keep information protected for private or legal reasons. Consequently, there is a strong need for a software environment that will help schools get control over the way important data is stored and distributed.

A DOCUMENT CONTROL ENVIRONMENT

As shown in Figure 2, the computer software system [3] consists of three main components: a Document Control Server (DCS), Author, and Viewer. These software components combine encryption, authentication, and authorization to protect important information while at the same time allowing the free exchange of ideas and data.

This system can be used in a variety of ways to secure confidential, copyrighted, or secure information while at the same time allowing users the access they need to get their job done. It provides access control that stays with documents and data after they are delivered. After information leaves the complex

world of TCP/IP, routers, switches, NICs, and port allocations, security must be applied on the ends where users are accessing it. If you are concerned about keeping information private and controlling who has access to important data, this system can help.

The system gives document authors total control over who has access to *what* data and *when*. For example, a document that contains the subject testing information might be divided into two sections: *questions* and *answers*. The document's author, the teacher, might want only students, who take this subject, to view the test questions before a specific date, and to be able to see the answers after such date. Under this system, the teacher is able to track who perform the test and when it has been done. In addition, the teacher has the ability to allow students to read the documents, and to prevent them from copying, pasting or forwarding the documents.

INCORPORATING THE ENVIRONMENT INTO E-LEARNING

After the teacher has finished editing electronic documents that he/she wants to control, he/she has to register the documents to the Document Control Server (DCS), as shown in Figure 2. Then, DCS generates keys used to encrypt the documents and stores the keys in itself (DCS) to decrypt such documents later. Only authenticated students with the proper rights are allowed to access DCS and the keys.

In the registration process, the teacher has to define a policy for controlling the document before delivering to students. In fact, a policy is a set of permissions that defines

- *who* can access a protected document,
- the network entities (i.e. IP address) from *where* they can access it,
- the date and times where they are allowed to access it, and
- activities such as read, print, copy and paste that are allowed to perform while accessing the document.

Before a student can view the protected document, he/she needs to connect to the Document Control Server (DCS) for proving his/her identity. After being authenticated, the student will be authorized access to keys that encrypt/decrypt specific documents. In general, this system can be used with any applications such as email and Web.

CONCLUSIONS

It has been widely accepted that almost all sensitive information is now in electronic form, and commonly stored in a network-based server. Naturally, once access is granted, information can be copied and distributed anywhere. In other words, authors lose control of their information after transmission. Unprotected documents can be forwarded, copied, printed or modified by any number of people.

In this paper, therefore, we proposed a document control environment mainly based on cryptography technologies. This enables teachers and students to track and control any academic documents after delivery. This environment consists of three main components: a Document Control Server (DCS), Author and Viewer. It can be simply integrated into any e-learning system.

REFERENCES

[1] C. Adams, and S. Lloyd (1999), Understanding Public-Key Infrastructure : Concepts, Standards, and Deployment Considerations, Macmillan Technical Publishing.

[2] E.G. Amoroso (1994), Fundamentals of Computer Security Technology, Prentice-Hall International, Inc.

[3] Authentica, Inc. (1999), PageVault Server, Available in:http://www.authentica.com.

[4] Lesley S.J. Farmer (2002), Seven Ways to BlackBoard, in 68th IFLA Council and General Conference, August 18-24, 2002.

[5] W. Ford and M.S. Baum (2001), Secure Electronic Commerce: Building the Infrastructure for Digital Signatures and Encryption, Prentice-Hall International, Inc.

[6] Duncan Lennox (2001), Managing Knowledge with Learning Objects – The Role of an E-Learning Content Management System in Speeding Time to Performance, Available in:http://www.wbtsystems.com, Access: September 28, 2002.

[7] M.K. Pinheiro, J.V. de Lima, N. Edelweiss, N. Layaida, and T. Lemlouma (2000), An Open E-Learning Authoring Environment.

[8] J.S.R. Subrahmanyam (2000), Future Trends of Content Management Systems (CMS) for E-Learning: A Tool Based Database Oriented Approach.

[9] W. Stallings (1999), Cryptography and Network Security : Principles and Practice, 2nd Edition, Prentice-Hall, Inc.

Situational and Task Characteristics Systematically Associated With Accuracy of Software Development Effort Estimates

Magne Jørgensen
Simula Research Laboratory, magne.jorgensen@simula.no, Telephone: +47 924 333 55, Fax: +47 67 82 82 01

Kjetil Moløkken, Simula Research Laboratory

ABSTRACT

Estimation skill is only one, out of many, factors that potentially impacts the accuracy of software development effort estimates. In this paper we examine how the size of the development task, the contract type (fixed-price versus per hour payment), the task priorities (time-of-delivery, quality, or cost), and the difference between estimating own and other peoples work, impact estimation accuracy. We found that an understanding of these factors could be important to explain the variance of estimation accuracy and, consequently, important when deciding on estimation improvement actions based on estimation accuracy measurement.

1 INTRODUCTION

Organizations developing software have, in general, a bad reputation for effort estimation. According to a survey carried out in 1998 by Standish Group[i] only 26% of the software projects completed on time, on budget and with the originally specified functionality. The characteristics of software projects, such as "one of a kind" activities, dynamic environments, changing requirements and carried out by humans, mean that we cannot expect zero effort overruns. There is however little doubt about that the improvement potential regarding estimation accuracy is large.

Most software effort estimation research studies seem to have a strong focus on the factors impacting the actual use of software development effort. Those factors are essential when building estimation models or providing the estimators with relevant information, but may not be sufficient for a proper understanding of the factors impacting the estimation *accuracy*. Standish Group, for example, reports that the main source of estimation accuracy improvement from 1994 to 1998 was the shift towards smaller projects, i.e., the estimation tasks were on average easier in 1998 compared with 1994.

The study reported in this paper is a follow-up study on our previous study of project experience reports at Ericsson Design Center in Norway (Jørgensen, Løvstad et al. 2002). In that study we found that a meaningful interpretation of the measured effort estimation accuracy required information about the project priority and properties of the requirement specification. For example, we found one project with a low priority on product quality (the software was meant to be a "demo") and a strong focus on not exceeding the cost budget. That project had very high effort estimation accuracy. However, it would be incorrect to attribute this high effort estimation accuracy only to good estimation skills. The experience report of that project indicated that the quality and completeness of the functionality had been adjusted to fit the available time and effort, i.e., that the requirement specification had been quite flexible. Similarly, there are several studies reporting different types of impact from the estimate on the project behavior, e.g., (Abdel-Hamid and Madnik 1986; Abdel-Hamid 1990). One type of project behavior impact from the estimate is the so-called "self-fulfilling prophecy" effect of software effort estimates, e.g., that an over-optimistic initial estimate and a high focus on estimation accuracy lead to actions that make that estimate more realistic.

To increase the confidence in the reported results and further extend our understanding of factors impacting the estimation accuracy we conducted a study of 60 software development tasks in a Web-development company. The hypotheses, which were based on our experience from earlier studies, tested were:

- H-1: Small tasks are typically over-estimated and large tasks under-estimated.
- H-2: Fixed-price tasks are typically over-estimated and tasks paid per hour typically under-estimated.
- H-3: Tasks where the customer prioritize quality or time-of-delivery have less accurate effort estimates compared with those with priority on cost.
- H-4: Tasks were own work is estimated are more accurately estimated than those where other developers' work is estimated.

The motivation for each individual hypothesis is described in Section 3. A study with the same goal, i.e., to increase our knowledge about factors impacting estimation accuracy, is described in (Gray, MacDonnell et al. 1999). That study found that over-estimation was connected with changes on small modules and development of screens, while under-estimation was connected with changes on large modules and development of reports. A potential explanation of these observations is that easy tasks (small modules and screens) typically are over-estimated, while complex tasks typically are under-estimated, i.e., an explanation consistent with our hypothesis H-1.

2 DESIGN OF STUDY

The company that participated in our study is the Norwegian branch of a large international web-development company. The role of the company is that of a contractor (McDonald and Welland 2001), producing web-solutions for its customers. Over a period of approx. 10 months we collected information about 60 software development tasks, i.e., most of the small and medium sized development tasks conducted by the company in that period. The median size of a task was 45 work-hours.

All tasks were estimated without the support of estimation models or databases of previous projects, i.e. "expert estimates". The practical difference between expert and model-based effort estimates is, in our opinion, much smaller then the "theoretical" difference. While expert estimates are based on non-explicit and non-recoverable reasoning processes, i.e., "intuition", the steps leading to a model based effort estimates are "in theory" explicit and recoverable. However, most estimation processes applied in practice have both intuitive and explicit (model based) reasoning elements (Blattberg and Hoch 1990). In fact, most formal software development estimation models requires expert estimates of important input parameters (Pengelly 1995), i.e., they require non-explicit and non-recoverable reasoning. The expert estimation-based accuracy results reported in this paper may, therefore, be valid for more model-based effort estimation.

Information collected immediately before the design and implementation of the task started, for each task:

- Name of the estimator
- Short description of the task (max 10 lines)
- Type of contract (fixed price, per hour). 43% of the tasks were fixed-price, 42% per hour, and 15% of unknown contract type.
- Customer priority (cost, time-of-delivery, quality). The customer prioritized in 22% of the tasks the cost (given an acceptable level of quality), in 48% the quality, and in 30% the time-of-delivery (given an acceptable level of quality).
- Proportion of the task planned to be completed by the estimator (zero, between 1% and 50%, more than 50%). 22% of the tasks were planned to be completed more than 50% by the estimator, 30% between 1% and 50%, and in 48% of the tasks the estimator was not supposed to participate in the development, at all.
- Estimated effort in work-hours. The estimated effort should be the "most likely" use of effort, not the effort accepted by the customer in the contract (the "price-to-win" effort). From the answers in the "reasons for high or low estimation accuracy"-field (see field description below) it is clear that there were tasks were the estimators were influenced by "price-to-win" effort when providing the effort estimates, i.e., there were situations with a poor separation of most likely and price-to-win effort estimates. The same lack of separation is reported in (Jørgensen and Sjøberg 2001) and (Jørgensen, Løvstad et al. 2002), i.e., this problem may be typical for software organizations.

Information collected immediately after the task was completed, to avoid hindsight bias (Stahlberg, Eller et al. 1995):
- Actual effort in work-hours.
- Unexpected problems during the task execution (free text). 18% of the tasks experienced at least one major unexpected problem. This is less than reported, on maintenance tasks of similar size, in (Jørgensen 1995). That study reported a proportion of 30% tasks with major unexpected problems
- Reasons for high or low estimation accuracy (free text). Almost all estimators wrote 20-200 words describing estimation accuracy causes. We use this information in the discussion of the data analysis presented in the result section.

3 RESULTS

3.1 Size of Task vs Estimation Accuracy

H-1 hypothesizes that small tasks are typically over-estimated and large tasks under-estimated. An argument for the size impact is the so-called "regression-toward-the-mean" effect (Jørgensen, Indahl et al. 2002). This effect implies that estimates tend to move closer to the mean[ii] effort with increasing uncertainty. This means that tasks smaller than the average task may be over-estimated and tasks larger than the average task will be under-estimated. In the extreme case, where the estimator knows very little about the effort usage of the new task, a rational estimation approach is to estimate effort usage close to the effort of the average task. The regression-toward-the-mean effect was first described by Sir Francis Galton (Galton 1997). There are studies (Kahneman and Tversky 1973; Nisbett and Ross 1980) demonstrating that the regression-toward-the-mean effect in real life situations can be large and that people tend to overlook it.

The median size of the tasks in our data set was 45 work-hours. We use this value as an indication on the effort usage on the average task in this analysis. To test H-1 we divided the tasks into two categories: SMALL (< 45 work-hours) and LARGE (>= 45 work-hours). A Kruskal-Wallis test on the difference in median relative estimation deviation, defined as $MRE0 = (actual\ effort - estimated\ effort)/Actual\ effort$, shows a significant difference (p=0.02). The median MRE0 for the small tasks was 0%, i.e., under-estimation was just as frequent as over-estimation, while the median MRE0 for the large tasks was 21%, i.e., the typical large task was under-estimated with 21%. The general tendency towards under-estimation (median MRE0 for all projects was 8% under-estimation[iii]) means that, although the hypothesized estimation deviation tendency is correct, our hypothesis is only partly supported. A better formulated hypothesis may be that the likelihood of underestimated tasks is much higher for large tasks compared with small tasks.

3.2 Contract Type vs Estimation Accuracy

H-2 hypothesizes that fixed-price tasks are typically over-estimated and tasks paid per hour typically under-estimated. An argument for H-2 is that,

when a company is paid per hour for a task, this induces less focus on not exceeding the estimate compared with the fixed-price situation. In the fixed-price situation the company loses money when exceeding the estimate, while the opposite may be the case in the payment per hour situation.

We tested H-2 applying the Kruskal-Wallis test on the median estimation accuracy (MRE0) of the tasks of the two contract types. The results were in the opposite direction of what hypothesized in H-2. The fixed-price tasks were more, not less, under-estimated (median under-estimation of 18%) than the tasks paid per hour (median under-estimation of 9%)[iv]. The hypothesis H-2 is therefore not supported.

An examination of the descriptions of unexpected problems and reasons for high or low estimation accuracy suggests that fixed price task estimates were frequently impacted by how much the customer was willing to pay. In particular, there were several examples of fixed-price tasks were the customer negotiations had pressed the estimate down very much. The consequence of this pressure was inaccurate, much too low, estimates. The relationship between contract-type and estimation accuracy is therefore more complex than we hypothesized. On one hand, there is a stronger incitement for not exceeding the estimate in the fixed-price situation. On the other hand, the customers' negotiation impact towards lower estimates may also be larger. We observed similar effects in the study reported in (Jørgensen and Sjøberg 2001).

3.3 Priority vs Estimation Accuracy

H-3 hypothesizes that tasks where the customer prioritizes quality or time-of-delivery have less accurate effort estimates compared with tasks where the customer prioritizes cost precision. The main argument for the hypothesis is that the developers try to optimize their behavior in accordance with the task priority, e.g., if time-of-delivery is priority one, there is less focus on actions to reduce the probability of exceeding the cost budget (Weinberg and Schulman 1974).

We applied the Kruskal-Wallis test on the median absolute relative estimation deviation ($MRE = |actual\ effort - estimated\ effort| / actual\ effort$). The median MRE was 11% on tasks with a priority on quality, 30% on tasks with a priority on time-of-delivery, and 18% on tasks with a priority on cost. The difference was significant (p=0.09). The difference was particularly large between the tasks with a priority on time-of-delivery and the other priorities, i.e., time-of-delivery seems to be an important indicator for high estimation deviations. The estimation accuracy (MRE) of tasks with a priority on quality was lower than those with a priority on cost. A closer examination of the described unexpected problems and reasons for high or low estimation accuracy suggests that the customers with a priority on cost were "more demanding" than the others, i.e., they negotiated lower fixed-price estimates or required more functionality than the developers had assumed when they estimated the task. An analysis of the MRE0, shows that a priority on cost had an impact on the level of under- and over-estimation. The median estimation deviation of the tasks with a priority on cost was 3% over-estimation, with a priority on quality the MRE0 was 11% under-estimation, and with a priority on time-of-delivery the MRE0 was 25% under-estimation. Clearly, the priorities of the task impact the estimation accuracy.

3.4 Estimation of Own Work vs Estimation Accuracy

H-4 hypothesizes that estimating own work leads to more accurate estimates than estimating other developers work. The main argument for this hypothesis is that the estimators estimating own work is more likely to use the estimate as a goal and that it is more difficult to predict the productivity on other people. This argument is supported by the software study reported in (Lederer and Prasad 1998). However, results reported other domains than software, e.g., in (Buehler, Griffin et al. 1994), suggest that estimating own work typically lead to more over-optimism compared with the estimation of other peoples work. A potential reasons for this over-optimism is the "I am above average"-bias (Klein and Kunda 1994), i.e., that far more than 50% of people believe they are above average skilled in work related tasks. The direction of the difference, stated in our hypothesis H-4, is based on the belief that the software study described in (Lederer and Prasad 1998) is the more relevant for our purpose than the studies reporting results from different estimation domains.

A Kruskal-Wallis test of the median MRE of the categories "Estimation of other developers work", "Less than 50% of the work conducted by oneself", and "More than 50% of the work conducted by one-self" resulted in a weakly significant (p=0.12) difference. The lowest estimation accuracy (median MRE of 31%) was, as hypothesized, achieved for those tasks where other software developers' work was estimated. The two other categories had median MRE of 16% ("Less than 50% of the work conducted by one-self") and 20% ("More than 50% conducted by one-self"), i.e., no large estimation accuracy difference between these two categories. The hypothesis H-4 is supported.

4 CONCLUSION

This paper reports that:

- Large software development tasks were typically under-estimated, while small tasks were just as frequently over-estimated.
- There was a complex relationship between contract type and estimation accuracy. Fixed price tasks experienced more frequently that a customer negotiation induced estimation pressure leading to less realism of the effort estimates. On the other hand, fixed price estimates led in some situations to more awareness of the importance of not exceeding the estimate, i.e., to better estimation accuracy.
- Tasks with a priority on time-of-delivery had lower estimation accuracy than those with a focus on quality or cost.
- Estimating own work led to more accurate estimates compared to estimating other peoples work.

There are several applications of these results. In order to understand the reasons for high or low estimation accuracy, and not automatically attribute it to good or poor estimation skills, it is important to know and apply information about the factors reported in this paper. Another application of the reported results is an increased awareness of the situations leading to high or low estimation accuracy. This is, for example, important information when assessing the uncertainty of an estimate or when deciding on actions to improve the estimation accuracy.

NOTES:

i) http://www.standishgroup.com/sample_research/chaos1998.pdf. Describes results from a survey of US companies.

ii) An estimator's interpretation of "mean effort" may depend on the size of tasks the estimator is used to estimate and on the "reference class" of task, i.e., the tasks that the estimator believes are relevant to compare with when estimating the new task.

iii) An earlier study in the same company (Moløkken 2002) found that the average under-estimated effort was 15%, as opposed to our 8%. That projects analyzed in that study, however, were on average larger than the tasks included in our study. This supports the finding that the size of the projects is an important factor when explaining differences in estimation accuracy.

iv) Amongst the tasks were the estimator did not know the contract type, the median MRE0 was as low as -6%, i.e., the median task was over-estimated.

REFERENCES

Abdel-Hamid, T. 1990. Investigating the cost/schedule trade-off in software development. *IEEE Software* 7(1): 97-105.

Abdel-Hamid, T. K. and S. E. Madnik 1986. Impact of schedule estimation on software project behavior. *IEEE Software* 3(4): 70-75.

Blattberg, R. C. and S. J. Hoch 1990. Database models and managerial intuition: 50% model + 50% manager. *Management Science* 36: 887-899.

Buehler, R., D. Griffin and M. Ross 1994. Exploring the "Planning fallacy": Why people underestimate their task completion times. *Journal of Personality and Social Psychology* 67(3): 366-381.

Galton, F. 1997. *Natural Inheritance*. New Mexico, Genetics Heritage Press (originally published in 1889 by Macmillan and Company).

Gray, A., S. MacDonnell and M. Shepperd 1999. Factors systematically associated with errors in subjective estimates of software development effort: the stability of expert judgment. *Sixth International Software Metrics Symposium*, IEEE Comput. Soc, Los Alamitos, CA, USA: 216-227.

Jørgensen, M. 1995. An empirical study of software maintenance tasks. *Journal of Software Maintenance* 7: 27-48.

Jørgensen, M., U. Indahl and D. Sjøberg 2002. Software effort estimation and regression toward the mean. *Accepted for publication in Journal of Systems and Software*.

Jørgensen, M., N. Løvstad and M. L 2002. Combining quantitative software development cost estimation precision data with qualitative data from project experience reports at Ericsson Design Center in Norway. *Empirical Assessments of Software Engineering (EASE)*, Keele, UK.

Jørgensen, M. and D. I. K. Sjøberg 2001. Software process improvement and human judgement heuristics. *Scandinavian Journal of Information Systems* 13: 99-121.

Kahneman, D. and A. Tversky 1973. On the psychology of prediction. *Psychological Review* 80(4): 237-251.

Klein, W. M. and Z. Kunda 1994. Exaggerated self-assessments and the preference for controllable risks. *Organizational behavior and human decision processes.* 59(3): 410-427.

Lederer, A. L. and J. Prasad 1998. A causal model for software cost estimating error. *IEEE Transactions on Software Engineering* 24(2): 137-148.

McDonald, A. and R. Welland 2001. Web Engineering in Practice. *Proceedings of the Fourth WWW10 Workshop on Web Engineering*: 21-30.

Moløkken, K. 2002. Expert estimation of Web-development effort: Individual biases and group processes (Master Thesis). *Department of Informatics*, University of Oslo.

Nisbett, R. E. and L. Ross 1980. *Human inference: Strategies and shortcomings of social judgment*, Englewood Cliffs, NJ: Prentice-Hall.

Pengelly, A. 1995. Performance of effort estimating techniques in current development environments. *Software Engineering Journal* 10(5): 162-170.

Stahlberg, D., F. Eller, A. Maass and D. Frey 1995. We knew it all along: Hindsight bias in groups. *Organizational Behaviour and Human Decision Processes* 63(1): 46-58.

Weinberg, G. M. and E. L. Schulman 1974. Goals and performance in computer programming. *Human Factors* 16(1): 70 - 77.

Basic Conceptualisation of a Resource Modelling Language

Dipl.-Inform. Juergen Jung

University of Koblenz, Universitaetsstrasse 1, 56070 Koblenz, Germany

phone: +49 261 287 2554, fax: +49 261 287 2521, e-mail: jjung@uni-koblenz.de

ABSTRACT

This paper presents the basic conceptualisation of a resource modelling language for business process modelling. This language is an extension to an existing process modelling language - MEMO-OrgML. The basic conceptualisation comprises basic resource types and their mutual relations. The resource modelling language aims at satisfying the needs of different user types. The language will be applicable by domain experts and offer domain specific resources and resource types for various domains by offering adequate abstraction on resources. Potential benefits of such a resource modelling language are outlined by an example.

1   MOTIVATION

The analysis, representation and management of knowledge related to an organisation and its processes have always been very important (Koubarakis and Plexousakis 2000). A lot of work has been done on the development and evaluation of ontologies for process modelling (Wand and Weber1989, Wand and Weber 1990a, Wand and Weber 1990b, Wand and Weber 1993, Weber 1997, Green and Rosemann 1999), the specification of process modelling languages (Eertink et al. 1999, Oberweis 1996, Sutton and Osterweil 1997, van der Aalst and van Hee 2002) as well as on business process modelling methods and concepts (Herbst 1997, Österle 1995). Business process models can be used for different purposes:

- documentation of processes of an organisation to foster communication (Frank 1999, Oberweis 1996)
- analysis of business processes (Eertink et al. 1999, Bergholtz and Johanneson 2001, Scheer 1999)
- simulation of processes (Baumgarten 1996)
- support for business process re-engineering (Curtis et al. 1992, Oberweis 1996)
- generation of workflow schemata (Curtis et al. 1992, Oberweis 1996)
- software development of process-oriented applications (Frank 1999, Scheer 1998, Scheer 1992, Österle 1995, Curtis et al. 1992)

The documentation of processes found in organisations (as well as other organisational aspects like structure or strategy) enables communication with recently hired employees or external consultants (Frank 1999, Oberweis 1996). An analysis of business processes relies on well formulated process descriptions. An analysis might help to find weaknesses in traditional processes (Eertink et al. 1999, Bergholtz and Johanneson 2000, Scheer 1999) and a business process re-engineering might follow (Curtis et al. 1992, Oberweis 1996). Simulation also supports the detection of weaknesses (Baumgarten 1996). In contrast to analysis, simulation works on prototypical instantiations of a process model. Typical instances of objects and their values (e.g. a specific processing time or accounting information) are added to the model and the execution of a process can be observed. Business process re-engineering supports the redesign of processes with respect to weaknesses identified by an analysis or a simulation (Curtis et al. 1992, Oberweis 1996). Business process models may also be a preliminary stage for an information system (IS) design. A workflow-management-system (WfMS) or proprietary corporate applications are alternatives for such an IS (Curtis et al. 1992, Frank 1999, Österle 1995, Scheer 1992, Scheer 1998).

Resources are essential for the modelling of processes (Podorzhny et al. 1999). Processes and their relationships only describe *what* has to be done. Resources assigned to processes specify *who* has to work on the process and *what* will be needed. Usually resources are not available in an unlimited quantity (Nübel 2001, Podorzhny et al. 1999). Modelling resources offers the opportunity to determinate the economic efficiency of a process. Hence, the usage of scarce resources has to be taken into account during the analysis or simulation of processes as well as the development of a workflow application or an information system. One application for the "rich in content" modelling of resources is business continuity planning (BCP). Bottlenecks resulting from scarce resources can be identified and supported by alternative resources which may replace the original resources in case of a failure.

The quality of analysis, simulation and system development depends on the conceptual power of the resource modelling language. Such a language should offer:

- domain specific concepts to be (re-)used by domain experts
- semantically rich resource types including integrity constraints
- support for analysis and simulation
- mappings to information systems

Many process modelling languages have been developed in the last years. Many of them also include the specification of resources on different levels of abstraction. Petri-nets offer a formal language for the specification of processes (Baumgarten 1996). In classical Place/Transition-Nets, resources (i.e. their states) can only be modelled by a subnet. Higher-level Petri-nets offer an extended expressiveness by using tuples as markings (instead of anonymous markings like classical Petri-nets). Oberweis (1996) developed a language based on Petri-nets but using complex relations as markings. Nonetheless these approaches only offer formal language features for the descriptions of resources. The term *resource* does not exist explicitly. Also Scheer's event-driven process chains (EPC) do not include dedicated resources (Scheer 1992, Scheer 1998, Scheer 1999). All entities participating at a business process have to be modelled by an entity-relationship-diagram (ERD). The current version of the Unified Modelling Language (UML) provides features for business process modelling (Bennet et al. 1999, Marshall 2000, Eriksson and Penker 2000). Like in all previously presented approaches, resources are not a dedicated language feature and have to be added by the user.

This paper represents a current work on the development of a resource modelling language for business processes. This language aims to satisfy the needs of different user types. The resource modelling language is an extension to an existing process modelling language - OrgML (Organisation Modelling Language) - which is part of an integrated enterprise modelling method called MEMO (Multi-perspective Enterprise MOdelling) (cf. Frank 1999).

2   DIFFERENT LEVELS OF ABSTRACTION

Many everyday terms are ambiguous with respect to their level of abstraction and can be interpreted accordingly. The term *resource* might be interpreted as *resource type* (i.e. a *resource class*) or just as likely as an instance of resource type (e.g. an existing database server in the corporate network). Ambiguities of interpretations should be avoided in the context of business process modelling to foster formal analysis, simulation or software development. Furthermore, concepts of the hereby described resource modelling language will be integrated into the existing process modelling language MEMO-OrgML.

Language features of a resource modelling language are specified by a meta-model. Instances of types in the meta-model are resource types such as a resource type representing a *database server*. The resource type *database server* may be classified from a technical or economical point of view. Technical

Figure 1: Part of the Meta-Model of Basic Resource Types

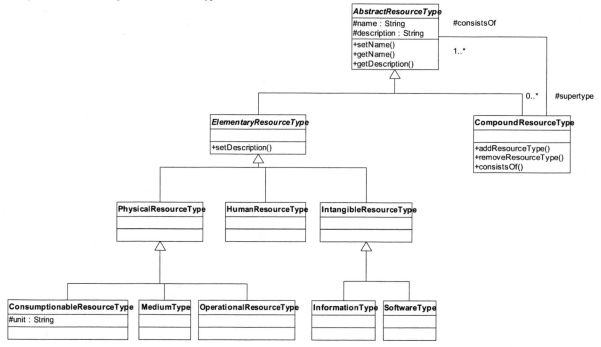

aspects are computer models, processor speed and maximum number of transactions per minute. These aspects determine the restrictions of usage for such a resource type within a certain context. Economic properties of a *database server* resource type address cost of operation and maintenance of a specific instance in a business process. Those aspects are described at different levels of abstraction by the same resource type.

A specific resource 'Oracle9i-server' is an instance of the resource type *database server* and can in turn also have instances (i.e. concrete installations of Oracle corresponding to a license). Consequently we have a multi-level type-instance-relationship for the description of database servers in a resource model. This relationship however is hard to handle when using business process models as the basis for information systems development.

Conceptual modelling usually prescinds from concrete objects (i.e. instances) and changeable aspects. Hence, only types are allowed in conceptual models. Nevertheless modelling of instances might be appropriate in certain situations:

• The modelling of - anonymous - instances is used to formulate relationships between resources in different processes. Such a relationship may be of the kind: The resource (instance) used in process A is also required in process B.

• A prototypical instance in a process model reflects the average property-values of a resource type. Costs for the usage of a resource are usually attached to the concrete resource instance and differ between instances. Hence, costs can not be assigned to resource types in conceptual modelling. But average costs of a certain resource type might be assigned to a prototypal instance which is used for formal analysis and simulation.

• Concrete instances are required to describe currently used resources. The first step of business process re-engineering is the modelling of existing business processes. This model includes processes and resources as they exist at the time being. This might also include dedicated resources like special servers, relevant machinery or technical engineers.

Hence, types and instances have to be modelled by a resource modelling language. This language should also allow different kinds of abstraction (technical and economical). Furthermore different levels of abstraction have to be available with respect to type-instance-relationships. We will present our first approach for resource modelling in the following section. This approach will cover some of the discussed aspects.

3 RESOURCE TYPES

The resource modelling language is specified by a meta-model. Such a meta-model defines basic concepts of the language, relationships between language elements and integrity constraints. An extract of the meta-model of the resource specification language is presented by the UML class-diagram in Figure 1.

3.1 Basic Meta-Model

At the top level of the type hierarchy we distinguish between compound and elementary resource types. A compound resource type is an abstract resource type, which is composed by other abstract resource types. Hence, a compound resource type may consist of several elementary or compound resource types. The design of compound resource types follows the *composite pattern* by (Gamma et al. 1998). Elementary resource types are specialised to human, physical and intangible resource types. A human resource type corresponds to an organisational unit or a role filled by an employee. Physical resource types comprise all tangible objects used within a business process. The distinction between human and physical resource types bases on the differentiation of human work (labour) on the one hand and man-made aids to further production on the other hand (Diederich 1992, Chrystal and Lipsey 1997). Subtypes of physical resource types are

• used for the completion of a process (OperationalResourceType),
• consumed by the completion of a process (ConsumptionableResourceType) or
• able to store information (MediumType).

Operational resource types are physical resource types, which are used within a process and are still available after its completion (Diederich 1992). Examples are machinery, tools and vehicles. They are all used for processing but remain available. In contrast to this, consumable resource types are a prerequisite for a process and are transformed during the execution of a process. Raw material as well as spare parts (both consumptionable resource types) are used by a business process and are transformed to a (partial) product (Chrystal and Lipsey 1997). They (individually) will not be available for other processes. Information containing media does not fit the differentiation between operational and consumable resource types. A medium or its information might be out-of-date after the completion of a process or it might be a prerequisite for subsequent processes.

Intangible resource types represent all resource types, which are neither physical nor human. Two subtypes have been identified up to now - information and software. They can not exist on their own, because they need a medium for representation - persistent or for transmission. The classification of software as an intangible resource is controversial and therefore problematic. Software is usually not regarded as an intangible resource or asset like human qualification, knowledge or business relationships. But from a computer scientist's point of view or in the context of project-management, software is no physical object; it is intangible. Hence, the current classification has only been done for evaluation purposes and will be changed whenever it seems not to be appropriate.

3.2 Information Types

Information types correspond to some kind of knowledge of an organisation (Chrystal and Lipsey 1997). Information types might be order, assembly list or invoice (Jung and Fraunholz 2002). Furthermore an information type reflects explicit knowledge, guidelines and regulations for the execution of business processes. All these kinds of information are covered by InformationType in the meta-model in Figure 2. An information type is characterised by its structure, as described by the following examples:

- An invoice consists of a date, sender, receiver and several positions.
- A guideline is structured by its format, the corresponding applicability and its contents.

This structure is encapsulated by the attribute structureDefinition. This definition is independent of a special data definition or medium. Information might be structured by a formal data definition but does not have to be. Consequently the structure definition of an information type is independent of a formal data definition. Such a data definition might be an XML-DTD, an SQL table definition or another structure definition language. If there is a formal structure definition, it might be assigned to the information type. Formal data-format type definitions are covered by DataFormatType in Figure 2. Every data-format type consists of the name of the format (formatType), the format's version (formatTypeVersion) and its formal specification (formatTypeDefinition).

3.3 Media Types

Information and data-format types represent a non-physical kind of resource. Every information type has to be stored on a medium representing the according information. We distinguish between human and electronically readable media in this paper. The distinction between those kinds of media is of special importance for business process modelling. Human readable media correspond to all representations of information to be interpretable by human

readers. Examples for such kinds of documents are a printed invoice, a paper-based product catalogue or any kind of paper-based documents. Information is represented in a form that humans are able to further process them. Electronically readable media are those which are based on an IT-system and allow a further processing by an information system. The conceptualisation of media types for the resource modelling language for the MEMO-OrgML is displayed in Figure 2. The class HumanReadableMediumType comprises all media readable by humans but not necessarily by automated information systems. This includes media-types like printed documents. ElectronicallyReadableMediumType comprises all kinds of media which are readable by information system components. Storage of information on an electronically readable medium is only allowed if a data-format for this information exists. Such a differentiation between human and electronically readable media will not be unambiguous for the future specification of resources. Some media are interpretable by human readers and IT-systems at the same time. Future research will prove or disprove adequacy of this classification.

Generally speaking, an information type does not change its readability with respect to human readers or information systems. All kind of readability might be reduced to the media containing information. The medium type determines the kind of reader: human readable media are restricted to the processing by humans and electronically readable media to information systems. Examples for human readable media are every kind of representation which maps formal structures of information types to a representation adequate to a human readable medium. Electronically readable media correspond to an information system containing a structured representation of information. Both representations base on the same type of information and its corresponding structure as presented in paragraph 3.2. The same kind of information might be represented on a human or electronically readable medium. Differences usually are based on the kind of media. Main goal of the differentiation of human and electronically readable media is the recognition of media clashes.

4 FURTHER CONCEPTS

This paper only presents a small subset of the meta-model of the resource modelling language of MEMO-OrgML. Further language features concern concrete resources related to types, economic aspects of resources and the allocation of resources to business processes (Jung and Fraunholz 2002). Concrete resources differ from general resource types (e.g. a database-management-system (DBMS)). They rather describe concrete instances of resource types. A DBMS developed by a specific manufacturer has as type the DBMS resource type but includes additional properties: product name, product version and manufacturer as well as system requirements. These properties do not necessarily apply to a general resource type DBMS. For example DB/2 version

Figure 2: Part of the Meta-Model of Information and Media Resource Types

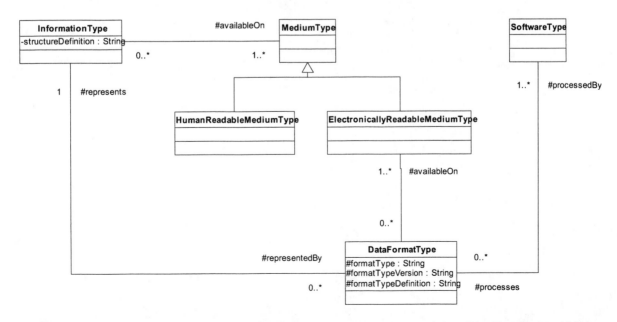

7.1 by IBM is a concrete resource of the type DBMS.

Economic aspects are very important properties of resources and resource types for the analysis and simulation of different process alternatives. Hence, the resource modelling language of the MEMO-OrgML includes the specification of costs related to the usage of a resource. This supports the mapping of different alternatives to monetary values. Beside other aspects like customer satisfaction, costs for the processing of tasks determine the quality of processes for an enterprise (Österle 1995). Additionally the allocation of resources to processes has to be taken into account. The allocation of resources determines the extent of a resource's use. The resource modelling language of MEMO-OrgML also includes this feature.

5 EXAMPLE

The application of the resource modelling language is demonstrated by an example given in Figure 3. An assembly list of a specific product type and its according data format types are presented. Additionally a database server running a DBMS managing the assembly list is modelled. An assembly list is a list of all parts of a physical product. Each part may either be an elementary part or a complex part specified by its own assembly list. The assembly list in Figure 3 is of the type InformationResourceType and therefore specified by a structure definition. This definition (structureDefinition in the rounded box labelled AssemblyList:InformationResourceType) is formulated in an abstract manner using the Extended Bacchus-Naur-Form (EBNF). The assembly list is stored in a corporate information system using a relational database and an XML document. The relational schema is represented by the data format type RDB and the document type definition expressed in XML. Both electronic incarnations of an assembly list are processed by a DBMS running on a dedicated server of the kind ElementaryResourceType. Benefits of such a modelling of the assembly list are the documentation of document structures, association to required resources and the specification of exchange formats.

An abstract definition of the structure of an information type fosters communication on this information type. Different communication partners can base their discussion on information types on a common definition. The specification of the assembly list might act as a reference for engineers and business administrators. It is also a specification for external partners producing subparts. The association with data formats like RDB or XML leads to a correspondence of an assembly list to computerised formats. These formats are not only used within a process but might also be used for the interaction with other information systems. Such information systems include other corporate information systems and systems of external partners as well. Data format type definitions are, thus, used as an inter-organisational reference system. They specify interfaces for the exchange of data.

Associating resource types to an information type supports the allocation of resources to a process. Some processes rely on the availability of information. Information classified as an intangible resource will not be available directly. There are other resources providing the required information. These might be media containing information or an elementary resource type providing information. Information systems in a broader sense fulfil this requirement. Hence, systems allowing the access to information are an important resource. Modelling these resources specifies the way of accessing the needed information.

6 FUTURE WORK

This paper presents the basic conceptualisation of a resource modelling language for an existing business process language. Core features of the meta-model of this language have been described and some other features have been mentioned. In the future the resource modelling language will be evaluated - in cooperation with other research groups and projects - fostered by modelling resources of different domains. Goals of this evaluation are the verification of the specified concepts and the determination of possible ambiguities in the language specification. Those ambiguities will be fixed in future versions of the resource modelling language. Furthermore the modelled resources and resource types will be integrated into the resource modelling language. They will be grouped by several domain-specific packages and made available to the user. We are planning to develop resource-packages for logistical processes, project management and IT-resources.

Up to now, tool-support for the modelling of resources using the resource modelling language is not available. An appropriate resource modelling tool will be developed after the end of the evaluation phase. This tool will be integrated into the process modelling framework of the MEMO-OrgML. It will support the definition of resources and resource types as well as the management of existing resources and resource packages.

REFERENCES

Baumgarten, B. (1996) *Petri-Netze: Grundlagen und Anwendungen*, 2nd edition, Spektrum Akademischer Verlag, Heidelberg (Germany)

Bennett, S., McRobb, S. and Farmer, R. (1999) *Object-Oriented Systems Analysis and Design using UML*, McGraw-Hill, London (UK)

Bergholtz, M. and Johannesson, P. (2000) 'Validating Conceptual Models - Utilising Analysis Patterns as an Instrument for Explanation Genertion', In: Bouzeghoub, M., Kedad, Z. and Métais, E. (eds) 5th International Conference on Applications of Natural Language to Information Systems, Versailles, France, June 28-30 2000, pp. 325-339

Chrystal, K. and Lipsey, R. (1997) *Economics for Business and Management*, Oxford University Press, Oxford (UK)

Figure 3: Example for the Usage of Information Resource Types

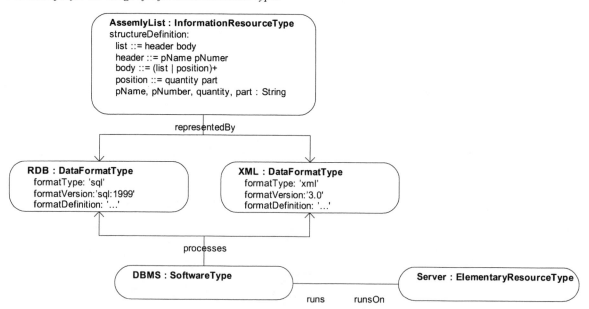

Curtis, B., Kellner, M. and Over, J. (1992) "Process Modeling" Communications of the ACM, Vol.35, No.9, September 1992, pp. 75-90

Diederich, H. (1992) *Allgemeine Betriebswirtschaftslehre*, 7th edition, Kohlhammer, Stuttgart (Germany)

Eertink, H., Janssen, W., Luttighuis, P.O., Teeuw, W. and Vissers, C. (1999) 'A Business Process Design Language', In: Wing, J., Woodcock, J. and Davies, J. (eds): Proceedings of the World Congress on Formal Methods in the Development of Computing Systems, Toulouse, France, September 20-24 1999, Volume I, pp. 76-95

Eriksson, H.-E. and Penker, M. (2000) *Business Modeling with UML - Business Patterns at Work* Wiley, New York (NY)

Frank, U. (1999) *MEMO: Visual Languages for Enterprise Modelling*, Research Report of the IS Research Institute, University of Koblenz, No. 18

Frank, U. (2001) *Organising the Corporation: Research Perspectives, Concepts and Diagrams*, Research Report of the IS Research Institute, University of Koblenz, No. 25

Gamma, E., Helm, R., Johnson, R. and J. Vlissides (1998) *Design Patterns: Elements of Reusable Object-Oriented Software* Addison-Wesley, Reading (Massachusetts)

Green, P. and Rosemann, M. (1999): 'An Ontological Analysis of Integrated Process Modelling', In: Jarke, M. and Oberweis, A. (eds): Proceedings of the 11th International Conference CAiSE'99, Heidelberg, Germany, June 14-18 1999, pp. 225-240

Herbst, H. (1997) *Business Rule-Oriented Conceptual Modeling*, Physica-Verlag, Heidelberg (Germany)

Jung, J. and Fraunholz, B. (2002) 'Resource Modelling in an object-oriented Process Modelling Language', In: Cybulsky, J.; Nguyen, L.; Lamp, J. and Smith, R. (eds): Proceedings of the Australian Workshop on Requirements Engineering, AWRE2002, Melbourne (Australia), 2-3 December 2002, CD-ROM edition

Koubarakis, M. and Plexousakis, D. (2000) 'A Formal Model for Business Process Modeling and Design', In: Wangler, B. and Bergman, L. (eds): Proceedings of the 12th International Conference CAiSE 2000, Stockholm, Sweden, June 5-9 2000, pp. 142-156

Marshall, C. (2000) *Enterprise Modeling with UML - Designing Successful Software through Business Analysis*, Addison-Wesley, Reading (MA)

Miller, B.B. (1988) Managing Information as a Resource, in: Rabin, J. and Jackowsky, E.M. (eds): Handbook of Information Resource Management, Marcel Dekker, New York (NY)

Nübel, H. (2001) "The resource renting problem subject to temporal constraints", OR Spektrum, Vol. 23, No. 3, 2001, pp. 359-381

Oberweis, A. (1996) *Modellierung und Ausführung von Workflows mit Petri-Netzen*, Teubner, Stuttgart (Germany)

Österle, H. (1995) *Business Engineering: Prozess- und Systementwicklung*, Springer, Berlin (Germany)

Podorzhny, R.M., Staudt Lerner, B. and Osterweil, L.J. (1999) 'Modeling Resources for Activity Coordination and Scheduling', In: Ciancarini, P. and Wolf, A.L. (eds): Proceedings of the ThirdInternational Conference, CO-ORDINATION '99, Amsterdam, The Netherlands, April 26-28 1999, pp. 307-322

Scheer, A.-W. (1992) *Architecture of Integrated Information Systems - Foundations of Enterprise-Modelling*, Springer, Berlin (Germany)

Scheer, A.-W. (1998) *Business Process Engineering - Reference Models for Industrial Enterprises*, Springer, Berlin (Germany)

Scheer, A.-W. (1999) *ARIS - Business Process Modeling* 2nd edition, Springer, Berlin (Germany)

Sutton, S.M. and Osterweil, L.J. (1997) 'The Design of a Next-Generation Process Language', In: Jazayeri, M. and Schauer, H. (eds): Proceedings of the 6th European Software Engineering Conference Zürich, Switzerland, September 22-25 1997, pp. 142-158

van der Aalst, W. and van Hee, K. (2002) *Workflow Management - Models, Methods and Systems*, MIT Press, Cambridge (MA)

Wand, Y. and Weber, R. (1989) An Ontological Evaluation of Systems Analysis and Design Methods, in: Falkenberg, E.D. and Lindgreen, P. (eds): Information Systems Concepts: An In-depth Analysis, North-Holland

Wand, Y. and Weber, R. (1990a) "An Ontological Model of an Information System", IEEE Transactions on Software Engineering, Vol. 16, No. 11, pp. 1281-1291

Wand, Y. and Weber, R. (1990b) Mario Bunge's Ontology as a Formal Foundation for Information System Concepts, in: Weingartner, P. and Dorn, G.J.W. (eds): Studies on Mario Bunge's Treatise, Rodopy, Atlanta

Wand, Y. and Weber, R. (1993): "On the Ontological exspressivness of Information Systems Analysis and Design Grammar", Journal of Information Systems, Vol. 3, No. 2, pp. 217-237

Weber, R. (1997) *Ontological Foundations of Information Systems*, Coopers and Lybrand Accounting Methodology, Monograph No. 4, Melbourne, Australia

zur Muehlen, M. (1999) 'Resource Modeling in Workflow Applications', In: Becker, J., zur Mühlen, M. and Rosemann, M. (eds) Proceedings of the 1999 Workflow Management Conference, November 9 1999, Münster, Germany, pp. 137-153

Time-Indexer: a Tool for Extracting Temporal References from Business News

Pawel Jan Kalczynski

Pawel.Kalczynski@utoledo.edu, Information Systems, Management, E-commerce & Sales Dept., College of Business Administration, University of Toledo, 2801 West Bancroft St., Toledo, OH 43606
phone: (419) 530-2258 fax: (419) 530-2290
Department of Management Information Systems, The Poznan University of Economics, Poznan, Al. Niepodleglosci 10, 60-967, Poland

Witold Abramowicz, W.Abramowicz@kie.ae.poznan.pl
Krzysztof Wecel, K.Wecel@kie.ae.poznan.pl
Tomasz Kaczmarek, T.Kaczmarek@kie.ae.poznan.pl
Department of Management Information Systems, The Poznan University of Economics, Poznan, Al. Niepodleglosci 10, 60-967, Poland

ABSTRACT:

The idea behind time-indexing is that documents, apart from for their semantic context, have a temporal context. The context places events described in documents on the time axis. One way of defining temporal contexts is to extract temporal references from documents. The article presents a tool for extracting time (temporal) references from news documents. It employs a set of simple rules and a finite state automaton to compute time indices of documents based on temporal references and publication dates. As distinct from other solutions this tool is based on pattern matching rather than on lexical-syntactical analysis. The paper describes the time indexer and the results of experiments conducted with the tool. The experiment consisted of computing time indices for a collection of business news documents. Preliminary results show that the time indexer produces satisfactory results in terms of its simplicity.

INTRODUCTION

Recent scholarly attempts of utilizing time constraints in document retrieval [Llido 1998] [Abramowicz 2001] [Abramowicz 2002] were based on the idea of event-time periods. A single event-type period is a calendar interval that represents the temporal coverage of information described by a single document. In current literature, the construction of event-time periods is based on the document publication date [Allan 1998] [Swan 2000] or on anchored and unanchored temporal references extracted from the document's content [Aramburu 2001] [Kalczynski 2003]. An anchored temporal reference is a time reference with a known location on the time axis. For example Jan. 1, 2002 and March 1999 are anchored references. Unanchored time references such as "in a month," "five days ago," do not have such location and must be resolved to calendar intervals. A typical event-time period is a contiguous calendar interval [Llido 2001]. Other representations include trapezoidal fuzzy numbers [Abramowicz 2002] and set of intervals [Kalczynski 2002].

Efforts to extract temporal information from documents are also presented in [Schilder 2001]. The significance of such information in the wide area of information systems [Pons 2002] was noticed with the development of temporal databases and data warehouses. The idea of linking time references with events described in documents was expressed in [Setzer 2002]. Time references extracted from texts help to index video content [Salway 2002], build temporal summaries [Allan 2001] and chronicles [Aramburu 1998], or analyze topic evolution [Berlanga 2001].

In general, current solutions to extract temporal information from textual content can be divided into the following areas: systems that annotate time expressions and systems that time-stamp event descriptions or focus on resolving temporal relations between events [Filatova 2001] [Wilson 2000].

In this paper we propose a time indexing tool based on the pattern-matching rather than on text understanding techniques.

TIME-INDEXER

To utilize temporal information included in the textual content stored in an IR system one has to index the documents temporally. This requires connecting extra information denoting its time meaning with each document. Such information will be further referred to as a time index. In order to create a time index for a document one needs to extract time references that occur in the content. As we mentioned earlier, there may be explicit or anchored time references e.g. dates – referred to as "strong references." Weaker or unanchored statements like "last week" or "a month ago" reference time intervals in the past or future but only if they can be properly resolved. In order to resolve a weak reference, a base date (or reference date) is required. This date can be extracted from document meta-data or, if it is not possible, the date is assumed to be the document's publication date. There are also some vague references (e.g.: "some time ago," "in the past"). These are not taken into account in the present implementation of the indexing tool. The temporal context of verb tenses is also not considered. Instead our idea of time indexing focuses on temporal references that may be resolved to calendar intervals.

Intuitively, a calendar comprises a finite number of time units (e.g. years, quarters, months, days) referred to as time granularities [Goralwalla 2001]. Time granularities are essential in analyzing temporal context of text documents because apart from the time intervals, they also define the importance (or weight) of references. For instance "last month" is less precise than "two days ago." In the proposed solution we assume that "day" is the finest granularity.

The proposed time indexer is based on meta-rules which represent patterns (rules) containing temporal references. Meta-rules comprise words (e.g. "ago" or "since") and variables (e.g. "[month]" or "[weekday]"). The variables are translated into words in the run-time. For instance "[number] [granularity] ago" is a meta-rule that enables finding multiple patterns in the document content like "2 weeks ago," "three months ago,", and "seven days ago."

Extraction of temporal references is a three-stage process. At the first stage, the textual content and reference date of the analyzed document are identified. This is performed by a dedicated parser that extracts necessary elements from the HTML code. As a result a set of XML documents emerges. The document has the following tag-hierarchy:

```
<DOC>
<REFDATE>
<TITLE>
<STORY>
```

At the second stage, sentences are extracted from documents' contents. We apply a simple set of sentence-parsing rules without employing semantic text analysis. The mechanism checks whether the punctuation mark is a part of floating point number (e.g.: 2.5), name (e.g.: Pawel J. Kalczynski) or one of the common abbreviations (e.g. U.S.). In general we assume that sentences do not end with any of the common abbreviations.

At the third stage, temporal references are extracted from sentences by means of meta-rules. The references are translated into symbolic representations which may be easily converted to calendar intervals. The proposed method of representing temporal references extracted from documents is described below.

TIME INDICES

The symbolic notation that we apply to represent temporal references builds upon the notation proposed in [Llido 2001]. The notation is based on dates, integer numbers and symbols representing temporal granularities: d – day, w – week, m – month, q – quarter, h – half and y – year. For instance "5d" denotes five days and "3m" three months. In addition to granularities we use symbols, which represent document publication dates on different granularity levels. And so, *rdd* denotes the actual publication date, *rdw* stands for the first day of the week, in which the document was published, *rdm* – the first day of the month, *rdw* – quarter, etc. For example if rdd=12/17/02 (Tuesday), then rdw=12/16/02, rdm=12/1/02, rdq=10/1/02, rdh = 7/1/02, and rdy=1/1/02.

Such a simple notation and two operators ("+" and "-") enable translating temporal references extracted from document contents into time intervals. For example "last week" may be translated into [rdw-1w,rdw-1d], and "next month" into [rdm+1m,rdm+2m-1d]. The main advantage of this notation is that it is human-understandable. This enables manual definition of meta-rules.

In the defined model, each reference has three properties: beginning of the interval, end of the interval, and the granularity level. For instance the reference "over the next two weeks" found in the document content would be resolved by the meta-rule "over the next [number] [granularity]" into {rdd, rdd+2w-1d, w}. Each reference is described by the interval and the granularity level. The granularity level is necessary to assess the importance (weight) of the extracted reference.

Finally, the symbolic representation of temporal references is translated into absolute calendar intervals. As a result a time index T={(b$_i$,e$_i$, g$_i$)} i=0..n is created for each document, where n denotes the number of temporal references in the document content, b$_i$ and e$_i$ denote respectively the beginning and end of a single time interval such that b$_i \leq$ e$_i$, and g$_i \in$ {d,w,m,q,h,y} represents the granularity level of the reference i.

In this way temporal references are stored in a structured format as records in a database. Below we describe the time indexer rules in more detail.

RULES

A single time indexer rule is a function that translates time-reference phrases extracted from a sentence into a symbolic representation. The meta-rules were created manually based on simple heuristics.

At the first stage, we manually searched for patterns in a small group of documents and built appropriate meta-rules. Then we processed the whole collection of documents with this small set of rules. Sentences containing specific words, which indicate potential time reference (e.g. "weeks" or "January") were marked as suspicious. The small fraction of suspicious references was processed manually and new meta-rules were added. Then we cleared the "suspicious" attribute and started the procedure all over again.

At the time we finished this paper, the procedure was still in progress due to the large number of suspicious sentences. Sample time-indexing meta-rules are given below.

```
yesterday → rdd-1d;rdd-1d

back in [month] [year] →
[year]+[month]m-1m;[year]+[month]m-1d

next [granularity] →
rd[granularity]+1[granularity];
rd[granularity]+2[granularity]-1d

today → rdd;rdd

year-ago [number] quarter →
rdy-1y+[number]q-1q;rdy-1y+[number]q-1d

in [month] [year] →
[year]+[month]m-1m;[year]+[month]m-1d
```

The variables represent different values depending on what side (input or output) of the rule they are located. For example [month] may represent "January" on the input side and "1" on the output side, [granularity]: "quarter"→"q," [year]: "2001"→"1/1/2001," and [number]: "second"→"2." The input and output values for all variables are stored in separate structures, which we call dictionaries. A fragment of a dictionary for [weekday] variable is given below.

```
<DICTIONARY name="weekday">
<Mapping output="1">
<Token>Monday</Token>
<Token>Mon.</Token>
</Mapping>
<Mapping output="2">
<Token>Tuesday</Token>
<Token>Tue.</Token>
</Mapping>
   . . .
</DICTIONARY>
```

The analysis of suspicious sentences resulted in about 100 meta-rules so far but also showed weaknesses of the proposed notation. Relatively strong references like "in the end of July" or "in the beginning of the fiscal year" could not be objectively resolved by the proposed mechanism.

Implementation of the time pattern-matching mechanism to extract temporal references from the documents' contents is based on the finite-state automaton (FSA).

FINITE-STATE AUTOMATON

The actual mechanism that searches for patterns in document contents is implemented using a finite-state automaton. The definition of automaton states:

A finite-state automaton (FSA) is a quintuple $M = (Q, \Sigma, \delta, i, F)$, where Q is a finite set of states, $i \in Q$ is the initial state, $F \subseteq Q$ is a set of final states, Σ is a finite alphabet and $\delta : Q \times (\Sigma \cup \{\varepsilon\}) \to 2^Q$ is the transition function. The transition function δ may be extended to $\hat{\delta} : Q \times \Sigma^* \to 2^Q$ to accept words over Σ as arguments.

In our implementation the alphabet consists of all tokens extracted from meta-rules and dictionaries. The transition function states whether the automaton should change its state after reading a particular input symbol. Out of many possible transitions, only one is arbitrarily chosen. If there are no transitions that match current input and current state (fail event) the automaton refers to the failure function. Given the last available state, the failure function changes the state of the automaton to the initial-state or other state in accordance with the previous input.

In our implementation the algorithm of Aho-Corasick, a multi-pattern matching automaton, was adapted [Aho 1975] to serve as a time-indexing tool. The algorithm works in two stages. At the first stage the automaton is constructed according to the set of meta-rules. At the second stage, the automaton is applied to process the input stream of tokens. As distinct from A-C, words, not characters, act as tokens in our time indexer.

In addition, a single state of the automaton may represent a particular word (e.g. "ago") or a variable (e.g. [month]). As distinct from A-C, our automaton produces output only for the last state. This means that only the longest patterns (in terms of the number of tokens) are recognized. For instance "in January" and "in January 2004" are two different references but classical A-C would find three references: "in January" in both strings and "in January 2004" in the second.

The algorithm for the indexing automaton can be expressed in the following pseudo-code [Aho 1975]:

```
state←0
 for i←1 to n do
 while g(state, a_i)=fail
 do state←f(state)
 state←g(state, a_i)
 if output(state)≠empty then
 write output(state)
```

Where:
- n is the number of processed tokens
- g(state,token) is the transition function
- fail is a fail event (no transition found)
- f(state) is the failure function
- output(state) is the output function that returns raw time indices.

The automaton algorithm is efficient as it enables matching multiple patterns at a time. It has a linear complexity [Aho 1975].

Given a document d, a set of content-parsing rules X, a set of time-reference-extracting rules Y, a set of time-index-elements weighting rules W and a document reference date t_0, the Time Indexer I = (d, X, Y, W, t) returns the time index T of the document d. [Kalczynski 2002]

Experiment

For the purpose of the experiment we chose CNN.com/business news documents – one-page HTML documents with mostly textual content, abstracts, navigation bars, logos, banners and semantic hyperlinks. Approximately 7,000 documents that contained significant textual content (bigger than 1KB) were acquired, with reference dates, extracted from their titles, ranging from February 2, 2001 to June 7, 2001.

The content was easily extracted thanks to the source-specific HTML-comment tags that wrapped the actual story. After pre-processing, the documents were stored in a simple XML-format. Most of the documents were from 1kB to 5kB in size. The sentence parser found about 161,000 sentences.

Based on the defined meta-rules, the time indexer created over 1,500 different rules (patterns) and found nearly 57,000 temporal references in the collection. This means that an average business news document contains 8 references. The distribution of the number of references in documents is illustrated in figure 1.

Figure 1. Distribution of the number of temporal references in documents

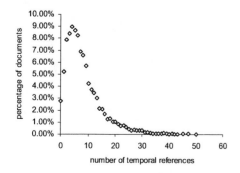

For 2.78% of documents the automaton did not produce any temporal references. 35% of all sentences in the collection contained at least one temporal reference. This indicates that temporal information is a significant part of business news documents.

Table 1 presents distribution of granularities in temporal references.

Table 1. Temporal granularities in business news

granularity	% docs
days	40%
years	24%
quarters	17%
months	13%
weeks	5%
halves	1%

It appears that 40% of all extracted references were the most precise in terms of the proposed model. Most of these references were weekdays. Thus, an average news document has 2-3 precise references, which refer to particular calendar days. Other references are less precise yet they still contain temporal information that may be used when searching for or analyzing business news documents.

With regards to document publication dates we divided temporal references into past, present and future. Past references are represented by intervals whose right boundary is before the publication date. Present intervals contain the publication date. The remaining references are future references. Table 3 presents percentages of future, present and past references in the analyzed collection.

Table 3. Past, present and future references

Past	Present	Future
42%	40%	18%

It is significant that 18% of all extracted references refer to the future. In terms of news archives such references will be less important than past references, because they address the unknown.

Preliminary verification shows that overall recall for the automaton is 55% and overall precision is 68%. However for the lowest granularity alone (days) recall = 73% and precision = 82%. Adding more rules and adjusting the existing ones should lead to better results.

The automaton is capable of precise indexing but it cannot find all references noticed by human-indexers.

Application to temporal retrieval

Information, especially business information, is relevant to its consumers only if they can put it in an appropriate temporal context. In the face of the information overload problem, precise information retrieval is essential for efficiency of knowledge workers [Zantout 1999]. The use of temporal references improves precision of information retrieval, as it provides additional constraints to be used in user queries. [Aramburu 1998] [Abramowicz 2002].

We define temporal retrieval as a two-stage retrieval. At the first stage user temporal needs expressed as time constraints are compared with temporal indices of documents. A document is considered relevant in terms of time constraints if any of its references intersect with user temporal needs [Abramowicz 2002]. This procedure narrows the answer set by rejecting irrelevant documents, i.e. such documents that do not match time constraints of the query. In the second stage a traditional keyword-based query is executed on the resulting subset.

Precision of information retrieval is generally defined as number of relevant documents retrieved (R) divided by the number of all documents retrieved (N).

$$P = \frac{R}{N}$$

The first step of the temporal retrieval reduces the number of documents

(N) returned by the query because documents irrelevant in time (hence generally irrelevant) will not be returned by the system. The number of relevant documents in the system's response remains the same, while the number of irrelevant ones is decreased. This leads to a better precision of the keyword-based retrieval performed at the second stage.

CONCLUSIONS

This article presents a pattern-matching tool for extracting time references from textual content. The tool has a satisfying performance in terms of its simplicity. Further improvement of the IR parameters of the tool and utilization of temporal context of information can lead to enhancement of a keyword-based information retrieval system. The time indexer uses a set of meta-rules and a finite state automaton. Yet, even with such a simple approach, without involving techniques of shallow text processing and text understanding, significant results can be obtained.

REFERENCES

[Abramowicz 2001] Abramowicz W, Kalczynski PJ, Wecel K (2001) Time Consistency Among Structured and Unstructured Contents in the Data Warehouse. In Managing Information Technology in a Global Economy, Proc. of IRMA 2001, Toronto. Idea Group Publishing, pp 815-818

[Abramowicz 2002] Abramowicz W, Kalczynski PJ. Wecel K (2002) Filtering the Web to Feed Data Warehouses, Springer-Verlag London

[Aho 1975] Aho A, Corasick M (1975) Efficient String Matching: An Aid to Bibliographic Search. Communications of AC, Vol 18(6)

[Allan 1998] Allan J, Papka A, Lavrenko V (1998) On-Line New Event Tracking, ACM Proceedings of the ACM SIGIR'98 Conference, pp 37-45

[Allan 2001] Allan J, Gupta R, Khandelwal V (2001) Temporal Summaries of News Topics, ACM Proceedings of the SIGIR'01 Conference, September 9-12, 2001 New Orleans, Louisiana

[Aramburu 1998] Aramburu M, Berlanga R (1998) A Retrieval Language for Historical Documents, Proceedings of the DEXA-2001 Conference, Springer Verlag, pp 216-225

[Berlanga 2001] Berlanga R, Perez J, Mrambury M, Llido D (2001) Techniques and Tools for the Temporal Analysis of Retrieved Information, Proceedings of DEXA'01, Springer-Verlag Berlin Heidelberg, pp 72-81

[Filatova 2001] Filatova E, Hovy E (2001) Assigning Time-Stamps to Event-Clauses. In Proceedings of ACL-EACL 2001, Workshop for Temporal and Spatial Information Processing, Toulouse, pp 88-95

[Goralwalla 2001] Goralwalla I, Leontiev Y, Ozsu M, Szafron D (2001) Temporal Granularity: Completing the Puzzle, Journal of Intelligent Information Systems 16, pp 41-63

[Kalczynski 2002] Kalczynski PJ (2002), PhD Thesis, The Poznan University of Economics, Poland

[Kalczynski 2003] Kalczynski P, Abramowicz W, Wecel K, Kaczmarek T (to appear in 2003) Time-Indexer: a Tool for Extracting Temporal References from Business News in M. Khosrow-Pour (ed.) Information Technology and Organizations: Trends, Issues, Challenges and Solutions, Idea Group Inc.

[Llido 2001] Llido D, Berlanga R, Aramburu M (2001) Extracting Temporal References to Assign Document-Event Time Periods, DEXA 2001 Conference Proceedings, Mayr H et al. (Eds) Springer Verlag, LNCS 2113 , Berlin Heidelberg, pp 62-71

[Pons 2002] Pons A, Berlanga R, Rumz-Shulcloper J (2002): Temporal - Semantic Clustering of Newspaper Articles for Event Detection Pattern Recognition in Information Systems (PRIS2002), Ed. ICEIS Press, pp 104-113

[Salway 2002] Salway A, Tomadaki E (2002) Temporal Information in Collateral Text for Indexing Moving Images, LREC 2002 Workshop on Annotation Standards for Temporal Information in Natural Language

[Schilder 2001] Schilder F, Habel C (2001) From Temporal Expressions to Temporal Information: Semantic Tagging of News Messages. In Proceedings of ACL'01 Workshop on Temporal and Spatial Information Processing, Toulouse, France, pp 65-72

[Setzer 2002] Setzer A, Gaizauskas R (2002) On the Importance of Annotating Event-Event Temporal Relations in Text, In proceedings of the Third International Conference on Language Resources and Evaluation (LREC 2002), Las Palmas, Canary Islands, Spain, Workshop on Annotation Standards for Temporal Information in Natural Language

[Swan 2000] Swan R, Allan J (2000) Automatic Generation of Overview Timelines, Proceedings of SIGIR'00, pp 49-56

[Wilson 2000] Wilson G, Mani I (2000) Robust Temporal Processing of News. In Proceedings of the 38th Meeting of the Association of Computational Linguistics (ACL 2000), Hong Kong, pp 69-76

[Zantout 1999] Zantout H, Marir F (1999) Document Management Systems from Current Capabilities toward Intelligent Information Retrieval: An Overview, International Journal of Information Management (19), pp 471-484

Using Innovative Teaching Techniques in Transition from Teacher-Centered to Learner-Centered Education

Volin Karagiozov, Ph. D.
American University in Bulgaria, Blagoevgrad 2700, Bulgaria
E-mail: vkaragiozov@.aubg.bg, fax: (359) 73 25-394, phone: (359) 73 88-443

INTRODUCTION

The concept and techniques of the Learner-Centered philosophy is an important process for the recognizing of any educational institution as a first-rate teaching institution.

Learner Centered Education is a strategy of education that places improvement of student learning at the center of decision-making processes and policies at all levels of the institution. It is characterized by the use of clear, measurable goals and student outcomes, and the direct involvement of learners in activities that produce deeper understanding of the content through the development of skills that are readily transferable to life and work. An additional central and very important goal is to prepare self-directed learners who can continue learning beyond their formal education.

The Seven Principles for Good Practice in Undergraduate Education [1] emphasize on:

1. Active Learning – students must discuss about what they are learning, write about it, relate it to past experiences, and apply it to their daily lives thus making what they learn part of themselves
2. Student-Faculty contact – the most important factor in student motivation and involvement is a permanent student-faculty contact in and out of classes.
3. Cooperation among students – good learning is collaborative and social, not competitive and isolated. Working in teams often increases involvement in learning. Sharing one's own ideas and responding to others' reactions improves thinking and deepens understanding.
4. Prompt and appropriate feedback on performance of the students – at various points during college, and at the end, students need chances to reflect on what they have learned, what they still need to know, and how to assess themselves.
5. Effective time management – allocating realistic amounts of time means effective learning for students and effective teaching for faculty. How an institution defines time expectations for students, faculty, administrators, and other professional staff can establish the basis for high performance for all.
6. Diversity of Talents and Ways of Learning - students need the opportunity to show their talents and learn in ways that work for them.
7. Holding high expectations – High expectations are important for everyone - for the poorly prepared and for the bright and well motivated students, for teachers and institutions as a whole.

TEACHER CENTERED V. LEARNER CENTERED INSTRUCTION

The educational goals for the twenty-first century are very different from the goals of earlier times. In the early 1800s, instruction in writing focused on the mechanics of making notation as dictated by the teacher, transforming oral messages into written ones. In the early 1900s, the challenge of providing mass education was seen by many as analogous to mass production in factories [2]. Teachers were viewed as workers whose job was just to pass the facts/knowledge to the students, but not understanding and to measure the progress and the costs through the standardized tests. This approach affected the design of curriculum, instruction, and assessment in educational institutions.

The traditional style of teaching has not been changed significantly since 1900. Many teachers still use the "I lecture; you listen and write" method of teaching. Despite the proliferation of electronic media and alternative methods of instruction, lecture is often the instructional tool of choice, forcing students to take notes and to listen carefully. The teacher-centered technique is characterized by involving this traditional type of instruction where the teacher lectures, uses the textbook, and sometimes promotes discussion.

Today, students need to understand the current state of their knowledge and to build on it, improve it, and make decisions in the face of uncertainty. The learner-centered instruction is non-traditional instruction where the students worked independently and in-groups on specific assignments. They discussed lessons in the text by focusing upon "real world" applications. The teacher uses visuals, field trips, guest speakers, and current events to teach the lessons. The role of the teacher in this case is to monitor the students and give advice or ideas so that they may draw conclusions and solutions independently or cooperatively.

INNOVATIVE TEACHING TECHNIQUES AND TOOLS OF TECHNOLOGY

Technology has become an important instrument in education. Computer-based technologies hold great promise both for increasing access to knowledge and as a means of promoting learning. Technology can help in establishing effective learning environments by: bringing real-world problems into classrooms through the use of videos, demonstrations, simulations, and Internet; increasing opportunities for learners to receive feedback from software tutors, teachers, and peers; to engage in reflection on their own learning processes; and to receive guidance toward progressive revisions that improve their learning and reasoning; providing "scaffolding" support to augment what learners can do and reason about on their path to understanding [2].

Technology has placed new demands on higher education. Institutions are challenged today with factors that include shifting demographics, rising student expectations, overburdened faculty resources, government mandates, and increased competition. Technology-enabled learning has opened a new world of opportunities. With the right strategy, advanced pedagogical tools, and technological framework, institutions can actually capitalize on this paradigm shift in higher education.

Various innovative teaching techniques can be used to improve the quality of the learning environment: web-based development and delivering of the course materials, electronic presentations, delivering and submission of tests, quizzes, assignments, examination papers and surveys. Even very simple mail-based agents can be of great help to enhance the faculty-student contacts and cooperation among students.

Many software systems exist promoting innovative teaching tools. Some of them provide tools useful just for a particular part of the teaching process, for example assignments and homework delivering, like WebAssign (http://webassign.net) that offers increased opportunity to practice skills, and the immediate feedback encouraging students to monitor their own progress and ad-

Transforming the Educational Experience

	Capability	Impact	Value
Administrators	+ Expands academic capacity + Student performance tracking	+ Student Retention + New Revenue Streams - Expense Management	+ Rapid ROI
Faculty	+ Course Management + Content Management + Assessment Tools	- Preparation Time + Content Availability	+ Increased Productivity
Students	+ Personalization + Academic Support	+ Content Sharing + Course Completion + Grades	+ Improved learning
IT Professionals	+ Scalability + Standards-based architecture	+ Campus-wide Deployment + Integration	+ Increased Efficiency

just the focus of their study accordingly. Other systems offer tools for creating an integrated learning environment suitable for on-line and distance education like WEBCT designed to address the needs of the entire educational enterprise - from administrators serving the needs of a broader student demographic, to students and faculty looking for ways to enhance teaching and learning. The following table taken from http://www.webct.com/transform summarizes the capability and impact of implementation of such systems on the entire educational enterprise:

TRANSITION TO LEARNER-CENTERED INSTRUCTION IN BULGARIAN UNIVERSITIES

The educational traditions in Bulgaria are rather old and their establishment began in the 1888 (October 1, 1888 is the birth date of Bulgarian university education) when the oldest Sofia University has been opened following the model of the famous European universities at that time. These traditions were and are still very close to teacher-centered style of teaching and although this approach had shown good results, now we have to recognize the drawbacks of this approach, mainly in applying the principles of active learning, an understanding the collaborative and social nature of the learning process, an appropriate feed-back on the student performance and assessing student learning.

The transition towards learner-centered teaching has been supported by the number of the ongoing pilot projects carried out together with the partners from other universities and funded through various programs like TEMPUS, NATO R&D projects, EU projects, Phare projects, etc. [3]:
- Intelligent Learning Environment for Course Telematics (INTELLECT) - This project aims at developing processes for transforming text/paper-based masters level course material into an interactive distance-learning environment based on the Internet, developing hypertext features, multimedia content and intelligent agents into a student-centered information system.
- Multimedia Applications for Telematic Educational Networks (MATEN) - The project attempts to combine the unique capabilities of different media with the power of computer networks in World Wide Web platform in order to design a rich educational environment for everyone. That environment removes the limitations and at the same time enhances the strong points of the traditional educational system. Multimedia application of computer networks provides people with the equal chances for life-long education, for flexible learning not only at the school, but as well as at home at work place. The Web is delivery distance medium, content provider, subject matter and "instructional designer" all in one.
- DEsign, implementation and MANagement of telematics based Distance education (DEMAND) – the project aims at developing a meta-level course for educational managers and practitioners at higher and further education level in order to be able to design and implement distance education courses using telematics. DEMAND itself will be implemented on the World Wide Web and will be delivered basically via the Internet. In settings for which this delivery option is not appropriate, an off-line version of the course will be offered.

The basic idea of these projects is to combine the strong points of the traditional education system with the innovative teaching techniques and modern methodological approaches and to disseminate the results in other Bulgarian universities. The implementation of these results affects the design of curriculum, instruction, and assessment at universities. The emphasis is set on getting an extensive feedback from the learners during the whole process of teaching and using this information in the pursuit of continuous improvement. Another very important issue is the assessment and self-assessment of the students, finding and applying the objective and measurable performance criteria for the evaluation of the learner's outcomes.

CONCLUSION

A scientific understanding of learning includes understanding about learning processes, learning environments, teaching, sociocultural processes, and the many other factors that contribute to learning. A truly effective learning solution must be aligned with an institution's mission and goals and designed to meet the needs of every constituency in the academic enterprise. The most successful educational institutions will be those who leverage emerging technology to: target, attract, retain, and cultivate students; continually improve the learning experience; maintain lifelong learning relationships with students; leverage institutional resources as efficiently and effectively as possible.

The transition towards learner-centered approach requires reformatting and keeping the courses up to date, implementing classroom innovations together with the adoption to different student learning styles. Applying modern IT techniques to the course design and development makes them suitable for distance learning education purposes also. This is extremely important nowadays taking into account the existing and foreseen budget cut constraints.

The latest achievements in the information technologies and communications create new opportunities and at the same time great challenges both for the educators and student.

REFERENCES

1. *New Directions for Teaching and Learning, Applying the Seven Principles for Good Practice in Undergraduate Education*, Arthur W. Chickering and Zelda F. Gamson Editors, Jossey-Bass, 1991.

2. *How People Learn: Brain, Mind, Experience, and School,* John D. Bransford,
Ann L. Brown, and Rodney R. Cocking, *editors,* National Academic Press, 1999

3. http://www.uni-sofia.bg/rdprojects/euprogrammes/index.html

Assimilation, Accommodation and Activism:How Women in the IT Workplace Cope

Sue Ellen Kase

Instructor, Department of Computer Science and Engineering, Doctoral Student
School of Information Sciences and Technology, The Pennsylvania State Unmiversity, 220 Pond Laboratory
University Park, PA 16802-6106, +1.814.865.-9505 (phone), +1.814.865.3176 (fax), **kase@cse.psu.edu**

Eileen M. Trauth

Professor, School of Information Sciences and Technology,The Pennsylvania State University, 002 Thomas Building, University Park, PA
16802
+1.814.865.6457 (phone), +1.814.865.6426 (fax), **etrauth@ist.psu.edu**

ABSTRACT

Women are under-represented in the information technology (IT) professions. A sufficient understanding of the underlying causes of gender under-representation in the IT profession is needed in order to develop effective educational policies and workplace human resource strategies to attract and retain more women. Unfortunately, few theories exist about how some women manage to survive and succeed in this male domain. One line of research critically analyzes marginalized groups coping and competing within the IT power structure. This paper continues in that tradition by developing a framework for the categorization of women's coping responses to gender issues found in the IT workplace. The framework integrates the findings from key multidisciplinary literature examining a variety of coping theories. The framework is based on the three types of women found in Trauth et al. (2000): *Assimilation, Accommodation*, and *Activism*. This coping responses framework will contribute to the development of new theories about the IT gender imbalance and provide a basis for interventions to promote change.

Keywords: Information technology, Workforce, Gender, Coping

INTRODUCTION

Despite significant growth in the information technology (IT) professions in recent years, there remain segments of the population that are under-represented in IT. Among those under-represented are women (Trauth, Nielsen, & von Hellens, 2000). A sufficient understanding of the underlying causes of gender under-representation in the IT profession is needed in order to develop effective educational policies and workplace human resource strategies to attract and retain more women (Trauth, 2002). Unfortunately, few theories exist about how some women manage to survive and succeed in this male domain. One line of research studied by Kvasny and Trauth (2002) describes patterns of coping behavior by under-represented groups competing within the power structure of the information society.

This paper continues in that tradition by developing a framework for the categorization of women's coping responses to gender issues found in the information technology workplace. The framework integrates the findings from key multidisciplinary literature that examines a variety of coping theories. The framework is based on the three types of women found in Trauth et al. (2000). In that study on the under-representation of women in the IT field, the authors explored the experiences of women who are in technical positions and who work in a range of industries throughout Australia. At the conclusion of the paper the authors suggested three types of women in the IT workforce. This paper begins where Trauth et al. left off by producing a framework of coping responses based on the three types of women identified in that study.

COPING THEORIES IN LITERATURE

In general, most coping studies appear to tap into three sorts of coping variables: direct action on the environment or self; interpretive reappraisal regarding the environment or self; and emotion-management. This section discusses several dominant viewpoints about coping that are found in the literature from non-IS disciplines. Two feminist identity theories are reviewed. This is followed by two investigations of coping behavior from psychology literature. Finally, several models of coping within occupational life are presented.

Women's Identity Coping Models

The Downing and Roush (1985) model of feminist identity development is derived from Cross's (1971) theory of Black identity development. The Downing and Roush model is based on the premise that women who live in contemporary society must first acknowledge, then struggle with, and repeatedly work through their feelings about prejudice and discrimination in order to achieve an authentic and positive feminist identity. Downing and Roush delineated a five-stage model. The first stage, *passive acceptance*, involves adherence to traditional sex roles and acceptance of male superiority. These women fail to acknowledge discrimination against women within society. The second stage, *revelation*, is exemplified by a consciousness-raising experience in which the individual develops anger through a questioning process resulting in an understanding of female culture. In the third stage, *embeddedness*, close affiliations with other like-minded women are formed. The relationships create a safe, women-friendly environment in which women process feelings of anger and betrayal. The fourth stage, *synthesis*, is characterized by the formation of a positive feminist identity that integrates the understanding that oppression has an impact on women. In the final stage, *acting commitment*, a culmination of the previous stages occurs in which the individual channels her feminist identity into activities promoting the creation of social change.

The Downing and Roush (1985) identity model is similar in certain aspects to another well-known women's identity model by Belenky, Chinchy, Goldberger, and Tarule (1986). In this model five perspectives outline how women view reality, define a male-dominated majority culture, and draw conclusions about truth, knowledge, and authority. The authors believe that most women can recall incidents in which either they or female friends were discouraged from pursuing some line of intellectual work on the grounds that it was "unfeminine" or incompatible with female capabilities (Belenky et al., 1986). Belenky et al. access conceptions of knowledge and truth that are accepted and articulated today and shaped throughout history by the male dominated majority culture. Men have constructed the prevailing theories, written the history, and set values that have become the guiding principles for men and women alike.

There are five perspectives in this model from which women know and view the world. The first perspective is *silence*. Women experience themselves as mindless and voiceless, and subject to the whims of external authority. They adhere to sex role stereotypes and have little awareness of their intellectual capabilities. In the second perspective, *received knowledge*, women conceive of themselves as capable of receiving, even reproducing knowledge. They are not capable of creating their own knowledge because all knowledge is obtained from the all-knowing external authorities. *Subjective knowledge* is the third perspective. In this perspective women conceive truth and knowledge as personal, private, and subjectively known or intuited. In the fourth perspective, *procedural knowledge*, women are invested in learning and applying objective procedures for obtaining and communicating knowledge. In the final perspective, *constructed knowledge*, women view all knowledge as contextual. They experience themselves as creators of knowledge, and value both subjective and objective strategies for knowing.

Both of these theories model the journeys of women through phases of psychological development from passive acceptance/silence to acting commitment/constructed knowledge in their realization of a gendered society. The destination is an individual who recognizes the social oppression of women and actively promotes the creation of social change in a positive way.

Psychological Coping Models

From a social-psychological perspective, Pearlin and Schooler (1978) investigate coping behavior as a protective function that mediates the impact that society has on its members. A fundamental assumption of their theory is that people are actively responding to the continuous strains built into daily roles. Pearlin and Schooler define coping responses as the behaviors, cognitions, and perceptions in which people engage when actually contending with their life-problems (Pearlin & Schooler, 1978).

Pearlin and Schooler (1978) categorize coping responses into three major types distinguished from one another by their functions. The first type of coping response changes the situation out of which the strainful experience arises. This response represents the most direct way to cope with life-strains. It aims at altering or eliminating the very source of the stress. Negotiation, discipline, and direct action are examples of coping responses that modify the conditions leading to the problem.

The second type of response controls the meaning of the strainful experience after it occurs but before the emergence of stress. This response recognizes that the meaning attached to an experience determines to a large extent the threat posed by that experience. Making positive comparisons, and selectively ignoring that which is noxious are examples of coping responses used to neutralize the problematic meaning of the experience.

The third type of response functions more for the control of stress itself after it has emerged. This type of coping neither alters the situation generating the stress nor modifies the perception of the strainful experience. The response functions more for the management of stress by helping people to accommodate without being overwhelmed by it. This type of coping response brings together a number of orientations to life-problems: denial, passive acceptance, withdrawal, a hopefulness bordering on blind faith, and belief that the avoidance of worry and tension is the same as problem solving (Pearlin & Schooler, 1978).

Unlike the previous theories, Pearlin and Schooler's (1978) coping responses do not propose a developmental timeline; instead they are influenced by general psychological resources. Psychological resources are the personality characteristics that people draw upon to help them withstand threats posed by events and objects in their environment. These resources reside in the individual's attitudes toward oneself. The psychological resources represent some of the things people *are*. Coping responses represent some of the things that people *do* in their efforts to deal with the strains they encounter in their different roles (Pearlin & Schooler, 1978).

An extensive research program by Lazarus and his colleagues (Lazarus & Folkman, 1984) distinguished between problem and emotion-focused coping. Problem-focused coping is defined as efforts aimed at altering the person-environment transaction and emotion-focused coping refers to efforts aimed at regulating the emotions. Problem-focused efforts are often directed at defining the problem, generating alternative solutions, weighting the alternatives in terms of their costs and benefits, choosing among them, and acting. In addi-

tion to problem-oriented strategies, problem-focused coping may include strategies that are inwardly directed (Lazarus & Folkman, 1984). Emotion-focused processes change the meaning of a stressful transaction without distorting reality, however, self-deception may become a consideration in this type of coping process. Lazarus and Folkman state that emotion-focused coping is used to maintain hope and optimism, to deny both fact and implication, to refuse to acknowledge the worst, to act as if what happened did not matter, and so on. In an earlier study, Lazarus and Folkman (1980) concluded that problem and emotion-focused functions were used by everyone in virtually every stressful encounter both facilitating and impeding each other in the coping process.

Workforce-Oriented Coping Models

A study by Menaghan and Merves (1984) examined the effectiveness of specific coping efforts for various problems in occupational life. Two different criteria of effectiveness were considered: the extent to which distress was reduced; and the extent to which occupational problems were reduced. The authors identified four major coping efforts: (1) direct action to resolve problems; (2) optimistic comparisons of one's situation relative to the past and relative to one's peers; (3) selective inattention to unpleasant aspects and heightened attention to positive features of the situation; and (4) a conscious restriction of expectations for work satisfaction and a focus on the monetary rewards from employment. Menaghan and Merves's (1984) coping efforts are similar to Pearlin and Schooler's (1978) coping responses in that they are largely interpretive strategies and emotion-management processes rather than direct efforts to change one's situation.

Other workforce-oriented models regarding the immediate reactions or coping strategies employed by women confronted with sexual harassment behavior identify a variety of classification schemes based on these women's reactions. Gutek's (1985) survey of victims of sexual harassment reported the following reactions: 9 percent of the women had quit a job sometime because they refused to grant sexual favors; 5 percent had transferred as a result of sexual harassment; and 23 percent had talked to coworkers after the instance of harassment. Crull (1982) reported that 42 percent of the victims in her survey had resigned from jobs because of sexual harassment. Also, a large number of the women tried to avoid the harasser. Jensen and Gutek (1982) provided more detail on the emotional reactions to sexual harassment. In their study the victims experienced depression 20 percent of the time, disgust 80 percent, and anger 68 percent. The victims labeled their responses as either inward-directed (hurt, sadness, and depression) or outward-directed (anger and disgust).

In response to the growing managerial concern about the detrimental effects of job stress, Latack and Havlovic (1992) present a conceptual evaluation framework in the form of a matrix that specifically focuses on coping processes in work organizations. They evaluated published coping theories and coping measures for *comprehensiveness* (defined as focus and method of coping) and *specificity* (defined as coping behaviors versus coping effectiveness; coping style; coping resources; and stress management applications). This coping processes matrix aids researchers in choosing and developing coping measures applicable to job stress.

COPING RESPONSES FRAMEWORK

The previous literature review was used to generate a framework of coping responses. The framework enables a researcher to take an analytical perspective on the many variations of women's coping responses in the IT workplace. This particular framework was tested on a set of in-depth interviews conducted with women practitioners and academics in the IT field.

Table 1 presents the framework. *Assimilation, Accommodation,* and *Activism* define the three categories of coping. A woman coping by *assimilation* denies that discrimination against women exists in the IT workplace. She successfully utilizes differing degrees of selective perception to operate in this male-dominated profession. An assimilating woman adheres to traditional sex roles and acknowledges male superiority in all aspects of life.

A woman who copes by *accommodation* accepts that gender discrimination is an integral part of the IT workplace, as simply the way things are. She internalizes oppression while skillfully avoiding confrontations within a male-dominated environment. Oftentimes, she manages both domestic responsibilities and a full time IT career. Due to impossible time constraints, the accommodating woman often chooses between scaled back professional aspirations and remaining childless.

The third type of woman uses *activism* to cope in the male-dominated workplace. She questions the inconsistencies and contradictions of the gender imbalance. The activist recognizes institutional barriers and expresses the need to be strong and fight the system. She networks with like-minded women while addressing discriminatory issues in hostile educational and work environments. The activist is proactive, often working as a radical or a champion to promote gender equality throughout society.

Table 1: Summary of Gender and IT Framework

Assimilation	Denies gender discrimination
	Selectively perceives oppression
	Adheres to traditional sex roles
Accommodation	Accepts gender discriminationInternalizes oppression
Activism	Questions male-dominated workplace
	Recognizes institutional barriers
	Aims to alter and resolve discrimination

CONCLUSION

This framework provides a conceptual tool that can be used for the analysis of transcripts produced from open-ended interviews, focus groups, participant observation, and other such data sets. The flexibility of the framework construction allows a wide range of scope useful from a high-level organizational view to a finely grained individualized analysis of specific coping experiences. The hierarchical structure of the framework lends itself to qualitative research software utilization through importation of coding trees.

Many promising possibilities for IS research emerge from the contents of the framework. Currently it is being utilized as an interpretative transcription analysis tool for several works in progress on gender and IT. This theoretical framework on how women in the IT workplace cope will improve our understanding as to why women are under-represented in the information technology sector and provide a basis for new interventions promoting change.

REFERENCES

Belenky, M. F., Clinchy, B. M., Goldberger, N., R., & Tarule, J. M. (1986). Women's Ways of Knowing: The development of self, voice, and mind. New York: Basic Books.

Crull, P. (1982). "Stress effects of sexual harassment on the job: Implications for counseling," American Journal of Orthopsychiatry. Vol. 52, pp. 539-544.

Downing, N., & Roush, K. (1985). "From Passive Acceptance to Active Commitment: A Model of Feminist Identity Development for Women," The Counseling Psychologist. Vol. 13, No. 4, pp. 695-709.

Folkman, S., & Lazarus, R. S. (1980). "An analysis of coping in a middle-aged community sample," Journal of Health and Social Behavior. Vol. 21, pp. 219-239.

Folkman, S., Schaefer, C., & Lazarus, R. S. (1979). "Cognitive processes as mediators of stress and coping," In V. Hamilton, & D. M. Warburton (Eds.), Human Stress and Cognition: An Information Processing Approach. New York: Wiley, pp. 265-298.

Gutek, B. A. (1985). Sex and the Workplace. San Francisco: Jossey-Bass.

Jensen, I. W., & Gutek, B. A. (1983). "Attributions and assignment of responsibility in sexual harassment," Journal of Social Issues. Vol. 38, No. 4, pp. 121-136.

Kvasny, L., & Trauth, E. M. (forthcoming). "The 'Digital Divide' at Work and Home: Discourses about Power and Underrepresented Groups in the Information Society," IS Perspectives in the Context of Globalization: Joint IFIP WG 8.2+9.4 Conference. Athens, Greece, 15-17 June 2003.

Latack, J., & Havlovic, S. (1992). "Coping with job stress: A conceptual evaluation framework for coping measures," Journal of Organizational Behavior. Vol. 13, pp. 479-508.

Lazarus, R. S., & Folkman, S. (1984). Stress, Appraisal, and Coping. New York: Springer Publishing, Inc.

Menaghan, E., & Merves, E. (1984). "Coping With Occupational Problems: The Limits of Individual Efforts," Journal of Health and Social Behavior. Vol. 25, pp. 406-423.

Pearlin, L., & Schooler, C. (1978). "The Structure of Coping," Journal of Health and Social Behavior. Vol. 19, No. 1, pp. 2-21.

Trauth, E. M., Nielsen, S. H., & von Hellens, L. A. (2000). "Explaining the IT Gender Gap: Australian Stories," Proceedings of the Eleventh Australasian Conference on Information Systems. Brisbane, December.

Trauth, E. M. (2002). "Odd girl out: an individual differences perspective on women in the IT profession," Information Technology & People. Vol. 15, No. 2, pp. 98-118.

Analysis of User's Behavior in Business Application Systems with Methods of the Web Usage Mining

Gamal Kassem, Jorge Marx Gómez, Claus Rautenstrauch
Otto-von-Guericke-Universität Magdeburg, Institute of Technical and Business Information Systems, P.O. Box 4120
D-39016 Magdeburg, kassem@iti.cs.uni-magdeburg.de

ABSTRACT

Navigation opportunities in modern business application systems[1] are various and complex. While navigating users leave traces, which can be used as an initial data for behavior analysis. Based on results of the analysis the application systems can be (re-) configured or (re-) customized in order to be more favorable for a user. The behavior analysis in the field of web application is supported by methods of Web Usage Mining. These methods can be assumed as a basis for the analyses in the field of business application systems. Proceeding from this, an aim of the present paper is a definition of approaches for a user behavior analysis in the field of business application systems. These methods should be derived from differences between web applications and business application systems. As a research in this field is not finished, this article is a research-in-progress paper.

1 INTRODUCTION

Today ERP-Systems[2] cover all task areas inside an enterprise. Besides, the systems continue to grow in size and complexity. The systems become more incomprehensible because of the functions and capabilities surplus. ERP-Systems offer a high amount of navigation opportunities, which enable users to perform tasks purposeful. Nevertheless, navigation through this system is not trivial. In an operating time users leave traces in the form of log-, protocol and trace data. These data can be pulled up and used as a main data source for user behavior analysis. The main purpose of the analysis is an extraction of a behavior patterns. The results of the user behavior analysis should support the correctness of the business processes structure examination of the enterprise on the ERP-System and the system settings (Customizing[3]). They also should simplify the personalization[4] of the system and enable the investigation of user's behavior with regard to work efficiency. In the field of web applications[5] the methods of Web Usage Mining [Ber02] are successfully used for investigation of user's behavior. The overall objective of users' behavior analysis is to support system designers in customization and personalization of systems.

Therefore, it might be possible to apply these methods in the field of business application systems, because here the same principles are used. To separate the examination of the user's behavior in the business application systems and web area, the concept of "Application Usage Mining" is introduced here. At the same time it indicates the relationship and similarity of both research fields. In order to designate the approaches for a user behavior analysis in the field of business application systems the description of the Application Usage Mining and comparison between web applications and business application systems take place in chapter 2. In chapter 3 a summary and perspective of future research activities in this field are given.

2 APPLICATION USAGE MINING

The attempt to apply basic approaches and methods of the Web Usage Mining in the field of business application systems and especially in ERP-Systems shows some significant differences, which have direct influence on aims of user's behavior analysis in the area of business application systems. These differences base on the fact that there are some fundamental logical as well as technical differences between a web application e.g. electronic shopping and a business application system. In a web application the connection between a guest and provider is not binding. The visitor is free to navigate on the providers' web pages. Moreover, he can access information and contents of the site and perhaps buy goods and services. However, there are some differences when a business application system is used. Here, the system user is not a visitor or customer, he is an employee of the enterprise and operates in the company's interests. Along with the usage of a business application system an employee should optimally perform assigned tasks and do not prevent business operations in the whole enterprise. These differences in intercommunications influence the application concept.

The following essential differences were identified during the comparison of the applications (see table 1):
• System access

In the business application systems a user identification takes place every time. Nevertheless, in the web area the user stays anonymous while accessing web pages. In web Usage Mining area it is very important to recognize users in order to be able to examine the traces in a long-run. The recognition can be done in the following way. The users' IP addresses can be identified, for example, by registration and with the help of the HTTP protocols. However, it is not simple because a computer can be used by several workers or a Proxy server is used for the allocation of temporary or dynamic IP addresses. Another solution is to check cookies. Although, there are some disadvantages: cookies can be deleted each time and also legal regulations about cookies usage are not completely clear.

Table 1: Technical and logical differences between the application types

Attribute	Web application	Business application system
System access	The visitor can stay anonymous	The user must be identified
Authorization	Usually, the visitor does not need an authorization	In the enterprise user receives an authorization according to performed function's
Protocol	Standard http	No standards
Software	Web application; (most of them) based on HTML-documents	Different software platforms are used
User's behavior	Free	Execution of predefined tasks and business processes
User's objective	Not defined	Optimal performance of tasks and business processes
Purpose of application	Reach a lot of visitors and customers	Efficient execution and automation of business processes

• *Authorization*

In a provider/customer relationship within a web application the role of the user is defined from the beginning, i.e. all visitors get the same authorization. In exceptional cases only some certain actions and sites, which the user can perform or see correspondingly, are allowed. In some cases a group of users can execute several actions or visit additional pages e.g. if they have been registered. Usually, a web page is a shop window, which is available for all users that want to get information or buy goods or services of a provider. In business application systems, for example in SAP R/3, each user must receive a certain authorization profile according to his functions or roles in the enterprise.

• *Protocol*

In the web area the HTTP protocol is a dominant application that serves the transfer of HTML pages. Besides it has a special meaning in the Web Usage Mining analysis. It presents data, which describe the user online behavior. In the business application field such information can be mainly collected from trace-, log- data and various protocol files. However in business application systems several protocols can be implemented, hence the information content and format of the data differ from system to system. Today there are no standard formats for such data in the field of business applications.

• *Software*

Web engineering methods [Mur01], which are applied for the web application development, are usually based on HTML, Java and XML technology. In the area of the business application systems different software platforms, software technologies and different system providers can be used. Therefore, it might be difficult in the future to obtain standardized software technologies for business application systems.

• *User's behavior, objectives and the purpose of application*

While reviewing a web page of a certain provider customer shows his interest in the content of the site. At this point it is not possible to determined what objectives the customer pursues and what pushed him to open the appropriate site. This can be only a curiosity or, for example, the customer bumped into the site just by chance. However, the goal of the provider is clear and unambiguous. By the supply of the web pages he wants to wake customer interest to the goods and services in order to sell them in the future. Thus, structure and presentation of the web pages play an important role. By the application of the Web Usage Mining methods one tries to analyze and value the patterns of customer behavior in order to design customized web pages.

There is another situation in the application field. While accessing a business application system a user declares his intention to perform tasks or business operations defined in the enterprise. The business processes of an enterprise, which have to lead the user in a proper way, is the center of the system.

The differences specified above influence the objectives and the procedure of the user's behavior analysis in the area of business application systems. As the user should perform tasks serviceable and purposefully, two aspects should be considered here.

1. Behavior of the users during the work performance

One tries to analyze the user's behavior by the application of the Web Mining methods in order to enable the user to perform his tasks serviceable and purposeful. For example, an application personalization is one of the possible solutions in this area.

2. Correctness of the execution of a business process and its activities

Another important goal of the analysis is the examination and if necessary an optimization of the business processes. By observation of the users' navigation the business process trend can be analyzed and valued.

It must be considered during the analysis what levels of the business processes are examined and whether it concerns the partial or the whole business processes.

3 SUMMARY AND PERSPECTIVE

Our decision to use the Web Usage Mining methods in the field of business application systems is based on the following fact: During the last years modern business application systems like SAP/R3 were introduced to the market. The business application systems offer users a lot of navigation opportunities in order to support users during performance of tasks and business operations. Hence, examination of the user's behavior can help to understand user needs and adjust the system, just like in the Web Usage Mining. However, at the beginning of our research we found out (chapter 2) that web application and business application systems differ logically and technically. Therefore, the objectives of the behavioral analysis in the Application Usage Mining and in the Web Usage Mining differ.

We are at the beginning of the research, thus it is a research-in-progress paper. The next stage of this research is the collection and examination of data about student's behavior during the usage of SAP R/3 at the Otto-von-Guericke-Universität Magdeburg, Germany.

ENDNOTES

1   Business application system means an installed software product, which supports the task settings in the business field [URL1].

2   The abbreviation "ERP" means Enterprise Resource Planning. This includes the application spectrum of the considered software for economical task settings in an enterprise and the public administration [Huf00].

3   Customizing [Kel99] enables for the customer to select and parameterize, on the basis of his aims and demands, the desired processes with the appropriate functionality from the various solutions of functions and processes.

4   Personalization means adjustment of a system so that it meets the work requirements of a specific user or user group. Personalization is aimed to accelerate and simplify the business transactions of the system processes [URL2].

5   Applications in the field of E-Commerce are called here web applications.

REFERENCES

[Ber02] Berendt, B.: Detail and Context in Web Usage Mining: Coarsening and Visualizing Sequences - Lecture notes in computer science. Springer, Berlin 2002.

[Huf00] Hufgard, A.: Definition und Abgrenzung des Begriffs ERP/ERM-Standardanwendungssoftware. IBIS Prof. Thome AG, Würzburg 2000.

[Kel99] Keller, G: SAP R/3 prozessorientiert anwenden: Iteratives Prozess-Prototyping mit Ereignisgesteuerten Prozessketten und Knowledge Maps. Addison-Wesley, Bonn 1999.

[Mur01] Murugesan, S.; Web Engineering: Managing Diversity and Complexity of Web Application Development. Springer, Berlin 2001.

[URL1] http://www-is.informatik.uni-oldenburg.de/lehre/Impl-IS/WS99-00/implementierung13/sld001.htm. 11.11.2002.

[URL2] http://help.sap.com. 23.09.2002.

Recreating Design Artefacts of Information Systems for Systems Evolution and Maintenance

Khaled Md. Khan
University of Western Sydney, Locked Bag 1797, Penrith South DC, 1719, NSW, Australia,
Tel: +61-2-9685-9558, Fax: +61-2-9685-9245, k.khan@uws.edu.au

Yi-chen Lan
University of Western Sydney, Locked Bag 1797, Penrith South DC, 1719, NSW, Australia,
Tel: +61-2-9685-9283, Fax: +61-2-9685-9245, yichen@cit.uws.edu.au

ABSTRACT

The paper presents an overview of the process of understanding existing information systems in order to aid system evolution and maintenance. The outcome of the paper is largely based on the experiences gather from a system maintenance project. The paper argues that the process of understanding existing systems involves four major design abstraction levels. To achieve the highest level of design abstraction in the hierarchy, maintainer programmers have to follow a defined process to gain a complete understanding of the system structure and semantics.

INTRODUCTION

Information systems (IS) always tend to change and evolve as technology and business rules change. Evolution of information systems is unavoidable, and it is a natural phenomenon. Organizations need to support systems evolution to take advantage of the new technology and to address the changing business rules. In the era of web-based systems and e-business, organizations need appropriate maintenance process and resources that are required to migrate their aging legacy information systems to web-enabled contemporary systems. The need for a system evolution emerges from various issues such as changes of business rules, emerging new technology, need for new functionality, or fixing defects in the systems and so on.

A major component of system evolution is to comprehend the underlying design rationale of IS at various levels. This paper explores issues of recreating design artefacts at various levels of abstractions. Current practices of system comprehension activities revolve around ad hoc patching which do not follow any defined methodology. A more defined formalism describing various levels of design artefacts and the abstraction process to recreate the underlying design knowledge is required to enable maintainers a clear understanding of the system.

The motivation of the work reported in this paper was actually generated from a maintenance project of a business application system. The candidate system was a small Inter Bank Reconciliation System (IBRS) used in a developing country in Asia. The organization later decided to transform the system into a more portable and efficient programming language platform keeping the entire functionality of the system intact. One of the authors of this paper was assigned the responsibility to lead the project. It involved considerable re-engineering task. The maintenance experience with the project reported in (Khan et al,. 1996; Khan and Skramstad, 2000; Khan et al., 2001) has motivated us to propose a program understanding process in this paper.

The paper proceeds as follows. In the next section, we outline the experiences with the maintenance process. We describe the issues related to program understanding process in section 3. The paper concludes in section 4.

EXPERIENCE WITH THE MAINTEANCE PROJECT

Beginning of the maintenance project with IBRS, it was learned that no design documents of the candidate system were produced during the development process. The system did not follow any coding standard, and no design documentation was available. One of the original programmers involved in the development of the system provided several informal diagrams about the system dependency. We combined the information gathered from her with the informal scenario that we already obtained to grasp the overall structure of the system. We tried to trace manually the flow of execution of the system to keep track of each function as reported in Khan et al., 2001.

First mental representation of the system we built was a program model as defined in (Pennington 1987; Mayrhauser et al.1994) by identifying the flow of control structures, call sequences, and scopes of global and shared variables found in the source code. We tried to map the relationships among all the scattered programming elements. This mapping process later allowed us to reconstitute the fundamental architecture of the system as well as the interaction of various programming components such as global and shared variables, function calls and branching structures.

PROGRAM UNDERSTANDING PROCESS

Based on the experience with the maintenance project, we have learned several lessons in program understanding process:
(a) Two types of *systems knowledge* are required to effectively understand an IS
(b) System knowledge can be recreated at four different *levels of abstractions*
(c) Maintainer programmers need to adapt defined *design recovery process*.

Each of the above three is discussed in the subsequent sections

System knowledge

In general terms, there are two major types of system knowledge found in a system: (1) syntactic knowledge (structure of the systems); and (2) semantic knowledge (program functionality).

Syntactic knowledge

This type of knowledge is the basic building block that is extractable from the source code. The syntactic knowledge includes for example, control structures, hierarchy of calling structures, programming patters, data structures. This type of information is very much programming language dependent.

Semantic knowledge

This type of knowledge comprises the ultimate intentions of program, and domain knowledge of the entire information system. This type of information is not always directly found in the source code and more difficult to be verified its correctness. We discuss the importance of informal linguistic information in understanding the semantics of a system in the latter sections.

Levels of abstractions

A system can appear to be in different levels of abstraction at different stages of its existence (Hausler et al., 1990). It is noted that the program understanding process gradually crosses different abstraction levels from implementation towards higher levels (Harandi and Ning, 1990). We can view a system conceptually at different levels in its existence. Program understanding is a knowledge intensive activity, and abstracting a higher level of representation requires abstracting of immediate lower level representation of the system in the hierarchy.

Figure 1 shows the hierarchical abstraction of an information system at four different levels such as: (1) implementation level, (2) structural level, (3) logical level, and (4) conceptual level.

Implementation level

To understand a system into its implementation level, one must be familiar with its language syntax and semantics. It can be derived in terms of an abstract syntax tree and a collection of program tokens. It is the lowest level of the system abstraction hierarchy.

Structural level

This level represents the dependencies among the program's different components. Control flow diagrams, control dependencies, procedure calls relationships, and structure charts are the examples of the structural level documentation. The syntactic knowledge specified in the previous section falls in this level.

Logical level

Logical level represents the logical relationship among the various components of a system. In program understanding, it is important to understand what function is provided by which part of the program. This level can be represented as data flow and data definition graphs.

Conceptual level

The conceptual level focuses on the application domain of the system. It includes the problem being solved, business rules, users' understanding of the problems and so on.

Design recovery process

Design recovery process has two phases: recreating syntactical knowledge from the source code; and recreating semantic knowledge. Maintainers first need to search for larger structural components of the system such as the subsystem structure, fundamental data structures, and module structures based on the analysis of source code and available design documents. Getting a conceptual view (a mental model of a program) of a system requires a representation of a program not as a text file but as a set of interrelated concepts. Syntactical knowledge provides maintainers enough information to recognize semantic knowledge of the system. Figure 2 shows the process on how the abstraction at the conceptual level can be achieved.

Recreating syntactical knowledge

The phase of recreating syntactical knowledge requires followings:
i)   Identifying the application domain
ii)   Understanding dynamic behaviour
iii) Composing the system into structural representation
iv)   Collecting informal linguistic information.

Identifying the application domain

Identifying the candidate system domain is the first step in system maintenance. Types of functionality and the profile of the environments in where the system being used indicates the application domain. These two ingredients are vital to perceive the system's application domain.

Figure 1: Hierarchy of program abstraction levels

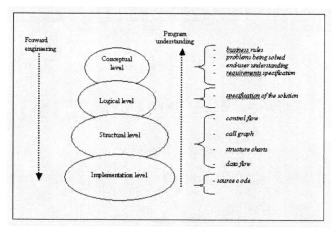

Understanding dynamic behaviour

The most important stage of recreating the system design is the comprehension of system functionality. The functionality of a program needs to be understood before attempting to extract the internal mechanisms of the system. This can be achieved by running the program with real data.

Composing the system into structural representation

It is important to compose the program into larger logical units. For languages which do not support the notion of module structure, the maintainer must depend on their intuition, experience and design documents to establish a conceptual boundary of the larger program structure. It is assumed that the functions in a source code file are semantically related, and constitutes a cohesive logical module (Choi and Sacchi, 1990). It is customized that program developers generally group related functions in one source file (Choi, 1989). The existing module structures could be constituted into larger chunk of the system structure to represent a wholeness of the related system functionalities. In this regard, program slicing is a well known technique that utilizes the properties of control flow to locate all instructions sets wherever in the control flow path that invoked an event across the module boundaries. This technique of slicing isolates individual computation threads within a program.

Collecting informal semantics information

It is quite useful to take into consideration the informal information structures scattered in the source code. Some natural language texts used in the source code as comments could be used to fill the gap between the conceptual level and the implementation level of the system. IS maintainers can retrieve a wide varieties of information from the combination of informal and formal linguistics structures in the source code. This type of information is helpful to identify the semantic knowledge of the program. The informal linguistic structures in the code such as comments, naming style and convention of data structures and functions provide vital information on the actual purposes of the data and function definitions.

Recreating semantic knowledge

Once the syntactic knowledge is created, maintainers experience and reasoning capabilities are used as an aid to recreate the semantic knowledge of the system. This practice heavily depends on the completeness of the syntactical knowledge recreated, programmers' experience, intelligent guessing, and their reasoning capabilities. Once semantic knowledge is reproduced, it is believed that maintainers' understandings reach at the conceptual level.

CONCLUSION

This paper focuses on the process of recreating the design rationale of existing IS. We have argued that system understanding is a pre-requisite for information systems evolution and maintenance. A system understanding process requires abstraction of system knowledge at various levels in the abstrac-

Figure 2: Design recovery process

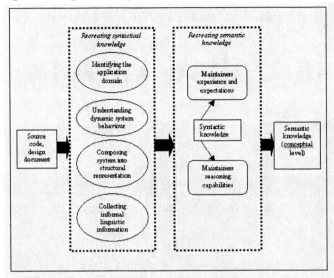

REFERENCES

Choi, S., Sacchi, W., (1990). "Extracting the Design of large Systems", IEEE Software, January, pp. 66-71.

Choi, S. (1989). "Softman: An Environment Supporting the Engineering and Reverse Engineering of Huge Software Systems", University of Southern California, Los Angeles 1989.

Hausler, F., el al., (1990), Using Function Abstraction to Understand Program Behaviour", IEEE Software, January 1990.

Khan, M. K., Rashid, M. A. and Lo, W. N. B. (1996). 'A Task-Oriented Software Maintenance Model', *Malaysian Journal of Computer Science*, Vol. 2, December 1996, 36-42.

Khan, K., Lo, B., and Skramstad, T. (2001). Tasks and Methods for Software Maintenance: A process oriented framework. Australian Journal of Information systems, Nol. 9., no. 1, September, pp. 51-60.

Khan, K., and Skramstad, T. (2000). Software Clinic: A Different View of Softare Maintenance. International Conf. On Information systems analysis and synthesis, Orlando, pp. 508-513.

Mayrhauser, A. von, Vans, A. M. (1994). 'Comprehension Processes During Large Scale Maintenance', *IEEE Proceedings Conference on Software Engineering*, 1994, 39- 48.

Pennington, N. (1987). 'Stimulus Structures and Mental Representations in Expert Comprehension of Computer Programs', *Cognitive Psychology*, Vol. 19, 1987, 295-341.

tion hierarchy. In an effective maintenance process, maintainer's understanding should reach at the conceptual level of the system knowledge. The paper also cites a design recovery framework to recreate the conceptual level of understanding of the system.

An Exploratory Study: Forecasting Winning Bid Prices in Online Auction Markets

Hong-Il Kim(itlime@ihanyang.ac.kr)[1], Bongjun Kim[2], Sungbin Cho[3], Seung Baek[1]

[1] College of Business Administration, Hanyang University 17 Haengdang-dong, , Seongdong-gu, Seoul 133-791, KOREA
Tel: +82-2-2290-1062 Fax: +82-2-2290-1169
[2] Electronics and Telecommunications Research Institute, [3] Konkuk University

ABSTRACT

To solve the information asymmetry problem in online auction markets, this study suggests and validates forecasting models of winning bid prices. Specially, it explores the usability of Neural network, Bayesian network, and Logistic regression in building the forecasting models. This research empirically shows that, in forecasting winning bid prices in online auction markets, data mining techniques such as Bayesian network and Neural network, have showed better performance that a traditional statistical model, Logistic regression. In addition, depending on the nature of data and the data transformation strategy, we have to select an appropriate data mining technique carefully.

1. INTRODUCTION

One of main problems in operating offline auction markets efficiently is the information asymmetry problem. The information asymmetry problem is caused by either lack of expertise (information regarding the product being auctioned) or lack of pricing information in the retail market[9]. If either buyers or sellers do not have a complete set of market information, they cannot guarantee that they get fair market prices for transaction items through auction. The online auction has solved the problem partially by providing powerful searching engines. However, online auction users have still suffered from the information asymmetry problem. Depending on what information online auction users have about transaction items, their perceived prices might have a huge gap. If the gap between the perceived prices of buyers and sellers is huge, it might take long time to negotiate the final price. The Revelation Principle of McAffee and McMillan[8] states that, by announcing the prices with which the seller wants to sell and the buyer to buy, auction markets can operate efficiently. In online auction markets, the online auction companies employ various methods to improve communication productivity between buyers and sellers. If sellers know fair market prices of their selling items before negotiating prices with buyers, the productivity of their price negotiation processes will be enhanced. In the case of buyers, if they know fair market prices of their buying items before negotiation, they can shortly reach to the final prices.

The objective of this research is to suggest and validate models to forecast the fair market prices of the products that are exchanged in online auctions. Since the transaction data in online auction markets normally has high noise, this study employs two AI-based forecasting techniques, Bayesian network and Neural network.

2. RESEARCH METHODS

2.1 Neural Network

Neural network emulates the human pattern recognition functions through a similar parallel processing structure of multiple inputs. It is designed to capture the causal relationships between dependent and independent variables in a given data set. Neural network has been applied widely in industries, from predicting financial series to diagnosing medical conditions, from identifying clustering of valuable customers to identifying fraudulent credit card transaction, from recognizing numbers written on checks to predicting the failure rates of engines[1].

Neural network generally consists at least a layer of input nodes, one or more layers of hidden nodes, and a layer of output nodes. Training the network is the process of setting the best weights among nodes in the network. Throughout the training process, Neural network produces weight where the actual output is as close to the forecasted outputs as possible for as many of the examples in the training set as possible[1]. One of the most popular training techniques is the back-propagation network, originally developed by John Hopfield. It is a supervised learning technique with the objective of training the network to map input vectors to a desired output vector[6]. Depending on Network structure, the performance of the Neural network is varied.

2.2 Bayesian Network

The Bayesian network consists of a set of probabilistic nodes and a set of directed arcs connecting the nodes. A central feature of the Bayesian network is to allow inference based on observed evidence on any of the nodes.

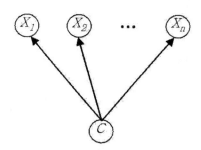

Figure 1. Naïve Bayesian Network

IF A and B are random variable, Bayes' rule states that

$$P(A \mid B) = \frac{P(B \mid A)P(A)}{P(B)}$$

Bayesian network, one of the most effective classifiers, is a rapidly growing field of research that has seen a great deal of activity in recent years[3]. It is a graphical representation of a probabilistic model that most people find easy to construct and interpret[5]. Over the last decade, the Bayesian network has become a popular representation for encoding uncertain expert knowledge in expert systems[4]. A key step in the Bayesian network is the computation of the marginal likelihood of a data set given a model[2]. In this study, the naïve Bayesian is used to predicting the winning bid prices.

3. RESEARCH METHODOLOGY

3.1 Data Collection

The data set used in this study consists of five hundred bid information of notebook computers from eBay which were collected in six weeks. The data collection has been restricted in four major notebook manufactures, *Compaq*, *Dell*, *IBM*, and *Toshiba*, which are popularly being auctioned on eBay. Drawing random samples from unbalanced populations is likely to yield biased samples, thereby adversely affecting the learning process of the models. As a result, the performance of the network and statistical model may be poor when tested in realistic situations[6, 7]. To solve the problem, each brand has been gathered equal population.

The data set consists of 12 variables. The product related information is notebook computer specification, for example, brand, TFT size, CPU type, RAM, HDD etc. The auction related information contains seller rating, bidding period, starting bid price. The input variables are summarized in Table 1.

Table 1. Input Variables

Category	Variables
Product related information (9)	Brand, TFT size, CPU Type, CPU Speed, RAM, HDD, Ethernet, Modem, CD drive
Auction related information (3)	Seller Rating, Bid Period, Starting Bid amount

3.2 Data Transformation

Before data transformation, data cleaning job has been performed firstly. The 71 data that have missing or incomplete information have been removed from the data set, as a result, total 429 data are left. To enhance the performance of forecasting models, two normalization strategies have been performed.

First, all the values of the data have been converted 0 to 1 ranges. Massaging the values to 0~1 range helps networks to recognize patterns in the input data. Second, by grouping the continuous values of data into several groups, the skewed distributed data is transformed into the symmetric distributed data [See Figure 1]. Although a major weakness of these data transformation strategies is losing information, many studies use these methods to enhance to model accuracy.

3.3 VARIABLE SELECTION

The choice of input variables used in the classification and prediction models is one of the important considerations in the design of Neural network and Bayesian network. In this research, to choose input variables for training networks, multiple regression analysis, stepwise method, discriminant analysis and decision tree are used. Through the analyses, nine variables (Brand, TFT size, CPU speed, RAM, HDD, Ethernet, CD drive, seller rating, and starting amount) are selected and three variables (CPU type, modem, and bidding

period) are removed.

3.4 Data Mining

The objective of this research is to suggest and validate models to forecast the fair market prices of the items that are exchanged in online auctions using Neural network and Bayesian network. *SAS Enterprise Miner 4.0* is used as a tool for Neural network and the macro function of *Microsoft Excel 2002* is used for Bayesian network.

3.5 Analysis of Results

Through twenty times simulation, averages of classification rates of the networks are computed. The results is showed in Figure 2. Neural network, Logistic regression and Bayesian network have showed 51.05%, 53.96% and 73.32% of average classification rate, respectively. In forecasting prices based on highly noisy data, such as online auction market information, Bayesian network showed best performance among three forecasting models. Many studies empirically state that, in handling highly noisy data, data mining techniques, such as Neural network or Bayesian network, outperform traditional statistical models. Surprisingly, in this study, a traditional statistical method, Logistic regression, outperformed a popular data mining technique, Neural network. This result might be caused by the data transformation. The information loss throughout the data transformation process undermines the performance of Neural network.

In order to investigate the information loss effect on forecasting model's performance, based on before-massaging training data, Neural network and Logistic regression are re-evaluated [See Figure 3]. The average classification rates of Neural network and Logistic regression are 57.47% and 55.79% respectively. The Neural network slightly outperforms Logistic regression. This result states that there is information loss effect on forecasting model's performance. This research empirically proves that, in handling noisy data such as online auction markets, data mining techniques, such as Neural network and Bayesian network, show better performance than traditional statistical methods. However, depending on the nature of data and the data transformation strategy, we have to select an appropriate data mining technique carefully.

4. CONCLUSIONS AND FUTURE STUDY

To solve the information asymmetry problem in online auction markets, this study suggests and validates forecasting models of winning bid prices. Specially, it explores the usability of Neural network, Bayesian network, and Logistic regression in building the forecasting models. This research shows that, in forecasting winning bid prices in online auction markets, data mining techniques such as Bayesian network and Neural network, have showed better performance that a traditional statistical model, Logistic regression.

As a future study, we will empirically investigate how differently sellers and buyers behave in online auction markets, if they know fair market prices before the actual negotiation process from our forecasting model.

Figure 1. Data Transformation

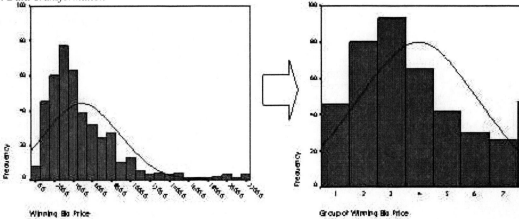

Figure 2. Classification Rate with Neural, Logistic, and Bayesian (After Data Massaging)

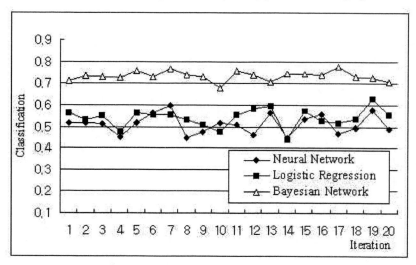

Figure 3. Classification Rate with Neural and Logistic (Before Data Massaging)

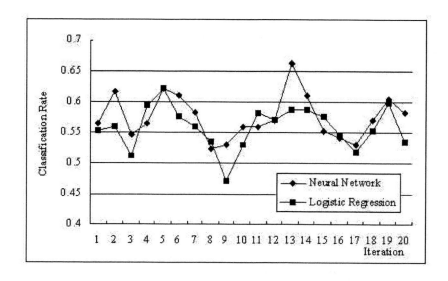

5. REFERENCES

1.   Berry, M.J.A. and Linoff, G., *Data Mining Techniques : for Marketing, Sales, and Customer Support*, 1997, Wiley Computer Publishing.

2.   Chickering, D.M. and Heckerman, D., "Efficient approximations for the marginal likelihood of bayesian networks with hidden variables", *Machine learning*, 1997, Vol. 29, Iss. 2, pp. 181-212.

3.   Friedman, N., "Bayesian network classifiers", *Machine learning*, 1997, Vol. 29, Iss. 2, pp. 131-163.

4.   Heckerman, D., Geiger, D., and Chickering, D., "Learning Bayesian networks: The combination of knowledge and statistical data", *Machine learning*, 1995, Vol. 20, Iss., pp. 197-243.

5.   Howard, R. and Matheson, J., *Influence diagrams*. Readings on the Principles and Applications of Decision Analysis, ed. J. Matheson, Vol. II, 1981, Menlo Park, CA, Strategic Decision Group.

6.   Jain, A.B. and Nag, N.B., "Performance Evaluation of Neural Network Decision Models", *Journal of Management Information Systems*, 1997, Vol. 14, Iss. 2, pp. 201-216.

7.   Korobow, L. and Stuhr, D., "Performance measurement of early warning models", *Journal of Banking and Finance*, 1985, Vol. 9, Iss. 2, pp. 267-273.

8.   McAffee, R.P. and McMillan, J., "Auctions and bidding", *Journal of Economic Literature*, 1987, Vol. 25, Iss. 2, pp. 699-738.

9.   Metha, K. and Lee, B., *An empirical evidence of winner's curse in electronic auction*, Proceeding of the 20th international conference on Information Systems, 1999, Charlotte, North Carolina, pp. 465-471.

Management of Document Versions in Workflow Systems

Yeongho Kim[†1)], Hyerim Bae[1)], Yong Tae Park[1)], and Woo Sik Yoo[2)]

[1)]Department of Industrial Engineering, Seoul National University; Seoul, 151-742, S. Korea; Tel: 82-2-880-8335, Fax: 82-2-889-8560; E-mail: yeongho@snu.ac.kr

[2)]Department of Industrial Engineering, University of Inchon; Inchon, 402-749, S. Korea; Tel: 82-32-770-8488, Fax: 82-32-770-8488; E-mail: wsyoo@incheon.ac.kr

ABSTRACT

This paper proposes a new method of document version management for workflow management systems. Recently, a workflow management system is considered as an essential element for automation of complex business processes, particularly for those in an e-Business environment. A core element of such processes is the documents that flow over the processes. Therefore, it is very important to have a systematic management of document changes along with the process execution. We propose a version model that can take into account the structure of the underlying process over existing version management techniques. In this model, the components of a document and a process are associated each other, and this becomes the basis for automatic creation of document versions and automatic configuration of relevant document for a certain user at a certain stage of process. A prototype system has been implemented, and the potential advantages of the approach have been discussed.

Keywords: Business process, Workflow, Version management, Electronic document management

1. INTRODUCTION

For the last several years, it has been conceived that WorkFlow Management System (WFMS) is an essential element for automation of complex business processes [1]. The WFMS is a software system that defines, controls and manages business processes [6], [7]. A business process usually involves documents, and in many cases, filling in the documents is considered as an important part of carrying out work in the process. Therefore, efficient handling of documents is of great significance in business process management.

A business process usually involves many participants who may deal with the same document on the process. As soon as one finishes one's task in the document, it is handed over to the next participant. This order of task sequence is specified in a process model. In a certain task, the responsible employee needs to work on a relevant version of the document, and updates it. This is repeated until the whole process is completed. In this setting, it is often very important to identify who is responsible for what part of the document contents. The importance may be doubled in e-Business environments in which many companies exchange documents.

Document management, as such, is an important part of business processes. Therefore, many commercial WFMS's provide functions dealing with document management to some extent. They, however, are limited to simple storage services and delivery of documents. A process execution usually accompanies document changes, such as adding, modifying, and deleting some of the document contents. This produces the necessity of managing document changes along with process execution. To the best of our knowledge, there is yet no system that can provide systematic management of document changes while taking into account the underlying process controlling the document flow.

To overcome the above limitation in conventional WFMS's, we propose a new version creation model. The essence of the proposed approach is at the fact that it takes into account the semantics of underlying processes. We modularize a document into several components, called workunits in this pa-

per, and associate each workunit with the activities that are supposed to handle it. We also propose a run-time model with which document versions can be created during process execution.

2. WORKFLOW AND VERSION MANAGEMENT

Workflow management is a term for a diverse and rich technology to support business process automation. In almost all WFMS's, defining a process model is prerequisite to automatic execution and control of the actual process. A process model is a coordinated set of activities, and an activity is a logical step or description of a piece of work. A WFMS first specifies a workflow process by defining activities that contribute to achieving the business objectives intended by the process and establishing the relations among the activities. While the process is being executed, the resources, like documents or application programs that are needed to perform each activity, are delivered automatically by the WFMS.

Version management, in its broadest sense, is a systematic method of dealing with changes of objects over time, and version is defined as a snapshot of an object that is semantically meaningful at a point in time [8]. The object changes are usually represented in a graphical form, and this is called version graph [8]. There are two different types of versions that are *revision* and *variant* [3]. Revision is a relation between two versions that are directly interlinked in a version graph. This is established when one of them is created by modifying the other. On the other hand, variant is the relation defined over two or more versions that are generated independently from the same previous version. This relation is not explicitly indicated in a version graph, but appears as a set of parallel paths.

There has been much research work in the field of version models [3], [8], and the version management has been successfully applied to such areas as software configuration management [3], engineering data management [5], [8], and temporal database. Although the application areas are different, the models used are similar to each other in that they manage the change of objects over the passage of time.

3. WORKFLOW-BASED VERSION MANAGEMENT

3.1. Process and Document Structure Models

A typical workflow system runs on a process model, like the example in Figure 1 (a). It, in general, represents activities, their relations, and attributes describing the process and activities. We can classify the process flow into serial, AND-parallel, and OR-parallel. A serial process is one that does not involve any split and merge, whereas an AND-parallel and OR-parallel process has split and merge. The latter two process types include more than one branches between the split and merge activities. Notice that a workflow process can be modeled with a combination of those types [7]. There is a huge body of literature in the process model, and readers can refer to [2], [10].

Business documents are usually very well structured, and the format is predetermined. Such a document is called form document. We partition a form document into a set of logical parts, each of which becomes a unit of work dealt with by an activity. The unit of work is called a 'workunit' in this paper.

Figure 1. Examples of process model and form document

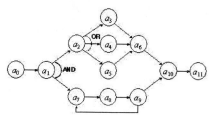

(a) Process model

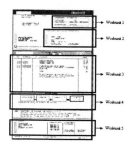

(b) Form document

Figure 1 (b) shows an example form document and its workunits. Once a process model and a document model are prepared, each workunit is assigned to some activities. The relation defined on the pair of workunit and activity is called assignment association. Every workunit has to be assigned to at least one activity, whereas an activity can have nothing to do with any workunit or deal with multiple workunits.

3.2. Document-Workunit Relations

In addition to the build-time models of process and document structures in the previous section, we need a run-time model that consists of version graphs and document-workunit relations. A version graph records the history of changes of an object that can be either a document or a workunit.

Creation of a new workunit version always leads to forming a new document version. In addition, a certain version of document can actually be considered as a collection of workunit versions. Document-Workunit Relation (DWR) represents such relations between a document version and a workunit version as follows.

Definition 1 (Document-workunit relations)

Consider a document d and its workunit w. The *DWR* relation, established between the p-th version of d and the q-th version of w, i.e., $v_p(d)$ and $v_q(w)$, is one of the following three types.

- The relation, $v_p(d) \leftrightarrow^I v_q(w)$, is an initialization relation (DWR^I) indicating that both $v_p(d)$ and $v_q(w)$ are the initial versions, that is, $p = q = 0$.
- The relation, $v_p(d) \leftarrow^G v_q(w)$, is a generation relation (DWR^G) stating that the workunit version, $v_q(w)$, generates the document version, $v_p(d)$.
- The relation, $v_p(d) \circledR^C v_q(w)$, is a composition relation (DWR^C) expressing that the workunit version, $v_q(w)$, is an element of the document version, $v_p(d)$.

4. TYPES OF VERSIONS

Based on the build- and run-time models described in the previous sections, we are able to manage versions while executing business processes. Since the operations of version creation are different depending on the types of process flow, they need to be described for each of the types. Due to the space limitation, a brief introduction to each of the type is presented below. A more detailed explanation is available in [3].

4.1. Serial Process

Activities in a serial process are all linearly connected. Such a serial process generates versions having revision relations. Consider the serial process in Figure 2 (a). The process deals with document d, and the document's workunits are assigned to the activities as indicated in the figure. The docu-

ment that has to be checked out in a serial process is always the latest version. The check-out procedure identifies the workunits that the latest document version consists of, and constructs it by simply putting them together. On the other hand, check-in procedure simple adds up a revision to the current version graph.

4.2. AND-parallel Process

An AND-parallel process allows multiple activities to be processed simultaneously. The split activities are independent of each other, and the workunits assigned to the activities also need to be dealt with in parallel. In this paper, AND-parallel processes are further classified into competitive split, cooperative split, and combined split. Depending on these split types, document versions are managed differently.

Competitive split

A competitive split is an AND-parallel process such that the same workunit is assigned to every branch of the split process. That is, after a process splits, all the branches check out the same document and work on the same workunit, but each of them generates its own version. Therefore, a competitive split produces several alternatives for one workunit. However, not all the alternatives are meaningful in the succeeding process. It can be considered that the branches compete to produce an alternative that is used in the final version. This is the reason why we call it a competitive split. The winning version could be automatically determined if the business logic is well understood and thus it can be codified. Otherwise, it is manually chosen. A simple example of competitive split is presented in Figure 2 (b).

Cooperative split

A cooperative split is a type of parallel process where each branch deals with different workunits. It is assumed that dependency doesn't exist among the workunits so that they can be processed in parallel. After finishing all the branches, the collection of the resulting workunits can form a document version. It can be seen that all the branches cooperate together to produce one

Figure 2. Process types and version creation models

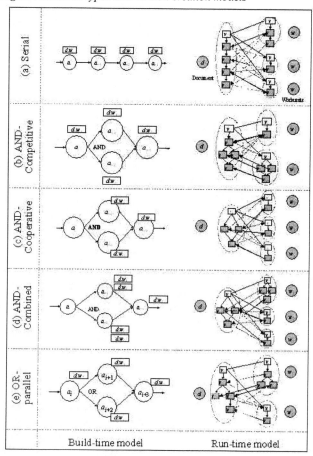

Build-time model · Run-time model

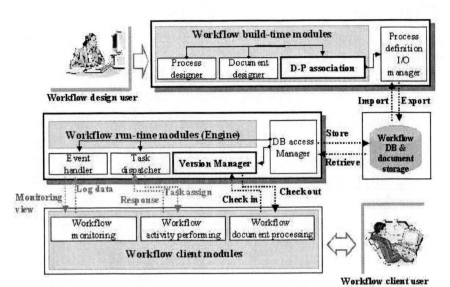

document version. This explains the name of the split. A simple example of cooperative split is shown in Figure 2 (c).

Combined split

A combined split is a combination of competitive split and cooperative split. Sometimes, the assignment of workunits to process activities cannot be explained by only one of the two split types. That is, some workunits are in a competitive split while the others a cooperative split. In such a case, the combined split is used. An example process of a combined split is presented in Figure 2 (d). Notice that every branch deals with workunit w_1. On the other hand, w_2 and w_3 are processed in different branches. While executing a combined split, the versions for w_1 is created based on the competitive split, and those for w_2 and w_3 follow the cooperative split.

4.3. OR-parallel Process

An OR-parallel process is similar to an AND-parallel process in terms of its process structure. It has split and merge activities and branches. However, not all the branches are meaningful at run-time. Some of the branches are selected and activated, and the process terminates when one of them finishes successfully. The branches that have not finished yet are simply canceled. At build-time, it is impossible to know which branch reaches to completion. Henceforth, in our version model, each branch maintains a version graph, but the one for successful branch becomes effective after merging the branches. An example of OR-parallel process is shown in Figure 2 (e).

5. PROTOTYPE IMPLEMENTATION

We have implemented a prototype system for the models proposed in this paper. The system is implemented on top of an existing WFMS, called SNUFlow [9], by adding component modules that provide version management functions. Some of the functions can be accessed at 'http://workflow.snu.ac.kr:8080/SNUFlow/client.jsp'.

The overall system architecture is presented in Figure 3. The system includes build-time, run-time, and client modules. The build-time modules include a process designer, document designer, and Document-Process (D-P) association component. The process designer and document designer provide interfaces for designing processes and documents and the D-P association component for establishing relations between processes and documents. These altogether describe how a process will be automatically executed at run-time. The specifications are imported from or exported to a workflow storage via an I/O manager.

In order for a user to easily carry out an activity, the prototype system identifies and delivers a right version of document to the user, so that the user can readily check out the document assigned to the activity. The user can simply click a mouse to check out the document version. On completion of the

activity, the user can check in the new version of the document, then the system automatically updates the versions of workunit and document.

6. SUMMARY AND CONCLUSIONS

The main purpose of our research is to develop a method of managing changes of documents in workflow processes. The essence of the proposed approach is that it takes into account the semantics of underlying processes. Our approach provides several advantages as follows. First, it helps workflow users by automatically checking out the right document version that the users have to work. Second, users can have a better understanding of the document changes. This is because the document changes are tightly associated with the underlying workflow processes, and our system can visualize it. Third, it is possible to recover a document into an earlier version that has been created before. When the process execution needs to be returned to a previous activity due to system errors or exceptional cases, it is required to recover the document at that activity. We think our version model can be a solution to the issue of workflow recovery. Fourth, since it is now possible to readily identify the content changes associated with a certain version creation, the approach would increase the responsibility of the employee in charge of the version creation.

An interesting further research issue is to support cooperative authoring in computer supported collaborative work environments. A cooperative authoring process involves multiple authors and thus many changes may take place even at the same time. It is important but not an easy task to support systematic versioning in the environment. Another issue is to develop standardized API's or standard versioning protocol for version management to interface with different WFMSs.

ACKNOWLEDGEMENT

This research was partly supported by the program of National Research Laboratory granted from Korea Institute Science and Technology Evaluation and Planning. It was also supported by the Korea Science and Engineering Foundation (KOSEF) through the Northeast Asian e-Logistics Research Center at University of Incheon.

REFERENCES

[1] W. M. P. van der Aalst, Process-oriented architecture for electronic commerce and interorganizational workflow, Information Systems 24 (8) (1999) 639-671.

[2] W. M. P. van der Aalst and A. H. M. ter Hofstede, Verification of workflow task structures: A petri-net-based approach, Information Systems 25 (1) (2000) 43-69.

[3] H. Bae, W. Hur, W. S. Yoo, and Y. Kim, "Document Versioning on Workflow Processes," Submitted to Computers in Industry, 2002.

[4]   R. Conradi and B. Westfechtel, Version models for software configuration management, ACM Computing Survey 30 (2) (1998) 232-282.

[5]   K. R. Dittrich and R. A. Lori, Version support for engineering database systems, IEEE Transactions on Software Engineering 14 (4) (1988) 429-437.

[6]   D. Georgakopoulos, M. Hornick, and A. Sheth, An overview of workflow management: from process modeling to workflow automation infrastructure, Distributed and Parallel Databases 3 (1995) 119-153 (also available at http://citeseer.nj.nec.com/georgakopoulos95overview.html).

[7]   D. Hollingsworth, Workflow management coalition specification: The workflow reference model, WfMC specification, WFMC-TC-1003, http://www.wfmc.org, 1995.

[8]   R. H. Katz, Toward a unified framework for version modeling in engineering database, ACM Computing Surveys 22 (4) (1990) 375-408.

[9]   Y. Kim, S. Kang, D. Kim, J. Bae, and K. Ju, WW-Flow: Web-based workflow management with runtime encapsulation, IEEE Internet Computing 4 (3) (2000) 55-64.

[10] G. Mentzas, C. Halaris, and S. Kavadias, Modelling business process with workflow systems: An evaluation of alternative approaches, International Journal of Information Management 21 (2) (2001) 123-135.

[11] E. Sciore, Versioning and configuration management in an object-oriented data model, VLDB Journal 3 (1994) 77-106.

A Risk-Trust-Control Perspective for Risk Management in the ASP Outsourcing Paradigm

Rajiv Kishore, Ph.D.

Department of Management Science and Systems, School of Management, The State University of New York at Buffalo, 310-B Jacobs Management Center, Buffalo, New York 14260-4000

Voice:(716) 689-2424, Fax:(716) 689-2424, E-mail: rkishore@buffalo.edu

Pauline Ratnasingam, Ph.D.

School of Business Administration, The University of Vermont, 314 Kalkin Hall, 55 Colchester Ave., Burlington, VT 05405-0158

Voice:(802) 656-4043, Fax:(802) 656-8279, E-mail: ratnasingam@bsad.uvm.edu

ABSTRACT

The ASP outsourcing paradigm, a special case of IT outsourcing, is fraught with risks of various kinds but the IS literature has not taken a risk management approach to IT outsourcing management. In this paper, we develop a risk taxonomy for the ASP paradigm and propose a risk management framework based on joint trust and control perspectives. This research has implications for potential vendors and customers of the ASP model. **Key words:** Application service provider, systemic risks, vendor risks, trust, controls, risk management framework.

1. INTRODUCTION

The Application Service Provider (ASP) outsourcing paradigm, also termed as the "Apps on Taps" model, is a new tool for strategic IT management. However, diffusion of this model has been quite slow despite its claims to provide several strategic benefits including accelerated speed of deployment of IT applications, seamless connectivity and integration among diverse business partners through shared web-based applications, scalability of IT infrastructure, and a lower and predictable total cost of ownership (2000). These advantages indeed have the potential to allow an enterprise to refocus on firm competencies and to provide flexibility in acquiring new business capabilities (1999).

While a lack of venture capital available to ASP vendors on account of the collapse of the Internet boom and the depressed business climate have undoubtedly resulted in several bankruptcies in this sector and have hampered growth on the supply side in this sector, the poor diffusion may also be attributed partly to the demand side of the equation. Potential customers of the ASP model are wary about adopting this paradigm on account of the risks involved in using this governance model. For example, clients lose control over their data – a vital corporate resource – because they reside on ASP servers in this model fueling new anxieties pertaining to data security and privacy.

However, the IS research literature has not paid much attention to the notion of risks and risk management for managing IS outsourcing arrangements, of which the ASP model is a special type. In fact, barring a few exceptions (Keil et al. 2000; Lyytinen et al. 1998) there are hardly any studies in the IS literature that deal with the notion of risks. This research seeks to fill that void. Its goal is to develop a risk taxonomy for the ASP paradigm, as it is important to understand fully the risks associated with this governance model to be able to make informed decisions about its adoption and to use it in an effective manner. Furthermore, this research also proposes to develop a risk management framework for the ASP paradigm based on a joint trust and control perspective (Das et al. 1998; Das et al. 2001) to provide mechanisms for risk mitigation and resolution.

2. INTRODUCTION

The diffusion of the Application Service Provider (ASP) paradigm, also termed as the "Apps on Taps" model, has been quite slow despite its claims to provide several strategic benefits including accelerated speed of deployment of IT applications, seamless connectivity and integration among diverse business partners through shared web-based applications, scalability of IT infrastructure, and a lower and predictable total cost of ownership (2000). These advantages indeed have the potential to allow an enterprise to refocus on firm competencies and to provide flexibility in acquiring new business capabilities (1999).

While a lack of venture capital available to ASP vendors on account of the collapse of the Internet boom and the depressed business climate have undoubtedly resulted in several bankruptcies in this sector and have hampered growth on the supply side, the poor diffusion may also be attributed partly to the demand side of the equation. Potential customers of the ASP model are wary about adopting this paradigm on account of the risks involved in using this governance model. For example, clients lose control over their data – a vital corporate resource – because they reside on ASP servers in this model fueling new anxieties pertaining to data security and privacy.

Yet, the IS research literature pertaining to the notion of risks and risk management for managing IS outsourcing arrangements of which the ASP model is a special type is limited. In fact, barring a few exceptions (Keil et al. 2000; Lyytinen et al. 1998) there are hardly any studies in the IS literature that deal with the notion of risks. This research seeks to fill that void. Its goal is to develop risk taxonomy for the ASP paradigm, as it is important to understand fully the risks associated with this governance model to be able to make informed decisions about its adoption and to use it in an effective manner. Furthermore, this research also proposes to develop a risk management framework for the ASP paradigm based on a joint trust and control perspective (Das et al. 1998; Das et al. 2001) to provide mechanisms for risk mitigation and resolution.

3. THEORY DEVELOPMENT

Major risks pertaining to the ASP model have been identified from practitioner literature and from first-hand discussions with ASP vendors and their clients. A preliminary classification containing two major categories is discussed below:

3.1 Risks

An event is generally considered to be risky if its outcome is uncertain and may result in a loss (Barki et al. 1993; Keil et al. 2000; Mellers et al. 1994).

2.1.1 Systemic Risks. These risks are endemic to the ASP paradigm and we, therefore, term them systemic risks. Regardless of which ASP vendor a client may choose, the client will face these risks and will have to utilize a combination of trust-control mechanisms to overcome them. Three risks are especially pertinent here:

3.1.1.1 Information Assurance Risks. Risks pertaining to security, privacy, and digital rights management with regard to the information assets of a firm are termed information assurance risks. The fact that client data reside on ASP platforms only exacerbates these risks, which exist even when data reside on client-owned IT infrastructure. ASP vendors may not provide adequate security mechanisms for client data, or may even misuse them by selling those to third parties including clients' competitors.

3.1.1.2 Quality of Service Risks. The ASP paradigm utilizes a complex value network as it aggregates products and services from a number of vendors, including telecommunications and network providers, hardware vendors, application vendors, software tools vendors, service firms, and distributors and resellers (Gillan et al. 1999). Moreover, the net-centric IT infrastructure is still evolving and, therefore, quality of service guarantees, often provided by ASP vendors, may not have much value as it is very difficult to pinpoint the source of errors and failures.

3.1.1.3 Application Standardization Risks. Because the ASP paradigm is essentially a one-to-many paradigm – one application to many clients – applications tend to be provided as standard vanilla applications rather than as customized solutions. While the "one size fits all" standardization is obviously good for the ASP vendor, who has to maintain single versions of various applications, it may not be such a good idea for clients who may want to have solutions that fit their business processes.

3.1.2 Vendor Risks

The second category of risks pertains to specific vendors and three risks are especially noteworthy. They include:

3.1.2.1 Survival Risks. Any business, if not managed effectively, runs the risk of poor performance and eventual extinction. ASPs are no exceptions. However, the risk of survival is quite pronounced in the ASP segment at the present time due to the current business climate and the comparatively nascent state of this industry. This is an extremely important risk to consider from a client perspective because the client may be left without data and an operational information system if the ASP vendor goes under.

3.1.2.2 Competence Risks. While ASP vendors may make tall claims about their capabilities to provide world-class application services, it is a risk clients ought to consider seriously because technical solution development and delivery competence is often difficult to gauge at the outset.

3.1.2.3 Opportunism Risks. Vendors may behave opportunistically both prior to contracting and during the course of providing contracted application services. This problem is more pronounced when the asset specificity of the contracted solutions is high, because customized solutions create a "lock-in" effect encouraging the vendor to engage in opportunistic behavior and in shirking contractual responsibilities.

We now briefly discuss the trust and control mechanisms that will help mitigate and control the above risks.

3.2 Trust and Control Mechanisms

3.2.1 Trust

Scholars have agreed that trust contributes to positive outcomes including lowering transaction costs (Gulati, 1995), reducing the extent of formal contracts (Larson, 1992), and facilitating dispute resolution (Ring and Van de Ven, 1994). This also known as a relevant factor in risky situations (Deutsch,

1962; Hosmer, 1995; Kee and Knox, 1970). For instance Boon and Holmes (1991: 194) defined trust *'as positive expectations about another's motives with respect to oneself in situations entailing risk'*. We adapt this definition of trust and apply it to institutional trust where one believes that there are impersonal structures that enable one to act in anticipation of a successful future endeavor (e.g., McKnight et al., 1998; Shapiro, 1987; Zucker, 1986). Zucker (1986) suggests that institutional trust is the most important mode by which trust is created in an impersonal economic environment where familiarity and similarity (commonality) does not exists. She identifies two dimensions of institutional trust; (1) third party certifications that define trading partners' trustworthiness, and (2) escrows that guarantee the expected outcome of a transaction. Thus, institutional trust serves as technology trust which is defined as *'the subjective probability by which organizations believe that the underlying technology infrastructure is capable of facilitating transactions according to their confident expectations'* (Ratnasingam and Pavlou, 2002). We identify two types of trust.

3.2.2 Types of Trust

2.2.1.1 Objective Technology Trust. We argue that objective technology trust measures and controls technical performances as its emphasis is on impersonal technical assurances embedded as security protocols and communication standards in the ASP IT platform. This kind of trust may serve to alleviate information assurance and quality of service risks.

2.2.1.2 Subjective Behavioral Trust. Subjective behavioral trust examines the credibility, ability, integrity, reputation, benevolence and goodwill of the ASP, vendors and customers. It refers to relationship trust as in open communications, in cooperation and, coordination among trading partners and improves the reputation of the vendor firms. This type of trust may serve to guard client firms against protect application standardization, survival, competence, and opportunistic risks.

2.2.2 Controls. Leifer and Mills (1996:117) define control as *'a regulatory process by which the events of a system are made more predictable through the establishment of standards in the pursuit of some desired objective or state.'* We identify two types of controls.

2.2.2.1 Technical Security Services. While technical solutions provide real-time tracking information for customers, it may also increase the extent of transparency that in turn increases information assurance risks. Technical security services include encryptions, digital signatures, and certified authorities and provide confidentiality, integrity and non-repudiation mechanisms that serve tov control the data residing on ASP platforms and serves to protect information assurance and quality of service risks.

2.2.2.2 Best Business Practices. Enforcing best business practices such as high quality standards, rigorous and regular audit checks that manage accountability will help to control application standardization, survival, competence and opportunistic risks. Similarly, the extent of top management commitment will influence best business practices that in turn increase the reputation of the ASP. Positive widespread reputations from referrals serve to control application standardization, survival, competence, and opportunistic risks. Table 1 presents the risk management framework and shows the relationship between risks, trust and controls.

4. CONCLUSIONS

In this research paper we have developed a preliminary risk taxonomy for the ASP paradigm and have proposed a risk management framework based on joint trust and control perspectives. This research not only contributes to

Table 1: The Risk Management Framework

Risks	Trust	Controls
Systemic Risks Information assurance risks	Objective technology trust	Technical security services
Quality of service risks	Objective technology trust	Technical security services
Application standardization risks	Subjective behavioral relationship trust	Best business practices
Vendor Risks Survival risks	Subjective behavioral trust	Best business practices
Competence risks	Subjective behavioral trust	Best business practices
Opportunistic risks	Subjective behavioral trust	Best business practices

the IS literature by providing a risk-trust-control based perspective for managing ement of the ASP paradigm, but it aalso This research contributes to practice as we have introduced some practical ways to mitigate using which how systsystemic and vendor risks in the an ASP paradigm can be mitigated. Our planned future research will utilize a qualitative research approach to conduct case studies at firms that use ASP services in order to validate the risk management framework being developed in this research.

5. REFERENCES

"Application Service Providers (ASP)," Cherry Tree & Co., pp. 1-20.

"e-Sourcing the corporation: Harnessing the power of web-based application service providers," in: Fortune, 2000, pp. S1-S27.

Das, T.K., and Teng, B.-S. "Between trust and control: Developing confidence in partner cooperation in alliances," Academy of Management Review (23:3), July 1998, pp 491-512.

Das, T.K., and Teng, B.-S. "Trust, control, and risk in strategic alliances: An integrated framework," Organization Studies (22:2) 2001, pp 251-283.

Deutsch, M "Trust and trustworthiness, and the F. Scale", Journal of Abnormal and Social Psychology, 61, 1962, pp 138-140

Gillan, C., Graham, S., Levitt, M., McArthur, J., Murray, S., Turner, V., Villars, R., and Whalen, M.M. "The ASPs' Impact on the IT Industry: An IDC-Wide Opinion," International Data Corporation, pp. 1-16.

Gulati, R. "Does Familiarity Breed Trust? The Implications of Repeated Ties for Contractual Choice in Alliances", Academy of Management Journal, (38:1), 1995, pp 85-112.

Hosmer, L.T. "Trust: The Connecting Link Between Organizational Theory and Philosophical Ethics", Academic Management Review, (20:2), 1995, pp 379-403.

Kee, H.W., & Knox, R. E "Conceptual and methodological consider-ations in the study of trust and suspicion, Journal of Conflict Resolution, 14, 1970, pp 357-366

Keil, M., Tan, B.C.Y., Wei, K.-K., Saarinen, T., Tuunainen, V., and Wassenaar, A. "A cross-cultural study on escalation of commitment behavior in software projects," MIS Quarterly (24:2), June 2000, pp 299-325

Larson, A "Network dyads in entrepreneurial settings: a study of the governance of exchange relationships", Administrative Science Quarterly, 5, 1992, pp 583-601

Leifer, R., and Mills, P.K "An information processing approach for deciding upon control strategies and reducing control loss in emerging organizations", Journal of Management, 22, pp 113-137, 1996.

Lyytinen, K., Mathiassen, L., and Ropponen, J. "Attention shaping and software risk - A categorical analysis of four classical risk management approaches," Information Systems Research (9:3), September 1998, pp 233-255.

Mcknight, H,D., Cummings, L.L., and Chervany, N.L "Managers as initiators of trust: An exchange relationship framework for understanding managerial trustworthy behavior", Academy of Management Review, (23:3), 1998, pp 513-530.

Ratnasingam, P., and Pavlou, P.A "The Role of Web Services in Business to Business Electronic Commerce," 8th American Conference in Information Systems, (AMCIS), August 9th-11th, Dallas, Texas, 2002, pp 889-907.

Ring, P.S and Van de Ven, A.H "Developing Processes of Cooperative Inter-organizational Relationships", Academy of Management Review, 19, 1994, 90-118.

Shapiro, D., Sheppard, B.H., and Cheraskin, L "Business on a Handshake", The Negotiation Journal, October, 365-378, 1996.

Zucker, L.G "Production of trust: Institutional sources of economic structure": 1840-1920. In B.Staw and L.Cummings, (eds) Research in organizational behavior, (8), 1986, pp. 53-111

Virtualisation as a New Trend of Applications of the Global Information Technology (IT) - Analysis on the Example of Transformation of Small and Medium Enterprises (SMEs) in the Global Market

Jerzy Kisielnicki, Warsaw University, Poland
jkis@wspiz.edu.pl, j.kisielnicki@mail.wz.uw.edu.pl

1. THESIS AND ITS REASONING

A new trend of applications of the global IT has appeared in the contemporary management that is called virtualisation. Virtualisation is such a process of transformation of an organisation that allows small and medium-sized enterprises (SMEs) to break through various limitations in their functioning. Most of them were difficult to overcome without application of IT. One of the existing barriers is limitation of the scale of SMEs functioning. Such enterprises were commonly associated with a local market, and their operation in the global market was a rarity. Even if they existed in it, their operation usually concerned specific products or services. Their operation in the global market was mostly restricted to operation as subcontractors of LEs.

The thesis to be justified in the paper is: Virtualisation changes dramatically the image of SMEs. Those enterprises, which use new trends of IT development for their own development, become fully competitive for large organisations. They may, *inter alia*, operate as equal organisations in the global market. Barriers of the economies of scale between them disappear. Thus, owing to virtualisation and the global IT connected with it, SMEs become flexible, new type organisations. They are often called 'modern organisations' in the literature. In organisations of this type, we deal with a very high speed of decision-making, and their functioning is based on economic criteria. In effect, opportunities to grow and to appear in the global market for SMEs are greater than if they operated as traditional organisations. Hence, it is a commonly assumed hypothesis that:

1. Virtualisation allows individual SMEs to enter strategic co-operative alliances with other similar businesses. A new organisational form, emerged in the form of virtual organisations, occupies a competitive position in the global market. For achievement of the goal outlined in such a way, SMEs use the opportunities, which the global IT provides. These opportunities mean creation of virtual organisations as well as creation of virtual branches for individual enterprises. Hence, we can say that an SME has today opportunities to grow in two planes:
   - horizontal (merging new organisations with the existing organisation),
   - vertical (creation of new branches for the existing organisations).
2. Large enterprises - LEs utilise IT quite differently than SMEs. They do not create virtual organisations, and they restrict the process of virtualisation to establishing new branches connected with the parent organisation.

Irrespective of the size of enterprise, we may assume that virtualisation is a significant element of a 'new economy'. Fundamentals of the theoretical process of virtualisation are yet under way of creation.

2. RELATIONS, PROBLEMS, QUESTIONS

Reasoning the previously put thesis, we want to discuss the relations occurring between the following elements:
- Virtualisation,
- SMEs,
- LEs,
- Global market.

The four elements specified may be discussed as a whole because of use of the global IT. An analysis of individual elements and of relations occurring between them requires answers to a number of questions. In the paper presented, we would like to focus on the following theoretical and practical research problems:

b. The notion of virtualisation and of virtual organisation, its framework and basic forms of implementation. Virtualisation as a new trend in business co-operation.
c. The notion of 'terminal point' as a theoretical construction, which achievement enables answering the questions:
   (i) When SMEs can be considered as functioning and having a significant position in the global market, and what is the role of global solutions of IT in it?
   (ii) What is the role of IT in liquidation of barriers between SMEs and LEs?
d. The practical case study. A specific construction enterprise, although it is in the class of SMEs, owing to application of the global IT and to creation of virtual organisation, was able to win an international tender for construction of a hotel complex. In result, it appeared in the global market for construction services. The enterprise in question won that tender having a renowned, large international enterprise as their competitors for construction of the said complex.

3. VIRTUALISATION – NOTIONS AND FORMS

Virtualisation, as we have already noted, is a herald of a new direction in sciences of organisation and management, having its theoretical and practical dimension. We understand it here as the process of continuous transformation. In the context of analysis carried out, this is a process, owing to which enterprises, irrespective of their size, may assume such a form that will allow them to become fully competitive in the permanently changing global market. The process of adjustment consists in a very quick adjustment of the enterprise to new requirements of the environment (Hendberg, 2000). This is done through alterations in the organisational structure as well as in the profile of products or services. These alterations are possible owing to a new direction of IT development. This direction is application of the global IT, and particularly application of global computerised networks, such as Internet (Keeny & Marshall, 2000).

From the theoretical point of view, we can separate the following three basic forms of virtualisation:
1. Extension of the function of enterprise activities, i.e. a vertical development of the organisation. This occurs when the enterprise wishes to be closer to the customer, and it does not have adequate resources, or when the economic calculus indicates that establishment of a traditional branch is profitless. For this purpose, the enterprise does create virtual branches or kiosks.
2. Creation of the virtual organisation, or the horizontal development. Such a development occurs through budding of the organisation, which is a virtual incorporation of other organisations in a given enterprise. There is lack of a

unanimous definition of this notion in the literature (Hendberg, 2000; Quinn, 1992; Scholzch, 1996). In an earlier publication, there was carried out an analysis of the definitions used (Kisielnicki, 1998). We assume, for the purpose of the analysis being carried out, that:

The virtual organisation is such an organisation that is being created by the principle of a voluntary nature of action, and its members enter with one another in relations of various types in order to achieve their common goal. Every member who creates the organisation fixes duration of the relation. That of the members, who first admits that the existence of that relation is unfavourable for them, may make the decision on its liquidation, and they withdraw from it as the first. The virtual organisation operates in the so-called cyberspace, and its functioning requires existence of the global IT. It is just because of functioning of solutions such as Internet activities of the virtual organisation in the global market are possible.

SMEs apply this form of development. LEs develop 'internally'. IT is used in them in order to strengthen their competitive position in relation to other enterprises. As Hammer and Stanton (1999) rightfully notice, IT becomes, for a certain class of organisations, a 'wall' that divides them from other enterprises.

3. Specialist structures being created in order to train and improve the future, and the present, employees. In physical terms, this is a computer or a network of computers equipped with specialist software. This form of virtualisation is used for raising qualifications of the personnel by both SMEs and LEs.

4. Virtualisation as an opportunity for SMEs to come to existence in the global market

Development of the global IT causes that more and more enterprises go out from the narrow framework of operating in the local market, and become global enterprises. Thus the global market, which over many years was only accessible for the chosen, thanks to IT and its growth, stands open to functioning of a wide class of enterprises, including also SMEs. An enterprise that wishes to come into existence in the global market should meet a number of conditions, such as, *inter alia*:

a. Possession of a well-known and reputable brand,

b. Built-up distribution and support service network,

c. Having at its disposal such a product or services provided, which, owing to quality and utility values, are unique and sought,

d. Possession of an up-to-date management infrastructure adjusted to supporting their activities in the global market, i.e. the global IT.

In order to meet the specified conditions, the enterprise must have at its disposal adequate financial, material and human resources. In confrontation of SMEs with large enterprises, the former are in a very difficult position. To come into existence in the global market, the enterprise must incur a definite outlay; or to exceed a certain volume of that outlay. Only having it incurred, we can say that the enterprise has chances to come into existence in the global market. We can describe an amount of that indispensable outlay as a 'terminal point'; sometimes, one may find the term 'barrier to entry in the global market' in the subject literature. Height of the 'terminal point' is determined by

volumes connected with:

1. Incurring costs for an advertising and promotional campaign in order to promote the enterprise or specific product(s) or service(s) in the global market.

2. Economies of scale, i.e. such volumes of production or services, which should be fulfilled below the market price, what will allow to occupy a favourable competitive position in the market.

3. A high quality of the product or service corresponding with international standards, such as, for example, in Europe, the ISO standards.

4. Having an access to the distribution channels existing in the global market or creation of alternative channels.

5. Observance of formal barriers, or adjustment of their activities to the regulations in force.

The specified parameters could only be met if the enterprise has got possibilities to use the global IT. Having such possibilities, it may make decisions under the conditions of full information, as well as reduce the risk of action. We should remember that functioning in the global market is much more difficult than in local markets, as it requires application of the global IT, and particularly of the global computer networks as well as an access to the international warehouses and data bases.

Enterprise's coming into existence and functioning requires still a greater outlay if it were to operate in the e-market. As the surveys carried out, *inter alia*, by Reichheld and Schefter (2000, 2001) have shown, the cost of winning the customer in this market is significantly higher than in the traditional market.

Fixing of the so-called terminal point requires carrying out empirical studies. Its magnitude depends on both the branch and degree of enterprise globalisation, as there are not many enterprises that are operating on all continents. In order to fix a height of the terminal point, we may use methods of the strategic analysis. For example, terminal point's height may be determined by definition of the outlay necessary if we want given enterprise's sales in the global market to be higher than 2%. Sometimes, as an organisation of such a type there can be considered the organisation, in which more than 50% sales value is connected with the global market. Because SMEs individually do not have such resources to be able to exceed the terminal point, that is why they create virtual enterprises with the use of the global IT. Graphically, such a situation is shown in Figures 1 and 2. Theoretically, development of the virtual organisation may be very great. Practically, extent of its development is connected with technical barriers (e.g., communication barriers), and with the need to create such an organisation that may achieve the fixed goal. Modification of the goal causes a very fast modification of the enterprise. In its simplified form, the procedure of creation of the virtual organisation is three-steps.

Point one - goal determination, i.e. the task that must be performed.

Point two - carrying out feasibility study of an independent implementation. In the case of negative result, there should be calculation whether creation of the virtual enterprise is feasible from the economic point of view.

Point three - creation of the virtual enterprise, which - with as high profit as possible for all the organisations forming it - can achieve it (in this step, there should be negotiated tasks for individual elements forming the enter-

Figure 1. Comparison of individual SMEs and LEs (LEs have a competitive advantage over individual SMEs)

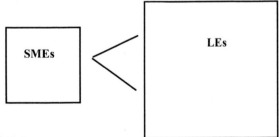

Descriptions:
< Relation of competitive
SMEs –Small and Medium-size Enterprises
LEs –Large Enterprises

Figure 2. Comparison of a virtual enterprise and LEs (a virtual enterprise – set of SMEs, is more competitive than LEs)

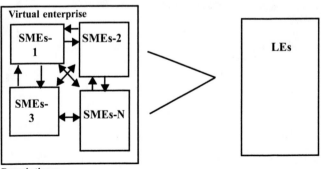

Descriptions:
> Relation of competitive
SMEs –Small and Medium-size Enterprises
LEs –Large Enterprises

prise, and conditions for settlement between them).

Having completed the task, dissolution of the virtual enterprise takes place. In practice, enterprises, having completed their tasks, are seeking for new goals and modifying the virtual organisation created earlier to new tasks. It sometimes occurs that the virtual enterprise transforms into various holding companies. Then, virtualisation can be treated as a preliminary stage in creation of traditional LEs.

The global IT constitutes a management infrastructure for the virtual enterprise. The global IT changes a nature of contact between the participants of the process of goal achievement, for which that enterprise has been set-up. This is not a traditional direct contact, for example, between the customer and the seller. Volumes of the necessary outlay on development of the IT infrastructure (and global networks in particular) are very high. Therefore, an adequate state policy is required in this respect, which should support development of the global IT. This is a problem going beyond the framework of this paper.

5. THE CONSTRUCTION S.A. ENTERPRISE AS A CREATOR OF THE VIRTUAL ENTERPRISE

In the subject literature, there are described many various types of virtual enterprises. Here, in order to support the thesis on the role of IT in creation of the global enterprise as well as its role in liquidation of barriers between SMEs, we shall present the problem of accomplishment of the project of construction of a hotel complex on the shore of the Mediterranean Sea. For the purpose of construction of that complex, tenderers were called to bid. The tendering procedure was held in accordance with the rules in force in the European Union. The Construction S.A. company won the tender. The value of the contract amounted to •160 million. The Construction S.A. company is a construction enterprise of a medium size. The basic size of employment is 180 people. A normal activity of the firm is designing and construction of housing estates and office buildings. Its assets are constituted by, among other things, an office building with a surface of 600 square metres, together with an adequate infrastructure and a multi-place computer network, technical background, comprised of heavy and light construction machines, cars and repair workshops. The enterprise has a very good opinion in the local market. They have also been awarded with international references for accomplishment of several contracts as subcontractors.

At the end of 1999, in the newsletter published by the International Federation of Consulting Engineers (FIDIC), and in accordance with the EU procedures, a tender was announced for completion of the said hotel complex. The Construction S.A. enterprise took part in the tender despite the fact they had had poorer experience and performance potential than other competitors. In order to take part in the tender, a special virtual enterprise was established that took part in the tender under the name of Construction S.A. That enterprise consisted of 15 organisations operating in various countries. They were such firms as:

1. The Construction S.A. firm,
2. A consulting enterprise that dealt with preparation of the tender bid,
3. An accounting and financial office,
4. An agency enterprise, in the area of labour and personal consultancy,
5. A specialist enterprise that was performing such tasks as, among other things, construction of swimming pools, facility protection, lifts, kitchen complex, air conditioning systems, greens arrangement.

The Virtual Construction S.A. enterprise (this name was nowhere used in the official materials) was created of both the firms that had been cooperating with Construction S.A. and with the use of IT.

The IT share in creating the enterprise that won the tender was as follows:

1. Finding out via Internet of specialist enterprises that had relevant references and expressed their wish to participate in the project.
2. Carrying out, also via Internet, of a partial employee recruiting campaign.
3. Operational management of project accomplishment, and exchange of information with the use of e-mail.
4. Management with the use of specialist software, such as the System Project, and systems of the MRP II/ERP class.

The firm's owner asked of the reasons for tender winning, said, among other things, that:

1. A very high contribution is at the side of global IT, and of Internet, in

particular. It allowed creating a strong virtual enterprise that was fully competitive for LEs.
2. A very serious treatment of the tender, and many hours lasting work of the team, Construction S.A. and collaborating firms, especially at the stage of tender preparation.
3. Luck that the companies selected for the purpose of creation of the virtual enterprise were fully competent.

At the same time, he uttered the following opinions:

1. Investors worse perceive the virtual enterprise than the traditional enterprise. These fears correspond with the above-specified characteristics of threats connected with functioning of virtual enterprises.
2. Firm's employees as well as the entire organisations creating the enterprise are exposed to an intense activity of 'head-hunters'.

6. FINAL REMARKS

The success of enterprise is decided by the whole complex of factors and adopted solutions. The global IT plays a very important role here. But to make it effective, even the best technology is not enough. IT must be supported with actions of the creative personnel. Obviously, IT is a very important factor that determines the strategy of firm's growth. It is also an initiator of a new direction of changes in the theory of organisation and management. Through virtualisation, it enables to create new organisational forms. Currently, the virtual enterprise, particularly in the global market, has yet not been treated in an equal way as large traditional organisations. The behaviour of the owner of Construction S.A. is characteristic, as he had some resistance in providing specific data related to his firm and to the virtual enterprise established. Such behaviour consists both in a business secret as well as in the fact that the entire tendering procedure did not contain the term 'virtual enterprise', though the enterprise created was an organisation of this type.

Analysing the role of global IT, one should pay attention to its two parallel directions of development:

The first of them concerns its role in SMEs. IT development acts towards an increase of the degree of cooperation of the entire organisation. It also reduces the barriers existing between individual enterprises, which form a single organism - the virtual enterprise. This enterprise, while seeking to achieve the common goal, behaves as a single organisation.

The second direction concerns large organisations. IT strengthens the existing management structure within them. A result is creation of LEs 'castles' separated from other enterprises by the wall of computer encryption systems.

One may only suppose that a more common creation of virtual enterprises in the future on the basis of the global IT will reduce differences between the potential of both types of organisations, and thus it will contribute to levelling barriers between SMEs and LEs.

REFERENCES

Hammer, M., Stanton, S., (1999). *How Process Enterprises Really Work*. Harvard Business Review, Nov-Dec, p. 108

Hendberg, B. & Dahlgren, G. & Hansson, J. & Olive, N., (2000): *Virtual organizations and beyond, discovering imaginary systems*, John Wiley & Sons, Ltd., Chichester, N-Y, Toronto.

Kenny, D. & Marshall, J.F., (2000). *The Real Business of the Internet*. Harvard Business Review Nov-Dec 2000, p.119

Kisielnicki, J., (1998). *Virtual Organization as a Product of Information Society*. Informatica, 22, p. 3.

Kisielnicki. J., (1999). *Management Ethics in Virtual Organisations*, in: Managing Information Technology Resources in Organisations in the Next Millennium, ed. M. Khosrowpour, IDEA Group Pub. Hershey, London.

Kisielnicki. J., (2001). *Virtual Organization as a chance for enterprise development*, in: Managing Information Technology in a Global Economy, ed. M. Khosrowpour, IDEA Group Pub. Hershey, London, p. 349.

Quinn. J. B., (1992). *The Intelligent Enterprise*, The Free Press, N-Y.

Porter. M. E., (2001). *Strategy and the Internet*, Harvard Business Review, March, p. 62.

Reichheld. F. F., (2001). *Lead for the Loyalty*, Harvard Business Review, July-August 2001, p. 76.

Reichheld. F. F. & P. Schefter., (2000). *E-Loyalty: Your Secret Weapon on the Web*, Harvard Business Review, July-August, p. 105.

Scholzch Ch., (1996). *Virtuelle Unternehmen - Organisatorische Revolution mit Strategischer Implikation*, Management & Computer, 2, p. 16.

Effort Estimation in Open Source Software Development: A Case Study

Stefan Koch

Department of Information Business, Vienna University of Economics and BA, Augasse 2-6, A-1090 Vienna, AUSTRIA
Telephone: ++43 1 31 336 5206, Fax: ++43 1 31 336 739, stefan.koch@wu-wien.ac.at

ABSTRACT

This paper presents first attempts at estimating the effort in open source software projects. First, the possible parties interested in the results of effort estimation, and both hindrances and advantages for effort estimation in this context are explored. Using data concerning an open source project retrieved from public data, several well-known estimation models from literature are applied, and their applicability for this type of development is discussed.

1. INTRODUCTION

Open source software development (Feller and Fitzgerald, 2002; Raymond, 1999) has generated increasing interest in the last years. This software is characterized by several rights given by the respective licence, including free redistribution, inclusion of the source code, possibility for modifications and derived works, and some others (Perens, 1999). The guiding principle for open source software development is that by sharing source code, developers cooperate under a model of rigorous peer-review and take advantage of "parallel debugging" that leads to innovation and rapid advancement in developing and evolving software products.

While the differences between the decentralized open source process and traditional software engineering practices have been debated (McConnell, 1999; Vixie, 1999), and also quantitative studies of development projects and communities have been undertaken (Dempsey et al., 2002; Ghosh and Prakash, 2000; Hermann et al., 2000; Koch and Schneider, 2002; Krishnamurthy, 2002; Mockus et al., 2002), some points remain to be explored. One of the most important questions remaining is the effort for developing open source software, which is not known even to the leaders of the respective project. As software engineering has dealt with the problem of estimating the effort for a software project for decades and has produced a multitude of methods to this end, their use seems a natural answer. Whether these models can indeed be used for open source software projects needs to be ascertained. If this were the case, the information delivered would have additional benefits even for the open source community and companies pursuing related business models.

2. CASE STUDY

For this research, data concerning a large scale open source project were needed. Therefore we chose to use data available to the public from the version control system CVS (Concurrent Versions System; Fogel, 1999) and discussion lists of the GNOME project. In particular, data concerning the participants' contributions to the project, their cooperation and the progression of the project in size and participants over time could be retrieved from these sources. For results concerning areas other than effort estimation see Koch and Schneider (2002).

The data retrieved from the CVS-repository included for every checkin programmer, file, date, LOC added and deleted, revision number and some comment. Using the conventions of CVS, a programmer is doing work on the project by submitting ("checking in") files, which is recorded with the changes in the lines-of-code and further information. The definition of this often disputed metric LOC is taken from CVS and therefore includes all types, e.g. also commentaries (Fogel, 2000). As the difference between the date of the first and the last checkin of a programmer includes all time elapsed, not necessarily

only time spent working on the project, this measure is not usable for predicting output. Therefore, a programmer is defined as being active in a given period of time if he performed at least one checkin during this interval.

In the GNOME project, 301 programmers were identified, who differ significantly in their effort for this software project, with a majority contributing only a quite small amount to the total work done, a result also found by Dempsey et al. (2002) and Mockus et al. (2002). The total size of the GNOME project in LOC has experienced a steady increase up to the size of 1 800 000 LOC at the end of the observed time period, with 1 230 000 LOC being the size at the time it became operational (first major release in March 1999). During this time, the number of active programmers has seen a staggering rise between November 1997 and the end of 1998 (see Fig. 1). During the year 1999 this number has been roughly constant at around 130 persons. One reason for this development could be taken from Norden (1960) and Putnam (1978) who argue that only a given amount of persons can be working in a productive manner at a given time. In the light of this interpretation, the peak manning of the project has already been reached and will only see a downfall from thereafter. A correlation of 0.932 was found between total of LOC added and number of active programmers each month, which confirms the usability of this number for effort estimation. Another interesting finding is that productivity (defined as the mean number of LOC per programmer) is strongly positive correlated with number of active programmers in each month, thus violating Brooks' Law (Brooks, 1995).

3. EFFORT ESTIMATION

3.1. General Discussion

Establishing effort estimation for open source projects has two reasons, with the first being to uncover how efficient this form of development is. In the last years, this topic has been the center of much debate, major points always having been the efficiency of finding and correcting bugs relatively late in the life cycle (McDonnell, 1999; Vixie, 1999), and the high overhead

Figure 1. Number of active programmers

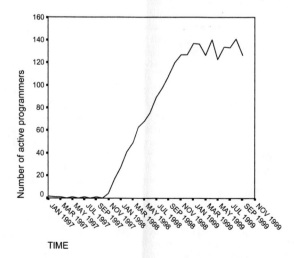

TIME

costs incurred for coordination and duplicated work. As the effort expended for developing open source software is unknown, these questions could not be answered. Therefore establishing retroactive effort estimation, thus arriving at a quantification for the effort expended for an existing software system, could help in deciding whether this development model should be pursued, abandoned or combined with traditional approaches into hybrid-models.

On the other hand, while the results of an effort estimation in commercial development are used for planning and control by management, there are also stakeholders in open source projects who could be interested in such results at early stages or during a project. These include the community itself, especially, dependent on the organizational form, the owner/maintainer, inner circle or committee (Fielding, 1999; Raymond, 1999), which need to monitor progress and plan for release dates, and programmers considering whether to join or to remain in a project. Further possible interested parties are current or prospective users, who need the functionality at a given date or with a given maturity level, especially corporations which are intending to pursue a business models based on this software, need it for their operations or plan to incorporate it in their products or services.

Several problems are associated with estimation for open source projects, in addition to the problems inherent in effort estimation. The first problem is the voluntariness of people's participation, which might also result in a high turnover of personnel and reduced productivity (Brooks, 1995). On the other hand, empirical data shows both that productivity is not necessarily declining (see above) and that the staffing for open source projects follows the postulated model for commercial software development (Norden, 1960; Putnam, 1978) closely (see below and Koch and Schneider, 2002). Vixie (1999) mentions the lack of a formal design and requirements definition as a problem, as necessary information for estimation will be missing. This information depends on the model employed and is thus discussed for each approach.

In addition, several assumptions of effort estimation models are inherently violated in open source development. For example COCOMO (Boehm, 1981) assumes a good management by both software producer and client, development following a waterfall-model and permanence of the requirements during the whole process. As there is no distinction between producer and client in open source development this seems no problem. The other two assumptions are both indeed violated, as the requirements are neither written down (Vixie, 1999) nor constant over time, and the software development follows are more spiral type of approach (Boehm, 1988), having been termed micro-spirals (Bollinger et al., 1999). COCOMO II (Boehm et al., 2000) on the other hand does not contain these assumptions but incorporates a more prototype-oriented type of development. The function point method also does not contain any assumption concerning the process model as it aims at being technology-independent and taking the user's viewpoint (Albrecht and Gaffney, 1983).

One main advantage is that all information concerning an open source project is available to the public. Therefore the data can be used by any interested party for estimation, which is not possible in commercial development.

3.2. Norden-Rayleigh

The first approach to estimating the effort for the GNOME project is based on Norden (1960) and Putnam (1978). A development project is modeled as an unknown but finite number of problems, which are solved by the manpower in events following a Poisson distribution. The number of people usefully employed at any given time is assumed to be approximately proportional to the number of problems ready for solution. Therefore, this number becomes smaller towards the end of a project as the problem space is exhausted. The learning rate of the team is modeled as a linear function of time which governs the application of effort. Following, the manpower function at a given time represents a Rayleigh-type curve governed by a parameter which plays an important role in the determination of the peak manpower. Using the relationship between time of peak manning and this parameter, the total manpower required can be determined once peak manning has been reached.

As the manpower distribution for the GNOME project has been retrieved from the data (see Fig. 1 above) and seems to follow a Rayleigh-type curve, this information can be used for estimating the effort. The peak manning of active programmers seems to have been reached between November 1998 and September 1999. Therefore the time elapsed between the beginning of the project (using January 1997) and the peak manning is set to 2.25 years, taking

Figure 2. Manpower function from data (FULL_PRO) and projected (VAR1 and VAR2).

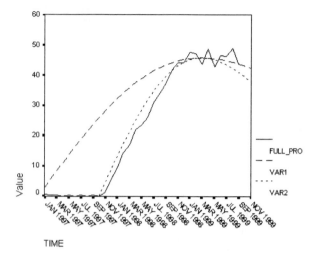

the middle of this range. The peak manning is set to 131.8 persons, again using the mean, but needs to be converted to full-time employees, as assumed in the model. For this conversion, some value for the time actually invested in the project is necessary. The study of Hermann et al. (2000), which shows at several points similar characteristics of the programmers questioned to the data retrieved from the GNOME project is used which gives 13.9 hours per week spent per programmer. This results in a peak manning of 45.8 persons (see Fig. 2 for the resulting manpower function for the GNOME project depicted as variable FULL_PRO). Using these values in the model, a total effort of 169.9 person-years is obtained. The projected manpower function derived is also shown in Fig. 2 (depicted as VAR1). As the manpower distribution retrieved from the data shows a small level of activity until October 1997, a second approach was taken using this point as start of the project. The time of peak manning then becomes 1.42 years and the total effort is estimated as 107.2 person-years. The resulting manpower function is again shown in Fig. 2 (as VAR2).

As Putnam (1978) has shown, the time of peak manning is close to the time the software becomes operational, while effort thereafter is expended for modification and maintenance. The first major release of GNOME has been in March 1999, which coincides with peak manning empirically determined. The effort expended until this date is estimated as 66.8 person-years by the first approach, as 42.1 by the second. The results of the effort estimation for the total project presented above therefore include modification and maintenance. But as the requirements are not fixed in open source projects over time, but are expanded according to the requests of programmers and users, the estimation presented might not give a complete forecast. As a result, models for effort estimation would have to be extended to incorporate this generation of new functionality, maybe using a stochastic process. Besides this, the fact that the Rayleigh-curve proposed for commercial projects decades before closely fits the curve for a contemporary open source project (at least until time of operation) is astonishing and hints at the fact that a self-regulating community follows the theory for efficient manpower application as well (or maybe even better) than commercial management. In addition this model builds the foundation of several other estimation methods including COCOMO, which therefore might also be applicable in this context.

3.3. COCOMO

The original COCOMO (Boehm, 1981) is one of most widely used models but two assumptions seem problematic. These are a development following a waterfall-model and the permanence of the requirements during the process. Therefore the applicability in the context of open source projects seems questionable. To confirm this, the work of Londeix (1987) is used, who details how an estimation in COCOMO can be transferred to the model by Putnam (1978), i.e. how the corresponding Rayleigh-curve can be determined. In this case the other direction is employed to find the parameters in COCOMO corresponding to the curve. As intermediate COCOMO has both the development mode and the values of cost drivers as parameters, there is no single solution. But nevertheless, even if organic mode, intended for small, in-house teams, is assumed, influence of the cost drivers would have to be more favorable than possible. Therefore the development of GNOME can not be modeled using original COCOMO, which states this development is more efficient than possible.

Therefore the successor COCOMO II (Boehm et al., 2000) seems to be a better choice, as it allows for both increasing and decreasing economies of scale, a prototype-oriented software process and flexibility in the requirements. When possible parameters are explored, the result is that once again this project is seen as very efficient as the cost drivers and scale factors replacing the modes of development in COCOMO II have to be rated rather favorably to obtain the estimated effort from the Rayleigh-curve, but this time the resulting combinations are within the range specified by the authors. If realistic values for the scale factors are used, the necessary value for the effect of the cost drivers is still within possible range.

For an additional effort estimation, the size of the GNOME project at time of operation is used with nominal values for all parameters, resulting in 612.5 person-years, and with realistic parameters resulting in 296.8 person-years, both of which are considerably higher than the results of the Rayleigh-curve. Nevertheless, while original COCOMO must be rejected in the context of open source development, COCOMO II provides for a modern type of software development and could be applicable, although it also deems this kind of development very efficient.

3.4. Function Point

While it is difficult, especially for an outsider, to correctly quantify the function points (Albrecht and Gaffney, 1983) for an open source project at the beginning, and also the requirements even from the user perspective can change during the progress, a quantification can be arrived at using the opposite way as in converting a function point count to LOC (Albrecht and Gaffney, 1983; Boehm et al., 2000). For this conversion, the mean number of LOC necessary to implement a single function point in a given programming language is provided. In GNOME, the most employed language is C, followed by Perl and C++. Therefore the overall conversion factor is estimated by using the factors from Boehm et al. (2000) for these languages with a weight of 0.7, 0.2 and 0.1, respectively, resulting in 100.5 LOC per function point. The size of GNOME at the time of operation thus corresponds to 12 200 function points.

In order to arrive at an effort estimation based on the function point count, either this measure is converted to LOC and another model like COCOMO is employed, or a relationship between function points and effort from historic projects is used. As the first approach has already been employed above, the second is taken. Using the equation provided by Albrecht and Gaffney (1983) results in an effort of 353.8 person-years. Different equations are provided by Kemerer (1987) resulting in 336.3 person-years, and by Matson et al. (1994) with a linear model resulting in 101.9 and a logarithmic model in 82.3 person-years. It seems interesting that the newer models estimate the effort as significantly less. This might be caused by the larger database containing larger projects of Matson et al. (1994) and the date of their study which allows for newer practices to be included in their results and thus resulting in stronger similarity to open source development. Nevertheless, the results which are in all cases higher than those of the Rayleigh-curve hint at a rather efficient mode of software development.

The main advantages for using function points are also of interest to their application in open source development. They are technology-independent, the user-viewpoint is considered and there is no assumption concerning the underlying software process. Therefore this metric can be used for comparisons of productivity and efficiency. Of course, additional data for open source projects need to be available.

4. CONCLUSION

In this paper we have discussed why effort estimation for open source development can be of interest. On the one hand, estimation of effort for completed developments is necessary for assessing their efficiency, and estimation at earlier stages can give important information to several stakeholders. The main problems in estimating this effort have been detailed, with some of them having been mitigated. Use of several approaches has been demonstrated us-

ing empirical data gathered for the GNOME project. Results indicate that open source development at least until time of operation seems to follow the model proposed for commercial projects very closely. In addition, this model can be used for estimating the effort for an open source project, although not right at the beginning, but including maintenance and modifications. The original COCOMO was dismissed both on theoretical and empirical grounds as being incompatible with open source development, while COCOMO II seemed applicable, as were function points, especially for providing a measure for technology-independent productivity comparisons. Both the results for COCOMO II and retroactive function point estimation showed that the estimations exceeded those of the Rayleigh-curve, hinting at a very efficient way of development from the viewpoints of these models.

REFERENCES

Albrecht, A.J. and Gaffney, J.E. (1983) Software Function, Source Lines of Code, and Development Effort Prediction: A Software Science Validation. *IEEE Transactions on Software Engineering*, 9, 6, 639-648.

Boehm, B.W. (1981) *Software Engineering Economics.* Prentice-Hall, Englewood Cliffs, New Jersey.

Boehm, B.W. (1988) A Spiral Model for Software Development and Enhancement. *IEEE Computer*, 21, 5, 61-72.

Boehm, B.W., Abts, C., Brown, A.W., Chulani, S., Clark, B.K., Horowitz, E., Madachy, R., Reifer, D.J. and Steece, B. (2000) Software Cost Estimation with COCOMO II. Prentice Hall, Upper Saddle River, New Jersey.

Bollinger, T., Nelson, R., Self, K.M. and Turnbull, S.J. (1999) Open-source methods: Peering through the clutter. *IEEE Software*, 16, 4, 8-11.

Brooks jr., F.P. (1995) *The Mythical Man-Month: Essays on Software Engineering.* Anniversary ed., Addison-Wesley, Reading, Massachusetts.

Dempsey, B.J., Weiss, D., Jones, P. and Greenberg, J. (2002) Who is an open source software developer? *CACM*, 45, 2, 67-72.

Feller, J. and Fitzgerald, B. (2002) *Understanding Open Source Software Development.* Addison-Wesley, London.

Fielding, R.T. (1999) Shared Leadership in the Apache Project. *CACM*, 42, 4, 42-43.

Fogel, K. (1999) *Open Source Development with CVS.* CoriolisOpen Press, Scottsdale, Arizona.

Ghosh, R. and Prakash, V.V. (2000) The Orbiten Free Software Survey. *First Monday*, 5, 7.

Hermann, S., Hertel, G. and Niedner, S. (2000) Linux Study Homepage. avaible online: http://www.psychologie.uni-kiel.de/linux-study/.

Kemerer, C.F. (1987) An Empirical Validation of Software Cost Estimation Models. *CACM*, 30, 5, 416-429.

Koch, S. and Schneider, G. (2002) Effort, Cooperation and Coordination in an Open Source Software Project: GNOME. *Information Systems Journal*, 12, 1, 27-42.

Krishnamurthy, S. (2002) Cave or community? an empirical investigation of 100 mature Open Source projects. *First Monday*, 7, 6.

Londeix, B. (1987) *Cost Estimation for Software Development.* Addison-Wesley, Wokingham, UK.

Matson, J.E., Barrett, B.E. and Mellichamp, J.M. (1994) Software Development Cost Estimation Using Function Points. *IEEE Transactions on Software Engineering*, 20, 4, 275-287.

McConnell, S. (1999) Open-source methodology: Ready for prime time? *IEEE Software*, 16, 4, 6-8.

Mockus, A., Fielding, R. and Herbsleb, J. (2002) Two case studies of Open Source software development: Apache and Mozilla. *ACM Transactions on Software Engineering and Methodology*, 11, 3, 309-346.

Norden, P.V. (1960) On the anatomy of development projects. *IRE Transactions on Engineering Management*, 7, 1, 34-42.

Perens, B. (1999) The Open Source Definition. In *Open Sources: Voices from the Open Source Revolution,* DiBona, C. et al. (eds.), O'Reilly, Cambridge.

Putnam, L.H. (1978) A general empirical solution to the macro software sizing and estimating problem. *IEEE Transactions on Software Engineering*, 4, 4, 345-361.

Raymond, E.S. (1999) *The Cathedral and the Bazaar.* O'Reilly, Cambridge.

Vixie, P. (1999) Software Engineering. In *Open Sources: Voices from the Open Source Revolution,* DiBona, C. et al. (eds.), O'Reilly, Cambridge.

Developing Intelligence-Based Threat Definitions for Global Information Security Management

Alexander D. Korzyk, Sr.

Department of Business, University of Idaho, Moscow, Idaho 83844, USA, akorzyk@acm.org, voice) 208-885-5958, **fax) 208-885-6296**

ABSTRACT

One of the major problems with global information security manage-ment is the piecemeal nature of pertinent information. An alert or item of interest might not mean anything in and of itself; however, combined with other items of interest and data, the last item might be the piece of the puzzle missing to uncover the nature of suspicious activity or unexplained problems. This research attempts to define how the pieces of data can be combined into information forming the basis of a possible scenario. Information systems using the database approach have generally failed to provide adequate infor-mation security because databases are not generally designed to discover facts or knowledge. Unlike databases, Model bases are generally integrative facili-ties that allow the capture of not just data, but the combination of data and information to form knowledge by storing combined data in a scenario. The proposed new threat definition model classifies the internal and external forces facing a trans-national organization from the relatively common operating en-vironment for many organizations and the intra-organization environment. Businesses using information systems need to continuously monitor their com-mon operating environment (COE). This threat definition model identifies the sources of macro-level potential threat forces and micro-level potential threat forces. These include nation-states, terrorists, hackers, and even soft-ware developers worldwide. Keywords: Threat Definition, scenario, military intelligence, information system security

I. GLOBAL THREAT SPECTRUM

A. Global Security Threats

Many governments have developed an information age threat spectrum for global security threats, shared threats, and local threats. Global security threats generally consist of eight critical infrastructures, information warfare, and global intelligence. The eight critical infrastructures that depend upon secure and survivable information systems (listed alphabetically) include: 1) Banking and Finance; 2) Electrical Power; 3) Emergency Services; 4) Gas and Oil Storage and Transportation; 5) Government Services; 6) Telecommunica-tions; 7) Transportation; and 8) Water Supply. The U.S. saw firsthand how Information Warfare can be carried out by criminals, organized crime, terror-ists, corporations, hackers, friendly governments and potential adversaries on Sept. 11, 2001. The global intelligence system did not detect the terrorist plot a priori even though there was a significant trail of information uncovered by the FBI, United States National Security Agency, Echelon, and United States Central Intelligence Agency in the weeks (Elliott, 2002). Perhaps had there been an integrative intelligence-based information security system that could have used current technology to thwart the attack, events might have been altered

B. Shared and Local Threats

The public and private sectors of a nation-state encounter several threats. The development and use of an integrative intelligence-based information se-curity system becomes even more important when the public and private sec-tor face the same common threats. Terrorists, hate organizations (such as the Aryan Nation, KKK, etc.), industrial espionage, organized crime, malicious mobile code, network failures, etc. can be used to acquire information to vali-date threats. Sources of information about local threats can provided acquired from insiders, vendors/contractors, consultants, institutional hackers, recre-ational hackers, natural disasters, accidents, and system failures. Any single security incident by itself might be meaningless but when security incidents are combined into patterns fitting a defined threat scenario, defensive options can be developed prior to the exploitation.

II. INTELLIGENCE-BASED THREAT DEFINITIONS

Prior to the use of an information system, a thorough assessment of vul-nerabilities given that certain threats exist, an in-depth risk assessment, and risk evaluation will allow the formation of scenarios. Management needs a method to determine which threats are most likely to exploit particular vulner-abilities and the impact of that exploitation on the information system. The creation of threat scenarios allows management to do "what-if" exercises, which simulate security incidents. Mitre Corporation has assembled an extensive list of common vulnerability exposures (CVE) (Mann and Christey, 1999). This CVE is a crude integrative facility that links intrusions to security inci-dents by the exploitation of a reported vulnerability. Unfortunately, the distri-bution of information about the CVE database is post facto and there is no scenario associated with the CVE, usually just a defect in the software or soft-ware design creating the vulnerability.

A. Environmental Threats

The High Level Global Threat Definition model (see Fig. 1) will allow information system designers to address threats given known vulnerabilities in the system design. It defines the threats that an information system faces and possible threat scenarios. All threats can be categorized into four types: environmental, exogenous, endogenous, and design-based (Sutherland, 1988). Environmental threats include climatic threats, primarily due to related severe weather, but can also come from extreme heat or cold exposure, and electrical surges from lightning strikes. . Natural disasters such as earthquakes, hurri-canes, floods, tornadoes, and landslides, give little warning before occurring. Enterprises should have disaster plans in place along with a backup facility ready to provide continuous service.

Figure 1. High Level Global Threat Definition Model
B. Exogenous Threats
Exogenous threats include the most often-sensationalized cyber crimes

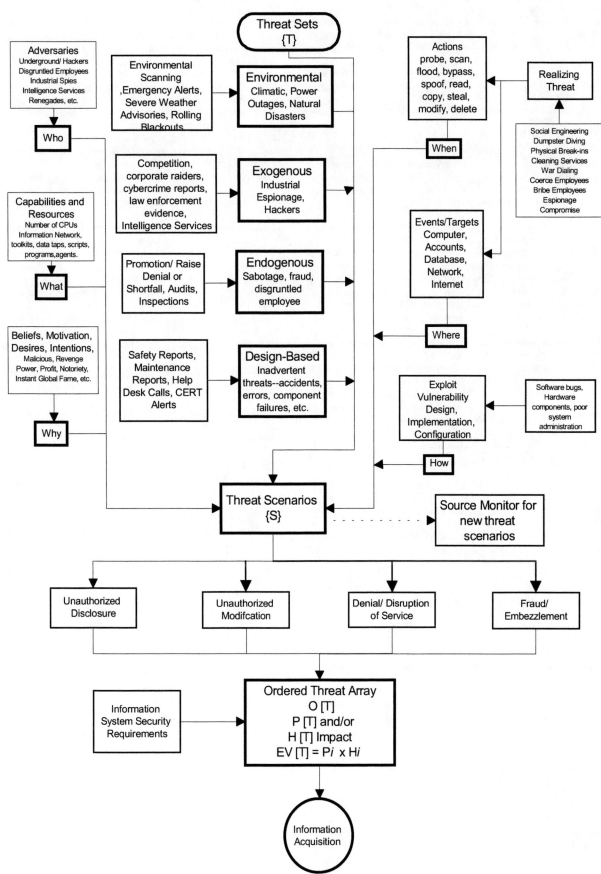

committed by hackers, criminals, and industrial spies. Despite efforts of the national governments to gain the cooperation of industry, many incidents do not get reported for fear of damaging publicity. Intense business competition often keeps enterprises from taking adequate countermeasures, as security generally is not considered essential for survival; however, enterprises report increasing numbers of cyber crimes daily to law enforcement agencies, even though the cyber crimes often get leaked to the media. The number of attacks from outside the organization is gradually equalizing with the number of attacks from inside the organization. Attacks had reportedly been generally occurring at 70% internal from 1985-1995. Since 1995 internal attacks have generally decreased to approximately 60% while external attacks have increased from 20 to 30% (CERT/CC, 2002

C. Endogenous Threats

Endogenous threats include many cover-ups committed by upper management to prevent embarrassing or reputation damaging information from reaching the media. Sabotage committed by disgruntled employees can be devastating, particularly to smaller enterprises with relatively few employees. A classic threat is the long-term employee who is passed over for promotion in favor a much shorter-term employee. Even a more common threat is the hardworking employee who receives no annual raise or a small raise of 2-3%, compared to a slack employee who receives an annual raise or large raise of 7-10%. One of the most common endogenous threats has been computer and wire fraud. Employees such as accountants with access to sensitive information or high dollar threshold limits are prime suspects for corporate espionage. Many companies monitor the Internet sites accessed by employees, but few monitor the content of electronic mail messages sent. An e-mail can easily contain sensitive information without the appearance of a sensitive message. Large business documents are a favorite tool within which to hide sensitive information. So unless the company monitors the content of each e-mail message and attachment to the email message to a fine level of granularity, a disgruntled employee can easily subvert the company by releasing sensitive information outside the company. Periodic inspections of employee e-mail have been ruled legal actions by an employer as have a full audit of documents transmitted by employees using company computer equipment (Daymont, 2002).. Unfortunately, security controls for endogenous threats has generally been much less emphasized than exogenous threats in the design and development of information systems.

D. Design-based Threats

Design-based threats include simple threats such as accidents destroying the physical computer or mistakes destroying the data or software due to poor system design or inadequate training of users. System administrators and database administrators often do not receive sufficient training for new or updated software and may end up deleting or modifying computer files unintentionally. Software bugs often do not become evident until after the release of software packages to the general public. Patches to correct the software bugs are not generally made until enough reports are made and the software bug is validated. Computer Emergency Response Team Alerts inform users of security related flaws that must be corrected to be protected from various other threats.

E. Elements of Threat Scenarios

Sets of threats together form threat scenarios consisting of who, what, why, when, where, and how. The threat sets combine to form threat scenarios. These scenarios consist of six types elements (Sengupta, 1992). The "who" elements include various adversaries, such as the computer underground, hackers, disgruntled employees, industrial spies, renegades, and foreign government intelligence services. The "what" elements include various capabilities and resources, such as the number of computers, an information network, hacking toolkits, data taps, scripts, programs, and software agents. The "why" elements include various beliefs, motivations, desires, and intentions, such as malicious retribution, revenge, power, profit, notoriety, and instant global-wide fame. Game Theory provides some mathematical foundations for what motivates the "who" element. A cooperative game is one in which the players communicate to plan strategy before taking action (Auman, 1967). In determining the rules of the game, the "when" elements include the specific times of various actions such as probing, scanning, packet flooding, bypassing, spoof-

ing, reading, copying, stealing, modifying, and deleting files or objects. Game theory describes the interactions between the players, which is essentially a choice of strategy determining the outcome of the interaction (King, 2001). If information technology, particularly the Internet, is considered a common property resource, one can call what is happening with crime and abuse on the Internet as a Tragedy of the Commons. Game theory considers the Tragedy of the Commons as a multiperson extension of the Prisoners' Dilemma, which points out that individually rational action results in both players made worse off in terms of their own agenda (Von Neumann and Morgenstern, 1974). The status of information system security can be considered in dominant strategy equilibrium as the "why" of the threats such as to defend when threatened. It is the interactions between the players which this research will try to manage. The "where" elements include various events/targets, such as computers, computer accounts, passwords, databases, networks, and the Internet. Prior to an information system threat or during the early stages of a realizing threat, the "who" may use several techniques to acquire more information about their target or to find a target. These techniques include social engineering, dumpster diving, physical break-ins, cleaning services, war dialing, coercing employees, bribing employees, espionage, and compromise. The "how" elements include the exploitation of a vulnerability, such as a design vulnerability, software bug, hardware component, insecure implementation or configuration of the system due to poor system administration. Multiple instances of any element type occur and the combination of all six element types normally combines into one threat scenario. Each threat scenario generally results in one of four outcomes: unauthorized disclosure, modification, denial or disruption of service, or fraud/embezzlement.

III. CONCLUSIONS AND RECOMMENDATIONS FOR FUTURE RESEARCH

There is information overload in the current global information security system causing international intelligence failures. By using intelligence-based threat definitions to classify threats for use by threat scenarios we may finally allow the global collaboration of intelligence to become a reality and prevent future intelligence failures. A model for acquiring the necessary information for the threat scenarios needs to be developed.

REFERENCES

Auman, Robert J. A Survey of Cooperative Games Without Side Payments, in Essays in Mathematical Economics, Princeton University Press, Princeton NJ, 1967.

CERT/CC. Security Incident Statistics. http://www.cert.org, 2002.

Daymont, Josh. EMAIL Security Juggling the Risks, SC InfoSecurity Magazine, Vol. 12, No. 5, May 2002.

King, William. Game Theory. http://william-king.www.drexel.edu/top/eco/game/. Dec. 6, 2001.

Mann, David E. and Christey, Steven M. Towards a Common Enumeration of Vulnerabilities. In the Proceedings of the 2nd CERIAS Workshop on Vulnerability Databases. Bedford, MA, January 8, 1999.

Reuters. Hackers could threaten airline safety. http://www.msnbc.com/news/468457.asp, September 27, 2000.

Sengupta (1992) Scenarios. In the Proceedings of the Hawaii Information Conference. Hawaii, 1992.

Sutherland, J. W. "Intelligence-Driven Strategic Planning." Journal of Technological Forecasting and Social Change, Vol. 34, pp. 279-303, 1988.

Von Neumann, John and Morgenstern, Oskar. Theory of Games and Economic Behavior. Princeton University Press, Princeton, NJ, 1974.

Influence of Geographic Dispersion on Control and Coordination for Management of Software Development Projects

Rajeev Sharma, and S. Krishna*
Indian Institute of Management Bangalore; Bannerghatta Road; Bangalore – 560076; Karnataka; India.
*Corresponding author: skrishna@iimb.ernet.in; Telephone No. 91-80- 6581906, 6993085; Fax No.: 91-80- 6584050

INTRODUCTION

Geographically dispersed projects are characterized by activities like coding and testing carried out at one geographical location while other activities like requirement analysis, implementation and testing are done at some other location. These projects are different from the co-located projects as there is a preponderance of electronic mediated communication and transactions.

Separation of resources in time and space can lead to problems in controlling and coordinating software development projects. It has also been mentioned in practitioner oriented literature that the cost advantage derived from employing cheap inexperienced manpower can vanish while managing the different aspects of a project in a remote location. Management of geographically dispersed activities so as to complete a project within the budgeted cost, time and quality parameters becomes much more demanding than those not so dispersed. Managers find it difficult to employ traditional means of controlling and coordinating team members with which they are familiar in the changed scenario (Piccoli, Powell and Ives, 2001).

THEORETICAL FOUNDATION

Control and coordination of activities has been an area of interest for researchers and practitioners for quite some time now. Control has found a mention in the management theories right from the beginning of scientific tradition of managing organizations (Henri Fayol, 1841-1925) to today's age of empowerment and downsizing (Jermier, 1998). At an organizational level, a failure to match controls with a firm's unique context is likely to lead to organizational decline in the long run (Ouchi, 1979).

Geographic dispersion has increased the complexity of managing software development. Some researchers have proposed that this complexity is the result of the struggle to negotiate place-space duality in the context of global software alliances (Krishna & Sahay, 2000). Place and space are the two central time-space configurations of modernity (Giddens, 1984, 1991) [1].

Geographically dispersed software development is carried over in "local", "global", and "shared" arenas (Krishna and Sahay, 2000). The "local" domain is one in which people work in their respective individual locales. The "global" represents the domain where individuals from a different location work on the same project. The "shared" electronic spaces enable developers to share messages, data or software programs with each other.

Global software outsourcing literature suggests that projects can be categorized into high and low structure projects (McFarlan and Nolan, 1995). High-structured projects are those in which the end outputs are clearly defined and there is little opportunity to redefine them. Low-structured projects are those in which the end outputs and processes are susceptible to significant evolution as the project unfolds. At the same time, research & development literature suggests that project characteristics such as risk, ambiguity and non-routineness determine to a large extent how the projects could be managed (Keller, 1994; Ettlie et al., 1984; Katz & Tushman, 1979). Accordingly, high and low structured software development projects should be managed differently.

We examine in this research the use of different approaches in the local, global and shared domains in high and low structured projects.

METHODOLOGY AND RESEARCH SETTING

A grounded research study uses a systematic set of procedures to develop an inductively derived theory about a phenomenon. In these studies, the concepts and relationships among them are not only generated but also provisionally tested. In these studies data is collected on the basis of theoretical sampling; it begins with studying some homogenous sample and then after developing a theory undertaking studies of heterogeneous samples. The rationale for studying a heterogeneous sample is to confirm or disconfirm the conditions under which the model holds (Creswell, 1998).

For conducting our study we have selected a set of organizations where we could observe both high and low structured geographically dispersed software development projects. High-structured projects form one homogenous group and low-structured projects form another homogenous group. The data collected from these two groups will be compared and contrasted to provisionally test the model.

Data has been collected in the forms of interviews, visits to the workstations and electronic documents, etc. For the purpose of collecting data, we interviewed the top management, project managers, and team members. For conducting the interviews, a brief interview guide was prepared so as to facilitate the interviewing process as well as ease the comparison of the data collected from different sources. A total of fourteen interviews have been held so far in few development centers located in India. This data collected from different sources is analyzed according to the processes described by Corbin and Strauss (1990) in their book on grounded theory procedures and techniques.

The data was collected from a company referred to as Orion in this paper, a pseudonym for a U.S. based global company that has a center in Bangalore, India for more than two years as on date. Its engineering center is not only involved in maintaining and servicing their proprietary software but also in developing some of the software products. The sustenance activities are being carried out from different geographical locations to provide year round 24-hour support. At the same time, software development activities are being carried out from different locations to take advantage of the local competencies and new business opportunities.

In the present context, sustenance activities are considered as high-structured activities and development activities as low-structured activities. Therefore to flesh out these differences, we decided to study one team working on sustenance activities and another team working on development activities. In the next few paragraphs we will present the findings of our study.

RESULTS

From the analysis of the data obtained so far, we find both formal and informal approaches being used in both sustenance and development projects. Formal control approaches like output control (project health meter, scope tracking, effort tracking, review status, etc.) and behavior control (in-house method for software development) are used. At the same time informal control approaches like peer-to-peer control and self-control also play an important role in software development. Similarly, organizations constitute committees (coordination-teams, product teams, implementation teams etc.) for formally coordinating the different activities while at the same time informal coordination gets facilitated through emails and teleconferencing.

Organizations have implemented certain new processes and tools that were not there at the beginning of the geographically dispersed work arrangements to facilitate better control and coordination of efforts. Some of these processes have been put in place formally whereas others have evolved informally over a period of time.

Most of the managers interviewed informed us that when they started working on the projects they had to put in more processes and rules, for example, definition of exit-entry criteria for moving from one phase to another or for changing the source code, etc. Some of these managers said that initially their counterpart in U.S. resisted imposition of these rules, as they also had to follow them but after using it for some time they realized that these rules lead to improvement in quality and productivity of the Indian team. Therefore the following proposition may be stated:

Proposition 1a: Geographically dispersed projects are structured to a greater degree than collocated projects.

As principles of software engineering relate quality to a higher degree of structure,

Proposition 1b: Increase in structures leads to improvement in quality and productivity of the geographically dispersed teams.

Geographically dispersed software maintenance and service activities require intense coordination on a day-to-day basis whereas software development activities need coordination only during some of the phases of a project. Cost of coordinating different activities includes real cost in terms of man-hours and telecommunication costs, and nominal costs of delay in providing a service or developing a product. Therefore to reduce the cost of coordinating different activities organizations use well-defined processes.

Proposition 2: Use of well-defined processes reduces the cost of coordinating geographically dispersed activities.

Software development activities were initially concentrated mainly in US and Europe as these places offer ample opportunity for interacting with the end customers. Over the last few years, some organizations have made an attempt to develop software from geographically dispersed locations. To a certain extent success of these ventures depends on the success of processes put in place for coordinating project activities. Organizations that have been successful in carrying out geographically dispersed sustenance activities are in a better position to ramp up software development activities. As the advantages of operating in India are primarily availability of a large number of skilled software developers, organizations that established their base are subsequently able to utilize this resource to quickly ramp up large projects.

Proposition 3: Organization that have well defined processes in place for coordinating the sustenance activities have shorter development times than organizations that do not have such processes in place.

Our initial results therefore point to the fact the global software development when implemented in the right manner lead to better quality and shorter development time.

We are continuing our studies with further interviews, data collection and analysis. Some more results of this research will be reported at the time of IRMA 2003 conference.

ENDNOTES

[1] Place refers to the experience of being in a bounded locality with unique qualities in which traditions are important determinants of behavior. In time-space configuration of place, there is a sense of being in place and of comfort in the familiar. Space, in contrast, refers to a time-space configuration experienced as being boundless, universal and infinite. There is a sense of freedom in a limitless expanse in which movement and change are welcome and possibilities are endless (Schultze & Boland, 2000).

REFERENCES

1. Corbin, J., and Strauss, A., Basics of Qualitative Research – Grounded Theory Procedures and Techniques, Sage Publications, London, 1990.
2. Creswell, J.W., Qualitative Inquiry and Research Design, Sage Publications, California, 1998
3. Ettlie, J.E., Bridges, W.P., and O'Keefe, R.D., 'Organization Strategy and Structural Differences for Radical versus Incremental Innovation', Management Science, Vol. 30, No. 6, 1984.
4. Giddens, A., The Constitution of Society: Outline of the theory of Structure, University of California Press, Berkeley, 1984.
5. Giddens, A., Modernity and Self- Identity: Self and Society in the Late Modern Age, Stanford University Press, Stanford, 1991.
6. Jermier, J.M., 'Introduction: Critical Perspectives on Organizational Control', Administrative Science Quarterly, Vol. 43, No. 2, 1998.
7. Katz, R., and Tushman, M., 'Communication Patterns, Project Performance, and Task Characteristics: An Empirical Evaluation and Integration in an R&D Setting', Organizational Behavior and Human Performance, Vol. 23, pp. 139-162, 1979.
8. Keller, R.T., 'Technology-Information Processing Fit and the Performance of R&D Project Groups: A test of Contingency Theory', Academy of Management Journal, Vol. 37, No. 1, 1994.
9. Krishna, S., & Sahay, S., 'An Empirical Investigation and Dialectical Analysis of a Global Software Alliance', Tech Report No. 1/2000, Center for Software Management, Indian Institute of Management Bangalore, 2000.
10. McFarlan, F.W., and Nolan, R.L., 'How to Manage and IT Outsourcing Alliance', Sloan Management Review, Winter 1995.
11. Ouchi, W.G., 'A Conceptual Framework For the Design of Organizational Control Mechanisms', Management Science, Vol. 25, No. 9, 1979.
12. Piccoli, G., Powell, A. L., and Ives, B., 'Virtual Teams: A Review of the Co-located Team Literature and Extensions to the Virtual Environment,' Working Paper, Cornell University, 2001.
13. Schultze, U., and Boland, R.J., 'Place, space and knowledge work: a study of outsourced computer systems administrators', Accounting, Management & Information Technology, Vol. 10, pp 187-219, 2000.

Discovering Valuable Patterns through InternetWeb-Log Access Analysis

Navin Kumar
Ph: (410) 455-8673

Aryya Gangopadhyay
(410) 455-2620

Department of Information SystemsUniversity of Maryland Baltimore County1000 Hilltop Circle, Baltimore, MD 21250{navin1,gangopad}@umbc.edu

ABSTRACT

This study outlines the usage of data mining techniques to analyze web log files. It shows the direction in which web mining can be performed to unearth concealed information in huge access log data. An attempt has been made to give an overview on how to derive association rules from web server data mining. Paper also discusses implementation of OLAP technology to perform web usage analysis.

Keywords. Web mining, web log analysis, usage analysis, association rules, OLAP cubes

1.0 INTRODUCTION

It is difficult to visualize the present market situation without taking World Wide Web (WWW) into consideration. Everyday new complexities are being faced in web site designing and site navigations. When the market is moving into internet, it is also a major concern for business industries to observe customer's interests. All these problems together seek for a rich-content and easily accessible site. To provide a better web designing, navigation through the web pages becomes an important input for analytical purposes. Here, Web mining refers to discovery and analysis of useful information from the World Wide Web. It also focuses its attention on user accesses data. Once the interesting patterns are recognized from web access log data, it will help the company in restructuring and better management of the web site, giving more effectiveness to it. Important point is that the web servers register a web log entry for every single access they get in which they save the URL requested, the IP address from which the request originated, and a timestamp, and with the rapid progress of WWW technology, and the ever growing popularity of the WWW, a huge number of Web access log records are being collected [3]. Frequently visited sites would easily end up with repository of hundreds of megabytes of log data. Here comes the issue of data mining considering colossal files of raw web log data where retrieving significant and useful information is a nontrivial task [3].

This study is an attempt to analyze web logs to dig information about session identification, user navigations, web usage analysis, and association rules between various pages. In order to show data mining techniques with examples, *a hypothetical company* (www.OnlineBookStore.com) is considered in this paper. The behavior of the web page readers is imprinted in the web server log files. Analyzing and exploring regularities in this behavior will significantly improve system performance, enhance the quality and delivery of Internet information services to the end user, and identify population of potential customers for electronic commerce. Thus, by observing people using collections of data, data mining will bring considerable contribution to company's web site designers.

2.0 ABOUT THE COMPANY

This hypothetical company hosts a website for online book shopping (*Site map is shown in appendix*) There are some web pages to provide the information about the company itself. Different categories of books include computers, children, sports, and fictions. A site navigation tree is presented below. Different categories of books are managed in their respective

directories e.g. computer books are kept in /Computer directory. /Home.html is the root file and all other files can be reached from this root node. Category files e.g. Sports.asp is accessible from SpecialOffer.asp. Moreover, users cannot directly access two files e.g. to reach Java2.asp from Java1.asp, user will navigate through /Computer/Computer.asp.

> *Note:*
> 1.*Every web page name is followed by a letter (A,B,C,...) in the site map. These letters have been used for derivation of association rules.*
> 2.*Access log data are randomly generated for analytical purposes, and so are **not** the actual data.*

3.0 STEPS FOLLOWED IN WEB MIINING

- Convert server log files into relational table format
- Data Preprocessing and Cleaning
- Session Identification
- Path Completion Analysis
- Transaction Identification
- Discovery of Association Rules
- OLAP Technology Implementation
- Characterization and Comparison (Web usage analysis)

ACCESS LOG FILE in text format:

130.85.253.114 — [05/Apr/2002:11:34:55 +0100] "GET /Home.html HTTP/1.0" 200 2048
130.85.253.114 — [05/Apr/2002:11:35:37 +0100] "GET /Category.html HTTP/1.0" 200 1536
130.85.253.114 — [05/Apr/2002:11:36:25 +0100] "GET /Computer/Computer.asp HTTP/1.0" 200 2048
....
....

The access log file is stored on server in ASCII format.
Log file contains following information about each navigation:
- *IP Address* of the computer the request is coming from
- *User ID* of the user who generated the request (if assigned any)
- *Date and time* of the request
- *user action* (GET or POST)
- *URL* of requested page
- *Name and version of the protocol*
- *Status code* (or error code) of the request e.g.
  - 200: successfully received
  - 400: bad request
  - 505: HTTP version not supported
- *Size of the page* in bytes

Table2: Identification of session from log files

Session Number	Session IP Address	Start Row number	End Row Number	Access Path
1	130.85.253.114	1	5	A-D-F-M-N
2	130.85.253.114	6	10	A-L-B-H-A3
3	207.46.230.220	11	13	B-H-A4
4	207.70.7.168	14	20	A-D-G-Q-T-R-W
5	209.96.148.192	21	22	C-E
6	144.92.104.37	23	33	A-E-L-F-O-P-I-A6-H-H-A2
7	170.248.128.30	34	37	D-I-A5-A7
8	199.171.55.3	38	40	E-J-K
9	198.82.162.11	41	45	A-D-I-A7-F

3.1 Step 1 - Convert The Raw Data From Access Log Files Into Relational Data Format.

A script is run to extract and put ASCII data into respective columns in a table. Table 1 (appendix) presents web usage data restructured in relational format. *(IE denotes Internet Explorer)*

3.2 Step 2 - Data Preprocessing and Cleaning

Data preprocessing is performed on relational data. At this stage, preprocessing and cleaning processes have been discussed taking discovery of association rules into consideration. Step 8 continues further with discussion on data preprocessing for OLAP implementation.

a) Data reduction: Remove undesired fields

Data set is reduced by avoiding some attributes which do not directly influence the web mining results. Hence, from current log data, *attributes User ID, User Action, and File Size are omitted.*

b) Data cleaning:

(i) HTTP protocol requires individual connection for every file. Hence even request for an ASP page may lead to several log entries on graphics/scripts written in log file. Concentrating on html/asp pages, records having file path ending with gif, jpeg, jpg, bmp are omitted. Here *row number 5,20,22,24,33,43,45, 46 and 54 are removed.*

(ii) Only successful requests are filtered.

If status code=200 ➔ request successful; record is retained.

If status code!=200 ➔ request unsuccessful; record is removed.

Here *row number 24, 37, and 56 are removed from the log data table.* These records are stored in "**error_info**" table to keep track of various errors occurring in web pages.

(iii) After removing error records, *status code and HTTP protocol fields are discarded requiring no attention for association rules derivation.* Table 2 (appendix) represents data after cleaning and preprocessing.

3.3 Step 3 - Session Identification

Discovery of association analysis from web log data starts with *transaction identification.*

Transaction can be identified by "a collection of user clicks to a single Web server during a user session". A criterion for identifying server session is implemented by examining if client has not surfed through the site for a reasonable long time.

Method used to identify unique user sessions If the time between page requests exceeds a certain limit, it is assumed that the user is starting a new session.

Let's assume that the **Timeout** (the session becomes inactive if not used for this specific time) is *30 minutes.*

Each log record *l* will contain this information:

l.ip: client IP address
l.uid: user id of the client
l.url: URL accessed
l.time: access time

Session can be identified by comparing all the tuples as described :

$$S = <ip_t, uid_t, \{(l_1^t.url, l_1^t.time),...,(l_m^t.url, l_m^t.time)\}>$$

$$where, for.1 \le k \le (m-1), l_k^t \in L, l_k^t.ip = ip_t, l_k^t.uid = uid_t, l_{k+1}^t.ip = ip_t, l_{k+1}^t.uid = uid_t$$

$$and, (l_k^t.time - l_{k+1}^t.time) \le W (= 30 Minutes)$$

By looking at table 2, we find that all IP addresses except 130.85.253.114 have unique user sessions. IP address 130.85.252.114 has two user sessions because time difference between row number five and six is (05/Apr/2002:13:14:37-05/Apr/2002:11:42:23) greater than 30 minutes. Hence 130.85.253.114 has two user sessions, one from row number 1 to 5, and another from row number 6 to 10. A summary **user session table** is shown below:

3.4 Step 4 - Path Completion Analysis

Even after unique user sessions are successfully identified, another problem remains if there are important accesses that are not recorded in the access log. We refer this problem as *path completion.* An approach is used here to identify missing web pages from the log file. ***This approach is explained as follows:***

If a page request is not directly linked to the last requested page, it is assumed that the page is already in user's recent request history, and so user backtracked with the "back" button available on browser. This in effect calls cached version of the pages until a new page was requested. Site map can be used here to identify the missing pages. If more than one page in the user's history contains a link to the requested page, assumption follows that the page closest to the previously requested page is the source of the new request. Missing page references inferred through this approach are added to the user session file.

Session number 1: Access path is A-D-F-M-N. There is no direct path from M to N. Hence, the user must have backtracked to reach N i.e. user would have used page F to reach page N. hence complete path would be A-D-F-M-F-N.

Session number 2: Access path is A-L-B-H-A3. Again there is no direct path to reach B from L That means user has once backtracked to reach B from L via A. Hence complete path would be A-L-A-B-H-A3.

Session number 3: Access path is B-H-A4. It does not require any further modification in the access path.

Session number 4: Access path is A-D-G-Q-T-R-W. There is no direct path from R to W, so user must have backtracked to G first and then has navigated to W. hence complete access path is A-D-G-Q-T-Q-G-R-V.

Session number 5: Access path is C-E. This is a complete path considering the fact that the site has common header with links to all first level pages.

Session number 6: Access path is A-E-L-F-O-P-I-A6-H-H-A2. There is no direct path from L to F suggesting backtracking. Navigation from A6 to H suggests I as the middle page. Page H appears twice indicating removal of one page reference from access path. Hence final access path would be A-E-L-E-A-F-O-F-P-F-A-I-A6-I-A-H-A2.

Session number 7: Access path is D-I-A5-A7. Final path is D-I-A5-I-A7.

Session number 8: Access path is E-J-K. Final path is E-J-E-K.

Session number 9: Access path is A-D-I-A7-F. To navigation from A7

Table 3: Identification of access path (path completion) from session file

Session Number	Session IP Address		Start Row number	
End Row Number				**Access Path**
1	130.85.253.114	1	5	A-D-F-M-F-N
2	130.85.253.114	6	10	A-L-A-B-H-A3
3	207.46.230.220	11	13	B-H-A4
4	207.70.7.168	14	20	A-D-G-Q-T-Q-G-R-W
5	209.96.148.192	21	22	C-E
6	144.92.104.37	23	33	A-E-L-E-A-F-O-F-P-F-A-I-A6-I-A-H-A2
7	170.248.128.30	34	37	D-I-A5-I-A7
8	199.171.55.3	38	40	E-J-E-K
9	198.82.162.11	41	45	A-D-I-A7-I-D-F

Table 4: Transaction table from session table (using Maximal Forward reference)

Session Number	Access Path	Transaction
1	A-D-F-M-F-N	A-D-F-M, A-D-F-N
2	A-L-A-B-H-A3	A-L, A-B-H-A3
3	B-H-A4	B-H-A4
4	A-D-G-Q-T-Q-G-R-W	A-D-G-Q-T, A-D-G-R-W
5	C-E	C-E
6	A-E-L-E-A-F-O-F-P-F-A-I-A6-I-A-H-A2	A-E-L, A-F-O, A-F-P, A-I-A6, A-H-A2
7	D-I-A5-I-A7	D-I-A5, D-I-A7
8	E-J-E-K	E-J, E-K
9	A-D-I-A7-I-D-F	A-D-I-A7, A-D-F

to F, there are two possibilities, reaching either from page A or page D. Because page D is the closest to the requested page, the final path would be A-D-I-A7-I-D-F.

3.5 Step 5 - Transaction Identification by Maximal Forward Reference

This approach divides large access paths into smaller ones to identify smaller transactions. *This technique works as follows:*

Users are apt to travel objects back and forth in accordance with the links and icons provided. This senses possibility of two types of references: backward and forward references. A *backward* reference is the revisit of previously visited resource; on the other end, a *forward* reference is the visit

of a new resource in user session path. Transaction is defined as the set of pages in the path from the first page in a user session up to the page before a backward reference is made. When backward references occur, a forward reference path terminates. New transaction starts with next forward reference. This resulting forward reference path is termed as a *maximal forward reference*.

Considering session data from table 4, for session number 1, access path is A-B-F-M-F-N. According to the rule, first transaction will end at A-B-F-M, and so another transaction will be A-B-F-N. *Table 5 presents all transactions.*

Each of the transactions represents a basket and each resource an item. ***Apriori algorithm*** is now applied to derive association rules.

Table 5

Transaction ID	Items	Transaction ID	Items	Transaction ID	Items
100	A-D-F-M	106	A-D-G-R-W	112	A-H-A2
101	A-D-F-N	107	C-E	113	D-I-A5
102	A-L	108	A-E-L	114	D-I-A7
103	A-B-H-A3	109	A-F-O	115	E-J
104	B-H-A4	110	A-F-P	116	E-K
105	A-D-G-Q-T	111	A-I-A6	117	A-D-I-A7
				118	A-D-F

Total number of transactions, N = 19
Let's assume that *minimum support level* = 15% = 2.85 ~ 3
   minimum confidence level = 50%

Itemset	Support count	Itemset	Support count	Itemset	Support count	Itemset	Support count
A	13	J	1	S	0	A2	1
B	1	K	1	T	1	A3	1
C	1	L	2	U	0	A4	1
D	8	M	1	V	0	A5	1
E	4	N	1	W	1	A6	1
F	5	O	1	X	0	A7	2
G	2	P	1	Y	0		
H	3	Q	1	Z	0		
I	4	R	1	A1	0		

3.6 Step 6 - Discovery Of Association Rules From Transaction Data

Because the **minimum support is 3**, the next picture shows frequent 1-itemset **L1** and subsequent analysis.

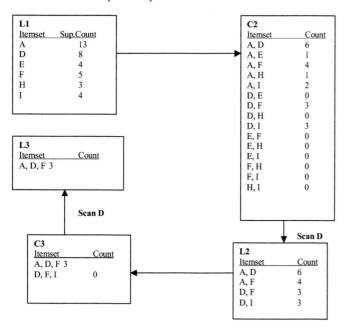

L1

Itemset	Sup.Count
A	13
D	8
E	4
F	5
H	3
I	4

C2

Itemset	Count
A, D	6
A, E	1
A, F	4
A, H	1
A, I	2
D, E	0
D, F	3
D, H	0
D, I	3
E, F	0
E, H	0
E, I	0
F, H	0
F, I	0
H, I	0

L3

Itemset	Count
A, D, F	3

Scan D

C3

Itemset	Count
A, D, F	3
D, F, I	0

Scan D

L2

Itemset	Count
A, D	6
A, F	4
D, F	3
D, I	3

Hence, Apriori algorithm provides these frequent item sets (resource sets) for the transaction data: {A}, {D}, {E}, {F}, {H}, {I}, {A, D}, {A, F}, {D, F}, {D, I}, {A, D, F}

Strong association rules for 2-itemsets:
Minimum confidence = 50%

Rule 1: $\forall x \in transaction, contains(X, A) \Rightarrow contains(X, D)$

$$Confidence = \frac{Support\,(A, D)}{Support\,(A)} = \frac{6}{13} = 46.15\%$$

Rule **cannot** be established.

Rule   2:

$\forall x \in transaction, contains(X, D) \Rightarrow contains(X, A)$

Confidence=75% i.e. *this rule is a **strong** rule. It implies that 75% of the users navigating page D (/Category.html) also are visiting page A (/Home.html).*

Rule   3:

$\forall x \in transaction, contains(X, A) \Rightarrow contains(X, F)$

Confidence=30.76%, rule **cannot** be established.

Rule 4: $\forall x \in transaction, contains(X, F) \Rightarrow contains(X, A)$
Confidence=80% i.e. *this rule is a **strong** rule.*

Rule   5:

$\forall x \in transaction, contains(X, D) \Rightarrow contains(X, F)$

Confidence=37.5%, rule **cannot** be established.

Rule   6:

$\forall x \in transaction, contains(X, F) \Rightarrow contains(X, D)$

Confidence=60%, *rule is established as **strong** rule.*

Rule   7:

$\forall x \in transaction, contains(X, D) \Rightarrow contains(X, I)$

Confidence=37.5%, this rule **cannot** be established

Rule   8:

$\forall x \in transaction, contains(X, I) \Rightarrow contains(X, D)$

Confidence=75%, *association rule is **strong**.*

Strong association rules for 3-itemsets:

Rule   1:

$\forall x \in transaction, contains(X, A)^\wedge contains(X, D) \Rightarrow contains(X, F)$

$$Confidence = \frac{Support\,(A, D, F)}{Support\,(A, D)} = \frac{3}{6} = 50\%$$

Strong *association rule is established. It infers that 50% of the time, if the client visits both /Home.html and /Category.html, he/she will also visit /Computer/Computer.asp.*

Rule   2:

$\forall x \in transaction, contains(X, A)^\wedge contains(X, F) \Rightarrow contains(X, D)$

Confidence=75%, so *this is a **strong** association rule.*

Rule   3:

$\forall x \in transaction, contains(X, D)^\wedge contains(X, F) \Rightarrow contains(X, A)$

Confidence=100%, so %, *it qualifies as **strong** association rule.*

3.7 Step 7 - OLAP Technology Implementation

Data Preprocessing:
To construct multidimensional cube technology, we first need to convert raw data into various dimensions with some defined to facilitate generalization and specialization.
* Access time is represented by **TIME** dimension with *schema hierarchy*.
    second<minute<hour<day<month<year<All
* **URL** stores file structure by server domain (if multiple servers running simultaneously), directory (where the file resides), file name, extension (.asp, .html, .cgi etc.). **Schema hierarchy**:
    file extension<file<directory<server domain<All
* **Client IP Address** defines organization name and domain with o*peration-derived hierarchy*.
    Organization name<domain name<All
* **Time Spent is** difference in access time for the current page and the next page. A *set-grouping hierarchy* would then be:
    If t = time spent (in seconds),
    *{very_short_stay,   short_stay,   moderate_stay, long_stay} ⊂ **all** (Time Spent)*
    {0<t<30} ⊂ very_short_stay
    {60<t<60} ⊂ short_stay
    {60<t<180} ⊂ moderate_stay
    {t>180} ⊂ long_stay
* **Range hierarchy** on **File_Size** (in bytes):
    *{tiny, small, medium, large, huge} ⊂ **all** (File Size}*
    {0<File_size<1000} ⊂ tiny
    {1000<File_size<2000} ⊂ small

$\{2000 < File\_size < 4000\} \subset$ medium

$\{4000 < File\_size < 5000\} \subset$ large

$\{File\_size > 5000\} \subset$ huge

- **Set-grouping hierarchy** for **Type_of_Resource**:

  {script, images} $\subset$ ***all** (Type_Of_Resource}*

  {asp, html} $\subset$ script

  {jpg, jpeg, gif, bmp} $\subset$ images

- **Browser type**

  Browser version < Type_of_browser < all.

We can construct OLAP cubes with abovementioned dimensions. OLAP operations drill-down, roll-up, slice and dice, can be performed to view and analyze web log data from different angles. One such *measure* is **"number of hits"** at a particular level of granularity. Step 8 explains more on OLAP operations.

3.8 Step 8 - Characterization and Comparison

a) Finding "TOP N" requested URLs

Selecting top N pages is achieved by performing drill-down on URL dimension to file, and **all** to other dimensions. For this sample data, top 6 pages in decreasing order of count would be

1) /Home.html, **2)** /Category.html, **3)** /Sports/Sports.asp, **4)** /CompanyInfo.html, and **5)** /Computer/Computer.asp, and **6)** /Fiction/Fiction.asp

b) Comparison of browser types for web site access

Web mining can be performed on the browser type to find out commonly used browsers, and more information on their compatibility for the web site can be further studied. Pie chart below presents web site usage by browser type obtained by drilling to browser dimension, and **"all"** for other dimensions.

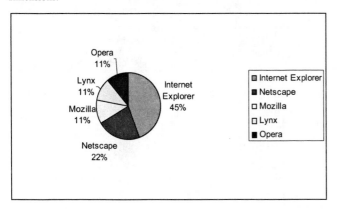

It explains that *Internet Explorer is the most frequently used browser.* Web site can be redesigned to provide maximum support for Internet Explorer and Netscape.

c) Comparison of various domains on web site access

The access log file is processed to convert the IP addresses into host names. E.g. www.umbc.edu has education domain.

It is easy to mine which kind of domains the web site is receiving the requests from. Pie chart explains that web site is mostly used by commercial sites (**37%**) and educational institutions (**37%**). It is obtained by drilling on IP address to 'domain name', and **"all"** along other dimensions.

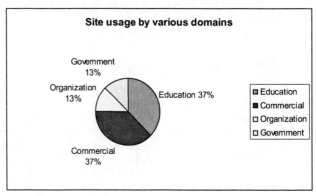

4.0 CONCLUSION

As web is a one of the biggest repositories ever built, analyzing web access logs can help us understand the user behavior and would lead to better web site management by making use of Web Usage Mining. Furthermore, more information about user agents and referring resources can be collected to reveal better information. Several tools like NetTracker, SAS Webhound, Analog, and WebTrends Log Analyzer can be used to explore web log data in efficient way.

REFERENCES

1.Cooley R., Mobasher B., and Srivastava J., Data preparation for mining World Wide Web browsing patterns , Knowledge and Information Systems, V1(1), 1999

2.Bartoloni G., Web usage mining and discovery of association rules from HTTP server logs, 2001 (http://www.prato.linux.it/~gbartolini/html/wum.html)

3.Jiawei Han, Man Xin, Osmar Zaiane, Discovering web access patterns and trends by applying OLAP and data mining technology on web logs, In Proceedings of the Fifth IEEE Forum on Research and Technology Advances in Digital Libraries, 1998.

4.White paper on Speed Tracer: A Web usage mining tool (http://www.research.ibm.com/journal/sj/371/wu.html)

5.Log File Basics (http://slis-two.lis.fsu.edu/~log/basics~1.htm)

6.WWW access statistics for the last 12 months (http://www.netstore.de/stats/www2002/frames.html)

7.Hits summary detail (http://www.ideva.com/reports/ideva/idevahitsummary.htm)

8.Request detail report (http://www.ideva.com/reports/ideva/idevarequests.htm)

IP Address	Host Name	Domain Type	IP Address	Host Name	Domain Type
130.85.253.114	www.umbc.edu	Education	144.92.104.37	www.wisc.edu	Education
207.46.230.220	www.microsoft.com	Commercial	170.248.128.30	www.accenture.com	Commercial
207.70.7.168	www.infotech.com	Commercial	199.171.55.3	www.sba.gov	Government
209.96.148.192	www.myvirginia.org	Organization	198.82.162.11	www.vt.edu	Education

872 Information Technology and Organizations

APPENDIX
Site map

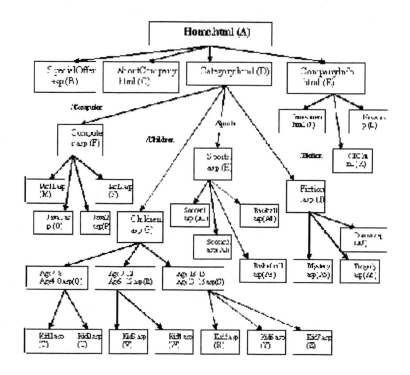

Table 1: Access log file in tabular format

Table 2: Web log data after preprocessing and cleaning

Row No.	Client IP Address	Access Time	File Path	Browser Type
1	130.85.253.114	05/Apr/2002:11:34:55	/Home.html	IE
2	130.85.253.114	05/Apr/2002:11:35:37	/Category.html	IE
3	130.85.253.114	05/Apr/2002:11:36:25	/Computer/Computer.asp	IE
4	130.85.253.114	05/Apr/2002:11:39:12	/Computer/Perl1.asp	IE
5	130.85.253.114	05/Apr/2002:11:42:23	/Computer/Per2.asp	IE
6	130.85.253.114	05/Apr/2002:13:14:37	/Home.html	Netscape 6.2
7	130.85.253.114	05/Apr/2002:13:15:55	/News.asp	Netscape 6.2
8	130.85.253.114	05/Apr/2002:13:17:13	/SpecialOffer.asp	Netscape 6.2
9	130.85.253.114	06/Apr/2002:13:18:21	/Sports/Sports.asp	Netscape 6.2
10	130.85.253.114	06/Apr/2002:13:20:51	/Sports/Basketball.asp	Netscape 6.2
11	207.46.230.220	06/Apr/2002:05:41:23	/SpecialOffer.asp	Opera 6.01
12	207.46.230.220	06/Apr/2002:05:43:45	/Sports/Sports.asp	Opera 6.01
13	207.46.230.220	06/Apr/2002:05:44:11	/Sports/Baseball.asp	Opera 6.01
14	207.70.7.168	07/Apr/2002:04:11:19	/Home.html	IE
15	207.70.7.168	07/Apr/2002:04:13:23	/Category.html	IE
16	207.70.7.168	07/Apr/2002:04:14:43	/Children.asp	IE
17	207.70.7.168	07/Apr/2002:04:17:17	/Children/Age4_8.asp	IE
18	207.70.7.168	07/Apr/2002:04:19:43	/Children/Kid1.asp	IE
19	207.70.7.168	07/Apr/2002:04:24:51	/Children/Age9_12.asp	IE
20	207.70.7.168	07/Apr/2002:04:27:55	/Children/Kid4.asp	IE
21	209.96.148.192	08/Apr/2002:19:23:49	/AboutCompany.html	Mozilla 4.0
22	209.96.148.192	08/Apr/2002:19:25:41	/CompanyInfo.html	Mozilla 4.0
23	144.92.104.37	09/Apr/2002:14:23:02	/Home.html	IE
24	144.92.104.37	09/Apr/2002:14:24:20	/CompanyInfo.html	IE
25	144.92.104.37	09/Apr/2002:14:27:53	/News.asp	IE
26	144.92.104.37	09/Apr/2002:14:28:52	/Computer/Computer.asp	IE
27	144.92.104.37	09/Apr/2002:14:29:09	/Computer/Java1.asp	IE
28	144.92.104.37	09/Apr/2002:14:32:53	/Computer/Java2.asp	IE
29	144.92.104.37	09/Apr/2002:14:35:39	/Fiction/Fiction.asp	IE
30	144.92.104.37	09/Apr/2002:14:37:50	/Fiction/Tragedy.asp	IE
31	144.92.104.37	09/Apr/2002:14:38:10	/Sports/Sports.asp	IE
32	144.92.104.37	09/Apr/2002:14:40:37	/Sports/Sports.asp	IE
33	144.92.104.37	09/Apr/2002:14:45:41	/Sports/Soccer2.asp	IE
34	170.248.123.30	11/Apr/2002:07:03:34	/Category.html	Netscape 6.2
35	170.248.123.30	11/Apr/2002:07:05:11	/Fiction/Fiction.asp	Netscape 6.2
36	170.248.123.30	11/Apr/2002:07:08:19	/Fiction/Mystery.asp	Netscape 6.2
37	170.248.123.30	11/Apr/2002:07:12:11	/Fiction/Drama.asp	Netscape 6.2
38	199.171.55.3	11/Apr/2002:20:33:10	/CompanyInfo.html	Lynx 3.83
39	199.171.55.3	11/Apr/2002:20:36:05	/Investment.html	Lynx 3.83
40	199.171.55.3	11/Apr/2002:20:39:55	/CD.html	Lynx 3.83
41	198.85.132.11	11/Apr/2002:08:49:11	/Home.html	IE
42	198.85.132.11	11/Apr/2002:08:51:06	/Category.html	IE
43	198.85.132.11	11/Apr/2002:08:52:27	/Fiction/Fiction.asp	IE
44	198.85.132.11	11/Apr/2002:08:54:33	/Fiction/Drama.asp	IE
45	198.85.132.11	11/Apr/2002:08:59:46	/Computer/Computer.asp	IE

Video Streaming Solutions for Web-Based E-Learning Courses

Karl Kurbel

European University Viadrina Frankfurt (Oder), Business Informatics
POB 17 86, 15207 Frankfurt (Oder), Germany
Telephone: +49-335-5534-2320, Fax: +49-335-5534-2321
E-Mail: kurbel@euv-frankfurt-o.de

ABSTRACT

The background of this work is the development of multimedia courses for an Internet-based master program in Business Informatics. This program is provided by a virtual organization. Delivering multimedia-based courses over the Internet is a challenging task. Low-cost multimedia technologies, in particular technologies for video production and delivery over the Internet, have just become available. Established rules and recommendations how to use those technologies effectively are still missing. In this paper an approach is discussed in which course material is divided into separate parts - one silent video file containing visual demonstrations, and another video with sound, with the instructor's explanations. We discuss approaches to achieve synchronization among two separate videos streams. Based on Microsoft Windows Media technology this problem can be solved but the solution is not straightforward. Problems encountered and the final solution to those problems are outlined.

Keywords: Streaming video, video-based e-learning courses, Windows Media technology, synchronizing playback, Virtual Global University

1 BACKGROUND OF THE WORK

The work reported in this paper is based on experiences from planning and operating a virtual master program in Business Informatics. This program was developed by the Virtual Global University (VGU), an organization founded by 17 professors of Business Informatics from Germany, Austria and Switzerland [1]. It is offered worldwide, leading to the degree of an "International Master of Business Informatics" (MBI). VGU as a private virtual organization has a cooperation agreement with a "real" state university - the European University Viadrina (EUV) in Frankfurt (Oder), Germany. While VGU provides expertise and teaching for the program, EUV is responsible for ensuring that the academic and educational standards of the program are maintained at an appropriate level.

Many courses and programs in today's virtual eduation are still text and paper based. We will refer to those as "traditional" virtual courses and programs. In Europe, rather advanced multimedia technologies for higher education have been investigated in research projects and prototypical courses over the past 10 years (e.g. [2]). Advanced tools for cooperative work are also being tried [3].

For the master program underlying this paper, multimedia technologies above the text-based level were intended to play a major role in the instructional design. The technologies for the MBI courses were chosen depending on the type and on the content of a course. A mix of technologies is actually used, while video and audio-based courses are the most important ones.

Section 2 outlines the use of video technology for e-learning. Subsequently, the front-end of a video-based e-learning course as it appeares to the user is discussed. Section 4 addresses the problems that have to be attacked to produce and deliver such a course over the Internet. In section 5, features and shortcomings of the Windows Media Player as observed in our work are described and the solution to the problems encountered is presented. Some conclusions from our experience with video-based courses are drawn in section 6.

2 VIDEO AS A BASIS FOR E-LEARNING

Web-based teaching and learning are becoming more and more popular as the numbers of virtual courses and virtual universities (like JIU [4], VGU [5], and VIROR [6]) are growing. While in the beginning static HTML pages, text, and graphics files were mainly used, animated and multimedia contents have significantly enhanced e-learning since then. Video clips are also found in web-based courses, but videos as the primary instructional medium are not very common yet. One reason for that is certainly that production and delivery of video-based courses are rather time consuming, requiring profound know-how about the technology.

On the other hand, video-based courses have one significant advantage. Many lecturers have years of experience giving "lectures", that is standing in a lecture hall or a classroom and explaining complicated matters to students, possibly using visual aids like overhead transparencies or Powerpoint slides. In computer-oriented subjects, online presentations on a video beamer may be another form of visualization. Using videos as the main instructional medium makes it possible to transfer this well-tried, though traditional method of teaching to the web age.

Common platforms to provide and distribute streaming video content over the Internet are Microsoft Windows Media [7], Real Media [8], and Apple QuickTime [9]. Windows Media technology was chosen for several reasons. First, the Windows Media Video V7 Screen codec (codec = coder/decoder for video and audio data) proved to be very good for online recordings from a computer screen. In our courses we need this feature because often things are explained by the lecturer online and real-time. Second, the Microsoft Media Server is included in the licence for Microsoft Internet Information Server (IIS) and that licence does not limit the number of client connections. The Real Media Server, for example, is free but only for 25 client connections at a time.

3 E-LEARNING USER INTERFACE WITH TWO VIDEO STREAMS

Following the paradigm of lecturing and visualizing, the user interface of VGU's video-based courses as it is presented to the student is outlined in figure 1. The crucial part of the web page is the Media Player in the upper right corner. In this corner a video of the lecture is running in a streaming compatible format.

The area left of the player is used to show visual materials accompanying the lecturer's explanations. In the simplest case these are text slides, tables, diagrams, charts, etc., similar to information that would be written on a blackboard or an overhead projector in a conventional lecture. In addition there are controls for user interaction with the course page, for example starting the lecture, advancing or going back to a certain topic, etc.

Basically there are two approaches to provide visual material plus video lecturing for such a course. The first one is fairly easy to achieve: Split up the lecture in separate topics and store the respective video clips in separate files. If the topics are associated with slides, then each topic, including the video clip, will be started separately.

Fig. 1: Functional diagram of a course page

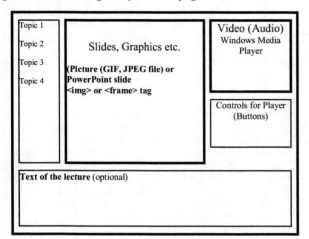

Fig. 2: Synchronization algorithm

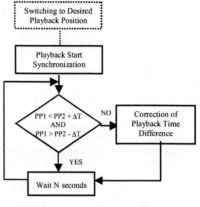

*PP = Playback Position

This solution is easy from a technical point of view, but it is not always feasible to split up a lecture in such a way. Moreover, only static images can be used as accompanying visual information. Displaying online recordings of program runs, for example, or videos shown by the lecturer is not posssible in this way; nor can recordings from two or more video sources be displayed at the same time. For example, it is not possible to do screen capturing on two ore more computers and record the pictures into one file. One more problem is that screen recordings cannot be merged with recordings from a video camera without serious loss of quality, or only at the cost of very large files.

As a possible solution for those problems one might think of using a pop-up window in which the second video runs. However, this is quite uncomfortable, requiring time for connecting to the media server and for preloading/ buffering some video data.

In some situations it is better, or even the only possible solution, to use two synchronized video clips. One example is the production of multilingual content. Here it is advisable to separate a video file with visual material from sound files for different languages. This solution saves space on the hard disk, proportional to the number of languages and to the size of the video file.

In the general outline of a course page as shown in figure 1 the area for visual material can be used for displaying a video stream as well. How this is achieved will be discussed in section 5. For the student there is no difference in the graphical user interface no matter whether static files or videos are displayed. Technology dependent peculiarities are hidden below the user interface.

4 INTEGRATING SEPARATE VIDEO STREAMS: FUNDAMENTAL PROBLEMES

Major problems in creating course pages like the ones in figures 1 and 2 result from limitations of the Windows Media Player object model. The available methods and properties do not provide mechanisms to control all stages of client-server interaction and to redistribute connection bandwidth among two players adequately. In other words, even if more connection bandwidth is available than required by the sum of bit rates of the two video streams, one cannot expect that the bandwidth will be divided in proportion to the bit rates of the streams, nor even equally.

This shortcoming implies that two video files will rarely start playing simultaneously even if they have exactly the same parameters (e.g. resolution, codec, file size). The synchronization task is thus left to the course creator.

To guarantee proper appearance and behavior of video-based courses we developed and implemented an algorithm for synchronizing and monitoring two video streams. It has the following components as shown in figure 2:
- Synchronizing playback start,
- Monitoring synchronized playback of two videos,
- Corrections if synchronization is off,
- Setting two players to specific positions on demand.

The problem that two players do not start at the same time is actually caused by the different data compression algorithms in the codecs used. The video file from screen capturing (with Matchware Screen Corder 2.0 [11]) is translated into streamable format with the Windows Media Video V7 Screen codec. The conventional camera recording is compressed with the Windows Media Video V8 codec.

Because of the particularities of these codecs a procedure is needed which checks the states of the players. When the first one is ready to play a video, the procedure checks the state of the second player and waits until the second one is also ready to start.

Once playback has started it is necessary to check in short intervals if the two videos are still in the correct positions. The playing times can be measured in seconds or frames from the start of the files. If a difference is detected and if that difference exceeds a certain limit a procedure is started that eliminates the time lag.

The procedure for correcting the differences in synchronization pauses the player that is running ahead and checks playback of the late player. This is done until the slower player has approximately caught up with the other one. Then the first player is released to continue playing.

One serious problem, however, needs to be observed. Due to various reasons the players can change their states (like playing, pausing, buffering, etc.) between individual calls of the procedure and even during the execution of the procedure. Reasons for this may be, for example, actions by the user, reaching a marker in the video file, or a state change in the connection with the Media Server. Therefore additional monitoring of the states of the two players not only at the beginning but also during playback is very important. Otherwise the procedure can crash or the user's web browser can get frozen.

As indicated in figure 2 the user may jump directly to a specific topic of the lecture forwards or backwards by clicking on a control on the left-hand side. In such a case both video files have to be advanced or set back to the desired positions in a synchronized way. Once this is achieved both players have to continue or start playing at the same time. This is basically the same problem as ensuring a synchronized start of two players in the first procedure, so that procedure can be adopted and reused.

5 INTEGRATING VIDEO STREAMS WITH WINDOWS MEDIA TECHNOLOGY

Providing two videos on the course page made it necessary to find a way to include two instances of the Windows Media Player (WMP) into one page. As stand-alone applications, two or more players cannot be started. Microsoft's technical documentation, on the other hand, does not specify whether it is allowed to use two or more WMP ActiveX controls in the same HTML page or not.

Therefore tests were performed to find out whether this is possible or not. Two WMP ActiveX controls were embedded in one page. In fact, both controls established a connection to the Media Server and started playback whenever the page was loaded. At the same time we found that a synchronization procedure is absolutely necessary because the playbacks never started simultaneously.

From the WMP versions available at the time the tests were performed, 6.4 and 7.1 [10], the latter one was chosen because more arguments seemed to be in favor of that version. Later when 9.0 became accessible we tested a prerelease of that version as well and found that its behavior was unsatisfactory.

In our initial work with WMP 7.1, two ActiveX controls where embedded into the HTML page with the help of the <object> tag. Synchronization procedures for playback as outlined above were developed in VBScript.

Testing the initial pages on six computers with different processors and connection speeds showed that program crashes occurred sometimes. The number of failures was inversely related with actual system load. Since the reasons for those system failures were neither obvious nor found in the technical documentation, a testing procedure had to be developed to allow for step-by-step execution of the synchronization procedures.

In a sequence of tests we found that all page crashes and browser hang-ups are occurring during or immediately after the first access to the properties or methods of the Media Player ActiveX control. However, when that control was accessed again after some time crashes rarely occurred. This behavior of the WMP 7.1 control gave rise to the assumption that for some reason the indicated state of a control (i.e. the value of the "PlayState" property) changes faster then the actual state of that control. In other words, the value of the properties is changed first and only afterwards all operations belonging to that state change are executed. This observation explains to some extent why the scripting procedures behave differently when executed on different computers.

A similar phenomenon can be observed on a conventional video tape recorder: When the "Play" button on the remote control is pressed the "Play" sign appears immediately on the recorder's display. However, before a picture from the tape appears on the screen the tape has to be stretched around the video head, and appropriate speeds of both revolving of the head and transporting the tape have to be established. The process may take up to several seconds. During that time the recorder displays the "Play" sign but no picture is visible on the screen. This problem has been known in the field of professional video editing for a long time. Today's video equipment has special functions that allow winding the tape back for several seconds to compensate for the difference between the indicated and the actual playback start.

However, solving the problem of delayed action in the underlying problem in an analogous way - by placing pauses after one player's actions - was not possible. Our findings from a long phase of testing and debugging efforts were that the Windows Media Player 7.1 version requires powerful computer systems to avoid the synchronization problems mentioned above. On many PCs the system performance demanded to play synchronized videos in a reliable and stable way is not available. Therefore the decision was made to go back to the Windows Media Player version 6.4 in order to obtain reasonable performance of the video material on average personal computers.

Adapting the synchronization procedures for WMP 6.4 required some deep changes because the object models underlying the versions 7.1 and 6.4 exhibit significant differences [10]. For example, the synchronization procedures responsible for playback start use the "BufferingProgress" property of the 7.1 version. This property helps to detect if a player is ready for playback or not. Once the value reaches 100 (%) then it is possible to start the playback. In the 6.4 version, however, this property always gets the value 100 when the specified time for buffering is over, no matter whether the buffering has really been accomplished or not. Therefore the procedure that checks the buffering progress had to be substituted by a procedure that watches the "BufferingStart" event. This event occurs at the start and the end of buffering.

Tests with the WMP 6.4 version were performed on the same computers as the previous tests with WMP 7.1. Results were excellent with respect to system stability, independently of actual system workload and bandwidth of network connection.

6 CONCLUSIONS

As a result of our work we found that video streams for e-learning can be synchronized using components of the Windows Media platform although this is not specified in the technical documentation. One solution to the synchronization problem is to use an HTML page with two ActiveX controls representing Windows Media Players. The 7.1 version of the Windows Media Player with many new features is only appropriate if it can be run on a sufficiently powerful computer to avoid the problems and program crashes encountered in our tests. WMP 9.0 in the prerelease version we tested did not satisfy the requirements with regard to playing two synchronized videos.

WMP 6.4 is compatible with all Windows operating systems including Windows NT, and with the Netscape Navigator web browser. This version plays two synchronized video streams correctly, practically on every PC that fulfills the minimum system requirements imposed by modern video codecs such as Windows Media Video V8 and Microsoft MPEG 4 V 3.

The synchronization procedures written in VBScript work correctly and robustly on any PC with that capacity. They provide satisfactory playback synchronization even if the available network bandwidth is too low to deliver both video streams simultaneously in real-time. In such a case some pauses will inevitably occur, due to additional buffering, but the videos will still run correctly. If it is known that the network bandwidth is smaller than the sum of the bit rates of the two video streams, then it might be considered to preload one of the files, store it, and synchronize playback with the video stream delivered real-time. The synchronization procedure does not require any changes in this case.

Taking into account that more and more ADSL connections with stable bandwidth of 400 - 700 Kbit/s are becoming available, this bandwidth is sufficient for uninterrupted delivery of a lecture video with 320 x 240 pixel resolution and 25 fps, compressed with Windows Media Video V8 codec, together with another video containing visual demonstration material with 800 x 600 pixel resolution and 10 fps, compressed with Windows Media Video 7 Screen codec. From our experience it can be concluded that the technical conditions for producing and delivering e-learning courses based on synchronized video streams already exist. In the project underlying our work - developing multimedia courses of the Virtual Global University (VGU) [5] - this approach has been successfully applied.

REFERENCES

[1] Kurbel, K.: A Completely Virtual Distance Education Program Based on the Internet - Case and Agenda of the International MBI Program; in: Hansen, H. R. et al. (Eds.), Proceedings of the 8th European Conference on Information Systems - ECIS 2000, A Cyberspace Odyssey, Vol. 2, Vienna, Austria, pp. 1363-1367.

[2] Bodendorf, F., Grebner, R.: Towards Virtual Universities - ATM-Based Teleteaching in Germany; in: Forcht, K. (Ed.), Information Systems Beyond 2000 - 1998 IACIS Refereed Proceedings, Cancun, Mexico 1998, pp. 67-74

[3] Kloeckner, K.: Preparing the Next Generation of Learning: Enhancing Learning Opportunities by WEB Based Cooperation; in: Proceedings of the Eden 10th Anniversary Conference, Learning Without Limits - Developing the Next Generation of Education; Stockholm, Sweden, 2001

[4] Jones International University (JIU); http://jiu-web-a.jonesinternational.edu/

[5] Virtual Global University (VGU); http://www.vg-u.org

[6] Virtual University in the Upper Rhine Valley (VIROR); http://www.viror.de

[7] Microsoft Windows Media; http://www.microsoft.com/windows/windows media/default.asp

[8] Real Media; http://www.realnetworks.com/

[9] Apple Quick Time; http://www.apple.com/quicktime/

[10] Windows Media Player; http://www.microsoft.com/windows media/players.asp

[11] Matchware Screen Corder; http://www.matchware.net/

[12] Feamster, Nicolas G., Adaptive Delivery of Real-Time streaming Video, M. Eng. Thesis, Massachusetts Institute of Technology, Cambridge 2001

[13] Wee, Susie J.; Apostolopoulos, John G., Secure ScalableVideo Streaming For Wireless Networks, IEEE International Conference on Acoustics, Speech, and Signal Processing, Salt Lake City, Utah 2001

Liberation and Domination: Understanding the Digital Divide from the Standpoint of the 'Other'

Lynette Kvasny

Assistant Professor , School of Information Sciences and Technology, The Pennsylvania State University, University Park, PA 16802
Voice: 814.865.6458, Fax: 814.865.6426, lkvasny@ist.psu.edu

ABSTRACT

In this paper, I present the competing perspectives of the digital divide that emerged from a study of African American inner city residents participating in a community technology center. A critical analysis of the participants' narratives about information technology and the digital divide was carried out. This analysis was informed by feminist standpoint theory, which posits that groups sharing a common location within hierarchical power structures also share collective experiences. The results demonstrate that participants viewed the digital divide from racial and class standpoints, and envisioned information technology as both liberating and dominating. These dual perspectives are used to identify policy implications for redressing the digital divide.

INTRODUCTION

In his Audubon address in 1964, Malcolm X offered the now famous line "We didn't land on Plymouth Rock; the rock landed on us." And in many respects, information technology (IT) has landed like a digital rock on economically oppressed inner cities. The US Department of Commerce (2002) has argued that a massive infusion of computers and broadband Internet connections into homes, schools, libraries and other neighborhood institutions may signal a closing of the digital divide. However, simply promoting access and basic training to improve the computer skills of marginalized individuals does not address the social forces that may limit these actions in the first place.

Prematurely proclaiming the closure of the digital divide may in fact monopolize a dominant ideology that socially constructs IT as an apolitical, unstoppable, and downright irresistible part of a common American culture. Privileged groups can safely imagine that IT is value neutral since the power they have traditionally asserted over inner city residents accord them the right to control the interpretation and reception of IT. From this perspective, the only problem is that some populations have been excluded from access and training.

This type of reasoning, however, fails to consider that inner city residents have been historically underserved in their quality of employment, degree of qualifications, level of income and education, and opportunities for consumption. The social inequalities that these disparities entail are longstanding and continue to cloud what could be an exhilarating moment for mankind (Postman 1992; Schiller 1996). Castells (1989), for instance, uses the term 'informational city' to describe emergent forms and processes of socio-spatial segregation that polarize highly valued groups on the one hand, and devalued groups on the other. 'Unskilled and uninformed populations' have become threatened with social and economic irrelevance, and have become isolated in inner cities (Wilson 1996). Scarce opportunities exist to overcome the vicious cycle of poverty, illiteracy, sporadic work, racial and ethnic discrimination, and criminal activity. In the informational city, IT becomes a contemporary mechanism for reproducing and deepening social structures and power relations (Moolenkropf and Castells 1991).

The digital divide, therefore, should not be explained as a gap in physical access to computers and the Internet, but rather as a political outcome rooted in historical systems of power and privilege (Patterson and Wilson 2000; Kvasny and Keil 2002). One question that emerges then is how do inner city residents make sense of the digital divide? To address this question, I offer the accounts of African American inner city residents participating in a community technology initiative. Through their narratives, I work to present the coexisting and directly competing points of view. While some informants assumed a standpoint that viewed IT as a tool for liberation, others believed that IT was a tool for domination. Informed by these rival narratives, the paper concludes with a set of policy implications that arise when the digital divide is examined from the perspective of the 'Other'.

THE SOCIAL CONSTRUCTION OF THE 'OTHER'

According to hooks (1995), to be objectified as the 'Other' is to be systematically subjugated by 'white supremacist, capitalist, patriarchal values' which maintain the oppression of African American women and other diverse peoples. Suppressing the knowledge produced by any oppressed group makes it easier for dominant groups to rule because the seeming absence of an independent consciousness in the oppressed can be taken to mean that subordinate groups willingly collaborate in their own victimization (Friere 1970).

Cheng (1997) argues that the institution of white supremacy requires diverse people to assimilate into the dominant group's values, aesthetics and attitudes, at the expense of negating their own unique cultural values. Grunell and Saharso (1999) caution that assimilation can lead to the development of a 'colonized mind', a mind that is restricted in its ability to question and transform existing systems of domination. Assimilation can also play a critical role in maintaining the invisibility of subjugated people and their ideas, and in structuring the patterned relations of race, gender, and class inequality that pervade the entire social structure (Hill-Collins 1990).

With respect to the digital divide, white supremacist ideologies come into play when people comfortable in and with IT unwittingly invest in the sense of IT as mystery. Marginalized groups are often reduced to abstractions and objects born out of the fantasies and insecurities of privileged members of society (West 1994; Fine 1998). Subjugated populations are typically believed to lack recognition, appreciation and understanding of the relevance of IT for their life situations. These types of fundamental assumptions conspire in the social construction of subjugated people as 'have nots', 'target communities', 'the Other'. Consequently, as the purveyors of knowledge, it is the job of the dominant to enlighten and demystify the Other by controlling their interpretations and receptions of IT.

The fact that inner city residents think critically about the digital divide and their relative position in the social hierarchy breaks the supposition that the Other lacks the capacity to comprehend and to embrace IT. Feminist standpoint theory provides a lens for understanding the ways in which inner city residents interpret and self-define IT and the digital divide.

RESEARCH APPROACH

Data Collection

In this study, I draw upon the narratives that emerged from a study of low-income African Americans participating in a community technology center located in an inner city. Unstructured interviews were conducted with participants to explore their life histories, and their perspectives on IT and the digital divide. These unstructured interviews were carried out over an eight-month period, and generally took the form of informal conversations in the break room, classrooms and labs.

Data Analysis

The data analysis was informed by feminist standpoint theory which is an interpretive framework dedicated to explaining how knowledge remains central to maintaining and changing unjust systems of power (Hill-Collins 1997). Standpoint theory is rooted in the power/knowledge framework that focuses on shared group experiences, history, and location in relation to power hierarchies. Standpoint theorists argue that collective experiences and histories lend a particular kind of sense making to a person's lived experience (Caraway 1991; Harding 1997; hooks 2000; Hill-Collins 1998).

Feminist standpoint theorists advocate for using people's everyday lives as a foundation for constructing knowledge and as a basis for criticizing dominant knowledge claims. The use of standpoint perspectives in organizational studies can help to increase knowledge, identify missing constructs, develop new relationships among concepts, and build more comprehensive theory (Allen 1996). Lived experiences of members of subjugated groups can also help to respond to criticisms that organizational research generally ignores the issue of race (Nmoko 1992) and social class (Cheng 1997).

Interpreting the Results

Historically underserved groups and individuals without access to IT critically assess the digital divide from a standpoint where IT is a privileged signifier. The participants in this study generally conceptualized the digital divide in two competing and contradictory ways. For some, IT signified hope and liberation; for others, IT signified pessimism and domination.

Liberation: "New Tools for Hope for the Future"

Many informants ascribed emancipatory power to IT. They believe in the possibility of upward mobility and collective progress enabled by IT. Even though they suffered in their daily lives, they also let themselves believe that times were changing. In this shared worldview, IT is highly prized as a mechanism for social advancement and inclusion in the information society. As one classroom facilitator states, "These people are coming here because they are hungry. They want to learn."

Beverly, a senior participating in the program, uses several metaphors that suggest movement – "the first step", "no longer left behind", and "the Internet is the mode of travel". Overcoming the digital divide is seen as an ascent along "the road of information freedom" that enables Black people to flee from the oppressive and menacing conditions of the inner city and to keep despair at bay. Developing IT skills is part of a larger struggle for wholeness and resilience.

Beverly: Through this program we are taking computer classes that have connected us with the great information divide, we are no longer left behind. We started our journey on January 8, 2001. We are still traveling on the road of information freedom and enjoying every minute of it. There is so much to be learned, and the information is available because we made the first step, receiving information and taking the steps to change our future in the usage of the computer in our everyday life. We now realize that the Internet is the mode of travel for today as well as tomorrow.

Ron, an adult male participant, juxtaposes "darkness" and "light" to construct a definition of the digital divide. He talks about a "growing divide among peers", and feeling "so left behind" due to his lack of IT skills. For him, redressing the digital divide is about "feeling connected" and "being part of what's going on". His desire is focused on connecting with people and institutions outside of his local community.

Ron: Technology is the thing of the future. My nieces and nephews tell me that I need to step it up some, so this is my first move to get out of the dark and into the light…I want to be more a part of what's going on. I want to feel connected…I was in the dark. Before I learned about the computers, it was hard to communicate with people. Without computer training, there will be a growing divide among peers. It is getting larger. I felt so left behind, out of it. I was not in the loop for communication. I had no email, so I couldn't keep in touch with my family on a regular basis. I had to use the phone. Now with email, I can communicate on a regular basis. It is also less expensive.

Another informant, Sean, believes that "conquering" the digital divide should be part of a broader "mission" aimed at improving the economic survival of not only individuals but of entire classes of poor people.

Sean: I will learn a lot of computer applications when I finish this class. I will be able to get a better job and better opportunities. I will conquer the digital divide. We all need to learn these computer applications. We will need this information to be successful in the business world. Afro-Americans have basically been left behind in this arena. We must make progress. The [community technology center] will help us to accomplish this mission.

Like Sean, Rose spoke from the standpoint of race and class to describe how IT has not been "prevalent in our community" because computers are unaffordable and intimidating. Her narrative also punctuates the need for the community to invest in and engage with IT. Rose not only saw the potential for community activism through technology education. She advised "those who have the ability to train" to "provide others with computer skills". Moreover, this learning should occur in a "comfortable setting".

Rose: There is definitely a digital divide in the area of technology when it comes to African-Americans mainly because many people cannot afford to obtain their own personal computers, and access to computer training have not been prevalent in our communities. Additionally, our older generations tend to feel intimidated by computer technology. It has become the responsibility of those who have the ability to train and provide others with computer skills to do so in a comfortable setting.

Participants such as Sean, Ron, Rose and Beverly, acknowledge the social and economic potential of IT. For them, redressing the digital divide has an urgency that goes beyond self-improvement and demystification. IT is perceived as a liberator of oppressed people. "People come in and pick up this spirit. It can't be measured in terms of money. We have to raise awareness and then it is boundless to where people can go." These individuals are not content to point out the source of their oppression. Instead they urged African Americans within the community to become active, self-reliant and independent.

Domination: "Technology Becomes a Nightmare for Us"

A few participants, however, believed that "technology becomes a nightmare for us". They spoke primarily from class-based standpoints that informed their narratives of IT and the digital divide. Yet, their pointed critiques of IT lacked a sense of activism or power to change unjust social structures. For these participants, IT was viewed as a contemporary mechanism for reproducing inequality.

Bill, for instance, expressed his views on why the government was now implementing digital divide initiatives. In his critique, he seeks to explain the benefits that accrue to the government for having a technologically educated population.

Bill: The plan was to perfect the technology with the rich people. Then when it is perfected it can be rolled out to the masses. The way to do this is to fund programs. The goal is to make us continue to make us buy things. They have to train us so that we can continue to buy. They also have to keep us in the workforce to avoid chaos. If too many people are not working, they will end up on welfare or in prisons. The rich people will have to foot the bill. They need low skilled people to keep the economy going, so they don't need to train us for the high paying jobs. It's all about economics, not humanity.

While Bill critiques the interests of the rich that underlie the formation of the community technology center, there is no sense of resistance or collective struggle against the established social order. Instead, Bill portrays "the masses" as naïve consumers at the mercy of producers that conspire to "make us continue to buy". The potential of IT as a tool to support grassroots organizing and community development is not explored. From Bill's perspective, the digital divide has much to do with being dominated and silenced. Established power structures and dominant ideologies effectively determine what people will receive computer training, and the conditions imposed on their use of IT (Kvasny and Keil 2002).

Roger, an adult participant, is faced with a similar dilemma. On the one hand, he would like to engage in IT training activities. On the other hand, he has generations of history to draw from which attest to the fact that wholehearted participation in education programs may not deliver on its promise of an enhanced quality of life (Gorard and Selwyn 1999).

> **Roger:** I don't expect much. I'm not here to get a job because I know that I am not learning enough. I am just getting a taste for technology. They keep raising the bar. Now you need to know more just to get an entry-level job. History tells me that this is the case. There is really nothing new about the technology.

Roger's pessimistic reading of the benefits that he will derive from IT training is informed by his class position. According to Brown (1974, p. 15) "Class involves your behavior, your basic assumptions about life. Your experience (determined by your class) validates those assumptions, how you are taught to behave, what you expect from yourself and from others, your concept of a future, how you understand problems and solve them, how you think, feel, act." Individuals such as Bill and Roger reproduce inequality by adopting the limited roles assigned to them by virtue of their membership in a subjugated class group.

IMPLICATIONS

In a world where people have multidimensional goals, all constrained within economic and social limits, policy interventions tend to improve and document the success of that one dimension, while ignoring the dimensions sacrificed. Most digital divide policy solutions to date have focused on the technical dimension of access. Substantially less attention has been paid to overcoming the societal structures that limit the social strivings of individuals who believe in the promise of IT, but are structurally barred from achieving their goals (Norris 2000).

The key policy implication derived from this study is the need to support not only the diffusion of the IT artifact, but to also support the hopes, aspirations and points of view of underserved groups. The digital divide will not be bridged with the delivery of computers, networks and other technology artifacts. Bridging the digital divide requires that we also deliver on the visionary ideologies and opportunity structures that we tend to associate with IT. Instead of imposing the meanings of the dominant, we should engage in dialogue with dominated groups in order to understand their perspectives, needs and desires. The learning that takes place through democratic dialogues can then inform the development of socially just and culturally relevant programs and stable local institutions that assist subjugated people in the use of IT to more fully realize their life chances.

CONCLUSION

This paper provides a micro-level analysis of how the digital divide is experienced and expressed through the narratives of African American inner city residents. I found that most informants saw themselves as agents of social change, not victims. They largely believed in the complex and transcendent nature of IT. However, calling upon inner city populations to be change agents only makes sense if we also look at the history, culture and social structures in which their agency is to be exerted (Sowell 1994; West 1994).

REFERENCES

Allen, B. "Feminist Standpoint Theory: A Black Woman's (Re)view of Organizational Socialization", *Communication Studies*, Volume 47, Number 4, 1996, pp. 257-271.

Brown, R. "The Last Straw", in C. Bunch and N. Myron (eds.), *Class and Feminism*. Baltimore: Diana Press, 1974, pp. 14-23.

Caraway, N. *Segregated Sisterhood: Racism and the Politics of American Feminism*, Knoxville: University of Tennessee Press, 1991.

Castells, M. *The Informational City: Information Technology, Economic Restructuring, and the Urban-Regional Process*. Oxford: Blackwell Publishers, 1989.

Cheng, C. "A Review Essay on the Books of bell hooks: Organizational Diversity Lessons from a Thoughtful Race and Gender Heretic", *Academy of Management Review*, Volume 22, Number 2, 1997, pp. 553-574.

Fine, M. "Working the Hyphens: Reinventing Self and Other in Qualitative Research", in N. Denzin and Y. Lincoln (eds.), *The Landscape of Qualitative Research,* Thousand Oaks: Sage Publications, 1998, pp.130-155.

Freire, P. *Pedagogy of the Oppressed*, New York: Continuum Books, 1970.

Gorard, S. and Selwyn, N. "Switching on the Learning Society? Questioning the Role of Technology in Widening Participation in Lifelong Learning". *Journal of Educational* Policy, Volume 14, Number 5, 1999, pp. 523-534.

Grunell, M., and Saharso, S. "bell hooks and Nira Yuval-Davis on Race, Ethnicity, Class and Gender", *European Journal of Women's Studies*, Volume 6, 1999, pp. 203-218.

Hekman, S. "Truth and Method: Feminist Standpoint Theory Revisited", *Signs*, Volume 22, Number 2, 1997, pp. 341-367.

Harding, S. "Comment on Hekman's "Truth and Method: Feminist Standpoint Theory Revisited": Truth and Method", *Signs*, Volume 22, Number 2, 1997, pp. 367-375.

Hill-Collins, P. *Black Feminist Thought: Knowledge, Consciousness, and the Politics of Empowerment*, New York: Routledge, 1990, pp. 19-40.

Hill-Collins, P. "Comment on Hekman's "Truth and Method: Feminist Standpoint Theory Revisited": Where is the Power?", *Signs*, Volume 22, Number 2, 1997, pp. 375-381.

Hill-Collins, P. *Fighting Words: Black Women and the Search for Justice*, Minneapolis: University of Minnesota, 1998.

hooks, b. *Feminism is for Everybody*, Boston: South End Press, 2000.

Kvasny, L. and Keil, M. "The Challenges of Redressing the Digital Divide: A Tale of Two Cities". *Proceedings of the International Conference on Information Systems (ICIS),* Barcelona, Spain, December 15-18, 2002.

Moolenkropf, J. and Castells, M. *Dual City.* Thousand Oaks: Sage Publications, 1991.

Nmoko, S. "The Emperor Has No Clothes: Rewriting 'Race in Organizations'", *Academy of Management Review*, Volume 17, Number 3, 1992, pp. 487-513.

Norris, P. *Digital Divide: Civic Engagement, Information Poverty, and the Internet Worldwide*, Cambridge: Cambridge University Press, 2001.

Patterson, R. and Wilson, E. "New IT and Social Inequality: Resetting the Research and Policy Agenda," *The Information Society*, Volume 16, 2000, pp. 77-86.

Postman, N. *Technopoly: The Surrender of Culture to Technology.* New York: Vintage Books, 1992.

Schiller, H. *Information Inequality: The Deepening Social Crisis in America.* New York: Routledge, 1996.

Sowell, T. *Race and Culture.* Basic Books: New York, 1994.

U.S. Department of Commerce, *A Nation of Millions: How Americans are Expanding their Use of the Internet.* National Telecommunications and Information Administration, 2002.

West, C. *Race Matters.* New York: Vintage Books, 1994.

Wilson, W.J. *When Work Disappears.* New York: Vintage Books, 1996.

UML Modeling for Cooperative Problem-Based Learning Situations: Towards Educational Components

Pierre Laforcade, Franck Barbier

Computer Science Research Institute of University of Pau et des Pays de l'Adour , LIUPPA, Université de Pau, BP 1155, 64013 Pau CEDEX FRANCE, Phone: (+33)5.59.92.33.43, Fax: (+33)5.59.80.83.74, E-mail: pierre.laforcade@univ-pau.fr

ABSTRACT

Problem-Based Learning Situations require accurate template models in which the roles of tutor and learner participate in varied codified cooperative activities. This paper discusses the use of the UML to first build such customizable models, and next to derive Educational Software Components from models. The paper contributes to reduce the lack of flexibility in open distance learning tools where distribution of components applies with some difficulty. It is on purpose introduced the designer role for problem-based learning situations. This designer aims to assemble educational components in order to offer computer-aided learning supports. Model examples and techniques to implement components are also briefly evoked.

Keywords: *Educational Component, Cooperative Learning, Problem-Based Learning Situation, UML.*

1 INTRODUCTION

Our work copes with learning situations involving cooperation between tutors and learners. Within this context, computer-aided learning hinges on software and platforms whose customization allows to implement scenarios embodying such cooperation. Because of the monolithic aspect of learning platforms and software, as well as the specificity of education based on Problem-Based Learning Situations (PBLS)(Meirieu, 1988), we propose in this paper an approach using the notion of Educational Software Component (Roschelle et al., 1999). PBLS rely on cognitive models of cooperative activities for tutors and learners. These cognitive models can be specified once for all and captured within components. By offering enough flexibility, namely parameterization to keep a good degree of tuning, and by naturally supporting distribution, Educational Components, when reused, allow to assemble new PBLS in software systems. Distance learning issues via distribution are especially associated with the idea of software component.

We focus in this paper on the UML specification of Educational Components. This formalism favors, at a conceptual level, the description of tutor/learner and learner/learner cooperation. At implementation time, UML supplies Component & Deployment Diagrams to package and deploy specification pieces into components. We sketch in this paper such cooperation and briefly discuss at the end of the paper, implementation based on a dedicated library. Indeed, we divide the modeling of pedagogical activities into Statechart Diagrams and therefore illustrate how to easily and quickly implement these dynamical models in Java.

2 EDUCATIONAL ENGINEERING

Educational Engineering covers techniques and tools that assist, and possibly automate in software, the universal and dual actions of teaching and learning. In this section, after describing our context of work and goals, we walk through current innovative projects in this domain.

2.1 Context of Work

Educational Components here described appear within the framework of a more general project: the specification of an environment allowing a teacher to implement cooperative learning situations. Our first goal is to help teachers to specify learning situations. PBLS are quite different from classic learning approach based on the notions of courses, exercises, assessments. PBLS are indeed based on the idea of cooperative activity and more exactly cooperative resolution of problems.

Recent works (Nodenot et al., 2002) describe stakes, actors and application principles of such learning activities. We pay attention on the definition of a system (called *Learning Management System* or *LMS*) that manages activities for distant user communities (learners and tutors). We also show that a pedagogy relying on cooperative activities conforms to normalization works carried out by international e-Learning consortia (AICC, 2000; ARIADNE, 2001; Dublin_Core, 2000; GESTALT, 2000; IMS, 2000; ISO/IEC_JTC1_SC36/WG2, 2001; LTSC, 2000; MASIE_Center, 2002; PROMETEUS, 2000; SCORM, 2000).

Previously, we worked on the specification of a role-component library enabling a designer to reuse learning scenarii (Sallaberry et al., 2002). This approach allows the assembling of new roles by combining pre-existent role-components.

2.2 Educational Components

Over years, research in Educational Engineering emphasizes the support of interoperable and reusable applications as well as "electronic" services (Wiley, 2000). The Educational Component (EC) approach is growing: *"having component developers collaborate with domain experts to build applications may be the future of software development"* (Roschelle et al., 1999).

The component paradigm used within the Educational domain has numerous objectives:
1. sharing learning resources between software tools and systems,
2. making interoperability between tools,
3. making interoperability between applications and learning resources,
4. reusing learning resources (by teachers),
5. reusing educational software (by developers).

As the word "Component" in Software Engineering, "Educational Component" has multiple meanings and may have very different interpretations. Thus, we cannot find out a generic definition of an EC. We point out the dual notion of Learning Object (LO). LOs are *"any digital resource that can be reused to support learning"* (Wiley, 2000) or *"Learning Objects are defined here as any entity, digital or non-digital, which can be used, re-used or referenced during technology supported learning"* (LOM, 2000). In fact, such a fine-grained component supports learning by means of its embedded learning content. So, research works on LOs rather correspond to points 1-3-4 above (ARIADNE, 2001; De_La_Passardière et al., 2001; IMS, 2000; Koper, 2001; LOM, 2000; SCORM, 2000) and relate to classical learning concepts as courses, exercises, assessments. LO approach is more convenient for the common learning approach than for the PBLS constructivist one (Deschênes et al., 1996) – learner build his own knowledge by doing.

2.1 Current Trends and Directions for Educational Software Components

We study different projects based on Educational Software Components that we split into two categories.

ESCOT (Educational Software Components Of Tomorrow) project (ESCOT, 2002) aims at the construction of a digital library containing educational software relating to Middle School mathematics. One of the ESCOT's goals is to have interactive JavaBeans-based content within an educational context. In the same way, ESCOT explores the process of distributed software-development with the specific objective to rapidly build and deploy reliable software (Repenning et al., 2001). It also deals with the EC stemming from AgentSheets (Agent_Sheets, 2001) and E-Slate projects (Birbilis et al., 2000). AgentSheets is an authoring-tool for the creation of reusable EC under the shape of applets, directly integrable on a Web page. These components can be used for exercises of simulation, demonstration, scientific modeling, etc. The technology used is simple and the integration on a Web page implies that the component is only a pedagogical element of a bigger one. In E-Slate, components are supplied in the form of prefabricated objects (card, clock, vector…). They possess a mechanism of interconnection (glue) and are configurable, customizable: they can contain features for a specific domain. They are connected together within the same global application which allows to visually assemble them according to "the puzzle's analogy"; they especially have an appropriate graphical interface.

The works on SimulNet (Anido et al., 2001) propose a layered component model for the support of Web-based interactive and collaborative applications (framework) as well as a development of an educational application based on this model. Every component aims at supplying a feature required in Web-based collaborative applications. In a similar way, the global objective of the PLACE project (PLAteforme à Composants Evolutive) (Peter et al., 2002) is the following study: how to realize flexible cooperative working environments based on models of standard components. In both SimulNet and PLACE projects, the Software Component principles are applied in the design and the realization phases: the creation of a Web environment dedicated to distant learning. For the PLACE project, the architecture is based on the use of the EJB / J2EE platform in order to build a CSCW (Computer Supported Cooperative Work) platform whereas SimulNet proposes a client / server architecture. At the structure level, the analogy between component and tool (auditing tool, e-mail, bulletin board, chat, whiteboard, agenda, project management, event delivering, producer-consumer manager…) is present in both projects.

The various researches previously quoted have in common a component approach based upon the Software Engineering. So, an Educational Component is close to the notion of tool. Like a Software Component, an Educational Component supplies services and has to be assembled with other ones in order to build an educational application.

3 EDUCATIONAL COMPONENT MODELING

This part describes first of all our viewpoint on EC, according to our project's requirements. Then, we detail how we may represent a pedagogical activity. This activity will be grounded on our EC notion. Then, we provide an illustrated approach in order to highlight EC main characteristics within a PBLS and then we show the building steps of such a component. Finally, we sketch an EC implementation example based on a Java library.

3.1 Properties of Educational Components

Like the PLACE and SIMULNET projects, our vision of Educational Component is close to a component / tool: a black box supplying services. However, our EC approach does not concern the architecture of the PBLS system. In contrast, it allows an EC manipulation (composition or extension) in order to *design new learning activities*. So, it will be possible to build opened and flexible cooperative PBLS, easily modifiable by the end-users: teachers / designers. Our EC concept does not embed educational contents like LOs but offers "pedagogical services": resources exchange service, synchronous communication service between tutor/learner, etc.

EC describes a small pedagogical activity process. It corresponds to a generic and reusable PBLS element:
- It supplies *pedagogical services* (monitoring, regulation, production…services).
- It describes *one or several views:* the learner's view, the tutor's view, …

(see following example).
- It is *configurable* during its use / assembly: some *generic* parameters have to be instantiated, insuring a better integration in the pedagogical activity. This configuration allow the EC to match specific learning situation.
- It is *customizable:* for example, the designer may choose between synchronous or asynchronous characteristic of a conversational EC.

On one hand, our EC model gives pedagogical services required by teachers. On the other hand, our model is supported by tool features: they can be supplied by any Software Components (chat, e-mail, diary…).

3.2 Modeling Method

Information System modeling based on UML is a central topic in recent papers. In (Nodenot et al., 2002; Sallaberry et al., 2002) we used UML to describe cooperative PBLS in terms of actions, roles, ressources, learning objectives and pedagogical activities. In this paper, we focus on the details of the pedagogical activity. To that extent, like (Bourguin, 2000), we refer on the Activity Theory (Engeström et al., 1998).

Our original contribution is our choice to represent pedagogical activities (learning or tutoring) with UML Statecharts. Such a Statechart represents the *expected progresses* for a user (learner and tutor) within the pedagogical activity. Here is the analogy between statechart elements and pedagogical activities:
- Any *state* of a diagram represents a *step* in the expected progresses of an activity.
- A *transition* represents a *pedagogical action* that a user can perform in its activity. The transitions also allow a *non-linear meshing* of progress possibilities within the activity. They are composed of:
- An *event*: it is raised by the user or the system in order to *validate an expected action*
- A *guard*: it represents a required condition whether the associated event is raised.
- *Action*: it is a call to a service provided by a tool – users have tools at their disposal.
- Generalization and aggregation of states allow to reliably divide a pedagogical activity into sub-elements. This insures a structural and hierarchical design.

During the execution stage, statechart models enable the LMS (*Learning Management System*) to provide users with context-sensitive tools: at each state of the users activity, the system will know which service calls are enabled / disabled by the designer. Consequently, the system will be able to enable / disable tools functionalities.

Statechart modeling also allows to manage a history (trace) of the various states, transitions, events, etc, that the users passed through. So, during the PBLS execution stage, it will be possible for both system and tutors to supervise *the actual pedagogical activity*. This allows to improve the tutoring and can be used in order to build a learner profile. This profile is used to regulate the pedagogical activity. It is also used in order to re-route a user towards another activity[1].

3.3 Illustration

The objective here is to highlight and to formally describe low level pedagogical activities. These activities will contribute to describe high level pedagogical activities. Thus, any pedagogical activity results from an assembly process of sub-activities.

In order to identify these reusable pedagogical activities, we are inspired of the "four-leaved clove" (David, 2001). This model presents four embedded spaces for the classification of cooperative work activities – production, communication, conversation and coordination. For example, some pedagogical activities which would inevitably appear in cooperative PBLS are: asynchronous or synchronous conversation between learner / learner or learner / tutor, collective production between learners, information pooling, information sharing, information research in a library / Web...

We describe in this part a simple example of our EC model. This component contains a monitoring pedagogical activity called "help on inquiry". This activity consists in giving the possibility for a learner to ask for some help to a distant tutor. This last one can then answer her/him.

Figure 1 : Example of pedagogical Statecharts into our basic Educational Component

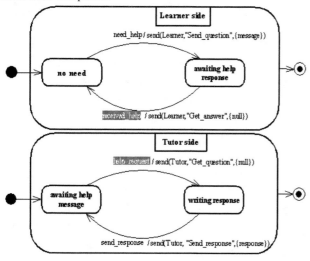

This pedagogical activity concerns two actors: a learner and a tutor. Thus, the pedagogical activity representation requires two Statecharts for each possible pedagogical treatments linked to one of the actors (Figure 1). The required precision for this component configuration is: who are the tutor and learner? The answer will enable the instanciation of the generic parameters "*Tutor*" and "*Learner*". During the design phase, the configuration may also concern the types of the messages: synchronous (*instant messaging*) or asynchronous *(e-mail)*. Moreover, this figure shows two different kinds of events: "*need help*" that corresponds to an event generated by the user "*Learner*"; "*received help*" (grayish event) that corresponds to an independent event of the "*Learner*", it is generated by the LMS or another user ("*Tutor*"). Every transition involves an action-element of this shape: *send (Target, Method, Parameters) - method* objects correspond to services provided by the *target*.

The following figure shows an example of assembly between the concern learner part ("*Yet designed Learner Side*") and a statechart ("*Yet designed Pedagogical Activity*") representing the pedagogical activity predicted by the PBLS designer. This second statechart is deliberately limited to one and only state ("in_progress") in order to hide pedagogical activity complexity. Both statecharts are assembled by aggregation into a new global state ("*My Final Pedagogical Activity*"). It means that both sub-statecharts can evolve separately during the actual realization of the pedagogical activity: while following sub-statechart activity, the learner may request some help and wait for the

Figure 2 : An assembly example between yet designed pedagogical activity and Statechart from EC

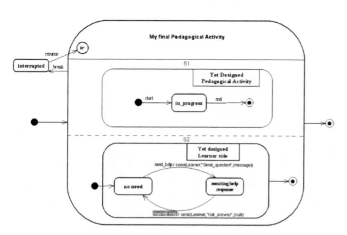

tutor answer. This "concurrent" mode is a pedagogical assembly possibility but other alternatives remain as direct chaining of two statecharts.

3.4 Implementations

We sketch here how our statecharts are implemented in order to become operational components. Here, the statechart of Figure 2 ("*My final Pedagogical Activity*") is build and execute in the same way as a simulation-tool in order to validate our model. To this end, we use the *PauWare* Statechart Java library.

```
protected Tutor _tutor;
…
protected Statechart _interrupted;
protected Statechart _S1;
protected Statechart _S2;
// Statechart_monitor extends Statechart class with new transition features
protected Statechart_monitor _My_final_pedagogical_activity;
…
_My_final_pedagogical_activity        =        new
Statechart_monitor((_S1.and(_S2)).xor(_interrupted));
// S1 & S2 states are concurrent à "and" assembling
// "interrupted" state is in exclusive or with the assembled S1&S2 à "xor" assembling
```

Events influence and conduct the way by which learning activities may run:

```
synchronized public void need_help() {
try {
        // transition "need_help" build between states from "_no_need" to "_awaiting_help_response"

_My_final_pedagogical_activity.fires(_no_need,_awaiting_help_response,true,_tutor,"Send_question", null);
        // simulation of the generated event à transition execution
        _My_final_pedagogical_activity.used_up();
}
catch(StatechartException se) {
System.err.println(se.getMessage());
System.exit(1);
}
}
```

4 CONCLUSION

In this paper, we introduce the idea of Educational Component in order to support computer-aided pedagogical activities. We review some current research works on this special concept of Educational Component. Our approach converges towards the modeling of Educational Components with the UML as well as the potential associated implementation of these components. Capturing learning/teaching activities that are in essence cognitive processes, comes up against inappropriate formalisms. We think that a suitable formalism is together helpful for representing all aspects of PBLS and easily leads to concrete software entities. We thus focus on the segmentation of activities in order to deliver components that can be readily assembled and deployed to provide opened and flexible distance learning activities.

Perspectives of our work rely on the use of component models like CCM (CORBA Component Model), EJB or .NET.

5 REFERENCES

Agent_Sheets. (2001). *Getting Started with AgentSheets*. Retrieved, from the World Wide Web: http://agentsheets.com/Documentation/windows/Getting-Started.pdf

AICC. (2000). *Aviation Industry CBT Committee (AICC). document #CMI001: CMI Guidelines for Interoperability v3.4; released* [WWW Document]. Retrieved, from the World Wide Web: http://www.aicc.org/

Anido, L., Llamas, M., Fernandez, M. J., Caeiro, M., Santos, J., & Rodriguez, J. (2001, may 1-5 2001). *A Component Model for Standardized Web-based Education*. Paper presented at the WWW'10, Hong Kong, ACM 1-58113-348-0/01/0005.

ARIADNE. (2001). *Alliance of Remote Instructional and Distribution Networks for EuropeAlliance of Remote Instructional and Distribution Networks for Europe.* Retrieved, 2001, from the World Wide Web: http://www.ariadne-eu.org/

Birbilis, G., Koutlis, M., Kyrimis, K., Tsironis, G., & Vasiliou, G. (2000). *E-Slate: A software architectural style for end-user programming.* Paper presented at the 22nd International Conference on Software Engineering (ICSE 2000), Limerick, Ireland

Bourguin, G. (2000). *Un support informatique à l'activité coopérative fondé sur la Théorie de l'Activité : le projet DARE.* Thèse de doctorat de l'Université des sciences et technologies de Lille. N°2753.

David, B. (2001). IHM pour les collecticiels. In E. Hermès (Ed.), *Les télé-applications* (Vol. volume 13).

De_La_Passardière, B., & Giroire, H. (2001). XML au service des applications pédagogiques. *Revue Sciences et Techniques Educatives, EIAO'01,* pp 99-112.

Deschênes, A. J., Bilodeau, H., Bourdages, L., Dionne, M., Gagné, P., Lebel, C., & Rada-Donath, A. (1996). Constructivisme et formation à distance. *DistanceS, Vol 1, num 1.*

Dublin_Core. (2000). *The Dublin Core Metadata Initiative.* Retrieved, from the World Wide Web: http://purl.org/dc/

Engeström, Y., Miettinen, R., & Punamäki, R.-L. (1998). Perspectives on activity theory. *(Eds.) Cambridge: Cambridge University Press.*

ESCOT. (2002). Retrieved, from the World Wide Web: http://www.escot.org/overview.html

GESTALT. (2000). *Getting Educational Systems Talking Across Leading Edge Technologies.* Retrieved April 1, 2000, from the World Wide Web: http://www.fdgroup.co.uk/gestalt/about.html

IMS. (2000). *The IMS Project.* Retrieved from the World Wide Web: http://www.imsproject.org/

ISO/IEC_JTC1_SC36/WG2. (2001). *Toward common understanding for Collaborative Learning - from the viewpoint of technical standardization.* Retrieved, from the World Wide Web: http://jtc1sc36.org/doc/36N0153.pdf

Koper, R. (2001). *Modeling units of study from a pedagogical perspective: the pedagogical meta-model behind EML. First draft, version 2*: Educational Expertise Technology Centre, Open University of the Netherlands.

LOM. (2000). *LOM (Learning Object Metadata) working draft v4.1.* Retrieved, from the World Wide Web: http://ltsc.ieee.org/doc/wg12/LOMv4.1htm

LTSC. (2000). *Institute of Electrical and Electronics Engineers (IEEE) Learning Technology Standards Comittee (LTSC).* Retrieved, from the World Wide Web: http://ltsc.ieee.org/

MASIE_Center. (2002). *Making Sense of Learning Specifications & Standards: A Decision Maker's Guide to their Adoption.*

Meirieu, P. (1988). Guide méthodologique pour l'élaboration d'une situation-problème. In P. E. e. éd. (Ed.), *annexe to : Apprendre... oui, mais comment ?* : Collection Pédagogies.

Nodenot, T., Marquesuzaà, C., Laforcade, P., Bessagnet, M.-N., & Sallaberry, C. (2002, 13-15 november). *Spécifications d'un environnement Web supportant des activités coopératives d'apprentissage.* Paper presented at the Technologies de l'Information et de la Communication dans les Enseignements d'ingénieurs et dans l'industrie, Lyon, pp. 253-262

Peter, Y., Vantroys, T., & Viéville, C. (2002). *PLAteforme à Composants Evolutive (PLACE).* Retrieved, from the World Wide Web: http://noce.univ-lille1.fr/~ypeter/PLACE/Place.pdf

PROMETEUS. (2000). *Promoting Multimedia access to Education and Training in European Society.* Retrieved, from the World Wide Web: http://prometeus.org/

Repenning, A., Loannidou, A., Payton, M., Ye, W., & Roschelle, J. (2001). Using Components for Rapid Distributed Software-Development. *IEEE Software, march/april,* pp 38-45.

Roschelle, J., DiGiano, C., Koutlis, M., Repenning, A., Phillips, J., Jackiw, N., & Suthers, D. (1999). Developing Educational Software Components. *IEEE Computer, 32*(9), 2-10.

Sallaberry, C., Nodenot, T., Marquesuzaà, C., Bessagnet, M.-N., & Laforcade, P. (2002, 27 - 30 May, 2002.). *Information modelling within a Net-Learning Environment.* Paper presented at the 12th Conference On Information Modelling and Knowledge Based, Krippen, Swiss Saxony, Germany

SCORM. (2000). *The Department of Defense Advanced Distributed Learning — ADL — Initiative Releases Version 1.2 of the Sharable Courseware Object Reference Model — SCORM 1.2 —.* Retrieved, from the World Wide Web: http://www.adlnet.org/Scorm/scorm.cfm

Wiley, D. A. (2000). *Connecting learning objects to instructional design theory: A definition, a metaphor, and a taxonomy* (In D. Wiley ed.): Bloomington: Association for Educational Communications and Technology.

(Footnotes)

[1] A re-routed activity is an individual pedagogical activity dynamically allocated; this allows the system to propose new pedagogical activities every time a user finishes an activity and is waiting for other ones, avoiding passive delay.

Identifying Security Threats and Mitigating their Impact: Lessons from Y2K and 9/11

Laura Lally
BCIS/QM Department, Hofstra University
Hempstead, NY 11549-134
516 463-5351
acslhl@hofstra

ABSTRACT

In the Post 9/11 environment, there has been an increasing awareness of the need for information security. This paper presents an analysis of the Y2K problem and 9/11 disaster from the perspective of Lally's extension of Perrow's Normal Accident Theory and the Theory of High Reliability Organizations. Insights into: 1) how characteristics of the current IT infrastructures make disasters more likely and 2) how IT can be used to identify future threats and mitigate their impact in the future, emerge from the analysis.

INTRODUCTION

In the post 9/11 environment, Information Technology managers have become more aware of the importance of security. Throughout the 1990s, IT security faced a wide range of new challenges. Yourdon (2002) places these challenges in three categories:

1) More organizations are dependent on the Internet for day-to-day operations.
2) An increasing number of computer systems, networks and databases make up a global IT infrastructure. Individuals, organizations and nations are "increasingly "wired," increasingly automated, and increasingly dependent on highly reliable computer systems" (Yourdon, 2002, p. 96).
3) IT managers faced more sophisticated and malevolent forms of attacks on these systems. Unlike the Y2K, problem, which was the result of an innocent bad judgement, "the disruptive shocks to our organizations are no longer accidental, benign, or acts of nature; now they are deliberate and malevolent." (Yourdon, 2002, p. 205).

This research will present an analysis of the sources, propagation and potential impacts of IT related threats. The Y2K problem and the information technology implications of 9/11 will be used to illustrate the analysis. The analysis will focus on both: 1) how the current IT infrastructure allows for the propagation of IT based threats, and 2) ways in which available IT tools can help identify potential threats and to mitigate their impact.

EXTENDING PERROW'S NORMAL ACCIDENT THEORY AND THE THEORY OF HIGH RELIABILITY ORGANIZATIONS

This analysis will draw on Lally's (2002) extension of Perrow's Normal Accident Theory (1984, 1999), as well as the Theory of High Reliability Organizations. Perrow developed his theory studying complex systems such as nuclear power plants. He distinguished characteristics of systems that would permit single failures, called "incidents" such as an operator error, to propagate into major accidents such as meltdowns. Systems that had these characteristics were likely to be subject to accidents in the normal course of their operation. Perrow concluded that accident prone systems are more:

1) **Complex**—with multiple versus linear interactions, and invisible interactions with only the "Tip of the Iceberg" visible, leading to the problem of "unknowability,"
2) Tightly coupled—with no slack time to allow incidents to be intercepted, and

3) Poorly controlled—with less opportunity for human intervention before problems spread.

Lally argued that Normal Accident Theory is a sound theoretical perspective for understanding the risks of Information Technology, because IT is:
1) **Complex**—The hardware that makes up IT infrastructures of most organizations is complex, containing a wide range of technologies. Software often contains thousands of lines of code written by dozens of programmers. Incidents such as bugs can, therefore, propagate in unexpected ways.
2) **Tightly coupled**—Both hardware and software are designed to increase the speed and efficiency of operations. Incidents such as operator errors can quickly have real world impacts.
3) **Poorly controlled**—Security features are often not built into systems. Testing of software is often inadequate in the rush to meet release deadlines.

Researchers in the Theory of High Reliability Organizations have examined organizations in which complex, tightly coupled, technologically based systems appeared to be coping successfully with the potential for disaster. Their studies of the Federal Aviation Administration's air traffic control system, the Pacific Gas and Electric's electric power system, including the Diablo Canyon nuclear power plant, and the peacetime flight operations of three United States Navy aircraft carriers indicate that organizations can achieve nearly error free operation (La Porte & Consolini, 1991; Perrow, 1994; Sagan, 1993).

High reliability organization theorists identify four critical causal factors for achieving reliability:
* Political elites and organizational leaders put safety and reliability first as a goal.
* High levels of redundancy in personnel and technical safety measures.
* The development of a "high reliability culture" in decentralized and continually practiced operations, and
* Sophisticated forms of trial and error organizational learning.

The two theories have been contrasted as "pessimistic" — Perrow's contention that disaster is inevitable in badly designed systems, versus "optimistic" — La Porte's pragmatic approach to achieving greater reliability. The theories, however, are in agreement as to which characteristics of systems make them more or less accident prone.

Lally applied these theories to various aspects of Information Technology including reengineering (Lally, 1996, 1997), the Y2K problem (Lally, 1999), and privacy in the hiring processes (Lally, 2000), (Lally and Garbushian, 2001). Lally concluded (Lally, 2002) that the rapid pace of **change** in Information Technology is a further exacerbating factor increasing the likelihood of disasters.

1) **Changes in Hardware**—According to Moore's Law, hardware doubles in power every 18 months. As a result, hardware continues to evolve rapidly. Furthermore, entirely new kinds of hardware appear and must be

integrated into existing systems.

2) **Changes in Software**—New software releases fuel revenue streams in the software industry, resulting in mandatory "upgrades" every two years. The changes create an additional learning burden on users. Programmers are again under time pressure that can result in poor testing and de-bugging (Halfhill, 1998), (Westland, 2000), (Austin, 2001).

In addition to these first order effect, Lally also argues that changes in IT create second order effects by enabling changes in organizational processes. These processes can also become more complex, tightly coupled, and poorly controlled, further increasing the problem of serious accidents. As a result, IT managers and users are faced with complex, tightly coupled, poorly controlled systems that undergo radical changes on a regular basis, making these systems more prone to "Normal Accidents".

LESSONS FROM Y2K

By the late 1990s, a significant number of researchers and IT professionals were highly concerned about catastrophic IT failures. They believed that the design flaw of representing years with only two significant digits would propagate throughout the global infrastructure causing widespread failures. Perrow (1999, p. 392) argued that "Y2K has the potential for making a linear, loosely coupled system more complex and tightly coupled than anyone had reason to anticipate". Perrow emphasized that Y2K made him more keenly aware of the problem of "unknowability":

One of the key themes of the theory, but not one formalized as much as it could have been, was the notion of incomprehensibility—What has happened? How could such a thing have happened? And What will happen next? This indicated that observers did not know what was going on and did not know what would happen next. The system was in an unknowable state (Perrow, 1999, p.293).

Not only were managers and users unaware, programmers were unlikely to know the real world impacts of the programs they wrote. One programmer who worked for the Federal Reserve System only became aware of what the Federal Reserve actually did during the Y2K crisis, "I read an article about how the Federal Reserve would crash everything if it went bad…I discovered we were kind of important" (Ullman, 1999, p. 4).

Lally (1999) also argued that the radical changes that IT programming, hardware and telecommunications had undergone in 40 years made the global infrastructure even more unknowable, and Y2K incidents even harder to isolate and their impacts harder to trace. Date representation errors were found in 40 year old COBOL code whose programmers had long since moved on to other careers and who, even if they could be located would be unlikely to still be able to read and de-bug the code.

By the late 1990s, computer systems were increasingly integrated and spanned organizational, and even global boundaries. Y2K failures in one organization, therefore, were likely to propagate to other organizations and to the economy as a whole. Y2K practitioners referred to this as the "ripple effect" (Kirsner, 1997).

One patched together, wrapped up system exchanges data with another patched together wrapped up system—layer upon layer of software involved in a single transaction until the possibility of failure increases exponentially (Ullman, 1999, p. 7).

On a global level, the lack of compliance by many countries lead airlines to consider practicing a form of fault isolation, establishing "no-fly zones" over non-compliant countries (Anson, 1999). Concern was also been expressed about potential cross border damage between countries that were Y2K compliant and those that were not. As a result of many countries' non-compliance, Ed Yardeni, Chief Economist at Deutsche Morgan Grenfell predicted that there was a 60% chance that Y2K will lead to a global recession (Golter & Hawry, 1998).

Isenberg (1999) argued that only "social coherence," the ability for individuals to pool their knowledge and work together for the common good, could minimize the impact of Y2K disasters. Having redundancy, in terms of backup systems, and slack, in terms of time and personnel needed to contain incidents and keep damaged systems running, is another key to survivability suggested by the Theory of High Reliability Organizations. Lally (1997), however, argued that organizations which have eliminated human labor during reengineering efforts in favor of computers would have fewer resources to keep the critical systems running manually, should computers fail. Other Y2K researchers agreed:

The "slack time" that could have been devoted to addressing the year 2000 issue before it became urgent has been deliberately cut out of the system in the search for leaner and meaner business processes. Furthermore, because they now lack the internal resources to handle the year 2000 problem, companies who have been through BPR downsizing will be forced to outsource the Year 2000 problem. Ironically, this contract could end up in the hands of the very consultants who advocated their BPR process in the first place (Gerner, 1998, p 144).

Y2K, therefore, was also characterized as a problem where poor control—the absence of redundancy, slack or the potential for social coherence—could exacerbate the damage.

Y2K came and went with a number of local failures but no major catastrophes. Failures happened within individual systems, but the "ripple effect" did not materialize as a serious threat. Y2K did succeed in raising the level of awareness on the part of managers regarding IT security. However, a number of managers who spent thousands of dollars preparing for Y2K only to have it be a minor problem, accused Y2K practitioner of "crying wolf," claiming catastrophic disasters were unlikely to happen.

9/11/01-WHAT HAS HAPPENED? HOW COULD SUCH A THING HAPPEN? WHAT WILL HAPPEN NEXT?

On September 11, 2001, a surprise terrorist attack left the world wondering,"What has happened? How could such a thing Happen? What will Happen Next?" The damage caused by the initial impact of the planes quickly spread destroying the World Trade Center and causing massive destruction and loss of life in lower Manhattan.

The Y2K problem was an innocent error, recognized ahead of time, and prevented from causing catastrophic failures. 9/11 was a deliberate, well organized, surprise attack that caused catastrophic damage before the military, the police, or the thousands of individuals who lost their lives could do anything to circumvent it. The prediction of the Y2K bug causing a worldwide recession did not come true. 9/11, however, will have serious global economic ramifications for years to come.

Responding to terrorism will be a more complex task,"…as John Koskinen, former head of the government's Y2K effort, remarked recently, "Unlike the Y2K Phenomenon, today's terrorist threat to IT is undefined, the response is difficult, and there is no known time frame," (Yourdon, 2002, p. 29).

A number of parallels, however, do emerge between the two events that can provide insight for preventing and/or mitigating the impacts of future terrorist attacks. Both emphasized the importance of planning for catastrophic failures. Some organizations indicated that their Y2K planning helped them mitigate the damage caused by 9/11 (Merian, 2001). Pressure is on from the business community to re-create the U.S. government effort in combating the Y2K problem as a means of combating terrorism (Thibodeau, 2001). This paper will argue that Y2K, therefore, provides a useful starting point in analyzing the 9/11 disaster.

RECOGNIZING AN INCIDENT AND UNDERSTANDING ITS POTENTIAL IMPACT

From a Normal Accident Theory perspective, a number of critical issues emerge regarding 9/11. First, what was the "incident" that needed to be recognized? Was it:

1) The first plane hitting the North Tower—at which point a serious problem became "knowable"?
2) The second plane hitting the South Tower—at which point a terrorist attack could be identified as occurring?

At this point there was no need to convince anyone that a serious problem existed. Here we can clearly distinguish between the "intellectual" threat of Y2K, which required large numbers of technical experts to convince the public of its seriousness and the "visceral" threat experienced by anyone viewing the 9/11 disaster. This paper will argue that although the plane crashes propagated into even greater destruction, the first plane crash was already an "accident" leading to massive destruction and loss of life. Incidents preceding this event, if intercepted, could have prevented its occurrence. Examples of such incidents include:

1) Terrorists boarding the planes.
2) Discovering the existence of the 9/11 plot.
3) Hearing a young man say he wishes to learn how to steer an airliner, but not how to take off and land.

However, recognizing a potential terrorist and uncovering a terrorist plot is a challenging intelligence task, which is likely to result in many "false positives" with serious implications for individual privacy. Individuals detecting these incidents will be in a much more difficult position in terms of convincing others that a serious problem exists. One approach is to adopt suggestions from High Reliability Theory to create a decentralized High Reliability culture where individuals are encouraged to report information they consider threatening. "..we need to make it easier for front line observers to communicate their warnings quickly and effectively, without worrying about being criticized as alarmists," (Yourdon, 2002, p. 199). More sophisticated IT based methods are also available (Verton, 2002). Customer Relationship Management software, such as that used by Amazon books to detect patterns in buyer behavior, can also be used to detect patterns of suspicious behavior. If initial fears are confirmed, collaborative projects can help make early warnings more widely available. Isenberg's theory of social coherence where individuals and organizations co-operate in sharing information also supports this approach.

MODELING THE UNTHINKABLE: MITIGATING THE IMPACT OF TERRORIST ATTACKS

On 9/11, many lives were lost after the initial impact of the two planes because bad judgements based on incomplete information were made by individuals working in the towers, as well as by firemen and police. This was particularly true in the North Tower. Individuals remained in the upper portion of the North Tower hoping to be rescued despite the fact that they were unreachable and that one stairway was still passable. Firemen continued climbing up into the lower portion of the North Tower despite the fact that the South Tower had collapsed and they were in imminent danger. Incompatible communication devices prevented critical information from reaching the firefighters (Dwyer, 2002). However, wireless communication devices, emails and other Internet communication did increase social coherence during the disaster. Victims said goodbye to loved ones, and the passengers on Flight 93 were able to mitigate the impact of the disaster they had become a part of. Regular business communication took place over employee cell phones and personal Internet accounts (Disabatino, 2002), (Kontzer, 2002).

Simulation models of the building, such as those designed afterward (see Nova's "Why the Towers Fell"), could be used to minimize the problem of "unknowability" that resulted in so many deaths. Office workers in all large complex buildings could use these models to develop optimal evacuation plans during an emergency. Firemen could train by simulating rescue missions in all large complex buildings in their area. Finally, in terms of social coherence, good communication between structural engineers, who are best able to determine the condition of the building, and the workers and firemen inside could also save hundreds of lives.

CONCLUSION AND IMPLICATIONS FOR FURTHER RESEARCH

IT based communication tools for improved Incident Detection and increased Social Coherence appear to have significant potential for preventing malicious attacks. Simulation models that would reduce Unknowability and further increase Social Coherence would help mitigate the impacts of attacks that have already occurred. Further research is needed as to how best to design and implement these technologies in a manner that is, technically and economically feasible, as well as being sensitive to individual privacy rights.

Finally, this analysis needs to be extended to other kinds of malicious acts. 9/11 was remarkable because of the relatively low degree of technologi-

cal sophistication needed to make it happen. A second kind of terrorist attack, E-terrorism, in which terrorists exploit their knowledge of the complex, tightly coupled, poorly controlled and continually changing global infrastructure to create disasters will be the focus of future research.

REFERENCES

Anson, R.S. (1999). 12.31.99. Vanity Fair, January, 80-84.

Austin, R. (2001). "The Effects of Time Pressure on Quality in Software Development" Information Systems Research, June, pp. 195-207.

Disabatino, J. (2001). "Internet Messaging Keeps Businesses, Employees, in Touch," Computerworld, September 17.

Dwyer, J. (2002) "Radio Problem Could Last Years", New York Times, September, 18.

Gerner, M. (1998). Five More Reasons Many Delayed From Year 2000: Best Practices for Y2K Millenium Computing. D. Lefkon, Editor. Upper Saddle River, New Jersey, Prentice Hall Publishers.

Golter, J. & Hawry, P. (1998). Circles of Risk. http://year2000.com/archive/circlesrisk.html.

Halfhill, T. (1998) Crash-Proof Computing. BYTE www.byte.com/art/9804/sec5/art1.html.

Isenberg, D. (1999). "SMART Letter $16." www.isen.com, February 1.

Kirsner, S. (1998). The Ripple Effect. http://www.cio.archive/y2k_ripple_content.html.

Kontzer, T. (2001). "With Phone Lines Bottlenecked, Internet Messaging Became Lifeline," Information Week, September, 12.

Lally. L. (1996). "Enumerating the Risks of Reengineered Processes," Proceedings of 1996 ACM Computer Science Conference, 18-23.

Lally, L. (1997). "Are Reengineered Organizations Disaster Prone?" Proceedings of the National Decision Sciences Conference, pp. 178-182.

Lally, L. (1999). "The Y2K Problem: Normal Accident Theory and High Reliability Organization Theory Perspectives," Proceedings of the 1999 National Decision Sciences Conference, pp. 234-237.

Lally, L. (2000). "Pre-Employment Screening for Reengineered Jobs: Issues in Information Access and Information Privacy," Proceedings of the National Decision Science Conference, 2000, pp. 371-373.

Lally, L. and Garbushian, B. (2001). "Hiring in the Post-Reengineering Environment:A Study Using Situationally Conditioned Belief," Proceedings of the International Information Resources Management Conference, pp. 234-237.

Lally, L. (2002). "Complexity, Coupling, Control and Change: An IT Based Extension to Normal Accident Theory," Proceedings of the International Information Resources Management Conference, upcoming.

LaPorte, T. R. & Consolini. P. (1991). "Working in Practice But Not in Theory: Theoretical Challenges of High Reliability Organizations" Journal of Public Administration, 1, 19-47.

Merian, L. (2001). "Y2K Plans Aided in Recovery, But More Planning Needed," Computerworld, September, 19.

Perrow, Charles. (1984) Normal Accidents: Living with High Risk Technologies, New York: Basic Books.

Perrow, Charles. (1999) Normal Accidents: Living with High Risk Technologies 2nd Edition, New York, Basic Books.

Sagan, Scott. (1993). The Limits of Safety. Princeton New Jersey: Princeton University Press.

Ullman, E. (1999). The Myth of Order Wired. http://wired.com/archive/7.04/y2k_pr.html.

Thibodeau, P. (2001). "Businesses Eye Y2K Effort as Model for Terrorism Fight," Computerworld, October 2.

Verton, D. (2002). IT Key to Antiterror Defenses at Nation's Sea Ports,"Computerworld, January 12.

Westland, J. C. (2000). "Modeling the Incidence of Postrelease Errors in Software" Information Systems Research, September, pp. 320-324.

Yourdon, E. (2002). Byte Wars: The Impact of September 11 on Information Technology, New Jersey: Pre ntice Hall.

Web Based Education to Prepare Health Information Management (HIM) Students in the Realm of Coding

Marcia M. Andrews
Rehoboth McKinley Christian Healthcare Services

ABSTRACT

For health care, trained personnel is increasingly important, especially health information management (HIM) professionals. Within this group of HIM professionals, the demand is great for in-patient International Classification of Diseases, Ninth Revision, Clinical Modifications (ICD-9-CM) certified coding professionals (coders). The use of an effective integrated information system (IS) is the basis for success in today's highly competitive health care market. Therefore, preparation of the workforce to handle complexities and sophistication of such IS and HIM is paramount for viability. The current environment for coding is computer based technology. Convergence taking place in computing and telecommunications plays a very important role in this endeavor.

INTRODUCTION

One of the circumstances causing great impact in the realm of computing is convergence, taking place with computing and telecommunications. Organizations in general are able to perceive the capabilities of combining the hegemony of computer based information and telecommunications networks (6) and the rapid evolution of the Internet and Intranet extant play a preponderant role in this new array. A primary user of computer based information and telecommunications is the health care industry, and in this sector, as with any industry utilizing these tools, it is emphasized that the drivers of the information revolution are cost, computing power, and convergence (5). These parameters are inter-related to computing infrastructure, new communication technology and the access to the technology. The research literature is rich in opinions regarding Nolan's Model, perhaps because he was a pioneer in relating computer technology and its use within the organizations and/or is a suitable approach to determine the stage of an organization in regard to computer technology. Nolan's Model is not universally accepted as he described it at the time of its inception in 1979, but neither is universally rejected (4). According to Nolan's Model the Institutions of High Learning employ a setting in which technology is a driving force to improve learning. Most of them are located in Stage IV: Integration. The most basic classroom topology regarding the use of technology is the one in which the instructor uses a computer, has access to a network connection and also to a projection system. A much better setting is the one in which the instructor uses a laptop, has access to the network connection and a projection system. In both settings described above, the students have a minor or no participation whatsoever. To obtain student participation, it is necessary to design a setup in which the end-user (students) will be able use a computer with network connections. The latter is the typical description of a computer lab. A better setting would be the one in which student has a laptop, network connection linked to the Internet and the teacher has direct interaction with the students (9).

For health care, available trained personnel is increasingly important, especially health information management (HIM) professionals. In particular, there is great demand for in-patient International Classification of Diseases, Ninth Revision, Clinical Modifications (ICD-9-CM) certified coding professionals (coders). The American Health Information Management Association (AHIMA) is the professional association that develops the testing and certifying of such professionals. However, the manner in which these professionals are trained is available through varying methods such as on-the-job, work-

shops, or in institutions of higher learning. Whatever the method, the field is requiring a greater level of hands-on training involving increasing sophistication in the areas of computing technology. Such interaction allows the teacher to interact with them on a one-to-one basis, or even in groups. Add to the latter, a software program with database capabilities and there will be ability to play scenarios, and sensitivity analysis to replicate real life situations in the classroom.

The use of an effective integrated information system (IS) is the basis for success in the highly competitive healthcare environment today. The Bureau of Labor Statistics cites health information technology (HIT) as one of the 20 fastest growing occupations in the US (2). Therefore, preparation of a workforce to handle the complexities of such IS and HIM is vital. It has been stated that factors preventing adoption of integrated healthcare IS may be a lack of user acceptance. The research literature concurs that as many as half of all IS fail because of user and staff resistance (11). Throughout the US, HIM instruction and training in the form of accredited (and some non-accredited) health information technology (HIT) programs, have begun to inculcate into curriculums, IS learning. Thanks to accrediting bodies, standards include requirements for this type of learning (8).

In the (HIT) classroom, more emphasis is being placed on providing situations with which the student will be faced in his or her day-to-day endeavors. Along with the hands-on type training, the student must learn the theoretical importance extant in choosing and implementing a successful IS in the realm of healthcare. As with most businesses, there must be a marriage of delivering a quality product with reduced costs. Although integrated information systems are vital to the delivery of high-quality care at a competitive price, many healthcare organizations have not yet implemented them. The primary factor limiting their implementation is cost (11).

Premise of the Paper

The purpose of this paper is to demonstrate the enhancement of learning using convergence to replicate in the classroom, situations that will educate and prepare students for professional roles within the Health Information Management (HIM) industry.

BACKGROUND

The dynamic professional association known as AHIMA represents more than 40,000 specially educated HIM professionals working throughout the health care industry (1). AHIMA traces its history back more than 70 years. At that time, the American College of Surgeons (ACS) established the Association of Record Librarians of North America (ARLNA) to "elevate the standards of clinical records in hospitals and other medical institutions." The association has undergone several name changes and is now known as AHIMA. This decision was based largely as a result of the health care industry ongoing restructuring and decision-making increasingly driven by data. AHIMA supports the common goal of applying modern technology to and advancing best practices in HIM (3). Credentialing and certification/registration offered by AHIMA today include Registered Health Information Administrator (RHIA), Registered Health Information Technician (RHIT), Certified Coding Specialist (CCS), Certified Coding Specialist – Physician-based (CCS-P), and Certified Coding Associate (CCA) (12.) The coding credentials have been developed most recently and are of great importance to a health care facility's financial viability. Hospitals or medical providers report coded data to third party payors, i.e., insurance companies, HMO's, Medicaid and Medicare for reimbursement of their expenses. The accuracy and validity of coding, then, directly impacts the revenues, as well as providing descriptions of the facility's health outcomes (7) through the gathering of data from patient records.

The literature describes coding as "transforming verbal descriptions of diseases, injuries, conditions, and procedures into numerical designations (codes)". In addition to the financial implications inherent in coding, it has enabled health care facilities and associated agencies to tabulate, store, and retrieve disease, injury, and procedure-related data (10).

Finally, coding for out-patient reimbursement purposes took on its greatest significance in 1983 with the passage of legislation requiring all Medicare visits to have some form of code attached to the encounter. Then, following legislation enacted the prospective payment system (PPS) utilizing diagnostic-related groups (DRGs- an inpatient classification scheme that categorizes patient who share similar clinical and cost characteristics) (10). DRGs are established based on the ICD-9-CM codes, reflecting the verbal descriptions of disease, etc. or diagnoses and procedures, that the coder is able to abstract from the medical record.

From the humble beginnings of AHIMA in 1928, the profession, and in particular, coding, has demanded increased education to produce qualified professionals with abilities in technology and computing convergence.

DISCUSSION

The current environment for coding is computer-based technology. Therefore, the main requirement for learning is a setting in which the appropriate tools are utilized. These must allow the student to transition smoothly from learning, to actual practice in which highly sophisticated information systems are extant. The tools must have the ability to present the student with realistic scenarios that he or she will encounter in the health care work place.

These situations should also lessen the barriers of utilizing advanced technology when the student begins his or her career.

In the classroom setting, utilizing remote server capabilities with internet-ready laptops, is demonstrating success as the type of learning environment described above. The paradigm common in the research literature defines computer information systems as being composed of the following: 1) hardware, 2) software, 3) data, 4) procedures, 5) personnel (end-user) and 6) communication links (in this particular case, Internet). These aforementioned components will be the framework to describe the learning setting. Hardware includes a wireless mobile computer lab containing 24 laptops providing portability enabling the instructor to set the learning environment anywhere. This provides flexibility for instruction due to the interaction with the students. Software utilized for this type of training is proprietary and resides on an Internet website. Usage is based on site licensing. However, the student may access the lessons anywhere there are Internet capabilities. The software provides self-paced instruction and self- assessment capabilities as feedback to the student on his or her progress. Hyperlinks give the required flexibility to enhance learning. There is a variety of HIT subjects available, including basic and advanced training to perform ICD-9-CM coding in particular. Because of the legislative nature of the subject involving Federal reimbursement of health care, the software provider annually upgrades the content to maintain the accuracy of the education. The software contains enough data to replicate actual ICD-9-CM coding scenarios. The data is embedded in the software. Procedures (instructions for use of the software) are self-explanatory. The end-user, in this case, the students, will have the ability to perform coding duties similar to those presented in actual practice. The high-learning institution is located

at Stage IV: Integration, therefore, the facilities provide radio wave wireless connection that allows the use of portable labs, ergo the use of the Internet which increases flexibility, accessibility, efficiency of learning and lowers cost.

Proficiency in coding is determined through the instructor's presenting scenarios in the form of case studies in which the student utilizes knowledge gained through the use of the software. This presents the student with the application of critical thinking to assign the appropriate coding nomenclature as would be presented in a real-life situation. Grading is assigned based on this ability to apply knowledge with skill and accuracy. The ultimate goal is for them to be able to pass one of AHIMA's coding examinations for certification in this field.

The latter makes the learning environment more realistic and creates the necessary motivation for the students' enhancement. Anonymous feedback from students involved in this type of e-learning indicates their appreciation of the use of advanced information technology and their feelings of adequacy when employed in the HIM field. The health care community is also eager to embrace his type of training for those already employed.

For the success of this type of training and educating, questions for the HIM educator and provider of software applications include, but are not limited to the following:

- How to keep continually updated and upgraded in the realm of HIM and health care in general due to the great fluctuation inherent therein?
- How to adequately provide a smooth transition from the educational environment to the workplace?
- How to network effectively within the community to encourage both students and health care employees to take advantage of educational resources pertaining to advanced computing technologies?

REFERENCES

1.   *About AHIMA.* (n.d.). Retrieved September 25, 2002, from http://www.ahima.org/about/main.htm

2.   *AHIMA Careers.* (n.d.). Retrieved September 25, 2002, from http://www.ahima.org/careers/growth01.html.

3.   AHIMA History. *(n.d.). Retrieved September 25, 2002 from http://www.ahima.org/about/history.htm*

4.   Anderson, D. & R. C. Reid (1998). A study of the growth of information system function and the Nolan development model. *Journal of Computer Information Systems*, Vol. XXXVIII, No. 3, Spring, 44-52.

5.   Bond, J. (1997). *Public Policy for the Private Sector.* The World Bank Group, Note No. 118, July.

6.   Carr, H. H. & C. A. Snyder. (1997). *The Management of Telecommunications: Business Solutions to Business Problems.* New York: Irwin McGraw Hill, 680-682.

7.   Certified coding specialist (CCS). (n.d.). Retrieved September 25, 2002, from http://www.ahima.org/certification/cert.cred.html

8.   Commission on Accreditation of Allied Health Education Programs. (1997). *Standards and guidelines for an accredited educational program for the health information technician & health information administrator.*

9.   Levine, L. (2002). Using technology to enhance the classroom environment. *T. H. E. Journal*, Vol. 29, Issue 6, 16-18

10.   Rogers, V. L. (1998). *Applying inpatient coding skills under prospective payment.* Chicago: American Health Information Management Association, 2.

11.   Wager, K. A. & F. W. Lee. (2002). Introduction to healthcare information systems. In M. Johns (Ed.), *Health Information Management Technology: An Applied Approach* (pp. 558-588). Chicago: AHIMA.

12.   *What are the credentials?* (n.d.). Retrieved September 25, 2002 from   http://www.ahima.org/certification/cert.cred.html

Mathematical Statistics in SW Engineering Education

Jaroslav Král, Michal Zemlicka
Dept. of Software Engineering
Faculty of Mathematics and Physics, Charles University, Prague
Malostranské nám. 25, 118 00 Praha 1, Czech Republic
Phone: +420 221 914 263, Fax:v+420 221 914 323
{kral,zemlicka}@ksi.mff.cuni.cz

ABSTRACT

The methods of mathematical statistics play an increasing role in SW engineering. Mathematical statistics is necessary to understand the functions of many applications as well as to mature SW development methods (proposed by CMM [CMM]). Mathematical statistics is the kernel of the analysis of software metrics. The analysis of software metrics must be used during the evaluation of the properties and impacts of software systems. The problem with mathematical statistics is that computer science students dislike it and are unable to use it. They like the simple Boolean (or black-and-white) world of computers too much. The importance of mathematical statistics and the attitude borrowed from experimental sciences is not even recognized by lecturers. The way to change this situation is discussed.

INTRODUCTION

SW systems grow, are more complex and support continually more complex functions using larger and larger data bodies. It is hardly possible without sophisticated methods of data analysis based on mathematical statistics. The complicated software systems cannot be developed or customized without modern management methods using data of software metrics (see the standard ISO 9126 and the recommendations CMM [CMM]).

It is well known (see e.g. [SG]) that the deficiencies in requirements specification and management errors during development customization are the leading triggers of the failures of SW systems, especially of information systems.

According to the experience of the authors gained via the development of SW systems and teaching at several universities the root reason of the failures is the improper (if any) use of the methods of mathematical statistics during requirement specification (offering proper management methods, the use of software metrics).

The solution of such problem is quite difficult as the computer professionals are not trained enough in mathematical statistics – and it is not recognized as important (compare [IS 2002, MSIS 2000]) although it is important (see [Král86]).

THE ROLE OF STATISTICS IN INFORMATION SYSTEMS

The growing data bodies collected by modern information systems (IS) and/or accessible via WWW cannot be analyzed properly without methods of mathematical statistics. The tools based on mathematical statistics must be also used if we want to measure the impacts and/or the effects (e.g. the financial ones) of modern software systems, especially of information systems. Statistical analysis should be included into the methodologies of the evaluation and testing of experimental laws and dependencies between software metrics like the dependency between the system development effort and the system size.

The tools of statistical analysis offered by many enterprise software systems (like workflow systems, production planning, and OLAP) are as a rule quite weak, if any. The methods of mathematical statistics are difficult to understand and/or to use for computer professionals as well as for many users. Many computer professionals strongly dislike statistical methods (and - more generally - the attitude of experimental sciences).

Modern SW development and software maintenance and/or use (SW processes) must include the collection and the analysis of software metrics. The maturity of a software firm can be - to a high degree – characterized by the quality of the collection and analysis of SW metrics (compare CMM maturity degrees).

Many software development techniques (e.g. the decision whether to stop testing and to release the system for distribution/use, the detection whether a system is "worn out" and should be cancelled/reengineered, [Rajlich, KZ02b]) depend on a proper use of the tools of mathematical statistics and the philosophy of experimental sciences (compare [Král98, KT2000]). The example of the Critical Chain method by Goldratt [Gold] indicate that there can be very surprising application of mathematical statistics in project planning.

Mathematical statistics should play an important, may be the crucial, role in software engineering, software science, and software use. It is not, however, generally recognized.

TEACHING OF MATHEMATICAL STATISTICS

Mathematical statistics is a science requiring a lot of mathematical knowledge and skills. If lectures on mathematical statistics are included into a curriculum a lot of lectures on mathematical analysis and probability theory must be included as well particularly in the case when mathematical statistics is presented as an abstract mathematical discipline. This implies that we must sacrifice some software-oriented lectures (e.g. lectures on latest programming languages). It is quite painful but it is not the main problem.

As the formal lectures on mathematical statistics must (should) be preceded by lectures on mathematical analysis and probability theory, they cannot be presented not earlier than third year of undergraduate curriculum (UC). It is quite unpleasant as it implies that we are unable to use mathematical statistics in software-oriented lectures in the first and second year and partially in the third year of UC. The result is that the students are not trained to use the methods of mathematical statistics during training basic software development skills. In fact it makes the lectures on mathematical statistics to a high degree useless due to student mental barriers and the lack of good inspiring examples. If the students learn computer-oriented lectures only they tend to consider all knowledge, problems, and skills not strictly related to computers useless and boring. We call such a narrow-minded attitude *hacker syndrome*. Hacker syndrome disqualifies computer professional for many upper level activities like the requirement specification with collaboration with users, teamwork, planning and audit, etc. Hacker syndrome disqualifies students from doing management. Even the lower management levels (like small team leadership) need a non-black-and-white way of thinking. The syndrome is very difficult to cure. Prevention is better. The prevention can be achieved via lectures on mathematical statistics and experimental sciences during the first study year. It would have some other advantages discussed below.

WHY COMPUTER PROFESSIONALS OFTEN DISLIKE MATHEMATICAL STATISTICS

Computer professionals often dislike mathematical statistics and are not able to use it. Some reasons for it are discussed in the previous paragraph. A further reason can be (with some simplification) characterized as a too strong emphasis on mathematical statistics as a mathematical discipline.

Software professionals tend like the black and white way of thinking. They dislike "gray" cases. In other words they are not happy if they must/may apply attitudes of experimental sciences like physics and to some degree economy and some humanities with experimental features like sociology or psychology.

We are convinced that the lack of knowledge and of paradigms of experimental sciences is a large drawback for computer professionals due to the following facts:

- It limits the application capability maturity principles from CMM.
- It is an obstacle for the application of modern management principles in the SW project management.
- The modern SW architectures like SW confederations [KZ02a, KZ02c] depend on the ability of developers to understand the functions of components and the functions often contain some function/knowledge of mathematical statistics.
- Optimality problems of SW confederations (i.e. peer-to-peer networks of applications/services) should be solved with the help of the tools of mathematical statistics.

It is interesting that in the Czech Republic many top information technology professionals are physicists.

In the long term the introduction of experimental/statistical paradigms could increase the adaptability of SW professionals in the changing world and to increase their chances to take part in well-paid and prestigious activities like requirement specification or management. The teaching of mathematical statistics can induce students to learn some experimental sciences (physics, sociology) to gain the paradigms common for all experimental sciences. It will increase the ability of the students to take part in the early stages of software development and to work and maintain the system during the system use. Last but not least it increases the ability of the students to work outside software firms. It can prevent the hacker syndrome and equip our students with useful knowledge and skills.

WHEN AND HOW TO TEACH MATHEMATICAL STATISTICS

The teaching of mathematical statistics should be based on a good theoretical background. But it implies that mathematical statistics cannot be taught early enough. If it is the case, the hacker syndrome can appear. It then results into resistance of students against mathematical statistics. This blind alley can be resolved in the following way:

We propose to teach mathematical statistics in two stages. The first step can be based on very elementary knowledge of probability theory and mathematical statistics (sometimes not too deeper than the knowledge obtained at grammar schools) an on the analysis of typical problems of the analysis of software metrics. Examples are: When to stop testing, when a system is to be reengineered, server capacity estimation, error prone components, software quality control, optimal project size, etc. Some tools from CASE systems like Together [Tog] can be used here. The teaching of the application of mathematical statistics should be accompanied by a lecture on some experimental science (sociology, financial controlling, experimental physics). Such lecture should include application of mathematical statistics on experimental data. The students can use a statistical software package.

The second stage can be based on more formal lectures on mathematical statistics discussed above. The formal lectures should again contain enough computer and software related examples. The mathematical statistics should be presented with the aim how to use it, not as an abstract mathematical discipline. This schema is about to be applied at some faculties of Masaryk University in Brno, Czech Republic.

CONCLUSIONS

The teaching of probability theory and mathematical statistics tend to be crucial part of the computer science education. Besides the points mentioned above (application in SW development, implementation of useful functions in applications, a greater adaptability of students, etc.) it forms a good background for the computer science research like probabilistic algorithms, simulations, relevance of software metrics, effectiveness of new software methods, quality of the software (e.g. reliability, effectiveness) etc. Moreover it can prevent the symptoms of the hacker syndrome or hacker like attitude. The importance of statistical methods is not pointed enough in the curricula [MSIS 2000, IS 2002].

The main aim is to change the attitude of the students to statistical methods as well as to experimental sciences. Note that while the trends in many professions increase the extension of the use of computers, for the computer professionals the trend could be "less computers, more common sense". Note that computer professionals often do not collect the data needed for later statistical research or metrics. People even do not care about generation and usage of log files and other easily available sources.

REFERENCES

[CMM] Carnegie Mellon University, Software Engineering Institute (Paulk, M.C., Weber, C.V., Curtis, B., & Chrissis, M.B.), *The Capability Maturity Model: Guidelines for Improving the Software Process*, Addison-Wesley Publishing Company, Reading, MA, 1995.

[MSIS 2000] Feinstein, D.L., Kasper, G.M., Luftman, J.N., Stohr, E.A., Valacich, J.S, & Wigand, R.T.: MSIS 2000 – Model Curriculum and Guidelines for Graduate Degree Programs in Information Systems. ACM, 1999.

[Gold] Goldratt, E.M.: *Critical Chain*, North River Press, Great Barrington, MA.

[IS 2002] Gorgone, J.T., Davis, G.B., Valacich, J.S., Topi, H., Feinstein, D.L., & Longenecker, H.E, Jr.: *IS 2002 – Model Curriculum and Guidelines for Undergraduate Degree Programs in Information Systems*. Association for Information Systems, 2002.

[Král86] Král, J.: Software Physics and Software Paradigms. In: Kugler, H.-J. (Ed.) *Information Processing 86*. Elsevier Science Publishers, B.V. (North-Holland), 1986. pp. 129-134.

[Král98] Král, J.: *Informaní systémy*, (Information systems, in Czech) Science, Veletiny, 1998, 356 pp.

[KT2000] Král, J., & Töpfer, P.: Education of software experts for a changing world. In: Pudlowski, Z., J. (Ed.): *Proceedings of 2nd Global Congress on Engineering Education*. Wismar, Germany, 2000.

[KZ02a] Král, J., & Zemlicka, M.: Component Types in Software Confederations. In: Hamza, M.H. (Ed.) *Applied Informatics*. ACTA Press, Anaheim, 2002, ISBN: 0-88986-322-9, ISSN: 1027-2666. pp. 125-130.

[KZ02b] Král, J., & Zemlicka, M.: Software Confederations and the Maintenance of Global Software Systems. In: *Software Maintenance and Reengineering*. Budapest, 2002. pp. 61-66.

[KZ02c] Král, J., & Zemlicka, M.: Global Management and Software Confederations. In: Khosrowpour, M. (Ed.): *Issues & Trends of Information Technology Management in Contemporary Organizations*. Idea Group Publishing, 2002. ISBN: 1-930708-39-4.

[Pressman] Pressman, R.S.: *Software Engineering: A Practitioner's Approach*. 5th edition. McGraw-Hill, 2001.

[Rajlich] Rajlich, V.: A staged Model of Software Evolution. In: *Proceedings of 6th European Conference on Software Maintenance and Reengineering (CSMR 2002)*, IEEE Computer Society Press, 2002.

[Som2000] Sommerville, I.: *Software Engineering*. 5th edition. Addison-Wesley, 2000. ISBN 0-201-42765-6.

[SG] http://www.standishgroup.com/chaos.html.

[Tog] http://www.togethersoft.com A Together company homepage.

Construction, Communication and Caring for Contextual Workflows: Scenarios from Homeland Defense

Edward J. Glantz and Sandeep Purao
School of Information Sciences and Technology, Pennsylvania State University
315 Beam Business Administration Building, 3F Joab L. Thomas Building, University Park, PA 16802
phone: 814-863-7243, fax 863-2381, 814-865-4461
ejg8@psu.edu, Sandeep-purao@psu.edu

INTRODUCTION

Exception handling[1] (van der Aalst, Basten et al. 2000) and adaptive workflows[2] (Rahm 2000) represent two prevalent directions to handling adjustments to workflows brought on by unexpected changes. The two directions suggest somewhat different approaches to workflow adjustments, the former involves direct adjustments at the case (instance) level, and the later addresses adjustments based on knowledge available at the definition (meta) level. The adjustment problems, however, can become severe, when the workflow instances occupy a large footprint in time and space. First, long-lived workflows need to withstand changes in the environment. Second, workflows spread across multiple organizations need to respect the decentralized, and sometimes, conflicting goals of the participants.

Issues that need attention to support such workflows include goal-articulation, goal-communication, and goal-sharing. Goal-based approaches[3] (Kuechler and Vaishnavi 1998) address some of these concerns. However, they fail to address these adequately in response to changes in environment. Nickerson (Nickerson 2003) describes a limited exploration of these issues by suggesting an alternative to workflow reference models (Hollingsworth 1995), with the use of sequence diagrams (to capture the distinction between human actors and machine processes). Luo et al (2002) suggest a bundled exception-handling approach that includes case-based intelligent reasoning and reuse of exceptions for cross-organizational exception handling processes to resolve workflow failures[4]. Both the Luo and Nickerson approaches, however, cannot account for important workflow components such as resource restrictions, roles, responsibilities, and explicit goal-articulation – concerns that become more relevant for large-footprint workflows. In a world, where long-lived workflows across organizational boundaries are likely to occur with some frequency, a comprehensive approach is necessary for their construction, communication and caring.

In this paper, we use multiple homeland defense scenarios (including one similar to that used by Nickerson (Nickerson 2003) with a view to *identifying key issues that need to be addressed in workflows that possess a large footprint in space and time*. Specifically, we focus on the articulation of goals, their evolution, and sharing across time and space to guide the monitoring of long-lived workflows that take place across multiple organizations.

PRIOR RESEARCH

Most current approaches to exception handling involve drawing on a knowledge-base stored at the meta-level. A few approaches allow dealing with these problems on a case by case basis, allowing human participants to intervene and adjust the workflow as desired, resulting in evolutionary changes that are ordered and result in universal changes (van der Aalst, Basten et al. 2000). Both can result in coordination and tracking problems referred to as dynamic change bugs (van der Aalst and Basten 2002). Dynamic change bugs cause errors either within the ability of a case to maintain its integrity or omissions that affect the ability to track and report changed processes (van der Aalst and Basten 2002). Inheritance-preserving transformation rules have been proposed for workflow processes, with the intention of eliminating the dynamic change bug (van der Aalst and Basten 2002). Situations exist, however, where the quality of the process implementation is not necessarily within the control of the workflow designer and their carefully devised workflows using inheritance. This is a typical situation for workflow processes that are spread across organizations, where goals are not likely to be aligned or shared (Zhuge). We present multiple homeland defense scenarios, which serve as specific instantiations of these types of workflows, which in turn allow us to identify and articulate important problems that must be tackled as important research questions.

Homeland Defense Scenarios

We describe and briefly analyze three specific homeland security scenarios to illustrate practical challenges to large-footprint workflow processes in a changing environment, and non-aligned or conflicting goals across participants in each scenario. The first scenario refers to the process used by the army for adjudicating security clearances. The second scenario introduces the early stages of an automated workflow process by the U.S. Immigration and Naturalization Service (INS) to assign and track student visas. The third involves the complex processes involving the coordination of public health, public policy and private health practitioners responding to bio-terrorism threats. Table 1 shows a summary of these scenarios[5].

Challenges to Workflow Support and Automation

The homeland defense scenarios outlined above suggest several interesting challenges. Each represents a long-lived workflow that crosses organizational boundaries. In the situations described, sharing of data across organizational boundaries is an important mechanism to support the overall workflow. However, such sharing, without clear communication of intent or goal alignment does not allow effective continuation of workflows. Each scenario reveals situations that include possible goal conflicts (scenario 3) or, at minimum goal indifference (scenario 2), seen from the perspective of the initiating organization. While several other traditional challenges continue to exist, including issues such as data formats for exchange, understanding task dependencies, and handing off of responsibilities, the important concern appears to be one of arriving at a shared goal structure that ensures that the workflow proceeds effectively.

Specifically, the key challenge consists of articulating goals and maintaining (or negotiating) their understanding as the workflow instances move across organizational boundaries, and in response to changes in the environment. Current work on operationalizing goals to specific tasks such as creating procedural paths to the goal states (Kuechler and Vaishnavi 1998), can be adapted and extended to address a part of this concern. However, including the human actors in the loop for the workflow process, allowing them to articulate, negotiate, map, share, and interpret goals; and create or change procedural paths from tasks to goals represents a key problem that has not been addressed by current research. Further, the problems that arise from a large-footprint workflow require that the goals in question must be adjusted in response to changes in the environment. This responsibility need not lie with the participant currently engaged in monitoring or executing the workflow but

Table 1: Challenges from Homeland Defense Scenarios

Scenario	Current Effort	Partners and Goals	Comments
Army Security Clearance	Integic Corp. e.Power WF/document management, Expedited "clean security clearance"	Currently, only 2 partners, with fairly aligned goals	Current partners, though represent different institutions, are under a central authority, easier to streamline other clearance types
INS Student Visa Tracking	Peoplesoft & EDS In process	37,000 + partners, Conflicting goals across universities and government agencies	Large number, though primarily two classes of partners: educational institutions and one government agency.
Public and Private health and Public response to bio-terrorism threats	Not really in process	Several and shifting (federal, state & local public officials; CDC, private health systems). Conflicting goals including compliance incentives, jurisdiction, respect, privacy, pride, etc.	Several and changing classes of partners, Limits on ability to support multiple/ parallel threats due to CDC limitations

may also include other, currently passive participants. Identifying mechanisms that allow such changes to be recognized constitutes the second important challenge.

Consider, for example, scenario 2 (see Table 1). The goals of participants may be broadly articulated as 'accurate tracking[6] of foreign students' for the initiating participant (Immigration and Naturalization Service), and 'ensuring a supportive and free environment for learning' for the responding participant (the Educational Institution). These goals, as articulated, can be in conflict[7]. However, a goal-decomposition strategy can suggest a sub-goal for the educational institution such as 'tracking students for billing' that may be more closely aligned to the goal articulated by the initiating institution. Articulating, identifying and mapping such goals can facilitate the execution of a workflow. Consider another framing for the same example. Without the benefit of the mapping suggested above, the task of tracking students for the purpose of reporting to the INS suggests extra work for the colleges with no corresponding, visible benefit. On the other hand, articulating a quid pro quo such as 'tracking alumni after they graduate' in return for 'tracking foreign students' may be articulated that will allow greater compliance with workflow tasks required by the initiating participant.

As a second set of examples, consider scenario 3 (see Table 1). The goals for a response to a bio-terrorism threat can be several and may require a satisficing approach. The complicating factor, however, involves monitoring the environment to ensure that the current goal articulation takes into account the most current environmental assessment. However, the triggering event, resulting from current environment monitoring, is often poorly implemented. The problem here is twofold. First, doctors do not typically track certain diseases as required, or even the myriad forms needed to report them. Compliance would even be problematic since the forms, even if completed, would reflect historically flagged events, and would not detect new threats. Physicians, therefore, report only a small percentage of new diseases. The largest percentage comes from infection-control nurses in hospitals and laboratories that have "been able to make reporting part of their routine." Although private practitioners are legally responsible for sending reports of specific infectious diseases to local health agencies, penalties are not usually enforced. This lapse exists even though it is not uncommon for doctors to complete medical records describing symptoms and treatments, often times in electronic formats. The second problem is diagnosis without context and risk. For example, the general medical community was basically unfamiliar with anthrax symptoms and treatment (antibiotics) was counter to currently accepted medical practices[8]. One approach to improving the overall workflow to monitor the environment can, therefore, include mapping the private medical community's sub-goal, 'accurate medical records,' with the public health community's sub-goal of 'tracking new and evolving health threats.'

Proposed Research Approach

We envisage a workflow modeling and support environment that allows workflow goal and sub-goal articulation, and mapping to tasks for each workflow participant. Instead of layering additional systems or processes, our objective translates to one of identifying intentions of participants, and mapping these at the closest common instance of alignment to facilitate workflow execution across organizational boundaries. By discovering and exploiting existent synergies and integrating a possible reward structure, we envision an environment that can create robust workflow processes, which can be resilient over time and distance. Our approach, therefore, does not preclude integration of existing research on exception handling and adaptive methodologies, but relegates them to a more appropriate "supporting" role rather than one of artificial enforcement. We are currently in the process of articulating the requirements for such an approach, and modeling the conceptual design of such a support environment.

ENDNOTES

[1] Exception handling refers to making changes, on-the-fly, to the workflow execution for individual cases as exceptions are encountered.

[2] Adaptive workflows refer to the "automation potential of knowledge bases to dynamically adapt the control and data flow of running instances" (http://dbs.uni-leipzig.de/de/Research/workflow.html)

[3] Goal-based inter-organizational workflows refer to a "high level specification of a desired system state that implicitly includes many (possibly an infinite number) of procedural paths to the goal state, termed extensions or instances." (http://www.cis.gsu.edu/~vvaishna/process/wits98.pdf)

[4] Cross-organizational workflow execution failures are attributed to "underlying application, controlling WfMS component failures or insufficient user input." (http://lsdis.cs.uga.edu/lib/download/LSKA02-TR.pdf)

[5] Descriptions of these scenarios are available at http://purao.ist.psu.edu/workflow/scenarios/homeland

[6] PeopleSoft student administration application, called PASS, automatically detects and reports changes in administrative information about students to immigration authorities.

[7] Examples of the multitude of INS/ University issues to be resolved: http://chronicle.com/colloquylive/2002/09/monitor/

[8] Thomas Morris, Jr. was a postal worker who died of inhalational anthrax after exposure at the Brentwood mail facility. His flu-like symptoms were not, per current medical practice, treated with antibiotics. Medical experts feel that the context and risk could not have been identified at the local level. (http://www.abcnews.go.com/sections/living/DailyNews/anthrax_misdiagnosis011120.html)

REFERENCES

Hollingsworth, D. (1995). The Workflow Reference Model, Workflow Management Coalition.

Kuechler, B. and V. Vaishnavi (1998). A Goal-based Model of Coordination in Interoperating Workflows. Proceedings of the 8th Annual Workshop on Information Technologies and Systems (WITS '98).

Nickerson, J. V. (2003). Event-based Workflow and the Management Interface. 36th Annual Hawaii International Conference on System Sciences.

Rahm, E. (2000). Adaptive Workflow Management, Institut für Informatik, Universität Leipzig.

van der Aalst, W. M. P. and T. Basten (2002). "Inheritance of workflows: an approach to tackling problems related to change." Theoretical Computer Science 270(1-2): 125-203.

van der Aalst, W. M. P., T. Basten, et al., Eds. (2000). Adaptive workflow On the interplay between flexibility and support. Enterprise Information Systems. Norwell, Kluwer Academic Publishers.

Zhuge, H. "Workflow- and agent-based cognitive flow management for distributed team Cooperation." Information & Management. In Press, Corrected Proof.

Speedup Learning for Text Categorization and Intelligent Agents

Jeffrey L. Goldberg, Ph.D. and Matthew L. Jenkins
Analytic Services Inc. (ANSER)
1000 Green River Drive, Suite 202
Fairmont WV 26554
(304) 534-5332, (304) 534-5368
Jeffrey.Goldberg@anser.org, Matthew.Jenkins@anser.org

ABSTRACT

Research in text categorization has been focused on off-line machine learning algorithms: a predetermined set of categories is learned prior to the operation of the system in which they are to be applied. Also, the learning from examples paradigm requires a training session in which a teacher, rather than the end-user, manually labels the training set of example documents. This is labor intensive, particularly for rare categories: and essentially all categories on the Internet are rare. We propose the use of a speedup-learning algorithm in which a user interacts directly with the machine learning algorithm, and thereby greatly reduces the amount of training documents that must be labeled for optimal performance of the system. It also places the training capability directly into the hands of end-users, which opens up new applications, e.g. to track breaking news events on the Internet. Other researchers have previously identified the speedup learning strategy; we extend the concept, implement an algorithm, and apply it to Intelligent Internet Agents and law enforcement.

ORGANIZATION

This paper is organized into eight sections: (1) Introduction; (2) Background, reviewing some relevant technologies; (3) Speedup learning: the algorithm; (4) FasTrac: the algorithm plus the user-interface; (5) Intelligent Agents: How might FacTrac technology be applied in Intelligent Agents (6) Future Work; (7) Conclusions; and (8) References.

1. INTRODUCTION

A lot of research has been done on text categorization. Text categorization is defined as the labeling of documents in accordance with previously specified categories. Several machine learning algorithms have been applied to learn text categorizers automatically from a set of positive and negative example documents. The text categorizers are then used to label new documents. [1]There are two problems with the above approach:

- A teacher, separate from the end-user, must exhaustively label the entire training set. As a rule of thumb, we attempt to maintain at least 50 positive examples in the training set for any category. For rare, or infrequent categories, categories that occur naturally less than ½ % of the time, this requires the user to label more than 10,000 documents.
- The algorithm is a priori. Two phases, separated in time, proceed in sequence as follows:
  o The training phase: a pre-determined set of categories is learned.
  o The performance phase: the text categorizers from phase one are plugged into and run as the classifier function in the end-user application.

But, to refine the performance of the categorizers themselves, the end-user is required to augment the training set of documents with additional examples, or to modify the training set with corrected examples, and then start the process from the beginning. It is non-incremental and non-adaptive in the sense that it cannot learn new categories chosen by the end-user at runtime.

2. BACKGROUND

Naïve Bayes Algorithm

Bayesian learning is relevant for our work in speedup learning, because when applied to text categorization, its output is of the form: $P(C_i|D_j)$; or the probability that a category C_i should be assigned given the occurrence of words in a document D_j. Naïve Bayes is a practical Bayesian learning algorithm that has been shown to be particularly effective when applied to natural language documents. The output probabilities are used to produce a ranking of documents according to how "like" they are to the set of positive examples from the training set.

The naïveness is due to its treatment of the features, in our case word roots or stems, and the assumption that they occur mutually independently in documents, which is what permits Naïve Bayes to be computationally feasible. This assumption is obviously false, for example the word "learning" is more likely to be found when the prior word is "machine" than it is at random. However, Naïve Bayes has been proven one of the best for text categorization.

The basic form of Naïve Bayes used by the speedup algorithm is:
$$P(C_i=1|D_j) = P(C_i)P_k\,P(F_k|C_i)$$

The formula reads as follows: the probability that a category occurs $C_i=1$ given the evidence in document D_j equals the product of the prior probability of the category and the product of the conditional probabilities of the occurrence of the features F_k in document D_j given the occurrence of category C_i. In other words: the problem of determining the probability that a category should be assigned is reduced to the product of the conditional probabilities that its features occur given the category. We have made some optimizations to Naïve Bayes for the problem of speedup learning that increase its performance by a few percent. The optimizations are related to higher weighting of the features of recently added examples to the increasing training set, because they are more likely to be near the borderline of the true optimal classifier function.

Speedup Learning

Lewis first introduced the strategy of a speedup learning algorithm for text categorization [2]. It is based on the notion that a machine learning algorithm learns the most from examples that are closest to the border that divides the positive from the negative examples in the training set. The algorithm knows what documents it needs the user to label at each stage of operation, those that are nearest the border defined by the classifier function, and measured by probabilities falling closest to 0.5.

Upon each iteration the current classifier function is applied to the entire unlabeled training set (step [iii] in Figure 3). The output of the Naïve Bayes algorithm is used to produce a ranking. The ranking is ordered by max uncertainty, i.e. closeness to the probability 0.5. The K most uncertain documents are removed from the unlabeled training set and the user is asked to identify the positives, or the documents that match the users criteria for membership in the category. The user can train an optimal categorizer for any category; it need not even correspond to a label, and can be totally abstract. The only necessity is that the user "recognizes" when a document should be included in the category.

3. THE SPEEDUP ALGORITHM

For each desired category:

[i] Index the unlabeled set of documents producing the vocabulary for learning.

[ii] Have the user create an initial test collection by moving N positive documents from the test collection into a folder and any uncovered negatives into another folder(s)

Repeat steps [iii] – [v] until a termination condition is reached: either M total positive documents have been placed in the positive folder; or the accuracy exceeds the performance threshold, L%

[iii] Apply the "current" classifier function to the entire "Unlabeled Set" to produce a ranking ordered by "max uncertainty".
Remove the top K most uncertain documents and put them into the "Candidate Set". The user will now be asked to label these documents.

[iv] Remove from the "Candidate Set" the documents the user identifies as positives, put them into the "Positives" folder of the "Test Collection". Remove the remaining documents from the candidate set, and place them into the "Negatives" folder.

[v] Train a new classifier function based on the "Test Collection"; at the same time use cross validation to produce performance statistics. This is done by dividing the "Test Collection" into two parts; a "Training Set" to produce the classifier; and a "Test Set" to produce the performance statistics. By using the current classifier to predict the labels of the documents in the "Test Set" an estimate of the performance on new/unseen documents can be determined.

Initial suggestions for the parameters M, and N are: M = 200; K = 20; and N = 5, and L is category dependant.

The performance of the current classifier is measured after each iteration and compared to several termination conditions: either the overall performance objective is met, or the maximum number of iterations the user is willing to execute is met.

Performance

The performance of the speedup algorithm on two categories related to terrorism is shown in Table 1 below. After 10 iterations the user has labeled 200 documents and the performance is already reasonable, around 90%. After 20 iterations the performance of the speedup algorithm is very high, around 95%. The performance of the Naïve Bayes algorithm on the entire training set was about this level. It is of concern that the performance of the speedup algorithm actually continued to increase beyond the "optimal performance." We are doing more extensive testing to determine what caused this unexpected result, the speedup algorithm is supposed to converge to optimal performance

Table 1: Performance of the Speedup Learning Algorithm

Iteration	Random's Errors = fp + fn	Random's Breakeven Performance	Speedup's Errors = fp + fn	Speedup's Breakeven Performance
1	565	71.03	576	70.8
2	460	76.63	467	76.0
3	352	80.16	408	78.9
4	533	72.11	372	80.5
5	467	74.17	314	83.4
10	656	63.37	194	89.2
15	447	73.57	138	91.8
20	281	82.34	81	94.9
25	257	82.76	42	97.2
30	205	85.43	46	96.9

Figure 1: The Architecture of An Intelligent Agent using Text Categorization via FasTrac

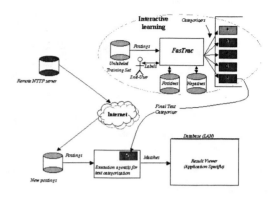

more quickly than the straightforward learning from examples approach, but it is not expected to exceed the performance on the fully labeled training set. Despite this, the effectiveness of the speedup algorithm is clear from the comparison to the algorithm that selects the candidate set documents randomly, rather than by max uncertainty.

4. FASTRAC

FasTrac is the user-trainable, reusable software module that uses the speedup learning algorithm for text categorization. Its dataflow diagram appears below in Figure 3: Appendix A. The steps of the algorithm were given in section 3. The algorithm is the smart one in this model of learning, as it knows what documents it wants the user to label at every step, and the user just does what it is told to do: provide the labels for the documents in the candidate set. The point of the speedup learning is twofold: to learn quickly, and to facilitate user-trainable categories.

In the upper right hand corner of Figure 1, the interactive learning component, FasTrac is shown. This produces the classifier functions, or text categorizers. For each desired category, the user produces an optimal text categorizer by interactively labeling the "Candidate Sets" of documents, extracted from the "Unlabeled Set" of documents by the speedup algorithm according to "maximal uncertainty." The output is the optimal (final) text categorizer for the category. Currently, the algorithms being applied for use with speedup learning are Naïve Bayes [3], Support Vector Machines (SVM) [4]. The optimal categorizer is then used by execution agents to recognize new documents.

In Figure 2, FasTrac's Candidate Document Window is shown. A document has been selected by FasTrac for labeling by the user according to the desired category. The user may choose the options in the panel at the bottom of the window labeled "Add to Training Set" to indicate the document is either an example of the category, by choosing "positive", or not, by choosing "negative". Alternatively, if the user wishes he or she may defer judgement on the document by choosing "skip", which returns it to the "Unlabeled Set"; or may remove the document from the system by choosing "delete."

Figure 2: FasTrac's User Interface

5. INTELLIGENT AGENTS WITH TEXT CATEGORIZATION

The initial application for FasTrac is to allow an Intelligent Internet Agent to be trained to track categories of immediate topical interest. We have several prototype Intelligent Agents in various stages of development: Newshound, Chathound, and Webhound. Newshound is most highly developed, is in actual use by law enforcement, and so we'll now describe its capabilities. Newshound, and the two agents in development, are described in more detail in a separate publication [5].

Newshound Requirements

The original purpose of Newshound is to look for specified, trainable content in Usenet newsgroups. By specified and trainable, we mean that given a set of (positive and negative) example postings, it must be able to discern a classifier function and find new postings that are 'like' the positive examples. Newshound is to operate as an intelligent agent. It must allow a human agent to specify the parameters of operation, including the news server, the newsgroups in which to look, and the categories of what to be on the look out for. After having the parameters of operation selected, the intelligent agent must then operate autonomously, only requiring interaction whenever the user desires to check the results of what has been matched so far, or to change the parameters of operation. Once a Newshound agent has found postings that match its category(s), the human agent instructs the Newshound agent as to which of the results are correct and which are not. This last requirement is called user-feedback and retraining and allows the originally learned text categorizers to be refined and personalized.

Newshound Implementation

Newshound is an intelligent Internet agent that recognizes postings of interest to a human user from Usenet newsgroups. It uses text categorization technology to train a classifier function for each desired category based on a set of examples. The classifiers, or text categorizers, are then used to recognize documents (Usenet postings), which are like the positive examples. It has been employed in a Pilot Program with an organization of the federal government and is being operationally tested by Special Agents.

Applying FasTrac to Newshound

Since text categorization has already been applied to Newshound, it already has an interface that allows a text categorizer to be plugged-in. The Intelligent Agent may now be used to recognize breaking events by simply archiving an adequate number of newspostings from Usenet news and running FasTrac. The user then can use FasTrac to train Newshound to retrieve new documents of the desired category. Since Usenet News has a high daily throughput, the amount of time to archive the required "Unlabeled Set" of documents required by FasTrac should be limited to hours or days for many typical categories. Applying Newshound with FasTrac to track categories related to breaking terrorist events would be of interest, but it remains to be seen how quickly useful Newshound Agents can be trained, and how well they will work.

6. FUTURE WORK

The infrastructure is in place, but the hard work has just begun. Requiring the end-user to be the trainer of an Intelligent Agent places a burden on both the user and the user-interface. If the user interface is too complicated for the prospective end-users to achieve acceptable performance; then the speedup algorithm is moot. Getting the right combination of technology and simplicity for use by non-technical, or at least non-programming end-users will require great skill beyond the realm of programming. All of this assumes that the Intelligent Agent technology is flawless, and that FasTrac is flawless, but they are currently prototypes and are therefore not flawless. Obviously, the user cannot be expected to tolerate difficulties with robustness in such a highly interactive, and dynamic system.

How to best apply the technologies of Newshound and FasTrac to monitor Usenet news will also be challenging. One question is whether it may be possible to apply text categorization to detect "first person" categories. These are categories where a perpetrator incriminates his or herself directly. And whether correlations can be found between threats made on the Internet and actual classes of criminal events or attacks? Also, how much "third person" information can be found in Usenet newsgroups or the rest of the Internet that

is of possible interest in intelligence in the hours or days immediately following breaking events?

And then, how can Newshound be combined with ANSER's other protocol agents, e.g. Webhound, and Chathound, to gather information on the same topic? How to answer questions like these using the technology of text categorization and Intelligent Internet Agents will be very challenging.

7. CONCLUSIONS

Speedup has been shown to work, it increases the rate of learning in text categorization by roughly one order of magnitude or greater. Unlike a pure learning from examples paradigm, it allows the training to be done by the end-user. It opens up new possible applications for text categorization, and some are highly relevant to the new war on terrorism..

8. REFERENCES

[1] J.L. Goldberg, "CDM: An Approach to Learning in Text Categorization," *International Journal on Artificial Intelligence Tools,* Vol 5, Nos. 1 & 2, pp. 229-253, July 1996.

[2] D.D. Lewis, "A Sequential Algorithm for Training Classifiers," In Proceedings of SIGIR'94 the 17th ACM International Conference on Research and Development in Information Retrieval, pp. 3-12, July 1994.

[3] David D. Lewis, "Naive (Bayes) at forty: The independence assumption in information retrieval," In *European Conference on Machine Learning*, 1998.

[4] N. Cristianini and J. Shawe-Taylor, *An Introduction to Support Vector Machines (and other kernel-based learning methods).* Cambridge University Press, 1999.

[5] J.L. Goldberg, and S.S. Shen, "Newshound Revisited: The Intelligent Agent that Retrieves News Postings," In V. Sugumaran, editor, *Intelligent Support Systems,* Idea Group Publishing, Hershey PA, In Press for Spring 2002.

APPENDIX A

Figure 3: Speedup Data Flow Diagram

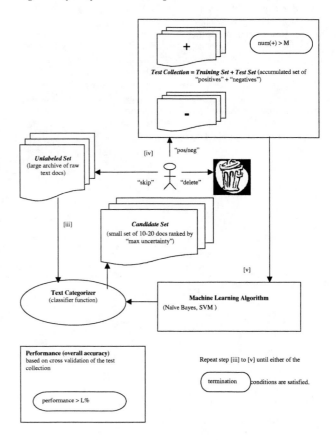

Analysis of Data Communication Aspects of Computer-Based Teaching

Dr. Anatoliy Gordonov

Department of Computer Science, College of Staten Island/City University of New York

2800 Victory Blvd., 1N-215, SI, NY 10314

Tel: (718) 982 2850

E-mail: Gordonov@postbox.csi.cuny.edu

ABSTRACT

The paper represents the results of an ongoing research aimed at investigating the data communications consequences of using network-based electronic classroom systems. We formulated practical recommendations that allow the instructor to optimize the network performance inside a classroom and minimize the influence on the network outside the classroom. These recommendations can be used by any instructor and do not require administrative network privileges.

INTRODUCTION: THE PROBLEM STATEMENT

The Electronic Learning Environments currently available can considerably improve teaching effectiveness. Networked multimedia computers enhance instruction by facilitating the distribution of text, graphics, sound and video images, providing communication links, and allowing continuous monitoring of student work. Benefits of employing networks in the classrooms include student access to sharable resources, enhancing communication between a student and an instructor, between students inside a working group, between working groups, etc. Transmission of information (especially video information) interferes with the local area network users outside of the classroom. It may considerably slow down all network activities, may affect other classrooms, research laboratories, faculty, and administrative offices.

In this paper we are going to consider one of the popular solutions for the [1]electronic classroom – "NetOp® School"[1]. We are going to focus on the analysis of data communication issues related to the employing of NetOp School and will try to give some recommendations that allow the instructor to optimize the network performance inside a classroom and minimize the influence on the network outside the classroom.

NetOp School supports the following operations:
- *Demo*
- *Monitoring*
- *Chat*
- *File Transfer*
- *Remote Control*
- Run Program

Table 1 shows the correlation between the operations mentioned above and various activities of the instructor.

Table 1

#	Instructor's Activities	NetOp Operations
1	Lecture	Demo
2	Individual Tutorial	Individual Demo, Individual Monitoring Remote Control, Individual Chat
3	Group Tutorial	Group Demo, Group Monitoring Group Chat (Conference), Run Program
4	Class Monitoring	Monitoring
5	Teaching By Example	Demo, File Transfer, Remote Control Run Program, Student's Demo

As we can see, all the instructor's activities fall into the category of synchronous teaching which means that all communicating parties must participate in any action in real-time.

Typically a NetOp classroom is a part of the Local Area Network (Figure 1). Any instructor's action generates additional network traffic. In other words, any action has some influence on the network load and, vise versa, the network load may affect the performance of the NetOp operations.

Depending on LAN features (such as topology, access method, protocols used, hardware and software characteristics), NetOP settings, and the instructor's activities NetOp operations may considerably degrade overall network performance and, as a result, prevent using NetOp.

OPTIMIZING NETWORK PERFORMANCE

There are several levels of optimization that may help avoid communications problems.
- Level 1: Automatic optimization imbedded in the NetOp software. This mode utilizes commonly used and default settings and may require minimum user involvement.
- Level 2: Allows the users to set some parameters manually in order to optimize network performance based on some specific features of the network, computers, and software.
- Level 3: Requires making changes in the network architecture, choosing another media and access method, and/or using a different type of network hardware.

In this paper we are going to consider the first two levels. These levels can be handled by an instructor and do not require network administrative privileges. Nevertheless, in many cases this optimization may enhance both NetOp and overall network performance.

Figure1. Possible Network Configuration

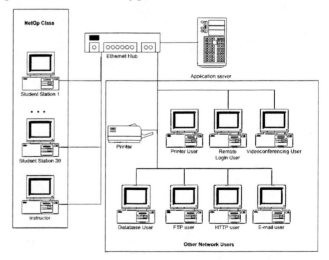

Level 1 Optimization

As it was mentioned above, Level 1 represents automatic optimization and is implemented by the NetOp School software. However, some parameters should be appropriately set to enable this mode. Generally, there are two groups of parameters that can be set by the instructor:

- Teacher station parameters – These parameters define the behavior of both the teacher station and the classroom as a whole. There are several of them that may influence network load:
  o If TCP (UDP)/IP profile is used for communication (which is the most common case), the maximum allowed packet size may affect the overall network performance. By default, the max packet size is 2600 bytes. Normally, the instructor should only change this setting if the default packet size is not supported by the TCP/IP setup. If the network settings allow only smaller packets, many IP packets will be fragmented which, in turn, will increase network load. In this case, the instructor may try to lower the packet size. If the instructor does not have enough information for setting the maximum packet size explicitly, the automatic option should be set allowing the NetOp software and communication system to handle the situation.
  o In the Monitor mode the teacher station will be connected to a student computer for a certain amount of time. The default value for the time interval is 15 seconds, which is acceptable for most students' activities. Nevertheless, the instructor should be aware that the traffic generated by monitoring also depends on the students' activities. Students watching full-screen high-quality video clips may create much higher traffic during monitoring as compared to those who work with word processors. In this case, the "waves" of different network loads will be generated. Increasing the time interval in this situation will not only increase monitoring time for the whole class but also prolong the interval with higher network traffic.

Note: NetOP features the Attention mode that allows the instructor to make the students stop working on their computers while listening to the teacher. This is done by locking the screen, keyboard, and mouse on the selected students' computers. On each student computer this mode is indicated by displaying text or bitmap on the student's screen. Either text or bitmap must be saved on each computer, which is done automatically by the NetOp software. Changing from text to bitmap or defining more advanced bitmap does not contribute to the network traffic each time the Attention mode is turned on.

- Student Options

The instructor may change student station settings remotely. Some of these settings may affect the network traffic. Level 1 optimization does not require any changes of the default values. Nevertheless, it is worth checking that the default parameters have been selected and automatic optimization may be provided by NetOp.

The default settings are:
  o Compression – *Automatic*
  o Desktop. Optimize screen transfer – *Always*
  o Desktop. Optimization parameters – *Full Optimization*.

Level 2 Optimization

At this level the instructor may change some default settings in order to minimize the influence on the network performance. As we have considered above, we are going to analyze two groups of parameters: for the teacher station and for student stations.

NetOp supports communication using TCP (UDP)/IP or Internet, IPX, NetBIOS. For each setup there is a communication profile that includes all the necessary information and makes it easy to quickly switch between communication setups.

Let us consider pre-defined profiles:
- TCP (UDP)/IP. NetOp School supports any 100% WinSock 1.1 compatible TCP/IP implementation.
  o As it was mentioned earlier, in case of necessity the default value of the *maximum packet size* can be changed. The allowed range is 512-5120 bytes. Changing the *maximum packet size* requires knowledge of the TCP/IP settings in the network. Either unreasonable

lowing or increasing the NetOp packet size setting may lead to extra traffic in the network.
  o When the TCP (UDP)/IP is used, NetOp School provides automatic browsing operations that allow the teacher computer to search for students and vise versa. By default, NetOp assumes that all the PCs are located on the same subnet (IP address of all 1s is used for local broadcast). It limits the number of IP addresses to be used during browsing. If students' PCs belong to different subnets, their IP addresses should be explicitly included in *IP Broadcast List*. At the same time, *Disable Local Subnet Broadcast* option should be chosen. It will prevent local broadcast.
  o If NetOp School is used through the Internet, the default packet size should be set to 1024 bytes. The *Optimize for the Internet communication* option should be chosen.

- When NetOp School is used in Novell Netware environment, the IPX communication profile must be used. Because the structure of Novell networks may include several sub-networks, three alternatives may be used:
  o Local network only
  o User defined list of networks
  o *Build list of known networks* (will be done automatically by NetOp software)

Being able to choose one of the settings, the instructor cannot change the physical network structure. NetOp allows the user to change the packet size between 512 and 5000 bytes, but this action is beyond the boundaries of the instructor's responsibility. As a result, nothing can be done on level 2 of optimization that may enhance IPX network performance.

- NetBIOS is a popular protocol for various LANs. The settings that the instructor can change will not affect network performance and will not be considered here (similarly to IPX, NetOp allows the user to change the packet size by configuring NETOP.INI file, but we do not recommend the instructor to do it without the network administrator).
- Student Options – As it was mentioned earlier, several student options that may affect network traffic can be set remotely from the teacher station.
  o Both the keyboard and mouse on a student computer may be controlled either by a student locally or by the instructor remotely. Remote control will introduce extra traffic and should be used only when it is necessary. The following options are available for the keyboard:
  Remote Keyboard – All keystrokes will be sent to a student computer.
  Local Keyboard – Special keystrokes will not be sent to a student computer
  No Keyboard Control
  o The following options can be set for the mouse:
  Remote Mouse – All the mouse events will be transmitted.
  Local Mouse – Only clicks and drags will be sent.
  No Mouse Control
  Display Student Mouse Movement – Controls transmission of all mouse events from a student station to the instructor
  o *Compression Level* – Normally, *Automatic* compression should be used. If the classroom activities include intensive transmission (ex: life video), the *High* compression level should be chosen. Being able to transmit data faster, this level also requires better processors to avoid bottleneck while processing compressed images. This level should be used when communication channels are not fast enough (ex: WAN). If the communication channel is fast and there are no high LAN activities unrelated to the NetOp class, the use of *Low* compression is preferable because it will decrease processing time and increase overall performance.
  o *Optimize screen transfer* – These settings allow the teacher to change some of the student desktop settings that are not necessary for the current session but, when being used, will increase network traffic. Among these settings are: wallpaper, screen saver, animation, etc. All changes will be automatically restored after the end of the session.

- On the student side, by setting communication options the instructor can change the way packets should be sent from the teacher's station to the student's station. The student's computer may accept either broadcast packets sent to a group of students or packets individually addressed to this computer. Individual addressing should be used only on the Internet or when broadcast is not possible. The unjustified use of the individual addressing will lead to increasing the number of transmitted packets and will dramatically low the network performance.

CONCLUSION

The paper represents the results of an ongoing research aimed at investigating the data communications consequences of using network-based electronic classroom systems. We formulated practical recommendations that al-low the instructor to optimize the network performance inside a classroom and minimize the influence on the network outside the classroom. These recommendations can be used by any instructor and do not require administrative network privileges. As it was mentioned in the paper, we emphasized three levels of optimization that may be employed to enhance the overall network performance. Two levels – Level 1 that requires minimum instructor involvement and Level 2 that requires changing and setting some of parameters by the instructor – were considered in this paper. Level 3 – that will include network modeling for various topologies and access methods – will constitute the next stage of this research.

ENDNOTES

[1]   NetOp® is the registered trademark of Danware Data A/S (Denmark).

Customization, Configuration, or Modification? A Taxonomy for Information System Specialization

Marc N. Haines
School of Business Administration, University of Wisconsin-Milwaukee
mhaines@uwm.edu, (414) 229-3773

Two key characteristics of Enterprise Systems (ES) - and many other types of packaged information systems (IS) - are: (1) ES are generic systems that may be used by a large number of organizations and (2) ES usually offer multiple mechanisms to make changes to the system to adapt the generic system to the specific requirements of an organization[1]. It is presumed that the goal of any changes - whether appropriate and successful or not - is to satisfy requirements that are specific to the organization implementing the ES.

To describe the nature of changes made to a system, practitioners and academics alike use a variety of terms. Most commonly the terms configuration, modification, and customization are used in this context. Unfortunately these terms are often used inconsistently across software vendors (i.e., SAP vs. Oracle) and articles discussing the issue. One software company (or article), for instance, may use the term customization for change activities that another software company (or article) describes as configuration. The problem is that there appears to be no commonly accepted framework that defines the terms and relates them to each other. This article first discusses the key dimensions that can be used to describe changes to a generic software system and then presents a proposal for a taxonomy that defines the key terms, and relates them to each other.

A change to a generic software system can be described from several viewpoints. One key dimension is the technical activity that is performed to accomplish the change. This includes, for example, setting software switches that enable or disable certain functionality, setting values in tables that drive business processes, or writing new source code that is added to the system. These technical activities vary in time and skill that is required to perform the change. Consequently there is also a cost dimension that differentiates the different change activities. But both of the above dimensions do not provide a base to categorize change activities into configuration, customization, or modification in general. For instance, changing a table entry can be considered a configuration activity or a modification depending on which kind of table is involved. Also the cost for the same type of activity may vary significantly from one organization to the other depending on the existing IS resources at the organization which is implementing the ES. For an IT department with an experienced group of Java programmers, adding a few lines of code may be as costly or even cheaper than hiring a consultant to make the right changes in the right tables of a complex database.

There is, however, a third important dimension: the support, which a software vendor provides for changes, made to a packaged system. The term configuration is generally used to describe activities, whether this is setting a software switch or changing a table entry, that lead to changes that are (or at least promised to be) supported in future releases and by the software vendor support facilities. If a change on the other hand is not supported at all it is usually described as a modification. The term customization is arguably the most ambiguous term. Sometimes it includes both configuration and modification, at other times just refers to either modification or configuration. Despite the existing inconsistency with which the terms are used, the dimension that leads to a clear and meaningful distinction between configuration, modification, or customization is the software vendor support. The support is important since it has significant implications for the development and mainte-

nance costs of a system. This is particularly important in the context of ES, for which the cost of making and maintaining changes are a substantial part of the overall project costs.

Software vendor support is not always an all or nothing matter. A software vendor can decide that only certain parts of a change are supported or that there are cost and time limits to the support. User exits for instance are defined interfaces to an ES. If functionality is added to a system by exploiting a user exit the interface is supported while the code that implements this functionality is not. Therefore user exits would be placed in the middle of the continuum that exists for software vendor support.

The taxonomy proposed in this article relates the following concepts: specialization, selection, customization, configuration, user exits, and modification.

The term specialization is used to describe any activity to achieve a better fit of the IS with the specific requirements of the organization. This may be achieved in two ways: (1) by selection and (2) by customization. The selection determines the initial specialization of an IS solution. A system, developed according to the requirements of a particular organization would have a high degree of specialization, while a generic ES "out-of-the-box" would have a low degree of specialization. A generic solution, however, may be further specialized by customization (see Figure 1).

Customization includes any activity that leads to a change of a process or data definition in a generic system. These activities may have varying support by the software vendor. Depending on the level of support three main categories are distinguished. Configurations, which have high level of support, user exits, which are partially supported, and modifications, which have a low level of support (see Figure 2).

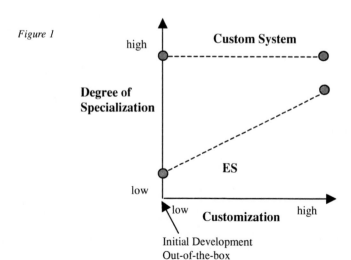

Figure 1

Figure 2

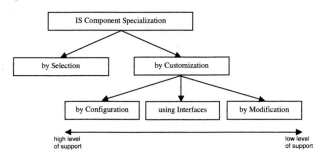

This taxonomy may provide helpful guidance in further research or practical applications. It could also be used to identify effective approaches to IS specialization in conjunction with other IS theories. For instance, the specialization for individual components of an ES may be examined by combining this framework with theories related to general asset specialization (asset specificity) and/or the resource-based view of the firm to determine the alignment of customization efforts with IS strategy.

ENDNOTES

[1] Note: This article does not discuss or make a judgement about the merits of a particular type of change applied to an actual system.

Investigating the Optimum Manager-Subordinate Relationship in Global Managerial Systems: A Case Study and Report of Key Findings for Practical Use in Global IT Management & Organizations: A Trend for the Future

Sergey Ivanov
School of Business and Public Management, The George Washington University
Address: 20101 Academic Way, Ste. 321, GWU-VA Campus, Ashburn, VA 20147
Phone: (703) 726-8314, fax: (978) 383-5856,
E-mail: sergey@gwu.edu

ABSTRACT

This research investigates the effective manager-subordinate relationship theoretically, and empirically tests the theoretical propositions using a global case study, conducted in North America and Eastern Europe. The original research started as an exploration of the effective manager-subordinate relationship in the IT companies and departments in the United States, but grew and extended to Eastern Europe, and included a wide variety of organizations.

THEORETICAL BACKGROUND

The seminal foundation for this study is the Requisite Organization theory developed by Dr. Elliott Jaques. The in-depth discussion of the theory is beyond the scope of this paper, though the major points of the theory are as follows. According to the Requisite Organization theory, human capability is discontinuous. The human capability[1] concept is different from IQ or any other 'intelligence-measures' – at the present time it is possible to evaluate the level of a person's capability, but not measure it precisely. This concept of capability extends far beyond the human species and encompasses all living organisms, discussed in detail in the "Life and Behavior of Living Organisms: A General Theory" book by Jaques published in 2002[2].

The main idea is that all living organisms have evolved to deal with discontinuous orders of information complexity to organize and influence the world around them to achieve their goals (intentions). Intentionality is what Jaques calls the basis and the major foundation of life, having found support in writings of St. Augustine, and ancient Greece[3] and China, where the same concept of 'intentional' time has apparently flourished and influenced the organization of thought and societies (also Kurt Lewin's[4] ideas of dynamics in psychology are very close to Jaques').

According to Jaques, there are five discontinuous orders of information complexity, and each order consists of four discontinuous levels how the living organisms deal with information. The following chart depicts the orders of information complexity as they relate to humans (see figure 1).

According to the theory, a person's capability grows over time depending on the speed of the development, and the current potential capability of an ordinary adult lies in one of the above strata. Having current potential capability in a certain stratum means that the person may at maximum work, plan and organize goals at the 'stratum's maximum time' into the future. For example, a person at stratum 1, at the present time may plan and execute goals under 3 months into the future, and will at a maximum present a declarative-style argument.

One of the major points of the Requisite Organization theory is that the discontinuous human capability gives rise to the layers of managerial hierarchy. Jaques writes, "The managerial hierarchy is the organizational expression of the hierarchical structure of human capability. The basic structure of managerial layers coincides with the layers of complexity of information processing."[5]

According to the theory, a manager should always work precisely one stratum above the subordinate, and the level of work of both, the manager and

Figure 1: Cognitive strata

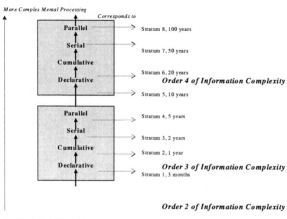

(Mental processing develops from declarative, to cumulative, to serial, to parallel modes, though the description of mental development is beyond the scope of this paper – see the "Human Capability" book by Jaques and Cason for a complete description of the human development process)

subordinate, is measurable with the ratio-scale time-span of the role measurement instrument. Thus, the requisite relationship is defined when the manager's role is one stratum higher than the subordinate's role. Each stratum is defined in precise periods of time, starting with Stratum 1 (1 day to 3 months), Stratum 2 (3 months to 1 year), and so on. To determine which stratum a person works at is an objective ratio-scale measurement, derived by interviewing the person's manager (via the time-span of the role measurement instrument).

EFFECTIVE AND NON-EFFECTIVE MANAGER-SUBORDINATE RELATIONSHIPS

The research question is whether there is a positive correlation between the Optimum Manager-Subordinate Relationship (OMSR) (this concept is defined in the next paragraph) and the requisite structuring of the managerial hierarchy (the manager's role is one stratum higher than the subordinate's). This phenomenon, in effect, constitutes the effective managerial relationship in the managerial hierarchy according to the Requisite Organization theory. Manager-Subordinate Relationship (MSR) describes how a subordinate, in a managerial hierarchy, feels towards the manager, and how the manager feels towards the subordinate – it is an empirical finding by Dr. Elliott Jaques of the criterion for effective management. OMSR is achieved when the subordinate feels 'just right' towards the manager – the subordinate is comfortable towards the manager's directions, communications, and overall feels that the relationship is as it should be. In OMSR, the manager also feels right towards the subordinate that the subordinate understands the manager's directives, and that the subordinate does not "pull the manager into the weeds."

In the non-Optimal Manager-Subordinate Relationship (non-OMSR) (non-effective management according to the theory), the subordinate reports either that the manager is 'too close', or 'too far'. When the subordinate feels that the manager is too close – the manager is breathing down the subordinate's neck. When the subordinate feels that the manager is too far, the subordinate feels that the manager is not providing the directions s/he should, and feels lost.

The manager, in non-OMSR, also reports either of the two conditions: that the subordinate is too close or too far. The manager feels too close when the subordinate does not listen nor need directions – the manager cannot set a context for the subordinate's work – the subordinate is ready to assume the manager's role. The manager feels too far, when the subordinate pulls the manager "down into the weeds" – the relationship feels uncomfortable because the subordinate's need for directions pulls the manager into the unnecessary levels of details to set the context for the subordinate's work – the manager feels that there should be another manager between him/her and the subordinate.

The study's hypothesis is that there is a positive relationship between the requisite working stratum of the manager and subordinate and the OMSR, and non-requisite structuring and the non-OMSR. Having collected data, determined the working stratum and the MSR, it is possible to draw a correlation between the requisite layering of manager and subordinate and the MSR. Finding/not finding the correlation would advance the Requisite Organization theory in its ability to predict (or not predict) the MSR in managerial hierarchies.

Additionally, the study has gone further and as an additional finding attempted to investigate the effects of the capability of manager and subordinate on the MSR as defined in the "Human Capability" book by Jaques and Cason . The investigative proposition is that OMSR will correlate strongly when not only the manager's role is one stratum higher than the subordinate's role, but also the manager's current potential capability corresponds with the manager's role's stratum, and the subordinate's current potential capability corresponds with the subordinate's role's stratum.

GLOBAL IT MANAGEMENT

Global IT management (in managerial hierarchies) is no different from local or national IT management, when attempting to manage people (not servers, and/or other technology investments). According to the Requisite Organization theory, any managerial hierarchy functions precisely on the same fundamental principles not depending on the culture, country, climate or any other factor – fundamentally, the global IT-management hierarchy depends solely on the organization of people and their capabilities in a most effective or non-effective way.

The researcher started this study concentrating on local IT companies, but the theory allowed a wider generalize-ability to include all managerial hi-

erarchies, not depending on any other elusive factor, such as culture or industry – even classifying what constitutes an IT-job/management versus a non-IT sometimes is blurry and not evident. The only resolution to creating an effective team and/or organizations within a global IT industry remains using a good and tested scientific theory, one aspect of which this study has attempted to validate.

CASE STUDY AND REPORT OF KEY FINDINGS

First preliminary analysis tests the strength of correlating the difference of strata (n) and Subordinate' MSR (S(MSR)). As an additional research question to this study, the researcher attempted to correlate the difference of strata (n) and S(MSR), where manager's current potential capability (M(p)), and subordinate's current potential capability (S(p)) corresponded to the level of work, or in other words, where M(p) = M(r) and S(p) = S(r).

Spearman's rho (on a confidence level of 95%) determines the strength of the four correlations above. A weak correlation would indicate a possible deficiency in the theory, while a strong correlation would confirm a possible validity of the theory, and will advance it by indicating whether or not MSR is possibly dependent on the level of work in managerial hierarchies, which altogether would provide useful theoretical and applicable advances into building more effective hierarchical accountability organizations.

This study does not use the random sampling technique because any sample represents the population, which is achieved using a universal measuring instrument, time-span of the role. The fundamental essence of having a random sample is to ensure that threats of unrepresentative samples do not bias the study and its outcomes to generalize to a population. There is no need for the random sampling technique in this study as any sample represents the population of managerial systems precisely. According to the Requisite Organization theory, all managerial hierarchies can be evaluated similarly on precisely the same measurements – the level of work of their employees, thus, allowing comparing various organizations throughout the world and a variety of different industries. Measuring the level of work of employees is universal, thus, any sample based on the principles of the Requisite Organization theory represents the population of managerial hierarchies – thus, making the study generalize-able to the entire population, including information technology teams and organizations.

29 cases were analyzed through SPSS statistical package. The 29 raw data cases constituted valid cases evaluating the strength of subordinate's MSR related to the difference of working strata; the correlation is significant at 0.05 level, and the correlation coefficient is 0.387, which indicates a relationship, but not as strong as the researcher might have expected. Interpreting this result might mean that the correlation between the MSR (of subordinate) with the requisiteness of roles need to be tested further and re-evaluated in light of new scientific evidence.

The researcher performed an additional test, also correlating the subordinate's MSR with difference of working roles' strata of manager and subordinate, but where subordinate's current potential capability corresponded with the subordinate's role stratum, and the manager's current potential capability corresponded with his/her role stratum. In this case, the preliminary data shows the strength of the correlation to grow to 0.545, indicating that there may be a significant correlation between the difference of working roles' strata and MSR, considering people's current potential capabilities matching their employment roles.

SUMMARY OF RESEARCH

This research studies the phenomenon of effective management as explained by the Requisite Organization theory, and tests it empirically. Preliminary data suggests that the phenomenon of better aligning the roles and people's capabilities makes a positive difference in effectiveness – when the manager is breathing down the subordinate's neck or when the manager feels "pulled down into the weeds" – are both cases hardly arguable that the team is effective. On the opposite, when the manager reports that s/he feels the subordinate is just right, and the subordinate reports that the manager is just the right distance from him/her – this is an important characteristic of effective management, which according to the Requisite Organization theory is related to the level of work of manager and subordinate, and, according to this study, additionally, people's capabilities' matching the working roles.

GLOBAL IT MANAGEMENT & THE FUTURE

Jaques writes in his book "The Life and Behavior of Living Organisms: a General Theory" (see endnotes for references) that St. Augustine understood in 500 A.D. that the future does not happen or come toward us, rather the future is here with us today – the future is our present goals and intentions we strive to realize now. It is this paper's prediction that global IT management, in time, will accept the principles of the Requisite Organization theory (unless a better theory is developed or the Requisite Organization theory does not withstand empirical tests) to build the most effective and efficient managerial IT systems to deal most effectively with the problems rising on the horizon. Technology will come and go and change, but it is people who make a difference by acting on their goals and doing, thus, the most effective organization of people's talents is urgently needed to arrive at better and brighter solutions and the overall success of the global IT and other endeavors. The Requisite Organization theory may be the scientific answer to organize people according to their talents and capabilities in a most effective way, though the overall effort requires a further learning and investment by the industry and IT academia into the applicability, feasibility and testability of the Requisite Organization theoretical principles to deploy them worldwide in the "production" mode.

ENDNOTES

1   Jaques, Elliot & Cason, Kathryn (1994). Human Capability. Rockville, MD: Cason Hall.
2   Jaques, Elliott (2002). The Life and Behavior of Living Organisms: a General Theory. Westport, CT: Praeger Publishers.
3   Jaques, Elliott (1982). The Form of Time. New York, New York: Crane, Russak & Company.
4   Lewin, Kurt (1935). A Dynamic Theory of Personality. New York, NY: McGraw-Hill.
5   Jaques, Elliott (2002). Social Power and the CEO: Leadership and Trust in a Sustainable Free Enterprise System. Westport, Connecticut: Quorum Books.

REFERENCES

Please contact the author, Sergey Ivanov, at sergey@gwu.edu or fax (978) 383-5856 or phone (703) 726-8314 for a complete list of references. If you would like to reach the author by mail, please write to Sergey Ivanov, 20101 Academic Way, Suite 321, GWU-VA Campus, Ashburn, VA 20147.

Frameworks for Emerging Mobile Data Services: Proposed Survey of GSM Operators

A.T. Jarmoszko
Central Connecticut State University, New Britain, CT USA
Telephone: (860)832-3298, Fax: (860)832-3267
jarmoszkoa@ccsu.edu

INTRODUCTION

Much is expected of the emerging mobile data services. Those mobile telephony companies – which have participated in 3G auctions and paid excessively for licensing – have indeed staked their future on the success of such services. However, this very future is still uncertain. The build-out of the 3G mobile infrastructure has been delayed by legal questions regarding licensing and by unmet deadlines for introducing network and handset equipment. Only recently have vendors of mobile handsets – PDAs, tablet PCs, mobile phones or combinations thereof – started to introduce devices that can be considered as appropriate for 2.5G and 3G mobile services. As the search for the killer mobile application continues, the expectation is that the coming months will bring a slew of new services.

This paper is a report on the early stages of a research project. In this project I have undertaken to study the process of introducing mobile data services by operators of GSM networks around the world. In October 2002, the GSM Association listed 660 such operators in 180 countries. The study is designed to take place in two phases. First, the largest operators in the most mobile-developed countries will be surveyed for the express purpose of validating proposed frameworks and for surfacing important research issues. Once this is accomplished, the second phase will expand the population of studied GSM operators to improve statistical validity and ability to generalize results. The results of conducted surveys should be available in time for the 2003 IRMA Conference, May 18-21, 2003.

LITERATURE REVIEW

The research stream focused on the subject of mobility and information systems is relatively new. Thus far few non-technical topics have been studied to any significant degree. It appears that the issue of culture and mobile-service use has generated a growing interest in the IS community. For example, Palen et al (2002) have studied the use of mobile phones in the context of cultural experience so users. Nurmi et al (2001), Aarnio et al (2002), Kim et al) and Carroll et al (2002) have studied adoption and use of mobile services in the Scandinavian, Australian and Korean contexts. Urbaczewski et al (2002) have proposed some reasons for the lower penetration and use of mobile services in United States when compared to Western Europe.

Hypothesis 1: Mobile data services which are location sensitive, time critical and customer initiated (pull) receive proportionally more attention both from service providers and customers than other categories of services in the service-dimension framework.

SERVICE-DIMENSION FRAMEWORK

Balasubramanian et al (2002) have proposed an interesting framework based on the concept of service dimensions: 1) location sensitivity, 2) time criticalness and 3) degree to which the service is initiated by the customer (pull) or by the provider (push). The three dimensions are used to generate eight different categories of services (Table 1). The conventional wisdom suggests the attraction of mobile services is directly related to the degree to which the service depends on location of provision, time-critical nature of service

Table 1: Service-Dimension Framework (adapted from Balasubramanian, et al (2002)).

Dimension 1	Dimension 2	Dimension 3	Example
Location Sensitive	Time Critical	Pull	Safety services (roadside, medical)
		Push	Local traffic updates
	Time Noncritical	Pull	Mobile Yellow Pages
		Push	Satellite-based agricultural yield-mapping
Location Insensitive	Time Critical	Pull	Stock quote request
		Push	Stock price alert
	Time Noncritical	Pull	Downloads of MP3s
		Push	Availability of chosen entertainment sources

need and users ability to control what is delivered. Pursuant to this perception, the study will examine Hypothesis 1.

SERVICE-ORIENTATION FRAMEWORK

Based on review of popular press and this author's own observations a Service-Orientation Framework for Mobile Data Services is proposed. The framework is a derivative of the traditional method for service classification – that which categorizes services based on service –types and characteristics of customers. The description of this framework is contained in Table 2.

In this context the following hypotheses will be studied (again, based on common perceptions of the current condition). Hypothesis 2 stems directly from the popularity of I-Mode applications in Japan.

Hypothesis 2: Mobile data services focused on personal communication and entertainment applications receive proportionally more attention both from service providers and customers than other categories of services in the individual segment of the service-orientation framework.

The conventional wisdom among planners of telecommunications services is that in the early stages of new service provision, one ought to exploit the early-adapters who are relatively price-insensitive. For most service providers price-insensitivity is linked to corporate accounts and organizational customers. Hypothesis 3 will test the validity of this notion.

Hypothesis 3: Mobile data services offered to organizational customers receive more attention from service providers than individual customers.

CONDUCT OF THE SURVEY

To validate the described frameworks and to gain new insights into the emerging mobile data service regime, I propose to survey the web sites of accessible GSM operators and to interview available operator personnel. The

Table 2: Service-Orientation Framework

INDIVIDUAL		
Service Type	**Service Examples**	**Description (if needed)**
Personal Communication	Multimedia Messaging	Sending of messages containing a variety of data types, including audio, video, text and image
	Video Telephony	One to one communication using audio and video
	Enhanced Telephony	Ability to attach and view data files in addition to audio
	Emobile-Postcard	
	Enhanced Chat	Interactive sending of text supplemented by sounds and image
Entertainment	Interactive Games	On-line games vs. virtual or real opponents, such as cards, board games, various video games, etc.
	Audio streaming	Continuous listening to audio -- such as music or books-on-tape – from a mobile device
	Video Streaming	Ability to watch on-demand movies or TV news on a mobile device
	Gambling	Mobile on-line gambling transactions on e.g. up to the last minute sporting events
	Ringing Tones and Handset screen savers	Ability to download data files to accomplish specific handset functions
Information and Education	Tele-learning	Ability to participate in interactive, on-line tutorial sessions with instructors and other students
	White and Yellow Pages	Consulting various listings of individuals and businesses
	EMobile-Library	Access to books, periodicals and databases
	Tourist Guides	Accessing information about the area being visited
	Location-Based Reference	Navigation services and reference information related to subscribers' location. E.g. where is the closest gas station
	Remote Consultation	Ability to consult professionals on issues related to health, engineering of particular products
	EMobile-Periodical	Accessing newspapers and magazines on a mobile device
Banking and Financial	EMobile-Banking	Conducting banking transactions from a mobile device
	EMobile-Billing	Paying bills
	EMobile-Financial Markets Trading	Buying and selling of securities
	EMobile-Cash	Ability to pay using a mobile device at vending machines
Shopping	Virtual Shopping	
	EMobile-Auction	
	EMobile-Ticketing	
Residence Management	Remote Monitoring	
	Security and Surveillance	
Home Office Management	Wireless LAN	
	Virtual Secretary	
	Video Conferencing	

ORGANIZATIONAL		
Service Type	**Service Examples**	**Description**
Organizational Communication	Sales Force Connectivity	
	Dispatch Communication	
Telemetry and Tracking	Monitoring of Devices or Meters	
	Safety Monitoring of people / animals	
	Fleet and Cargo Management	
Retail and Distribution	POS Tracking	
	Mobile Credit Card Authorization	
	Inventory Management	
	Virtual shops and showrooms	

study will take place in two phases. First, the largest operators in the most mobile-developed countries will be surveyed for the express purpose of validating proposed frameworks and for surfacing important research issues. Once this is accomplished, the second phase will expand the population of studied GSM operators to improve statistical validity and ability to generalize results.

The surveys will attempt to identify which services have been introduced, which are in the planning stages, and which are not even considered. The results are likely to contribute our understanding of the emerging mobile services and their impact on the communications industry.

REFERENCES

1) Aarnio, A., Enkenberg, A., Heikkila, J. & Hirvola, S. (2002), *Adoption and Use of Mobile Services, Empirical Evidence from a Finnish Survey*, Proceedings of the 35th Hawaii International Conference on Systems Sciences, 2002.

2) Balasubramanian, S., Peterson, R.A., Jarvenpaa, S.L. (2002), *Exploring the Implications of M-Commerce for Markets and Marketing*, Journal of the Academy of Marketing Science, Vol. 30, No. 4, pp. 348-361.

3) Carroll, I., Howard, S., Vetere, F., Peck, J. & Murphy, J. (2002), *Just what do the youth of today want? Technology appropriation by young people*, Proceedings of the 35th Hawaii International Conference on Systems Sciences, 2002.

4) Kim, H., Kim. J., Lee, Y., Cha, M. & Choi, Y. (2002), *An Empirical Study of the Use Context and Usability Problems in Mobile Internet*, Proceedings of the 35th Hawaii International Conference on Systems Sciences, 2002.

5) Palen. L, Salzman, M. Aoungs. E. (2000), *Going wireless: Behaviour & Practise of New Mobile Phone Users*, Conference paper CSCW 2000. Dec. 2-6 Philadelphia, PA.

6) Oliphant, M. *The Mobile Phone Meets the Internet*, IEEE Spectrum, August 1999.

7) Vahinen, J. And Tuunainen, V.K. (2002), *Mobile Business: Channel Capabilities and Requirements*, available on www.mobiforum.org/proceedings/papers/06/6.1.pdf (February 6, 2003)

8) Varshney, U. and Vetter, R. (2002), *Emerging Wireless and Mobile Networks*, Communications of the Association of Computing Machinery (ACM), June 2000.

9) Varshney, U. & Vetter R. (2001), *A Frameworks for the Emerging Mobile Commerce Applications*, Proceedings of the 34 Hawaii International Conference on System Science, 2001.

10) Urbaczewski, A., Wells, J. Sarker S., and Amattikorkeakoulu M., *Exploring Cultural Differences as a Means for Understanding the Global Mobile Internet: A Theoretical Basis and Program of Research*. Proceedings of the 35th Hawaii International Conference on Systems Sciences, 2002.

Effects of Informal Networks on Knowledge Management Strategies

Tony Jewels, Helen Partridge, and Alan Underwood
Queensland University of Technology, Australia
t.jewels@qut.edu.au, h.partridge@qut.edu.au, a.underwood@qut.edu.au

ABSTRACT

The application of a knowledge management strategy does not take place in a vacuum. Successfully meeting objectives of a knowledge management strategy may depend not only on the efficacy of the strategy itself or of the team that is responsible for its implementation, but also on the environment into which it is being introduced. Research carried out with an application service provider (ASP) indicates that existing informal communication networks will continue to operate independently of any formal strategy introduced. It is important therefore for management to recognise the existence of such informal networks and to understand how they are likely to affect the success of any formal knowledge management strategy.

INTRODUCTION

In 1998 an application service provider (ASP) with the assistance of a major international consultancy company acting as its implementation partner, had coordinated the simultaneous implementation of SAP R/3 across five government agencies. Three years later, this ASP, like several other organisations following the spate of Enterprise Systems (ES) implementations prior to the turn of the century, was facing its first major upgrade. The ASP General Manager (GM) appreciated the need to recall the lessons and practices from these initial projects as the extent and cost of these major upgrades were likely to match or exceed that of the initial implementation. The GM had long recognised the importance of knowledge capture, access, sharing and re-use, both for the current upgrade process and for future upgrades, and university researchers had already been engaged with the ASP in a number of research projects in the area of knowledge management within an ES environment (Timbrell and Gable, 2001), (Chang et al., 2000), (Chan and Rosemann, 2000).

Based partly on its experiences with the original implementation partner, for its forthcoming upgrade, the ASP had decided to "go it alone", choosing to employ just a few key individual contractors to work with its internal staff. Knowledge of the forthcoming upgrade and the awareness of a newly published paper, *Theory of Knowledge Reuse: Types of Knowledge Reuse Situations and Factors in Reuse Success (Markus, 2001)* provided an opportunity to test the validity of the paper's typology of knowledge reuse and to concurrently provide research data that might assist the ASP in providing conditions under which successful knowledge reuse was likely to occur. In its conclusion, the original study, (Timbrell and Jewels, 2002) supported the *Theory of Knowledge Reuse* whilst also indicating the prevalence of informal knowledge sharing networks operating within the organisation. A cursory examination of the original research provided some preliminary evidence that this informal knowledge sharing activity may somehow relate to the ultimate effectiveness of any formal knowledge management strategies implemented.

The original study tested a published knowledge re-use theory by matching the expected and actual responses to a set of predetermined questions linked to that theory. Responses originally conducted from a knowledge re-use perspective in the original study were carefully re-examined from a perspective of informal network knowledge sharing and findings subsequently compared to the current literature. The purpose of this paper is to examine the effect of informal knowledge sharing networks on formal knowledge management practices of an organization.

RESEARCH PROCESS

Semi-structured interviews were conducted over a period of six days with all twenty-eight employees within the ASP. The interviews were taped for later transcriptions and relevant notes taken to highlight key issues. Interviews, held in an office provided specifically for the purpose by management were planned for 30 minutes duration, commencing at 0830 and finishing at 1700 each working day until completion.

The interview technique used was a combination of the standardized, otherwise known as structured interview (Fontana and Frey, 1998 p.47) and guided interviews. The research team prepared a semi-standardized set of questions that would take about three quarters of the interview time and the remainder of the scheduled time was used to revisit issues that had arisen during the more structured questioning, by referring to the question topic guide. The interviewer's technique was based on the styles described by Fontana and Frey, (1998 pp.52-53) as "balanced rapport" and "interested listening", meaning that a casual yet impersonal attitude that neither evaluated nor judged the interviewees responses was maintained.

An assurance that responses would be kept confidential may have contributed to the candid nature of responses. To ensure that it was not possible for individuals or definable groups to be identified by the published data, identity numbers were allocated to each interviewee, which was used for report analysis rather than names. Names with matching identity numbers were kept in a separate database table and were kept strictly confidential, available only to the researchers.

REVIEW OF THE LITERATURE

Knowledge Requirements

In explaining the knowledge required in a project Frame (1999), suggests a three stage approach by asking,

- What skills should we possess in order to do the job?
- Do we have them?
- How can we acquire them?

According to Chan, (1999), Chan and Rosemann, (2000) ES implementations require a wide range of knowledge including, project knowledge, technical knowledge, product knowledge, business knowledge and company-specific knowledge.

Where an organisation believes that it does not have the requisite expertise, it will seek knowledge-based resources from third-party providers such as consulting firms (knowledge vendors), which act in the capacity of implementation partner (Timbrell and Gable, 2001). The GM believed however that his organisation was already experienced enough in all the identified knowledge areas to execute the upgrade without the assistance of an implementation partner.

The Contributors

For the purposes of examining knowledge dynamics within an organisation it is important to understand the roles played by each of the types referred to by Frame (1999), in contributing to competence

- The individual
- The team
- The organisation

The traditional and popular view is that it is the individuals within organizations, and not the organizations themselves that learn, (Weick, 1978), (Simon, 1976). Although new knowledge is developed by individuals, organizations do play a critical role in articulating and amplifying that knowledge. (Nonaka, 1994). The literature is increasingly discussing the use of "teams" and "communities" according to Ferrán-Urdaneta (1999), whose work discusses the differences between these two types of group. From an organisational learning perspective Andrews and Delahaye (2000) also adds the group level to that of the individual and the organization. We may, (for the purpose of this study), define a team (or community) simply as more than one individual collaborating together. It might be more controversial to suggest that for knowledge sharing purposes a team need not necessarily be part of the same organization.

Informal Networks

Whereas formal organizational structures are able to handle easily anticipated problems, when unexpected problems arise, (Krackhardt and Hanson, 1993) suggests that an informal organization kicks in. The phenomenon is discussed by Bhatt (2002), who states that employees often form their own informal communities of expertise from where they can get necessary pieces of knowledge.

It should be emphasised that the informal structures that are being referred to in this paper do not directly relate to the informal transfers of tacit knowledge described by Nonaka, (1994) occurring between employees, (although this type of informal transfer might still occur within an informal structure). Informal networks are relationships developed between individuals independently of any formal structure (although an informal structure might occur within a formal structure), and are not the chance meetings at the water cooler or cafeteria that Davenport and Prusak (1998), discusses, but carefully conceived personal "networks of knowing", built up over time and used as complementary knowledge sharing alternatives to an organization's formal strategy. They are described by Krackhardt and Hanson (1993), as being highly adaptive, moving diagonally and elliptically, skipping entire functions to get work done. In much of the type of work that 'symbolic analysts' perform, frequent and informal conversations are used as neither problem nor solutions can be defined in advance, (Reich, 1991). The development and prominence of informal networks could be related to the culture state within an organization.

Organisational Culture

Culture, according to McDermott and O'Dell (2001), is often seen as a key inhibitor of effective knowledge sharing. A wide body of evidence exists to indicate that organizational or corporate culture is critical to the success of most, if not all ES implementations. There are four hypothesized categories of organisational obstacles in information systems development, according to Jin (1993) namely,

- Bureaucratic complexity
- Personality conflict
- Technical complexity
- Acute resource scarcity

The effect that organisational culture has on knowledge management strategies is being increasingly recognised as a major barrier to leveraging intellectual assets according to De Long and Fahey (2000), who consider four ways in which culture influences the behaviour central to knowledge creation, sharing and use,

- Culture, and particularly subcultures, shape assumptions about what knowledge is and which knowledge is worth managing.
- Culture defines the relationships between individual and organisational knowledge, determining who is expected to control specific knowledge, as well as who must share it and who can hoard it.
- Culture creates the context for social interaction that determines how knowledge will be used in particular situations.
- Culture shapes the processes by which new knowledge, with its accompanying uncertainties, is created, legitimated and distributed in organisations

Certain types of identifiable culture have the potential to affect an ERP environment, (Stewart et al., 2000). Although these culture states can affect different types of organizations in different ways and each can be more prevalent in certain types of organization, they may best be identified by comparing how closely the organization meets the following principles,

- Genuine user empowerment that produces internal as well as external commitment.
- Acceptance of "risk-taking" as a necessary factor in planning, which does not punish failure, and the move away from non-competitive or even anti-competitive cultures to true market competitive cultures.

Formal organization charts have little relevance to the true sources of power in the high-value enterprise, according to Reich (1991), "Power depends not on formal authority or rank (as it did in the high-volume enterprise), but on the capacity to add value to enterprise webs" (p99).

Knowledge Sharing Choices

The role that individual-level processes play in organisational learning is examined by Andrews and Delahaye (2000), in terms of how knowledge inputs and outputs are mediated by individuals. Knowledge inputs are discussed in terms of the individuals' social confidence and their perception of the credibility of the knowledge source. Knowledge outputs are discussed in terms of what knowledge would be shared with whom, determined by the perceived trustworthiness of the recipient. The term "psychosocial filter" is used to describe the cluster of factors that influence knowledge sharing processes, and is described as working at the 'micro-level'.

OBJECTIVES

The purpose of this study is to investigate the nature of informal knowledge sharing within the organization, a rationale for its existence and its possible affect on the operation of the organisation's formal knowledge management policy. In seeking to better understand the dynamics of informal knowledge sharing, our objective is to inform academe and practitioners on ways of improving the effectiveness of knowledge management strategy.

FINDINGS

Informal Networks

There was evidence from the interviews that knowledge sharing was occurring in at least two identifiable modes. Management had introduced a range of knowledge sharing initiatives that could be considered as a formal top-down approach. It was however clearly evident that employees' were using an alternative method of knowledge sharing to the one created by management. Individuals had formed their own personal networks and had developed their own "communities of interest" in what could be considered as an informal bottom-up approach.

What was interesting in our research was that management, although recognising the existence of informal networks, had had no direct role in either creating or nurturing them and had little idea of their extent and frequency of use.

The following examples were typical of the responses:
"Who I use (as experts) and the people on the formal experts list are different"
"I network with people that I have worked with in the past"
"I use my personal network of contacts if I can't readily find appropriate documentation"
"I have an extensive personal collection of books that I use"

The manner in which the "hidden" teams engaged in knowledge sharing practices was however strictly informal and consequently management would not have been reasonably expected to be aware of how they operated. Interestingly, although the management executives themselves had indicated that they were using their own informal knowledge sharing structures, they still did not fully appreciate that similar practices operated extensively at other levels within their organization.

Organizational Barriers

Although evidence of all four categories of obstacle referred to by Jin was identified in the research, it appeared that when confronted with these obstacles employees would merely find an alternative way to reach their objectives. There was a general feeling that these organizational obstacles, although considered annoying, could be bypassed, if necessary. One of the common methods employees used to circumvent organizational obstacles was to marshal their own informal structures.

However the barriers that De Long refers to are not as easily bypassed. These are the ones that appear able to be controlled only by organizational initiatives. The barriers referred to by Stewart et al are either similarly organizationally controlled or are deeply personalised in the individual, (Stewart et al., 2000).

System security appeared to be an issue that was affecting knowledge sharing activities. One contractor admitted,

"I don't know of any contractors that have had direct access to the Knowledge database"

while one relatively new full time employee commented that,

"I wasn't even told about the existence of the knowledge data base"

There was a policy that employees should only be given access to the specific areas that they were working in, and subsequently lessons learnt from one part of the system were seldom able to be formally shared with those that did not have access to that part. Remarks such as,

"No-one would be interested in what I am doing"
"I only bother formally documenting for myself because I am the only person who would need to use this type of information"

indicated a general under-utilisation of formal knowledge sharing practices.

Formal KM Strategies

The importance of formal team building and creating a sense of shared purpose as described by Senge, (1992) was clearly evident to management as they had embarked on a range of formal initiatives to harness its potential.

By his introduction of such initiatives as a free text knowledge database and the championing of specific knowledge transfer sessions the GM appeared typical of the sort of individual that Skyrme, (1999) and Health Canada, (2000) refer to when they suggest that the appointment of a senior executive responsible for knowledge initiatives appeared to be a prerequisite to a successful KM strategy.

Yet the knowledge transfer sessions were not well regarded with comments such as,

"Skill transfer sessions were not popular, they were seen as a waste of time and irrelevant"

Although it was evident that management understood the rationale for these sessions it was uncertain whether there was an understanding by employees of their raison d'tre.

What was made unambiguously clear in the interviews was that the knowledge sharing that was intended to take place with the original implementation partner (IP) did not occur properly. Comments such as,

"(The IP) knew very little regarding SAP and the Government's business rules".
"(The IP) kept public servants at 'arm's length' or possibly didn't have the required knowledge themselves".

indicated a lack of trust and confidence in the IP.

CONCLUSIONS

There was a clear indication that informal knowledge sharing was taking place throughout the organisation. No pattern was evident to suggest that the knowledge sharing structures were anything but randomly formed. It appeared that many, but not all, of the individuals who were most actively involved in informal knowledge sharing groups were those people who had been with the organization, (or ones similar to it), the longest.

It was evident that individuals within these informal structures maintained their links, after job changes, or even after leaving the organisation in which the original structure was formed. This would suggest that the organization itself may have little impact in how informal knowledge sharing structures are formed and are operated.

There was evidence to suggest that wherever there was a perceived failure to provide a process for adequate individual or organizational learning, although some individuals merely complained, many automatically engaged in alternative strategies to ensure that they would be able to do their work. One of the main strategies used was that of engaging in informal networks.

It is likely that once any appropriate knowledge sharing strategy (formal or informal) is securely in place, the widespread adoption of any alternative strategy (formal or informal) will need not only to prove its own worth but also to prove itself more effective than any existing strategy, in order to take a pre-eminent position. It would appear logical to assume therefore that the prevalence and strength of any informal network would impact the internal acceptance of a newly introduced formal knowledge management strategy. Evidence of robust informal network activity within the subject organization would at least partly explain the relatively unenthusiastic acceptance by staff of formally introduced knowledge management initiatives.

REFERENCES

Andrews, K. M. and Delahaye, B. L. (2000) Influences on Knowledge Processes in Organizational Learning: the Psychosocial Filter, *Journal of Management Studies*, 37(6) pp797-810.

Bhatt, G. D. (2002) Management Strategies for Individual Knowledge and Organizational Knowledge, *Journal of Knowledge Management*, 6(1) pp31-39.

Chan, R. (1999) 'Knowledge Management for Implementing ERP in SMEs', proceedings of 3rd Annual SAP Asia Pacific SAPPHIRE 1999 Singapore 1-2 November

Chan, R. and Rosemann, M. (2000) 'Managing Knowledge in Enterprise Systems', proceedings of Americas Conference of Information Systems Boston, USA 3-5 August

Chang, S.-I., Gable, G. G., Smythe, E. and Timbrell, G. T. (2000) 'A Delphi examination of public sector ERP implementation issues', proceedings of International Conference of Information Systems Brisbane, Australia 10-13 December

Davenport, T. H. and Prusak, L. (1998) *Working Knowledge: How Organizations Manage what they Know*, Harvard Business School Press, Boston MA.

De Long, D. W. and Fahey, L. (2000) Diagnosing Cultural Barriers to Knowledge Management, *Academy of Management Executive*, 14(4) pp113-127.

Ferrán-Urdaneta, C. (1999) 'Teams or Communities? Organizational Structures for Knowledge Management', proceedings of SIGCPR '99 New Orleans

Fontana, A. and Frey, J. (1998) Collecting and Interpreting Qualitative Materials In *Interviewing: The Art of Science* (Eds, Denzin, N. and Lincoln, Y.) Sage, Thousand Oaks, CA, pp. 47-78.

Frame, J. D. (1999) *Project Management Competence*, Josey-Bass, USA.

Health Canada (2000) *Vision and Strategy for Knowledge Management and IM/IT for Health Canada* Health Canada URL http://www.hc-sc.gc.ca/iacb-dgiac/km-gs/english/vsmenu2_e.htm

Jin, K. G. (1993) Overcoming Organizational Barriers to System Development: An Action Strategy Framework, *Journal of Systems Management*, 44(5) pp28-33.

Krackhardt, D. and Hanson, J. R. (1993) Informal Networks: The Company Behind the Chart, *Harvard Business Review*, (July-August).

Markus, M. L. (2001) Toward a theory of knowledge reuse: Types of knowledge reuse situations and factors in reuse success, *Journal of Management Information Systems*, 18(1) pp57-93.

McDermott, R. and O'Dell, C. (2001) Overcoming Cultural Barriers to Sharing Knowledge, *Journal of Knowledge Management*, 5(1) pp76-85.

Nonaka, I. (1994) A Dynamic Theory of Organizational Knowledge Creation, *Organisational Science*, 5(1).

Reich, R. B. (1991) *The Work of Nations*, Vintage Books, USA.

Senge, P. M. (1992) *The Fifth Discipline: The Art and Practice of the Learning Organization*, Random House Australia, Adelaide, Australia.

Simon, H. A. (1976) *Administrative Behaviour: A Study of Decision Making Processes in Administrative Organization 3rd ed.*, Free Press, New York NY.

Skyrme, D. J. (1999) *Knowledge Management: Making it Work* David Skyrme Associates URL http://www.skyrme.com/pubs/lawlib99.htm

Stewart, G., Milford, M., Jewels, T., Hunter, T. and Hunter, B. (2000) 'Organisational Readiness for ERP Implementation', proceedings of AMCIS 2000 Long Beach CA August

Timbrell, G. and Jewels, T. (2002) 'Knowledge Re-use Situations in an Enterprise Systems Context', proceedings of IRMA 2002 Seattle WA

Timbrell, G. T. and Gable, G. G. (2001) 'The SAP Ecosystem: A Knowledge Perspective', proceedings of Information Resources Management Association International Conference Toronto, Canada 20-23 May 2001

Weick, K. E. (1978) *The Social Psychology of Organizing*, Addison-Wesley, Reading MA.

Content Presentation in a Four Factor E-learning Model

Rhoda Joseph
Baruch College, City University of New York
One Bernard Baruch Way, Box B 11-220
New York NY 10010-5585
(646) 312-3393   (Office)
Rhoda_Joseph@baruch.cuny.edu

ABSTRACT

E-learning has received significant attention as organizations attempt to reduce costs and streamline operations. A four-factor model is proposed to describe the critical elements in the e-learning environment. The four elements are product, service, channel and synergy. The traditional learning environment viewed learning as a function in a social context that involved a variety of components such as teachers, learners and tools. This paper focuses on the way that the content is presented in the e-learning environment with a focus on the organization. The focus on the content presentation addresses issues pertaining to the individual user needs, and argues that there needs to be a fit between the content presentation format and the user's cognitive description of the problem. Content presentation is not the single factor that affects the success or failure of an e-learning strategy. However, discussion of content presentation can provide a basis to examine the underlying components that are relevant to successfully selecting and implementing e-learning initiatives.

E-LEARNING ENVIRONMENT

There are many challenges and issues facing the organization in today's environment. Efficient management and accountability; revenue generation; competition and global responsive; are a few of the issues that come to mind. In a technology driven marketplace new issues are emerging and need to be addressed. One such item that has received increasing interest and relevance over the last few years is organizational e-learning initiatives.

A skeptic can argue that by placing an "e" in front of an established idea or construct does not automatically make it a new and innovative one. However, the e-learning landscape presents and environment for discussion and development that would not have previously been relevant, in the context of traditional learning.

In the most generic sense, a *book* is the tool most frequently associated with learning. Books vary in many different dimensions including topic, type, context and overall function. The book, teacher and student represents the traditional context of learning, with the book viewed as the technological component (Bruckman 2002). In the e-learning environment, shifts have redefined this traditional structure and now placed a network with supporting material as the main technological component.

E-learning is defined as learning that has a significant involvement with computers and interactive networks simultaneously (Tsai et al. 2002). The world-wide-web is the prototypical example of an interactive network involving computers. The definition of e-learning also encompasses learning on local networks such as Intranets.

In an attempt to reduce costs associated with employee training and education several businesses today are investing in e-learning technologies (Dorai et al. 2001; Goodridge 2002; Pantazis 2002). However, many organizations are realizing that cost reduction cannot be the major determinant for the implementation of e-learning. The new focus of e-learning includes increased worker productivity, improved operational efficiency and streamlining corporate training (Goodridge 2002).

There must be a careful assessment of the needs of the organization in terms of its training needs, and an honest analysis of what can feasibly be transferred to this platform. It is unrealistic to suggest that all training needs within the organization can at some point be transposed to an e-learning environment. The selection of e-learning tools involves consideration of factors such as: functionality, customization and support.

This paper identifies four critical factors that affect the choice of the e-learning tool that will be implemented in an organization. These four factors are: product, service, channel and synergy. E-learning consists of both product and service components.

The product component can be viewed as largely a function of the design team. However, just as schools, colleges and other learning institutions invest time and effort into selecting the best books, the product that supports the e-learning environment also needs attention. Learning is a social artifact that involves many different elements. These combine to create a "learning environment". This paper pays particular attention to the product component of the e-learning environment.

E-LEARNING COMPONENTS MODEL

The organizational super highway is littered with companies that attempted to introduce new technological initiatives and failed. For the successful implementation and adoption of any new technology the correct infrastructure must be in place.

The infrastructure that must exist to support the successful implementation of the e-learning product includes personnel and a commitment by the organization to support its implementation. There is a strong dynamic with e-learning initiatives that links learning, people and organizational performance (Pantazis 2002). This triad highlights the social context of e-learning.

Moving one step beyond the social phenomenon and service, is the discussion of the product. One of the strong selling points of the e-learning product is the promise of customization. In the traditional learning environment, the teacher, the tools and the methods were usually immutably fixed. There is now a shift from the classroom group mode in the traditional environment, to the individual learner mode in the e-learning environment. The learners can access material on their own time and develop a Just-In-Time delivery format for training (Pantazis 2002).

The three main components forming the e-learning environment are the product, the channel and the service. The product is created from knowledge acquired for the particular topic. The channel refers to how the material is delivered and distributed. The service refers to all the promises that the product will deliver. The service components include user satisfaction; improved organizational performance and the creation and development of learning communities. The three components converge to establish organizational synergy – derived from within a social context.

Figure 1 (The E-learning Components Model) illustrates the four main components of the e-learning environment. The primary component of the product is content presentation. Consider the similarity as we look at two textbooks that cover the identical topic. The large difference between how users react to the content will be based on how the material is presented. With the absence of a live teacher or trainer content presentation becomes more critical.

The components proposed in the e-learning model are relevant irrespective of if the product is being custom designed or purchased off-the-shelf. A four-step method for the selection of an off-the-shelf product involves 1. Iden-

Figure 1 (The E-learning Components Model)

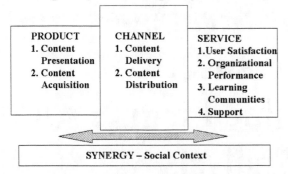

SYNERGY – Social Context

tifying selection criteria and constraints; 2. Select shortlist of vendors; 3. Select and Test Courses; 4. Package and Implement (Lewis et al. 2002). Each of these steps involves or relates to components that have been outlined in the four-factor e-learning components model. A customized product involves more input on accurate content acquisition.

CONTENT PRESENTATION

E-learning includes the use of various tools such as video conferencing, satellite delivered learning and virtual educational networks (Pantazis 2002). This paper takes a very focused view and concentrates primarily on web-based instruction.

The management of content in the e-learning infrastructure is a major issue that must be addressed when such systems are to be adopted and implemented (Goodridge 2002). Content management involves determining what format is best for the needs of different users. The presentation of the content provides a great opportunity to customize the product to fit the specific needs of the end-users.

The media transfer channel has historically limited presentation of content on the web. The emergence of broadband has helped to significantly minimize the channel distribution problem. With web-based instruction material is downloaded to the user machines. The speed of downloads is a key design factor that can discourage many first time e-learners from returning to the system (Hartley 2002). The use of broadband introduces more options to support non-text content presentation for the e-learning environment.

The e-learning environment presents a great opportunity for more use of stunning two and three-dimensional visualizations. A main strength of three-dimensional graphics is that it can be used to impress a user and bring more "real-world-effects" to the desktop. Presentation formats affect a user's decision-making process and the attitude that they have towards the product (Tractinsky et al. 1999).

THEORETICAL FOUNDATIONS

The cognitive fit theory states that for a general problem-solving mode there must be a "fit" between the problem representation and the problem task (Vessey 1991). The initial application of the cognitive fit theory dealt with users that were completing problem-solving task with both graphical and tabular data items. This discussion applies the foundation concepts of that theory to the e-learning environment, with the goal of completing a learning task. It is proposed that in a learning environment there must also be a fit between the data representation and the learning task.

The content must be presented in a manner that will be coherent with the user's underlying mental model and understanding of the material. One of the main principles adhered to in this paper is that the e-learning environment primarily supports the individual learner or trainee. For the user to obtain the best results, and continue to user the product, there must be components that they can relate to on the interface level.

Some of the seven intelligences (Gardner 2000) can be easily applied to content presentation on-line. However, in the attempt to bring about a fit between the content presentation and the user, a determination of the users intelligences and learning preferences can be a step in that direction.

Graphical content in the e-learning environment can be a very attractive feature. Knowledge represented for the purpose of learning can be either presented in a literal or figurative format (Boland Jr. et al. 2001). The figurative component for learning encompasses graphical items in one, two and three dimensions. The argument that is purported here is that for effectiveness in our e-learning environment a critical building block from the individual perspective is that the content presentation matches the user's learning model. The ability to present data in a variety of formats supports this objective.

FUTURE DIRECTIONS AND IMPLICATIONS

This paper presents a four-factor e-learning components model. The main objective of this model is to isolate the constituents of the e-learning environment. The categorization of these four factors provides a framework for further work to be developed in each of the four groups.

The focus on the product and the content presentation of the product was necessary. Too many discussions about e-learning have focused on the end result and promised service that was not delivered, and ignored some of foundation items that are critical. A textbook is taken for granted in many academic and learning environments. However, it receives significant negative attention if it does not present the material in a manner that can easily be understood and assimilated by the student.

E-learning is still in its infancy and many advances have already been made E-learning provides a window of choices to all involved and can transform learning from an organizational domain to an individual domain (Wallhaus 2000). Cognitive issues become relevant in a discussion about individual domains in the e-learning environment. Different cognitive characteristics can influence the user's decision to return to the product and continue to use it in the manner for which it was designed. This research can be further extended to actually test the influence of the different content presentation formats and how users respond to the different environments.

CONCLUSION

E-learning can be a formidable alternative to some traditional learning environments. E-learning initiatives, when successfully implemented, present many advantages and opportunities for an organization. These benefits range from tangible cost reductions to more intangible items such as streamlining organizational training.

Computer training has had a long history in supporting organizations. Behavior modeling, when compared to lecture training and independent study produced better results with respect to knowledge retention, transfer of learning and end-user satisfaction in an experimental setting (Simon et al. 1996). Behavior modeling involves combining elements of the lecture mode and the independent study mode with individual user characteristics. The e-learning environment is a hybrid for behavioral modeling that can potentially recoup substantial gains for the learning organization.

The components model proposed in this paper highlights some of the main concerns involved in defining the e-learning landscape. The selection of content presentation as a focal point highlights the need for users to be able to relate to the content they must learn and assimilate. Presentation format of the content can have an impact on whether the individual user is motivated internally to re-use the system. Many business users view the use of graphics as a way to disseminate an idea and convince an audience about the product (Tractinsky et al. 1999). The use of two and three-dimensional visualizations in the presentation can also enhance the user's experience.

This paper in no way makes the case that the content presentation component of the product is the most significant factor. However, this issue might be overlooked as there is a very strong focus on the organizational needs of e-learning and to a lesser extent the needs of the individual user. Focusing on content presentation addresses the concerns of the individual that will be responsible for using the tool.

For future studies it would be very helpful to empirically test these ideas and isolate each of the four factors presented in the model. E-learning has many areas to explore and it will continue to be an issue of interest and relevance to organizations.

REFERENCES

Furnished upon request.

Environment, Generic Strategies, and Resource-Based Perspective On Performance In Online Firms : An Empirical Analysis

Chulmo Koo, Kichan Nam, and Jae Beom Lee
Sogang University
Shinsu-Dong 1, Mapo-Ku, Seoul, Korea
Tel: 82-2-705-8710, Tel: 82-2-705-8710, Tel: 82-2-705-8538
Fax: 82-2-703-8224, Fax: 82-2-703-8224, Fax: 82-2-717-9773
helmet@sogang.ac.kr, knam@ccs.sogang.ac.kr, jblee@sogang.ac.kr

Chang E. Koh
University of North Texas
College of Business Administration
P.O. Box 305249, Denton, TX 76203-5249
Phone & Fax: (940) 565-3625
E-mail: kohce@unt.edu

ABSTRACT

In these days, fims have recognized the potential and the importance of electronic commerce to survive in this increasingly complex and competitive market. Electronic commerce can be used to create and enhance competitive strategies by all types and sizes of firms. Today all types of firms are squaring off for a dominant position in a virtual market. However, firms should carefully consider various factors such as the size of a firm, its access to resources, and the industry in which it competes.

The resource-based theory is one of attempts to explain how firms acquire a strategic advantage emphasizes the availability of various internal resources for sustainable competitive advantage. The resource of the dot.com was usually augmented by on or more of a network of joint ventures, strategic alliances and venture capital consortia, but the surviving dot.coms are usually led by new and more realistic wealth creators. This paper integrates environment, generic strategies, and the resource-based perspective on performance in online firms. More theoretically the results will imply the environment factors and the resource factors which can influence the strategic choices and the selected strategies make a direct impact on the performance. And also the resources of firm are another in determining performance. And the practically, managers in online firms must consider firms assets and environment simultaneously to firm success.

I. INTRODUCTION

For the past few decades we have been witnessing unprecedented technological changes and increasingly turbulent market conditions. Information technologies(IT) and management techniques are readily available to all businesses that transcend geographic boundaries, that served customer within 24 hours business time . Porter (2001) suggests that the Internet can help organization achieve competitive advantages by either improving operational effectiveness or enhancing its strategic position in the market. In this time, new players more easily to enter the traditional market — either physically or virtually — and consequently increases the level of complexity of market dynamics and intensifies competition. Therefore, many traditional firms couldn't ignore the potential and the importance of electronic commerce to survive in this increasingly complex and competitive market. By effectively adopting electronic commerce, a traditional firm may improve its profitability by increasing its market share while reducing costs (Amit and Zott, 2001). For example, companies like Kmart entered into a partnership with bluelight.com and Banz and Noble Inc. launched another online firm(www.banzandnoble.com) in an attempt to add an electronic channel to their existing "bricks-and-mortar" channel to counter emerging online firms like eBay, Yahoo!, Amazon and LookSmart. Even though the electronic commerce still makes up a small part of all commerce, it is growing rapidly. Forrester Research estimates that electronic commerce will reach $ 3.2 trillion in 2003 (www.forester.com).

Today all types of firms are squaring off for a dominant position in a virtual market. Technically savvy online startups like amazon.com took advantage of Internet technologies to break into the market that would have been considered impenetrable. Many of these online firms quickly became a significant force to reckon with. Their flexible organizational culture and entrepreneurial sprit often make these upstarts more apt to rapidly evolving technologies and changing market environments (Yoffie and Cusumano, 1999). In response, traditional firms like Barnes & Noble counter not only with added online channels but also by linking new online business to their existing brands and physical presence and services(Strategic Change, 1999). While technology plays an important role in almost every aspect of business, increasingly competitive market is forcing firms to look for ways to utilize technology to gain strategic advantages.

Previous studies have looked into technology can provide competitive advantages such as requiring superior cost structure (Porter, 1980), offering different products and services (Caves and Williamson, 1985), offering superior products through innovation (Miller and Friesen, 1984) and establishing strategic alliance with business partners (Kogut, 1988). It means that firms should carefully consider IT based on various factors such as the size of a firm(Wright, 1987), its access to resources(Porter, 2001), and the industry(Porter, 1980) and environment(Miller, 1988) in which it competes.

The resource-based theory is one of attempts to explain how firms acquire a strategic advantage emphasizes the availability of various internal resources for sustainable competitive advantage. It argues that a firm's performance is a function of how well it establishes itself in the market around resources that are valuable, rare, inimitable, and substitutes (Barney, 1991). These resources may include not only tangible but also intangible assets such as management skills, organizational processes and routines, and information and knowledge it controls (Barney et al, 2001).

Recently many firms have formed strategic alliance to strengthen their strategic position in the market and to compete with new online players that pose a serious threat. The resource of the dot.com was usually augmented by on or more of a network of joint ventures, strategic alliances and venture capital consortia, but the surviving dot.coms are usually led by new and more realistic wealth creators (Business Horizons, 2002)* working to more robust business plans and info-technology platforms for product and service distribution (Strategic, 2001) and brand strength (Coltman et al, 2002).

This paper integrates environment(Miller, 1988), generic strategies(Porter, 1980) and the resource-based perspective on performance in online firms. Previous research identified empirically that environment can influence choices of strategy within an industry or across industries(Miller, 1988). And Spanos and Lioukas (2001) studied both perspectives' strategy, firm-assets effects and industry forces on firm performance. This paper introduces a composite model by integrating different theories as discussed above. The research framework will be tested on online firms. Subsequent sections present the model development and hypotheses, and then the expected results.

II. THEORY

The Competitive Strategy and Performance

The theory advanced by Porter (1980, 1985, 1990, 1991) departs markedly from the traditional IO theory. Porter focuses on the performance of individual firms rather than the performance of the industry. Furthermore, he considers the industry structure to be neither wholly exogenous nor stable, as commonly viewed in the traditional IO theory (Bain, 1968; Caves, 1972). Porter's two perspectives are the role of firm's conduct in influencing performance and industry structure still central role in explaining firm performance. Competitive strategies generically embody and implement the firm's desire to achieve cost leadership, product differentiation, and focus (Porter, 1980; 1985). Within this overall strategic orientation, the firm has the choice to develop products to satisfy a wide range of commercial and industrial demands, or products which focus on specific market segments.

Environment and Strategy

Traditional contingency theorists have argued that the uncertain environment that seem to necessitate the innovation (Miller, 1988), require organic (Burns and Stalker, 1961), decentralized, differentiated (Lawrence and Lorsch, 1967), and intensively integrated (Galbraith, 1973; Thompson, 1967) structures. According to the literature, strategies as necessary responses to environments more than as influencers of environments. Business strategy has strong relationship with environment (Miller, 1988; Burns and Stalker, 1961; Dess and Beard, 1984; Hambrick, 1983b, 1985; Miller and Friesen, 1983; Zaltman et al, 1973). Innovation and marketing differentiation are typically more necessary in dynamic and uncertain environments (Burns and Stalker, 1961; Porter, 1980; Miller, 1988). Miller (1988) argued that the matching of strategy and environment can influence performance whereas the poor match can hurt performance. The environmental unpredictability (Khandwalla, 1977)-the difficulty of forecasting the behavior of competitors and customers, and the environmental dynamism- product and practices change quickly (Duncan, 1972) have associated with the strategy.

The Resource-Based View Perspective

Edith Penrose (1959) has been credited by several authors espousing a resource-based perspective of the firm as having been instrumental to the development of this perspective. Wernerfelt (1984) and Teece (1982) cited Penrose's (1959) work: 'the idea of looking at firms as a broader set of resources', 'the optimal growth of the firm involves a balance between exploitation of existing resources and development of new one.' The RBV distinguishes between resources that can be acquired in factor markets and those developed inside the firm. To confer competitive advantage, resources must not be possessed by all competing firms, they must be difficult to imitate or duplicate through other means, and contribute positively to performance (Barney, 1991). The Resource Based View of the firm focusing on the relationships between firm internal characteristics and performance. Firm may be heterogeneous in relation to the resources and capabilities on which they base their strategies, and these resources and capabilities may not be perfectly mobile across firms, resulting in heterogeneity among industry participants (Barney, 1991)

The Complementary Relation with RBV and Strategies

Besides the apparent conflicting views between the two perspectives outlined above, it has been recently recognized that the "competitive strategy" and resource-base perspectives complement each other in explaining a firm's performance. The two perspectives have made significant and complementary contributions in the field of strategic management (Foss, 1996, 1997a; Amit and Schoemaker, 1993; Peteraf, 1993; Mahoney and Pandian, 1992; Conner, 1991). As Barney and Zajac (1994) have argued, the examination of strategy implementation skills (i.e., resources and capabilities) cannot be understood independently of strategy content and the competitive environment within which the firm operates. Spanos and Lioukas (2001) studied the Porter framework of competitive strategy and the resource-based view of the firm.

The Resource Based View and the Other Areas' Studies

(1) Information Technology

Mata, Fuerst and Barney (1995) showed the resource-based theory as a means of analyzing sustainability. They justified IT RBV such as capital requirements, proprietary technology, technical IT skills, and managerial IT skills. And the managerial IT skills is the only one of these attributes that can provide sustainability. Powell and Dent-Micallef (1997) investigated between IT and firm performance. The findings show that IT alone have not produced sustainable performance advantages but have gained with intangible, complementary human and business resources such as flexible culture, strategic planning, IT planning, and supplier relationships.

(2) Human Resources Management

Wright et al (2001) investigated that a firm's success has contributed to the interaction and convergence of strategy and HRM (Human Resource Management) issues. They provide a preliminary framework that suggests core competence, dynamic capabilities, and knowledge serve as a bridge between the strategy and the HRM such as the process of attraction, development, motivation, and retention of people.

(3) Marketing Research

RBV in marketing research needs to identify precisely how customer value in the form of specific attributes, benefits, attitudes and network effects is intended, generated, and sustained. RBV research has been important in suggesting that local firms are interested in using foreign alliances to acquire advantages over their domestic rivals, in emphasizing the importance of network ties as an intangible resource for entrepreneurial start-ups. Schroeder,

(4) Manufacturing Strategy

Bates and Junttila (2002) examines manufacturing strategy from the perspective of the RBV of the firm. The resources and capabilities are formed by employees' internal learning based on cross-training and suggestion systems, external learning from customers and suppliers, and proprietary processes and equipment developed by the firm.

III. HYPOTHESES

Our research extends previous research into the cyber market of online firms. The composite model include P environment, Porter's generic strategies, and resources within firm associated with competitive sustainable performance.

Environment, Strategy and Performance

Porter (1980) distinguished three generic strategies: differentiation, cost leadership, and focus. Miller (1986) noted that there are at least two different types of differentiation strategies: those based on product innovation and those based on intensive marketing and image management. Miller (1988) suggested environments that are unpredictable or subject to much change will create severe diseconomies for firms trying to pursue cost leadership. Product innovation is generally more prevalent and useful in dynamic environments. Without innovation, firms in such settings fall behind, losing market share and sales. When innovations induce competitors to retaliate, the result is a still more dynamic and unpredictable environment and the need for further change to maintain effective differentiation (Scherer, 1980). Marketing differentiation is likely to invite competitive responses, thereby increasing not only unpredictability but market dynamism as well. Focus can reduce the information-processing burden of managers, allowing a depth of knowledge that enhances predictability. Therefore, there are many narrowly focused firms operating in highly unpredictable settings.

Yoffie and Cusumano (1999) told that conventional and e-commerce environment may be fundamentally different. The competitive e-commerce environment is considerably shaped by developments in hardware, software, and networking technologies and therefore inextricably liked to the rapid cycles of change in these enabling technologies. The phrase Internet time has been used to describe the heightened pace of operations and rapid cycles of decision making required to exploit extremely short windows of opportunity to gain competitive advantage (Yoffie and Cusumano, 1999). The current environments are characterized by considerable volatility and are described as a parallel universe(Fox 1999) requiring radically different organizational strategies and managerial mindsets. So here we infer the hypothesis based on the literatures.

Hypothesis 1-1: The cyber environment of unpredictability and dynamism will make an impact on the firms' strategic choices.

Hypotheses 1-2 : The selected strategies influence on the firm performance directly.

A Resource-Based View of Online Firm and Performance.

General definition of resource are broadly categorized such as assets, knowledge, capabilities, and organizational processes. Grant (1991) distinguishes between resources and capabilities and provides a classification of resources into tangible, intangible, and personnel-based resources. Tangible resources include the financial capital and the physical assets of the firm such as plant, equipment, and stocks of raw materials. Intangible resources encompass assets such as reputation, band image, and product quality, while personnel-based resources include technical know-how and other knowledge assets including dimensions such as organizational culture, employee training, loyalty etc. Firms create competitive advantage by assembling resources that work together to create organizational capabilities. Capabilities is an organization's ability to assemble, integrate, and deploy valued resources (Amit and Schoemaker, 1993; Russo and Fouts, 1997). Castanias and Helfat (2001) present two resource characteristics for firm performance. One is managerial abilities such as leadership quality or functional area experience, the other is fundamental resource-based characteristics such as scarcity, immobility, and inimitability. The authors argue that managerial resources, which cannot be imitated quickly or which may have imperfect substitutes. Online firms tend to be technology-driven and have significant capabilities related to Internet technologies(Yoffie and Cusumano, 1999).

(1) Technological Resource

EC technologies have received very much attention from both academia and practice in the last few years (Chircu and Kauffman, 2000). EC technology investments might be understood and evaluated form a similar perspective, and shows how one might link impacts in a business process to firm outcomes at the market level. Kauffman et al (2000) argued that the value of an electronic banking network as a combination of firm-specific value and networking-generated value, and showed that banks participating in shared networks can reap more benefits from electronic banking systems than banks with proprietary systems. Clemons (1991) and Clemons and Row (1991) pointed out a firm can obtain a sustainable competitive advantage if it uses IT to exploit specific organizational characteristics. When other firm resources are both specialized and indispensable to a specific IT, they become co-specialized assets (Teece, 1987). Amazon has developed sophisticated internal search engines to make product search very easy and precise. The online bookseller also offers additional search features, such as pointing the customer to related books of interest. At Books.com can compare prices with other vendors. Books.com's own search engine will ping Amazon.com and Barnesandnoble.com Inc (Sloan Management Review, 2000)*. Since these resources may be unique or hard and costly to imitate, other firms may not be able to acquire or build them fast enough. E-business success depends on continually monitoring state-of-the art Internet features to make sure a website incorporates them ahead of competitors. Also important is having up-to-date development expertise –either in-house or through an outside partnership. Developers need to be able to design and upgrade the back and front ends of their e-business using languages and tools that are universally accessible to a complete range of customers with varying operating systems, software, and Internet browsers (USA Today, Mar 2002)*. So here we infer the hypothesis based on the literatures.

Hypothesis 2-1: The firm performance will depend on the technology resources and capabilities directly.

Hypothesis 2-2: The technology resources and capability will make an impact on firm's strategic choices and then the selected strategies influence the firm performance indirectly.

Figure 1. <Conceptual Framework>

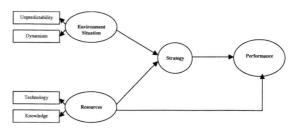

Knowledgeable Resources

Today, most assume that e-business stands for browser-accessible applications of many flavors and their necessary infrastructure. What has been added to this description are the business-process changes and organizational commitments necessary for success. If a company wants to deploy an agent portal with handy access to renewal information, it will need to realize that business processes will need to change-sometimes radically. If departments within a company-marketing, sales, customer service-fail to realize the scope of these nontechnology e-business requirements, they may find themselves alone at the launch party (Best's Review, Jan 2002).

Charles Schwab and Fidelity Investments have found significant success with their online trading services. Schwab was a very early mover to the online trading area. Therefore, it has long-held competencies in serving a customer base from a distance. Its telephone trading system was in place long before the Internet existed, and its information and data systems made it relatively easy to make the transition to the Web. Schwab's corporate culture has supported its "serving a customer at a distance" strategy. These in-place competencies and assets transferred efficiently and effectively to the Web, and gave Schwab an advantage over its counterparts. (Sloan Management Review, 2000). Banding resource will be important, too. The actual EC vendor band is important to the extent that it signals reliability and customer service. The opportunity for new EC bands has arisen, however, in the commodity and quasi-commodity segments. Hence, we see the rise of Amazon, Buy.com Inc. and Travelocity.com Inc. (Sloan Management Review, 2000). In an Ernst & Young survey on e-commerce, 69% of respondents stated that brand names played a significant role in their online buying decisions. Online users continue to gravitate toward brands for two basic reasons: first, band names act as substitutes for information gathering by helping online buyers locate specific products and thus reduce search costs; and second, consumer attitudes regarding brand trust, security, and expectations regarding product quality (Coltman et al., 2002). So here we infer the hypothesis based on the literatures.

Hypothesis 3-2: The knowledgeable resources and capability will make an impact on firm's strategic choices and then the selected strategies influence the firm performance indirectly.

Hypothesis 3-1: The firm performance will depend on the knowledgeable resources and capabilities directly.

EXPECTED RESULTS

Overall our results will testify a composite framework for online firm performance. More theoretically the results will imply the environment factors and the resource factors which can influence the strategic choices and the selected strategies make an direct impact on the performance. And also the resources of firm are another in determining performance. And the practically, managers in online firms must consider firms assets and environment simultaneously to firm success.

FOOTNOTES

* Business Horizons; Greenwich; Jan/Feb 2002
* John M. de Figueiredo, "Finding Sustainable Profitability in Electronic Commerce," Sloan Management Review, summer 2000. http://www.findarticles.com
* Mark Pinsley, How to survive in e-business

REFERENCES

References are available upon request from authors

From the Ground Up: An E-Learning Designer's Experience with the Development, Deployment, and Assesment of E-Learning

Vincent F. Kwisnek
Duquesne University
224 Universal Road, Apartment A-1
Pittsburgh, Pennsylvania 15235-3758
412-247-5163
vkwisnek@ppg.com

EXECUTIVE SUMMARY

I worked for one year as an independently contracted E-learning Designer with a Fortune 500 Company located in Pennsylvania. I utilized my expertise to develop safety and health e-learning modules that could be utilized on the various computers and operating systems within the company and could be modified to meet the specific needs of each of the company's locations. Since the company had no formal method for assessing the effectiveness of e-learning modules, I developed and implemented a research study that would pilot the concept of evaluating the educational effectiveness of e-learning modules. The research study was comprised of a Pre-Module and a Post-Module Survey that could be used as "bookends" to an e-learning module. The Pre-Module Survey, Driving Readiness Module, and Post-Module Survey were joined by a series of linear links and placed on the company's intranet. At the heart of the Pre-Module and Post-Module Surveys existed the questions that formed a Know, Want to Know, Learn Chart. The research study is currently a work in progress, but I have already learned valuable lessons about lesson design and research study development.

THE COMPANY'S FIRST ATTEMPTS TO DEPLOY E-LEARNING

The Instructional Technology Graduate Program at Duquesne University provided me the experience I needed to realize that I wanted to move from public education to the corporate realm; therefore, I resigned my teaching position and sought to make my way in the corporate world. From the fall of 2001 to the fall of 2002 I was an independently contracted E-learning Designer with a company located in Western Pennsylvania. To place my role as an E-learning Designer into the proper context, I have provided below a summary of the company's efforts to purchase and develop e-learning.

To remain in accordance with OSHA's and its own high standards, the company's policy is to operate the safest possible workplace environment. To best meet the requirements stated in this policy, the company has utilized face-to-face instructor-led training to convey safety and health practices and requirements. During the late 1990s, the company began searching for a way to reduce the cost of training and the expense incurred due to lost productivity. Such safety and health training would also need to provide flexibility so that employees could begin, continue, or complete training at their convenience. E-learning was seen as the solution, so the company began purchasing and developing safety and health modules.

After years of unchecked e-learning purchasing/development and deployment, the company informally examined the perceptions of e-learning among its employees. Most employees generally saw e-learning as ineffective, unavailable, unsupported, cost-prohibitive, and too high-tech for the hardware that was available at the company's locations. In reaction to these negative perceptions, the company formed an Action Team that was comprised of employees who supported the utilization of e-learning. The Action Team spent three months examining the possibilities of improving the purchase/development and deployment of e-learning. By March of 2001, the Team concluded that the best solution would be to purchase and deploy commercially available training provided by outside vendors.

Because of this conclusion, the company spent the spring of 2001 evaluating various types of commercial training products, including: web-based training (WBT), CD-ROM, video, and pay-per-view. After two months of evaluating a variety of products, the following discoveries and conclusions were reached. First, content providers typically lease training through a per-user or yearly fee, and these fees proved cost prohibitive for the company. Second, content providers tend to distribute basic, generic content so that they may maximize their profits by offering the content to a variety of businesses, and such content had little or no specific connection to the company's employees. Third, each vendor that was evaluated utilized proprietary technology, and the company saw the use of proprietary technology as limiting in regard to the ways that training could be developed and deployed.

Due to the conflicting findings of the Action Team and the commercial training product evaluations, the company contacted a distance education professor at a university located in Pittsburgh, Pennsylvania. After numerous meetings, the professor advised that the internal development of e-learning, though challenging, over time would be the most economical and effective method to deploy safety and health e-learning within the company. This recommendation was made because internally developed content could be modified and improved for little expense to best meet the needs of the learners. Based on this recommendation, the company spent the summer of 2001 developing and demonstrating internally created e-learning modules created with various e-learning development software.

These demonstrations validated the need for further internal development of e-learning, so the company sought an Independent Contractor who had a background in education and experience with technology. Their search yielded me, a former fourth grade teacher who wanted to utilize my experience as an educator and my new skills in the area of Instructional Technology to assist businesses with the development of e-learning. As the fall of 2001 began, I began laying the foundation of an e-learning development process.

AN E-LEARNING DEVELOPMENT PROCESS

As winter approached, I set out to develop learner-centered e-learning that would seamlessly integrate with the existing and upcoming technology platforms so that all employees could utilize the developed e-learning within their locations.

To develop e-learning that met the training needs of the employees, I collaborated with the locations that requested the development or modification of an e-learning module. Content creation began when a supervisor identified a training need and requested the development of e-learning to meet this need. Throughout the development process, the supervisor and content experts were allowed to view the status of development. Before any e-learning module was deployed for employee use, the module was informally piloted. Feedback from the pilot was used to further improve the e-learning module. An e-learning module was deployed for employee use only when it proved to contain properly communicated content and was grammatically and navigationally correct. Each development effort resulted in an e-learning module that was designed to meet the specifications of the requesting location and meet the needs of the learners.

E-learning proved useless if the company's locations could not utilize the modules in accordance with the existing technology; therefore, each e-learning module needed to integrate with the various technologies utilized throughout the company. Knowing that the only feasible e-learning development and deployment solution would be the one that worked on the oldest computing hardware and software in use, I created two versions of the first e-learning module I developed. One version was authored with e-learning development software, and the other was created with HTML and JavaScript.

The version of the module authored in the e-learning development software failed to function on many of the company's computers, but the version that was created in HTML and JavaScript worked on all computers; therefore, the use of this HTML and JavaScript format was approved. Over time, informal pilots of the first e-learning module provided feedback about the module's interface, and I utilized this feedback to create a set of module template pages. I also enhanced subsequent e-learning modules with features such as an automated slide show that could demonstrate various health and safety processes.

THE RESEARCH STUDY

As I finished the development of the first e-learning modules I realized that the company had no formal method of assessing the effectiveness of these e-learning modules. In an effort to correct this, I developed a research study that would pilot my first attempt at creating a standardized method of assessing the e-learning that I developed. I decided that the research study would focus on the effectiveness of the *Driving Readiness Module*.

I drafted my research project with two objectives: analyze the educational effectiveness of the Driving Readiness Module, and prove the concept of evaluating the educational effectiveness of e-learning modules. To meet these objectives, I created a Pre-Module and a Post-Module Survey that can be used as "bookends" to the *Driving Readiness Module* or any other e-learning module. Embedded into these surveys are three questions that will form a Know, Want to Know, Learned (KWL) Chart. The three questions that comprise the KWL Chart ask:
1. What do you already know about "Driving Readiness?"
2. What do you want to learn about "Driving Readiness?"
3. What did you learn about "Driving Readiness" by completing the *Driving Readiness Module?*

The Post-Module Survey also contains two questions that can be used to compare the learner's wants garnered from the Pre-Module Survey against what expected learning was and was not covered in the e-learning module. The two questions are:

1. What things that you expected to learn were covered by the *Driving Readiness Module?*
2. What things that you expected to learn were not covered by the *Driving Readiness Module?*

Once the surveys were created and the Institutional Review Board approved the research study, I randomly selected 10 potential participants from a pool of approximately 30,000 employees. The 10 potential participants will receive an invitation email. For those potential participants that decline participation, I will randomly select additional potential participants and send each one the invitation email. This process will conclude when 10 potential participants agree to participate in this study. In conjunction with this process, I began researching the history of Distance Education and the previous efforts to evaluate the effectiveness of e-learning and traditional learning.

The Pre-Module Survey, *Driving Readiness Module*, and Post-Module Survey were joined through a series of linear links and placed on the company's intranet. Upon the consent to participate, I will send each participant a welcome email that provides a link to the Pre-Module Survey. Once the Pre-Module Survey, *Driving Readiness Module*, and Post-Module Survey are completed, the participant will automatically be linked to a thank you page from which s/he can close the web browser to complete his/her participation in the research study.

To participate in this research study, each participant must have access to a multimedia computer that has an operating system no older than Windows 95, which has access to the company's intranet. Each participant must also have an email account provided by the company so that s/he can receive the invitation to participate, the consent to participate letter, and the welcome letter. A printer, video card, sound card, and set of speakers or headphones are optional hardware that will enhance the training experience.

CURRENT CONCLUSIONS

As of this writing, I have received five signed Consent to Participate forms, and I am continuing to research of the history of Distance Education and the previous efforts to evaluate the effectiveness of e-learning and traditional learning. By the end of January, I hope to receive five additional signed Consent to Participate forms and all ten Pre-Module and Post-Module Surveys. Along with gathering all forms and surveys, I will complete my research of Distance Education's history and previous evaluations of e-learning and traditional learning. By the beginning of March, I will conclude the data analysis of the Pre-Module and Post-Module Survey and produce a brief report of my research study.

Though the research study is still underway, I have already gained valuable knowledge and experience. Looking back upon my experiences, I now see that there are things that I could have done differently and better. Before creating another research study, I will first conduct a literature review, for such a review will have a positive influence on the creation of the research study. Also, the next research study that I create will be drafted so that it meets Institutional Review Board (IRB) approval the first rather than the third time I submit the research study's documents. In conclusion, I am excited by the prospect of concluding this research study and assimilating the collected data.

Web-STAR: A Survey Tool for Analyzing User Requirements for Web Sites

Jonathan Lazar, Adam Jones, and Kisha Greenidge
Department of Computer and Information Sciences and
Center for Applied Information Technology, Towson University
8000 York Road, Towson, Maryland 21252
Phone: 410-704-2255, Fax: 410-704-3868
jlazar@towson.edu, ajones5@towson.edu, kgreen10@towson.edu

ABSTRACT

The main goal of the Web-STAR (Web-Survey Tool for Analyzing Requirements) project is to provide a standardized survey tool which developers can use to determine the user requirements for existing or new informational web sites. The Web-STAR will allow this most vital stage in the development process to take place within a convenient, tested, and cost-effective framework. Based on existing work in user evaluation design, Web-STAR will take sound development practices and apply them to user requirements in the design of informational websites. This paper presents the research-in-progress development and testing of Web-STAR.

INTRODUCTION

User involvement in the development stage is critical to the success of a new information system (Hoffer, George, & Valacich, 2002). However, due to tight timelines for web development projects, users typically have been left out of the development process. Organizations are beginning to involve users in many different stages of their web development projects, as it has clearly been shown to improve the user experience. This can lead to an increase in repeat visitors and, in the case of e-commerce sites, higher sales. Examples of well-known companies and organizations that include user involvement in web development projects include Eastman Kodak, Indiana University, the National Institutes of Health, IBM, and the National Football League (Clarke, 2001; Corry, Frick, & Hansen, 1997; Lazar, 2003; Tedeschi, 1999; Yu, Prabhu, & Neale, 1998). This user input is necessary to determine user needs, both relating to the user interface (usability), and web site content (functionality). In certain types of web sites, namely e-commerce, search engines, and newspapers, tasks may be well defined (Lazar, Ratner, Jacko, & Sears, 2003). However, for the majority of informational web sites the user tasks are not well-defined and data collection (requirements gathering) needs to be done in order to determine what tasks the users actually need to perform. There are a number of different methods for user involvement in requirements gathering. Surveys are of interest here because they allow data to be collected from a large number of people in a short amount of time. A recent study found that the two methods used most often for requirements gathering for web site development are surveys and interviews (Lazar, Ratner, Jacko, and Sears, 2003). One of the strengths of surveys is that they can be distributed to a wide participant base and in a variety of formats such as paper, email, web site, or telephone (Lazar & Preece, 2001). However, one challenge in using surveys is the start up time required for creating, testing, and validating a survey. The goal of this paper is to present the research-in-progress development and testing, of a standardized survey tool that can be utililized in user requirements gathering for informational web sites.

THE CHALLENGE OF REQUIREMENTS GATHERING

It takes more time and money to involve the users and understand their usability and task needs but the end result is a more appropriate system. The time required to create a survey for requirements gathering can be challenging. Part of the key to improving usability and user involvement for web sites is to make the process easier for designers, by providing a toolkit (pre-tested surveys, interface guidelines, etc.) to assist them with user involvement. It is not as useful to tell designers to "build an interface that is easy to use," as it would be to say, "follow these 10 guidelines to make a good interface." Popular sets of interface heuristics, such as "Shneiderman's 8 Golden Rules of Interface Design" (Shneiderman, 1998), can help translate the large concept of interface design into something more concrete and manageable. Telling designers to "find out what the users need," is quite vague and difficult, but a survey tool that will help with understanding user needs is helpful to designers, and easy to implement.

The best way to encourage user involvement in the requirements gathering stage is to lower the cost (in time and effort) of doing so. Providing well-written surveys that have already been developed and tested can increase the likelihood that surveys will be utilized for user involvement. A number of surveys have already been developed in the field of human-computer interaction for evaluating existing user interfaces : QUIS (Harper, Slaughter, & Norman, 1997), WAMMI (Kirakowski, Claridge, & Whitehand, 1998), Information Quality Survey (Zhang, Keeling, & Pavur, 2000) and WEBMac, a series of surveys (Small & Arnone, 2000). While all of these surveys can assist with evaluating a system after it has been built, a review of the literature shows that no surveys have been created for assisting with the requirements gathering stage of web site development.

The goal of this research is to develop a survey tool that can be used for user requirements gathering in websites, and we have named this project Web-STAR, the **Web S**urvey **T**ool for **A**nalyzing **R**equirements. Though there are different types of web sites, such as e-commerce, informational, and entertainment (Lazar, 2003), the goal of Web-STAR is to assist with requirements gathering where it is needed most: for informational web sites where tasks are relatively undefined.

SURVEY DEVELOPMENT METHODOLOGY

While no standardized survey tool exists for requirements gathering for web sites, there are a number of case studies where surveys were used for requirements gathering. This existing knowledge, as well as research on what influences people to return to web sites, was used to create the Web-STAR survey tool. Web-STAR can be used for both existing sites and sites under development. This is an important distinction as many web sites were not originally developed with user involvement, but include user involvement as they are redesigned (Lazar, 2003). The following topics were examined to find key areas in providing a good user experience on a web site: Web usability (Lazar, 2003; Nielsen, 2000), Motivational quality of a web site (Small & Arnone, 2000), User satisfaction (Harper et al., 1997), Information Quality (Zhang et al., 2000), Survey design (Oppenheim, 1992; Dillman, 2000), and Web accessibility (Paciello, 2000; Sullivan and Matson, 2000). The Web-STAR survey tool was developed in order to address the issues described in the above topical areas. In addition, based on examinations of web site re-design projects (Dong & Martin, 2000; Yu et al., 1998), it was determined that while some questions would apply to both new web sites and re-designed sites, some questions would be unique to each. For example, it is important to evaluate the existing web resources for possible improvements, but this is by definition impossible if web resources have not yet been developed. Therefore, 50 informational web sites were examined by the research team to look for possible content categories, which could be helpful in determining what content might be useful on a site that does not currently exist. The 50 sites that were examined were chosen based on their inclusion in a previous research study (Lazar, Beere, Greenidge, & Nagappa, 2002), and the web sites represented 10 different categories of informational sites. Based on the content categories that were offered on those sites, the Web-STAR offers possible content categories for new sites.

The Web-STAR was designed with three main sections. The first section addresses data about the technological environment, browser version, and download speed of the users, as well as demographic information and previous computer experience. This data is important, regardless of whether a site is new or already exists (Lazar, 2003). The second section of Web-STAR addresses new web sites, by asking users what types of content would interest them on a new web site for an organization. There are three different types of responses in this section. Users are given the opportunity to examine the content categories from other representative web sites (such as schedule of events and contact information), to see if any would be useful. The designer can suggest possible content specific to this site (which would be written into the survey), to see if the users would be interested in such content. In addition, the users can suggest their own content, in an open-ended question. The third section of Web-STAR addresses currently-existing web sites. Users are asked to indicate how often they visit the currently-existing web site, their overall perceptions of the web site, as well as how they found out about the web site. In addition, there is a section where the developers can indicate existing content, giving users the opportunity to comment on how useful that content is, through the use of a likert scale.

CURRENT RESEARCH STATUS

A prototype for Web-STAR has been created. This survey tool is currently being tested with 5 web development projects. From using the Web-STAR tool in a real-world setting, feedback will be available to improve the tool and validate its usefulness. In addition, information will be available on how the Web-STAR is used in web development projects. It is expected that, by the time of the IRMA 2003 conference, data on the usage of Web-STAR will be available for presentation.

REFERENCES

Clarke, J. (2001). *Key factors in developing a positive user experience for children on the web: A case study.* Proceedings of the Human Factors and the Web 2001, Available at: http://www.optavia.com/hfweb/index.htm

Corry, M., Frick, T., & Hansen, L. (1997). User-centered design and usability testing of a web site: An illustrative case study. *Educational Technology Research and Development, 45*(4), 65-76.

Dong, J., & Martin, S. (2000). *Iterative Usage of Customer Satisfaction Surveys to Assess an Evolving Web Site.* Proceedings of the Human Factors and the Web, Available at: http://www.tri.sbc.com/hfweb/

Harper, B., Slaughter, L., & Norman, K. (1997). *Questionnaire Administration via the WWW: A Validation & Reliability Study for a User Satisfaction Questionnaire.* Proceedings of the WebNet97: International Conference on the WWW, Internet and Intranet, Toronto, Canada,

Hoffer, J., George, J., & Valacich, J. (2002). *Modern systems analysis and design* (3rd ed.). Reading, MA: Addison-Wesley.

Kirakowski, J., Claridge, N., & Whitehand, R. (1998). *Human centered measures of success in web site design.* Proceedings of the Human Factors and the Web, available at: http://www.research.att.com/conf/hfweb/

Lazar, J. (2003, in press). *User-Centered Web Development* (2nd edition). Sudbury, MA: Jones and Bartlett Publishers.

Lazar, J., Beere, P., Greenidge, K., & Nagappa, Y. (2002). Web Accessibility in the Mid-Atlantic United States: A Study of 50 Web Sites. *Submitted to the Universal Access in the Information Society.*

Lazar, J., & Preece, J. (2001). Using Electronic Surveys to Evaluate Networked Resources: From Idea to Implementation. In C. McClure & J. Bertot (Eds.), *Evaluating Networked Information Services: Techniques, Policy, and Issues.* Medford, NJ: Information Today.

Lazar, J., Ratner, J., Jacko, J., & Sears, A. (2003). User Involvement in the Web Development Process: Methods and Cost-Justification. Under Review.

Nielsen, J. (2000). *Designing web usability: The practice of simplicity.* Indianapolis: New Riders Publishing.

Oppenheim, A. (1992). *Questionnaire design, interviewing, and attitude measurement.* London: Pinter Publishers.

Paciello, M. (2000). *Web Accessibility for People with Disabilities.* Lawrence, KS: CMP Books.

Shneiderman, B. (1998). *Designing the User Interface: Strategies for Effective Human-Computer Interaction* (3rd ed.). Reading, Masssachusetts: Addison-Wesley.

Small, R., & Arnone, M. (2000). Evaluating the effectiveness of web sites. In B. Clarke & S. Lehaney (Eds.), *Human-Centered Methods in Information Systems: Current Research and Practice* (pp. 91-101). Hershey, PA: Idea Group Publishing.

Tedeschi, B. (1999, August 30, 1999). Good Web Site Design Can Lead to Healthy Sales. *The New York Times.*

Yu, J., Prabhu, P., & Neale, W. (1998). *A user-centered approach to designing a new top-level structure for a large and diverse corporate web site.* Proceedings of the 1998 Human Factors and the Web Conference, available at: http://www.research.att.com/conf/hfweb/

Zhang, X., Keeling, K., & Pavur, R. (2000). *Information quality of commercial web site home pages: an explorative analysis.* Proceedings of the International Conference on Information Systems, 164-175

Developing a Framework for SME E-Commerce: A UK Perspective

Marie Quinn, Brian Lehaney, Peter Every
School of Mathematical and Information Sciences,
Coventry University
Priory Street, Coventry, CV1 5FB, UK
Tel: +44 (0)24 7688 7762
Fax: +44 (0)24 7688 8080
Email: m.quinn@coventry.ac.uk

ABSTRACT

Whilst there has been work on e-commerce development, much of the work has been about large organisations and much has been USA-based. This research focuses on SMEs in the UK, and it considers how much of the existing published literature is applicable in this context. A prototyping approach is being developed to create a framework that will be based on benchmarks and that may be used by SMEs to assist in the creation of successful e-commerce web sites.

INTRODUCTION

SMEs are often perceived as having special needs because of their limited resources, especially in terms of personnel and finance. The introduction of e-commerce puts an extra strain on these resources. SMEs do have some advantages when considering new technology and new methods of conducting business, particularly that they tend to be more entrepreneurial, flexible, and innovative than large, more formally structured businesses.

There are several definitions of the term SME. In practice, schemes that are nominally targeted at small firms adopt a variety of working definitions depending on their particular objectives. In February 1996, the European Commission adopted a single definition of SMEs that would apply across Community programmes and proposals (Snaith and Walker, 2002). To qualify as an SME, both the employee and the independence criteria must be satisfied, and **either** the turnover or the balance sheet total criteria (see Table 1). The EC definition will be used for the purposes of this research.

The next section explains what is meant by the term 'e-commerce' in this context and why usability is an issue.

E-COMMERCE AND USABILITY

The UK Department of Trade and Industry (DTI) recommend their preferred definition of the term e-commerce for adoption within the UK to be as follows: 'Electronic commerce is the exchange of information across electronic networks at any stage in the supply chain, whether within an organisation, between businesses, between businesses and consumers, or between the public and private sectors, whether paid or unpaid'.

There are two main sub-divisions of e-commerce, business-to-business (B2B) and business-to-customer (B2C). Many SMEs move into B2C e-commerce without careful consideration of the implications this may have. The main driver seems to be fear that they will be 'left behind' if they are not seen to have the same web presence and facilities as their competitors. Whereas other projects undertaken in business will usually be preceded by favourable

feasibility studies, a significant number of companies have been found to enter into e-commerce regardless of projected returns on investment (Damanpour, 2001). Entry into the e-commerce arena may therefore be viewed as a strategic move by business owners – a calculated risk that they hope will one day pay off.

SMEs with a desire to implement e-commerce enabling customer interaction, i.e. B2C e-commerce, are shown to face more barriers than those who implement e-commerce for B2B solutions. B2C-oriented SMEs are therefore expected to grow at a smaller rate than their B2B peers (Woods, 2000). From these findings it can be deduced that SMEs considering – or in the early stages of – implementing e-commerce may require more practical assistance than B2B SMEs.

Usability refers to the extent to which a product is designed to fit users' needs, or the extent to which a product is easy to use (Rhodes, 2001). In software design it has been recognised that every $1 spent on usability testing provides a payback of between $10 and $100 (Nielsen cited by Rhodes). These figures take on added significance when applied to web design; in other software developments the customer traditionally pays first and then experiences usability – whereas on the web users experience usability first and pay later.

There are many issues for consideration under the general heading of usability. At one level there are factors that affect the success rate of users in achieving particular tasks on a website; these may include page design, information design, multimedia content, navigation, and search capabilities.

When a website is implemented for the purpose of e-commerce, other issues arise. Trust, security and privacy may influence customers' decisions on whether or not to purchase online. Staff within the organisation of an SME may also have responsibilities for processes involving the e-commerce website. As end users, they may also need to be considered with regard to usability.

An e-commerce website cannot succeed without customers, therefore user-centred design ought to be the priority of e-commerce developers – in other words, website functionality should be determined by its impact on the user rather than what the developer may find easier to implement technologically. For example, a customer looking for a product on a site may choose to use a search box option. Products may be stored on more than one database according to type or function. The easier implementation option would be to provide a search box for each database – requiring the user to type the same search criterion more than once. User-centred design would consider this unnecessarily burdensome on the user; a single search box, while possibly requiring more engineering, would be the easier solution for the user (Vividence, 2000).

The following two sections of this paper provide an overview of the concerns mentioned above, while a third section discusses methods of evaluating the usability of an e-commerce website.

Design Factors

There is no way of knowing how individual customers will access websites – even assuming that most access will be via standard PCs, monitor sizes vary greatly as do modem bandwidths. There is also no guarantee that users have recent versions of browsers installed. These factors should ideally be taken into account when designing web pages. This may make life more difficult for

Table 1: EC Definition of SME

Criterion	Micro	Small	Medium
Max. no. of employees	9	49	249
Max. annual turnover	-	7m Euros	40m Euros
Max. annual balance sheet	-	5m Euros	27m Euros
Max. % owned by one, or jointly by several enterprise(s) not satisfying the same criteria	-	25%	25%

the designer, but the purpose of usability is to put the needs of the user first. It is estimated that 10% of users employ old software and low-spec hardware, and 10% of a potential customer base is a lot to risk losing (Nielsen, 2000).

Nielsen also suggests that fast initial loading of a page may minimise the risk of losing customers' attention. This can be achieved by ensuring that the top of the page contains less images and more text; providing text attributes for images so users know what they are waiting for to download and can make faster decisions based on that information; and by producing several smaller, less complex tables rather than one large table. Images should preferably be used only to represent concepts not easily presented in a text format.

Where media other than text are employed (e.g. video or sound files) it should not be assumed that all users have access to the necessary playback software. If a user is required to download plug-ins to view site content, they may decide to go elsewhere. Where these media formats are employed, it is a good idea to provide an alternative text-based explanation of what they offer, thereby enabling the user to make an informed decision on whether or not it is relevant to their needs. Another issue is playback times via low-bandwidth access. Providing an indication of file size/download time also facilitates usability (Nielsen, 2000).

Users are affected by delays in Internet responsiveness, and delayed documents containing text and graphics are viewed less favourably than delayed documents containing text only (Sears, Jacko and Borello 1997, cited by Lee 1999). Where graphics are required thumbnail images can be employed, whereby a small version of an image is downloaded with the web page and the user has the option to click on a picture to enlarge it for a clearer view. Text should never be presented as an image.

Users will usually have a specific goal in mind when they alight on a web page – they need to know that they can achieve that goal within a very short time of arriving. It is good practice to present all important information at or near the top of the page to prevent the need for scrolling, although recent studies show that users are more willing to scroll now than they were in the early years of the Web (Nielsen, 1996). Web users on the whole also tend to scan web pages rather than read them word for word (Nielsen, 1997). For this reason, it is important to present information clearly and concisely – e.g. highlighting keywords enabling users to quickly determine page relevance. Bulleted lists break up blocks of text and ensure that information can be scanned and comprehended relatively quickly.

Search engines use page titles to display results, therefore it is important to name each page clearly and appropriately. This enables users to make informed decisions on whether they wish to visit a site or not and may encourage more visitors to your site.

These users will not necessarily arrive on site via the home page; many will arrive on a page that is specific to their goals (via deep linking). These users must also be accounted for when making user-centred design decisions. Including the company name or logo on each page along with a clearly recognisable link direct to the home page enhances usability by passing control of navigation to the user. It is suggested that these users may in fact be the most important visitors an e-commerce website will receive, as they have a current, specific interest in the product they have searched for (Nielsen, 2002).

The user should always have the freedom to navigate a site at will. While the company may like to ensure that all visitors see specific pages of a site, this may be at odds with the user's goals. In order to navigate successfully, the user must always know where he is within the site. Breadcrumbs are increasingly being used as navigational aids (e.g. Home > Products > Perfume). Each breadcrumb may also be used as a link to another page. Links are arguably the most important feature of the World Wide Web; they enable the user to navigate within websites and to access a wide range of information from other sources if what they want is not in their current location. To best meet the users' needs, links should be descriptive without being over-wordy (Nielsen, 2000). Many browsers offer the option of a pop-up explanation of a link when the mouse is positioned over it; this again promotes usability by enabling the user to make a decision on a link's suitability to their needs before visiting it.

Although no navigation standard exists as such, there are conventions that have become established over time. The primary navigation bar tends to be placed across the top of the page, with secondary navigation categories listed down the left side. Many users will look for this familiar layout, so deviance from this format may counteract usability. Studies of e-commerce usability show that between 27% and 40% of users experience difficulty in finding the required page/information from within a website (Nielsen, 2002,

Vividence, 2000). Increasing user success on navigational tasks can increase their likelihood to return to a site by 25% (Vividence, 2000).

Trust, Security and Privacy

Trust is of major concern for e-commerce websites – it is a critical factor not only in attracting new customers, but also when it comes to maintaining the loyalty of existing customers (Lee, J., Kim, J., and Moon, J.Y., 2000). With regard to new customers, 70% of American users in 2000 were concerned that hackers may be able to access their credit card details, and 86% worried that their personal details may be passed to other people or companies once registered with one organisation (Fox, 2000). Improving usability can go some way toward overcoming these issues of pre-purchase trust, as people tend to trust web sites that are well-presented and more usable (Rhodes, 1998). Bricks and mortar stores have a human face to present to the customer that enables a relationship of trust to be established via a two-way interaction. On the Internet, the interface is the only medium presented to the user. The interface must deliver a sense of trustworthiness.

First impressions count, and good content with a simple design and few grammatical errors are factors that encourage the onset of trust from the user – findings that were confirmed by a survey of Internet users (Rhodes, 1998). The survey also concluded that users were more likely to trust sites that provided information with regard to when the content was last updated, sites that were easy to access, and sites that were easy to search. Users do not approve of promotional writing style with boastful claims (e.g. "best ever"): they prefer plain facts. Trust has been shown to suffer when the site exaggerates (Nielsen, 1997).

For established companies venturing into e-commerce, a prominent logo and/or slogan may assist the pre-purchase user to invest a level of trust in the website. This transference of trust can be extended by ensuring that the appearance of the website (e.g. colour schemes) matches up to that presented by the company in other media – sales literature, etc. A professional looking website can convey the impression that a company has invested considerably in the website and is therefore less likely to take opportunistic advantage of the user. Another factor of professionalism that may favourably influence the trust of the user is to have a domain name for the website that is consistent with the company name (Egger, 2001).

When trust has been established to the degree that the user feels comfortable enough to make an online purchase, the e-commerce website must maintain that trust in order to maintain customer loyalty. Feedback at all stages of the transaction provides reassurance to the user and improves the usability of any interface. An effective after sales service which makes it easy for users to return products and obtain refunds if necessary helps to build the environment of trust further.

Security of transaction was cited as a concern of 70% of American users in 2000 (above). To overcome this concern, clear information must be provided within the website on measures that are taken to ensure the integrity of data transfers. External links to organisations who provide hardware or software enabling secure transactions are another element of trust-building. Prominent links to security policies that address issues of liability in case of fraud and redress mechanisms can be used to complement textual reassurances that the page currently displayed is a secure page (Egger, 2001).

Not all users may differentiate between security and privacy. Providing links between security policies and privacy policies, or presenting them on the same page, may prevent some users from leaving a site when they are unable to find answers to their concerns (Snyder, 2001).

86% of American users questioned (above) were worried that their personal details may be passed to other people or companies once registered with one organisation. Privacy policies that state how personal information will be stored and utilised establish an environment of trust for the user. Good usability would also require that all personal information asked for is justified, can be easily amended and modified, and is requested at a relevant point in the transaction (Egger, 2001).

A usable website is more likely to inspire trust than one with poor usability, as ease-of-use may be interpreted by the user that a company understands its customers and cares for their needs (Egger, 2001).

Methods of Evaluating Usability

Methodologies for evaluating usability can either incorporate actual users or be carried out by the website developer/usability personnel. Each methodology has it's own costs dependent on resources needed, and may be implemented at various stages of the development cycle.

Methodologies include the following.
- Task analysis – evaluates how people actually accomplish things with software. Interviews and observations with users enable user goals to be established; tasks that support these goals are then determined and prioritised according to importance of goal and frequency of performance. Usability experts may then suggest ways to make the task more efficient from the perspective of the end-user.
- Cognitive walkthroughs – whereby users' goals are broken down to individual tasks to determine level of complexity. This methodology attempts to emulate the thought processes of a novice user to determine usability, and may be carried out on a prototype or working interface.
- Focus groups – enable an interface to be evaluated by more than one user at a time. Evaluating with more than one focus group provides a measure of integrity, with each focus group having a leader responsible for writing up comments and recommendations for improvement.
- Usability inspections – the review of a system based on a set of usability guidelines, carried out by usability experts. Issues such as consistency, navigation and error minimisation are analysed. When problems are discovered, the experts recommend solutions (usabilityfirst.com).

Testing with actual users identifies specific areas of poor usability within websites; the users chosen for testing should always be representative of the target audience. Evaluating usability need not be particularly costly; it has been shown that testing with five users provides the most reliable results (Nielsen and Landauer 1993). The first user observed will reveal a third of all usability problems with the design; the second user will repeat some of the first users actions and add some of his own. Each new user reveals less new data, therefore usability budgets are best spent on more tests with less users. More users may need to be tested when there are distinct user types for a system – e.g. e-commerce consumers and staff within an SME who have responsibility for processes involving the site.

CONCLUSIONS

SMEs are an important part of the UK economy and e-commerce is a growing area that cannot be ignored if SMEs want to be competitive. There are a number of barriers to successful B2C e-commerce, and these appear to remain unresolved. These barriers include design factors, trust, security, and privacy. This research involves the development of an approach for SMEs to develop e-commerce and these factors will be incorporated within the prototypes. The methodology outlined indicates that hands-on testing of sites will be combined with concepts and principles to establish a sensible framework that SMEs can use in e-commerce development.

REFERENCES

Damanpour, F. 2001, E-business E-commerce Evolution: Perspective and Strategy, Managerial Finance, 27(7).

DTI cited by e-commerce@its.best.uk Cabinet Office [Online], 1999, Available: http://www.cabinet-office.gov.uk/innovation/1999/ecommerce/ec_body.pdf [2002, October 6].

Egger, F.N., 2001, Affective Design of E-Commerce User Interfaces: How to Maximise Perceived Trustworthiness. Proceedings of the International Conference on Affective Human Factors Design, Asean Academic Press, London.

Fox, S., 2000, Trust and Privacy Online: Why Americans Want to Rewrite the Rules. Available from www.pewinternet.org [Accessed: 15 November 2002].

Lee, J., Kim, J., and Moon, J.Y., 2000, What Makes Internet Users Visit Cyber Stores Again? Key Design Factors for Customer Loyalty. CHI Letters, vol 2, issue 1, pp 305-312.

Nielsen, J., 1996. Top Ten Mistakes in Web Design. Alertbox [May 1996]. Available from http://www.useit.com/alertbox [Accessed: 7 November 2002].

Nielsen, J., 1997. How People Read on the Web. Alertbox [October 1997]. Available from http://www.useit.com/alertbox [Accessed: 8 November 2002].

Nielsen, J., 2000, Designing Web Usability. New Riders Publishing, Indiana, USA.

Nielsen, J., 2001. Did Poor Usability Kill E-Commerce? Alertbox [August 2001]. Available from http://www.useit.com/alertbox [Accessed: 16 October 2002].

Nielsen, J., 2002. Deep Linking is Good Linking. Alertbox [March 2002]. Available from http://www.useit.com/alertbox [Accessed: 7 November 2002].

Nielsen, J., and Landauer, T., 1993. A Mathematical Model of the Finding of Usability Problems. Proceedings of ACM INTERCHI'93 Conference (Amsterdam, The Netherlands, 24-29 April 1993), pp. 206-213.

Rhodes, J.S., 1998. How to Gain the Trust of Your Users. Available from http://webword.com/moving/trust.html [Accessed 5 November 2002].

Rhodes, J.S., 2001. A Business Case For Usability. Available from http://webword.com/moving/businesscase.html [Accessed 5 November 2002].

Sears, A., Jacko, J.A., and Borello, M.S., 1997 cited by Lee, Alfred T., 1999. Web Usability: A Review of the Research. SIG CHI Bulletin, vol. 31, no. 1, pp 38-40.

Snaith and Walker, 2002. The Theory of Medium Enterprise [Online], Available: http://www.missingmiddle.com/pdf/paper19.pdf [2002, October 6].

Snyder, C., 2001. Seven Tricks that Web Users Don't Know. Available from http://www-106.ibm.com/developerworks/usability/library/us-tricks/ [Accessed 15 November 2002].

Usability First, Usability Methods, [Online]. Available: http://www.usabilityfirst.com/methods/

Vividence, 2000. How To Make Customers Happy on the Web. Available from: http://www.vividence.com/resources/public/What+We+Do/BestPractices/HappyCustomers.pdf

Woods, Bob, 2000 cited by Karakaya F. and Charlton, E. (2001), Electronic Commerce: Current and Future Practices, Managerial Finance, 27(7).

Establishing Trust in a Business-to-Business Collaboration: Results from an International Simulation

Yvonne Lederer-Antonucci,Ph.D. and Penelope Sue Greenberg,Ph.D.
School of Business Administration
Widener University, Chester, PA 19013
(610) 499-4310   Fax: (610) 499-4614, (610) 499-4475   Fax: (610) 499-4614
Yvonne.L.Antonucci@Widener.edu, Penelope.S.Greenberg@Widener.edu

Michael zur Muehlen, Ph.D.
Stevens Institute of Technology
Hoboken, NJ 07030
mzurmuehlen@stevens-tech.edu
(201) 216-8293, Fax: (201) 216-5385

Ralph Greenberg, Ph.D.
Temple University
Philadelphia, PA USA
rgreen@sbm.temple.edu
(215) 204-6830

ABSTRACT

Businesses in the 21st century have extended to a process oriented, e-business world that is increasing in business-to-business, web-centric interactions. The geographical dispersion of participants in this new process oriented e-business world introduces challenges of building a degree of trust needed for effective collaboration. Yet, examining the correlation of various trust manifestations to the success of business-to-business collaboration remains a challenge. This paper examines trust as a factor in successful business-to-business process implementations. Based on an international collaboration between two universities that address issues of new e-centric business practices, results in the form of students' perceptions of trust manifestations are presented.

INTRODUCTION

In recent years, we have seen tremendous worldwide growth of process-oriented e-Business relationships between organizations. In 1999 Forrester Research analyzed inter-organizational trade (e-business) of goods and services and predicted that business-to-business (B2B) spending would surpass consumer spending worldwide (Intelligent Enterprise, 2001; Beximco, 2001). Recently the Gartner Group predicted worldwide B2B spending to reach 7.9 trillion by 2004, and several other research organizations have also revised their forecasts to be higher than predicted in 1999.(Intelligent Enterprise, 2001). As a result, corporations are leveraging their investment in their Enterprise Resource Planning (ERP) solution by extending the existing ERP system to support inter-organizational transactions and e-commerce applications. Despite the fact that increased collaboration is being conducted in a B2B setting, little is known about the factors that affect the effectiveness of such collaboration.

Effective B2B process implementations are constrained by inter-organizational collaboration methods. In fact, the ability to collaborate between organizations may be as important as the ability to deploy appropriate technology in maintaining a competitive advantage (The Economist, 1999). Yet, establishing effective collaboration methods for this new process oriented e-business world remains a challenge. The geographical dispersion of participants in a B2B endeavor can introduce challenges of building trust without a face-to-face interaction (Jarvenpaa, Knoll and Leidner, 1998). Trust has been defined by Mayer et al. (1995) as "the willingness of a party [trustor] to be vulnerable to the actions of another party [trustee] based on the expectation that other [trustee] will perform a particular action important to the trustor, irrespective of the ability to monitor or control that other party." It has been revealed that a degree of trust is needed in order to engage in cooperative behavior (Cassell and Bickmore, 2000). Recent research has begun exploring the impact of trust on both B2B (e.g., Welty and Becerra-Fernandez, 2001) and B2C (e.g., Torkzadeh and Dhillon, 2002) relationships. Bhattacherjee (2002)

points out that the importance of trust as a key facilitator of electronic commerce is increasingly being recognized in academic and practitioner communities. Three dimensions of trust identified are ability (expertise, information, competence, expertness, dynamism), integrity (fairness in transaction, fairness in data usage, fairness in service, morality, credibility, reliability, dependability), and benevolence (empathy, resolving concerns, goodwill, responsiveness) (Bhattacherjee 2002, McKnight, Choudhury and Kacmar 2002). However there is still a lack of research that examines the correlation of various trust manifestations to the success of B2B collaboration.

The research reported in this paper examines trust as a factor in successful B2B process implementations. Data was collected from an international collaboration between two universities that addressed these issues of B2B process implementation. Similar classes of the two universities, one located in the US and one located in Germany, participated in joint projects involving the negotiation, analysis, design and implementation of B2B processes. Specifically, each project group was composed of 8-10 students, 4-5 from each university. Thus, the groups from each University simulated the geographical dispersion of participants in a B2B collaboration. An online forum was created by the course instructors and used by the project groups throughout the semester as a collaboration medium. A post-course survey was utilized to measure the trust manifestations.

HYPOTHESES AND METHODOLOGY

This research builds upon other studies that explored the impact of trust in collaborative activities between geographically dispersed participants. Jarvenpaa, Knoll, and Leidner (1998) argue that collaboration between remote participants introduces the challenge of building and maintaining trust without face-to-face interaction. Because trust is essential to a relationship, creating trust during the implementation process is critical to successful collaboration endeavors. Several manifestations of trust during interactions such as good rapport, politeness, technical knowledge, comfort, use of pictures, and confidence in the other party to meet deadlines, have been identified by Cassell and Bickmore (2000), and Tractinsky and Rao (2001).

In order to examine the role of trust, data collected from a B2B collaboration between two university classes, one in Germany and one in the U.S., were analyzed. Faculty from these universities collaborated in the development and deployment of five case scenarios that were used to simulate a business-to-business integration project. Kalakota and Robinson (1999) discuss two implementation methods of inter-organizational process integration. The first method involves a shared process where both organizations are interdependent upon each other within the process, requiring extensive collaboration among the organizations to ensure success. In the second method each organization maintains their own independent process, designed to invoke each other's process when needed (Hayami et al., 2000). The second method was used to design the case scenarios. The case scenario method of collaboration allowed the simulation of business-to-business process development between university class teams, which formed a two-stage supply chain. Student teams from the American university assumed the role of the customer/client enterprise and teams from the German university assumed the role of the service provider (see Figure 1).

The collaboration between these two Universities began with a pilot of one scenario in 1999. Based on the results of that pilot, improvements were made for the collaborations conducted in 2000 and 2001. The collaboration methods included a web forum created by the course instructors that allowed the students to communicate non-verbally and discuss project details. The classes were divided into 5 project groups, each assigned to a different B2B scenario. The forum included student pictures in order to provide some level of personal communication. Students were required to utilize this forum to establish contact with their virtual partners and meet several required milestones evolving around the negotiation of process details. The students were also encouraged to negotiate with their counterparts from the other university and create a project web page.

Analysis of the students' perception of the collaboration effectiveness from the 2000 class revealed there was a significant difference between the five scenarios (Antonucci and zur Muehlen, 2001). This supported the assumption that other possible factors, such as trust, contribute to collaboration effectiveness. This paper thus hypothesizes that trust is a determinant of collaboration effectiveness.

H1: Geographically dispersed participants in a B2B collaboration who establish a high level of trust will have greater collaboration effectiveness.

This preliminary hypothesis is designed to identify correlation in perceived trust and collaboration success. Perceived trust was measured using student perception data from a post-course survey, which was designed using the trust manifestations identified by Cassell and Bickmore (2000), and Tractinsky and Rao (2001). Collaboration success was based on the ability of the scenario teams in accomplishing the required milestones. Regression analysis and Analysis of Variance was used to initially examine this hypothesis.

Based on the same rationale as H1, the following was hypothesized:

H2: The level of trust during the collaboration among the German students will be significantly different to the level of trust during the collaboration among the US students.

This hypothesis was designed to examine possible differences in trust as a factor of collaboration success between the German and US Cultures. The following manifestations of trust were included in the post-course survey and were compared between the German and US student responses:

Figure 1: Basic Construct of Business-to-Business Case Scenarios

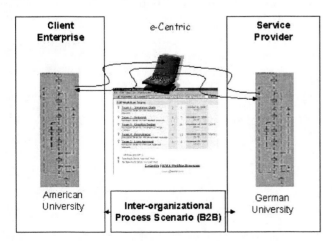

Good rapport, politeness, technical knowledge, comfort, use of pictures, and confidence in the other party to meet deadlines.

These hypotheses were designed to examine the ability of the various trust items identified by Cassell and Bickmore (2000), and Tractinsky and Rao (2001) to predict the effectiveness of a simulated B2B collaboration.

DATA ANALYSIS AND DISCUSSION

A 5-point Likert-type scale was used to assess the students' perceptions of the trust manifestations with their virtual team counterparts. A Likert value of 1 represents a very low trust level, a value of 2 represents a moderately low trust level, a value of 3 represents a neutral trust level, a value of 4 represents a moderately high trust level, and a value of 5 represents a very high trust level.

The raw data, gathered from the 26 students, were analyzed using SAS™. The analysis of student demographics (age, major, gender) showed no significance. H1 hypothesized that a high level of trust led to greater collaborative effort. Analyzing H1 is not possible since in each of the four scenarios, the teams were all successful in the collaboration. They were all able to meet the milestone requirements. Although there was no significance in the correlation of collaboration success and trust manifestations, there are some interesting observations. The recruitment and insurance teams were outstanding in completing the required milestones where the loan approval team was very good and the graphics team was good. Overall perceived trust was slightly higher for the recruitment and loan approval teams.

H2 hypothesized that there were no overall differences between the German students' perceptions and US students' perceptions of trust during the collaboration. Table 1 shows the results of t-tests between all the US and all of the German students' collaboration perceptions for the trust manifestations. For most of the trust manifestations, there was no significant difference found between the German students' perceptions of trust and the US students' perceptions of trust, however there was an indication of difference in the trust manifestation, technical knowledge. The means suggest that the German students felt they had a higher level of technical knowledge than the US students and the US students agreed. There was also a marginal difference in the trust manifestation, comfort of collaboration. US students tended to be more comfortable collaborating with German student. The overall results present some similarities between the US and German teams such as both felt the presence of pictures did not enhance the collaboration experience, suggesting that the use of pictures does not affect their level of trust in the collaboration. Also the German team seemed to have an overall lower perceived level of trust than the US students.

Table 1: Analysis of Variance between US and German students for trust factors

Item	N	Sig.	Mean of Response	
			US	GERMAN
(A) I feel our collaboration group was able to establish a **good rapport** with our counterparts.	26	.82	4.19	3.56
(B) I feel our counterpart team was very **polite**.	26	.92	4.50	4.20
(C) The presence of our **pictures** on the web site enhanced the collaboration experience.	26	.77	3.25	3.00
(D) I feel the level of **technical knowledge** of our counterpart team is higher than ours.	26	.00	4.25	1.20
(E) I feel very **comfortable** collaborating with our counterpart team.	26	.10	4.13	3.67
(F) I felt as though I had **confidence** in our counterpart team to meet the milestone due dates.	26	.92	2.44	2.78
(G) I feel video connections would increase the effectiveness of the collaboration.	26	.84	3.67	3.88
(H) Overall I have a high level of trust for our counterpart team.	26	.47	3.88	3.44

924 Information Technology and Organizations

Table 2: Analysis of Trust Measures by Scenario

Trust Items		Scenarios			
		Insurance Claim	Graphics Design	Recruitment	Loan Approval
(A) I feel our collaboration group was able to establish **good rapport** with our counterparts.	Germany	5.00(0.0)*	3.00(0.0)	2.50(0.71)	3.67(1.15)
	US	4.75(0.5)	4.25(0.5)	4.00(0.82)	4.25(0.96)
	P	.39	.32	.12	.52
(B) I feel our counterpart team was very **polite**.	Germany	5.00(0.0)	4.33(1.15)	4.00(0.0)	3.67(0.58)
	US	5.00(0.0)	4.50(0.58)	4.25(0.58)	4.25(0.96)
	P	------------	.83	.39	.36
(C) The presence of our **pictures** on the web site enhanced the collaboration experience.	Germany	3.50(0.71)	3.00(0.0)	Does not matter**	2.50(2.12)
	US	3.00(0.82)	3.75(0.96)	3.00(1.83)	3.25(1.26)
	P	.51	.36	.00	.33
(D) I feel the level of **technical knowledge** of our counterpart team is higher than ours.	Germany	1.00(0.0)	1.00(0.0)	1.00(0.0)	1.67(1.15)
	US	4.75(0.5)	4.00(0.0)	4.25(0.96)	4.00(1.15)
	P	.00	-	.01	.05
(E) I feel very **comfortable** collaborating with our counterpart team.	Germany	4.00(0.0)	4.00(0.0)	3.50(0.71)	3.30(0.58)
	US	4.00(0.82)	4.00(0.0)	4.50(0.58)	4.00(1.15)
	P	1.0	-	.25	.37
(F) I felt as though I had **confidence** in our counterpart team to meet the milestone due dates.	Germany	2.00(0.0)	2.50(0.71)	3.50(0.71)	3.00(0.0)
	US	1.75(1.5)	2.25(1.26)	2.75(1.26)	3.00(1.41)
	P	.76	.77	.41	1.0
(G) I feel video connections would increase the effectiveness of the collaboration.	Germany	4.00(0.0)	3.00(0.0)	4.00(0.0)	3.00(0.0)
	US	4.00(1.15)	3.25(2.06)	3.33(1.53)	3.00(1.41)
	P	1.0	.82	.85	.55
(H) Overall I have a high level of trust for our counterpart team.	Germany	3.00(0.0)	3.50(0.71)	3.00(0.0)	4.00(0.0)
	US	4.00(0.82)	3.75(0.96)	3.75(0.5)	4.00(0.82)
	P	.09	.74	.06	1.0

* Notation is MEAN(STANDARD DEVIATION)

** All of the subjects in this cell felt that pictures had no effect on trust.

Out of the five different scenarios, only four were usable for this study. One scenario team did not have participation at all from the German group, therefore this scenario was not used. Since combining the scenarios may obscure some interesting insights, Table 2 presents the results for each trust manifestation for each of the scenarios. A general observation is that the levels of the trust manifestations usually differed for each of the scenarios. Both German and US students felt a high level of rapport was established in the Insurance claim scenario, German students felt a lower level of rapport than US students.

SIGNIFICANCE OF RESEARCH AND FUTURE DIRECTIONS

Understanding the role of trust in collaboration during inter-organizational process implementation can potentially increase the probability of achieving a successful B2B implementation that leads to a productive longer-term relationship. Identifying specific trust manifestations early in the collaboration may introduce the ability to intervene during an unsuccessful collaboration and ensure success. These results could impact both industry relationships and University class collaboration teams that are designed to simulate real world project environments. This study extended the current research (Cassell and Bickmore (2000); Tractinsky and Rao (2001)) by identifying possible relationships between trust items and their ability to contribute to successful B2B collaborations.

Future studies are needed to incorporate measures of collaboration success. Our follow-up study uses the student's perceptions of success and the instructors' evaluation of success. This study only analyzed the students' perceptions of various trust manifestations. Additional factors that can contribute to trust include small talk, self-disclosure, and the use of technical jargon (Cassell and Bickmore 2000). This study only used single items on the post-

course survey to measure the manifestations of trust, which limits the reliability of the measurements. Our follow-up study uses multiple items and also includes other items under the dimensions of ability, integrity, and benevolence. Future studies should analyze these factors by analyzing the content and frequency of the teams' communications that were captured through sanctioned channels, such as the web forum. In addition, small talk, self-disclosure, and the use of technical jargon should be compared between the US and German students as disclosed through the analysis of the web forum discussions.

REFERENCES

Antonucci, Y.L. and zur Muehlen, M. "Deployment of Business to Business Scenarios in ERP Education: Evaluation and Experiences from an International Collaboration". In *Seventh Americas Conference on Information Systems*, (Boston, MA, 2001), AMCIS 2001 Proceedings, 998-1004.

Beximco, "B2B: The Big Bazaar; The Phenomenon", *Beximco Research Brief (an ERC Research Magazine)*, No. 8, February 2001.

Bhattacherjee, Anol, "Individual Trust in Online Firms: Scale Development and Initial Test," *Journal of Management Information Systems*, Vol. 19, No. 1, Summer 2002, pp. 211-241.

Cassell, J., and Bickmore, T., "External manifestations of trustworthiness in the interface," *Communications of the ACM*, 43 (12), December 2000, pp. 50-56.

Hayami, Haruo; Katsumata, Masashi; Okada, Ken-ichi: Interworkflow: A challenge for business-to-business electronic commerce. In: Fischer, Layna (Ed.): Workflow Handbook 2001, Future Strategies, Lighthouse Point, 2000, pp. 145-160.

Intelligent Enterprise. "The B2B Market 2 B", *Intelligent Enterprise*, February 2001.

Jarvenpaa, S. L., Knoll, K., and Leidner, D. E., "Is Anybody Out There?: Antecedents of Trust in Global Virtual Teams," *Journal of Management Information Systems*, 14 (4), Spring 1998, pp. 29-64.

Jarvenpaa, S. L., and Leidner, D. E., "Communication and Trust in Global Virtual Teams," *JCMC*, 3 (4), June 1998.

Kalakota, R, and Robinson, M., *e-Business: Roadmap for Success*, Addison-Wesley, Reading, MA, 1999.

Ludwig, H. and Whittingham, K., "Virtual Enterprise Co-ordinator – Agreement-Driven Gateways for Cross-Organsational Workflow Management," *Proceedings of the International Joint Conference on Work Activities, Coordination, and Collaboration*, 1999, pp. 29-38.

Massey, A. P., Montoya-Weiss, M., Hung, C., and Ramesh, V. "Global virtual teams: Cultural perceptions of task-technology fit", *Communications of the ACM*, 44(12), 2001, 83-84

Mayer, R. C., D. J Davis, and F. D. Shoorman, "An Integrative Model of Organizational Trust," *Academy of Management Review*, 20(3), 1995, pp. 709-734.

McKnight, D. Harrison, Vivek Choudhury, and Charles Kacmar, "Developing and Validating Trust Measures for e-Commerce: An Integrative Typology," *Information Systems Research*, Vol. 13, No. 3, September 2002, pp. 334-359.

Torkzadeh, Gholamreza, and Gurpreet Dhillon, "Measuring Factors that Influence the Success of Internet Commerce," *Information Systems Research*, Vol. 13, No. 2, June 2002, pp. 187-204.

Tractinsky, N., and Rao, S., "Incorporating social dimensions in Webstore design," *Human Systems Management*, Amsterdam 2001.

Warkentin, M.E., Sayeed, L., & Hightower, R., "Virtual teams versus face-to-face teams: An exploratory study of a web-based conference system", *Decision Sciences*, vol. 28, no. 4, pp. 975-996, 1997.

Welty, B., Becerra-Fernandez, I., "Managing Trust and commitment in collaborative supply chain relationships". *Communications of the ACM*, 44(3), June 2001, pp. 67-73.

A Holistic Approach for Initial Acceptance and Continuance Model in Website Stickiness

Chulmo Koo, Kichan Nam, and Jae Beom Lee
Sogang University
Shinsu-Dong 1, Mapo-Ku, Seoul, Korea
Tel: 82-2-705-8710, Tel: 82-2-705-8710, Tel: 82-2-705-8538
Fax: 82-2-703-8224, Fax: 82-2-703-8224, Fax: 82-2-717-9773
helmet@sogang.ac.kr, knam@ccs.sogang.ac.kr, jblee@sogang.ac.kr

Sang-Gun Lee
University of Nebraska-Lincoln
252B CBA, University of Nebraska, USA
Tel: 1-402-472-0630
Fax: 1-402-472-5855
sglee@unlserve.unl.edu

ABSTRACT

How much do you pay to attract each customer to your Website? Some of the new e-commerce businesses are paying hundreds of dollars to attract one customer who will actually make a purchase, without a guarantee of a return visit. Until now, most research has focused on attracting customers or initial acceptance of Information Technology. However, as we know, attraction costs or initial acceptance cost are more expensive than retention costs or re-visit costs. Thus, this paper investigates the causal relationships between initial acceptance and the continuance process on Website visits. Specifically, it will examine from a holistic perspective the stickiness mechanism of Websites.

1. INTRODUCTION

Information Technology and its applications have been used widely in businesses of various industries, and specifically, the Internet has had a profound impact on a number of industries (Evans and Wurster, 1997). The number of users engaging in electronic commerce (EC) activities on the Internet such as financial investments, banking, gaming, and shopping has dramatically grown at an annual rate of greater than 50 percent (Liang and Ku, 1999). Simultaneously, Web technology for EC has developed broadly and been used widely in organizations by firms (business-to-business: B2B) and by individual users (business-to-customer: B2C; Hoffman et al., 1995; Zwass, 1996).

Despite the impressive growth of EC, there is compelling evidence to suggest that users' Website revisiting intentions are not subsequently a sure thing. According to a 2000 Boston Consulting Croup study (Shop.org & Boston Consulting Group, 2000), the proportion of consumers who buy out of those who visit a Website remains low ranging between 2.8% and 3.2%.

Therefore, the preceding evidence regarding Web business has prompted many firms to reassess and redesign their service quality, system use, playfulness, and design quality (Liu and Arnett, 2000; Wan, 2000) of their associated Websites as well as attempting to understand the growing numbers of customers (Kalakota 1997), consumer reactions to electronic shopping, product perceptions, shopping experiences, and customer service (Jarvenpaa and Todd, 1996). Palmer and Griffith (1998) propose that a change is needed for organizations to concentrate on not only the technological characteristics of their Website, but also to address customer concerns (Jarvenpaa and Todd, 1996) for Web usage.

In Web business, information technology determinants may lead consumers to engage in information system usage, while marketing determinants may facilitate one-time purchasing or repeat repurchasing behavior. Smith and Sivakumar (2002) explored conditions under which different dimensions of Internet shopping behaviors (browsing, one-time purchases, and repeat purchases), consumer related factors, the nature of the product, and the nature of the purchase occasion influenced user behavior. Forrestor research (1999) suggested that the perceived price of a product is a key attribute that most consumers consider in Web usage.

However, prior studies of Websites have articulated that consumer behavior of IT acceptance is separate from consumer characteristics or product characteristics. The willingness of customers to use Websites needs to be considered together with technology, products or services, social, and human factors. Actually, in Internet-based EC, why people decide to shop online, what kind of people want to use the Internet, and how people keep using Web sites have increasingly become important to web service providers.

In this paper, our conceptual model of Web usage is introduced from a holistic perspective. The research model proposes to investigate not only the relationship between the initial technology acceptance factors such as social influence, human, and marketing factors in predicting not only Web usage, but also the continuance of Web usage. In order to achieve the study's objectives, our Web usage model integrates initial-acceptance models such as TPB (Ajzen and Fishbein, 1980), TAM (Davis, 1989; Davis et al., 1989), Marketing Determinant (Rayport and Sviokla, 1994), and Individual Characteristics (Venkatesh, 2000; Klein, 1998; Compeau et al., 1999; Stewart, 1999), continuance models such as Online Repurchase Intention Model (Shim et al., 2001), and SERVQUAL & Behavioral Model (Dabholkar et al., 2000; Zeithaml et al., 1996; Homburg and Giering 2001; Oliver 1997; Anderson et al 1994; Marr and Crosby 1992; Ostrom and Iacobucci 1995), and post acceptance models (Bhattacherjee, 2001; Karahanna et al., 1999). Based on the literatures, we identify the key predictors of initial Web usage and continuance of Web usage through a survey of Web visitors.

2. LITERATURE REVIEW

The theoretical model for the study combines the initial acceptance models and the continuance models. The initial acceptance factors are based on the aspects of technical factor (Ajzen and Fishbein, 1980; Davis, 1989; Davis et al., 1989), social factors (Beard et al, 1986; Burnkrant and Cousineau, 1975; Handelman and Arnold, 1999), human factors (Compeau et al., 1999; Currall and Judge, 1995; McKnight et al., 1998), and marketing factors (Rayport and Sviokla, 1994). The continuance factors are based on satisfaction (Zeithaml et al., 1996; Bailey and Pearson, 1983) and stickiness (Beddoe and Stephens, 1999; Bush, 1999).

2.1. Initial Acceptance Constructs: Technology Dimension

Theories of IS use research have examined through the TRA and TPB, which has been proven successful in predicting and explaining behavior across business areas (Adams et al., 1992; Agarwal and Prasad, 1997; Christensen, 1987; Davis, 1989 and 1993; Mathieson, 1991; Moore and Benhasat, 1996; Pavri, 1988; Sheppard et al., 1988; Taylor and Todd, 1995; Thompson et al., 1991), Based on TRA, Davis (1989) introduced the technology acceptance model (TAM) which provided an explanation of the determinants of computer acceptance to end users (Chau, 1996; Hu et al., 1999; Sznjna, 1996; Venkatesh and Davis, 1996 and 2000).

2. 2 Initial Acceptance Constructs: Social Dimension

According to institutional theory (Handelman and Arnold, 1999), the institutional environment contains taken-for-granted social and cultural meaning systems, or norms, that define social reality. Rogers (1976) insisted that social factors are closely related to the communication network aspects of IDT (Innovation Diffusion Theory), which lie at the heart of the diffusion process. There are two types of social influence: (1) informational influence, which occurs when individuals accept information as evidence of reality, and (2) normative influence, which occurs when individuals conform to the expectations of others (Bearden et al., 1986; Burnkrant and Cousineau, 1975; Handelman and Arnold, 1999).

First, Word-of-Mouth (WOM) communications might be a highly important external variable. WOM messages may be a powerful determinant of the adoption of technology. Consumers were affected more by WOM messages than by any other factor overall (Webster, 1991). Based on prospect theory, several studies (Kahneman and Tversky, 1979; Einhorn and Hogarth, 1981; Aharony and Swary, 1980, Lang and Litzenberger, 1989; Michaely et al., 1995) detect stronger effects when information about a product is unfavorable rather than favorable, and when information is verbal rather than written (Herr et al., 1991). In addition, face-to-face WOM messages have proven to be powerful influences on consumer attitudes and behavior.

Second, possible salient referents for the social normative component with respect to individuals' adoption of IT could be friends (Brancheau, 1987; Cale and Eriksen, 1994) and near peers of the potential adopter through their own personal experiences (Brancheau and Wetherbe, 1990).

2.3 Initial Acceptance Constructs: Human Dimension

In a learning electronic environment, individuals who are comfortable with technology may have positive attitudes (Jonassen, 1985). The concept of self-efficacy (Bandura, 1986) has been incorporated into IS research on technology adoption and use (Compeau and Higgins, 1995a and 1995b; Marakas et al., 1998; Staples et al., 1999). It has also made its way into the literature through the theory of planned behavior (Ajzen 1985), which considers perceived behavioral control and social norms as predictors of attitude (Mathieson, 1991). This research has shown that self-efficacy is an antecedent of Web usage (Compeau et al., 1999).

In addition, the failure of the Web as a retail distribution channel has been attributed to the lack of trust consumers have in Web security and privacy in general (Stewart, 1999). Currall and Judge (1995) defined trust as an individual's reliance on another party under conditions of dependence and risk. Mayer et al (1995) further clarified the relationship between trust and risk: trust is the willingness to assume risk, while trusting behavior is the assumption of risk. When the trustor does not have firsthand knowledge of electronic commerce, trust is important, given that there is some risk involved in using an electronic channel for financial transactions. This research has shown that trust is an antecedent of Web usage.

Klein's 1998 investigation found that prior experience with Internet shopping influences the next behavior. Liang and Huang (1998) found that consumer's prior experience had a moderating effect in predicting their acceptance of Internet shopping. This research has shown that prior experience is an antecedent of Web usage

2.4 Initial-Acceptance Constructs: Marketing Dimension

Hoffman and Novak (1996), as well as Berthon et al. (1996) suggest several uses for Websites including presence, promotion, sales, and customer research. In addition, the opportunity for users to examine or test the product or service and receive technical support can be provided through the Website. Rayport and Sviokla (1994) developed a framework for creating new values for customers. A customer's perceived value of a product or service consists of the three basic elements, the content of the product or service that companies are offering, the context of how companies are offering the product or service, and the infrastructure that enables the transaction to occur. Rayport and Sviokla (1994) developed a framework representing customer behavior in the marketspace using TRA. Customers' beliefs about a particular brand's content, context, and infrastructure have impacts on their attitude toward repetitive transactions for the product or the service associated with it.

Moreover, the price of product is an important aspect of online shopping. Price power is evident in the ranking of store formats. Some shoppers are highly price sensitive and consequently look for bargains. Such individuals will actively search and buy products on the Internet in order to obtain lower prices because lower prices are a main reason why online shoppers shop on the Web (Forrester Research, 1999).

In an Ernst & Young survey on e-commerce, 69% of respondents stated that brand names played a significant role in their online buying decisions. Online users continue to gravitate toward brands for two basic reasons: first, band names act as substitutes for information gathering by helping online buyers locate specific products and thus reduce search costs; and second, consumer attitudes regarding brand trust, security, and expectations regarding product quality (Coltman et al., 2002).

2. 5 Continuance Constructs: Satisfaction

According to SERVQUAL and satisfaction theory (Zeithaml et al., 1996; Bailey and Pearson, 1983; DeLone and McLean, 1992; Ginzberg, 1979, Kettinger and Lee, 1999, Klenke, 1992; Melone, 1990), the concept of end user satisfaction has been exclusively researched as a surrogate of system success. DeLone and McLean (1992) introduced a comprehensive taxonomy to organize diverse research in this area, as well as to present a more integrated view of the concept of information system success and posited six major dimensions or categories of success: system quality, information quality, use, user satisfaction, individual impact and organizational impact. Ives, et al (1983) developed a 13-item instrument, which was later confirmed by Baroudi and Orlikowski (1988). They defined end user satisfaction as felt need, system acceptance, perceived usefulness, MIS appreciation, and feelings about a system. Bailey and Pearson (1983) evaluated overall satisfaction, which they suggested is affected by 38 items, measured on a 7-point likert scale where "1" indicates users strongly agree with his/her present computer experience, and "7" indicates that they strongly disagree. Lee and Ulgado (1997) investigated the relationship between perceived SERVQUAL value and customers' overall satisfaction in the fast-food industry.

In this paper, the four-dimensional conceptualization of satisfaction is used, including satisfaction through usability, satisfaction through personalization, satisfaction through content, and satisfaction through privacy. These dimensions will be explained in detail later.

2.6 Continuance Constructs: Stickiness

Even though stickiness is a relatively new concept, according to the latest academic literature, there are several definitions in the concept of stickiness. Some definitions are as follows.

Beddoe-Stephens (1999) defined Stickiness as "a company's ability retain end users and drive them further into a site." Bush (1999) emphasize that Stickiness is clearly based on providing unique content and specialized services to vertical market niches. According to Devenport (2000), Stickiness is a measure of how much attention a Web site receives over time. By term definition, Website Stickiness is measured by the average minutes per month visitors spent at a site or network (Marketing terms.com), and Stickiness is anything about a Web site that encourages a visitor to stay longer. A Web site is sticky if a visitor tends to stay for a long time and to return (searchwebservices.com).

HYPOTHESES

On the basis of literature review, we seek to derive the causal relationships between initial-acceptance constructs and continuance constructs. Most research models are discontinuous and have not considered a causal relationship between initial-acceptance and continuance. Therefore, in this paper, we integrate two acceptance models to better explain end users' Websites usage from a combined or holistic perspective rather than from each perspective separately.

Our literature review suggested that technology, social, human, and market dimensions strongly affect end-users' intention to use Web sites based on TRA, TAM, TPB, IDT, Institutional theory, Prospect Theory, and WOM.

From this general statement, the degree of intention to use Websites will be measured within the four initial constructs. Hence, we propose the following hypotheses:

H1~4: Intention to use Web sites is determined by Technology, Social, Human, Marketing dimensions.

It is expected that if this hypotheses are proven true, then these new initial-acceptance constructs could be commonly used to test internal validity and statistical conclusion validity.

Theory of Reasoned Action (Ajzen and Fishbein, 1980; Ajzen, 1985) suggested that intention (behavior) affects behavior, and Shim and Drake (1990) also insisted that a strong intention to use a PC affects the use of PCs. Hartwick and Barki (1994) hypothesized that intention to use determines system use. According to the IT diffusion process model (Straub, 1994; Straub et al., 1995; Gefen and Straub, 1997), the perception of usefulness, the perception of ease of use and Gender differences may be related to intention to use which directly affect actual use. Hence, the following hypothesis is suggested:

H5: Intention to use directly affects actual use.

The second part of our research demonstrates the mediating role of satisfaction in Web site stickiness, and investigates the idea that end user Web continuance is channeled through satisfaction.

Klein (1998) found that prior experience with Internet shopping influences the next behavior. Similarly, Liang and Huang (1998) found that consumers' prior experience had a moderating effect in predicting their acceptance of Internet shopping. In prior experience, customer satisfaction is an essential factor regarding the reuse or revisitation of a Website.

Zeithaml et al. (1996) developed SERVQUAL and then insisted that service quality relates to retention of customers at the aggregate level. Kettinger and Lee (1994) demonstrated that knowledge and information, information products and information system staff and service improve user satisfaction with an information service function.

Bowman and Narayandas (2001) showed that customer satisfaction influenced repetitive buying behavior. Satisfaction research has typically defined satisfaction as a post choice evaluative judgment concerning a specific purchase decision (Bearden and Teel 1983; Churchill and Suprenant 1982; Oliver 1979, 1980; Oliver and DeSarbo 1988). Parasuraman et al. (1994) conceptualized the idea that transaction satisfaction contained evaluation service quality, evaluation production quality and evaluation price.

Based on SERVQUAL, we adapt and develop IT's Post-Acceptance Model (PAM) to ascertain why end-users stick to using certain Websites. PAM is based on Expectation-Confirmation Theory (ECT), which is adapted from consumer behavior literature (Anderson and Sullivan, 1993; Oliver, 1980; Petterson and Johnson, 1997). The process of repurchase-intention on the PAM framework is as follows (Bhattacherjee, 2001):
1. End-users form an initial expectation of a specific IT, and expect usefulness.
2. They accept and use the IT, and then form perception of its usefulness.
3. They assess their satisfaction with the IT.
4. Finally, satisfied end-users form an IT continuance intention.

The PAM model is different from TAM on at least three counts: 1) PAM explains continuance behavior while TAM focuses on initial acceptance; 2) PAM is a richer model from the perspective of post acceptance variables because these variables are in greater temporal proximity to continuance behaviors; and 3) TAM cannot provide a reasonable explanation of the acceptance-discontinuous anomaly based on a common set of pre-acceptance variables (Bhattacherjee, 2001).

As theorized and validated by ECT and PAM, end-users' continuance behavior is determined by their satisfaction with prior IT use (Trevino and Webster, 1992). Bhattachejee's 2001 study indicated that end users' satisfac-

tion level is positively associated with their IT continuance intention.

According to Northwestern University's Integrating Marketing Communication research group (IMC: http://www.medill.northwestern.edu/imc/studentwork/projects/ Sticky/stickiness.htm), a Website's stickiness comes from Usability, personalization, and content. Walczuch et al. (2001) insisted that stickiness is affected by content, privacy, incentives schemes, online special events, Brand loyalty, personalization, reminders and navigation. Barnes and Vidgen (2001) suggested that Web quality is determined by information quality, interaction quality and an integrated view of Web site quality.

Based on previous research, in this paper we consider the satisfaction factors that increase stickiness to be usability, content, personalization, and privacy.

Satisfaction relates to customer evaluations of product usability based on such characteristics as durability, technical sophistication, and ease of use (Parasuraman, 1994). Usability explains the process of designing an e-commerce Website and compares it to designing a store in the offline world. It states that companies need to have a deep understanding of their consumers; how they shop, browse, and purchase (http://www.medill.northwestern.edu/imc/studentwork/ projects/Sticky/usability.htm).

IMC also defined personalization such that a personalized Website recognizes repeat visitors, offers them a unique set of alternatives based on their past behavior or stated preferences, and continues to learn from the users' interactions so as to remain relevant and tailored to meet their individual needs and wants. Some researchers (Hagel and Armstrong, 1997; Hof, 1998; Luedi, 1997) insisted that personalization attracts more people and keeps them on the Web site for longer, creates customer loyalty, and generates stickiness. According to Kotwica (1999), 81 percent of respondents to her survey have visited a site that uses some form of Web site personalization, and 64 percent found it useful.

According to Walczuch (2001) and his partners, tailoring content to the individual user is one of the important factors in creating stickiness. They suggested three different types of content, depth of content, breadth of content, and frequent updates. Hegal and Armstrong (1997) insisted that the greater the vertical integration of functional content, the stickier the Web site is for end users. Davenport (2000) emphasizes a broad offering of content because the wide range of information options builds stickiness. For example AOL users more spend substantial amounts of time in the site due to a self-contained world of content. Another important factor for achieving stickiness is rapid updates in content. Users visit a Web site, and when they are satisfied with the site content they revisit the site.

According to Brenner (1998), respecting the privacy of users has a positive effect on stickiness. When privacy is respected, end-users may have loyalty to the site. When users feel that the sole owner of any information collected on a site sells, shares, or rents their information to others, they will not revisit or reuse the Web site. Kotwica (1999) also found that many respondents voiced concerns about privacy. That is, Web users feel that Big Brother is watching their information.

All four elements must work in unison in order for a site to achieve a sufficient degree of stickiness required to repeat transactions. This leads to the hypotheses.

H6-9: Stickiness in Web continuance usage is positively affected by satisfaction through Usability, Personalization, Content, and Privacy

4. EXPECTED CONCLUSION

Our research model lays down a conceptual framework for continuance of Website visits by users. The holistic model between initial acceptance and continuance helps provide a better understanding of Web stickiness. Even though current research suggests a concept of stickiness, there is little empirical evidence. This study tries to investigate the causal relationships from initial acceptance to continuance.

This research also has limitations. Future research should consider specific types of Web sites as research subjects because there are likely many important deviations between Web site types, such as news sites, BC sites, and portal sites.

REFERENCES
References are available upon request from authors

Figure 1. Research Model

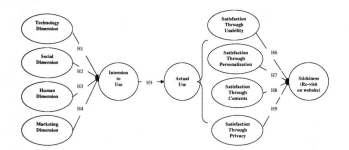

The Influence of Web Usability on Online Shopper's Repurchase Intention

Jeongil Choi
Department of Management
College of Business Administration
University of Nebraska-Lincoln
Lincoln, NE 68588-0491, USA
Phone: 402-472-0630
Fax: 402-472-5855
jichoi@unlserve.unl.edu

Sang-Chul Jung
Department of Management
College of Economics and Management
Chungnam National University
Daejeon 305-764, Korea
Phone: +82-42-821-5586
Fax: +82-42-823-5359
scjung@cnu.ac.kr

Dahui Li
Department of Finance and MIS
School of Business
University of Minnesota Duluth
Duluth, MN 55812-2496, USA
Phone: 218-726-7334
Fax: 218-726-7516
dli@d.umn.edu

ABSTRACT

Website plays an important role as a "cyber store" through which online shoppers have their initial and on-going interactions with the Web retailers. Therefore, Web usability becomes an important determinant of productive online transaction in the B2C e-commerce. The concept of Web stickiness in B2C e-commerce along with Web usability has drawn much attention from the practitioners and researchers. We believe Web usability and Web stickiness affect online shopper's repurchase intention in B2C e-commerce. In this regards, from the investigation of the relationship between the website and website users, this study explores the effects of Web usability, Web stickiness, online shopper's repurchase intention and the strengths of the relationships between different variables.

INTRODUCTION

As Internet is becoming a powerful channel in e-commerce, the website plays an important role as a "cyber store" through which consumers have their initial and on-going interactions with the Web retailers. In business to consumer transactions environment, website has become a major information source and cyber store to purchase online.

Up to now, numerous studies have focused on the design principle of websites and the measurement of Web usability. Unlike the previous research, this study concentrates on the relationship among usability of the website and stickiness of potential online shopper toward Web retailers from the B2C e-commerce perspective, because it has been suggested that elements of human-computer interface design have a significant influence on customer attitudes and perceptions of trustworthiness of a supplier (Kim and Moon 1998; Cheskin Research 2000; Nielsen and Norman 2000; Egger 2000).

From the relationship marketing perspective, since it always costs more to attract new customers than to retain current customers, customer retention is more critical than customer attraction. Increasing customer retention could improve long-term profitability in the business (Reichheld and Sasser 1990; Reichheld and Teal 1996; Reichheld and Schefter 2000). The key to customer retention is customer satisfaction (Zhang and M. von Dran 2001-2002). Consequently, if a customer is satisfied with the use of a specific website, he/she will continuously use the website to purchase online. Reichheld and Schefter (2000) found that acquiring consumers on the Internet is more expensive than on conventional channels and that if consumers cannot stick to the business' website, the e-business model will collapse. Therefore understanding consumers' expectations and how they feel about the website they use is becoming very important concern in the B2C e-commerce (Zhang and M. von Dran 2001-2002). Nonetheless, it is little known about the effect of human-computer interaction on the sticky behavior of website users to purchase online.

The purpose of this research is to explore the relationship between Web usability and users' repurchase intention and to identify the effect of Web stickiness constructs in the relationship. Based on the research purpose, the following research questions are raised: To what extent does a useful website lead online shopper's repurchase intention from the website? To what extent does a useful website lead online shopper's Web stickiness? Can online shopper's Web stickiness finally lead to online shopper's repurchase intention?

THEORETICAL BACKGROUNDS AND LITERATURE REVIEW

Web Usability

The usability of website has received attention in the human computer interaction (HCI) literature. Prior to widespread use of the web, usability of information systems was equivalent to a set of design principle (Palmer 2002). According to Nielsen (1993), the key element is (1) consistency of the interface, (2) response time, (3) mapping and metaphors, (4) interaction styles, and (5) multimedia and audiovisual. As the Web became a robust channel in the e-commerce, usability research began to focus more specifically on extending the basic usability principles into the Web environment (Shneiderman 1998; Nielsen 2000; Palmer 2002). Nielsen (2000) extends the following principles for Web design: (1) navigation, (2) response time, (3) credibility, and (4) content.

Some previous research has shown the impact of website design on the customer's initial perception of the company (Roy et al. 2001). The website in the B2C e-commerce is a web retailer's face to the consumer. Potential customers look at web retailer's online presence before doing any business with it. Since the Web is a strong medium in the context of online transaction, Web retailers are pursuing the most effective and competitive web design to communicate with potential consumers, motivate them to access or purchase their products and services, and engender consumers' trust. The website is an entry facilitator or barrier in achieving these goals in a Web-based transaction environment (Zhang and M. von Dran 2001-2002).

Unlike the physical store, the switching costs on the Internet are low. If consumers don't find what they want, cannot figure out how to purchase, or do not feel safe giving their personal information, they will leave the site by only a mouse-click. The initial visit to the website can be triggered by the advertising or other promotional methods. But If the website doesn't have usability, the percentage of those who complete a purchase after visiting the site will not be increased (Nielsen and Norman 2000).

Web Stickiness

The concept of stickiness in the Web world is currently defined multiple ways. Media Metrix, the leading digital media measurement company, measures stickiness solely on the average time spent at a site per usage month. Nemzow (1999) divided stickiness into short-term stickiness and long-term stickiness. Short-term stickiness is easily replicated by competitors. Long-term stickiness needs to grow even stickier over time, creating a financial hurdle that discourages customers from switching to competitors. Davenport (2000) points out that stickiness is critical on the e-commerce and that its main concern is how much actual viewer attention they attract over time. From the perspective of information technology, stickiness is the "first indication that companies are focusing not just on information distribution but on usage as well" (Davenport 2000, p.58). Dahui and Yadav (2001) suggested that user satisfaction, lack of motivation to switch, and perceived switching cost may lead stickiness toward a website.

In marketing research, stickiness might contribute to the evolution from customer acquisition to customer retention. Relationship marketing theories propose that the development of customer relationship follows a continuum from transactional to relationship orientations (Dwyer et al. 1987). Morgan and Hunt (1994) suggested that consumer stickiness might be one of the behavioral facets of the consumer's loyalty and commitment toward the long-term relationship with a business. We considered the definition of stickiness in terms of customer loyalty (Oliver 1999) as a deeply held commitment to reuse a preferred website consistently in the future, thereby causing repetitive same-web site visiting and using, despite situational influences and marketing efforts having the potential to cause switching behavior.

Online Shopper's Repurchase Intention

Social Exchange Theory (Thibaut and Kelley 1959; Homans 1961; Blau 1964) states that people are likely to apply social exchange rules developed and reinforced in past interactions with other individuals. This principle can be reasonably applied to the context of continuous IS use. In this study, website can be an example of an IS (Isakowitz et al. 1998). Initially, the user has certain needs and goals in browsing the Internet. After he finds a website that is useful and can satisfy his needs, the user may feel dependent on the website and keep returning to this website. If during the ongoing interactions the website can fulfill the user's need constantly, the user may have intention to repurchase a product or service at a specific website. Thus, the user may feel more dependent on the website and interact more with the website.

In a recent study, Bhattacherjee (2001) has developed a continuous IS use model based on expectation-confirmation model and investigated the significant effect of satisfaction on an individual's intention to use an IS continuously. The outcome of the research model is online shopper's repurchase intention at a web site, which is jointly determined by perceived usefulness and satisfaction with the browsing of website. His empirical study found that satisfaction and perceived usefulness are salient predictors of continuous IS use intention. Baroudi et al. (1986) also found that user satisfaction is a strong predictor of system use.

RESEARCH MODEL AND PROPOSED HYPOTHESES

Based on the relevant literature, we propose the research model for web usability and IT continuous use. The proposed model consists of 6 constructs: four dimensions of web usability, and one for web stickiness and IT continuous use, respectively. The constructs and their relationships are presented in Figure 1.

The theoretical hypotheses to be tested, grounding on each of the relations, are as follows:

H1: Each Web usability dimension will increase online shoppers' Web stickiness.
H1a: Ease of navigation will increase online shoppers' Web stickiness.
H1b: Consistency will increase online shoppers' Web stickiness.
H1c: Easy to learn will increase online shoppers' Web stickiness.
H1d: User guidance will increase online shoppers' Web stickiness.

H2: Online shoppers' web stickiness will have a positive impact on online shoppers' repurchase.

RESEARCH METHODOLOGY

An experiment will be conducted to evaluate the proposed research model. The constructs in the research model will be measured respondents self-reported perceptions after experiencing different websites. Participants' percep-

Figure 1. Proposed Research Model

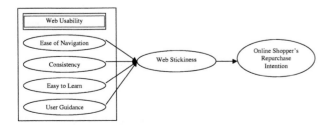

Table 1. Constructs and Operationalization

Construct	Operational Definition	Reference
Web Usability	Ability of a website to assist users perform tasks.	Adapted from Lin et al. (1997) index of usability.
Web Stickiness	Users' perception to satisfy the use of website and want to visit at the website again.	New scale will be developed.
IT Continuous Use	Users' continuous purchase behavior from the specific website.	Extended from Mathieson's (1991) behavioral Intention Scale.

tion can be gathered utilizing questionnaires. The unit of analysis in this study is the perception of an individual user about using a website in B2C e-commerce. Students from several undergraduate business classes can be asked to participate voluntarily in this study. The use of student subjects is a pragmatic choice for controlled experimental research (Miranda and Bostrom, 1993-1994). For adequate statistical power, data from many subjects will be collected. However it needs to be very careful when interpreting the results of the experiment because of the mental constructs involved (Kumar and Benbasat 2001).

Measurement

A questionnaire was used to collect data on user evaluation on the constructs proposed in the research model. The first part of the questionnaire will be designed to collect general demographic information and previous Internet use experience of subjects. The second part will contain questions based on five-point Likert scale, comprising questions adapted from the previous studies and newly developed for this study. For evaluating website usability, index of usability developed and validated by Lin et al. (1997) can be used. The dimensions of web usability proposed by Neilsen were latter integrated into a general index of usability by Lin et al. (1997). Table 1 provides operational definitions and sources for the constructs.

Data Analysis and Hypothesis Testing

Structural equation modeling is considered a powerful second generation multivariate analysis technique for studying causal model. It also superior to tradition regression and factor analysis because of the measurement model is assessed within the context of the theoretical structural model (Fornell 1982). Partial least squares (PLS) and LISREL are the most widely known implementation of structural equation modeling. PLS, developed by Wold (1982), was the preferred technique for data analysis in this study because PLS is considered more appropriate for the relatively small sample size (Thong et al. 1996).

EXPECTED OUTCOME AND LIMITATION

Web usability becomes an important determinant of productive online transaction in the B2C e-commerce. In this regards, from the investigation of the relationship between the website and website users, this study explores the effects of Web usability, Web stickiness, online shopper's repurchase intention and the strengths of the relationships between different variables. We expect this study will provide both theoretically and practically useful implications. This study includes a very important mediating variable such as Web stickiness in the relationship between web usability and online shopper's repurchase intention. Therefore, the study will provide the conceptual development in the website-user relationship and the additional applicability of social exchange theory and expectation-confirmation model in the B2C e-commerce. For the practice of human-computer interaction, this study expects to suggest that new features of website such as customization and personalization have the potential to change the roles of IS from merely tools to social actors and relationship partners. The findings of this study will also help companies analyze the efficacy of new interface technologies in impacting their target customers' perceptions.

However, this study has a number of limitations. First, it is difficult to control the possibility that Web stickiness and online shoppers' continuous use can be both influenced by a third components, undefined by the measurement items. Second, because this study will be conducted in a laboratory setting, the results make it becomes less applicable to the real world situations.

REFERENCES

References are available upon request from authors.

Integrated Domain Model for Digital Rights Management

Eetu Luoma, Saila Tiainen, and Pasi Tyrväinen
Department of Computer Science and Information Systems
University of Jyväskylä
Tel: +358-14-260-4632, Tel: +358-14-260-4632, Tel: +358-14-260-3093
eetu.luoma@jyu.fi, saila.tianen@jyu.fi, pasi.tyrvainen@jyu.fi

ABSTRACT

Digital Rights Management (DRM) is an issue of controlling and managing digital rights over intellectual property. Currently, the domain has an essential problem: lack of models on an appropriate level of abstraction needed to support research and system development. This paper contributes in recognizing the principal entities by using the existing frameworks of the domain and our observations of the definitive characteristics of these entities. Modelling, identifying and describing the core entities enable the DRM functionalities. Our analysis distinguishes the evolution stages of digital content processed through the value chain and separates the different offers and agreements through which the rights are traded between the value chain participants. Definition of the differing characteristics is evidently important in specifying the requirements for a comprehensive DRM system.

1. INTRODUCTION

Traditional management of intellectual property rights in digital environment is based on prohibiting access to the content if customer has not presented the proper considerations. This is facilitated by encryption and security measures, and forces the content providers to select business models according to the available technology. Since success in electronic commerce seems to depend on the companies' business models, it is conceded that the equilibrium between technology and the way of doing business should be vice versa (Rosenblatt et al., 2002).

Currently, associated under the term Digital Rights Management (DRM), the domain has developed from an immature consideration of digital products' protection to identification, description, trading, protection, monitoring and tracking of rights permissions, constrains, and requirements over assorted assets, either tangible or intangible by limiting content distribution (Iannella, 2001).

Fulfilling such tasks with the intention of providing comprehensive solution sets high requirements to the development of an effective holistic information system, which shall be integrated with current operational systems. Moreover, the assignment of these requirements is challenging as the domain lacks sufficient framework, which has a level of abstraction applicable in multiple situations and which describes the definitive characteristics of the domain elements. We therefore attempt to provide a depiction of an integrated domain model in relation to the current research and standard development activities. Our scope to the rights management issues is on electronic assets - the content's straightforward creation, management and trade in the digital environment.

2. EXISTING FRAMEWORKS

An existing work for describing DRM entities and their relations is presented in the framework of the <indecs> project (Rust & Bide, 2000). Their contribution is based on the assumption that the complexity of intellectual property rights information could be handled through generic models identifying the fundamental concepts with high-level attributes. The generic framework divides and identifies the principal entities that include parties, rights and content. From a commercial point of view, their relationships are: parties *hold and trade* rights *over* content, and parties *create and use* content.

This abstract presentation provides a basis for further discussion by clarifying what must be identified and described (parties, rights and content itself), what is traded in the domain (content and related rights), what we should

protect (content and rights for infringements), and what is necessary for monitoring and tracking (usage of content and honouring the rights). Thus, identifying and describing the entities facilitate the DRM functionalities.

The International Federation of Library Associations (IFLA) has provided a valuable framework for observing and modelling the content's development throughout its evolution stages (Plassard, 1998). IFLA's model enables the creation to be identified through four dimensions, beginning from the most abstract: work, expression, manifestation, and item dimensions.

A work corresponds to the most abstract level of a creation, thus, a work is not an identifiable entity and it can be caught only throughout its expressions. An expression together with a specific media and format embodies a manifestation of that particular creation. An item is the entity, which finally ends up into the consumers' hands. Each of the items is individual even if they would exemplify the same manifestation.

Despite the acknowledged contribution of these frameworks, they by definition cannot be used to capture and analyze the requirements of the development of a DRM system. Data collection, processing and management needs for DRM may be elaborated as the commercial view is considered with the evolution aspect and the definitive characteristics of the domain's entities.

3. THE PROPOSED DOMAIN MODEL

In the attempt to provide an integrated domain model, we make use of the basic notions in the object-oriented discipline. Constructing the domain model is one of the fundamental tasks of the object-oriented analysis methods. We do not suggest object-orientation to be the most suitable for the implementation of DRM systems, but rather it provides a valuable tool for illustrating and visualizing the substance of the domain. In the domain model below, we

Figure 1 - Four Dimensions of the Creations and Their Relationships

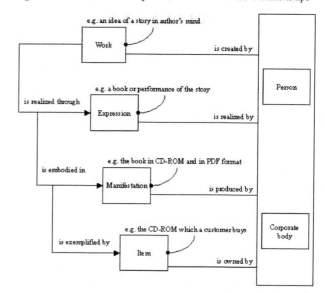

use a notation of UML class diagram (Jacobson et al., 1999). Entities in the domain model represent the basic actors, different realizations of a creation and rights descriptions evolving from offers to agreements describing permissions and obligations. Figure 2, presenting the integrated domain model, entails different entity categories organized in three columns, as these differentiate the evolution stages of digital creations and agreements created, processed and used through the value chain. The notion of these different dimensions offers valuable considerations for content identification, description and trading.

The entity characteristics are demonstrated as attributes consisting of the metadata describing the content, the details and the roles of organizations and individuals as well as the details of offers and agreements expressed in digital rights expression language. Associations between entities generally follow the straightforward rules of the <indecs> framework. Accordingly, there are parties holding and trading rights over content, which is created and used by the parties.

3.1 Identification and Description of Content

Within its lifecycle, a creation serves several purposes, being at first a realization of its creator's intellectual effort. Then, creation is transformed into a product available for utilization, and at last, the copy of the product is offered to the customers as something concrete and an experience worth of paying. Therefore, associated with the creation, we need to separate identification and description schemes for different dimensions. Moreover, at different stages of evolution, diverse rights holders can be distinguished. Therefore, reflecting the right level of abstraction for creations, we may classify the subjects to different agreements and further justify the different agreements in our model.

Techniques used for identification in the traditional environments cannot be directly transferred to the digital world. One downside of the traditional identifiers is that they consider creations at the manifestation dimension – an identifier is assigned as creation is transformed into products. Nevertheless, in the digital environment a need emerges to identify creations both at expression and item level to enable monitoring and tracking functionalities. Another point of consideration is the unique identification of the parts in composites consisting of several unique content entities.

Figure 2 – The Integrated Domain Model for Digital Rights Management

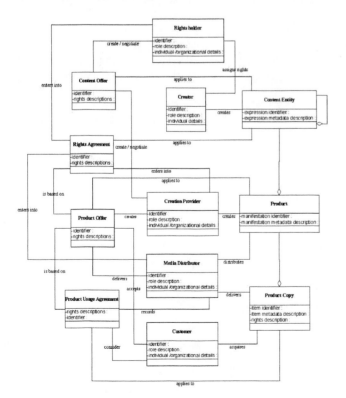

For describing the content, the complicated issue is not the selection of metadata standard or scheme to apply. Similarly, it is a question on how a scheme should by applied with different dimensions of the creation. Moreover, as the creation consists of several individual parts, different metadata on expression and manifestation levels exist.

3.2. Identification and Description of Parties

To approve both the individuals and agents to perform their role specific operations, actors of a system have to be identified and their roles recognized. At present, a few recognized standards for such purposes prevail. In rights management, the roles represent the basic activities in the trading of intellectual property rights by initiating or facilitating the flow of rights, payments or other information (IMPRIMATUR, 1999).

A creator wishes to circulate her creation and, as a result, assigns her rights to exploit the creation to the creation provider with an agreement. Optionally, the creator may have assigned her rights to some other legal entity; thus, the agreement will be made between the third party rights holder and the content provider. IMPRIMATUR suggests that the defining characteristic of the creation provider is responsible for making a creation available for exploitation or use, namely, making products. Additionally, the creation provider operates in various functions concerning the control and management of the creation, payments and intellectual property rights.

Media distributor's task is to establish the trade of creations on behalf of the creation providers in order to meet the needs of the customers. Media distributor's role may take responsibilities in packaging the product for distribution and delivery, in facilitating and reporting on sales and payment transactions and in providing marketing functions towards the customers. However, the basic responsibility of the media distributor is to deliver product copies to the customer. Finally, value to the chain is returned as customers acquire the product copies.

3.3. Identification and Description of Rights

Negotiation on the terms of the trade will be carried out as parties choose to circulate and acquire the content – offers between parties are created and possibly modified. Once parties accept the terms of the offering, they enter an agreement specifying who (party) acquires what (content) on which terms (rights descriptions). Rights descriptions consist of permissions, constraints and requirements of material utilization. Permissions consider the usage of the material, the downstream transfer of the material, content management and to the reuse of the material. Permissions can have constraints such as assigning the permission to a group of individuals, to some IP address space or for a period of time. Moreover, the rights holder may set some requirements concerning the utilization of material, for instance pre-use or per-use payments.

The terms above reflect the possibilities of a currently evolving rights description language, Open Digital Rights Language (Iannella, 2002). One similar development activity is in progress: eXtensible Rights Markup Language (ContentGuard, 2001). Like its competitor for the standard, XrML attempts to provide "a general-purpose language in XML used to describe the rights and conditions for using digital resources."

Maintenance of the described data improves rights clearances and trading of rights over content in different situations. Moreover, digital rights data in the delivery channel confines consumers to use the material in the way defined in the rights descriptions. Such enforcement and possible tracking of digital rights through special technologies strives to govern digital rights data in a reasonable way.

Although the description of rights relating to the content has become one of the most attractive single research areas, the issue of identification should not be neglected here. Unique identification of rights descriptions enables mechanisms to build an association between the content and the rights descriptions regarding that particular content.

4. CONCLUSION

The constructed domain model presents data collection, processing and management needs for DRM. It is therefore a valuable tool in specifying requirements for a comprehensive management system. Additionally, the model clarifies the need for separate identification and characteristics description of offers, agreements, value chain participants and creations through their life cycle. Processes and business models related to exchange of digital content and products are subject to further research. The integrated domain model of digital rights management facilitates this examination.

REFERENCES

ContentGuard, I. (2001). eXtensible rights Markup Language (XrML) 2.0 Specification. Available: http://www.xrml.com, [26.8.2002].

Iannella, R. (2001). Digital Rights management (DRM) Architectures. D-Lib Magazine, 7(6).

Iannella, R. (2002). Open Digital Rights Language (ODRL) Version 1.1. IPR Systems Pty Ltd. Available: http://www.odrl.net/1.1/ODRL-11.pdf, [31.8.2002].

IMPRIMATUR. (1999). Synthesis of the IMPRIMATUR Business Model.

Jacobson, I., Booch, G., & Rumbaugh, J. (1999). The unified software development process. Reading (MA): Addison-Wesley.

Plassard, M.-F. (1998). Functional Requirements for Bibliographic Records. Final Report., IFLA Study Group on the Functional Requirements for Bibliographic Records. Available: http://www.ifla.org/VII/s13/frbr/frbr.pdf, [6.8.2002].

Rosenblatt, B., Trippe, B., & Mooney, S. (2002). Digital Rights Management: Business and Technology. New York: M&T Books.

Rust, G., & Bide, R. (2000). <indecs> metadata framework: principles, model and dictionary, Indecs Framework Ltd,. Available: http://www.indecs.org/pdf/framework.pdf , [6.8.2002].

Assessing E-Commerce Technology Enabled Business Value: An Exploratory Research

M. Adam Mahmood, Leopoldo A. Gemoets, Laura L. Hall, Francisco J. Lopez, and Ritesh A. Mariadas

Department of Information and Decision Sciences, University of Texas at El Paso, El Paso, TX 79968-0544

t: (915) 747-7754, t: (915) 747-7763, t: (915) 747-7743, t: (915) 747-7741, t: (915) 747-5496, [fax]: 747-5126

mmahmood@utep.edu, lgemoets@utep.edu, lhall@utep.edu, fjlopez@utep.edu

INTRODUCTION

Despite the recent demise of a considerable number of dot-coms, many traditional brick-and-mortar companies have invested and continue to invest heavily in eCommerce technologies. These companies will spend by 2002, according to one source, over $200 billion dollars on eCommerce business projects (Stuart 1999). While sizeable investments in eCommerce enabled initiatives are being made, it is extremely difficult to measure the benefits received from these initiatives mainly because of the difficulty involved in collecting data.

Anecdotal evidence in the information technology (IT) productivity and business value literature suggests that these firms have achieved enormous performance and productivity gains by integrating eCommerce channels with their existing brick-and-mortar channels and thereby transforming themselves into a click-and-mortar business. Cisco Systems, Dell Computers, and Boeing Corporation are examples of large click-and-mortar organizations that have achieved a significant economic benefit by using eCommerce technologies. Cisco claims it is the single largest user of eCommerce in the world, with 90% of its 2000 sales which amounts to about $18.9 billion, coming online It also says that 82% of its customer inquiries are handled online (McIlvaine, 2000). Cisco's revenues and net income have increased significantly since 1992 and its stock prices soared to the point that made Cisco a company with the highest market capitalization in the world in the early 2000 (Kramaer and Dedrick, 2002).

Dell Computer reported over 250% return on invested capital from its logistics and order fulfillment systems (dell.com, November 2000). It makes more than $1 million dollars in PC sales online every day. Boeing's electronic intermediary, PART online, allowed it to process 20 percent more shipments per month in 1997 than in 1996 with the same number of data entry people and resulted in elimination of 600 phone calls per day to telephone service staff (Teasdale, 1997).

In spite of these anecdotes and others, there is no systematic empirical evidence in the IT productivity or business value literature regarding the payoffs from eCommerce business initiatives, especially for large click-and-mortar companies (Brynjolfsson and Kahim, 2000). The fundamental objective of the present research is to assess the eCommerce technology enabled business value. The research will investigate whether firms using eCommerce technology are successful in generating business value and, if they are, what eCommerce drivers determine such success and how best to use these drivers. An exploratory model of e-Commerce business value is proposed depicting the possible effect of management support for eCommerce enabled initiatives, efficient eCommerce support systems (e.g., automated data transmittal and retrieval system, automated order processing system, and online procurement system), and effective eCommerce presence on business operational efficiency and financial success. The model is fully grounded in IT business value and productivity literature (Kauffman and Kriebel 1988, Mahmood and Mann, 1995).

The contribution of the present research, once completed, will be an empirically validated eCommerce business value model that can function as a reference framework for strategic managers by offering guidelines for eCommerce based business initiatives. The constructs developed in the model can serve as a foundation for further investigation of different eCommerce drivers and their relationships with business value measures. To the best of our knowledge, this is the first empirical study to address the business value of eCommerce enabled initiatives.

The paper proceeds as follows. The next section discusses the relevant prior literature to provide the background information and theoretical perspective for the present research study. This is followed by a presentation of the research model describing different drivers that affect the performance of a eCommece initiative. The theoretical rationales for relationships among the drivers and relevant hypotheses are also presented in this section. The following sections, once the empirical study is completed, will present hypotheses testing results, discussion of relevant results, and conclusions and directions for future research.

LITERATURE REVIEW

While there are no empirical studies on the economic payoffs from eCommerce initiatives, a significant amount of research has been conducted in the IT business value area. We will review the relevant IT business value literature to provide background information and a concrete theoretical support for the present research. Please be advised that, at this stage of the research, the literature review is preliminary and incomplete.

Organizational Alignment

This driver measures the level to which the strategic managers support eCommerce initiatives by helping IT align its goals and strategies with organizational goals and strategies. The presence of an IT manager with executive authority goes a long way towards achieving this goal. Teo & King (1996, 1997) established that the business knowledge of the IT executive is important in completing this integration successfully. Reich and Benbasat (2000) found that communications between IT and business executives lead to better alignment of IT and business strategies. Teo & King (1996, 1997) found that integration of business planning and information systems planning results in IT being able to support business strategies more effectively.

eCommerce initiatives always involve additional learning on the part of a company. The presence of a training mechanism and top management's willingness to invest in employees' time for training are, therefore, very important. Teo & King (1996, 1997) established that top management support acts as a facilitator in the development of IT applications that have a strategic impact on the organization. Ginzberg (1981) identified management commitment as a key factor in the success of information systems.

Integration Factors

One way in which eCommerce adds value to an organization is by automating many low-skilled tasks. Measuring the extent to which eCommerce has helped integrate the systems and made workflow easier is an important indication of the value derived from eCommerce. Kauffman and Dai (2002) suggested that one way that firms can conduct successful B2B transactions is through the creation of inter-organizational systems. Barua, Konana, Whinston and Yin (2001) indicate that business partners and their readiness to implement eCommerce technologies is critical to achieve business excellence and operational efficiency.

Bakos (1991) found that electronic marketplaces reduce search costs for customers. The mechanisms that enable this value to the customer also strategically affect the company's performance by dramatically improving inter-organizational coordination. Benjamin and Scott Morton (1988) cite anecdotal evidence on how electronic integration provides significant cost advantages and how technology creates new integration possibilities.

Online Presence Factors

'The ability to market products and services through an eCommerce site directly to the customers worldwide on a 24/7 basis is a huge value-adding attribute of eCommerce. According to Moon and Kim (2001), measuring online presence effectiveness through the eCommerce site design and availability aspects is similar to the Technology Acceptance Model's (TAM) "perceived ease of use" component.

A survey of 661 webmasters selected from Fortune 1000 companies by Liu, Arnett, and Litecky (2000) pointed towards the attractiveness, the quality of design, and information available on the eCommerce site as being the most important factors that influence the ultimate purchase decision of a customer. Keeney (1999) stresses the importance of identifying value propositions that concern customers and developing a value model for the customer.

Operational Efficiency

Setting up uniform operating mechanisms through eCommerce technologies normally results in better operational efficiency ultimately ensuing in crucial cost savings. Setting up online customer service in terms of FAQ's, chat rooms, and a link to the call centers indicates a higher operational efficiency level. Barua, Konana, Whinston, and Yin (2001) show that business partners and their readiness to implement eCommerce technologies is critical to achieve business excellence and operational efficiency. Banker, Kauffman, and Morey (1990) emphasize the importance of distinguishing between impacts of IT investment on competitive efficiency (e.g., ROI and STA) and operational efficiency (e.g., impact on value chain components).

eCommerce Business Success

Continuing support for eCommerce strategy is key to success with eCommerce initiatives as initial costs are high. This happens only when an e-commerce implementation is producing viable financial returns. This is similar to measuring the impact of information technology (Bryjolfsson and xxx 199, Mahmood et al, 1993, 2000, 2001).

RESEARCH MODEL

An eCommerce enabled business value model for understanding the drivers that determine the success of an eCommerce initiative is proposed in Figure 1. The model suggests that organizational alignment, integrations factors, and online presence variables interact together and affect operational efficiency and ultimately financial performance of a business involved in eCommerce business. In this section, we discuss the independent and dependent constructs and suggest some research hypotheses that will be tested, once the data is collected. Each construct is operationalized using a number of items asking the respondents to rate the extent of agreement or disagreement with each statement on a seven point Likert scale, with anchors ranging from 1 (Strongly Disagree) to 7 (Strongly Agree).

Organizational alignment refers to the alignment of information technology strategies, goals, and objectives to organizational goals, objectives, and strategies. This construct is operationalized using five items about IT strategies being aligned with top management strategies, IT being a part of long-term organizational strategies, IT executives having decision making roles, IT structure, and overall organizational learning environment (see Appendix 1).

Integration factors refer to the extent to which eCommerce has helped integrate the different systems and made workflow easier. This is an important indication of the value derived from eCommerce. This driver is operationalized using six items The questions related to whether an Internet-enabled system exists for information sharing, order changing, transmitting and processing of data, inventory and purchase tracking, and online procurement system.

The Online presence construct point to online presence effectiveness through the eCommerce site design and availability aspects. It is operationalized

using five items about the security, attractiveness, navigationability, flexibility, and availability of the eCommerce site.

Operational efficiency refers to setting up uniform operating mechanisms using eCommerce technologies. The construct is operationalized using three items about online business, customer service, and highly automated order tracking system availability; and two items about whether customer requests can be resolved online, and whether continuous monitoring of orders is available.

eCommerce business success refers to the business value gained by a brick-and-mortar company through its eCommerce initiatives. This construct is measured by performance, productivity, and perceptual measures. The performance criterion is best measured by gain in four financial performance measures: return on investment (ROI), return on sales (ROS), growth in revenue (GINR), and net income over invested capital (NIC). Cron and Sobol (1983) and Dos Santos, Peffers, and Mauer (1993) employed ROI while NIC was utilized by Barua, Kriebel, and Mukkhopadhyay (1995) and Hitt and Brynjolfsson (1994). ROS was used by Hitt and Brynjolfsson (1994) and Mahmood and Mann (1993). Woo and Willard (2000) used GINR in their research. Two ratios were used to indicate an organization's level of productivity: sales by total assets (STA) and sales by employee (SE). A variable similar to STA, total sales, was used by Brynjolfsson and Hitt (1993) while SE$ was used by Strassman (1990). The perceptual criterion is measured using four customer loyalty related measures in terms of company's image, customer satisfaction, product service innovation, and number of return customers. First three items contribute to customer loyalty. Customer loyalty is one of the most significant contributors to business profitability (Turban, King, Lee, Warkentin, and Chung, 2002). Customer loyalty can also reduce costs. It costs five to eight times more to acquire a new customer than to keep an existing one

Research Hypotheses

In summary of eCommerce business success model, we propose the following hypotheses:

H1: *Businesses with higher level of organizational alignment will achieve operational efficiency.*

H2: *Businesses with higher level of integrated online systems will achieve better operational efficiency.*

H3: *Businesses that have a better online presence will have a better chance of achieving operational efficiency.*

H4: *Businesses with higher operational efficiency will be more successful in achieving eCommerce business success.*

METHODOLOGY

An instrument for gathering relevant information was designed based on the existing academic and practitioners literature. It consists of a total of 31 items. A seven-point Likert scale was used with anchors ranging from 1 (Strongly Disagree) to 7 (Strongly Agree). The respondents were asked whether they agreed or disagreed with each statement. The items were developed on the basis of prior work.

A copy of the instrument has been mailed to 250 click-and-mortar companies within the United States of America. These firms were selected from those published in Informationweek.Com. The respondents were told, to minimize potential biases, that their identity and responses will remain confidential and that only aggregate information will be published.

The responses, once received, will be analyzed using the LISREL software tool. The results will be used to empirically validate the model and critically test its reliability.

RESULTS

The results of our research will either support or refute the belief that business operational efficiency and value are generated by eCommerce initiatives. Our study will provide insights into whether eCommerce technologies are likely to be effective and how these technologies can be used efficiently to derive most businesses value.

REFERENCES

References will be provided upon request.

A Method to Implement a Workflow Management Process: The Case of University "Federico II"

Paolo Maresca, Antonino Mazzeo
Università di Napoli Federico II, Via Claudio 21, Napoli (Italy)
Tel.+39 0817683168, Tel.+39 0817683184, Fax +39 0817683816
Paolo.maresca@unina.it mazzeo@unina.it

ABSTRACT

The **workflow** *can be defined as the flow and the control of the information that enter to belong to a productive process. The workflow management represents the efficient management and the control flow of information in a process of a firm.*

In this paper the authors show a methodology for the description of the very complex workflow processes of a large university. The process was described in his essential parts, then represented in unified manner using UML (Unified Modeling Language) and was conducted into Workflow and Security Laboratories (WSL) of DIS at University of Naples. The case study of the University Federico II is composed of many offices. In this job, for the sake of the brevity, we will show one of them. The workflow description has involved many employees with a lot of interviews. Currently we are facing with the validation phase and the identification of the unusual and critical processes.

INTRODUCTION

The *workflow* [3,4,20,21,22] can be defined as the flow and the control of the information that enter to belong to a productive process. The workflow management represents the efficient management and the control flow of information in a process of a firm. Every firm possesses a core business and a lot of the business units of the core business are crucial for the growth and for the survival of the firm. Making more efficient the business units processes, the firm reduces his costs improving the product and the service to the client, becoming so more competitive on the market [32,35,39].

The architecture of a company reflects the whole of its objectives and therefore of the own business units. Only that often this complex infrastructure is not documented it is "wired" in the way with which people work in a certain office; this "modus operandi" is learned as a young boy usually does in a Renaissance shop: "the elderly teachs to the more youth." In this process of job when an element abandons the structure near which the person that will replace him works will be trained equally and that is with the technique "what you see is what you learn.". It is needless to say that this architecture of firm is that more exposes him to a series of well documented problems in literature [1,2,10,14,15,17,18], if the objective is that to make a firm more efficient the witticism is: *"first documents so that then what you have documented can be seen again and used for the management of the workflow.*

A lot of firms manifest the slowness of some of their inside procedures and they look to them with the eyes of the optimization in the sense of speed and efficiency. More one is able, to make better and efficient a business unit and fast the company grows and it holds the competition. *In short it seems that the competitiveness and the workflow managements are tightly correlated.*[19].

The *workflow* has at least three dimensions: the process, the organization (the mens) and the infrastructures (on which it leans the process and the organization). The *process* is constituted by activities and subactivities [13,16]. For the various activities it needs to specify the control and data flow. And also it is usual to specify the application programs that process needs to use inside an activity (es. word processor, databases, spreadsheets, etc.). The *organization* is constituted by the men that are employed inside the process. For each

of them it is necessary to define the role, the level as well as the levels of authorization (if you introduce one) possessed in the informative system. The *infrastructures* are the technological substratum of which need is had for implementing the workflow (net, telephone connections, calculating, servers, etc.). In this three dimensions vision safety is an activity distributed and transversal [12] it can be disseminated in everybody the three sights. In other words to have a some meaningful improvement in safety terms the safety engineer and software engineer should work together in an iterative and enhancement activity of dissemination of the safety in the product and in the process rather than to separately try to work in maintenance operation that they would make only to degrade the state of the process (and of the product) [11 ,18]. We try to set another question. Why the workflow management is useful ? There are many motives for which a big firm should equip him with a workflow management [9,14]. I bring someone of it:

1. Make faster the execution of the process
   a. To increase the productivity through the automation
   b. To improve the service to the client reducing the costs of it
2. To make the process more solid so that to pilot it toward a certification of quality (ISO 9000 compliances)

To do this we have necessity to face the followings points:
   a) to define and to document the process
   b) to perform the process of which to the point 1) to the purpose of
      a. to support the people that work inside it,
      b. to fully automatize those activities of the process that don't ask for the human intervention.
   c) to administer the workflow

The next paragraph will show the process definition, Documentation and Implementation

1. PROCESS DEFINITION, DOCUMENTATION AND IMPLEMENTATION

Looking more from near an example of business process, that of an office of a great University as the Federico II is, to define and to document a process there are a lot of things that it needs to wonder. But the first thing that we probably wonders us it is: from where to start ? It is often begun hiring an advisor that recommends their what there is to do. Naturally is not the correct movement because no one advisor will be able to understand a process that there is not or that has not been described because is in the head of few people! *Therefore the first step to implement the workflow is to analyze the processes of business.* This is what we will do in the next paragraph.

Following a methodology will be illustrated for analyzing the processes of business. It is composed of three phases
1. To identify and to denominate the company business processes
2. To identify the processes of business that don't work
3. To assign a priority to that processes of business that don't work

Tab. I The Federico II Offices

Division/direction	office	New Code	Administration code
D	Segreteria Direzione Amministrativa	2	99006
D	Organi collegiali	3	99008
D	Economato	4	99031
II	Personale docente e ricercatore	29	99104
II	Personale tecnico amministrativo	30	99035
II	Pensioni	31	99049
II	Stipendi	32	99099
III	Affari Generali	33	99028
III	Affari Speciali	34	99095
III	Dottorati ed assegni di ricerca	35	99046
III	Statuto regolamento e documentazione	37	99119
IV	CEDA	38	99027
IV	Pianificazione Strategica	39	99116
IV	Protocollo e Archivio	41	99117
V	Legale	42	99010
V	Contratti	40	99009
V	Patrimonio	43	99034
V	Relazioni Internazionali	44	99118
V	U.C.A.F. (ufficio fiscale)	45	99069
VI	Ragioneria	46	99086
VII	Ufficio Speciale	47	99114
VII	Sicurezza e Protezionistica	48	99111
VII	Ufficio Tecnico Servizi di ingegneria ed architettura	49	99121

1.1 Identification of the Company Business Processes

A good method of business processes identification is suggested by [9]. Their method analyzes the list of the processes to the purpose to assign them a name that expresses their initial and final state.

This method is a good way to begin the first iteration of the business processes identification for a specific application dominion. As it regards the dominion of the University "Federico II", is constituted from offices whose list is brought in Tab. I. Every office is responsible for the carrying out of activity (or processes) to develop which the office has available human resources and technological infrastructures to be conducted. For convenience every process is encoded both to make it distinguishable from others both to synthesize it; for instance the process " 3-0-1 " is a process that belongs to the collegial organs (office 3), it doesn't have sub-offices (number 0) and it is particularly the first process in the temporal order to be performed in the office (Preparation of the memo for the Board of directors).

Every process is divided in phases (or subprocesses) also them sequential, every of which is still encoded and is hinged on a number of employees and can produce documents (structured and not, signed and not) at the end of its phase. It is worth to underline how such subprocesses, in the almost totalities of the cases, appear to be simple from the point of view of the inside states in how much they often develop a simple assignment that finishes with the issue of a document. They are the so-called two states (beginning and term) subprocesses. To codify the subprocesses is added a further field for which "X-X-X-X." Then" 3-0-1-1" it represents the first subprocess (Acceptance proposed data) of the activity " 3-0-1." If an office produces a document of this type there are also listed the following characteristics:

- it is structured or less;
- Its characterization in comparison to the process/subprocesses (I-Input,O-Output, IO- Input and Output);
- The signature typology if, eventually, exists;
- The reachability of other offices (inside or external to the dominion of affiliation of the document).

The characterization of the data that crosses the processes and the subprocesses is very important and it is an essential point for the analysis of the document flow belonging to every application dominion.

1.2 Identification and Priorities Assignment for the to the Process that don't Work and their Improvement

After to have identified the processes of business it is necessary to identify those that don't work for esteeming them through objective criterions. The objective criterions are often factors of quality of process and/or of product [5,6,7] that is necessary that the processes in operation possesses. Criteria could be: Quality, Accuracy, Cost, Speed, Customer Satisfaction, Flexibility, etc. After to have identified that processes of business that don't work, prob-

Fig. 1 G/Q/M Paradigm to Select the Process that doesn't Work

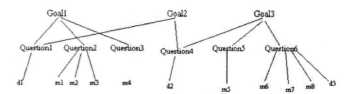

ably the first question that sets us is: from which process we start for the improvement ? From the moment that all the processes belong to the category of those that need improvement they are all **candidates** to the improvement but only one of these will come **"selected"**. *The selection happens through some factors of quality chosen by the management of the firm on the base of the objectives that is established.*

The qualities factors have to come down from the strategic objectives of the firm through a paradigm of quantification of the objectives that is denominated Goal/Question/Metric (GQM) [8]. This paradigm doesn't furnish a specific collection of objectives but rather a structure to define the objectives and refines it in specific quantifiable questions about the software process and product. Such questions help to pick up the data that serve for the attainment of the objectives places. The quantification of the objectives should be mapped, therefore, in a set of data which can be disseminated in the product and in the process. The data collected should be validated in function of their accuracy and the results interpreted in the respect of the objectives. For this reason that for the harvest and the evaluation of such data often are also necessary tools for the objective metric evaluation.

In the fig.1 is shown the tree of the paradigm GQM in which we specify three goals. Goal1: Critical factors; **Question1**: Which processes of business are critical for your company **Question 2:** What is the quality of the product ? **Question3**: Which is the speed of the release of the product ?
These processes of business are all critical factors to which it owes a priority of intervention to be in partnership. **Goal2**: Strategical factors **Question4**: Which processes of business are critical for the future of the company and which are strategic ? Naturally for the process that are essential to the future direction of the firm it needs to assign greater priority. To observe that there can be question common to more objectives as understands for the question 1 of the goals 1 and 2 in (fig. 1) **Goal3**: Factors of Core Business, **Question5**: Which processes of business to the core business of the firm ? **Question6**: Which processes improve the core business of the firm ?

For the processes that increase the core business they should have a priority in comparison to the others.

The tree of fig.1 turns him into the document xml named *BusinesProcessImprovement.xml*. Such document can be used for different purposes (harvest of the data, validation of the data, metrics, identification priority, documentation of the processes, etc.).

Fig. 2 The Main Use Case Diagram of the Patrimony Office

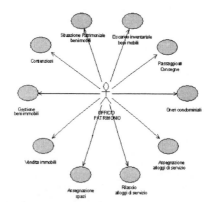

Tab II Patrimony Office: Activities and Destination

	Activities	Destination
1	Situazione patrimoniale beni mobili	Ufficio Ragioneria (n°-46)
2	Discarico inventariale beni mobili	Strutture dell'Amministrazione (n°-2)
3	Passaggio ci consegne	Strutture dell'Amministrazione (n°-2)
4	Oneri condominiali	Ufficio Economato (n°-4)
5	Assegnazione alloggi di servizio	Personale con qualifica di custode
6	Rilascio alloggi di servizio	Personale con qualifica di custode
7	Assegnazione Spazi	Strutture dell'Amministrazione (n°-2)
8	Vendita immobili	Soggetti o Enti interessati all'acquisto
9	Gestione beni immobili	Enti, Ufficio Ragioneria, Ufficio Legale (n°-42)
10	Contenziosi	Soggetti Enti esterni all'Amministrazione

2. THE DOCUMENTATION OF A COMPLEX WORKFLOW PROCESS

We have two problems to resolve in the description of the workflow of a complex system. The first one is that to understand inside a process of business as to identify univocally the elements that constitute it and as a process that describes the workflow of an office is related to that of the other offices. The second is to choose the correct level of abstraction from which to start to describe the process. Probably the simplest way to define the level of abstraction taller for the description of the workflow of the University Federico II is that to give a recursive definition of process: **The University Federico II is an empty process or it is constituted by the process of the office X connected to the process of University Federico II.**

This type of approach allows meanwhile to describe a complex reality for repeated and improved steps of the process of an office without worrying about what it happens elsewhere.

2.1 A Case Study: An Office of Federico II University

The case study illustrated in this paper is the *Patrimony office* of the university "Federico II", its number *is 43* and its Administration Code *is n°-99034*. The problem has been faced through the description of the process using the language *UML* [23]. The use case, activities, sequence, collaboration and state diagrams have been adopted. Before observing the fruit of such job some informative data on the office Patrimony are brought.

Fig. 3 Situation Property Mobile Good

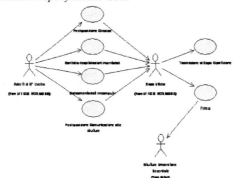

Fig. 4 Diagram of General Collaboration

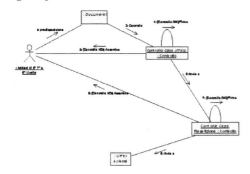

Fig. 5 General Diagram of the States

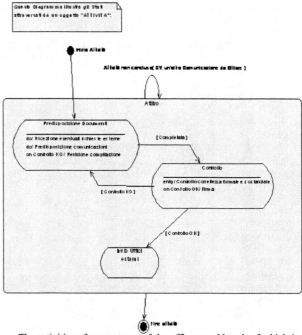

The activities of competence of the office *are 10* each of which is divided in phases and each activity have a destination. We bring the summary table in tab. II.

How example of static description of the system we show the UML [23,24] main use case diagram brought in fig.2. It is necessary to underline that besides the main diagrams exist other use case diagrams that constitutes the static sight of the system from other points of view and therefore from some or all the actors involved in the process. Particularly that diagrams are interesting that show all the use cases for an assigned actor. In the fig. 3 are for instance shown an activity of the system denominated "situation property mobile good" as seen by an employee of 6.o level and by his manager.

Other diagrams of the interesting use cases are those that show the use cases implemented during an iteration of the process of iterative enhancement, still that diagrams are important that shows a use case and all of its relationships. Naturally, accompanied to the static description, a dynamic sight of the system it is also necessary.

As it regards the dynamic sight of the process two of them are the meaningful diagrams respectively brought in Fig. 4 and Fig. 5. Particularly in the Fig. 4 are brought the diagram of collaboration among all the use case. In it the simplicity of the process of the office is deduced. In the fig.6 are shown a sight of detail that concerns every process instead: its states diagram. Every activity of the tab. II follows the diagram of the states of Fig. 5 The following step would be that to identify the processes and the subprocess of the office *43* that don't work and to assign a priority to these on the base of objective criterions as described in precedence. Nevertheless this is not the objective of this paper that has the purpose to describe only the process.

CONCLUSIONS

In this paper we have shown a methodology for the description and maintenance of the business processes. The methodology has been applied to all the offices of a large university. The documentation has been represented by means of UML diagrams and the picked data of the process was validated.

As future development we have the aims to face with simulation of the processes described in order to discover "critical processes" that will be tested in a "clean room". The clean room testing could serve us to identify the process variables that could be modified in order to improve it. Successively the same critical process could be tested in a real case and the result could be correlated with the 'clean room' results. The methodology adopted is currently under experimentation in the workflow and security laboratories at DIS of University Federico II and has involved all the offices and many employees of the same university.

BIBLIOGRAPHY

[1] Frank Leymann, Dieter Roller, Production Workflow: Concept and Techniques, New Jersey, Prentice Hall PTR, 1999.

[2] Frank Leymann, Dieter Roller, Workflow-based Applications, IBM System Journal 36, n. 1, pp. 102-123, 1997.

[3] Workflow Management Coalition. Workflow Management Coalition - The Workflow Reference Model. Document No. TC00-1003, Issue 1.1, 19-Jan-95.

[4] Rob Allen, Workflow: An Introduction, Open Image System Inc., http://www.wfmc.org, 1999.

[5] FCD 9126-1.2, Information Technology-Software product quality - Part 1: Quality model, ISO/IEC JTC1/SC7 n. 1949,1998.

[6] WD 9126-4, Software Engineering- Product quality - Part 4: Quality In Use Metrics, ISO/IEC JTC1/SC7 n. 2208, 1999.

[7] WD 9126-3 – Information Technology – Software Quality Characteristics and Metrics – Part 3 : Internal Metrics, ISO/IEC JTC1/SC7 n. 1713, 1997.

[8] H. D. Rombach, V. Basili, Quantitative Assessment of Maintenance: An Industrial Case Study, 1987, IEEE.

[9] Michael Hammer, James Champy Reengineering the Corporation - A Manifesto for Business Revolution. Nicholas Brealey Publishing, London, 1993.

[10] Wil van der Aalst, Jorg Desel, Andreas Oberweis Business Process Management: Models Techniques and Empirical Studies Lecture Notes in Computer Science 1806, Spinger-Verlag, 2000.

[11] W.M.P. van der Aalst and S. Jablonski. Dealing with Workflow Change: Identification of issues and solutions International Journal of Computer Systems, Science, and Engineering, 15(5):267-276, 2000.

[12] A. Bernstein How can Cooperative Work Tools Support Dynamic Group Processes? Bridging the Specificity Frontier. CSCW'00, December 2-6, 2000, Philadelphia.

[13] Sergio C. Bandinelli, Alfonso Fuggetta, Carlo Ghezzi Software Process Evolution in the SPADE Environment. IEEE Transactions of Software Engineering, Vol 19, No, 12. December 1993.

[14] The Butler Group. Workflow: Integrating the Enterprise, 1996, Butler Report.

[15] F. Casati, S Ceri, B. Pernici, G. Pozzi. Workflow Evolution. Proceedings of the 15th ER'96 international Conference, Oct 7-10, Cottbus, Germany, Springer Verlag Lecture Notes in Computer Science, 1996.

[16] Davenport Thomas Process Innovation: Reengineering work through Information Technology. 1993, Harvard Business.

[17] C. A. Ellis, L. Keddara A Workflow Change is a Workflow. W van der Aalst et al. (Eds.) Business Process Management, LNCS 1806, pp.16-29, 2000.

[18] Michael Hammer Reengineering Work: Don't Automate, Obliterate. Harvard Business Review, July August 1990.

[19] Gerrit K. Janssens, Jan Verelst, Bart Weyn. Techniques for Modelling Workflows and Their Support of Reuse. Business Process Management - Models, Techniques and Empirical Studies. Lecture Notes in Computer Science 1806. Wil van der Aslst, Jorg Desel, Andreas Oberweis (Editors) Springer Verlag. 2000.

[20] Workflow Management Coalition. The Workflow Management Coalition Terminology and Glossary. Document No WFMC-TC-1011. Issue 2.0. Jun 1996.

[21] Workflow Management Coalition. (1999) The Workflow Management Coalition Specifications – Terminology and Glossary Document No. WFMC-TC-1011, Feb-1999, 3.0

[22] Workflow Management Coalition. The Workflow Management Coalition Interface 1: Process Definition. Interchange Process Model. Document No WFMC-TC1016-P Oct 1999.

[23] I. Jacobson, G. Booch, J. Rambaugh, *The Unified Modeling Language*, user Guide, 1999

[24] I. Jacobson, G. Booch, J. Rambaugh, *The Unified Software Development Process*, 1999.

Knowledge Creation Process: Evolving Knowledge Process (EKP) Model

Win Maung
Department of Information Systems
University of Technology, Sydney
PO Box 123 Broadway, NSW 2007, Australia
Email:winmg@it.uts.edu.au

"Knowledge is experience. Everything else is just information." – Albert Einstein

ABSTRACT

Nonaka and Takeuchi (Nonaka, 1995) define knowledge creation as a spiraling process of interaction between explicit and tacit knowledge. However, their theory is to be made concrete to integrate into business process. To do this, the author proposed the Evolving Knowledge Process (EKP) model for a systematic approach for capturing and managing knowledge. The proposed model consists of knowledge resources and knowledge activities for creating and capturing knowledge.

1. INTRODUCTION

The main goal of research on knowledge management is to design processes that an organization can use to learn to improve its ways of working and to create value for its customers and community (Choo, 1999). Such research must address ways to integrate knowledge management into business processes. These activities should not be seen as separate. Nonaka's knowledge creation process is often broad and abstract and needs to be made concrete to integrate into business processes. We propose a systematic approach to knowledge management. This must include a systematic way of finding, selecting, organizing, and presenting information within business processes. This often requires appropriate and effective technology to support the process. In this paper author proposes a concrete process that follows a set of concrete steps. This process is called the Evolving Knowledge Process (EKP) model.

The EKP model has a sequence of knowledge activities that create and capture knowledge in a business context. The model is finally defined all consists of five activities: knowledge accumulation, filtering knowledge, domain knowledge analysis, knowledge consolidation and knowledge modification. Knowledge resources are captured knowledge object, time & space, filtered knowledge object, transitioned knowledge object and consolidated knowledge.

The paper describes a use-case design approach to show business to consumer process as an example how to integrate EKP model into business process.

2. DATA, INFORMATION AND KNOWLEDGE

It is important to differentiate between data, information and knowledge. Data are just facts and have no meaning unless one understands the context in which the data was gathered. Information has been packed with data in a useful and understandable way. Knowledge is the richness of personal learning, insight and experience. Knowledge provides the background that allows one to make the best decision. Knowledge can be in people's heads (tacit knowledge) or it can be written down or recorded (explicit knowledge).

3. EVOLVING KNOWLEDGE PROCESS (EKP) MODEL

The following notations are used to the presents the EKP model, shown in Figure 1. The activities are knowledge accumulation, filtering knowledge, domain knowledge analysis, knowledge consolidation and knowledge modification and resources are captured knowledge, time & space, filtered knowledge object, transitioned knowledge object and consolidated knowledge.

Knowledge Asset: Knowledge asset is some combination of context sensing, personal memory and cognitive processes. Measuring the knowledge as-

EKP Symbols:

☐	activities
⬭	resources
⇨	knowledge or information between sources and activities

set, therefore, means putting a value on people, both as individuals and more importantly on their collective capability, and other factors such as the embedded intelligence in an organization's computer systems (Skyrme 2002).

Explicit Knowledge: Explicit knowledge is codified knowledge, which is usually documented in the form of publication or stored as electronic formats. The explicit knowledge may be collected from internal or external resources. Internal knowledge resources may be various recorded documents or stored databases of the organization. The common resources of external knowledge include external publications, government agencies, consultants and alliances.

Tacit Knowledge: Tacit knowledge is the form of knowledge possessed by individuals and not usually stored. It can only be obtained through sharing the ideas and concepts and collaboration among the group of people. It is especially useful in using previous experiences to analyze existing information and take actions in current circumstances.

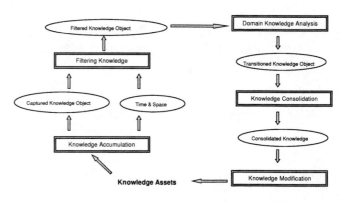

Figure 1. Evolving Knowledge Process (EKP) Model

Knowledge Activities

Knowledge Accumulation: Knowledge accumulation is a process of collection and collation of useful knowledge from various external and internal knowledge assets such as documented processes, structures, strategy, goal setting, direction and resources of the business organization.

Filtering Knowledge: Creating knowledge assets is the task of selecting or filtering information in order to make it relevant to the organization. Figure 2 describes filtering knowledge process. If information is relevant, it is to be retained or memorized in knowledge base. If information is not relevant, it is to be rejected or ignored (Godbout, 1996). Some information may be retained in memory for recall when necessary.

Domain Knowledge Analysis: The process which analyses the given set of tacit and explicit knowledge based on predefined domain rules and norms are called domain knowledge analysis. It first acquires prerequisite knowledge of business domain that is the basic know how of the business and its transformation methods into activities which is the relevant in the specific context of business domain and further uses it to analyze the provided case of application.

Knowledge Consolidation: Knowledge consolidation accumulates transitioned knowledge objects into consolidated form of knowledge.

Knowledge Modification: Knowledge modification is a process of updating or modifying the existing knowledge assets.

Knowledge Resources

Captured Knowledge Object: Knowledge accumulation produces *Captured Knowledge Object* which is a desired level of knowledge use in practice and application.

Time & Space: *Time* is important to situate the business plan in the context of time. *Space* is the location that can be validated in the situation of knowledge.

Filtered Knowledge Object: Filtered knowledge object is the quality of synthesized knowledge and is determined by its accuracy and appropriateness. It can be used to interpret the reality and can provide means for predicting the behavior of resources or person in the business system.

Transitioned Knowledge Object: Transitioned knowledge object is a set of transformed object, which is produced by domain analysis process. It is a new level and/or updated knowledge. This contains sufficient amount of modified and updated form of existing knowledge of business process.

Consolidated Knowledge Object: Consolidated knowledge object is a verified, validated and comprehended transitioned knowledge object for the intended purpose. This knowledge object is embedded into long and short term organizational memory. It can be utilized for analysis of business situation and helping management in taking decisions.

4. DISCUSSION

In this section, the author applies use-case approach to the EKP model in a business process. The paper describes the business to consumer process. In the example, activities and resources of the EKP model are shown the square bracket in italics. A use case diagram shows in Figure 3.
* the system boundary-
  a box that separates the systems from its environment defines the behavior of the system
* each external actor-
  an actor may be person, a computer, or an organization the type of the actor may be shown in guillemets << >> the name of the actor is show with the actor

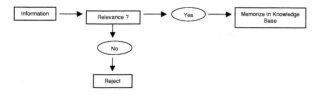

Figure 2. Filtering Knowledge (Godbout, 1996)

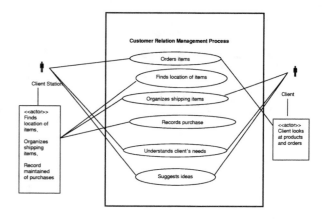

Figure 3. Use case diagram for business to consumer

* each enterprise use case-
  an oval with a name
  one use cases may include other use cases
  several use case may share some actions
  scenarios live inside use cases
* the actor's goal-
  a line between an actor and a use case (no direction) indicates a message into or out of the system

The elements of a use case diagram are-
* system name and boundary
* actors (picture or small box)
* communicate with (line)
* use cases (oval with name)

Business to Consumer (B2C) are systems that provide services when purchasing goods and services from the organization. The computer makes it easier to promote and sell electronically on the Internet. Clients can find what they need on the Internet that is retrieves information. Then they can order item and purchase it. Figure 3 describes the customer relationship management. The objective is to maintain and even raise the level of service to a client through finding out what the clients' current and future requirements will be. The goal is to use information that about the client's requirement to customize services and products to the needs of the clients. Clients can use the systems to follow orders and negotiate changes as new information becomes available.

(a) Client

The organization has a database of client profiles and produces that match these profiles in order to attract clients using the Internet [*knowledge assets*]. Clients find the products [*captured knowledge object*] that they need to buy. They can compare the quality and prices of the items from other organizations [*space*]. Most clients prefer a quick response [*time*] service to information about what they need. They find and consider the item that matches their requirement [*filtered knowledge object*] to order and purchase. Before they decide to order, they have knowledge about that product [*domain knowledge analysis*] which is most suitable for their needs. Then they decide to order the item [*transitioned knowledge object*] and notes [*knowledge consolidation*] the purchase this item [*consolidated knowledge*]. In the future, clients can find new updated item, they can consider new ideas [*knowledge modification*] to order and purchase.

(b) Client Station

The client station supports clients and their requirements using a database such as client information, transactions, supplier information, products and price lists [*knowledge assets*]. When client station receives orders from clients then organization has to find out and contact the supplier [*space*] and respond as quickly as possible to clients [*time*] so that clients can purchase the items. Organization ships the goods to clients and maintains records of purchase of the clients into their database [*knowledge assets*].

Organization can accumulate client requirements such as queries and quotes, customer feedback, FAQs, payment details and orders [*knowledge accumulate*] and service [*captured knowledge object*] as well as suppliers [*space*] and respond time to both suppliers and clients [*time*] in minimum time. To better customer service and good relationship with suppliers, organization has to find out which product is the one most clients prefer [*captured knowledge object*] where can get it [*space*] and how long it take to order to suppliers and respond to clients orders and shipping that item to clients [*time*]. Management can better understanding [*filtering knowledge*] the client needs and developing alternative solutions with the client responding quickly about price and delivery schedules [*filtered knowledge object*]. Organization analyzes and considers providing time and cost saving, exchanging transactions electronically with their business partners to reduce transaction processing costs [*domain knowledge analysis*] and creating new processes that take advantage of new business opportunities such as mass customizations, or joint product design in business [*transitioned knowledge object*] The existing system can be updated or modified to the new system when necessary changes in business processes are made [*knowledge modification*].

4. SUMMARY AND FUTURE WORK

This paper described the knowledge evolving process, which includes capturing filtering and transforming knowledge from explicit and tacit knowledge resources to consolidated knowledge specific to an application. The author proposed the knowledge evolving process model in business organizations, which is based on Nonaka's process, then integrates the model with a business process using use-case approach.

Further research is the application and implementation of this model in a business process. In this case, the author needs to investigate case studies.

ACKNOWLEDGMENT

The work reported in this paper has been funded in Faculty of Information Technology Doctoral Research Scholarship from the University of Technology, Sydney, Australia. The author would like to thank Igor Hawryszkiewycz, Julia Prior and reviewers for their comments on draft of this paper.

REFERENCES

Davenport, T.H and Prusak, L (1998) "Working Knowledge, How Organization Manage What They Know", Harvard Business School Press.

Godbout, M (1999) Filtering Knowledge: "Changing Information into Knowledge Assets", Journal of Systematic Knowledge Management, January 1999. www.it-consultancy.com/extern/systemic/knowfilter.html

Nonaka, I and Takeuchi, H. (1995) "The Knowledge Creating Company", Oxford University Press.

Plotkin, H (1994) "The Nature of Knowledge", Allen Press-Penguin, London.

Sellers, B and Unhelkar, B (2000) "Open Modeling with UML", ACM Press Book, Oxford, UK.

Skyrme, D. (2002) "The Knowledge Assets", www.skyrme.com.insights/11kasset.htm

Soo, C.W, et al (1999) "The Process of Knowledge Creation in Organization", Working Paper Series, AGSM, UNSW, Sydney, Australia. Spring 1999, 00125-145.

Introducing Mobile Computing: Student Built Mobile Databases

W. Brett McKenzie
Gabelli School of Business
Roger Williams University
One Old Ferry Rd., Bristol, RI 02809
(401) 254-3534 (O), (401) 254-3545 (F)
wmckenzie@rwu.edu

ABSTRACT

This study reports on using Personal Digital Assistants (PDA) as supplemental tools for student projects in an introductory database course. The course has traditionally been taught using a relational database in a PC. This modified course builds on the design approach and adds a Palm based relational database as the deployment component.

PURPOSE

The structure of the introductory database course devotes about eight weeks to database design issues (ER diagrams, normalization, defining business rules) and about eight weeks on application of the theoretical content in building a project. The educational model faculty use for this and most courses in the department is a constructivist approach (Gallagher and Reid, 1981), where students learn the tools then implement those skills in a project. The faculty teaching the introductory course on database design had found that students were limited in applying the concepts to novel situations. To solve this problem, faculty attempted using real-clients. These, however, were found wanting because few projects were of a viable scale for novices to complete during a fifteen week undergraduate course. Additionally, many real world projects involved repeated tasks, such as creating multiple transaction forms or reports, which detracted from the instructional objectives.

Integrating a PDA with database software was proposed to enable students to think differently about database implementation and design. The questions of interest were:

- How would the students implement the Palm as a solution to their database project?
- Would students develop more appropriate databases by incorporating the Palm?
- What was the student satisfaction with the Palm as a component of the course?
- Would the students use the Palm in other ways in support of their academic program?

Given the constructivist model, the primary measure of success in the program was the types of projects the students decided to undertake. Usually students' proposals are wildly ambitious, such as the management database for the student lab services, which would require access to university records for full implementation, or acutely personal, such as a CD or video collection. The course designers, by integrating the Palm hoped to shift the focus to meaningful projects, with a chance of implementation, and possible real-world piloting within the confine of the semester long course. A student survey focused on usage served as a secondary measure.

Rational for a PDA

Two criteria led the decision to integrate a PDA into the database design course. First, it introduced students to field or mobile computing, a growing issue for IT professionals (Hamblen, 2002). Interestingly, a student who worked part-time for a medical billing services company was issued a T-Mobile Sidekick, demonstrating to the class that PDAs were likely in their futures. Second, a PDA introduced students to alternative interaction with computers.

The selection of the Palm was driven by primarily by its dominance in the marketplace (Rubinstein, 2002), its simplicity (Butter and Pogue, 2002),

and its positioning as an inexpensive accessory to a PC. The market dominance meant there were a number of database options and some students were already familiar with the device. Three students already owned Palm OS devices. The Palm's simplicity would minimize the training time. The minimal expense would diminish the costs to implement.

A secondary consideration was to introduce students to an alternative operating system. All courses in the university program use WINTEL computer labs and Microsoft publishes the majority of the software that the students use. With the prerequisites of the course, enrolled students have taken at least three courses all using the WINTEL platform so are familiar with the interface but not necessarily aware of its conventions, limitations, and advantages. The Palm forced students to be cognizant of displaying information in a limited screen size, interacting without a keyboard or mouse, and interacting in an environment without specific file management which required integration with a host computer.

IMPLEMENTATION

The class comprised twenty-two students, of whom three were female and nineteen male. Four of the students had taken part of the course previously but had withdrawn prior to completing; two when the course had been built upon using *Oracle* and two when it focused exclusively on *Access*.

All students were issued a Palm M105 with the basic Palm software (date book, contact list and so on) and additional software including *Giraffe*, a Tetris-like game to teach and practice text input with graffiti (the stylized script for text entry on the Palm), *Tap*, an arts project funded by the DIA foundation (Buckhouse, 2002), and *thinkDb* a database program (DataViz, 2002).[1] Each student had access to a personally owned computer to serve as a host for the Palm. All students were given the Palm desktop synchronization software and *dbSync*, a conduit which allows *thinkDB* databases to synchronize with an *Access* database on a host computer.

Two teams of two students each were designated to assist with the Palm implementation. One team managed the devices and software licenses and served as a helpdesk to answer operational issues, such as performing a "soft reset". The other team served as a helpdesk for *thinkDb* application specific questions including synchronization. Both teams developed and maintained databases for their respective areas.

Familiarization

The *Tap* application, which emulates a tap dancer by selecting from a set of tap dance steps, was used to introduce the Palm devices. This application was selected because it required fundamental Palm concepts, such as tapping to execute commands or select from a list, and beaming to exchange information. Additionally, *Tap* allowed students to think more broadly about the concept of a data than the traditional text and numerical examples, such as a name and address in a phonebook. Each of the steps is a data element and the combinations of data create a specific dance, or information. One student noted that because of *Tap* he considered including images of contracts in his database.

To familiarize the students with *thinkDB* the database software in the Palm, and to make them aware of the differences between it and *Access*, class examples used the same datasets for both applications. In particular, this brought

Table 1: Summary of Student Projects

Project	Description
Fleet Racing	Shows the rotation of boats and crews in a fleet race; includes the results of races, taking into account protests.
Yearbook Production	Records the completion of yearbook pages including the drafting and editorial approval of the final version.
IT Department Trouble Calls	Records and assigns trouble calls to technicians
Truckers Log	Records trucking details for a shipping company.
Real Estate Management	Records tenant agreements and apartment maintenance
Hotel Management	Assigns cleaning duties to maids and records room damage. Field tables in Spanish.
Religious Affiliations	Records religious affiliation and participation for international students
Palm Database	Inventory and help call database
thinkDb database	Help call database

up the differences between the Query By Example (QBE), a unique model for *Access*, and the model for thinkDB which uses categories, filters, and views.

Integration

The project required the students to develop and application with a field component as a means to integrate the Palm into the database design. The architecture of *DbSync* did not permit updating multiple tables in a single synchronization of the Palm and the desktop database. To accommodate this limitation, only one table needed to be deployed on the Palm. This required students to think about the usefulness of the table and its integration with the database. The table could be based either upon the table or the query objects in the *Access* database.

RESULTS

The student databases were developed in teams to build upon collaborative learning and to encourage team relations. Table 1 gives a brief description of each project.

Of these projects, only one, the Yearbook Production, did not include a field component. A modification suggested that a photographer's log would provide a field component. All other projects included a field component and the "Palm" and "thinkDB" databases were implemented as field databases exclusively with the *Access* version serving as a backup.

The Hotel Management project became the most interesting project as it brought up unanticipated issues. The maids in the hotel are all Spanish speaking, while the management speaks English. For this project, the Palm tables were deployed in Spanish with the synchronized tables in the *Access* database in English. This is the first instance of any student project requiring language localization.

Survey Results

The survey attempted to determine student usage patterns and acceptance of the Palm PDAs. Of the twenty-two students, sixteen (73 %) used the Palm for personal use, such as maintaining a calendar or contact list. Nine (41%) reported using the Palm more than once during the day with four reporting that they used it more than five times per day. Ten students (45%) reported adding software in addition to the given software, most of them games. Only three students (14%) felt that the Palm should not have been included in the database class; one commented "not enough time for use" and another commented that it was "too hard to browse." Of the nineteen students (86%)

who were supportive of the Palm, eight commented that it gave them a better understanding of databases and six commented that it was a valuable introduction to the Palm. (Note, not all respondents included a comment).

CONCLUSIONS

The student projects showed greater variety than in the past. The field component did seem to have a positive effect on the projects the students chose and caused them to work with real world problems and real world data. Only one project did not include a field component. One student was sufficiently motivated by the project that he requested use of the Palm during the winter break to develop a fishing log as a Palm database. His goal is to upload the completed database to the Sports area of the DataViz website.

Additionally, students responded positively to the experience with the PDA, despite it being a low end model, with gray scale screen and limited power. Comments such as "...helps students understand real world scenarios" and "...won't be long before palms & databases are always linked together. Important we know how to use" indicate that students found the experience purposeful.

The implementation had three drawbacks. First, the course would be better served if *thinkDB* were able to synchronize multiple tables to allow for reinforcement of the relational concepts. Second, an implementation with a synchronization server through a product such as *iAnywhere* or *DB2 Everyplace* would better model the business environment for students. Third, a full SQL engine in the Palm, as is available for the iPaq/Windows device, would increase flexibility and reinforce those concepts, although at the expense of introducing an alternative operating system.

It was fortuitous that the implementation actively involved the students to provide support to their classmates because the sale by the publishers in early November led to degraded vendor support at a critical time. DataViz now packages desktop development tools along with the conduit, which is an improvement for students who struggled with developing on the Palm itself.

While Johnson et. al. (2002) concluded that handhelds are not yet ready for the college classroom as a substitute for a laptop computer, this study indicates that as development devices, handheld computers may bring benefits at minimal costs and provide better preparation for our students in their careers.

ENDNOTE

[1]   ThinkingBytes, which generously provided a software grant, sold *thinkDb* to DataViz in November 2002 who re-released the product as *Smart Lists To Go*.

REFERENCES

Buckhouse, J. 2002 *Tap* (Palm Software) http://www.diacenter.org/buckhouse/

Butter, A. and D. Pogue, (2002) *Piloting Palm: The Inside Story of Palm, Handspring and the Birth of the Billion Dollar Handheld Industry* John Wiley: New York, NY.

DataViz, (2002) *Smart Lists to Go*, http://www.dataviz.com/products/smartlisttogo/index.html

Gallagher, J. M. and K. M. Reid, (1981) *The Learning Theory of Piaget and Inhelder*, Brooks/Cole Publishing: Monterey, CA.

Hamblen, M. *Taking Control of the PDA Phenomenon*, ComputerWorld, June 29, 2002 Retrieved December 03, 2002 from http://www.computerworld.com/mobiletopics/mobile/story/0,10801,73019,00.html

Johnson, D. W., Jones, C. G., and Cold, S. J., "Handheld Computers: Ready for Prime-Time in the College Classroom?" Proceedings of the Eighth Americas Conference on Information Systems, 2002, pp 756-762.

Rubinstein, J. Gartner: *Palm Losing Ground to Pocket PC*, Software Developer Times, June 15, 2002. Retrieved December 03, 2003 from http://ww.sdtimes.com/news/056/story3.htm

Knowledge Creation and Competitive Advantage

Patricia C. Miller
Information Science, University at Albany
34 Greentree Dr. N., Hyde Park, NY 12538
(845) 229-6246, Patricia@compuwise.us

ABSTRACT

Knowledge management enables organizations to better utilize their current stock of knowledge and position themselves to recognize opportunities to create knowledge faster than their competitors, thus increasing an organization's value and competitive standing. Economic value is increasingly related to an organizations ability to innovate and innovation requires that the organization engage in learning on a continuous basis.

This research in progress paper investigates the relationship between an organization's structure and its ability to create knowledge and increase value. The author suggests that any organization can gauge its potential to create new knowledge by giving careful consideration its intellectual bandwidth for knowledge creation and discusses the key enablers of knowledge creation.

INTRODUCTION

Interest in knowledge management as a crucial organizational resource has grown dramatically over the past decade as refinements in technology have enabled instant communication and access to information on a global scale. Knowledge management enables organizations to better utilize their current stock of knowledge and position themselves to recognize opportunities to create knowledge faster than their competitors, thus increasing an organization's value and power. The ability to transform information to make it more productive is critical to an organization's ability to maintain a competitive advantage [Drucker, 1998]

Information is data that has been transformed and is actionable; it is easy to duplicate and it is codifiable. Knowledge goes a step further; Knowledge is information that has meaning and is always in a state of becoming. It is the result of taking existing information that is inert and static and transforming it by giving it new meaning. [Bhatt, 2000] "Knowledge is information possessed in the mind of individuals' it is personalized information that is related to facts, procedures, concepts, ideas and judgments." [Alavi & Leidner, 2001] Knowledge is a justified belief system, held by individuals and groups, that leads to action. [Nonaka & Takeuchi, 1995] How one characterizes knowledge is intimately related to the perspective of knowledge held by the organization. Understanding knowledge perspectives and its implications for action is of critical importance to an organization's ability to harness its power and create new knowledge. New knowledge should lead to innovative products or services that increase the organization's stature, revenue stream or profits and enhance its ability to acquire or maintain a competitive advantage.

TACIT AND EXPLICIT KNOWLEDGE

Knowledge can broadly be categorized as either explicit or tacit. Explicit knowledge can be codified, communicated without difficulty, recorded, written, and transferred into other formats or embedded in technology. [Davenport & Prusak, 1998] Organizations make use of explicit knowledge in best practices, manuals, specifications and routine, programmed activities. Tacit knowledge is content specific, abstract, difficult to articulate, with cognitive, intuitive and technical components. [Nonaka and Takeuchi, 1995, Bhatt, 2000, Alavi & Leidner, 2001] Tacit knowledge is flexible, fluid and self-fortifying. It builds on an individual's experiences and mental models, combining them and giving new meaning as the context changes. Organizations need to be able to draw on the tacit knowledge found in individuals and transform it into tacit knowledge held by a group or into an explicit form. This is a difficult task

since tacit knowledge results from life experience, which include the social, cultural, emotional and cognitive backgrounds of individuals, therefore, the ability to externalize this knowledge so that others might directly learn from it may not be possible. [Polyani, 1998, Nestor-Baker & Hoy, 2001] Hence, organizations must provide the environmental accouterments that will enable individuals to utilize their tacit knowledge and expertise to increase organizational performance and productivity.

INNOVATION & KNOWLEDGE IDENTIFICATION

An organization must be able to leverage knowledge to create value consistently. "Innovation is essential to competitive advantage and the chances of survival will be enhanced when the organization attends and responds to more and different stimuli." [Belardo & Belardo, 2002] Innovation requires that the organization engage in learning on a continuous basis. The process of learning and creating value can be viewed as a time line, in which the process moves through four distinct but continuous phases, identification, elicitation, dissemination and utilization. [Huber, 1991, Nevis et al, 1995, Belardo, 2001] Identification entails determining what the knowledge needs of an organization are, elicitation involves extracting the knowledge from the source(s), dissemination involves making sure that all who need to know do know and utilization is the process of making the knowledge one's own to improve organizational performance. [Belardo & Belardo, 2002] The identification stage is crucial to knowledge creation, both from a macro perspective, which helps the organization develop its strategy, and from a micro perspective, so that the right knowledge gets to the right person at the right time. [Belardo & Belardo, 2002]

INTELLECTUAL BANDWIDTH FOR KNOWLEDGE CREATION

The concept of an intellectual bandwidth has been discussed in conjunction with an organization's ability to create value. [Nunamaker et al, 2001] Opining on this concept and building on previous literature on knowledge creation, absorptive capacity, and innovation, the author suggests that any organization can gauge its potential to create new knowledge by giving careful consideration to the key enablers, leadership, culture, knowledge creators and

INTELLECTUAL BANDWIDTH FOR KNOWLEDGE CREATION

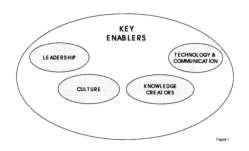

Figure 1

technology and communication, described in Figure 1, which comprise the Intellectual Bandwidth for Knowledge Creation [Cohen & Levinthal, Von Krogh, et al, 2000, Belardo & Belardo, 2002]

- **Leadership**

Leadership plays a critical role in identifying the knowledge that an organization will acquire and use. Leadership determines whom the organization listens to externally and to what degree this knowledge is disseminated inside the organization. Knowledge creation is often chaotic and disorderly but if managed correctly can result in the creation of new skills and competencies. [Bhatt, 2000] The relationship the organization has with its external and internal environment must critically examined to identify and correct assumptions and behaviors that are not value adding. Leadership must also examine the basis for rewarding employee performance and a fine balance must be struck between rewarding units or teams for the sharing of knowledge and rewarding individuals in cases where their tacit knowledge leads to innovations.

- **Culture**

Culture is a reflection of the values and practices of the organization. One cannot ignore the role culture plays in knowledge seeking as it can serve to facilitate or restrict knowledge. "Organizations and parts of organizations develop particular cultures and particular practices. They may have originated for good reasons, or simply by chance, but they tend to become accepted and, indeed, unseen" [DeLong, 2000] Organizations may have difficulty identifying the true culture as there are usually two cultures in an organization, "the espoused culture" and the "true culture." [Schein] It is the apparent demonstrations of the "true culture" and the realities that it presents, i.e. behavior that it supports and norms that must be transformed. Strategies for change need to be grounded in a clear understanding of where the organization is now, where it wants to be and what it will take to get there.

While culture has a major influence in the management of knowledge, the ability of an organization to put together teams of individuals with diverse but complementary experiences can serve to ignite sparks of creativity where they might otherwise lie dormant. Socialization and activities where individuals can informally share knowledge with teammates and other colleagues is vital. [Davenport & Prusak, 1998, Von Krogh et al, 2000]

- **Knowledge Creators**

The capability of building on existing knowledge is affected by an organization's intellectual capacity. "The ability to evaluate and utilize outside knowledge is largely a function of the level of prior related knowledge." [Cohen & Levinthal, 1990] Therefore, it is important that the organization employ individuals whose experience will enable them to recognize and assimilate new sources of information, produce something unique and innovative or contribute to team productivity.

Knowledge creators are individuals who have a role in seeking out knowledge sources, who recognize the potential of information to be reused in a novel way or who are able to create new or improved products and services by working individually or in groups with other knowledge creators. When an organization realizes the importance of having individuals who function as gatekeepers, constantly spanning the external environment for sources of new information, and the need for individuals who can absorb this information, it will seek to employ individuals with this potential. It will also provide the intellectual sustenance needed within the organization to allow this potential to develop more fully. [Davenport & Prusak, 1998]

- **Technology & Communication**

One of the biggest misconceptions about knowledge management is the belief that technology plays a major role in the success of any knowledge management initiative. Getting the right information to the right people at the right time is important, and technology is a key enabler in disseminating information throughout the organization. However information technology is limited and its ability to facilitate teammaking, elicit tacit knowledge or build trust. [Davenport & Prusak 1998, Belardo & Belardo, 2002] As knowledge creation has more to do with "relationships and community-building then databases …investments in information technology alone cannot make the knowledge-creating company happen." [Von Krogh et all, 2000]

Technology can be used to design systems to support collaboration and communication, and to facilitate the flow information throughout the organization. There are knowledge management tools and technologies that support the identification of new knowledge opportunities, such as sophisticated GroupWare, web retrieval software and recommender systems. [Resnick & Varian, 1997, Stenmark, D., 2001]

Communication should be multi-dimensional; formal, informal, social, oral and written; it must initiate at all levels within the organization. The ability to express and share ideas must be encouraged and fostered. When people trust that what they say will not result in negative criticism, they will feel free to communicate their ideas. When communication is encouraged and varied opportunities to foster dialogue are facilitated by the organization, people learn to understand each other and develop relationships, which are important to the sharing of tacit knowledge. [Davenport and Prusak, 1998, Von Krogh et al, 2000, Belardo & Belardo, 2002]

RESEARCH METHOD

My study is will explore knowledge creation in organizations. Three organizations identified in current literature as engaged in knowledge management and who have demonstrated superior performance over time, as indicated by revenue, market capitalization and recognition, will form the source of case study research. The study will involve interviews, observations and review of documents, to determine the characteristics and factors that facilitate knowledge creation in the organization. Particular inquiry will focus on the role played by the four key enablers, leadership, culture, knowledge creators and technology and communications. The author purports that the degree to which an organization possesses these key enablers, correlates closely with the level of knowledge creation occurring within the organization.

The study will add to the body of knowledge in the field of knowledge identification by identifying characteristics found in organizations that are widely recognized as leaders in this area. It will provide support to the importance of the four key enablers in the role of knowledge creation and may lead to the discovery other factors that may also play a significant role in this area.

The study will seek to identify similarities in knowledge creating activities across organizations. The study will draw on inferences from documents, interviews and observations, to give both depth and validity to the results. The subjects in the study will initially be identified by organizational leadership as individuals engaged in knowledge creating behaviors and/or in knowledge management positions. Additional subjects will be identified for inclusion through information gained in interviews and through observations.

REFERENCES

Alavi, M. and D. E. Leidner (2001). "Knowledge Management and Knowledge and Knowledge Management Systems: Conceptual Foundations and Research Issues." MIS Quarterly 25(1): 107-136.

Belardo, S. (2001). Learning Organizations and Knowledge Management: A Conventional and Alternate View. Advanced Information Systems Techniques Course Lecture Series. Albany.

Belardo, S. and A. W. Belardo (2002). Innovation Through Learning. Albany, Whitston Publishing Company, Inc.

Bhatt, G. D. (2000). "Information dynamics, learning and knowledge creation in organizations." The Learning Organization 7(2): 89-90.

Cohen, W., M., and Levinthal, Daniel, A. (1990). "Absorptive Capacity: A New Perspective on Learning and Innovation." Administrative Science Quarterly (35): 128-152.

Davenport, T. H. and L. Prusak (1998). Working Knowledge. Boston, Harvard Business School Press.

DeLong, D., and Fahey, L. (2000). "Diagnosing cultural barriers to knowledge management." The Academy of Management Executive 14(4): 113-127.

Drucker, P. F. (1998). The Coming of the New Organization. Harvard Business Review on Knowledge Management. Boston, Harvard Business School Press: 1-19.

Huber, G. (1991). "Organizational Learning: The Contributing Processes in Literature." Organization Science 2: 88-115.

Kogut, B., and Zander, U., (1992). "Knowledge of the firm, combinative capabilities, and the replication of technology." ORGANIZATION SCIENCE VOL 3(NO 3): 383-397.

Nestor-Baker, N. S. and W. K. Hoy (2001). "Tacit knowledge of school superintendents: Its nature, meaning and content." Educational Administration Quarterly 37(1): 86-129.

Nevis, E. C., A. J. DiBella and J.M. Gould (1995). "Understanding Organizations as Learning Systems." Sloan Management Review: 73-85.

Nonaka, I. and H. Takeuchi (1995). The Knowledge-Creating Company: How Japanese Companies Create the Dynamics of Innovation. New York, Oxford University Press.

Nunamaker J. F., B., R. O. , de Vreede, G. R., (2001). Value Creation Technology. Information Technology and the Future Enterprise: New Models for Managers. G. W. a. G. D. Dickson. New York, Prentice-Hall: 102-124.

Polyani, M. (1998). The Tacit Dimension. Knowledge in Organizations. L. Prusak. Boston, Butterworth-Heineman: 135-146.

Resnick, P. and H. R. Varian (1997). "Recommender Systems." Communications of the ACM 40(3): 56 - 58.

Schein, E. H. (1999). The Corporate Culture Survival Guide: Sense and Nonsen about Culture Change. San Francisco, Jossey-Bass.

Stenmark, D. (2001). "Leveraging Tacit Knowledge." Journal of Management Information Systems 17(3): 9 - 24.

Von Krogh, G., Ichijo, Kazuo, and Nonaka, Ikujiro, (2000). Enabling Knowledge Creation. New York, Oxford University Press.

Information Technology is Thriving in Yugoslavia! Case Study of Delta Holding

Lakshmi Mohan, Ph.D. and Jakov Crnkovic, Ph.D.
School of Business, University at Albany
State University of New York
BA 332, 1400 Washington Avenue, Albany, NY 12222
tel: (518) 442-4927, tel: (518) 442-5318
Fax: (518) 442-2568, Fax: (518) 442-2568
l.mohan@albany.edu, yasha@albany.edu

OVERVIEW

The research was initiated as a result of a one-week intensive course on IT Strategy and E-Business conducted by the authors at the invitation of the Faculty of Economics, University of Belgrade. The participants were drawn from the various subsidiaries of Delta Holding, a private conglomerate company founded in 1991. The learning from the course was applied by the participants to their respective companies in the form of presentations by 3-4 participants on the last day of the course. The presentations revealed the extensive use of IT in Delta Holding, which would be impressive by any standard, but especially so in Yugoslavia. The decade-long political upheaval in the country has left its economy in shambles, dimming the likelihood of IT being used as an integral part of operations in Yugoslavian companies. The sophisticated nature of IT applications in Delta Holding, in particular, the use of the Web, triggered the research to address the question: What are the factors that create the environment for successful deployment of IT in a company despite the adverse economic climate in which it operates? The course participants are providing a valuable conduit into Delta Holding for the purpose of this study. The findings from this case study will be juxtaposed with another case study on Cemex, the Mexican cement company which has been hailed as a "digital innovator" and has become the most profitable cement company in the world, surpassing the European multinationals, LaFarge and Holcim.

COMPANY BACKGROUND

Delta Holding was launched in February 1991, a time that was unfavorable for private enterprises in Yugoslavia due to the Bosnian War. The after-effects of that war coupled with political instability have ripped the country apart making it a shadow of its former self. The early years of Delta Holding showed modest growth of revenues from USD 7.5 million in 1991 to USD 27 million in 1995. The real spurt in the company's growth came in 1996 when the company tripled its revenues. The company has kept growing through all the tumult in the country to reach the level of USD 550 million in 2001. Its workforce has expanded from 8 employees in 1991 to 537 in 1995 and 8,000 in 2001.

Delta Holding is comprised of five divisions, the largest of which is the Delta M Group. This division is again a mini-conglomerate of 10 business units in industries ranging from agribusiness, to chemicals, automobiles and retail, and includes a majority ownership in a Russian pulp and paper mill that exports raw materials to Asian, European and African markets. Another division of Delta Holding is the Delta Banka Group, which has been ranked by *Finance Central Europe* as the best private bank in Yugoslavia in 2001.

INFORMATION TECHNOLOGY TODAY IN DELTA HOLDING

Our study will examine the status of IT in the Delta M Group and the Delta Banka Group. Delta M was selected for the study since it is the largest division in Delta Holding and is also a conglomerate with a diversity of businesses. The IT unit is a separate "non-profit" center at the corporate level, and has played a proactive role in setting up a global communications network. Starting with an internal network inside the corporate headquarters building, the IT unit went on to link through a WAN the branches in the country to the corporate office. With the advent of the Internet, the Corporate Website was created for connecting with customers and with the international branches of the company.

Aside from the global communications network, an Intranet portal has been created in Delta M which has reduced paperwork and minimized the time and cost of getting information. A simple application is the ordering of business cards through the portal, which aggregates small orders and gets a volume discount that yields a cost saving of over 500%.

The IT unit at corporate also addresses the requirements of the individual businesses within the Delta M Group. An example is Maxi Diskont, a chain of supermarkets and the market leader in its class in Yugoslavia. On-line shopping has been introduced to differentiate it from competitors and add value in terms of convenience to customers. The inventory control application links the cashiers at the checkout counters and the online site to the suppliers to ensure minimum level of stocks to meet demand.

The other division selected for the study, the Delta Banka Group, has made continuing investments in IT to not only improve existing systems but also provide modern electronic banking services to its clients. Delta Bank has improved its competitive standing to rank among the top three private banks with regard to gross profit, assets and return on equity.

Both these divisions are moving forward with aggressive plans for broadening the application of IT to B2B E-Commerce, Customer Relationship Management, and the like.

CEMEX: IF CEMENT CAN, ANYONE CAN

Cemex is perhaps the most unlikely of today's digital innovators. Its roots are in a single cement plant founded in Hidalgo, Mexico, in 1906. Cemex has taken a commodity-based asset-intensive, low-efficiency business, and enhanced its profitability by adding a brilliantly integrated layer of IT – a "bits" factory designed to complement and support the "atoms" factory.

The Cemex case demonstrates that, in today's business world, anyone can play. Even if a company has a remote location with no special advantages in terms of talent base or IT infrastructure, it can perform at a world-class level if the quality of its thinking to devise and implement a "digital business design" is world-class. The major success factors in Cemex were:

(a) Bench-marking the best world-class practices for systems that sense the environment and respond quickly;

(b) Re-structuring the organization based on lessons learned from best practices;

(c) Investing in IT infrastructure;

(d) Exploiting the potential of IT to support and grow the business; and,

(e) Bringing about change in IT culture and management style.

Above all, the key was the powerful partnership between the CEO, who was attuned to the strategic value of IT and the CIO hired by him, who had a genuine understanding of business. This type of teamwork has become a characteristic of many of today's successful digital businesses.

FOCUS OF OUR STUDY

The purpose of our study is to examine the factors that foster investments in IT even in a depressed economic climate in a country like Yugoslavia that has been buffeted for over a decade with political turmoil. For example: How is IT organized in Delta Holding, the parent company, and in the Delta M Group and Delta Banka Group, two of its major subsidiary companies? Who is the champion of IT in the business units? How are the business units connected to the IT group? What makes Delta Holding's culture different from that of other private companies in Yugoslavia? The Cemex case will provide a backdrop for evaluating the findings of the Delta Holding study.

The Evolution of a Global Information System Course: Case Study at Southern Connecticut State University

Robert L. Mullen
Southern Connecticut State University
Management Department; School of Business
501 Crescent Street, New Haven, CT 06515
203-392-5856 phone, 203-392-5863 fax
MULLENR1@SOUTHERNCT.EDU e-mail

ABSTRACT

The education of a computer systems analyst in today's business environment requires exposure to the unique issues for dealing with information systems which cross country boundaries. One popular software package to deal with such issues is SAP R/3. This paper discusses the evolution of a course taught at Southern Connecticut State University in global information systems. The course is offered for the second time in the Spring 2003 semester at Southern and has 16 students currently enrolled.

INTRODUCTION

The writer participated in an MBA team-taught graduate course in global business operations. This experience led the writer to develop a new course, MIS400, Global Information Systems. This course is designed for undergraduate MIS students. A requirement for a program to become a major at Southern is that it have its own focused course on international issues for its field. This paper presents the experience to-date of that course.

CASE STUDY RESULTS

The first offering of the course was in the Spring 2002 semester at Southern. The schedule of topic for that course is shown as Figure 1. Lessons learned are discussed as the next generation of the course for Spring 2003.

Figure 1

Lessons learned from figure 1 include the following:
- Undergraduates need more guidance in research project work.
- Students seemed to like the opportunity to contribute research work to the class.
- Text book is too dated to use next semester. Need to find a new one.
- Include more coverage of SAP R/3 as example of global ready software.

Other future issues include:
- This would probably be a possible summer course that would attract the required ten students if offered in the late afternoon or early evening.
- This would probably be a good course to design for OnLineCSU to offer in the future in a distance learning situation allowing MIS students from sister schools in the Connecticut State University system to take this course for credit at their school.

Figure 2 represents the schedule for the upcoming Spring 2003 version of the same course demonstrating the changes from above analysis of the ex-

Figure 2

SOUTHERN CONNECTICUT STATE UNIVERSITY-Spring 2002
MIS400-01 GLOBAL INFORMATION SYSTEMS
Meets:**Tues.6:00-8:30PM** Instructor: Dr. Robert Mullen

TEXTBOOK: Deans, P. Candace and Karwan, Kirk R.; **Global Information Systems and Technologies**;Idea Group Publishing.; 1997.

WEEK/DATE	TOPIC	READING	RESEARCH-WORK
1- 1/22	The Globalization of Business	Ch 1,2	
2- 1/29	Impact on Marketing Systems	Ch 3,4	
3- 2/5	Impact of the European Community Ch 5		Team 1 Report
4- 2/12	Impact on Financial Systems	Ch 6,7	Team 2 Report
5- 2/19	Impact on Financial Services	Ch 9	Team 3 Report
6- 2/26	Impact on Accounting Systems	Ch 10,11	Team 4
Report			
7- 3/5	**EXAM #1 (WEEKS 1-6)**		
8- 3/12	Impact on Manufacturing Systems	Ch12,13,14	Team 5 Report
9- 3/19	Impact on Logistical Systems	Ch 15,16	Team 6 Report
10-3/26	**SPRING BREAK - NO CLASS**		
11-4/2	Impact on R & D Systems	Ch 17,18	Team 7
Report			
12-4/9	Impact on Human Resource Systems	Ch20,21,22	Team 8
Report			
13-4/16	Impact on entire enterprise	Ch 24,25	Team 9
Report			
14-4/23	New issues since 2001	Ch 26,27	Team
10Report			
15-4/30	Future issues		
16-5/7	**EXAM #2 (WEEKS 8-15)**		
NO FINAL EXAM			

SOUTHERN CONNECTICUT STATE UNIVERSITY-Spring 2003
MIS400-01 GLOBAL INFORMATION SYSTEMS
Meets:**Tues.6:00-8:30PM** Instructor: Dr. Robert Mullen
TEXTBOOKS: - Dadashzadeh, Mohammad, **Information Technology in Developing Countries,** IRM Press,2002; Nah, Fiona Fui-Hoon, **Enterprise Resource Planning Solutions and Management,** IRM Press, 2002; Tan, Felix, **Global Perspective of Information Technology Management,** IRM Press; 2002.

WEEK/DATE	TOPIC	READING	RESEARCH-WORK
1- 1/22	The Globalization of Business	Ch 1 (2)	
2- 1/29	Impact on Human Resource Systems	Ch 2	
3- 2/5	Global Software Outsourcing	Ch 4	Team 1
Report			
4- 2/12	Undergraduate Global Education	Ch 6	Team 2
Report			
5- 2/19	ERP in a Global Company	Ch 9	Team 3
Report			
6- 2/26	Three-Tiered Global E-Commerce	Ch 10	Team 4
Report			
7- 3/5	**EXAM #1 (WEEKS 1-6)**		
8- 3/12	ERP and E-Business	Ch1 (1)	Team 5
Report			
9- 3/19	Evolution of ERP Systems	Ch 3	Team 6
Report			
10-3/26	**SPRING BREAK - NO CLASS**		
11-4/2	A Case Study of ERP Implementation	Ch 5	Team 7
Report			
12-4/9	The Next Wave of ERP Implementation Ch 8		Team 8
Report			
13-4/16	ERP in Brazil	Ch 10	Team 9
Report			
14-4/23	ERP in Australia	Ch 12	Team
10Report			
15-4/30	ERP in New Zealand	Ch 15	
16-5/7	**EXAM #2 (ERP)**		
NO FINAL EXAM			

perience gained from the 2002 offering of the course. New textbooks were selected from IRM Press which provided three soft-cover books dated 2002 to overcome the outdated issue of the 1997 text used in 2002. The concept of students conducting research based on articles from one of the books will continue as the research assignment is thought to be important to this senior level course but which required more guidance for undergraduates. A third difference is the coverage of Enterprise Resource Planning software, in general, and SAP R/3 in particular, as examples of fully integrated packaged software ready for global implementation.

There appears to be enough students registered so far that the course will be offered. It is scheduled in one of the new classroom which will present an excellent environment for the course in a modern setting. Students will be informed that it is still considered a pilot offering of the course and their comments and suggestions for future versions will be sought and welcomed at the end of the course.

When this paper is presented in May 2003, experience from the Spring 2003 version will be available to compare to 2002 version. Suggestions for the 2004 version will also be available.

CONCLUSIONS

Courses in the MIS field need to undergo three iterations before they settle down into an acceptable pattern. Student input is critical to the evolution process.

REFERENCES

1. Ananthanpillai, Raj; Implementing Global Networked Systems Management; McGraw-Hill; 1997.

2. Dadashzadeh, Mohammad; Information Technology in Developing Countries; IRM Press; 2002.

3. Deans, P. Candace and Karwan, Kirk R.; Global Information Systems and Technologies; Idea Group Publishing.; 1997.

4. Nah, Fiona Fui-Hoon; Enterprise Resource Planning Solutions and Management; IRM Press; 2002.

5. Tan, Felix; Global Perspective of Information Technology Management; IRM Press; 2002.

The Evolution of an MIS Program: Case Study at Southern Connecticut State University

Robert L. Mullen
Southern Connecticut State University
Management Department, School of Business
501 Crescent Street, New Haven, CT 06515
203-392-5856 phone; 203-392-5863 fax
MULLENR1@SOUTHERNCT.EDU e-mail

ABSTRACT

The education of a computer systems analyst remains in high demand. Support of this education has been provided by Southern Connecticut State University for twenty-five years. However, the extent of the support has increased during the last ten years which will eventually culminate with a major in MIS. This case study described the process of evolving the program into its present status.

INTRODUCTION

Computers have been used for a variety of applications in business since the 1950s. In the early years the focus of education of a computer professional was in learning languages to program the computer. In the 1960s, business began to recognize a different form of education for computer systems analysts who design computer systems but do not build them. The difference was knowledge needed in the nature of business itself rather than how computers are programmed. Business schools began offering programs in MIS, as this new field was known. Computer programming was taught by the Computer Science Department usually found in the school of Engineering at a University rather than the School of Business.

BACKGROUND OF THE PROGRAM

In the 1970s, the School of Business Economics (title of the current School of Business of Southern Connecticut State University in the 1970s) began offering a few courses in business applications of computers to support the growing Computer Science program in another area. Southern increased its stature to a university rather than a college by increasing the breadth of its program offerings. The number of MIS courses offered to support the applications track of the Computer Science increased during the 1980s from four to eight but all were electives. In the early 1990s, The author was hired from industry where he held the position of Director of MIS into a full-time tenure-track faculty member with the specified purpose of developing a more extensive program in MIS in the School of Business. Although never specifically written by the then dean, Dr. Alan Leader, his vision was MIS taking over the Computer Science program itself. The author had a different vision, one with a separate major but existing alongside of the Computer Science major. MIS majors could minor in Computer Science and Computer Science majors could minor in MIS.

THE TEN YEAR EVOLUTION

During the early 1990s, my focus was on updating the catalog descriptions of the courses to modern computer system technology (removing references to batch vs. on-line systems). The second step was to organize the existing courses in the catalog into a program allowing students to specialize in MIS within their major of Business Administration along with the other disciplines – accounting, finance, economics, marketing, and management. The third step was to grow the program into a size (over 60 students) that justified the hiring of a third full-time faculty member (a requirement for any major program).

CURRENT STATUS

In 2002, we revised the program for a specialization in MIS to include more elective credits for Computer Science courses (four courses allowed) and encourage students to select two more courses from Computer Science to receive a minor in Computer Science to support their MIS specialization. We modified the program to encourage internships for MIS work experience. There are now 80 students in the program. In 2003, we revised the program for a specialization in General Management to include electing our MIS Global Information Systems for their international requirement and allow up to three MIS courses for their six courses in management.

FUTURE PLANS

By the end of the current academic year in May 2003, we expect to have in place a degree program in the School of Business at Southern Connecticut State University for a major in Management Information Systems with a minor in Computer Science. This plan requires the hiring of a third member of the MIS department to have sufficient faculty to teach the required ten courses in the major. The author is currently Chair of the School of Business Curriculum Committee so is in a good political position to accomplish this end goal.

REFERENCES

1. Beerel, Annabel (2000): Expert Systems in Business: Real World Applications; Ellis Forwood Publishing; New York.
2. Chandler, John S. (1998): Developing Expert Systems for Business Applications; Merrill Publishing; Columbus, Ohio.
3. Durkin; John (1999): Expert System Design and Development; Maxwell McMillan Publishing; New York.
4. Edwards, John S. (1998): Building Knowledge-Based Systems: Towards a Methodology; Halsted Press, New York.
5. Guida, Giovanni. (2000): Design and Development of Knowledge Based Systems; Wiley and Sons, New York.
6. Harmon, Paul (1999): Creating Expert Systems for Business/Industry; Wiley and Sons, NY. Vol. 13, No. 3; pp 78-80.
7. Southern Connecticut State University catalog 2002-2003.

E-Pizza USA: A Web-Based Pizza Ordering System for a Statewide Pizzeria

Dr. Yousif Mustafa
Department of Computer Information Systems, School of Business
Central Missouri State University
Warrensburg, MO 64093
Mustafa@cmsu1.cmsu.edu

ABSTRACT

We have been inspired by the success of implementing the concept of e-commerce in domains such as car rentals, Avis.com and Hertz.com just to mention few examples, where customers have the ability to reserve a car via the internet any time around the clock. Our system, e-PizzaUSA, is a web-based system developed to enable customers, after becoming registered users of the system, to view all meals, deals and specials, then make their our selection.

Customers have the option of making an order from one address and have it delivered to a different address within the state of Missouri. They also have the choice of making the order and have it delivered after one hour, for example, or one week.

Customers will get a 10% discount of the advertised price when they order via the web. The e-PizzaUSA system rewards its users by giving them 1 point for each dollar they spend. Each time a customer accumulates 100 points, he or she gets a $10 discount on his/her next order.

e-PizzaUSA periodically surveys customers to get their feedback and identify their preferences. The system rewards its customers with various incentives when they respond promptly to those surveys.

Finally, the system maintains an up-to-date database of its customers and is equipped to handle different credit cards.

Country as Brand – A Marketing Information System for Developing Countries Case Study of Ethiopia

Margaret Crossman O'Connor
Robert Morris University
P.O. Box 201, Ringtown, PA   17967
570.889.5001, oconnor1@epix.net

ABSTRACT

This paper explores a marketing information system to help Ethiopians market their diverse goods and services to Ethiopians living in the United States (U.S.).   It is a work-in-progress submittal.   This system begins with the development of a positive brand identity strategy for Ethiopian goods and services.   It then tests this strategy with Ethiopians living in the U.S.   Once validated, the brand identity strategy is overlaid into a web-based prototype to be used for e-commerce of Ethiopian goods and services by Ethiopians living in the U.S.   This is defined by the author as a Country of Origin website. The project includes user task analysis and survey data to develop Ethiopia's brand identity by Ethiopians who currently live in the United States.   The paper suggests a new strategy to help developing countries find markets for their unique products and services.

INTRODUCTION

The topic of branding countries, while controversial, has lead to new studies that warrant consideration. Holt (2002, p.87) discusses brands as "citizen-artists" and their focus as a "cultural resource." Papadopoulos and Heslop (2002, p. 296) state that people have a need to "chunk" information due to potential overload and that there is an image associated with places that sometimes is beyond the marketer's control. Van Ham (2001, p.3) argues that essential elements of brand equity are reputation and image. Unfortunately, there are countries in the world that are stigmatized globally. Higginson (1999) discusses regional stigmas and notes that companies are "tarred with the territorial brush of the country…". The purpose of this study is first, to execute a brand equity study with Ethiopians that live in the United States to determine positive perceptions and attitudes about the country and its products and services. Brand equity as defined by Braunstein and Levine (2000, p.26) is "an indelible mark made on the mind of a stakeholder." Other synonyms include "brand assets", "brand inventory", "brand hierarchy" and "brand positioning". The study will include a user task analysis and survey that will translate into a prototype design of branding elements for Ethiopia. According to Braunstein and Levine (2000, p. 36), elements included in branding strategies are what are "meaningful", "unique", and emote "passion" by the group served with products or services.   Those elements will then be incorporated into a web-based prototype to be used for e-commerce of Ethiopian goods and services by Ethiopians living in the U.S.   A discussion about the conceptual considerations for this marketing information system, Ethiopia's challenges, products, and technological considerations are highlighted.

CONCEPTUAL CONSIDERATIONS

Change Agent

There is a thrust to look at culture as an integral consideration of global

information systems. Myers and Tan (2002, p.13) suggest that researchers in IS view "culture as contested, temporal and emergent." It is time to think out of the box for developing countries. The current system of industrialization does not work for many of them, such as Ethiopia. Lodge (2002, p. 14) states that poverty is unable to be eradicated by globalization. He argues that a "new means" is needed to ensure that poverty's causes are attacked. Could there be other ways to help countries help themselves? Furthermore, is it possible to translate what companies are experiencing and doing to help countries? Currently, corporations are seeking alternate ways of competing. Hamel (2002, p.25) refers to "discontinuous change" where companies use creative, new methods that are unconventional to develop competitive advantage.

This paper addresses a way for Ethiopians that live in the United States to be able to exchange goods and services for money that is needed by people in Ethiopia. It creates a knowledge community via the Internet. Afele (2003, viii) describes knowledge communities as a place where "talents and ideas are identified; creativity is nourished, capitalized, and translated into tangible services and products for the primary impact zone." With in this marketing information system, people that have wants and needs related to Ethiopia's brand unique meanings, such as symbolic, experiential or functional (Hsieh, 2001, p. 48) have a means to access those wants and needs. This access will, in turn, contribute to the welfare of individuals and groups living in diverse regions of Ethiopia. Hsieh (2001, p. 63) states the Internet will aid in "cross-national exposure" to the message and programs of brands.

Ethiopia- Challenges

Ethiopia has a stigma in the United States and is perceived as a country of poverty, famine and disease. Clearly, much of what is perceived is media-driven. However, the facts validate the perception. Over 6 million people are facing food shortages after a severe drought. Its population is estimated at 66 million of which half are considered chronically poor. Life expectancy is 45 years. Furthermore, overall literacy is 35.5%. Ethiopia is an extensively fragmented society. It is made up of 168 different tribes possessing their own culture and language. Its leadership is inconsistent and its government is unstable. (The World Fact Book, 2002.) Given its many challenges, Ethiopia must consider other means of development and assume that current constraining factors of economic development are not going to change in the near future.

Ethiopia- Products

Currently, *coffee* is the most important product, earning $260 million in 2000 through exporting. (The World Fact Book, 2002.) It is the place of origin for organic coffee (Coffee Production, 1999.) Ethiopia is also known for its *fabrics*, hand made *jewelry*, and *artifacts*. There has been a strong increase in jewelry consumption by the Middle and Far East. (Duncan, J. 2000.) Ethiopia currently has four state owned *beer* breweries and four new breweries currently under construction. Most of the breweries produce for the export market. (Economic and Commercial Office, 2001.) The textile industry is the largest manufacturing industry in Ethiopia. The industry employs 30,000 workers, which is 36% of the manufacturing industry. The textiles produced include cotton and polyester with consumption of 93 million pounds in 2001. The principle importers of cotton are Indonesia, Mexico, Russia, and Thailand. (Raines, 2002). Other valuable exports of Ethiopia are livestock products. Ethiopian highland sheepskin has gained an international reputation in glove manufacturing. A few other exports of Ethiopia are seeds and pulses, tea, and natural gum. Tourism is also growing. There are 40 agencies available to give tours in Ethiopia. Ethiopia has three primary Resort areas, Sodere, Rift Valley Lakes and Wando Genet. There are closely 22 hotels in Ethiopia including a Sheraton and a Hilton. There were 693 million tourists traveling worldwide in 2001 of which 28% visited Africa (The World Tourism Organization, 2001.) Furthermore, Ethiopia's main exporters include Germany (6%), Japan (13%), Djibouti (10%), and Saudi Arabia (7%). The major importers are Saudi Arabia (28%), Italy (10%), Russia (7%), and the United States (6%).

Ethiopia also has many organizations and countries that are interested in aiding them. According to the 1998 Agency Performance Report, The United States ranked first among bilateral donors to Ethiopia, followed by Germany, Japan, Ireland, the Netherlands, and Italy. Major multilateral donors include International Development Association, the United Nations Development Program, the World Food Program, and the World Bank. There are many organizations that donate food, water, shelter, medical care, and educational support.

TECHNOLOGICAL CONSIDERATIONS

The sole provider for Internet services within Ethiopia is The Ethiopian Telecommunications Corporation (ETC), established in 1996. The ETC handles the operation, expansion and development of telecommunications throughout Ethiopia, while the Ethiopian Privatization Agency (EPA) handles its regulation. In late 1999, the EPA announced its search for an internationally recognized consulting firm for guidance regarding the privatization of the ETC. It is hoped that this development might lead to more connections and lower prices for Ethiopian users. Ethiopia also has the ability to use wireless communications. Other African nations are developing computer technology to aid country growth. Ghana hopes to have at least 100,000 computer jobs throughout the country. More Ghanaians own computers, televisions, radios, cell phones, and satellite dishes than ever before. They hope to increase their living standard with IT (Zachary, 2002.) Another nation that has greatly benefited from a surge of technology is Mauritius, situated in the Indian Ocean. Due to a fiber optic cable placement strategically located near Mauritius, it has taken to marketing itself as a Cyber Island (an information technology hub for Africa and the Middle East.) (In Mauritius…, 2002.)

RESEARCH QUESTIONS
1) What are the positive brand-unique meanings (symbolic, experiential, functional) that Ethiopians living in the U.S. have in demanding the products and services and cultural aspects of their homeland?
2) How can these positive meanings be translated into a brand identity strategy for Ethiopian goods and services?
3) Can this Ethiopian brand identity strategy then be translated into a prototype design for a Country of Origin website?

RESEARCH DESIGN

A user task analysis of 10 Ethiopians living in the United States will first be conducted to provide an in-depth understanding of those positive meanings most identified by Ethiopians. This analysis will use a contextual design, incorporating ethnographic interviews. (Harvey, 1997, p. 132-146.) Once complete, a survey will be distributed to a larger sample of Ethiopians living in the U.S. (approximately 300) in order to validate those positive symbolic, experiential and functional benefits derived from Ethiopian products and services by Ethiopians living in the U.S. The survey will be designed using existing brand equity questionnaire techniques. Key findings will be translated into an Ethiopian brand identity strategy. That brand identity strategy will be illustrated using prototype concept boards and shared with the 10 Ethio-

pians living in the U.S. involved in the user task analysis. Once validated, concepts will be translated into a Country of Origin website.

TIME FRAME

The results of the user task analysis and survey will be available summer of 2004. The Country of Origin web-based prototype design is expected to be available summer of 2005.

CONCLUSIONS AND IMPLICATIONS

Countries around the world are looking at branding to help create positive perceptions for world markets. Current studies include New Zealand, Australia, Korea, Ireland and the U.S. Developing countries such as Ethiopia that face extensive internal challenges such as leadership, fragmented cultures, famine, disease and war must look at alternative solutions to develop unique competitive advantage. A Country of Origin website with positive Ethiopian brand identity that finds people to serve with its vast array of culturally rich products and services may be a long-term solution. This research intends to advance those efforts to help Ethiopia help itself develop within its current environmental frame.

REFERENCES

Afele, J. (2003). *Digital Bridges*. Hershey: Idea Group Publishing.

Braunstein, M. and E. Levine (2000). *Deep Branding on the Internet*. California: Prima Publishing.

Central Intelligence Agency. *The World Fact Book*. Retrieved December 2, 2002. http://www.cia.gov/cia/publications/factbook/ethiopia.

Coffee Production (1999). *Ethiopia: Coffee Production*. Retrieved November 22, 2002. http://www.tradeport.org/ts/countries/ethiopia/mrr/mark0056.html.

Duncan, J. (2000). Gold Jewelry Demand Remains Strong. Retrieved December 2, 2002. http://www.professionaljeweler.com/archives/news/2000.

Economic and Commercial Office (2001). *Beer Brewing: Big Business in Ethiopia*. Retrieved December 2, 2002. http://www.telecom.net.et/~usembet/wwwhebeer.htm.

Hamel, G. (2002). *Leading the Revolution*. New York: Penguin Group.

Harvey, F. (1997). National cultural differences in theory and practice: Evaluating Hofstede's national cultural framework. *Information Technology & People*, (10(2), 132-146.

Higginson, S. (1999). Ireland: From Rags to Riches. Retrieved December 29, 2002. http://www.insuranceireland.com/live/papers/text/pr1999.html.

Hsieh, M. (2001). Identifying Brand Image Dimensionality and Measuring the Degree of Brand Globalization: A Cross-National Study. *Journal of International Marketing*, (10 (2), p. 46-67.

Holt, D.B. (2002). Why Do Brands Cause Trouble? A Dialectical Theory of Consumer Culture and Branding. *Journal of Consumer Research, Inc.* 29, 87-88.

In Mauritius, the silicon hills of Africa. (2002). *USA Today.com*. Retrieved November 1, 2002. http://www.usatoday.com/tech/news/techinnovations/2002-10-28-cyber-island_x.htm

Lodge, G. (2002). The Corporate Key. *Foreign Affairs*. 81, p.13-18.

Myers, M. and F. Tan (2002.) Beyond Models of National Culture in Information Systems Research. *Journal of Global Information Management*, 10 (2), article 3.

Papadopoulos, N. and L. Heslop (2002). Country equity and country branding: Problems and Prospects. *Brand Management*. 9, 296.

Raines, G. (2002). Outlook for the Cotton Market. 14th EFS System Conference. Retrieved December 2, 2002. http://www.cottoninc.com .

The World Fact Book (2002). Ethiopia. Retrieved December 20, 2002. http://www.cia.gov/cia/publications/factbook/geos/et.html#Econ.

The World Tourism Organization (2001). *Latest Data*.

Retrieved November 23, 2002. http://www.world-tourism.org/market_reserch/facts&figures/latest_data.htm.

Van Ham, P. (2001). The Rise of the Brand State. *Foreign Affairs*. 80, p.3.

Zachary, G. (2002). Ghana's Digital Dilemma, *Technology Review*, July/August 2002, Retrieved July 3, 2002. http://www.technologyreview.com/articles/pring_version/zachary0702.asp

Human Factors in the 'System Selection' Stage of Library Automation

Nasrine Olson
Lecturer/doctoral student
The Swedish School of Library and Information Science
501 90 Borås, Sweden
Ph.: +46-301-19193; +46-33-164318
Fax: +46-33-164005
Nasrine.Olson@hb.se

ABSTRACT

Since the late fifties and early sixties when computers and computer-based systems were introduced in the libraries in modest forms, use of IT within libraries has evolved greatly[1]. Libraries of today use various automated systems to take care of a vast range of simple and complex tasks. The term automation has been loosely used to refer to vastly differing levels of adoption and use of IT in great many different settings. Just within libraries, this term has been used to refer to anything from utilizing a simple PC, to most sophisticated use of technology in automating all aspects of library work. To remove repetitive clarifications however, the term 'automation' and 'library automation' in this paper are hereafter solely used to refer to the adoption and use of Automated Library Systems[2] (ALS) within libraries.

BACKGROUND

Since the emergence of ALS, a large amount of literature has been accumulating on various fronts. According to Storey (1992: 1), the two lines of approach excessively found in the library automation literature are the " machine side" and "what we did in our library to install a system". Like others (e.g. Fine 1986:84), Storey finds the amount of literature written on "human aspects" less frequent. Only in the more recent years the human aspects of automation have begun to receive more attention (e.g. in Sykes 1991; Döckel 1992; Morris and Dyer 1998; Clarke and Morris 1998; and Farley, Broady-Preston et al. 1998).

However, despite the vast range of literature and guidelines available regarding library automation, costly mistakes are still made and problems are still recurring on a daily basis.

The fact that people have a pivotal role in organizations of libraries and in the process of automation is discussed and accepted widely (Jordan and Jones 1995; Clarke and Morris 1998; Olsgaard 1989; Farley, Broady-Preston et al. 1998). For example it is stated that "Libraries spend more than half their budgets on staff salaries" (Jordan & Jones 1995: 1) and that "system migration results in large scale changes which will affect all levels of staff" (Clarke and Morris 1998: 153) or that "research indicates that 90 per cent of change initiatives that fail do so because human factors were not taken adequately into account" (Goulding 1996). Similarly, Olsgaard (1989) indicates that 85% of all failures in systems implementation can be attributed to people problems.

However, research-based studies on the human factors that are of significance in the process of adoption and use of automated library systems are still minimal (e.g. see Clarke and Morris 1998).

Based on this background, the following study is just a fraction of a doctoral research project, which includes a study of the human factors affecting the process of library automation and the relationship between these factors and the outcome of the automation project and management of change.

As such, this short paper only looks at the 'system selection' phase of library automation and tries to identify possible significant factors that can have a bearing on the selection of ALS.

As a preparation for this study, a list of factors that can be of importance in the 'system selection' phase of library automation has previously been put together based on a literature review and work-related experiences. Due to the length of this paper, that literature review and the related references are not included here. However it should be noted that some of the areas that were looked at were: literatures that examine the role of system specification documents; case studies that explain the process of system selection at libraries; models of evaluation methodology for information systems; aspects of selection and evaluation software packages; technology acquisition; human behavior and decision making process; models as a basis for investigating the acceptance and use of IT e.g. Technology Acceptance Model (TAM), Theory of Reasoned Action (TRA), and Diffusion of Innovation theory (more specifically organizational innovation adoption; factors affecting individual innovation; factors affecting new product success and failure; variables influencing inter and intra firm adoption decisions; etc).

AIM AND OBJECTIVES

The aim of this study is to complement and/ or modify the above mentioned list firstly with the factors that are seen to be of importance according to ALS vendors and library decision-makers and secondly with possible factors that could be identified as significant by listening to the story of system selection as told by library workers.

Therefore a couple of study questions have been formulated as follows:
- What do library system vendors and library decision-makers see as being the significant factors in the system selection phase of automation?
- What factors can be identified as being of significance by listening to the story of system selection as told by library workers?

METHOD

This study includes two sets of interviews:
1) The first set comprises four approximately one-hour long semi-structured interviews with:
    - a sales person with involvement in more than 200 sales of ALS,
    - a system developer/ vendor with double role of being head librarian at an academic library,
    - a head librarian at an academic library, which now runs its third ALS,
    - a systems librarian who has been involved in a major purchase of an ALS for use by a consortium of five different academic libraries.

In these interviews, the emphasis was placed on the possible factors that had seemed of significance to the informants.

2) A different approach was used in an additional interview with a library worker at a public library where the informant was asked to tell the story of how and why they had chosen their particular ALS and to relate her experiences of this system selection process to any relevant past experience in her life as she would see appropriate. Unlike the first approach, in this life-history-like interview, the emphasis was placed on the infor-

mant and her experiences and she was not directed to account for possible factors. The aim with inclusion of this different approach was to see if the data gathered could be enriched and a new perspective added.

When analyzing the first set of interviews a comparative perspective was used while for the latter interview a more hermeneutic approach was called for[3].

RESULTS AND DISCUSSION

Although, due to the scope of this paper, no epistemological considerations and discussions are included, it should be noted that this study has had a qualitative nature, where the aim of the work done has not been to produce results that could be generalized; the aim has rather been to form an insight that would aid a better formulation of the questionnaires that are to base a future quantitative study. As such, many elements were identified as possible significant factors, but as inclusion of a long list of these is not possible in this paper, the following presents just a few of the more interesting findings.

- According to all respondents in the first group of interviews, price and technical platform could be the deciding factors but only in a fraction of cases.
- According to the system vendors, system specification documents are not used constructively and in fact it was said that in many cases libraries seem to make up their minds about the system of their choice and then write the specifications to match this choice.
- According to the head librarians and the systems librarian, system functionality and functions specified in the system specification documents are the most important factors in the selection of a system. However, even they admitted that testing of all the potential systems against these system specifications is not possible and that at the time of purchase one cannot be sure as to whether the chosen system is the best match to the specifications made.
- According to all, the head and systems librarian's views can have a strong affect on the other library workers' views and thus on the choice of the system.
- Factors such as vendor company's reputation, location, language or system's innovativeness, openness, level of support offered, etc, all make deciding factors, but in both directions (positively or negatively) depending on the libraries involved.
- Sex and age of the people involved were not viewed as having a bearing on the choices made.
- In the story told by the last interviewee, only two library systems were considered. These are the two largest Swedish systems on the market that by far have the largest share of the Swedish market. No thought was even given to considering any other system. In that particular library, no system specification document was written and instead two library workers were assigned to look at possible choices and although both were in favor of one system, the other alternative was chosen and purchased by the head librarian. It seems that the price of the system has been one of the major factors in this decision but one cannot rule out the influence of personal networks that seem to have had a major bearing on the decision on several different levels. The importance of these personal contacts and their effects on the final decision was highlighted in a much stronger way in this story telling than it was in the first set of interviews.

The results of these interviews, as hoped, helped in the modification of the list of possible significant factors previously put together. Furthermore they have lead to several thought-provoking indications that require further consideration in designing the data gathering instruments of the wider doctoral research. An example that would highlight this is the role of the system specification documents as a basis for testing the suitability of potential systems. These documents are emphasized by many library decision makers as an important instrument in choosing an ALS. However, in deeper investigations, the feasibility of detailed examination of potential systems based on these documents becomes questionable. This gives rise to the question as how to design the data gathering instruments to capture such hidden contradictions between the actual cases and the initial perceptions of library workers.

Based on this study, the data gathering instruments need to be designed in a way that this and similar issues (e.g. the role and the extent of the influence of key people, social and professional networks, and previously formed personal preferences on decisions made) can be investigated in a suitable way.

ENDNOTES
[1]   For some historical accounts see Duval and Main (1992) or Tedd (1993).
[2]   For a definition of ALS refer to Duval and Main (1992:1)
[3]   For more details on the analysis methods used see e.g. Andersson (1986)

REFERENCES
Andersson, S. (1986). Hermeneutikens två Traditioner - om skillnaden mellan Schleiermacher och Gadamer. Kunskapens villkor en antologi om vetenskapsteori och samhällsvetenskap. S. Selander. Lund, Studentlitteratur.

Clarke, L. J. and A. Morris (1998). "Library system migration: A case study of change management at Oxford University." LIBRI 48(3 (SEP)): 153-162.

Duval, B. K. and L. Main (1992). Automated Library Systems: A Librarian Guide and Teaching Manual. Westport. London, Meckler.

Döckel, H. (1992). "Managing the impact of automation on library personnel." Mousaion 10(2): 83-92.

Farley, T., J. Broady-Preston, et al. (1998). "Academic libraries, people and change a case study of the 1990s." Library Management 19(4): 238-251.

Fine, S. F. (1986). "Technological Innovation, Diffusion and Resistance: An Historical Perspective." Journal of Library Administration 7(1): 83-108.

Goulding, A. (1996). Managing change for library support staff. Aldershot, Avebury.

Jordan, P. and N. Jones (1995). Staff management in library and information work. Aldershot, Gower.

Morris, A. and H. Dyer (1998). Human aspects of library automation, Gower.

Olsgaard, J. (1989). "The physiological and managerial impact of automation on libraries." Library Trends 37(4): 484-494.

Storey, C. (1992). "Great expectations: the human aspects of library automation." Journal of Library and Information Science 18(2): 1-15.

Sykes, P. (1991). "Automation and Non-Professional Staff: The Neglected Majority." Serials 4(3): 33-43.

Tedd, L. (1993). An Introduction to Computer-based Library Systems. Chichester, John Wiley.

Motivations and Barriers to the Adoption of 3G Mobile Multimedia Services: An End User Perspective in the Italian Market

Margherita Pagani
Bocconi University
Viale Filippetti, 9 - 20136 Milan (Italy)
tel: ++39 02 58366920
fax: ++39 02 58363714
margherita.pagani@uni-bocconi.it

Danilo Schipani
Valdani Vicari&Associati
Corso Italia, 13 - 20122 Milan (Italy)
tel: tel: ++39 02 727331
fax: ++39 02 72733350
schipani@valdani-vicari.it

1. INTRODUCTION

As telecommunications move into an era where the distinction between voice, video and data will be blurred, convergence of communications, information, entertainment, commerce and computing will lay the foundation for the development of an Information Society.

Over the last five years there have been a number of significant developments in multimedia computing power, CD-ROM technology, digital television, the Internet/Intranet, and IP-based services and terrestrial and satellite mobile communications, which could have a profound impact on our society. These technologies and systems may enable dramatic changes to take place in working practices, entertainment, education and healthcare.

Many organisations within the computing, entertainment, and communications industries are now looking to identify and capitalise on the promise of new market opportunities in multimedia created by these developments.

However, demand for multimedia services, should they be successful, is unlikely to be constrained to the fixed network. Greater pressure on time, and the need for flexibility and responsiveness in business, will lead to a growing demand for access to these services anytime, anywhere.

In order to meet the evolving needs of customers, and to capture the opportunity which this evolution represents, the mobile industry is looking to define and develop a third generation of mobile technology which will take the personal communications user into the Information Society by delivering voice, graphics, video and other broadband information direct to the user, regardless of location, network or terminal.

The purpose of the paper is to provide an end-user perspective on mobile multimedia services that are likely to emerge with the roll out of Third Generation Mobile Services (3G).

The remainder of this paper is organized into the following four section. The first section provides a brief review of the literature on the technology acceptance model. Next we present our research model based on a qualitative exploratory survey conducted in six markets. Then we test the proposed model on the Italian market and present the analysis and results of our study. Finally we make conclusion by discussing the implication of our study, followed by presenting future research direction.

2. TECHNOLOGY ACCEPTANCE MODEL (TAM): THE THEORETICAL BACKGROUND

Information Systems (IS) researchers have made significant efforts in building theories to examine and predict the determinant factors of information technology (IT) acceptance (Agarwal and Prasad, 1998; Agarwal and Prasad, 1999). Existing model of IT acceptance have their foundations from several diverse theories, most noticeably innovation diffusion theory, where individual's perceptions about using an innovation are considered to affect their adoption behavior (Agarwal and Prasad, 1998; Moore and Benbasat, 1991; Rogers, 1995). Other important theoretical models that attempt to explain the relationship between user beliefs, attitudes, intentions, and actual system use include the theory of reasoned action (TRA) (Ajzen and Fishbein, 1980), the theory of planned behavior (TPB) (Ajzen, 1991), and the technology acceptance model (TAM) (Davis, 1989; Davis et al., 1989). In the Information System literature on IT adoption, researchers have conducted several studies to examine the relationship between perceived ease of use, perceived usefulness, and the usage of other information technologies (Davis, 1989; Davis et al., 1989, Mathieson, 1991; Adams et al., 1992; Szajna, 1996; Hendrickson and Collins, 1996; Chau, 1996). Their researches have supported the Technology Acceptance Model (TAM) proposed by Davis (1989) which posits that perceived ease of use and perceived usefulness can predict the usage of technology.

TAM was derived from the Theory of Reasoned Action (TRA). According to Davis (1989), perceived usefulness and perceived ease of use are the two determinants that influence people's attitude toward IT usage intention and actual IT usage. Perceived usefulness is defined as "the degree to which a person believes that using a particular system would enhance his or her job performance" and perceived ease of use is defined as "the degree to which a person believes that using a particular system would be free of effort" (Davis, 1989, p.320) Davis and his colleagues (Davis, 1989; Davis et al., 1989; Davis et al., 1992) demonstrated that perceived ease of use affected usage intention indirectly via perceived usefulness.

In an extension to TAM, Davis and his colleagues examined the impact of enjoyment on usage intention (Davis et al., 1992). They reported two studies concerning the relative effects of usefulness and enjoyment on intention to use and usage of computers. As expected, they found enjoyment had a significant effect on intention. A positive interaction between usefulness and enjoyment was also observed.

Originally evaluated with email, word processing and graphics applications, TAM has been extended to other applications such as voice-mail (Adams et al., 1992), spreadsheets (Mathieson, 1991), DBMS (Saajna, 1994), GSS (Chin and Gopal, 1995), mobile computing (Zhu and Fui-Hoon, 2002). Various constructs such as cultural differences (Straub, 1994) and gender differences (Gefen and Straub, 1997) have also been suggested.

In this research our goal is to extend the TAM model to study motivations and barriers to the adoption of 3G mobile multimedia services. In the following sections the research is divided into two stages: an exploratory qualitative stage followed by a quantitative stage focused on the Italian market.

3. RESEARCH FRAMEWORK

3.1 Methodology

Many factors positively or negatively influence user's adoption of multimedia mobile services. In this section we identify several variables that influence adoption of 3G mobile multimedia services. The variables are derived from an exploratory qualitative stage conducted by Nokia through 24 focus groups in 6 markets (Brazil, Germany, Italy, Singapore, UH, USA).

The second stage of the analysis concentrates specifically on a quantitative marketing research conducted on a sample of 1.000 Italian users of mobile. It tries to describe behaviors, roles and test variables influencing adoption of mobile computing. We consider Italy because it is the European country with the higher penetration of mobile phones and profitability, it is also prone to market innovation.

3.2 Exploratory Qualitative Stage

The fieldwork has been carried out face to face in the first and second quarters of 2001 through 24 focus groups conducted by Nokia Networks in 6 markets (Brazil, Germany, Italy, Singapore, UK, USA). The interviews focused in on the core target for the 3G offering, namely, teenagers, young adults and family adults, all currently using mobile phones for personal usage. The sample was segmented by age, 16-19, 20-29 and 30-45 and by life-stage.

The research looked primarily at the following mobile multimedia services: photo messaging, mobile e-mail, video messaging and postcard messaging. However, the research also briefly touched on rich text messaging, and on video calling.

Of utmost importance in the study was to ensure that the respondents concentrated on the messaging format, and did not allow previous misconceptions about service or delivery of the service. They were therefore told to imagine that there would be no network problems, and not to concentrate on pricing.

The prompted statements offered to the sample as motivations for usage of the future multimedia mobile services can be classified to form eight broad segments of usage (Table 2):

1) Business
2) Formality
3) Urgency
4) Function
5) Price
6) Discretion
7) Personal Contact
8) Fun

The research model to be empirically tested in the Italian market is illustrated in Figure 1. The model is derived from the theories and hypothesis described in the preceding section. The relationship constituting the model also have support from prior theoretical and empirical work in the exploratory qualitative stage.

3.3 Exploratory Quantitative Stage

A following stage of analysis concentrates specifically on a quantitative marketing research conducted in the second quarter of 2002 through questionnaires on a sample of 1.000 Italian users of mobile (sampled among over 18 Italians).

Table 1 – Fieldwork details

Country	Sample	Field times
Brazil	Nationally representative of adults aged 18-64, who are economically active	6th – 20th March 2001
Germany	Nationally representative of adults aged 14+	23rd March – 5th April 2001
Italy	Nationally representative of adults aged 15+	23rd March – 5th April 2001
Singapore	Nationally representative of adults aged 15-64	13th – 26th April 2001
UK	Nationally representative of adults aged 15+	23rd March – 5th April 2001
USA	Nationally representative of adults aged 18+	21st – 30th March 2001

Table 2 – Motivation segmentation

- **Business**
- for business purposes
- **Formality**
- When I want to send a formal message
- **Urgency**
- When I need to know the message has arrived
- When I want to send urgent communication
- As a rapid way to stay in touch
- **Function**
1. To send a long piece of text
2. To send an attachment
3. When I don't feel like talking
4. Practical reason (like to show something I want to buy)
- **Price**
- When I want to communicate cheaply
- **Discretion**
1. Need to be discret and quiet
2. When talking would disturb people around me
3. Might disturb the person I'm trying to contact
Personal contact
• To keep in touch with friends/family abroad
• To send an intimate message
• To contact people I don't see very often
• As a personalised way to send a message
• To increase the feeling of contact
• To share an experience
• Nice for people to see me if they haven't done so for a while
• For longer greetings
• When I don't want to talk, but need to communicate
- **Fun**
• Joke or chit-chat with friends
• As a novel way to message
• To share an experience
• As it is just great fun
• To send pictures from my holiday
• To show something like a view
• To express creativity

1.000 interviews provide a sampling error (at 50%) of 3,1% (with a probability level of 95%).

The research, managed through telephone calls, tries to describe behaviors, roles and variables influencing adoption of mobile computing.

The results of the quantitative marketing research are now summarized. This research was structured in order to deepen the motivations and barriers towards the innovative services delivered through 3G mobile services, the eventual levels of demand and usage and the content types and formats that consumers express opinion for.

Figure 1 - Adapted TAM Model on the Adoption of multimedia mobile services

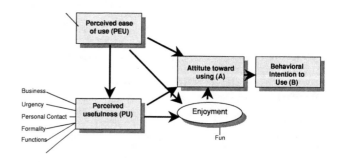

Figure 2 - Composition of the sample

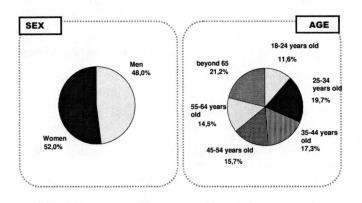

Table 3 – Features preferred

	Importance	
	Ranking	%
Usefulness	1°	31,3%
Easy of use	2°	26,7%
Price	3°	23,8%
Speed of use	4°	18,2%

Key items in the questionnaire used for analyzing the survey are as follows:

1. **Degree of service innovation** perceived by consumers. Respondents selected their answers from a list of innovative services categories;
2. **Interest** for the services categories under scrutiny;
3. **Preference** for means/platforms through which selected services can be accessed (portables, phone and/or Tv);
4. **Analysis** of key features of services (ease of use, speed, cost and usefulness);
5. **Ranking** of services features.

The services considered in the questionnaire are the following:
• interactive and real-time entertainment;
• data exchange among people and among people and various electronic devices;
• contextual and real-time shopping;
• portfolio and personal funds management;
• safety-related services;
• location-based services.

All the services have been considered rather innovative (the average is 7,1 on a 1-9 scale).

In terms of the interest expressed towards these services, the sample distributes as follows (see Figure 3).

Table 3 shows the mean features preferred by the people to be attracted to use these services.

"Usefulness" and easy of use are considered the most important variable in order to access the segments of population and, as shown in figure 4 and 5, there are different meaning assigned to these words.

Figure 4 – The meaning of usefulness

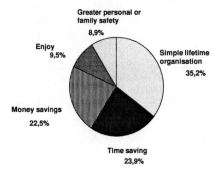

Figure 5 – The meaning of easy of use

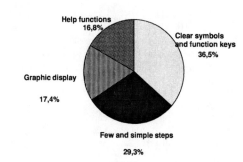

Figure 3 – Interest expressed towards multimedia mobile services

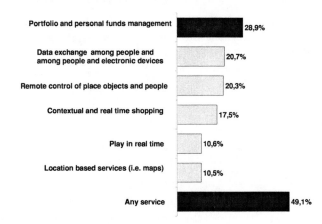

The final objective of the research was to identify the key descriptive elements of homogeneous segments of the population. This is relevant in order to define the right strategies to offer the new services in the proper and differentiated way.

The most statistically powerful variable in order to distinguish the behaviors of people is the degree of interest towards the innovative services.

If we then clusterize the sample using this variable, and cross it with the socio-demo data, it turns out that the kind of activities performed in life by the consumers is the strong predictor of their future use of the new services.

In particular, it is possible to describe two different segments as indicated in the following figure:
• cluster 1 is composed by people who declared they are not interested in the new services;
• the remaining 51% can be divided in two groups which are different in terms of the way firms should approach them to sell the new services.

The two segments are:
• the "professionals", that is people who mainly are managers or entrepreneurs in life, who are 38% of the interviewed base;
• the "students", who account for the remainder 13%.

Figure 6 – Main clusters of mobile users in the Italian market (base 1000 Italian mobile users)

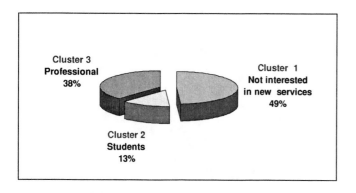

The purpose is now to identify the variables network operators can use to access the identified clusters. This is an essential piece of information for crafting the right strategies in order to "catch" the segments.

The "professional" segment is made of people who look for *usefulness* as the almost exclusive variable in order to access and pay for the service.

The "students" segment is made of people who look mainly for *low-cost* and *convenience*.

For all the interviewed base, an interesting relationship emerges: the degree of interest is inversely related to the degree of knowledge of the service. In particular it has been noticed that people who declare a low level of interest in these services, are those who actually know least the main features and potential outcomes of these services, even though the interviewer deeply explained the meaning of each service.

4. CONCLUSION

In this research, we attempt to identify valid factors that predict a user's adoption of 3G mobile multimedia services.

The findings show key characteristics and factors playing decisive roles in the development of strategies for the launch of multimedia mobile services.

The findings of this study have significant implications also in the perspective of research on mobile consumer behavior. Our study provides further evidence on the appropriateness of using the TAM model to measure the different dimensions of actual multimedia mobile usage and it provides empirical evidence that PEU (perceived easy of use), PU (perceived usefulness) are important factors that influence the user's adoption of 3G multimedia mobile services.

The findings of the study suggest important practical implications for businesses currently providing mobile multimedia services as well as that are planning to do so. It is evident from this study that to influence adoption of 3G multimedia services, perceived ease of use (PEU) and perceived usefulness (PU) must be enhanced.

ENDNOTES

1   The authors wish to acknowledge Massimo Farioli for his cooperation in the data processing phase

REFERENCES

Adams, D. A., R. R. Nelson, and P. A. Todd. (1992). "Perceived Usefulness, Ease of Use, and Usage of Information Technology: A Replication," *MIS Quarterly* 16 (2), 227-250.

Agarwal, R. and J. Prasad. (1997). "The Role of Innovation Characteristics and Perceived Voluntariness in the Acceptance of Information Technologies," *Decision Sciences* 28 (3), 557-581.

Agarwal, R. and J. Prasad. (1998). "A Conceptual and Operational Definition of Personal Innovativeness in the Domain of Information Technology," *Information Systems Research* 9 (2), 204-215.

Agarwal, R. and J. Prasad. (1999). "Are individual differences germane to the acceptance of new information technologies?," *Decision Sciences* 30 (2), 361-391.

Ajzen, I. (1991). "The Theory of Planned Behavior," *Organizational Behavior and Human Decision Processes* 50 (2), 179-211.

Ajzen, I. and M. Fishbein. (1980). *Understanding Attitudes and Predicting Social Behavior*, Eaglewood Cliffs, NJ: Prentice-Hall.

Chau, P. Y. K. (1997). "Reexamining a Model for Evaluating Information Center Success Using a Structural Equation Modeling Approach," *Decision Sciences* 28 (2), 309-334.

Chin, W. W. and P. A. Todd. (1995). "On the Use, Usefulness, and Ease of Use of Structural Equation Modeling in MIS Research: A Note of Caution," *MIS Quarterly* 19 (2), 237-246..

Davis, F. D. (1989). "Perceived Usefulness, Perceived Ease of Use, and User Acceptance of Information Technology," *MIS Quarterly* 13 (3), 319-340.

Davis, F. D., R. P. Bagozzi, and P. R. Warshaw. (1989). "User Acceptance of Computer Technology: A Comparison of Two Theoretical Models," *Management Science* 35 (8), 982-1003.

Gefen, D. and D. W. Straub. (1997). "Gender Differences in the Perception and Use of E-mail: An Extension to the Technology Acceptance Model," *MIS Quarterly* 21 (4), 389-400.

Moore, G. and I. Benbasat. (1991). "Development of an Instrument to Measure the Perceptions of Adopting an Information Technology Innovation," *Information Systems Research* 2 (3), 192-222.

Nokia (2002) 3G Market research Mobile Messaging: An End user perspective, Nokia Report

Rogers, E. (1995). *Diffusion of Innovations*, 4th ed., New York, NY: Free Press.

Mathieson, K. (1991). "Predicting User Intensions: Comparing the Technology Acceptance Model with

Theory Planned Behavior," *Information Systems Research* 2 (3), 192-222.

Straub, D., M. Limayem, and E. Karahanna-Evaristo. (1995). "Measuring System Usage: Implications for

IS Theory Testing," *Management Science* 41 (8), 1328-1342.

Szajna, B. (1994). "Software Evaluation and Choice: Predictive Validation of the Technology Acceptance

Instrument," *MIS Quarterly* 18 (3), 319-324.

Szajna, B. (1996). "Empirical Evaluation of the Revised Technology Acceptance Model," *Management*

Science 42 (1), 85-92.

VVA (2002). "Osservatorio Marche: Le Telecomunicazioni", VVA Report

Zhu W. and Fui-Hoon Nah (2002) "Factors Influencing Adoption of Mobile Computing" Issues and Trends of IT Management in Contemporary Organizations – IRMA Conference Proceedings

The Critical Role of Digital Rights Management Processes in the Context of the Digital Media Management Value Chain

Margherita Pagani
I-LAB Research Centre On Digital Economy
Bocconi University
Via Filippetti, 9 - 20136 Milan (Italy)
tel: ++39 02 58366920, fax: ++39 02 58363714
margherita.pagani@uni-bocconi.it

ABSTRACT

This paper set out to analyze the impact generated by the adoption of Digital Rights Management (DRM) processes on the typical Digital Media Management Value Chain activities and try to analyze the processes in the context of the business model.

Given the early stage of the theory development in the field of DRM the study follows the logic of grounded theory (Glaser and Strauss, 1967) by building the research on a multiple-case study methodology (Eisenhardt, 1989). The companies selected are successful players which have adopted DRM processes. These companies are Endemol, Digital Island, Adobe Systems, Intertrust, and the Motion Picture Association. In this paper we provide in-depth longitudinal data on these five players to show how companies implement DRM processes. Twelve DRM solution vendors are also analyzed in order to compare the strategies adopted.

After giving a definition of Intellectual Property and Digital Rights Management (section 1) the paper provides a description of the typical Digital Media Management Value Chain Activities and players involved along the different phases examined (section 2).

An in-depth description of Digital Rights Management processes is discussed in section 3.

Digital Rights Management processes are considered in the context of business model and they are distinguished into content processes, finance processes and Rights Management processes.

We conclude with a discussion of the model and main benefits generated by the integration of digital rights management and propose the most interesting directions for future research (section 4).

1. INTRODUCTION

The burgeoning market for information and entertainment over TV, PC and mobile devices is forcing media operators and content providers to develop their businesses in order to remain competitive. With the availability of more sophisticated content, and the increasingly popular trend of peer-to-peer distribution, the requirement for Digital Rights Management (DRM) is becoming essential and the early movers in the operator community are aware of the opportunities they will miss if their DRM solutions are not in place.

Digital Rights Management poses one of the greatest challenges for multimedia content providers and interactive media companies in the digital age in order to make profitable their interactive products and service catalogues and to face information security management issues.

The importance of protecting digital contents is crucial for content and media rights holders looking to distribute and re-distribute their digital contents over more and more digital channels (TV, radio, Internet).

The definition of Digital Rights Management (DRM) adopted in this study covers the description, identification, trading, protection, monitoring and tracking of all forms of rights uses over both tangible and intangible assets including management of rights holders relationships. DRM technologies enable secure management of digital processes and information.

The purpose of the study is to analyze the impact generated by the adoption of Digital Rights Management (DRM) processes on the typical Digital Media Management Value Chain activities trying to analyze the processes in the context of the business model.

Given the early stage of the theory development in the field of DRM we followed the logic of grounded theory (Glaser and Strauss, 1967) by building the research on a multiple-case study methodology (Eisenhardt, 1989). The companies selected are successful players which have adopted DRM processes. These companies are Endemol, Digital Island, Adobe Systems, Intertrust, and the Motion Picture Association. In this paper we provide in-depth longitudinal data on these five players to show how they implement DRM processes. Twelve DRM solution vendors are also analyzed in order to compare the strategies adopted.

After giving a definition of Intellectual Property and Digital Rights Management (section 1) the paper provides a description of the typical Digital Media Management Value Chain Activities and players involved along the different phases examined (section 2).

Digital Rights Management processes are considered in the context of business model and they are distinguished into content processes, finance processes and rights management processes (section 3).

We conclude with a discussion of the model and main benefits generated by the integration of Digital Rights Management and propose the most interesting directions for future research (section 4).

2. INTELLECTUAL PROPERTY: DEFINITION

Intellectual Property refers to all moral and property rights on intellectual works. Intellectual Property Rights (IPRs) are bestowed on owners of ideas, inventions, and creative expressions that have the status of property[1]. Just like tangible property, IPRs give owners the right to exclude others from access to or use of their property.

The first international treaties covering Intellectual Property Rights were created in the 1880s and they are administered by the World Intellectual Property Organisation (WIPO), established in 1967.

The newly revealed physics of information transfer on the Net has changed the economics and ultimately the laws governing the creation and dissemination of Intellectual Property.

The Net poses challenges both for owners, creators, sellers and users of Intellectual Property, as it allows for essentially cost-less copying of content. The development of Internet dramatically changes the economics of content, and content providers operate in an increasingly competitive marketplace where much content is distributed free (see the Napster phenomenon).

There are many issues that organisations need to address to fully realise the potential in their Intellectual Property. They can be summarised in the following:

- *Ownership:* clear definition of who owns the specific rights and under what circumstances;
- *Distribution*: definition of the distribution strategy (small trusted group or the mass market);
- *Protection*: definition of the content the organisations need to protect and the level of protection required;
- *Globalisation*: because of the slow harmonisation across countries regarding protection of Intellectual Property Rights what is acceptable in one country may have legal implications in another;
- *Standards*: understanding what standards are in development and how these may affect system development.

3. DIGITAL RIGHTS MANAGEMENT: FUNCTIONAL ARCHITECTURE

Digital Rights Management (DRM) covers the description, identification, trading, protection, monitoring and tracking of all forms of rights uses over both tangible and intangible assets, including management of rights holders relationships.

At the heart of any DRM technology is the notion of a rights model.

Rights models are schemes for specifying rights to a piece of content that a user can obtain in return for some consideration, such as registering, payment, or allowing her usage to be tracked.

Digital Rights Management (DRM) can be defined as the secure exchange of Intellectual Property, such as copyright-protected music, video, or text, in digital form over channels such as the Web, digital television, digital radio, the much talked 3G (third-generation) mobile or other electronic media, such as CDs and removable disks.

The technology protects content against unauthorised access, monitors the use of content, or enforces restrictions on what users can do with content[2].

Digital Rights Management (DRM) allows organisations that own or distribute content to manage the rights to their valuable Intellectual Property and package it securely as protected products for digital distribution to a potentially paying, global audience.

DRM technologies provide the basic infrastructure necessary for protecting and managing digital media, enterprise-trusted computing, and next generation distributed computing platforms, and they allow content owners to distribute digital products quickly, safely, and securely to authorised recipients.

The Digital Media Management Value Chain can be described by the following main areas which play a key role in building digital rights-enabled systems:

1. *Intellectual Property (IP) Asset Creation and Acquisition*: This area manages the creation and acquisition of content so it can be easily traded. This includes asserting rights when content is first created (or reused and extended with appropriate rights to do so) by various content creators/providers. This area supports:
   - **rights validation**: to ensure that content being created from existing content includes the rights to do so;
   - **rights creation**: to allow rights to be assigned to new content, such as specifying the rights owners and allowable usage permissions;
   - **rights workflow**: to allow for content to be processed through a series of workflow steps for review and/or approval of rights (and content).
2. *Intellectual Property Media Asset Management*: After the finished content is bought, this area manages and enables the trade of content. The digitalisation of the television signal and the storage of the materials that have been purchased need to manage the descriptive metadata and rights metadata (e.g., parties, uses, payments, etc.). This area supports:
   - **repository functions**: to enable the access/retrieval of content in potentially distributed databases and the access/retrieval of metadata;
   - **trading functions**: to enable the assignment of licenses to parties who have traded agreements for rights over content, including payments from licensees to rights holders (e.g., royalty payments).

3. *Intellectual Property Asset Delivery Management*: This area manages the distribution and usage of content through different platforms (TV, radio, Web, 3G mobile) once it has been traded. This includes supporting constraints over traded content in specific desktop systems/software. This area supports:
   - **permissions management**: to enable the usage environment to honor the rights associated with the content (e.g. if the user only has the right to view the document, then printing will not be allowed);
   - **tracking management**: to enable the monitoring of the usage of content where such tracking is part of the agreed to license conditions (e.g., the user has a license to play a video 10 times).

4. DIGITAL RIGHTS MANAGEMENT: VALUE CHAIN ACTIVITIES

After defining the functional architecture, we can describe at a first level the DRM Value Chain identifying the activities supported by each segment and the players involved. At a second level we try to understand the DRM processes in the context of the Digital Content Management Value Chain and the impact of these processes on the business model.

The data provided refer to an in-depth longitudinal survey on five players (Endemol, Digital Island, Adobe Systems, Intertrust, and the Motion Picture Association) trying to understand how they implement DRM processes.

The Digital Rights Management Value Chain can be described by six main segments: contract & rights management, rights information storage, licence management, persistent content protection, clearing house services, billing services.

Each segment along the Value Chain is characterised by specific activities:

1. *Contract and Rights Management*: the registration of contract terms and rights, tracking of usage, and payment of royalties (residuals);
2. *Rights Information Storage*: the storage of rights information (e.g., play track five times) and usage rules (e.g., if they have a UK domain and have paid) as well as rights segmentation and pricing structures;
3. *Licence Management*: the management and issuing of licences in line with the Rights and Conditions. Without a licence the consumer can't use the content;
4. *Persistent Content Protection*: the use of encryption, keys, and digital watermarking to securely package digital content;
5. *Clearing House Services*: managing and tracking the distribution of the packaged content and the license in line with the defined Rights Information;
6. *Billing Services*: charging consumers for purchased content and payment to parties within the Value Chain.

Various players in the market are affected by Digital Rights Management, in particular all those operators involved with ideation, creation, realization, enabling and handling of contents. The role of these operators is to provide contents successively broadcast on the networks channels, radio, the Internet and other media. The different players involved along the Value Chain can be summarised in the following (see p. 963):

Figure 1. Typical Digital Media Management Value Chain Activities

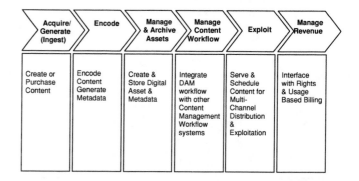

- *Content Author/Creator* (e.g., Canal+, Reuters) or any other media or non-media company that produces content for internal or external use;
- *Content Publisher/Aggregator* (e.g., IPC Magazines, Flextech Television, BskyB) it buys various content and aggregate it into channels aimed at a particular lifestyle or niche;
- *Content Distributor*, e.g. W.H. Smith News, BskyB, NordeaTV;
- *Service Provider/eTailer*, e.g., T-Online.com, Yahoo.com.

In the first phase of the DRM Value Chain (*Contract&Rights Management*) after the author has created the content, the aggregator packages it in a container which provides persistent protection, enforcing the rights which the author has granted. This may be written as an applet that travels with the content which will be encrypted.

In the second phase (*Rights Information Storage*) the aggregator specifies the rights which apply to the content using products such as IBM, EMMS or Microsoft which encode the rights using an XML-based standard such as XrML or XMCL.

In the third phase (*Licence Management*) the consumer purchases the rights to use the content, the eTailer obtains the content from the distributor and requests a license from the content clearing house. The license may well be written in XML and may travel with the packaged content or separately.

The fourth phase is *Digital Asset Protection*. The consumer cannot access the content without the license. The Media Player, e.g., Real Video Player, interprets the license and enforces the rights granted to the consumer. That may include how many times or for how long time they can access the asset, whether they can duplicate it or 'rip' CDs from it.

With reference to the Digital Content Management Value Chain described above, DRM processes play an important role in the encode activity (Contract Management& Rights Storage), management and archive assets (Encrypt / PackageContent Asset Protection), management workflow (Key & License Generation) and exploit (Key/License Management & Clearing-houseServices) (Figure 2).

Figure 2. *DCM Value Chain Activities & DRM processes*

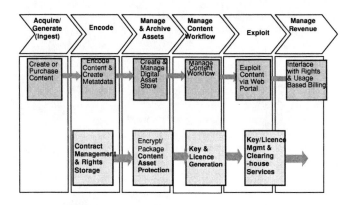

At a second level of analysis, we try to understand Digital Rights Management processes, described above, in the context of the business model.

All the processes analysed can be grouped in three broad categories (Figure 3):
1. **Content Processes**: include all systems and processes that enable the creation/capture, formatting, packaging, protection and storage of trusted channel content, control of when and how content is released, where and when it gets used and how long it remains there;
2. **Finance Processes**: include all systems and processes (payments) between the Financial Clearing House and the other players along the Value Chain (author/creator, publisher, distributor, consumer);
3. **Rights Management Processes**: include all Content Clearing House services which authorise the usage of rights to distributors, service providers, and consumers.

Figure 3. *The Processes in the Context of the Business Model*

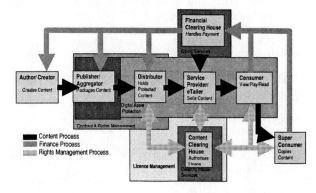

5. DIGITAL RIGHTS MANAGEMENT BENEFITS

There are many benefits generated by Digital Right Management.

The survey has been carried out through questionnaires on a sample of successful players which have adopted DRM processes. These companies are Endemol, Digital Island, Adobe Systems, Intertrust, and the Motion Picture Association. Twelve DRM solution vendors are also analyzed in order to compare the strategies adopted.

The first main area concerns all benefits related to Contract & Rights Management.

Digital Rights Management allows a better management of bought-in content rights to maximise return on investment, and it avoids potentially expensive misuse.

A better management of content is allowed also by means of the creation of what-if scenarios for potential new revenue streams on the basis of the cost and ownership of content rights[3]. New contents can no longer constrained to budget on a cost basis but they can now budget on the basis of forecast rights revenue.

Digital Rights Management generates benefits also with reference to the sale of rights, allowing a retained control of the sale of content rights and the conditions of sale in mass or niche distribution environments.

DRM allows the establishment of flexible business models for digital content sales (e.g., rental or purchase, play or edit, burn to CD, or just play online).

Segmentation of content allows to create different versions with different rights and conditions for different markets.

Information that has previously been stored in a vast number of separate databases can now be merged, sorted, and analysed, resulting in the creation of a personal profile or data image of a subject based on his or her electronic data composite[4].

Consumer acceptance will determine the success of the market. The critical factor for vendors is to address the right market (publishing, audio, video and software).

6. CONCLUSIONS

Digital Rights Management allows organisations to manage the rights to their valuable Intellectual Property and package it securely as protected products for digital distribution.

It's not solely about technology; Digital Rights Management works across the people, processes and technology boundaries.

The key issues include:
- handling of complex sets of rights within each asset;
- rights licensing and management, and digital rights protection;
- understanding and design of revenue generation and collection models;
- standards - flexible rights languages and content formats;
- globalisation – territorial issues, both legal and commercial;
- ownership of rights.

Digital Rights Management is emerging as a formidable new challenge, and it is essential for DRM systems to provide interoperable services. Industry and users are now demanding that standards be developed to allow interoperability so as not to force content owners and managers to encode their works in proprietary formats or systems.

The market, technology, and standards, are still maturing Digital Rights Management should be considered an integral part of company's Digital Media Management framework.

ENDNOTES

[1] G. Scalfi, *Manuale di Diritto Privato,* UTET 1986 p. 61

[2] Forrester, 2002

[3] See also D.C. Burke, "Digital Rights Management: from zero to hero?" Cap Gemini Ernst & Young, speech at IBC Nordic Euroforum Conference held in Stockolm (Sweden) on 20th February 2002

[4] Tapscott, D., (1999) "Privacy in the Digital Economy" in *The Digital Economy*, McGraw-Hill, p.275

REFERENCES

Alattar, A. M. (2000), 'Smart Images' Using Digimarc's Watermarking Technology', *Proceedings of the IS&T/SPIE's 12th International Symposium on Electronic Imaging* San Jose, CA, 25ᵗʰ Jan, Volume 3971, Number 25

Association of American Publishers Copyright Committee, (2000), *Contractual Licensing, Technological Measures and Copyright Law.* Washington, DC: Association of American Publishers

Association of American Publishers Rights and Permissions Advisory Committee, (2000), *The New & Updated Copyright Primer: A Survival Guide to Copyright and the Permissions Process.*

Burns, C. 1995, *Copyright Management and the NII: Report to the Enabling Technologies Committee of the Association of American Publishers.*, Association of American Publishers, Washington, DC

Burke D.C., (2002) *"Digital Rights Management: from zero to hero?"* Cap Gemini Ernst & Young, speech at IBC Nordic Euroforum Conference held in Stockolm (Sweden).

Chaudhuri, Abjihit K., et al. (1995), 'Copyright Protection for Electronic Publishing over Computer Networks' *IEEE Network*, Volume 9, Number 3 , May-June 1995, pp. 12 -20

Gervais, D. J. (1997), 'Electronic Rights Management and Digital Identifier Systems' *Journal of Electronic Publishing*, Volume 4 Number 3, Ann Arbor, MI: University of Michigan Press.

Iannella R. (2001), Digital Rights Management (DRM) Architectures in D-Lib Magazine Vol. 7 N.6

Interactive Multimedia Association (1994), ed. *Proceedings: Technological Strategies for Protecting Intellectual Property in the Networked Multimedia Environment.* Annapolis, MD: Interactive Multimedia Association.

Kahin, B. and Kate Arms (1996), eds. *Forum on Technology-Based Intellectual Property Management: Electronic Commerce for Content.* Special issue of *Interactive Multimedia News*, Volume 2.

Lyon, G. (2001), *The Internet Marketplace and Digital Rights Management.* National Institute for Standards and Technology.

Risher, C. and Rosenblatt B. (1998) "The Digital Object Identifier - An Electronic Publishing Tool for the Entire Information Community." *Serials Review*, Volume 24 Number.3/4, Dec. 1998:13-21. Stamford, CT: JAI Press, Inc.

Rosenblatt, B. (1996) "Two Sides of the Coin: Publishers' Requirements for Digital Intellectual Property Management." Inter-Industry Forum on Technology-Based Intellectual Property Management, Washington, DC.

Rosenblatt, B. (1997) "The Digital Object Identifier: Solving the Dilemma of Copyright Protection Online." *Journal of Electronic Publishing*, Volume 3 Number 2, Ann Arbor, MI: University of Michigan Press.

Scalfi, G., (1986) *Manuale di Diritto Privato, UTET,* Torino, p.61

Silbert, O. et al. (1995), "DigiBox: A Self-Protecting Container for Information Commerce." Proceedings of the First USENIX Workshop on Electronic Commerce, New York, NY.

Souzis, A. et al. (2000) *ICE Implementation Cookbook: Getting Started with Web Syndication.*

Stefik, M. (1999) *The Internet Edge: Social, Technical, and Legal Challenges for a Networked World.* Cambridge, MA: MIT Press.

Tapscott, D., (1999) "Privacy in the Digital Economy" in *The Digital Economy*, McGraw-Hill, p.275

Vaidhyanathan, S. (2001) Copyrights and Copywrongs: The Rise of Intellectual Property and How It Threatens Creativity. New York: NYU Press.

Van Tassel, J. (2001) Digital Content Management: Creating and Distributing Media Assets by Broadcasters.

Washington, DC: NAB Research and Planning Department. Available from National Association of Broadcasters at (202) 429-5373

Vonder Haar, S. (2001) Digital Rights Management- Securing New Content Revenue Streams. Yankee Group Report.

Supplier Integration in Web-Based Supply Chains

Somendra Pant, Rajesh Sethi, and Anju Sethi
Clarkson University, School of Business
Potsdam, NY 13699-5790
(315) 268-7728, pants@clarkson.edu.

EXTENDED ABSTRACT

It is increasingly being argued that in today's competitive marketplace, an important way of securing strategic advantage for companies or original equipment manufacturers (OEMs) is the use of highly integrated supply chains. In such chains, the OEM, its key suppliers, and distributors operate as one integrated unit to effectively serve the customer. Integrated supply chains are expected to enhance productivity, lower costs, reduce response times, and lead to the development of superior new products. More and more OEMs are either already implementing or are planning to embrace such integrated Web-based Supply chains (Teach, 2002).

The main responsibility for the creation of an integrated supply chain falls on OEMs. They decide which of their suppliers should become the primary or main partners in the chain and which will be secondary suppliers. The trend is to have few key suppliers for a particular part or material. Thus, suppliers who are included in the supply chain get a large share of the OEM's business. However, OEMs, in turn, expect quite a bit from these suppliers by way of technological infrastructure, commitment, and identification with the supply chain. Generally such suppliers are expected to install sophisticated Web-based supply chain systems that are compatible with the OEM's systems and provide open access to the OEM to their information systems, databases, drawings, and documents.

However, suppliers may not share the same view that OEMs have regarding integrated Web-based supply chains. They may see a number of risks in joining an integrated supply chain and thus may hesitate to do so. From the suppliers' perspective, they are being asked to tie their future with that of the OEM in a major way. Providing the OEM a great deal of access to their information systems, databases, drawings, and documents makes suppliers feel vulnerable. In addition, often suppliers are small or medium in size and are subject to price and other pressures from the OEM. Another cause for concern is that while suppliers often do not have the technical infrastructure to implement a fully integrated supply chain management system, they are pressured by the OEM to do so. This ends up increasing costs and eroding supplier profitability. In view of the above, suppliers face a real dilemma. On the one hand they have the concern of being exploited by the OEMs in integrated supply chain systems; on the other hand they run the risk of being left out by the OEMs and falling behind competition.

Some key factors that are likely to make suppliers reluctant in joining integrated supply chains are information technology infrastructure (Wagner, 2001), lack of embeddedness of information systems (Uzzi, 1996), business process redesign (Grover, 1993), and low level of trust between suppliers and OEMs (Munson, 1999; Hart, 1997; Premkumar et al 1994, 1995). We also expect that there are likely to be several additional important considerations that can make suppliers particularly hesitant in joining integrated supply chains. The purpose of our research effort is to identify many such considerations that have escaped the attention of supply chain researchers. We briefly discuss one such issue below.

Suppliers' Willingness to Acquire Supply Chain Identity. If a supply chain has to work successfully in an integrated manner, it is important that its members work toward the interest of the overall chain rather than their own interests. This requires that members identify with the supply chain rather than merely with their respective organizations and perceive a stake in the success of the chain (Mackie and Goethals 1987). High chain-based identity enhances the perception of intra-chain similarities and leads to psychological acceptance of individuals from other partner organizations and their work methods

(Ashforth and Mael, 1989; Mackie and Goethals, 1987). In other words, a feeling of psychological ownership of the supply-chain arises among individuals from different partner organizations, which enhances cooperative behaviors. However, individuals in supplier organizations are likely to have separate deep-rooted organization-based identities. Since individuals tend to behave in ways that enhance their organizational identities, they prefer the work methods, goals, and time horizons of their own organization over those of others (Ashforth and Mael 1989). Also, some suppliers can have a fear that if they integrate themselves very strongly with supply chains of OEMs, it can affect their identity. Thus, unless suppliers are highly motivated to join the supply chain and merge their identity with the supply chain identity, and unless they have carefully thought through how they will maintain their own organizational identity while still participating in the chain, they may have problems getting integrated into the supply chain. Thus issues of interest that emerge are: how does organizational identity of suppliers affects their involvement in OEMs Web-based supply chain initiatives, and, furthermore how does the level of identification of suppliers with that of OEMs affects their commitment to the OEMs Web-based supply chains.

Research Method We propose to adopt the grounded theory approach to study the implementation of integrated supply chain systems at a few firms and their suppliers' though intensive interaction and close observation. We have already identified a major distributor of industrial goods in the US that is implementing an integrated web-based supply chain system with its key suppliers. Over the duration of this research we will visit the distributor and its suppliers and observe the phenomena of its integration into the supply chain system, hold discussions with people involved, carry on structured and semi-structured interviews with managers and IT personnel, and participate in their planning sessions or meetings. We will then analyze the information so gathered and triangulate different sources of information to draw conclusions. Interviews will be content analyzed to identify themes that emerge, which, in turn are expected to lead to new theoretical insights into supplier-OEM relationships in highly integrated chains. Since the proposed research adopts a grounded theory approach with a view to gaining new theoretical perspectives, these perspectives will need to be subsequently tested through detailed surveys.

REFERENCES

Ashforth, Blake, E. and Fred Mael (1989), "Social Identity Theory and the Organization,"
Academy of Management Review, 14 (January), 20-39.

Grover, V. An empirically derived model for the adoption of customer-based interorganizational systems, *Decision Sciences* 1993; 24 (3), 603-649.

Hart, and Saunders, C. (1997). Power and Trust: Critical Factors in the Adoption and Use of Electronic Data Interchange, Organization Science, January-February, 23-42.

Mackie, Diane M. and George R. Goethals (1987), "Individual and Group Goals," in *Review of Personality and Social Psychology*, C. Hendrick, ed. Newbury Park, CA: Sage Publications, 144-66.

Munson, C. L., Rosenblatt, M. J., and Rosenblatt, Z. (1999). The Use and Abuse of Power in Supply Chains, *Business Horizons*, January-February, 55-68.

Premkumar, G. and Ramamurthy, K. The role of interorganizational and organizational factors on the decision mode for adoption of interorganizational systems, *Decision Sciences* 1995; 26 (3): 303-335.

Premkumar, G., Ramamurthy, K., and Nilakanta, S. (1994). Implementation of Electronic Data Interchange: An Innovation Diffusion Perspective, *Journal of Management Information Systems*, Vol. 11, No. 2, 157-176.

Teach, E. (2002). Working on the Chain, CFO Magazine.

Uzzi, B (1996). The source and consequences for embeddedness for the economic performance of organizations: The network effect, *American Sociological Review* 61: 674-498.

Wagner, M. (2001). Customers warming to Oracle11i. *InternetWeek*, November 26, 2001, p. 12.

Campus-Wide Faculty Development: No "Mission Impossible." Results from Implementation of Intensive Summer Workshops Programs

Katia Passerini, Kemal Cakici, and William Koffenberger
The George Washington University
(202) 994 2770 (w) (202) 994 0454 (m)
pkatia@gwu.edu, cakici@gwu.edu, billkoff@gwu.edu

OVERVIEW

Faculty development is the key enabling strategy for the successful introduction of technology in the classroom and at a distance, required as universities strive towards achieving campus-wide technology competencies. Motivating the entire faculty to acquire new technology skills and to experiment with applications in their area of competence has been regarded by many as "mission impossible." Technology training and its curriculum implementation often require a time investment that may discourage faculty commitment.

To foster technological innovation, the Instructional Technology Laboratory (the center which provides pedagogical and technological support to faculty at the George Washington University) created an intensive development program supported by partnerships across several university departments. Faculty participating in the summer development institute and undertaking new projects (as a result thereof) receive incentives and rewards (release time, student assistance, monetary and resource support).

The paper will present the success of the institute evaluated on a series of criteria: faculty needs and satisfaction, ability to meet faculty time-constraints with an intensive program format, and short-term and long-term benefits in terms of new initiatives implementation. It also highlights lessons learned on successful, and less successful, incentives.

The paper does not address how faculty development programs impact students' learning and satisfaction. Effectiveness questions on classroom technology initiatives are elaborated in several other studies, and are out of the scope of this review.

THE FACULTY DEVELOPMENT PROGRAM ORGANIZATION

Summer Intensive Workshop Initiative (SIWI), is a faculty development program designed to significantly increase faculty competency with advanced instructional technologies. Unlike other approaches that focus primarily on a technical skills 'boot camp', the SIWI seeks to provide faculty a progressive series of experiences that sequentially build on different skill levels and abilities and that include both pedagogical and technical experiences and training. Additionally, it incrementally adds new direct staff support to assist faculty during design and implementation of instructional technology projects started as part of the SIWI. The initiative involves units across the University community to provide complete solutions and tap existing expertise and resources.

The SIWI accomplishes the goal of increased faculty proficiency and use of instructional technologies through a series of intensive three-day long workshops and seminar summer institutes. Since 1999, each summer, at least three of these summer institutes - comprising the yearly Summer Intensive Workshop Initiative - are flexibly offered to faculty in the form of learning tracks/modules. The tracks/modules are designed to provide a progressive series of experiences ranging from basic computer skills, through computer based research skills, including productivity and classroom presentation tools and skills, and progressing to elaborate pedagogically sound multimedia and mediated

learning projects. Pedagogical, technical, and content specialists provide year-long support and assistance to faculty, as they implement effective instructional technologies and approaches learned through the SIWI.

THE "WHY "OF FACULTY DEVELOPMENT

Several colleges and universities in the US currently offer faculty instructional and technology support services. Regardless of the services availability, the core problem faced by faculty often remains the lack of time and funds to undertake technology-based projects. Simultaneously, students' expectations surrounding faculty use of technological resources to support learning increased exponentially. In the last few years, scholars often find themselves openly challenged in exploiting the new pedagogical opportunities and advantages of Web-based course delivery. An on-line survey conducted on faculty members at the George Washington University showed that over 80% of the 79 respondents surveyed felt a higher than average need for additional support to use information communication technologies, such as the World Wide Web (Figure 1).

These numbers show the importance of initiatives for faculty development. Results from the survey conducted in 1999 assisted in increasing University Official's awareness of faculty needs and garnered support for the launch of the SIWI program.

THE "HOW" OF FACULTY DEVELOPMENT

Intensive three-day sessions that provide faculty with opportunities to experiment with new technology, assist in demonstrations, discuss curricular impacts, and submit grant proposals for technology-based projects in the class-

Figure 1

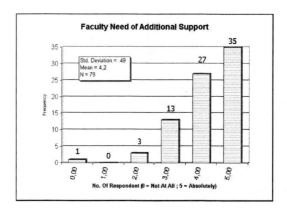

Figure 2

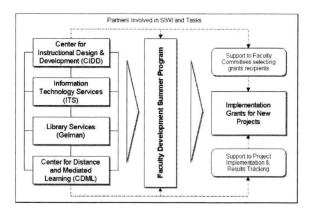

room are component of successful development programs. The SIWI development plan differs from similar efforts in its reliance on a partnership based management model In terms of implementation, the SIWI experience shows the importance of partnership and coordination across university centers (university teaching centers, libraries, instructional technology labs, computer resource centers) to provide the full spectrum of services needed by faculty in their technology-based curriculum innovations (Figure 2). This model brings increased success due to synergistic efforts, and offers the ability to serve the diverse need of instructors in different fields. The partnership model also brings opportunities for program cost sharing across different units, while achieving an enhanced level of content variety and *ad hoc* support for each participant.

THE "WHAT" OF FACULTY DEVELOPMENT

A successful development program must not only answer the question on how to use technology, it must also explain the benefits of different instructional technologies. To this end, the SIWI seeks to encourage and support exchange of ideas, experiences, practical tips, and interactions coupled with skill based activities. Success stories from faculty in the same field inspire innovation. Luncheon scholar showcases encourage sharing of research findings among participants. Guest speakers and key figures in technology-based instruction also provide knowledge and lessons learned. Discussions occur about project partnerships supported by the institute through grants and awards. Opportunities for hands-on experience, assisted projects, and demonstrations in two-hour blocks focus on both curriculum issues and software skills during the program.

The application software used in the summer workshops includes the MS Office suite, Web-authoring software, and graphical software packages for image scanning and editing, such as Adobe PhotoShop. Other packages include: Adobe Acrobat, Adobe Premiere, RealProducer and the web-based courseware applications. Future edition of SIWI may present full multimedia development workshops, - using Macromedia Director, Flash and Authorware - and video production workshops.

THE "WHEN" OF FACULTY DEVELOPMENT

A faculty development institute offered during the summer sessions reduces faculty time constraints by creating a pedagogical and technical support system available to participating instructors during less demanding months of the year. The institute approach proposes a track-by-track progression of skills, building competencies on the basis of a phased approach, from basic to advanced skills. Faculty enjoy an intensive exposure to technology and computer mediated instruction in the summer institutes. They then conduct hands-on activities and receive project support throughout the academic year. An Instructional Technology Lab and content experts provide assistance on field-specific implementations. Teaching assistants are also assigned to support academic projects. Although the preferred progression to higher-level tracks is on a year-to-year basis, faculty can complete all tracks during the same summer.

THE "WHERE" OF FACULTY DEVELOPMENT

A final evaluation form was completed at the end of the 3-day event. Participants agreed and strongly agreed with the statements in the final evaluations. The only statement that participants disagreed strongly with was the proposal that SIWI should be held off-campus. Participants seemed to enjoy the ability to go to their offices during breaks. The rationale for the proposal was related to the organizers' fear that there would have been a high "mortality" rate for specific seminars and workshops. There were in fact some cases in which attendance to specific workshops was lower, but faculty appreciated the flexibility to choose not to attend specific events if constrained by their schedules.

RESULTS FROM IMPLEMENTATION

The evaluations conducted after each edition witness a success story with highly encouraging results. Overall, participant satisfaction was very high: (scale out of 5.0)

- Participants reported that they were satisfied with SIWI (mean=4.76)
- They found that SIWI motivated them to participate in other learning tracks (mean=4.75)
- They found that SIWI encouraged collegiality (mean=4.70).

Several comments recognized and praised the organizers for a job well done. Partners had organized the initiative with clear expectations, but had several concerns:

- Faculty would not find the time, nor the motivation, to participate in SIWI
- Limited grants and incentives would discourage participation
- Attendance might be discouraged because program participation and often classroom innovation are not generally included in tenure criteria
- It was not clear how self-selection would impact successful faculty completion of a learning track.
- It would be difficult to forecast whether any of SIWI endeavors would be transformed into specific products and projects by participating faculty

Many of these concerns proved unsubstantiated. Faculty participation was very high, with a fair distribution across academic roles (as represented in Figure 3). Faculty enthusiasm was high throughout the workshops, in spite of the intensive schedule and the amount of new material presented.

A number of new projects were started as a result of ideas and skills attained in SIWI. While specific impacts on classroom effectiveness are difficult to measure, faculty indicates that skills acquired in the SIWI have made a positive impacts on their teaching. Analysis of walk-ins at the Instructional Technology Lab facilities shows that at least 20% of participants repeatedly used faculty support facilities after SIWI, and they used applications that were demonstrated at the workshops (scanning, narrated PowerPoint, HTML, CD-ROM burning, and video digitization). In addition, many participants started using web-based applications in their courses (e.g. use of streaming technol-

Figure 3

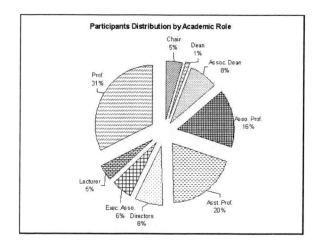

ogy and Adobe Acrobat), or moved to an advanced level of on-line course implementation using pedagogical strategies demonstrated in the workshops.

LESSONS LEARNED

SIWI feedback clearly portrays a success story. The responses range between the levels 3 to 5, which are values above the mean. Participants were satisfied with the events and with the organization. The lessons learned in this initiative are therefore less a result of faculty concerns than reflective of troubleshooting and administrative hurdles that the organizers encountered.

The main reason why the SIWI programs ran smoothly is related to the staff efforts in troubleshooting computer hardware problems. Staff undertook last minute installations of software not available on the computer network. Often, the number of computers properly functioning in a given lab was less than the number of participants. Several computers appeared infected with viruses. Although all the problems were successfully addressed, careful testing of hardware and software prior to faculty development events is critical.

As new and advanced learning tracks are added, evaluation of faculty skills and subsequent assignment to learning tracks, will become much more important. In some instances, self-selection disrupted the pace of instruction because a few participants did not have prior Windows experience. With advanced sessions, problems associated with overconfidence in prior skills may have significant impacts on the program's success and faculty satisfaction.

Although speakers were well received, the luncheon presentations were often regarded with less enthusiasm. Future programs should reduce luncheon presentations and while increasing networking, information exchange and opportunities to share experiences and build research partnerships.

Strategies for follow up activities should be carefully integrated in the development of a faculty development program. Faculty should be made aware that participation entails the initiation of a project, often extending over an entire semester that will draws upon the skills and the resources made available in the summer workshops. This goal could be better achieved if participation was competitively based on willingness to start new projects. Faculty would apply to SIWI on a competitive basis by submitting an outline of their projects and highlighting their training and resource needs.

Implementing this approach would also allow SIWI partners to have a clearer vision of audience needs, background and objectives. A needs assessment was indeed one of the most crucial missing elements of SIWI. The inability to select audiences with competing project proposals led to the inability to target objectives and needs. By making registration to SIWI more competitive and based on project proposals, audience needs would be identified and the emphasis would move towards the realization of specific products, rather than short-term technology training.

An Exploratory Study on how Double Majors, MIS Internship, and GPA Influence Job Opportunity

Wayne Huang, Hao Lou, and John Day
Department of MIS, College of Business
Ohio University, Ohio 45701
huangw@ohio.edu, lou@ohio.edu, dayj@ohio.edu

INTRODUCTION

About two years ago, most MIS majors had multiple job offers, even before their graduation. Now, due to the current economic downturn, some MIS graduates don't find a job six months or even one year after their graduation. According to the National Association of Colleges and Employers (NACE) survey of 230 companies, 2002 has been a difficult year for college graduates seeking employment (Hames, 2002), and many firms are slashing their entry-level hires by 20% this year compared with 2001 (Dash, 2002). In this slow economy, employers are selectively choosing their campus recruits — including entry-level IT applicants.

Many MIS departments are reviewing and revising their curricula in order to equip their graduates with the most marketable knowledge and skills for future job markets. Educational policy makers need to understand the key factors influencing the placement of their graduates. They need to know how their majors can increase their chances of placement in a very competitive job market. Some potential factors include taking a double major, receiving a high GPA or doing an internship. Traditionally, GPA has been considered to be the single most important factor influencing a graduate's job hunting success (Hames, 2002). As business environments have changed substantially in the last decade, industries don't look for graduates who have only perfect GPA scores. MIS curricula have also changed with more options being available to the students including the ability to take a double major or an internship, which can be important vehicles for securing a job after graduation. However, there is relatively little empirical research in the MIS research literature that can determine if these factors really have an impact on placement.

This research intends to explore the affect these factors have on placement. A survey instrument was used to collect data in order to evaluate the importance of double majors, GPA and internships on the placement of MIS graduates.

LITERATURE REVIEW

Historically, larger corporations have valued academic achievement and typically look for students who graduated from top schools and/or universities with top grade point averages (GPAs) of at least 3.5 out of 4.0. An excellent GPA may normally reflect a high level of material mastery, but real-world skills and experience can make a recent college graduate stand out from the crowd (Hames, 2002).

Prior studies suggest that recently, GPA is not the only important factor influencing placement of university graduates. Internships are another important option for graduates to increase their chances for receiving job offers (Goo, 2002; Knouse, Tanner, and Harris, 1999; Neimeyer, Bowman, and Stewart, 2001). Internships provide students an opportunity to break free from classroom theory and practice what they've learned in the business community. Internship programs also help students to confirm whether they are on the right career path. As they gain knowledge, some elect to focus on a particular aspect of a career, while others opt to change course entirely (Ben-David, 2002). University students might also benefit from their internship experience by increasing their chance of securing a job after graduation (Knouse 1999; Schambach and Kephart 1997). However, the positive effect of an internship on job placement has not been found in research with large samples (Fuller and Schoenberger 1991), but only in research with small samples and limited controls on factors such as ability (Sagen 2000).

Another emerging trend is that students are able to take more than one major (normally double majors) to increase their marketability. For example, SNL Securities LLC Inc. will hire four or five entry-level IT graduates who have a mix of Web development, Web design and technical support skills, according to Barbara Kessler, human resources director at the financial publishing firm. As an additional example, some accounting knowledge is a big plus for someone who wants to work at a financial services firm (Dash, 2002).

Statistical evidence about the affect of GPA, internships, and double majors on the number of job offers is scare, especially in MIS research literature. Therefore, this research intends to explore whether the factors of GPA, internship and double major could be used to leverage job opportunities for MIS graduates.

RESEARCH METHODOLOGY

MIS Seniors in the business school of a large state university were the subjects in this survey. A survey instrument measuring relevant dependent variables was used. Students were asked for demographic background information, the number of majors completed, when they declared their MIS major, whether they completed internships, and whether they have received full time job offers.

There were 360 students in the MIS program, and 120 were seniors who will graduate in 2003. A cover letter written by the MIS department chair was sent to all MIS seniors, inviting them to participate in the survey. The survey questions were put on a website so that the subjects could fill in the questionnaire anytime within one week following the distribution of the cover letter. 65 students volunteered to fill in the questionnaire, which represented a 54% response rate. Of the 65 filling in the questionnaire, 58 of them were usable. 34% of the valid subjects were female and 66% were male.

RESEARCH FINDINGS

Figure 1 indicates that most of the students surveyed (55%) have a GPA ranging from 3.1-3.49, 33% of them have a GPA ranging from 3.5-4.0, and 12% have a GPA ranging from 2.5-3.0. Therefore, the majority of the surveyed students have GPAs above 3.1.

Figure 2 shows that most students (41%) believe that internship experience is the single most important factor influencing the success of finding a full time job after graduation. This is very interesting because it is very different from the traditional view that GPA is the single most important factor in finding a full time job (Hames, 2002). In fact, only 2% of the surveyed students think that a high GPA is the most important factor in finding a full time job. Further, 24% of them think that communication skills are the most important factor for them in finding a full time job, and 21% consider technical skills as the most important factor. These findings reflect prevailing views of current MIS students, which may have an impact of future MIS curriculum.

From the student perspective, the internship experience has now become the most important factor influencing job placement for MIS graduates. Moreover, as shown in Figure 3, 30% of the students expect to obtain full time job offers from the company where they had their internships; whereas 70% expect to find a full time job in companies other than the company offering the internship.

Figure 4 shows that nearly half of the MIS majors (47%) are taking two, three, or more majors. Random interviews with those taking more than two majors indicate that most of them plan to do double majors, but either (1) they are not sure whether they could cope with the core courses required to do the preferred double major, or (2) they don't know which two majors would be most welcome in job market in the near future. As a result, they are taking more than two majors for the time being but will probably not complete all of them.

It is interesting to note that, while nearly half of the MIS seniors realized the importance of double major (see Figure 4), only less than 7% of the surveyed students thought that the double major was the most important factor in finding a full time job (see Figure 3). It seems that a double major is not perceived as an important factor for job hunting, but rather is perceived as an important factor for providing more career options which has could also have an affect on placement.

However, perception may not always reflect reality. Figure 5 shows that 45% of the students received job offers that were not MIS-related. This indicates that 45% of the jobs offered require knowledge and skills other than MIS, which could indicate the importance of double majors in job hunting.

Additional information was gathered about internships. Figure 6 shows that the factors students considered important in obtaining an internship were different than those they perceived as important in finding a job. Figure 6 shows that student believed that communication and technical skills were the most important factor. These seem like reasonable perceptions but while students did not feel that GPA was important in job placement, 18% felt that GPA was the most important factor in obtaining an internship.

In addition to the factors relating to obtaining an internship, students were also asked about the interaction between internship experience and what they learn in the classroom. As Figure 7 shows, more than half of the students felt that an internship either helped some (19%) or a great deal (44%) in their classroom learning subsequent to the internship experience.

DISCUSSION AND IMPLICATIONS

This exploratory investigation reported some interesting research findings. Contrary to the traditional belief that GPA is the single most important factor in finding a full time job for students, in this study students felt it was the least important factor among the seven factors studied. Instead, internship experience was perceived as the most important factor by MIS seniors. Further, a double major may be another important factor in helping MIS graduates find a full time job, but its importance in job hunting has not been recognized by these MIS majors.

It seems that these MIS students believe that a high GPA is not very important to their future career development, while internships and double majors are becoming more and more important. Hence, MIS programs should consider if curriculum changes are needed help students secure internships and to integrate with other programs (typically with other business programs such as accounting, finance, and marketing) to offer double major programs. In this way, MIS programs may be able to strengthen their ability to successfully place their graduates.

Further, communication skills and information technology related technical skills were considered as very helpful in finding a full time MIS job as well as an MIS internship (see Figures 2 and 6). How-

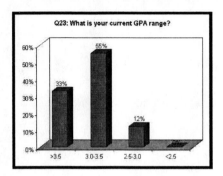

Figure 1. GPA Range of Surveyed Subjects

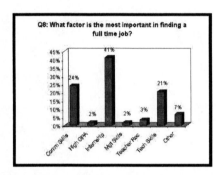

Figure 2. The Perceived Most Importance Factor Influencing Job Hunting

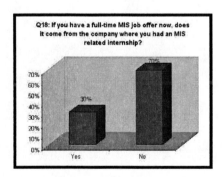

Figure 3. The Percentage of Job Offers from the Company Providing an Internship

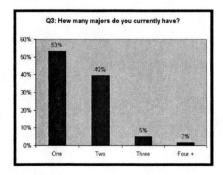

Figure 4. Number of Majors Taken by MIS Students

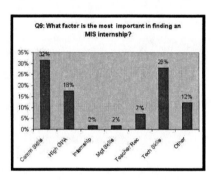

Figure 5. Percent with MIS-related Job Offers?

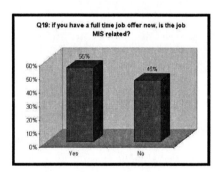

Figure 6. The Most Important Factor in Finding an MIS Internship

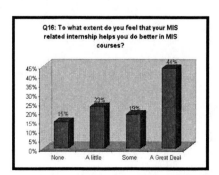

Figure 7. Does an Internship Help You Do Better in MIS Courses?

ever, Figure 8 shows that nearly 40% of the students did not feel that current MIS courses did much to help them in their MIS related internships. Hence, some MIS courses may need to be revised to add in more components that require communication skills. Also to support the student belief that technical skills are important, courses or content could be added into existing MIS programs, such as Java, C++, ASP, Networking, UML, and eCommerce.

On the other hand, even though internships are considered the most important factor by the students, there are still some potential issues to be considered. For example, Figure 7 reveals that more than one third of the students think that their MIS related internship does not help their learning in MIS courses at all (15%), or only helps a little (23%). Another important issue is that 13% of the MIS students could only find an internship that is not MIS related at all. Therefore, given the importance of internships to MIS graduates, a better MIS internship system should be in place in MIS programs so that MIS students can find MIS related internships that would be more closely related to their MIS courses.

MIS programs face new challenges ahead. Traditional emphasis on a high GPA will not help MIS students in the current job market. Many existing MIS programs may have to change to help MIS students locate internships, complete double majors, and improve communication and technical skills.

ACKNOWLEDGMENT

The authors would like to thank Professor S. Lee from Miami University for his help with the survey instrument.

REFERENCES

(Due to the limit of words on the paper, the references will be available upon the request)

The Role of the Information Technology Executive in Chilean Firms

Gloria E. Phillips-Wren
Loyola College in Maryland
4501 N. Charles Street, Baltimore, MD 21210
tel: 410-617-5470; fax: 410-617-2006
gwren@loyola.edu

Osvaldo M. Ferreiro
Universidad Alberto Hurtado
Erasmo Escala 1835 (Casa Fernando Vives), Santiago, Chile
tel: 671 7130; fax: 698 6873
ferreiro@uahurtado.cl

ABSTRACT

Interviews were conducted with information technology (IT) executives in Chilean firms. The interviews revealed a positive business climate, advanced hardware and software infrastructure within the firm, and utilization of computing resources throughout the organization. The use of information technology for strategic planning and decision support was more limited. In general, the information technology executive reported to a senior manager, who in turn reported to the chief executive officer. Studies suggest that even greater business value could be obtained by aligning information technology and the strategic objectives of the firm.

INTRODUCTION

The Gartner Group provides a description of the Chief Information Officer (CIO) as providing "technology vision and leadership for developing and implementing IT initiatives that create and maintain leadership for the enterprise in a constantly changing and intensely competitive marketplace" (Gartner Group, 2002). The position is viewed as a senior management position, reporting to the CEO of the company, and responsible for both IT policy and strategy (Gartner Group, 2002). Studies have found that the degree to which CIOs participate in top management teams influence the success and use of IT initiatives in the firm (Amstrong and Sambamurthy, 1999). Best-practice studies suggest that a firm will obtain greater business value from IT by creating a senior management position, often called the Chief Information Officer, with broad responsibilities that include alignment of the company's information technology with the company's strategic goals (CIO Executive Research Center, 1999; Kearns and Lederer, 2001). The CIO may initiate and lead knowledge management initiatives, business reengineering processes, customer relationship management activities, and Internet uses (CIO Executive Research Center, 1999).

Previous studies of Chilean business and government efforts have shown that infrastructure for IT and ecommerce applications is developing (Davis, 1999; Grandon and Mykytyn, 2002), and that IT adoption is growing (Montealegre, 1998). The use of mobile and wireless technologies is increasing in Latin America, in general, and Chile, in particular (Deans, 2002). Some studies have focused on the adoption of information and communication technologies (ICTs) in developing countries and applied the research to Chile to increase adoption rates (Silva and Figueroa, 2002). Our interviews confirmed these general trends for IT adoption in Chile and focused on the role of the IT executive within the Chilean company.

PROPOSED RESEARCH METHODOLOGY

This study focuses on the role of the senior IT executive in Chilean firms in order to identify opportunities for increased business value from IT investments. Formal interviews were conducted with approximately 40 senior IT executives in the summer of 2002 to determine the responsibilities and reporting level of the position in firms in Chile. Approximately five interviews were in-depth, and the companies represented some of the largest firms in Chile. The pilot study targeted large firms with advanced technology with the expectation that these firms represented the leading edge of IT strategy in Chile. The responses to the interview questions were used to provide qualitative descriptions of the role of the IT executive in Chilean firms and the use of IT for decision support. A follow-up questionnaire will be used to provide quantitative results.

RESULTS OF INITIAL STUDY

An industry description of the firms that agreed to participate in an interview is shown in Table 1. Most of the organizations are large companies in Chile, with several of the consulting companies being medium size. Large, international companies are classified by their primary activity.

The interviews revealed advanced technology such as enterprise systems, current releases of enterprise software, excellent computing architectures, and knowledgeable IT executives in the large companies. In one company, the IT executive had completely overhauled the entire enterprise software system in one year with minimal use of outside consultants. On the other hand, sectors such as a public service hospital lacked infrastructure and computer hardware.

In general, the IT executives interviewed described their responsibilities as shown in Table 2. It should be noted that several companies are multinational corporations, so that the senior IT executive was outside of the country. Most IT executives (approximately 80%) described their primary responsibility as highly-technical administration. It should be noted that the administration is high-level and entails significant responsibility for the company's IT. Less than 5% of the reporting companies utilize the IT executive position as a strategic management resource.

Table 1. Industry sector of Chilean companies participating in an interview.

Type of Industry	Number of Companies
Government	6
Finance	4
Education	2
Retail	2
Medical/Pharmaceutical	4
Food/wine	2
Utility/telecomm	4
Construction/engineering	2
Manufacturing	6
Mining	2
Racing	1
Consulting	6
Advertising	1
Other	1
TOTAL	43

Table 2. Description of IT executive responsibilities.

Responsibilities	Number of Companies
Administration, technical management, user support, evaluate new technologies, sourcing	36
Reporting to higher-level IT executive outside country	4
Coordinating outsourced functions	1
Strategic planning with CEO	2
TOTAL	43

Table 3. Organizational reporting structure for IT executives interviewed.

IT executive reports to:	Number of Companies
Director of Finance	13
Manager; IT executive not part of senior management team	17
Manager; IT executive part of senior management team	5
CEO	4
Outsourced or no information	4
TOTAL	43

These observations are reinforced by the organizational reporting structure shown in Table 3. About 70% of the IT executives are not considered senior managers, reporting to either the director of finance or to a line manager. Approximately 20% of the IT executives are considered senior management, with only 9% reporting directly to the CEO.

DISCUSSION

Information systems strategic alignment can be described as the fit between the strategic orientation of the business and the strategic orientation of the information systems used in the business (Chan, Huff, Barclay and Copeland, 1997). Previous studies have suggested that the firm's IT becomes more effective with alignment, and, concurrently, that the business itself becomes more effective by better utilizing its IT (Chan, Huff, Barclay and Copeland, 1997; Kearns and Lederer, 2001). These studies suggest that significant business value can be obtained by aligning IT and business management strategies.

Best-practice studies have indicated that a firm can obtain value by expanding the role of the IT executive to a CIO, a position that has a senior management perspective, in order to develop alignment between its IT and business strategies (Gottschalk and Taylor, 2000). IT can then become an integral player in developing and obtaining a firm's strategic objectives. Chan (1999) describes the relationship through strategic and structural alignment. An antecedent of strategic alignment is a close linkage between business and IS plans, and an antecedent of structural alignment is the direct report of the CIO to the CEO (Chan, 1999). In general, as indicated in Table 2, these types of relationships are not evident in Chilean firms, suggesting that an opportunity exists for Chilean businesses to capitalize on their investment in IT infrastructure by expanding the role of their IT executive to a senior management position.

ACKNOWLEDGMENTS

The authors would like to thank the Chilean companies in Santiago, Chile, who made the visitations and interactions possible. The anonymous reviewers are acknowledged for their comments and helpful suggestions on the manuscript.

REFERENCES

Armstrong, C. and Sambamurthy, V. (1999). Information technology assimilation in firms: the influence of senior leadership and IT infrastructures. *Information Systems Research*, December, 10(4), 304-327.

Chan, Y. (1999). IS strategic and structural alignment: Eight case studies. *Proceedings of the Association of Information Systems*, Atlanta, GA, 390-392.

Chan, Y., Huff, S., Barclay, D. and Copeland, D. (1997). Business Strategic Orientation, Information Systems Strategic Orientation and Strategic Alignment. *Information Systems Research*, June, 8(2), 125-150.

CIO Executive Research Center (1999, 23 April). What is a CIO? Accessed from http://www.cio.com/research/executive/edit/description.html.

Davis, C. (1999). The rapid emergence of electronic commerce in a developing region: The case of Spanish-speaking Latin America. *Journal of Global Information Technology Management (JGITM)*, 2(3), 25-40.

Deans, C. (2002). Global trends and issues for mobile/wireless commerce. *Proceedings of the Eighth Americas Conference on Information Systems*, Boston, MA, 2396-2402.

Gartner Group (2002). Mission of the CIO. Accessed from http://www.cio.com/research/executive/edit/gartner_description.html.

Gottschalk, P. and Taylor, N. (2000). Strategic management of IS/IT functions: The role of the CIO. *Proceedings of the 33rd Annual Hawaii International Conference on System Sciences*, Maui, HI, 4-7 January, 2811-2820.

Grandon, E. and Mykytyn, P. (2002). Developing an instrument to measure the intention to use electronic commerce in small and medium sized businesses in Chile. *Proceedings of the Eighth Americas Conference on Information Systems*, Boston, MA, 1524-1537.

Kearns, G. and Lederer, A. (2001). Strategic IT Alignment: A Model for Competitive Advantage. *Proceedings of the Twenty-Second Conference on Information Systems*, New Orleans, LA, 1-12.

Montealegre, R. (1998). Waves of change in adopting the Internet: Lessons from four Latin American countries. *Information Technology & People*, 11(3), 235-260.

Silva, L. and Figueroa, B.E. (2002). Institutional intervention and the expansion of ICTs in Latin America: The case of Chile. *Information Technology & People*, 15(1), 8-25.

Web-Based Multimedia Educational Application for the Teaching of Multimedia Contents: An Experience with Higher Education Students

Alcina Prata
Departamento de Sistemas de Informação
Instituto Politécnico de Setúbal
Campus do IPS, Rua Vale de Chaves, 2914-503 Setúbal, PORTUGAL
Telephone: +351.265.551726, Fax: +351.265.709301
aprata@esce.ips.pt

Pedro Faria Lopes
Departamento de Informática
Instituto Superior de Ciências do Trabalho e da Empresa
Av. das Forças Armadas, 1649-026, Lisboa, PORTUGAL
Telephone: +351.21.7903907
Pedro.Lopes@iscte.pt

ABSTRACT

This paper describes an experience undertaken with higher education students, which consisted in utilizing a Web-Based Multimedia Educational Application to serve as an aid in the teaching of Organizational Multimedia. This course is taught to students on the 4th year at Escola Superior de Ciências Empresariais (Higher School of Managerial Sciences, Setúbal, Portugal), where the first author teaches.

Briefly referred to in the paper, the model used for the planning, development and evaluation of the above-mentioned application. In relation to the resulting application, the way it was applied and its evaluation are also presented. The results obtained are interpreted and future developments are proposed.

1 INTRODUCTION

The utilization of Information Technologies, is presently part of the day-to-day of the majority of public and private institutions. The traditional education system also had the necessity to adapt to this new society [4] and has benefited quite a lot from the contribution of these types of technologies/applications [3,9]. Simultaneously, the "professional philosophy" has also evolved to life long learning [18] and professional careers are becoming increasingly demanding, implying a rapid adaptation and constant education in less time, and preferably without dismissal of employees [1,5]. This leads us to E-learning, a teaching method, which utilizes Internet technologies to supply, by distance, a set of solutions for the acquisition and/or updating of knowledge [11,17,18].

The main reason for the growing popularity of this teaching method is due to the fact that it combines the advantages of using Information Technologies in education [3] with the advantages of distance learning [11,17], namely, access to the information using the new instructional model "anytime, anyplace and anybody" [2]. This was therefore the main reason which led us to chose on using a Web-Based Multimedia Educational Application (WBMEA) to serve as an aid in the teaching of Organizational Multimedia, a course taken by 4th year students at the Escola Superior de Ciências Empresariais. As it is an obligatory course, the resulting classes were very heterogeneous, collecting students from five different academic areas witch, naturally, implied difficulties in teaching the classes.

The model used for the WBMEA planning, development and evaluation resulted from the integration of the model presented in the first author's Master's thesis [15,16] with other methods [21], methodologies and guidelines proposed by other authors [6,7,8,10,12,13,14,19,22,23,24]. The final model is composed of 9 grouped phases in three different stages and, in very general terms, implies the initial development of a prototype which, if proven efficient, will serve as the basis for the subsequent development of the final WBMEA.

2 WEB-BASED MULTIMEDIA EDUCATIONAL APPLICATION (WBMEA)

Students witch could not attend classes were considered to be the target group for the WBMEA. That is why the most important factor was to develop a WBMEA, which would best compensate for a student's absence. All classes are laboratorial and last 3 hours. The first hour and a half is theory and the reminder dedicated to practice. Given that the model used for the planning, development and evaluation of the WBMEA assumed the initial development of a prototype, the WBMEA will be designate as prototype. The prototype comprises 3 different sections: the section with the content of a laboratorial class about animation (the practical part of the class), the Frequently Asked Questions (FAQ's) section and the exercises section (including resolution).

3 EVALUATION METHOD

Some students of the course participated in the final evaluation made to the prototype (68 out of 90), which consisted in an experiment and in the application of a questionnaire:

3.1 The Experiment

- 68 students participated in a one hour and a half theoretical class about animation;
- After being characterized they were distributed into two groups of 34 students each. Each group occupied a separate classroom;
- One of the groups was submitted to the other hour and a half class, which corresponded to the practical part of the laboratorial class. Meanwhile, in the other group, each student had, during an hour and a half, access to prototype which was meant to be a substitute for the practical class;
- The prototype was installed on a public server and each user achieved speeds similar to that of a 56Kb-modem connection (the most frequent type of connection speed achieved amongst the student population);
- Afterwards all students were submitted to individual practical exercises.
- In a general way, all students easily resolved the exercises. However, the results obtained by the students who initially attended the practical class and the results obtained by students who initially only used the prototype, were different. The results obtained amongst:
  - students without a lot of previous experience in using the Internet (18) were the same for both groups;
  - students with experience in using the Internet but without previous knowledge of animation (34) were more or less the same for both groups;
  - students with experience in using the Internet and previous knowledge of animation (16) were very good and better amongst those who sat in for the attended class. These students already had previ-

ous knowledge on animation and participated quite actively in class by posing several questions and doubts, which were immediately clarified. Those who used the prototype could also have had their doubts but as they were not immediately clarified (they had to use the FAQ's section) the result was a slightly worse score.

3.2 The Questionnaire

After finishing the above-mentioned exercises the group that had the practical class, was asked to consult and evaluate the prototype. Meanwhile, the group which had used the prototype was lectured a practical class. Afterwards, all students were invited to fill out a questionnaire where they could freely and anonymously express their opinions on the prototype. The answers are resumed in Table 1.

As verified in the table, the majority of the students considered the prototype good in general terms. However, some attention needs to be paid to the results related with the prototype lack of speed.

We also noted that although all students considered this type of prototype to be a good (59) or medium (9) substitute for attended classes, only 49 considered it sufficiently good to substitute the class. This indicates that there are still some improvements to be made to the prototype in order to make it more efficient and personalized.

In relation to the open questions, students were asked to identify the strong points, the weak points and to suggest ways to improve the prototype. Strong points mentioned were that it helped students who could not attend classes (58), it was accessible from anywhere at any time (61), motivating (62) and a different and original study method (36). Weak point mentioned was slowness (47).

4 DISCUSSION

In order to facilitate the access to information from any place at any time, a WBMEA was developed to serve as an aid in the teaching of Organizational Multimedia, a course taken by 4th year students at the Escola Superior de Ciências Empresariais. The final evaluation made to the prototype of the WBMEA consisted of two parts, an experiment and a questionnaire, both with the participation of 68 students.

The experiment showed us that the majority of the students feel quite enthusiastic using this type of WBMEA. In relation to weak points the only problem pointed was the slowness in downloading the prototype. In general, the obtained results are very encouraging and show us that the production of these types of applications should be encouraged. The enthusiasm/results achieved with the usage of the prototype justifies that this work is further developed, and at the time the prototype is being perfected, especially the referred access speed problems. Another incentive to continuing this work is the fact that the School is currently developing an e-learning project which,

will be implemented in the short term, and will, benefit from these types of studies and resultant WBMEA.

REFERENCES

1. Abbey, B., Instructional and Cognitive Impacts of Web-Based Education (Idea Group Publishing, 2000).
2. Aggarwal, A., Web-Based Learning and Teaching Technologies: Opportunities and Challenges (Idea Group Publishing, 2000).
3. Azevedo, B., *Tópicos em Construção de Software Educacional.* Estudo Dirigido, 1997.
4. Chambel, T., Bidarra, J. and Guimarães, N., Multimedia Artefacts That Help Us Learn: Perspectives of the UNIBASE Project on Distance Learning, Workshop on Multimedia and Educational Practice, ACM Multimedia'98 (Bristol, UK, September 1998).
5. Chute, A., Thompson, M. and Hancock, B., The McGraw-Hill Handbook of Distance Learning (McGraw-Hill, New York, 1999).
6. Drener, D., Áudio, Video and Digitizing Sound and Video Clips for Various Languages Courses. Toronto: Multimedia Lab of University of Toronto, CHASS, 1998.
7. Driedger, J., Multimedia Instructional Design. University of Alberta Faculty of Extension. Academic Technologies for Learning, Canada, 1999.
8. Fernandez, J., Learner Autonomy and ICT: A Web-based Course of English for Psychology, *Educational Media International* 37 (2000) pp. 257-261.
9. Hartley, K., Media Overload in Instructional Web Pages and the Impact on Learning, *Educational Media International* 36 (1999) pp. 145-150.
10. Lynch, P. and Horton, S., Web Style Guide - Basic Design Principles for Creating Web Sites (Yale University Center for Advanced Instructional Media, 1999).
11. Machado, S., E-Learning em Portugal (FCA, Lisboa, 2001).
12. McGloughlin, S., Multimedia - Concepts and Practice (Prentice Hall, New Jersey, 2001)
13. Nielsen, J., Designing Web Usability (New Riders Publishing, USA, 2000).
14. Olsina L., Godoy, D., Lafuente, G. and Rossi, G., Assessing the Quality of Academic Websites: a case study, *The New Review of Hypermedia and Multimedia*, 5 (1999) pp. 81-103.
15. Prata, A., Planeamento e Desenvolvimento de um CD-ROM para apoio ao Estudo da Multimédia, Tese de Mestrado, apresentada no ISCTE - Instituto Superior de Ciências do Trabalho e da Empresa, em 2 de Maio de 2000.
16. Prata, A., Lopes, P., How to Plan, Develop and Evaluate Multimedia Applications – A Simple Model, *Proceedings VIPromCom-2002 (International Symposium on Video/Image Processing and Multimedia Communications)*, Croatian Society Electronics in Marine - Elmar, Croácia (Zadar), (2002) pp.111-115.
17. Rosenberg, M., E-learning - Strategies for Delivering Knowledge in the Digital Age (McGraw-Hill, New York, 2001).
18. Ryan, S., Scott, B., Freeman, H. and Patel, D., The Virtual University - The Internet and Resource-Based Learning (Kogan Page, London, 2000).
19. Salmon, G., E-Moderating - The Key to Teaching and Learning Online (Kogan Pge, London, 2000).
20. Santos, A., Ensino a Distância & Tecnologias de Informação (FCA, Lisboa, 2001).
21. Sutcliffe, A. G., A Design Method for effective information delivery in multimedia presentations, *The New Review of Hypermedia and Multimedia* 5 (1999) pp. 29-57.
22. Tsai, C., A Typology of the Use of Educational Media, with Implications for Internet-Based Instruction, *Educational Media International* 37 (2000) pp. 157-160.
23. Vaughan, T., Multimedia - Making It Work (McGrawHill, California USA, 1998).
24. Vrasidas, C., Principles of Pedagogy and Evaluation for Web-Based Learning, *Educational Media International* 37 (2000) pp. 105-111.

Table 1. Answers Obtained in the Questionnaire

About the prototype:	A Lot	More Or Less	A Little	Very Little
1. Has an attractive design	47	18	3	0
2. The information is well organized	60	7	1	0
3. Simple and intuitive navigation	58	8	2	0
4. The subjects are exposed clearly	61	7	0	0
5. Easy to use	56	10	0	0
6. Motivating	63	5	0	0
	Good	Medium	Weak	Bad
7. Number of examples	60	7	1	0
8. Number of exercises	19	36	13	0
9. FAQ's section	57	6	5	0
10. In terms of speed, the result was	0	21	37	10
11. Is a good method of substituting the attended class	59	9	0	0
12. Global evaluation	44	15	9	0
	Yes		No	
13. Good enough substitute for the attended class?	49		19	

The Open Source Software Model and a Business Case for Open Source Software Implementation: Creating a Symbiotic Open Source Solution

Alan I Rea, Jr.
Business Information Systems Department
Western Michigan University, Haworth College of Business
1903 West Michigan Avenue, Kalamazoo, MI 49008
Phone: 269.387.4247, Fax: 269.387.5710
e-mail: rea@wmich.edu

INTRODUCTION

Open Source Software (OSS) was once purely the realm of geeks and techies. However, businesses depend daily on various Open Source-based technologies such as HTTP (Web) and SMTP (e-mail) to conduct transactions and maintain client contacts. Apache and sendmail (not to mention BIND, Linux, Perl, etc.) are the lifeblood of the Internet economy, yet programmers created this software without a traditional business software development model. Instead, it was developed, debugged, maintained, and distributed by volunteers. It's only recently that companies, such as Red Hat, have formed to profit from OSS.

It might stand to reason that businesses would also rely on OSS for their other needs, such as desktop applications, servers, and databases. However, in this arena businesses have long relied on commercial off-the-shelf software (COTS). Whether it's Microsoft or mainframe systems, COTS still has a stronghold in the corporate environment.

This trend is changing as more business and corporations are turning to OSS, such as Linux, to run servers. IBM is a long-time supporter of Linux on its architecture and Sun has recently joined in Linux support as well. Others have implemented Linux on the desktop. Red Hat Linux 8.x is specifically targeted for the desktop market. Initial news reports show that it's being well received by desktop users.

BUSINESS AND OPEN SOURCE

Why is this happening? Is OSS ready for "prime time"? Or have businesses found methods to implement OSS effectively? In 2001, MITRE released a business case study for OSS adoption for U.S. military program managers. MITRE argues that managers need to take five steps when considering OSS implementation:

1. Assess the supporting OSS developer community (e.g., Linux, Apache).
2. Examine the market.
3. Conduct a specific analysis of benefits and risks.
4. Compare the long-term costs.
5. Choose your strategy. (Kenwood, 2001)

Using the MITRE model as a benchmark, this research looks to create a new business case for OSS assessment and deployment in variegated business environments. The research develops a heuristic tool that businesses—no matter what their size or function—can use to determine what OSS implementation (full, partial, none) works best for their mission.

THE BUSINESS OF OPEN SOURCE

In the MITRE model, the first two steps involve an assessment of OSS offerings available to business. In the past, most OSS software was acquired for low to no cost and then configured by each business, as it deemed necessary. While the front-end costs are low, the development and maintenance costs can become quite high. Most businesses cannot afford to train and re-train programmers with each new OSS implementation, nor can they afford to lose programmers' time that must be devoted to mission-critical tasks.

In order to fill the gaps between OSS purchase, implementation, and maintenance, businesses have begun to move to a service-oriented model. This is how OSS vendors such as Red Hat Linux make a profit. In some cases, the OSS service contract—also termed a "paid support network"—is less expensive than an outright COTS purchase. It remains to be seen if businesses will opt for a long-term service model.

However, does the service model look to be a viable component of OSS software development companies and business who use the OSS? While software is available for free as a download are businesses willing to at least purchase CDs and manuals for extremely reduced costs than COTS? Can OSS developers provide quality software for low cast and make a profit with various service models?

BUSINESS AND OSS SYMBIOSIS

Although businesses are sometimes ready to adopt OSS in terms of technological advantages and cost savings, the OSS model does conflict with competitiveness and business knowledge practices. Most businesses guard their intellectual property and software that embodies knowledge in order to remain competitive and/or show a profit by selling it. The OSS model requires it to be shared.

Some corporations, such as HP, have adopted a model of "Progressive Open Source" (POS). In POS, the OSS is layered into a three-tiered structure (Dinkelacker, et. al., 2002):

Inner Source: Open Source concepts, such as collaboration, sharing of code, and open modification are only available to employees. All collaboration takes place via the HP intranet protected by a firewall and other security measures.

Controlled Source: The source code is placed outside of the firewall, but this code is only shared with authorized partners on a necessary basis.

Open Source: The software is released to the Open Source community under a limited license. Only select pieces of software are selected for this level.

The HP model may be one that corporations adopt in order to use OSS yet retain a competitive advantage. This model can be effective if two items take place:

1. The POS model allows for enough sharing of OSS so that OSS developers can use the source code to improve existing applications and develop new offerings.
2. The POS model insures that all OSS develop of the source code remains open source and does not divert back into the inner or controlled source levels.

PRODUCT VERSUS SERVICE MODEL

The POS model has yet to be proven on a larger scale adoption, but it does attempt to bridge what is a large gap in synthesizing OSS and business—disparate culture. Most OSS is not developed for profit in the more traditional sense such as COTS. Whereas COTS has a high front-end cost, OSS can be downloaded for free or purchased on CDs for a marginal cost (compare the cost of Red Hat CDs versus Microsoft XP CDs).

This paradigm shift from product to service model suggests a change in software development. Instead of considering software a product, OSS is moving toward software development as a service. Paid support networks are emerging in OSS and are usually more cost-effective than a combination of COTS and service contracts.

This move to a service model in software development and implementation benefits both developer and business. As Feller and Fitzgerald (2000) note:

More important than sticker-price, OSS allows companies developing and implementing systems to share both the risks and long-term costs associated with a system. By shifting the locus of value from protecting "bits" of code to maximizing the gain from software use and platform development, OSS redefines software as an industry.

CONCLUSION

This research explores the changing OSS model of software development as seen in large OSS companies such as Red Hat Linux, traditionally COTS companies like IBM, and smaller operations offering OSS alternatives to popular applications, such as Ximian's Evolution: a Microsoft Exchange program for Linux. In the research, the author looks forward to see what market niches OSS development companies can fill for businesses and if OSS can significantly displace COTS in business (or if it should).

Ultimately, the question we must answer is if a viable OSS symbiosis between OSS developers and venders with businesses can be fostered and maintained. This research sheds light on the debate. While no definite conclusions can be determined without further study, some type of OSS symbiosis looks to be a part of the business climate in the foreseeable future.

SELECT WORKS

Dinkelacker, J., Garg, P., Miller, R., & Nelson, D. (2002, May 19-25). *Progressive Open Source*. Paper presented at the JCSE, Orlando, FL, USA.

Feller, J., & Fitzgerald, B. (2000). *A Framework Analysis of the Open Source Software Development Paradigm*. Paper presented at the 21st International Conference in Information Systems (ICIS 2000).

Hecker, F. (2000). *Setting Up Shop: The Business of Open-Source Software*. Retrieved October 4, 2002 from http://www.hecker.org/writings/setting-up-shop.html.

Kenwood, C. (2001). *A Business Case Study of Open Source Software*. Bedford, MA: The MITRE Corporation.

Open Source Initiative. (2002). *Open Source Case for Business*. Retrieved October 4, 2002 from http://www.opensource.org/advocacy/case_for_business.php.

Raymond, E. S. (2001). The Cathedral & the Bazaar (2 ed.). Sebastapol, CA: O'Reilly.

Three Types of Data for Extended Company's Employees: A Knowledge Management Viewpoint

Michel Grundstein and Camille Rosenthal-Sabroux
LAMSADE–Paris – Dauphine University
MG Consei, 75775 Paris Cedex 16, l4, rue Anquetil
Tel: 01 48 76 26 63, Tel: 01 44 05 47 24
Fax: 01 48 76 26 63, Fax: 01 44 05 40 91
mgrundstein@mgconseil.fr, sabroux@lamsade.dauphine.fr
http://www.mgconseil.fr, http://www.lamsade.dauphine.fr

ABSTRACT

This paper introduces a reflection on the types of data to accessed by be extended company's employees from the Knowledge Management viewpoint. This leads us to distinguish between three types of data: main-stream-data, shared-data, *and* source-of-knowledge-data. *In that way, as distinguishing crucial knowledge is a key factor, we propose to use a specific approach so-called* GAMETH framework, *the aim of which is to identify and locate crucial knowledge for the Company.*

1. INTRODUCTION

The concept of information system covers two notions: on the one hand, the reality of the organization that evolves and undertakes, communicates and records information; and on the other hand, the digital information system, the artificial object conceived by humans to help them acquire, process, store, transmit and restore the information that allows them to carry out their activities within the context of the organization [Reix, 95]. We will refer afterwards to the digital information system.

In the first part of this paper, we draw up a brief description of the Extended Company's digital information system and we introduce a reflection on the evolution of the employee's role within the Extended Company. This leads us to make an attempt at positioning Knowledge Management. Next, taking into account the new role of employees, we analyze the new employee's information needs when placed at his computerized desktop. And finally, we introduce the GAMETH framework.

2. THE EXTENDED COMPANY

Under the influence of globalization and the impact of Information and Communication Technologies (ICT) that modify radically our relationship with space and time, the company increasingly develops its activities in a planetary space with three dimensions: a global space covering the set of the organization that are the geographic places of implantation, a local space corresponding to the subset of the organization situated in a given geographic zone, and a space of influence that covers the field of interaction of the company with the other organizations. The hierarchical company locked up on its local borders is transformed into an Extended Company, without borders, opened and adaptable. Furthermore, this Extended Company is placed under the ascendancy of the unforeseeable environment that leads towards uncertainty and doubt .

The Extended Company meets fundamental problems of information exchange and knowledge sharing among, on the one hand, its formal entities distributed in the world (offices, core competencies, business units, projects), and on the other hand, the company's employees (nomadic or sedentary), bearers of diversified values and cultures according to the places of implantation.

Two networks of information overlap:
- An internal and external formal information network between the entities in which circulate data and explicit knowledge. Theses networks are implemented under intranet and extranet technologies.

- An informal information network between members, nomadic or sedentary employees, that privileges information exchange and tacit knowledge sharing. These networks are implemented through Communication Technologies.

3. THE EVOLUTION OF THE EMPLOYEES ROLE WITHIN THE EXTENDED COMPANY

« *What makes knowledge valuable to organizations is ultimately to make better the decisions and actions taken on the basis of knowledge* [Davenport & Prusak, 98]. » In the Extended Company which is taking place, initiatives and responsibilities are increasing, whatever the individuals hierarchical levels and roles are. Employees are placed in situations in which they need to take decisions. They become decision-makers who use and produce more and more knowledge as a basis for their efficiency. Their knowledge is the crucial factor enabling them to enhance their competencies, and thus improve their decision-making processes. To answer their missions, these individuals, commonly pointed out as « Knowledge-Workers», have to access knowledges and know-how widely distributed in the global and influence spaces of their organization. They must rely on the formal and the informal information networks of the company through their sedentary or mobile computerized workstation. The computerized workstation becomes a window opened on the company's planetary space of activities. Thus, the essential role of the digital information system is to provide relevant information to each employee at all levels of the hierarchy, so that he can control, make decisions and undertake actions.

Beyond the technical infrastructures that are implemented, the digital information system has to bring, to each individual, useful information. Moreover the digital information system has to supply means to share the knowledge with distant colleagues, and to enable access to essential knowledge in order to solve problems out of routine. Knowledge Management offers a way to answer these problems, may the employee be nomadic or sedentary, and whatever his geographic location and his mode of connection to the network (computerized workstation, laptop, personal assistants) are.

4. THE KNOWLEDGE MANAGEMENT

Today, the expression *Knowledge Management* has become a current expression that covers many different meanings according to the own perspective of the person who uses it. We make an attempt at clarifying the positioning of *Knowledge Management* as one facet of the general problem of capitalizing on company's knowledge assets.

4.1. The Multifacets Problem-Solving Approach to Capitalizing on Company's Knowledge Assets

When capitalizing on company's knowledge assets, many problems appear. We group them into a five facets model described as follows (see figure 1):

The first facet of the problem deals with **the location of crucial knowledge**, that is knowledge (explicit knowledge) and know-how (tacit knowledge) that are necessary for decision-making processes and for the progress of the essential processes that constitute the heart of the activities of the company: it is necessary to identify them, to localize them, to characterize them, to make cartographies of them, to estimate their economic value and to organize them into a hierarchy.

The second facet of the problem deals with **the preservation of knowledge and know-how**: it is necessary to acquire them with the bearers of knowledge, to model them, to formalize them and to conserve them.

The third facet of the problem deals with **the added-value of knowledge and know-how**: it is necessary to enhance their value, to put them at the service of the development and of the expansion of the company, that is to make them accessible according to certain rules of confidentiality and safety, to disseminate them, to share them, to use them more effectively, to combine them and to create new knowledge. Here is the link with innovation processes.

The fourth facet of the problem deals with **the actualization of knowledge and know-how**: it is necessary to appraise them, to update them, to standardize them and to enrich them according to the returns of experiments, the creation of new knowledge and the contribution of external knowledge. Here is the link with business intelligence processes.

The fifth facet of the problem deals with the interactions between the various problems mentioned previously. It is there that **the management of activities and processes, allowing the mastery of knowledge in organizations to be insured**, takes place. It is often called *Knowledge Management* in numerous publications. In fact, the expression *Knowledge Management* covers all the managerial actions aiming at answering the problem of capitalization of knowledge in general. It is necessary to align the knowledge management on the strategic orientations of the organization; to make people sensitive; to form, to encourage, to motivate and to rally people's interest; to organize and to pilot activities and specific processes leading towards more mastery of knowledge; to arouse the implementation of favorable conditions to the cooperative work and to encourage the sharing of knowledge; to elaborate indicators allowing the follow-up and the coordination of launched actions to be insured, to measure results and to determine the relevance and the impacts of these actions.

In this way, we can define Knowledge Management as: « *The management of activities and processes that enhance creation and use of knowledge within an organization, aim at two strongly linked goals: a patrimony goal and a sustainable innovation goal with economic, human, socio-cultural and technological underlying dimensions* ».

We will refer to KM abbreviation afterwards.

4.2. The KM Prism Analysis Model

The above definition generates the need for a Knowledge Management Framework "*which can act as a meaningful and practical guide to the context of KM initiatives – economic, technical, structural, socio-cultural – within the enterprise, and the interplay between these elements.*" [CEN/ISSS, 02]. This partially refers to the Knowledge Management Prism Analysis Model that is described hereafter.

The KM Prism Analysis Model is aimed at describing the different aspects that have to be taken in consideration when studying Knowledge Man-

Figure 1: The Multifacets Problem-Solving Approach

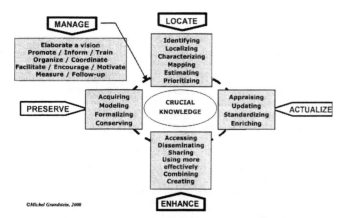

©Michel Grundstein, 2000

agement activities and processes with enhancing the company efficiency as the final goal. Activities and processes must be analyzed under economical, organizational, socio-cultural and technological viewpoints, and on how they interact. So that we have to consider:

*   Socio-organizational interactions, that is legal status, leadership, power distribution, management style, incentive and rewards, professional culture, ethic and values;
*   Socio-technical interactions, that is digital information system linked to individuals (needs, self autonomy, and competence);
*   Technico-organizational interactions, that is digital information system linked to organization (missions, structure, processes, relationship network).

These two last points of view are central in order to conceive relevant computerized knowledge-worker desktops needed by Extended Company. The digital information system, centered on the knowledge-worker, requires a human centric design approach to place the knowledge-worker into the heart of the design process [Rosenthal-Sabroux, 96] [Kettani *et al.*, 98]. The design must not dissociate the knowledge-worker, stakeholder of different functional and organizational groups and lines of business or projects, from the professional processes in which he is engaged, the actions he performs, the decisions he makes, the relations he has with his company environment (persons and artifacts).

Furthermore, beyond the conventional information system, the digital information system must bring to each computerized workstation three natures of information put in light by our research works on Information System, Knowledge Management and Decision Aid.

5. THE KNOWLEDGE-WORKER AT HIS COMPUTERIZED DESKTOP

Our researches focused on knowledge management and the knowledge-worker at his computerized desktop have led us to distinguish three general categories of data to be processed by the digital information systems: the *main-stream data*, the *source-of knowledge data*, the *shared-data* [Grundstein & Rosenthal-Sabroux, 01].

5.1. The Three General Categories of Data

When considering the notion of *Knowledge Portal* that has emerged as a key tool for supporting knowledge work [Mack *et al.*, 01], we observe that the analysis has been done from a specific point of view, that is "*a fundamental aspect of knowledge management is capturing knowledge and expertise created by Knowledge-Workers as they go about their work and making it available to a larger community of colleagues.*" Our research are more focused on the problematic that is set down above. Therefore we have been led to distinguish three general categories of data as described below.

The Main-Stream-Data

The *main-stream-data* makes up the flow of information that informs us on the state of a company's business process or working information needed by each individual to act. If the digital system information is itself a company's production system (for example, a bank's digital information system), the *main-stream-data* informs us on the state of the information-related material to be transformed, and on the state of the digital information system that carries out this transformation. If the company's production system involves physical materials, *the main-stream-data* will provide information on the state of that material before and after the transformation, and will give information on the whole environment that makes this transformation possible.

The Source-of-Knowledge-Data

The *source-of-knowledge-data* is the result of a knowledge-engineering approach that offers techniques and tools for acquiring and representing knowledge. This knowledge, encapsulated in computer programs capable of reconstructing it as information immediately understandable to human beings, thus becomes accessible and manipulable. This leads us to integrate into the digital information system specific modules called *source-of-knowledge-data* systems, that both in their conception and in the techniques used to implement them influence the results produced through new orientations in knowledge engineering research [Charlet *et al.*, 00].

The Shared-Data

Moreover, the information and communication technologies have caused a rupture with older technologies, a rupture linked to the relationship of human beings to space, to time and to the capacity to be ubiquitous which take us from the real world to a virtual one, from the manipulation of concrete objects to abstract ones. The instantaneous transfer of digitalized multimedia documents that include texts, images and sounds, the possibility of asynchrony of information exchanges that transforms our relationship with time and space, electronic conferences that allow us to be in different places at the same time, engender a transformation in our behavior at work. They accelerate the publication and dissemination of documents, they facilitate working in groups, they modify our means of communication, and above all, they speed up the transmission and sharing of tacit knowledge that, until now, operated from person to person on a master-apprentice basis. In short, they generate processes of information exchange that were unbelievable with previous technologies. Information processed by these technologies is called "*shared-data*".

5.2. The Knowledge-Worker Desktop

Within the Extended Company, Knowledge-Workers find themselves confronted to situations that go beyond daily routine, situations in which they must evaluate all possible choices in terms of criteria relevant to a given set of goals. Taking into consideration all available information (*main-stream-data, shared-data, source-of-knowledge-data*), their own intentions, any restrictions that influence their decisions and their knowledge and know-how, they must analyze and process information in order to make these choices. We have materialized this vision under an empirical model form described below (see figure 2).

The Knowledge-Worker engaged in business or project lines processes is subjected to constraints inherent to these processes (available financial and human resources, cost, delays, quality, security, specific objectives to achieve). He uses physical resources (working environment, tools). He possesses knowledge and skills. Through the "*Main-Stream-Data System*", he receives and gets "current data", *i. e.*, data relative to the tasks he has to execute (data on the status of the work he is achieving, data on evolving events to take in charge, management and technical data). Through the "*Shared-Data System*", he communicates in real time with the other actors, he exchanges information and shares tacit knowledge. To make a decision and act, he activates a cognitive process that shows his capability to put together his knowledge, his skills, his ethical attitude, under constraining conditions of his task situation. Here, we refer to his competence.

His knowledge and skills can prove to be insufficient to solve the out-of-routine problem he is confronted with. In that case, and according to his intention that depends on his freedom of action, he needs to get additional data stored in the "*Source-of-Knowledge-Data System*". This data, by interaction with his cognitive system, becomes new knowledge, enabling him to solve the problem, make decision and act. During this process, there is production of new knowledge. This new knowledge, on the condition of being acquired and formalized, can update and complete the "*Source-of-Knowledge-Data System*" [Grundstein & Rosenthal-Sabroux, 01].

Figure 2: The Knowledge-Worker as a Decision-Maker

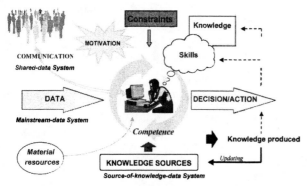

Adapted from Michel Grundstein, MCX Poitiers, 1997

What is essential in this vision of things is the creative relation, between the knowledge-worker and his activity, taking into account his "intention", the end purpose of his action, and the orientation of knowledge towards an operational objective [Grundstein, 00].

Consequently, when considering the multifacets problem-solving approach to capitalizing on company's knowledge assets, we can envisage the digital information system as an essential instrument to provide Knowledge-Workers with crucial knowledge that is required to accelerate and improve the reliability and the quality of their decisions. The problem consists of being aware of what is known and what is crucial for Knowledge-Workers in order to achieve their tasks and respond to the functional, organizational, business lines and project lines overall goals aligned on the company's strategic orientations. This is the aim of the GAMETH framework that is briefly described in the following section.

6. THE GAMETH FRAMEWORK

As pointed out by Richard Collin [Collin, 01],

today, the knowledge management mainly amounts to store, to organize, to extract, to analyze and to spread information in the company. The role of the actors is underestimated and the knowledge management is mostly oriented towards "contents" : information stock is privileged with regard to the dynamics of knowledge sharing. People looking for information are lost, while they are the source of the value: loss of orientation facing a vast and heterogeneous stock of information; loss of energy caused by the necessity of repeating requests to find the reliable solution; loss of sense bound to the absence of visibility concerning the operational utility of the information. The holder of information is not really mobilized: one asks him to give his knowledge without being paid for that. Information is little shared, little updated, badly exploited.

In fact, while since 1991 Thomas A. Stewart has made us sensitive to the necessity of considering the knowledge of the company as the essential resource and has announced a new challenge « *The challenge is to find out what you have - and use it* » [Stewart, 91], in his last work the same author notices the fatal effect of "contents" oriented processes that were not subjected to advisability studies: « *Companies waste billions on knowledge management because they fail to figure out what knowledge they need, or how to manage it* » [Stewart, 02].

Beyond the incentive organizational ways, methods and indispensable tools, the implementation of Knowledge Management points out a real need: the need to locate crucial knowledge for the company. This last point is developed below.

6.1. A Brief History of the GAMETH Framework

The GAMETH framework is one of the results of the CORPUS project initiated and led from 1991 to 1995 into the Framatome Group[1]. The scope of CORPUS was to elaborate a set of concepts, methods and tools aimed at contributing to capitalizing on company's knowledge assets.

At the beginning, CORPUS deliverable was a complementary approach to manage the advisability phase of an information project with the aim of integrating knowledge capitalization functionalities into the specifications [Grundstein, 96]. As an example, for a quotation improvement project, this approach leads to highlighting a problem that we had decided to call "*knowledge traceability*", that is a generic problem based on the following needs: the need to refer to earlier facts, the need to refer to analogous cases, the need to ask questions about earlier choices, and the need to rely on experience feedback. Beyond a system that helps to prepare quotations, the solution implemented the functionality necessary for "*knowledge traceability*". This functionality responded to the problematic of capitalizing on company's knowledge assets defined above.

Later on, we have considered that this approach could be generalized, and since 1997, it has been consolidated as a Global Analysis Methodology, the so-called GAMETH framework.

6.2. General Description of GAMETH framework

The GAMETH framework is described below. The GAMETH framework consists of looking more directly at the production processes. The GAMETH framework relies on three postulates, suggests three guiding principles, induces an approach that has three specific characteristics and consists of three main stages. A detailed description has been given in [Grundstein *et al.*, 02].

The postulates
The approach is based on the following postulates:
1) Knowledge is not an object, knowledge exists in the interaction between a person and data.
2) Knowledge is linked to the action.
3) Company's knowledge includes two main categories of knowledge: explicit knowledge – the specific know-how that characterizes the company's capability to design, produce, sell and support its products and services - and the individual and collective skills that characterize its capability to act and to evolve.

The guiding principles and the characteristics
The approach is characterized by three main characteristics:
1) It is a problem-oriented approach: the problems are located, the required needs for knowledge that allow their resolution are clarified, the knowledge is characterized and then, the most adapted solutions to solve the problems are determined.
2) It is a process-centered approach that connects knowledge to the action: the analysis is not based on a strategic analysis of the company's goals, but instead on the analysis of the knowledge needed by the value-added activities of functional, production, business and project processes.
3) It is a constructivist approach that allows collective commitment. The aim of this approach is to build from partial knowledge of the actors through their activities, the representation of the process. This representation allows to identify informal links between the actors that are not described in the documents.

The main stages
The approach is aligned on the company's strategic orientation, and the deliverable is an Advisability Analysis Report that notably includes:
- A repertory of the crucial explicit knowledge, associated with a document presenting a description and a classification of these knowledges.
- A repertory of agents, the bearers of crucial tacit knowledge, associated with a document presenting a description and a classification of these knowledges.
- An index of the agents possessing knowledge elicitable, associated with a descriptive card of their competences, the persons who might solicitate them and the events that determine this solicitation.
- A document defining the tacit elicitable knowledges that should be shared, completed with a grid establishing the formal and informal relations between the agents, bearers of these knowledges, and the agents who might use them.
- Recommendations concerning the acquisition and the formalization of tacit elicitable knowledges.

In short, the GAMETH Framework Approach consists of the following steps:
- inventorying the goods and services for which a knowledge capitalization initiative is envisaged;
- modeling the units (functions, organs, and communication links) that supply these goods and services;
- delimiting the production processes concerned and specifying the phases and steps of the production cycles corresponding to these processes;
- analyzing the role of the poles of expertise in the satisfactory operation of each phase and each step of the production cycles;
- analyzing the risks and determining the critical activities;
- identifying the constraints and dysfunctions that weigh on these activities;
- distinguishing the determining problems;
- locating and characterizing the knowledge necessary to solve these problems;
- measuring the value of this knowledge and determining the crucial knowledge;
- drawing up a map of the knowledge to be capitalized, based on the inventory of the actors;

- cross-checking with the crucial knowledge, for each phase of the production cycles concerned.

In this way, the fields of knowledge, their locations, their characteristics and their influence on the operations of the company and its strategic orientations are detailed. At the end of the advisability analysis, the elements enabling the justification of a knowledge capitalization exercise will have been gathered, making it possible to decide upon and undertake the feasibility study.

7. RESEARCH PROSPECTS
Our research has two prospects in view.
1) When practicing the GAMETH framework approach, we are led to consider capitalizing on company's knowledge assets as a part of the digital information system project specification. Thus, customer's requirements are studied in depth during the advisability phase. The study emphasizes the required needs for knowledge that allow the resolution of well-posed problems. People are involved in the construction of the solution. As such, when considering integrating into a digital information system project, functionalities that will support knowledge management, the GAMETH framework approach can be useful. In particular we think about the establishment of a link with the inception phase of the development cycle as defined in the Rational Unified Process (RUP) [Kruchten, 99].
2) When speaking of crucial knowledge, the problem of finding good criteria arises. We are working in this way with a large automotive company which wants to justify investment in knowledge management initiatives.

The GAMETH framework has been implemented into a methodology developed by Alexandre Pachulski during his doctoral studies [Pachulski, 01]. The GAMETH framework partially underlies the KDE project[2] [Esprit project, 01]. It is the basis for another doctoral study specially focused on knowledge qualification [Saad *et al.*, 02]. At this point, this methodology is not completely validated as it has not been tested in a scientific protocol way.

ENDNOTES
[1]   French Nuclear Power Plant Company, first transformed into Framatome ANP, then integrated into AREVA Group in September 2001.
[2]   Esprit-IV Project 28678. Participants are Bureau Veritas, Eutech, Intrasoft, Salustro-Reydel Management, TXT and the University of Amsterdam.

REFERENCES
[CEN/ISSS, 02] Knowledge Management Workshop, European Committee for Standardization / Information Society Standardization System, Brussels, June 2002.

[Charlet et al., 00] Jean Charlet, Manuel Zacklad, Gilles Kassel, Didier Bourigault: *Ingénierie des connaissances, Evolutions récentes et nouveaux défis*. Editions Eyrolles et France Télécom-CENT, Paris 2000.

[Collin, 01] Richard Collin: *Connaissances, Compétences et Technologies: Pourquoi l' homme est la mesure de toute information*, Séminaire SIGECAD, Université Paris-Dauphine, avril 2001.

[Davenport & Prusak, 98] Thomas H. Davenport, Laurence Prusak: Working Knowledge. How Organizations Manage What They Know. Harvard Business School Press, Boston, 1998.

[Esprit project, 01] Esprit project 28678: *Final report on the BV test applications*, KDE Workpackage 7.4., September, 2001.

[Grundstein & Rosenthal-Sabroux, 01] Michel Grundstein, Camille Rosenthal-Sabroux: *Vers un système d'information source de connaissance*, chapitre 11, pp. 317-348, dans Ingénierie des Systèmes d'Information de Corine Cauvet et Camille Rosenthal-Sabroux, Hermès sciences Publications, 2001.

[Grundstein et al., 02] Michel Grundstein, Camille Rosenthal-Sabroux, Alexandre Pachulski: *Reinforcing Decision Aid by Capitalizing on Company's Knowledge: Future Prospects* EJOR 2002.

[Grundstein, 00] Michel Grundstein: *From capitalizing on Company Knowledge to Knowledge Management*, chapter 12, pp. 261-287, in *Knowledge Management, Classic and Contemporary Works* by Daryl Morey, Mark Maybury, Bhavani Thuraisingham, The MIT Press, Cambridge, Massachusetts, 2000.

[Grundstein, 96] Michel Grundstein: *"CORPUS," An Approach to Capitalizing Company Knowledge*. AIEM4 Proceedings, The Fourth International Workshop on Artificial Intelligence in Economics and Management, Tel-Aviv, Israel, January 8-10, 1996.

[Kettani *et al.*, 98] Nasser Kettani, Dominique Mignet, Pascal Paré, Camille Rosenthal-Sabroux: *De Merise à UML*. Editions Eyrolles, Paris, 1998.

[Krutchen, 99] Philippe Krutchen: *The Rational Unified Process, An Introduction*. Addison Wesley Longman, Inc., 1999 (first printing, November 1998).

[Mack *et al.*, 01] Robert Mack, Yael Ravin, Roy J. Byrd: *Knowledge Portals and the Emerging Digital Knowledge Workplace*, IBM Systems Journal, Vol. 40, N° 4, 200, pp. 925-954.

[Pachulski, 01] Alexandre Pachulski: *Le repérage des connaissances cruciales pour l'entreprise: concepts, méthode et outils*. Thèse de Doctorat, 2001, Université Paris-Dauphine.

[Reix, 95] Robert Reix: *Systèmes d'information et management des organisations*, 3ème édition, Librairie Vuibert, Paris, 2000.

[Rosenthal-Sabroux, 96] Camille Rosenthal-Sabroux: *Contribution méthodologique à la conception de systèmes d'information coopératifs: prise en compte de la coopération homme/machine*, Mémoire HDR, Université Paris-Dauphine, Paris, 1996.

[Saad *et al*, 02] Inès Saad, Camille Rosenthal-Sabroux, Michel Grundstein et Patrick Coustillère: Une démarche de repérage de connaissances cruciales conduisant à l'identification des compétences. Papier présenté au 1er colloque du Groupe de Travail Gestion des Compétences et des Connaissances en Génie Industriel (GCC-GI), Nantes, 2002.

[Stewart, 02] Thomas A. Stewart: *The Wealth of Knowledge: Intellectual Capital and the 21tst century Organization*, to be published in 2002 by Currency Doubleday. Excerpt by Business2.0 from Thomas A. Stewart's.

[Stewart, 91] Thomas A. Stewart: *BRAIN POWER: How Intellectual Capital Is Becoming America's Most Valuable Asset*, FORTUNE, June 3, 1991.

Discovering the Causes of IT Project Failures in Government Agencies

Mark R. Nelson and Diana Thomas
Lally School of Management - Summer Undergraduate Research Fellow
Rensselaer Polytechnic Institute
110 8th Street, Pitt 2216 -Buck 3001, 1999 Burdett Avenue, Troy, NY 12180
Phone: 518-276-2768, Fax: 518-276-8661
nelsom@rpi.edu, thomad@rpi.edu

ABSTRACT

This project used an extensive collection of longitudinal project-related documents to gain a better understanding of project failure in large-scale government IT projects. The study focused on the Tax System Modernization (TSM) project at the U.S. Internal Revenue Service (IRS), primarily from 1986 to 1997. During that time period, the agency spent over USD $3.5 billion on the TSM project, which was terminated at the end of the time period having failed to achieve several major objectives. Using a qualitative approach and working with a large volume of project-related documentation, this study found factors not previously reported in the literature that may inhibit the success of large-scale IT projects in government agencies. The findings from the study introduce several new questions for future research.

INTRODUCTION

This project focused on large-scale systems implementation. In this study we examined measures of IT project success and failure across a set of government documents using formal research methods and specialized software tools. While we were unable to completely code the entire data set during the time we had available, we were able to identify several hypotheses that are both new to the literature and suggest the need for further research in this area. Although the IRS experienced technical difficulties that resulted in problems for the Tax Systems Modernization Project (TSM), it is important to note that their lack of system advancement could symptomatic of deeper-rooted problems. The source of these problems could be management practices and the organizational structure resulting from years of hierarchical structure changes and changes in top management control. However, there appears to be another phenomenon that is occurring as it relates to information capacity. The IRS is continuously being bombarded with recommendations from external agencies and committees, who may prove to be more harmful than helpful to large-scale IT projects.

RESEARCH QUESTION AND SIGNIFICANCE

Project Context: The Internal Revenue Service (IRS), like many government agencies, deals with massive amounts of information associated with different individuals and organizations. For example, a person's basic data such as his/her name, address, telephone number, are just a few of the many bits of data that compile one's identity in the whole scheme of tax collecting. In addition, like many agencies, the IRS has an antiquated data and system architecture, consisting of over 50 databases across several platforms, some of which date back to the 1950s! Audits by the General Accounting Office (GAO) have uncovered serious weaknesses within the agency's financial systems, including cumulative discrepancies in excess of $30 billion in a given year. The situation seems inevitable as humans and technology interact for a common purpose, only to find that their goal has been distorted by human error in numerous forms, or technical disintegration. Whatever the case, the IRS has attempted to implement IT projects that would remedy the problem, such TSM which began in 1986 and ended in 1997. The IRS required the modernization to keep pace with a growing volume of tax returns. Unfortunately, after costing up to $3.5 billion after ten years the project failed to meet its intended goals and was largely considered a failure in most documented sources.

Practical Significance: The IRS scenario is not uncommon in federal and state government agencies where the aggregate costs of failed IT projects are estimated to be over several billion dollars (CSTB, 2000). In fact, an estimated 70 percent of large-scale IT projects fail, many before implementation is completed (CSTB, 2000). We now face an exciting challenge to find a cure for a recurring "disease" that presently seems dangerously incurable. Indeed, the IRS or other federal agencies cannot stop their functions while this research goes on, but must continue to operate as a federal agency. However, by studying the past attempt to solve this problem through the research that has already been done on the Tax System Modernization project, we are trying to find new ways of implementing large-scale IT projects that ultimately will be effective.

Academic Significance: Most of the existing research on IT project implementation fails to capture the process-based and contextual dimensions that lead to success or failure (Montealegre, 1996). The lack of process-oriented, longitudinal studies and case-studies in this area has recently been noted by an NSF-appointed panel as a critical shortcoming of existing research on large-scale systems implementation (CSTB, 2000). The study reported in this paper was designed to specifically address issues raised by the NSF study by focusing on an individual case with a longitudinal data set. In doing so, we hope to build new understanding of how factors present in the case change in relation to one another, in relation to major events and episodes during the lifetime of the TSM project, and in relation to a standard set of project outcome metrics.

METHODOLOGY USED

For this project, we used an in-depth case study approach and used grounded theory guidelines described by Strauss and Corbin (1990) to assist with the analysis. Prior to starting our work on the SURF project, over 750 project-related documents spanning the lifetime of the IRS TSM project were collected. We began our process by selecting "potentially important" variables from the literature, specifically from two studies: Lyytinen and Hirschheim (1987) whose study focused on defining failure notions and failure types; and, Willcocks and Griffiths (1994), which defines a set of outcome measures applied to large-scale projects in the public sector. Because the study was exploratory and theory-building in nature, an effort was made to work, as Eisenhardt (1989:536) described, "as close as possible to the ideal of no theory under consideration and no hypotheses to test."

To ensure increased reliability among our findings, we conducted coding experiments and came to "negotiated agreement" as to the proper way in which to code the variables in the data set. To facilitate the coding process, we used a software package called NVivo, which is specifically designed to support the grounded theory approach to qualitative data analysis. In addition, consistent with recommendations by Strauss and Corbin (1990), we kept journals throughout the project to identify observations of patterns in the data that might lead to new hypotheses or theories about what makes large-scale IT projects succeed or fail in the public sector. We had frequent meetings to discuss our observations, to classify and interpret our analyses, and to verify that our coding of concepts remained consistent among the researchers.

The result of this approach to research is a set of hypotheses and suggestions for future research. We did not attempt to validate the hypotheses at this stage, as that would require additional data, and more case environments at a minimum. The IRS TSM project was selected initially because of the easy access to documentation from a variety of sources, the public interest and attention to this particular IT failure, and the fairly universal agreement among different sources that this project was indeed a failure along most measures. From this project we hoped to gain some new insight into possible causes of failure in large-scale IT projects in federal government and learn which sources of documentation are most useful in studying these projects. In subsequent research we hope to validate these hypotheses and confirm the generality of the current findings. To date, we have identified nearly a dozen similarly documented large-scale projects that are failing or have failed across a variety of federal and state agencies that should be useful in the validation process.

FINDINGS AND DISCUSSION

Based on the research conducted, we observed several factors that may have contributed to the failure of the Tax Systems Modernization Project. Overall, the findings were consistent with current literature, which suggests that the most significant challenges to large-scale IT projects are more managerial and organizational than technical in nature. Most of the issues identified related to the basic management of IT projects, with the added twist of complexity and overload introduced by project size and duration. While reviewing the coded outcome variables and searching for patterns, some unexpected issues arose from the data set. Among the issues we found most interesting is the potential impact that the General Accounting Office (GAO) has on project failure. Gaining a better understanding of these issues and phenomena may help federal agencies like the IRS, as well as other organizations, better manage large-scale IT projects.

One theme that persists throughout the documents is the inability of IRS to manage large-scale and long-term IT projects. Documents generated by the GAO continuously emphasize the need for the IRS to be able to plan, prioritize and schedule projects so that they do not run over budget and over time. Therefore, we can hypothesize that project failure is due in part to the inability of management to organize projects and treat them as meaningful investments. However, this surface observation has an underlying pattern that raises question about the role that the GAO plays in the success or failure of the TSM project. Indeed, patterns show that GAO points out the same managerial faults of IRS across different projects. Furthermore, paired with their observations are a series of recommendations, which sometimes conflict with one another, that could possibly add to the information overload and complexity that the IRS already faces on the TSM project. In reality, despite the numerous suggestions that the GAO has made on different projects, IRS has not shown significant improvement in managing them.

As a result of the GAO recommendations, IRS often formed committees to alleviate the problems raised. However, the birth of committees appears to be an easy solution to a large mass of technical and business requirements that are not being met by the existing or planned information systems. These committees are thought of as taking care of the situation, but in reality may further diminish the agency's information capacity by making additional recommendations that are also rarely put into practice. Therefore, these groups may act as a deterrent to future progress of TSM.

Ultimately, the weaknesses that GAO continuously points out about management cannot be ignored. In our research, we observed that bureaucracy runs deep within IRS culture. Indeed, we believe that the IRS tried to implement a new organizational structure without establishing new rules to support the changes. Consequently, critical players were not empowered to make valuable decisions that would affect the planning and budgeting of TSM, which resulted in the changes being somewhat ineffective and futile.

DIRECTIONS FOR FUTURE RESEARCH

A goal of our research was to identify possible explanations or hypotheses as to why large-scale IT projects fail, since existing literature in this area is sparse and incomplete. From the discussion above, we have identified several important directions for further research.

First, information overload and project complexity negatively affect the success of large-scale IT projects. We termed this concept "information capacity" to suggest that there is a certain amount of information and complexity that can be processed in relation to an agency or a project, and when that is exceeded, the likelihood of project success decreases. However, we are not yet certain as to *how* this relationship plays out specifically in the IRS context.

Second, the processes by which agencies like the IRS incorporate or fail to incorporate recommendations into their project management techniques,

particularly in cases where recommendations are to change existing management practices, are not well understood and appear to be ineffective. It would be important to see why those changes are not being implemented and who is responsible for driving those changes in the agency. If these recommendations could be used in management methods perhaps it can improve the overall efficiency of the IRS, and further facilitate the success of large-scale IT projects.

Third, the role that the GAO plays as an oversight agency in large-scale IT projects in federal agencies may have some negative consequences for the success of these projects. It is important for future research to take a closer look at the roles that GAO and other oversight organizations play in large-scale IT projects in federal agencies like the IRS. Although they are external to the IRS, do they take on a more internal role as they become more involved in the culture of the IRS? And if they do, how does it affect their evaluation of the IRS and consequently their recommendations? It would be worthwhile to know exactly how they operate and how they actually affect large-scale IT projects like TSM.

Fourth, the role of agency internal committees in the management and resolution of recommendations and problems should be studied further. It would be useful to know why they are formed and if they are useful to the IRS in managing projects like TSM, since evidence in the documentation suggests this may not be the case. For both committees and the GAO, we believe there may be detrimental effects to the IRS's information capacity and likelihood of project success.

RESEARCH AND PROJECT LIMITATIONS

It is hard to pinpoint the exact causes of the problems that surrounded the TSM project failure. The enormity of such a task with endless amounts of information and people involved suggests many different reasons for its failure. From a research perspective, there have also been drawbacks to studying potential causes for failure. Firstly, the limited timeframe handicapped our efforts to code and analyze the entire data set. Therefore, our hypotheses are limited to a subset of the available data. In addition, some researchers involved in this study did not have time invested in fully understanding and learning the background of the IRS. This yielded a narrow view of the organization, which is just based on the documentation, which affected the way we chose variables for the coding scheme.

Secondly, although we spent a good deal of time creating and negotiating a coding scheme and structure, we did not achieve the amount of interrater reliability that we would have liked for select variables. Consequently, it made it more difficult to detect patterns with the data set that could have potentially weeded out problems. This also could have been a result of some researchers in the study lacking background knowledge of the IRS.

Lastly, since most of the documents were intended for public view and consumption, there are details that may be missing from the reports. As a result, the data may be biased in order to make it presentable to such a wide audience. In reality, a lot of truth about what happened at those specific times may have been left out of the picture. For these reasons, we were only able to form general hypotheses at this point which will require further research to validate.

CONCLUSIONS

Despite the limitations of the data set, there were patterns that emerged from the research that were notable. For example, the role of external agencies like the GAO may prove to play a critical role in the outcome of large-scale projects because of its overwhelming auditing presence in the IRS. The GAO is constantly providing suggestions for improvement to the IRS who in turn takes the time to agree or disagree with the recommendations, but no worthwhile change has occurred. Therefore, the recommendations may prove to be in excess and may even slow down IRS functions as the information capacity of the project and agency managers becomes overwhelmed. The same idea can also be applied to the creation of committees whose formation may just be a justification for resolving some of the IRS's project problems. Furthermore, among these problems may be the organizational structure and bureaucratic culture that deters top management from leading critical project ideas and acting as a stimulus for proper planning and budgeting for IS projects. These findings and observations are insufficiently explained and discussed in the existing literature and represent potentially important ideas worth further investigation.

As an exploratory research effort focusing on one in-depth case study, we were successful at identifying some new hypotheses and ideas around what leads to project failure in large-scale IT projects in the public sector. In subsequent stages of this research, we hope to further demonstrate the generality of the findings and verify their contribution to the success or failure of large-scale IT projects.

REFERENCES

CSTB, *Making IT Better: Expanding Information Technology Research to Meet Society's Needs*," Committee on Information Technology Research in a Competitive World, Computer Science and Telecommunication Board, National Research Council, National Academy Press, 2000.

Eisenhardt, K. "Building Theories from Case Study Research," *Academy of Management Review*, (14:4), 1989, pp. 532-550.

Lyytinen, K. and Hirschheim, R. "Information systems failures—a survey and classification of the empirical literature," *Oxford Surveys in Information Technology*, (4), 1987, pp. 257-309.

Montealegre, R. "What Can We Learn from the Implementation of the Automated Baggage-Handling System at the Denver International Airport?" 1996 Americas Conference, Association for Information Systems, Phoenix, AZ, August 16-18, 1996.

Strauss, A. and Corbin, J. *Basics of Qualitative Research: Grounded Theory Procedures and Techniques*, Newbury Park, CA: Sage Publications, 1990.

Wilcocks, L. and Griffiths, C. "Predicting Risk of Failure in Large-Scale Information Technology Projects," *Technological Forecasting and Social Change*, (47), 1994, pp. 205-228.

Adding Economic and Information Theory to Technique – The Case of Using the Uniform Chart of Accounts for Building Entrepreneurial Nonprofit Organizations

John F. Sacco
Department of Public & International Affairs–3F4
George Mason University
Fairfax, VA
Tel: 703 993 4569, fax: 703 993 1399
jsacco@gmu.edu

Odd J. Stalebrink
Division of Public Administration
West Virginia University
213 Knapp Hall, PO Box 6322, Morgantown, WV 26506-6322
(304) 293-2614 Ext. 3155, fax: 304-293-8814
Odd.Stalebrink@mail.wvu.edu

BACKGROUND

Integral to entrepreneurship in nonprofit organizations is finding more earned income to balance traditional philanthropy. An entrepreneurial context for nonprofit entities, however, tends to challenge the effectiveness of traditional nonprofit accounting systems. Frequently, these systems have lacked both uniformity and flexibility in organizing financial data at desired level of detail.

Touted among the accounting reforms for entrepreneurial entities is the Uniform Chart of Accounts (UCOA). The UCOA allows for tracking various types of revenues and expenses by category such as grants, programs and departments. The level of detail permits a closer look at where cost or revenue problems might be located. The UCOA is also designed to automatically take account information (e.g., contributions, salaries and supplies) and report it according to Generally Accepted Accounting Principle (GAAP) as well as Internal Revenue Service reporting requirements, namely, Form 990.

Recalling the accounting equation (Assets = Liabilities + Net Assets [revenues –expenses]), here is a simple outline of the UCOA for coding nonprofit transactions.

1xxx where 1= assets
2xxx where 2= liabilities
3xxx where 3=net assets
4xxx-xxx to 6xxx-xxx = revenues and associated activities
7xxx-xxx to 9xxx-xxx = expenses and associated activities

The additional 3xs for the revenues and expenses are for programs and operations. The account numbers 7xxx-100 might be an expense for an adoption program. Following the same format, the account number 7710-100 might be a supplies expense for the adoption program, indicated by the 100. Revenues for the adoption program could also be tracked. Thus, with UCOA, a positive or negative change in net assets ("profit or loss") can be assessed for the adoption program.

THE ENTREPRENEURIAL NONPROFIT

Since at least the 1980s nonprofit organizations have sought to become more enterprising. Among other things, this means adding earned income to philanthropic donations. Some of the larger nonprofit entities have remained classical hierarchical organizations, adding royalties, licensing fees, some products and affinity cards. Some mid-size nonprofit operations have sought to operate more like loosely connected organizations with franchises and partners. In these mid-sized entities, the national or headquarter office can generate ideas, products and cover start up costs. These national offices are some-

times called "angels." They fly in, offer start up cost and support and then leave, hoping the franchise or partner will succeed and share some of its returns with the national office. Regardless of the mode, this more energetic, risk taking venture needs a sound accounting and financial reporting system. UCOA is a part of that sound accounting system.

THEORY BUILDING

While the UCOA adds necessary details for entrepreneurial management, it is still a technical foundation without the benefit of theoretical guidance. With respect to suggestions for nonprofit entreprenuership there is no lack of ideas. Examples are the use of royalties, affinity cards, and changes in the organizational culture to one that is more entrepreneurial, including shifting or discharging employees who cannot or will not fit the new earned income thrust. Given that the focus is entreprenuership, theories from economics ought to be considered in developing approaches or guides for those nonprofit entities that wish to be oriented to what is called earned income. One broad theory that can help is Austrian Economics. Unlike classical economics, it does not make the operating organization a black box and has entrepreneurship as one of its main foci. Another important economic idea for entrepreneurial nonprofit entities is that marginal cost should equal marginal revenue (MC=MR). The next element borrowed from economics is agency theory. Agency theory is very important in the discussion of nonprofit entrepreneurialship since nonprofit entities operate on the notion of trust and agency theory goes against faith in trust. The last economic element is transaction cost economics (TCE). Costs associated with negotiations and contracts among parties can become high and must be included in any earned income plan. With this dispersion of efforts as a possible important vehicle for the entrepreneurial nonprofit, an information technology (IT) theory is important. The direction here is to have sufficient robustness in IT so that it can accommodate both coordination and individuality. The last element in this theoretical model is a value added accounting tool. The tool interjected is activity based accounting (ABC).

FINDING A STRATEGY, PRODUCT OR PRODUCT NICHE FOR EARNED INCOME

To produce earned income a nonprofit needs to find a strategy, product or product niche. Here is where the lists of ideas can play a role. Does it have something valuable to franchise? Can it license its logo? Can it provide research and development of value to a client sector? With the exception of Austrian Economics and some other non-classical economic theories, few economic theories provide guidance to entrepreneurship. Austrian Economics is built, in part, on learning from information and feedback. It focuses on change, uncertainty and risk. As a result, the starting point is usually the openness of the nonprofit to new ideas, tests of those new ideas and more openness about earning signals. In a case study underway, the nonprofit has a successful model and products for civic education for youth that has been franchised. Further, the companies that make the products place the nonprofit's civic education logo on the products and pay the nonprofit for use of the logo.

The Main Role of MC=RC

Table 1, "Stop Production when MC=MR", shows the important role of the equation, MC=MR, in earned income strategies. The proclivity of a nonprofit might be to push production too far on the grounds that the product fits achievement of the social mission. Notice in the Table 1, "Stop Production when MC=MR," profit is at a maximum at 140 units. Continuing production can advance the social mission but leave the nonprofit with insufficient resources to find the next niche. Moreover, once the nonprofit gets itself into the market where earned income is central, other producers will see the profits being made and jump into production, increasing the supply and lowering the price that can be charged. Thus, MC=MR will change, with MC=MR coming at a lower profit level.

TRANSACTION COST ECONOMICS

If it is the propensity of entrepreneurial nonprofit entities to have diverse structures or products to gain those earned incomes then transaction cost economics (TCE) becomes important. One main issue in TCE is whether to go to the market to buy the product or to do it "in-house." This decision was sometimes called the make-buy decision or more broadly the market versus hierarchy with the hierarchy meaning the organization. The TCE issue becomes complicated as nonprofit operations include a loose structure that includes franchises and partners. In this case, nonprofit operations are confronted with deciding whether to keep production at headquarters, spin some to a franchise or partner or go directly into the market. A number of criteria have been developed to help with this decision. One is asset specificity. If the asset, fund raising operations for instance, is not ordinarily available in the market place, then the nonprofit is best to keep that function in-house. Otherwise, the firm chosen to do the fund raising might constantly haggle and inflate the transaction costs. Fund raising, however, seems not to be a unique asset and thus some can be placed in the market for competitive bidding.

AGENCY THEORY

The underlying assumption in nonprofit organizations even when they move to be entrepreneurial is that trust was and remains integral to operations. As the social mission begins to clash with the so-called double bottom line approach where the pressure for earned income is as or nearly as important as donations, workers may pursue their own self interest for self protection rather than the goals and mission of the nonprofit organization. Under such heavy pressure for earned income, job security becomes an issue with a new entrepreneurial attitude and self interest may over take trust. If that is the case, then greater monitoring might be needed. Accounting systems, such as UCOA, become relevant again as a means to track workload, production and earnings. The delicate issue is to determine how much monitoring is needed. Nonprofit organizations can be destroyed with too little or too much monitoring. One

option is better record keeping (use of the accounting system again) and more frequent use of internal and external auditors. Another option is better tracking of bottom line issues. Accountants and auditors have a variety of ratios available for identifying problem spots. Good tracking of how quickly pledges and receivables get collected are examples of such indicators.

INFORMATION TECHNOLOGY (IT) THEORY

The main point vis a vis IT theory as it relates to entrepreneurial nonprofit operations is to avoid seeing IT as a tool solely used for coordination. Take an intranet for instance. It can be set up to be an excellent coordination tool by placing documents and forms online for all to use. However, the intranet must allow individuals to share (i.e., post) draft documents and ideas. A relatively open ended intranet can provide a place for experimentation for what to place on the intranet.

Intranets have the potential for this dual capacity. One definition of an intranet is that it is "a private network that uses Internet software and standards to deliver information to an internal audience." A focus on the employees does not mean that employees cannot use the intranet to train clients or demonstrate products. It can be used for training either by direct use of the intranet or by spinning off software from the intranet to the market. While the intranet logic as well as the various tools included can cut across different organizations, organization culture can play a role. For instance, if units within the organization are accustomed to some independence then the intranet needs to allow for that independence in the form of allowing units to add their own material. Thus, the coordination and individuality capacity must be built into the intranet from the beginning.

VALUE ADDED THROUGH ACTIVITY BASED ACCOUNTING

Activity based accounting (ABC) is designed to provide a picture of which program activities are consuming the most resources. Here is an example of assigning object expenses from the UCOA to program activities. Table 2, "Activity Based Accounting for Better Program Management," shows the process.

Unit Cost from the Matrix

One piece of potentially important information that can be derived from this matrix is the cost to train teachers. Assume that four (4) teachers were trained. At a total cost of $1200, cost per unit or the cost to train one teacher is $300. If such information were done in budget or proposal form, it could be used to price any cost to teachers (or schools), not covered by donor money.

SUMMARY

Accounting tools such as UCOA and ABC as well as IT tool such as intranets are important to the progress of entrepreneurial nonprofit operations. However, they are techniques that need to be placed in a theoretical context for guidance. This paper suggests the use of economic and IT theory for this context.

Table 2, Activity Based Accounting for Better Program Management

Salary	Training	Taxes	Supplies	Rent	Phone	Services	Total
$2,000	$400	$100	$1,300	$400	$100	$500	$4,800

Allocation to Activities

	Salary	Training	Taxes	Supplies	Rent	Phone	Services	Total
Recruiting								
30%	0	0.3	0	0.3	0.5	0.2		
600	0	$30	0	$120	50	$100		$900
Training teachers								
30%	0.4	0.3	0.1	0.4	0.2	0.2		
600	160	30	130	160	20	100		$1200
Investigating								
20%	0.2	0.2	0.1	0.1	0.1	0.2		
400	80	20	130	40	10	100		$780
Implementing								
10%	0.3	0.1	0.7	0.1	0.1	0.2		
200	120	10	910	40	10	100		$1390
Learning laws								
10%	0.1	0.1	0.1	0.1	0.1	0.2		
200	40	10	130	40	10	100		$530

Table 1, Stop Production when MC=MR

Weekly Production	Price	Marginal Cost	Total Cost	Total Revenue	Profit
100			1250	1500	250
	15	10.5			
110			1355	1650	295
	15	11.55			
120			1470.5	1800	329.5
	15	12.61			
130			1596.6	1950	353.4
	15	14.61			
140			1738.2	2100	361.8
	15	15.23			
150			1890.5	2250	359.5
	15	16.81			
160			2058.6	2400	341.4

Virtual Reality In Education

Nicoletta Sala
Academy of Architecture
Largo Bernasconi- CH 6850 Mendrisio
University of Italian Switzerland – Switzerland
Tel: + 41 91 640 48 77 Fax: + 41 91 640 48 48
Email: nsala @arch.unisi.ch

ABSTRACT

Virtual reality (VR) is a technology which permits its users to become immersed in a computer generated virtual world. This paper presents some potential application of VR to education, in particular in two undergraduate courses of Mathematics (Mathematics 1 and Mathematics 5) at the Academy of Architecture of Mendrisio, Switzerland (University of Italian Switzerland). In our courses, we have organized the lectures using multimedia technologies, for example: scientific documentaries, hypermedia, 2D Computer Aided Design (CAD). To introduce the connections between mathematics, nature, and architecture we have also utilised some virtual objects, created using VRML (Virtual Reality Modelling Language). In our case, we have observed that virtual reality is not only an educational tool but it is introductory for a correct students' background.

1 INTRODUCTION

New technologies of communication (hypertext, hypermedia, the Internet) can help to modify our teaching methods [1, 2, 3, 4, 5]. Virtual Reality (VR) is a technology, but can virtual reality aid in education? To answer to this question we have to present some considerations. Recently, the term "Virtual Reality" has been applied more widely to include graphics applications that allow users to walk through a simulated environment and, possibly, to interact with objects in it. In a 1998 study titled Educational Uses of Virtual Reality Technology, Christine Youngblut says of educational curriculum available for use by VR, "The range of educational subjects covered is quite broad, showing a fairly equal split between the arts and sciences." In addition, Youngblut says that VR "applications are fairly equally split between those designed for elementary and middle school levels, those for high school students, and those for college students (undergraduate and graduate)" [6, p. 29]. Virtual Reality is strictly defined in this paper as a specific technology, in agreement with other works [7, 8]. This technology is computer based and gives the illusion of being immersed in a 3-D space with the ability to interact with this 3D space. The interface hardware components consist of a visual display apparatus, some sort of input device, and a position sensor. Typically, the visual display that is used is a helmet that places a television-like screen over each eye, blocking one's view of the physical world. Instead, of the physical world, one sees a 3-dimensional rendition of a place that is created by computer graphics [9, 10]. Input devices can range from a keyboard to a mouse (2D or 3D) to a head-mounted display (HMD) to a motion-sensing data gloves. The purpose of the input device is to allow the human participant to give electrical signals to the computer which can be interpreted as specific commands. Depending on how the software was programmed, one mouse button or hand gesture might represent "fly forward" while another button or gesture means "fly backward." Virtual reality has emerged as a revolutionary human/computer interface, challenging everything to which we are accustomed. Research institutes around the world have demonstrated the potential of VR systems as a visualization tool and, as technology continues to improve, VR systems will become pervasive as tools for research and education [11]. Three primary requirements of a virtual reality system are [12]:

- immersion (that requires physically involving the user, both by capturing exclusive visual attention and by transparently responding to three – dimensional input. For example, through a head – tracker, 3D mouse, wand, data glove, or fully instrumented body suit);
- interaction (through the three – dimensional control device to investigate and control the virtual environment);
- visual realism (that is an accurate representation about the virtual world).

In this paper we describe some applications of the virtual reality in the educational process in two different undergraduate courses of Mathematics at the Academy of Architecture of Mendrisio (Switzerland). The paper is organized as follows: section 2 presents VR in educational process; section 3 describes our educational examples of the virtual reality; and in the section 4 we have our conclusions.

2 VIRTUAL REALITY IN EDUCATION

The potential of VR supporting education is widely recognised. Many researchers believe that Virtual Reality offers strong benefit that can support education. For some, VR's ability to facilitate constructivist learning activities is the key issue. Others focus on the potential to provide alternative forms of learning that can support different types of learners, such as visually oriented learners. Still others see the ability for learners, and educators, to collaborate in a virtual class that transcends geographical boundaries as the major benefit.

In traditional instructional environments, students learn by assimilation, for example, by listening to an instructor lecture about a subject. Current educational thinking is that students are able to master, retain, and generalize new knowledge in a learning-by-doing situation. This philosophy of pedagogy is called constructivism and its supporters vary, ranging from those who see it as a useful complement to teaching – by – telling to those who argue that whole curriculum should be reinvented by students through gently guided discovery learning [6]. The major distinction between traditional instructional design and constructivism is that the former focuses on design instruction that has predictable outcomes and intervenes during instruction to map predetermined conception of reality onto the student's knowledge, while the latter focuses on instruction that fosters the learning process instead of controlling it [13]. Educational theory and cognitive science support the exploration of VR as an educational tool. In the field of educational theory, the concept of constructivism powerfully articulates an effective strategy for teaching children. Its proponents advocate that students should be fully involved in their education instead of playing the role of passive sponges waiting to be told the correct answers. The actual methods that constructivist teachers may use vary greatly. At one extreme, teachers may propose that there are no correct answers and that individual students must discover their own truths [14]. At the Human Interface Technology Lab (HITLab), a part of the Washington Technology Center at the University of Washington in Seattle, several pilot studies had been performed to examine VR's potential in the field of education. The Pacific Science Center studies used 10 to 15 year old students who were attending a week-long summer day camp. Some of these students had extensive computer knowledge, while others were novice computer users. As part of their camp, they learned about VR. In groups of 10 or so students, they brainstormed virtual world creations. In sub-groups of 2 to 3 students, they created objects for their world along with specifications as to how the objects should be placed and move in the virtual world. An example of constructivist teaching method is "The Adventures of Jasper Woodbury," a videodisk program for teaching math that was developed by The Cognition and Technology Group at Vanderbilt (CTGV). "Jasper" consists of 4 adventure stories designed to provide students with real-world, open-ended problems that do have correct mathematical solutions. CTGV believes "that the realistic nature of our Jasper problems (including their complexity) helps students construct important sets of ideas and beliefs and refrain from constructing misconceptions" [15]. Using constructivist theory, Byrne (1996) has created a virtual chemistry world to encourage students to learn by exploring and interacting with the information. Instead of sitting in a classroom and passively viewing images of atomic orbitals, students can place electrons into a atom and see the atomic orbital appear as the electron buzzes [16]. Cognitive science is another field of knowledge that guided the use of VR and multimedia technologies as educational tool [17]. Since cognitive scientists study how the human mind works, their theories can address how VR can help students learn. According to cognitive theories, VR can help humans process information and therefore learn, by making abstract concepts more concrete. According to many cognitive scientists humans think symbolically [18, 19]. VR can present abstract information in concrete forms that humans have been processing by immersing people in a visual computer-generated world.

3 VIRTUAL REALITY OUR EXAMPLES

In our case, we have used VR inside two different courses of Mathematics (first and fifth year). In this paper the term "virtual reality" is used broadly to cover both immersive and non-immersive VR. For example, in the course of Mathematical Thought (first year) VR is a good medium for making abstract concepts concrete [20]. To illustrate our idea, we needed a subject area to examine. The topic dedicated to the polyhedra and their interconnections between nature and architecture is an excellent example of an abstract topic that is difficult to learn [4]. The difficulty of understanding scientific concepts is well researched [21]. "Students' misunderstandings and misconceptions in school sciences at all levels constitute a major problem of concern to science educators, scientist-researchers, teachers, and, of course, students" [22, p. 1054]. This difficulty is attributed to the abstractness of the scientific topics [11, 23, 24].

Virtual reality has been used by our students in different way [25]:
- to observe and to rotate the platonic solids and the polyhedra from the different points of view (outside and inside the virtual objects),
- to create some virtual object using VRML (Virtual Reality Modeling Language),
- to observe and to manipulate the fullerreni molecules (C_{60}),
- to observe and to manipulate the geodesic domes,
- to study the symmetry presents in the crystals.

In the course of Mathematics 5, the VR has been analysed as a medium to create the virtual towns, and to virtual world. VR is also connected with the Internet and the cyberspace [9]. There are some interesting topics on the virtual communities and the virtual cities with their sociology implications [26]. During our course we have emphasized the connection between virtual reality a fractal geometry, to realize the virtual worlds, for example to create trees using fractal algorithms, mountains, special effects. Figures 1 and 2 show an example of VR application to generate virtual landscape using fractal procedures.

Figure 1 Virtual landscape generated using fractal procedures (grid phase)

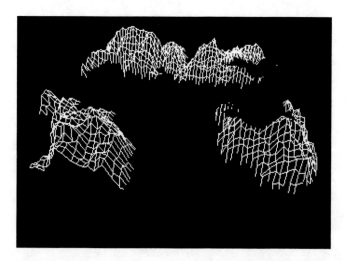

Figure 2 Virtual landscape generated using fractal procedures (texture phase)

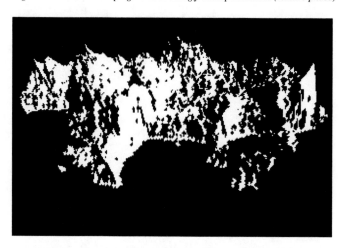

Virtual Reality in our teaching process is a good tool to train our students to use this technology inside an architectural project (e.g., to realise a virtual building in 3D or a virtual set designing). VR is also integrated with the Web and the cyberspace, for example to realise a Geographic Information System (GIS) [25].

Already there are several browsers on the web that can be used for non immersive viewing of virtual worlds, although these browsers only support very minimal interaction with virtual worlds. Virtual worlds can be designed for single inhabitants, such as a solo flight trainee, or for many, simultaneous participants. When a virtual world supports multiple users, it can give rise to a virtual community. Inhabitants of a virtual community have a heightened sense of presence in this artificial world, since they can communicate with each other in the context of the simulated world. Virtual communities can provide the settings for effective teleconferencing, and for productive, remote cooperative work. We have also analysed VR as a medium to create virtual cities. For this reason, our students have researched virtual worlds on the Web (e.g., Alphaworld). AlphaWorld is an urbanised virtual world where each piece of land is owned by individually registered users (citizens of the virtual world), and where people, represented as avatars, can meet and interact. The world is rendered in fully three-dimensional graphics. As time goes by, this world has been further developed. In the future we will use an immersive virtual reality to create virtual visit in the buildings in agreement with other researchers [27, 28].

4 CONCLUSIONS

Virtual reality technology may offer strong benefits in education not only by facilitation of constructivist learning activities but also by the potential to provide alternative forms of learning that can support different types of learners such as visually oriented learners. VR promotes the best and probably only strategy that allows students to learn from non-symbolic first-person experience, and it permits to the students to see the effect of changing physical laws, observe events at an atomic or planetary scale, visualize abstract concepts, and visit environments and interact with events that distance, time, or safety factor normal preclude [16, 29, 30, 31, 32]. Most educational applications for VR are designed to make use of some characteristics which include:
- Allowing students to gain a greater understanding of abstract concepts through the creation of visual metaphors,
- Allowing students to directly manipulate and scale virtual objects or environments for clearer understandings,
- Allowing students to visit places and interact with events that distance, time, or safety concerns would normally prohibit [6, 33]

These characteristics allow virtual worlds to support a wide range of types of experiential learning that is otherwise unavailable [6]. Based on data collected from thousands of students of different ages, using different applications with different interfaces, there is overwhelming evidence that students enjoy both experiencing pre-developed applications and developing their own virtual worlds [34].

Virtual Reality has a definite role to play in education, if merely from a motivational viewpoint. However, this should not be extrapolated to the idea that VR should be used for every aspect of education. While VR may offer something for every subject, the cost of the system, especially at current prices means VR is a heavy resource sink.

We have observed that the use of virtual reality for teaching offers a series of advantages learning, for example the efficacy, and a high level of interactivity, in agreement with other researches [32, 35]. We are sure that VR will be an important tool to organize learning environments in the 21st century.

REFERENCES

[1] R.B. Kozma, Learning With Media, *Review of Educational Research*, 61, (2), 1991, 179-211.

[2] R.E. Mayer, *Multimedia Learning* (Cambridge: University Press, 2001).

[3] M.J. Rosenberg, *E-Learning: Strategies for Delivering Knowledge in the Digital Age* (New York, McGraw-Hill Professional Publishing, 2000).

[4] N. Sala, Multimedia Technologies in Educational Environment: An Overview, *Proceedings International Conference on Computer in Education (ICDE)*, Seoul, Korea, 2001, 404 – 411.

[5] J.D. Wilhelm, P. Friedemann, & J.Erickson, *Hyperlearning : Where Projects, Inquiry, and Technology Meet* (Stenhouse Pub, 1998)

[6] C. Youngblut, Educational Uses of Virtual Reality Technology, Institute for Defense Analyses, IDA Document D-2128, (1998, January (Available as online: http://www.hitl.washington.edu/scivw/youngblut-edvr/D2128.pdf)

[7] P. Weishar, *Digital Space: Designing Virtual Environments* (New York, .McGraw-Hill Professional Publishing, 1998).

[8] W. Sherman & A. Craig, *Working with Virtual Reality* (New York, Morgan Kaufmann Publishers, 2002).

[9] N. Sala, L'informatica: scenari presenti e futuri. in *Didattica delle scienze e informatica*, n° 208, Casa Editrice la Scuola, Brescia, 2000, 45- 54.

[10] L. Jacobson, *Garage Virtual Reality* (USA, Sams, 1994).

[11] D.E. Brown, Using Examples and Analogies to Remediate Misconceptions in Physics: Factors Influencing Conceptual Change, *Journal of Research in Science Teaching*, 29, (1), 1992, 17-34.

[12] L.J. Rosemblum & R. A. Cross, The Challenge of Virtual Reality (In Earnshaw W. R., Vince J., Jones H. (Eds.) *Visualization & Modeling*, San Diego: Academic Press, 1997, 325 - 399)

[13] D.H. Jonassen, Thinking Technology, *Educational Technology*, April, 1994, 34 – 37

[14] D.H. Jonassen, Evaluating Constructivistic Learning, *Educational Technology*, 1991, September, 28-33.

[15] Cognition and Technology Group at Vanderbilt (CTGV), Some Thoughts About Constructivism and Instructional Design, *Educational Technology*, 1991, September, 16-18.

[16] C.M. Byrne, *Water on Tap: The Use of Virtual Reality as an Educational Tool* (Ph.D. Dissertation. University of Washington, Seattle, WA. 1996).

[17] N. Sala, Constructivist Approach In The Learning Using Hypermedia Solution, *Multimedia Modelling MMM 2000* (Singapore, World Scientific, 2000, 107 – 122).

[18] P. N. Johnson-Laird, *Mental Models* (Cambridge: Harvard University Press, 1983)

[19] A. Newell, *Unified Theories of Cognition* (Cambridge: Harvard University Press, 1990).

[20] N. Sala, Teaching mathematics using the new media, *Proceedings CIEAEM53: Mathematical Literacy in the Digital Era*, Ghisetti e Corvi Editori, Verbania, Italia, 2001, 56 – 63

[21] P. J. Garnett & D. F. Treagust, Conceptual Difficulties Experienced by Senior High School Students of Electrochemistry: Electrochemical (Galvanic) and Electrolytic Cells, *Journal of Research in Science Teaching*, 29, (10), 1992, 1079-1099.

[22] U. Zoller, Students' Misunderstandings and Misconceptions in College Freshman Chemistry (General and Organic), *Journal of Research in Science Teaching*, 27 (10), 1990, 1053-1065

[23] A. H. Johnstone, Why is science difficult to learn? Things are seldom what they seem, *Journal of Computer Assisted Learning*, 7, 1991, 75-83.

[24] R. Millar, Why is science hard to learn? *Journal of Computer Assisted Learning*, 7, 1991, 66-74.

[25] N. Sala, From Virtual Reality to the Virtual Cities, *Proceedings International Conference on New Educational Environment 2002*, Lugano, Switzerland, session 2.3, pp. 21 - 24

[26] H. Rheingold *The Virtual Community* (USA: MIT Press, 2000).

[27] M. Engeli, Agents – Enhanced Reality (Schmitt G., *Architektur mit dem Computer*, Wiesbaden: Vieweg Verlag, 1996) 110 - 111.

[28] D. Kurman, N. Elte & M. Engeli Real Time Modeling with Architectural Space (In Junge R. *CAAD Future 1997*, Dordrecht: Kluwer Academic Publisher, 1997) 809 – 819.

[29] J. R. Brown, Visualization and Scientific Applications (Earnshaw W. R., Vince J., Jones H. (Eds.) *Visualization & Modeling*, San Diego: Academic Press, 1997) 1-11.

[30] R. A. Cross & A. J. Hanson, Virtual reality performance for virtual geometry, *Proceedings Visualization '94* , Washington DC, Oct. 1994, 156 – 163.

[31] J. H. Kim, S.T. Park, H. Lee, K.C. Yuk & H. Lee, Virtual Reality Simulations in Physics Education, *Proceedings World Conference on Educational Multimedia, Hypermedia & Telecommunications EDMEDIA 2001*, Tampere, Finland, 2001, 964 – 965.

[32] A. Antionietti , E. Imperio, C. Rasi, & M. Sacco Virtual Reality in Engineering Instruction: In Search of the Best Learning Procedures, *Proceedings World Conference on Multimedia, Hypermedia & Telecommunications ED-MEDIA 99*, Seattle, Washington, 1999, 663 - 668.

[33] W. Winn, *A conceptual basis for educational applications of virtual reality*. (HITL Technical Report No. TR-93- 9). Seattle, WA: Human Interface Technology Laboratory. (Available as online HTML document: http://www.hitl.washington.edu/publications/r-93-9)

[34] S.M. Ervin & H.H. Hasbrouck, *Landscape Modeling*, McGraw-Hill, New York, 2001.

[35] R.L. Jackson, W. Taylor & W. Winn, Peer Collaboration And Virtual Environments: A Preliminary Investigation Of Multi-Participant Virtual Reality Applied In Science Education, *Proceedings World Conference on Multimedia, Hypermedia & Telecommunications ED-MEDIA 99*, Seattle, Washington, 1999, 1050 – 1055.

The Impact of Unsolicited Online Help on the Usability of Software Applications

Suzanne Sackstein and Renata Sanfona
School of Economics and Business Sciences
University of the Witwatersrand, South Africa
P.O. Box 29609, Sandringham, 2131
Tele: 27-11-717-8158, Fax: 27-11-717-8139,
suzannes@isys.wits.ac.za

ABSTRACT

This paper will report on work in progress aimed at exploring whether unsolicited online help, within a software application, provides the end user satisfaction and ease of use. Using the theory of the field of Human Computing Interaction (HCI) and a classification of end users into different skill levels, the impact on each skill level will be investigated. Empirical data is currently being collected and will be used to illustrate that the more skilled an end user is, the less satisfaction there will be with unsolicited online help.

INTRODUCTION

The area of HCI is a vast "multi-disciplinary" field that incorporates many other fields of study: these include psychology, ergonomics, art, engineering, design and many others (Faulkner, 1998; Preece, 1993). "HCI is the study of relationships which exist between human users and the computer systems that they use in the performance of their various tasks" (Faulkner, 1998). Preece (1993) suggests that the aim of HCI research is to improve the usability of software applications. This is achieved when the software application can be used both easily and effectively by its intended end users (see Shackel, 1991).

Contributing to this research area a study is currently underway, that examines how unsolicited online help, specifically the MS Paper Clip, affects end users differently based on their skill level in terms of user satisfaction and usability of the software application. The following two sections of the paper describe the study's key concepts.

Usability and User Satisfaction

Usability is the "capability of the computer in human functional terms to be used easily and effectively by a specified range of end users, given specified training and user support, to fulfill the specified range of tasks, within a specified range of environmental scenarios" (Shackel, 1991).

According to Schneiderman in a survey of 6 000 computer users, it was found that an average of 5.1 hours per week were wasted trying to use computers. Many authors have discussed the benefits of improved software usability; these include reduced user errors, increased user satisfaction and software utilization, improved productivity and user performance and reduced user frustration (Preece, 1993, Henneman, 1999). If software applications are not usable, the number of errors that users encounter increases, thus resulting in reduced user satisfaction and increased user frustration. So, usable applications are those that aim to reduce the number of possible errors that users are able to make (Norman, 1990).

User satisfaction is "a feeling of happiness or pleasure because you have achieved something or got what you wanted" (Longman English Dictionary). In order to provide for the above benefits, software designers must take into account effective design of error messages, online help and user manuals (Bolton, 2001).

Online Help

"Help and usability are intertwined" (Kalk, 2001). "Online help is a necessity for all users, whatever their skills, knowledge, cognitive capabilities and type of use". It should help users learn and master the use of the software through helping them achieve the tasks they are required to perform (Capobianco & Carbonell, 2001).

Dix et al., (1998) suggest that any form of online help should fulfill certain requirements; these include, availability, accuracy and completeness, consistency, robustness, flexibility and unobtrusiveness. Many authors agree that good online help systems are those that describe the error clearly, are understandable, offer constructive guidance, take on a positive tone and are represented in a user-centered style, i.e. it should allow users to feel in control of the software application and should never blame the end user when an error occurs (Schneiderman, 1987; Gaine, 2000; Bolton, 2001; Nielsen, 2001; Seebach, 2002)

There is a difference between online help that is searched out by the user and online help that comes up on the screen when the software application detects an error that the user is about to make or is able to suggest a better way to achieve the task currently being performed. The latter referred to, as 'unsolicited help' is the focus of the current study. Dix describes these as adaptive help systems, which monitor the activity of an end user and construct a model of the specific end user.

All adaptive systems must have some knowledge of the system itself, in order to provide the correct and relevant assistance to the end user. One way that this can be achieved is through domain and task modelling, which allows the help system to select the appropriate advice for the end user. Overlay models of the system hold a record of known user errors and the user's actual behaviour is compared with these. "Potential errors may be matched when partially executed and help given to enable the user to avoid the error" (Dix, 1998). Unsolicited online help should be able to offer user support without being obtrusive, i.e. that the software application should be designed to avoid errors, and should solve errors without disturbing the user (Bolton, 2001).

The issue of who holds the initiative in the request for online help is an area that also needs to be addressed i.e. who is in control of the system activity? As adaptive help systems can be intrusive to the user. The majority of authors agree that there should be a mix of initiative i.e. the user should be able to question the system at any time, and the system can offer hints to the end user, this should be done in a sensitive manner and the user should be able to switch off the help is desired (Dix, 1998).

The unsolicited online help to be tested in this study is the Microsoft (MS) Office Assistant Paper Clip, affectionately known as 'Clippy', which offers tips on tasks that you perform as you work. For example when you write a letter, the MS Paper Clip automatically displays topics to help you create and format the letter. Research has shown that many people curse when they mention the animated MS Paper Clip. "But it is a big mistake to attribute user aggravation to the cutesy graphic. The problem is not the messenger. It is the message: MS thinks it knows what you want better than you do" (Postrel, 1998). Postrel also makes the claim that if applications display intelligence then they should do what the user requires them to do and not what they want to. She likens the changes and suggestion of the MS paper Clip to your car suddenly reconfiguring the pedals or rearranging the dashboard.

THE STUDY

The authors' hypothesis is that the more skilled the end user is, the less satisfaction and ease of use the unsolicited online help will provide.

Classification of end users in the study is based on the combination of categories as described by Dix, Schneiderman & Prescott and Crichton. Usually the designer will have a 'typical' user in mind and will build the interface accordingly. In most cases, the user model assumes that all users are essentially the same and have the same help requirements (Dix, 1998).

Schneiderman suggests a generic separation of end users into 3 categories; novice or first time, knowledgeable-intermittent, and expert-frequent users, and suggests that different software design goals will be more or less appropriate for each user category. Prescott and Crichton et al. group end users into the following categories according to skill level; Beginner i.e. a user who has never been in front of a computer or has extremely limited experience; Intermediate i.e. a user who is comfortable with the basic operations of the computer and; Advanced i.e. a user who has above average knowledge in computer usage. These groupings will be used to evaluate the user population that will be questioned in this study.

The term "user" will refer to South Africans working in a corporate environment who have a need to use computers. A cross section of the population will be examined.

The method in which the required information is to be collected is a questionnaire, which consists of open and closed ended questions that will evaluate the experience of the different user categories together with the software usability and user satisfaction associated with the presence of unsolicited online help i.e. MS Paper Clip.

The results of this study will be available online at http://www.isys.wits.ac.za/hci.

REFERENCE LIST

Bolton, M. (2001). *A review of Error Messages*, available online http://home.earthlink.net/~mbolton/AreviewOfErrorMessages.html

Capobianco, A., Carbonell, N., (2001). *Online Help: a Potential Contribution to Universal Access*, in proceedings of CHI 2001 conference, Seattle, USA

Dix, A., Finlay, J., Abowd, G. and Beale, R. (1998). *Human Computer Interaction*. Second Edition, Prentice-Hall

Faulkner, C. (1998). *The Essence of Human-Computer Interaction.* Prentice-Hall

Gaine, J. (2000). *Effective Error Messages*, available online http://infocentre.frontend.com

Henneman, R.L., (1999). *Design for Usability: process, Skills, and Tools.* Information Knowledge Systems Management, Vol 1, No. 2, pp 133-145

Kalk, J. (2001). *Help and Usability*, in Proceedings of CHI-SA 2001 Human Computer Interaction Conference, Pretoria, South Africa

Nielsen, J., (2001). *Error Message Guidelines*, available online http://www.useit.com/alertbox/20010604.htm

Norman, D., (1990). *The Design of everyday things*. MIT Press, New York.

Postrel, V., (1998). *Some software features are so helpful, they're actually undesirable*. Forbes, Vol. 162, Issue 7, pg. 128

Preece, J. (1994). *Human-Computer Interaction- Concepts and Design.* Addison-Wesley.

Seebach, (2002). *The Cranky User: could you repeat that in English.* IBM Developer Works, available online: http://www.106.ibm/developerworks/library/us-cranky14.html.

Shackel B., Richardson S.J., (1991). *Human Factors for Informatics Usability.* Cambridge University Press.

Shneiderman, B. (1998). *Designing the User Interface*. Third Edition. Addison-Wesley.

A Hypothetical Wireless Network with Mobile Base Stations in Urban Areas

G. Sampath
Department of Computer Science
The College of New Jersey, Ewing, NJ 08628
sampath@tcnj.edu

ABSTRACT

A wireless network is proposed for densely populated areas served by public transportation units (PTUs) in which the base stations are mounted on the PTUs and are thus themselves mobile. The advantages of having such mobile base stations are pointed out, and the proposed architecture is studied, first for a simple geometry, and then for more complex layouts as are found in urban areas. The features of the transportation model, the propagation model, and the communication model are discussed. Results for the simple model with a rectangular geometry and line-of-sight (LOS) propagation are given, work is ongoing on a more general model with non-LOS propagation, various quality-of-service (QoS) properties, and resource allocation and the associated cost analysis, for two wireless technologies, CDMA and TDMA.

1. OVERVIEW

In a conventional cellular network, base stations (BS) are laid out in a hexagonal pattern with each BS serving a hexagonal cell whose side decreases inversely with the size of the population covered [4]. In dense urban areas a macrocell is replaced by a larger number of microcells with lower power base stations, usually located at the intersections of streets. In downtown areas with a large number of multistoried buildings, a microcell is overlaid with a network of picocells with very low power base stations on the floors of a multistoried building. The ongoing work reported here describes a model of urban wireless communication at the street level using base stations that are themselves mobile. These moving base stations (MBS) are mounted on public transportation units (PTU) that move along fixed paths in an urban transportation grid. Initially the transportation model restricts the PTU routes to a rectangular grid; this restriction is removed in a subsequent more detailed model. Likewise the propagation model initially assumes signal propagation paths to be line-of-sight (LOS) through a set of MBSs, this too is later relaxed. For the simple model, conditions for continuous communication between two MTUs are derived. The extended propagation model considers non-line-of-sight propagation, including reflection, diffraction, and propagation through buildings [1]. The communication model of the network looks at two technologies, CDMA and TDMA. Analysis of different aspects of radio resource management [5] including load factor, various quality-of-service (QoS) parameters for voice, and dependence on PTU service patterns is ongoing.

2. A NETWORK OF MOBILE BASE STATIONS

Wireless communication in an urban area is modeled with a dynamic non-cellular network overlaid on the fixed macrocellular network. It consists of mobile base stations (MBSs) that move along fixed routes in an urban transportation system. A MBS can be implemented with a transceiver and antenna mounted on a PTU such as bus, tram, cable car, and surface (and possibly subway) train. At the street level an MTU communicates with another MTU in the urban area directly through the MBSs without going through a macrocell BS. (It has still to go through one of the latter to communicate with an MTU outside the MBS coverage area or with the backbone.) In a dense urban area, this could have several potential advantages:
1) the lower cost of serving dense MTU clusters on the street;
2) the corresponding savings in power and bandwidth at the macrocellular BSs (the latter are involved only in billing and security operations); and
3) ease of maintenance of the MBSs.

Figure 1. Simple Wireless Network Geometry

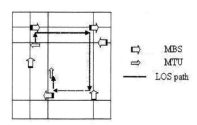

Interestingly, the service patterns of the PTUs tend to intrinsically reflect MTU density in space and time in an urban area. Since the routes followed by MTUs on the streets are fixed and generally along the lines of the urban transportation grid, the communications properties of such a network are easy to study for simple propagation models.

The following are examples of questions that are of interest in modeling and design of such a network:
1) What are the required conditions for two MTUs A and B to communicate with each other?
2) What are the movement patterns of the MBSs (equivalently the service patterns of the PTUs on which they are mounted) in order for A and B to have uninterrupted service?
3) What is the minimum number of MBS's required for different propagation assumptions?
4) For a given number of MBS's how many MTUs can be served at any given time?

Answers to some of these questions have been obtained; others are currently the object of this ongoing study. They are based on techniques from computational geometry [3], mobile communication [2], and radio resource management [1, 5].

Figure 2. Example of Extreme LOS Path

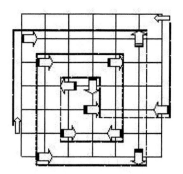

Figure 3. Minimum Coverage Example

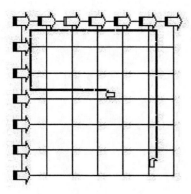

Figure 4. Multipath example

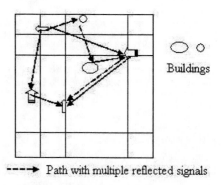

3. A SIMPLE MODEL

The following assumptions are made:
1) an MBS moves along a horizontal path or vertical path only (but not both) at all times;
2) the mode of propagation is line of sight (LOS);
3) the grid is a lattice with integer addresses (x, y); $1 \leq x, y \leq N$.

None of these conditions is necessary; they are used only to simplify this first model and its analysis. The following results can be derived using simple network analysis and computational geometry techniques:
1) At any given time MTU A at (x,y) can communicate with MTU B at (w,z) if there is a LOS path through one or more MBSs such that each pair of MBSs communicate through LOS.
2) The maximum communication delay along a path with distinct MBSs between A and B is of order $O(N^2)$.
3) The minimum number of MBSs for full coverage at all times is 2n-1.
4) Given a set of MBSs they can be partitioned into connected subsets where a connected subset is one in which any two MBSs can communicate through a LOS path. A can communicate with B if and only if both are connected to at least one and the same partition of the MBSs. When A is connected to (that is, communicates with an MBS in) partition X and B to partition Y, $X \neq Y$, the minimum number of connections required for A to be able to communicate with B is also a shortest path from X to Y.
5) An MBS (on a PTU) moves along a grid line and is always visible along the line. It becomes visible along a perpendicular grid line when it crosses an intersection, with the duration of visibility determined by the time it remains in the intersection (which may include the time it may stand at a service point such as a bus stop or tram stop). This behavior is modeled with a visibility function $V_{X (or Y)}$ (y (or x), t), which, for a uniform grid size, is (approximately) a rectangular periodic pulse train. Then the vis-

Figure 5. Example of multipath with reflections

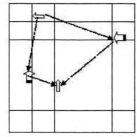

ibility pattern function V(t) for the set of all MBSs is the boolean AND of all the individual visibility functions. A call between two MTUs will complete if and only if V is unity over the duration of the call.

4. A MORE COMPLEX MODEL WITH NON-LOS PROPAGATION

The assumption of full coverage through a set of PTUs being present at intersections at all times (which is necessary in the simple model for an unbroken call) is of course not realistic. Also, PTU routes usually do not pass over all streets. However, with sufficient signal levels at an MTU and sufficient link power at the MBSs these problems are circumvented. Thus radio signals on direct non-LOS paths (typically passing through buildings and other obstacles) can have sufficient strength to provide full coverage at all times whenever and wherever PTU service is available. When such service ceases or is reduced (usually after normal business hours) communication can switch to the underlying cellular network. Since this change occurs along with a drop in call density (mirroring the lower off-peak usage seen in land-line usage) an overall savings in bandwidth and power over a 24-hour period can be expected.

An extended analysis that is ongoing includes the following:
1) Transportation model: a) PTU service is assumed not to blanket the entire area, and b) PTU service patterns are used to coordinate service with the above mentioned step of switching to the cellular network.
2) Propagation model: properties studied include multipath (including reflection and diffraction), fading (slow and fast, due to mobility of both MTU and MBS), path loss in open air and wall penetration, and required link budgets. Two urban radio propagation models are appropriate: Walfisch and Ikegami's COST, and IMT2000 [1].
3) Communication model: effects considered include channel coupling due to interference between multiple MBS transmissions and the near-far effect from nearby MTUs. Two technologies are considered: CDMA and TDMA.

Based on the above analysis appropriate parameters for radio resource management (capacity management and resource allocation for a desired QoS) will be derived and a cost model constructed. It is hoped that tangible results will be available shortly.

REFERENCES
[1] V. K. Garg. Wireless Network Evolution: 2G to 3G. Prentice-Hall, 2001.
[2] W. C. Y. Lee. Mobile Communications Engineering. McGraw-Hill, 1982.
[3] F. P. Preparata and M. I. Shamos. Computational Geometry. Springer-Verlag, 1985.
[4] W. Stallings. Wireless Communication Systems. Prentice-Hall, 2001.
[5] J. Zander and S.-L. Kim. Radio Resource Management for Wireless Networks. Artech House, 2001.

The Communication in the Communities of Practice: Is there a "Best" Tool?

MOISIG[1]
Rua Dr. Jaime Lopes de Amorim
4465-111 S. Mamede Infesta – Portugal
tel: +351 919 497 331, fax: +351 229 025 899
moisig@moisig.iscap.ipp.pt

INTRODUCTION

Communities of practice (CoP) are described as "groups of people who share a concern, a set of problems, or a passion about a topic, and who deepen their knowledge and expertise in this area by interacting on an ongoing basis" [Wenger, McDermott and Snyder, 2002:4]. Additionally, we recognise that knowledge has become the key to success as well as a source of competitive advantage. Organizations are recognizing that the need to nurture the development of "communities of practice in strategic areas is a practical way to manage knowledge as an asset" [op. cit.:6]. These communities are not bound to an organization. They can be constituted by elements "from different organizations as well as across independent business units" [op. cit.:6]. These communities can be, though, collocated or distributed. For example, "[s]cientists have long been forming communities of practice by communicating across the globe (once by letter and now by e-mail). Some communities meet regularly[2] (…). Others are connected primarily by e-mail and phone and may meet only once or twice a year. What allows members to share knowledge is not the choice of a specific form of communication (face-to-face as opposed to Web-based, for instance), but the existence of a shared practice" [op. cit.:25].

Although these communities are not built around a certain technology, in some cases it is needed in order to help the group to be developed. Some CoP's grow because they use the "right" tools. They help the members of the community, for instance, to be in touch, to share ideas and opinions, to solve problems together, to socialize, to work in the same document at the same time.

Due to a great effort of the Software Engineering, there are several tools available to help to improve collaborative work. As time goes by, these tools have acquired great usability and thus allowing users to overcome difficulties in its use and improving satisfaction and productivity.

Nevertheless, these tools are not all the same nor have they the same potentialities or functionalities. Some follow a peer-to-peer approach, while others are web-based.

In this communication, we present a CoP – MOISIG – and its characteristics as well as its communication needs. We also describe the tools experienced - (a) a mailing list (yahoogroups); (b) Groove – a peer-to-peer tool; (c) WebCT – a platform of e-learning. Finally, we analyse the cross relation between CoP's needs and tools' functionalities and draw some final remarks.

FOOTNOTES

[1] The members of MOISIG are: Anabela Sarmento (ISCAP-IPP), Joao Batista (ISCA-UA), Leonor Cardoso (FPCE-UC), Mário Lousã (ISPGaya), Rosalina Babo (ISCAP-IPP) and Teresa Rebelo (FPCE-UC)

[2] One example of such community is the MOISIG – Management, Organization and Information Systems Interest Group. For further information about this community, please see the articles Cardoso et al., 2000; Batista et al., 2001; Sarmento et al., 2002.

Knowledge Management: A Rewarding Challenge for SME's?

Anabela Sarmento
Instituto Superior Contabilidade Administração Porto
Instituto Politécnico Porto
R. Dr. Jaime Lopes de Amorim
4465-111 S. M. Infesta, Portugal
Sarmento@iscap.ipp.pt
Tel: + 351 228322925, Fax: +229025899
Algoritmi R&D Centre, Information Systems Group
University of Minho, Portugal

Ana Maria Correia
Instituto Superior de Estatística e Gestão de Informação
Universidade Nova de Lisboa
Campus de Campolide
1070-124 Lisboa, Portugal
acorreia@isegi.unl.pt

INNOVATION AND COMPETITIVENESS

In contemporary knowledge-based society, where organizational environment is changing at a rapid pace, information and knowledge to promote innovation are the keys to competitiveness and success.

This was recognised in the conclusions of the Lisbon European Summit [Lisbon ... 2000], which were then extended in the Barcelona European Summit [Barcelona ... 2002]. The latter state that one of the goals of Europe is to attain a "competitive knowledge-based society" based on education and training systems, adapting quickly to the "demands of the knowledge society and the needs for an improved level of quality of employment". Furthermore, every citizen must be equipped with the skills needed to live and work in this rich information environment. These goals would be attained, for instance, by improving the "mastery of basic skills, development of digital literacy and lifelong learning" [Barcelona ... 2002:18-20]. The same concerns are expressed in the UNICE Benchmarking Report 2000 [UNICE, 2000].

KNOWLEDGE MANAGEMENT

The emergence of interest for Knowledge Management (KM) lies in the confluence of many factors and aspects, which bring all branches of knowledge to the fore including historical, intellectual/philosophical, economic, technological and cultural areas [Despres and Chauvel, 2000:4]. Little, Quintas and Ray [2002] state that the interest for knowledge, as an area of research and practice in the field of management, has its origins in the convergence of different perspectives including information management, organizational learning, strategic management, management of innovation, and the measurement and management of intangible assets. Thus, KM emerges as a pluri- and interdisciplinary area.

Furthermore, Davenport and Cronin [2000] consider that KM is being used differently across different domains with each claiming that its partial understanding represents a definitive articulation of the concept. These domains are library and information systems (LIS), process engineering (PE) and organizational theory (OT). To the LIS, KM is seen as management of know-how, which corresponds to the "coding and classification of recorded material (content) embedded in artefacts, structures, systems and repositories", without trying to understand how business value is perceived and created. In process engineering, KM is perceived as the discovery and extraction of value when existing processes are analysed. This "process approach does not do justice to the application of individual competencies, skills, talents, thoughts, ideas, intuitions, commitments, motivations and imaginations, in short, the realm of tacit knowledge". None of these perspectives takes into consideration the knowledge that cannot be codified, or tacit knowledge. Nevertheless, there is a growing recognition that the "knowledge of experts is an accumulation of experience – a kind of residue of their actions, thinking, and conversations – that remains a dynamic part of their ongoing experience" [Wenger et al., 2002:9]. Knowledge is simultaneously tacit and explicit and its creation is the result of the interaction between them. It is in this context that the third domain emerges, where KM is perceived as a capacity, which allows organizations to develop, to innovate and to be more competitive. Thus, in the perspective of OT, KM is not the management of resources but of the context where knowledge is used. It is argued that to achieve sustainability, firms should focus on methods to build knowledge as well as providing a stimulating organizational culture, as these are the crucial and differentiating factors, difficult to imitate by competitors [Pfeffer, 2002].

Examples of large corporations implementing KM initiatives proliferate in the specialised and professional literature. Among these, one finds Ford Motor Company, Chevron, Texas Instruments, Canadian Centre for Management Development, Health Canada [Bontis, 2002], Microsoft, Coca-Cola, Merck, Intel, Skandia [Snyder and Pierce, 2002].

Taking into account that the large majority of firms worldwide are small and medium ones (SME's) [EUROSTAT, 2002], why is it that the literature does not offer as many references to applications of KM in this sector? Is KM of any relevance to SME's? If so, are their KM needs analogous to those of large corporations?

One could argue that the solution to KM lies in the training and preparation of a particular kind of worker – the knowledge worker. However, it should be recognised that the biggest contributors to GNP in Europe are the SME's, who cannot afford the resources to formally "compartmentalize the information gathering and use functions, nor do they have the resources to develop the infrastructure necessary to access and use the information" [Rosenberg, 2002:2]. It is argued that these competencies should be developed by all employees, regardless of the dimension of the enterprise in which they are working in. We believe that educational institutions should prepare professionals able to contribute to and manage knowledge across the organisation. Moreover, information literacy must be part of the "skill set of almost every employee who works with information" in a business [Rosenberg, 2002:3]. Furthermore, firms should provide training opportunities to their employees to enhance their KM skills and foster an environment where knowledge is created and disseminated through the organization [Zack, 2002].

THE CREATION OF A KNOWLEDGE AND INFORMATION ECONOMY: THE PORTUGUESE SCENARIO CONCERNING SME'S

Taking into consideration the importance recognised by the European Union concerning KM, being aware that knowledge and its management is at the confluence of some disciplines and can be approached by several perspectives, we have undertaken our research, acknowledging the goals and strategies drawn up by the Portuguese government, in order to help Portugal move towards a knowledge driven society. In the following paragraphs, the results of this research are outlined. A search of the Portuguese official sites (Programa do XV Governo - The Programme of the XVth Government of Portugal – http://www.portugal.gov.pt; Sociedade da Informação em Portugal - Information Society in Portugal – http://www.si.mct.pt; Instituto de Apoio às Pequenas e Médias Empresas e ao Investimento - IAPMEI - Portuguese Institute for SME – http://www.iapmei.pt) shows that the main Portuguese concerns regarding the development of the Information Society are:

a) to provide online access to all the public services;
b) to create the portal called "Portugal online" for centralised provision of Government information services;
c) to create other portal, under the same philosophy of the described above, addressing specific needs of SME's;
d) to connect to the internet every library and post-offices existing in the country;
e) to increase the ratio of computers at school regarding students numbers;
f) to include in the budget of each school the acquisition of didactic contents in the internet;
g) to increase the ratio of home computer ownership among the population
h) to create a competitive information technologies sector ,
i) to modernise the Portuguese Public Administration,

An analysis of the political aims set out in that Programme, reveals that the interpretation of the knowledge driven society outlined in the European Summits is mostly a technological one. Concerns are still linked to the development of infrastructures, bandwidth, access cost to the Internet, equipment in schools and numbers of domestic computers.

Specifically, regarding Internet use by the SME's, one can see that, although a commission named Unidade da Missão Inovação e Conhecimento (*Mission towards the Knowledge and Innovation Society*) has been created (www.si.mct.pt), its strategies and measures that will be taken in order to accomplish its goals are not yet clear (and available) to the public. On the other hand, the *IAPMEI* aims to promote the creation of packages that include electronic business, social security, the generalization of the electronic transference of data between enterprises and public administration, stimulation for the creation of web sites, the creation of support centres, the development of e-commerce, the regulation of digital signature and the dissemination of its use and the improvement of internet domain registry. Finally, the PME Digital (*Digital SME*) - *Portugal Digital* initiative of the Ministry of Economy (http://www.poe.min-economia.pt) aims to help SME's to use the Internet and develop e-business.

COMPETENCES AND SKILLS IN KM FOR SME'S

Despite this scenario, which has a rather technological focus, we claim that there is scope, within the current Programme of Government, for the modernization of the SME's sector, through a Knowledge Management approach. In order that the alteration will have a lasting effect, it needs to be grounded in managers that are aware of the importance of knowledge management principles in managing knowledge intensive firms and in knowledge workers that are urgently needed to achieve the innovation and competitiveness that will enable the country's economy to converge with other EU partners.

To prepare these professionals, some training is required to update their management skills. We claim that such training should address the topics shown in figure 1.

In the six areas of study every contribution to KM, described above, is approached in a way that avoids any partial perspectives. The topics covered in each area are briefly explained in the following paragraphs. These are only illustrative and, by no means, an extensive list of what has to be addressed:

i) Knowledge resources – the knowledge manager should be able to understand how information and knowledge resources – e.g., databases, web-based and other information and knowledge resources, usually available through library and information services - are created, organised, accessed and retrieved to enable him/her to fully exploit all the information that is being made available, both internally and externally, to the organization.

ii) KM systems (KMS) – these are seen as the enabling technologies for an effective and efficient KM. These tools and systems can be categorized as (1) basic functionalities (support communication, storing, exchanging, search and retrieval of data and documents, discussion among groups and organizational processes); (2) integrative KMS (support codification, search and retrieval); (3) interactive KMS (support KM processes), and (4) bridging KMS (providing contextualized knowledge repositories) [Maier, 2002:20].

iii) Organizational knowledge – the notion that while individuals learn so also do groups and organizations has gained wide acceptance in the last decade [Bood 1998:210; Nahapiet and Goshal, 2002], together with the idea that organisational knowledge can be stored, retrieved and recollected. As Karreman [2002] points out "organizational (collective) memory is socially constructed, culturally maintained and dispersed, and as indeed is indicated by the concept of knowledge management – a possible target for managerial efforts"; within organizational knowledge, "Competitive Intelligence" (CI) is also referred to as competitor intelligence, business intelligence or environment scanning. It covers numerous sectors of intelligence (e.g. competitor, technology, product/service, environment, economy) [Fahey, 1999] and its goal is to stimulate the organization's creativeness, innovativeness and willingness to change. "Social intelligence", which is the process by which a society, organization or individual scans the environment, interprets what is there and constructs versions of events that may afford competitive advantage [Cronin and Davenport, 1993:8], falls also within Organizational Knowledge.

iv) Organizational context and culture –how people are managed, effectively motivated and the effects of this on their behaviour and skills are becoming vital [Pfeffer, 2002:62 - 66]. Furthermore, knowledge creation implies, besides information codification, the development of a "knowledge culture" that can be translated into the nurturing of communities of practice [Wenger, McDermott, Snyder, 2002]; [Davenport and Hall, 2002], trust among people, rewards, incentives, motivation [Hall, 2001] as well as the establishment of communication channels and organizational structure [Maier, 2002].

v) Intellectual capital – knowledge creation by business organisations is now recognised as the most important source of organizational competitiveness, at international level. The importance of intangible resources gave rise to a growing interest in developing methods and tools that enable companies "to analyse their intellectual capital stocks" and "organizational learning flows" [Bontis, 2002:623]. Intellectual Capital includes the human, structure and relations. Measurement methodologies of Intellectual Capital, within plan of study to convey KM skills, will contribute to the understanding of the role intangible assets have in an organization and will address the measures and metrics to assess and evaluate the IC.

vi) Innovation management – those who are going to perform the Knowledge Management function should be able to identify KM resources to support a knowledge strategy for technical/scientific innovation, contribute to the writing of a development plan for an innovative product or service in a scientific or technical organisation, search for developments funds, contribute to the strategic understanding of the regulatory and standards environment of scientific and technical organizations and identify and evaluate knowledge markets opportunities; it is these subjects that this area of study aims to address.

These areas of study should not be seen as independent of each other, or as mutually exclusive.

CONCLUSIONS

This paper highlights the European strategy towards a knowledge-based society where innovation and competitiveness are the goals to attain. Knowledge management is, also, briefly, introduced by presenting some approaches contributing to an understanding of the scope of this discipline. The elements contained in the Portuguese Government's strategy towards a knowledge driven society allow us to see that it is primarily based on technology. We agree that technology is an essential issue, in the access to the internet by firms and citizens at large in public places or at home. However, KM is much more than infrastructures. We also have the involvement of people, the building of communities and contexts where the sharing of knowledge is promoted, intellectual capital is developed and inter- and intra-organization communications are stimulated.

Although not underestimating the infrastructure aspect in KM, we think there is scope within the current Government Programme to embark on complementary perspectives to accelerate the pace at which Portuguese SME's are embracing KM. In our opinion, the way ahead is to offer education programmes on KM (formal degrees, lifelong learning opportunities, etc.). This would contribute to the development of adequate competences and skills that will allow the emergence of KM in SME's.

BIBLIOGRAPHY

Barcelona European Council (2002). *Presidency Conclusions* 15-16 March 2000. URL: http://ue.eu.int/pressData/en/ec/71025.pdf. [Retrieved in 20 Dec 2002].

Bontis, N. (2002). "The Rising Star of the Chief Knowledge Officer", *IVEY Business Journal*, March / April, p. 20-25

Bood, R. (1998). "Charting organizational Learning: a Comparison of Multiple Mapping Techniques". *In* Eden, C. and Spender, J. (eds.) *Managerial and Organizational Cognition*. London: Sage, p. 210-230.

Cronin, B. and Davenport, E. (1993). "Social Intelligence". *In* Williams, M. (ed.). *Annual Review of Information Science and Technology (ARIST)*, 28, p. 3-43.

Cheuk, B. (2002). "Information Literacy in the workplace context: issues, best practices and challenges". White Paper prepared for *UNESCO*, the *U.S. National Commission on Libraries and Information Science*, and the *National Forum on Information Literacy*, for use at the *Information Literacy Meeting of Experts*, Prague. URL: http://www.nclis.gov/libinter/infolitconf&meet/papers/cheuk-fullpaper.pdf [Retrieved in 20 Dec 2002].

Davenport, E. and Cronin, B. (2000). *Knowledge management: semantic drift or conceptual shift?* Proceedings of the *ALISE (Library and Information Science Education) Conference*. URL: http://www.alise.org/conferences/conf00_Davenport-Cronin_paper.htm [Retrieved in 20 Dec 2002].

Davenport, E. and Hall, H. (2002). "Organizational Knowledge and Communities of Practice", *in* Cronin, B. (Ed.) *Annual Review of Information Science and Technology*, Medford, NJ: Information Today, p. 171-228.

Despres, C. and Chauvel, D. (2000) *Knowledge Horizons: the Present and the Promises of the Knowledge Management*. Oxford: Butterworth Heinmann, quoted in Kasinskaite, I. (2002). "Managing Knowledge Assets: Between the Global and the Local". *Informacijos Mokslai*, 21, p. 33-42.

EUROSTAT (2002). *SMEs in Europe: Competitiveness, innovation and the knowledge-driven society*. Luxembourg: Office for Official Publications of the European Communities (CAT No KS-CJ.02-001-EN-N).

Fahey, L. (1999). *Competitors: Outwitting, Outmanoeuvring, Outperforming*. New York: Wiley.

Governo da República Portuguesatugal Gove (2002). *Programa do XV Governo Constitucional. URL:* http://www.portugal.gov.pt/pt/Programa+do+Governo/programa_p023.htm [Retrieved in 20 Dec 2002].

Hall, H. (2001). *Social exchange for knowledge exchange*. Paper presented at the *International Conference on Managing Knowledge*, University of Leicester, April 10-11 2001. URL: http://www.bim.napier.ac.uk/~hazel/esis/hazel1.pdf [Retrieved in 20 Dec 2002].

Karreman, D. (2002). "Knowledge management and "organizational memory" - remembrance and recollection in a knowledge intensive firm".

Paper presented at *OKLC/ALBA*, APRIL 2002 URL: http://www.alba.edu.gr/OKLC2002/Proceedings/pdf_files/ID312.pdf [Retrieved in 20 Dec 2002].

Lisbon European Council (2000). *Presidency Conclusions*. 23-24 March 2000. URL: http://ue.eu.int/Newsroom/LoadDoc.asp?BID=76&DID=60917&LANG=1 [Retrieved in 20 Dec 2002].

Little, S., Quintas, P. and Ray, T (2002). *Managing Knowledge: an essential reader*. London: Sage Publications.

Maier, R. (2002). "State-of-Practice of Knowledge Management Systems: Results of an Empirical Study", *Informatik / Informatique – Knowledge Management*, 1, p. 14-22.

Ministério da Economia - IAPMEI (2002). *Economia Digital*. URL: http://www.iapmei.pt/iapmei-art-03.php?id=549 [Retrieved in 20 Dec 2002].

Ministério da Economia (2002). *Programa Operacional da Economia – Programa -Missão*. URL: http://www.poe.min-economia.pt/0001.htm. [Retrieved in 20 Dec 2002].

Nahapiet, J. and Ghoshal, S. (2002)." Social Capital, Intellectual Capital, and the Organizational Advantage", in Choo, C. W. and Bontis, N. (Eds.) *The Strategic Management of Intellectual Capital and Organizational Knowledge*, New York: Oxford University Press, p. 673-698.

Pfeffer, J. (2002), "Competitive Advantage through People", *in* Henry, J. and Mayle, D. (Eds.), *Managing Innovation and Change*, London: Sage, p. 61-73.

Presidência do Conselho de Ministros (2002). *Unidade de Missão Informação e Conhecimento*. URL: http://www.si.mct.pt [Retrieved in 20 Dec 2002].

Rosenberg, V. (2002). "Information Literacy and Small Business," White Paper prepared for *UNESCO, the U.S. National Commission on Libraries and Information Science, and the National Forum on Information Literacy*, for use at the *Information Literacy Meeting of Experts*, Prague, URL: http://www.nclis.gov/libinter/infolitconf&meet/papers/rosenberg-fullpaper.pdf [Retrieved in 20 Dec 2002]

Snyder, H. and Pierce, J. (2002). "Intellectual Capital", in Cronin, B. (Ed.), *Annual Review of Information Science and Technology*, 36, Medford, NJ: Information Today, p. 467-500.

UNICE (2000), *Stimulating creativity and innovation in Europe: the UNICE benchmarking report 2000*. URL: http://www.unice.org/unice/docum.nsf/all+by+description/35E8D63071BCD394C12568EA002FECB0/$File/Innov-5.pdf. [Retrieved in 20 Dec 2002].

Wenger, E., McDermott, R. e and Snyder, W. (2002). *Cultivating Communities of Practice*. Boston: Harvard Business School Press.

Zack, M. (2002). "Developing a Knowledge Strategy". *In* Choo, C. W. and Bontis, N. (Eds.). *The Strategic Management of Intellectual Capital and Organizational Knowledge*. New York: Oxford University Press.

Key Factors in Establishing Successful E-Government Services[1]

Khalid S. Soliman
Hofstra University
Hempstead, NY 11549, USA
khalid.soliman@hofstra.edu

John F. Affisco
Hofstra University
Hempstead, NY 11549, USA
acsjfa@hofstra.edu

ABSTRACT

Local, state, and federal governments around the world have realized that the Internet represents a great tool for providing government services that can significantly impact internal operations and external relationships with businesses and citizens. The literature reveals that there are three key success factors in establishing a successful e-government environment: Quality customer service as a focal point, government internal process reengineering to integrate with the front-end interface, and adoption of information technology throughout the whole process. Creating the best fit among these three factors is a basic ingredient for providing successful e-government services.

INTRODUCTION

The advancements of information technology (IT) in the past few years have made many organizations reform their businesses in order to utilize IT for competitive advantage. Furthermore, governments around the world have realized that utilizing the Internet to deliver government services would have a significant impact on internal operations and external relationships with businesses and citizens. Electronic government (e-government) can be defined as "the process of transacting business between the public and government through the use of automated systems and the Internet network," (Brannen, 2001).

Governments around the world have put aside a significant IT budget to implement e-government environment in their countries. For example, the U.S. federal government is expected to put aside 28% of its IT budget for e-government by 2005 (Taft, 2001). Moreover, according to the Gartner Group, by the end of 2005, the public sector total spending is expected to reach a total of $6.5 billion. North of the border, the Canadian federal government's 2000 budget allocated CAN$160 million over two years to design and implement government-online, an initiative that will allow the government to serve more Canadians (Chenery, 2001). Moreover, the federal government is pledging to make all services available electronically by 2004 (Doucet, 2001).

E-government initiatives are not limited to federal governments around the world. Local and state governments are also racing to create an e-government service for residents. According to the Gartner Group, it is expected that state and local government will spend almost CAN$58 billion by 2005, up from CAN$44 billion in 2000 (Taft, 2001). For example, Ontario province government is targeting 2003 to move to e-government (Doucet, 2001). In the U.S., a recent survey reveals that 85.3% of 1,471 surveyed local governments have their own websites and 57.4% have adopted Intranets (Moon, 2002).

This paper is to explore the different evolutionary stages of e-government and to highlight key success factors in implementing a successful e-government environment.

E-GOVERNMENT SUCCESS TRIANGLE

Gartner Group has classified e-government services offered online into four evolutionary phases: publishing (web presence), interacting, transacting, and transforming. These four phases are evolutionary and each phase represent a significant improvement from the previous one.

Publishing is the earliest stage where static information about the agency mission, services, phone numbers and agency address are provided for further communication. *Interacting* goes one step further by enhancing the site's features with search capabilities and intentions-based programs, host forms to download, and linkages with other relevant sites, as well as e-mail addresses of offices or officials. *Transacting* represents a full featured online service that allow users to conduct and complete entire tasks on-line. Typical services that are migrated to this stage of development include tax filing and payment, driver's license renewal, and payment of fines, permits and licenses. Moreover, many government agencies put requests for proposals and bidding regulations online as a precursor to e-procurement. *Transforming* is considered to be the long-term goal of almost all e-government services. It is characterized by redefining the delivery of government services by providing a single point of contact to constituents that makes government organization totally transparent to citizens. It involves re-engineering internal processes in order to create smooth integration between different government agencies for the purpose of providing transparent service to citizens and businesses. Also, this phase relies on robust customer relationship management tools and new methods of alternative service delivery capabilities. Table 1 summarizes the phases, key capabilities, and major challenges.

According to recent research published by the North Carolina Information Resources Management Commission (2001), most of the 50 states in the U.S. are either at the interacting phase or in transition to some degree to the transacting phase. Both the transacting and the transforming phases are difficult because they involve the adoption of new technologies and the development of new business practices. Reaching and maintaining operations at the transforming phase requires a major cultural leap in business practices, organizational structures, and governance processes. To that end, an e-government strategy should be adopted in order facilitate the transition from one phase to another and to develop the goal of reaching the transforming phase.

E-government strategy, or success triangle, revolves around three critical elements: customer service, business processes, and technology. These are key elements in delivering a successful e-government environment.

Customer Service: The first step toward delivering high quality customer service is to realize that the nature of customer needs is different depending upon their primary relationship to government. Three classes of customers for services provided by the government have been identified – government-to-citizen (G2C), government-to-business (G2B), and government-to-government (G2G). The objective of G2C initiatives is to allow citizens to use the web for accessing services such as benefits, loans, recreational sites and educational materials. The objective of G2B initiatives is to reduce the burden on businesses by adopting processes that enable collecting data once for multiple uses and streamlining redundant processes. Online procurement, or e-procurement, with the government is an area that appeals to many solution providers and vendors. In fact, the U.S. government's interest in e-procurement led Washington-based eFederal company last year to start an electronic store for government buyers making micro-purchases up to $2500 (Taft, 2001). The objective of the G2G initiatives is to share and integrate federal, state, and local data. Examples of G2G initiatives are the ones establish by the U.S. government such as E-Grants managed by the Health and Human Services Administration and Disaster Assistance and Crisis Response managed by the Federal Emergency Management Agency.

Business Processes: While G2C, G2B, G2G applications may be different, all enterprise-based e-government initiatives generally have a common vision – a single entry point to government services that allows constituents to get everything they need without the cyber equivalent of long lines and bureaucratic red tape. Such an entry point, or portal, should be "intentions-based",

Table 1: E-government Phase

Phase	Key Capabilities	Major Challenges
Web presence for offering information	• Online content • Information presentation and retrieval	• Content management • Presentation hierarchy • Roles and responsibilities
Interactions with the public for exchanging information	• Search engines • Form/document transmission • Simple data collection	• Content management • Support staff • Public records management
Online transactions for providing public services	• Technical infrastructure for licenses, permits, filings, reservations, etc. • Integration with legacy systems • 24 x 7 operations support	• Privacy and security • Backup and recovery • Funding sources • Transaction fees • Business process reengineering • Staffing skills • Interagency cooperation
Transformation of government – new processes as well as movement to e-democracy for citizen-participation in the democratic process	• Telecommuting • Data sharing • Integration of applications • Mobile computing • Wireless technology • Video conferencing • Broadband networks	• Ongoing funding stream • Intergovernmental cooperation • Program performance and accountability

Source: Baum and DiMaio (2001)

that is the portal is service driven and customized based on customer class. So instead of being presented with a list of agencies and having to guess their way through the list to determine where and how to obtain the services they are interested in, users simply have to know which service they require. A well-designed enterprise portal offers value in two basic ways. One is by taking away the need for citizens to understand the complexity of government. The other is by enabling users to save time (example: the U.S. Federal e-government system is through the FirstGov portal that was launched in September 2000)

Technology: As is the case for any implementation of technology, the application of even the best IT to poorly designed processes will only make matters worse. Therefore it is important to ensure that all processes are reviewed and reengineered where necessary to support a new way of doing business. Any IT solution should be designed as part of the improved process. A broad government-wide perspective on business processes may lead to aggregation in many cases. Aggregation of like transactions from all agencies can lead to increased efficiency and cost-effectiveness for e-government initiatives. Aggregation of demand can lead to lower purchase prices and economies of scale that can reduce unit costs.

E-government initiatives must be supported by a shared integrated technology infrastructure across agencies and applications. This infrastructure should include reusable technical components, which will reduce redundancy and increase the reliability of processing. As part of the design process an analysis of the existing infrastructure and legacy systems must be conducted with an eye towards their improvement and integration into the new-shared e-business architecture. The e-business architecture must adhere to widely accepted standards to allow for compatibility of systems and ease of expansion.

MANAGEMENT ISSUES

Establishing a working e-government environment presents several challenges to governments. Regulatory and privacy issues that are more easily overcome by commercial businesses represent major challenges for governments (Taft, 2001). Unlike commercial businesses that can choose their customers,

government agencies have to provide services to all citizens. To that end, in today's environment, governments are more concerned than ever with the question of who is using the services. Proof of ownership and data security concerns are magnified as governments are moving toward interacting and transacting e-government services (Soliman and Affisco, 2002). On the other hand, citizens are concerned about how well protected is their private information. According to a recent study, 56% of Canadians feel that the information highway is decreasing the privacy level in Canada (Chenery, 2001). Another challenge to e-government implementation is unifying data and systems that operate differently in each agency (Barr, 2001). Over the years, federal, state or local government agencies have developed information systems in isolation. The main factor for successful Internet-based government services is establishing a standardization of data definition and procedures.

CONCLUSION

E-government initiatives are all about serving citizens electronically. Governments around the world are taking advantage of the rapid growth of Internet usage. However, in order to establish a successful e-government environment, governments need to develop strategies that revolve around the three key factors. First, provide high-quality, added-value service. Second, reengineer internal processes with a new vision. Finally, adopt emerging technologies to ensure seamless integration between front-end interface with customers and back-end operations.

ENDNOTE

[1] This paper appears in the Proceedings of the 2003 Information Resources Management Association (IRMA) International Conference, Philadelphia, PA, May 2003.

REFERENCES

Barr, S., "President Searching for a few good e-gov. ideas," *The Washington Post*, Aug. 10, 2001, pp. B2

Baum, C. & DiMaio, A., "Gartner's Four Phases of E-Government Model," http://www.gartner3.gartnerweb.com/public/static/hotc/00094235.html

Brannen, A., "E-government in California: Providing services to citizens through the Internet," *SPECTRUM*, Spring 2001, pp. 6-10.

Chenery, J. "Seamlessly Serving Citizens," The Business of Public Sector Procurement, Summit, March 2001, pp. 19

Doucet, K. Canada ranks first in e-government services. *CMA Management*, 2001, (6), 8.

Moon, M. J., "The evolution of the E-government among Municipalities: Rhetoric or Reality?" *Public Administration Review*, Vol. 62, No. 4, July-August, 2002, pp. 424-433.

North Carolina Information Resource Management Commission, "*E-Government: Using Technology to Transform North Carolina's Governmental Services and Operations in the Digital Age, Report for the General Assembly,*" Report for the General Assembly, February 2001.

Soliman, K. S. and Affisco, J. F., "Reporting on e-Government initiatives in Canada and the United States," *Proceedings of the 3rd Annual Global Information Technology Management World Conference*, Long Island, New York, June 23-25, 2002.

Taft, D. K., "Raising the e-government banner," *CRN*, March 19, 2001, pp. 32-38.

Assessing Impact of Organizational Culture in The Transformation of IT into Business Value

Li Xiao and Subhasish Dasgupta
George Washington University
Monroe 403, 2115 G Street, NW, Washington, DC 20052
Tel: (703) 248-9642, Tel: (202) 994-7408
Fax: (202) 994-4930, Fax: (202) 994-4930
lilyxiao@gwu.edu, dasgupta@gwu.edu

ABSTRACT

The process of turning IT investment into realized business value is long and complex. According to Soh and Markus (1995) process theory, there are three stages during this process: IT conversion, IT use, and competitive process. Successful completion of each stage will enable the organization to pursue the next stage in the process. Moreover, the execution of each stage is dependent on a number of factors. Organizational culture is generally regarded as one of the most important factors influencing IT success in organizations. This research seeks to analyze the role played by organizational culture in the process-based creation of IT business value using the process theory proposed by Soh and Markus (1995).

INTRODUCTION

Organizations that decide to invest considerable amount of financial, human and other resources on an IT project expect to see improved organizational performance. This improved performance, in many cases, is realized after years of continued investment. After significant allocation of resources to a project, management may find out that the project greatly improved organizational performance. On the other hand, it may find that the project improved organizational performance only slightly, or had no improvement at all. No organization wants to see that huge investment on IT became waste of resources but such situation occurs every day.

Large IT projects require months and years to implement and there are many uncertainties in the process from initial IT investment to final improved/unimproved organizational performance. Soh and Markus (1995) proposed a process theory on how IT creates business value. According to this process theory, there are three stages in the process that IT creates business value in organizations: IT conversion process, IT use process, and competitive process. A number of factors influence successful completion of these stages. One of them, organizational culture has been regarded as being among the crucial factors that influence IT implementation in organizations. Studies have researched on relationship between organizational culture and general information system success (Harper, 2000, Harper and Utley, 2001) and between organizational culture and knowledge management success (Ribiere 2001). Those studies, however, have addressed IT success as a general construct without considering the temporal dimension of IT projects. This research seeks to empirically validate Soh and Markus's (1995) theory with data collected from organizations, and investigate the role of organizational culture during each stage of IT implementation.

This research will provide valuable insight into understanding the role of organizational culture in the process of IT creating business value. From a theoretical perspective, this research brings a new approach to look at relationships between organizational culture and IT. Instead of looking at broad IT success as most previous studies did, this study looks in depth at different stages of the process of IT creating business value, which more accurately reflect the reality of IT in organizations. From a practical perspective, determining the impact of organizational culture on IT conversion process, IT use process, and competitive process will enable organizations to focus on differ-ent cultural attributes during different stages of IT implementation. It will also help in ensuring success at each stage and in making more efficient decisions to abort IT projects at early stages if necessary.

The organization of the paper is as follows. In the next section, we will present our theoretical framework and research questions. And then we will discuss about our research model and research methodology. Finally we will report on our current progress in this research.

THEORETICAL FRAMEWORK

The impact of information technology (IT) on organization performance has been a topic of interest for IS scholars for many years. Does IT really improve organizations performance? Does IT investment yield satisfactory payoff? How should we measure IT payoff? These issues draw a lot of debate among IS researchers. In 1990s alone, there had been at least 66 studies on IT investment payoff (Kohli and Devaraj, 2002). In recent years, because of accelerating increase in IT investment, the issue of IT investment payoff has become a critical issue for both practitioners and researchers.

Although significant amount of research has been done in this area, results have been mixed, and this has made IT payoff issue even more controversial. As Kohli and Devaraj (2002) pointed out, studies on IT payoff differ greatly on sample size, process-orientation, and analysis methods, which are a few reasons that caused these inconclusive results in establishing a relationship between IT investment and organization performance.

Among the key issues in IT payoff research brought up by Kohli and Sherer (2002), the lag effects of IT investment are an important one. There are several steps between initial IT investment and improved/unimproved organization performance. Soh and Markus (1995) synthesized previous studies on IT investment payoff and proposed the process theory, which well addresses the lag effects of IT investment payoff. According to this theory, the process that IT creates business valued involves three stages: IT Conversion process, IT use process and competitive process (Figure 1).

The process theory synthesizes previous studies and addresses the lag effect of IT payoff, however, it has not been verified with empirical evidence, which is one of the objectives of this study. This study will involve 2 steps. First, we will test this theory with empirical data. After empirically validating this theory, the second step in this study will be to examine the influence of organizational culture at each of the three stages during which IT investment yield payoff. Here, we will use the Managerial Grid theory developed by Blake and Mouton (1964) as theoretical framework for organizational culture.

There are two main research questions to be answered in this study:
1. Does empirical data support the process theory that during the three processes of IT business value realization, the success of each process will lead to success in the next process and finally lead to improved organizational performance?
2. Is there relationship between organizational culture and IT implementation at different stage of the process of IT business value realization?

Figure 1 Process Theory of how IT creates business value (Soh and Markus, 1995)

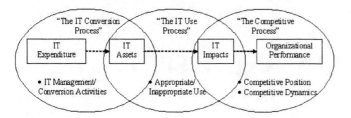

RESEARCH MODEL

In determining the role of organizational culture in the process of turning IT investment into realized business value, the research model was proposed as follows (please refer to figure 2):

H1: There is some relationship between organizational culture and success of IT conversion process.

H2: There is some relationship between organizational culture and success of IT use process.

Figure 2 Research Model

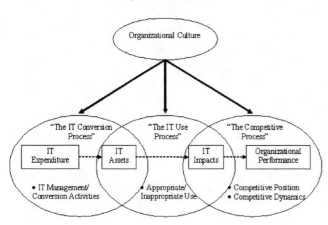

H3: There is some relationship between organizational culture and success of competitive process.

METHODOLOGY

In an attempt to verify the process theory, we will develop a questionnaire for survey organizations. This questionnaire will be developed based on the operational, managerial and strategic variables of organizations (Kohli and Devaraj, 2002). And then we will develop a questionnaire based on Organizational Culture Profile (OCP) instrument to measure organizational culture. Regression methods will be used to examine the relationships between organizational culture and the dependent variables at each stage of IT implementation.

STATUS OF THE RESEARCH

Currently we are working on developing the survey questionnaire and identifying subjects for data collection. We will use operational, managerial and strategic variables to measure IT assets, IT impacts, and organizational performance. As for organizational culture, we will use the tested, theory-based instrument Organizational Culture Profile (OCP) by O'Reilly, Chatman and Caldwell (1991) to measure organizational culture.

REFERENCES

Blake, R. R. and Mouton, J. S. *The Managerial Grid*, Houston, TX, Gulf Publishing Co., 1964.

Harper, G. R., *Assessing Information Technology Success As a Function of Organization Culture*, PhD Dissertation, The University of Alabama in Huntsville, 2000

Harper, G. R., Utley, D. R. Organizational culture and successful information technology implementation, Engineering Management Journal, Rolla; Jun 2001; Vol. 13, Iss. 2; pp. 11-15

Kohli, H. and Devaraj, S. Measuring Information Technology Payoff: A Meta-Analysis of Structural Variables in Firm-Level Empirical Research, *Information Systems Research*, 2002, forthcoming

Kohli, H. and Sherer, S. A. Measuring Payoff of Information Technology Investments: Research Issues and Guidelines, *Information Systems Frontiers*, 2002, forthcoming

O'Reilly, C. A. III, Chatman, J. A. and Caldwell, D. F., People and Organizational Culture: A Profile Comparison Approach to Assessing Person-Organization Fit, *Academy of Management Journal*, Vol. 34, No. 3, 1991, 487-516.

Ribiere, V. M. Assessing Knowledge Management Initiative Success as a Function of Organizational Culture, PhD Dissertation The George Washington University, 2001

Soh, C. and Markus, M. How IT Creates Business Value: A Process Theory Synthesis. *Proceedings of the Sixteenth International Conference on Information Systems, Amsterdam*, The Netherlands, 1995.

Towards an Effective Organizational Knowledge Management Strategy

Theophilus B. A. Addo, Zsuzsa-Klara Barna, and Murray Jennex
Information & Decision Systems Department
San Diego State University, San Diego, CA 92182-8234
Tel: (619) 594-3013, Fax: (619) 594-3675
taddo@mail.sdsu.edu, zbarna@hotmail.com, mjennex@mail.sdsu.edu

OBJECTIVE

The main objective of this study is to develop a comprehensive strategy for effective knowledge management in organizations, based on the best practices used by organizations (private and public) that have successfully implemented knowledge management systems (KMS). A set of knowledge management success factors is developed, which should help organizations focus their efforts and resources on those issues that are most likely to lead to success in knowledge management implementation projects.

THE IMPORTANCE OF A KNOWLEDGE MANAGEMENT STRATEGY

In today's "new" economy, it is becoming increasingly apparent that organizational performance depends less on tangible assets and more on intangible ones, notably knowledge. The reverse was the case just a couple of decades ago. As stated recently by Norton (2001), "the source of value has shifted from tangible to intangible assets." Citing studies conducted by The Brookings Institute, among others, Norton notes the declining trend in market value attributed to tangible assets (62 percent in 1982, 38 percent in 1992, and 15 percent in 1998) and a corresponding increase in market value attributed to intangible assets (38 percent in 1982, 62 percent in 1992, and 85 percent in 1998). Other authors have made similar observations. For example, Drucker (1993) asserts that knowledge has become the only meaningful resource today, relegating the traditional "factors of production" to a secondary level of importance. Therefore, to the extent that an organization is able to harness and successfully utilize its knowledge resources will it be able to improve its competitive position in the new economy. This calls for a comprehensive, meaningful, and deliberate strategy for organizational knowledge management (Jennex et al., 2003).

Knowledge management poses a significant challenge to many organizations. For one thing, the concept is relatively new, and for another, there is very little direction (in the form of strategy) that organizations can follow in their quest to implement effective knowledge management systems. Citing KPMG's "Knowledge Management Report 2000," in which 137 companies were surveyed, Barth (2000) noted that companies practicing knowledge management were generally better off than those that were not, however, the benefits did not always fulfill the respondents' expectations. The main reasons given for this failure to meet user expectations are as follows: (1) lack of user update due to inadequate communication; (2) KMS not integrated into normal everyday working practice; (3) lack of time to learn a complicated system; (4) lack of training; (5) users not seeing any personal benefits; (6) senior management not standing behind the project; and (7) unsolved technical problems.

At the present time, there is tremendous interest in knowledge management in the information systems literature. Numerous articles have been written on the subject. However, almost invariably, each article has come with its own classification system for the various aspects of knowledge management; there is no single source that pulls all the information together into a comprehensive taxonomy of the salient aspects of knowledge management and its implementation.

The issue of knowledge management is not just a matter of "managing" some "knowledge" that resides in some known place. It also includes the ability to recognize the different *types* of knowledge, as well as the establishment of policies, procedures, and processes for extracting, codifying, storing, and maintaining the knowledge. Several authors, notably Nonaka and Takeuchi (1995), have identified two main types of knowledge—*explicit* and *tacit*. The former consists of relatively "structured" knowledge that is easily verifiable and readily available in the form of paper documents and/or electronic files (e.g., corporate policies). The latter comprises knowledge that typically resides inside the heads of individual experts—needless to say, this is also the more difficult type of knowledge to extract and manage. Tacit knowledge is more likely to provide a competitive advantage to an organization, if harnessed effectively and managed properly. Therefore, it deserves special attention by organizations.

With respect to organizational knowledge management, Nonaka and Takeuchi (1995) assert that "the essence of strategy lies in developing the organizational capability to acquire, create, accumulate, and exploit knowledge. The most critical element of corporate strategy is to conceptualize a vision about what kind of knowledge should be developed and to operationalize it into a management system for implementation" (p. 74).

Liebowitz (2001) identifies the knowledge management lifecycle as comprising the following stages: *knowledge capture; knowledge sharing; knowledge application;* and *knowledge creation*. Therefore, an effective knowledge management strategy should provide guidelines to address each of these stages.

THE CASE STUDIES

Several case studies of successful, as well as unsuccessful, knowledge management projects were analyzed for this study. The companies examined include the following: Best Buy Company, Xerox Corporation, Frito-Lay, IBM, Pillsbury, and a Washington D.C. lobbying organization. These companies embarked on their knowledge management projects with different objectives, ranging from increasing company profitability to consolidating information/ knowledge that was dispersed throughout the organization. All but two of these companies were successful in their knowledge management implementation. Of the two failures, one was rectified mid-stream and changed into a success.

SUCCESS FACTORS IN KNOWLEDGE MANAGEMENT

Based on the analysis of the case studies mentioned in the preceding section, several factors for the successful implementation of an organizational knowledge management system begin to emerge. These factors are grouped below into three categories: *managerial success factors, design/construction success factors,* and *implementation success factors.* Collectively, they address issues at each of the four stages of the knowledge management life cycle identified by Liebowitz (2001).

Managerial Success Factors

- Create and *actively* promote a culture of knowledge sharing within the organization. This includes:
  - clearly articulating and sharing a corporate vision of knowledge management
  - rewarding employees for knowledge sharing activities
  - creating communities of practice to improve communication among people with common interests
  - involving multiple departments and levels within the organization in KM projects to further encourage cross-functional knowledge sharing
  - encouraging, and even championing, the creation of a "best practices" repository
- Create an environment that encourages and rewards experimentation and creativity.
- Create a learning organization.
- Provide the necessary training for employees who will use the KMS.
- For a given KMS project, correctly define the problem at hand, and identify it as one that *requires* a KMS solution, as opposed to some other technology.
- Precisely define the KMS project objectives.

Design/Construction Success Factors

- Approach the problem not as a technical problem, but as an enterprise-wide problem, whose solution will most likely involve a realigning of people, processes, and technologies.
- Create and standardize a knowledge submission process.
- Create methodologies and processes for the codification, documentation, and storage of structured knowledge in relevant databases.
- Design processes for capturing and converting individual tacit knowledge into organizational knowledge; this can include the use of apprenticeship programs, workshops, and demonstrations by recognized experts to reveal their tacit knowledge.
- Aim to capture knowledge that has the following characteristics:
  - is relevant to the intended user's daily activities and is easily accessible

  - has value (i.e., produces some real benefit to the user and the organization)
  - is accurate, reliable, and up-to-date
- Use formal design methodologies.
- Creating relevant and easily accessible knowledge-sharing databases.
- Create a system for cataloging the team members' strengths and expertise.

Implementation Success Factors

- Use a pilot approach to manage complexity and demonstrate success.
- Measure the benefits of the pilot system by means of appropriate and valid metrics.
- Utilize operational knowledge during implementation.
- Involve subject matter experts for content management.
- Use formal implementation methodologies.
- As much as possible, use advisory boards and steering committees, comprised of relevant players, to further ensure buy-in and implementation success.
- Use appropriate knowledge management tools and technologies, such as portals and intranets, where necessary.
- Acquire requisite expertise by using external consultants and/or other strategic partners where necessary.

SELECTED REFERENCES

Barth, S. (2000). "KM horror stories: These tales from the dark side of knowledge initiatives may keep you up at night." *Knowledge Management,* Volume 3 (October), Number 10 (37 40).

Drucker, P. (1993). *Post-Capitalist Society.* New York: Harper Business.

Jennex, M., Olfman, L., & Addo, T. (2003), "The Need for an Organizational Knowledge Management Strategy." *Forthcoming in Proceedings of the Hawaii International Conference on Systems Science, January.*

Liebowitz, J. (2001). *Knowledge Management: Learning from Knowledge Engineering.* Boca Raton: CRC Press LLC.

Nonaka, I., & Takeuchi, H. (1995). *The knowledge-creating company: How Japanese companies create the dynamics of innovation.* New York: Oxford University Press.

Norton, D. P. (2001). *"Measuring and Managing the Value of Information Capital."* BSCol NetConference, September 21.

Legalization of On-Line Gambling

Mario Alba Jr., Louis J. Papa, Anthony Basile, Stuart Bass, and Eugene Maccarone
Hofstra University, 600 Old Country Rd., Suite 327, Garden City, NY 11530
Tel. 516.222.1912; Fax. 516.222.1851; E-mail. maz524@msn.com

INTRODUCTION

Gambling has always been legal in the United States. The gaming industry continues to grow as more Americans view gambling as entertainment rather than a vice (Edward M. Yures, *Gambling on the Internet: The States Risk Playing Economic Roulette as the Internet Gambling Industry Spins Onward*, 28, Rutgers Computer & Tech. L.J. 193, 196, 2002). In recent years, Internet gambling, which exists without any significant regulation, has exploded in popularity (David Goodman, *Proposals for a Federal Prohibition of Internet Gambling: Are There Any Other Viable Solutions to This Perplexing Problem?*, 70, Miss. L.J. 375, 379, 2000). As a result, politicians have struggled with laws that limit or ban the use of Internet gambling (Craig Lang, *Internet Gambling: Nevada Logs In*, 22, Loy. L.A. Ent. L.J. 525, 526, 2002). To date, all attempts at controlling or eliminating on-line gambling have been unsuccessful. The more prudent option would be for the government to place its seal of approval on Internet gambling so that it can draw gamblers away from unregulated sites and generate substantial tax revenues.

HISTORY AND GROWTH OF INTERNET GAMBLING

Despite scorn by Puritan settlers, gambling quickly became popular in the colonies (Lang, *supra*, at 528). While there has been great opposition to all forms of gambling at various times, increased regulations have never amounted to a total ban on gambling activities (*Id.*). Today, gambling is as popular as ever. One study found that approximately 86 percent of Americans have gambled at least once during their lifetime (Yures, *supra*, at 195). In 1999 alone, there were over 58 billion dollars in legal wagers, and that figure was expected to grow rapidly in subsequent years (*Id.* at 196, 197). As legitimate gambling continues to grow, it is no surprise that Internet gambling is also growing at a healthy rate. Current statistics estimate the number of on-line casinos at 2000, all of which are off-shore (Goodman, *supra* at 379.). The amount of money pouring into Internet casinos has skyrocketed from 2.2 billion in 2000 to over 4 billion in 2002 (Ira Sager et al., *The Underground Web*, *BusinessWeek*, Sept. 2, 2002, pg. 66). This is a major concern for politicians because at least 80% of the on-line gambling done in the U.S. is illegal (*Id.*). Politicians cite both a threat to America's youth and rampant fraud as reasons to prohibit on-line gambling (Lang, *supra* at 534).

IS BANNING ON-LINE GAMBLING FEASIBLE?

Through the implementation of The Wire Act and The Travel Act, Congress has been unsuccessful in regulating on-line gambling. Proposed laws, such as the Internet Gambling Prohibition Act (IGPA), in conjunction with credit card agencies have deterred these illegal activities.

The Wire Act

The Wire Act prohibits the use of wire communication outlets, in either interstate or foreign commerce, by persons engaged in the business of betting and wagering on any sporting event or contest (Goodman, *supra* at 386). The Wire Act has been proven ineffective against Internet gambling because individual gamblers are not "engaged in the business of betting or wagering" and the Act is unclear as to whether non-sports related gambling fall within its reach (*Id.*).

The Travel Act

The Travel Act provides in part that, "…whoever…uses the mail or foreign commerce, with intent to (1) distribute the records of any unlawful activity … or (3) otherwise promote, manage, establish, carry on or facilitate the promotion, management, establishment or carry on, or any unlawful activity … shall be fined under this title or imprisoned not more than five years, or both" (Beau Thompson, *Internet Gambling*, 2, N.C. J.L. & Tech. 81, 91-92, 2001). The Act includes a prohibition against "any business enterprise involving gambling" (*Id.*) The Act, while it could presumably punish individual gamblers, has similar shortcomings as the Wire Act in that they involve primarily supply-side regulation (*Id.* at 93). Individual bettors seemingly have very little to fear from these laws, so they will continue placing bets. Additionally, web-site operators will continue to provide the services if they feel that the benefits outweigh any potential sanctions.

The Internet Gambling Prohibition Act

Congress has made several attempts to enact new legislation or update the Wire Act to specifically target on-line gambling. The IGPA has yet to pass as legislators voice worry over the amount of regulation the law would create for Internet users (Lang, *supra*, at 535-536).

The Attack on Payment Mechanisms

The latest, greatest attempt to shut down illegal on-line gambling sites has lawmakers and regulators targeting what has been called Internet gambling's "Achilles' heel—its heavy reliance on credit cards" (Linda Punch, *Are All Bets Off for Online Gambling?*, Credit Card Management, Sept. 2002). Already seven of the top ten credit card issuers refuse on-line casino transactions (David Colker, *Net Casinos Find They Can't Bet on Plastic*, L.A. Times, Sept. 1, 2002, pt.3, pg. 1). This desire to stay out of the market does not stem from gambling being harmful, or even illegal; rather card companies are hesitant to involve themselves in a field where it may be possible for customers to avoid their debts (*Id*; See Also *In re Mastercard*, 132 F. Supp. 2d at 468 (1999)). Authorities have also targeted companies such as PayPal, a payment service widely used to gamble on-line (Matt Richtel, *PayPal and New York in Accord on Gambling*, The N.Y. Times, August 22, 2002, C8).

To attack the gambling problem, card companies are refusing to sign up merchants that knowingly offer Internet gambling (Punch, *supra*). This pull out of the market, while certainly depressing the industry's growth, is not likely to halt it (Colker, *supra*). European banks seem all too eager to enter into a consistently growing four billion dollar industry (Punch, *supra*).

Additionally, alternative payment methods such as wire transfers, money orders, traveler's checks, bank drafts, cashier's and certified checks are already being used; as well as "e-cash" which is in development (William Jenkins, Jr., *Internet Gambling: An Overview of the Issues*, GAO Reports, Dec. 2, 2002).

WHY LEGISLATION FAILED

By trying to regulate or eliminate on-line gambling, greater evils have been created. Strict laws in the U.S. prohibiting on-line gambling are proving as powerful a deterrent as Prohibition was to drinking in the 1920s (Sager et al., *supra*).

The cost of policing on-line gambling far outweighs the benefits received in outlawing the activity. At the same time, the government loses the potential tax dollars it could have received by legalizing these sites (Thompson, *supra*). Legislators, with the aid of most of the major credit card companies, tried to eliminate on-line gambling by policing illegal gambling websites and by blocking money transfers to these sites. However, these attempts have two main weaknesses: lack of personal jurisdiction and the creative circumvention of the website owners.

Lack Of Personal Jurisdiction

The biggest obstacle that legislators face with regards to regulating Internet gambling is obtaining personal jurisdiction over statutory offenders (*Id.* at 95). Since most sites are located abroad, the most obvious concern with any proposed legislation is whether or not such casinos can be effectively prosecuted in American courts.

There are two major related jurisdictional problems in the area of the Internet: 1) Is jurisdiction based upon where the bet is received or where it is placed; and 2) Are offshore casinos subject to jurisdiction in American courts? If both parties to the transaction reside in states which allow gambling, then the solicitation and placing of the bet is permissible. The jurisdictional determination becomes relevant, however, when the bettor, who is from a state that allows gambling, accesses a web-based casino operated from a state in which gambling is illegal, and vice versa. However, American bettors can mask their location by dialing to an offshore Internet service provider ("ISP") before logging into a cybercasino. This allows the gambler to appear to be located in an area where gambling is legal. Essentially, a conflict of laws problem arises and the question then becomes which jurisdiction is proper (*Id.* at 96-97).

Some cases appear to provide a conclusive answer that any company that advertises on the Internet will be subject to personal jurisdiction in every state where people can access the company's website and conduct business. Other courts find the mere operation of a website too tenuous of a connection with a state to grant personal jurisdiction. (*N.Y. v. Lipsitz*, 174 Misc.2d 571, 663 N.Y.S.2d 468 (1997)).

The Rise Of The Black Market

The creation of legislation such as the Wire Act and the uncertainty of litigation surrounding on-line gambling led credit card companies such as American Express and Discover to develop company wide policies that restrict the use of credit cards for Internet gambling (Jennings Jr., *supra*). Illegal website owners have devised ways to allow patrons to deposit money in their on-line accounts. These "merchants" have accomplished this in many ways. First, they disguise transactions by miscoding them (*Id.*). Second, they attempt to circumvent the system by using on-line payment providers, and other non-credit card payment methods (*Id.*). Third, Internet merchants are able to circumvent the coding system by engaging in factoring (*Id.*). Factoring occurs when a merchant submits credit card transactions through another merchant's terminal by using that merchant's identification number and category code, and pays that merchant a percentage of the submitted transactions. (*Id.*).

ARGUMENTS FOR LEGALIZATION

There are many arguments in support of the legalization of on-line gambling. First, gambling is simply a form of entertainment and American consumers are free to spend their entertainment dollar on a product from which they derive the most utility (Thompson, *supra*, at 86). Second, Internet gambling allows computer users the opportunity to partake in casino activities from the comforts of their home without going on vacation (*Id.*) Third, they can avoid the numerous traps that the onsite casino experience entails such as the glitz and glamour of the Las Vegas Strip or the Atlantic City Boardwalk, which induces people to spend money they otherwise may not have spent (*Id.*).

The creation of these web sites will also generate substantial revenues and job opportunities that are of great benefit to local communities (Thompson, *supra*, at 87). The major benefit to the communities is the increased tax revenues received from gaming operations. Casinos generate millions of dollars of revenue each year that are used to subsidize government programs that benefit the community as a whole (*Id.*). By making the activity illegal, hundreds of millions of dollars will be lost each year, and this money will remain in the hands of those website operators who are able to evade the law (*Id.* at 102).

Credit card companies will also benefit. Cardholders use alternative methods to deposit funds in their accounts while others use European or Caribbean banks. While consumers might be hesitant to deposit funds in a Caribbean bank, they don't have a concern depositing money in German, French, Dutch or English banks (Punch, *supra*). These card issuers that feared losing potential revenue can now compete and reap the benefits of one of the fastest growing industries in the world.

In addition, where some companies refused to get involved in such a high-risk industry, others like VISA and MasterCard did not have such a restriction (Jenkins Jr., *supra*). Instead, both associations have developed procedures that enable member banks to block Internet gambling transactions (*Id.*). Officials from both associations explained that since some members are located in countries where Internet gambling is legal reaching a global, blanket policy among members would be difficult (*Id.*) With legalization, companies can compete in an expanding business market and save money on trying to police merchants who were previously miscoding or factoring..

Creation Of An SEC-Like Organization

It is easy to draw parallels between the stock exchange and gambling, especially sports gambling. Unlike the market maker who takes a percentage on both ends of the transaction, the bookmaker only adds the "VIG" when the gambler loses. However, gambling is looked upon as a vice while stock traders are viewed as entrepreneurs. So, if the entrepreneurs have the SEC looking over their shoulder, then on-line gambling should mirror its brother.

The need for regulation is great. For example, Las Vegas slot machines usually are required to pay back from 90 percent to 98 percent of all of the money played; in cyberspace, however, there is no regulatory regime to impose such a requirement (Goodman, *supra*, at 383). With Internet gambling, the house develops and manipulates the odds and controls the account of the player without oversight from any regulatory body (*Id.*). Hence, there are real concerns that the odds on various games are rigged in favor of the house. Even if the player does win, the uncertainty surrounding the legality of Internet gaming sites have allowed disreputable site operators to refuse payment because they face no uniform legal consequences (Thompson, *supra*, at 89). Not only must players worry about the deck being stacked against them from the outset, they have to consider the possibility that they will never receive their winnings from the website proprietor. Additionally, even if the gambling website is honestly run, computer hackers may intercept the gambler's credit card or other financial information (Goodman, *supra*).

CONCLUSION

There is a legitimate concern that Internet gambling may pose a potential for addiction even greater than that associated with traditional gambling activities (Goodman, *supra*, at 384). Prior attempts to eliminate or even criminalize this behavior have failed. Proposed legislation has led to lost revenues, increased policing costs, and money filtering to offshore merchants and foreign banks. Therefore, the federal government should be allowed to make their own assessments in wholesale fashion about the desirability and legality of Internet gambling rather than have the states decide the issue. Their assessments should lead to legalizing Internet gambling, not only to increase revenues for the public and private sector, but will allow the government to regulate an industry that it has let run wild.

Socioeconomic Environment and Technological Change: The Case of California

Rasool Azari and James Pick
School of Business, University of Redlands
1200 E. Colton Avenue, Redlands, CA 92373
(Azari) P: 909-748-6252, (Pick) P: 909-748-6261, F: 909-335-5125
rasool_azari@redlands.edu, james_pick@redlands.edu

ABSTRACT

This paper examines the influence of socioeconomic factors on the receipts and payroll of three technology sectors for 13 counties in California. Based on correlation and regression analyses, the results reveal that factors that are important correlates of several technology sectors are professional/scientific/technical services, other services, and educational services workforce, ethnicity, and college education. As a whole, the findings emphasize the importance of the association of socioeconomic factors with the per capita magnitude of the technology sectors. The paper suggests steps that can be taken by the state of California and its county and local governments to reduce the digital divide.

INTRODUCTION

The continued existence of the "digital divide" and the increasing inequality of wages in the U.S. during the last two decades poses considerable challenges to policy makers. California with its incredible diverse workforce has a unique role in this equation. It has been recognized as one of the leading high-tech exporting and job creating states in the U.S. In the year 2000 it ranked first in high-tech employment, first in venture capital investment, and second in high-tech average wage. Furthermore, 77 of every 1,000 private sector workers were employed by high-tech firms (AEA, 2001). Therefore its economic activities and slowdown, which include the Silicon Valley, much of the entertainment industry, and 48 federal government research labs, have repercussions on a global basis. In 2001 the high-tech industry grew in California only by one percent, down sharply from 1999 and 2000 and this rate of growth varied from county to county. "California is lagging behind other states in workforce readiness. If California cannot meet industry's demand for skilled labor, it could lose science and technology jobs to other states" (Conrad, 1999, p. 1). The technology leadership of California could be threatened.

This paper has the objective to better understand the relationship between socioeconomic factors and the information technology sectors for the counties in California. It raises some relevant questions that may help policy makers and experts to identify and address potential and already developing social and economic problems based on the recent budget shortfall. It may also help to increase dialogue among different stakeholders.

BACKGROUND

The term "digital divide" entered the American vocabulary in the mid-1990s and refers to the unequal access to information technology (Light, 2001). It is not limited to consumer (household) access to technology but is also used to define and distinguish the level of penetration and diffusion of ICT in large and small and medium size enterprises (OECD, 2000). Furthermore, Lentz (2000) argued that the concept of the digital divide should be used in broader terms than merely describing end user problems and should extend also to community development. Other researchers have applied the term to business, economy, and/or society levels, rather than the individual level (OECD, 2000; Baker, 2001). Baker points out that the policy problem of the digital divide is best addressed through multiple dimensions, i.e., policies that address disparities in information technology diffusion at different geographic, economic, social, and organizational levels.

The uneven distribution of IT benefits across the U.S. is frequently reported. Major reports from the National Telecommunications and Information Administration (NTIA, 2000, 2002) utilized U.S. Census national data to examine household distribution of access to technology including computers, phones, and the Internet. It defined "digital divide" as the divide between those with access to new technologies and those without. This report concluded that even though the utilization of electronic tools and computers expanded dramatically in the last two years for all groups in the U.S., a digital divide remained and in some cases grew slightly.

Another issue that widens this gap is the phenomenon of wage divergence and inequality related to technological change. This has received the attention of many labor and trade economists (Feenstra, 1997). It is widely believed that the development of the new technology increases the demand for skilled workers, thereby increasing the wage differential between skilled and unskilled workers. Even though empirical evidence from the literature on wage inequality is inconclusive and fragmented (Deardorff, 1998, p. 371), there is a wide consensus among many economists that technological change is the primary explanation for the widening gap in inequality of wages in the United States. The World Employment Report (2001, p. 56) writes "that the issue of a digital divide between developed and developing countries has come to top the joint policy agenda of the world's wealthiest countries, many developing countries, as well as intergovernmental and development organizations worldwide."

We consider digital divide and wage inequality as a broad concept that includes economic, educational, and social aspects. For instance, a rich economy is better able to afford technology and a highly educated community can better use technology. Furthermore, social issues may also stimulate technology use. For example, socioeconomic characteristics influence consumer uses of technology. In turn consumers with scientific and technology skills provide technology employees for businesses. Those employees contribute to corporate receipts and payrolls. Corporate results add up to constitute technology sectors in counties.

Literature on the digital divide does not address wage inequality. It avoids discussing the broader social problem of this division and focuses mainly on the technical aspect of the issue. But the widening gap in wages in the long run directly or indirectly influences the digital divide in a region, county or country and vice versa. In other words, they are interrelated. It is obvious that technology does not develop by itself but in context with predisposing characteristics of the environment. Today technology has become so intertwined with our everyday life that a broad understanding of its utilization and distribution requires a thorough examination of the socioeconomic environment. Paying attention to the relationship between socioeconomic factors and the changes in the high-tech sectors may further shed some light on the problem and help to alleviate it.

RESEARCH QUESTIONS

This paper has two research questions:

1. What are the most important socioeconomic factors overall that influence the per capita economic sizes of the information, information services/data processing, telecommunications/broadcasting, and motion

Figure 1.

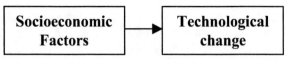

picture/sound recording technology sectors for counties in California?; and

2. How do these three sectors differ with respect to the most important socioeconomic factors that influence their economic sizes?

METHODOLOGY

Our research framework is based on the unidirectional relationship between the socioeconomic factors and technological change as depicted in Figure 1. These factors are one of the most important variables in social study. The socioeconomic position of a person affects his/her chances for education, income, occupation, and health (Miller, 1991).

We are aware that this framework may also flow in a feedback way in the opposite direction, in that larger county technology sectors may attract population with certain socioeconomic characteristics. We are not ready to present a comprehensive framework of these different dimensions and their linkages. Rather, in this paper, we focus on unidirectional linkage as shown in the figure above.

To measure technological change we used the size of payroll and receipts (dependent variables in our regression models) of the main components of the 2000 Economic Census of the Information sector. Data for the Census are published based on the North American Industry Classification System (NAICS); the report presents sources of receipts data for establishments with payroll by kind of business. The three main components of information sectors selected for this study are: Information Services/Data Processing [IS/DP], Broadcasting/Telecomm [B/T], and Motion Picture/Sound Recording [MP/SR]. Following are several reasons why we selected the information technology sectors: 1) The universal use of computers and modern information communication technology in all form of works, 2) IT has increased the productivity of our institutions, shortened the product life cycle, and reversed the composition of our labor force, 3) it diminished the importance of distance and globalized the markets and economies, and 4) it contributes nearly 60 percent to the American gross national product.

We explored the association of twelve socioeconomic factors with six variables that measure the size of industry sectors. The socioeconomic factors are: professional/scientific/technical, other services, and educational services workforce, median household income, college graduates, change in population 1990-2000, and proportions Black, Asian, Latino, and female. Our unit of analysis was the county, because it is the smallest geographical unit for which a wide range of statistical data can be obtained and its unit applies across the entire state, has accurate and extensive variables collected through the U.S. Census and other sources, and is stable geographically over time. It also represents a governmental and policy unit, so policy suggestions from research can inform governmental decision-making. Correlation and linear regression analysis were conducted to test our models. Data were collected from the U.S. Census and the American Electronic Association (AEA).

FINDINGS

The regression findings demonstrate that for the overall aggregated category of information industries, the two most important variables are the professional, scientific, technical (PST) workforce, followed by median household income. For the information services-data processing (IS-DP) information industry sub-category, the most informant associated variable is PST. Education services payroll per capita is also significantly associated with IS-

DP payroll. Likewise, for the broadcasting-telecommunications (B-T) information industry subcategory, PST is the most important predictor. Also significant are federal funds per capita (associated with B-T employees per capita) and proportion Black (associated with BT payroll per capita). For the motion picture – sound recording (MP-SR) sub-category, PST is not significant. Instead, for MP-SR employees per capita, educational services is the most important, and for MP-SR payroll per capita, college graduation and percent population change are significant.

Overall, then, the most important single predictor of technology industry sector sizes per capita is PST per capita, followed by household income. The implication is that wealthier California counties with significant intensity of scientific and professional institutions and workforces tend to have larger per capita high tech sectors. An example is the Silicon Valley area near San Jose, located in the midst of substantial scientific workforce and institutions including such famous universities as Stanford and U.C. Berkeley. Lower profile but also important for information systems and telecommunications technology to thrive are presence of educational services, federal funds, and black ethnicity. The finding that black ethnicity is associated with B-T is also in line with recent studies that associate workforce diversity with technology advance (Florida and Gates, 2001). For motion picture sound recording, college graduation and educational services are the most significant.

CONCLUSION

In summary, the findings support both of the research questions. This study for California corresponds with our earlier findings at the national level. The results suggest that California counties need to plan for and invest in building a scientific and professional workforce and related educational and scientific institutions; stimulate great diversity in the workforce; and encourage development of educational services, as well as support services.

REFERENCES

American Electronics Association. (2001). *Cyberstates 2001: A State-by-State Overview of the High-Technology Industry.* Santa Clara, CA: American Electronics Association.

Baker, P. M. A. (2001). Policy Bridges for the Digital Divide: Assessing the Landscape and Gauging the Dimensions. *First Monday* 6(5), located at www.firstmonday.org.

Conrad, A.C. (1999). Industry Sector Analysis of the Supply and Demand of Skilled Labor in California. *A Report to the California Council on Science and Technology.*

Feenstra, R.C. and G. H. Hanson (1997). Productivity Measurement, Outsourcing, and its Impact on Wages: Estimates for the US, 1972-1990. *NBER Working Paper*, No. 6052, June.

Florida, R. and G. Gates (2001). "Technology and Tolerance: The Importance of Diversity to High-Technology Growth." Washington, D.C.: The Brookings Institution.

Lentz, R.G. (2000). "The E-volution of the Digital Divide in the U.S.: A Mayhem of Competing Metrics," *Info*, 2:4, August, pp. 355-377.

Light, J. (2001). Rethinking the Digital Divide. Harvard Educational Review, 71(4): 709-733.

Miller, D.C. (1991). *Handbook of Research Design and Social Measurement.* Fifth Edition, Sage Publication.

National Telecommunication Information Administration (NTIA). (2000). "Falling Through the Net: Towards Digital Inclusion," *US Department of Commerce*, Washington, D.C.

National Telecommunication Information Administration (NTIA). (2002). "A Nation on Line: How Americans are Expanding the Use of Internet," *US Department of Commerce*, Washington, D.C.

OECD. (2000). *OECD Small and Medium Enterprise Outlook,* Paris.

Web-Based Consumer Research Surveys: An Essential Addition to the Undergraduate Marketing Curriculum

Susan A. Baim, Assistant Professor of Business Technology
Miami University Middletown, 4200 E. University Blvd., Middletown, Ohio 45042
(voice) 513-727-3444, (fax) 513-727-3462, baimsa@muohio.edu

ABSTRACT

This paper provides an overview of the emerging trend of using electronic or Web-based surveys to provide marketing research data. Constraints facing researchers who elect to employ these newer techniques are presented as a preamble for designing an approach to properly introduce electronic surveys into the research tool section of an undergraduate marketing class. Suggested uses beyond a traditional marketing curriculum are noted.

INTRODUCTION

Mention the desire to conduct a consumer- or business-focused survey in marketing circles today and someone will immediately ask whether or not the survey is being conducted online. Electronic surveys are becoming so popular that many large corporations are turning to this sub-classification of studies to provide the majority of research answers needed to stay in tune with consumers. Generally, executing surveys "online" will simplify a number of the logistical steps undertaken by the researcher. Nevertheless, it must also be stressed that use of the Internet for consumer research presents an entirely new set of challenges of which many seasoned research professionals may not be fully aware.

Students entering the marketing workplace after receiving their undergraduate degrees are likely to encounter Web-based survey techniques in use across a broad range of real-world research situations. Unfortunately, many undergraduate marketing programs, particularly those that confer a two-year degree, limit discussions of survey techniques to the familiar mail, phone and mall intercept procedures that have formed the backbone of the industry for decades. Incorporating the study of Web-based survey designs into the undergraduate marketing curriculum will greatly increase the ability of marketing students to compete effectively in their chosen careers.

Students enrolled in the Marketing program within a two-year Business Technology (BTE) program at Miami University (Miami of Ohio) have, for a number of years, been exposed to traditional survey techniques and customarily participate in mail survey research projects each semester. The skills acquired have meshed well with the expectations of local and regional employers who hire BTE graduates at the end of their programs. As a higher percentage of local and regional businesses move to establish a presence on the Web, however, BTE faculty have received numerous requests for assistance in setting up online customer databases, handling customer satisfaction issues over the Internet and moving time-consuming, manual research efforts to Web-based approaches. The drive to incorporate Web-based survey techniques into the BTE Marketing curriculum is thus driven not only by a desire to keep students abreast of the latest research trends but also to provide the practical skills that are in demand today.

USING WEB-BASED SURVEY TECHNIQUES

Web-based surveys introduced into an undergraduate marketing class should be designed to help students develop basic application skills. Typical research problems may include preference testing between two or more products, opinion research on potential advertising concepts or general research on consumer attitudes and lifestyles. Specific objectives to be achieved at the student level are:

1. Develop a basic understanding of the procedures for conducting a survey over the Internet and conducting a survey through traditional mail, phone or intercept means.
2. Be able to use and apply common Web-based survey software packages, like automated, personalized e-mail software and automated data retrieval software designed to eliminate manual tabulation of incoming results.
3. Learn how to assist marketing professionals in the interpretation of data outputs from Web-based surveys.

During the present semester (Fall, 2002), three different Web-based surveys are being fielded within the BTE program at Miami University. Two out of three surveys involve consumer attitudes regarding specific new BTE programs that are planned for introduction over the next academic year while the third survey is designed to capture general consumer needs and wants regarding undergraduate two-year business programs in general. These three surveys, collectively, are serving as important "test mules" for the teaching modules on Web-based surveys currently being incorporated into the BTE 105 Introduction to Marketing course. Initial feedback from both students and faculty shows a highly positive response to the "online" surveys. Response rates are not yet official, but early indications show a higher rate of survey return than that experienced by other departments using a similar content, but mail-based, survey design.

WEB AND INTERNET SURVEYS: CONSTRAINTS FACING THE RESEARCHER

Inherent in teaching students how to execute electronic surveys is the process of helping them differentiate between the proper use of direct Web or Internet surveys and e-mail surveys that are individually sent to pre-selected recipients. Web and e-mail surveys are often lumped together for purposes of discussion. These technologies are, however, actually distinct with each offering its own advantages and challenges to a skilled researcher. Fortunately, the choice of which technology to apply customarily may be made based on the need of the researcher to reach either a general or a carefully-selected population—provided that the population of interest is known to use e-mail and the Internet.

According to research conducted by Don Dillman over a 20 year period, Internet and e-mail users are not quickly migrating to a single set of universal hardware, software and connectivity standards (Dillman, 2000, pp. 357-358). Such standards would potentially make it much simpler for the researcher to design survey questionnaires and data capture regimens that work in exactly the same manner on each individual computer system. Software is similarly limiting. Questionnaire designs are thus often forced to fit the "lowest common denominator" in terms of hardware and software configurations in order to ensure the highest accessibility for respondents.

Dillman's research also indicates that the design of questionnaires and other survey materials for Internet and/or e-mail use requires some additional considerations not normally of concern in traditional paper-based surveys (Dillman, 2000, pp. 358-373). One of the simplest concerns, and also one of the most often overlooked, is the process of navigating through and responding to a series of questions presented on a computer screen as opposed to on a traditional sheet of paper. Dillman notes, surprisingly, that some people will become frustrated when they attempt to click on any underlined text and it turns out not to be a hyperlink (Dillman, 2000, p. 359). Conversely, other people will "forget momentarily that they are operating a computer" and continue to read right past hyperlinks and other branching instructions, or even forget to hit "Reply" to an e-mail survey before trying to fill in their responses (Dillman, 2000, p. 359). While these situations are easily prevented by a little more attention to up front details on the part of the researcher, failure to do so can cause potential survey participants to quickly become non-participants due to the frustrations encountered. Mick Couper, Michael Traugott and Mark Lamias investigated how many of these parameters truly can affect the response rate of Web surveys under a variety of conditions. Of particular concern to this group of researchers were survey participants who began in good faith to complete an electronic survey, but then abandoned it part way through for any one or a number of reasons (Couper, Traugott and Lamias, 2001, p. 231-232). Although results were hard to quantify reliably, these researchers found a positive correlation between the rate of abandonment and the complexity of the survey screens—particularly when survey designers placed so much on-screen that respondents needed to scroll excessively to read and respond to questions.

A particularly good overview of other common constraints, along with current thinking on how to manage the survey process, is given by Zeki Simek and John Veiga in their comprehensive work on organizational surveys (Simek and Veiga, 2001, pp. 218-235). Generalizing their comments to move beyond organizational surveys and into the world of marketing research is not difficult and this work is highly recommended as a guide for researchers who have already decided to move their work to the Internet. Based on all summary of the authors' work, researchers should keep in mind the following bulleted list as they begin the process of designing surveys specifically to be placed online:

- Common sense rules regarding good question design, survey layout, etc., still apply.
- Selection criteria for the desired sample population can proceed as usual, but the researcher must then ask whether or not the earmarked participants are reachable by electronic means.
- Electronic surveys of any type require extra consideration when it comes to their appearance and the means through which participants will record and transmit answers. Extra care is needed in this area in order to produce a functional survey that is easy to answer on as broad of a range of computers as possible.
- Personalization of the invitation to participate is just as critical for electronic surveys as it is for traditional paper-based surveys. The use of "listservs', "bcc's" and other mass-mailing techniques over the Internet should be avoided in favor of personalized invitations to the participants' private e-mail addresses.

- Electronic surveys can generate very good response rates because of their ease of use—provided that they are well designed. To assist in achieving the highest possible response rate, always give participants an "out" if they encounter difficulties while trying to complete the survey. In many cases, it is sufficient to provide an address where participants can mail a copy of the survey if they encounter problems and elect to print the questionnaire and fill it out by hand.

Finally, follow up is every bit as important to the success of electronic surveys as it is to traditional mail surveys. Personalized e-mail alerting participants to an upcoming survey, a quick note at the top of the survey introducing the study, a phone number and/or e-mail address for questions, a reminder copy of the survey sent at an appropriate later time and an electronic "thank you" note, perhaps with a small gratuity such as an electronic coupon, all can help to generate the best possible response rate.

WORKING WITH STUDENTS TO DESIGN ELECTRONIC SURVEYS IN MARKETING AND BEYOND

When incorporating any form of electronic survey into an undergraduate marketing class, it is imperative to make sure that students first have a basic understanding of how to generate simple mail or phone interview survey questionnaires. Students who are familiar with basic research survey design issues and the layout of an easy-to-follow questionnaire can concentrate more readily on the unique challenges of executing an electronic survey without needing to master research fundamentals at the same time. Students should be instructed in how to set up the electronic survey using a straightforward software package (SumQuest and StatPac both work well at the undergraduate level) and then given the opportunity to pre-test and "debug" the questionnaire thoroughly before actual use. It is also advantageous to cover the design and roll-out of survey questionnaires as a separate topic that is distinct from the tabulation and analysis of data that are returned by respondents. While the two topics do go hand-in-hand, data analysis is best taught in conjunction with basic survey statistics and the procedures commonly used to draw meaningful conclusions from an analyzed data set.

Electronic surveys, whether in Web-based or e-mail formats, are applicable in a broad range of situations that range well beyond traditional marketing/consumer research studies. The principles covered here are equally relevant to management or organizational surveys, engineering surveys covering product design or defects, or many other topics. As long as the desired survey population has access to and uses computers on a regular basis, carefully designed and executed electronic surveys can offer high quality information in a timely manner.

REFERENCES

Couper, M. P., Traugott, M. W. and Lamias, M. J. (2001, Summer). Web survey design and administration. *Public Opinion Quarterly,* 65(2), 230-253.
Dillman, D. A. (2000). *Mail and Internet Surveys.* New York: John Wiley & Sons.
Simek, Z. and Veiga, J. F. (2001, July). A primer on Internet organizational surveys. *Organizational Research Methods,* 4(3), 218-235.

Safety of Data in Computer Systems: Introduction to the Study of the Cryptography – Methods and Algorithms

Rômulo Cássio Reginaldo Bezerra and Aluízio Ferreira da Rocha Neto

Faculdade Natalense para o Desenvolvimento do Rio Grande do Norte – FARN, Rua Prefeita Eliana Barros, Brazil

Tel: +55(84) 215-2918, Fax: +55 (84) 211-8688, rmurdock@mail.com, aluiziorocha@hotmail.com

ABSTRACT

The importance of the study of the cryptography feels in one moment in that the electronic trade grows exponentially in Internet and it is done necessary a middle of protecting the data that freely in Internet. This document offers a general vision of network security softwares and related methods for the professionals of network security of the present time. The approached topical principal will be: protection of networks through the cryptography and cryptographic softwares. We will present an abbreviation historical notes of the cryptography making a comparison with the systems of the present time.

INTRODUCTION

After September 11, 2001, the world understood that it lived under constant threat of some attack type. The concern with this new reality surpassed the governments' ambit and financial institutions and it also reached the organizations that noticed the significant increase of the threats and of the vulnerability the one that is exposed, mainly in what refers the discharge vulnerability of the digital atmosphere.

The need to protect your assets and to assure the continuity of the operations, it has been taking the companies they develop a system of administration of information security to implement controls based on analyses of the risks to the business and in legal and compatible requirements with the nature of your activity.

For your time, the users of information systems were more alert and cautious in the hour of accomplishing operations on-line.

In agreement with Módulo consulting (Módulo, 2002) of 547 Brazilian companies interviewees, 72% of those companies suffered some attack type to October of 2002. Of those, 19% had inferior loss the US$ 15 thousand, 8% had losses between US$ 15,000 and US$ 400,000 and 1% above US$ 400,000.

Another study of Gartner Group (Barbosa, 2002) showed that swindle them in stores on-line in 2001 they arrived to 700 million dollars.

For Santos (2002), one of the problems for the lack of safety of the companies, is the system administrators' unpreparedness that not always they are willing to install all the "patchs" and updatings that appear every day. The speed with that the technology moves forward and the easy access to the "hackware" in Internet is another added difficulty.

CRYPTOGRAPHY: AS EVERYTHING BEGAN

Before introducing to the study of the cryptography, we will have a fast vision on the history of the cryptography.

In agreement with Terada (2000), the cryptography flows of the words Greek "kriptó" that it means "hidden" and "logos" that means "word." Soon cryptography means hidden word.

The cryptography, in agreement with Burnett (2002) it is so old when the writing but it is not known for sure in that time the cryptography became used for ends of safety; what is known for sure it is that the cryptography began to be used for military ends. A classic example and one of the oldest cryptographic systems documented (Carvalho, 2002), it is Caesar's System, of the Roman emperor Julios Caesar. The system consisted of substituting a letter of the alphabet for an another in such a way that this substitution relationship was fixed; in this case the key ch is a whole number between 0 and 25 and each letter L it was encrypted using the following equation:

$$L'=(L+Ch) \bmod 26$$

and for decrypt it is had:
$$L=(L'-Ch) \bmod 26$$

This cryptography method is known as system of substitution word by word and it is shown extremely simple given that only have a maximum of 26 possible keys; although extremely fragile it was used with success during the empire.

As the Cryptography Works Today

The cryptography today is the half more used for the sending of secret information through insecure communication lines (Carvalho, 2001). Your use is going of safe e-mails to protocols of safety. Several techniques exist to use the cryptography efficiently but the key cryptography is one of the more used. For Terada (2000), key secretes of cryptography it is a mechanism that seeks to maintain the safety of what it was encrypted and of the user's only knowledge. It works as an additional protection to the cryptography.

According to Burnett (2002), one problem of this system is in the choice of the key that if it goes very easy or of easy deduction, it doesn't increase safety any and the algorithm will be easily "broken."

In agreement with Terada (2000), the systems of key cryptography are divided and, systems of symmetrical and asymmetric key; symmetrical when it uses the same key for encrypt and decrypt; asymmetric when the key that was used for encrypt is not necessarily made necessary for decrypt.

The cryptography of stronger symmetrical key today, meets in the level of 128 bits.

For understanding ends, we will see how the cryptography key works. See an example below with a key with three bits:

000 001 010 011 100 101 110 111

now, adding one more bit, we see that the number of possible keys is bent:

0000 0001 0010 0011 0100 0101 0110 0111
1000 1001 1010 1011 1100 1101 1110 1111

Breaks and Attacks in Cryptography

Several ways exist of breaking the cryptography. The algorithm can be attacked or to attack the cryptography key. For break of cryptography key, one of the attacks more used it is the attack of rude force.

Table 1. A worse scenery than the worst of the situations: How long an attack of rude force would take with relationship to the several key sizes (Burnett, 2002)

Bits	1% of the space of the key	50% of the space of the key
56	1 second	1 minute
57	2 seconds	2 minutes
58	4 seconds	4 minutes
64	4.2 minutes	4.2 hours
72	17.9 hours	44.8 days
80	190.9 days	31.4 years
90	535 years	321 centuries
108	140.000 millennia	8 million of millennia
128	146 billion of millennia	8 trillion of millennia

In agreement with Burnett (2002), a method of attack of rude force consists of trying all the possible keys until that the correct is identified. To proceed, a very simple algorithm of attack of rude force:

```
/ * Algorithm of Rude Force * /
1. Begin
        a. Y := 0;
        b. I := 0;
        c. Read (k);
        d. While (Y <> K) of the
                i. Y := I +1;
        e. Write (" The Key is: ", Y);
2. end.
```

That method takes a long time in normal computers but computers exist created exclusively to break cryptographic systems. One of them is DeepCrack. A computer of the American government capable to test one billion keys a second (Terada, 2000).

For Burnett (2002), essentially 50% of the key are researched before being broken. To proceed, we have a table with a worse scenery than the worst of the situations with relationship at the time of an attack of rude force would take with relationship to the several sizes of the keys (see Table 1).

In fact, the technology of cryptography key has been advancing in a such way that is very unlikely that hackers get to break an alone key.

In recent challenge proposed by RSA Securities, they were necessary four years and more than 331 thousand computers working daily to decipher the secret key RC5-64 of 64 bits. In agreement with Alexandre Cagnoni, general manager of RSA Security in Brazil, RC5-64 has combinations of 18 million of trillion of keys. An alone hacker or in small group it would take many years the plus, or even some decades, to get to find the correct key. (Santos, 2002).

CONCLUSIONS

The security data in computers network it has been critical factor in the executives' of IT calendar in the whole world. In fact, the technology has been moving forward to wide steps and it doesn't get to be the largest problem. As it was seen, network's administrators' unpreparedness is that causes the largest index of attacks with success in the nets of computers; it doesn't advance to place an algorithm with key of 512 bits if the used key is something like 123456.

In fact, it is quite unlikely that the size of symmetrical key surpasses the 512 bits; what generates a size of such big key that she cannot list in that document.

However the cryptography is not and nor it should be the only middle of maintaining secret data; it is just a tool as several other existent ones.

Is the alert so that the cryptography community and of safety of the information it announces telling your researches and the flaws found in the cryptography algorithms. The success of those tools depends of as they are explored.

REFERENCES

BARBOSA, Alexandre. Security e-business. Internet Business Magazine. São Paulo, Brazil: v.XVII, n195, jun. 2002., pg. 25/37.

BURNETT, Steve, PAINE, Stephen. Cryptography and security: The official guide RSA. Rio de Janeiro: Campus, 2002.

CARVALHO, Daniel Balparda de. Security data with cryptography: methods and algorithms. 2ed., Rio de Janeiro: Book Express, 2001.

MÓDULO, Security Magazine. 8th National research of information security. [online] Available in Internet through WWW.URL: http://www.modulo.com.br/comum/docs file captured on November 05, 2002.

SANTOS, Teresa. Chances exist of winning the hackers. Information Week Brazil Magazine. São Paulo, Brazil: 12/04/2002, Y.04 N.83, P.27, DEC. 2002.

TERADA, ROUTO. Security data: Cryptography in computers networks. São Paulo, Brazil: Edgard Blücher, 2000.

Strategic Utilization of Choice-Board Technology: A Conceptual Framework

Pratyush Bharati
University of Massachusetts Boston
100 Morrissey Boulevard, Boston, MA 02125-3393
P: 617 287 7695, F: 617 287 7877, pratyush.bharati@umb.edu

Abhijit Chaudhury
Bryant College
1150 Douglas Pike, Smithfield, RI 02917
achaudhu@bryant.edu

INTRODUCTION

The advent of the new millennium has witnessed an increasing skepticism about the powers of information technologies (IT) to create business value, leading to sluggish investment in new IT. Generating business value using IT is a challenge in this environment. A critical element in this environment is the necessity to create a satisfied and an empowered customer. This paper describes an emerging technology, choice-boards, that allows customers to design their own product and services. More specifically, choice-boards are interactive, online systems that permit individual customers to custom design their own products by choosing from a menu of attributes, components, prices and delivery options [4]. Dell provides a popular instance of choice-board at its site, *Dell.com*. It is an important part of the firm's web-based direct ordering system. Customers start with a basic configuration defined by a processor model and speed, and then go on to specify the full configuration of a personal computer with their choice of hard-drive size, memory, and add-ons such as CD-ROMs, multi-media, monitors and printers.

1) This paper provides a framework called choice-board pyramid that businesses can use to acquire competitive advantages in the market by successfully using the technology of choice-boards as a differentiating factor. The framework relates four factors: company strategy, consumer characteristics, systems and the service that is offered.

The remainder of the paper will focus on choice-board systems, our framework and the hypotheses.

UNDERSTANDING CHOICE-BOARDS

Choice-boards are becoming popular in a wide variety of industries. They are being used in industries as varied as toys, recruitment, finance, wireless phones, travel, apparel and telecommunication gear. While choice-boards are all designed to help users customize their choices, they do so using differing focuses such as providing product information, advising customers, and even letting users have a vicarious experience with the product they have customized.

On *VermontTeddyBears.com*, for example, children are offered many options from which they can select various add-ons to the teddy-bears, e.g., in terms of shoes, glasses, and color. At travel sites such as *Travelocity.com*, customers are provided with information for choosing not only their flights, but also hotels and rentals cars. Choice-boards systems are used in learning and training of individuals in which users make choices and are provided with feedback as to the consequences of their choices. Similar sites are available at GEFinancialLearning.com and in *Cisco.com*. The Cisco site employs a tool, Product Advisor, which assists users in network design and installation using Cisco products and solutions.

While choice-board systems such as *Dell.com* began with providing information to customers, some systems have graduated to providing advice as to the most appropriate choice to make. Point.com uses a choice-board system to help customers buy service plans and wireless phones based on their budget and service profile. Vicarious experience of the product is another option that these systems are beginning to embody. At *landsend.com*, customers spend a few minutes answering questions on weight, height and body-shape. They can select colors, styles and pocket options for the apparel they desire to purchase. The system then generates a picture of the person wearing the apparel. The firm is gearing up its choice-board system to help customers order custom-made jeans in a few-months time, with slacks, shirts and swimsuits following

thereafter. Similarly, at *lanebryant.com*, customers can generate 3-D models of themselves using a virtual model technology called *3D@LB*, which can then be used for trying out, in a virtual sense, tops, jeans and career-wear available at the site.

Benefits of Choice-Boards

Choice-boards offer many advantages to customers and businesses. For businesses, the technology is becoming a significant mode for differentiation in the crowded market place [4]. In product markets, customers are product-takers, i.e., they are offered a fixed set of products from which they are constrained to choose. Customers are typically allowed some variation as to add-ons and features. Buying cars is a good example of a market where customers are product-takers. Choice-boards allow customers to migrate from being product-takers to becoming product-makers. They are able to interact with the system to precisely describe what they want so that suppliers can deliver the product with minimum delay. They cease to be passive recipients and become active designer; in other words, they are product-makers.

For businesses, choice-boards are becoming a source of accurate and real-time data on consumer preferences. Since the configurator records every customer's preferences, Dell, for example, is able to capture buying patterns in real time. The basis of decision-making at Dell moves away from speculating to actually knowing what the customer wants. The choice-board system allows the firm to manufacture against an actual order, vis-à-vis other PC suppliers who manufacture to forecasts, which are apt to be inaccurate. Dell has a pull-based system where customers "pull" their orders in contrast to other PC makers who have a push-based delivery system. In push-based systems, companies make the best guess as to what might appeal to their customers, and plan on delivering the merchandise months ahead of the actual sale to its distributors and retailers. Forecasting is an inaccurate process leading to a huge inventory of goods that buyers often refuse to purchase. This leads to firms engaging in sales and offering rebates, dealer incentives and give-aways to get rid of unsold goods. The pull-based system has allowed Dell to integrate its production line with those of its suppliers. The cross-firm integration has shifted away from silos to a system where information in real time is collected and distributed across the process-chain, and services are delivered to customers in the shortest possible time [5].

Finally, the service model has now shifted from supplier-provided service to self-service. Customers make their own designs and express their customized choices without any other human intervention. Firms save on labor and in processing the entire transaction. Customers feel empowered and firms save on costs.

The choice-board pyramid framework is related to Karl Albrecht's Service Triangle [1] and Parasuraman's Service Marketing Triangle [2]. It is composed of four factors (1) Strategy (2) Customers (3) Service (4) Systems (Figure 1):

Strategy. Strategy is a distinct formula for delivering a unique service that helps a firm differentiate itself in the market [3]. It is built around asking such basic business questions as: (1) In what business is the firm engaged in? (2) Am I selling PCs or am I selling business solutions that use computer software and hardware? (3) Am I selling apparel or am I trying to make my customers feel good about themselves in the context of dresses? The differentiation is achieved in the context of some particular customer segment.

Customers. A strategic conception in the context of choice-boards leads to questions such as: (1) Who are my customers? (2) How sophisticated are

Figure 1. The Choice-Board Pyramid

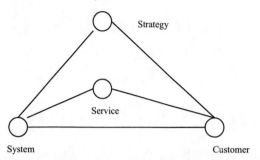

they in using computerized tools? (3) What are their needs, e.g., are they children buying toys using PCs from homes or are they engineering professionals considering networking gear using high-speed connection from their offices? (4) What makes them come to my business? (5) What makes them go to my competitors? (6) What value elements are important to my customer? The most important selection in strategy building is deciding what markets to serve with what products. The first step in market selection is the division of the market according to some scheme that is relevant to the industry. A market segment is set of customers who are alike in the way they perceive and value a product. The segmentation can be done along several dimensions: demography (e.g., income, age, education, tastes and consumption pattern), geography (e.g., location and culture specificity), lifestyle (e.g., career-oriented women versus at-home moms) and product-use patterns.

Service. A strategic conception defines not only a market segment, but also the nature of service that needs to be delivered. The uniqueness and the differentiation power reside in providing a value element that the particular customer segment values highly and considers superior to that delivered by other firms. The service delivered by a choice-board is of self-service type and the benefits are intangible. The experience needs to be positive so that the firm stands from its competition.

Systems. The system delivers a particular service to a specific customer segment. The system consists of an information processing and manufacturing component that produces products customized for each customer. The discussion of this system is beyond the scope of this paper.

RESEARCH IN PROGRESS

Choice-boards provide the foundation for a new business model that is characterized by a user selecting product and service features from a computerized menu of choices. Firms employing this technology are offering a new value – proposition in which the customer is empowered to become a product-maker instead of being a product-taker. Not only can customers implement their choices, but, depending on the application, can experience how that choice would work. Firms that do not offer these systems are at a competitive disadvantage.

This paper described choice-board systems and their diverse applications. It provided a framework that managers can use to target the technology to create business value. The framework has four elements: strategy, customer, service and systems. This research is currently in progress. Hypotheses are being developed to test this framework using a survey and/or experimental method. Constructive feedback from fellow researchers would benefit in further strengthening this framework.

REFERENCES

1. Albrecht, Steve, "Service, Service, Service," Adams Media Corporation, Holbrook, MA, 1994.
2. Bitner, Mary Jo and Matthew L. Meuter, "Technology Infusion in Service Encounters," Journal of Academy of Marketing Science, vol. 28, no. 1, pp. 138-149.
3. Henderson, Bruce, "Nature of Business Strategy," in Perspective on Strategy from the Boston Consulting Group, edited by Carl W. Stern and George Stalk Jr., John Wiley and Sons, New York, 1998.
4. Slywotzky, Adrian J., Clayton M. Christensen, Richard S. Tedlow, and Nicholas G. Carr, "The Future of Commerce," Harvard Business Review, January–February 2000.
5. Slywotzky, Adrian J. and David J. Morrison, "How Digital is your Business?" Crown Business, New York, 2000.

Micro- and Small-to-Medium Sized Enterprises in the Austrian Computer Software Industry: Their Economic Importance, Software Process Characteristics and ICT Utilisation

Edward W.N. Bernroider
Department of Information Business
Vienna University of Economics and Business Administrations
T: (+43) (1) 31336-5231, F: (+43) (1) 31336-739, edward.bernroider@wu-wien.ac.at

ABSTRACT

This paper reports on results from an empirical investigation of the Austrian computer software industry. A questionnaire was used to interview a random sample of key executives in 174 Austrian software enterprises. Firstly, the important role of micro- and small to medium software enterprises is outlined. Secondly, the article focuses on specificities of micro- and small to medium software enterprises regarding inquired software process characteristics and in the utilization of new information and communication technologies for the development of new products and services.

RESEARCH OBJECTIVES

Scholars in economic sciences have focused on the role of smaller enterprises, especially SMEs, in economic development (Pavitt, Robson et al., 1987; Acs and Audretsch, 1988; Keeble, 1996). While these references contributed to an economy in general, I firstly want to present the economic value of micro- and small-to-medium enterprises (MEs and SMEs) (topic i) for the Austrian software industry. Secondly, the article focuses on differences observed between MEs, SMEs and large enterprises (LEs) for the following two important areas of software companies: Differences of software engineering process characteristics between MEs, SMEs and LEs as perceived by the management of Austrian software companies (topic ii). And finally, differences in the utilization rates of new information and communication technologies (ICT) in the companies' product and service portfolios (topic iii).

METHODOLOGY

The methodology employed to investigate these research topics is an empirical study of the Austrian computer software industry, which was carried out in the year 2000. The results shown in this paper represent only a part of the wider field of research topics considered by the undertaken empirical survey.

For both, the preliminary (for screening purposes) and the main analysis, the design of a questionnaire which was validated in several pre-tests was necessary. For the preliminary phase random sampling was employed and the 600 chosen companies were contacted by telephone. The achieved response rate was 70.4. On completion of the preliminary analysis structured face-to-face interviews followed in the main step of analysis, which based on a stratified and disproportional sample with subgroups according to company size. The rate of return for the second step of the study was 55.6%. The non-response analysis revealed no significantly different characteristics between non-respondents and respondents. Of the 174 data sets received, 91 belonged to MEs, 50 to SMEs and 33 to LEs.

EMPIRICAL RESULTS

Economic Importance

While Austria's MEs and SMEs account for 25% of the whole target populations' sales (including non-software), the contribution to R&D investments (49.08%) and especially to employee education and training (88.0%) investments is much higher (see Table 1). This high contribution to employee education and training of smaller software organizations in Austria shows their significant role in building up knowledge resources. LEs often obtain these resources by buying and integrating technology from smaller organizations or by utilizing the high mobility of human resources (Porter, 1990) and thereafter embracing the proportion of exogenous organizational knowledge which is embedded in the minds of the individual employees. Thus, the value of MEs and SMEs in terms of knowledge contribution to the Austrian software industry can be rated as very high.

Austria's software companies employ a workforce of approximately 40.000 software specialists on a permanent basis and 13.000 as software freelancers, not fully integrated in the company. SMEs employ 31.8% of the permanent software workers, LEs employ 63.4%. Both categories, SMEs and LEs, employ the same share of freelancers for software related tasks (44%). But MEs and SMEs rely more intensively on their non-permanent work force than LEs. The empirical data showed a strong overbalance of smaller software enterprises in Austria: Micro-enterprises (ME) account for 55.7% of the Austrian software organizations. 32.2% can be attributed to SMEs and 12.1% to large enterprises (LE). Classification was performed following the definition proposed by the European Community (EC, 1996) (see Table 1). In Austria the average firm size has declined in line with smaller firms entering the industry.

Inquired Software Process Criteria

The development of software is known to be a complex task and routinely breaches the effort, quality and functionality targets (Van Genuchten, 1991; Kautz and Larsen, 2000). This work seeks to reveal the current focus of the Austrian software industry in seeking to overcome the limited success of software projects as reported in academic literature.

During the interview, the companies assessed 14 different variables according to their perceived application in their software engineering processes. Therefore only companies which provide either packaged or custom software were considered for analysis in this section (144 enterprises).

The questioned factors were divided into two different groups: programming languages and criteria applicable to the software engineering process as a whole. The data showed that object-oriented program languages are most commonly used and that companies have recognized project management tech-

Table 1. Distributions of industry characteristics

Size	Employees	Turnover (Mio. €)	In-dependency[1]	No. of Companies (rel.)	No. of Companies (abs.)
ME	1-9	< 7	< 25%	**55.7%**	1.082
SME	10-249	< 40	< 25%	**32.2%**	625
LE	> 250	> 40	> 40	**12.1%**	235
Total				100%	1.941

[1] Capital share in external ownership.

Size	Distribution of Sales	Distribution of R&D Expenses	Distribution of Employee Education and Training Investments
ME	4.0 %	5.6 %	50.5 %
SME	20.6 %	43.4 %	37.7 %
LE	75.4 %	50.9 %	12.0 %
	100 %	100 %	100 %

Total sales p.a. (including non-software related sales): € 11 billion
Software-related sales p.a.: € 5 billion

All data are based on own estimation referring to the year 1999

niques including a unified process and project controlling as the most important aspects of the software engineering process. To improve software development, software managers achieve greater leverage from the management of people and the cross-functional processes than with the use of CASE tools, which were rated as relative unimportant.

To test the independence of responses between MEs, SMEs and LEs, the Kruskal-Wallis H-Test was applied, which is a non-parametric equivalent to one-way ANOVA. The strength of a relationship was analyzed with Spearman rank correlation coefficients, which is used when ordinal scaled variables (in this case the size of the company) are involved. The study identified six out of the 14 criteria that showed differences in how they were rated by managers between company sizes (see Table 2). The highest correlated relationships (either positive or negative) with high significances were "Case-Tools" and "Distributed Object System Technology (CORBA, COM/DCOM)". The perceived importance of all identified characteristics correlates positively with the size of the organization, i.e., the importance increases with the size of the organization.

To examine the effect demonstrated by the six criteria as a whole a multiple discriminant analysis (MDA) based on the split-sample or cross-validation approach (Green and Carrol, 1978; Perreault, Behrman et al., 1979) was applied. The results of MDA show that using these six factors in a simultaneous estimation approach, 69.8% of all cases in the analysis sample could be correctly grouped in MEs, SMEs and LEs, while 54.1% of all cases in the holdout sample could be correctly classified. The calculated discriminant functions are statistically significant (p=0.05), as measured by the chi-square statistic, and the first function accounts for 94.4% of variance explained by the two functions. This also affirms the significance of the six variables for classifying the company's size. Using the group sizes for the reduced sample, the proportional chance criterion (Hair, Anderson et al., 1998) is 0.424. Comparing this chance criterion with the prediction accuracies presented shows that they are acceptable.

Table 2. Identified discriminating software process characteristics

No.	Variable	Mean (MEs)	Mean (SMEs)	Mean (LEs)	Mean (all)	Significance (H-Test)	Correlation Coefficient (Spearman)	Significance (Spearman)
1	CASE-Tools	2.00	2.79	3.29	2.42	0.000	0.378	0.000
2	Distributed Object System Technology (CORBA, COM/DCOM)	1.94	2.64	3.33	2.34	0.001	0.368	0.000
3	Software Project Management Practices	3.47	4.22	4.33	3.83	0.000	0.347	0.000
4	Software Project Controlling	3.26	3.84	3.83	3.53	0.008	0.307	0.000
5	Unified Modeling Language (UML)	1.60	2.01	2.48	1.83	0.007	0.285	0.001
6	Formal Software Testing Routines	3.20	3.67	3.79	3.43	0.037	0.193	0.024

Variables rated by managers on a scale between one (not important) and five (very important) as perceived in their own organizations

Table 3. Identified discriminating ICTs

No.	Variable	Mean (MEs)	Mean (SMEs)	Mean (LEs)	Mean (all)	Significance (H-Test)	Correlation Coefficient (Spearman)	Significance (Spearman)
1	Digital signatures & auth.	1.72	2.29	2.39	1.99	0.002	0.263	0.001
2	New encryption mechanisms	1.68	2.08	2.42	1.90	0.013	0.260	0.001
3	WAP	1.45	2.00	2.12	1.71	0.003	0.229	0.003
4	New HTML-extensions	2.47	2.98	3.36	2.74	0.003	0.219	0.004
5	Bluetooth	1.21	1.58	1.09	1.31	0.000	0.195	0.011

Variables rated by managers on a scale between one (not important) and five (very important) as perceived in their own organizations

ICT Utilisation

The inquired information and communication technologies (ICT) can be divided into the following groups: security and e-commerce ("new encryption mechanisms", "Digital signatures and Authentication", "smart cards"), convergence of media and ICT ("new multimedia standards" such as the moving picture experts group-4 standard), Internet ("new HTML extensions" such as XML or CSS2 and "WAP") and new communication techniques ("voice over IP", "bluetooth"). The utilization of these technologies in the design of the companies' ICT products and services had to be rated by managers of Austrian software companies on a scale from one (not important) to five (very important) as perceived in their own organization. Another inquired variable corresponded to the use of new technologies in general. For the data analysis in this section the non-software developing companies were allowed back into the sample resulting in the original number of 174 data sets.

The data showed that although new technologies in general were utilized by the Austrian software companies regularly, the specific ICT technologies inquired were not classified as very relevant. An exception are the HTML extension such as XML, CSS2 or VRML. On second place follow the security technologies which need to be considered with every e-commerce application.

To find differences between MEs, SMEs and LEs, again first the Kruskal-Wallis H-Test and second, Spearman rank correlation coefficients were analyzed (see Table 3) prior to the MDA analysis. Again, the calculated discriminant functions are statistically significant (p<0.01) and the first function accounts for 82.1% of the variance explained by both functions. The comparison with the proportional chance criterion (which is 43% when including all companies in the analysis) yields a acceptable prediction accuracy only for the analysis sample (57.7%). The cases could not be successfully classified in the holdout sample (42.7%).

CONCLUSION

The median firm operating in the Austrian software industry has become smaller through time. Although MEs and SMEs together contribute for only a quarter of the whole industry sales, they already account for nearly half of the R&D investments and nearly 90% of costs attributed to employee education and training in the Austrian software industry showing the value of MEs and SMEs in terms of knowledge contribution. It seems that the Austrian software companies have a stronger focus on software project management practices than on technology-driven approaches to strive for high-quality software development. The statistical analyses employed showed several factors differing between different sized companies out of which the importance of Case-Tools is valued most differently, resp. highest by LEs. According to the empirical findings the inquired new IT technologies are more often utilized for products and services in larger enterprises.

REFERENCES

Acs, Z. J. and D. B. Audretsch (1988). "Innovation in large and small firms: an empirical analysis." *American Economic Review* 78(4).

EC (1996). Empfehlung der Kommision betreffend die Definition der kleinen und mittleren Unternehmen. Brussels, Commission of the European Community.

Green, P. E. and J. D. Carrol (1978). *Mathematical Tools for Applied Multivariate Analysis*. New York, Academic Press.

Hair, J. F., R. E. Anderson, et al. (1998). *Multivariate Data Analysis*. London, Prentice Hall.

Kautz, K. and E. A. Larsen (2000). "Diffusion theory and practice - Disseminating quality management and software process improvement innovations." *Information Technology & People* 13(1): 11-26.

Keeble, D. (1996). Small Firms, Innovation and Regional Development in Britain in the 1990s, ESRC Centre for Business Research.

Pavitt, K. L. R., M. Robson, et al. (1987). "The size distribution of innovating firms in the UK: 1945-83." *Journal of Industrial Economics* **35**(3).

Perreault, W. D., D. N. Behrman, et al. (1979). "Alternative Approaches for Interpretation of Multiple Discriminant Analysis in Marketing Research." *Journal of Business Research* 7: 151-173.

Porter, M. (1990). *The competitive advantage of nations*. London and Basingstoke, The Macmillan Press LTD.

Van Genuchten, M. (1991). "Why is software late? An empirical study of reasons for delay in software development." *IEEE Transactions on Software Engineering* 17(6): 582-590.

Ethics and Students in the Information Professions: A Survey of Beliefs and Issues in Information Ethics Coursework

Elizabeth A. Buchanan, Ph.D.
School of Information Studies, University of Wisconsin-Milwaukee
PO Box 413, Milwaukee, WI, USA
T: 414.229.4707, F: 414.229.4848, buchanan@sois.uwm.edu

INTRODUCTION

The ideas of computer or information ethics are not novel; the formal use of the term "computer ethics" dates to 1976 with Walter Maner, while somewhat more recently in the late 1980s, Robert Hauptman in the US and Ralphael Cappura in Germany began using the term "information ethics." What these terms mean in both theory and practice varies across information-related professions and disciplines, as well as professional organizations. One commonality, however, is emerging, and this is the fact that many computer and information professional organizations want or require students to have some training and education in ethics as part of their curricula prior to assuming job responsibilities in the "real world." The university classroom is the ideal place to build an understanding of ethical theories, to introduce a growing array of topics surrounding computer/information ethics, and to conduct case studies and role playing around ethical dilemmas.

Such professional organizations as the ACM have recommended that all computer science students receive required coursework in ethics totaling 16 hours, with 10 Social/Professional/Ethical units. Others, such as the ALA, has a code of ethics but does not require students in library and information science programs to take ethics courses. While codes of ethics exist across professional organizations, they are often not adequate tools to assist professionals when they are facing ethical dilemmas in the workplace. Thus, many computer/information studies programs have elective courses in ethics. The remainder of this paper will discuss student perspectives on information ethics, and it will conclude with brief recommendations for developing an information ethics course.

CONTEXT

The perspectives reflected in this paper are based on informal surveys conducted in an Information Ethics course, comprised of both graduate and undergraduate students. Surveys were collected from 64 students, from four sections of the course taught over two years, beginning in 2000. Thus, this population is fairly small, and future research will present on greater numbers of students across longer spans of time. The students are either pursuing a Bachelor of Science degree in Information Resources or a Master of Library and Information Science. Students are asked as part of their first session to respond anonymously to a brief survey, which includes the following questions:

1. What does "ethics" mean to you?
2. Do you consider ethics to be the same as religion? As law? Why or why not?
3. What do you hope to gain from taking an ethics course?
4. Identify the single most important ethical issue facing information professionals today. Why is this important?
5. Have you ever encountered an ethical issue in your work or personal life? How did you resolve it?
6. Should an ethics course be required for information professionals? Why or why not?

Responses were coded, using qualitative coding techniques, and tallied, and are presented in percentages; due to space limitations, not all survey questions are described herein.

WHAT ARE ETHICS?

The area of philosophy known as ethics deals with morality, how to make moral decisions, and how to lead a "good life." Ethics, more specifically, is the formal study of morality and what we do and how we act as rationale human beings.[1] For simplicity's sake, ethics can be broken into three major realms: *Descriptive ethics*, which focus on existing situations, for example, "Joe is a computer hacker." *Normative ethics* take us into the realm of evaluation, what ought to be. For example, "Joe should not be a computer hacker because computer hacking is wrong." It is between the descriptive and the normative where most of the discussions in computer and information ethics occur. The third area of ethics is *meta-ethics*, which is the "logical analysis of moral language and the aim to make precise the meaning of moral terms and clarify the moral arguments that are at stake" (Buchanan, 2000, p. 524). For instance, what does it mean to say hacking is wrong?

Understanding student beliefs on ethics helps frame formal coursework. Coming into an information ethics course, the students surveyed here represented some interesting views in their understanding of ethics. The question "What do ethics mean to you" elicited the following responses[2]:

Right/Wrong	32%
Moral Code/Rule/Guideline/Principle	26%
Way of Acting/Thinking	24%
Belief/Value System	13%
Moral Standard	4%
Other	1%

WHAT ETHICAL ISSUES ARE MOST IMPORTANT?

Areas of coverage in computer/information ethics courses vary among institutions. Typically, such areas as privacy, intellectual property issues, intellectual freedom, computer crime and security, and professional ethics are included for discussion and study.

In keeping with many American's concern for privacy, the largest area stated was privacy, followed by censorship. Given these students' disciplines, this is not a surprising report. In sum, students reported the following areas of concern in response to this question:

Privacy	41%
Censorship/Freedom of Information/Access	28%
Copyright	9%
Surveillance	5%
Data Integrity	3%
Filtering	3%
Data Mining	2%
Plagiarism	2%

Illiteracy	2%
International/Global Policies	2%
Don't Know	3%

SHOULD ETHICS COURSES BE REQUIRED?

Overwhelming, students believed that an ethics course should be required for the information professions. Of the 64, 59 (92%) believed an ethics course should be required, two (3%) held it should not be, while three (5%) were not sure. A recurrent comment, too, suggested that not only information professionals be required to take an ethics course, but any degree-seeking student should be aware of the ethical issues surrounding the uses of technologies today. This is encouraging, given the complexities of technologies and the many ways in which breeches of ethics are occurring vis-à-vis technologies. If our upcoming professionals feel strongly that ethics are indeed important, our future looks hopeful.

One student succinctly stated: "The world is becoming more complex yet more accessible at the same time. Information professionals will be faced with difficult ethical decisions. The right thing may not always be readily apparent. By requiring that IP's take an ethics course, it will help to guide us in future situations by providing us with the knowledge of where to look and how to determine the ethical connotations of the situation."

The students surveyed here represent only a small group of forthcoming information professionals, but show great promise for the future of our professions, as they reveal an awareness and an interest in ethics. While not described in this paper, most of the responses to the question "What do you hope to gain from taking an ethics course" revolve around a desire to understand and know how to respond appropriately to ethical challenges. From an instructor perspective, it is encouraging to have an audience of students want to engage with ethics and their professional work. Given the responses to the surveys, which are ongoing, a number of lessons for teaching information ethics can be described.

LESSONS LEARNED FROM DEVELOPING AND TEACHING INFORMATION ETHICS

When the IE course was first conceived in 1998, I thought I would spend the majority of time on professional ethics and codes of ethics. After one semester with this focus, it became evident that this was too narrow and not as preparatory for students as I had hoped. The course was revised to include a thorough introduction to ethical theory, after which applied ethics were introduced. Since most students in the IE course do not have philosophy backgrounds, or any knowledge of ethical theory, presenting complex theories as presented in primary philosophical texts proved difficult and impractical. Thus, secondary texts such as Baase (2002), Johnson (2001), or Tavani (forthcoming) are useful in presenting both theory and practical issues.

What should be covered in an IE course? As mentioned above, typical coverage includes such areas as privacy, intellectual property, intellectual freedom, computer crime and security, and professional ethics and codes of ethics. Given the rich landscape of ethical dilemmas current in the news, using current events and real-world examples proves beneficial in elucidating the theory behind these areas while highlighting the practical significance of ethical issues. A common example has been Napster, with which most university student are familiar. Through a discussion of Napster, one can look at an array of issues, including copyright, ownership, theft, technological distance from a crime, and whether technology crimes, where there is no tangible object, are different from "physical" crimes, for instance.

IE courses benefit greatly from case studies and role playing, where students have the opportunity to debate ethical dilemmas and engage in ethical decision making. Spinello's (1997, 2003) case study text is useful, as it provides scenarios representing various areas of computer and information work, and affords thoughtful, provoking questions for discussion. Giving students the opportunity to engage in such decision making will assist them when facing ethical dilemmas in the workplace.

Finally, spending time on professional ethics, including codes of ethics and organizational statements helps students understand their roles as members of a profession. While breaching a code of ethics in such professions as librarianship or computing does not mean lose of licensure or ability to work, as with law or medicine, it is highly important to instill a sense of professional responsibility in students. As we see in this day and age of corporate scandal, irresponsibility, and ethics violations, instilling a sense of ethics and responsibility is a necessity, not an elective. It is my hope that information ethics courses ground students in an ethical framework from which they make decisions, choose their actions, and serve their profession and the public.

CONCLUSION

It is my belief that computer and information ethics education begins well before students enter a university classroom. Students in the K-12 settings need to be introduced to the complexities of computer and information technologies, including ethical complexities (see Lipinski and Buchanan, 2002). By introducing ethics to our youngest students, we can instill a sense of ethical responsibility that parallels technical know-how: Ideally, while students continue to learn the latest programming language or technique in information organization as they progress through schooling, too they continue to learn and practice ethics. As professionals in the computing and information fields, we owe it to our students, who are our future, to assist them in identifying, understanding, and making sound ethical decisions around the complexities of computer and information work.

ENDNOTES

[1] For more on the distinction between ethics and morality, see Buchanan, 2000.

[2] If students responded with multiple answers, all were included in the coding for this question.

REFERENCES

Baase, S. (2002). A gift of fire: Social, legal and ethical issues for computers and the Internet. Upper Saddle River, NJ: Prentice Hall.

Buchanan, E. (2000). Ethical considerations for the information professions. In *Readings in Cyberethics*. Edited by Herman Tavani and Richard Spinello. Sudbury, MA: Jones and Bartlett.

Johnson, D. (2001). Computer ethics. Upper Saddle River, NJ: Prentice Hall.

Lipinski, T. and Buchanan, E. (2002). There's a place for us(e): Incorporating the responsible application of new technologies into the K-12 curriculum: Results of a study assessing the level of knowledge, preparation and dissemination among educators. Paper presented at ETHICOM 2002. Lisbon, Portugal.

Tavani, H. (Forthcoming). Ethics and technology: Ethical issues in an age of information and communication technology. New York: Wiley.

It's Never Too Soon: Responsible Technologies in K-12 Education

Elizabeth A. Buchanan and Tomas A. Lipinski
Center for Information Policy Research, School of Information Studies
University of Wisconsin-Milwaukee
T: 414.229.4707, F: 414.229.4848
buchanan@sois.uwm.edu, lipinski@sois.uwm.edu

WHAT IS RESPONSIBLE TECHNOLOGIES?

Some are beginning to ask a very important question of K-12 education: "Should we be teaching reading, writing, and copyright?" (Slind-Flor, 2000). We believe the answer to this question is a straightforward yes, and to this end, the "Responsible Technologies" (RT) project, funded by the University of Wisconsin System, is underway. RT is the understanding, knowledge, and uses of technologies in ethical and legal ways.

Why is it more important now than ever to teach responsible technologies? There are many reasons: Firstly, technology use in K-12 settings has grown exponentially. Relatedly, students are not learning responsible use along with technical skills, and this must change. Secondly, such high profile cases as Napster are raising awareness of legal and ethical dilemmas in technology use for all users, not simply computer professionals. Thirdly, many states are now mandating standards which include a component of legal and ethical competence in technology use. For instance, in Wisconsin, where the RT study is underway, the Model Academic Standards for Information and Technology Literacy (WMACITL, 1998, p. 14-15) dictate that:

"By the end of Grade 4 students will ... Use information, media, and technology in a responsible manner, by the ability to demonstrate use consistent with the school's acceptable use policy, understand concepts such as etiquette, defamation, privacy, etc. in the context of online communication ... Respect the concept of intellectual property rights, by the ability to explain the concept of intellectual property rights, describe how copyright protects the right of an author or producer to, identify violations of copyright law as a crime ...

By the end of Grade 8 students will ... Use information, media, and technology in a responsible manner by the ability to describe and explain the applicable rules governing the use of technology in the student's environment, demonstrate the responsible use of technology, recognize the need for privacy and protection of personal information ... Respect intellectual property rights by the ability to explain the concept of fair use, and that the application of the concept may differ depending on the media format, relate examples of copyright violations, explain and differentiate the purposes of a patent, trademark, and logo...

By the end of Grade 12 students will ... Use information, media, and technology in a responsible manner by the ability to assess the need for different informational polices and user agreements, understand concepts such as misrepresentation and the need for privacy of certain data files or documents ... Respect intellectual property rights by the ability explain why fair use is permitted for educational purposes but not in for profit situations, and the conditions under which permission must be obtained for the use of copyrighted materials ..."

Thus, various reasons exist to support a systematic and systemic program to educate K-12 teachers, administrators, media specialists, and technology coordinators—and their students—about emerging legal and ethical issues in technology use.

RT is a multi-year project developed with these overarching goals:

1. To assess the current state of knowledge and perceptions of a sample of K-12 teachers, media specialists, technology coordinators, and administrators from a five county population in Southeastern Wisconsin surrounding legal and ethical implications of technology use in the classroom;
2. To teach this sample about legal and ethical uses of technologies in the classroom;

3. To work with participants to develop resources about legal and ethical uses of technologies in the classroom and make these resources widely available;
4. To assist K-12 educators become aware and knowledgeable about law and ethics in order to better instruct their students so they become responsible users and consumers of technologies.

It is with this last goal that we hope the RT project begins to facilitate systemic change in the attitudes and actions of children and young adults in regards to technologies. Only educated individuals can make truly informed ethical and legal decisions.

ASSESSING RT BELIEFS AND KNOWLEDGE

This paper reports briefly on the first goal and the results from year one, which assessed perceptions and knowledge of technology ethics and law, in particular, copyright and fair use of media and information technologies in school settings. Twenty-seven individuals representing 20 schools completed a pre and post assessment survey.

One survey area polled participants about their beliefs surrounding technology law and ethics, asking, for example, in a Likert scale format (1=strongly disagree to 5=strongly agree) such statements as:

- My school has a policy about ethical uses of technology (computers, World Wide Web, software, etc.).
- I am familiar with ethical uses of computer technology.
- I understand what an acceptable use policy is.
- I teach my students why copying software or committing other copyright violations is wrong.
- I teach my students about the social implications of technology use.
- Technology ethics should be taught distinct from the regular curriculum.
- Copyright or other legal concepts are too impractical to teach to K-12.

In addition, a battery of legal questions and scenarios was presented for responses. Here, questions spanned a wide range of copyright issues: "Can a teacher make a copy of a pre-recorded music CD or videocassette for personal use?", "Is there a blanket exception for educational reproductions of copyrighted material, in other words is every educational use a fair use under the copyright law?", "Can a student scan a photograph from National Geographic into a word processing document and use it as an illustration in a class term paper?", "Could a student take two minutes of the Johnny Depp movie *Sleepy Hollow* and use it in a multi-media presentation in a class on American authors of the Romantic Period?", "Under Sections 512 and 1201, could a teacher refer in class to a web site that is likely to contain infringing material, such as one that has over 1,000 theatrical videos downloadable for free, or one that has available for downloading anti-circumvention technology on it such as DeCSS that would allow users to 'crack' a protection code on a DVD?" This paper does not report on the battery results.[1]

Overall, the goal of the survey was to determine the extent of knowledge and beliefs of this sample of K-12 educators in order to proceed to stage two of the project—the development of teaching and curricular resources, which is a major area of need. Few teacher education programs have specific courses or course content on legal and ethical issues in technology use, and educators must often rely on in-service sessions or grant projects such as these to gain knowledge and skills to both understand and practice RT and to develop curriculum to use with their students to instill a sense of responsibility in them.

Results were reviewed to compare differences between the pre-survey and the post-survey responses. Comparisons were also reviewed between the following groups[2]:

- Those who taught library or technology-related subjects and those who did not;
- Those who taught primary grades (K-6) and those who taught secondary (7-12) (in the instances where a teacher taught in both categories, he/she was placed in the category that he/she taught more; i.e., a teacher who taught Grades 4-8 was placed in primary since Grades 4, 5, 6 represent a majority of the grades.); and
- Those who taught greater than 15 years and those who taught less than 15 years.

SUMMARY OF OPINION QUESTION RESULTS

Regarding the levels of agreement with the school's and teacher's knowledge of, enforcement of, and support of legal and ethical use of technology, the post-survey responses indicated a decrease in confidence. In the post-survey, fewer participants indicated that their school had a copyright policy (73.1% to 63.0%), that they were familiar with the content of such a policy (66.7% to 40.7%), and that their school administrator was supportive of responsible use (88.5% to 66.7%). It is notable that more non-library/technology teachers disagreed that they were familiar with the school's copyright policy (75.0%) than library/technology teachers (50.0%) in the post-survey.

An interesting finding regarding the support of RT within the school was that none of the participants agreed that their school as a whole punishes teachers for the infringement of copyright in either the pre- or post-survey, which conflicts with the fact that the majority of them (greater than 50%) said that their administrator was supportive of responsible use. However, the number of participants who agreed that their administrator was supportive of responsible use did drop approximately 22% (88.5% to 66.7%). On a related issue, a majority (greater than 50%) strongly believed (level of 4-5) that their school as a whole punishes students for unethical or inappropriate use of technology.

A greater number of participants' reported a greater understanding of ethical uses of technology, the meaning of intellectual property, and the definition of an Acceptable Use Policy (AUP) in the post-survey. A large number of people reported that they enforce AUPs in their classroom in the pre-survey, 80.7% chose level 3, 4, or 5, but it is worth pointing out that in the post-survey, 100.0% chose level 3, 4, or 5. There was also an increase in the levels participants indicated regarding what they teach their students (why plagiarism is wrong, why copying software is wrong, respecting others in online environments, privacy rights, and using technology responsibly). It is worth mentioning, however, that the levels of agreement in the pre-survey were considerably high (more than 50% reporting levels 3, 4, or 5) in these areas as well. It seems that more participants learned the need to also teach the social implications of technology. 44.4% indicated a level of 1 or 2 in the pre-survey while 88.8% indicated a level of 3 or 4 in the post-survey regarding social implications.

Not many participants were aware of the "Ten Commandments of Computer Ethics" (Computer Ethics Institute, 1992) before the inservice (63% indicated level 1), with 0% indicating level 4 or 5. However, in the post-survey, 48.1% indicated a level of 4 or 5.

More people indicated a higher level of confidence in teaching technology ethics in their classroom. Before and after the inservices, participants felt that technology ethics should not be taught distinct from the regular curriculum (greater than 70% indicated level 1 or 2), and that it is appropriate to teach ethics and legal issues to K-12 students (greater than 60% indicated level 1). However, in both of these areas, the number of people indicating a level of 4 or 5 jumped from 3.7% to 14.8% and 0.0% to 7.4%, respectively.

CONCLUSIONS

While small, this sample of educators reveals that much needs to be learned and attitudes do need to be changed in regards to RT. Our belief is that RT should not be looked at from the punitive perspective; that is, technology ethics and law violations are occurring in the schools not due to malicious intent, but to ignorance, and while punishment may be necessary, a preventative program would benefit both educators and their students greatly. If we change the ways in which educators receive information about technology law and ethics within their preparatory programs, they will be better suited to practice RT within their classrooms. Students will then see RT in practice, and learn RT from their educators both by example and within the curriculum.

ENDNOTES

[1]   For discussion, see Lipinski and Buchanan (2002).
[2]   Few significant differences were found among these distinctions.

REFERENCES

Computer Ethics Institute. (1992). Ten commandments of computer ethics. Available on the WWW: http://www.brook.edu/dybdocroot/its/cei/overview/Ten_Commandments_of_Computer_Ethics.htm.

Lipinski, T. and Buchanan, E. (2002). There's a place for us(e). Incorporating the responsible application of new technologies into the K-12 curriculum: Results of a study assessing the level of knowledge, preparation and dissemination among educators. Paper presented at ETHICOM, 2002. Lisbon, Portugal.

Slind-Flor, V. (2000), Students flunk IP rights 101, The National Law Journal, March 13, 2000, at B6.

WMASITL (1998), Wisconsin Department of Public Instruction, Wisconsin's model academic standards for information and technology literacy.

Management Theory Based Critical Success Factors in Enterprise Resource Planning Systems Implementation

Joseph Bradley
Central Washington University-College of Business
Ellensburg, Washington
T: (509) 963-3520, F: (509) 963-2875
bradlejo@cwu.edu

ABSTRACT

This study proposes to identify critical success factors in Enterprise Resource Planning Systems implementation. ERP systems promise to provide an off-the-shelf solution to the information needs of organizations. Despite this promise, implementation projects are plagued with much publicized failures and abandoned projects. These software products require most organizations to change existing business processes to adopt the standardized process provided by the ERP systems. As economic resources and management time are scarce in most organizations, the results of this study should aid management in controlling those factors that are most important to project success.

The current study utilizes a framework developed by Sneller (1986) in the study of critical success factors in MRP implementation. Various proposed CSFs will be subjected to a factor study to identify variables relevant to ERP outcomes.

INTRODUCTION

ERP systems promise to meet the information needs of organizations with an off-the-shelf solution for replacing legacy information systems. Worldwide annual expenditures on ERP systems in the late 1990s are estimated at $10 billion for software and another $10 billion for consultants to install the software. (Davenport, 1998) A survey conducted by AMR Research confirmed that ERP will remain the biggest segment of large and mid-sized company IT applications budgets through 2004 (Seewald, 2002). Despite these huge expenditures by firms adopting ERP, implementation projects are plagued with much publicized failures, abandoned projects, and general dissatisfaction. Upon completion, this research will determine the management-based critical success factors leading to successful implementation of ERP systems.

This study examines the critical success factors (CSFs) (Bullen & Rockart, 1981; Drucker, 1973) for implementing enterprise resource planning systems in the framework of classical management theory. An earlier study (Sneller, 1986), identified management based critical success factors in the implementation of materials requirements planning systems (MRP). Since Sneller's study, software vendors enhanced the functionality of MRP systems, first by developing manufacturing resource planning systems (MRP II) and subsequently by developing enterprise resource planning systems (ERP). As a result of expanded functionality, implementation of such systems affects a wider portion of the business enterprise than the operations and logistics functions affected by MRP.

Prior studies of CSFs in ERP implementations are largely based on anecdotal practitioner observations or case studies of a few implementations. A recent summary of ERP literature states that while ERP implementation difficulties and failures are widely cited, "research of critical success factors (CSFs) in ERP implementation is rare and fragmented" (Nah, Lau, & Kuang, 2001). More rigorous academic studies were directed to CIOs. The present study partially replicates and expands Sneller's work to determine the critical success factors for ERP systems. Sneller surveyed material managers, as MRP dealt with their functional areas. This study surveys functional managers to reflect the wider organizational impact of ERP functionality. Questionnaires will be directed to CEOs, CFOs, COOs, CIOs and other functional managers.

RESEARCH PROBLEM

This research seeks to discover the critical success factors for ERP. The study will follow Sneller's (1986) methodology for determining CSFs in MRP implementation and determine whether his methodology works on larger, more complex implementation projects. Sneller's study combined the identification of proposed CSFs from a literature review with a factor study to determine variables relevant to ERP implementation outcomes.

LITERATURE

ERP and IS literature were reviewed using the lens of the five functions of management theory. Possible critical success factors were identified in the areas of planning, organizing, staffing, leading, and controlling.

Planning. The integration of business planning and IS planning is one of the top problems reported by executives and IS systems managers (Reich & Benbasat, 1996). An A.T. Kearney study demonstrates that firms that integrate business plans with IS plans outperform other firms (Das, Zahra, & Warkentin, 1991). This literature suggests that the higher the level of integration of ERP planning with business planning the more likely the implementation will be successful.

H1. The level of integration of ERP planning and business planning is related to implementation project success.

Organizing. Organizations must deploy resources to attain goals. A common view is that a user must head up the project team and that it must be a full time job (Wight, 1974). Another view is that systems knowledge is the least important skill of a PM (Flosi, 1980).

H2. Organizing the ERP implementation project under the direction of a project manager whose sole responsibilities are the project is related to implementation project success.

H3. An organizational structure in which the project manager reports to the business unit's senior manager is related to implementation project success.

Staffing. Recruitment, selection, placement, appraisal, and development of appropriate employees affect the firm's ability to perform any tasks including the implementation of ERP systems. The perception of the importance of the consultant is demonstrated by expenditures of $10 billion per year (Davenport, 1998). One practitioner states "the success of the project depends strongly on the capabilities of the consultants..." (Welti, 1999). Yet, Sneller (1986) found no significant relationship between the use of consultants and MRP project success.

H4. Staffing the ERP project manager position with an individual with extensive business experience is related to implementation project success.

H5. Use of an ERP consultant for guidance in the implementation project is related to implementation project success.

H6. The quantity and quality of training are related to implementation project success.

Leading. Executive support is generally been regarded as critical to the implementation of management information systems. Senior management's role in ERP implementation is described as communicating direction, allocating resources, delaying conflicting projects and dealing with organizational resistance (Laughlin, 1999). Executive support consists of both participation and involvement (Jarvenpaa & Ives, 1991). Champions can be critical to new systems by using their abilities to bring about organizational change (Beath, 1991).

H7. CEO involvement in planning and implementing the ERP system is related to implementation project success.

H8. The existence of a champion is related to ERP implementation project success.

H9. Management's effectiveness in reducing user resistance to change is related to implementation project success.

Controlling. Steering committees are a common method of control in IS projects, although the "membership, chairmanship, reporting level, procedure and frequency of meeting" may vary significantly (Gupta & Raghunathan, 1989).

H10. The use of a steering committee that: (a) is headed by the CEO and (b) meets at least every four weeks is related to implementation project success.

Success Measurement. Peter Keen identified the measurement of success as one of the key issues that needed to be resolved to establish coherent research in IS. Subsequently, researchers reviewed 180 articles published between 1981 and 1987 and developed a six dimensional model of IS success-systems quality, information quality, use, user satisfaction, individual impact and organizational impact (DeLone & McLean, 1992). This success model will be used in this research.

METHODOLOGY

This research will use both a questionnaire and case studies. A questionnaire was designed which measures project success and the use of the proposed CSFs in the implementation project. This questionnaire will be sent to functional managers at approximately 1,500 manufacturing companies selected from the Harris Manufacturing database or similar sources. Companies with over $100 million in sales volume will be selected as they are more likely to have implemented ERP than smaller firms.

Respondents will complete thirteen questions to determine the success of the project. Questions have been developed using the DeLone and McLean model assessing systems quality, information quality, use, user satisfaction, individual impact and organizational impact (DeLone & McLean, 1992). The remaining questions concern the project management practices used to operationalize the hypotheses defined above. The respondent's reported success measurements will be used to classify implementation projects at respondent's firm into one of two groups, successful or unsuccessful. Both a continuous composite success variable and nominal success/failure variable will be developed and used in the statistical treatment described below.

Implementation practices used by these firms and based on management theory in the area of planning, organizing, staffing, leading and controlling will be related to project success using regression analysis. Data for testing each hypothesis will be evaluated using the following statistical techniques. First, responses from successful and unsuccessful implementation projects will be compared using the t-test for significance. Next, the data will be subjected to a multivariate regression analysis using a composite success variable as the dependent variable. Finally, a multivariate discriminant analysis will be used to identify the ability of the independent variable to predict membership in the successful or unsuccessful group.

In the management area of planning, survey questions will concentrate on the integration level of ERP planning and business planning. In organizing, the use of a project manager (PM), the time the PM allocates to the project and importance of the project compared with other business objectives will be examined. The organizing area further considers the reporting level of the PM and use of a matrix organization. In staffing, the study examines the business experience and project management experience of the PM as well as how the PM was motivated and rewarded. Staffing investigates the use of consultants and the amount, quality, and timing of training provided in connection with the project. Leading considers the role of the CEO in the project, the effect of a champion, and management's effectiveness in reducing user resistance. Finally, Control examines the use of a steering committee or other means of controlling the implementation project.

The case study part of this research involves interviews with functional managers of two or more firms who implemented ERP systems. These case studies are expected to provide richer and deeper information to supplement the questionnaire findings.

CONCLUSIONS

Upon completion of the survey and case studies, management of firms implementing ERP systems should have a better understanding of the underlying factors leading to successful ERP implementation projects. The earlier Sneller (1986) study concluded that unsuccessful projects failed to follow good management practices. In the seventeen years since Sneller completed his dissertation, the IT community gained experience in implementing complex systems such as ERP. The results of this study should indicate whether organizational learning was offset by the increasing complexity of systems implementation projects.

REFERENCES

Beath, C. M. (1991). Supporting the Information Technology Champion. *MIS Quarterly* (September 1991), 355-372.

Bullen, C. V., & Rockart, J. F. (1981). Appendix: A Primer on Critical Success Factors, *The Rise of Managerial Computing*.

Das, S. R., Zahra, S. A., & Warkentin, M. E. (1991). Integrating the content and process of strategic MIS planning with competitive strategy. *Decision Sciences, 22*, 953-984.

Davenport, T. H. (1998). Putting the Enterprise into the Enterprise System. *Harvard Business Review, 76*(4, July-August), 121-131.

DeLone, W. H., & McLean, E. R. (1992). Information Systems Success: The Quest for the Dependent Variable. *Information Systems Research, 3*(1), 60-95.

Drucker, P. F. (1973). *Management: Tasks, Responsibilities, Practices*. (Harper Colophon 1985 ed.). New York: Harper & Row.

Flosi, T. (1980). *How to Manage an MRP Installation*. Paper presented at the Management Seminar.

Gupta, Y. P., & Raghunathan, T. S. (1989). Impact of Information Systems (IS) Steering Committees on IS Planning. *Decision Sciences, 20*(4), 777-793.

Jarvenpaa, S. L., & Ives, B. (1991). Executive Involvement and Participation in the Management of Information Technology. *MIS Quarterly, 15*(2), 205-227.

Laughlin, S. P. (1999). An ERP game plan. *Journal of Business Strategy, 20*(1), 32-37.

Nah, F. F.-H., Lau, J. L.-S., & Kuang, J. (2001). Critical factors for successful implementation of enterprise systems. *Business Process Management, 7*(3), 285-296.

Reich, B. H., & Benbasat, I. (1996). Measuring the Linkage Between Business and Information Technology Objectives. *MIS Quarterly (March 1996)*, 55-81.

Seewald, N. (2002, September 11). Enterprise Resource Planning Tops Manufacturers' IT Budgets. *Chemical Week*, 34.

Sneller, M. L. (1986). *Application of Classical Management Approach to the Implementation of Material Requirements Planning Systems*. Unpublished Ph.D. Dissertation, Claremont Graduate School, Claremont. CA.

Welti, N. (1999). *Successful SAP R/3 Implementation: Practical Management of ERP Projects*. Harlow, England: Addison-Wesley.

Wight, O. (1974). *Production and Inventory Management is the Computer Age*. Boston, MA: CBI Publishing Co.

Towards a Framework for Distributed Collaboration: A Study of Technology Impact on Isolation in Distributed Extreme Programming.

Dedric Carter
Nova Southeastern University
P.O. Box 2489 Fairfax, Virginia
T: +1 703.267.8710, F: +1 703.267.2222, dedric@nova.edu

INTRODUCTION

Over the last decade, the notion of contained systems has decreased significantly with the globalization of networks, systems and businesses of varying forms. With the increased scope of traditional networks comes a wealth of new opportunities for utilizing a more virtual presence in teamwork in order to facilitate distributed collaboration (DeMarc, Hendrickson, & Townsend, 1998).

For purposes of this research, the terms distributed collaboration and virtual teams will be used interchangeable to represent the aggregation of personnel in an organization for the accomplishment of a specific and designated task of prescribed and measurable duration at a distance. A systems approach is applied to a case study of distributed extreme programming teams

This research focuses primarily on gaining an understanding of the issues faced in building a distributed software product development organization (virtual software development team).

METHODOLOGY

Firm X is a 30 year old publicly traded professional services firm. Over the course of the last year, the firm has experienced a significant amount of turbulence. The organization is introducing further perturbations by developing horizontal service offerings that cut across existing virtual business groups. One of these groups will continue to develop the firm's flagship credit and risk collections products. The group will represent the deconstruction of at least three existing businesses spread across a number of states and two countries.

In addressing distributed collaboration environments in this firm and working towards a framework for understanding the issues and opportunities that such an exercise presents, the researcher will use an interpretive, nomothetic, case study approach which applies systems level framework analysis with no *a priori* hypotheses. The researcher is working to develop an initial framework on which to evaluate the efforts of the virtual team built upon the team dispersion work of Cummings and O'Leary (2002). Using the notion of isolation, the research will examine the impact of spatial dispersion in the virtual team on the use of special technologies for development. The unit of analysis is the entire virtual team at a professional services firm with the measurable outcome being a comparison of the connectedness of the individual groups initially (prior to the horizontal group formation) and post group formation as determined by a representative group sample survey. The framework will further build on a combination of the Levitt Rhombus model and Quershi (1995) systems level distinctions for evaluating activities in the virtual team.

Although many have focused on technology in the past, the people and process and association aspects of the complex distributed system are often more important that the implementation of technology (Hendrickson & Strader, 1998; Reinsch, 1997; Bui, Higa, Sivkumar, & Yen, 1996; Evaristo & Munkvold, 2002; Spinks & Wood, 1996; Sia, Tan, Teo, & Wei, 1998). This work will build on the Quershi (1995) case study model to examine Technology, People, Process, and Associations. It is assumed that the charter of a virtual team will have a clear statement of the task (mission) and timeline, therefore, these aspects of the analysis are considered attributed of the virtual teams and not necessarily areas of review in the research. The impact of the constraint of the attribute, however, may be a point of discussion in the conclusion of the case study.

The focusing element of the research builds on the emerging area of distributed extreme programming. A limited body of work in this young area has been developed over the last two years (Maurer, 2002; Cursaro, Jain, Kircher, & Levine, 2001)

INITIAL FRAMEWORK COMPONENTS

Technology. Technology involves a number of issues in the virtual team. Primarily these items are infrastructure and application dependent.

People. People aspects are sometimes the most difficult aspects to resolve. In several early pilots, the people issues have been overlooked. A key theme in the recent writings of James Champy has been on the omission of people in the haste to implement technologies.

Process. Process aspects are key to understanding the readiness and strategies of the organizations that contain virtual teams. It is important to remember that process is present in all facets of the organization. The purpose of examining process is to understand the intersections of actions and the virtual teams purpose.

Association. Association manages the interconnections between the virtual team an other entities. These other entities could be other virtual teams, traditional teams, or other organizations.

This work will be undertaken in a limited active researcher environment to better ensure the objectiveness of the research. A mediating third party will work to develop a pilot for technology implementation on the virtual team. The researcher serves as an expert advisor to the pilot formation and operation, while simultaneously using the pilot as a data collection vehicle for the research.

The principles of the interpretive case study will be modeled on the work of Klein and Meyers (1999), which calls for some definition in the interpretive case study even though a pure interpretive study would not employ any mechanisms such as surveys which are traditionally held as conventions of positivism.

LITERATURE

For the most part, work in this space has focused on collaboration and computer-mediation in the academic research organization. Nazer (2001) performed a psychological/sociological-focused thesis that examines the dynamics of a virtual organization and the ability to transfer those behaviors to traditional paradigms. Some research has focused on collaboration and discussion in distributed environments (Burnishe, 2001; Scott, 2002). Other work has been centered on specific technical implementations that facilitate collaboration (Dorochenceanu, Marsic, & Wang, 1999; Greenberg & Roseman, 1996;

Gupta, Grudin, & Jancke, 1999). Additional technical work has been completed in the formulation of generalized technical frameworks (Beca, 2002; Begole, Rosson, & Shaffer, 1998; Brave, Dahley, Ishii, 1998; Lauwers, 1990). Although some have done work in the organizational structures that support distributed collaboration (Ang & Slaughter, 1995, Bailyn, 1989; Nazer, 2001, Schmidt, 2000) and the overall impact of these programs (Burnishe, 2001; Henrickson & Strader, 1998; Scott, 2002, Spinks & Wood, 1996), very little work has been done in holistic frameworks which take into account technical and functional requirements for a robust evaluative distributed collaboration environment classification taxonomy.

STAGE OF RESEARCH

This dissertation work is in the very early stages of the idea paper. Work refining the topic is currently underway in conjunction with initial coursework in information systems at Nova Southeastern University, where the author is in the second semester of coursework in the Graduate School of Computer and Information Sciences.

EXPECTED BENEFITS FROM SYMPOSIUM PARTICIPATION

The researcher seeks feedback on methods for strengthening the outcomes of the research while preserving the objective and non-assumptive nature of the research process. Most researchers have conducted laboratory-like studies of distributed collaboration with hard distinctions between distributed and non-distributed teams using surveys as the major vehicle. In this research, an amalgam of a number of data collection mechanisms will be employed, including surveys, however, the survey is not the primary and vehicle for data collection. Given this diversion from the traditional path, it is important to understand as early as possible in the research any mitigating circumstances that may reposition the survey as a more primary vehicle and thus force the research to take on a more positivist role. Particular feedback on interpretive case studies in IS is sought.

REFERENCES

Ang, S., & Slaughter, S. (1995). Alternative employment structures in information systems: A conceptual analysis. *Proceedings of the 1995 ACM SIGCPR Conference on Supporting Teams, Groups, and Learning Inside and Outside the IS function Reinventing IS, 181*-193.

Bailyn, L. (1989). Towards the perfect workplace? *Communications of the ACM, 32*(4), 460-471.

Beca, L. M. (2002). A methodology and platform for building collaborative environments on the Web. *PhD Dissertation*. DAI - B 63/03.

Begole, J. B., Rosson, M. B., & Shaffer, C. A. (1998). Supporting worker independence in collaboration transparency. *Proceedings of the 1998 ACM Symposium on User Interface Software and Technology (UIST '98)*, 133-142.

Brave, S., Dahley, A., & Ishii, H. (1998, November). *Tangible interfaces for remote collaboration and communication*. Paper presented at CSCW '98. Retrieved October 2, 2002, from http://tangible.media.mit.edu/papers/inTouch_PSyBench_CSCW98/inTouch_PSyBench_CSCW98.pdf

Bui, T. X., Higa, K., Sivakumar, V., & Yen, J. (1996). Comparison of telework in the US and Japan: A cultural contingency model. *Proceedings of the 1996 Conference on ACM SIGCPR/SIGMIS Conference*, 351-359.

Burnishe, R. W., Jr. (2001). Fostering exploratory discourse in global, telecollaborative learning projects. *PhD Dissertation*. DAI-A 62/03.

Computer Science and Telecommunications Board, & National Research Council. (2002). *Broadband: Bringing Home the Bits*. Washington, DC: National Academy Press.

Corsaro, A., Jain, P., Kircher, M., & Levine, D. (2001). Distributed eXtreme Programming. *Proceedings of XP-2001*, 66-71.

Cummings, J. N., & O'Leary, M. B. (2002, January). *The Spatial, Temporal, and Configurational Characteristics of Geographic Dispersion in Work Teams* (Paper 148) [Center for eBusiness at MIT Technical Report]. Cambridge, MA: Massachusetts Institute of Technology.

DeMarie, S. M., Hendrickson, A. R., & Townsend, A. M. (1998). Virtual teams: Technology and workplace of the future. *Academy of Management Executive, 12*(3), 17-29.

Dorohenceanu, B., Marsic, I., & Wang, W. (1999, October). *Design of the DISCIPLE synchronous collaboration framework*. Paper presented at IASTED International Conference on Internet and Multimedia Systems and Applications. Retrieved October 3, 2002, from http://www.caip.rutgers.edu/disciple/Publications/iasted-99.pdf.

Fitzpatrick, G., & Kaplan, S. (1997). *Designing Support for Remote Intensive-Care Telehealth using Locales Framework*. Retrieved October 1, 2002, from http://www.dstc.edu.au/Research/Projects/EWP/Papers/DIS97-kaplan.pdf.

Greenberg, S., & Roseman, M. (1996). TeamRooms: Network places for collaboration. *Proceedings of ACM 1996 Conference on Computer-Supported Cooperative Work (CSCW '96)*, 325-333.

Gupta, A., Grudin, J., & Jancke, G. (1999, September 13). *Presenting to Local and Remote Audiences: Design and Use of the TELEP System*. Retrieved October 2, 2002, from http://www.research.microsoft.com/research/coet//TELEP/TRs/99-71.pdf.

Hendrickson, A., & Strader, T. (1998). From silicon valley to silicon prairie: A long distance telecommuting case study. *ACM SIGPCR Computer Personnel, 19*(3), 20-33.

International Telecommunications Union[ITU]. (2002, March). *World Telecommunication Development Report*. Retrieved September 27, 2002, from http://www.itu.int/ITU-D/ict/publications/wtdr_02/material/WTDR02-Sum_E.pdf.

Klein, H. K., & Myers, M. D. (1999). A set of principles for conducting and evaluating interpretive field studies in information systems. *MIS Quarterly, 23*(1), 67-94.

Lauwers, C. (1990). Collaboration transparency in desktop teleconferencing environments. *PhD Dissertation*. Technical Report CSL-TR-90-435, Computer Systems Laboratory, Stanford University.

Maurer, F. (2002). Supporting Distributed Extreme Programming. In *Lecture Notes in Computer Science: Vol. 2002. XP/Agile Universe 2002* (2418th ed., pp. 13-22) Berlin: Springer-Verlag.

Munkvold, B. E., & Evaristo, J. R. (2002). Collaborative infrastructure formation in virtual projects. *Journal of Global Information Technology Management, 5*(2).

Nazer, N. (2001). Operating virtually within a hierarchical framework: How a virtual organization really works. *PhD Dissertation*. DAI-A62/04.

Qureshi, S. S. (1995). Organisations and networks: Theoretical considerations and a case study of networking across organisations (Unpublished PhD Dissertation). *London School of Economics*. London School of Economics Department of Information Systems, http://is.lse.ac.uk/Research/rescomp2.htm#QURESHI.

Reinsch, N. L., Jr. (1997). Relationships between telecommuting workers and their managers: An exploratory study. *Journal of Business Communication, 34*(4), 343-369.

Schmidt, B. L. (2000). You can go home again: Successful telecommuting for the technical communicator. *Proceedings of IEEE Professional Communication Society International Professional Communication Conference and ACM Special Interest Group on Documentation Conference on Technology and Teamwork*, 25-37.

Scott, D. M. (2002). Group collaboration in web-based distance education: The effect of computer-mediated communication and personality traits on student productivity, participation, and technology preference. *PhD Dissertation*. DAI-A62/09.

Sia, C.-L., Tan, B. C., Teo, H.-H., & Wei, K.-K. (1998). Examining environmental influences on organizational perceptions and predisposition toward distributed work arrangements: A path model. *Proceedings of the International Conference on Information Systems*, 88-102.

Spinks, W., & Wood, J. (1996). Office-based telecommuting: An international comparison of satellite offices in Japan and North America. *Proceedings of the 1996 Conference on ACM SIGCPR/SIGMIS Conference*, 338-350.

U.S. Federal Communications Commission. (2000, August). *Deployment of Advanced Telecommunications Capability: Second Report* (FCC 00-290, p. 3). Washington, DC.

A Comparison of CRM Implementation Across Internet and Wireless Channels

Susy S. Chan
DePaul University, Chicago
T: (312) 362-8723, F: (312) 362-6116, schan@cs.depaul.edu

Jean Lam
IBM
jeanlam@us.ibm.com

INTRODUCTION

This research-in-progress paper outlines our current research in comparing the deployment of customer relationship management (CRM) features on the wired and mobile Internet. Our study examines the current practice of 15 selected e-commerce sites. From this research, we expect to identify strategies and research questions regarding cross-channel coordination of CRM services, content mapping, and interface design.

PRIOR RESEARCH

CRM involves the deployment of strategies, process, and technologies for strengthening a firm's relationship with customers throughout their lifecycle — from marketing, sales, to post-sale services. The goal of CRM is to optimize a firm's revenue, profitability, and customer satisfaction. Internet technology has transformed CRM into electronic CRM (eCRM) because it can be used to capture new customers, track their preferences and online behaviors, and customize support and services. Furthermore, the convergence of wireless communication and mobile Internet forms a new, mobile channel for CRM (mCRM).

Many researchers believe that the wireless channel offers the potential to strengthen relationships with customers. Four factors make the mobile Internet an ideal channel to implement customer relationship management (CRM) for its ability to: (1) personalize content and services, (2) track consumers or users across media and over time, (3) provide content and service at the point of need, and (4) provide content of highly engaging characteristics (Kannan et al., 2001). Services that deliver strong mobile values make the wireless channel particularly important (Anckar & D'Incau, 2002). The challenge is the coordination of user interfaces and contents across multiple channels so the experienced users and repeat customers can handle multiple media and platforms with satisfaction.

However, at present, business and consumers are still hesitant in adopting the wireless channel because of many technology and usability barriers (Ernst & Young, 2001; Chan & Fang, 2001, 2003; Zhu, Nah, & Zhao, 2002). Consumer adoption of m-commerce has been slow, even in countries that have broadly adopted wireless technology (Anckar & D'Incau, 2002). Poor usability of mobile Internet sites and wireless applications for commerce activities stands out as a major obstacle for the slow adoption of mobile solutions (Chan, Fang, Brzezinski, Zhou, Xu, & Lam, 2002) or choosing m-commerce as a distribution channel (Shim, Bekkering, & Hall, 2002).

A recent study has found that most mobile sites were designed primarily to support existing users (Chan et al., 2002). Prospective customers may be discouraged from exploring a new mobile site by the inherent difficulty in the current wireless technology, such as limited bandwidth and poor connectivity, and in the wireless handheld devices, such as small screen display and difficult input formats. The study by Anckar and D'Incaur (2002) indicates that e-commerce users are more likely to adopt m-commerce services. Furthermore, consumers are most interested in services with high mobile values that meet spontaneous and time critical needs.

The technology's capability for personalization seems to be the strongest argument for establishing a wireless channel. Mobile CRM is likely to be one of the first areas to embrace wireless solutions. A careful mapping of tasks, data, form factors, and the CRM process will become essential for user inter-face design. Location technology and personalization of services and content are critical for content presentation, navigation, and search. Differences between novice and experienced users will also be important, as well as approaches for development and usability testing.

OBJECTIVES

Our proposed study intends to: (1) articulate a framework for evaluating CRM deployment over the Internet and the mobile channels, (2) compare the deployment of eCRM and mCRM in terms of CRM components (marketing, sales, and service), (3) determine the relationship between eCRM and mCRM, and (4) propose new ways wireless technology can be used for mCRM.

RESEARCH METHODS

We will perform site walkthrough of 15 sites on the Web and on the mobile platforms, using two wireless devices — Palm-OS PDAs (Personal Digital Assistants) and WAP (Wireless Application Protocol) phones. These two platforms are the most popular in the North America market. The 15 sites will include travel, financial services, news, shopping, and portal sites. A checklist will be developed for the content analysis. Questions on the checklist will address strategies for marketing (personalization, push email), sales (search, order, and payment), and post-sale support (tracking shipment, customer service, and account management).

RESEARCH QUESTIONS

Building on our initial observation and prior research, this study seeks answers to the following questions

- How do companies implement components of CRM over the Internet channel?
- To what extent are CRM components implemented in the mobile channel?
- To what extent is consistency in content, functionality, and interface retained over the two channels?
- Do companies use eCRM and mCRM in a complementary or a redundant manner?
- How are CRM components implemented for different wireless handheld devices?
- What roles mobile portals and wireless service providers play in supporting mCRM strategies?
- How should CRM be deployed in the Internet and the wireless environments in order to optimize customer acquisition and retention?
- What unique features of wireless/mobile technology can be explored to enhance mCRM?

SIGNIFICANCE

This research would provide empirical evidence for understanding how eCRM is extended to the wireless channel and how companies can optimize CRM through leveraging the unique characteristics of Internet and wireless technologies. At this early stage of mobile commerce development, this study will make significant contribution to the understanding of mobile commerce technology and strategies.

REFERENCE

Anckar, B. & D'Incau, D. (2002). Value creation in mobile commerce: Findings from a consumer survey. *Journal of Information Technology Theory & Application*, 4(1), 43-64.

Chan, S. & Fang, X. (2003). Mobile Commerce and Usability. In K. Siau & E. Lim, Eds. *Advances in Mobile Commerce Technologies*. Hershey, PA: Idea Group Publishing (in press).

Chan, S., & Fang, X. (2001). Usability issues for mobile commerce. *Proceedings of the Seventh Americas Conference on Information Systems*, 439-442.

Chan, S., Fang, F., Brzezinski, J., Zhou, Y., Xu, S., & Lam, J. (2002). Usability for Mobile Commerce Across Multiple Form Factors. *Journal of Electronic Commerce Research (JECR)*.

Ernst & Young. (2001). *Global online retailing: an Ernst & Young special report*. Unpublished report. Cap Gemini Ernst and Young.

Kannan, P., Chang, A., & Whinston, A. (2001). Wireless commerce: Marketing issues and possibilities. *Proceedings of the 34th Hawaii International Conference on System Sciences*. Los Alamitos, CA: IEEE Comp Soc.

Shim, J. P., Bekkering, E., & Hall, L. (2002). Empirical findings on perceived value of mobile commerce as a distributed channel. *Proceedings of the Eighth Americas Conference on Information Systems*, 1835-1837.

Zhu, W., Nah, F., & Zhao, F. (2002). Factors influencing adoption of mobile computing. *Proceedings of the 2002 Information Resources Management Association Conference: Issues & Trends of Information Technology Management in Contemporary Organizations*, 536-539.

The Strategic Impact of Enterprise Systems: A Dynamic Capabilities Study

Ying-Hueih Chen
Eric Sprott School of Business, Carleton University, Canada
(613) 520-2600, Ext. 7490, yhchen@business.carleton.ca

RESEARCH BACKGROUND AND OBJECTIVE

The move to enterprise systems (ES) and its extended applications is a prominent issue in the field of information systems (IS) (Kumar and Van Hillegersberg, 2000; Markus and Tanis, 2000). Featuring a central database, open system architecture, and business reference models, ES is a process-based commercial system that aims to integrate transactional information and business processes in a distributed business environment. Its implementation has influenced business operations in two significant ways. First, the integrated central database and open system architecture comprise an application information technology (IT) infrastructure that affects scope, feasibility, and flexibility in long-term organizational information support and system deployment. Second, ES imposes standard business models regardless of the idiosyncratic practice of the firm. The increasing ubiquity of ES, then, indirectly homogenizes operational processes within an industry and opens new avenues for electronic inter-organizational interaction and cooperation (Davenport, 2000; Kumar and Van Hillegersberg, 2000).

The ES-imposed generic processes and the trend toward a single industrial IT application have caused great strategic concern to researchers and practitioners alike. Tom Davenport, one of the pioneers of ES and BPR research, speculates that homogeneous best practice in a single industry might lead to a lessening of the value of innovation in business process design (Davenport, 1998). Weill and Broadbent (2000) also question the strategic impact of standardized IS packages. While these questions imply that the pervasiveness of ES undermines any extraordinary advantage, empirical research has revealed various outcomes of ES adoption (Davenport, 2000; Kumar and Van Hillegersberg, 2000; Markus and Tanis, 2000; Bermudez, 2002). Yet despite increasing concerns about the business value associated with ES, systematic research on the strategic implications of ES is lacking. Most research on ES consists of anecdotal case studies that focus on system implementation processes and critical success factors, or deals with the multi-faceted impact of ES on business operation. Seldom, however, does the research examine the implications of ES transition.

The objective of this study is to address this research issue through formulating and validating a research construct to analyze ES-enabled organizational capabilities and their impact on firm performance. The position taken in this research is that ES does not provide a source of competitive advantage. The adoption of a single system within industry, however, does not mean that system outcomes will be homogeneous, as firms may not be equally capable of capturing the strategic benefits of ES. Based on this assumption, a key to understanding the strategic implications of ES is the identification and assessment of system-enabled capabilities.

LITERATURE REVIEW

The dynamic capabilities perspective, combining ideas from both resource-based theory and evolutionary theory, focuses on the source of competitive advantage in a rapidly changing environment (Teece, Pisano et al., 1997). Such an approach is particularly relevant to this research because it highlights the strategic implications of management processes and organizational structure through which firms develop and renew their competences.

The Conceptual Framework of Dynamic Capabilities

As ES-imposed best practice becomes an industrial standard, strategy is fast becoming a dynamic process of system utilization toward innovative competence deployment and exploitation (Eisenhardt and Martin, 2000). The strategic implication of this process can be understood from the perspective of dynamic capabilities—*the firm's ability to integrate, build, and reconfigure internal and external competences to address rapidly changing environments* (Teece et al., 1997, p. 516). This capability is dynamic because it constantly modifies the leverage of competence to achieve congruence with the harsh competitive environment.

The dynamic capabilities study supplements resource-based analysis in two ways. First, rather than focusing on the issues of resource appropriateness and sustainability, dynamic capability highlights the value of resource portfolio configuration and integration (Kogut and Kulatilaka, 2001; Makadok, 2001). In essence, dynamic capabilities posits that the perpetually changing environment will frequently alter the strategic value and the life span of core resources (Eisenhardt and Martin, 2000; Barney, 2001; Barney, Wright et al., 2001). Thus, the capability for plural competence deployment and exploitation of resources overshadows the characteristics of those resources (Lengnick-Hall and Wolff, 1999).

Second, the characteristics of dynamic capabilities are idiosyncratic in detail yet common in key features (e.g., best practice), a notion that departs markedly from the usual view of RBV regarding the idiosyncratic features of strategic resources and capabilities (Eisenhardt and Martin, 2000). Compared with RBV researchers, advocates of this theory hold a relatively conservative view as to the value of organizational best practice. However, the observation of organizational routines as dynamic capabilities offers an operational foundation for empirical study.

The dynamic capabilities perspective contributes to IT research in two distinct ways. First, it repositions IT capabilities as competitive necessities. Rather than being the source of competitive advantage, IT capabilities are stepping-stones to advanced competence creation and leverage. Second, the concept of dynamic capabilities provides an overarching framework within which the implications of IT-enabled flexible competence leverage, organizational learning, and business transformation can be recognized and analyzed (Porter and Millar, 1985; Clemons and Row, 1991; Venkatraman, 1994; Lee and Lee, 2000; Zello and Winter, 2002).

ES and Dynamic Capabilities

With respect to competitive advantage, the roles of ES as IT infrastructure, knowledge management mechanism, and BPR catalyst have been discussed favorably in the literature (Davenport, 2000; Lee and Lee, 2000; Markus and Tanis, 2000; Weill and Broadbent, 2000). The dynamic capabilities perspective provides unique insights into the strategic influence of these ES roles.

IT Infrastructure

As part of an IT infrastructure, ES is an organizational backbone and operational mechanism providing an integrated communication platform for functional applications. Its capabilities are often measured in terms of system-enabled reach and range (Keen, 1991). Modularity, compatibility, integrity,

Figure 1. Dynamic ES capabilities and business value

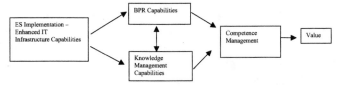

and IT personnel skills are assessment indicators of the flexibility of the IT infrastructure (Byrd and Turner, 2001). These capabilities are essential because they determine the firm's ability to add, modify, and remove application systems; the effectiveness of information sharing and control; and the functional competence of ES deployment and exploitation to support business strategies (Broadbent and Weill, 1997; Willcocks and Sykes, 2000; Byrd and Turner, 2001). IT flexibility, then, influences organizational performance in terms of market responsiveness and innovative action.

Business Process Reengineering

As a viable instrument of business processes reengineering, ES is positioned as processware (Davenport, 2000). Business process reengineering is a socially complex procedure that involves radical change in organizational culture, structure, and business processes (Hammer and Champy, 1993). While the concept of process is not new, ES is the major driving force bringing the concept into institutional practice (Davenport, 2000). Researchers have identified several key aspects of the impact of IT on process management: IT leadership, process integration and disintegration throughout value systems, information bundling and unbundling, culture fit, management competence, and strategic thinking (Feeny and Willcocks, 1998; Davenport, 2000; Scheer and Habermann, 2000; Soh, Kien et al., 2000; Willcocks and Sykes, 2000).

Knowledge Management

The proposition that organizational routines and processes represent firm-specific skills and capabilities has made knowledge management a focal point of concern in dynamic capabilities research (Pisano, 1994; Grant,1996). The ES-embedded business model provides a formal vehicle for knowledge retention and distribution (Zello and Winter, 2002). Lee et al. (2000) investigated the processes of ES implementation and suggested that the ES-embedded reference model offers a viable learning mechanism for communicating tacit business process knowledge across functional areas. While the reference model provides codified tacit knowledge to adopting firms, the level of knowledge internalization and its further application to process innovation may be subject to the firm's absorptive ability, comprehensive understanding of internal resource characteristics, and commitment to the application of knowledge to resource reconfiguration (Cohen and Levinthal, 1990; McGrath, MacMillan et al., 1995).

Summary

The literature addressing IT infrastructure, BPR, and knowledge management sheds considerable light on ES capabilities analysis. Synthesizing the foregoing discussion, we propose the research construct shown in Figure 1.

RESEARCH METHODOLOGY

This research will combine both case study and survey methods for theory building and empirical validation. Traditionally, IS research is dominated by a single methodology paradigm and rarely explores the analytical benefits of a multi-method application. Yet despite the limited application, the value of utilizing a multi-method approach in a single research design is recognized (Lee, 1991; Gable, 1994; Henderson and Cockburn, 1994). The qualitative and quantitative methods, while drawing on different sources of evidence and ideas, serve a complementary purpose at different phases of IS research.

Secondary Cross-Case Analysis for Issue Identification

The qualitative research method, or case study, is a context-rich and empirically valid approach in IT research. This method collects descriptive phenomenological data from on-site observation, internal document assessment, and in-depth personal interviews. By means of extensive access to organizational information, the case study seeks to describe and explore the con-

text of the research object. Orlikowski (1993) suggests that such an interpretive and explorative approach provides an effective instrument for theory building and testing (Orlikowski, 1993). Gable (1994) also highlights the contribution made by observational information to the identification of problems and issues.

There are two ways of collecting qualitative data. One is the pilot case study based on a carefully designed research protocol. This method delivers specific information for a purposeful investigation. The other is the published case study that is ready for advanced hermeneutical interpretation. Such public data usually contains rich contextual information and can serve a broad range of research purposes. As an alternative lens enabling a different focus on the research question, secondary data offers a viable avenue to the discovery of business issues, patterns, and ongoing research trends. This rich source of data also simplifies the demand for cross-referencing of issues and problem verification.

Given the abundance of ES case reports, it is believed that the copious amount of empirical information will provide a rich source of insight for proposed ES capabilities analysis and testing. Although the validity of such an approach is questionable in terms of the research theme, it is reasonable to propose that a hermeneutic approach to secondary case analysis is not only valid but also provides insight equivalent in value to that derived from primary investigation (Lee, 1991; Lee, 1994). Furthermore, by cross-referencing multiple case studies, the concern over methodological legitimacy is resolved. Building on this vein of thought, the first stage of this research plan is to enhance the content of proposed ES capabilities on the basis of 15 published case studies focusing on ES implementation and utilization. Descriptive data has been collected from the *Journal of Information Technology, Harvard Business Cases,* and *CIO Magazine.* The outcome of this research stage will be an empirically verified measurement construct and a research questionnaire derived from assessments of case analyses.

Survey Methods for Hypotheses Testing

The survey method refers to quantitative analysis where the research data is collected by mail questionnaires, telephone interviews, or published statistics. Essentially, this method provides a snapshot of the research context and yields statistically descriptive information for research models. As well it offers a scientific technique for testing the reliability and validity of the research model and variables.

According to Gable (1994), the quantitative method supplements the qualitative approach by improving the generalizability of the research model. Therefore, the second stage of this research will test the proposed research model using a questionnaire survey. More specifically, the second phase of the research targets 1000 ES adopters recognized as major players in the business community to serve as research informants. In this way, this research will be able to capture the business consequences of ES adoption that are unavailable for qualitative assessment.

DISCUSSION AND FEEDBACK SOUGHT

This research is still in the preliminary stage. Building on dynamic capabilities, this study expects to provide theoretically rigorous and practically relevant guidelines for effective ES deployment and exploitation. The research outcome is expected to reveal the link between ES adoption and business value through identifying the ES-enabled dynamic capabilities. For the research purpose of enhancing operationalization of the RBV paradigm, the author seeks comments on the potential drawbacks of the multi-method approach in research design. Furthermore, identification of missing pieces in the proposed research questions and construct, and suggestions for enhancement, are equally important to further development and refinement of the research.

REFERENCE

Barney, J. B. (2001). "Resource-Based Theories of Competitive Advantage: A Ten-year Retrospective on the Resource-Based View." *Journal of Management* 27: 643-650.

Barney, J. B., M. Wright, et al. (2001). "The Resource-Based View of the Firm: Ten Years after 1991." *Journal of Management* 27: 625-641.

Bermudez, J. (2002). Enterprise Applications: Are They the Solution or Part of the Problem? AMR Research.

Broadbent, M. and P. Weill (1997). "Management by Maxim: How Business and IT Managers Can Create IT Infrastructure." *Sloan Management Review* Spring: 77-92.

Byrd, T. A. and D. E. Turner (2001). "An Exploratory Examination of the Relationship between Flexible IT Infrastructure and Competitive Advantage." *Information & Management* 39: 41-52.

Clemons, E. K. and M. C. Row (1991). "Sustaining IT Advantage: The Role of Structural Differences." *MIS Quarterly* September: 275-292.

Cohen, W. M. and D. A. Levinthal (1990). "Absorptive Capacity: A New Perspective on Learning and Innovation." *Administrative Science Quarterly* 35: 128-152.

Davenport, T. H. (2000). "The Future of Enterprise System-Enabled Organizations." *Information Systems Frontiers* 2(2): 163-180.

Davenport, T. H. (2000). *Mission Critical: Realizing the Promise of Enterprise Systems*. Harvard Business Press.

Eisenhardt, K. M. and J. A. Martin (2000). "Dynamic Capabilities: What are they?" *Strategic Management Journal* 21: 1105-1121.

Feeny, D. and L. P. Willcocks (1998). "Core IS Capabilities for Exploiting Information Technology." *Sloan Management Review* 39(3): 9-21.

Gable, G. G. (1994). "Integrating Case Study and Survey Research Methods: An Example in Information Systems." *European Journal of Information Systems* 3: 112-126.

Grant, R. M. (1996). "Prospering in Dynamically-competitive Environments: Organizational Capability as Knowledge Integration." *Organizational Science* 7(4): 375-387.

Hammer, M. and J. Champy (1993). *Reengineering the Corporation: A Manifesto for Business*. New York, Harper Business.

Henderson, R. and I. Cockburn (1994). "Measuring Competence? Exploring Firm Effects in Pharmaceutical Research." *Strategic Management Journal* 15: 63-84.

Keen, P. G. W. (1991). *Shaping the future: Business design through information technology*, Harvard Business School Press.

Kogut, B. and N. Kulatilaka (2001). "Capabilities as Real Options." *Organizational Science* 12(6): 744-758.

Kumar, K. and J. Van Hillegersberg (2000). "ERP Experiences and Evolution." *Communications of the ACM* 43(4): 23-26.

Lee, A. S. (1991). "Integrating Positivist and Interpretive Approaches to Organizational Research." *Organization Science* 2: 342-265.

Lee, A. S. (1994). "Electronic Mail as a Medium for Rich Communication: An Empirical Investigation Using Hermeneutic Interpretation." *MIS Quarterly* 18(2): 143-157.

Lee, Z. and J. Lee (2000). "An ERP Implementation Case Study From a Knowledge Transfer Perspective." *Journal of Information Technology* 15: 281-288.

Lengnick-Hall, C. A. and J. A. Wolff (1999). "Similarities and Contradictions in the Core Logic of Three Strategy Research Streams." *Strategic Management Journal* 20: 1109-1132.

Makadok, R. (2001). "Toward a Synthesis of the Resource-Based and Dynamic Capability Views of Rent Creation." *Strategic Management Journal* 22: 387-401.

Markus, M. L. and C. Tanis (2000). The enterprise system experience—from adoption to success. *Framing the Domains of IT Management: Projecting the Future through the Past*. R. Zmud. Cincinnati, Ohio, Pinnaflex: 173-207.

McGrath, R. G., I. C. MacMillan, et al. (1995). "Defining and Developing Competence: A Strategic Process Paradigm." *Strategic Management Journal* 16: 251-275.

Orlikowski, W. J. (1993). "Case Tools as Organizational Change: Investigating Incremental and Radical Changes in Systems Development." *MIS Quarterly* 17(3): 309-340.

Pisano, G. P. (1994). "Knowledge, Integration, and the Locus of Learning: An Empirical Analysis of Process Development." *Strategic Management Journal* 15: 85-100.

Porter, M. E. and V. E. Millar (1985). "How Information Gives You Competitive Advantage." *Harvard Business Review* July-August: 149-160.

Scheer, A.-W. and F. Habermann (2000). "Making ERP a Success." *Communications of the ACM* 43(4): 57-61.

Soh, C., S. S. Kien, et al. (2000). "Culture Fits and Misfits: Is ERP a Universal Solution?" *Communications of the ACM* 43(4): 47-51.

Teece, D. J., G. Pisano, et al. (1997). "Dynamic Capabilities and Strategic Management." *Strategic Management Journal* 18(7): 509-533.

Venkatraman, N. (1994). "IT-Enabled Business Transformation: From Automation to Business Scope Redefinition." *Sloan Management Review* Winter: 73-87.

Weill, P. and M. Broadbent (2000). Managing IT Infrastructure: A Strategic Choice. *Framing the Domains of IT Management: Projecting the Future through the Past*. R. Zmud. Cincinnati, Ohio, Pinnaflex: 329-353.

Willcocks, L. P. and R. Sykes (2000). "The Role of the CIO and IT Function in ERP." *Communications of the ACM* **43**(4): 32-38.

Zello, M. and S. G. Winter (2002). "Deliberate Learning and the Evolution of Dynamic Capabilities." *Organizational Science* 13(3): 339-351.

Evolving Learning Environments in Information Technology Education

Kuan C. Chen, Ph.D.
Department of Information Systems and Computer Programming
Purdue University Calumet, Hammond, IN 46323-2094
P: (219) 989-3195, F: (219) 989-3187, kchen@calumet.purdue.edu

ABSTRACT

The information technology instructional model involves not only the knowledge convey, but also the skills training. Information technology learning requires that students have opportunities to comprehend what they hear and read as well as express themselves in meaningful assignments or products. From the instructor standpoints, creating a learning environment for students becomes an import part of the course instruction. Evolving a learning environment for information technology classes adopting the cooperative learning approach is demonstrated in this paper.

Cooperative learning is the instructional use of small groups so that students work together to maximize their own and each other's learning. Cooperative learning helps build strengthened individual and team performance which in information technology class and helps produce more high quality graduates for tomorrow's information technology workforce.

In cooperative learning, the instructor acts as a facilitator, a tutor, a resource, but is not the source of the course's content—the students are, through their own research and analysis. The aim: fostering independence and critical thinking.

INTRODUCTION

Teaching information technology courses involves three main elements: logic training, theory instruction and hands-on practices. Thus, the information technology instructional model involves not only the knowledge convey, but also the skills training. Information technology learning requires that students have opportunities to comprehend what they hear and read as well as express themselves in meaningful assignments or products. Creating a learning environment for students becomes an import part of the course instruction. Generally speaking, in the traditional approach to information technology teaching, most class time is spent with the professor lecturing and the students watching and listening. The students work individually on assignments in the campus lab or at home, and cooperation is discouraged. However, lecturing is the most common, the easiest, and the least effective. Unless the instructor is a real spellbinder, most students cannot stay focused throughout a lecture: after about 10 minutes their attention begins to drift, and for longer intervals their minds are totally flying in the air and hard to catch up the contents.

Students' backgrounds and learning curves in information technology are very diverse. Some students can catch up the content in a one hour; some students may need one week to figure the contents. Creating a flexible and diverse learning environment in information technology instruction is the best way to assist students' study. Cooperative methods are very flexible and can be adapted for students with special needs. In diverse IT background settings, differences in students' computer skill proficiencies makes it necessary for teachers to modify the methods to ensure that information technology learners can participate fully with fellow team members. For example, teachers may ask one member of each team to be a project leader who helps students work together. In addition, activities that focus on skill development and teambuilding should be used frequently to facilitate problem solving and understanding among team members.

In this paper, creating a student learning environment—cooperative learning in information technology education is presented. Cooperative learning is a successful teaching strategy in which small teams, each with students of different levels of ability, use a variety of learning activities to improve their understanding of a subject. Each member of a team is responsible not only for learning what is taught but also for helping teammates learn, thus creating an atmosphere of achievement. Cooperative groups increase opportunities for students to produce and comprehend language and to obtain modeling and feedback from their peers. Much of the value of cooperative learning lies in the way that teamwork encourages students to engage in such high-level thinking skills as analyzing, explaining, synthesizing, and elaborating.

COOPERATIVE LEARNING

This paper will provide a general case discussion of a different information technology course using cooperative learning to evolving learning environments. The general case will be presented in four phases: pre-planning, planning, implementation and evaluation.

Pre-planning

The most important concept of the cooperative learning is the instructor plays a variety of roles—curriculum designer, tutor, resource, and evaluator. The difference between traditional lecture and cooperative learning is the instructor's task in cooperative learning is guiding without leading and assisting, without directing.

The role of students is also different from traditional lecture classroom setting. They must become team players with peers to grab the concept and learn the skills. They cannot afford to sit passively in the classroom and collect the information provided by the instructor (LaLopa, Jacobs and Countryman, 1999).

Planning

Team Building

When you assemble a team, you will bring together people who represent diverse experiences, skills, personalities and social backgrounds. Had you not brought these people together, they may not have naturally gravitated to one another to from friendships or social interaction. Yet now these people must work together to achieve a specific objective. Your job is to manage the interaction and unite these very different people to get the desired results.

The advantage is that the different experiences and skills provide you with tremendous opportunities to devise innovative solutions to the problem or task you face. The disadvantage is that the differences, if not managed properly can create endless stumbling blocks and make it difficult to achieve any results.

To this extend, the first stage is to form teams. Although there are many good models to form a team, the general rules of thumb are skill and knowledge diversity, and personality. Skill and knowledge diversity can be found from student background checking in the first day of class. Managing a diverse group, particularly one that contains individuals with strong or abrasive personalities, can be broken into three steps:

1. Identify basic psychology/emotional needs that are common to all team members.
2. Establish limits and ground rules that will help you manage future problems.
3. Minimize differences and maximize shared interests and needs to build cohesiveness among

In the first two weeks, students did not get into the main topics of the course. Instead, the first two weeks are spent building team and a team learning environment. Students learn how to build a team, build up team goal and how to work on the team activities as well as use the problem-solving tool and techniques. Instructor can take advantage of this stage to give students some pre-assessment to review the pre-knowledge they should have prior to take this course.

The Syllabus

The syllabus can follow the traditional syllabus structure. However, the team rule and the cooperative learning instructional model have to be included in the components. The team rule includes the team building approach, team goal, team activities implementation and grading method.   Students new to the team style may get frustrated by what they perceive as lack of structure, direction, and information. The cooperative learning instructional model section must clearly communicate goals and expectations to student. It must also provide the guidance and structure in order to have students learn process skills and how to effectively function in teams.

Implementation

Having taught at Purdue University, Davenport University and Lansing Community College, the author develops and implements the information technology cooperative learning methods to the following courses: Introduction to Computer Information Systems, Network Administration, E-commerce, Project Management as well as C++, Visual Basic and Web Programming. After the pre-planning and planning stage, the following procedure shows the implementation within the class.

1. Give students a short, well-formatted handout covering lecturing material, a case study or example, or a summarized text. Ask them to read silently. The study team works best when the material is moderately challenging or open to widespread interpretation.
2. Provide each group a team in-class assignment and ask them to work together. The main purpose of the team assignment is to help students to grab the concepts, systematically organize the key points and application disciplines. To this extent, the team in-class assignment should include the following five directions:
    a. Assess how well you understand the material.
    b. Clarify the contents.
    c. Crate examples, illustrations, or applications of the information or ideas.
    d. Identify points that are confusing or you disagree with.
    e. Argue with the text; develop an opposing point of view.
3. Reconvene the total class and do one or more of the following:
    a. Review the material together
    b. Quiz students
    c. Obtain questions
    d. Ask students to assess how well they understand and material
    e. Provide an application exercise for students to solve.

Evaluation

Grade will base on team performance and also adjusted for individual performance. Two peer performance assessments, three team exams, 10 in-class assignments as well as self-assessment journal have to be developed.

The peer performance assessments are administrated at the middle and end of the semester. It can be developed as the Likert scale or open-end questions. The important idea is that it has be able to quantified later on.

An in-class team assignment is a good tool for equipping students to deal with specific puzzling problems that may surface. For example, in the programming language course, syntax debug and logic design are always the bid headache to students. Thus put give the team assignment and give them a few minutes to brainstorm strategies which any idea to implement the language and logic design. List their ideas on the board, throwing in one or two of your own if you have any input, and put the students back in their groups to try and reach consensus on the best strategies for what to do. Also, in-class team assignment serves as the individual attendance and contribution to the team. Students miss class a total of five times, including the ones they had accrued to that point. Each additional absence beyond the fifth would result in the student having his or her grade dropped one full letter grade unless the absence was due to illness and accompanied by a doctor's excuse or a legitimate school function that was accompanied by official explaining the dated and purpose of the event. Attendance improved dramatically from that point forward.

Often group conflicts stem from different expectations team members have for one another. To get teams off to a good start, have them prepare the self-assessment journal. In a few weeks into the semester, have the teams revisit their lists and evaluate how well they are doing in meeting the expectations the set for themselves. A self-assessment journal is a good tool for equipping students to deal with specific interpersonal problems that may surface. For example, after the instructor has gotten a few complaints about the slackers, the instructor might ask each team member to submit the self-assessment journal and review it with the whole team. Then, it can easy toe expose the problem and also build up the communication within the team members.

REFERENCES

1. Deutsch, M. (1962). Cooperation and trust: Some theoretical notes. In M. R. Jones (Ed.), *Nebraska symposium on motivation*, 275-319. Lincoln, NE: University of Nebraska Press.
2. Felder, R. M. & Brent, R. (2001) Effective strategies for cooperative learning. Journal of Cooperation & Collaboration in College Teaching, 10(2), 69-75.
3. Johnson, D. W. (1993). *Reaching out: Interpersonal effectiveness and self-actualization* (6th ed.). Needham Heights, MA: Allyn & Bacon.
4. Johnson, D. W., & Johnson, R. T. (1989). *Cooperation and competition: Theory and research*. Edina, MN: Interaction Book Company.
5. Johnson, D. W., & Johnson, R. T. (1995). *Teaching students to be peacemakers* (3rd ed.). Edina, MN: Interaction Book Company.
6. Johnson, D. W., Johnson, R. T., & Holubec, E. J. (1993). *Cooperation in the Classroom* (6th ed.). Edina, MN: Interaction Book Company.
7. LaLopa, J. M., & Jacobs, J. W. (1998) Utilizing student teams to facilitate an introductory tourism course in higher education, *Journal of Hospitality and Tourism Education* 10(1), 26-31.

A SSM Driven Knowledge-Portal Design

Chan Cheah

School of Information Management and Systems, Monash University

Caulfield Campus, Caulfield East, Victoria 3145, Australia

T: +61 412 107 280, F: +61 3 9903 2167, chancheah@aol.com

ABSTRACT

Portal design, regarded as a human-activity centric process, defines: (a) what users want in the context of their activity flows and information-resources; and (b) how information systems can be designed to address these needs. On this basis, the Breast Cancer Knowledge On-line (BCKO) project is trialling soft system methodology (SSM) in transforming its system development lifecycle (SDLC) approach into a human activity centric system design model to develop a user sensitive and intelligent knowledge-portal.

INTRODUCTION

The BCKO project (http://www.sims.monash.edu.au/research/eirg/BCKprojectdescr.html) is a two-year action-research program between Monash University, BreastCare Victoria and Breast Cancer Action Group.

The portal resolves the lack of availing relevant, quality and in-time information for the Australian Breast Cancer (BC) communities. Its characteristic features are marked by its user sensitive and intelligent knowledge management functionality that would help users find what they expect to know, as and when required, and in a form that would effectively empower them to make and take appropriate decisions and actions (Fisher, Burstein, McKemmish, Manaszewicz, Anderson & Williamson, 2002).

LITERATURE REVIEW

The literature review on portal definitions, human-computer interaction, information systems, knowledge and service management paradigms concluded that:

1. Portals are not just evolutionary representations of information systems (IS) that are built on newer technologies, but are also human-activity system solutions that connect people, process and technology for resolving users problems and realising opportunities that enhance their lives.
2. Design is a process that concerns the ability of people to use their experiences, skills and knowledge to change their environments for meeting their living needs, and involves the use of rationale logic and linear structure to build design artefacts, systems and environment changes (Bilton, 2002).
3. User centricity is an emerging concept of and success factor for designing and delivering IS for supporting people to carry out their work efficiently and effectively (Dix, 1998 and Preece, Rogers, Sharp & Benyon, 1994). Dix views portal design as a process that not only specifies the task decomposition of human based knowledge activity flows, but also the socio-technological system framework of how they are represented and effected by system artefacts.
2. The SSM approach of Checkland and Scholes (1999) is a suitable user-centric problem solving technique for probing the notion of purposeful human activities, social roles and political drivers in defining user requirements and for guiding the logical and physical architecture-designs of systems.

RESEARCH METHODOLOGY

This section examines why and how SSM is currently being tried in the BCKO project.

Why?

The project team views the BCKO project as an iterative-prototyping based action-research that would deliver a portal that is capable of helping users locate and find web resources in a manner and form that they want, as and when (and where) required.

User needs analysis has been carried out using socio-oriented, qualitative methods to describe the problem situation and confirmed through interpretative research that the portal is the problem resolution. From an IS perspective, this user analysis lacks vigour in system context that developers can effectively use for designing the portal's logical and physical system architectures. This instigated exploring SSM and the literature review concluded that it is most suitable because SSM:

1. Uses system-modelling concepts that developers can easily relate to in defining user requirements in terms of human activity flows.
2. Enhances project success by revealing critical success factors that lie hidden in stakeholders' cultural and political drivers, which relay to their different expectations of and preferences for development approaches, project scope and management drivers, and portal functionality.
3. Provides an effective management approach for supervising a multidisciplinary team, which according to Denley and Long (2001), brings about as many benefits as there are problems. These problems arise from differences in team-members' opinions, interests, language, communication styles, entrenched training, skills and knowledge, etc. SSM not only enables multidisciplinary team members to view their different definitions and ideas, but also foster them to collaborate and agree on common views of human activities, social roles and political motivators that constitute problem situations and solutions. This approach would result in a defendable model of user requirements that BCKO developers can rely on during system development (Lane & Galvin, 1999).

How?

The project's research methodology uses SSM during its project planning and iterative SDLC process execution.

During project planning, SSM is used to scope the problem situation by modelling the CATWOE-definition to specify user requirements.

This first level of user requirements is then translated into theory-based conceptual models that describe the macro and micro interactions of individual human and enterprise activities (because individual stakeholders use the portal services for engaging personal and/or enterprise activities).

Established muli-disciplinary theories are used to describe user requirements as follows:

- **Personal requirements** concern how a user uses the portal to locate, organise, share and use web information to address decision-making or action-taking. *Knowledge management* (such as that of Alavi's knowledge activity model (1997)) and *human-computer interaction* principles can be used to describe these knowledge flows and conative styles of users.
- **Enterprise requirements** expressed in terms of:
  • Customer service provisioning when enterprise users use the portal or refers their customers to use the portal to access reliable BC information resources. *Service management* paradigms can be used to model how enterprise users service their customers on-line.
  • Strategic leverage of the portal to increase operational efficiency and effectiveness, and manipulate competitive and share-market advantage. *Industry structures, value chain, financial systems, e-business design* and *strategic thinking* paradigms can be used to model the integration of enterprise workflows (in the context of value chains), industry structures and financial systems for competitive positioning.

A work-in-progress framework of modelling user requirements in the manner described as in Figure 1.

Integration of these individual and enterprise activity interactions provide the micro to macro views of user requirements for developers when executing SDLC activities. They would specify what and how individual and enterprise activities interact, including revelations of their consequential socio-economic-political dynamics.

These user models provide the complete "*cause and effect*" framework of modelling and verifying user requirements that developers can use when designing and carrying out other SDLC activities.

INTERMEDIATE SSM OUTCOME

Root Definition

The BCKO knowledge-portal alleviates the issues of the Australian Breast Cancer communities in accessing in-time, relevant and quality information for supporting their critical health and lifestyle management activities.

CATWOE Descriptions

Three SSM analysis iterations worked out the general, cultural and political dimensions of the problem situation to describe the CATWOE elements.

Analysis 1 describes the CATWOE elements as follows:

1. The Customers are the:
- BC users and their support communities, who would use the portal solution for deciding and effecting critical health care choices and lifestyle changes
- Enterprise users, i.e., the small and institutional service providers, who would leverage the portal for servicing their customers and fulfilling other enterprise purpose/s.
2. The Actors are the project team (Monash University) and the two sponsors (BreastCare Victoria & the Breast Cancer Action Group) who would respectively develop and market/deploy the portal. All parties are joint financiers. The sponsors are also candidate portal owners.
3. The Transformation process enables the project's customers to access in-time, relevant and quality on-line information, as and when (and where) required, throughout different disease stages.
4. The Weltanschauung (worldwide) view that would make the transformation possible when:
- Monash University can leverage the project as their action-research process.
- The project delivers a prototype that the:
  - Sponsors can *take to market* the portal to a small group of BC users in 2004
  - The selected BC users can use to locate, store and share information regarding disease management and their experiences, and apply the knowledge acquired to make appropriate decisions and take effective actions.
  - Enterprise users (who service the selected users) can leverage the portal for improving their customer servicing, financial bottom-lines and other enterprise purposes.
5. The Owners are the sponsors. They are also prospective enterprise users and portal owners, who play a major role in referring the Australian public to use the BCKO portal. Without these parties, long term economic and referral support of the portal is not easily viable.
6. The Environment is servicing people affected by breast cancer in finding WWW information to support them in decision-making and action-taking regarding matters of critical health care and lifestyle management.

Cultural Analysis 2 expands the CATWOE-description by profiling the social roles played by the stakeholders and generalises their behavioural norms and value-standards, which help in identifying expectations and mindset drivers. The social roles are those of university, government, non-profit making community care, small to institutional health servicing organisations, and the people communities of breast cancer.

Political Analysis 3 finalises the CATWOE-description by revealing the stakeholders' vested interests and how they can potentially leverage power from their inter-relationships, processes and resources. In doing so, the analysis discloses that the critical success factor of the project requires the development process and the portal functionality to show support for and value-adds:

1. The research agendas of the project team/Monash University

Figure 1. A SSM and theory based user modelling framework

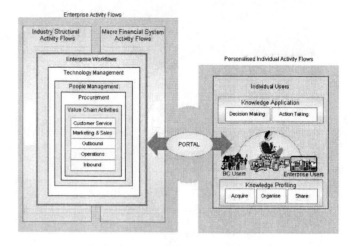

Figure 2. CATWOE rich picture summary

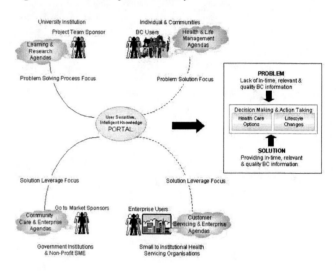

Figure 3. Overview of the BCKO research methodology

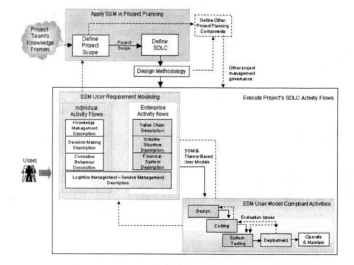

2. The personal decision-making and action-taking of the BC users and their support communities
3. Delivering customer servicing and enterprise (including financial) benefits for the:
- Enterprise users
- Other two sponsors.

CONCLUSION

Through continuous advances in technology, information systems have transformed to become portal-solutions that not only meet the information needs of users, but also support and enhance their human activities, social roles and political aspirations. As part of this new paradigm shift, user centricity is an emerging important design concept and success factor. The concept views portal design as a human activity centric system development process that identifies what users need and how a socio-technical system can be designed (and deployed) to meet these needs.

The BCKO project is incorporating SSM into its research methodology as a strategy of adopting a human activity centric design approach for building its portal system. The research methodology uses SSM for increasing user requirement clarity and design focus during

- Project planning, where the project scope is enhanced by the CATWOE-definition and better guides project managers in crafting their SDLC and other project management frameworks.
- SDLC execution, where the CATWOE root definition is translated into conceptual user models that use theories from different business and technology management disciplines to describe user requirements. The descriptions would make logical and/or theory-based sense to all stakeholders, especially providing a system-modeling context that developers can easily understand and use for guiding their system design and other SDLC activities.

REFERENCES

1. Fisher, J., Burstein, F., McKemmish, S., Manaszewicz, R., Anderson, J. and Williamson, K. (2002). Building A User Sensitive Intelligent Portal to Breast Cancer Knowledge To Meet Diverse Information Needs. A proceeding of the 13th Australian Conference on Information Systems – Enabling Organisations & Society Through Information Systems. School of Information Systems, Victoria University, Australia.
2. Bilton, J. (2002). An on-line paper (http://atschool.eduweb.co.uk/trinity/watdes.html) "What is design?" issued by the UK Technology Centre found as an URL link of the University of Colorado at Denver, School of Education website http://carbon.cudenver.edu/~mryder/itc_data/idmodels.html.
3. Dix, A, et al. (1998). The Human-Computer Interaction. Prentice Hall Europe, Second edition.
4. Preece, J., Rogers, Y., Sharp, H. and Benyon, D. (1994). Human-Computer Interaction. Addison-Wesley.
5. Denley and Lane (2001). Multidisciplinary Practice in Requirement Engineering: Problems & Criteria for Success. Joint Proceedings of HCI and IHM 2001, edited by Blandford, A., Vanderdonckt, J. and Gray, P. Springer.
6. Lane and Galvin, K. (1999). Methods for Transitioning from SSM Models to Object Oriented Analysis developed to support the Army Operational Architecture and an Example of its Application. www.dodccrp.org/1999CRTS/pdf.files/track-6/092galvi.pdf, December 2001.
7. Checkland, P. and Scholes, J. (1999). Soft Systems Methodology in Action. John Wiley & Sons Ltd.
8. Alavi, M (1997). Knowledge Management and Knowledge Management Systems - Workshop at ICIS'97 12/19/97, [on line] http://www.mbs.umd.edu/is/malavi/icis-97-KMS/index.htm.

Measuring Information Security: Combining the SSE-CMM with the ISO 17799 Standard

Vaughn Christie and James Goldman
Department of Computer Technology, Purdue University
vrchristie@tech.purdue.edu, jegoldman@tech.purdue.edu
(Christie) 765-495-1312, (Goldman) 765-494-9525

ABSTRACT

Information security (IS) incidents are on the rise with new attacks reported daily. How have system administrators and security professionals reacted to these new threats? Traditionally, system owners have rushed to "acquire the latest cure" (Nielsen, 2000). They have implemented today's fix with little thought to the benefit truly gained from such tools. This historical approach to system security is yielding to a model of increased accountability. In short, IS professionals are being asked, "How secure are we?" (Payne, 2001).

Answers to this and similar questions are not easily derived (Payne, 2001). Dating back to the late 1970's and early 1980's, when the annual loss expectancy (ALE) calculation was being developed, security professionals have attempted to define security by a single distinct value: ALE (Fletcher, 1995). Since that time, additional IS management documents, defined by Fletcher (1995) as third-generation information security tools, have been developed, including a number of guidance documents, which have been published to assist organizations in establishing and maintaining their IT security programs. Examples include the NIST Handbook, the CSE Guide, ISO 17799, etc. (Hopkins, 1999). Unfortunately, problems reside in these guidance tools; specifically, they lack the ability to measure defined IS parameters easily, effectively or efficiently (Payne, 2001).

This research has yielded a metric-based IS maturity framework constructed from the combination of the ISO 17799 standard and the Systems Security Engineering Capability Maturity Model (SSE-CMM). The study has illustrated the complementary nature of the SSE-CMM and ISO standard and shown how the SSE-CMM can be leveraged to assess the maturity of the practices implemented according to ISO 17799 standard specifications. The end result is a self-facilitated metrics-based security assessment (MBSA) framework, which will allow organizations to assess the maturity of their IS processes. By using the SSE-CMM to measure the maturity of industry accepted IS process standards, the findings of this study enable professionals to measure, in a more consistent, reliable, and timely manner, areas for improvement and effectiveness. Furthermore, the findings allow a more dependable qualitative measurement of the returns achieved through given IS investments. Ultimately, this research has provided professionals an additional, more robust self-assessment tool in answering: "How secure are we?"

THE PROBLEM

Sparked by a combination of 9/11, the mounting complexity of online attacks, and the increasing realization that network surveillance, intrusion detection and real-time response strategies are organizational responsibilities, IS has come to the forefront of organizational agendas (Dargan, 2002). However, even with mounting media attention and increases in IT spending, data reported by Ultima Business Solutions suggests that IT teams are increasingly failing to protect organizations from attack (Dargan, 2002).

As such, IT security projects are coming under greater scrutiny, and IS managers are increasingly being asked to demonstrate a return on the investments being made. In brief, (Payne, 2001):
- "Are we more secure today than we were before?"
- "If so, how do we know?"
- "How do we compare to our competition?"
- "How secure are we?"

How will these questions be answered? In recent years, guidance documents have evolved that have attempted to qualitatively guide corporations in addressing these questions (Hopkins, 1999). While each differs from its peers, in structure, culture and organization, each seeks the common goals of explicitly documenting, in a single framework, the various facets of the system, such as the system's behavior, structure, and history (Craft, 1998). Unfortunately, industry has cited the following broad-level weaknesses with such frameworks.
- Independence from actual risks, which may lead to:
  - Over- or under-securing information assets (or both)
  - Difficulties in measuring the efficiency of security procedures (Chuvakin, 2002)
  - Measurement of security investment effectiveness is largely ignored (Payne, 2001)
  - Answers to the aforementioned questions are difficult to determine (Payne, 2001)

Jamie Carroll (2000) has proposed a potential solution to these weaknesses: metrics. With metrics, a number of advantages are realized (Carroll, 2000):
- Processes become repeatable, more manageable, and may be carried out more frequently on specific systems
- Risk assessments can be performed immediately
- System targeting can be performed more frequently
- Risk assessment processes and results between service providers may become more standardized
- Threat, risk and impact baselines, for similar functional systems, may be created
- Planning, programming and budgeting system inputs, for acquisition and development, may realize improvements

By finding a middle ground between the highly quantitative measures of the late 1970's and the qualitative frameworks currently being used, this research has attempted to broach a topic currently in its infancy (IS metrics) and taken a step toward the fourth generation of IS paradigms (Fletcher, 1995).

FRAMEWORK:
METRICS BASED SECURITY ASSESSMENT

The first steps in building the MBSA required a compare and contrast of the SSE-CMM and ISO 17799 standard, resulting in the following tables:
- A matrix defining the areas of overlap
- A matrix defining the strengths and weaknesses of each
- Matrixes illustrating where one model mitigated specific weaknesses of the other
  - The primary SSE-CMM weakness mitigated is that of a lack of defined standards for which to measure against
  - The primary ISO 17799 weakness mitigated is that of a lack of measurement and assessment

Once all tables had been created, the author framed ISO 17799 processes in the SSE-CMM framework, and identified where, within the SSE-CMM process model, the MBSA best fit. The framework is illustrated in Figure 1.

Figure 1. MBSA architecture

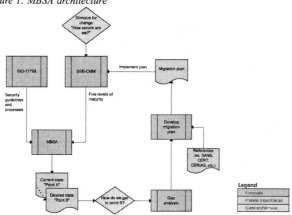

Table 1. Metric sample

Metric	Terms and conditions of employment state employee responsibilities regarding IS and (where appropriate) are continued for a period of time after the employment period
Maturity Level Goal	Level 3
Scale/Rating	0—1—2—3—4—5 N/A Unknown
Frequency	Current Date: Frequency: Next Assessment Date:
Implementation Evidence	Sample Only
Data Source	Sample Only

Constructing the metrics required framing each ISO process in the form of specific, measurable quantities and developing a response scale inline with SSE-CMM parameters. A sample MBSA template and metric is illustrated in Table 1.

Assessing each control is straightforward; for each baseline control, a response indicating the degree to which the control has been implemented is recorded. The two extreme responses are 0 and 5:

- Score a baseline control as 0 if the baseline control is required but has not been implemented in the organizational entity for which responses are being sought and there has been no effort put forth that might ultimately lead to implementation.
- If the control is not required or the question is not applicable to the organization, score it as N/A.
- Score a control as 5 if the baseline control has been fully implemented in the organizational entity for which responses are being sought and the assessor is satisfied with the quality and completeness of that implementation.

Generally, values between 0 and 5 should reflect the extent of implementation. For instance, if the security policy is 20% of the way towards Level 5 maturity, score the control as 1. If the security policy is 60% of the way towards Level 5 maturity, score the control as 3.

Scores can be influenced by varying degrees of implementation within the organizational entity. If one part of the entity has completely implemented a security policy, while another part has rejected that policy and has no plans to develop their own, the control should by scored as a 2 (rounding down to limit the potential for a 'false feeling of security') for the entire organization. Note fractional values are not defined in the MBSA; this promotes a more straightforward alignment with the SSE-CMM.

Assigning scores to controls is most straightforward if they are thought of in the following manner: score 0 being 0% of the way towards full and complete attainment of Level 5 maturity and 5 being 100%. Scores between 0 and 5 signify only partial implementation of the ideal maturity level (Level 5).

Averaging the values of each metric within a given process area (PA), the assessor may report (e.g., to management) their overall assessment and therefore readily identify the level of maturity for each PA within the SSE-CMM. Should the organization elect to assess each process area on an annual basis, the following legend may prove useful; it allows the organization to easily indicate up to four years of maturity within a single assessment document.

- 2002 – Underlined
- 2003 – Highlighted
- 2004 – Box
- 2005 – **Bold**

Within Table 1, the 'Scale/Rating' can be marked according to the previous list, such that past assessments can visually be identified. For instance, in Table 1, the assessor can clearly see the maturity levels attained for the metric; indicating that in 2002 and 2003, the entity was at Level 1. In 2004, the system progressed to Level 2; and in 2005, the goal of Level 3 maturity was attained. Note a similar legend is easily applied to the averages calculated when reporting PA assessments.

Due to time constraints, validation and testing of the MBSA has been delimited from the scope of the research; future scholars should attempt to more thoroughly test and validate this work. To assist in the process, Figure 1 illustrates the MBSA architecture; for which the following six steps have been defined.

1. Enter the SSE-CMM maturity model – the stimulus for change is the question: "how secure are we?"
2. Combine the strengths of the SSE-CMM and ISO 17799 standard – through the areas of identified mitigated weaknesses, the MBSA attempts to account for the SSE-CMM's lack of defined processes and the ISO 17799 standard's lack of measurement and assessment.
3. Determine current and desired state – conducting the MBSA results in a current state definition of IS maturity. Activities such as benchmarking or consultation with local system, environment and technological requirements, should be considered to define a desired state.
4. Conduct gap analysis – a gap analysis should be considered as a means for identifying the processes and requirements to get from the current state to the desired state.
5. Develop migration plan – based on the gap analysis findings, a migration plan should be developed and implemented (per the SSE-CMM process model) according to business need.
6. Re-evaluate IS maturity – after implementing the migration plan, and continuing its progress through the SSE-CMM process model, the organization reaches the step of 'analysis and evaluation,' where it should, again, conduct the MBSA, assess the results (i.e., the 'New current state' after implementing the migration plan) against the 'desired state' maturity level, defined in the initial stages of the framework, and identify potential future actions, resulting in an iterative approach to IS maturity. Note that conducting the full MBSA may not be required; depending on the business drivers at hand, the organization may chose only to assess the changes that were implemented and identify the level of maturity attained by such projects.

Certainly, this is a work in progress that must be cost justified and tested prior to implementation. The research is seen as a point of entry toward the fourth-generation of IS, and may benefit those organizations seeking a measurement tool to finally answer: "How secure are we?"

REFERENCES

Carroll, J.M. *A Metrics-based Approach to Certification and Accreditation*. BTG Inc. July 6, 2000.

Chuvakin, A. (2002, Jan. 28). *Approaches to Choosing the Strength of Your Security Measures*. LinuxSecurity.com. Ret. April 4, 2002, from: http://www.linuxsecurity.com.

Craft, R. et al. (1998, Aug. 6). *An Open Framework for Risk Management*. National Institute of Standards and Technology. Ret. Aug. 27, 2002, from: http://csrc.nist.gov/nissc/1998/proceedings/paperE6.pdf.

Dargan, L. (2002, Aug. 24). Smashing the Milestone. SC Info Security Magazine. Ret. July 2002, from: http://www.scmagazine.com/scmagazine/sc-online/2002/article/32/article.html.

Fletcher, S., Jansma, R., Lim, J., Halbgewachs, R. Murphy, M., Wyss, G., *Software System Risk Management and Assurance*, Proc. of the 1995 New Security Paradigms Workshop, Aug. 22-25, 1995, San Diego, CA.

Hopkins, J.P. (1999). *The Relationship Between the SSE-CMM and IT Security Guidance Documentation*. EWA-Canada Ltd., 1-7.

Nielsen, Fran. (2000). *Approaches to Security Metrics*. Ret. August 25, 2002, from: http://csrc.nist.gov/csspab/june13-15/metrics_report.pdf.

Payne, S. (2001, July 11). *A Guide to Security Metrics*. SANS Institute. Ret. March 16, 2002, from: http://rr.sans.org/audit/metrics.php.

Open Source Business Solutions:
A Case Study and
Application of SQL & PHP

Dan Clark and Alan I.Rea, Jr.
Haworth College of BusinessWestern Michigan UniversityKalamazoo, MI 49008
(Clark) P: 989.714.2456, (Rea) P: 269.387.4247, F: 269.387.5710
dan.clark@wmich.edu, alan.rea@wmich.edu

PHP (PHP: Hypertext Preprocessor) is a powerful scripting language that is designed to allow web developers to quickly and easily create dynamic web sites. PHP is among the most widely used scripting languages on the web. It is often used to create web-based database front-ends to simplify database administration. Many business problems can be addresses effectively and efficiently using open source solutions based on PHP and SQL. The three characteristics of PHP that make it a highly desirable choice for many web developers follow:
1) It is a free, open-source project
2) It is a server-based scripting language
3) PHP's relative ease of use

When PHP is combined with HTML (Hypertext Markup Language) and an SQL (Structured Query Language) based database, the possibilities are nearly endless for professional web developers. One popular application based on PHP and SQL is trouble-ticket software for help desk or problem tracking. The final paper will focus on the benefits, problems and requirements for successfully implementing a PHP driven front-end to an SQL database; specifically a database designed to track help desk trouble tickets. This paper will allow us to better understand the challenges and opportunities facing a business when implementing an open source system.

HISTORY OF PHP

PHP was created in the fall of 1994 by Rasmus Lerdorf. Initially, Rasmus designed PHP to create a simple page counter and track who was viewing his online resume. The initial public release (known then as Personal Home Page Tools) was made available in 1995. This version of PHP consisted mainly of a simple parser engine that understood a few special macros. Also included were a guestbook and visitor counter. The parser was rewritten in mid-1995 and renamed PHP/FI Version 2 (Personal Home Page tools/Form Interpreter). Rasmus combined the Personal Home Page tools scripts with a Form Interpreter and added mSQL support to create PHP/FI.

The next major revision of PHP was PHP 3.0. PHP 3.0 was created by Andi Gutmans and Zeev Suraski in 1997 as a complete rewrite of PHP/FI. In an effort to cooperate and start building upon PHP/FI's existing user-base, Andi, Rasmus and Zeev decided to cooperate and announced PHP 3.0 as the official successor of PHP/FI 2.0.

The current version of PHP is PHP 4.0, officially released in May 2000. This most recent version of PHP improved performance of complex applications and improved the modularity of PHP's code base. PHP 4.0 also includes support for a wider variety of Web servers, HTTP sessions, output buffering, more secure ways of handling user input and several new language constructs.

BUSINESS SOLUTIONS USING PHP AND SQL

Many business problems can be addresses effectively and efficiently using open source solutions based on PHP and SQL. One of the more popular applications developed using PHP and SQL is a shopping-cart system for eCommerce sites. Product information is pulled from a database, then parsed using PHP script to compute quantities, order totals and update inventory records.

Another popular application is trouble-ticket software for help desk or problem tracking. A trouble-ticket solution will be the main focus of the final report. I plan to investigate the hardware and software requirements needed to implement such a system. I will focus on both the technical needs of such a system, as well as the general usability of the system. This process of evaluation will allow us to better understand the challenges facing a business when implementing an open source system.

PROS AND CONS

The final paper will deal with the many of the challenges and opportunities facing a business developing and implementing a PHP and SQL application. Among the opportunities are low-cost or no-cost solutions to complex business problems. Because PHP and SQL are both open-source projects, the initial cost to business is essentially free. Another opportunity that exists is the ability of PHP to work with a wide variety of databases, from mySQL to Microsoft Access. This gives businesses much needed flexibility when developing applications using PHP. One potential challenge is convincing decision-makers that an application based on open standards is a viable replacement for a proprietary application. These challenges and opportunities will be further discussed in the final submission.

REFERENCES

Bretthauer, D. (2002). Open source software: A history. *Information Technology & Libraries 21, no. 1,* 3-10.

Burger, E. F., & Soreide, N. N. (2002). A web based news distribution system using PHP and MySQL. *International Conference on Interactive Information and Processing Systems for Meteorology, Oceanography and Hydrology, 18ᵗʰ,* 50-51.

Gardner, M., & Pinfield, S. (2002). Database-backed library websites: A case study of the use of PHP and MySQL at the University of Nottingham. *Program: Electronic library and information systems 35, no. 1,* 33-42.

Ross, D. (2000). DB Forms: PHP, MySQL, and PHPLIB. *Dr. Dobb's Journal 25, no. 8,* 98-104.

Royappa, A. V. (2000). The PHP Web Application Server. *Journal of Computing in Small Colleges 15, no. 3,* 201-211.

Environmental, Organizational and Managerial Determinants of Strategic IS Plan Implementation

Jason F. Cohen
School of Economic and Business Sciences
University of the Witwatersrand, South Africa
T: +27117178157, jasonc@isys.wits.ac.za

ABSTRACT

This paper reports on an empirical study which examined the effect of various environmental, organizational and managerial determinants on strategic IS plan implementation success. The paper presents the theoretical underpinnings of the study, together with the study's hypotheses and results. Data collected from 106 organisations in South Africa revealed that, amongst other factors, the external business and IT environments, as well as the level of CIO influence and the significance of IS within an organisation, are all variables which effect IS plan implementation.

INTRODUCTION TO THE STUDY

Strategic information systems plan implementation is the process of introducing into an organization the selected systems, applications and infrastructures identified in the long term strategic IS plan. The process also includes the implementation of the policies related to the governance and management of the IS function, and ideas related to the long term role and expected contribution of IS within the organization (Gottschalk, 1999). Associated with this implementation process is the concept of change (Markus and Benjamin, 1996) and the corresponding issues of organizational resistance together with external constraints imposed by budgetary and technical realities.

Earl (1993), however, indicates that even when the planning process is "judged successful...resultant plans are not always followed up or fully implemented." Others, e.g., Chan *et. al.* (1998) and Ward and Peppard (2002) also describe how IS strategies are not always realized (implemented) as intended. Failure to implement strategic IS plans can result in significant wasted resources, poor investment decisions and numerous lost opportunities for the competitive use of IS (King and Raghunathan, 1987; Lederer and Sethi, 1991; Edwards *et. al.*, 1991). In addition, failed implementation also leads to lack of integration or alignment between IS and the business (Lederer and Sethi, 1998; Reich and Benbasat, 2000), lost confidence by business management in the IS function and consequently their reluctance to support future IS efforts and to consider IS as a potential source of advantage. Moreover, the validity of IS strategic planning (ISSP) as a managerial activity is severely undermined if the implementation of resultant strategic IS plans cannot be assured. Implementation is thus a necessary and desirable outcome of an organization's ISSP process (Lederer and Salmela, 1996).

Yet despite its importance and recent reminders that IS researchers not overlook implementation in IS strategy research (Chan and Huff, 1992), a review of the literature reveals that attention to implementation remains limited and is in need of advancement. Some noteworthy progress has, however, been made in uncovering implementation problems (Lederer and Mendelow, 1986; Lederer and Sethi, 1991; Lederer and Sethi, 1992), identifying barriers to implementations (Wilson, 1991), and defining planning process variables, organizational practices and mechanisms that facilitate plan implementation (e.g., Premkumar, 1992; Premkumar and King, 1994; Lederer and Sethi, 1996). In addition, implementation is being recognized as a measure of planning success (e.g., Segars; 1994; Doherty *et. al.*, 1999), and its importance in linking planning to performance has been examined (Raghunathan and King, 1988).

Furthermore both theoretical and empirical works have also begun to consider the relationship between plan content and implementation (e.g., Lederer and Salmela, 1996; Gottschalk, 1999).

While it is important to continue with these efforts, much also needs to be learned about the effect of other factors (environmental, organizational and managerial in nature) on the strategic IS plan implementation process, which hereto have remained untested. Gottschalk, for example, found that 81 percent of variation in implementation extent was left unexplained in his study of plan "content predictors" of implementation. This suggests the need to identify other important *determinants* of strategic IS plan implementation successes and failure. Implementation success may thus be influenced by factors not only in direct control of the ISSP process but also that lie outside of it. The purpose of this study is to explore those factors.

DEVELOPMENT OF HYPOTHESES

Drawing on various perspectives from strategic management and organization theory, this study recognizes the potential influence of selected environmental, organizational and managerial factors on strategic IS plan implementation. It is recognized that since the IS function and its management team are no longer "buffered" from the effects of the external business environment (see Lederer and Mendelow, 1990), the characteristics of the organization's external environment must be recognized for their possible effects of IS plan implementation. The ever changing external organizational environment, together with trends and developments in the "technical base" of IS (Venkatraman, 1986), and the corresponding need for constant change and flexibility, quickly make IS plans obsolete and hamper organizational efforts to implement IS plans. In addition to the external environment, the internal characteristics of the host organization, such as its size, complexity and strategic orientation, must be recognized together with the characteristics of the IS function as potential factors influencing IS plan implementation. Furthermore, the nature of the IS business relationship and demographic characteristics of the IS management team may also be important explanatory variables. Such variables play important roles in determining the ability of the IS management team to secure funding, gain organizational support and cooperation, and exercise the necessary influence required for effective implementation (see Enns *et. al.*, 2001).

Thus the hypotheses of this study are as follows:

*H1: The greater the level of uncertainty, dynamism and hostility in the organization's **external business environment**, the lower will be the level of strategic IS plan implementation success.*

*H2: The greater the level of perceived dynamism in the **external IT environment**, the lower will be the level of strategic IS plan implementation success.*

*H3: The greater the level of **organizational complexity**, the lower will be the level of strategic IS plan implementation success.*

*H4: The more prospector oriented the **organization's business strategy**, the lower will be the level of strategic IS plan implementation success.*

*H5: The **larger** and more **experienced the IS function**, the greater will be the level of strategic IS plan implementation success.*

*H6: The more **significant IS is to current and future organizational success**, the more complex will be resultant plans and thus the lower will be the level of strategic IS plan implementation success.*

*H7: The greater the **business orientation (education), experience and length of organizational tenure** of the top IS management team, the greater will be the level of strategic IS plan implementation success.*

*H8: The more **influential the CIO**, the greater will be the level of strategic IS plan implementation success.*

*H9: The greater the level of top managerial **commitment to IS**, the greater will be the level of strategic IS plan implementation success.*

*H10: The greater the degree of **shared vision** between IS and business management, the greater will be the level of strategic IS plan implementation success.*

*H11: The greater the **focus of the IS strategic planning process on implementation**, the greater will be the level of strategic IS plan implementation success.*

DATA COLLECTION

A pilot tested questionnaire measuring the study's constructs was mailed to the directors of IT in over 650 companies listed in the 2002 edition of "Who Owns Whom in South Africa" (a comprehensive publication of information on major listed and unlisted companies). As of January 2003, 118 questionnaires were returned for an 18% response rate. Questionnaires with missing data were eliminated, yielding 106 useable responses.

Measurement

Where possible, the study's explanatory variables (contextual determinants) were measured using multiple items adopted from the IS, organization theory and strategic management literature. Implementation was measured using multiple items capturing the extent to which the strategic IS plan is as a whole was being implemented as planned as well as in terms of the adequacy of resources provided. For all multi item variables, composite values were calculated except for IS managerial demographics (hypothesis 7), which were examined individually. Due to the number of respondents providing incomplete data on IS function size and number of years computing experience, hypothesis 5 was dropped from the study.

RESULTS

Based on a mean split, the sample was classified into two groups representing high and low levels of strategic IS plan implementation success. There were 63 cases in the successful implementers group and 43 in the unsuccessful group respectively. Step wise discriminant analysis was performed on the data with 12 environmental, organisational and managerial variables as predictors of membership in the high and low implementation success groups.

A significant discriminant function, Wilks' Lambda = .768, χ^2 (10) = 21.97 (p<0.01), was extracted. All variables, except "strategic orientation" and the demographic variable measuring "tenure", entered the discriminant function (enter criterion of F=1.0). Thus providing some level of support for all but hypothesis 4. Sixty-seven percent (67%) of the cases were correctly classified by the discriminant model. This is high enough above the chance criteria of 51.8% for the model to be considered useful for predicting implementation success. Although most of the study's variables entered the analy-

sis, which suggests they were important for distinguishing between successful and unsuccessful implementers, the most significant variables were the strategic significance of IS to the organisation, CIO influence, external business environment and ability to cope with external IT dynamism, followed by a focus on implementation during ISSP. Organisational complexity and IS managers' business experience surprisingly related negatively to implementation success, a finding which deserves further exploration.

Correlation analysis reveals that the composite implementation success score is related, at p<0.1 or better, to all independent variables except for "strategic orientation", "organisational complexity", "business experience of IS managers" and "length of organisational tenure". These variables may thus be less important in predicting implementation success. Although "CIO influence" also did not correlate significantly with the composite implementation success score, the successful and unsuccessful implementer groups differed significantly on this variable (F=4.99, p<0.05) thus confirming its importance.

From a practical perspective, these results provide IS managers with an understanding of the relative impact of environmental, organisational and managerial variables on strategic IS plan implementation. Specifically, the results show the important effect that factors, both within and outside of the control of IS managers, can have on IS plan implementation. Although it may not be possible for IS managers to influence many of the environmental or organisational variables, they must make themselves aware of the mechanisms through which these factors influence IS plan implementation, i.e., understand the inherent problems that context presents, and thus be in a position to respond accordingly. IS managers wishing to improve plan implementation should ensure they are more comfortable with and able to reconcile external IT trends with their strategic plans. Furthermore, they should work on improving the strategic significance of IS and their own influence within their organisations. IS managers should also focus on implementation during their ISSP process and create an environment that facilitates shared vision with and commitment from business managers.

CONCLUSION

It is hoped that this study will add to the growing strategic IS plan implementation research stream by demonstrating that factors in the environmental, organizational and managerial context can influence strategic IS plan implementation. This research has thus helped to identify those contexts that are more conducive to strategic IS plan implementation and will benefit organizations looking to improve their strategic IS plan implementation efforts. Although not specifically addressing actions that can be taken to influence context or mitigate implementation problems it is hoped that results will help influence the development of contextually sensitive methodologies for strategic IS plan implementation. In addition, similar to other studies that address plan implementation, these results will aid researchers attempting to understand implementation successes and failures. This study included only selected variables, future research would do well to identify the effect of other environmental, organizational and managerial factors not included in this study.

REFERENCES

Available from the author on request.

OSS for Vital Public Projects

Amanda Dambrouckas

Bay Path College/Rensselaer University/Stanpak Systems

53 Lakeview Hgts., Tolland, CT 06084

P: (870) 871-6547, amanda@stanpak.com

I believe that open systems are the key to increasing the rate of information availability and technological progression in our global society. I am convinced that a concentrated effort in open development will benefit society as a whole. I consider open development to be especially valuable in the context of vital projects. By vital, I refer to causes that contribute to the well being of society as a whole. Examples of these critical causes include medical research, defense, communications, and environmental resource maximization. My theory is that if we can achieve the progressive speed, quality, and reliability that past open source projects have in working for these causes, we will see an overall improvement in human life. This is the ultimate goal. I am not the first person to see open source advantages:

"Benefits are manifold... for education, non-profits, people/groups who simply can't afford them."[1]

My plan for open advocacy involves four major steps:

1. Spread awareness about the possibilities of open development for vital projects. Concentration should include educating a team/community of open developers, and then government/ influential organizations.
2. Communicate with members of government/organizations to determine their goals.
3. Develop prototype projects within the open community in order to prove the validity/possibilities of open projects to organizations associated with vital projects (AMA, Nasal, NIH, NSF, DOD, etc.).
4. Begin open development for vital projects (medical research, alternative energy sources, communications).

RESEARCH QUESTIONS

1. What is the best way to apply open software to information availability and progression of the productivity of society?
2. What types of software do we need?
3. What is the most efficient way to spread awareness of the benefits of open source?
4. How can we convince people (and corporations and government) to break old habits and embrace open systems? We must clarify the benefits of open development tools, but what is the most efficient way for doing so?

PRODUCTIVITY

Progress yields feelings of accomplishment and self-worth for humans. The leaders of our society should support this concept in order to better the lives of our global community. After all, productive individuals comprise a progressive society.

My theory is that open source software embraces human productivity. Briefly, my evidence includes the facts that:

1. OSS[2] projects promote code reuse. This means that society produces progressive technology, without having to reinvent the wheel with each for each step forward. (Efficiency)
2. The economic advantages that OSS offers business include cost efficiency, which ideally can be passed to consumers. (Economical)
3. OS projects are a collaborative learning experience. Developer communities yield skilled programmers, project designers, communicators, and project managers. These individuals can be critical members of government, academic, corporate, and entrepreneurial organizations. (Intellectual enrichment/training)
4. Open source projects follow the goals of a representative sector of society rather than those of a single firm. These goals are likely to mirror those of the public. (Objectives)
5. Open projects undergo rapid development, while showing fast turnaround time from request to implementation. These efforts are also very flexible in meeting customer needs. (Customization)
6. These projects incorporate the ideas and creativity from many backgrounds. Such diverse talent bases tend to produce creative and innovative tools. These tools will help create a progressive movement for vital projects. (Diverse talent base)
7. Open projects tend to yield products that are creative, have a low error tendency, and are created with care. These projects are subject to communal testing. This situation reveals weak points, possibilities for enhancement, and errors in the code. Coding errors have no place to 'hide' within compiled code as they would in commercial products. (Quality, security and reliability)

OPEN SOURCE AND QUALITY

In my opinion, open development yields quality products. This is due to the fact that bugs can be eliminated, ideas can be incorporated, security holes can be patched, and a community can perform comprehensive testing. These facts are clear in my mind, so I see that vital public projects as efforts that require the attributes I associate with open projects. I believe that we will find a consensus opinion that such projects must be secure, reliable, creative, bug-free, and demonstrate a high level of quality. There are four primary reasons why I believe that OSS products are inclined to a high quality.

1. Open developers are not assigned specific tasks that they may or may not enjoy, instead concentrating in areas where they are interested and talented. Most people tend to excel at that which they enjoy.
2. Open developers are typically end users of their products. When project designers/implementation teams understand the needs of a finished product, requirements are likely to be addressed attentively.
3. Discovery of errors in open software is shared and conducted within the community. When a bug is discovered, there are individuals available to correct the problem.
4. Corporations take credit for commercial products. A hired developer has no incentive to perform above the requirement (even knowing that a project is flawed). In contrast, open developers are associated with their work. Peer review is extensive, and developers will go out of their way to ensure quality of work before releasing code to peers.

BUG IDENTIFICATION AND REPARATION

Bugs are eliminated rapidly under open developmental models. This is due to the fact that errors in code are not hidden within compiled (locked) code when source available. When program logic is visible, and developers can examine errors, bugs are accessible for remedial efforts. I will argue that bugs are fixed within commercial products no sooner than when a manufacturer has capital, initiative, and time to fix them. In open source, a capable developer before the "wrong person discovers them" can identify problems.[3]

SECURITY

Open Software is inclined to foster secure products. Security breaches are often possible via the bugs, or overlooked holes in software. In open code these holes are visible and reparable. It is harder to conceal an entity from a community than it is to hide it from a corporate department. There is greater volume of testing in a community than there is time/capital for within a business. We can look to many documented facts that exemplify the high level of security in Open Software:[4]

1. There are companies that insure corporate technology assets. For example, J.S. Wurzler Underwriting Managers provides "hacker insurance" against system downtime and site defacement. The firm charges up to 15% higher premiums when customers use Windows rather than a GNU Linux system.

2. The Bugtraq database suggests that the least vulnerable OS is OSS and that proprietary systems can have as many as twice the amount of reported holes.

3. SecurityPortal compiled a list showing the average amount of time that it takes for distributors to address security issues.

Vendor	Reparation Time
Red Hat Linux	11.23 days
Microsoft	16.1 days
Sun Microsystems	93 days

4. CERT reports more IIS alerts than OSS flaws. (2001 Statistics)

Platform	# Attacks
IIS	31 million
Apache	22 million

RELIABILITY

Open software is reliable. Peer review is effective for refining a product. Several research efforts have been targeted toward comparing the relative reliability of OSS and commercial products.[5]

1. A 10-month ZDnet experiment found that GNU Linux is more reliable than Windows NT. Identical machines were loaded with Caldera Open Linux, Red Hat Linux, and Windows NT respectively.

Platform	Crash frequency	Repair time
NT	Once every six weeks	1/2 hour
Linux	Never	N/A

2. Bloor Research conducted a year long trial, comparing GNU Linux with Windows NT. In the end, GNet summarized the experiment's results with, "The winner here is clearly Linux."[6]

SUCCESS IN OPEN DEVELOPMENT

Open source projects have proven to yield successful products that are used extensively in our society. Such projects include several Internet services as DNS, sendmail, Apache, and Mozilla. One must recognize that these products have kept pace with the rapid pace of the development of Internet technology. To me, this suggests that open projects can keep a fast pace and likely undergo efficient development cycles.

Current Open Projects

1. The "eEurope" project aims to achieve an "information society for all" incorporates the validity of open source work for public projects. The plan claims that, the EC and Member States will promote using "open source software in the public sector and e-government." This will include the central government departments and agencies, local government, volunteers, the public sector and the National Health Service. [7]

Success in Medicine

I think that software is so important to our near future due to recent explorations in medical technology (ie-genetics). Humans are not quite as capable with working with such exact data. We need powerful processing (hardware and intelligent software) to understand the possibilities of this science. Can we imagine the possibilities of extending the availability of medical care if the process can be successfully, and cost effectively automated? We could avoid harsh, expensive, and dangerous drugs in many cases. We could provide care for people in remote or underdeveloped areas. Several examples of vital OSS pieces can be viewed in the medical field today.

1. The Integ Hospital Info System is and integrated hospital IS. Its functions include service to surgery, nursing, wards, labs admission, schedulers and communications.

2. ezDICOM is a medical viewer for MRI, CT and ultrasound images. It reads and presents images in many incompatible proprietary formats.

3. Open Microscopy Environment is a database backend program for creating five dimensional analytical biological microscopy and cell-based screening.[8]

4. OmniGene is a project centralized at the whitehead institute. This project aims to standardize biological data interchange, in hopes of streamlining communication between researchers.[9] OmniGene uses the web to store, access, share, and display collective stores of data. Students and professionals can add to, maintain and interchange this collective data.[10]

5. SBaGen is what I consider to be a revolutionary open public project. This project explores the use of binaural brain waves in easing medical ailments. This effectively has eased pain, sleeping troubles, and helped stabilize moods in test patients.[11]

Current Open Projects – Space/Robots/Navigation

In addition open tools have been developed in the fields of robotics, astronomy, and geographical information systems.

1. The Autonomous Systems Development Platform aims to develop navigation and behavioral software for real robots.

2. GCollider is a simulation package for analyzing the possibility of a collision of two galaxies.

3. The Geographical Information System Toolkit provides the tools for s GIS system according to OGIS standards.[12]

ECONOMIC CONCERNS

I feel the need to address the economic concerns associated with open projects. I was asked, "it is unclear how society can immediately benefit from simply having free software (when so much of the world doesn't even have reliable electricity." I don't associate open software with a lack of profit opportunity anymore. Open software does not have to be unprofitable just because the source code is available/free. For example, there is an opportunity for making money in supporting software. Open code is no exception. I have recognized several other methods in which to explore opportunity from open projects.

There are at least a handful of proven business models for pulling in a profit via open projects.[13] These include:

1. Companies can market supporting services/merchandise for open (and free) code. These include distribution media, brand names, documentation, and support. Red Hat Linux sells distributions for consumers, small business, and corporations. This company also sells technical support to customers.

2. Commercial firms use open source projects in order to earn a place in the market. With the validity of OSS projects proven, the firm may see a bright outlook for commercial sales. Netscape freely distributes software while building a position in the market for commercial products.

3. When software is a necessary component for a commercial product, yet not the primary profit channel, businesses can also use open software. This firm has found that their interface cards and other products can use open source drivers at a lower cost than in house commercial tools.

4. Companies utilize an earning process via "accessorizing." Companies market books, complete/turnkey systems configured with open software, or trivial items such as mugs, and t-shirts. O'Reilly Associates sells literature geared toward the open source community

CASE EXAMPLES USING OPEN PROJECTS

I have learned of several corporations, as well as governments that have recognized the appeal of open software.

Private Sector

There are Fortune 500 companies that have undergone open initiatives.[14] While my main concern in advocating OSS is not in the interest of the business sector, I do feel that it is necessary to recognize OSS here. My thoughts are that OSS has proven beneficial to large agendas, and these are the variant of project that the public sector initiates.

1. IBM: Apache within WebSphere suite.

2. Apple Computer: Partner with Apache, FreeBSD, NetBSD and other OSS developers for the Mac OS X platform.

3. Corel: Linux vendor, Wine project.

4. Netscape: Release Netscape Communicator and Netscape Navigator as open source software.[15]

Corporate Decisions

Different firms express a decision for open source tools in many ways:

1. "The change from proprietary software to open source software will be as significant as the change from mainframe technology to personal computers...This will affect both home and business computing00luting and change the way the world works."

2. "Traditional software development methods claim that open source...can not result in something reliable and well suited to customer needs. They are."[16]

COMPARATIVE ANALYSIS: OPEN SOURCE VS. COMMERCIAL FIRM

A convincing argument for the move to open source software for mass public projects must address the performance of communal vs. commercial project results. I have not learned of any study fairly comparing the performance of open source projects with commercial firms in a controlled environment. Thus, I turn to the history of the industry for an analysis. It is not uncommon for business to imitate successful open works, nor is it uncommon for the open community to create projects mirroring successful (yet somehow flawed) commercial products. This happens, for example, when a firm is slow to fix various bugs in a product. I find it quite interesting to note the areas in which OSS has been so successful, that commercial firms have not even attempted to compete for market share. Sendmail is the number one MTA on the Internet.[17] The product is so successful that there is no incentive to develop a non-OSS tool.

1. A 2001 survey by K.J. Bernstein found that:

% Internet email servers	Platform
42%	Sendmail
18%	MS Exchange

2. The bind package is used in over 95% of domain name services on the Internet.[18]

OS Market

The OS market is an area in which we can examine competition between communal and commercial products. The popular search engine google.com uses gnu/Linux, while yahoo.com uses FreeBSD. Many ISPs also use OSS. Providers tend to host as many sites on one machine to cut costs. These examples are indicative of the overall picture of the industry.

Web Server OS Market

GNU/Linux is the number two serving OS on the Internet[19]

Web Server Market

This phenomenon of real life product comparison is visible in the web server market as well. In reality, the most 'popular' web server has always been an open source product. Netcraft's surveys find that Apache currently has twice the market share of the #2 product. Before Apache (prior to 1996), NCSA was the most popular product. (09/02)

Platform	Market share
Apache	66.04%
Microsoft	24.18%

Public Sector Beneficiaries

Many public/government bodies have explored the possibilities/benefits of OSS. This phenomenon seems to have been concentrated in Europe and in Asia. A recent New York Times article reported that, "more than two dozen countries in Asia, Europe and Latin America include china and Germany, encouraging government agencies to use open source software — developed by communities of programmers who distribute the code without charge and donate their labor cooperatively debug, modify and otherwise improve the software." The following organizations have all explored/implemented Open Software in their mission: [20]

1. National Health Service of the United Kingdom
2. United Nations Food and Agriculture Organization
3. International Atomic Energy Agency
4. Canada has used OSS in the public Health service sector
5. Germany signed a deal with IBM via the country's Interior Minister, to use OSS to cut costs, lower dependence on a single vendor, and improve the nations' network security
6. The US consumer Project on Technology (lead by Ralph Nadir) gives reasons that the US government should support future OSS support
7. In addition, the governments of Peru, the UK, South Africa and Taiwan have expresses an interest in OS development
8. The German Ministry of the Interior forged a deal with IBM to standardize the German government on Linux and open source IT
9. China's post office runs on the platform; so too do France's culture, defense and education ministries[21] [2223]
10. A European FLOSS study found that in Europe, Open Source software is utilized by:

   43.7 % - German establishments
   31.5 % - British 17.7% Swedish
   The study claimed that the OSS rates in public sector were above average.[24]

MILITARY OSS APPLICATION

Military and intelligence agencies in North America, Europe and Asia — including the U.S., Canada, Germany, France, England, Spain, China and Singapore — have invested in Linux systems. MITRE Corporation has done research in OSS in a military context. "A Business Case Study of Open Source Software," advocates OSS applicability in government software. In this paper, researchers claim that: "OSS encourages significant software development and code re-use, can provide important economic benefits, and has the potential for especially large direct and indirect cost savings for military systems that require large deployments of costly software products." [25]

1. In a separate report issued by MITRE for the DOD Information System (DISA) concluded that the abolishment of OSS would have "immediate, broad and strongly negative impacts on the ability of many sensitive and security-focused DoD groups to defend against cyber attacks." This report also claimed that the use of OSS in the Department of Defense is "widespread and should be expanded." [26]

2. The OSPR (Open Source Prototype Research) project aimed to analyze the performance of OSS in technical on site tests. The project conclusion claims:
   "Open Source Software development is a paradigm shift and has enormous potential for addressing government needs. Substantial technology leverage and cost savings can be achieved with this approach...." [27]

4. The paper "Open Source and These United States" by C. Justin Seiferth argues that open software may signify advantages in the US Department Defense. Seiferth claims that: "The Department of Defense can realize significant gains by the formal adoption, support and use of open licensed systems. We can lower costs and improve the quality of our systems and the speed at which they are developed...[and] increase interoperability among our own systems and those of our Allies."[28]

PROJECT MANAGEMENT: CENTRALIZATION

I do believe that the long-term plan for productive open projects must include structure and organization. There should be a clearly identified central management team overseeing the project. With the benefit of many minds comes the opportunity for chaos. I don't see communication or group collaboration, as issues due to the fact OSS communities have had to collaborate using the Internet since the beginning. These communities have had to engineer effective communication models, and succeed in-group decision-making. I do feel that the issue of standardization could help streamline the development cycle for large/public projects. I would stress that it is important that this standardization cannot impede the creativity of production.

REALISM

When one considers the amount of effort that must go into large software projects, he/she will see that the monetary and time investments are substantial. The end result is that OSS projects get the job done faster, cheaper and more efficiently. For example, Red Hat Linux 7.1 contains over 30 million lines of source code. This effort represents an estimated 8,000 years of programming time and over one billion dollars. The release of Windows XP is also approximately 30 million lines of source code.[29]

REFERENCES

[1] Abort, Retry, Fail? A weblog on technology and software development. ON OPEN SOURCE. October 28, 2002. www.dynamicobjects.com/~diego/weblogs/arf/archives/

[2] Open Source Software

[3] www.opensource.org/advocacy/case_for_business.php Open Source Case for Business

[4] Wheeler, David A. Why Open Source Software / Free Software (OSS/FS)? Look at the Numbers! December 5, 2002. www.dwheeler.com/oss_NFS_why.html

[5] Wheeler, David A. Why Open Source Software / Free Software (OSS/FS)? Look at the Numbers! December 5, 2002. www.dwheeler.com/oss_NFS_why.html

[6] Wheeler, David A. Why Open Source Software / Free Software (OSS/FS)? Look at the Numbers! December 5, 2002. www.dwheeler.com/oss_NFS_why.html

[7] ukonline Cabinent office , open source software, draft for public consultation 10/12/01 europa.eu.int/comm/information society/eeurope/documentation/index en.htm. www.govtalk.gov.ulk/library

[8] OSDN Open Source Development Network. SourceForge.net: Software Map – Medical Science Applications. http://sourceforge.net/softwaremap/trove_list.php?cat=266. 2002.

[9] omnigene.sourceforge.net

[10] Bioinformatics Open Source Conference. Talk Abstracts. Jason Stajich duke University

[11] SBaGen Binaural Brain Wave Experimenter; www.uazu.net/sbagen/

[12] OSDN Open Source Development Network. SourceForge.net: Software Map. http://sourceforge.net/softwaremap/trove_list.php. 2002.

[13] Open source.org. Open Source Case for Business.http://www.opensource.org/advocacy/case_for_business.php.12/6/02.

[14] Minoru Corp. Open source goes mainstream. www.minoru-development.com/en/opensource.html

[15] opensource.org. "The Open Source Initiative–Products." www.opensource.org.ac.uk/mirrors/www.opensource.org/docs/products.html

[16] Minoru Corp. Open source goes mainstream. www.minoru-development.com/en/opensource.html

[17] opensource.org. "The Open Source Initiative–Products." www.opensource.org.ac.uk/mirrors/www.opensource.org/docs/products.html

[18] opensource.org. "The Open Source Initiative–Products." www.opensource.org.ac.uk/mirrors/www.opensource.org/docs/products.html

[19] Wheeler, David A. Why Open Source Software / Free Software (OSS/FS)? Look at the Numbers! December 5, 2002. www.dwheeler.com/oss_NFS_why.html

[20] Minoru Corp. Educational Services and Seminars. www.minoru-development.com/en/products.html

[21] National Advisory Council on Innovation: Open Software Working Group. "Open Software & Open Standards in South Africa". January 2002.

[22] Weiss, Todd. Chrysler adopts Linux for Vehicle Crash Testing. October 21, 2002. Computer World. http://www.computerworld.com/softwaretopics/os/linux/story/0,10801,75294,00.html

[23] http://www.aspnews.com/news/article/0,,4191_1276831,00.html

[24] Wheeler, David A. Why Open Source Software / Free Software (OSS/FS)? Look at the Numbers! December 5, 2002. www.dwheeler.com/oss_NFS_why.html

[25] MITRE corp. A Business Case Study of Open Source Software. http://www.mitre.org/support/papers/tech_papers_01/kenwood_software/kenwood_software.pdf. July 2001.

[26] Mitre Corp. "Use of Free and Open-Source Software (FOSS) in the US Department of Defense. http://www.egovos.org/pdf/dodfoss.pdf. 2002.

[27] OSSIM. OSPR Report. http://ossim.org/documentation/ospr.html. 05/03/02

[28] C. Justin Seiferth. "Open Source and these United States." http://skyscraper.fortunecity.com/mondo/841/documents/99-184.html

[29] Wheeler, David A. Why Open Source Software / Free Software (OSS/FS)? Look at the Numbers! December 5, 2002. www.dwheeler.com/oss_NFS_why.html

Wireless Cryptographic Systems

Amanda Dambrouckas

Bay Path College/Rensselaer University/Stanpak Systems

53 Lakeview Hgts., Tolland, CT 06084

(870) 871-6547, amanda@stanpak.com

The science of cryptology has been the center of research projects for decades. As we know, the explosion of sophisticated mobile devices is a much more recent event. Now, we are facing the task of fusing these two technologies to implement secure mobile communications. As we will see, there are many constraints to implementing secure encryption for wireless devices. While many of these issues lie in the area of hardware capabilities, we must consider the public transmission medium used in these networks. Despite these obstacles, I do believe that we can have working, secure encryption for mobile devices in the near future. I think that this task can be solved via communal development and testing, new calculation methods, processing/storage efficiency, and forethought.

FORETHOUGHT

Corporations tend to get overly anxious when preparing to release a new product. This often leads to situations in which security is left to an afterthought (or even worse, seen in hindsight). This is especially common in the tech industry where it is essential to be the first, and the newest innovator. Due to the types of information that we are using wireless technology to transmit/store (e-cash, stock quotes, mail, conversation, account access), we must pay special attention to information security.

A developer and consultant for the US Department of Justice described the Internet surge in late 90's as having only security as an afterthought. She explained that security should be "woven into entire lifecycle." She pointed out that right now, wireless transmissions are not as fast as wired communication. This causes wireless networks to be less attractive targets for hackers. If we wish to enjoy improved mobile technologies, we will have to concentrate on security in order to counteract attacks. [1]

It may seem ironic that encryption algorithms are publicly available. However, not only is the publication of encryption algorithms independent from security, it drives extensive testing and validation of a cryptographic process. The more access cryptanalysts have to these algorithms, the more they can attempt to surpass them. As we have learned from open source projects, more minds yield superior accomplishments. Any person who requires validation of this fact will find proof in the recent advent of AES. The Advanced Encryption Standard was made possible via the efforts of many researchers who shared information and worked collectively to produce the technology.

What does matter in terms of security of cryptographic processes is the key. If the key is private, and it is impossible to fabricate key generation, the algorithm can be publicly available. In fact, experienced cryptographers make the assumption that cryptanalysts will have access to algorithms when designing encryption processes. My theory is that we can improve wireless security practices by concentrating on encryption keys rather than the overall crypto processing. We already have well known blueprints for encryption in wired environments. Now, we can modify these existing methods by replacing tools within the process and customizing for the wireless arena.

Cryptography is a science that offers us humans two main benefits. The first is the ability to conceal the meaning of messages. Second, cryptography allows us to authenticate parties. Wired encryption can only give us message security during storage and transmission. We will see that there are ways in which we can implement ad-hoc network encryption during processing as well.

THE WIRELESS ARENA

When we consider the technological implications of wireless connectivity, we must realize that there are effects on encryption. The process of signal interpretation processing and communications can be encrypted in addition to the usual states of storage and communication. As there are always drawbacks associated with capabilities, the open-air transmission achieved in wireless environments creates more opportunity for interception than we see in wired networks. These added points of possible attack increase the opportunities for malicious eavesdroppers to gain knowledge of the key, and/or message.

WLANS

In order to truly understand the complications of security, and thus the cryptography implemented in wireless settings, we should understand how the environmental architecture differs from that seen in wired networks. A standard (IEEE802.11) WLAN contains a set of radio transceivers, various clients (PCs, workstations, printers, PDAs), access points and other equipment. The base stations (access points) act similarly to the wired bridge, connecting network segments. One of these segments may be a wired LAN, via which the WLAN obtains Internet access.

What makes wireless transmissions vulnerable to security breaches is the medium of transmission. Rather than constraining packets within a protected wire, mobile devices transport packets over untrusted/public mediums. These may include radio frequencies. This leaves the possibility for eavesdroppers to listen to transmissions, simply because the communications take place over a public medium. This point exemplifies the importance of cryptography in wireless settings. We must have some way to conceal data when the transmission channel provides no security. Theoretically, we should feel confident transmitting confidential information over insecure mediums if we know that the information is unintelligible.

WIRELESS ENCRYPTION EQUIPMENT

We can approach the task of implementing strong wireless cryptography with a specialized toolset. Our tools work with keys, rather than with the cryptographic process. We can replace symmetric and asymmetric tools that are in place inside wireless networks. In this toolset, we can include ECC where RSA is currently in place. We can use Rjindael in place of DES and WTLS in place of SSL.

Tool Table *(Example)*

Old Tool	New Tool
MD5	*SHA1*
RSA	*ECC*
DES and RC4	*RJINDAEL*
SSL	*WTLS*

REAL ENCRYPTION

There are two primary variants of cipher text generation. These entail symmetrical (single shared key) and asymmetrical (two different yet related keys) encryption. We can refer to an encryption algorithm as being "strong" when the possible number of keys makes a brute force attack unreasonable. We must note the "unreasonable" element in this determination is derived from available processing power, not from human capabilities. Even the long standard DES algorithm has seen the last of its days as a "strong" algorithm. This is because of the fact that the 70 quadrillion possible keys (56bit) are no match for current (and future) processing power. [2]

NEW TOOLS

1. (Symmetric tool) Rjindael is a symmetrical cryptographic technique that gives implementers of the algorithm a great deal of flexibility. Rijndael has been implemented in various dedicated hardware environments, and in smart cards. [3]

2. (Symmetric tool) TDEA (Triple Data Encryption Algorithm) key consists of two or three distinct DES keys. The initial plaintext message is encrypted three times using these keys and the standard DEA/DES logic. This is more secure than its DES ancestor.

3. (Asymmetric tool) Elliptic Curve Cryptosystem (ECC) addresses the issues of processing, storage, and bandwidth limitations faced in wireless devices. This is important because wireless devices tend to provide relatively low memory, processing and storage capabilities. This makes ECC a hopeful method in which to implement secure cryptography (signatures or entire messages) in smart cards, PDAs, ATM machines, remote access systems, electronic cash, and cellular phones.[4]

4. (SHA1). The SHA algorithm produces a fixed length digest, regardless of the plain text message that is input into the function. The length of input is always equal to 2^{64} bits, and the resulting digest is 160 bits in length. The message digest is unique for the initial message; that is, no two messages will produce identical hash values. The "Secure" in Secure Hashing Algorithms is due in part to the fact that the logic is designed to prohibit the generation of plain text messages from the message digest.

WIRELESS SOLUTIONS: FOCAL POINTS

I believe that the keys (no pun intended) to successful and practical wireless encryption methods fall into two main categories. Specifically, realistic wireless encryption must be computationally efficient, and require minimal storage capacity. Techniques including hashing algorithms such as SHA-1 and mathematical methods can be of aid to wireless security engineers. These topics address two primary complications of wireless communications, namely processing/bandwidth capabilities and storage capacity.

1. *Mathematics*

We can overcome many of the limitations imposed by wireless device capabilities through the implementation of mathematical routines that best fit the wireless environment.

ECC offers us an alternative method for public key, and for digital signature generation. ECC systems implement a variant of DLP (Discrete Logarithm Problem) using groups of points on elliptical curves. These points are used in formulas to determine the private/public key relationship.

ECC is able to provide a high level of security to these devices without creating unreasonable computational overhead.

This is vital for resource restrained wireless hardware.

A study of ECC efficiency concluded that RSA and DSA would need a 1024 bit key while ECC needed only a 160bit key to perform strong encryption. Furthermore, we can significantly increase the security provided using ECC in small key size increments.

Key Size Equivalency Table

RSA	ECC
1024	160
2048	210[5]

Implementation
a) 3com's palm computing division (palm VII)
b) Motions's Blackberry pager[6]

All of these facts lead one expert to say: "You will start to see people adopt ECC as an option, after it's a pretty common option, it will start to become the default."[7]

2. *Hashing Algorithms*

Hashing algorithms reduce the size of the data that must be transmitted in enciphering routines. This reduces the burden on bandwidth. Message digests produced via hashing reduce the computation time/resources required for mobile devices to perform private key signing and public key authentication. This becomes especially important when we consider public key encryption, which is inherently slower than private key encryption (yet ever so common in e-commerce).

The message summary is a compressed "image" of the original message. It is far faster to perform encryption operations on these summaries than it is to encrypt entire messages. From a security standpoint, hashing algorithms such as SHA-1 are very attractive, due to the fact that they operate in a uniform direction.

Implementation

SHA-1 has already found a niche in the arena of wireless encryption services. HORNET is an efficient stream cipher that implements the SHA-1 algorithm in key generation and has been implemented in ASICs for wireless phones.

HORNET family routines have been implemented to form impressive security measures when teamed with ECC mathematical routines and the Rjindael encryption algorithm.

There are no documented cases of breaches in SHA-1 security. The two most likely attack methods have both failed to break SHA digests. [8]

OLD TOOLS

1. *(Symmetric tool) DES*

DES takes 64 bits of plain text and transforms them into a different 64 bits. The transformed bits comprise the cipher text. First, the Initial Permutation (IP) is applied to the 64bits of plain text to be encrypted. The initial 64 bits of plain text are simply rearranged.

The Problem

Today, it is far too easy for diligent hackers to break 56 bit keys. We simply cannot rely on this level of security for anything more than trivial transmissions. This is where the ECC alternative shines.

2. *WEP*

The Wired Equivalent Protocol WEP (is a security standard used in WLAN environments. WEP implements symmetric keys and is configurable on an 802.11 network.

The Problem

The secret key for WEP implementations ranges from 40-128 bits, and is generally physically typed into the hardware device. This stored key is retained for continued use. Due to the fact that each mobile device associated with a WEP WLAN uses the same key, if one device is compromised then all devices must alter their keys. [9]

CASES FOR IMPROVEMENT

We can examine many cases in which we can improve wireless security. Most of the weak points in these scenarios are obvious or explained below. We can look to our tool table and replace the 'old tools' with the 'new tools' for our new wireless environments.

1. *Bluetooth*

Bluetooth is an inexpensive, short-range radio link for mobile devices within WANs. Cryptography in Bluetooth communications is performed symmetrically with SAFER+ (block cipher) and E0 (stream cipher). *The Problem*

SAFER+ keys cannot exceed 128bits, which has been proven insecure in WEP. The E0 cipher also users a 128bit (max) key, and is quite vulnerable to divide and conquer attacks. "Bluetooth is simply scrambled, spreading its data over numerous different spectrums, rather than encrypted in complex algorithms."[10] This leaves privacy/integrity to a game rather than a dependable method of information security.

Experts have identified four main areas of concern in Bluetooth technology:[11]

Device address discovery — authenticate device, not user.
Key management — transmission in plain text
Pin code attacks — could fix with public key crypto (ECC)
No user authentication — could fix with robust symmetric ciphers Rjindael

2. *VPNs*

The IPSEC Protocol is an addition to the standard IP protocol, intended to provide security and privacy for TCP/IP sessions. IPSEC is the most widely used protocol for VPNs. Virtual Private Networks are implemented today in many wireless (and wired) networks in order to fill in for the loopholes of WEP. [12]

Current	*Replacement*
1. Key exchange is handled via RSA or D-H	1. ECC
2. Session protection is delegated to DES or triple DES (3DES)	2. Rijandael
3. HMAC-MD5 algorithms provide data integrity	3. SHA-1

3. WLANS

The core of WEP logic lies in RC4, a stream cipher symmetric key algorithm. Developers chose this algorithm due to the fact that it was inexpensive to license, and relatively easy to implement. Today, RC4 is not the state of the art encryption algorithm that it once was, but it is still regarded as reasonably secure. RC4 uses a variable length key (1-256 bytes). A psuedo random stream is generated and XORed with the plain message text. Due to export restrictions, the RC4 key is often limited to 40 bits. However, the algorithm can utilize keys from any length between 1 and 2048 bits.

The Problem

Berkley researchers discovered that WEP could be compromised via passive attack strategies. The researchers discovered that a 128-bit WEP key could be recovered using such an attack. This is quite indicative of the amount of processing power that is available to the public today. A 128-bit key generated with high entropy can pose a possible 3.4028236692e38 keys for crackers.

One of the major reasons that the Wired Equivalent Privacy technique faulted was the use of RC4 for multiple WLAN functions. Specifically, the RC4 stream cipher was used for both the authentication and privacy functionality. RC4 warns never to use identical key material repeatedly, because it is a simple XOR stream cipher. [13]

Current	Replacement
RC4 (authentication)	Rijandael/RC5
RC4 (privacy)	Rijandael/RC5

CONCLUSION

We have seen that there are solutions available to implement wireless security. I think that we will see a pattern of public attitude modification, in the area of confidence in ad-hoc technologies. Just as the number of consumers willing to participate in wired e-commerce has grown, I believe that the number of wireless financial transactions will increase. Hopefully, efficient encryption designs will aid in this process. We have discussed several techniques that show great potential in reaching this goal. In my analysis, these methods tend to fall into the computational and hashing/compression paths. In any case, I think that we can indeed have truly secure ad-hoc networks in the near future. The outcome of this project will depend on communal development/testing, and in exploring new tools and techniques.

ENDNOTES

[1] Gaudin Sharon. "Wireless security lesson to learn." Bluetooth IT management. www.earthweb.com/secu/article.php 10/22/02

[2] US Department of Commerce and The National Institute of Standards and Technology. Data Encryption Standard (DES).

[3] Daemen, Rijmen. Proton World & COSIC. "Rijndael: Vincent meets Joan." ProtonWorld, NISSC 2000. October 23, 2000.

[4] Certicom. The Elliptic Curve Cryptosystem: Current Public-Key Cryptographic Systems. July 2000.

[5] Ntru Press Room. Fastest, Smallest Security Toolkit for Palm. 3G Strategies for operators. Issue 5.

[6] Lee, Tom. The Industrial Physicist. The American Institute of Physics. August 2000.

[7] IBM Developerworks. What's what in wireless surveying the wireless landscape victor marks software engineer. IBM May 2001.

[8] IBM schedules TeleHubLInk's wireless encryption microchip for manufacturing. www.semiconductorfabtech.com/sit-global/news

[9] Nichols, Lekkas. Wireless Security Models, Threats, and Solutions. McGraw Hill TELELCOM. 2002. 226-241.

[10] Nichols, Lekkas. Wireless Security Models, Threats, and Solutions. McGraw Hill TELELCOM. 2002. 415.

[11] Nichols, Lekkas. Wireless Security Models, Threats, and Solutions. McGraw Hill TELELCOM. 2002. 415.

[12] Cisco Technologies Documentation. IPSec Network Security. www.cisco.com/univercd/cc/td/doc

[13] Nichols, Lekkas. Wireless Security Models, Threats, and Solutions. McGraw Hill TELELCOM. 2002. 415.

A B2C Development Model for Electronic Commerce in Less Developed Countries: The Peruvian Case

Antonio Díaz-Andrade

Escuela de Administración de Negocios para Graduados

P.O. Box 1846, Lima 100, Perú

T: +(511) 317-7200, F: +(511) 345-1328, adiaz@esan.edu.pe

INTRODUCTION

Despite the sudden fall of the NASDAQ composite index in April 2000, drawn by the collapse of the–until then–promising dotcoms, UNCTAD foresees information and communication technologies (ICTs), especially the Internet, will continue driving international economic growth (World Trade, 2002). In this sense, ICTs and e-commerce emerge as the tool to expanding corporate and country competitiveness and improving their people's living standards (UNCTAD, 2002). In the US, 30% of total economic growth has been attributed to ICTs (Schlögl, 2001).

Nevertheless, unequal growth of the Internet, in particular, and ICT, as a whole, across the world's social groups in the last decade has created the so called digital divide (Norris, 2001) that threatens less developed countries.

OBJECTIVE

This research paper explores a business to consumer (B2C) e-commerce development model for less developed countries. Evidence is presented from a survey on e-commerce in Peru.

METHODOLOGY

A wall-to-wall review of the literature on e-commerce in less developed countries led to identifying three sectors involved in developing e-commerce in Peru. Semi-structured interviews were conducted separately with e-commerce policy and regulation makers, Internet Service Providers (ISPs) and managers and executive officers of companies involved in e-commerce.

Analysis of results identified shared traits to outline a development model for e-commerce in developing countries. *A priori* the model was proposed to consider the condition of the national technological infrastructure, penetration of mediums of payments, the logistics of goods' distribution, and on line shopping culture in Peru.

CONCEPTUAL FRAMEWORK

Created in 1969 as a network for military and academic use, the Internet later evolved into a commercial application that brought among other developments the unforeseen spread of electronic mail. Since the invention of web browsing in 1993 it has been possible to carry a wide range of message types over the web including photos, text, video and audio (Westland & Clarke, 1999). Later, the first web-based transactions started.

E-commerce is defined as "the purchase and sale of goods through digital means, specifically […] the web that allows the restructuring of businesses, markets and provides a competitive advantage" (Kalakota & Robinson, 1999: 23). Three major forces explain the development of e-commerce: digitalization, or more powerful computers and wider bandwidth available at increasingly lower prices; globalization that makes the world an ever smaller place but an increasingly larger market; and deregulation, driven by the perception that free markets are the best resource allocators (Arroyo, Herrera, Temoche, Vilches & Whittembury, 2001). These three forces suffice to change the value chain of any business, regardless of its size.

An 'e-business' uses information technology, specially real time networks for its transactions. E-companies are not only to those selling products on line, but more broadly those resorting to networking technologies in production, supply chains, marketing, and sales and customer care automation (Choi & Whinston, 2000).

The way companies use the web may make the difference between failure and success. According to Porter (2001) the sources of their competitive edge have remained invariable. Although the way Internet technology is integrated into their business strategy may be key in strengthening the roots of their competitive advantages, it cannot replace them. Electronic commerce is definitely one way to do business (Borenstein & Saloner, 2001), although it modifies the way business creates value; "time to market , innovation and quality have become requirements for the survival of organizations" (Westland & Clarke, 1999: 53). We are now able to exchange and spread data anywhere around the globe at a negligible cost, giving business the opportunity to create alliances and to distribute information without the traditional burdens imposed by geography (Lekse & Olivas-Luján, 2001). Although in the short term developed country businesses may derive the greatest benefit, as time passes businesses from less developed countries may reap the greatest advantages as they leapfrog many stages of the developed nations' long learning curve (Panagariya, 2000).

Moreover, the performance of 'e-business' companies will be reflected on states through improved tax collection or greater job creation, an outcome that demands consideration. Some authors hold e-commerce may help to substantially improve country competitiveness (Sprano & Zakak, 2000); from there the need for states to take the relevant actions to overcome the burdens of deficient education and poor technological infrastructure common to less developed countries, in order to make them more competitive in the global scene. Governments' role is to refit regulations not only to not obstruct, but to promote e-commerce, specially taking into account that more often than not governments are the main consumers in many countries.

Finally, Internet Service Providers (ISPs) have a major responsibility in developing e-commerce given that their service offering ranges from hardware and software through network access thus making them indispensable for the existence of 'e-business' companies.

E-COMMERCE IN PERU

Business communities in less developed countries must overcome major roadblocks to growth within their domestic markets and to access international markets. The number of companies that do on line business in Peru is still minuscule; even if 96% of the 2000 largest companies have an Internet connections, and only 50% have a website. Scarcely 18% do electronic business transactions of which 88% are B2B transactions[1] and 38% are B2C business (Apoyo, 2001, as cited in Telefónica, 2002). Besides, just five companies account for 90% of all on line retail transactions[2] (E. San Román, speech, November 21, 2002).

In order to develop electronic business three elements are necessary: Internet access, availability of payment mediums and, for tangible goods, the

Figure 1. Building blocks for e-business

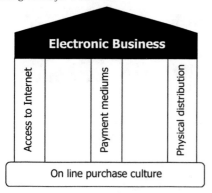

physical distribution of products (Mann, 2000), all of them supported by a culture of on line purchases. Figure 1 shows the proposed model for developing electronic business.

Internet Access

Peru's information and communications technology (ICT) infrastructure is weak as shown in Table 1. However, the figures also show that the ratio of Internet users to either the number of fixed or mobile telephone lines, the number of personal computers or the number of hosts, is very high compared to other countries. This is explained by the phenomenon of access to Internet through Internet kiosks, a business model developed in the mid-90s by the Red Científica Peruana ISP. From 580 Internet kiosks in December 1999, Peru went to 1,740 in June 2001 and the figure is growing; currently Peru ranks 13 among countries with the higher rates of public access to Internet (Harvard University, 2001, as cited in Telefónica, 2002).

Means of Payment

Scarce Internet-based payments means continue to hamper the expansion of electronic business in Peru. Bank penetration is extremely low as is the number of credit card holders compared to more developed countries. At the end of 2001, only 24.96% of GDP went through Peruvian banks (ASBANC, 2002) and even as recently as 2000, only 9% of households in Lima, the capital city and Peru's largest and more developed city, held a credit card (INEI, 2000). Some local banks have created Internet-only purchase cards, such as the viaBCP card of Banco de Crédito del Perú (www.viabcp.com) and the NETACTIVA24 card of Interbank (www.interbank.com.pe), both linked to savings accounts. Banco Wiese Sudameris (www.wiese.com.pe) launched the Pagum MasterCard that does not require a link to a bank account. ViaBCP card is the most accepted of these, probably because Banco de Crédito del Perú is the largest bank in the country, has the largest number of clients, and conducts intensive promotion campaigns. Still there are only some 27,000 ViaBCP card users who buy US$ 350.00 a month; 97% of these transactions are carried out with foreign establishments (R. Dasso, speech, November 21, 2002).

Table 1: Main ICT indicators (for every 100 people)

Countries	Fixed telephones	Mobile telephones	Personal computers	Internet users	Hosts (per 1000 people)
United States	66.5	44.4	62.3	34.6	292.8
European Union	57.5	60.5	24.4	38.0	75.0
Scandinavian countries	65.0+	66.0+	60.0+	50.0+	100.0
Argentina	21.6	18.6	5.3	5.3	12.4
Brazil	21.8	16.7	6.3	3.5	9.5
Chile	23.9	34.0	8.4	11.8	7.9
Colombia	17.1	7.6	4.2	1.7	1.3
Mexico	13.7	21.7	6.9	2.3	9.1
Peru	7.6	5.9	4.8	12.0	0.5
Uruguay	28.3	15.5	11.0	11.1	21.1
Venezuela	11.2	26.4	5.3	5.0	0.9

Source: ITU, CIA, CyberAtlas, INEI, OSIPTEL
Prepared by the author

Besides scarce payment means, the diversity of payment channels also poses a problem. Many bank and business credit cards have created proprietary payment infrastructures, further hampering operations. Some companies allow the buyer to pay in cash on delivery of the purchased goods; however, this option requires prior certification in order to avoid transaction repudiation and the subsequent delivery expenditures for returned merchandise.

Physical Distribution

Peruvian on line companies mostly outsource the physical distribution of tangible goods. Delivery rates are based mainly on the distance from the distribution hub to the address of delivery indicated by the buyer. Most e-commerces are located in Lima, and goods are rarely delivered to the provinces of the interior as delivery expenses would be prohibitively high. Some business have started opening stores in cities around Peru to simplify distribution of orders by merging on-line and off-line operations.

Little progress has been made in terms of electronic commerce as a channel for export sales. An assessment is still required of Peru's potential for Internet-based export sales and the most appropriate business model. Some Peruvian e-businesses have successfully developed sales abroad for locally-distributed goods (Santana & Díaz, 2002).

On Line Purchase Culture

In contrast to more developed countries, catalog shopping in Peru is not widespread. Internet shopping arrived with a public unfamiliar with remote purchase selection and ordering. Lima users asked about their personal use of the Internet mentioned from e-mail through video downloading but failed to include web-based shopping among their Internet practices (Telefónica, 2002).

Another study to determine Internet user profiles in Lima found that only 4% of users who access the web at Internet kiosks (more than 70% of all users) had bought by Internet once, compared to 15% of those who access the web from their homes (9% of the total) and 13% of those who join the web from work or school (17% of the total). These figures reveal 92% of users have never carried out an Internet-based purchase. Among users never having shopped on the web, 18% cite lack of confidence as 38% think this channel is unsafe (Apoyo, 2002, as cited in Telefónica, 2002).

National administrations must contribute to creating an environment of confidence that will induce economic agents to develop on line business, including a regulatory environment providing enhanced transaction security (Goldstein & O'Connor, 2001). Peru's legal system is however a tangle of complex regulations shown in Appendix A. Most of them have only been recently enacted and some experts even suggest that regulations may have moved faster than on line commercial practices in Peru.

DISCUSSION

As Kirkman and Sachs (2001) say, to benefit effectively from the advantages offered by information technologies, electronic commerce included, a determined political will from the state and adequate business leadership are needed.

Government regulations enacted in Peru for privatizing telecommunications services, promoting these services in rural zones, the projected use of information technology in education through the Huascarán Program (www.huascaran.gob.pe)-the government's IT project-forums on the information society organized by the government and the norms which to promote Internet use as a commercial toll all signal the political will to promote the information society where electronic commerce is an important component.

Moreover, the will of private business to become major players in the moving to the Internet world, on line business initiatives already underway, including electronic banking and Internet purchase cards, the proposed Puyhuán Plan to create a sustainable development model for rural areas supported by greater IT use (www.setinedic.edu.pe/proyectoPuyhuan/modeloplan.htm) and the increasing number of Internet kiosks, among others.

Although Peruvians show interest in accessing information technologies, doubts linger on the convenience of using the web as a channel for their commercial transactions Hopefully, the multiplier effect of initiatives mentioned in the foregoing paragraphs may increase consumer comfort with and confidence in transacting from a computer.

Given the particular present conditions in a less developed country like Peru where economic inequalities and a notorious digital gap subsist, it is not likely that an e-commerce model similar to that of developed countries will succeed. In those countries, Internet access and payment means are widespread, as well as adequate physical distribution services, while growth builds on a tradition of catalog shopping.

In Peru, an already large and still growing network of Internet kiosks could serve not only as a way to access the web but also as payment centers for on line orders. The Peruvian government is already planning to turn Internet kiosk managers into fee collectors for on line government services to citizens, with an undeniable impact on developing e-commerce. Business could likewise enter into agreements with select authorized Internet kiosks for collecting revenues from goods and services commercialized on line. These Internet kiosk owners would benefit from an edge against strong competition which prevents them to generate surpluses to make their business profitable in the long term while business which trade on the web would be able to offer an additional purchase channel to clients and so reach new markets.

In this on line work scheme, logistic operators may increase their now reduced volume of operations, and thus cut distribution costs. Internet services providers should be prepared to meet the need for enhanced connectivity and may find it interesting to expand their service network to cover larger geographic coverage where they identify a market opportunity.

ENDNOTES

[1] Mining companies and their suppliers account for the greatest volume of B2B transactions in Peru.

[2] E. Wong Supermarket (www.ewong.com), virtual store and travel agency on web-based information service peru.com (www.peru.com), Rosatel florist (www.rosatel.com), SAGA-Falabella department store (www.sagafalabella.com.pe), and virtual store of the El Comercio Newspaper portal (www.ec-store.com).

REFERENCES

Arroyo, J.A., Herrera, G.A., Temoche, L.F., Vilches, F.J. & Whittembury, J.T. (2001). *Transición de las empresas peruanas hacia el comercio electrónico*. Lima, Peru: ESAN.

ASBANC-Asociación de Bancos del Perú. (2002). Retrieved October 15, 2002 from http://www.elcomercioperu.com.pe/Texto/Html/2002-09-26/Econom4683.html.

Borenstein, S. & Saloner, G. (2001). Economics and Electronic Commerce. *Journal of Economic Perspectives, 15*(1), 3-12.

Choi, S.Y. & Whinston, A.B. (2000). *The Internet Economy: Technology and Practice*. Austin, TX: SmartEcon Publishing.

Goldstein, A. & O'Connor, D. (2001, January). Navigating between Scylla and Charybdis. *OECD Observer, 224*, 72-74.

INEI. (2000). *Tecnologías de Información y Comunicaciones en los Hogares en Lima Metropolitana*. Lima: Instituto Nacional de Estadística e Informática.

Kalakota, R. & Robinson, M. (1999). *E-Business Roadmap for Success*. Reading: Addison-Wesley.

Kirkman, G. & Sachs, J. (2001, January-February). Subtract the Divide. *World Link*, 60-65.

Lekse, W.J. & Olivas-Luján, M.R. (2001, August-September). Getting Firms in Developing Countries on the E-Commerce Highway. *International Journal of e-Business Strategy Management, 3*(1), 45-53.

Mann, C.L. (2000). Electronic Commerce in Developing Countries: Issues for Domestic Policy and WTO Negotiations. Retrieved July 23, 2002, from http://www.iie.com/CATALOG/WP/2000/00-3.pdf.

Norris, P. (2001). *Digital Divide? Civic Engagement, Information Poverty, and the Internet Worldwide*. Cambridge: Cambridge University Press.

Panagariya, A. (2000). E-Commerce, WTO and Developing Countries. *World Economy, 23*(8), 959-978.

Porter, M.E. (2001, March). Strategy and the Internet. *Harvard Business Review, 9*(3), 63-78.

Santana, M. & Díaz, A. (2002). Inca Foods: Reaching New Customers Worldwide. In M. Raisinghani (Ed.), *Cases on Worldwide e-Commerce: Theory in Action*. Hershey, PA: Idea Group Publishing.

Schlögl, H. (2001, January). Digital lessons for digital policies. *OECD Observer, 224*, 41-42.

Sprano, E. & Zakak, A. (2000). E-Commerce Capable: Competitive Advantage for Countries in the New World E-Conomy. *Competitiveness Review, 10*(2), 114-122.

Telefónica del Perú. (2002). *La sociedad de la información en el Perú: Presente y perspectivas 2003-2005*. Lima: Servicios Editoriales del Perú.

UNCTAD-United Nations Conference on Trade and Development. (2002). E-Commerce and Development Report. Internet version prepared by UNCTAD Secretariat. Retrieved December 4, 2002 from: http://r0.unctad.org/ecommerce/docs/edr02_en/ecdr02.pdf.

Westland, J.C. & Clarke, T.H.K. (1999). *Global Electronic Commerce: Theory and Cases*. Cambridge: The MIT Press.

World Trade (2002, April). E-Commerce Yet to Improve Developing World. *World Trade, 15*(4), 14.

APPENDIX A: REGULATIONS GOVERNING TELECOMMUNICATIONS, IT AND E- COMMERCE

Legislative Decree N° 681	Regulates digital document archiving
Legislative Decree N° 702	Promotes private investment in telecommunications
Supreme Decree N° 013-93-TCC	Enacts the Telecommunications Act
Supreme Decree N° 011-94-TCC	Approves the concession contract between the Peruvian government, and ENTEL-Peru and CPTSA
Ministry Resolution N° 250-97-MTC	Approves the National Plan for of Bandwidth Allocation
Supreme Decree N° 020-98-MTC	Assigns OSIPTEL exclusive competence on interconnection of telecommunication services
Guidelines for free and fair competition	OSIPTEL decides against cases of abuse of dominant position and restrictive practices
Interconnection regulation	OSIPTEL regulates interconnection between businesses
Law N° 27291	Allows the use of electronic means to communicate declarations of will
Law N° 27309	Includes computer crime in the Criminal Code
Law N° 27419	Accepts serving notice by e-mail
Law N° 27269	Creates an infrastructure of digital certificates and signatures
Directive Council Resolution N° 015-2001-SC/OSIPTEL	Establishes the conditions to use Internet public services
Supreme Resolution N° 292-2001-RE	Gives INDECOPI the administration of Peru's domain name
Supreme Decree N° 66-2001-PCM	Defines outlines for Internet expansion
Ministry Resolution N° 266-2002-PCM	Creates e-Government Project Office
Regulations of Law N° 27269	Regulations pertaining to the law for digital signatures and certificates
Supreme Decree N° 67-2001-ED	Initiates Huascarán Program
Emergency Decree N° 67-2001	Creates the National Fund for the Use of New Information Technologies (FONDUNET)
Law N° 27806	Transparence and access to public information

Source: Various
Prepared by the author

Information Security Policies in Large Organisations: Developing a Conceptual Framework to Explore their Impact

Neil F. Doherty and Heather Fulford
The Business School, Loughborough University, Loughborough, UK,
T: + 44 (0) 1509 223128, F: + 44 (0) 1509 223960, n.f.doherty@lboro.ac.uk

ABSTRACT

Whilst the importance of the information security policy (ISP) is widely acknowledged in the academic literature, there has, to date, been little empirical analysis of its impact. To help fill this gap a study was initiated that sought to explore the relationship between the uptake, scope and dissemination of information security policies and the accompanying levels of security breaches. To this end a questionnaire was designed, validated and then targeted at IT managers within large organisations in the United Kingdom. The aim of this paper is to provide a progress report on this study by describing the objectives of the research and the design of the conceptual framework.

INTRODUCTION

It has been claimed that 'information is the lifeblood of the organisation' [CBI, 1992], as it is the critical element in strategic planning and decision-making, as well as day to day operational control. Consequently, organisations must make every effort to ensure that their information resources retain their accuracy, integrity and availability. However, the increasing integration of information systems both within and between organisations, when coupled with the growing value of corporate information resources, have made information security management a complex and challenging undertaking [Gerber et al., 2001]. Indeed, the high incidence of security breaches suggests that many organisations are failing to manage their information resources effectively [Angell, 1996; Gaston, 1996]. One increasingly important mechanism for protecting corporate information, and in so doing reducing the occurrence of security breaches, is through the formulation and application of an information security policy (ISP) [Hone & Eloff, 2002]. Gaston [1996; p. 175] defines an ISP as:

"broad guiding statements of goals to be achieved; significantly, they define and assign the responsibilities that various departments and individuals have in achieving policy goals."

Whilst the high incidence of security breaches and the importance of information security policies are both areas that have attracted significant attention in the literature, there is little evidence that these topics have been explicitly combined. To help fill this gap a research study was initiated that sought to empirically explore the relationship between the uptake and application of information security policies and the incidence of security breaches. The aim of this paper is to provide a progress report on this study by describing the objectives of the research and the design of the conceptual model. The remainder of this paper is organised into three sections: a discussion of the research objectives and method, a description of the conceptual framework, and the conclusions and recommendations for future research.

RESEARCH OBJECTIVE AND METHODS

The aim of this section is to describe the study's broad objective before reviewing the methods by which it is to be explored. Given the lack of empirical research in the area it was felt that an exploratory piece of work that em-braced a wide range of issues would be most appropriate. To this end the aim of the study was to explore how a variety of issues relating to the uptake and application of information security policies impacted upon the incidence of security breaches, within large organisations. This broad objective was ultimately broken down into a number of distinct research hypotheses, which are fully described in Section 3 and graphically presented in Figure 1.

To effectively explore the research hypotheses, it was necessary to develop a series of measures that, when incorporated into a questionnaire, would adequately describe an organisation's information security activity. To this end, the questionnaire was designed through an iterative process of review and refinement. It sought to capture a significant amount of information with regard to the respondent's organisation, in addition to the information required to explicitly address the six research hypotheses. The initial draft of the questionnaire was developed from a thorough review of the literature. The first phase of the 'review and refinement' process was accomplished through a series of pre-tests with four academics, each of whom had an interest in information security. The questionnaire was then modified accordingly before a further series of pre-tests was conducted with five IT practitioners. To complete the validation process a pilot study of 10% of the sampling frame was conducted. Together, these validation exercises resulted in a number of significant changes that greatly enhanced both the content and wording of the questionnaire, before the full survey was ultimately distributed.

In terms of the sampling frame, we wanted to target senior IT managers as these were most likely to be responsible for the formulation and application of an ISP. Moreover, only large organisations [firms employing more than 250 people] were targeted, as previous research has found that small firms tend to have few, if any, dedicated IT staff [Prembukar & King, 1992]. To this end, a list of the addresses of IT directors, from large UK-based organizations, was purchased from a commercial market research organization. Each of the sample of 2838 IT directors was mailed a questionnaire, with an accompanying letter, that explained the study, and a pre-paid envelope.

THE CONCEPTUAL FRAMEWORK

The aims of this section are to describe and justify the conceptual framework, discuss the proposed analysis strategy and then review the anticipated results and their importance.

It was anticipated that a number of distinct aspects of the ISP might influence the incidence of security breaches. Each of these was explicitly covered by the questionnaire and is described below:

- **The existence of a policy:** The questionnaire sought to determine whether the responding organisation had formulated a documented ISP. Consequently, this question was operationalised as a simple dichotomous variable. If the organisation did have a policy the following questions were also then asked.
- **The age of the policy:** If an ISP was in use, respondents were asked to specify the number of years that it had actively been in operation.
- **The updating of the policy:** Respondents were also asked to identify the frequency with which the policy was typically updated, using a five

point, ordinal scale [< every two years; every two years; every year; every six months; > every six months].

- **The dissemination of the policy:** Policies are of little use unless all employees are made aware of their rights and responsibilities, in relation to it. In addition to explicitly asking whether policies were disseminated via a *company intranet* or the *staff handbook*, respondents were asked to stipulate any *other* dissemination mechanisms.
- **The scope of the policy:** Policies may vary greatly in their scope. Consequently the questionnaire included a list of eleven distinct issues, such as disclosure of information, Internet access and personal usage of systems, that might be covered by the policy. For each issue, the respondent was asked whether it was covered by the policy document, a stand-alone procedure, by both policy and procedure, or neither.
- **The adoption of success factors:** It has been suggested that organisations will only be successful in the adoption of their ISP if they apply a range of success factors [BSI, 1999]. The British Standard identifies eight distinct factors, such as *ensuring the policy reflects business objectives* and *conducting a risk assessment*. For each factor, the respondent was asked to assess their importance, using a five point Likert scale, and identify how successful his / her organisation had been in its adoption, also using a five point Likert scale.

The '*incidence of security breaches*' was operationalised as a multi-dimension construct. A number of potential risks to the security and integrity of computer-based information systems were identified from the literature [e.g. BSI, 1999], and included in the survey. A total of eight distinct threats, including computer viruses, hacking, human error, fraud and natural disasters, were identified and ultimately included in the research instrument. Each of these threats were operationalised in the following two ways:

1) **Occurrence of threat:** Respondents were asked to estimate the approximate number of occurrences of a specified threat that they had experienced in the previous two years, using a four item ordinal scale [0; **1-5;** **6-10;** >10].
2) **Severity of threat:** Respondents were also asked to estimate the severity of the worst incident, over the same two year period, using a five point Likert scale [**1** = fairly insignificant; **5** = highly significant].

It is anticipated that there may be important relationships between each of the six independent variables, relating to the uptake and application of the ISP, and the dependent variables: '*incidence of security breaches.*' Moreover, it is envisaged that the data will be analysed using either ANOVA or Pearson correlation, depending upon whether the independent variables have been operationalised as ordinal or metric scales. The anticipated results of the analysis can best be described as a series of hypotheses [see also Figure 1]:

H1: Those organizations that *have a documented ISP* are likely to have fewer security breaches, in terms of both frequency and severity, than those organisations that *don't.*
H2: Those organizations that have had an ISP in place for *many years* are likely to have fewer security breaches, in terms of both frequency and severity, than those organisations that *haven't.*
H3: Those organizations that update their ISP *frequently* are likely to have fewer security breaches, in terms of both frequency and severity, than those organisations that *don't.*
H4: Those organizations that *actively disseminate* their policy are likely to have fewer security breaches, in terms of both frequency and severity, than those organisations that *don't.*
H5: Those organizations that have a policy with a *broad scope* are likely to have fewer security breaches, in terms of both frequency and severity, than those organisations that *don't.*
H6: Those organizations that have been adopted a wide variety of *success factors* are likely to have fewer security breaches, in terms of both frequency and severity, than those organisations that *haven't.*

Whilst the hypotheses have been formulated to represent the outcomes that the researchers believed to be the most likely, it was recognised that in some cases alternative, yet equally plausible results, might be produced. For example, it might be that the existence of an ISP is associated with a high incidence of security breaches, in circumstances in which the policy has been implemented in direct response to a poor security record.

CONCLUDING REMARKS

At this point in time, the full survey has now been distributed and a follow-up mailing is underway, in an attempt to generate more responses. It is envisaged that the statistical analysis of the research hypotheses will begin in the near future and should generate some very interesting results. In terms of future work, a series of follow-up interviews is planned to provide deeper insights into the nature of any significant relationships that the quantitative analysis might uncover. As the project unfolds, it is anticipated that the findings will help organisations to better understand the value of security policies and to pinpoint the policy areas for prioritisation.

REFERENCES

Angell, I. O. (1996) Economic Crime: Beyond good and evil. *Journal of Financial Regulation & Compliance*, **4** (1).
B.S.I. (1999) *Information security management -BS 7799-1:1999*, British Standards Institute, London.
C.B.I. (1992) *IT The Catalyst for Change*, Confederation of British Industry, London.
Gaston, S. J. (1996) *Information Security: Strategies for Successful Management*, CICA, Toronto.
Gerber, M., von Solms, R. and Overbeek, P., (2001), "Formalizing information security requirements." *Information Management and Computer Security*, **9** (1), pp. 32-37.
Hone, K. & Eloff, J. H. P. (2002) "Information security policy- what do international security standards say?," *Computers & Security*, **21** (5), pp. 402-409.
Premkumar, G. and King, W. R. (1992) An empirical assessment of information systems planning and the role of information systems in organisations. *Journal of Management Information Systems*, **19** (2), pp. 99-125.

Figure 1.

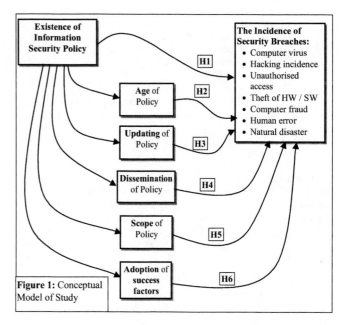

Figure 1: Conceptual Model of Study

Monitoring Accounting Information via Control Charts

Richard B. Dull, PhD
Clemson University, School of Accountancy & Legal Studies
Clemson, SC 29634
T: 864-656-0610, F: 864-656-4892, rdull@clemson.edu

David P. Tegarden, PhD
Virginia Tech, Pamplin College of Business
Blacksburg, VA 24061
T: 540-231-6099, F: 540-231-2511, dtegarde@vt.edu

INTRODUCTION

Currently, there is a lot of interest in supporting the continuous assurance of financial statements (Vasarhelyi, 2002). The current research suggests using control charts to assist decision-makers in the identification of patterns in the underlying processes that produce financial statements. Once interesting patterns are identified, decision-makers may focus on the processes that generated the patterns. The objective of continuous monitoring is detecting abnormalities as near as possible to the time of occurrence of the underlying event that generated the data. If an error or irregularity occurs, the situation can be corrected, and the effect mitigated. Overall, the purpose for monitoring financial information is to gain confidence that systems are operating as intended through the ability to identify and resolve of errors, irregularities, or inconsistencies.

CONTROL CHARTS

Manufacturing processes have been monitored through the use of control charts (Shirland, 1993). Viewing, metaphorically speaking, the creation of financial statements as a manufacturing process, control charts can be applied to determine whether the "financial statement creation process" is going "out of control." If a process is in control, the control chart will appear as if the variation in the line graph is randomly distributed between the control limits. If a process is out of control, the data will appear to have a pattern or some abnormality.

Through the application of the manufacturing metaphor, it is possible to potentially identify problem areas within the financial accounts using control charts. The accounts we investigate are based on suggestions by Mulford and Comiskey (2002) and Schilit (2002). The control charts may provide auditors with a method of monitoring information identified as "high risk" to the financial health of an organization.

METHODS

The data used do develop the control charts in this paper were collected from Compustat. The authors selected financial information relating to WorldCom, Inc., because of the scope and variety of accounting irregularities that have surfaced with the financial information they have reported over the past few years. For demonstration purposes, the authors extracted quarterly information for a ten year time period, providing forty data points for each graphic. In practice, an individual monitoring the accounts ideally should have access to the actual account values in a more continuous manner.

Several procedures were used to standardize the data extracted. For demonstration purposes, we only show the analysis with regards to the Cost of Goods account. Table 1 gives the first two years worth of values for the Cost of Goods and Net Sales accounts (see Actual Values in Table 1). First, following Schilit (2002), the data was "common sized" by dividing the selected accounts by the total sales, for the income statement accounts, or total assets, for the balance sheet accounts, for the same period. In this example, Cost of Goods Sold was divided by Net Sales (see Common Size Values in Table 1). Second, a moving average of four data periods (quarters) was used to provide the base line for the control chart. In this case, the first period in which a moving average was computable was for Dec-91 (see Moving Averages in Table 1). Third, we used a "z-transformation" of the data to set the base line to zero and standardize the periodic data. Next, we computed a moving standard deviation that in conjunction with the moving average could be used to compute a

Z-score for each of the "4-period windows." An example of a control chart using ten years of data for the Cost of Goods sold account using this approach is shown in Figure 1.

A second approach is to common-size the accounts choosing a specific year's account values as the baseline and divide the other years' accounts by the baseline year's accounts' values (Schilit, 2002). Using this approach, we chose Mar-91 as the baseline period. In this case, we again used the Cost of Goods account (see Actual Values in Table 2). All other periods were divided by the Mar-91 value (see Common Size Values in Table 2). Once this transformation has been done, a moving average, a standard deviation, and z-transformation can be executed to create the values on which to base the control charts (see Moving averages, Moving Standard Deviations, and Z-Score Transformations, respectively, in Table 2). A control chart using this method for the Cost of Goods account is shown in Figure 2.

There are many different rules on which to base the control chart analysis. Currently, we are investigating the use of rules regarding runs in z-transformed account values to identify areas for additional investigation. For example, if the z-transformed value of a specific account has a set of seven positive (or negative) values above (or below) the moving average in seven consecutive time periods, there could be a problem with the underlying process. The probability of seven values in a row being above (or below) the mean is less than two percent. This is the so-called "rule-of-seven." In Figures 1 and 2, data points that fall under this rule are identified with an oval. Other rules that may be investigated include:

- If the values trend in the same direction (increasing or decreasing) for seven periods, then it is likely that the underlying process is out of control.
- If the values for two or more periods are greater than two standard deviations ($Z = 2$), but within the actual control limits, then it is likely that the underlying process is out of control.
- If the values for four or more periods are greater than one standard deviation ($z = 1$), but within the actual control limits, then it is likely that the underlying process is out of control.

Through the application of control charts to monitor the accounts, we believe that it is possible to potentially identify problem areas within the financial accounts, in a manner that it has been applied in manufacturing, before the accounts go "out of control."

CONCLUSION

In this research, we suggest that control charts may provide a way to continuously monitor business and financial processes. Control charts have been successfully used to monitor manufacturing processes and to identify processes when they become "out-of-control." We believe that they may also be beneficial when monitoring financial processes.

There are potential limitations in applying control charts to financial processes. Since this is a new domain for this application, the rules to interpret the charts and identify "out-of-control" systems may need to be modified. Alternatively, new rules may need to be developed. Consideration should be given to the frequency of reporting; are standard control charts as useful when monitoring accounting processes at all reporting frequencies, including continuous reporting.

REFERENCES

Mulford, Charles W. and Comiskey, Eugene E. (2002) *The Financial Numbers Game: Detecting Creative Accounting Practices,* John Wiley, New York.

Schilit, Howard (2002) *Financial Shenanigans: How to Detect Accounting Gimmicks & Fraud in Financial Reports*, 2nd Ed., McGraw-Hill, New York.

Shirland, Larry E. (1993) *Statistical Quality Control with Microcomputer Applications*, John Wiley, New York.

Vasarhelyi, Miklos A. (2002) Chapter 12: Concepts in Continuous Assurance, in Researching Accounting as an Information Systems Discipline, Vicky Arnold and Steve G. Sutton (Eds.), American Accounting Association, Information Systems Section, Sarasota, FL.

Table 1. Sample values

	Mar-91	Jun-91	Sep-91	Dec-91	Mar-92	Jun-92	Sep-92	Dec-92
Actual Values								
Net Sales	40.638	43.704	57.534	80.061	82.109	183.748	197.815	205.78
Cost of Goods Sold	22.097	25.074	33.763	48.63	49.622	105.252	112.311	116.821
Common Size Values								
Cost of Goods Sold	54.38%	57.37%	58.68%	60.74%	60.43%	57.28%	56.78%	56.77%
Moving Averages								
Cost of Goods Sold				57.79%	59.31%	59.28%	58.81%	57.82%
Moving Standard Deviations								
Cost of Goods Sold				0.03	0.02	0.02	0.02	0.02
Z-Score Transformations								
Cost of Goods Sold				1.105289	0.714374	-1.24137	-0.98211	-0.59309

Table 2. Baseline sample values

	Mar-91	Jun-91	Sep-91	Dec-91	Mar-92	Jun-92	Sep-92	Dec-92
Actual Values								
Cost of Goods Sold	22.097	25.074	33.763	48.63	49.622	105.252	112.311	116.821
Common Size Values								
Cost of Goods Sold	100.00%	107.54%	141.58%	197.01%	202.05%	452.16%	486.77%	506.37%
Moving Averages								
Cost of Goods Sold				136.53%	162.05%	248.20%	334.50%	411.84%
Moving Standard Deviations								
Cost of Goods Sold				0.44	0.46	1.39	1.57	1.42
Z-Score Transformations								
Cost of Goods Sold				1.368614	0.879116	1.470449	0.973004	0.667410

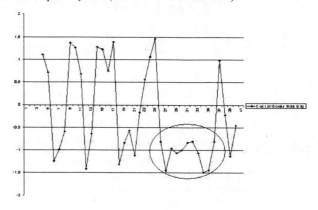

Figure 1. Control chart for the cost of goods sold account WorldCom quarterly data (March 1991-December 2000)

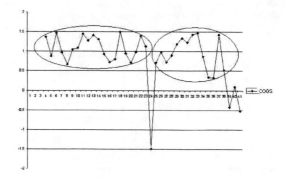

Figure 2. Baseline control chart for the cost of goods sold account WorldCom quarterly data (March 1991-December 2000)

Buttons, Sliders and Dials:
Implementing Metrics in DSS

William K. Holstein, D. Hollins Ryan Professor
The College of William and Mary
T: (757) 221-2920, F: (757) 221-2937
william.holstein@business.wm.edu

Jakov Crnkovic, Associate Professor
University at Albany, State University of New York
T: (518) 442-5318, F: (518) 442-2568
yasha@albany.edu

INTRODUCTION

This paper follows our paper last year, which dealt with metrics and measurement in Decision Support Systems (DSS). This year we turn our attention to implementation details–how metrics can be implemented in DSS, with particular attention to the features that managers want and need, and what, in our view, are the 'indications for the future' in DSS user interfaces.

As our title suggests, the implementation of metrics and measurements in a Decision Support System relies heavily on display and data manipulation techniques and the functions and features available in the system. Many authors have stated that data is THE issue in DSS, and we do not disagree–without good data there is no basis for good decision support. But we go a step further, to state that the CONVERSION of data into meaningful information that can serve as the basis for action is the REAL issue in DSS. This statement brings us squarely to the questions of how data is portrayed, what models are used to organize, parse, and interpret data, and the analytical methods that will be used by the decision maker.

A statement attributed to Gideon Gartner, founder of the Gartner Group and the Giga Information Group, captures the main idea:

Many companies will develop more explicit strategic intelligence systems, with a bias towards converting information to action.

There are several important concepts embedded in this short quote:

Explicit: Implies clear, unequivocal information that enables decision-makers to act quickly and with confidence and knowledge.

Strategic: Points toward the opposite of short-term, mundane, and operational. Rather, managers need information that helps with long-term decisions and issues that are important to future success; information that supports conceptual and visionary leadership activities.

Intelligence: Indicates aptitude, brainpower and acumen when thought of in the context of individual intelligence. More importantly for this discussion, intelligence implies collecting, processing and disseminating information about the future environment, e.g., the enemy's resources and capabilities in a military environment, or a competitors resources, capabilities and skills, and likely future moves in a competitive marketplace.

Converting: Involves information that can assist in planning change, in adapting to new circumstances, in altering procedures or processes, or translating from one (known) context to another about which there is considerable uncertainty. In the context of decision support, we often want to convert or change historical data into information about the future, e.g., convert a series of data points on quarterly sales for the past three years into a forecast of quarterly sales for next year. The data are clear, but how to interpret and convert the data points often is not. Is there seasonality that should be considered? Are the products represented in the historical sales figures the same ones that we will carry into the future? Is the competitive environment the same as in the past? Are we stronger or weaker with the current product line in that environment? One can think of many examples where simple extrapolation or regression against dependent variables would lead to nonsense.

Action: In a decision support context, action implies change. All management decisions eventually lead to change of some sort–a manager whose decisions never change anything is just occupying (expensive) space, s/he can always be replaced with a cheaper do-nothing. Change is the critical determinant of the value of information in a decision support system–the converted information must lead the manager to a decision that leads to, or perhaps a path or series of actions that, in the end, will change something. Thus, actionable information is an essential ingredient that must assist the manager and lead to appropriate conclusions.

To make the point about the importance of action more forcefully, we quote our paper from last year's IRMA International conference:

If the information from a decision support system cannot serve as the basis for action (i.e., cannot first **help the decision-maker to decide to do something, and then help to decide what to do**) *the information will not be used and the system will therefore be useless.*[1] *(Boldface emphasis added.)*

In the following sections, we delve into specific examples of several different techniques and models for portraying and interpreting data.

SENSITIVITY

Consider first a straightforward example of a homeowner who is transferred and must sell a house and buy a new one. For most of us, on a monthly budget that approximates our total income, the principal focus in this decision would be on the difference between the old mortgage payment and the new one. This difference is created by several interacting values; the selling price of the old house and the purchase price of the new one, the mortgage rate on the new mort-gage, whether a real estate agent is used to sell the old house, etc. But again, for most of us, all of these factors come together in a single 'target value' that is the only thing that the decision-maker is interested in: the monthly payment difference.

Figure 1 shows the main screen of a 'mortgage calculator' to assist with a home sale and purchase decision as described above.[2] Here we see basic data entered in the cells to the upper right, the amount due on the current mortgage and the current monthly payment.[3] The key indicator, the payment difference, is prominently displayed under the new mortgage payment in the upper right. The model is currently set with the following assumptions:

Old house will sell for $195,000
New house will cost $250,000
New mortgage will be 25 years at a rate of 6.5%
Real estate fee to list and sell old house will be 6%

In Figure 2, the report accessed by the 'View Report' button in Figure 1 shows that these assumptions lead to a net for the old house (after the real estate agent's fee is deducted) of $183,300 and $62,242 of equity after the mortgage for the old house is paid off.

In this decision, an important consideration is the sensitivity of the target variable to the assumptions that have been set. Note that the model makes it easy for the decision-maker to test sensitivity by simple sliding the scroll bars for the decision variables. Understanding the sensitivity would be important, for example, if the $302.99 monthly payment increase is simply too much. Imagine that the decision-maker says "not a penny more than $150 more per month!"

What if the old house is sold without a real estate agent–is that enough to bring the difference down to no more than $150 per month? Sliding the scroll bar to a zero real estate fee with all other assumptions the same indicates a difference of $223.99 per month as shown in Figure 3, a significant reduction, more than most people would think, but not enough.

How about a 30-year mortgage rather than a 25? That will reduce the monthly payment on the new house, but will it be enough? As we see in Figure 4, a 30 year mortgage just makes it!

As one last example, let us assume that our homeowner has found a dream house, but it is $260,000. What interest rate will make it possible to keep the monthly payment difference under $150? Sliding the new house price scroll bar up to $260,000 starts the process. Then, as shown in Figure 5, sliding the new house mortgage rate scroll bar down until the monthly payment difference drops below $150 answers the question; in this case a rate of just under 6% does the trick.

In summary, what we see in this example is not so much models or conversion of data, but *tools* to permit the user to quickly and easily *explore* the sensitivity of the decision variables, in an attractive, environment that needs little or no explanation. Despite the simplicity of this proto-type, it produces interesting, perhaps even powerful, results to assist the decision-maker.

EXCEPTIONS

Exception reporting and analysis is the basis for much management decision-making. Managers love exceptions because, once they find one, they know what to do–ask 'WHY?' and start digging for answers. The following example is an Executive Information System (EIS) prototype for a national chain of retail stores.[1] Metrics and reports in this system are based on the Balanced Scorecard methodology.[2] Exception reporting in this system is highlighted with color formatting on performance indices that are below a set performance level. Figure 6 shows the opening screen of the EIS.

Choosing the Financial Scorecard selection from the opening screen, the user is led to the screen shown in Figure 7. The data is clear and comprehensive, with break-outs of data for different divisions and store categories. Note the buttons to the left of the screen–the user can easily drill down to regional data screens, and from there to state screens. A drill-down through the South-east Region to the screen for Virginia is shown in Figure 8. Note that individual store data is shown at this detail level, but layout, formatting and exception reporting is similar to that of the top-level screen, a helpful feature to build user familiarity, comfort and acceptance.

Accessing the Help file at the bottom of the financial scorecard screen leads to the screen in Figure 9. Definitions for 'exceptions' are found here. Such help files and definitions are useful to users, but are appropriately placed like this–easily accessible but not intrusive to regular users of the system.

The button at the bottom of the screen in Figure 7, Top and Bottom Five Stores, is particularly interesting. Results of pushing that button are shown in Figure 10. If managers want exceptions to work on, this feature gives it to them. With the push of one button, the manager sees the top and bottom performing stores. We encourage our students and clients to build such features into their systems. Indeed, our vision of the ultimate DSS would have permanent Top 5 and Bottom 5 buttons on every screen. If the manager was looking at sales by region, the buttons would display the top and bottom sales regions. Sales people? The buttons would lead to top and bottom performers. Products? Package sizes? Margins? Each would automatically lead to the correct top and bottom list. This is true decision support–make exceptions, rankings, sorts, etc., immediately available in whatever category the manager is looking at in real time.

Space restrictions prevent us from describing many other features of this rich prototype, but we highlight one of the other scorecards that focus on internal processes. A DSS should focus the user's attention on a small number of metrics that relate to critical success factors. In this company, there are essentially two ways to go wrong at the store level–have the wrong mix of merchandise available for sale (e.g., too many red, small, not enough blue, medium) or mismanage the store process and end up with too many damaged, unsaleable goods. The Process Score-card screen shown in Figure 11 gives data on these variables with color coding similar to the Goal Performance Index: In this case, store process rates of greater than 2.5% and ordering rates of less than 90% are formatted in bold red.

A summary of this example is an easy task–give the user the kinds of features that we see here: clarity, focus on only the most relevant data, straight-forward navigation with no confusion cul-de-sacs or alleys, attractive, easy-to-understand screens with help when needed, and clear, relevant metrics.

AGGREGATE INDICATORS

We end with one more example that has no detail, only a suggestion of future opportunity. Figure 12 shows the opening screen from an early beta version of another Balanced Scorecard DSS, with the four Balanced Scorecards

in an attractive multi-screen display. This screen is more than a pretty picture or just a general menu of choices. Each individual screen has three 'lights,' and each light can take on one of four colors, red, yellow, green or grey (off). The idea is that the lights on the four screens will be a 'dashboard,' sometimes called a 'cockpit,'[1] for the user, available immediately on opening the application. As in other color-coded decision support systems, red will be a warning that there are significant exceptions; or that trends are deteriorating, yellow will mean little or no change from previous values, green will mean an improving situation. An off, or grey, light will mean 'no current values' or 'not available' or 'not measured' or perhaps 'data is not conclusive.'

A dashboard usually portrays the status of a few key variables or, in more recent systems, a weighted average other combination of key variables that have meaning to the business. In this case the three lights on each scorecard are indented to, together, portray an overall impression of the status of that scorecard, ranging from three green lights to three red lights. Combinations of green, yellow, grey and red would signal lower-level areas that need review and invite the user to dig or drill further. Imagine, for example, that there is a measure of corporate performance in each scorecard area for the last year, for the last six months, and for the last month, and each can be compared to the previous period. Three green lights might indicate improved performance in all three time periods, yellow, yellow, green might indicate the last year and last six months are flat compared to the previous periods, but the last month is up–a hopeful trend. A manager would likely want to drill down to find the source of the recent up-tick in performance, and maybe send a note to the responsible manager.

This is only blue-sky thinking–the particular protocols and models behind the lights are not yet worked out. But this example points us towards the future, when DSS dashboards, with just a glance, will assist managers to determine where to look and the severity of problems they are likely to encounter in their analysis and exploration.[1]

We end with a quote from our 2002 IRMA International Conference paper: *There are many unknowns, but one thing is sure: rapid progress in DSS will be made, with or without those of us in the academy who are interested in contributing.*[2] Managers need help to cope with contemporary problems, and it is an exciting time to contribute.

ENDNOTES

[1] *Metrics and DSS: Do we have the DSS cart ahead of the measurement horse?* William K. Holstein and Jakov Crnkovic, Proceedings of the 2002 Information Resources Management Association International Conference, May 19-22, 2002, Seattle, Washington.

[2] This DSS Prototype was developed in Excel by a team of undergraduate students at The College of William and Mary in 1999. The team members included Qianqian Guo, Ben Alexander, Joseph Zapf, Rey Pascual and Mathew Talley.

[3] The assumption here is that the home seller/buyer will invest all of the equity from the old house into the down payment for the new house, and will neither add nor withdraw any cash from the two transactions.

[4] This EIS Prototype was developed in Excel by a team of MBA students at The College of William and Mary in 1999. The team members included Beth Bacon-Williams, Linda Broll, Dawne Galdi, Cathy Grady, Mark Letchworth and Susan Nootnagel

[5] For further information on the Balanced Scorecard, see www.bscol.com, the web site for the Balanced Scorecard Collaborative, hosted by the originators of the idea.

[6] Much recent discussion in DSS has centered around General Electric's effort to install cockpits in all of their operating divisions. See, for example, "GE Capital's Dashboard Drives Metrics To Desktops," InformationWeek, Apr 22, 2002, http://www.informationweek.com/story/IWK20020418S0005.

[7] For more general information on dashboards and cockpits, see the web site of the Global Rhythm Institute at http://grinstitute.mougayar.com/Dashboard.

[8] See Endnote 1.

Figure 1. Mortgage Calculator with sliders and pull-down menu

HOME PURCHASE ASSISTANT
Note: Red numbers with prenthesis are negative numbers: ($1,000) = - $1,000
How much more (or less) will you pay per month?
Summary
Current Mortgage Due
$121,058.00
New House Monthly Payment ....
$1,267.76
Current Monthly Payment
$964.77
Monthly Payment Difference ....
$302.99
Data required for the computation of new monthly payment:
Min
Indicate your values
Max
Current House Selling Price
$195,000.00
$195,000.00
$250,000.00
Current House RE Fee %
6.0%
0.0%
6.0%
New House Price
$250,000.00
$220,000.00
$260,000.00
New House Mortgage Rate
6.5%
4.0%
8.0%
Length of Payment (year)
25
<-Click to view your complete Home Purchase report!
View Report

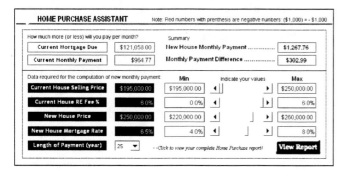

Figure 2. Report Screen for mortgage calculator

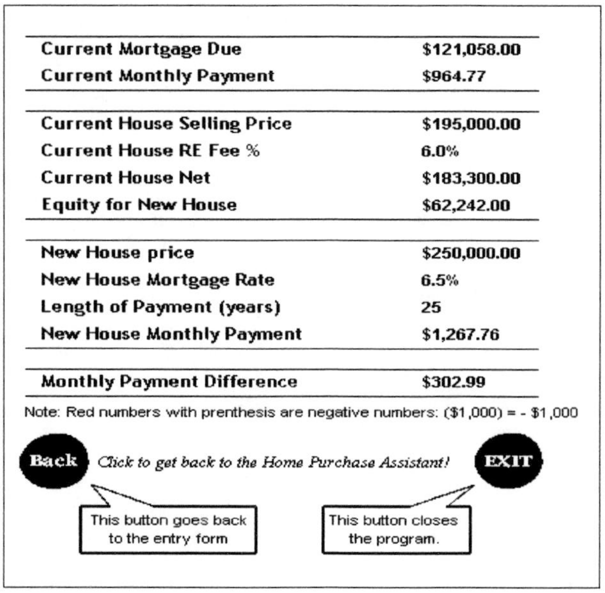

Current Mortgage Due
$121,058.00
Current Monthly Payment
$964.77
Current House Selling Price
$195,000.00
Current House RE Fee %
6.0%
Current House Net
$183,300.00
Equity for New House
$62,242.00
New House price
$250,000.00
New House Mortgage Rate
6.5%
Length of Payment (years)
25
New House Monthly Payment
$1,267.76
Monthly Payment Difference
$302.99
Note: Red numbers with prenthesis are negative numbers: ($1,000) = - $1,000
Back
Click to get back to the Home Purchase Assistant!
EXIT
This button goes back to the entry form
This button closes the program.

Figure 3. Mortgage Calculator with revised assumptions

HOME PURCHASE ASSISTANT
Note: Red numbers with prenthesis are negative numbers: ($1,000) = - $1,000
How much more (or less) will you pay per month?
Summary
Current Mortgage Due
$121,058.00
New House Monthly Payment ....
$1,188.76
Current Monthly Payment
$964.77
Monthly Payment Difference ....
$223.99
Data required for the computation of new monthly payment:
Min
Indicate your values
Max
Current House Selling Price
$195,000.00
$195,000.00
$250,000.00
Current House RE Fee %
0.0%
0.0%
6.0%
New House Price
$250,000.00
$220,000.00
$260,000.00
New House Mortgage Rate
6.5%
4.0%
8.0%
Length of Payment (year)
25
<-Click to view your complete Home Purchase report!
View Report

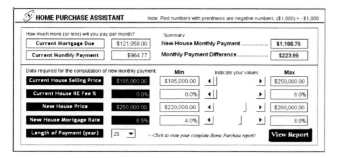

Figure 4. Mortgage Calculator with further revised assumptions

HOME PURCHASE ASSISTANT
Note: Red numbers with prenthesis are negative numbers: ($1,000) = - $1,000
How much more (or less) will you pay per month?
Summary
Current Mortgage Due
$121,058.00
New House Monthly Payment ....
$1,112.81
Current Monthly Payment
$964.77
Monthly Payment Difference ....
$148.04
Data required for the computation of new monthly payment:
Min
Indicate your values
Max
Current House Selling Price
$195,000.00
$195,000.00
$250,000.00
Current House RE Fee %
0.0%
0.0%
6.0%
New House Price
$250,000.00
$220,000.00
$260,000.00
New House Mortgage Rate
6.5%
4.0%
8.0%
Length of Payment (year)
30
<-Click to view your complete Home Purchase report!
View Report

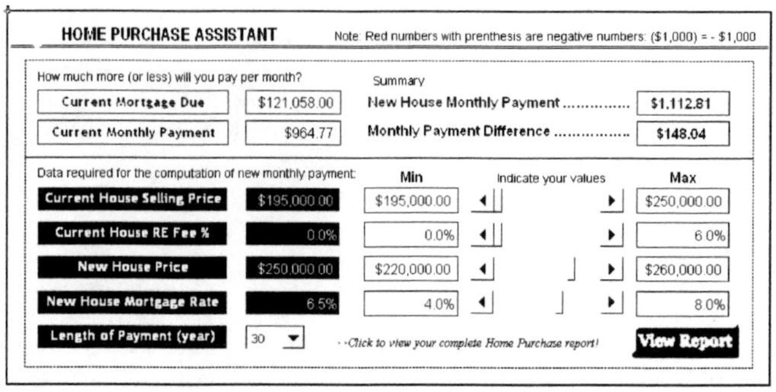

Figure 5. Mortgage Calculator with still further revised assumptions

HOME PURCHASE ASSISTANT
Note: Red numbers with prenthesis are negative numbers: ($1,000) = - $1,000
How much more (or less) will you pay per month?
Summary
Current Mortgage Due
$121,058.00
New House Monthly Payment ....
$1,114.32
Current Monthly Payment
$964.77
Monthly Payment Difference ....
$149.55
Data required for the computation of new monthly payment:
Min
Indicate your values
Max
Current House Selling Price
$195,000.00
$195,000.00
$250,000.00
Current House RE Fee %
0.0%
0.0%
6.0%
New House Price
$260,000.00
$220,000.00
$260,000.00
New House Mortgage Rate
5.990%
4.0%
8.0%
Length of Payment (year)
30
>>Click to view your complete Home Purchase report!
View Report

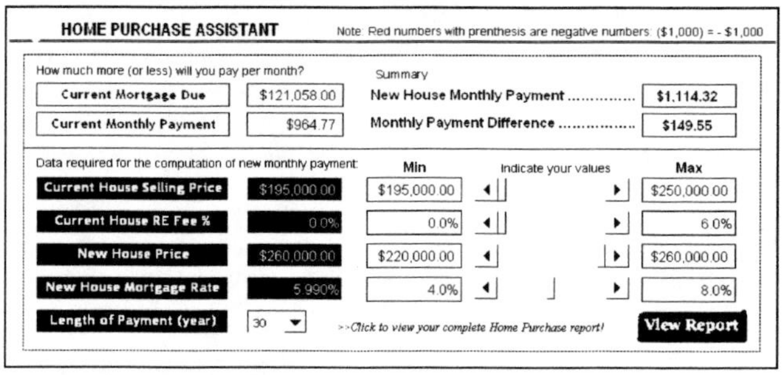

Figure 6. Opening screen for an EIS based on Balanced Scorecard Metrics

Balanced Scorecard
Executive Information System
Financial Scorecard
Processes Scorecard
Customer Scorecard
Innovation/Learning Scorecard
Return to Cover

Figure 7. Top-level financial Scorecard

Financial Scorecard - April 30, 2003

	YTD Actual Sales	YTD Goal	GPI	Sales Last Week	Goal Last Week	GPI
Nationally	$1,893,640,000	$1,690,000,000	1.12	$633,500,000	$519,470,000	1.22
Northeast	$425,000,000	$500,000,000	0.85	$250,000,000	$300,000,000	0.83
Southeast	**$29,140,000**	**$47,000,000**	**0.62**	$23,500,000	$9,400,000	2.50
Southwest	$682,000,000	$620,000,000	1.10	**$310,000,000**	**$465,000,000**	**0.67**
Midwest	$705,000,000	$470,000,000	1.50	$23,500,000	$12,925,000	1.82
Northwest	$49,500,000	$50,000,000	0.99	$25,000,000	$25,000,000	1.00
International	$3,000,000	$3,000,000	1.00	$1,500,000	$1,425,000	1.05
Co.-Owned	$662,774,000	$676,000,000	0.98	**$221,725,000**	**$292,677,000**	**0.76**
Franchises	$416,600,800	$507,000,000	0.82	$139,370,000	$104,527,500	1.33
Division 2	$530,219,200	$338,000,000	1.57	$177,380,000	$168,511,000	1.05
On-Line Sales	$284,046,000	$169,000,000	1.68	$95,025,000	$57,015,000	1.67

Top and Bottom Five Stores | Back to Scorecard Menu | Help

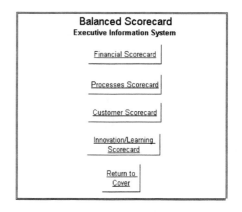

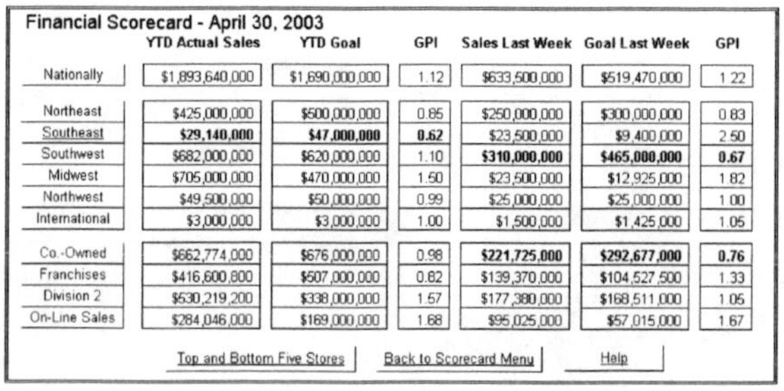

Figure 8. Drill down to State of Virginia Financial Scorecard screen

Virginia Financial Scorecard by Store						
	YTD Actual Sales	YTD Goal	GPI	Sales Last Week	Goal Last Week	GPI
Center Mall	$192,437	$181,746	1.06	$33,004	$37,013	0.89
Dulles Village	$398,073	$403,880	0.99	$78,423	$82,250	0.95
Oak Fair Mall	**$74,042**	**$100,970**	**0.73**	$22,974	$20,563	1.12
Eisenhower Center	$237,982	$242,328	0.98	$42,971	$49,350	0.87
Potomac Center	$152,078	$161,552	0.94	$31,600	$32,900	0.96
Newport Village	$187,635	$181,746	1.03	**$24,050**	**$37,013**	**0.65**
Tysons City	$522,087	$565,433	0.92	$160,600	$114,793	1.40
Reston Valley	$161,974	$181,746	0.89	**$18,050**	**$30,000**	**0.60**

Back to Southeast

Figure 9. Help file accessed from Financial Scorecard with definitions of exceptions

Financial Scorecard

The Financial Scorecard values represent the Goal Performance Index.

Goal Performance Index (GPI): Defined as the Current Performance / Financial Goal.
This is set to monitor weekly and fiscal year performance.

GPI=1	Goals are being met exactly.
GPI<1	Goals are not being met.
GPI>1	Goals are being exceeded.

As a warning indicator, all GPIs less than 0.76 are color-coded in **bold red text**.

Back

Figure 10. Financial Scorecard data on Top and Bottom Five Stores, accessed from Financial Scorecard screen

Financial Scorecard Top and Bottom Five Stores

	YTD Actual Sales	Percent of Average
National Average	$315,606,667	
TOP FIVE		
South Coast Plaza (Costa Mesa, CA)	$473,410,000	150%
Westlake Center (Seattle, WA)	$394,508,333	125%
First City Center (Dallas, TX)	$347,167,333	110%
Port Authority (New York, NY)	$315,606,667	100%
Colonial Mall (Myrtle Beach, SC)	$252,485,333	80%
BOTTOM FIVE		
Maine Mall (South Portland, ME)	$126,242,667	40%
Glenbrook Square (Fort Wayne, IN)	$123,086,600	39%
Southgate Mall (Missoula, MT)	$119,930,533	38%
West Acres Mall (Fargo, ND)	$63,121,333	20%
The Summit (Birmingham, AL)	$31,560,667	10%

Back

Figure 11. Process Scorecard screen

PROCESSES SCORECARD

	Store Process-Reject %	Ordering Process-Sale %
Nationally	2.1%	92.3%
Geographically:		
Northeast	5.0%	75.0%
Southeast	2.5%	90.0%
Southwest	1.5%	95.0%
Northwest	1.0%	99.0%
Midwest	1.0%	97.5%
International	6.0%	72.0%
Business Units:		
Co. Owned	1.9%	95.0%
Franchises	2.4%	90.0%
Division 2	2.0%	88.0%

Back to Scorecard Menu

Help

Figure 12. Opening screen of a DSS with 'dashboard lights'

The Determinants of Web-based Instructional Systems' Outcome and Satisfaction: A Causal Model

Sean B. Eom, Michael A. Ketcherside, and John Cherry
Southeast Missouri State University, Cape Girardeau, MO 63701
sbeom@semo.edu, jcherry@semo.edu

INTRODUCTION

The landscape of distance education is changing. This change is being driven by the growing acceptance and popularity of online course offerings at universities, and in some extreme cases, complete online programs are being offered. *U.S. News and World Report* recently reported that "70 percent of American universities have put at least one course online, and by 2005 that may grow to 90 percent" (Shea & Boser, 2001, p. 44). Further, the growth of 'distance learning' programs gives students a wider choice of schools without regard to location. The trend towards more online offerings may not, and will not, remain only unique to the United States, but is being exhibited internationally.

The primary objective of this study will be to determine what are the primary factors (independent variables) that influence learning outcomes and user satisfaction of online courses (dependent variables). The study aims at determining the level of correlation of those relationships, thus allowing us to make recommendations to online instructors about which factors, if focused on, will yield the greatest results in terms of user satisfaction and perceived learning outcomes. Therefore, this research helps educators manage the critical factors, by maximizing factors with the greatest positive relationship to learning outcomes and user satisfaction. This will help to increase the learning outcome while simultaneously increasing user satisfaction. Ideally, this will allow online instructors, faculty members, department chairs, and computer service departments in learning and teaching institutions, to design, implement, and facilitate online courses in a style that enhances these positive factors.

Furthermore, class surveys and instructor survey assessments could be created around the identified factors where applicable. Thus, creating an assessment tool more closely aligned with the factors that must be positively managed in order to most efficiently implement effective online classes that enhance user satisfaction while delivering quality learning outcomes. Such feedback would be most beneficial to instructors seeking to improve the overall satisfaction and learning outcomes for their online students' semester over semester.

DATA COLLECTION

In an effort to survey students using technology enhanced teaching tools, we focused on students enrolled in online (Web-based courses). An online course can be defined most simply as being a distance education course with no or limited on campus meetings. We collected the email addresses from the student data file archived with every online courses delivered through the online program of a university in the Southeast Missouri area. We used email addresses from all courses taught from fall 1999 through and including the spring 2002 semester. From these, we generated 2,131 unique email addresses. These addresses were the original target group. Valid unduplicated responses numbered 408.

RESEARCH METHOD

This study uses structural equation modeling (SEM), which will allow us to determine if our theoretical model successfully accounts for the actual relationships observed in the survey data. If not, we will reassess the model and make the necessary adjustments to get the data to fit a given model. SEM is generally applied to latent factors (unobserved) to discover their linear, casual relationships. Each of our latent factors is measured by multiple indicator variables (individual survey question responses) with the general rule being that at least two variables must load on each latent factor. However, most researchers prefer three to four indicator variables, with some believing that the more the better (Marcoulides, 1998).

We attempt to illustrate the casual relationships between the eight latent variables as well as making a determination as to which exogenous factors (independent) influence the endogenous factors and to what degree. For example, the original model has student satisfaction and perceived learning outcome as the endogenous, non-recursive factors. On the other hand, our original model has content, feedback, integration, self-motivation, and learning style as exogenous factors. These are variables that we make no predictions about what influences them, nor are these factors affected by other factors in the model (see Figure 1).

The initial research model is constructed based on the review of the literature (Arbaugh, 2001; Graham & Scarborough, 2001; Jiang & Ting, 2000; Piccoli, Ahmad, & Ives, 2001; Saltzberg & Polyson, 1995)

Model Assessment and Modification

We have specified a tentative initial model. Our goal was to not only find a model that fit the data set well from a statistical point of view, but also had the property that every parameter of the model can be given a substantively meaningful interpretation. The re-specification of each model may be theory-driven or data-driven. We chose the data-driven method to redesign the model. We use the generally weighted least squares (WLS) method as this is the method implemented by LISREL. We examine the correlation matrix to assess possible future model changes and to draw general conclusions.

The correlation matrix is show below.

CONCLUSIONS

We are still in the process of refining our model. The better results will be presented at the conference. Several intermediate findings so far will be briefly discussed here. First, several known latent constructs were reaffirmed as being pivotal in the online education process such as content, feedback, interaction,

Table 1. Correlation matrix

	Satis-faction	Out-come	Inter-action	Content	Feed-back	Instuctor	Moti-vation	Style
Satisfaction	1.000							
Outcome	.885	1.000						
Interaction	.925	.716	1.000					
Content	.903	.735	.945	1.000				
Feedback	.902	.649	.985	.863	1.000			
Instructor	.954	.730	1.017	.846	1.008	1.000		
Motivation	.997	.922	.965	.861	.802	.874	1.000	

Figure 1. Research model

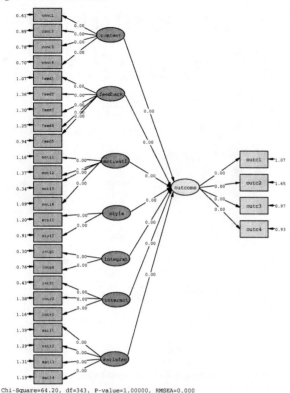

Chi-Square=64.20, df=343, P-value=1.00000, RMSEA=0.000

and motivation. Of these four latent factors, motivation quite possibly was our most underrated factor as we discovered motivation to be the common thread throughout the model as it was significantly correlated to all other factors in our study. In other words, we can draw the conclusion that if all other constructs are in place, but motivation is lacking, then learning outcomes and satisfaction will be adversely affected. Therefore, future research in developing an online education casual model will want to clearly define motivation, possibly into two parts: intrinsic and extrinsic. Furthermore, motivation load upon all other defined factors will need to be examined as we have hypothesized that it will have a significant, direct path loading on all other factors.

Second, the importance of interaction in the learning process needs to be analyzed. The correlations matrix exemplified high levels of correlation between interaction and three other factors: content, instructor input, and feedback. We believe that the interaction factor is the process factor. In other words, all other factors, except satisfaction and outcome, flow through interaction. As many researchers before have proven, we will reaffirm that interaction is a necessary component for online learning just as it is in traditional face-to-face learning environment. Successful online learning has to be more than an individual completing assignments alone and reading materials assigned daily/weekly in a silo setting. Interaction is the pivotal process that facilitates students learning and understanding into a deeper level. Third, we have not conclusively proved that a student's personality and learning style should not be included in future causal models, but we have our doubts. None of our data suggested strong correlations between this factor with any other factors in our model. Furthermore, significant path loadings did not materialize. Our conclusion is that an online student with sufficient motivation will learn regardless of their personality or learning style.

And finally, the construct of instructor input, which became evident late in the research process, appears to bear relevance in the online education process. The premise that the instructor's role decreases in an online environment appears to bear no weight. We believe that strong possibilities exist for the instructor's input to significantly affect motivation and interaction, which are necessary for online learning to occur. It is our final conclusion that the importance of the instructor is as important to online education as it is for traditional classroom settings.

REFERENCES

Arbaugh, J. B. (2001). How Instructor Immediacy Behavior Affect Student Satisfaction and Learning in Web-based Courses? *Business Communication Quarterly, 64*(4), 42-54.

Graham, M., & Scarborough, H. (2001). Enhancing the learning environment for distance education students. *Distance Education, 22*(2), 232-244.

Jiang, M., & Ting, E. (2000). A study of factors influencing students' perceived learning in a web-based course environment. *International Journal of Educational Telecommunication, 6*(4), 317-338.

Marcoulides, G. A. (1998). *Modern Method for Business Research*. Hillsdale, New Jersey: Lawrence Erlbaum Associates.

Piccoli, G., Ahmad, R., & Ives, B. (2001). Web-based Virtual Learning Environments: A Research Framework and A Preliminary Assessment of Effectiveness in Basic IT Skills Training. *MIS Quarterly, 25*(4), 401-426.

Saltzberg, S., & Polyson, S. (1995). Distributed Learning on the World Wide Web. *Syllabus, 9*(1), 26-28.

Shea, R. H., & Boser, U. (2001). So Where's the Beef? There is High Quality Online, But It Takes Real Work to Find it. *U.S. News & World Report, 131*, 44-54.

User Acceptance of Online Computer Games: A Two-Model Comparison

Yuan Gao, PhD
Assistant Professor of Information Systems
Ramapo College of New Jersey, Mahwah, NJ 07430
P: (201) 684-7819, F: (201) 684-7957, ygao@ramapo.edu

INTRODUCTION

User interface design makes an important contribution to the effective presentation of the products. For web-based products in general and online entertainment in particular, attributes like the navigational structure, the interactive media, online help functions, and search mechanism are significant factors contributing to visitor and player retention. The relationship between such features and the effectiveness of the presentation of online computer games has not been widely explored in the literature. This paper explores the application of two distinct streams of research, the consumer behavior theories in marketing research, and the technology acceptance model (TAM) in information systems. It compares the predictive power of the two models in user attitude toward a computer game, and their intentions to return to the game.

THE TECHNOLOGY ACCEPTANCE MODEL (TAM) (MODEL 1)

In information systems research, a user's attitude toward technology is addressed in the Technology Acceptance Model (TAM) (Davis, 1989; Davis et al., 1989). TAM finds its root in the theory of reasoned actions (TRA) (Fishbein & Ajzen, 1975; Ajzen & Fishbein, 1980), and proposes that perceived ease of use and perceived usefulness of technology are antecedents to user attitude toward the use of technology and subsequent behavior. TAM has been adopted in numerous studies testing user acceptance of various types of information technology, e.g., word processors (Davis et al., 1989), spreadsheet applications (Mathieson, 1991), e-mail (Szajna, 1996), and websites (Koufaris, 2002). This study applies the two constructs of the TAM model to online computer games and looks at the predictive power of each to user experience, reflected in his/her attitude toward the site and intention to play the game again.

H1a. Attitude toward the game is positively associated with perceived ease of use.

H1b. Intention to return to the game is positively associated with perceived ease of use.

H1c. Attitude toward the game is positively associated with perceived usefulness.

H1d. Intention to return to the game is positively associated with perceived usefulness.

CONSUMER BEHAVIOR MODEL (MODEL 2)

The World Wide Web is a valuable communications channel founded on a hypermedia system. The design and presentation of products and services, such as entertainment, are critical in influencing online visitors' attitude and intentions to return. Factors related to consumer behavior, attitude, and perception in the online environment have been gradually explored in recent research (Ducoffe, 1996; Chen & Wells, 1999; Eighmey, 1997; Koufaris, 2002). Attitude in turn mediates the effect of systems characteristics on behavioral intentions such as intention to revisit and intention to purchase products from the sponsoring companies.

Entertainment

An online game's entertainment effect is an important source of value for visitors and players of the game, just like entertainment provides value to consumers through its ability to enhance the experience of visitors to a website (Ducoffe, 1996). Pleasant messages impact attitude positively (Mitchell & Olson, 1981). Uses and gratifications research indicated that the entertainment value of a communications exchange lies in its ability to fulfill the audience's needs for escapism, diversion, aesthetic enjoyment, or emotional release (McQuail, 1983). Jupiter Research (1999) finds 36% of respondents engage in entertainment activities, like viewing videos, listening to audio, playing fantasy games, and visiting movie or sports sites. This paper proposes that the entertainment of an online computer game similarly nurtures a favorable attitude in the player toward the computer game, and in turn provides incentive to coming back in the future, and thus the following hypotheses.

H2a. Attitude toward the game is positively associated with perceived entertainment.

H2b. Intention to return to the game is positively associated with perceived entertainment.

Informativeness

Consumers consider information a major benefit of being exposed to any type of commercial messages (Ducoffe, 1996). Information is one of the need-satisfying functions derived from media communications, according to the extended uses and gratifications theory (McQuail, 1983). Consumers in the online environment value information just like in the traditional media, with 48% of respondents in a Jupiter Research survey citing their major use of the Web for product research and gathering information (1999). Eighmey (1998) finds that website users benefit from information that adds value in and of itself. In this study, we adapt the informativeness construct to online computer games in terms its informativeness in various aspects of the game clarity, progress report, performance updates, and related help functions.

H2c. Attitude toward the game is positively associated with perceived informativeness.

H2d. Intention to return to the game is positively associated with perceived informativeness.

Irritation

Irritation is an unintended outcome from visiting a website. It can be caused by tactics employed by advertisers and site or game promoter that annoy, offend, insult, or are overly manipulative (Ducoffe, 1996). It can also be a result of visitor feelings of confusion, distraction, and messiness due to the way a website or online game is presented and features incorporated (Chen & Wells, 1999). In the traditional media, an irritating commercial is one that provokes and causes displeasure and momentary impatience (Greyser, 1973; Aaker & Bruzzone, 1985). In the Web context, irritation may arise from the negative feelings about the organization, a feature of the site, or the visitor's frustration with the computer game. Thus we hypothesize the following.

H3e. Attitude toward the game is negatively associated with perceived irritation.

H3f. Intention to return to the game is negatively associated with perceived irritation.

METHODOLOGY

Research has been done in getting consumer reactions to their shopping experience with real world commercial sites. Jarvenpaa and Todd (1997) gathered consumer comments and responses to questions about electronic commerce after their visits to a real world website. Koufaris (2002) conducted a field study to understand online consumer attitudes and behavior. Chen and Wells (1999) developed an attitude toward the site (Ast) construct through gathering visitor evaluations of websites. An advantage of studies using real websites is the higher level of external validity obtained. We adopted three real online computer games in our field study. The games include a card game Black Jack, in a realistic table and chips environment, a simulated arcade game Supertris (like the video Tetris game), and a somewhat literally challenging Word Painter game (a word puzzle). Subjects were recruited through a gift incentive from undergraduate students, the majority of whom were computer-savvy, with most having played online games more that 20 times in the recent month, and who regularly spent over 10 hours a week surfing the Net. Each participant played two games and filled out a single-page questionnaire containing 7-point semantic differential scales for test variables. Sample demographic information with respect to age, gender, and prior experience with the net and online games was also taken. On average each participant spent 10 minutes trying out a game and filling out a survey for that game.

RESULTS

The two proposed models were separately tested. Within each model, two multiple regression analyses were conducted based on 105 useable data points collected from the field study. One model considered attitude toward the game as the dependent variable, and the other treated intention to return as the dependent variable.

In Model 1, perceived ease of use and perceived usefulness of the game explained about 34% of the variance (adjusted R-squared) in attitude toward the game. Both variables are significant at p< .01 as predictors of attitude. About 57% of the variance in intention to return to the game were explained by the same two variables, with each again significant at p< .01. An immediate observation is that the two variables seem to be better predictors of intention to return to the game (play the game again). Thus we conclude that hypotheses H1a, H1b, H1c, and H1d were supported in this study.

In Model 2, both perceived entertainment and perceived irritation were significant predictors of attitude toward the game, at p< .01, while perceived informativeness is not significant (p> .10). The model explained 64% of variance in attitude. In the mean time, the three variables in Model 2 explained 80% of the variance in intention to return, with both perceived entertainment and perceived informativeness significant predictors of such intentions, while perceived irritation is not a significant predictor of intention to return (p >.10). In summary, we conclude that hypotheses H2a, H2b, H2d, and H2e were supported, and H2c and H2f were not.

DISCUSSION

Model 1 based on TAM seems to provide a consistent framework to consumer acceptance of technology, including online computer games such as those tested in the field study. On the other hand, the three perceptual antecedents to online consumer behavior as a whole seem to explain a significant portion of variance in attitude and behavioral intentions, but did not serve as consistent predictors in the two regression runs. Replication of this study should further examine the roles played by each factor.

This study used college students (between ages 16 and 25, and some between 25 and 30) as participants, who are deemed appropriate subjects in that they make a significant of the Internet population (GVU's 10th Survey). However, whether the general public will respond in the same way as the student sample did in this study is unknown. The games selected for this study were as broad as possible with the inclusion of three distinct types of games. Nonetheless, factors such as the amount of animation and interactiveness could potentially influence the results.

Findings of this study are encouraging. Perceptual antecedents to consumer attitude toward traditional communications and advertising media were compared to TAM in this study, and the majority of the relationships were validated via hypotheses tested. Like much prior research in consumer behavior and technology acceptance, this study was observational. Future research should explore experimental designs to study the effects of content factors, such as color, animation, and audio, on attitudinal consequences. As the population of online game players grows dramatically in the next few years, the line of research connecting online game design and user behavior is promising.

REFERENCES

1 Aaker, D.A., and Bruzzone, D.E. (1985). Causes of irritation in advertising. *Journal of Marketing*, 49, 47-57
2 Ajzen, I., and Fishbein, M. (1980). Understanding attitudes and predicting social behavior. Englewood Cliffs, NJ: Prentice-Hall
3 Chen, Q., and Wells, W.D. (1999). Attitude toward the site. *Journal of Advertising Research*, 39(5), 27-38
4 Davis, F.D. (1989). Perceived usefulness, perceived ease of use, and user acceptance of information technology. *MIS Quarterly*, 13, 319-340
5 Davis, F.D., Bagozzi, R.P., and Warshaw, P.R. (1989). User acceptance of computer technology: comparison of two theoretical models. *Management Science*, 35(8), 982-1003
6 Ducoffe, R.H. (1996). Advertising value and advertising on the Web. *Journal of Advertising Research*. 36(5), 21-34
7 Eighmey, J. (1997). Profiling user responses to commercial Web site. *Journal of Advertising Research*, 37(3), 59-66
8 Fishbein, M., and Ajzen, I. (1975). *Belief attitude, intention and behavior: an introduction to theory and research*. Reading, MA: Addison-Wesley
9 Greyser, S.A. (1973). Irritation in advertising. *Journal of Advertising Research*, 13(1), 3-10
10 GVU's 10th Survey (1998). *GVU's 10th WWW User Survey*. Available at http://www.cc.gatech.edu/user_surveys/survey-1998-10/
11 Jarvenpaa, S.L., and Todd, P.T. (1997). Consumer reactions to electronic shopping on the World Wide Web. *International Journal of Electronic Commerce*, 1(2), 59-88
12 Jupiter Research (1999), Inside the mind of the online consumer — increasing advertising effectiveness, by Johnson, M., Slack, M., and Keane, P. *Jupiter Research* @ http://www.jupiter.com, Volume 18, Aug. 19,1999
13 Koufaris, M. (2002). Applying the technology acceptance model and flow theory to online consumer behavior. *Information Systems Research* (forthcoming)
14 Mathieson, K. (1991). Predicting user intentions: comparing the technology acceptance model with the theory of planned behavior. *Information Systems Research*, 2(3), 173-191
15 McQuail, D. (1983). *Mass Communication Theory: An Introduction*. London: Sage Publications
16 Mitchell, A. A., and Olson, J.C. (1981). Are product attribute beliefs the only mediator of advertising effects on brand attitudes? *Journal of Marketing Research*, 18, 318-332
17 Szajna, B. (1996). Empirical evaluation of the revised technology acceptance model. *Management Science*, 42(1), 85-92

IT-Labor Intensities and Firm-Level Productivity

Stephan Kudyba, MBA, PhD
Assistant Professor, Department of Management
New Jersey Institute of Technology
43 Toms Point Lane, Lincoln Park, NJ 07035
P: (973) 769-6318, skudyba@nullsigma.com

The continued growth in US productivity which began in the mid-1990's and continues today, attracted the attention of economists and analysts who conducted empirical studies to identify the fundamental underpinnings behind this noteworthy trend. The results of these works largely attributed this new productivity pulse to investment and utilization of new forms of technologies, largely classified as information technologies. The incredible increases in economic growth from 1995 to 2000 had involved significant investment in information technologies including, hardware, software, and telecommunications, as companies augmented existing business processes with the purpose of increasing productivity, profitability and market share.

This investment resulted in a more technologically intensive corporate infrastructure which quickly changed the required activities of the corresponding organizational labor force as firms were increasingly dependent on employees who possessed hi-tech intensive skills. The new corporate labor force increasingly required a combination of IT employees; individuals who could develop and implement software applications and build and maintain IT networks, along with existing less IT skilled employees. In order to extract the fullest productivity potential from newly acquired technologies, firms were required to incorporate an employee base that included an appropriate balance between IT skilled and non-IT skilled workers.

This study focuses on identifying the ramifications investment in IT and Non IT employees have on firm output. Utilizing data from large IT intensive organizations over the years from 1995 to 1997 in a production function, this analysis concludes that higher intensities of IT employees in the overall employee base results in increased productivity at the firm level. The period from 1995 to 1997 is particularly insightful as it captures the initial period of increased productivity in the US but avoids the IT "bubble" period, which began towards the year 1998. The results of this study therefore are not affected by the potential adverse ramifications of misallocation of factor inputs and questionable financial reporting practices by organizations that transpired during the "bubble" period. This work is therefore particularly insightful as it incorporates detailed firm level data over a period of time that avoids potential adverse events affecting the performance of organizations. It also analyzes the changing characteristics of evolving firm level labor given increased investment in Information Technologies and utilizes established economic theory (a Cobb-Douglass production function) to estimate changes in productivity resulting from different IT skilled worker concentrations.

PRODUCTIVITY AND THE INFORMATION ECONOMY

As investment in information technology increased across industry sectors of the economy, analysts began to study the effects this new technology would have on corporate productivity. A number of benchmark studies addressed this topic in detail. Earlier works by Lichtenberg (1995) and Brynjolfsson and Hitt (1996a, 1996b) concluded that investment in IT led to increased productivity at the firm level. These early conclusions were further support by their later works (Brynjoffson, 1998) and (Lichtenberg, 1998) and more recently by (Kudyba and Diwan, 2002) who identified increasing returns to investment in IT as the information economy began to progress.

However when taking a detailed look at individual IT initiatives, it is evident that not all IT investments were a success, as failed projects were many times the result of inappropriate resource allocations and organizational struc-

ture. Firms realized that in order to effectively implement new technologies to enhance business processes, they were required to incorporate a workforce with greater concentrations of IT skilled labor which also involved interaction between technically skilled labor and less technically skilled business, managerial labor. Accordingly, this study analyzes whether increases in IT skilled labor to the overall employee base results in increased productivity at the firm-level by utilizing a standard Cobb-Douglas production function.

ECONOMIC THEORY AND PRODUCTIVITY

In order to achieve increased efficiencies in their operations, firms seek to optimize the use of inputs and invest in an input such as labor, until the output it generates adds no more value than the last unit added. To estimate payoff of factor inputs, investment in an input is maintained to the point where marginal input cost is equal to the value of marginal output. Given the changing character of organizational labor, production theory can be applied to measure the impact of IT intensive labor on corporate output. This work utilizes the Cobb-Douglas production function since this form facilitates the estimation of elasticity of production function inputs through linearization of the equation. The Cobb-Douglas function in this study takes the simple form:

$Q = (L^\beta, K^\beta)$ where Q is output and (L, K) are Labor and Capital.

The linearized version becomes:
$ln(Q)_{ij} = \beta 1 ln(L)_{ij} + \beta 2 ln(K)_{ij}$

where the (β) values are the parameters that denote the elasticity of each of the input factors.

Accordingly this paper attempts to test the following hypotheses:
$Q = f(L, K)$

H1. *IT skilled intensive labor results in increased productivity at the firm level.*
$dQ/dL > 0$

DATA SOURCES

The primary source of data for this study utilizes the information available in *InformationWeek*'s 500 survey published on an annual basis from the years 1994–1997. It includes firm level attributes including revenue, number of workers employed and number of IT skilled employees of the top 500 corporate users of information technology. Data was also gathered from corporate disclosure reports, which contained information on firm level Capital along with financial related information to determine firm level value added output. Generally, production function inputs in this study consist of Capital and Labor:
1) Capital
2) Labor

Where output is measured by economic Value Added.

Variable Inputs

Capital is defined as Net Property Plant and Equipment (PP&E), which adjusts total plant property and equipment for accumulated depreciation. Net PP&E includes expenditures on information technologies.

Table 1.

(1995 – 1997) IT Skill Labor Intensity Regression Results   Output (Value Add)

Parameters	Low Coefficient (t-stat)		Normal Coefficient (t-stat)		High Coefficient (t-stat)	
Labor	0.152 ***(4.78)		0.331 ***(10.19)		0.526 ***(12.51)	
Capital	0.415	(11.1)	0.399	(13.5)	0.253	(9.09)
Adj R^2	.60		.72		.75	
N-Observ	190		257		200	

*** Significant at the 0.01 level

Unit labor skill intensities involved classifying the pool of firm level labor according to the ratio of the number of IT workers to non-IT workers. The resulting ratios depict the corresponding IT skilled intensity of the overall firm level labor pool.

Value Added refers to firm level gross sales less variable costs, where variable costs includes CGS and SG&A for corresponding firms in the data base.

RESULTS

The Cobb Douglas equation was estimated over the entire period from 1995 through 1997 and the corresponding results are given in Table 1.

The results indicate that labor forces with higher IT skill concentrations have made statistically significant increased contributions to firm level output measured by Value Added.

A possible explanation of this increased productivity of higher concentrations of skilled labor pools follows from the assimilation of the significant increased investment and implementation of software, hardware and communications equipment by organizations that began in 1993. This investment had transformed existing corporate infrastructures to higher "IT technological" infrastructures. As a result, firms who incorporated a higher concentration of IT skilled labor achieved increased efficiencies as they were better able to take advantage of the process enhancement capabilities these new technologies introduced to their organizations (e.g., CRM, Supply Chain Networks and the like).

Future work could involve a more detailed analysis of the type of IT skills that are essential to driving corporate productivity and business efficiency and perhaps the returns to IT labor outsourcing.

REFERENCES

Brynjolfsson , E. and L. Hitt. "Productivity, Profitability and Consumer Surplus: Three Different Measures of Information Technology." *MIS Quarterly*, (0:2), (1996).

Brynjolfsson, E. and L. Hitt. "Beyond the Productivity Paradox," *Communications of the ACM,* Aug. 41 (8), (1998) 49-55.

Kudyba, S. and R. Diwan. *"Increasing Returns to Information Technology,"* Information Systems Research, March (2002).

Kudyba, S. and R. Diwan. *"The Impacts of Information Technology on US Industry,"* Japan and the World Economy, August (2002).

Lehr, W., and F. Lichtenberg. *"Computer Use and Productivity Growth in US Federal Government Agencies"* 1987–1992, Journal of Industrial Economics, (June 1998).

Lichtenberg, F. *"The Output Contributions of Computer Equipment and Personnel: A Firm-Level Analysis."* Economic Innovation and New Technology, (3), (1995).

Women and Minorities in Technology: With Focus on Local Schools

Guity Ravai
Department of Computer Technology
Purdue University
West Lafayette, IN 47907-1421
P: (765) 496-6005, F: (765) 496-1212, gravai@tech.purdue.edu

ABSTRACT

This is an ongoing project that will take several years to complete. The core of this study is to look at four local junior and senior high schools and find out the factors that affect female and minority groups in choosing their future education and career path. One way to accomplish this task, is to look at the guidance the students get from their counselors, existing programs in schools, and the way students' interests change as they move on to higher grades. The lack of females and minorities going to scientific and technological fields requires more proactive attention nation wide.

INTRODUCTION

As a woman growing in a male dominant society, I was troubled by the discriminatory attitude towards women. Gender based bias was embedded in every aspect of women's life, from their marriage, to proper behavior, and suitable jobs. Birth of a baby girl was never a cause for great celebration! Some families kept bearing children until they had a son! In such a society, I decided to go to an engineering school, and continued my education in computer science. I was determined to prove that girls could do whatever boys did and even more. When I married and moved to U.S. 25 years ago, I found out that the western culture has similar stereotypes for women! I also realized that because of lost opportunities there were very few minorities in colleges, especially in science and technology. Things have changed since, but minorities and women still have a long way to go to.

BACKGROUND

The gender and race schema (the preset attitude about gender and race) has been woven into the minds and hearts of the society including parents and teachers who have a direct impact on young children and transfer their own biases to the next generation. Gender schema exists even among those who consider themselves equalitarian. From very early age teachers and parents encourage boys' competitive and aggressive behavior by giving them special attention, but for girls such behavior is discouraged and not acceptable (Valian, 1999).

Parents do treat their children similarly in many domains, but in the area of gender they do not. Their own gender schema makes them blind to the specific ways they perceive and treat children differently. This is true with regards to the race schema as well. Many parents transfer their own biases about race to their children merely to protect them from discriminatory hurts in society! The data available since 1947 throughout 1980 on standardized testing in Grades 8 through 12 shows a dramatic decline in sex difference in test results (Feingold 1988). In 1947 for example, tests of verbal reasoning, abstract reasoning, and the ability to deal with numbers showed higher performance by boys. In 1980, those differences had been decreased, and numerical ability showed higher performance by girls. By 1980, similar tests in which girls were superior to boys in 1947, showed declining sex differences. This diminution is good evidence, that some portion of cognitive differences is socially constructed (Valian, 1999).

Some educators and sociologists suggest that women and minorities suffer in groups where they are present in small numbers. Significant improvement in performance appears as the ratio of minority to majority members improve (Etzkowitz, Kemelgor & Uzzi 2000).

DESCRIPTION

This project focuses on four local junior and senior high schools in Lafayette, and West Lafayette, Indiana, where I reside. These two cities are separated by Wabash river, and share a lot of resources. Having the Purdue University's main campus located in West Lafayette, makes a big difference in the quality of education in West Lafayette schools. My goal is to analyze the existing programs, and give suggestions to schools to encourage the girls and minorities' participation in scientific and technological fields. To find out more about the existing programs, and determine the factors that play a role for girls and minorities in making a decision, I have designed a questionnaire to be given to the counselors in local schools.

The Questionnaire For Counselors

1. How many students are registered in your Junior and Senior high school?
2. What percentage of your students goes to college after graduation?
3. What percentage of the graduating students are girls?
4. What percentage of the graduating students are minorities?
5. What percentage of the graduating students goes to college to pursue science and technology?
   a. What percentage of these students are girls?
   b. What percentage of these students are minorities?
6. Do you have programs designed for women and minorities' advancement in science and technology?
7. How do you advise students to decide the fields of studies?
8. In computer programming course(s), what percentage of students are girls or minorities?
9. In accelerated math and science courses, what percentage of students are girls or minorities?
10. In your opinion, what are the fields in which girls will most likely succeed?
11. In your opinion, what are the fields in which minorities will most likely succeed?

The West Lafayette high school has provided me with answers. I am awaiting the responses from other schools.

I have also designed a questionnaire for students. This questionnaire will be given to all the girl and minority students in 8th grade, this year. A follow up questionnaire will be given to them, each year as they move on to higher grades until their senior year. This way one can observe the changes in this group's thought process as they approach their graduation from high school.

The Questionnaire For Students

1. What subjects are you interested in?
2. Are you good in math?
3. Are you good in science?
4. What do you think of those students who are good in math or science?
5. Are you planning to go to college after graduation?
6. If you are not planning to go to college, is financial constraint a factor in that decision?
7. Would you be interested in continuing your education in a scientific or technical field? If your answer is no, please give a brief explanation.
8. Do you have a clear idea about what you would like to study once you enter college?

9. Do your teachers/counselors help you determine your academic goals?
10. What kind of job would you like to do when you finish your studies?
11. What kind of job does your family like you to do?

CONCLUSION

In summary, parents and teachers perceive the children with their own race and gender schema, which affect the perception of the children from what they can achieve in life. This in turn influences children's ability and interests in academics. It is crucial for the educators to be aware of the biases that exist in society about race and gender. Having programs that promotes the participation of female and minority students in scientific and technological fields will encourage these students by giving them a chance to interact with other members of their own minority group and form their future goals. It is impera-tive to invite women or minorities in technical fields to go and talk to these students in high schools, and share their experiences and accomplishments with them. Purdue University's main campus located in West Lafayette pro-vides a good source for such programs. Girls and minority groups deserve getting the attention that they have been denied for decades. We as educators play a big role in achieving this goal.

REFERENCES

1. Virginia Valian (1999) "Why So Slow?" MIT Press.
2. Feingold, A. (1988) "Cognitive gender differences are disappearing".
2. Henry Etzkowitz, Carol Kemelgor, and Brian Uzzi (2000) "Athena Un-bound". Cambridge University Press.

The Availability of Domain/Key Normal Form

Robert A. Schultz, Professor
Computer Information Systems, Woodbury University
7500 Glenoaks Blvd., Burbank, CA 91510
P: 818-767-0888, F: 818-504-9320, bob.schultz@woodbury.edu

INTRODUCTION

In my earlier paper, "Understanding Functional Dependency" (2002), I distinguished intensional and extensional characterizations of functional and other dependencies used in defining the Normal Forms for relational databases. In that paper, I left incomplete my discussion of how this distinction applies to Domain/Key Normal Form (DK/NF). In this paper, I will continue that discussion.

Extensional characteristics are those which remain the same through substitution of terms with the same reference, whereas intensional characteristics do not. In a database context, extensionality means that the only features of fields appealed to is the frequency of their appearance with other fields, with the same or different values. Meanings or connotations of field names or values, and connections between fields having to do with knowledge about the meanings or business rules or conventions connecting field values are intensional and therefore have no place in extensional database considerations. In my earlier paper (2002), I showed that the first three normal forms can be done on an extensional basis (and Boyce-Codd, fourth and fifth normal forms as well). Although many texts mention intensional elements in defining functional dependency, this is not necessary.

Normal Forms exist in order to produce well-behaved database designs that avoid the occurrence of anomalies, unexpected difficulties with deleting, adding, or modifying data. If a database is in DK/NF, it is provable that no anomalies can occur. Whereas, the other Normal Forms (First, Second, Third, Boyce-Codd, Fourth, and Fifth), were designed to avoid certain anomalies, and there is no guarantee that some further anomaly may pop up not prevented by these Normal Forms. Unfortunately, there is no effective procedure for putting a set of tables into DK/NF. As David Kroenke (2002, 134) puts it, "Finding, or designing, DK/NF relations is more of an art than a science."

Ron Fagin's original paper (1981) on DK/NF is done squarely within standard mathematical set theory, which is completely extensional in character. This implies that his characterization of possible anomalies and his proof that tables in DK/NF avoid them are also extensional. If they are reflected in patterns of repetition in the data, then one would want to know why they, or their absence, could not be detected by a simple (but possibly extended) search of the data for repetitions or their absence. This is in fact how "automated" procedures for doing first, second, and third normal form work. So offhand it seems as though DK/NF and its accompanying anomalies must not be reflected solely in patterns of repetition in the data.

In this paper, I will discuss:
1. The basis for the claim that all possible anomalies are prevented by DK/NF;
2. Why there is no effective procedure for producing DK/NF.

DK/NF AND THE ANOMALIES

Fagin defines *insertion anomaly* as follows:
(1) Relation schema R* has an *insertion anomaly* if there is valid instance R of R* and there is a tuple t compatible with R such that R$\dot{E}$\{t\}, the relation obtained by inserting t into R, is not a valid instance of R* (i.e., violates a constraint of R*)(391).

If we replace 'relation schema' with 'table structure' (a relation schema is a set of attribute names plus some constraints on possible values for those attributes), 'relation' with 'table' (understood as with all its values), 'tuple' with 'record,' (1) reads as (1)':

(1)' A table structure R* has an *insertion anomaly* if a table with the structure R* can have a record added which by itself satisfies the constraints of the structure but the resulting table violates a constraint of the structure R*.

Fagin is almost always working at the level of generality of what I call table *structures* rather than tables themselves. Usually when anomalies are discussed in database textbooks, they are presented in terms of a few examples of tables without any attempt at a general formal characterization. So, how does Fagin's formal definition square with intuitive examples of insertion anomalies?

Intuitive examples of insertion anomalies involve a nonkey field which has another functionally dependent field; thus it is not possible to add a record exhibiting a new nonkey dependency until a record with the key and nonkey fields is added. An example in Kroenke is a StudentActivity table with StudentID, Activity, and ActivityCost fields. Since StudentID functionally determines Activity and Activity functionally determines ActivityCost, there is no way to insert a record with a new Activity and ActivityCost until some student decides to engage in the activity (Kroenke, 126).

Fagin's definition does not apply; and in fact his example of an insertion anomaly is different. The table structures are the same, but in terms of the above example the anomaly would be a new student with an existing activity who was assigned a different cost for that activity (Fagin, 392). On Fagin's approach, the intuitive insertion anomaly is simply an attempt to insert an ineligible record. In fact, Fagin, in a discussion of Codd (1972), seems to view as illegitimate the attempt to restructure tables to capture information such as a student activity fee in the absence of a student (401).

Fagin's definition of deletion anomaly is:
(2) Relation schema R* has a *deletion anomaly* if there is a valid instance R of R* and a tuple t in R such that the relation obtained by removing t from R is not a valid instance of R* (i.e., violates a constraint of R*)(395).

Replacing terms as above, (2) reads as (2)':
(2)' A table structure R* has a *deletion anomaly* if a table with the structure R* can have a record deleted which results in the table violating a constraint of the structure R*.

Intuitive examples of deletion anomalies involve nonkey fields with others functionally dependent on them; thus information about the dependency can be lost when the record is deleted. In the example StudentActivity(*StudentID*, Activity, ActivityCost), information about ActivityCost can be lost if all students are deleted who happen to be engaged in that activity (Kroenke, 126). Fagin's examples of (DK) deletion anomalies are based on domain dependencies (396). In this case, Fagin's example is similar to the intuitive one. Information about the relation of value of two fields is inadvertently lost because of the table structure. The difference is the nature of the dependency between the fields.

Also, Fagin's definition of insertion and deletion anomaly supposes that the constraints mentioned in (1), (1)', (2) and (2)' are Key Dependencies and Domain Dependencies only, and not functional dependencies (FDs), multivalued dependencies (MVDs), and join dependencies (JDs). So Fagin's insertion anomalies should more appropriately be called "domain key insertion anomalies," and similarly his deletion anomalies should be called "domain key deletion anomalies." So understood, the actual theorem stating that table schemata are in DK/NF if and only if they have no DK deletion or DK insertion anomalies seems perhaps less dramatic. Fagin himself notes that this theorem is "not deep" (398), presumably for similar reasons.

However, later in the paper he proves that DK/NF implies the traditional normal forms defined in terms of functional dependency multivalued dependency, and join dependency (403-409). The DK/NF theorem together with the implication of traditional normal forms does still show that DK/NF prevents whatever anomalies the traditional normal forms do, plus any DK anomalies.

FAGIN'S PROOF THAT DK/NF IS FREE OF ANOMALIES

If a table structure is in DK/NF, any table with that structure has no (DK) insertion or (DK) deletion anomalies. Fagin shows this by appealing to the definitions. A table derived from the original by deleting or inserting a tuple also satisfying the DK constraints, will satisfy any constraint the original does. So no anomalies.

If a (consistent) table structure is not in DK/NF, then it has anomalies. Fagin shows this by constructing an anomaly. If a table structure is not in DK/NF, there is a "bad" table for which a constraint fails when the set of DK constraints holds. Since the table structure is consistent, there is a "good" table which does satisfy the constraints. He constructs a sequence of tables starting with the "good" one, deleting one row at a time until all are gone. Then add one row from the "bad" table until we have the complete "bad" table. Somewhere in this sequence, the table goes from "good" to "bad". If it is in the first part, we have found a deletion anomaly. If it is in the second part, we have found an insertion anomaly.

AN EFFECTIVE PROCEDURE FOR DK/NF?

Fagin closes his discussion of how to put a database into DK/NF with a warning:

In the general case, it is not useful to think in terms of mechanical procedures for conversion to DK/NF, since we immediately run into undecidability results. For example, it is not even decidable as to whether a sentence of first-order logic is a tautology (this is Church's theorem). (Fagin, 403)

To determine whether a table structure is in DK/NF, we have to determine that every constraint can be *inferred from* key dependencies and domain dependencies alone. The question is what rules of inference can be used. As long as we allow at least first-order predicate calculus (quantification theory), it is know that no decision procedure exists for what can be inferred from what. If an inference is valid, that can be proved. But for an arbitrary inference, it cannot be decided whether it is valid or not (Quine 1966, 212).

Fagin deliberately refuses to restrict constraints only to formulations in quantification theory (389). Quantification theory (or predicate logic) does seem to be a bare minimum because otherwise we cannot formulate constraints mentioning fields or attributes. Even though a restriction to quantification theory will not help, Fagin also raises the question of restricting domain and

key dependencies to allow decidability for DK/NF (403). But such restrictions on domain and key dependencies may also invalidate the proof that all (DK) anomalies are prevented by DK/NF.

CONCLUSION

My original suspicion that the extensional/intensional distinction by itself might help understand the status of DK/NF turned out to be incorrect. Fagin makes only one explanatory statement about DK/NF using intensional considerations: "A 1NF relational schema is in DK/NF if every constraint can be inferred by simply *knowing* the DDs (domain dependencies) and the KDs (key dependencies)" (397, my italics). However, the rest of the paper is completely extensional in character. So help with my two puzzles about DK/NF lies elsewhere.

On the basis for the claim that all possible anomalies are prevented by DK/NF, there are two facts: DK/NF prevents all DK insertion anomalies and DK deletion anomalies; and DK/NF implies the traditional normal forms. Thus all DK insertion and deletion anomalies are prevented, and whatever anomalies prevented by the earlier normal forms are also prevented by DK/NF. However, some intuitive anomalies are not recognized as DK anomalies, even though they will also be prevented by DK/NF.

On why there is no effective procedure for producing DK/NF, I found that DK/NF is defined in terms of very general kinds of inference, including classes of inference known to be undecidable. My conclusion was that it was probably not workable to restrict allowable *inferences* to avoid undecidability, and that a restriction of allowable *dependencies* would have unpredictable effects on whether all anomalies can be prevented by DK/NF.

Taken together, both points suggest that the theoretical claims for DK/NF are probably unassailable. However, the practical difficulties in achieving DK/NF also can probably not be ameliorated.

REFERENCES

Codd, E. F. (1972) "Further Normalization of the Relational Database Model." in *Data Base Systems*. Englewood Cliffs, NJ: Prentice-Hall.

Fagin, Ronald (1981) "A Normal Form for Relational Databases that is Based on Domains and Keys," *ACM Transactions on Database Systems,* v.6 no.3, pp. 387-415.

Kroenke, David (2002) *Database Processing*. Upper Saddle River, NJ: Prentice-Hall.

Quine (1966) "Church's Theorem on the Decision Problem", *Selected Logic Papers*. New York: Random House.

Schultz, Robert (2002) "Understanding Functional Dependency," *2002 Proceedings of IRMA*. To appear in *Effective Databases for Text and Document Management,* ed. Becker.

Learning Outcomes in Web Based Synchronous and Asynchronous Learning Environments - A Comparative Analysis

Chayan Rattanavijai, Sushil K. Sharma
Ball State University, Muncie, Indiana
(Rattanavijai) P: 765-285-3523, F: 765-285-5308, crattana@bsu.edu
(Sharma) P: 765-28505315, F: 765-285-5308, ssharma@bsu.edu

ABSTRACT

As the web-based synchronous and asynchronous learning environments are used by many schools to deliver courses, the need for the systematic impact evaluation of these new learning environments of learning outcomes becomes more significant. This paper presents an analysis of synchronous and asynchronous learning based instructions that were used for graduate courses for both on-campus (full time) and off-campus students (distance learning). The paper presents preliminary findings about learning outcomes of students in these information systems courses. The study although is limited to one schools but findings could contribute significantly to generalizability to other institutions.

BACKGROUND

In the educational environment of the 21st century, it is necessary to create educational programs that are student-centered rather than classroom or university centered (Jackson, 2000). While research has demonstrated that many students respond favorably to web-based innovations and such techniques can be highly effective (Shea and Boser, 2001; Zhao, 1999). Schools offer many different types of web-based synchronous learning environment. The common features of web-based synchronous (real-time) are browser-based, IP-based two way audio (usually half duplex), collaborative application sharing, whiteboard and synchronized web browsers. Currently, offering courses through asynchronous mode such as blackboard or web environment has been increasing in schools over the years. Many faculty members post their lectures on the web and students download the material to supplement their lectures and enhance their learning. Faculty members use newsgroups and discussion boards for students' interactions apart from conventional e-mail interactions.

Online technologies, specifically web-based applications, are increasingly being utilized as a delivery mechanism in higher education. It is the capability of the web to facilitate communication and collaboration between/ among students and instructors that could overcome the increasing barriers to effective teaching and learning in higher education (Lockyer, Patterson & Harper, 2001). Web-based programs have been growing in popularity and there is every indication that the trend will continue for the foreseeable future (Holstein, 1997). Many schools have started offering web-based programs partially or fully online at the university and college level (Awalt, 1998; Dziuban et al. 1999). It encompasses a variety of media including videoconferencing, web-based training, satellite broadcast, streaming media, and audio conferencing in asynchronous as well as synchronous mode (Becker & Dwyer 1994; Mioduse et al. 2000). In asynchronous e-learning training takes place in different time frames and trainees access information at their convenience. Some examples of asynchronous training include self-paced computer-based training (CBT), web-based training (WBT), bulletin boards, and email. On the other hand, synchronous distance learning takes place for all students at the same time and information is accessed instantly. This form of distance learning provides more interactivity. Examples of synchronous e-learning include

video teleconferencing, whiteboard, Internet conferencing, and chat rooms. All of these technologies extend learning beyond traditional classrooms to encompass homes, museums, libraries, and workplaces anytime, anyplace, for anyone (Boroni et al. 1998; McManus, 1996).

Few studies have been conducted for assessing online learning (Dziuban et al. 1999). However, the research literature on the use of assessing web-based programs is short of analytical as well as qualitative studies (Burge, 1994; Chalk, 1999; Chalk, 2000; Gunawardena, 1995). Also, there have not been many studies conducted to examine how effective the current web-based, asynchronous and synchronous learning programs are. Our study used the data on social interaction that occurs during the course or project, and the effects of the experience on individuals in web-based learning environment. The study also examined instructional delivery modes, interaction and speed of course development/ adaptation. The study although is limited to one schools but findings could contribute significantly to establish new standards for student-centered learning oriented framework, a major conceptual advancement in student learning, that can serve a foundation for a revolutionary graduate learning experience.

METHODOLOGY ADOPTED

In this study, we investigated the learning outcomes delivered by synchronous learning and asynchronous learning methods. The methodology adopted was based on students' involvement, interactions and participations in courses, and their performance in graduate programs. Detailed structured as well as non-structured interviews were conducted involving IS students. The data was collected through various methods such as observations, structured questionnaires, interviews and pre and post test results of students. Furthermore, informants validated each interview transcript and interpretation. The evaluation is done using quantitative as well as qualitative techniques. The data was collected from multiple classes totaling more than 500 students.

DATA ANALYSIS AND FINDINGS

The data analysis and findings in detail would be presented in the conference since some work is still in progress. A comparative analysis of four different web-based instructional models would be presented. However, few broad highlights of findings on web-based instructions in general found are;

Positive Attitude

Students were observed to have a highly positive attitude toward web-enhanced instruction. The web provides a better environment than the traditional classroom does. As a result, even students who are separated by time and place will be better off than students sitting in lectures given by professors through teleconferencing. Asynchronous learning provides convenience and effective communication. The delays among students' discussions provided group members the opportunity to reflect and think/rethink about a problem and examine it thoroughly than is provided in a synchronous environment.

The chat room was the least used web component, possibly because it required the students to log on at specific times (Sanders et al. 2001). Due to convenience factor, students preferred asynchronous environment than synchronous environment.

Motivation/Self Responsibility

The study found that students fared poor in taking self responsibility and found hard to motivate them in a asynchronous environment than synchronous environment. Students lacked in time management, in control of their studies and maintain an image of self-worth and self-efficacy more in asynchronous environment than synchronous environment.

Learning Outcomes

There is no significant difference in performance of students using asynchronous or synchronous environment. There is no significant difference in performance among students who used deep learning strategy in either web format or lecture format. Students with similar learning strategy and motivation performed equally well irrespective of web or lecture format (Sankaran, & Bui, 2001). However, technology difficulty experienced in asynchronous environment for participation did affect students' learning outcomes. The poor internet access also was experienced an obstruction for the real-time communication.

Effectiveness

Findings from this study suggest that students showed preference to use the web for the posting of course syllabi, grades, quizzes, questions, and materials that encourage student-to-student and student-to-faculty interaction. There was mixed opinion among students about posting questions through web bulletin boards and chatting through the web. Those students who did post regularly to the bulletin board were better able to answer questions on tests, showed a higher level of critical thinking in class assignments, and were more likely to download the critical-thinking questions than those who did not participate (Sorg et al. 1999).

Achievement

Research study indicates that the achievement and satisfaction of students in asynchronous learning and synchronous learning environment is not significantly different than the achievement and satisfaction of students in traditional classrooms. One major difference across these two learning environment was that students' experiences in shaping their learning behaviors were found to be different (Poustie, 2001). For example, students in asynchronous learning environment found more isolation and less involved in team projects. Also, asynchronous learning based students missed advising from instructors' environment that affected their learning experience.

Critical Thinking

The web component primarily allowed asynchronous learning outside the classroom and increased student-to-student interaction. Students could use the web site, access chapter outlines, grades, critical-thinking and problem-solving questions, self-grading quizzes, and the course syllabus. It was found that the web component of asynchronous environment had a highly positive effect on student learning, problem-solving skills, and critical-thinking skills (Sanders et al. 2001).

Participation and Collaboration

The online discussions and participation among the instructors and students and between students was found to be poor in both but comparatively poorer in asynchronous learning environment. Although, few instructors promoted discussions and participation by provoking students on number of occasions but students were more interested to hear from the instructors and did not actively participate in effective discussions. The course lacked to increase learner-learner interactions that include group assignments, group projects, and online group debates. Communication that took place in online environments was often found to be lacking in richness as compared to traditional face-to-face classrooms.

CONCLUSION

The study indicates that students are ready for the web technology for learning environment. However, students prefer asynchronous over synchronous learning environment, since they do not have to be online at a specific time. Students showed more concern about their convenience. Their learning is more effective in asynchronous environment because they feel they have more time to think and rethink carefully about assignments. In synchronous learning environment students have to response to given questions. Further, study indicates that students have positive attitude toward synchronous learning environment although students are still not friendly to using teleconferencing, whiteboard and chat-room.

REFERENCES

Awalt, M. (1998) The Internet Classroom (http://sunsite.unc.edu/horizon/mono/CDITECH-HTML)

Becker, D. and Dwyer, M. (1994) Using hypermedia to provide learner control, *Journal of Educational Multimedia and Hypermedia*, 3(2) 155-172.

Boroni, C. M., Goosey, F. W., Grinder, M. T., and Ross, R. J. (1998) A paradigm shift! The Internet, the Web, browsers, Java, and the future of computer science education *Proceedings of the 1998 SIGCSE Symposium* Atlanta, 145–152.

Burge, E. J. (1994). "Learning in computer conferenced contexts: The Learners' perspective," *Journal of Distance Education*, 9(1), 19-43.

Chalk, P. (1999). Survey of web worlds for software engineering education, *Proceedings of the 7th Annual Conference on the Teaching of Computing, Belfast*, August 25–27, 37–41.

Chalk, P. (2000). Web worlds-Web-Based Modeling Environments for Learning Software Engineering, *Computer Science Education*, 10(1), 39–56.

Dziuban, C. D., Moskal, P. D., and Dziuban, E. K. (1999) Learning styles go on-line. Unpublished manuscript, University of Central Florida.

Gunawardena, C. N. (1995). Social presence theory and implications for interaction and collaborative learning in computer conferences, International Journal of Educational Telecommunications, 1, 147–166.

Holstein, W. J. (1997). The new economy: Winners and losers are being created with a vengeance. *U.S. News & World Report*, 122(20), 42-48.

Jackson, L. (2000). Applying Virtual Technology: A Joint Project Between The University Of Queensland And Townsville State High School, *Australian Science Teachers Journal*, 46(2),19-23.

Lockyer, L., Patterson, J. and B. Harper (2001), ICT in higher education: Evaluating. Outcomes for health education, *Journal of Computer Assisted Learning*, 17, 275-283.

McManus, T.F. (1996). Delivering instruction on the World Wide Web (http://www.edb.utexas.edu/coe/depts/ci/it/projects/wbi/wbi.html)

Mioduser, D., Nachmias, R., Lahav, O., and Oren, A. (2000) Web-Based Learning Environments: Current Pedagogical And Technological State, Journal of Research on Computing in Education, 33(1), 55-77.

Poustie, M. (2001) Engaging Students and Enhancing Skills: Lessons from the Development of a Web-supported International Environmental Law Conference Simulation, International review of law computers, & Technology, 15(3), 331–344.

Sanders, D. W., Morrison, S., and Alison, I., (2001) Student Attitudes Toward Web-Enhanced Instruction In An Introductory Biology Course, *Journal of Research on Computing in Education*, 33(3), 251-263.

Sankaran S. R., and Tung Bui, (2001). Impact of Learning Strategies and motivation on Performance: A Study in Web-based instruction, *Journal of Instructional Psychology*, 28(3), 191-198.

Shea, R. H. and Boser, U. (2001). So where's the beef? There's high quality online but it takes real work to find it. *U.S. News & World Report*, 131(15), 44-54.

Sorg, S., Davis, B. T., Dziuban, C., Moskal, P., Hartman, J. and Juge, F. (1999). Faculty Development, Learner Support and Evaluation in Web-Based Programs, *Interactive Learning Environments*, 7(2–3), 137–153.

Market Share as a Determinant of Making Profit in the E-Commerce Industry - An Empirical Enquiry

Ramesh Dangol and Sushil K. Sharma
Ball State University, Muncie, Indiana
(Dangol) P: 765-285-5323, F: 765-285-5308, ardangol@bsu.edu
(Sharma) P: 765-285-5315, F: 765-285-5308, ssharma@bsu.edu

ABSTRACT

Researchers, business analysts and practitioners are trying to determine the relationship between market share and profitability for e-commerce companies. We hypothesize that market share has a positive exponential relationship with profitability. This paper investigates the market-share/profitability relationship among 50 out of 173 publicly traded e-commerce companies.

INTRODUCTION

Since January 2000 nearly 10% of Internet-based companies have shut down or declared bankruptcy. In fact, e-commerce companies account for more than fifty percent of companies that failed in this industry. During the Internet boom, the majority of investors assumed that low operating costs in this sector would eventually lead to higher profits. The potential earnings that can be derived from Internet technology prompted many individuals to invest in newly formed e-commerce companies. As a result, in 2000 NASDAQ stock market reached the peak and closed at above 5,000 points. Since then more than four hundred e-commerce companies have shut down or gone bankrupt; a few are struggling to stay afloat. According to Webmergers.com, a total of 423 e-retails went out of business between January 2000 and April 2002, which constitutes 51% of overall online business shutdowns (Miller, 2002). Although the majority of e-commerce companies share similar business models, only a few of them have been able to realize any profits.

In 1999, retailers and venture capitalists were energized and excited about the prospect of capturing market share. Currently, the struggle for profitability weighs heavily on most online merchants. Failed e-commerce companies, falling stock prices, loss of venture capital and pressure from stockholders are forcing Internet companies to take a hard look at profitability. Companies with lower costs will obtain larger profit margins because profitability is a function of cost-efficiency (Gimeno and Woo, 1999). A study conducted by McKinsey-Salomon Smith Barney found that the cost of receiving orders online is lower than the cost of acquiring and distributing goods to customers. Despite low operating costs, the majority of e-commerce companies have not reached a break-even point or generated profits. This may be a result of the relatively smaller market share each company enjoys in this industry. Therefore, we believe that e-commerce companies can generate significant profits if they focus their energy on gaining a larger market share in the industry.

BACKGROUND

Over the years, numerous studies have been conducted to determine the market-share/profitability relationship (Buzzell et al. 1975, Hergert 1984, Markell et al. 1988, Woo, 1984). The results of these studies vary from no significant correlation to a strong positive correlation between market share and profitability. Studies of Buzzell and Woo found a strong positive relationship between market share and profitability. Markell et al. concluded that the link between market share and profitability is an occasional phenomenon rather than a universal law. Hergert's study concluded that although market share and profitability appear to be positively related on average, the relationship is weak overall and non-existent in many industries (Hergert 1984). However, these studies have been conducted on non-Internet-based companies.

The business models of Internet-based e-commerce companies are based on network reach, intangible assets such as relationships, knowledge, people, and brands (Boulton et al., 2000, McGarvey, 2001). Many of these factors will contribute to e-commerce companies' profit margins; however, we believe that market share would make a more significant contribution to profitability. To determine this market-share/profitability relationship, we studied publicly traded e-commerce companies. The study argues that market share is the primary requirement to earn profits and to succeed in this industry.

Thomas (1973) pointed out that larger companies have monopolistic power thus enabling them to bargain more effectively with suppliers compared to those with smaller market shares. Therefore they can obtain goods and services at discounted prices. Similarly, large companies benefit from economies of scale because they can spread their fixed costs over a larger volume of production. Economies of scale and market power can increase companies' overall profits by reducing costs. In the e-commerce industry, 75% of cost savings come from economies of scale and companies' abilities to bargain with suppliers (Morton et al. 2001). Thus, this study hypothesizes that a percent increase in market share will result in more than a percent increase in profitability (Fraering and Minor, 1994).

METHODOLOGY

We randomly selected 50 out of 173 publicly traded e-commerce companies. Financial data for each company was obtained from *www.hoovers.com*. According to *The Market Share Reporter*, the e-commerce industry sold $26.1 billion worth of goods and services in the year 2001. This figure was divided by each company's sales to determine its relative market share in the industry. For example, in 2000 E-bay Inc. occupied 2.87% of total e-commerce market share, which was calculated by dividing total industry sales by the company's revenue of $748.8 million. This relative market share was regressed against the operating profit margin. A similar method was used by Porter to determine the relationship between market share and profitability.

We hypothesized that a unit increase in market share would result in more than a unit increase in profitability. In order to test this relationship, we used regressed relative market share data against a company's operating income (see Equation 1).

Equation 1.

$$\pi = \alpha(MS)^{\beta}$$

π = *Operating Margin*
α = *Constant*
MS = *Relative Market-Share*
β = *Market-Share Parameter*

Equation 1 suggests that there is a positive exponential relationship between the operating margin (dependent variable) and market-share (independent variable). Once the constant and the parameter of market-share are determined, we can calculate the minimum market-share required to break even (see Equation 2).

Equation 2.

$ln\pi = \alpha + \beta lnMS$

$Or\ ln\hat{\pi} - \hat{\alpha} = \hat{\beta}\ lnMS + \varepsilon$

$Or\ e^{\pi} - \hat{\alpha} = MS^{\beta}$

Replacing the predicted profitability with zero and dividing both sides by the power of $1/\hat{\beta}$ will enable us to calculate the minimum market-share required to break even.

RESULTS

Using the above mentioned equations, the study found a positive linear relationship between market-share and profitability in non-Internet companies. However, in the e-commerce industry we observed an exponential relationship between market-share and profitability. This type of relationship is observed because as market-shares for a given company increase, fixed costs will decline at a faster rate compared to non-Internet companies. Also, variable costs tend to increase at a declining rate because large e-commerce companies can reduce costs through economies of scale and bargaining power.

A regression output showed a significant exponential relationship between market-share and operating margin. The relationship between the dependent variable profit margin and independent variable market-share is significant at a 1% confidence level (see Table 1).

When the predicted values for the constant and the coefficient of market-share were substituted in Equation 2, we obtained:

Equation 2.

$e^{\pi} - \hat{\alpha} = MS^{\beta}$

$Or\ e^{o} - (-0.639) = MS^{0.473}$

$At\ a\ breakeven\ point\ \pi = 0$

$Or\ (1 + 0.639)^{1/0.473} = MS$

$Or\ MS = 2.84$

By solving Equation 2, we determined that e-commerce companies must have 2.84% of market-share to break even. In other words, companies with a market-share of greater than 2.84% are likely to enjoy operating profits.

The average market-share and operating profit margin in the e-commerce industry was 0.55% and –1.3995 respectively for the year 2000. ADS Systems Inc., a Texas based computer software and Web hosting company, held the smallest market-share with 0.01%. The company posted a loss of $18 million for the same year. On the other hand, eMerge Interactive Inc., which provides online information and services to livestock producers controlled the highest share with 4.58% and a loss of $33 million.

Table 2 shows that companies with less than 2.84% market-share posted negative net income before taxes of $64 million on average. On the other hand, companies with equal to or more than 2.84% of market-share reported net income before taxes of $32 million on average.

DISCUSSION

As predicted, there is a significant exponential correlation between profit margin and market-share. A percent increase in a market-share leads to more than a percent increase in profit margin. E-commerce companies that wish to become profitable should aim to capture a market-share of greater than 2.84% of the industry. Companies with a market-share of less than 2.84% are unlikely to have market power to bargain with suppliers to purchase goods at discounted prices and will not be able to benefit from economies of scale. As a result, they would not be able to realize substantial profits. As discussed in the preceding section, profitability is a function of cost efficiency. Companies that have lower operating costs in any industry will enjoy higher profits. Companies with higher market-shares can reduce their operating costs by spreading fixed costs over a larger volume of sales and by bargaining with suppliers to obtain goods and services at a discounted price. In the e-commerce industry, market-share plays a significant role in determining a company's profitability because receiving orders online and helping customers using "self help" websites, such as frequently asked questions, costs very little (Tillet, 2001). Further research needs to examine the correlation of market-share and multiple product offerings as well as other factors that influence the success of e-commerce companies.

REFERENCES

Boulton, R.E.S., Libert, B.D. and Samek, S.M. (2000) A business model for the new economy, *The Journal of Business Strategy, vol. 21, Issue 4, p. 29-35.*

Buzzell, R.D., Gale B.T., and Sultan, R.G.M. (1975) Market share – A Key to Profitability, *Harvard Business Review*, vol. 53, pp. 97-106.

Fraering, J. M. and Minor, M.S., (1994), "The Industry-Specific Basis of the Market Share – Profitability Relationship," *Journal of Consumer Marketing*, vol. 11, pp. 27-37.

Gimeno, J., Woo, C.Y. (1999) Multi-market Contact, Economies of Scope, and Firm Performance, *Academy of Management Journal*, Vol. 43, Issue 3, pp. 239-259.

Hergert, M., (1984), "Market Share and Profitability: Is Bigger Really Better?" *Business Economics*, vol. 19, pp. 45-48.

Markell, S.J., Neeley, S.E. and Strickland, T.H., (1988), "Explaining Profitability: Dispelling the Market Share Fog," *Journal of Business Research*, vol. 16, pp. 189-196.

McGarvey, R. (2001) New corporate ethics for the new economy, *World Trade*, vol. 14, Issue 3, p. 43.

Miller, T. (2002) A Statistical Summary of the Dot Com Shakeout, *Business Plan Archive*.

Morton, F.S., Zetteelmeyer, F., Silva, R.J. (2001) Internet Car Retailing, *Journal of Industrial Economics*, vol. 4, pp. 501-520

The Market Share Reporter (Detroit, MI: 2002)

Thomas, B. (1973) The Structure of Retailing and Economies of Scale, *Bulletin of Economics*, Vol. 25, Issue 2, pp. 122-128.

Tillet, L. 2001. Self-Help Saves Money, *Internet Week*, Issue 846, pp. 21

Woo, C.Y. 1984. Market Share Leadership Not Always So Good, *Harvard Business Review*, Jan-Feb, pp. 50-54.

www.hoovers.com

www.webmergers.com

Table 1.

Model		Coefficients	t	Sig.
		Beta		
1	(Constant)	-0.639	-1.820	.075*
	Log Market-share	0.473	2.845	.0007**
$R^2 = 0.447$				
* = Significant at 10% confidence level				
** = Significant at 1% confidence level				

Table 2.

Market-share	Number of Companies	Number of companies reported loss	Number of companies reported profits	Average Loss or Profit
MS < 2.84	47	46	2	-64
MS > 2.84	3	2	1	32

The Concepts of Class and Object as Presented in Selected Java Textbooks

Robert Joseph Skovira, PhD
Robert Morris University, PA
rjskovira@worldnet.att.net

INTRODUCTION

In object-oriented programming languages, and in particular Java, the most elemental concepts are those of class and object. Yet, in many textbooks that are the basis of teaching and learning Java, ideas are not clearly presented. Textbooks that are used to introduce students to object-oriented programming in Java, ought to be clear about the Java structures of class and object and how they are constructed and used. There is a problem with most textbooks purporting to be the learning platform for object-oriented programming in Java. The problem is the breadth and depth of the discussion and presentation of the class and object structures. These structures are concepts introduced and discussed, but the discussion is spare and sparse. There is a reliance on using the syntactical structures to enhance and extend the explanations of what classes and objects are, but the explicit coupling of syntax to concept is weak. The cognitive model of class and object is usually fragmented and not clearly drawn. Object-oriented textbooks in Java do not sufficiently link, in a descriptive or explanatory way, the conception with the syntax. A great burden of understanding of how things go together and work in regards to class and object rests upon the individual reader. Consequently, this essay is a study and analysis of Java textbook presentations of class and object concepts and how these ideas are modeled and implemented. In other words, the paper is a study of the cognitive models of class and object. The paper discusses various ways in which the class and object concepts are represented to students of the Java language.

OBJECT-ORIENTED PROGRAMMING

All of the textbooks say something about object-oriented (O-O) programming, or the object-oriented paradigm. They, in some fashion, try to set the context, but not very well. In most cases, the object-oriented paradigm is presented as a natural way of dealing with what most of the authors call "the real world." Programming in the O-O paradigm is modeling entities of real world environments.

One author writes that O-O programs are "models" of "real world system" The program consists of "objects" representing "entities," customers, vendors, reports, transactions, in the world (Hughes, 2002, 31). Another author states that object-oriented languages "model objects in the real world" and that classes are "representations" of things in the world (Cornelius, 2001, xiii-xiv). Another text states that another O-O feature is its "natural" way of perceiving and thinking about things. Problem solving is identifying "objects" in problematic situations and any necessary "actions" (Garside & Mariani, 2003, 29).

But, even so the O-O paradigm is not clearly conceptualized in the textbooks. For example, one author states that object orientation is about objects and sending and receiving "messages" (Morelli, 2000, 58). The same text describes object oriented programming in terms of the principles or rules such as divide and conquer, encapsulation, interface, information hiding, generality, and extensibility (Morelli, 2000, 8-9). Thus, a text states that "object definitions" and "instances of actual objects" are features of the O-O paradigm (Garside & Mariani, 2003, 35).

For several other textbooks, the O-O paradigm refers to how "data" and "procedures" are packaged in "objects" or "encapsulated," effectively "hiding" them (Shelly, Cashman & Starks, 2001, JI.10; Deitel & Deitel, 2002, 380). Finally, one text, usually used as a support text in trying to understand object-oriented programming, states that O-O paradigm is about joining functions and data to simplify a program (Holzner, 1998, 15).

GENERAL NOTION OF OBJECT

Some of the texts begin the discussion of what an "object" is by alluding to examples of experienced objects in the everyday world. Am object is thought of as a conceptual structure or a module of code. Objects are representational of things we deal with (Savitch, 2001, 211). But, one author sees an object in relation to activity and tasks. Classifying things or objects in the world is a natural way of thinking about the world and its things. Objects are grouped based on some differentiating attribute (Morelli, 2000, 60). Objects are inanimate things about which we have difficulty thinking that they send and receive message. However, objects are animate things in the world which do naturally communicate and interact with one another by sending and receiving messages (Morelli, 2000, 7). Another text, for example, states that, "Object is a broad term that stands for many things. For example, a student, a desk, a circle, and even a mortgage loan can all be viewed as objects. Certain properties define an object, and certain behaviors define what it does (Liang, 2000, 142)."

For at least one text, the idea of object is a useful device for modeling complexity in systems. "We can use the concept of objects to model quite complicated real-world systems that consists of many different kinds of objects and many instances thereof" (Garside & Mariani, 2003, 30).

SPECIAL NOTION OF OBJECT

From an instructor's, and student's, points of view, the penultimate idea to grapple with in O-O programming is the special notion of object. This idea is dealt with in all of the texts, as would be expected. But, as perhaps, not expected, the idea is not as well presented as it ought to be, in my estimation. One text states that an object is "module" "encapsulating" a program's behavior (Morelli, 2000, 7). Another text states that an "object" has "data" and "actions" (Savitch, 2001, 210). An object is a complex entity (Savitch, 2001, 213) that has callable operations (Garside & Mariani, 2003, 30). Further attempt at clarification is when a text states that an object has a "state," i.e., its data and procedures (Garside & Mariani, 2003, 29). The ultimate clarifying note is that an object is a "noun" (Shelly, Cashman & Starks, 2001, JI.12).

One of the most repeated explanatory sentences in all the textbooks is the one that simply states that an object is an instance of a class (Liang, 2000, 144; Morelli, 2000, 64; Liang , 2000, 143; Cornelius , 2001, 43, 50; Bishop, 1998, 23).

The most intriguing explanation is to be found in two texts. This is that an object is a "black box" (Garside & Mariani, 2003, 30; Shelly, Cashman & Starks, 2001, JI.12).

Another explanatory attempt views an object as a modeling piece, perhaps like a Lego block. The interesting thing here is that the explanation leads to the notion of a class as a category of objects sharing behavior. A class defines shared behavior. So, instead of dealing with the idea of what an object is, we move to what defines it. The text states that objects are "model elements" (Anow & Weirs, 2000, 4).

CLASSES AS CONSTRUCTS AND DEFINITIONS

One text states that classes are "constructs" defining objects by specifying variables and methods (Liang, 2000, 143; Holzner, 1998, 15; Bishop, 1998, 80; Morelli, 2000, 63, 65).

Other texts discuss class as a definition encapsulating an object's information and behaviors (Morelli, 2000, 61, 78 ; Schildt, 2001, 130; Garside & Mariani, 2003, 40; Savitch, 2001, 211-212).

One text states that a class is a "category" of objects, a way of classifying common properties and behaviors (Shelly, Cashman & Starks, 2001, JI,12).

One text suggests that a class is set of elements or declarations about information and processes (Anow & Weirs, 2000, 4; Hughes, 2002, 250).

Other texts discuss the notion of class as a way of defining "types" of things, the things beings objects as instances of the class (Cornelius, 2001, 44, xix, 23; Schildt, 2001, 130). This idea of a class-defining-new-type of entity is an way of extending objects and the scope of Java (Adams, Nyhoff & Nyhoff, 2001, 70).

One text states that a class is an "abstract entity" or an "abstraction" (Morelli, 2000, 77; Garside & Mariani, 2003, 43).

EXPLANATORY METAPHORS

An interesting aspect of the various texts studied here is that they all try to describe the function, and perhaps, nature, of a class by certain metaphors. These metaphors are blueprint, template, model, pattern, recipe, and cookie cutter. While we all commonly understand what these metaphors say, they still do not bring the instructor or the student any closer to the notion of class.

One metaphor for describing what a class is blueprint (Liang, 2000, 143). Another author uses the same metaphor of blueprint and creates a synonym in the form of the template metaphor (Morelli, 2000, 63; Garside & Mariani, 2003, 43). Another author uses the template metaphor (Schildt, 2001, 130). Still, another text manages to use template, blueprint, and extend the metaphoric range to include pattern, and model. (Adams, Nyhoff & Nyhoff, 2001, 70). Some flip places; the main metaphor is template, followed by blueprint (Morelli, 2000, 61). Another metaphor is the recipe (Liang, 2000, 143). A text uses the model metaphor to describe a class; here a class is a representation something. (Anow & Weirs, 2000, 2, 57). Another author uses a cookie cutter to cookie metaphor (Holzner, 1998, 14-15).

CONCLUSION

The burden of explaining the natures, and not merely the syntax, of class and object, and their relationship is the instructor's in almost all cases to bring things together coherently. The syntax for creating a class which defines objects is straight forward. But, it takes awhile to realize that not all classes produce objects. Thus, the sense of the relationship between class and object shows up in the discussion and understanding of how instance variables and class variables function within a program. That is, what an instance variable is and what a class variable is refers to what they do or can do in a program. The same holds for the discussion of instance methods and class methods. Understanding how these two kinds of methods work, and are allowed to work, shows up in understanding the relationship of class and object. It also shows up in the understanding that not all classes produce instances, are used to produce instances, or objects. This explanatory burden extends to the discussion of abstract classes and to interfaces as they appear in the object-oriented world of Java. And, this leads us to a consideration of the analysis and design of systems in an object-oriented manner. While we may experience, at the level of detail, things and stuff we can turn into objects, we must ultimately think, or program, the experienced objects as classes. We must do a classification turn, and create the conceptual versions of the actual things, the actual objects. This classifying turn is not discussed at all in any of the textbooks reviewed in this essay.

REFERENCES

Adams, Joel, Nyhoff, Larry R. and Nyhoff, Jeffrey. (2001). *Java: An introduction to computing.* Upper Saddle River, NJ: Prentice Hall.

Anow, David M. and Weirs, Gerald. (2000). *Introduction to programming using Java: An object-oriented approach.* Reading, MA: Addison Wesley Longman.

Bishop, Judy M. (1998). *Java gently.* Harlow, England: Addison Wesley Longman.

Cornelius, Barry. (2001). *Understanding Java.* Harlow, England: Pearson Education.

Deitel, H.M. and Deitel, P.J. (2002). *Java: How to program,* 4e. Upper Saddle River, NJ: Prentice Hall.

Garside, Roger and Mariani, John. (2003). *Java: First contact,* 2e. Pacific Grove, CA: Brooks/Cole Thomson Learning.

Holzner, Steven. (1998). *Java 1.2: In record time.* San Francisco: Sybex.

Hughes, David. (2002). *Fundamentals of computer science using Java.* Boston: Jones and Bartlett.

Liang, Y. Daniel. (2000). *Introduction to Java programming with Microsoft Visual J++ 6.* Upper Saddle River, NJ: Prentice Hall.

Morelli, Ralph. (2000). *Java, Java, Java: Object-oriented problem solving approach.* Upper Saddle River, NJ: Prentice Hall.

Savitch, Walter. (2001). *Java: An introduction to computer science and programming,* 2e. Upper Saddle River, NJ: Prentice Hall.

Schildt, Hebert. (2001). *Java 2: The complete reference,* 4e. Berkeley: Osborne/McGraw-Hill.

Shelly, Gary B., Cashman, Thomas J. and Starks, Joy L. (2001). *Java programming: Complete concepts and techniques.* Boston: Course Technology.

Constructing a Java Programming Syllabus: Some Observations

Robert Joseph Skovira, Ph.D.
Robert Morris University, PA
rjskovira@worldnet.att.net

Putting a syllabus together for any course or class is always an experience and an intellectual struggle. A syllabus, especially in a programming course, is not merely (or should not be) a copying of the book chapter titles. A syllabus is a means of getting knowledge in the head (or perhaps in textbooks) out into the world, of creating and sharing knowledge in the world. A syllabus is a conceptual structure of a subject area. This essay discusses the construction of a syllabus for a class on Java programming as an example of the dimensionalities of a course syllabus.

For some, a course syllabus is a legal document. Some of the legalities show up in "policy" statements. For example, "Policies: Attendance policy follows the C&IS department's policy (25% missed). Attendance will be taken every session. The student is responsible for obtaining any missed notes and materials and assignments. Make arrangements (phone numbers or email) with other people to do this for you, should you need to miss a session."

For others, it is a plan, a pathway through a discipline, area of study, or subject matter. It is a template for, a conception of, significant notions of a particular subject matter. This plan or way through the thicket of a particular subject matter shows up in the weekly topics of study and discussion. This is usually the bulk of any syllabus. For example:

1. 27 August   *Introduction to Course*
2. 3 September   *Java Introduced*
    Chapter 1 Introduction to Java and Visual J++, 3-44
    Geography Lessons in Visual J++
        JAR 1 due
3. 10 September   *Basic Elements & Structures*
    Ch 2 Java Building Elements, 45-78
    Ch 3 Control Structures, 79-109
4. 17 September   *Object-Oriented Thinking*
    Ch 4 Methods, 111-138
    Ch 5 Programming with Objects and Classes, 139-183
        JAR 2 due

A course syllabus is an intentional document, a rhetorical device to alert an audience, the students, to the shape and form, the profile of a subject. As a rhetorical means, a syllabus may operate as a tool of discovery, a map of already explored parts, or a codified repository of elements to be learned anew by a new generation. This intentional approach first shows up in the course description and in the course objectives. The course description for the undergraduate Java course is: "INFS3151 Java Programming provides the opportunity for students to learn an object-oriented language and to learn object-oriented programming. The course is aimed at learning how to program in Java and developing Java applications and applets. Topics included are Object-oriented Programming, Classes, Objects, Instances, Methods, Applets and Applications, Control Structures in Java, Java Arrays (as Objects), Strings and Characters, Graphics, Multimedia, Exception Handling, Multithreading, Files and Streams, Networking." The objectives of the course are: "To study and learn object-oriented programming, To study and learn object-oriented program design concepts and techniques, To study and learn the object-oriented programming language, Java 2 (JDK 1.2.2), To study and learn about JDK (Java Development Kit, Sun Microsystems), To study and learn about the IDE Visual J++, To gain an understanding of self."

A syllabus is an existential document because it is created with an audience in mind, but one that is situated in a set of circumstances. It is a dynamic state-of-affairs. How it is an existential document shows up in ways much like the following statement: "Any part of this syllabus may changed by the professor at any moment in time, depending on where you are, and if there is a valid reason, including the whim of the professor."

A course syllabus reflects a context, and represents situations of performance within that context. The context is an educational one, not merely a training context. There is a different sense as to the reasons why someone may be studying the subject matter, in this case Java. This does not mean that "training" is not addressed, because these concerns commonly show up in the definitions of the situation according to the students. They are studying Java for a variety of reason, from "required" to "want to use it in the workplace". Situations of performance show up in any syllabus in terms of the assignments developed and given and in the manner in which a student's performance is reported on. For example, in this case, a student, when asked to do an assignment, which is commonly a programming assignment, is required to submit the results of the assignment in a report. The report details the assignment problem picked (usually a student has a choice of one from several problems), the algorithm designed to accomplish the task, the code of the Java program, screen shots of the output, and a discussion of any and all problems the student encountered, including error messages, on the way to completing the assignment. This report is designed to insure the engagement of the student in the learning process of doing any assignment. It is integral to the nature of the course.

A course syllabus is also a model of a particular subject matter, purporting to reflect or represent a body of knowledge, a logical space of known objects or propositions, processes, procedures, and vocabularies.

A course syllabus is also an abstract list of things known to practitioners or a community of practice, but represents things to be learned.

A syllabus is a representation of how a professor sees the subject matter and how he or she thinks things ought to be understood.

A course syllabus is a definition of a subject. A course syllabus models the known states-of-affairs of a subject area. The modeling of the known state of affairs in a discipline or area of study is difficult to do, and depends upon and uses other recognized models. These other models commonly show up in textbooks. Usually, one these models is picked to be the basis for a course, but to design a course appropriately, many other models as possible ought to be consulted. For example, the textbook used in this Java course is: Liang, Y. Daniel. (2000). *Introduction to Java programming with Microsoft Visual J++ 6.* Upper Saddle River, NJ: Prentice Hall. However, these other textbooks were used to build the syllabus, and to understand the subject matter behind the categories found in the syllabus: Adams, Joel, Nyhoff, Larry R. and Nyhoff, Jeffrey. (2001). *Java: An introduction to computing.* Upper Saddle River, NJ: Prentice Hall; Anow, David M. and Weirs, Gerald. (2000). *Introduction to programming using Java: An object-oriented approach.* Reading, MA: Addison Wesley; Longman, Cornelius, Barry. (2001). *Understanding Java.* Harlow, England: Pearson Education; Garside, Roger and Mariani, John. (2003). *Java: First contact,* 2e. Pacific Grove, CA: Brooks/Cole Thomson Learning; Hughes, David. (2002). *Fundamentals of computer science using Java.* Boston: Jones and Bartlett; Savitch, Walter. (2001). *Java: An introduction to computer science and programming,* 2e. Upper Saddle River, NJ: Prentice Hall; and Wigglesworth, Joe and Lumby, Paula. (2000). *Java programming: Advanced topics.* Cambridge, MA: Course Technology/Thomson Learning

A syllabus is a management tool of a project of learning. A course syllabus is a cultural artifact, for it exists within institutions, and a social setting. It represents something of value within the social scene. So, it is a social fact which spawns other facts of behavior (grades for example). These other facts are emotional and cognitive facts.

A course syllabus is a philosophical treatise because it rests on ontological and epistemological assumptions. It is an ontology of a worldview. In this case, it is the world of Java and the world of object-oriented programming.

A course syllabus is a lexicon, an introduction to a vocabulary. The vocabulary is the vocabulary of Java programming language, and its semantics and syntax. It is also a taxonomy of categories. The categories name and collect experiences, things, events, and bric-a-brac into coherent classification systems. A syllabus is an information architecture of a subject matter. In most (if not all) instances, a particular syllabus is only one of many possible architectures of a subject. Usually, specific textbooks offer a specific architecture to follow. A syllabus represents in the view of its creator an architecture designed to optimally traverse the subject matter.

Peer-to-Peer Corporate Resource Sharing and Distribution with Mesh

Ramesh Subramanian
Quinnipiac University – School of Business
275 Mount Carmel Avenue, Hamden, CT 06518
P: 203-582-5276, F: 203-582-8664
ramesh.subramanian@quinnipiac.edu

Brian Goodman
IBM – Advanced Internet Technology
150 Kettletown Road, Mail Drop 121
Southbury, CT 06488
bgoodman@us.ibm.com

INTRODUCTION

Currently, much of the corporate data and content within "global" organizations are distributed by replicating and distributing such data and content using centralized content repositories. That is, the data is globally distributed, but made available within a location or geographical area by using a "central" server that is responsible for serving the content to clients located within the area.

The advent of peer-to-peer (P2P) computing has changed this approach. The term "P2P computing" emphasizes the shift away from centralized and client/server models of computing to a fully decentralized, distributed model of computing.

During the last couple of years, the term "P2P," or "peer-to-peer" has aggressively moved to the center-stage of the computing field. According to Clay Shirky, "P2P is a class of applications that takes advantage of resources – storage, cycles, content, human presence – available at the edges of the Internet…" **(Shirky, 2000)**. A report on P2P technology by Gartner Consulting **(Gartner Consulting Report, 2001)** states that "half of the current server-based content management vendors will add Data Centered P2P functionality to their product offerings by 2005 (0.7 probability)."

With P2P computing, the accent has shifted from storing content in, and serving from, centralized servers to storing and serving (at least some of) the content from the client-side. In this model, the content provider manages his/her content in a local client, and shares the content with anyone who is allowed to access the content. Responsibility for content creation, storage and security dwells on the client side. This has a lot of ramifications for the way in which corporate data is distributed.

There are several advantages to using the P2P approach to resource sharing in organizations. By shifting the responsibility for content to the client side, server-side management of diverse resources can be vastly reduced. Server managers need not be responsible for the integrity of the content. Problems arising from centralized distribution of content could possibly be averted.

The disadvantages include factors such as reduced security and reduced integrity of content arising from client-side mismanagement.

In this paper we discuss the architecture and implementation details of Mesh, a P2P system for corporate resource sharing. In section 2 we discuss current P2P architectures, their strengths and weaknesses. In section 3 we discuss some prime issues in P2P computing. In section 4 we present the primary design considerations underlying Mesh. In section 5 we present the Mesh architecture and discuss how Mesh works. In this section, we also specify certain generic characteristics for P2P systems. Section 6 contains implementation notes, and section 7 presents our conclusions.

P2P ARCHITECTURES: CURRENT ART

Several P2P implementations have been proposed in recent months. Most of the P2P applications are *file-centric*, and facilitate either synchronous or asynchronous file sharing. Newer applications also provide access to resources other than files. Almost all of the P2P systems that have been implemented use either a central-server based approach (e.g., Napster) or a "pure" P2P approach (e.g., Gnutella-based implementations. Gnutella is discussed in a later section).

We discuss below, the main architectural approaches to peer-to-peer resource sharing systems: P2P with centralized control, *pure* P2P, and a hybrid approach that incorporates aspects of the former two approaches.

Napster

A good example of P2P with centralized control is *Napster*. *(Note: In July 2000, Ninth Circuit U.S. District Judge Marilyn Hall Patel, issued the first of two injunctions that closed down the Napster service (from King, 2002). The Napster company and web site (http://www.napster.com), which in late 1999 boasted of 80 million registered users, is now defunct)*. The Napster system uses a central server to maintain a list of connected clients. Every client connects to the central server, which scans the clients' disks for shared resources, and maintains directories and indexes of the resources. The central server responds to search queries from connected clients by sending back information on which of the clients hold the resources. Once a client knows where to find the resources that it is seeking (i.e., which client has the files it is searching for), it makes a direct connection to the appropriate client and transfers the resources.

Napster is not web-based, and does not run in a browser. It is a stand-alone application that runs on each individual client, and uses TCP/IP for its data-communication and data transfers. Since Napster depends on a central server that acts as a collector and regulator of information, the clients are not guaranteed anonymity. The Napster system is also vulnerable if the central server fails.

Gnutella

A good example of *pure* P2P is *Gnutella* (http://gnutella.wego.com). Gnutella is a generic term used to identify those P2P systems that use the gnutella protocol **(Kan, 2001)**. This is a reverse-engineered version of a P2P protocol that briefly appeared in AOL's system around March 2000, as a means for sharing recipes. Thus, there is no single interpretation of what the protocol is, actually. However, there are certain common elements that manifest in Gnutella-based systems. Chief among those is that Gnutella does away with the central server. In this system, each client continuously keeps track of other clients by pinging known clients in the system. Searches are propagated from one client to its immediate neighbors in ever-increasing circles until answers are found, or the search times out. Search responses are propagated back to the searcher in the same manner.

Like Napster, Gnutella-based systems are also not web-based, and run as stand-alone applications in client environments.

Gnutella is a truly anonymous resource sharing system. The searcher does not know the identity of the responder, and vice-versa. Trust is implicitly assumed.

A serious problem of Gnutella-based systems is their reputation for being unreliable. Lacking a central server that keeps track of which client is connected, and which is not, there is no way for a particular client to know if all its neighbors are alive and connected. This leads to less than reliable performance.

Web Mk

The *third* approach to P2P systems is what is referred to as *Web Mk*. This is more of an approach than an actual product, and is described in a Gartner Group Report **(Gartner Consulting Report, 2001)** on the emergence of P2P computing.

This is a web-based approach that uses web servers and web browsers. The web browsers would be configurable by users and would integrate resource-sharing features. The servers will maintain multiple indexes and allow access to different forms of data. This type of system would use software agents or Bots to provide services such as extraction and consolidation of multiple resources, chat facilities, and notifications of changes. Search requests could be stored in the server and set to run in real-time or as a batch process, and alert the appropriate clients of the results.

The Gartner Report article does not mention any specific product that uses this approach. It is likely that a few products that incorporate some of the features described in the report will be released in time.

JXTA

A fourth approach to P2P computing is JXTA. Sun Microsystems has recently offered a new P2P application framework called JXTA (pronounced 'juxta') **(Gong, 2001)**. The framework offers a set of protocols, each of which is defined by a message. Each message has a predefined format and includes various data fields. The protocols offered are:
- Peer Discovery Protocol: Enables a peer to find another peer, peer group or advertisement.
- Peer Resolver Protocol: Enables peers to send and receive generic queries.
- Peer Information Protocol: Enables peers to learn more about other peers.
- Peer Membership Protocol: Enables a peer to join other peer groups, get information about or membership into groups, etc.
- Pipe Binding Protocol: Allows a peer to bind a pipe advertisement to a pipe end-point, thus indicating where messages actually go over the pipe.
- Endpoint Routing Protocol: Enables a peer to get routing information to route messages.

JXTA is transport-independent and can utilize TCP/IP as well as other transport standards. It is meant to be a conceptual framework that provides some protocols and mechanisms using which one can implement either a centralized or decentralized P2P system. In our opinion, JXTA offers a robust and flexible P2P solution framework. However, it must be noted that the protocols it offers are not standard.

ISSUES IN P2P FRAMEWORKS

Issues about the performance of Gnutella have been widely studied and discussed in available P2P literature **(Hong, 2001)**. Since JXTA is a relatively new, with a limited number of P2P implementations based on it, we not have much by way of prior studies. However, we believe that both Gnutella and JXTA, at their core, share certain basic traits. We discuss these traits, with the associated issues related to performance.
- **Effort expended:** Both approaches primarily offer frameworks for a "pure" (or almost pure) P2P architecture, which disposes of the need for a "central" server. Since there is no central server to maintain a master index, it takes more effort to query the system. Since each search requires a hop, this adds to the total bandwidth load and increases the search time. The lack of a central server also requires that a peer be aware of at least one other connected peer. Several recent Gnutella-based systems have tried to solve this problem by including a central server, which plays a limited role, such as providing some seed-IP numbers to a peer joining the network – thereby moving away from a "pure" P2P implementation.
- **Participation base:** Both approaches to building P2P communities are synchronous, and thus depend on the presence of a sufficient base of connected clients in order to function successfully.
- **Connection speed:** Connection speed dominates processor and I/O speed as the bottleneck. Due to the highly parallel nature of P2P, a connection fast enough to talk to one remote peer quickly becomes less so for ten of them trying to connect simultaneously. This problem will affect both Gnutella and JXTA systems, as they are inherently synchronous systems.
- **Free rider:** According to a recent analysis by E. Adar and B.A. Huberman at Xerox PARC **(Edar and Huberman, 2000)**, nearly 70 percent of current Gnutella users may be sharing no files at all. This may not be a big issue with central-server systems like Napster, since all the files and directories are indexed in the central server. But in a Gnutella system, where searches are propagated to each peer, this may consume more bandwidth and contribute to performance decline. (This problem may have been solved in JXTA, through the introduction of the "Endpoint Routing Protocol").

OUR APPROACH TO P2P RESOURCE SHARING: PRIMARY DESIGN CONSIDERATIONS

We propose a hybrid approach to P2P resource sharing within a corporate environment. The approach is code-named *Mesh*. Mesh is a hybrid system for P2P resource sharing. It consists of both a server and a client component. It supports the features of the three existing P2P architectures described above, as well as certain some additional characteristics.

The Mesh client is an application running in the client computer, and will be a modified Gnutella client. While building upon the base protocol we integrate a reliable IP repository, security integration through enterprise systems, an enhanced client side database for better search results and some basic network activity reduction. Together these qualities provide better P2P services for the corporate environment.

Specific characteristics of Mesh:
- **Reliable IP Repository** – Unlike Gnutella, each client first "announces itself" to a Mesh server, and requests a list of IP addresses of connected clients. The Mesh server sends a seed list of the connected clients. (We call this a "seed" list because each client needs only a limited number of other connected clients to get started). The Mesh server maintains a "current" list of connected clients by maintaining a list of clients, and pinging each client periodically.
- **Metadata** – Most of the currently available P2P systems do not provide the facility for client-side metadata description. Mesh will provide for client-side metadata description. Client-side metadata description allows an easy way to search for different types of content based on types (i.e., spreadsheet, audio, video), content subject (i.e., annual report, benefits plan, etc), content keywords, etc.
- **Authentication and Authorization** – The metadata could also consist of simple file descriptions as well as security and access control information. The security checks can be local account based or enterprise level security such as the corporate LDAP directory.
- **Enhanced Client Database** – Each Mesh client maintains a database of resources that it shares. The database will not only contain names and characteristics of the files, but also user-defined metadata describing the files.
- **Reduced Network Activity** – Unlike Gnutella, each client does NOT ping the other clients continuously. Instead, a client maintains awareness of other connected clients by downloading the list of IP addresses from the Mesh server periodically. Each client sends a Gnutella handshake to each of the clients in the list received. If a Gnutella acknowledgement is received from another client, that client is added to the original client's list.
- **Gnutella Protocol Based** – Like most of the packet communications, search and search response is accomplished among clients using the Gnutella protocol **(CapnBry, 2002)**.

This approach enables us to use the central server concept within a P2P environment that results in a highly enhanced P2P resource sharing system. This system thus builds upon existing P2P approaches and provides additional functionality.

MESH ARCHITECTURE

The Mesh architecture is illustrated in Figure 1.

Explanation of the Architecture
- Like Gnutella clients/servers, Mesh receives three types of messages, GET, SEARCH and PING. In the figure these low level packets are represented as components (boxes). The code in a Mesh client that handles "message routing" is labeled "Event Dispatcher."
- The Event Dispatcher takes the incoming packet and routes it to the correct message handler (i.e., PING, GET or SEARCH handler). Items in the figure marked in gray represent the components that are Mesh specific. These are the Reliable IP components, and the Authorization and Authentication components.
- In Figure 1, it should be noted that GET and SEARCH cannot be reached directly. A user may choose to share files without any required security checks. However, if a security check has been specified, if there is a security violation, then the remote client's request is never handed off to

the GET and SEARCH handlers. Basically, this means that the GET and SEARCH are hidden behind a custom firewall.

- The PING handler uses the "Reliable IP subsystem" (see figure above), and is not behind any security wall. It thus functions like a handler in any typical Gnutella client/server. In fact, the GET, PING and SEARCH handlers appear to a remote client as "available." The remote client does not know if a particular action is possible on a Mesh client or not. If a remote client initiates an action (i.e., PING, SEARCH or GET), and does not get any response, it simply means that the Mesh client's resources were protected against unauthorized searches and GETs. When there is a failed authorization or failed authentication, the remote client initiating the action does not receive any response from the search (i.e., it does not receive a response such as: "No items found"). Thus the remote client has not way of knowing if the items requested were protected or if they were non-existent.

Generic Architectural Attributes of P2P Resource Sharing Systems

Based on the prior work and our own work described above, we list below some attributes that we believe should be generic to P2P resource sharing systems. It is important to note that these attributes are not all available in current P2P systems. Some of the attributes have been incorporated into our Mesh system implementation.

- P2P systems should provide mechanisms for providing a reliable set of IPs to each connected peer. For example, each peer could first "announce itself" to a central server, and request a list of IP addresses of other connected peers. The server would send a seed list of the connected peers' IPs. (We call this a "seed" list because each peer needs only a limited number of other connected peers to get started). The central server maintains a "current" list of connected clients by pinging each client periodically – thus providing a reliable IP repository of connected peers.
- Each peer should maintain an enhanced database of resources that it shares. The database should not only contain names and characteristics of the files, but also user-defined metadata describing the files – thus providing an enhanced client database that is easier to search
- The metadata could consist of simple file descriptions as well as security and access control information. The security checks can be local account based or enterprise level security such as the corporate LDAP directory – thus providing enhanced authentication and authorization in the P2P resource sharing environment.
- Every peer need NOT ping the other peers continuously. Instead, a peer can maintain awareness of other connected peers by downloading the list of IP addresses from the central server. Each peers will then send a handshake to each of the peers in the list received. If an acknowledgement is received from another peer, that peer is added to the original peer's list. This "handshake" is also repeated while initiating a search, and defunct IPs are discovered and removed – a process that would lead to reduced network activity and decreased bandwidth usage.
- The central server can be enhanced to maintain a list of previous searches done by a specific peer, so that when the peer that actually has the resource comes online, it can be informed about the search.

IMPLEMENTATION

The Mesh implementation consists of two parts: the Mesh server and the Mesh client. The Mesh server was implemented in Java™. The Mesh client was implemented in Sash™. Sash Weblications for Windows is a dynamically configurable programming environment for rapidly building and deploying platform-integrated desktop applications using JavaScript and DHTML. This programming environment enables Web programming beyond the browser, and the resulting applications are integrated seamlessly into the common desktop environment and take advantage of the latest standards in Web services (http://www.alphaworks.ibm.com/tech/sash).

Figures 2 through 4 present some representative screenshots of the Mesh implementation.

CONCLUSION

In this paper, we have described a P2P system that is built using a hybrid approach, combining the features of pure P2P and central-server-oriented P2P systems. This approach enables us to use the central server concept within a P2P environment that results in a highly enhanced P2P resource sharing system. This system thus builds upon existing P2P approaches and provides additional functionality.

We have also provided a generic set of attributes for P2P systems, such as providing reliable IPs for P2P interaction, providing extensions to enhanced searches, providing enterprise level security and reducing network activity.

Preliminary tests indicate that the prototype and architecture is viable, and future work will involve enhanced architectures and testing for scalability.

REFERENCES

CapnBry 2002. "The Gnutella protocol," available online at http://capnbry.net/gnutella/protocol.php.

Edar, E. and Huberman, B.A. 2000. *"Free Riding on Gnutella,"* First Monday, Issue 5_10, October 2000, available online at http://firstmonday.org/issues/issue5_10/adar/index.html.

Gartner Consulting 2001. "The Emergence of Distributed Content Management and Peer-to-Peer Content Networks," GartnerGroup Report # 010022501, January 2001.

Gong, Li 2001. "JXTA: A Network Programming Environment," IEEE Internet Computing, Vol .5, No. 3, May/June 2001, available online at http://computer.org/internet/v5n3/w3jxta.html.

Hong, Theodore 2001. *"Performance,"* in Peer-To-Peer: Harnessing the Benefits of a Disruptive Technology, pp 203-241, Edited by Andy Oram, O'Reilly & Associates, California, 2001.

Kan, Gene 2001. *"Gnutella,"* in Peer-To-Peer: Harnessing the Benefits of a Disruptive Technology, pp 94-122, Edited by Andy Oram, O'Reilly & Associates, California, 2001.

King, Brad 2002. *The Day the Napster Died,"* Wired News, May 15, 2002. Available at http://www.wired.com/news/mp3/0,1285,52540,00.html.

Shirky, Clay 2000. *"What is P2P..And What Isn't,"* November 2000; available online at http://www.openp2p.com/pub/a/p2p/2000/11/24/shirky1-whatisp2p.html.

URLS CITED

The Napster home page, http://www.napster.com
The Gnutella home page

Figure 1. Mesh architecture

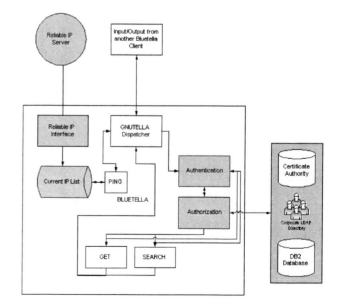

Figure 2. Mesh main screen

Figure 4. Mesh search results screen

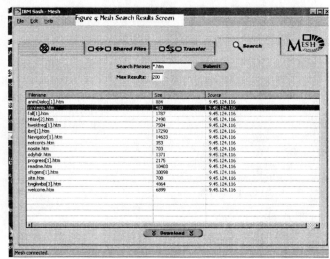

Figure 3. Mesh shared files screen

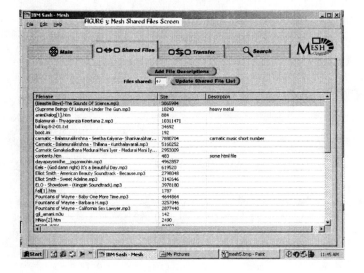

Meeting Industry's Changing IT Needs

Dewey Swanson, Nancy Wilson Head, and Julie Phillips
Purdue University School of Technology
4601 Central Avenue, Columbus, IN 47203
dswanson@puc.iupui.edu, (812) 348-7238
nhead@puc.iupui.edu, (812) 348-7211
japhillips@puc.iupui.edu, (812) 348-7207

INTRODUCTION

Purdue University's School of Technology has long been a proponent of responding to the industry and business needs in order to enhance the social and economic development of the state.

One of the strong partnerships that has developed over the years is between the Purdue University location in Columbus, IN and Cummins Inc. a leading worldwide designer and manufacturer of diesel engines and related products for trucks and other equipment. Purdue University entered into a joint venture with Cummins Inc. in 1997 in an attempt to benefit Purdue, Cummins and the local community. The program named Advanced Information Technology Training Program (AITTP) started as a one-time effort that has evolved into a program offered twice a year since the initial offering in 1997.

The Advanced Information Technology Training Program (AITTP) is a program where Purdue University offers six credit courses and a project delivered in a compressed format for Cummins Inc. employees and individuals from the community. These courses have focused in the database area developing skills for application developers or database administrators by providing a strong foundation for new hires and retraining current employees. Students go through the program as a cohort group. Since its inception there have been over seventy graduates of the program. According to Cummins the normal IT attrition rate is estimated at 15%. For the AITTP graduates this rate is approximately 8%.

The AITTP has been used as a prototype by the CPT department as an external source of funds and a means to acquire new faculty.

SYSTEMS/BUSINESS ANALYST PROGRAM

Cummins Inc. approached Purdue University School of Technology in the summer of 2002 with a proposal to develop a program to educate/train Systems/Business Analyst. The program was initially based on the AITTP program that currently existed between Cummins Inc. and Purdue University School of Technology. However after many planning meetings it was determined that this program would be vastly different.

Program Development

Cummins Inc. Information Technology management, two Purdue University School of Technology CPT associate professors, an OLS associate professor, and the director of the Columbus location met to brainstorm the development of a Business Systems Analyst training program. Cummins Inc. shared with the group an "IT Functional Excellence Skills Matrix", a document that they use to determine the skills necessary for a specific IT Function and then to determine how to deliver this training to their employees, hence our involvement. The Purdue School of Technology Professors shared syllabi of what existing CPT courses and OLS courses could meet these skill needs.

After many brainstorming sessions and renditions of the material, it was determined that the following four skills were critical at this point in the Systems/Business Analysts training: Systems Analysis/Information Technology Awareness, Facilitation/Team Building, Basic Business Knowledge, and Communication. It was also determined that these courses would be noncredit, with pieces taken from existing courses.

Content, Format, and Delivery

The content of the Systems/Business Analyst Program would consist of the four following skills sets:
1. Systems Analysis/Information Technology Awareness
2. Facilitation/Team Building
3. Basic Business Knowledge
4. Communication Skills

The training will be completed in two weeks, 8:00 am - 5:00 pm, with approximately 20 participants in attendance. The material will be delivered by associate professors, an assistant professor and an adjunct faculty based on their area of expertise. The Systems/Business Analyst skills identified above will be dispersed through the entire two week period, with all of the professors present throughout, hence creating a team approach to training. The application based training will be delivered through mini lectures, exercises, and activities. Based on Cummins Inc.'s request for student assessment, case studies and exams will be included in the training.

Purdue University Issues

The Systems/Business Analyst program is completely different in format from its predecessor, the AITTP program. AITTP consisted of six Purdue University credit courses being taught by individual instructors in a six to eight day delivery time for each class. The Systems/Business Analyst program is non-credit material taught over two weeks by a team of five instructors. Administratively, this posed some new challenges in addition to the old challenges that had been addressed in the AITTP.

Pricing the Program

The first challenge was to price the program. The methodology used to price the Systems/Business Analyst Program would be different from the methodology used for the AITTP program. Some costs would be consistent with both programs such as administrative overhead costs and textbook fees. The format of the new program required reworking the pricing model that had been in place for several contracts with Cummins. The major issue affecting pricing was the non-credit content of the program. While all credit courses are offered through an academic department, like CPT, non-credit classes must be offered through the Purdue's Continuing Education Department. The development and delivery costs of the program involved considerably different pricing methods from those used for the AITTP program. For the AITTP program each course was priced to include normal tuition fees for students along with an estimate for each professor's salary. The salary was estimated as one-month's pay for the anticipated instructor (similar to Purdue's pay for an overload course or a course during summer school). With the new program the number of instruction hours was approximately the same as for a three credit hour class. For this reason we estimated faculty salary similar to the faculty salary for teaching a three credit hour class in Summer school.

Another issue was developing a method to recover the cost of course development. In the AITTP program the development costs were paid in advance. For subsequent offerings there was no development costs budgeted. For the new non-credit program Cummins did not want to pay development costs up front. Instead Cummins asked for quotes based on the number of offerings. This would allow the development costs to be absorbed over the number of sessions Cummins chose. This would also require adding a clause to the letter of agreement with Cummins. That clause specified that if Cummins decided not to offer all of the agreed upon sessions they would still need to pay the development costs. With five different instructors (three associate professors, one assistant professor and one adjunct) the development pricing was not as straightforward as in the past. For the AITTP program development cost was estimated at one month's salary development time for each course. Working with Continuing Education we estimated development time as a ratio to delivery time, or two hours development time for one hour delivery time. Purdue felt it was important to estimate development costs on the low side. This would allow us to stay competitive with an outside contractor that Cummins was also negotiating with to deliver a similar program. To simplify the model for development costs Continuing Education chose one instructor's salary to base this cost on.

Scheduling the Faculty and Facilities

The second challenge was scheduling of faculty and the location of the program. The goal with the program was to use a team approach with instructors available at any time. Since Cummins intended for at least one of the sessions to be offered during the regular semester, the OLS and CPT departments had to work together to plan the regular semester course offerings. This required assigning most of the faculty involved to evening instead of daytime classes in their regular program to avoid conflicts with the Cummins non-credit daytime classes.

Scheduling the facility was relatively easy since IUPUC is a commuter campus most facility scheduling problems arise for classes offered in the evening. A classroom with lab facilities was reserved for the spring semester between 8:00 am - 5:00 pm which was the anticipated program time.

Faculty Salaries

The third challenge was faculty salaries. Instead of one month's salary as was paid instructors for each class taught in the AITTP program a new method would have to be determined. With the help of Continuing Education it was decided the faculty salary estimate along with the development cost for each session would be divided among participating faculty based on their participation in the program. The percentage each faculty was lead instructor would be calculated and salaries would be based on that percentage of the overall allotment for faculty salaries. All faculty agreed to this method.

Effect on the Purdue Program in Columbus

The next step in program planning was to consider the impact (both positive and negative) of the Systems/Business Analyst Program on the mission and existing programs at Purdue University School of Technology in Columbus. It was immediately obvious that this program could provide many positives. Primarily, it could provide the opportunity to engage a Fortune 500 company and the leading employer in the community. We believe that faculty involvement in engagement and discovery activities are necessary to enhance faculty development and to help integrate the effective use of technology in business and industry. Secondly, the program could provide a renewed source of outside funding, for individual faculty members and for the CPT program as a whole. In lean times of reduced academic funding, this type of engagement program is ideal to augment departmental budgets.

However, early in the program planning stages, Purdue Columbus recognized that implementing a program of this type could result in facing more than one challenge. One challenge could be described as "faculty drain". Faculty teaching loads are strictly controlled by University regulations in an attempt to avoid overload situations. Any time-intensive engagement activity can potentially drain the faculty from their classrooms and teaching of the normal credit courses in their program. Classes that faculty members would normally have taught might have to be cancelled, or adjunct instructors would need to be hired to fill in for those faculty. That could put the quality of the credit programs at risk and impact student retention. We soon realized that removing three tenured professors from the normal classroom to deliver non-credit coursework could have a strong negative impact on a growing program.

FUTURE ISSUES TO ADDRESS

As planning for the Cummins/Purdue Columbus Systems/Business Analyst Training Program reached its final stages, a new challenge arose. Cummins Inc. is a global operation. Although headquartered in Columbus, Indiana, Cummins serves its customers through more than 500 company-owned and independent distributor locations in 131 countries and territories. These include large operations in Canada, Mexico, and Europe. Cummins had identified a need to take the Systems/Business Analyst Training Program to their other locations. Their past training model had been to bring international employees to the Columbus headquarters for training. Their new training model was moving toward making training programs portable enough to take them to all international locations. In the final stages of the program planning, Cummins worked with Purdue Columbus to devise a method to "train the trainer" and provide those trainers with the materials required for program portability to other locations.

As a final step, planners explored a Phase II program for Cummins IT employees. This program would consist of a subset of Cummins employees who had successfully completed the Systems/Business Analyst Training Program. Tied closely with this phase would be Cummins' effort to "standardize" the tools they would require all analysts to use for project documentation. Phase II would devote more time to the skills required to document project specifications for projects sent off-shore to be developed. It was predicted that Phase II would be delivered beginning in fall of 2003.

SUMMARY

The development of a Systems/Business Analyst Program offers Purdue University an opportunity to build on a strong partnership with a Fortune 500 company that can benefit both partners. To be successful it has been necessary for the university to be flexible in its approach. Format, content, pricing and resource issues for this program created unique problems and opportunities from its predecessor the AITTP program. At the time of this writing, Purdue is awaiting word from Cummins Inc. on whether they will proceed with the program.

Engaging Industry to Benefit Industry and Academia

Dewey A. Swanson
Associate Professor, CPT
Purdue University
4601 Central Avenue, Columbus, IN 47203
dswanson@puc.iupui.edu
P: (812) 348-7238, F: (812) 348-7258

Erick Slazinski
Assistant Professor, CPT
Purdue University
West Lafayette, IN 47907
edslazinski@tech.purdue.edu
P: (765) 496-7582, F: (765) 496-1212

ABSTRACT

Partnerships between universities and industry can often bring much needed rewards to both parties. This paper outlines the details of an attempt to take the lessons learned from a successful partnership between one company and Purdue University and extend that model into a statewide program that can benefit Purdue University, industry and local communities in the state of Indiana.

INTRODUCTION

Purdue University entered into the Advanced Information Technology Training Program (AITTP) with Cummins Inc. in 1997. In this venture the company provided Purdue funding to: purchase a state-of-the-art computer lab, purchase software, pay for a faculty position for the Computer Technology Department, and develop a set of courses using the latest software. Purdue University in return provided: a cost effective training alternative, a nearby source for training information technology personnel, college credit toward a Purdue degree and college instructors to teach courses. What started as a one-time effort that has evolved into a program offered twice a year since its initial offering.

The AITTP is a program where Purdue University offers six credited courses and a project delivered in a compressed format for Cummins Inc. employees and individuals from the local community. These courses were focused on developing skills crucial for individuals wishing to become application developers or database administrators. Students go through the program as a cohort group. Each cohort group consists of new hires and current employees desiring retraining. Cummins is responsible for filling the seats in the program. Demand is for entrance into the program is high and Cummins has strict entrance criteria that employees must meet before being allowed into a cohort's candidate pool. The courses making up the program are given sequentially, meeting Monday through Friday from 8:30 am to 5:00 pm, with each course being delivered over the course of one to one and a half weeks. Since its inception there has been over 70 graduates of the program.

Clearly the need for trained professionals is not just a need for Cummins. Many of the fastest growing occupations are computer related. Universities have not been able to keep up with this growing demand. Industry will need to come up with answers as their needs worsen.

Last year the Computer Technology Department (CPT) started to look into development of a program based on the highly successful AITTP program. Initially, this was rather informal review of the existing program and investigation over the course of two semesters. The results of the preliminary investigations were promising. A feasibility study was undertaken during the past summer. The rest of this paper reports on the progress has occurred and where the program is headed in the future.

ENGAGEMENT PROGRAM

The term Purdue University uses for business and industry collaboration is engagement. The School of Technology defines engagement as technology transfer and application, responding to business and industry needs, and enhancing social and economic development.

Although our program it is based on AITTP model, it has several differences. The most significant is how the program is funded. The AITTP was completely funded by Cummins (including all startup costs). This program

would be supported by the selling of individual seats or groups of seats to the program. Financially this involves either getting the startup costs or building them into the early year of the program. Building the costs into the early years makes it difficult to keep the price of the program competitive. Marketing the program to industry is required – a task that many departments are not equipped to handle. The AITTP focused mainly on a database curriculum. The CPT department would like to expand these offerings to include the different tracks/specialties that are available within CPT baccalaureate degree: database, telecommunications and networking, application development and systems integration.

The format of the program would be similar to the AITTP program, which has Purdue faculty delivering credit courses in a condensed format to a cohort group over an eight to 12 week period. The program could be delivered at any of Purdue's locations which have sufficient resources available to support the courses taught – many of the courses have a hand-on component which requires specific hardware/software.

Based on the relationship we have developed with Cummins over the last five years, as a result the AITTP program, the potential for new, significant, long-term relationships is promising. Instead of building isolated one-to-one relationships, we are looking to develop multiple relationships simultaneously.

FRAMEWORK OF THE PROGRAM

Based on the experience with the AITTP initiative and brainstorming with CPT faculty, it was decided that we would offer specialized educational certificate programs that matched the areas of specialization that existed within the CPT baccalaureate program.

We evaluated condensed format programs for pricing and determined that our certificates would be competing with programs in the $10,000 range. Our goal is develop a program that will fall into that competitive price range. Initially, we looked at four, five and six as the potential number of classes to offer in each track. To get the depth in a concentration area and still stay close to the desired price point, the five-class format was selected.

Initial offerings would include the network and database certificate tracks. Demands for the skills these tracks represent are high. The database track has the added benefit of having several classes already formatted for condensed delivery – classes used in the AITTP program. The next phase would include the systems integration (systems analysis) track. The application development track would be implemented last based on the application development faculty's concerns of offering their classes in the condensed format.

The classes that each certificate track will include are shown in Table 1.

ISSUES IDENTIFIED

With a basic format and content the program developed there were issues that were identified and need to be addressed to successfully implement the program. The issues that will need to be resolved and potential solutions and aids in resolving the issues in order create a viable program:

A source of funding for the programs' startup costs must be found. The most expensive items are a set of laptops to be loaned to students and the cost to compress existing courses into the compressed format. Potential sources of startup funding include grants, or a set of founding organizations (companies) who, for an annual fee, would receive some benefit (i.e., reduced cost per student or right of first denial for seats in offered courses).

Table 1.

Database	Network
CPT 272 Database Fundamentals	CPT 176 Information Technology and Architecture
CPT 372 Database Development	CPT 230 Data Communications
CPT 392 Database Design and Implementation	CPT 330 Local Area Networking and Systems Administration
CPT 487 Database Administration	CPT 343 Advanced Systems Administration
CPT 488 Data Warehousing	CPT 430 Wide Area Networking
Systems Integration	
CPT 280 Systems Analysis and Design Methods	
CPT 380 Requirements Discovery and Modeling	
CPT 385 Advanced Design Techniques	
CPT 480 Managing Information Technology Projects	
TECH 581B Information Technology Quality and Productivity	

The CPT department and our school, the School of Technology, have little experience in the type of mass marketing that such a program requires.

The time commitment required of their employees to complete the coursework. In the AITTP program, the students spend up to 12 weeks dedicated entirely to learning. This proves to be quite a strain to the departments/organizations where the students came from. This is partially mitigated in this proposal since there are only five courses per certificate – however this is still an eight week commitment on both the students and company. Other alternatives include:

- Reducing the number of courses to four per certificate. While this reduces the time required by the students, there are other ramifications that require investigation (i.e., increased cost per student).
- Splitting the certificates into an introduction (two courses) and an advanced (three courses) certificate. The total time commitment is the same (eight weeks, but they are not necessarily contiguous).
- Adopting a weekend master's-like approach with courses being held over weekends (versus during the work week).

Due to the laboratory equipment required for the Networking courses, offering this certificate at any location other than West Lafayette may be impossible. This is a limiting factor when trying to engage the entire state of Indiana.

POTENTIAL BENEFITS OF PROGRAM

In order for the program to be successful it must provide benefits to all parties involved. A program of this type would offer Purdue and specifically the CPT department the following opportunities:

- Develop funding source for CPT department for:
  - faculty
  - faculty development
  - labs
  - software
- Utilize labs and classrooms at times when they are typically under-utilized
- To engage different companies in state of Indiana that can result in:
  - Additional partnerships between Purdue and industry
  - Grants and gifts for department and university
  - Aid in student placement for jobs and internships

Benefits for industry include:
- Cost effective training alternative
- By utilizing Purdue's main and statewide campuses a nearby source of training
- Potential of college credit
- Classes taught by college instructors
- Building a relationship with the university that can be used for recruitment of employees

STATUS OF PROGRAM

The program has been merged with several other initiatives as part of a Course Modules Task Force. This task force seeks to fulfill the educational needs of industry. Not only does it include the certificate programs mentioned here, but also individual courses, course modules (parts of existing classes) and workshops. With the creation of the task force, the momentum of this initiative has been stymied. The current goal is to have a program in place in the next year.

SUMMARY

With the current economic climate, many universities face unreliable funding, any possibilities for additional income are enticing. However, that same economic climate presents difficulties with securing the initial start-up funding from within the university or with industry.

Seamless Multiparty Videoconferencing System

T. Lertrusdachakul, A. Taguchi, T. Aoki, and H. Yasuda
Research Center for Advanced Science and Technology, The University of Tokyo
4-6-1 Komaba Meguroku, Tokyo 153-8904, JAPAN
T: +81-3-5452-5277, F: +81-3-5452-5278
{pom, taguchi, aoki, yasuda}@mpeg.rcast.u-tokyo.ac.jp

ABSTRACT

In this paper, an innovative multiparty videoconferencing system supporting eye contact and synchronous pointing based on the combination between human image and shared workspace is presented. We propose an idea to establish multiple eye contacts by representing each participant's eyes with a small video camera. Therefore, participants are able to be aware of who is visually attending to them. All participants' images are displayed as the image layer which is naturally merged with the shared workspace. With this method, the proposed system has the advantage of serving synchronous pointing of more than one site at a given time. The basic idea is to make camera's view overlapped with pointing area by using the technique of camera's angle and position. Therefore, multiple target points can be recognized simultaneously.

INTRODUCTION

Although the conventional videoconferencing systems are very effective as a means of remote person-to-person communication, they still do not totally fulfill the need of actual meetings. Since they generally present a variety of problems such as lack of eye contact, limited of viewing and no finger pointing. It can be seen that eye contact, facial expression and gesture provide a variety of non-verbal cues that are essential in human-human communication. Eye contact means that the eyes of one person meet those of the other person while talking or gazing at each other. The lack of eye contact in typical VC systems comes from the fact that when participants talk with each other, they look at image of remote site on their display rather than into the camera, which is typically mounted above, below, or beside the display. This spatial separation between camera and display has introduced a serious problem of unrealistic during the conference.

In addition, typical videoconferencing system still cannot support the presence of finger pointing since display's content does not overlap with camera's view and shared workspace is displayed as the separated window with participant's image.

We have developed the two-way videoconferencing system that supports eye contact and presence of pointing with seamless control between human image and shared workspace. The underlying concept behind this system is to place a small video camera at a common point of gaze direction between display and camera. The system makes it possible to support the finger pointing since camera's view is overlapped with area of display's content and by offering the seamless between image and shared workspace rather than placing them in the individual and arbitrarily separated window as in the conventional system. With the closer consideration, the system reveals a number of various problems in supporting multiparty videoconference. In this paper, we focus on the specific problems of multiple eye contacts and synchronous pointing. The proposed idea of seamless integration with the method of preserving eye contact and synchronous pointing by using technique of camera's position and angle will be described.

SEAMLESS INTEGRATION

One obvious problem on the conventional videoconferencing system is that it breaks down as the number of remote sites increases due to the decreasing size of the tiled images and shared workspace. Therefore, we propose an idea of seamless integration which human image and shared workspace are

naturally merged. It can be considered that all participants' images and shared workspace are the primary layers of a seamless screen. This technique has the advantage that all parties can see each other as the full screen. In addition, this method also makes it possible for the users to freely control the seamless level according to the various situations during a conference. Seamless integration also has another main advantage of serving pointing and synchronous pointing for multiparty conference since participants can use their finger to indicate any point in the shared workspace.

MULTIPLE EYE CONTACTS

It could be realized that the eyes of users are an important cue for a decision making process and in increasing the feeling of presence between participants in a videoconference meeting. The participant will never perceive eye contact unless the gaze direction between camera and display are synchronized. Based on this fact, we realized that looking at camera can convey the feeling of perceiving eye contact or being attended at. Therefore, we represent eyes of each participant with a small video camera in front of his image. Each site will receive the video signal from the camera that placed at his position of all other sites. For example, in three-way videoconference, as illustrated in Figure 1 (a), the video image for site A comes from a video signal of a camera placed at A position of site B and C. The same manner is applied for site B and C. Then each participant is able to perceive the feeling of being attended at from the person who is looking at his image.

SYNCHRONOUS POINTING

Simple user interface such as finger pointing is considered to be one of significant parts to improve the efficiency of a conference. The underlying concept for supporting synchronous pointing is to make camera's view overlapped with pointing area. The technique of camera's angle and position has been introduced. The various methods of how to display human image for multiparty videoconference have been investigated. The method that provides the effective point of view for synchronous pointing, is to display all participants in the shifted position. The display will be divided into n vertical parts; where n is the total number of participants. Each participant has own area to display his image on the screen which is one of those n parts. All participants have their own space in front of the display during a conference.

Firstly, we define a pointing area and camera position. The pointing area is an area that parallels to the display's content and has the distance about 40 cm from the plane of participant's position. The position of camera is in the middle of each remote participant's area on the display. We make the camera's view overlapped with the pointing area by turning a camera to direct at the center of pointing area with a relatively small angle between plane of camera's view and display. As illustrated in Figure 1 (b), if the distance between display and participant is larger, the angle difference x between plane of camera's view and display will become smaller. If the angle x is small enough, a required point can be approximately to be a target point in the shared workspace since distance a and b are approximately to be the same as shown in Figure 1 (a). It can be seen that a vertical line at the middle of display is exactly with a vertical line at the middle of camera's view. The other positions can be approximately to be the same if the angle x is small enough. With this method, the upper-part body and target point of each participant can be observed clearly and simultaneously.

Figure 1. (a) Three-way videoconference with the technique of camera's angle and position, (b) The comparison of different angle between plane of camera's view and display

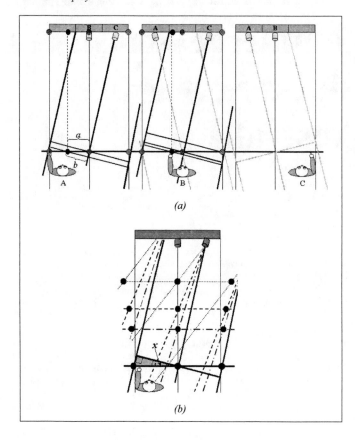

(a)

(b)

Figure 2. The view of site A in three-way videoconference (a) C is attending at A, (b) B is attending at A

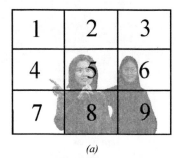

(a)

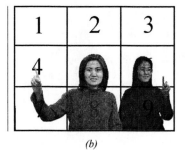

(b)

EXPERIMENTAL RESULTS

We conducted the experiments to prove the proposed idea based on three-way videoconference. The plasma display's size of 90 cm×110 cm is used with the distance between display and pointing area of 150 cm. The angle x is about 13.5 degree. Figure 2 shows the system with supporting of synchronous pointing and multiple eye contacts from the view of site A according to three-way videoconference in Figure 1 (a). Figure 2 (a) shows that C is pointing and looking at A while B is pointing at B's area. We can see that A can perceive the feeling of eye contact with C and recognize that he is not attended from B. Figure 2 (b) shows that B is looking and pointing at A while C is pointing at C's area. It can be seen that A can perceive the feeling of eye contact with B and recognize that C is not looking at A. Moreover, the seamless level can be freely controlled according to the various situations during a meeting as shown in the difference transparent level of participant's image between Figure 2 (a) and Figure 2 (b).

CONCLUSION

We focus on the particular problems of supporting multiple eye contacts and synchronous pointing for multiparty videoconference. The method is based on the seamless integration and technique of camera's position and angle. Camera is considered to be the eyes of remote participants so that gazing toward someone can be effectively conveyed. By turning camera direct to the center of pointing area with relatively small angle between camera's view and display, participants are able to user their finger as a simple user interface to indicate the required point in the share workspace. The experimental results proved that the proposed idea has a good potential of serving synchronous pointing and multiple eye contacts. Developing the system for a large number of participants is the subject of our future work.

REFERENCES

[1] Terumasa, A., Kustarto, W., Nobuki, S., Masanori, Y., and Hiroshi, Y. (1999). Next-Generation Videoconference System with Sense of Reality. International conference on computer communications'99 (ICCC'99).

[2] Liyanage, C. De Silva, Mitsuho, T., and Kiyoharu, A. (1995, August). A Teleconferencing System Capable of Multiple Person Eye Contact (MPEC) Using Half Mirror and Cameras Placed at Common Points of Extended Lines of Gaze. IEEE Transaction on circuits and systems for video technology, vol. 5, no.4.

[3] Ken-ichi, O., Fumihiko, M., Yusuke, I., and Yutaka, M. (1994). Multiparty Videoconferencing at Virtual Social Distance: MAJIC Design. Proc. of CSCW'94.

[4] Ishii, H., Kobayashi, M., and Grudin, J. (1993, October). Integration of Inter-personal Space and Shared Workspace: ClearBoard Design and Experiments. ACM Transactions on Information Systems (TOIS), ACM, Vol. 11, No. 4, pp. 349-375.

Information Need and Its Impact on the Adoption of E-Commerce Tools in the Small Business Sector in Western Australia

V. S. Venkatesan
Graduate School of Management, University of Western Australia
35 Stirling Highway, Crawley 6009 WA, AUSTRALIA
P: 61 8 9380 1349, F: 61 8 9380 1072, vvenkate@ecel.uwa.edu.au

BACKGROUND

Despite the demonstrated advantages of Information Technology (IT) and e-commerce, worldwide evidence suggests that the adoption of e-commerce is uneven among businesses. While the varying degrees of adoption of IT and the ensuing digital divide issues generally have been widely debated (Chanda 2000; Hoffman, Novak et al. 2000; NOIE 2000), much less research has been done into the factors that moderate the adoption of these tools by the business sector.

For businesses, the assumption appears to be that operational efficiency will mandate the use of computers and business and market forces will dictate the use of the Internet. Broad-based information suggests that adoption of computers and Internet connectivity have been high among Australian businesses but such connectivity has not translated into business transactions (Venkatesan & Fink 2002). Among small businesses, studies show there is still a low level of adoption of e-commerce (Poon & Strom 1997; Akkeren & Cavaye 2000).

Like most OECD countries, Australia has a dominant small business sector and this sector is the backbone of its economy in terms of innovation and employment generation (ABS 1997). Thus, the adoption or non-adoption of e-commerce by this sector has the potential to significantly impact on the overall use of e-commerce. Data from Australian business sector suggests a higher rate of computer usage and Internet connectivity compared to UK and Europe (NOIE 2000). However, there is concern within national agencies about the poor uptake of e-commerce and possible loss of business opportunities (CSIRO 1999).

Poor adoption of e-commerce in the 'Business-to-Consumer' (B2C) sector worldwide has been largely attributed to security issues and lack of consumer confidence. However, Business-to-Business (B2B) transactions are often confined to larger businesses and their supply chains and horizontal transactions between small firms have been infrequent in Australia (Venkatesan and Fink 2001).

Driven by the tenet that information is power, existing Internet solutions have focused on providing massive volumes of information on the World Wide Web (www), without an understanding of what information is needed, resulting in information overload. This is exacerbated by the open structure and accessibility of the Internet.

While large volumes of information may be a requirement for big businesses, questions remain on whether small businesses need such information and whether they are capable of analysing such information. Little is known about what information is needed, how it is accessed and what impact new technologies have had on such access. Thus, these have become crucial questions impacting on how businesses use IT.

Small and medium sized businesses, by their very nature, are localized in their operation, have limited market impact and face significant resource constraints (Venkatesan 2000). Studies reveal that they engage in limited market research and take an unprofessional approach to gathering and implementing market information (Carson 1985). Such businesses are usually owner managed and their time and knowledge limitations hinder their ability to search for information on the Internet.

Given the paucity of data on the information needs and access patterns of businesses, a study was carried out in a regional Australian town and the results are presented below. The findings are based on a quantitative study using mail survey to collect data. Parallel studies reveal that many of the findings are also applicable to small and medium businesses located in metropolitan areas of Australia.

RESULTS

Business Profile

The majority of businesses surveyed were home-based and involved in primary production. Almost all were owner-managed and met the Australian Bureau of Statistics (ABS) criteria for classification as small businesses. The number of retail and service based businesses was small[1]. The median annual turnover of these businesses was around A\$100 000 (range \$50000 - \$250 000).

Responding businesses were predominantly production oriented with little emphasis on aspects such as marketing, accounting or financial planning. Almost half of the businesses serviced local markets and about 30% serviced statewide. Though their products were sold to a wider market through intermediaries, these businesses viewed marketing as too involved and time consuming. Minimal impact on the market and the long lead-times between producing a product and sales also discouraged their marketing efforts. Other studies demonstrate that localised operation and lack of need for marketing appear to be generally applicable to small businesses (Carson 1985; Carson & Cromie 1990; Venkatesan 2000).

About 50% of businesses used computers and less than 30% were connected to the Internet. The frequency of use was low to moderate with most computers being used for administrative tasks.

Information Need

To examine the need for different types of information, importance of such information and frequency of access of such information, respondents were asked to use a five-point scale to rate the importance of a range of information in their everyday activities.

Mean values suggested that, in relative terms, businesses considered banking and agriculture information to be more important than leisure and financial information. Employment and educational information were considered relatively unimportant. Because of their narrowly defined business activities and restricted scope for diversification, businesses sought information directly relating, and of immediate relevance to, their business. Because of the long planning cycle and local markets, businesses had more need for locally oriented information. Other studies on metropolitan city-based small businesses have shown that small businesses use little market intelligence (Venkatesan & Soutar 2001). This could be one reason for their minimal adoption of the Internet.

As can be inferred from the mean values (Table 1), weather, which directly impacts on primary production operations, was the most accessed information, followed by banking and price of products. This was not surprising

Table 1. Type of information accessed

	Mean	S.D
Banks	3.28	1.191
Accountants / financial planners	4.37	0.925
Government services	4.43	0.893
Weather	2.42	1.655
Health	3.84	1.221
Agriculture information	3.42	1.490
Price of products	3.18	1.341
Stock markets	4.07	1.363
Others	2.55	1.508

(1-Daily; 2-Twice a week; 3-Twice a fortnight; 4-Once or twice a month; 5-less than once a month)

Table 2. Frequency of information access through different media

Medium	Mean	Median	S.D
Phone	1.46	1.00	0.746
Fax	2.69	2.00	1.407
Internet	3.59	4.00	1.500
Email	3.50	4.00	1.551
Radio	2.97	3.00	1.542
TV	2.99	3.00	1.590

(1-Always; 2-Often; 3-Sometimes; 4-Rarely; 5-Never)

Table 3. Information access and sources of information

Source	Mean
Local sources	2.62
From regional centers	3.25
Perth and whole of WA	3.21
Whole of Australia	3.71
Internationally	4.15

(1-Always; 2-Often; 3-Sometimes; 4-Rarely; 5-Never)

given the preponderance of primary producers in the sample. However, it should be noted that even weather information was accessed about twice a week or less. Stock market and other information were accessed much less. Dealings with accountants/financial planners are also less frequent. This demonstrates that instantaneous access to such information may not be critical for small businesses.

Medium of Information Access

To examine the use of Internet as an information-gathering tool, businesses were asked to rate how frequently they used different media to communicate in their business. A five-point scale was used for rating the frequency. The mean, median and standard deviation values are given in Table 2.

Telephone appeared to be the most used communication medium followed by fax and personal contacts. Mass media such as Radio and TV also found frequent use. Use of email, the Internet and other computer-mediated tools was less frequent. The Internet seemed to have had minimal to moderate impact on information access by regional businesses. Conventional media continued to be preferred ahead of computer related information channels.

This is likely to be due to lack of need for information, relevance of information from the www to the local community, the nature of the business activity and lifestyle as well as slow technological diffusion.

It should be noted that, while the adoption of the Internet and the www has been relatively rapid in large cities both by businesses and the community (about 80% adoption of computers and 50–60% adoption of the Internet by businesses), studies (Venkatesan & Fink 2001) show that businesses still use the computer for administrative and accounting purposes and the Internet was mainly used for gathering information and not for transacting any business. The adoption of email to contact other businesses or clients was also at a low level. Consequently, it is not surprising that regional or rural businesses have a low level of adoption of the Internet.

Progressively increasing mean values in Table 3 (comparable standard deviations) suggests the local nature of the information sought by respondents with the frequency reducing as the information horizon expanded from local to international arena.

Table 3 also demonstrates that regional communities/businesses have a higher need for local information and supports the argument that one reason for lack of Internet use is the lack of need to access general worldwide information. The www does not offer locally tailored information and anecdotal evidence suggests that www information is generalized and not current and specific local information can be obtained from other sources such as regional radio without logging onto a computer. While specialized sites are available for specific information, most such sites require payment and the total cost can be prohibitive.

Ease of access, lack of need for global information and limited availability of local information seem to be three key factors limiting the use of computers and the Internet.

Respondents were asked to rate the extent to which Internet was useful in their business.

Of the Internet users, over 60% considered it highly useful. Less than 10% found it to be not useful.

CONCLUSION

The results of the study suggest that businesses in regional Australia need more localised information better tailored to their needs. While the www was useful for generalised information, key business information needed a local focus to be of any relevance.

Businesses preferred conventional media such as phone and radio and relied more on local experts than on information available on the Internet, mostly because local experts could modify the general information to meet individual business needs. Criticality of information and speed of access was not of major concern to these businesses.

Overall, it appears that conventional and global IT solutions could have limited value in regional Australia and generally in the small business sector and more tailored solutions may be needed.

ENDNOTES

[1] The town surveyed was an agriculture based town and hence the small number of retail businesses. However, in metro areas and non-agriculture based towns the proportion of retail and service based businesses has been shown to be high.

REFERENCES

ABS (1997). Characteristics of Small Business 1997. Canberra, Australian Bureau of Statistics.

Akkeren, J. v. and A. L. M. Cavaye (2000). *Factors affecting the adoption of E-commerce technologies by small business in Australia - an empirical study.* ICSB Conference.

Carson, D. and S. Cromie (1990). "Marketing Planning in Small Enterprises: A Model and Some Empirical Evidence." *The Journal of Consumer Marketing* 7(3): 5 - 18.

Carson, D. J. (1985). "The Evolution of Marketing in Small Firms." *European Journal of Marketing* 19(5): 7 - 16.

Chanda, N. (2000). "The Digital Divide." *Far Eastern Economic Review* (October 19): 50-53.

CSIRO (1999). Caught in the Web: The Not-So-Lucky Country. Canberra, CSIRO.

Hoffman, D. L., T. P. Novak, et al. (2000). "The Evolution of the Digital Divide: How Gaps in Internet Access may Impact Electronic Commerce." *Journal Of Computer Mediated Communication* 5(3).

NOIE (2000). The Current State of Play - July 2000. Canberra: 1-49.

Poon, S. and J. Strom (1997). *Small Businesses' Use of the Internet: Some Realities.* The Seventh Annual Conference of the Internet Society, Kuala Lumpur, Malaysia, *http://www.isoc.org/inet97/proceedings/C2/C2_1.HTM.*

Venkatesan, V. S. (2000). The marketing orientation of Small and Medium Enterprises: An Australian Study. *Ph.D Thesis.* Edith Cowan University, Australia: 300+.

Venkatesan, V. S. and D. Fink (2001). Joondalup Region Business Audit. Perth, Small and Medium Enterprise Research Centre, Edith Cowan University: 162.

Venkatesan, V. S. and D. Fink (2002). *Adoption of Internet technologies and e-commerce by Small and Medium Enterprises (SMEs) in Western Aus-tralia*. 13th IRMA International Conference, Seattle, Washington USA, Ideas Publishing Group.

Venkatesan, V. S. and G. Soutar (2001). "Market research in Australian SMEs: An empirical study." *Small Enterprise Research 9*(2): 17-31.

Community Based Approach to E-Commerce: An Alternative E-Commerce Model for Small Communities

V. S. Venkatesan
Graduate School of Management, University of Western Australia
35 Stirling Highway, Crawley 6009 WA, AUSTRALIA
P: 61 8 9380 1349, F: 61 8 9380 1072, vvenkate@ecel.uwa.edu.au

BACKGROUND

Portrayed as the panacea for businesses in the late nineties, Information Technology (IT) is fast maturing into realistic business tool integrating with business processes to make an impact on business performance. The Internet has lowered barriers and provided access to the world market while IT generally has made the core functions of business more efficient. However, has it transformed business practices?

Early exponential growth in Internet use was driven by the simplistic view that Internet presence would automatically lead to business transactions and this has resulted in the Internet becoming a 'cyber junkyard'. With millions of businesses on the worldwide web, the promised competitive advantage of Internet presence has either failed to materialise or been short-lived. While large businesses are able to use conventional media to promote their web presence, small and medium-sized enterprises (SME), because of resource constraints and limited promotional activities (Carson 1985), are unable to take advantage of the web. Studies reveal that the volume of business generated for SMEs through the Internet is small (Venkatesan and Fink 2001; Venkatesan, Fink et al. 2001). Consequently, questions such as 'How do people know about my business?' become relevant to SMEs.

Given the importance of the SME sector in many OECD economies (ABS 1998; Chetcuti 1998; Flynn, Heidi et al. 1998), the adoption or non-adoption of e-commerce tools by this sector will significantly influence the impact of IT revolution in different economies. Several studies acknowledge the low level of adoption of e-commerce by SMEs (Dekleva 2000; Venkatesan and Fink 2001; Venkatesan, Fink et al. 2001).

Experience suggests that the digital revolution has had limited impact in regional Australia (Foreshaw 2000). A study in regional Western Australia (WA) identified several problems that potentially widen the digital divide between city and regional areas (Venkatesan & Robinson, 2002). Limited market, distance and other related factors limited the usefulness of IT based solutions in regional areas.

Apart from technological barriers such as communication networks, speed of access and poor service, non-technical barriers such as knowledge, time and resource constraints of business owners/managers can also limit the use of IT tools. Most small businesses are owner-operated and these owners/managers, unlike their counterparts in large firms, have to be experts in several areas (Carson 1985), thus adding to their knowledge and time constraints.

A major obstacle regional businesses (most of which are SMEs) encounter is their inability to respond to business opportunities quickly. Further, because of their isolation, businesses in one rural community rarely communicate with the next.

Thus, for regional businesses, conventional solutions such as improving the networks, producing websites and joining portals alone cannot provide the competitive advantage. A next generation business tool that enables smarter use of existing network infrastructure is needed. This paper discusses a community based e-commerce business model and examines various issues associated with its implementation. Such a development is in progress in Western Australia.

A HUB AND SPOKES MODEL

Fundamentally, this model takes a community approach to e-commerce. Conventional solutions focus on maximizing revenue for software solution providers and target individual business oriented software. However, small businesses in regional communities require a cooperative rather than a competitive approach. While individual businesses make their own decisions on transactions, they become a collective while searching for business opportunities.

Conceptually, businesses in a town or community are connected to a local hub. Several such hubs are connected to a central hub which provides intelligence, technology and support. The local hub uses basic technology which every business has access to. Local hubs act as a conduit for information flow between businesses and the central hub and store information useful to the local community (such as the member listing). A conceptual schematic is shown in Figure 1. Businesses connect either directly to the local hub or through other service providers. Technically, the central hub can link directly to businesses but the local hubs are being deliberately introduced so that this becomes a true cooperative effort between communities and industry.

Information flow is automatic, from the hub through the node to businesses with little human intervention. The hub will respond to manual queries and suggestions, add new websites for searching and will grow in tune with the needs of regional businesses. Part of the hub will also make use of existing business networks within small rural areas (e.g. Telecentre networks).

Operation of the System

Any small/medium business in regional Western Australia will be able to join the network free of cost for three to five years by completing their basic profile on-line, the type of business they are in, opportunities they are looking for etc. Such details are entered into the system and modified when necessary. Absence of log-ins and passwords is a key feature of the system. Businesses will have the option to revise their details at any time in future.

Technical issues such as security are dealt with at the central hub. Business information is automatically fed into the central hub and stored in a database. The system uses a variety of filters based on geographic and business parameters.

The central hub continually searches for business opportunities at local, regional, state, interstate and international levels depending on the summary profile of businesses. Using key words and web addresses, the intelligent system seeks and extracts information on market opportunities from a variety of sources on the www, in a progressively widening circle. Such information is then stored in a database.

Using a database matching system, market opportunities are filtered, matched to local business profile and fed back to relevant businesses alerting

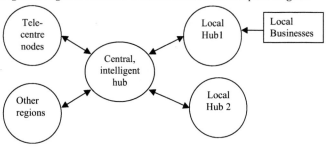

Figure 1. Regional Electronic Business Network - A conceptual diagram

them about suitable market opportunities, through email and similar channels available to regional communities. A business will automatically get the message once its computer is switched on.

For example, if a landscaping business wants to operate only in one specific town, the system will identify all the landscaping business opportunities, filter them and email information on specific town-based jobs to that business. In contrast, if a construction group operates throughout Australia, then all the Australian market opportunities identified by the system will be relayed to that business. The system will continuously learn and expand its capabilities.

The system will also encourage horizontal transactions between businesses in the regions. Each participating business will be able to post their requirements on the system through a series of templates. Instead of acting as a simple bulletin board, the hub will filter the message and relay it to businesses meeting that profile.

At present, this system is being designed to relay the information selectively through the network and no transactions are processed. This is deliberately done because transaction systems are still evolving and there is no standardisation in the market. Further, the theme behind the project is to make smarter use of existing networks and not to compete with the market.

It may be noted that this central hub is not a website, is not in competition with other portals and is not directly visible to businesses. It remains in the background and works through local hubs such as the local Chambers of Commerce. The design of the system is such that local hubs are continually promoted. Essentially the network will go to businesses and deliver information rather than businesses having to struggle with systems and interfaces to extract information.

KEY ADVANTAGES OF THE PROPOSED NETWORK / SYSTEM

- The system is dedicated to businesses in Western Australia.
- It acts as a technology buffer and minimises the effect of rapidly changing technology.
- Resource burdens associated with changing technology is eased. Upgrading of software, need to keep up training and local availability of expertise to solve problems add to ongoing cost. Most regional businesses, being small, can ill-afford such a cost.
- Current portals and web sites are generalised and not intelligent.
- Substantial time is saved for businesses in searching new opportunities.
- The system overcomes the complexity of websites - Some large websites are created by technologists and are not user friendly. The skill and time requirements can be high.
- It is dynamic and grows with the needs of the business community.
- It is in the public domain where business information and profile is confidential and is managed by the local community for their benefit but cooperating with other areas in the interest of regional growth.

- The intelligent hub will substantially reduce the load on the physical network in the regions, resulting in faster access, reduced dropouts etc.
- The same tool can be later used to provide community information through community portals.
- The model will be the first step towards a publicly owned, national e-commerce platform and the hub will be the central element of the regional electronic business network.

Why an Intelligent System for Regional Businesses Only?

Despite significant improvements in the technical infrastructure, information access continues to be a major issue for regional Australia. IT adds another layer of digital divide to existing problems faced by businesses. Thus the need is more acute for regional businesses.

A business may spend considerable time using the Internet without identifying any opportunity. Low success rates, lack of time, financial and knowledge resources to update their technology all exacerbate the situation. Some of these problems are unique to regions and rarely felt in major cities. For example, a major software change will have a lot more impact on a regional small business as compared to its metropolitan counterpart purely because of the lack of access and knowledge. Having a broadband connection has very little effect if the software is not updated or cannot be better implemented. In such cases, the regional hub can be a technological buffer and ensure that businesses use the networks more efficiently.

A regional business network for business to business (B2B) also has a better chance of success because unlike any consumer site, a business hub can be better regulated, the information can be streamlined and in the long run such a network can be self-sustaining using a fee for service mechanism. In such a network, information overload can also be avoided. For the same reason, the regional network will be limited to regional or rural businesses.

COMMUNITY ORIENTED E-COMMERCE TOOL

The technical solution that was discussed earlier is not new and is within the reach of existing technology. However, similar solutions offered by private service providers in the past have failed due to the business motives of such providers, customer perceptions and lack of community ownership. The focus of these software solutions has been on developing a solution that will maximise profit for the IT company rather than meeting community needs. Further, the ownership of such solutions has never rested with user groups. In contrast to conventional solutions, the proposed hub and spoke model will have full community participation and ownership.

REFERENCES

ABS (1998). Small Business in Australia. Canberra, Australian Bureau of Statistics.

Carson, D. J. (1985). "The Evolution of Marketing in Small Firms." *European Journal of Marketing 19*(5): 7-16.

Chetcuti, V. (1998). Small is Big News in Exporting. *Government of Canada Information Supplement.*

Dekleva, S. (2000). "Electronic Commerce: A Half-Empty Glass?" *Communications of the Association for Information Systems 3*: 1-68.

Flynn, J., D. Heidi, et al. (1998). Startups to the Rescue - Throughout the Continent, small companies are where the action is. *Business Week - Industrial / Technology Edition*: 50.

Foreshaw, J. (2000). Regions miss out as IT keeps to big cities. *The Australian.* Melbourne: 46.

Venkatesan, V. S. and D. Fink (2001). Joondalup Region Business Audit. Perth, Small and Medium Enterprise Research Centre, Edith Cowan University: 162.

Venkatesan, V. S., D. Fink, et al. (2001). Moving into New Economy: Strategies for SMEs in the Wangara Industrial Park. City of Wanneroo, Small and Medium Enterprise Research Centre, Edith Cowan University: 170.

Distributed Object Based SCM Simulator: LOSIMOPU

Hiroshi TSUJI, Takefumi KONZO, Ryosuke SAGA
Graduate School of Engineering, Osaka Prefecture University
1-1 Gakuen-cho Sakai, Osaka, Japan 599-8531
P: +81-72-254-9353, F: +81-72-254-9915, tsuji@ie.osakafu-u.ac.jp

INTRODUCTION

Under the current Internet era, many companies are interested in supply chain management (SCM) in order to rebuild their business process [1]. Especially, constraints theory on throughput [2] that requires the managers to detect the bottlenecks in the business process has impacted many industries. On SCM, there are two research approaches: (1) OR/MS technology such as mathematical programming that optimizes the objective function in order to allocate resources such as persons, machines, and money [3], and (2) IT technology such as workflow management and electronic payment that integrates the enterprise systems [4].

These researches have been done independently. However, not only to assess the risk and the chance of the business process reengineering but also to evaluate the implementation issues, the SCM designers require the means that integrate both OR/MS technology and IT technology. Therefore, we plan to develop software simulator called LOSIMOPU (LOgistics SIMulator by Osaka Prefecture University) by the distributed object technology [5]. This paper describes the target, the system overview and the design issues of our LOSIMOPU.

TARGET OF SCM SIMULATOR LOSIMOPU

Our purpose is to develop the software simulator designed for the internet based supply chain management that assigns the value of system parameters as stochastic variables and presents the simulation result visually. Although the spreadsheet based risk simulator is well known [6], it is difficult for the designer to express the concurrent and complex supply chain shown in Fig. 1 into the computational model.

Essentially, SCM is an autonomous and distributed system. There are varieties of players for the business: customers, vendors, manufactures, and parts suppliers. While they hide their internal information and behave actively and/or passively, they keep the same information structure such as company property and balance, and the same activity such as "buy" and "sell". Sometimes, they exchange information asynchronously in order to collaborate with each other and update the status for the trade. Each player has its own policy on trade and its own capacity for manufacturing and inventory.

Our strategy for the development is as follows:
(1) We first develop LOSIMOPU as the learning system that teaches the general users what the supply chain management is;
(2) Next we enhance it as the research platform that the experts can include the supplemental components and the special functions in the simulator;
(3) Finally, we expect it can be used in industry.

To realize our strategy, the distributed object oriented modeling technology is suitable to express the supply chain model. In fact this technology is beneficial on the following items [5]:
(1) Improved availability,
(2) Flexible configuration,
(3) Localized control and management,
(4) Incremental system expansion.

To follow the steps, we design LOSIMOPU as follows:
(1) It has basic model that any users can runs easily;
(2) It opens its application interface in order that researchers can implement their OR/MS idea;
(3) It adopts the international standard protocol/interface for the practical use.

SYSTEM CONFIGURATION OF LOSIMOPU

Let us analyze use cases in the SCM model first. In general, the player in the supply chain has the common actions as shown in Figure 2: request, reply, sell, buy and manufacture. Of course, according to the core competence of the player, some activities should be added and the others should be omitted. For example, the customer does not have the function "sell" while the end supplier does not have the function "buy".

Further, each player has the property and the account data in time series. Thus, the participants are expressed as class-subclass relation as shown in Figure 3.

There are five player subclasses in our simulator: (1) Customers, (2) Intermediate suppliers, (3) End suppliers, (4) Electronic payment servers, and (5) Transportation servers. Each player objects in the supply chain runs concurrently [5]. Communication protocol among objects is built in standard formula such as XML and SOAP. Note that the activities strategy of a player is different from each other according to its capacity and policy and is hid in the object. The strategy is often designed by OR/MS technology. Individual information is as follows:

(1) Intermediate Supplier Class
It has information on components that constitutes each goods and information on capacity for manufacturing and inventory. Such information is used to control the inbound of the supply chain. It has the mechanism for the economic order quantity and material requirement planning [1]. On the other hand, it has sales log and customer information that controls the outbound of the supply chain. It has mechanism for the customer relationship management. Further, it keeps management index such as cost, income, real estate and so on. Those are indispensable for calculating the interest, the throughput, and the loss of sales chances.

(2) End Supplier Class
In general, there are the competitors for the parts supply. They have price table and lead time information on parts delivery. For LOSIMOPU, the latter is assigned as stochastic variable.

(3) Customer Class
They play roles for the demanders. The demand information includes goods identification, volumes, and time-limit for the delivery. LOSIMOPU should allow the user to assign a variety of random value for the customer order arrival.

(4) Electronic Payment Server Class
They play roles for the electronic payment among the players. It simulates the time delay on the account DB as business process and charges the payment.

(5) Transportation Server Class
It delivers parts to the manufacturer and delivers goods to the customers. It has price table that is a function of transportation lots and distance.

WORKFLOW IN LOSIMOPU

Let us describe the concept of the workflow in LOSIMOPU. Each player receives the requests from its customers. Then it makes decision whether it accepts the request and replies to the requester.

LOSIMOPU has an e-Market place engine. It received the message from the players, records audit and transferred to the other players. The action of e-Market place is shown in Figure 4. The e-Market place has function that visualizes goods flow, money flow and information flow for the analysis. The visualized information also includes the management index and the risk.

Figure 1. Example of concurrent and complex supply chain

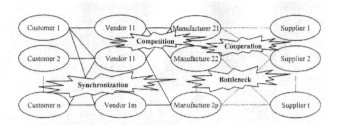

Figure 2. Use Case for intermediate supplier

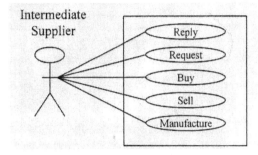

Figure 3. Class diagram of players

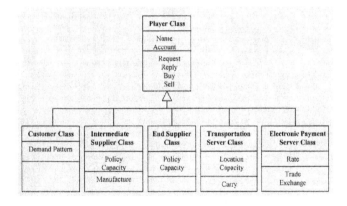

Figure 4. Action of e-Market place

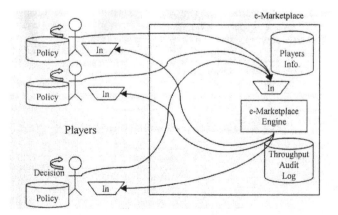

Figure 5. Statechart for transaction

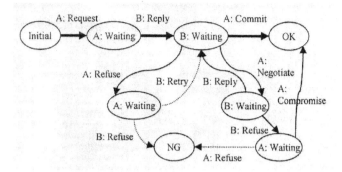

Each transaction has the state in LOSIMOPU and it starts as "initial" state. If the trade is established, the transaction finalizes as "OK" state, otherwise as "NG" state. The state chart for the transaction is shown in Figure 5. The basic idea in this statechart is borrowed from Language/Action theory [7].

CONCLUSION AND DISCUSSION

We have described the target and overview of LOSIMOPU. The project is now on going. We have gotten the use cases, class structure and state chart for the conceptual design. To develop the basic model of LOSIMOPU, the design issues are as follows:

(1) Dynamic modeling (object interaction modeling, dynamic analysis);
(2) Software architecture design (system decomposition, subsystem structuring criteria);
(3) Detail software design (user interface design, object state visualization, performance).

Other issues are to develop the open interface for the following research:

(a) Agent behavior that negotiates between buyers and sellers are implemented as an application model of LOSIMOPU.
(b) It simulates the tracking system that monitors the status of the goods that were ordered by the customers. It is possible to analyze the complexity between the manufacturer and the others by implementing the cancel protocol.
(c) In the case that the demand is greater than the supply, LOSIMOPU detects the bottleneck of the supply chain and presents the alternatives that dissolve the bottleneck. Therefore, LOSIMOPU can be also the infrastructure for analyzing the chain.
(d) It can be platform that the user develop and analyze the campaign model and the pricing model.

Those are application examples of LOSIMOPU. Adding the concurrent and distributed objects (for examples, warehouse and wholesalers objects) to the basic model, the user of LOSIMOPU can continue to enhance the SCM simulator.

REFERENCES

[1] J. Coyle, et al.: The management of Business Logistics, West Publishing Company (1996).
[2] E. Goldratt, J. Cox: Goal: A Process of Ongoing Improvement, Penguin Highbridge Audio Published (1993).
[3] F. Karaesmen, et al.: Integrating advance order information in Make-to-stock production systems, Vol.34, pp. 649-662 (2002).
[4] S. Knoshafian and M. Buckiewica: Introduction to Groupware, Workflow, and Workgroup Computing, John Wiley & Sons, Inc. (1995).
[5] H. Gomaa: Designing Concurrent, Distributed, and Real-time Applications with UML, Addison Wesley (2000).
[6] J. R. Evans and D. L. Olson: Introduction to Simulation and Risk Analysis, Prentice Hall, Inc., (1998).
[7] T. Winograd: A Language/Action Perspective on the Design of Cooperative Work, In: I. Greif (ed.), Computer Supported Cooperative Work: A Book of Readings. Morgan Kaufmann, San Mateo (1988).

Interactive URL Correction for Proxy Request

Kai-Hsiang Yang, Chi-Chien Pan, and Tzao-Lin Lee
Department of Computer Science and Information Engineering
National Taiwan University, Taipei, Taiwan, R.O.C.
{ f6526004, d5526001, tl_lee}@csie.ntu.edu.tw

ABSTRACT

Proxy servers are getting more and more important today. They provide web page caches for users to browse quickly, and also reduce unnecessary network traffic. However, users can't browse web pages with the wrong URL. Sometimes we just want to get some information about some subjects, the proxy server couldn't help us at all. Most people often use search engines to find data, but they still have to type the correct URLs of search engines. We actually need the proxy server with the ability of "Interactive URL Correction", which means the proxy server could correct the URL request, and take the users to where they want to browse, or send back some possible URLs. Users simply enter one word "google", or even "goggle", and then will eventually be taken to "www.google.com". To accomplish the URL correction, we have applied URL preprocess and approximate URL matching technique into proxy server. In this paper, we implement the system on the "squid" proxy system, and use "edit distance" as the URL error measurement. Additionally, we also list the limitation of proxy parameters and the benefits of our system.

INTRODUCTION

With the rapid expansion of the World Wide Web (WWW) too many web-based applications had caused serious performance degradation on the Internet. Caching is the process of storing web elements (pages, files, images) on proxy servers. The use of caching has proliferated because it reduces bottle-necks. The Internet Caching Resource Center (www.caching.com) estimates that caching can reduce the need for bandwidth by at least 35 percent. Consequently, the proxy servers had been widely deployed to reduce the bandwidth for the same "web page" requests; proxy server could accelerate the browsing rate by storing current web pages for the future requests. When some web pages are very popular, the proxy server only needs to download them once, then users could quickly browse these pages from the proxy. Nowadays, proxy server becomes necessary for the WWW community.

When proxy server receives a web page request (called "URL request"), it first matches all web pages in its native database. If the URL request is correct (by the DNS lookup), the proxy server immediately sends the requested page back to the user. Otherwise it has to access the requested page through the Internet, and then sends the page back and stores it in its native database. However, this is inconvenient and insufficient for users. When users browse web pages, they sometimes enter the wrong URL or just guess one URL for the product or company name. For example, we often enter the URL ("www.starbucks.com") for the company "Starbucks". But when we enter the word with some errors, for example "www.starbuck.com", the proxy will return error messages to us, and doesn't help us any more. Users have to correct the URL by themselves.

Most people often use search engines to find data, but they still have to enter correct URLs of search engines. We actually need to have the proxy server with the ability of "Interactive URL Correction", which means the proxy server could correct the URL request, and take the users to where they want to browse, or send back some possible URLs for users to choose the correct URL by simply one click. Users could just enter one word "google", or error word "goggle", and then will be taken to "www.google.com".

To accomplish the URL correction, we have applied URL preprocess and approximate URL matching technique into proxy server, so that users could just enter some important names (maybe with some errors) to browse the web pages they want. Normally, the proxy server works as usual when the URL request is correct. However if proxy server discovers the URL request is non-existent, it first performs the URL preprocess to get the important part of URL, and then performs the approximate URL matching to obtain some approximate URLs, and sends back to the users. Users could see the approximate URLs listed in their browsers and just simply click the correct URL to browse the web page. This is very convenient for users to browse on the Internet.

In this paper, we choose "edit distance" as the URL similarity measurement of two URLs, because it has a clear definition and is also widely used in many fields of applications. Furthermore, we have designed one algorithm to utilize three filter conditions [14] based on n-gram technique to perform the URL correction.

This paper is organized as follows: Section 2 presents related work, Section 3 lists some basic concepts about our method, Section 4 outlines the design of the URL correction, Section 5 presents the implementation environment and results, and the last section is the conclusion.

RELATED WORK

Web tracking and caching is highly active research area. A lot of tracking studies analyze the request rate, number of requests, the effects of cookies, aborted connections, and persistent connections on the performance of proxy caching [2, 3].

There has also been extensive work on cooperative Web caching as a technique to reduce access latency and bandwidth consumption. Cooperative Web caching proposals include hierarchical schemes like Harvest and Squid [4, 5], hash-based schemes [6], directory-based schemes [7] and multicast-based schemes [8].

For the approximate matching field, many researches have been published. For two strings of length n and m, there exists a dynamic programming algorithm to compute the edit distance of the strings in O(nm) time and space [9], and improvements to the average and worst case have appeared [10, 11].

In [1], they solve the problem of approximate string joins in a database, using n-gram as index stored in database and using three filter conditions for quickly joins. In the field of database, several indexing techniques proposed for the "approximate string matching" problem, however, such techniques have to be supported by the database management system [12].

BASIC CONCEPTS

In this section, we briefly describe some basic concepts about URL preprocess and URL approximate matching technique.

Edit Distance (The URL Similarity Measurement)

The edit distance $d(x,y)$ between two URLs x and y is the minimal cost of a sequence of operations that transform x into y. The cost of a sequence of operations is the sum of the costs of the individual operations. In this paper we use three standard operations of cost 1 such as follows.

Insertion: inserting the letter a, Deletion: deleting the letter a, Replacement or Substitution: for $a \neq b$, replacing a by b.

URL Preprocess

Before we have to introduce the index (called n-grams) for each URL, we perform one preprocess. The preprocess procedure prunes some common prefixes or suffixes of each URL, such as: "www.", ".com", ".org", ".gov", ".tw", etc. For all URLs in proxy native database we must perform this prepro-

Figure 1. The preprocess prunes URL strings into some important keyword

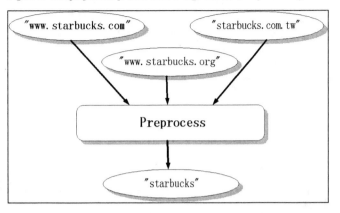

Figure 3. Matching process

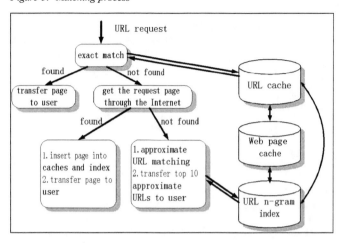

cess first, and then start to make the n-grams of the pruned URLs. On the other hand, we also perform the same preprocess for all URL request before matching. The benefit of the procedure is that users could just type some important parts of the URL, and they don't need to consider what the prefix or suffix is. The following example shows the influence.

Example [Preprocess] As Figure 1 shows, assume proxy server has three URL strings about "starbucks" (such as: "www.starbucks.com", "www.starbucks.org", "starbucks.com.tw",) then the preprocess prunes the three URLs to the same string "starbucks". Therefore users could just enter "starbucks" to find these three URLs. The improvement is very convenient for users.

N-Grams: Indices for Approximate URL Matching
For a given pruned URL s, its n-grams are obtained by "sliding" a window of length n over the characters of s. Since n-grams at the beginning and the end of the string have fewer than n characters from s, we introduce new characters "#" and "$", and conceptually extend the string by prefixing it with occurrences of "#" and suffixing it with occurrences of "$". Thus, each n-gram contains exactly n characters. The concept behind using n-grams is that when two strings a, b are within a small edit distance of each other, they must share a large number of n-grams in common.

For any string s of length |s|, we can easily find out the number of its n-gram is |s| + n − 1. For example, the pruned URL s is "DIGITAL", and then its n-grams are: "##D", "#DI", "DIG", "IGI", "GIT", "ITA", "TAL", "AL$", "L$$". The number of 3-grams: 9 = 7 (length) + 3(n) − 1.

Filtering Technique Using N-Gram
For a large URL cache in proxy, we use three filter conditions [1] to quickly filter out impossible URLs having edit distance less then k (k is the error threshold of proxy). The key objective here is to efficiently identify approximate URLs before we use the "expansive" distance function to compute their distance. These three filtering conditions are as follows:

Count Filtering: Consider strings s_1 and s_2, of lengths $|s_1|$ and $|s_2|$, respectively. If the equation $d(s_1, s_2) \leq k$ holds, then the two strings must have at least (max($|s1|$) − 1 − (k − 1)*n) the same n-grams.

Position Filtering: If strings s_1 and s_2 are within an edit distance of k, then a positional n-gram in one cannot correspond to a positional n-gram in the other that differs from it by more than k positions.

Length Filtering: The last condition is that string length provides useful information to quickly prune strings that are not within the desired edit distance. If two strings s_1 and s_2 are within edit distance k, their lengths cannot differ by more then k.

URL CORRECTION DESIGN
In this section we introduce our method and new proxy architecture for the URL correction.

New Proxy Architecture
We modify the proxy architecture to perform approximate URL matching, and Figure 2 shows the new architecture of proxy server. We need to make

a new "URL N-gram Index" in addition to the "web page cache" and corresponding "URL cache"; the "URL N-gram Index" is the set of all n-grams of each URL in proxy. Especially, we apply the approximate URL matching into the situation when proxy server couldn't get the requested page, then the proxy server returns top 10 approximate URLs back to the user.

Index Architecture
For each web page, proxy server stores it into inside web page cache and URL cache. Furthermore, we create the n-grams for each URL and use the set of n-gram (G_s) as the URL indices. We put the indices G_s into a large table (called "URL N-gram Index"). The URL N-gram Index contains four fields: 1.n-gram 2.URL string length (denote L) 3.position (the position which n-gram appears) 4.URL_ID (the unique identification of each URL).

Example [URL N-gram Index] Assume that URL string D_s = "HELLO", Length(D_s)= |Ds| = 5, and we use the 3-grams as indices(n = 3,) then we get the following 3-grams:

$G_{3,1}$ = "##H", $G_{3,2}$ = "HE", $G_{3,3}$ = "HEL", $G_{3,4}$ = "ELL", $G_{3,5}$ = "LLO", $G_{3,6}$ = "LO$", $G_{3,7}$ = "O$$"

Matching Processes
The URL correction processes using n-gram are as follows:
1. For each URL string D_s, we produce all the n-grams of D_s.
2. Retrieve each filter list in the URL N-gram Index corresponding to each n-gram.
3. In all filter lists, we sum the records having the same URL_ID. When the sum is greater then the **Count Filtering**, the record with the URL_ID maybe is the answer; then we check it for the **Length Filtering**, and insert it into the last result list when it passes the condition.
4. Use the distance function to compute the edit distance for the records in the last result list.

Figure 2. The new proxy architecture

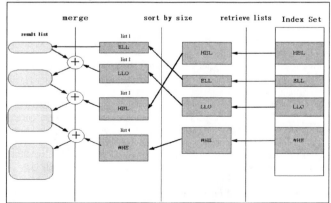

Some serious problems arise during these processes, especially when the amount of record in filter lists is very large. Therefore we need an efficient method for these merge processes. We sort records in each filter list by URL_ID field, like the merge-sort algorithm. The following j iterations present the method:
1. List 1 => Result List (initiation).
2. List 2 + Previous Result List => new Result List (because we sort the records by URL_ID in lists, we can do the counting linearly in time O(n)).
3. List j + Previous Result List => new Result List.

During the merge iterations, we can easily observe that the preceding list records also appear in the latter lists, and the space and time used for counting increases quite substantially. For the purpose to reduce the space and time, we sort all lists by size beforehand, and the first list has the smallest size. Figure 3 shows our searching processes and data structures.

Rank and Return
After these matching processes, we have the real distances of last few possible URLs. Then we rank the approximate URLs by its similarity with the requested URL; we report error messages and the top 10 URLs back to users.

IMPLEMENTATION AND RESULTS
In this section, we present the implementation environment, browser setting, and parameter limitation of proxy server. Furthermore, we also describe the performance and benefits of our implementation.

Environment
We implement our proxy server on the Linux platform (Red Hat Linux release 6.2,) and choose the "squid" proxy system to apply URL correction technique, because the system is an open source and widely used under most network infrastructures. Besides, we also use the DB library developed by the University of Berkeley to perform the b+ tree structures for the URL N-gram Index.
Our implementations contain two parts:
(1) *Index Generation*
The part is responsible for generating n-grams of all URLs and making the sorted URL N-gram Index mentioned above, and sorting lists, etc. We use 3-gram (n=3) as default in our implementation.
(2) *Filter and Matching*
Programs could match approximate URLs under k edit distance, and we set k = 2 in the proxy settings.
For the distance function, we use the Levenshtein distance algorithm [13] to compute the real distance between two URL strings.

Browser Setting
In order to have faster efficiency on browsing the web, it is necessary for the user to set the proxy server in the web browser. This helps to make more efficient use of bandwidth and reduce the chances of getting duplicated copies of the same data from overseas. Two common browsers, Netscape Navigator and Internet Explorer, have to be configured to use the proxy server; especially in the IE browser, we have to check the check box of "*Access the Internet using a proxy server*" and cancel "*Bypass proxy server for local (Intranet) addresses*". The later action is very important, because the IE browser would automatically append local domain to the requested URL when it is just one word; if we don't cancel the later check box, the proxy server would not receive any URL request.

Parameter Limitation
In our implementation, the proxy server could select different parameters (n-gram, k error threshold) to work, however, the filters would lose their functionality when we choose unsuitable parameters. The limitation comes from the **Count Filtering:** $L - 1 - (k - 1) * n > 0.$. That is, our filters will lose functions when the inequality doesn't hold. In experiments, we choose k = 2 and n = 3 for proxy server, therefore, the filters work well for the pruned URL strings of length L > 4. For strings of length L <= 4, we have to directly compute their edit distances.

Experimental Results
We used about 500,000 URL strings to evaluate the performance of approximate URL matching, and produce more then 5,000,000 n-gram data. In our experiments, almost approximate URL matching processes had finished in one to three seconds; the performance of the filtering is acceptable. As our previous research [14], we use the matching processes to perform the filtering. However, the n value is very important for search performance. If n is too large, the filters lose its functions, then we have to use brute force method to check each string, and the performance decreases. If n is too small, the index size increases, and the performance also decreases. Therefore, it is very important to one suitable n value, and in our experience, n (three to five) is suitable for common situations.
We could change the proxy parameters for various approximate levels depending on different needs. On the other hand, users could just enter some important keywords to find what they want because we first perform the URL preprocess, and maybe users would discover some other URLs containing the information they are interested in.

CONCLUSIONS
We successfully applied the URL correction technique into proxy server, and this kind of proxy server will take users to a convenient environment for browsing on the Internet. Even though users enter error URLs, they still will be taken to the correct web pages. This is our major contribution.
To perform the URL correction technique, we make and sort the n-grams of all URL strings, and archive a well URL correction performance. Furthermore, we list the limitation of the proxy parameters for administrators to customize the system. Most of all, we make users a lot easier to browse the web.
To increase the practicality of the system, it should be deployed on one bigger proxy server, such as some ISP's proxy servers, which has a lot of web pages and a lot of user requests.

REFERENCES
[1] L. Gravano and P. G. Ipeirotis and H. V. Jagadish and N. Koudas and S. Muthukrishnan and D. Srivastava. Approximate String Joins in a Database (Almost) for Free. In *Proceedings of the 27th VLDB Conference, 2001.*
[2] R. Caceres, F. Douglis, A. Feldmann, G. Glass, and M. Rabinovich. Web proxy caching: The devil is in the details. In Workshop on Internet Server Performance, pages 111-118, June 1998.
[3] A. Feldmann, R. Cacres, F. Douglis, G. Glass, and M. Rabinovich. Performance of web proxy caching in heterogeneous bandwidth environments. In *Proceedings of IEEE INFOCOM '99, March 1999.*
[4] A. Chankhunthod, P. B. Danzig, C. Neerdaels, M. F. Schwartz, and K. J. Worrell. A hierarchical Internet object cache. In *Proceedings of the 1996 USENIX Technical Conference, pages 153-163, January 1996.*
[5] Squid internet object cache. http://squid.nlanr.net.
[6] D. Karger, T. Leighton, D. Lewin, and A. Sherman. Web caching with consistent hashing. In *Proceedings of the 8th Int. World Wide Web Conference, May 1999.*
[7] R. Tewari, M. Dahlin, H. Vin, and J. Kay. Design considerations for distributed caching on the Internet. In the 19th IEEE Int. Conference on Distributed Computing Systems, May 1999.
[8] J. Touch. The LSAM proxy cache – a multicast distributed virtual cache. In *Proceedings of the 3rd Int. WWW Caching Workshop, June 1998.*
[9] T. F. Smith and M. S. Waterman. Identification of common molecular subsequences. In *Journal of Molecular Biology*, 147: pages 195-197, 1981.
[10] R. Cole and R. Hariharan. Approximate string matching: a simpler faster algorithm. In *Proceedings of ACM-SIAM SODA '98*, pages 463-472, 1998.
[11] W. Chang and E. Lawler. Sublinear approximate string matching and biological applications. Algorithmica, 12(4/5):327-344, 1994. Preliminary version in FOCS'90, 1990.
[12] T. Bozkaya and Z. M. Ozsoyoglu. Distance based indexing for high dimensional metric spaces. In *Proceedings of String Processing and Information Retrieval Symposium (SPIRE'99,)* pages 16-23, 1999.
[13] Levenshtein Distance. http://www.merriampark.com/ld.htm
[14] Chi-Chien Pan and Kai-Hsiang Yang and Tzao-Lin Lee. Approximate String Matching in LDAP based on edit distance. In *Proceedings of the IPDPS2002 Conference, 2002.*

Adapting UP for CORBA Application Development

Bencomo, N. Matteo, A.
Laboratorio TOOLS – Centro ISYS
Escuela de Computación, Facultad de Ciencias, Universidad Central de Venezuela
Apdo. 48093, Los Chaguaramos 1041-A, Caracas, Venezuela.
Phone number: 0058-212-6051659, Fax number: 0058-212-6051131
e-mail: nelly@acm.org, amatteo@isys.ciens.ucv.ve

ABSTRACT

The design of distributed applications in a CORBA based environment can be carried out by means of an incremental software process, which starts from requirements specification and leads to architectural design and implementation. In such a process, activities related to communication and integration mechanisms defined in the CORBA standard have to be executed. This paper discusses an adaptation of the Unified Process (UP) for the developing of CORBA applications. The adaptation proposes a clear traceability from the Use Case model through Analysis, Design, Deployment and Implementation models.

INTRODUCTION

During the past decade, distributed computing has gained increasing importance in the Information Technology domain. One of the most important results in this field is the Object Management Group (OMG) Common Object request Broker (CORBA) [13]. CORBA provides the mechanisms by which objects transparently make requests and receive responses. The heart of the architecture is an Object request Broker (ORB) which fulfils this function. The OMG has also specified a complete architecture (OMG/OMA) addressing both general issues and particular needs of application domains (e.g., Telecom, Banking, and Medicine) by defining high level library modules and frameworks. However, OMG mainly addresses the technological aspects in O-O distributed computing with little emphasis on the development process or notation.

On the other hand, the concept of software process has evolved over the past few years. Nowadays, it is accepted that a process has to focus not only on such aspects as workflows, devices, and activities, but also on other aspects such as the nature of the company and technology to be used in the project. Generally speaking, a process is defined to be adapted by an organization considering its culture, social dynamics, abilities, clients, complexity of the project, tools, techniques, and the application domain, among others. In O-O software, a generic process known as Unified Process (UP) [7] has been defined. UP can be adapted by taking into account the aspects mentioned above.

This paper reports our experience in specifying an adaptation of UP for the development of CORBA applications. The adaptation focuses on use cases, which are used to establish a clear traceability among analysis, design, deployment and implementation models. In this sense, control objects of the analysis have a direct correspondence with distributed components in implementation and deployment models. Currently, the adaptation affects Analysis, Design and Implementation workflows by tailoring and introducing activities and artefacts. We are also interested on studying how Requirements workflow can be adapted to fulfil CORBA applications development.

The reminder of this paper is organized as follows: in section 2 we present an overview of the adaptation and section 3 draws some preliminary conclusions and the research directions we plan to explore in the future.

ADAPTATION

Overview

Figure 1 shows an overview of the adaptation. CORBA icons highlight the activities affected by the adaptation. CORBA has a strong influence on the architecture of a system; this is the reason why Architectural Design activity is

Figure 1. Adapted workflows and activities

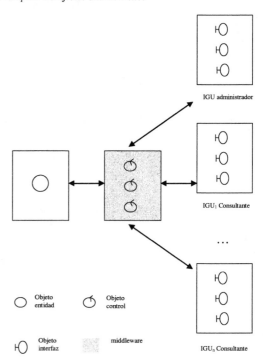

adapted in all workflows. In the Use Case Analysis activity, control classes responsible for remote communication are identified and specialized. These control classes are given the name of Remote Communication Control Classes (RCCC) and are the abstractions of components in charge of remote communication in the implementation. In Use Case Design, Subsystem Design and Class Design activities, the design classes corresponding to the specialized control classes in analysis and their IDL interfaces are specified. Finally, in Subsystem Implementation and Class Implementation activities, are the steps related to the implementation of the IDL interfaces in design, and the mapping of components onto nodes.

1.1 Workflows

In this section we briefly explain the adaptations done in the Analysis, Design and Implementation workflows.

Analysis

The adaptation is tailored to aspects related to control classes. A control class plays the role of intermediary. The adaptation mainly proposes the identification of control classes responsible for remote communication among the analysis classes; this has to be done for each relevant use case in the Use Case Model. These RCCCs are specializations or adaptations of common control classes in the Use Case Model.

Design

In Design, some classes can be initially sketched from analysis classes; this is the case of design classes that deal with remote communication. A RCCC associated with a use case i in analysis will correspond to a pair of design classes, see Figure 2. Corresponding objects related to this pair of design classes will be intermediaries for remote component communications in the implementation.

Each design class in Figure 2 traces to a CORBA object in the implementation. These classes expose basically two kinds of interfaces; one is a common UML semantic interface and the other is an IDL interface. IDL interfaces let CORBA objects in the implementation send/receive the (remote) messages. The common UML interfaces let components on each end to send/receive the messages without taking care of CORBA communication mechanisms.

The methods of both kinds of interfaces are specified using the interaction diagrams that were specified early in design.

Implementation

In implementation, we have to program the code associated with CORBA objects and components based on the IDL interfaces in design. Currently, we are working on the definition of CORBA Components Diagrams to describe the functionality and interactions among CORBA components.

Figure 2: Trace relationship between Use Case Model, Analysis Classes (RCCC) and Design Classes

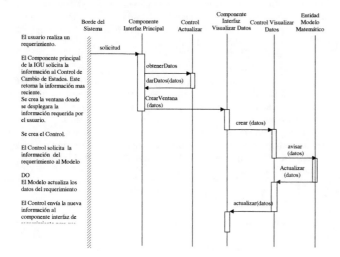

3. CONCLUSIONS

Currently, the specification of the adaptation is almost finished, leading to a formal adaptation named CORBAdapted-UP. The adaptation is based on practical experience, [1][2][3]. One such successful experience has been the development of a distributed graphical interface for a Real-Time system.

One of the issues we are refining is the formal notation of new stereotypes, artefacts and diagrams related to CORBA to be included in UP. Another issue is the application of this adaptation for the development of new applications based on legacy applications.

We are also extending the adaptation to include Requirements workflow and to specify a list of parameters tailored to CORBA application development.

One of the most difficult issues in this work has been describing our adaptation of a process that is so detailed. For this reason, we are also interested on developing a formal specification of a template UP adaptation specifications.

4. REFERENCES

Bencomo, N,.: Interfaz Gráfica Basada En Objeto Distribuidos Para Un Sistema En Tiempo Real, Tesis de Maestría, Postgrado en Ciencias de la Computación, UCV, Venezuela, (1998)

Bencomo, N., Blanco, A., Correa, E., Matteo, A.: An experience using OOSE for a Graphical Multi-User Interface based on Distributed Objects, 5th. International Conference on Information Systems Analysis and Synthesis ISAS'99, Proceedings de la Conferencia, Volumen II, Orlando, Florida, USA, (1999)

Bencomo, N., Correa, E., Matteo, A.: An experience using CORBA and OOSE in the construction of a Graphical multi-user Interface based on Distributed Objects, Proceeding of Practical Experience Segment of Objetos Distribuidos 2000, Sao Paolo, Brazil, (2000)

Bencomo, N., Correa, E., Matteo, A.: Comparación de CORBA y X Web en el Desarrollo y Desempeño de Una Interfaz Gráfica Multiusuario, Publicado en Memorias XXVI Conferencia Latinoamericana de Informática CLEI200, (2000)

Finkelstein, A., Kramer J., Nuseibeh, B.: Software Process Modelling and Technology, Research Studies Press LTD (1994)

Fowler, M., Scott, K.: UML Distilled Applying the Standard Object Modelling Language, AW, (1997)

Jacobson, I., Booch, G., Rumbaugh J..: The Unified Software Development Process, Addison-Wesley (1999)

Jacobson, I., Magnus, C., Patrik, J., Gunnar, O.: Object-Oriented Software Engineering: A Use case driven Approach, Addison-Wesley (1993)

Kendall, S.: Modern Systems Analysis & Design, Prentice Hall, Tercera Edición (2002)

Leszek, A. Maciaszek: Requirements Analysis and System Design Developing Information Systems using UML, ADDISON WESLEY, (2001)

OMG Unified Modelling Language Specification, Version 1.4, OMG, (2001)

Shatz, S.: Developing of Distributed Software, Macmillan Publishing Company, (1993)

Slama, D., Garbis J., Russelm P.: Enterprise CORBA, Prentice Hall, (1999)

Stevens, P., Pooley, R.: Using UML Software Engineering with Objects and Components, AW, (2000)

K_SERVICES: From State-of-the-Art Components to Next Generation Distributed KM Systems

Frank Laskowski1
OFFIS e.V.
Department of Business Information Systems
Escherweg 2; 26121 Oldenburg; Germany
tel.: +49 441 9722 157
fax: +49 441 9722 202
frank.laskowski@offis.de

Norbert Gronau
University of Oldenburg
Chair of Business Information Systems
Escherweg 2; 26121 Oldenburg; Germany
tel.: +49 441 9722 150
fax: +49 441 9722 202
gronau@wi-ol.de

ABSTRACT

The information architecture of an organization is the way individuals, groups and the organization itself handle information and hence is a central issue in knowledge management. Knowledge management software assembled in knowledge management systems reflects and influences information architecture in parts or as a whole. Yet insufficient flexibility prevents knowledge management systems to be used effectively as a tool to conduct the ongoing evolution of an organizations information architecture. In this paper we first describe results from the TO_KNOW project regarding the integration of components in current knowledge management systems. These experiences we base on the K_SERVICES project proposing a consequent component-oriented approach to build knowledge management software to enable the support of dynamic strategies in knowledge management.

1. INTRODUCTION

The term "knowledge management" comprises methods to improve organizational capabilities and rise the efficiency of the implementation of the organizational strategy by the consequent use of knowledge as a resource. Knowledge can be defined in this context as the totality of experience and capabilities which people use for solving a problem ([1], [2] etc.). An important task in this context is to analyze the use and demand of knowledge of the individual members of the organization as well as of the organizational units of different size up to the complete organization by itself - i.e. to grasp the "information architecture" of an organization. ([3])

Knowledge management systems (KM systems) implement an information architecture hereby delivering direct support to users who have "knowledge-related" problems. For this purpose a wide variety of methods and technologies is integrated into a fully fledged KM system - from database systems over CSCW tools up to WWW portals with the intention to support „knowledge-intensive" processes. (e.g. [4], [5], [6]) Figure 1 shows a typical KM system and subdivides the KM specific functional sections and components embedded in a layered architecture.

In the following sections we give an overview about our research in progress regarding component-based KM systems: In the project TO_KNOW ([7]) we study the possibilities to extend typical KM systems using state-of-the-art concepts and technologies. As part of the project a case-based reasoning component is being developed and integrated into an existing KM system.

Fig. 1: Architecture of a KM system

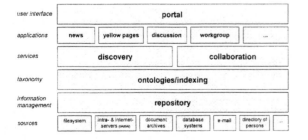

The comprehensive experiences on conceptual and technical aspects lead us to start the project K_SERVICES. Here we investigate into a consequently component-oriented architecture for KM systems: A proper component-oriented design in terms of software-engineering standards is a technical necessity. But far more is needed to make the vision of a KM system combined of knowledge-oriented building blocks become a reality.

2. TO_KNOW: A COMPONENT INTEGRATING CBR TECHNOLOGY INTO A KM SYSTEM

Knowledge oriented methods and technology are well-known from the field of artificial intelligence (AI). Hence various AI methods and technology are part of KM systems, among those case-based reasoning ([8]). Basically cased-based reasoning (CBR) means to solve new problems based on available experiences. These experiences are expressed as "cases" that include a description of a problem and an appropriate solution. If a new problem can be solved by applying and modifying the experiences from the "case base", the problem and the new solution make up a new case, a new experience. (See [9] for an introduction to CBR.)

Looking at a KM system from a birds eye view there are obvious parallels: The users might not expect the system to solve their problems but they use it as a case-base, learn from the experiences with similar problems they retrieved from it and they add new experiences. Typically a main part of the information involved has the form of documents. These can be looked at as experiences and with his or her initial search query a user just tries to describe his or her current problem. This extends the parallels to information retrieval (IR) (see [10], [11]) that is part (sometimes core) of typical KM systems. (For the combination of CBR and IR see [12], [13].)

As part of the project TO_KNOW a CBR component is designed (and implemented) to fit into a typical KM system (referring to the illustration in fig. 1). This task served as example to develop an architecture-based approach to figure out appropriate interfaces between the KM system and a component to be integrated. As result we found five types of correspondences between the component's special functionality and the KM system's general realm, as listed below and illustrated in figure 2.

- *replace:* Do data or tasks play a similar role as well in the component as in the KM system?
- *use:* Can any technical aspect of the KM system be used to implement the component's functionality?
- *mapping:* Real KM systems can not be expected to be sufficiently open to support every eligible replacement or usage seamlessly or completely. In these cases a loose coupling should be possible, rather than ignoring a possible synergy.
- *add:* How is the exclusive, core part of the component to be integrated into the KM system? (This is the most basic type of correspondence. The concepts of replacement, usage or mapping do not apply here.)
- *feedback:* The component might produce results that are of general interest (in the KM system) even where the special functionality of the component is not needed.

While correspondences of the first three types listed ("replace", "use", "mapping") enable efficient implementation and execution, relationships of

Fig. 2: Five types of correspondences between a KM system and an component

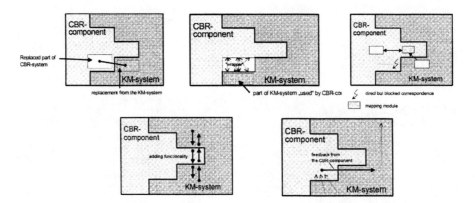

the other types ("add", "feedback") improve effectiveness (i.e. quality of the provided support for knowledge-oriented tasks).

3. K_SERVICES: A COMPONENT-ORIENTED FRAMEWORK FOR KM-SYSTEMS

KM systems have no special qualities that would justify to exclude them from the major trend of building information systems using a component-oriented approach (see [14]) to reduce the cost of development as well as enhance flexibility and hence achieve sustainable architectures resp. long running systems. In fact these issues affect especially KM systems for they are not "primary" systems in two ways: a) KM systems have to integrate, mediate and enrich "basic" information that comes from technically different components, namely from the "standard" information systems of an organization. b) The later include the "first priorty" systems of a company, while KM systems are usually rated rather as "useful" but "necessary" – therefore a KM system's financial requirements should be "moderate" at the latest after deployment.

The TO_KNOW approach discussed in the last section provides a roadmap to design efficient and effective components for integration into typical KM systems. But the results also show that there is need for a more detailed "domain specification" for knowledge management software support: Developing a component for a KM system still rises too many questions regarding entities that should be easily recognized as common business objects or vertical facilities with clearly understood positions in a typical components framework for knowledge management systems.

As part of the project K-SERVICES such a framework is developed by abstracting from correspondences found by applying the TO_KNOW approach to different component candidates. Elaboration of the framework covers two main aspects:

- Interfaces for a KM systems information sources, services and applications: What are the basic and extended mechanisms that these types of components offer or need and that should and can reasonably be unified?
- Core components of a KM system: Some features are necessary to run a KM system that integrates a variety of components and changes over time (e.g. user profiles). Others are candidates for "common knowledge facilities" because of their high potential to increase the overall quality delivered by many components (e.g. metadata and internal association services). Of course a complete KM framework includes such functionalities. But it is conceptually crucial that the core system provides unified and logically centralized access points to these facilities, while the implementation might reside in external components as well.

To fully exploit the advantages of the component-oriented approach KM systems have to operate distributedly. A KM system should be able to integrate components externally provided by using the emerging web-services technology ([15]) and it should be able to cooperate with other KM systems. The option to integrate a variety of external knowledge-oriented services like ontologies, analysis-tools or community support with reasonable effort facili-

tates the vision of an evolving KM system: Not only the accessible information sources but the complete functionality of the KM system can adopt to changes in the information architecture of an organization. This is of specific interest in knowledge management, because KM systems implement knowledge management strategies and thus are expected to influence the way individuals, organizational units and an organization as a whole handle information. (In most standard information systems flexibility is mainly needed to adopt to externally caused "drift effects" in user or technical requirements but change is not inherent to their purpose.)

This vision imposes a bunch of problems to be coped with from different fields, e.g.:

- Technical problems: Which additional web-services standards (like [16], [17]) are useful and which are still inadequate or missing?
- Application barriers: Some external components of a KM system might need extensive access to sensitive data. Both appropriate business models and feasible tools to grant just the access needed are required.
- KM specific aspects of distribution: In case of an external component dropping out a KM specific rules can enable more tolerant reactions compared to standard information systems.

With extended (and affordably priced) flexibility a local setup and maintenance of KM systems becomes a more common scenario, e.g. local KM systems in departments that have very special and important knowledge intensive tasks in a company. To prevent counterproductive "knowledge islands" to emerge, in the design of the core KM system resp. the "common knowledge facilities" there has to be a major focus not only on integration but on cooperation as well.

4. CONCLUSIONS & FUTURE WORK

Developing a state-of-the-art component and integrating it into an existing KM system lead us to the vision of a consequently component-oriented

Fig. 3: Outline of the K_SERVICES architecture for KM systems

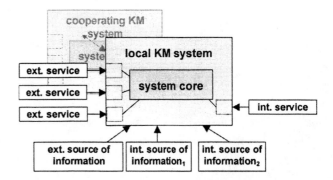

approach addressing the shortcomings we experienced working with current knowledge management software. Starting to design a suitable framework in the K-SERVICES project we came to a first intermediary result: It is not sufficient just to define appropriate business objects and implement these using a current component software standard. The design of the K_SERVICES framework will additionally include knowledge management specific issues regarding integration and cooperation into the design of a framework for KM systems. As we outlined above this can significantly improve a KM systems suitability to evolve interactively and dynamically with an organizations information architecture.

REFERENCES

[1]   Probst, G., Raub, S, Romhardt, K.: Manage the Knowledge. How companies optimally use their most valuable resource. 3rd Edition Frankfurt (Main) 1999 (in German).

[2]   Krallmann, H.; Gronau, N. (Hrsg.): Wettbewerbsvorteile durch Wissensmanagement - Methodik und Anwendungen des Knowledge Management. Stuttgart 2000

[3]   Allen, B.R.; Boynton, A.C.: Information architecture: In search of efficient flexibility. In MIS Quarterly, Vol. 15, No. 4, p. 435-445, 1991

[4]   Harvard Computing Group Report : Knowledge Management – Return on Investment, http://www.kmadvantage.com/docs/KM/KM_—_ROI.pdf, (Nov. 15 2001)

[5]   Versteegen, G.: Knowledge Management. Architektur für das Firmenwissen. i'X (1999) 3, S. 113-119

[6]   Lawton, G.: Knowledge Management: Ready for Prime Time?, IEEE Computer 34, February (2001), 12-14.

[7]   Gronau, N.; Laskowski, F.: An architecture for integrating CBR components into KM systems. In: Mirjam Minor, Steffen Staab (Hrsg.): Proceedings of the 1st German Workshop on Experience Management. Bonner Köllen Verlag, 2002, S. 92-97

[8]   Aha, D.W.; Muñoz-Avila, H. (Hrsg.): Exploring Synergies of Knowledge Management and Case-Based Reasoning: Papers from the AAAI 1999 Workshop. Washington, DC: Naval Research Laboratory, Navy Center for Applied Research in Artificial Intelligence, 1999

[9]   Aamodt, A., Plaza, E.: Case-Based Reasoning: Foundational Issues, Methodological Variations and System Approaches. AI communications 7 (1994), 1, S. 35-39

[10]   van Rijsbergen, C.J.: Information Retrieval. Second Edition, Butterworths, London, 1979

[11]   Homepage of the ACM Special Interest Group on Information Retrieval Http://www.acm.org/sigir/, 3.12.2001

[12]   Rissland, E.L.; Daniels, J.J.: Using CBR to Drive IR. In Proceedings of the Fourteenth International Joint Conference on Artificial Intelligence (IJCAI-95), 400-407, 1995

[13]   Wilson, D.; Bradshaw, S.: CBR Textuality. In Proceedings of the Fourth UK Case-Based Reasoning Workshop, 1999

[14]   Szyperski, C.; Gruntz, D.; Murer, S.: Component Software - Beyond Object-Oriented Programming, Second Edition, Addison-Wesley/ACM Press, 2002

[15]   Vasudevan, V.: A Web Services Primer: A review of the emerging XML-based web services platform, examining the core components of SOAP, WSDL and UDDI. O'Reilly XML.COM, 2001
http://www.xml.com/pub/a/2001/04/04/webservices/

[16]   http://www.w3.org/TR/xkms/

[17]   http://www.gotdotnet.com/team/xml_wsspecs/xlang-c/default.ht

Challenges for Curriculum Design in IT Education

Wai K. Law
College of Business and Public Administration
University of Guam
UOG Station, Mangilao, Guam 96923
Tel: (671) 735-2520, Fax (671) 734-5362
wlaw@uog.edu

Jeffrey Hsu
Silberman College of Business Administration
Fairleigh Dickinson University
285 Madison Avenue M-MS2-04, Madison NJ 07940-1099
Tel: (6973) 443-8861, Fax: (973) 443-8377
jeff@fdu.edu

INTRODUCTION

Widespread applications of computer technology prompted the adoption of "Introduction to Computers" course in many college curriculums. Many business schools provided the computer literacy training through Information Systems curriculums. Growing popularity of the basic computing course created pressure in both computing facility and staffing support. The rapidly changing technology posted major challenges for designers of Information Systems (IS) curriculum. Careful decision must be made to select the appropriate technological platform, and to balance the technological capability with a shrinking budget. A greater challenge was to design IS courses for students who had no intention of pursuing the vigorous IS professional training. These students lacked the same motivation of those choosing a career in IS, and experienced great difficulties in adjusting to the pace of a traditional IS courses. At the same time, the course designer must consider the prior computing experiences of the students, and changing expectation of students, faculty, and other stakeholders. The huge discrepancy in technical backgrounds and career interests posted challenges in instructional delivery. The course designer must be selective in bundling relevant materials into the limited time of a single course, while providing sufficient challenge and learning experience relative to the prior technical backgrounds of students.

This paper reports research findings of an exploratory survey seeking answers to some of these questions. We originally planned to apply an identical survey instrument at both the University of Guam and at the Fairleigh Dickinson University, each campus with approximately 200 students enrollment for the "Introduction to Computers" course. However, only a portion of the data collected from the University of Guam was available prior to the proceeding publication. We expected a much larger sample size with updated results.

SURVEY INSTRUMENT

Students were asked to complete a questionnaire to indicate their experience with a list of fifteen areas of computing, communication and network technologies. The list was chosen to ensure common knowledge of the technologies, although it would be difficult to ensure a common definition among the respondents for each particular technology. The students were asked to indicate years of experience with each technology, and whether the technology was used at work. The respondents next answered whether they had easy access to technologies, and those they planned to own or subscribe to. They were then asked to indicate the importance of each technology in their career, and whether the technology should be a mandatory training in high school or college curriculum. Lastly, they were asked to express their feeling toward computing activities. The survey was designed for voluntary participation, and thus aimed at collecting exploratory data that could give better insight toward design of IT training.

PRELIMINARY SAMPLE DESCRIPTIONS

The survey was conducted among University of Guam students enrolling in IS courses. This ensured that the students had adequate understanding of the technical terminology, and a fresh experience with the usage of technology. Over ninety-five percent of the students participating in the survey did not pursue a career in IS, and over forty percent of the enrolled students were from outside the College of Business and Public Administration that offered the course. We chose to allow voluntary participation in the survey study with full disclosure under the human research subject guidelines, thus reducing the possibility of random responses or potential harm to the respondents. A usable sample of 85 responses was used to compile this preliminary report.

REEXAMINE THE OBJECTIVE OF AN "INTRODUCTION TO COMPUTERS" COURSE

As the first course in an Information Systems curriculum, the "Introduction to Computers" course was frequently designed to prepare students for more vigorous computer and technical training. As a result, the emphasis tends to be on the depth of knowledge on technical details, compared to the productivity deployment of computers in general applications. This strategy began to fail with multiple platforms of technology, and especially when students enrolled in the course had diverse career interests. Many students must be motivated to learn computing, as a mandatory requirement rather than a study of personal choice. Other students might have a preference for a technology platform other than the selected platform, and some might have advanced beyond introductory computing concepts. There was also increasing pressure to ensure that students acquire computing capability besides a basic conceptual understanding of computing.

Table 1 summarized the voting results on the array of technology that should be adopted as mandatory training. Over half of the respondents believed that a broad spectrum of technical training should be required for students either at high school or at the college level. A majority of them believed that word processing, spreadsheet, Internet, email and chat room should be required in a high school program. Twenty percent agreed that college level training would be desirable in these areas. This immediately raised the research question whether colleges should use their limited resources to provide training in these areas. A relevant question to ask is whether students would have acquired the adequate levels of skills at the high school level. An informal survey among IS instructors concluded that students were not sufficiently prepared to handle tasks requiring these skills at the college level. Future research should provide more insight for IS curriculum designers.

The unexpected findings were the large ratio of respondents expecting college training in programming, web design, groupware, networking, database, PCS, and high-end application software such as CAD/CAM and Desktop Publishing. The findings were significant especially for the fact that a majority of the respondents did not choose a program of study in Computer Science (CS), Computer Information System (CIS), or Information Systems. At the University of Guam, the Computer Science department offers a separate "Introduction to Computers" course for CS and CIS students. Further research should investigate the real interests of the general body of students, and how non-professional track technical training could benefit them.

DESIRABLE OUTCOMES FOR COMPUTER TRAINING

Course contents in a curriculum were normally packaged to support outcomes of specific degree programs, designed by IS faculty. However, there

Table 1: Perceived Required Technology Training

Perceived Required Training	During High School	In College
Word Processing	91%	18%
Programming	25%	66%
Electronic Presentation	61%	42%
Internet	88%	20%
Web design	39%	58%
Groupware	28%	54%
e-mail	88%	18%
LAN	24%	64%
Network Administration	15%	74%
Spreadsheet	75%	32%
CAD/CAM	24%	64%
Desktop Publishing	28%	61%
Chat room	72%	19%
Database	35%	54%
PCS	27%	56%

Table 2: Skills Important for Career

Technical Skill	Considered important for career	Required College Training
Word Processing	91%	18%
Programming	52%	66%
Electronic Presentation	72%	42%
Internet	79%	20%
Web design	51%	58%
Groupware	28%	54%
e-mail	78%	18%
LAN	25%	64%
Network Administration	42%	74%
Spreadsheet	84%	32%
CAD/CAM	27%	64%
Desktop Publishing	46%	61%
Chat room	25%	19%
Database	49%	54%
PCS	34%	56%
Graphics	60%	n/a

could be a mismatch between the intended outcomes of an individual course, compared to the desired outcomes of individual students, as increasing number of students outside of the academic program enrolled in the course. Table 2 showed the perceived importance of various technical skills. It was interesting to observe that, with the exception of programming and web-design, respondents did not expect to receive college training for technical skills considered important to their career. It was also interesting to observe that many technical training considered mandatory requirements at college level were not considered important to the career of the respondents. The important research question to ask would be whether students consider technical training as important enrichment experience for their career development, or that students were not aware of the growing importance of technology in the various career paths. Additional research should help to make technical training more assessable; to debate the role of IT training as foundation skills, similar to language and mathematics; and for improving the IT awareness of career counselors.

PRIOR EXPERIENCE WITH TECHNOLOGY

With the prevalence of technology, students were expected to receive early exposure to information technology during their high school years. Students were asked to indicate the years of experience they had with the use of each technology, and whether the technology was used at work. Table 3 sum-

Table 3: Prior Experience with Technologies

Technology	With some experience	More than 1 year experience	More than 5 years experience	Use at work
Word Processing	94%	82%	51%	36%
Programming	31%	12%	2%	5%
Electronic Presentation	59%	35%	7%	14%
Internet	92%	86%	54%	27%
Web design	25%	11%	2%	1%
Groupware	14%	4%	2%	4%
e-mail	92%	85%	53%	31%
LAN	26%	15%	5%	7%
Network Administration	21%	8%	4%	7%
Spreadsheet	72%	51%	22%	27%
CAD/CAM	14%	5%	2%	0%
Desktop Publishing	16%	9%	6%	5%
Chat room	68%	52%	20%	6%
Database	32%	18%	7%	9%
PCS	24%	13%	4%	7%
Graphics	38%	18%	7%	11%
Communications	55%	39%	20%	15%

marized the results. The low ratio of those with more than 5 years of experience with various technologies indicated the slow progress in exposing students to technology at their early age. It is hope that the ratio would improve with subsequent research studies. Most of the respondents did not receive an early exposure to areas of technology with significant applications. These areas include electronic presentation, spreadsheet, and database. The low awareness of web-based technology signaled a potential gap in preparing the future workforce for electronic business environment. Less than 25% of the respondent reported experience with PCS technology, while 86% of them reported easy access to cellular telephones. The knowledge gap was disturbing given the trend toward a full digital environment.

EQUIPMENT SUPPORT FOR IT EDUCATION

For many years, IT education had been hampered by the limited training facility and equipment. Ninety-four percentage of the respondents claimed easy access to personal computer and Internet, and 67% of them reported easy access to cable TV network and fax machine. Sixty-five percent of this group planned to own a personal computer and subscribe to Internet service. This prompted the research question of whether IT curriculum should be planned around the limited resources of educational institutions. Innovative design practices could take advantage of the accessibility of technology resources to students for more flexible instructional programs at greatly reduced infrastructure supporting costs.

CONCLUSION

A closing question asked the respondents to rate statements on a five points scale, with 1 represent strongly agree, 3 for neutral, and 5 for strongly disagree. The average response was 3.9 to the statement "Working with computers is so complicated it is difficult to understand what is going on", with a standard deviation of 0.9. Despite the small sample size, this was beginning evidence of a new generation that would incline to embrace the complexity of technology. The expressed desired for advanced IT training, and the readiness of students to ensure availability of computing resources suggested the need to revise model for the planning and delivery of IT education. The expanded data collection would improve our understanding of the observed challenges for IT curriculum design. Our goal would be to compare student preparedness, geographic environment, and other educational factors for the adjustment of IT curriculum design for global delivery.

REFERENCES

Available on Request.

ICT Supported Learning: A New Institutional Approach

Paola Bielli and Stefano Basaglia
I.S. Department, SDA Bocconi, Italy
paola.bielli@uni-bocconi.it, stefano.basaglia@sdabocconi.it

ABSTRACT

ICT diffusion at any level of society is offering a great opportunity to promote innovation in teaching and learning.

This paper presents the experience of Bocconi's Information Systems department in the field. Bocconi's I.S. Department has been an early adopter of any innovative teaching methods and of ICT in its courses both at the undergraduate and postgraduate levels.

Since the Spring semester 2000 it adopted Learning Space as pilot environment for one of the Management Information Systems classes (undergraduate level) and some of the executive courses of the Business Schools.

After three years of use and having a relatively big research sample (about 300 users) the research team can now sum up some of the most interesting results, which are the focus of this paper.

The analysis of the field experience bases on a research model which identifies the variables influencing the adoption and use decision of both students and instructors. Among the most interesting results of the research project it is worthwhile to mention the institutional variables which affect the first adoption decision and the successive decision to continue the use. Institutional variables include tangible factors, such as technical infrastructure or financial incentives, and intangible variables, such as friends' or colleagues' pressure.

INTRODUCTION

Information and Communication Technologies permeate everyday life [Drucker, 1993; Negroponte, 1995; Galimberti, 1999; Varian, Shapiro, 1999; Evans, Wurster, 2000] and education also experiences this trend [E.U., 1995; E.U., 2001; OECD, 2001], even if up to now it is not as advanced as other branches of society.

This statement leads to a logical conclusion: the use of ICT in education is no longer an option, an alternative to traditional education approaches, but it is a "must".

In other words, teachers and professors can no longer discuss whether it is worthwhile to use or not to use ICT in their courses, but they have to concentrate on how to use technology.

Even if relevant from any perspective (practice and pedagogy, to mention but few), the debate about how to introduce ICT in education has not reached a commonly agreed approach, yet.

Experiments and pilot studies have been launched in several countries and the first results are published and discussed.

This paper presents the experience of Bocconi's Information Systems department in the field. Bocconi's I.S. Department has been an early adopter of any innovative teaching methods and of ICT in its courses both at the undergraduate and postgraduate levels.

Since the Spring semester 2000 it adopted Learning Space as pilot environment for one of the Management Information Systems classes (undergraduate level) and some of the executive courses of the Business Schools.

After tree years of use and having a relatively big research sample (about 300 users) the research team can now sum up some of the most interesting results, which are the focus of this paper.

The first paragraph proposes an overview of the most recent literature about ICT based learning, with emphasis on factors influencing the use of ICT within courses. The review of dominant literature leads to the design of the research model (paragraph 2) that the research team developed to support

data analysis. Paragraph 3 gives an overview of Learning Space experience in Bocconi. Eventually in the last paragraphs the main conclusions are discussed and some of the open questions are listed.

THEORETICAL BACKGROUND

Several theoretical approaches influenced the research project. In particular, they can be divided into two different classes:
- Pedagogical approaches regarding new learning models and the role of ICT in education, which influence the implementation and management of Learning Space course;
- Literature about Information Systems use and New Institutional theory, influencing the analysis of Learning Space experiences.

Pedagogical Approaches

The changing philosophical paradigm (from "Modernism" to "Post-modernism") is also deeply modifying the pedagogical approach of Western education. This evolution is consistent with the approach envisioning that the turn into the Post-modern stage is demonstrated by the reinforcement of "weaken structure" (opposed to the "strong structures" of the Modern Era). Therefore, rationality itself is less rigid, is softer [Vattimo, Rovatti, 1983; Vattimo, 1999].

Education also experiences this change, as its main objective is no longer to transfer technicalities or rules, but to teach how to learn. This implies being able to cope with ambiguity, diversity, uncertainty.

The traditional objectivist model of learning is being replaced by the constructivist model of learning (Figure 1) [Leidner, Jaarvenpaa, 1995; Van Baalen, 1999].

The objectivist model of learning considers reality an external variable, independent from the interpretative scheme of each individual. The first task of instructors is to structure objective reality into abstract and/or generalized representations. Then he/she tries to efficiently and effectively transmit these representations to the learner. Under this perception, learning coincides with an uncritical absorption of objective knowledge by the learner.

The teaching and learning style consistent with the basic assumptions of the model are, respectively, top-down and passive.

Figure 1– Relationship between the reason's crisis and learning models

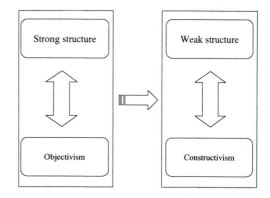

The constructivist model considers the existence of an objective world, but, unlike the objectivist model, denies the existence of an external reality independent of the interpretative scheme of each individual's mind. The learner, not the instructor, constructs the "reality" which is his own subjective representation of the objective

world. This poietic process is based on particular learner's experiences and biases. In this sense learning is the formation of abstract concepts to represent reality, while the task of teaching is to enable this creative process[1]. The objectivist model is instructor-based because the instructor has control over the learning environment, while the constructivist model is learner-based because the learner is the protagonist of the learning process. Then, according to the principles of the model the learning style and the teaching style are respectively active and bottom-up (Bielli, Basaglia, 2000).

Constructivism has two main offsprings [Leidner, Jarvenpaa, 1995]: the cooperative model of learning and the cognitive information processing model of learning.

In the basic constructivist model the learning process has an individual dimension, in fact the learning process bases on the interaction between the individual (with his/her own experiences and biases) and the objective world. The collaborative model substitutes this individual dimension with a group dimension in which knowledge emerges as a consequence of the interaction of individual with other individuals. In this sense the goal of teaching is to facilitate group dynamics [Bielli, Basaglia, 2000].

The cognitive information processing of learning focuses on cognitive processes which characterize each students involved in the learning process. The main assumption of the model is that students differ in terms of cognitive styles. Different cognitive styles imply different learning techniques and tools because cognitive styles influence the impact of instructors' inputs on mental model, that is the degree with which students recall or process instructors' inputs. The relationship between cognitive styles and learning techniques suggests the need for a personalization of learning processes (in terms of presentation form or contents) [Bielli, Basaglia, 2001].

Some authors[2] argue that technology *per se* is neither good nor bad in education; its use might produce positive or negative effects depending on its consistency with the learning and teaching objectives and on the interaction between education system and its environment.

Information Systems Use and New Institutional Theory

Adoption and use of ICT in learning (i.e. e-learning) can derive reference models from the literature field which observes in general the adoption and use of ICT. In particular, the research model is influenced by reflections on the decision process in ICT and on the factors explaining why some users keep on using ICT systems, while others reject them.

Beside this research stream which usually takes an individual's perspective (the decision maker or the adopter is often considered as an individual isolated from the environment), the authors considered both literature on diffusion of innovations and new institutional theories which focus on the environment (social, economic, technological sphere) as one of the key explanations for adoption or non adoption.

The main references influencing the research model are listed and briefly commented in the following table (Table 1)

RESEARCH MODEL

The research model identifies two main decision stages: the Acceptance

Figure 2 – ICT Acceptance model: students' perspective

stage and the Continuance stage. Each stage is split into two levels: the student level and the instructor level.

At the first level of the acceptance stage, the framework identifies the variables affecting the process of acceptance and use of I.S for the students. The core idea is that the student's decision is mainly influenced by the expectations – positive (that is benefit) or negative (that is risk) - of the course which in turn derive from technical skills or from the social and institutional pressures (i.e. internal marketing campaigns promoted by the university, and so on) (figure 2).

The instructor's decision to accept and to adopt (use) I.S. is similarly influenced by his/her expectations (benefits and/or risk) of the course which are again influenced by the instructor's previous experience with multimedia or innovative teaching/learning, by

social and institutional pressure (i.e. department policies, colleagues, etc.) and by technical and pedagogical skills. Moreover, previous experience is influenced by technical and pedagogical skills (figure 3)

In the second stage (continuance phase), the student's decision to continue to use e-learning is largely influenced, from one side by the same variables of the first stage, but with different intensity or factors (in terms of research methods it means same variable, but different operators); at the same time decision is also influenced by a new variable, previous experience. Previous experience influences expectations and technical skills, in particular, it improves students' technical skills (figure 4).

Figure 3 - ICT Acceptance model: instructors' perspective

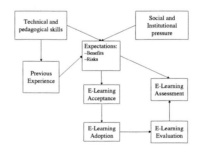

Figure 4 – ICT Continuance: students' perspective

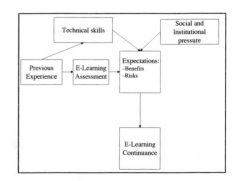

Table 1 – Literature review

Authors	Theory, Model, Content	Relevance for our research model
Bhattacherrjee, 2001.	Post-Acceptance Model of Information Systems Continuance	The distinction between Acceptance and Continuance ("acceptance and continuance are two temporally and conceptually distinct and possibly incongruent phases of I.S. use", p. 357).
Davis, Bagozzi, Warshaw, 1989.	Technology Acceptance Model (TAM)	The suggestion of variables influencing Acceptance of I.S.
Compeau, Higgins, Huff, 1999.	Social Cognitive Theory	The linkage between cognitive factors, affective factors and usage.
Rogers,1995.	Diffusion of Innovations; The innovation-decision process.	The role of earlier adopters; the distinction between Adoption and Continued Adoption.
Meyer, Rowan, 1977; Powell, DiMaggio, 1983; Scott, 1987; Powell, DiMaggio, 1991; Scott, 2000.	New Institutional Theory	The role of institutional environment and institutional pressures.

Figure 5 – ICT Continuance: instructors' perspective

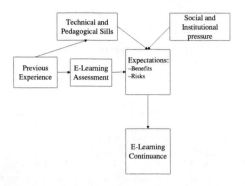

The instructor decision to continued use is influenced by the same variables of the first phase, but there exists a difference from an operational point of view (i.e. now previous experience regards past L.S. experience, not only general multimedia experience) (figure 5). In fact, the results of the evaluation process taking place after the first L.S. experience strongly influence the instructor's expectations, that is his/her perception of benefits and risks.

LEARNING SPACE EXPERIENCE AT BOCCONI UNIVERSITY

In 1999 Bocconi decided to heavily invest in ICT to develop learning platforms for its undergraduate and MBA programs. The committee for innovative teaching methods agreed on promoting pilot courses using Learning Space (L.S.) as test environment[3]. Bocconi's approach to ICT in education considers technologies as enabling factors to improve effectiveness and efficiency of in class lessons. In fact, Bocconi decided not to enter the pure Open and Distance Learning (ODL) environment[4] as it is not consistent with Bocconi's mission.

In Bocconi, a first group of four courses per semester was selected and the chairpersons were expected to select his/her colleagues ready to lead the experiment. Management Information Systems (a third year compulsory exam in the Management track, with five parallel classes of about 250 students each) was one of the four candidates in the Spring semester 2000 (A.Y. 1999 – 2000). Experimentation has continued during A.Y. 2000 – 2001 and A.Y 2001 – 2002.

Technological Infrastructure

Aware that infrastructure and support play a critical role in innovative teaching projects, Bocconi University had made the following decisions:
- Lotus and IBM would provide L.S. experts on a 5 day presence per week;
- An internal expert team would be set up with 3 full time people and 1 part time person supporting and counseling professors;
- IBM would install in Bocconi 3 dedicated servers;
- Bocconi would install 4 classrooms exclusively dedicated to L.S. students (each classroom with LANs of about 60 PCs Pentium III 733, 64 Mb, Word Millenium Edition, connected to the Notes Server and to Internet);
- The pilot courses used Learning Space 3.0 as SW platform;
- Each professor adhering to the project would receive a lap top computer with L.S. client on it and would attend one day training course;
- Each student would attend a training course (with certificate at the end of the course), would enter the computer classrooms any time and without duration constraints five days a week.

After the experience in year 2000 also in the following academic year the initiative took place with 23 Courses involved (around 5000 students and 45 professors)[5].

To complete the overview of the technical platform adopted, L.S. is shortly described in its main functions. L.S. includes four main sections: schedule, media center, course room and profiles.

The Schedule is the *road map* for students throughout the course: it lists the sessions of the course with the topic of each session and can be ordered by date or subject.

The MediaCenter includes all teaching materials for the course (such as readings, articles, web sites, video clips, graphics, presentations).

The CourseRoom is the asynchronously interactive, virtual classroom of the course supporting discussions among students and between students and instructors, information sharing for project works and assignments filling in or grading.

Eventually the Profiles area contains information about course participants and instructors (personal data, areas of interest, projects, groups, contact information).

Learning Space Implementation

Learning Space implementation is influenced by:
- The principles of Constructivism as regard relationship between instructor and student;
- The statements of Cooperativism as regards relationship among students;
- The ideas of Cognitivism as regards the design of multimedia content.
As stated at the beginning, L.S. was considered as support to traditional lectures. The role of the SW platform was to:
- Enable the students to access as many real cases and projects as possible;
- Provide an environment to communicate with professors and colleagues in structured and unstructured ways (through assignments, forum, case discussions);
- Stimulate the active search for additional material (paper, newspaper articles, video, films) referring to study topics;
- promote projects and personal study.

Learning Space Use by Students (Methodology to Evaluate Students' Participation/Use)

Learning Space students' use is measured through students' participation to Learning Space activities. Learning Space activities are: discussions (for instance forum) and comments. Students can start a discussion or continue a discussion (comment) within the Course Room. Each discussion and/or comment is considered as a document. Students' participation was analyzed from a quantitative point of view (number of documents produced by students) and from a qualitative point of view. In order to satisfy qualitative analysis, all the documents were divided into two classes: Value-added documents and not – value – added documents. A Value-added document is a text with an original content, that is the product of critical reasoning.

The Main Problem

Students' participation during the second and third year of experimentation was greatly lower (both from a quantitative point of view and from a qualitative point of view) than that of first year (table 2).

Comparison Among First Year, Second Year and Third Year

L.S. implementation process was the same in the first year, second year and third year, in fact the professor was the same. Moreover, the same pedagogical methodologies and techniques were applied.

Students participating to L.S. activities have expressed an high degree of ex-post satisfaction, both at the end of A.Y. 1999 – 2000 and at the end of A.Y. 2000 – 2001 (table 3).

It is necessary to distinguish between adhering to the pilot class and participating to L.S. activities. The first decision is a formal use of I.S., while the second decision represents a real use of I.S. (decoupling "form" and "substance"[Meyer, Rowan, 1977]). Students of the A.Y. 2001 – 2002 can only decide if participate or not participate to L.S. activities, because they have been assigned accidentally to the pilot course (figure 6).

Table 2 – Students' participation

	I year	II year	III year
Number of class students	180	120	130
Number of participating students	141	77	7
Number of Discussions, Comment and Assignment	1071	436	11
Value added Discussion and Comment	296	41	0
Document per student	7,6	5,66	1,57
Percentage of value added documents	28%	9%	0%
Value added documents per student	2	0,5	0

Table 3 – Students' satisfaction

Question	MIS A.Y. 1999-2000	MIS A.Y. 2000 - 2001
	scores: 1 to 10	scores: 1 to 10
Overall assessment of L.S. as support tool	7,78	7,61
Contents	7,43	7,23
Link between lecture and L.S. contents	7,17	7,91
Students' interaction	6,79	6,57
Students' - professors interaction	7,35	7,27
Interface	7,49	6,7
Browsing	7,51	6,55
At the end of the L.S. experience:		
You have improved your business knowledge	7,41	7,44
You have improved your business trends	6,92	6,55
You have improved your technical trends	7,65	7,45
You can better use PC	6,57	6,6
Would you suggest to your colleague to attend a L.S. course?		
	MIS A.Y. 1999 - 2000	MIS A.Y. 2000 -2001
yes	98%	85%
Would you attend another L.S. course?		
yes	77,3%	76,5%

The students of the first L.S. course are different from the students of the second L.S. course in terms of previous experience and technical skills. In fact, first year experimentation is consistent with the Acceptance model, while second year experimentation is consistent with the Continuance model.

The continuance occurs inside different courses: students cannot attend twice the same course, therefore they can decide to look for another course which uses the same e-learning platform. Different courses mean different professors, different learning techniques and different L.S. implementation processes. So the main difference between the first and the second year is students' experience developed within different courses, an environment on which M.I.S. professors have not any form of control. The satisfaction degree of a course influences the students' expectations regarding another course.

LESSONS LEARNED

The preliminary results deriving from the comparison of successive courses using Learning Space allow the research team to draw some conclusions.

First of all, the empirical evidence clearly showed students' high expectations towards ICT in learning, but at the same time it focused that students have not a precise idea of what benefits and risks can be. Therefore, decision to attend an ICT based course is mainly a matter of personal curiosity or a social choice (groups of friends candidate themselves together). Once they experience what ICT offer in practice, a small part of the participants remains, as the additional effort required by the course does not fit with the updated expectations.

At the instructor's level, first adoption decision is partly due to previous experience in teaching innovation (also independently from ICT propensity or use) and partly to institutional pressure (university projects, department decisions, incentives, etc.).

Continuance is strongly influenced by the first test assessment, which in turn can be reinforced or weakened by institutional variables. In this case, institutional variables include quality of the technical and support infrastructure, availability of guidelines and experts supporting the instructor, interest of the institution to assess results, etc.

ENDNOTES

1 Von Glaserfeld [1984] defines constructivism: "a theory of knowledge in which knowledge does not reflect an objective ontological reality, but exclusively an ordering and organization of a world constituted by our experience".

2 This field is known as Interpretive-hermeneutic approach (Lee, 1994; Van Baalen, 1999) of ICT in education.

3 Literature [Calvani, Rotta, 2001] classifies technical learning environments with respect to four learning models: Time-independent learning model; Real-time learning model; Simultaneous learning model; Autonomous learning model. Each learning model requires specific tools and

infrastructure with functionalities and performance consistent with learning requirements. The first learning model requires environments oriented to manage community and to share resources, the second group needs environments oriented to situational simulation and problem solving; the third class asks for environment oriented to manage one-to-many synchronous situations and to provide interactive lessons and the last model requires tools oriented to provide structured material. According to this synthetic classification, Learning Space belong to the first category.

4 Open Learning might be defined as [E.U., 1995]: "any form of learning which includes element of flexibility which make it more accessible to students than courses traditionally provided in centers of education and training. This flexibility arises variously from the content of the course and the way in which it is structured, the place of provision, the mode, medium or timing of its delivery, the pace at which the student proceeds, the forms of special support available and the types of assessment offered (including credit for experiential learning). Very often the openness is achieved, in part at least, by use of new information and communication media". While Distance Learning is [E.U., 1995] "any form of study not under the continuos or immediate supervision of tutors, but which nevertheless benefits from planning, guidance and tuition of a tutorial organization. Distance learning has a large component of independent or autonomous learning and is therefore heavily dependent on the didactic design of materials which must substitute for the interactivity available between student and teacher in ordinary face to face instruction. The autonomous component is invariably supported by tutoring and counseling systems which ideally are provided at regional/local study centers and to an increasing extent by modern communication media".

5 During year 2000 the initiative took place with 9 courses (around 1000 students and 15 professors).

REFERENCES

Bhattacherjee, A. (2001). Understanding Information Systems Continuance: an Expectation-Conformation Model. *MIS Quarterly*, Vol. 25, No. 3, pp. 351-370.

Bielli, P. and S. Basaglia (2000). Multimedia case studies: development and use in management education. In Proceedings of the VIIIth European Conference on Information Systems, Wien, July 2000.

Bielli, P. and S. Basaglia (2001). ICT and Learning Models: the Learning Space Experience. ITP Conference, Stern Business School, New York, July 2001.

Calvani, A., Rotta, M. (2000). *Fare formazione in rete – manuale di didattica online*, Erickson, Trento, 2000.

Charmaz, K. (2000). Grounded Theory – Objectivist and Constructivist Methods, in Denzin, Lincoln (edited by), Handbook of Qualitative research.

Compeau, D., Higgins, C.A., Huff, S., (1999). Social Cognitive Theory and Individual Reactions to Computing Technology: a Longitudinal Study. *MIS Quarterly*, Vol. 23, No. 2, pp. 145-158.

Davis, F.D., Bagozzi, R.P., Warshaw, P.R. (1989). User Acceptance of Computer Technology: A Comparison of Two Theoretical Models. *Management Science*, Vol. 35, No. 8, pp. 982 - 1003.

DiMaggio, P.J., Powell W. (1983). The Iron Cage Revisited: Institutional Isomorphism and Collective Rationality in Organizational Fields, American Sociology Review, No 48, pp 147-160, 1983.

Druker, P.F. (1993). *Post Capitalist Society*, Butterworth Heinemann, Oxford, Milano.

E.U. (1995). *Open and Distance learning in the EU member states: synthesis report*, May 1995.

E.U. (2001). *The eLearning Action Plan – Designing tomorrow's education*, Communication from the Commission to the Council and the European Parliament, March 2001.

Evans P., Wurster P. (2000). *Blown to Bits: How the new economics of Information Transform the Strategy*, Harvard Business School Press, Boston.

Galimberti, U. (1999). *Psiche e Techne – L'uomo nell'età della tecnica*, Feltrinelli, Milano.

Glaser, B.G., Strauss, A.L. (1967). *The Discovery of Grounded Theory: Strategies for Qualitative Research*, Aldine Publishing Company, New York.

Leidner, D. E., Jarvenpaa, S.L. (1995). The use of information technology to enhance management school education: a theoretical view. *MIS Quarterly,* September 1995, pp. 265 - 291.

Meyer J.W., Rowan B. (1977). Institutional Organizations: Formal structures as Myth and Ceremony, American Journal of Sociology, Vol. 83, No 2, pp 340-363,1977.

Meyer J.W., Scott W.R. (1983). Organizational Environments – Ritual and Rationality, Sage, Newbury Park, 1983.

Negroponte N. (1995). *Being Digital,* Knopf, New York.

OECD (2001). *E-learning – The Partnership Challenge.*

Powell, W.W., DiMaggio, P.J., (1991). *The New Institutionalism in Organizational Analysis,* University of Chicago Press, Chicago.

Scott, W.R. (1987). The Adolescence of Institutional Theory, *Administratively Science Quarterly*, Vol. 32, pp. 493-511, 1987.

Scott, W.R. (2001). *Institutions and Organizations*, Sage, Thousand Oaks.

Van Baalen, P. (1999). *Is the medium the message? Three theoretical perspective on the use new learning technologies: the non-neutrality of technology information richness theory interpretative-hermeneutic approach,* Management report series, Rotterdam school of management, management report NO. 22.

Van Baalen, P., van der Linden, R. (1998). *Models of learning and medium choice in MBA-education,* Management report series, Rotterdam school of management, Management report NO.33.

Varian, Shapiro, (1999). *Information Rules – A Strategic Guide to the Network Economy,* Harvard Business School Press, Boston.

Vattimo G., Rovatti P.A. (1983). *Il pensiero debole,* Feltrinelli, Milano.

Vattimo, G (1999). *Tecnica ed esistenza - una mappa filosofica del Novecento,* Paravia, Torino.

Von Glaserfeld, E. (1984). "An introduction to radical constructivism", *The invented reality*, Norton and Comp., New York.

Yin, R.K. (1989). *Case Study Research – Design and Methods*, Sage Publications, Newbury Park, 1989.

Confirming an Industry Certification Examination as an Outcome Assessment for Information System Programs

Andrew Borchers, DBA
Kettering University
1700 W. Third Ave, Flint, MI 48504
(810)-762-7983
aborcher@kettering.edu

INTRODUCTION AND LITERATURE

Since the mid-1980's educational institutions have been under increasing pressure to demonstrate measurable outcomes from academic programs (Marchese, 1998). At the same time a "parallel postsecondary universe" has evolved in a rich mosaic of industry certification programs in information technology (Adelman, 1998). This parallel world has "brought competency based education and performance assessment to a status they have never enjoyed within traditional higher education." (Adelman, 1998). For IS educators these parallel worlds have created troubling questions of exactly what role each should play in preparing future IS professionals. At the same time, there is potential for the two worlds to work together. This paper examines one possible point of sharing in the use of certification exams to assess the outcomes of traditional academic programs.

Some industry certifications are proprietary (such as Microsoft MCSE, Novell CCNA and Cisco CCNA). One certification, the Institute for the Certification of Computer Professionals (ICCP)'s Certified Computer Professional (CCP), however, is vendor neutral. The ICCP is backed by seven constituent societies, including AITP (Association of Information Technology Professionals, formerly DPMA) and ACM (Association for Computing Machinery). Some 55,000 IS professionals have completed certification through the ICCP.

The ICCP exam suite includes a core exam and a set of specialty exams. A review of the core exam reveals a broad coverage of IS topics that matches much of the course work in typical BS and MS programs in Information Systems. Review material from the core exam includes references from frequently used textbooks in IS programs (www.iccp.org).

The questions that this study addresses include "Do the results of ICCP certification exams correlate with measures of academic achievement in IS programs?" and "To what extent do undergraduate GPA, quality of undergraduate institution and years of work experience correlate with ICCP test results?"

The importance of understanding the relationship of ICCP exam scores, academic performance, undergraduate quality and work experience is clear. Educators need to demonstrate that their academic programs have measurable outcomes. Initial attempts at many schools have "remain(ed) a thin veneer on most campuses", done to please soon to arrive accreditors (Marchese, 1998). Schools, in many cases, are unable to measure students against published standards. To the extent that certification programs, such as the ICCP's, reflect industry needs, they can serve a valuable role in measuring whether academic programs impart important skills to students. Given ICCP's roots in industry, their exams certainly are certainly candidates for use by academic institutions. At the same time the ICCP can benefit from understanding what factors lead to success in their certification program.

A secondary aspect of this study comes from the perspective of faculty and administrators leading MSIS programs. Among their concerns are how to assess applicants. Which of the typical admission factors – undergraduate grades, quality of undergraduate institution and/or work experience – correlate most highly with academic success at the graduate level and, ultimately, success on ICCP exams?

A somewhat parallel situation exists in the area of graduate management admissions. The GMAT (Graduate Management Admission Test) has been administered for many years to students entering graduate study in management. The GMAC (Graduate Management Admission Council) has repeatedly conducted studies to ascertain the correlation between achievement on the GMAT, undergraduate GPA and first year grades in MBA programs (Manning, 1998). GMAC has consistently shown a positive correlation between these variables. This study is somewhat different in that the ICCP exam comes after the academic program, not before. Further, this study considers the quality of undergraduate institution and years of work experience. However, the need to establish correlation between the exam and academic performance is similar.

METHODOLOGY

Data to perform this study comes from MSIS graduates of a Midwestern U.S. university that were required to take the ICCP Core exam (but not to score at any particular level) as a graduation requirement. The sample is unique in its rich mixture of U.S. born and international students at three campus locations. The sample size is 195 students and covers graduates from 2000 to 2002.

For each student the following data was collected:

ICCP Core exam scores – Researchers recorded an overall score and five component scores (Human and Organizational Framework, Systems Concepts, Data and Information, Systems Development, Technology and Associated Disciplines) from the official ICCP exam profile.

MSIS grades – Researchers recorded an overall GPA and specific grades in database management, systems analysis, networking and capstone courses for all students. Grades were measured on a 4.0 score.

Campus location – Students in this sample attended three different campus locations. Researchers recorded data on which campus the students attended.

Undergraduate grades and degree – The researchers secured undergraduate GPAs (on a 4.0 scale) for all students who attended U.S. colleges and universities. Undergraduate major was also collected and categorized two ways. Majors were categorized into four groups – "In field majors" including computer science and information systems, business, engineer-

Figure one: Proposed model

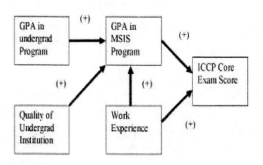

ing and other. A second 0/1 variable was created that indicated "In-field majors" (computer science and information systems) and "out of field majors" (all others). No attempt was made to scale grades from students who attended non-U.S. schools.

Quality of Undergraduate institution – The researchers located the peer assessment score as recorded in U.S. News and World Reports annual college ranking guide for all students who graduated from U.S. schools. According to U.S. News "A school's peer assessment score is determined by surveying the presidents, provosts, and deans of admissions at institutions in a single category." (2003).

Work Experience – Researchers recorded years of work experience in the Information Systems field and total years of work experience. These were based on experience prior to matriculation in MSIS program and were recorded for students that submitted a resume to the institution.

Traditional admission decisions into graduate programs in business and information systems have focused on factors including GPA in undergraduate study, quality of the undergraduate institution and work experience. Figure one above shows the author's proposed model along with the expected signs for correlations. To test the model correlation analysis was conducted between all variables. Further, the author created three regression models and ANOVA model.

FINDINGS

Correlation Results
Correlation results are summarized in table 1.

Several points should be noted. First, there is a significant correlation between grades in the MSIS program, and to a lesser extent undergraduate program, and ICCP test scores. Quality of undergraduate institution was significantly correlated with MSIS GPA. Finally, work experience scores were significantly correlated with ICCP scores, but not graduate GPA. The infield indicator was significantly correlated with ICCP scores, but not with graduate GPA.

Regression Model Results
The authors constructed three regression models to test the relationships in the model shown in figure one. The first regression model views the data from the perspective of academic administrators and faculty trying to predict success in an MSIS program.

Model 1 – Graduate GPA model (* denotes variables retained in the final model)

Dependent Variable: MSIS GPA
Independent Variable: Undergraduate GPA *, Work Experience, Quality of Undergraduate institution *, in-field indicator
Sample size: 36

Table 1 - Correlations

		TOTICCP	MS_GPA	UND_GPA	QUALITY	YRSWORK	YRSIT	INFIELD
ICCP Score	Pearson Correlation	1.000	.416	.376	.289	.329	.277	.292
	Sig. (2-tailed)	.	.000	.014	.079	.010	.031	.044
	N	196	195	42	38	61	61	48
MSIS GPA	Pearson Correlation	.416	1.000	.329	.437	.013	.006	.083
	Sig. (2-tailed)	.000	.	.033	.006	.920	.963	.573
	N	195	195	42	38	61	61	48
UNDER GRAD GPA	Pearson Correlation	.376	.329	1.000	-.065	-.317	.028	.162
	Sig. (2-tailed)	.014	.033	.	.702	.056	.868	.377
	N	42	42	42	37	37	37	32
UNDER GRAD QUALITY	Pearson Correlation	.289	.437	-.065	1.000	.120	-.076	-.016
	Sig. (2-tailed)	.079	.006	.702	.	.486	.659	.933
	N	38	38	37	38	36	36	30
YRS WORK EXP	Pearson Correlation	.329	.013	-.317	.120	1.000	.467	-.095
	Sig. (2-tailed)	.010	.920	.056	.486	.	.000	.549
	N	61	61	37	36	61	61	42
YRS IT EXP	Pearson Correlation	.277	.006	.028	-.076	.467	1.000	.224
	Sig. (2-tailed)	.031	.963	.868	.659	.000	.	.153
	N	61	61	37	36	61	61	42
INFIELD (Y/N)	Pearson Correlation	.292	.083	.162	-.016	-.095	.224	1.000
	Sig. (2-tailed)	.044	.573	.377	.933	.549	.153	.
	N	48	48	32	30	42	42	48

** Correlation is significant at the 0.01 level (2-tailed).
* Correlation is significant at the 0.05 level (2-tailed).

Final R square: .362
F Ratio: 9.643

The second and third models view the data from the perspective of academic administrators and faculty trying to predict success on the ICCP exam. The second model looks at the entire sample of 195 students and considers only their graduate GPA and campus location.

Model 2 – ICCP Test Score model (* denotes variables retained in the final model)

Dependent Variable: ICCP Test Score
Independent Variable: MS GPA *, campus location *
Sample size: 194
Final R square: .305
F Ratio: 9.643

The third model seeks to predict ICCP test scores, but focuses only on main campus students with work experience:

Model 3 – ICCP Test Score model (* denotes variables retained in the final model)

Dependent Variable: ICCP Test Score
Independent Variable: MS GPA *, Work Experience *, undergraduate GPA, quality of Undergraduate institution
Sample size:
Final R square: .303
F Ratio: 12.58

Finally, the author used the undergraduate degree major variable in an analysis of variance (including a Bonferroni post hoc analysis) on ICCP scores and graduate GPA. This was an effort to see if any of the four degree majors were identified with significantly higher ICCP scores or GPAs. Neither ANOVA resulted in a significant finding.

DISCUSSION

This paper examines a number of variables associated with students in MSIS programs, including antecedents (undergraduate GPA, quality of undergraduate program and work experience) and outcomes (scores on the ICCP exam). The research is limited in several ways. First, this project is an attempt to confirm what is generally held to be true, namely that success in graduate school and professional certification is based on undergraduate and work experience. Such an approach can have inherent bias and needs additional theoretical foundation. Second, the work was conducted at a single Midwestern university. Third, traditional academic measures, such as grades, are by their nature imprecise. Fourth, student performance on the ICCP exam may be largely influenced by their personal motivation to do well. Students at this institution were required to sit for the exam, but not to achieve any particular score. Further study could be conducted to overcome these and other limitations.

The results are significant, however, in showing significant correlation between the variables and general support for the model shown in Figure 1. This information provides a preliminary result that should be of use to academic administrators and faculty that manage and teach in MSIS programs.

For admission to a graduate MSIS program, undergraduate GPA and the quality of the institution attended appear to be the most significant factors. For success in the ICCP exam, grades (both undergraduate and graduate) and work experience are significant factors. As is common with research of this type, however, the correlations are statistically significant, but not strong. Indeed, as much as 70% of the variation in the data is not explained by the predictors. This raises the question "what other factors drive academic and certification test success?"

BIBLIOGRAPHY

Adelman, C. (1998). *A Parallel Post Secondary Universe: The Certification System in Information Technology*. Jessup, MD: U.S. Department of Education.

Marchese, T.J. (1998, September/October). Assessment and Standards. *Change*. Manning, W. H. (1998, Spring). Test, Technology and the Tender Ship. *Selections*. 37-42.

www.usnews.com (2003). America's Best Colleges.

www.gmat.com How Valid is the GMAT? Retrieved October 3, 2002.

www.iccp.org Textbook and Materials. Retrieved October 4, 2002.

The Effect of Culture and Environmental Context on Strategic Use of Decision Support Systems in Local Authorities: A Comparative Study of Egypt and the UK

Ibrahim Elbeltagi
Information Management Division
De Montfort University
The Gateway, Leicester, LE1 9BH, UK
Ieb@dmu.ac.uk

ABSTRACT

This article draws on a survey among CEO and IT mangers in local authorities in the UK and Egypt to explain the similarities and differences in the cultural and environmental dimensions that affect using Decision Support Systems (DSS) in making strategic decisions. The astronomical global growth of Information Technology (IT) has inspired IT practitioners, researchers, developers, and innovators to seek new, more sophisticated, and more effective methods to use DSS strategically. This interest in the subject has been manifested in the abundant research and studied carried out to identify the factors that lead to successful adoption and use of IT in general and DSS in particular (Agarwal & Prasad, 1998a; Davis, 1989; Davis, Bagozzi, & Warshaw, 1989; Rose & Straub, 1998; Thompson & Rose, 1994). Unfortunately, little research is currently available about the state of IT management in developing countries in comparison to developed countries. Furthermore, with the increased globalisation of the world economy, many organisations interested in entering the promising marketplace of developing countries may need to get a sense of the particulars of the cultural dimension that affect DSS usage in these countries in comparison to the developed countries where these technologies is developed and designed. Mangers should be aware of these findings and should take it into consideration in the planning, design, introduction, and usage of DSS in making strategic decisions in local authorities.

INTRODUCTION

As investments in IT, in general and DSS in particular, by organisations all over the world continue to grow at a rapid pace, However, regardless of potential technical superiority and promised merits, an unused or under-utilised DSS cannot be effective (Markus & Keil, 1994). So determining the cultural and environmental related factors that affect the strategic use of DSS will be a critical issue to increase the utilisation of DSS.

This paper presents, as far as I know, one of the few in-depth analyses of the cultural and environmental factors that affect use of DSS in Strategic Decision Making (SDM) comparing one of the developing countries (Egypt) with another developed country (UK) and one of the few non-sole Euro-American field study.

Literature Review of the Cultural and Environmental Factors that Affect DSS Usage

The adoption and usage of IT in general, and DSS in particular, is a social process, determined largely by the attitudes of people and the culture and environmental factors. There is a growing theme of research regarding culture and adoption of IT other than concentrating on the technical issues

(Kanungo, 1998) (Lin, 1994) (Pliskin, Romm, Lee, & Weber, 1993; Straub, Loch, Hill, & El-Sheshai, 1998; Straub, Loch, Evaristo, Karahanna, & Srite, 2002). Organisational culture has been mentioned as a critical success factor in IS implementation (Bradley, 1993; Pliskin et al., 1993).

With the aim of helping local authorities to improve their operations by promoting IT enhancement, both central and local governments provide consulting and advice at the request of a particular authority or helping some sort of arising problem. In addition to that government in both developed and developing countries to increase the utilisation of IT, they invest a lot of money to achieve this goal. So the researcher need to understand the variables relating to these dimension to increase the utilisation of DSS in making SD.

Components and their Operationalisation

To measure what the CEO in local authorities think about the possibility of effect of DSS on SDM, the respondents requested to indicate, on a five-point scale, their degree of agreement or disagreement with each item of the previous framework (5 being strongly agree and 1 strongly disagree)

RESEARCH METHODS AND DATA COLLECTION

The unit of Analysis for this research is the chief executive officer or his delegate in the local governments in both the UK and Egypt. To ensure that the respondents understood the meaning of DSS and strategic decision-making and did not mistake MIS or operational decisions with DSS or strategic decisions, DSS and strategic decisions were carefully defined at the beginning of the questionnaire. To help ensure the validity, Huber and Power (1985) suggest, if a single key informant is to be used, it should be a person most knowledgeable about the issue of interest. For the present study, key informants were those who made or participated actively in making strategic decisions but directly or indirectly use DSS.

A pre-test was conducted among number of the academics who are interested in the area of DSS in number of universities in America, Australia, UK, Israel and Egypt. Then a pilot study conducted on a number of senior executives and IT mangers in local government in both the UK and Egypt. Some alterations made on the questionnaire according to the feed back that returned from the academics and practitioners. Revised questionnaires were then sent out around mid of January 2000 and data collection was completed within the next six months.

The sampling frame includes Municipal yearbook for 1999 and directory of local government on the web by Tagish for the UK sample and the directory of DSS units in the local governments in Egypt issued by Information and Decision Support Centre (IDSC).

A package that was mailed to senior executive officers in both Egypt and the UK contains two items: a covering letter explaining the importance of the study, the questionnaire with stamped return address on the back. The covering letter requested the respondent to return the completed questionnaire within two weeks. The respondents were assured of the confidentiality of their responses. Follow-up phone calls were made to the local authorities that had not responded two weeks after sending out the questionnaire.

A randomly selected list of 200 Chief Executive Officer of the five different types of local authority: County Councils, District Councils, Metropolitan Districts, Unitary Authorities and London Boroughs which make up the total number of councils in the United Kingdom which is 467. Seventy-nine usable responses were received (about 40 %) from the UK sample. But if we taken a way the 32 councils who refuse to participate in the study for different reasons (16 don't use DSS at all, 3 don't use DSS in strategic decision making but use it in operational decisions and 13 councils use it but not willing to respond for limited staff resources) from the UK sample the response rate will be 47 %.

Of the 309 questionnaires that were returned from Egypt sample, 294 (about 73.5%) were valid, 12 incomplete and 3 returned by post-office due to incorrect addresses. To ensure that the valid responses were representatives of the larger population, a non-response bias test was used to compare the early and late respondents. χ^2 tests show no significant difference between the two groups of respondents in either of the UK or Egypt sample at the 5% significance level, implying that non-response bias is not a concern.

The researcher made some interviews with CEO and IT managers in some local authorities to validate the results from the questionnaire.

RESEARCH RESULTS AND DISCUSSION

The researcher, before using the multiple regression to analyse the data, tested the different assumptions related to linearity and multicollinearity. The following results in both groups were found:

(1) Cultural characteristics: -

As the results of this research showed there are culture gaps between DSS and IT people from one side and decision makers from another side in both research groups. This result is consistent with Hattens when they notice that this gap may be due to that professionals do not speak the language of business. And from another side the business people are to often separate from IS by what many perceive as priesthood IS, off limits to mortal managers (Hatten & Hatten, 1997).

To understand the differences in the effect of culture on DSS usage in SDM, the researcher will illustrate how the prevailing philosophies, values and beliefs of western and Egyptian societies have led to these different patterns. There is a dominant and resolute Western belief that human being has individual rights and a legitimate appetite for private property. This in turn has spawned specific forms of democracy, capitalism and technological development (Hall & Ames, 1993). Similarly, although the increasing business role of MIS has been enabled by technological advances, this development has hinged on the acceptance of a specific set of a assumptions. The rational for using MIS stems largely from the cultural values and attitudes that are associated with Western and particularly Anglo-American) philosophical beliefs. Theses beliefs have been crystallised in the Weberian bureaucratic idealisation (Weber, 1947), considerable effort has been made to organise economic activities into an orderly system. This system has a well define purpose and is governed by rational and impersonal set of rules. This impersonalism is critical. The organisation takes on a distinct identity, separate from that of its owners, with a structure based on an abstractly ordered set of positions. The relationships among these positions result from the need to achieve specific and objective business goals. Information, which as Drucker points out is objective, logical, formal and specific, naturally supports the achievement of these goals (Drucker, 1973). Such a cognitive model diminishes the relevance of individuals and personal relationships. A bureaucratic tradition also promotes formalism. Organisational rules are codified into systematic policies, procedures and regulations. As a result, a formal and impersonal MIS is needed to monitor and control a large number and wide range of activities. The IT application provides the manager with compressed and/or filtered symbolic data on a timely and frequent basis.

From another side, management science techniques are also used to enhance business decision-making. This assumes a rational and logical process that can be effectively modelled and quantified (Miller & Feldman, 1983). Quantitative methods are used to develop a better understanding of complex relationships between organisational and environmental variables. These methods require extensive data collection and analysis, and so their efficiency can be greatly enhanced by computers. Meanwhile, the multi-faceted and complex nature of the modelled relationships encourages integration of the resulting information systems.

The use of scientific methods further implies that nature is subject to man rather than vice versa. The environment is considered to be explainable, predictable, and controllable. As Thomas Jefferson stated, "a man's future is in his own hands" the natural world can be investigated and analysed, enabling individuals to forecast the future and make decision accordingly. This logic can also be extended to business planning. Business managers assume that they can influence environmental events and circumstances. Uncertainty may be hard to eliminate, but it can be mechanistically reduced. The assumed relationship between uncertainty and a lack of information suggests that with sufficient data there is a basis for predicting the future.

The mainstream American management literature further implies that using information processing to reduce uncertainty simply requires obtaining sufficient data to solve the focal problem (Lin, 1994). This is confirmed by the results of this research where there was a significant relationship between uncertainty avoidance (extent to which people feel uncomfortable with uncertainty) and DSS usage in SDM. DSS meets the analytic need of the decision makers to ease the risk of the unpredictable future. So DSS from this cultural viewpoint is inevitable.

From another side the Egyptian culture are less inclined to use systematic and formal planning procedures than their Western counterparts. Instead they will rely more on extrapolations from experience and intuition. This was clear from one of the interviews with one of the head of city council, he stated:

DSS and IT in general is like a sledge hammer waiting to fall on our heads. We have mangers that thy think they know how to use it and don't. We deal with people interest in their daily and future life and this system could be very dangerous if we depend on it in making our SD. They trained the IT staff to use this system but the city managers. And if any one is going to train me around its use, it is better to be an experienced head of city council who has used the system. I don't understand why we needed it, what it can do for us, so I have no intention to use it.

As the results of this research showed there was a significant relationship between DSS usage and individualism. Strategic decisions, in most of the cities, made by powerful individuals (rather than group) who frequently rely on personal knowledge and intuition rather than objective criteria or formal and quantitative method. As one of the DSS staff expressed his negative feelings about the way that decision makers made their decisions, he stated

Most of managers seek the information that they need by their own personal way. Much of this information remains in a soft form, in the mind of the manger, and is verbally communicated mainly in private meetings rather than written memos or reports. In the formal meeting, employees will compete for privileged confidence of the boss and manoeuvre to get close to him by showing the agreement with what he is saying and the decision will be at the end what the boos think is right and suitable according to his viewpoint.

So in most of the cases head of city councils in Egypt are widely perceived to have natural right to determine the strategic direction to their cities according to their individual interpretation of the general policy of the state.

This results agree with two of Hofstede dimensions which is power distance where "less powerful should be dependent on the more powerful", Subordinates expect to be told what to do" and individualism where individual interests come first (Hofstede, 1997).

(2) Environmental characteristics: -

Different environments experience different types of DSS applications and development problems. In relation to the UK group, mangers are characterised with uncertainty avoidance and this make them use DSS tools to alleviate this uncertainty that prevailing in SDM. It is notable that there is a significant relationship between DSS usage and availability of favourable government policies in both groups. Favourable government policies was noted as a facilitator for the strategic use of IT in either developed or developing countries (King & Teo, 1996). In Egypt the government dominate the shape of IT development in the country, so control over the computing infrastructure has frequently been associated with the political control of information, particularly to reinforce the power of the government (Nidumolu, Goodman, Vogel, & Danowitz, 1996). Although the results showed the importance of government policies in the two groups, there is a difference in the applications and the outcomes. The government in Egypt is highly centralised and the public administration system is dominant. So the head of cities ought to closely follow the central government plans and priorities and therefor most of the important decisions made centrally. This views were formed based on the interview results that researcher made with the head of cities that don't use DSS in their SDM. The most important reasons for this were as follow:

1. There are very few important decisions to be made. Most of the decisions have always made by the centralised government.
2. Most of the decisions are quits simple and we used to it for long time, so that required evaluation can be done mentally.
3. Important factors affecting SDM are qualitative in nature; therefore, they can not be incorporated into computer mode as the results of this research showed earlier in the task characteristics.

While in the UK local authorities is much decentralised and this give the CEOs more room to evaluate the benefits of DSS and use it according to the requirements of the situation.

In relation to Egypt group the research results showed a relationship between DSS usage and competition among local government. This result is in consistent with Nidumolu et al., where they found that although the governors perceived that putting a long term investments in computerising the governorate's information and decision making processes as a low priority, and there was a lack of clarity of benefits, it is nevertheless noteworthy that only because adopting DSS in the governorates will give the governors a considerable political and symbolic value as a rational decision maker on the governorates and on the national levels, they chose to go for the adoption of this systems (Nidumolu et al., 1996).

CONCLUSIONS

1. As expected, there was a direct relationship between DSS usage and complexity of analysis and evaluation of alternatives in the UK group, while in Egypt group managers perceived SDM as too person centred and too complex to be computerised. This result reflected on the utilisation of DSS usage where it was higher in the UK than Egypt. This result could be of importance to the local authorities in the UK and Egypt. For the UK, the DSS should be design considering specific characteristics to extend its use to the intelligence phase of strategic decision process and not limited its use to only analysis and evaluating the alternatives as it now the case. For Egypt it is recommended to involve decision makers from the early stage of developing DSS, this will make them relies the possibilities of using this system in SDM and it is capable of supporting the 'intelligence' and design phases of the problem solving process rather than later 'choice phase' (Chung, Lang, & Shaw, 1989).
2. As highlighted by the results of this research that organisational culture plays an important role in the effective implementation and usage of DSS in SDM. So high culture differences between IT people and decision makers which may cause culture clash between the two groups and reflect on the effective usage of the system. Therefore it is highly recommended that local authorities in both countries should pay as much attention to issues of cultural fit during the implementation of DSS.
3. This study clearly demonstrate that favourable government polices play an important role in using DSS in SDM in both research groups. But this government policy should be different in both countries according to the current situation of each. For example, in Egypt the way DSS is man-

aged centrally by the CIDSS which affect the effectiveness of managing and using the systems for the local authorities located far away from Cairo because of longer response time and excessive control by CIDSS. So the government policy need to change to be more decentralised which will allow the local decision makers more room for making strategic decision and use the systems more effectively.

REFERENCES

Agarwal, R., & Prasad, J. (1998a). A Conceptual and Operational Definition of Personal Innovativeness in the Domain of Information Technology. *Information Systems Research, 9*(3), 204-215.

Bradley, S. P., ; Hausman, J. A. and Nolan, R. L. (1993). *Globalization, Technology, and Competition.* Boston, MA: Harvard Business Press.

Chung, C. H., Lang, J. R., & Shaw, K. N. (1989). An Approach for Developing Support Systems for Strategic Decision Making in Business. *OMEGA International Journal of Management Science, 17*(2), 135-146.

Davis, F. D. (1989). Perceived Usefulness, Perceived Ease of Use, and User Acceptance of Information Technology. *MIS Quarterly, 13*(3), 319-340.

Davis, F. D., Bagozzi, R. P., & Warshaw, P. R. (1989). User Acceptance of Computer Technology: A Comparison of Two Theoretical Models. *Management Science, 35*(8), 475-487.

Drucker, P. (1973). *Management: Tasks, Responsiblity, Practices.* New York: Harber and Row.

Hall, D. L., & Ames, R. T. (1993). Culture and the Limits of Catholicism: a Chinese Response. *Journal of Business Ethics, 12*(12), 955-963.

Hatten, M. L., & Hatten, K. J. (1997). Information Systems Strategy: Long Overdue—and Still Not Here. *Long Range Planning, 30*(2), 254-266.

Hofstede, G. (1997). *Cultures and Organisations: Software of the Mind.* New York: McGraw-Hill.

Kanungo, S. (1998). An Empirical Study of Organizational Culture and Network-Based Computer Use. *Computers in Human Behavior, 14*(1), 79-91.

King, W. R., & Teo, T. S. H. (1996). Key Dimensions of Facilitators and Inhibitors for the Strategic Use of Information Technology. *Journal of Management Information Systems, 12*(4), 35-53.

Lin, T. (1994). An integrated model of user resistance in information systems: The Taiwan case. *Journal of Information Technology Management, 5*(3), 47-58.

Markus, M. L., & Keil, M. (1994). If we Build it, they will come: Designing Information Systems that People Want to Use. *Sloan Management Review, 35*(4), 11-25.

Miller, J. R., & Feldman, H. (1983). Management Science- Theory, Relevance and Practice in the 1980s. *Interfaces, 13*(5), 18-25.

Nidumolu, S. R., Goodman, S. E., Vogel, D. R., & Danowitz, A. K. (1996). Information technology for local administration support: The Governorates Project in Egypt. *MIS Quarterly, 20*(2), 197-221.

Pliskin, N., Romm, T., Lee, A. S., & Weber, Y. (1993). Presumed Versus Actual Organisational Culture: a Managerial Implications for Implementation of Information Systems. *The Computer Journal, 36*(3), 1-10.

Rose, G., & Straub, D. (1998). Predicting General IT Use: Applying TAM to the Arabic World. *Journal of Global Information Management, 6*(3), 39-46.

Straub, D., Loch, K., Hill, C., & El-Sheshai, K. (1998). *Transfer of Information Technology to Developing Countries: A Test of Cultural Influence Modelling in the Arab World* (Working Paper).

Straub, D., Loch, K. D., Evaristo, R., Karahanna, E., & Srite, M. (2002). Toward a Theory-Based Measurement of Culture (10: 1, January-March, 2002), 13-23 (with Karen D. Loch, Roberto Evaristo, Elena Karahanna and Mark Srite). Working paper version. *Journal of Global Information Management, 10*(1), 13-23.

Thompson, R., & Rose, D. (1994). *Information Technology Adoption and Use.* Paper presented at the Administrative Sciences Association of Canada, Canada.

Weber, M. (1947). *The theory of social and economic organisation* (T. P. a. A. M. Henderson, Trans.). New York: Free Press.

Collaborative Knowledge Sharing: A Case Study for an Academic Portal (*University Knowledge Cluster*)

António Serrano and Paulo Resende da Silva
Center for Studies and Training in Management
Evora University, Largo dos Colegiais, 2
7000-803 Évora, Portugal
phone: 351-266-740892
fax: 351-266-742494
amss@uevora.pt, pfs@uevora.pt

Leonilde Reis and Ana Mendes
Information Systems Department
College of Business Administration
Setúbal Polytechnic, Campus do IPSEstefanilha, 2914-503 Setúbal, Portugal
phone: 351-265-706427, phone: 351-265-706431
fax: 351-265-709301, fax: 351-265-709301
lreis@esce.ips.pt, amendes@esce.ips.pt

ABSTRACT

The higher education institution, like others organisations, receive some pressure to change your organisational and management methods, to answer to the new demands by society - life long learning, elearning, distance learning, quality of learning process, etc. The information communication technologies create news opportunities and facilitate the global communication process, the creation of new knowledge and the global access to information. So, news forms of sharing and access information and knowledge are needed. The goal of this communication is present the development of particular website. The mission of the website is sharing knowledge on university management and others subject on university field, and promote the scientific and technical interchange about Portuguese higher education system. The main issue is the creation the university knowledge cluster.

1 INTRODUCTION

The challenge derived from the "new economy", which models are oriented to the services, demands a new re-orientation of the Organizational Information Model. This new model is essential to the future viability of organization and to define a new process of conception and implementing service.

The recent trends of information and communication technology and the constant change at the economic and social activities induce new framework reference of the society, in general, and in academic society.

The higher education institution (HEI), are complexes social organization, and they having some pressures to re-think her role. This new role has some consequences: building new strategies, the activities development, news products and services, and news training and learning process.

New solution to the Information Management and, in specially, to the Knowledge Management needs to be developed. This new solution and management structure is important to maintain I degree of quality, good learning process and adequately research management to capture and manager the collective knowledge.

The great challenges to the academic community and to the institution are the competency informal networks management, which should be efficient. To be efficient they needs to have a sharing environment culture between all actors, intra and inter organization and between the higher education institutions.

This means, management and the sharing of know-how, skills, knowledge and information are the key factor to develop and execute new projects and research program.

The position of the HEI on society, face to the actual relational context, should be open to the exterior. This position is the best place to answer to the demand of market and society.

The cultural and science space are so closed to society and in most time surprisingly closed inside of the institution. We need to open the doors of culture and science to the community to attract the actors and partners.

This new partner and actor are essential to promote and develop new ideas, new innovative process and sharing knowledge and resources.

The aims of this new relational culture should humanize and socialize the old and the new skills and abilities, should have find an new equilibrium between creation and research with learning and training process. This new equilibrium is important, not only to the traditional learning process, to the professional's qualification competencies and to the civic and social learning [UTL 2002].

This papers is to present an university portal that have the aims of sharing knowledge between researchers on field of management, information and knowledge applied to the university and college institution.

2 THE INFORMATION AND COMMUNICATION TECHNOLOGY TO THE SERVICE OF KNOWLEDGE MANAGEMENT

Technology supported strongest the diffusion of knowledge because they can diffuse and disseminate in organisation all kind of information in real time or just very near in real time to people, however the local, space and distance where they are.

The knowledge is tacit or explicit [Nonaka and Takeuchi, 1995]. Tacit knowledge are thinks, values and others or capacities, this means knowledge not separated from individual, stored in human brain of each us, including conviction, competencies, talents, abilities, etc.; technically "*wetware*" is the word associated to this kind of knowledge. For other hands, explicit knowledge, from this authors are experiences stored in documents, electronic mail message, etc.; or ideas, this means codified knowledge stored in external support – outside from human brain, is the software knowledge. [Nonaka and Takeuchi, 1995; Nélson e Romer, 1996 in Conceição e Heitor, p. 78]

To Davenport and Prusak knowledge management in organisation should attend some aims [Davenport e Prusak 1998]: create a repository of knowledge (internally or externally), improve the access to knowledge (network links and personal contact) and develop an environment and organisational culture that stimulate the creation, transfers and uses of knowledge.

The technology evolution occurred in recent years directed the computer science and the informatics to a high capacity of processing and storage information and knowledge.

The HEI while institution of knowledge creation is one the privileged actors in conception and user of informational portals that support her activities, creating, diffusing, supporting, maintaining and actualising information, documents and dates.

The appearing of the communication networks the capacity to linked organisation inside and between them, for one side, and the capacity to create networks (more or less) informally between HEI, permit the development of news partners research teams, projects and the development of common strategies.

When people collaborate between them the sharing of knowledge is more efficient, making the collaborative technology supported by web essential to promote the organisation competitiveness and to create a competitive organisation. The knowledge not shared is loosely knowledge.

In this way, the web technology is the single and friendly form to support the business process and the work of all actors that have a connection with the process. This improvement is possible because web technology promote the access to different source of information and knowledge.

The web services are systems software, with distinction to object oriented architecture, which commended new service-oriented architecture (SOA - Service Oriented Application). This architecture is based in interaction between two principles intervenient. One of them is the client, who asks for the service. The other is the suppliers, who offer the service. In this architecture is possible to exist a third intervenient, the broker or mediator, which have the role of promoter in interaction links between the intervenient.

In figure 1 are identified the components of the service-oriented application:

- Service provider: who have the responsibility to furnish the service through the net and publish the service in a broker;
- Service requester: are entities that request a service in a broker, intermediate, and connected between him to a service provider;
- Service broker or/and service registry: have the responsibility to make the connection between service provider and service requester.

3 AN APPLICATION TO HIGHER EDUCATION INSTITUTIONS – CLUSTER OF KNOWLEDGE

The development and adoption of web service systems by HEI will be a value to these institutions. This conviction defines the intention of the promoters of this paper to develop a portal to support knowledge sharing and some services for the institutions and university management and technology researchers applied to HEI context.

Figure 1 – Web services Architecture (adapt from Gunzer, 2002)

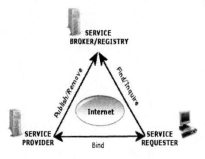

The empirical conceptualisation of Knowledge Management, sharing Known and Knowledge, the collaboration between HEI and Knowledge society are expressed across the information systems and information and communication technology potentiality.

The access portals to information sources permitting translate the empirical conceptualisation in application realities.

Facing to new roles and the appeal of new models that explain the organisational reality, the HEI needs to develop new strategies that consolidate and development your activities, products/services and your training and learning offer, and also your creativity and innovative capacity.

The introduction of information and communication technology and the marriage between the two technologies (information and communication) accelerating the development of electronic communication process to planetary scale, in creation new knowledge and in the accessing to this knowledge.

In study of HEI this reality is also present, i.e., the creation of known and new knowledge or applied to this institutions, permitting the publicity of research works and innovation in the educational field (learning, management of learning, university management, organisational model that explain the university systems), and others type of work.

The exponential increase in master of science, master business administration (master thesis in general) and doctoral thesis in the HEI area, create some difficulty to access this kind of sources.

This reality create an opportunity, derived from new needs, to build some kind of way that facilitate the access to this works and sources. Another possibility is communicate the different initiatives, knowledge and information between discussion groups, researchers partnership, sharing experiences, knowledge and information with others kind of association.

The portal UniversitasOnline have some objectives, but the most important are: facilitating and create a culture of sharing knowledge. Our proposal is create the architecture that facilitate the process sharing and been a web bro-

Figure 2 - UniversitasOnline Portal

ker between higher education institution, in some HEI or researchers publicity yours works and document (best practice and benchmarking) or some service provider they have, and others institution, research and others person are "clients", service request (document, works, etc.).

In this way, we try to build a university knowledge cluster [Porter, 1990] to support the Knowledge Sharing Society. The building of this architecture of sharing try to concentrate in a single gateway researchers and institutions, in different spatial-geography, connected in a virtual net.

To build an efficient portal we need define the technological structure plan, the information access requisites, the application integration and reengineering the explicit business process to share ideas, thinks and opinions.

4 CONCLUSION

The uses of information and communication technologies are today a key factor in knowledge society. They are useful to knowledge management in way that facilitate the integration of people, facilitate in eliminating of boundaries redundancy between organisation, helps in prevention of information fragmentation and permitting the creation of global networks to share knowledge.

The management and the sharing of knowledge and information are a determinant factor to execute and develop actions and projects in all areas of knowledge.

Seeking the Knowledge Sharing Society through the conception of the Cluster of University knowledge, about the reality of the HEI organisational and management, we need implement and development two specific slopes: this knowledge information systems and a portal.

This project (portal universitasonline) are in your primary objective the promotion of scientific and technical interchange about the Portuguese higher education across the divulgation of information and knowledge in your different fields (scientific, pedagogical, organisational and informational).

Figure 3 - Portal development

Process integration

People's

Information access

Application integration

5 REFERENCES

Conceição, Pedro. Heitor, Manuel V. "Perspectivas sobre o papel da universidade na economia do conhecimento". Colóquio/Educação e Sociedade, pp. 70-98.

Davenport, T. e Prusak, L., 1998. *Working Knowledge: how organizations manage what they know*. Boston, MA: Harvard Business School Press.

Gunzer, H., 2002. Introduction to Web Services. Borland Enterprise. URL: http://www.devx.com/javaSR/Whitepapers/borland/12728jb6webservwp.pdf

Nonaka, I. Takeuchi, H. 1995. *The knowledge-creating company*. New York: Oxford University Press.

Porter, Michael. 1990. *The competitive advantage of nations*, The MacMillan Press.

UTL - Universidade Técnica de Lisboa, "A organização do Ensino Superior e o Poder Académico", http://www.utl.pt/Orgoverno/21032002/OrganizaoEnsinoSuperiorePoderAcademico.doc, em Abril 2002.

A Metamodel for Specifying Design Patterns in UML

Reza Jaberi and Mohammadreza Razzazi
Software Research and Development Laboratory
Computer Engineering Department
Amri-Kabir University of Technology
jaberi@b-et.com, razzazi@ce.aut.ac.ir

ABSTRACT

UML considers a pattern as a parameterized collaboration between objects replaced by their actual values during the pattern application phase. However, a design pattern differs from a simple design construct described by the collaboration mechanism. A pattern does not express a fixed and accurate structure. Rather, it defines a generic template whose different aspects can be changed in different applications. In this paper, UML is extended to provide the linguistic infrastructure that specifies design patterns. Most of the existing pattern specification approaches consider a specific solution of the pattern problem to describe the pattern. However, a pattern should be considered as a family of solutions and applications of the pattern problem; since, an unbounded number of concrete solutions and real applications may conform to it. In this paper, four models are presented to describe the general specifications of a pattern, its essence, its solutions and its instances, respectively. The main construct used in these models is the role concept that defines a family of classes. This paper also proposes a model to specify the definitions related to this concept. This model uses three relations to define the binding between the roles specification level and their implementation level. These relations define the implementation of roles, satisfying the structural relationships between roles and conforming to the behavioral specifications of roles, respectively. Finally, the semantics of the proposed models are precisely defined. This paper ends up presenting the definitions needed to support the pattern-oriented features including the pattern specification, application, validation, recognition and discovery.

1. INTRODUCTION

Design patterns are considered as an approach to encapsulate design experiences in the software development. Each pattern expresses a relation between a certain context, a problem and a solution [1]. According to the object-oriented software design, it can be viewed as a description of communicating objects and classes that are customized to solve a general design problem in a particular context [2]. Design patterns are mostly described in the form of a specific solution using object-oriented diagrams.

The current version of the Unified Modeling Language [3] has defined a mechanism to support design patterns. This mechanism considers a pattern as a parameterized collaboration whose parameters are replaced by their actual values during the pattern application phase. Two conceptual levels are provided in this mechanism. Collaboration diagrams are used to describe design patterns and the collaboration usage notation is used to represent their applications.

The UML proposed mechanism has many problems in specifying design patterns that some of them are discussed in [5]. Most of these problems originate from the fact that UML has not considered the design pattern as a distinct language construct. However, there is a point that differentiates a design pattern from a simple design construct described by the collaboration mechanism. A design pattern does not express a fixed and accurate structure. Rather, it defines a generic template whose different aspects can be changed in different contexts.

Another problem is that collaboration diagrams are used as the tools of the behavioral modeling of a system. Restricting pattern specifications to collaborations generally means that the modeling of a system does not need any structural diagrams and behavioral diagrams are sufficient. Moreover, most of the known pattern specification templates, such as the one presented in the

catalog of design patterns [2], consider distinct sections for the structural and behavioral features.

Our goal in this paper is to extend UML to provide the linguistic infrastructure for specifying design patterns. Most of the existing pattern specification approaches, including the one proposed by UML, have a fundamental weakness in their view. They consider a specific solution of the pattern problem to describe the pattern. Nevertheless, a pattern is not restricted to a particular solution; rather, unbounded number of concrete solutions and real applications may conform to it. It is better to consider a pattern as a family of solutions and applications of the pattern problem. This view is compatible with the definition of patterns in [6].

The mentioned view leads to a 3-layer structure presented in [7] to describe design patterns. The first layer describes the essence of a pattern. A family of solutions implements this essence in the second layer. A family of real applications in the third layer applies each of these solutions. Based on this structure, we present four models that respectively describe the general specifications of a pattern, its essence, its solutions and its applications. We also introduce a mechanism to represent design patterns based on this approach.

The main construct used in these models is the *role* concept, which has been introduced by the object-oriented methods such as OORam [9]. While a class is a complete description of objects, a role is a specific view a client object holds on the other object. In this paper, we propose a model that specifies the required definitions related to this concept. We define the binding between the roles specification level and their implementation level by three relations. These relations define the implementation of roles, satisfying the structural relationships between roles and conforming to the behavioral specifications of roles, respectively.

Finally, we precisely define the semantics of the proposed models and present the required definitions in order to the pattern-oriented features. These features according to [8] include the pattern specification, application, validation, recognition and discovery.

2. UML PROPOSED MECHANISM

In order to support design patterns, UML defines two conceptual levels that are discussed in this section.

2.1. Collaborations in UML

A collaboration is a description of a collection of objects that interact to implement some behavior within a context [4]. A collaboration is defined in terms of *roles* whose definitions has correspondence with the concepts discussed in the object-oriented methods such as OORam [9]. A role is a specific view a client object holds on the other object. It is the client that defines what constitutes the role [10]. An object can play different roles at different times, and may also play more than one role at the same time [11].

Roles are specified using *ClassifierRoles* and *AssociationRoles* in UML. A ClassifierRole represents a description of the objects that can participate in an execution of the collaboration. ClassifierRoles are connected to each other by means of AssociationRoles. A ClassifierRole does not specify the complete features of an object; it only specifies the features required to play that role. An object conforms to a ClassifierRole if it provides the required features of the role. Thus, each ClassifierRole is a distinct usage or a restriction of some

Classifiers in the context of a collaboration. These Classifiers are considered as the *base* of that ClassifierRole. Instances of the base Classifiers or their descendants can play that role.

2.2. Specifying Design Patterns

UML considers a design pattern as a parameterized collaboration between objects. A parameterized collaboration represents a design construct that can be reused in various designs. The structural and behavioral aspects of a pattern solution are modeled as a collaboration and the elements that must be bound to the elements in a particular context are considered as its parameters. According to the definitions of the collaboration elements in UML, the base classifiers of each role are turned into parameters of the collaboration.

2.3. Applying Design Patterns

A design pattern is instantiated by supplying the actual classifiers for the parameters in the pattern definition. Each instantiation yields a collaboration among a specific set of classifiers in the model. The instantiation of a pattern is showed by means of the collaboration usage notation. This notation is a dashed ellipse containing the name of the pattern. A dashed line is drawn from this symbol to each of the classifiers participating in the pattern and each line is labeled with the role of the participant.

2.4. Existing Problems

The UML proposed mechanism to describe design patterns has many problems that some of them are mentioned here and other ones are discussed in [5].

An important point is that a collaboration defines the features needed for an object to participate in an interaction with some other objects and specifies how the interaction is done. Parameterized collaborations are as well used to produce collaborations in different contexts by assigning different values to the template parameters. Thus, these collaborations do not define any new structural specifications. Restricting pattern specifications to collaborations generally means that the modeling of a system does not need any structural diagrams and behavioral diagrams are sufficient. It is quite clear that it is not true and structural diagrams, such as class diagrams, are required to model a system. Most of the known pattern specification templates, such as the one presented in the catalog of design patterns [2], allocate distinct sections to structural and behavioral features.

At last, most of the existing pattern specification approaches, including the one proposed by UML, have a fundamental weakness in their view. They consider a specific solution of the pattern problem to describe the pattern and provide concrete diagrams intended to present the specific solution. However, a pattern is not restricted to a particular solution and an unbounded number of concrete solutions and real applications may conform to it. Patterns community explicitly introduced the *"used twice rule"* as follows: A pattern is a pattern, if and only if it has been used in more than one application [12]. Thus, a pattern is never the result of a single analysis, but only of a cross-project analysis. It is better to consider a pattern as a family of solutions and implementations of the pattern problem, which is compatible with the definition of patterns in [6].

3. SELECTED STRUCTURE

This section illustrates the structure used to describe design patterns based on the mentioned view.

3.1. Main Construct

A participant of a pattern defines the features required in the pattern context. According to the definitions of the role concept discussed in the section 2.1, it seems that the participants of a pattern description are more compatible with roles rather than classes. In fact, describing design patterns requires a design construct that specifies a family of classes and the role concept is more appropriate for this purpose.

Gamma et. al proposed the *"program to an interface, not an implementation"* principle in their catalog as follows: "Don't declare variables to be instances of particular concrete classes. Instead, commit only to an interface defined by an abstract class."[2] They note that this principle is a common theme of the design patterns they describe. This principle is very close to the role concept. Pattern community has also noted that roles are the true struc-

tural primitives upon which most patterns rely [13] and classes are only used because a role modeling primitive is not yet established.

3.2. Family of Solutions and Applications

The 3-layer structure presented in [7] has been selected to describe a design pattern as a family of solutions and real applications. Role and class diagrams are used at different levels of abstraction in this structure. Role diagrams are specification-oriented, while class diagrams are implementation-oriented. Both are needed, since a good design pattern should comprise a clear problem solution as well as efficient ways of implementing it.

The first layer describes the essential properties of a design pattern without any additional property and is common between all of its solutions. This common core for all possible variants of a design pattern is called its *essence* in [14]. Different variations of a pattern are special instances of its essence. Role diagrams are used to present the essence of a pattern, since they do not prescribe a certain class design, but only set up constraints in such a way that the actual core of the solution is maintained.

A pattern specified by a role diagram can be made more concrete by a class template, which in turn can be instantiated in numerous applications. Thus, a role pattern specifies and abstracts from a family of class patterns, which in turn specify and abstract from a family of concrete implementations. The third level has another interpretation and based on the template presented in [2], it can be considered as the samples of the pattern.

4. PROPOSED ROLE MODEL

The current specification of the role concept in UML has some problems that are mentioned in this section and a model is proposed to solve them.

4.1. Current Problems

The most important problems of the UML role support are the following three:

- *Independent Definition*: The UML specification does not allow a classifier role to exist with no base classifier. Nevertheless, there are many cases, such as the RUP method [15] and the design pattern specifications, in which roles are defined before classes and then classes are introduced to implement them. So, roles should be defined independent of base classifiers.
- *Base Classifier*: A classifier role has no feature from its own. It defines a subset of those available in the base. In fact, roles in UML are mappings between collaborations and their instances. However, implementing roles is wider than this simple mapping idea and the references such as [16] and [18] discuss different views in this area. So, it is better to define roles with their own features and force classes to implement them.
- *Association between Roles*: An association role is a specific usage of at most one base association and is defined dependent on that. However, it is possible that some different and general associations satisfy the conditions stated in that usage. So, association roles should be independently defined and satisfying them should be considered a distinct concept as the implementation of roles.

4.2. Revised Generalization Model

The UML specification defines the inheritance relationship using an instantiable metaclass named *Generalization* [3]. In order to get all of the parents of a given element, all of the Generalization instances must be found in which the mentioned element is defined as the specialized one. Such a question is much needed in our proposed models. Accordingly, another model is taken from [17] and [19] to define the inheritance relation. This model defines a new relation named *generalizes* by which a class or a role specifies the classes or the roles inherited from.

4.3. The *RoleModel* Package

A package named *RoleModel* is introduced to solve the mentioned problems. It is shown in figure 1 and is the linguistic infrastructure that specifies the role concept, the structural relationships between roles and the behavioral specifications of roles.

A new metaclass named *Role* is defined to specify roles. Each role has its own features and can be defined independent of its implementing classes. The *implements* relation specifies the relationship between a role and the imple-

Figure 1: The structure of the RoleModel *package*

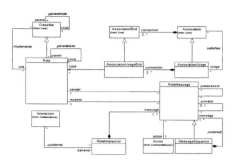

Figure 3: Pattern role model

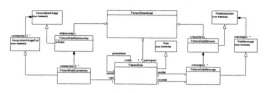

menting classes. This relation relates classifiers to the roles that can be played by their instances.

The structural relationships between roles are defined using associations between them. An association role is specified independent of its base by means of the *AssociationUsage* metaclass. The scope of an association is wider than that of its usage in an association role. A new relation, named *satisfies*, relates an association to its specific usage.

Each communication between two roles is done by means of sending a message between them and is specified by the *RoleMessage* metaclass. An interaction between a set of roles involves a set of communications among them to carry out a particular purpose and is specified by the *RoleInteraction* metaclass. It imposes some behavioral constraints on the implementing classes. Its implementation by an actual interaction between the implementing classes is specified using a new relation named *conforms*.

5. PATTERNMODEL PACKAGE

This section extends the UML metamodel to provide the linguistic infrastructure that specifies design patterns based on the approach discussed in the previous sections. The proposed models are contained in a package named *PatternModel.*

5.1. Pattern Model

Figure 2 shows the model suggested to describe the specifications of design patterns. It is based on the features presented in the catalog of design patterns [2]. The features such as the role model, solution, samples and related patterns are determined by the relationships between the model elements. The features such as the name, intent, motivation, applicability and consequences are considered as the attributes of the pattern.

Figure 2: Pattern model

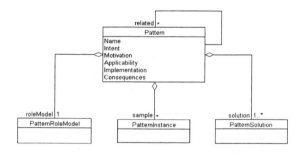

5.2. Pattern Role Model

Each pattern has a role model that defines the pattern essence and figure 3 shows the required model to describe it. A pattern role model is specified by the *PatternRoleModel* metaclass and involves some roles specified by the *PatternRole* metaclass. These roles must be implemented by the classes participating in the pattern solution model.

Pattern roles are connected to each other using some relationships specified by the *PatternRoleRelationship* metaclass. Some of these relationships indicate the static features of roles and some of them exist only in the context of the pattern to provide a behavioral communication path.

Pattern roles communicate with each other by sending messages specified by the *PatternRoleMessage* metaclass. A pattern role model contains some interactions specified by the *PatternRoleBehavior,* which define the sequences of messages and the control flow of the role model.

5.3. Pattern Solution Model

Each pattern has some solution models that implement the pattern role model and figure 4 shows the model required for describing them. A pattern solution model is specified by the *PatternSolution* metaclass and involves some participants specified by the *PatternClass* metaclass. As mentioned in the section 3, these participants are not true classes, they are roles that implement the roles defined in the pattern role model. They are called classes because their tendency is towards the implementation.

The behavioral features of a pattern class are of two kinds named *Template* and *Hook* methods in [20]. They relate to some pattern core functionality and application specific functionality, respectively. Template methods have specific implementations and provide a general skeleton for the pattern behavior. The functionality of this skeleton is changed in particular contexts by hook methods. Hook methods are called in the implementation of template methods and are defined when the pattern is applied.

Pattern classes are related to each other using some relationships specified by the *PatternRelationship* metaclass. The establishment of these relationships when applying the pattern depends on how its connections become visible and includes these kinds: association relationship, method parameter, local scope, global scope and the class itself. The first type is a static relationship in the application model and the others are transient relationships that provide a path for sending message. Accordingly, the static relationships of the pattern role model must be satisfied by an association type relationship in the solution model; however, the other relationships of the role model can be satisfied using each type of the relationships in the solution model.

The behavior of a pattern solution is described by means of some interactions specified by the *PatternBehavior* metaclass. Each interaction involves some messages specified by the *PatternMessage* metaclass that are passed between the pattern classes to carry out a specific pattern purpose. Each of these interactions must conform to one of the interactions in the pattern role model.

There is a difference between the structural and the behavioral constraints on a solution. The solution structure must satisfy all of the structural constraints somehow, but all of the solution behaviors must conform to one of the behavioral constraints. The structure of a role model makes it possible to take place different behaviors and the behavioral specifications specify the valid ones between them. The pattern solution must present some valid behaviors and not necessarily all the valid behaviors.

5.4. Pattern Instance Model

A pattern is instantiated in a particular application by implementing one of its solutions. Figure 5 shows the required model to describe the instantiation

Figure 4: Pattern solution model

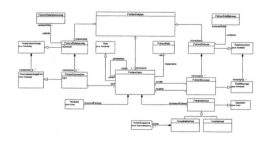

of a pattern in an application model. A pattern instance is specified by the *PatternInstance* metaclass. An application model involves some *classifiers* that implement pattern classes.

Application classifiers are related to each other by means of some *associations* that can be static or dynamic. The static ones are relationships that exist outside the pattern context too, and satisfy the pattern relationships whose types are specified as association in the pattern solution model. The others are transient relationships that are only established in the pattern context and can be used to satisfy the other kinds of the pattern relationships.

The behavior of the instances of application classifiers is specified by some *interactions* between them. Each interaction must conform to one of the pattern solution behaviors.

Further details discussed in the pattern solution model about implementing roles, satisfying structural relationships and behavioral conformance are also applicable here and we avoid repeating them.

6. SEMANTIC DEFINITION

This section defines the semantics of the proposed models. At first, the conditions required to implement a role model are expressed and at the end of this section, precise definitions are presented for instantiating a design pattern.

Figure 5: *Pattern instance model*

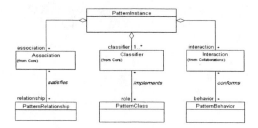

6.1. Implementing Roles

Definition 1: Implementing a Role
A class *C implements* a role *R*, if and only if
? $allAttributes(R) \subseteq allAttributes(C)$
? $allOperations(R) \subseteq allOpertions(C)$
? $R.parent \subseteq (C.role \cup C.parent.role)$

The attributes and the operations of the role must be a subset of those of the class. The class must also be able to implement the generalized roles of the role.

Definition 2: Implementing a Set of Roles
A set of classes *CS implements* a set of roles *RS*, if and only if
- $\forall R \in RS, \exists C \in CS$ where *C implements R*

6.2. Satisfying Association Roles

Definition 3: Satisfying a Role Connection
A connection *CC* to an association between classes *satisfies* a connection *RC* to an association between roles, if and only if
-   *CC.type implements RC.type*
   OR
   $\exists C \in CC.type.child$ where *C implements RC.type*
-   $RC.isNavigable \Rightarrow CC.isNavigable$
-   $RC.cardinality \subseteq CC.cardinality$

The definition says that the corresponding class of the class connection or one of its subclasses must implement the corresponding role of the role connection and the navigability and cardinality constraints of the association between classes must be saved in its specific usage in the role model.

Definition 4: Satisfying a Set of Role Connections
A set of connections *CCS* to an association between classes *satisfies* a set of connections *RCS* to an association between roles, if and only if
? $\forall RC \in RCS, \exists? CC \in CCS$ where *CC satisfies RC*
? $\forall CC \in CCS, \exists? RC \in RCS$ where *CC satisfies RC*

Definition 5: Satisfying an Association Role
An association between classes *CR satisfies* an association between roles *RR*, if and only if
-   *CR.connection satisfies RR.connection*

6.3. Conforming to Behavior of Roles

Definition 6: Conforming to a Message
A message *CM* from a behavioral model of classes *conforms* to a message *RM* from a behavioral model of roles, if and only if
? $\exists CR \in allAssociations(CM.sender) \cap allAssociations(CM.receiver)$,
    $\exists RR \in allAssociations(RM.sender) \cap allAssociations(RM.receiver)$ where
     CR satisfies RR
?   *CM.sender implements RM.sender*
?   *CM.receiver implements RM.receiver*
?   *CM.action = RM.action*

The definition indicates that the sender and the receiver must provide the path required to send the message. They must also implement the sender and the receiver roles, respectively. The executed action upon receiving the message must be the same.

Definition 7: Conforming to a Message Sequence
A sequence of messages $CM_1, CM_2, ..., CM_n$ sent in a behavioral model of classes *conforms* to a sequence of messages $RM_1, RM_2, ..., RM_m$ sent in a behavioral model of roles, if and only if
? $n = m$
? $\forall i \in \{1..n\}$, CM_i *conforms* RM_i

Definition 8: Conforming to an Interaction Role
An interaction *CI* from a behavioral model of classes *conforms* to an interaction *RI* from a behavioral model of roles, if and only if
-   $\exists MS \subseteq CI.message$ where *MS conforms RI.message*

The definition says that a subsequence of the class messages must conform to the sequence of the role messages. A role model indicates a general behavior and a high-level control flow that can be more complex in an actual application.

6.4. Implementing a Role Model

Before defining the implementation of a role model, the following definitions are considered for class models and role models:

Definition 9: Class Model
A set of classes *CS* along with their structural relationships in a set *CRS* and their behavioral specifications in a set *CIS* is considered as a class model represented as *<CS, CRS, CIS>*. Class model is also known as application model.

Definition 10: Role Model
A set of roles *RS* along with their structural relationships in a set *RRS* and their behavioral specifications in a set *RIS* is considered as a role model represented as *<RS, RRS, RIS>*.

Now, the implementation of a role mode is defined as below:

Definition 11: Implementing a Role Model
A class model *CM<CS, CRS, CIS> implements* a role model *RM<RS, RRS, RIS>*, if and only if
?   *CS implements RS*
? $\forall RR \in RRS, \exists CR \in CRS$, *CR satisfies RR*
? $\forall CI \in CIS, \exists RI \in RIS$, *CI conforms RI*
In this case, the class model can be considered as an *instance* of the role model.

Namely, the classes of the class model must implement the roles of the role model, each relationship of the role model must be satisfied by one of the relationships of the class model and each interaction of the class model must conform to one of the interactions of the role model.

6.5. Instantiating a Design Pattern

Definition 12: Pattern Solution
A pattern solution model *PS* is a solution of a design pattern *P*, if and only if
?   *<PS.participant, PS.relationship.nonTransient, PS.interaction> implements*
    <P.roleModel.participant,   P.roleModel.relationship.static,
P.roleModel.interaction>

This definition indicates that the given solution model must implement the pattern role model.

Definition 13: Pattern Instance
A pattern instance model *PI* is an instance of a design pattern *P*, if and only if
? $\exists\,PS \in P.solution$ where
$<PI.classifier, PI.association.nonTransient, PI.interaction>$ implements
$<PS.\,Participant, PS.relationship.nonTransient, PS.interaction>$

This definition indicates that the given instance model must implement one of the solutions of the design pattern. The above definitions implicitly consider the non-static relationships of the pattern role model and the transient relationships of the pattern solution model as one of the message conformance conditions during the behavioral checking of the solution and the instance, respectively.

7. PATTERN-ORIENTED FEATURES

This section presents the required definitions in order to support pattern-oriented features. It uses the definition of a pattern instance given in the previous section. According to [8], pattern-oriented features include specification, application, validation, recognition and discovery.

Definition 14: Pattern Specification
A design pattern is *specified* by a pattern model *P*, a pattern role model *RM*, a set of pattern solutions *PSS*, a set of pattern instances *PIS* and a set of related patterns *RPS*. It is represented as $<P, RM, PSS, PIS, RPS>$.

Definition 15: Pattern Application (Instantiation)
Given a design pattern *P*, an *application* generates or modifies a pattern instance *PI* such that *PI* is an instance of *P* based on definition 13.

Definition 16: Pattern Validation
Given a design pattern *P* and a pattern instance *PI*, a *validation* answers the question whether *PI* is an instance of *P* based on definition 13.

Definition 17: Pattern Recognition
Given a design pattern *P* and an application model *M*, a *recognition* gives all pattern instances *PI* in *M* which are instances of *P* based on definition 13.

Definition 18: Pattern Discovery
Given a set of application models *MS* and a set of known patterns *PS*, a *discovery* is a search for pattern instances $S<P, RM, PSS, PIS>$ such that
? $S \notin PS$
?   *PIS* is a set of submodels of *MS* having at least two members and contains the instances of *P* based on definition 13.

The last definition is based on the "*used twice rule*" that indicates a pattern must be used in more than one application.

8. CONCLUSION

In this section, the proposed models are evaluated and the benefits of the presented approach regarding the UML proposed mechanism are mentioned.

1. As mentioned, collaborations are behavioral modeling tools. Accordingly, the structural specifications of design patterns are not explicitly considered in UML. The proposed role and pattern models consider the structural specifications as distinct parts.

2. A generalization relationship in a collaboration does not necessarily force such a relationship between the base classifiers. It only indicates that the child role inherits the parent features. The proposed role and pattern models explicitly consider the generalization between participants.

3. UML assumes that the bases of association roles can be automatically deduced from the existing associations among the corresponding base classifiers when the pattern is bound. The proposed role model considers satisfying association roles as a distinct concept. The proposed pattern model defines different kinds of satisfying a pattern relationship. It also considers the usage of derived associations for satisfy a relationship.

4. Classifier roles are not allowed in UML to have any features of their own. They only repeat some parts of the features of their bases. The proposed role model drops this restriction and gets rid of the base alto-

gether. Roles are allowed to define the needed features within themselves.

5. UML does not define how the pattern interactions are involved in the binding process. The proposed role and pattern models consider the interactions as a new kind of constraint. The actual participants must conform to these behavioral constraints.

6. In the UML proposed mechanism, the existing elements of the application are mapped on the elements of the pattern. Applying design patterns is more than this simple mapping idea and may generate or modify some elements. The proposed role model defines a role as a general description for a family of classes and there is no need to a preexisting structure.

7. The essence of a pattern can not be described by the UML proposed mechanism. The proposed pattern model considers a distinct level for the pattern essence and describes it using role diagrams.

8. UML does not support pattern-oriented features appropriately. It has only considered pattern specification and application. Pattern-oriented features, including specification, application, validation, recognition and discovery are well supported in this paper.

REFERENCES

[1]   Christopher Alexander, *The Timeless Way of Building*, Oxford University Press, New York, 1979.

[2]   Erich Gamma, Richard Helm, Ralph Johnson, John Vlissides, *Design Patterns: Elements of Reusable Object-Oriented Software*, Addison-Wesley, Reading, 1995.

[3]   UML Revision Task Force, *OMG Unified Modeling Language Specification v. 1.3*, Document ad/99-06-08, Object Management Group, June 1999.

[4]   Grady Booch, Ivar Jacobson, James Rumbaugh, *The Unified Modeling Language Reference Manual*, Addison-Wesley, 1999.

[5]   Gerson Sunyé, Alain Le Guennec, Jean-Marc Jézéquel, "Design Patterns Application in UML", ECOOP'2000, *LNCS 1850*, pp. 44-62, 2000.

[6]   Ralph Johnson, "An Introduction to Patterns", *Report on Object Analysis and Design*, vol. 1, no.1, SIGS Publications, 1994.

[7]   Dirk Riehle, "Describing and Composing Patterns Using Role Diagrams", *Proceedings of the 1996 Ubilab Conference*, pp. 137-152, 1996.

[8]   Amnon Eden, Yoram Hirshfeld, "Towards a Formal Foundation for Object Oriented Architecture", *Proceedings The 3rd ACM SIGSOFT Workshop on Formal Methods in Software Practice*, 2000.

[9]   T. Reenskaug, P. Wold, O. Lehne, *Working with Objects*, Greenwich, Manning, 1996.

[10] B. Kristensen, K. Osterbye, "Roles: Conceptual Abstraction Theory and Practical Language Issues", *Proceedings of Theory and Practice of Object Systems*, 1996.

[11] Barbara Pernici, "Objects with Roles", *Proceedings ACM-IEEE Conference of Office Information Systems (COIS)*, 1990.

[12] J. Vlissides, M. Linton, "Unidraw: A Framework for Building Domain-Specific Graphical Editors", *ACM Transactions on Information Systems* 8, 3, pp. 237-268, 1990.

[13] Frank Buschmann, "Falsche Annahmen (Teil 2)", *OBJEKTspektrum*, pp. 84–85, 1998.

[14] Amnon Eden, "Giving "The Quality" a Name", *Journal of Object Oriented Programming*, Guest column, SIGS Publications, 1998.

[15] Grady Booch, Ivar Jacobson, James Rumbaugh, *The Unified Software Development Process*, Addision-Wesley, 1999.

[16] Friedrich Steimann, "On the Representation of Roles in Object-Oriented and Conceptual Modeling", *Proceedings of* Data & Knowledge Engineering 35, pp. 83-106, 2000.

[17] Friedrich Steimann, "A Radical Revision of UML's Role Concept", *Proceedings of «UML» 2000 - The Unified Modeling Language*, Third International Conference, 2000.

[18] Martin Fowler, "Dealing with Roles", PLoP'97, *Conference Proceedings*, 1997.

[19] Bernd-Uwe Pagel, Mario Winter, "Toward Pattern-Based Tools", PLoP'96, *Conference Proceedings*, 1996.

[20] Wolfgang Pree, *Design Patterns for Object-Oriented Software Development*, Addison-Wesley, Reading, 1995.

Cultural Influences on Information Technology Skills Acquisition: An Australian Perspective

Anita Greenhill
The University of Salford
Salford, Greater Manchester, M5 4WT, UK

ABSTRACT

This paper advocates the engendering of a learning environment that reduces, potential barriers to IT access and equity rather than seeking to identify individuals who experience inequalities as the cause of the problem. Information technology (IT) holds the promise of enabling unlimited access to information irrespective of a person's social situation. To realize this promise particular considerations must be given to the issues of IT access and equity during the primary and secondary education experience (Bors 1987,56). In addition, strategic planning which has as its aim the reduction of existing social barriers that lead to these inequalities must be addressed at the outset by policy and planning decisions. Therefore, considerations of IT access and equity must address the barriers, as well as the opportunities that IT creates. Some of the existing barriers to participation and access in IT are discussed in this paper. Particular attention is given to issues surrounding the access and equity potential of those groups identified by Australian governments as requiring special attention.

INTRODUCTION

Men, women and children are most likely to be willing to cross boundaries and assume more flexible identities not only when they understand where they fit in the great scheme of things, but also when they are free from oppression, when what they say, do and believe, is not ignored or trivialized.
(Ryan 1997, 51)

Particular groups of students have a greater likelihood of experiencing disadvantage with the introduction of IT into the classroom than others. Existing studies suggest that female students, for example, may not be receiving the benefits of IT in the classroom to the same extent as their male peers (Fletcher-Flinn & Suddendorf, 1996; Comber et. Al, 1997; Reinen & Plomp, 1997). While this observation is significant in itself and identifies an issue among this group of students, it does little to address, or alleviate, the source of inequality and access. This identification also implies this group is in some way the source of the problem, diverting attention from the broader and, usually, systemic sources of the problems. Of crucial importance to addressing inequalities and access to IT is the identification and the minimization of broader influences that assist in the perpetuation of these socially constructed barriers. Being identified as a girl does not causally imply that the student will be disadvantaged in accessing IT (Leah & O'Brian 1992). Some girls will experience inequality, however, in the form of barriers such as scarce resources and their relationship to the construction of gender — "girls don't do that" (The Women in Science, Engineering and Technology Advisory Group, 1993; Fletcher-Flinn & Suddendorf 1996, 371). Discriminatory barriers are maintained and largely function in an external relationship to those groups being disadvantaged (Dwyer 1997, 72-76). The classification of women, ethnic minorities, students with disabilities, indigenous students, gay students and students from disadvantaged socio-economic backgrounds and other arbitrary groupings are defined by a relationship to an assumed 'norm' which possesses none of these identifications.

For the purpose of this paper the barriers to access and equity are grouped into the four broad areas of resources, the curriculum, the classroom setting and attitudes. It should be stressed that in selecting these four categories they are just that, categories, and that the key element of this discussion is to shift emphasis regarding the sources of inequality and access from those experiencing inequality to situations and structures which enables the existence of these barriers. The effect of this approach is to require the identification of the sources of disadvantage in order to advocate strategies for the minimization of their influence within the classroom environment.

Resources

Resourcing is a key element in the provision of access to IT. Educational providers obtain IT equipment at varying rates, in what are described as fast and slow tracks. The rate at which equipment is obtained impacts upon an individual's ability to gain access to information technologies, especially in an educational setting (Marginson 1993, 91-101). The maintenance of discrepancies in the availability of IT resources is a significant barrier to equitable educational practice and consequently the even development of IT skills among all students.

Educational environments, when appropriately managed and funded, can alleviate the disparities that exist among the personal ownership of resources (see Bourdieu & Passeron, 1977). Differing domestic situations, the priority given to IT and education in this environment and the availability of home-based educational resources, is beyond the scope of direct government intervention, however, addressing inequality within educational environments can contribute to more equitable distribution of IT equipment for those students. IT tools remain high cost items and require a significant domestic contribution to become an element of the domestic environment. It is well documented both within Australia and overseas, that current information technologies are not equitably distributed through all levels of the student's educational experience (Clark & Ramsay 1990, 238; Reinen & Plomp 1997, 71). Compounding this situation inequality can be experienced at many levels. The unequal distribution of IT resources is experienced between different schools, between individual students and individually between the school and domestic environments.

Resources between Schools

The disparity in IT resources between schools is anticipated to compound as an increased reliance upon the entrepreneurial skills of each school becomes necessary for the acquisition or updating of IT equipment. Not surprisingly, it is those schools situated in more socio-economically affluent areas, and supported by more affluent parents who are leading the private acquisition of high cost equipment that permits a fuller range of IT possibilities (O'Chee 1988, 13). This position, for those other schools who are less socio-economically affluent, can only be achieved when suitable funding enables adequate resourcing to occur. Additionally, there is an increasing tendency to prioritize access to IT resources within a school. The students privileged with greater access to IT equipment tend to have better access to all of a school's valued resources (Hodges Persell & Cookson 1987, 126). This is revealed with the placement and utilization of computers in maths and science courses before being placed in English or art classes. (Hanson 1985, 79-80). Given the necessity, and wisdom, of introducing computers gradually into classrooms and the burden of limited resource consideration must be given to the equity implications of a school's approach instead of simply perpetuating existing protocols, agendas and assumptions regarding IT.

In a recent international study (Reinen & Plomp, 1997) support was found for the proposition that females "know less about information technology, enjoy using the computer less than male students, and perceive more problems with software" (Reinen & Plomp 1997, 65) and that these differences were evident both inside and outside school. Based on analyses of the results, the authors concluded, that the reasons for the disparity between the sexes, in experience of information technology, might include "parental support, access to computers (in terms of availability and use), amount of female role models and (the type of) activities carried out with computers in school". The disparity of access to IT that individual students' experience at school is further compounded by the variation in the domestic consumption of IT equipment. In Canada, in 1996, the 20% of households with the highest income were four times more likely to have a home computer than the 20 % with the lowest household income (56.6% compared to 13.7%) (Laferriere, 1997). This emphasizes the difference of experience in IT access beyond the school environment and, if left to operate alone, could further contribute to the definition of the information 'rich' and information 'poor'. This disparity would become exasperated if students were encouraged to utilize IT outside the classroom, to access information on the Web, for example.

Information technology has transformed and continues to transform the schooling experience for children living in rural and remote areas (Whiston 1988, 31). Children living on properties or attending small or isolated schools have gained access to an expanded range of courses through the combination of IT and distance education. This development makes it possible for children in remote and isolated regions to remain with their families throughout their secondary education.

Despite the considerable improvement in opportunity that IT has provided to children in these situations not all children are benefiting from access to new technology and improved communications infrastructures. Distance can exasperate the barriers to acquiring appropriate IT resources. For students attending suburban or rural schools in low-income areas, this situation may be repeated, especially when the demand for access to IT resources exceeds the capabilities of funding sources.

Consideration must be given to developing the most equitable strategies for funding IT in schools. This strategy must proceed cautiously to avoid privileging schools that already have, potentially self-funded, technology resources and are considered 'technologically ready'. Considering 'who is ready' in isolation may exacerbate inequities and inhibit providing wide access to the greatest number of students (Fletcher-Flinn & Suddendorf 1996, 369).

CURRICULUM / PEDAGOGY

The four areas identified as impediments to generalized access and equity to IT must necessarily be addressed as a coherent group. Barriers constructed and maintained in relation to resourcing will permeate through to the possibility of a student receiving both access and equitable position in the education sector Dwyer 1997, 72). A discussion about student's access to educational tools obviously impacts to some degree on the curriculum and course development that the students receive. Though it is important to disentangle the differences of inequalities students experience if they do not gain adequate access to the tools to participate in IT as opposed to the knowledge and information that is encapsulated by the area of IT.

Producing quality software which guide students towards curriculum outcomes is an expensive process. When resourcing is inadequate purchasing software of this quality becomes problematic. When the purchase of software of any type becomes problematic purchasing specialized educational software is not a reasonable option. Developing a reliance upon donated or non-customized tools that are devoid of Australian content can also result in the use of American or other culturally inappropriate material. This possibility has direct consequences on curriculum development and the substantive content that may be taught to Australian students.

The Australian education sector, in this sense, is not only constrained by the allocation of resources to IT but also the pedagogical considerations that its use implies (Hansen & Olson 1996, 669). Therefore, as well as requiring software that complements Australian realities, pedagogically sound software is required. For these reasons, policy and benchmarking consideration must be

made to ensure that software utilized in the classroom respects the Australian situation of cultural diversity as well as maintaining a cultural sensitivity. In this way the lessons that have been learned about inclusive curriculum development are reflected in educational settings that utilizes new communications technologies.

Innovative IT practices has also assisted non-English speaking students to improve their English language acquisition while keeping up with their peers in other subjects. Where this technology has been used effectively, it has encouraged non-English speaking background (NESB) students to take risks in practising their English and has fostered increased cross-cultural understandings among students (Ryan 1997, 44-45). The utilization of the new and interesting teaching practice and the way a lesson is presented may assist all students in their acquisition of language skills and it is this element this element that needs stressing. The presentation of lessons in an interesting and challenging manner results in the acquisition of better skills and not necessarily its information technology packaging (Hansen & Olson 1996, 673). To highlight this educationalists involved in this area, have suggested that care needs to be taken in selecting software for NESB students as the software currently on the market is often of poor quality (Kersteen et al 1988, 322). Information technology may provide a remedy to inequalities if educators can enable the distribution of content of equal pedagogical quality. Alternately, if this condition of quality is not met, IT may increase the discrepancies of formal learning environments (Dwyer, 1997).

ENVIRONMENT/ CLASSROOM SETTING

Appropriate reflection of the existent success stories of the utilization of IT to overcome barriers to access and equity exist. For example, some of the most exciting results of IT usage in schools has been in the enhancement of learning for students with a disability through the use of various assistive technologies (Curriculum Corporation 1994, 8). If Australia is to stay at the forefront of developments in the area of the utilization of IT in education both practical and creative utilization of the technology is needed. For instance in the US the Corporation for Public Broadcasting is developing retrofitted televisions, closed captioning, synthesized speech, and digitally delivered radio to assist students in their particular environment setting. The utilization of such sophisticated equipment requires both access to an existing body of knowledge as well as forward planning which necessarily equates to an alteration in the existing classroom setting. Assistive technologies when appropriately integrated into the classroom can provide all students with both a dynamic and interesting environment from which to learn.

The classroom setting provides the very important environment in which learning and skill acquisition occurs. The classroom setting incorporating IT into its makeup therefore can either benefit or restrict the individual students learning experience. The wide variety of student life experience, histories and therefore skill's levels and confidence is particular to each and every classroom. To adequately provide access to all students is a challenging task for the educators in these settings. Disparity between social composition in the forms of gender, socio-economic situation (SES), disability, ethnicity, sexuality and such are unique to each classroom. It is for this reason that it is suggested that appropriate blanket style benchmarks should be developed and utilized so as to reduce the barriers associated with access and therefore providing a situation where maximum student inclusion is sort. Awareness of the barriers to equitable distribution of resources and a strategy of targeting such barriers can therefore result in maximum participation and therefore access for students.

The development and maintenance of classroom culture is a dynamic process where group interaction, management and the organization of the classroom are ever changing (Ryan 1997, 37). The introduction and use of IT will have varying repercussions for these sights, it is therefore impossible to predict the outcome for all such settings. Recommendations made from above, which alone target the numbers of computers that should exist in each classroom, or impose specific time allocations to the tools of information technology, do not take into consideration the complexity of the classroom environment. They therefor will not provide an appropriately broad-based approach to skills acquisition and learning for the students involved. However the introduction of IT into the classroom setting in the aim of reducing or at least addressing existing barriers to access and equity is more likely to achieve a goal of maximum participation for all students.

ATTITUDES

Both overt and covert discrimination resulting from attitudinal behaviors continues to be a cause of disadvantage for many students in the classroom (Ryan 1997,39; Dwyer 1997, 71). Government policy makers are particularly concerned in addressing such inequalities for Aboriginal and Torres Strait Islanders (ATSI), NESB and students with a disability. Anecdotal evidence suggests that when schools commence the integration of IT in classrooms, the first classrooms to be equipped are the higher grades, and for math and science. The rationale for such decisions as previously discussed rests on the notion of those students who are 'technologically ready', however this scenario has little room for the possible existence of barriers to becoming 'ready'.

A shift in attitudinal position, to achieve broad-based inclusion and a shift away from problem group targeting, will result in a reduction of barriers and greater utilization of IT by more students. It is the barriers that are created by attitudes of exclusivity, fear and ignorance which result in many students receiving lower levels of equity and access to IT resources and equipment. Attitudinal changes must be addresses at a number of levels including teacher's, parent's and student's.

CONCLUSION

Existing educational practices target specific interest groups who have been identified as problem areas. These groups are largely calculated using traditional sociological group categories. The continuing use of this approach miscalculates the people in these groups as the source of a problem. To realise the promise of enabling unlimited access to information irrespective of a person's social situation a shift in emphasis must occur. The barriers socially constructed to reinforce social situations perpetuate inequalities and therefor must be addressed as such. These barriers are not necessarily constructed around the sociological categorisations of people according to their, ethnicity, gender, socio-economic situation, age or class. Therefor by addressing and minimising, potential barriers to IT access and equity rather than seeking to identify individuals who experience these inequalities as the cause of the problem may indeed better fulfil the promise of enabling unlimited access to information irrespective of a person's social situation.

REFERENCES

Bourdieu P. and Passeron J.C. 1977 *Reproduction in Education, Society and Culture*, Sage: London.

Bors D. A. 1987 "Introducing Microcomputers into Schools: A Social-Political Issue" in *Education and Society*, 5, 1&2, 55-63.

Clark E. and Ramsay W. 1990 "The Importance of Family and Network of Other Relationships in Children's Success in School" *in International Journal of Sociology of the Family*, 20, 2, 237-254.

Comber, C. Colley, A. Hargreaves, D.J. and Dorn L. 1997 "The effects of age, gender and computer experience upon computer attitudes" in *Educational Research*, 39, 2, Summer, 123-133.

Curriculum Corporation 1994 "Technology as an area of learning" in *A statement on technology for Australian schools*, Australian Education Council, Curriculum Corporation: Carlton VIC.

Dwyer P. 1997 "Outside the Educational Mainstream: foreclosed options in youth policy" in Discourse: studies in the politics of education, 18, 1, 71-85.

Fletcher-Flinn, C. M. and Suddendorf, T. (1996) "Computer Attitudes, Gender and Exploratory Behaviour: A Development Study" in *Journal of Educational Computing Research*, 15(4), 369-39.

Hansen K.H. and Olson J. 1996 "How teachers construe curriculum integration: the Science Technology, Society (STS) movement as building" in *Journal of Curriculum Studies*, 28, 6, 669-682.

Hanson M. 1985 "The Microcomputer Revolution: another attempt at educational reform" *in Education and Society*, 3, 1, 75-81.

Hodges Persell C. and Cookson P.W. 1987 "Microcomputers and Elite Boarding Schools: Educational Innovation and Social Reproduction" in *Sociology of Education*, 60, 123-134.

Kersteen, Z.A., Linn, M.C., clancy, M., & Hardyck, C. (1988). Previous experience and the learning of computer programming: The computer helps those who help themselves. Journal of Educational Computing Research, 4, 321-334.

Laferriere, T. (1997). Towards well-balanced technology-enhanced learning environments: Preparing the ground for choices ahead. Paper prepared for the *Council of Ministers of Education*, Canada.

Leah, M. and O'Brian B. 1992 "Post Modern tensions: femininity and reality" in *Femininity and Reality: factors that affect girls learning*, Department of Employment, Education and Training, Canberra, 32-46.

Marginson S. 1993 *Education and Policy in Australia*, Cambridge University Press: Cambridge.

O'Chee A. 1998 "Computers come into Classroom" in Courier Mail, Saturday, January 24.

Reinen I.J. and Plomp T. 1997 "Information Technology and Gender Equity: A Contradiction in Terms?" in *Computers Education*, 28, 2, 65-78.

Ryan J. 1997 "Student Communities in a Culturally Diverse School Setting: identity, representation and association" in Discourse: studies in the cultural politics of education, 18, 1, 37-53.

The Women in Science, Engineering and Technology Advisory Group 1993 *Women in Science, Engineering and Technology*, Office of Chief Scientist, Department of the Prime Minister and Cabinet, Canberra.

Whiston T.G 1988 "Education, Science and Technology: Co-Ordinating Policies and Plans in Developing and Western Countries" in *Bulletin of the International Bureau of Education*, April-June, 247, 9-38.

Distance Learning as a Tool to Support a Classroom Based Learning: College of Business Administration Challenge

Leonilde Reis, Ana Mendes, José Gaivéo and Vasco Silva
Information Systems Department, Escola Superior de Ciências Empresariais, Instituto Politécnico de Setúbal
Campus do IPS – Estefanilha, 2914 – 503 Setúbal, Portugal
Telephone: +351 265 709 300, Fax: +351 265 709 301
lreis@esce.ips.pt, amendes@esce.ips.pt, jgaiveo@esce.ips.pt e vsilva@esce.ips.pt

ABSTRACT

Technology is now revolutionizing the way we teach and learn allowing new learning methods, tools and techniques, and other benefits for life long learning.

E-learning is becoming a very important tool for the learning organisations and also for academic organisations. This paper will review College of Business Administration e-learning project and describe our approach for e-learning as an effective teaching tool in Higher Education programs curricula.

We'll present how ESCE/IPS will use e-learning as complement tool for the traditional classroom education, which means a hybrid approach – blended learning.

INTRODUCTION

The change rhythm that organisations are actually confronted has been increasing with globalisation and technological evolution. Communication and Information Technologies (CIT) came to contribute to organisations regeneration, increase information sharing, open to external world, and increase their action ray (Mendes, et al. 2002). In this context of digital economy and e-commerce explosion, the organisations and people development are influenced by CIT (Gaivéo, 2001). Distance Learning using possibilities takes us to consider the relief paper that Higher Education Institutions (HEI) can assume face to actual change context imposed by globalisation.

HEI, as complex organisations, also come across with some difficulties at a management level, need to rethink their environment position. They have been pressed to alter their management and organisation methods as a consequence of the new roles that are requested them by Society: life long training, distance learning, quality of supplied teaching, and larger approach to social and economic realities (Mendes and Silva, 2002).

In accordance with its mission and strategy, the College of Business Administration (before referred as ESCE – *Escola Superior de Ciências Empresariais*) intends to position its activity area, developing their educational and social functions governed by quality patterns, and also as an entity that is recognised as a well-founded partner in economic activity. For that, ESCE seeks with an enlarged use of new CIT, the development of their activities as a modernization and differentiation form in its environment.

DISTANCE LEARNING – THE NEW TRAINING WAVE

In this accelerated change environment, where social nature subjects (employing, training, and self-esteem) are put in a pertinent way, it is necessary to find an answer to people needs. Distance Learning can play a fundamental part allowing each individual to reach its own purposes.

CIT potentialities should be used in several ways of education/training. In this extent Urdan and Weggen identified several Distance Learning subsets: Computer Based Learning, On-line Learning, e-Learning and Distance Learning, see "Figure 1".

When teaching is supplied through computer use, is designated by Computer Based Learning. Another learning form is Online Learning, where edu-

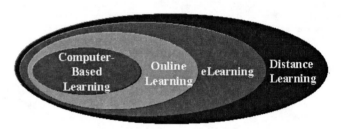

Figure 1. Distance Learning subsets, in Urdan and Weggen, 2000

cation contents are provided by Internet, Intranet or Extranet. The e-Learning method collects a united square of applications and processes as Online Learning, Computer Based Learning, virtual classes and digital collaboration. This includes contents availability through Internet, Intranet or Extranet, audiocassettes and video, satellite communications, interactive television and CD-ROM. Distance Learning method is more embraced and is used when teacher and students meet separate for time, location/space or both. Teaching is made remotely through synchronous and asynchronous sessions including correspondence change, texts, graphs, audiocassettes and video, videoconferencing, interactive television, fax. This is a method that includes all of electronic and non-electronic means.

Like this, in a basic level, Distance Learning happens when teachers and students, separated for physical distance (Santos A., 2000), they use technology to establish processes that allow neutralise or reduce that distance. Teaching methods types above referred, gives to students' a support system to traditional teaching, once relative limitations at time, distance or derived of physical deficiencies, stop being impeding factors of its constant actualisation and increase of knowledge base. In a subsequent phase of development, this system can facilitate to adults renewing its knowledge base, acquired updates in traditional system, or a second opportunity in higher education.

Independently of the used method, teaching process includes at least seven basic elements: (1) motivate student, (2) explain what should be learned, (3) help student reminding him their previous knowledge, (4) supply pedagogic material, (5) make available orientation and attendance from teacher, (6) test his understanding, and (7) contribute for his enrichment (Dick and Reiser, 1989).

Is essential to enhance the importance of a clear and perceptible adaptation of contents that will be available, in way to guarantee that students build a mental connection between the acquired information and some information that has been kept already in his memory, fruit of his involvement in sessions they had attend (Gagné, 1985).

Students' relationship with CIT means can be translated in positive results since these meet the created expectations. Dodge prosecutes eight specific strategies based on (Marzano, 1992) work, which can be attributed to assure that students produce results of its knowledge. These strategies request that students compare, classify, induce, deduce, analyse mistakes, build a maintenance theory, make abstractions, or analyse different perspectives of knowledge that find in pedagogic materials that are supplied them through web (Dodge, 1995).

Is also necessary that, the prospective Distance Learning users acquire competences to create HTML pages or use other tools to support contents availability. So, is crucial to stimulate the use of several services, that Internet makes available, to foment the debate with students and teachers, trying to motivate them for learn, making available orientation and necessary attendance simultaneously to optimise virtual teaching system potentialities use.

Distance Learning allows to increases flexibility and enlargement of training geographical covering. However, its use as support system to teaching can only be seen as advantageous if it obtains an improvement of traditional teaching pedagogic results.

In broader terms e-Learning benefits can be several (Rosenberg, 2001):
- **Lower costs** – an investment optimisation in training, when reducing the costs associated to dislocation, as well as costs associated to traditional teaching infrastructures;
- **Solid and coherent contents, depending on the needs** – exists a larger uniformity and consistence in the form as contents are made available and introduced to students;
- **More actual contents** – it passes the simplest and fast being the renewing of pedagogic contents made available;
- **Possibility to learn it any hour** – Distance Learning makes possible the learning in any hour at any place;
- **New communities' emergency** – foments virtual communities' emergence, where pedagogic contents are discussed even after teaching program finish.

DISTANCE LEARNING AND PORTUGUESE HIGHER EDUCATION INSTITUTIONS

In Portugal, and not only, Distance Education/Training don't have a prominence room in business calendars of most organisations. This tendency was confirmed in Training Director's Forum (TDF, 2002), where the elected training method for most organisations in 2001 continues to be room training (about 75% of preferences).

However, according to same study, it is expected that this tendency lose temper in next years, originating the search of a method that combines traditional method with on-line method (training offered through technology). So, the new tendencies, that will occupy a prominence place, in most organisations will be - distance learning.

Some organisations, which come across budget problems and difficulties with improving their resources, relegate usually training for second plan. For this purpose, Rosenberg defends the implementation (Elliot Masie works) of a mixed solution - blended learning (b-learning), attending to costs decreasing in organisations (Rosenberg M., 2002).

It is necessary that organisations innovate and motivate Human resources, for competences development of their human assets (Senge P., 2002). HEI plays an important role in this subject. Is necessary to rethink education, according to Marçal Grilo, they must improve flexibility to allow individuals to face any challenge along their life (Grilo, M., 2002).

The Technology adoption, by different HEI in Portugal, for training/education as tool for traditional training or for distance learning, is growing up. Platforms like WebCT, TWT or Learning Space are the elected. We verify that preferences are in most cases for tools that presents a smaller cost for the HEI.

Untraditional training/education of our HEI has begun in the ends of the 80s' with Open University emergence. Their population goals are essentially "adults, endowed with maturity and motivation". To the similarity of Open University, also Catholic University, has distance training courses, attributing a specialisation diploma to individuals that its.

More recently (2001), Institute for Statistics and Information Management (ISEGI) of Lisbon New University, makes available a Master's degree Course totally at distance, except the dissertation defence that takes place in the Institution.

Other HEI are using a mixed method (b-learning) as complement to tra-

ditional teaching, retrieving from CIT advantages to acquirement of knowledge. Examples are, Aveiro University, Évora University, Minho University, Porto University, Porto Polytechnic Institute and Viseu Polytechnic Institute, and in a close future Setúbal Polytechnic Institute (IPS).

HEI approach to business tissue has been a part of delineated strategies by these institutions. Aveiro University and Viseu Polytechnic Institute are examples. They have an organism that provides adults professional training allowing the acquisition of needed competences independently of its location.

Nowadays, HEI have conditions to define a strategy to create a Distance Learning system, contributing to the development and improvement of new learning paradigm and business world connection.

COLLEGE OF BUSINESS ADMINISTRATION AND REASONS FOR DISTANCE LEARNING

The College of Business Administration (ESCE) is one of the five IPS Schools, born in 1994 December. The main function is intervening in Business Sciences areas, complementing the slope Education and Technology presented by the other IPS Schools, Education School, Technology School of Setúbal and Barreiro and Health School.

ESCE has as mission: to Teach, to Investigate and to Research the Business Sciences, dignifying the Man and promoting Setúbal region and country development.

In the academic year of 2002/2003, ESCE counts with a 100 teaching staff, with superior academic graduation, approximately 2000 students and 25 employees.

About facilities, ESCE has the conditions, underlying to their strategies, for the accomplishment of a b-learning or Distance Learning initiative. It is essential to refer that, about technological resources, school and students have a free use computer science rooms (24 hours a day, 7 days a week), with Internet access, and whole software and equipment needed to prosecute their academic activities.

ESCE in its youth is watchful to deep technological changes and fast modifications in job market conditions, and knowing that superior education system is constantly challenged to increase the supply of education opportunities, obtaining as compensation successive budget cuts.

Looking to School region, Distance Learning constitutes today an alternative to knowledge democratisation, in normal learning process, in along life learning process (life long learning), in continuous professional improvement. ESCE intends to adopt Distance Learning, in slope Online Learning, as a support tool to traditional teaching way, to optimise supplied teaching and also to foment a larger use of new CIT, by students and teaching staff.

ESCE is characterized by possessing an own organisational culture, where participation, democracy and human values are an acting pillars, trying to stimulate the involvement of their members in several activities, promoting a narrow connection with community. Through a Distance Learning program, ESCE seeks, besides geographical base enlargement, a larger opening to its involving community, increasing the offer of teaching actions along life, creating a complementary mechanism to traditional room based learning.

CONCLUSION

According with analysis concerning CIT advantages to support new learning forms, and looking to actual competitive context, where people and organisations are included, becomes necessary to HEI find appropriate answers to its position as knowledge repository and transmission.

According with ESCE mission and its objectives prosecution, Distance Learning becomes an important contribution for increasing process efficiency, that interactive teaching-learning is intended, in a way that is possible to accomplish its important functions as HEI – the knowledge spread.

In this way, our perspective is that ESCE will adopt a Distance Learning system, initially in b-learning approach, as complement to traditional teaching, seeking to increase value to actual model.

REFERENCES
Dick, W. & Reiser, R. (1989). Planning effective instruction. *Englewood Cliffs*, NJ: Prentice Hall, 1989.

Dodge, B. (1995). Some thoughts about WebQuests. San Diego State University.

Gagné, Ellen D. (1985). The Conditions of Learning and Theory of Instruction, International Thomson Publishing.

Gaivéo, José (Março 2001). As organizações e as pessoas perante os desafios da globalização e do comércio electrónico In IX Encontro Nacional de Sociologia Industrial das Organizações e do Trabalho, APSIOT, Lisboa.

Grilo, E. M. (2002). Desafios da educação: Ideias para uma prática educativa no século XXI. Oficina do livro.

Marzano, R. J. (1992). A different kind of classroom: Teaching with dimensions of learning, Alexandria VA: Association for Supervision and Curriculum Development.

Mendes, A., Teixeira, I. e Marques, F. (Maio 2002). Organizações e Sistemas de Informação centrados em torno de processos In Conferência Científica e Tecnológica em Engenharia – *CCTE'2002*, ISEL, Lisboa.

Mendes, A. e Silva, P. (Maio 2002). Universitas On-line Poster. In Conferência Científica e Tecnológica em Engenharia – *CCTE'2002*, ISEL, Lisboa.

Rosenberg, Marc J. (2001). E-Learning: Strategies for Delivering Knowledge in the Digital Age, McGraw-Hill.

Rosenberg, Michael (2002) http://www.e-learningcentre.co.uk/

Senge, P. – As pessoas não são recursos. In http://gurusonline.tv/pt/conteudos/senge_rh.asp. 05 Julho 2002

Training Director's Fórum (Novembro 2002) .http://www.trainingdirectorsforum.com

Urdan, T. E Weggen, C. (Março 2002) "Corporate e-learning: Exploring a new frontier", WR Hambrecht +Co,

http://www.digitalpipe.com/pdf/dp/white_papers/e_learning/corporate_elearning_H_Q.pdf.

Using Scripting to Investigate Perceptions of the IT Helpdesk

Neil McBride, Ibrahim Elbeltagi and Paravhjoyt Dosanjh
Centre for IT Service Management Research
De Montfort University
Leicester LE1 9BH, UK
nkm@dmu.ac.uk

ABSTRACT

This paper describes the application of script theory to the assessment of IT helpdesk service quality. Scripts are cognitive structures which organise sequences of events in a particular context. IT helpdesk operators and IT helpdesk users were interviewed to assess their attitude to the service. They were also asked to write down the sequence of events they would expect to take place during a service interaction. Participants were given guidance as to the structure of a script using example scripts from common service interactions. A qualitative analysis of the scripts identifies some significant gaps between the expectations of the IT helpdesk customer and service provider. The study suggests that scripting may be a useful tool in other areas of information systems research, particularly in examining interactions between software developers and users.

INTRODUCTION

Increasingly IT departments are seen as deliverers of services to their host organisations. These services involve the provision of information to support business decision-making and development, the provision of operational systems to enable business processes and the development of information systems which enable efficient production and delivery of the organisation's products and services. The focus of the IT department moves away from the technology towards the whole service. The use of IT becomes a means to an end rather than an end in itself. IT systems are seen as tools that support the delivery of business services for which the IT department is responsible. An increasing amount of the work of the IT department then revolves around service strategy, design, development, and implementation, rather than software design, development and implementation. The focus of quality improvement activity then moves towards services quality and away from software and technology quality.

In such a service-oriented IT environment, issues of quality concern the quality of the overall service of which the actual technology quality, to which traditional software metrics may apply, is a small element of the overall quality. Hence IT departments need to look to the service industries for approaches to measure and improve service quality (Rand, 1992). The judgement of service quality relies on the perceptions and expectations of IT department customers, whether internal or external. Service quality methods examine the gap between expectations of a service to be delivered and perception of what has been delivered and provide approaches for closing the gap. (Pitt et al, 1995; Pitt et al, 1998) Such gaps may be closed both by improving the actual service delivery to match it more to the customer's expectations and altering the expectations through, for example, marketing activities (Watson et al, 1993).

This paper examines the use of scripting, a technique that documents consumer and provider expectations of the service process. The theory and practice of the technique of scripting is discussed. The results of a pilot study which applied scripting in an IT environment to study expectations of the IT helpdesk are described. Using scripting provides a dynamic approach to judging the quality of a service encounter. The results of the pilot study suggest that scripting could usefully be applied in a variety of IT service management situations within and beyond the IT helpdesk

SCRIPT THEORY

In order to make sense of the world, people develop cognitive structures to describe what they expect to happen in a particular situation. For example, on entering a McDonalds restaurant, the customer uses a script to act appropriately in the situation. This involves queuing at the counter, ordering, and receiving the meal on a tray. If the customer was approached by a smartly-dressed waiter and ushered to a table, the customer would be confused because such service provider's behaviour did not agree with the customer's script. Similarly, if the customer entered a McDonalds restaurant and asked for a shoe fitting, the customer's script would clearly be wrong. Scripts are knowledge structures which are organised around routinized goal-oriented activities.

Script theory was developed by Schank and Abelson (1977) as a means of encoding knowledge structures in computer programs. It has been applied in management studies as a way of mapping knowledge of processes. Leigh and McGraw (1989) applied script theory to industrial sales personnel's activities. More recently, Greenwood (2000) has applied scripting in nursing and Hibbert et al (1995) applied script theory to hairdressing as an example of a service industry.

A script involves a location where the activity takes place, defined roles and props, entry conditions, expected outcomes and a number of scenes (Schank and Abelson, 1977). Activity is targeted at achieving a goal. That goal may be divided into sub-goals.

The script will usually require exchanges between several actors taking on roles. The typical analysis occurs at the level of the dyadic interaction between the customer and the service provider (Solomon et al, 1985). The exchange that takes place between customer and provider will depend on the scripts of the participants.

Scripts are triggered by instantiating events and depend on entry conditions. For example, if one was hungry, hunger would be the instantiating event and ones goal would be to satisfy ones hunger. However, entry conditions for a restaurant will require hunger and the possession of a means to pay by the customer. If entry conditions are satisfied, a script may be invoked from the customer's memory. Similarly, a script may be invoked by the provider in response to the customer's request. In a restaurant, roles may include customer, waiter, cook, cashier, and owner - all acting according to their own scripts. The customer selects a script according to the type of restaurant.

The use of scripting in service quality involves the comparison of customer and provider scripts, the analysis of the differences and the implementation of changes to close the gaps. Understanding the customer's script and point of view will increase service quality. Scripts may differ in content and elaborateness. Frequently, provider scripts are more elaborate and detailed than customer's scripts. If some actions appear in more detail in the customer script than in the provider script this may point to a potential reduction in service quality. Scripts may start and end at different points, again creating service quality gaps. Hibbert et al (1995) found that the customer's script started before the provider's script. While the hairdresser considered that the service interaction started when the customer entered the salon, customers considered the script to begin when an appointment was booked.

Scripts may be strong or weak. Strong scripts include expectations of sequence as well as occurrence of events. Weak scripts do not include sequence expectations. Schank and Abelson (1977) defined a situational script as one where, in a particular context, participants have interlocking roles and share an understanding of what's supposed to happen. The focus of service industry scripting studies is on strong, situational scripts which are examined for mismatches.

THE ROLE OF IT HELPDESKS

In IT service delivery, the internal helpdesk has a pivotal role in delivering IT services within the organisations and determining service quality. The traditional role of the IT help desk is in providing technical IT solutions for non-technical users. It provides the key interface between users and IT professionals and is the hub of IT services activity. The support of existing information systems and the introduction of new information systems may be managed and monitored from the help desk. Indeed IT help desks may have a strategic role in the take-up and management of information systems (Marcella and Middleton, 1996). Critically, internal helpdesks will be the link to external maintenance providers. The speed and accuracy of diagnosis, together with the identification of the supplier and the time-to-contact, will all be integral parts of any mission-critical system (Czegel, 1998; Bruton, 2002). However, despite its key role at the heart of the IT department, the helpdesk tends to have a poor image.

User interaction may start with the help desk when hardware and software is installed at the user's desk. The help desk will support and manage the installation process, help the user get started on the company's network and support application training. The help desk has also traditionally focussed on reactive support, receiving requests for help, filtering requests and allocating technical resources to resolving problems arising out of the requests. However, IT help desks may be moving towards a more proactive role, becoming the 'human face' of IT, servicing requests for new systems, arranging user training, monitoring business benefits of delivered information systems and negotiating and evaluating service level agreements (Bruton, 2002).

The perception of IT helpdesk service quality will be significantly influenced by the quality of the service encounter between the internal customer and the helpdesk technicians. Indeed, the IT helpdesk service encounter provides an ideal candidate for examining service quality gaps using scripting. Differences in scripts between the helpdesk customer and the service provider may have a significance influence on the perception of the service.

METHOD

Helpdesk staff and end users in a city council were interviewed. The IT services department of the council comprised some 104 staff. As part of the Town Clerk's Department, it provided a variety of IT support services. It operated a help desk for internal customers which looked after the front office activities and directed requests to technical services. The help desk was managed using a Quetzal system. Calls were classified according to three levels of priority and the help desk was run on the basis of service level agreements developed by the customer service manager. Four staff ran the help desk, supported by a manager.

All help desk staff and three end users were interviewed. The structured interviews explored the interviewee's attitude to the help desk. Following the interview, respondents were ask to write a script describing their interaction with a the helpdesk as customers, or the steps they undertook in delivering the service as IT staff. Respondents were given examples of scripts for a visit to a hairdresser, attending a lecture and going to a restaurant. The small size of the sample precludes any quantitative analysis. Scripts were compared using a small database to identify similarities and differences.

ANALYSING THE INTERVIEWS

Both helpdesk workers and end-users expressed a positive attitude to the helpdesk. The interview data helped identify the goals of stakeholders in the helpdesk process. Both customers and providers were focused on resolving the query in as short a time as possible. The concerns of helpdesk staff centred on the quality of the supporting technology and staffing issues, particularly levels of staffing and staff turnover. Themes of customer care, communication and efficient response were highlighted.

The end users interviewed were generally satisfied with the helpdesk. They were positive about helpdesk personnel's levels of understanding, aware of the importance of IT, and focussed on the importance of efficient and speedy resolution of queries The end-users involved in this pilot study all attempted to resolve problems before contacting the help desk, although their level of technical knowledge was generally low. While a small sample may be biased in favour of the helpdesk, the interviews functioned to elicit context for the scripts. The similar level of understanding of IT purpose and of the goal of the service

interaction between helpdesk personnel and end-users may suggest that differences in scripts reflect different cognitive models of the service interaction process, rather than conflicting goals or attitudes.

ANALYSING THE SCRIPTS

Schank and Abelson (1977) focused on how a script is developed and used approaches derived from artificial intelligence to enable the encoding of scripts in a form which could be represented in a computer program. Hibbert et al (1995) analysed scripts in terms of sub-goals and derived a master list of sub-goals. Their analysis was very much statistically focussed, examining frequencies of sub-goals and quantifying elaborateness using chi-square analysis. We take a more qualitative view, drawing out interpretations from individual scripts, highlighting qualitatively significant differences and drawing some conclusions. Scripts may be treated as texts, which can be analysed as a form of literature. The following sections analyse some scripts from helpdesk operators and end users individually. The analysis will then focus of differences between helpdesk service provider and end-user scripts.

Helpdesk Operator Script 1

SCRIPT TYPE: HELP DESK

MAIN GOAL: RESOLVE QUERY

SUBGOALS:

CUSTOMER CALLS
ANSWER PHONE
ASK QUESTIONS
OPEN CALL
ADD DETAILS
GIVE CUSTOMER RESPONSE TIME
ALLOCATE CALL
TECHNICIAN CALLS CUSTOMER
FIND RELEVANT SERVER
RESET PASSWORD
ADVISE CUSTOMER PASSWORD RESET
CHECK CUSTOMER OK
END CALL

The helpdesk operator imagines a specific call to reset a password, in itself a very common activity. The script splits into three scenes: receiving the call, technicians calling the user, and the helpdesk operator checking with the customer before closing the call. Receiving the call itself splits into interactions with the customer and with the computerised helpdesk system. The script indicates that interaction with the helpdesk computer system is important, but not necessarily a driver of the call.

Helpdesk Operator Script 2

SCRIPT TYPE: HELPDESK

MAIN GOAL: RESOLVE QUERY

SUBGOALS:

SWITCH PC ON
LOG INTO PC
OPEN UP CALL SYSTEM
LOG INTO PHONE SYSTEM
PICK UP UNFINISHED WORK
ANSWER PHONE
GREET CUSTOMER
TAKE CUSTOMER DETAILS
OPEN CALL
CUSTOMER DETAILS APPEAR
ASK QUESTIONS

ADD CUSTOMER DETAILS
ADD MACHINE DETAILS
CONFIRM CUSTOMER DETAILS
CONFIRM MACHINE DETAILS
AGREE PRIORITY
CALL REF
RESPONSE TIME
ALLOCATE CALL

In this case the helpdesk operator's script starts with logging on to the helpdesk system. There is a great deal more elaboration on the use of the helpdesk system. Indeed it may be suggested that the script is being driven by the computer system's requirements. The script ends once the call is allocated. This script includes agreeing priority, which script 1 does not mention.

Helpdesk Operator Script 3

SCRIPT TYPE: HELPDESK

MAIN GOAL: RESOLVE QUERY

SUBGOALS:

ANSWER PHONE
GREET CUSTOMER
ADD CUSTOMER DETAILS
ADD MACHINE DETAILS
ADD DEPT DETAILS
ADD LOCATION DETAILS
ASK QUESTIONS
ADD CUSTOMER COMMENTS TO CALL
AGREE PRIORITY
THANK CUSTOMER
ALLOCATE CALL
END CALL

This third example script also elaborates on the computer system dialogue and suggests that the help desk system dialogue is an important driver. Both agreeing priority and communicating a response time are mentioned, but again the script ends once the call is allocated.

Helpdesk Operator Script 4

TYPE OF SCRIPT: HELPDESK

MAIN GOAL: RESOLVE QUERY

SUBGOALS:

ANSWER PHONE
GREET CUSTOMER
LISTEN TO PROBLEM
ASK QUESTIONS
LISTEN TO ANSWERS
PROBE CUST FOR MORE INFO
OPEN CALL
ADD CUSTOMER DETAILS
ADD MACHINE DETAILS
AGREE PRIORITY
CALL REF
RESPONSE TIME
END CALL

This final example of a helpdesk operator's script is less elaborate in terms of computer interaction and somewhat more customer-focused. It is the script only that includes listening to the customer. Again, the call ends once the response time has been communicated. It makes no reference to closing the call.

End User Script 1

SCRIPT TYPE: END USER

MAIN GOAL: RESOLVE QUERY

SUBGOALS:

CALL HELPDESK
WAIT FOR REPLY
GIVE NAME
GIVE LOCATION
EXPLAIN PROBLEM
REPLY TO SECONDARY QUESTIONS
AGREE PRIORITY
CALL REF
WAIT
ENGINEER ARRIVES
DESCRIBE PROBLEM IN DEPTH
LEAVE ENGINEER TO RESOLVE PROBLEM
RESPOND TO SECONDARY ENQUIRY BY ENGINEER
NOTE WHEN PROBLEM FIXED
WAIT(LATER)
RECEIVE CALL FROM HELPDESK
GIVE SATISFACTION RATING
END

The end user script contains three scenes. Firstly, the call is made, next the engineer visit is received and finally the call is closed. Furthermore, three wait events occur. The script may indicate that waiting is considered a significant issue. The end-user specifically notes down when the problem is fixed.

End User Script 2

TYPE OF SCRIPT: END USER

MAIN GOAL: RESOLVE QUERY

SUBGOALS:

LOG CALL IN CENTRAL REGISTER
CALL HELPDESK
GREET OPERATOR
EXPLAIN PROBLEM
AGREE PRIORITY
CALL REF
CHECK DETAILS OF CALL WITH HELPDESK
END CALL
ASSIGN CALL REF IN CENTRAL REGISTER

Significantly, this end-user script involves a user-maintained log, the Central Register, maintained by the Central Payroll. The script begins an ends with the Central Register. The script does not refer to problem resolution or call closure. The interview suggested that the respondent was not particularly concerned with call resolution since she would just do other work while waiting for the call to be dealt with. Furthermore, it may be that interaction with the Central Register is seen as the point at which ownership of the problem ceases for this user and becomes someone else's responsibility.

End User Script 3

TYPE OF SCRIPT: END USER

MAIN GOAL: RESOLVE QUERY

SUBGOALS:

PICK UP PHONE

CALL HELPDESK
EXPLAIN PROBLEM
AGREE PRIORITY
CALL REF
RESPONSE TIME
ENGINEER ARRIVES
DESCRIBE PROBLEM IN DEPTH
LEAVE ENGINEER TO RESOLVE PROBLEM
GIVE SATISFACTION RATING

The third end user script includes interaction with the engineer and a return call either to or from the help desk to give a satisfaction rating.

DISCUSSION

Understanding and interpreting scripts

Scripts provide a rich source of material for examining service interactions. Analysis of their content will identify interesting themes, key issues and problems and suggest where service improvement may be found. The following discussion illustrates the types of issues that may arise.

Studying scripts involves identifying differences and similarities. Differences may indicate divergent underlying concerns between customers and providers. When a script starts and ends may be significant. Omissions from scripts and sub-goals that occur rarely should be looked for. The particular concerns of participants may be indicated by scenes or sub-goals which get elaborated. Participants may attend in more detail to elements of the service encounter which cause them particular concern. Dependencies between provider and customer scripts should be considered. Scripts may indicate key interaction points and concerns common to providers and customers which will need careful attention in improving the service encounter.

It is also useful to consider the overall encounter. How is the script structured? What are the underlying scenes? What other roles are involved? If individual scripts are missing scenes or sub-goals within scenes this may indicate a service encounter problem.

Understanding the Helpdesk Operator's Scripts

The helpdesk script's ideal overall structure consists of three scenes: the call, the problem resolution and the call-back to check for problem closure. Completion of these three scenes will fulfil the goal of rapid problem resolution. The main means of communication is the telephone, although increasingly, communication with the helpdesk takes place through e-mails (Hahn, 1998). Besides the internal customer and the helpdesk operator, other roles may include the support technicians and support managers. The principle prop is the helpdesk support system. Entry conditions include knowledge of the availability of the helpdesk by the customer, and the occurrence of a computer problem the customer cannot mend. The outcome should be that the problem is resolved and the customer can resume full work activities. Preferably the customer should be pleased with the service received.

Helpdesk operator scripts start with taking a call. Operator 2 adds a scene logging on to the call system, which would occur at the start of the day. Three out of four end the script when the call is allocated, only one extends the script to include the call-back scene, checking that the customer's call has been dealt with adequately. This may suggest a lack of attention to customer satisfaction and a possible area for training. Three out of four scripts involve greeting the customer. However, only one operator was sensitive to the need to listen to the customer. Clearly in any service encounter, listening is a key skill which may need to be highlighted. Agreeing a priority and giving a response time may be key interaction points.

Scripts that extend into the domains of other actors may indicate more awareness of the overall process. Helpdesk operator script 1 includes the technician's action in resolving the problem, which the other helpdesk operator scripts do not. This scene is of interest to all end-users. The absence of this scene suggests that helpdesk operators do not address the whole process of problem resolution. This may result in a lack of empathy with the customer who is clearly interested in what is actually done to their PCs. Helpdesk operators should be encouraged to extend their scripts to include all scenes which concern the end-users.

Three of the scripts contain a significant number of sub-goals concerning data input into the helpdesk computer system. In one script the extent of elaboration of the computer system dialog suggests that the system is the focus of the script and the script may be driven by the computer system. Such sub-goals are not of interest to end-users. Information elicited by the helpdesk operators may be seen as a 'Reply to secondary questions' sub-goal by the end-user or part of 'Explain the problem'. Service encounters which are effectively driven by the supporting computer systems carry a number of risks. The information required by the computer system may not be central to the service encounter and may not be in tune with the customer's concerns. Gathering information seen as irrelevant to the customer may slow down the service interaction and be perceived as time-wasting by the customer. It will be necessary in the service encounter to ensure that dialog is effectively conducted with the computer system and is not inhibiting the flow of the service encounter. These scripts suggest that the information requirements of the computer system can have a significant effect on the service encounter. Therefore it is important that information systems designers elicit customer and provider scripts before defining the computer dialog.

Understanding end-user scripts

Where the end-user retains responsibility for the problem, a scene involving interaction with the support technician appears. Importantly, the end-user describes the problem twice and differentiates between the detail of problem description. In the interview, end-users indicated that repeating the problem to several people was annoying.

For end-user 2, ownership of the problem is relinquished once the problem is recorded on the Central Register. The script also suggests a concern as to whether the helpdesk has understood her and recorded the problem correctly. This may also indicate a wish to relinquish responsibility for the call as quickly as possible by assuring the problem is properly logged and then becomes the concern of the owner of the Central Register.

The end-user scripts also suggest that 'Agree Priority' is a pivotal point in the service encounter. It may be that further investigation is required to see if there is a possible conflict at this point.

Examining the Service Interaction

Comparing the content of helpdesk operator and end-user scripts raises some significant points. Firstly, end-user scripts end when a satisfaction rating has been given and not when the call has been allocated. This suggests a need to educate helpdesk operators to extend the scope of their scripts.

Secondly, interaction with the support engineer to resolve the problem is part of the end-user script. Helpdesk operators need to be aware of this in order to provide an empathic service.

Thirdly, waiting is not part of the helpdesk operator's script, but is implicitly or explicitly part of the end-user's script. Customer sub-goals which are not visible to the provider may be important in delivering good service quality.

Fourthly, the extent to which the computer system is driving the interaction needs to be considered. This may be adding unnecessary sub-goals to the script which are not concerned with the main goal of rapid problem resolution.

Finally, comparison of the scripts identifies key interaction points which may act as sources of conflict and dissatisfaction with the service. This study suggests that agreeing the priority is pivotal.

Uses of Scripting

This study illustrates the value of scripting in teasing out important issues in a service interaction which may affect service quality. Script analysis can play a useful role in improving the helpdesk service interaction. However, it may also be of value in other areas of the IT department where service interaction take place and customers or users interact with IT staff. For example, it may be particularly useful in analysing the systems development process and defining developer and user expectations. Moves towards rapid application development, joint application development, client-led system development and extreme programming will result in extended service interaction between users and developers. Understanding expectations using scripting may point to valuable changes in systems development processes.

This study also suggests that scripting may be valuable as a system development tool for supporting the design and development of information systems to support service interactions. Understanding service provider and customer scripts may enable the development of a common script that would raise service quality (Mohr and Bitner, 1991). Script analysis may enable the development of computer dialogs which support the flow of the service interaction. The role of the computer system in the service interaction is itself an area for further research. In this study the scripts suggested that the computer system was not adequately supporting the service encounter and may have been imposing an additional stress on what was already a stress-laden interaction.

REFERENCES

Bruton, N. (2002), How to Manage the IT Help Desk, 2nd Edition, Butterworth-Heinemann, London.

Czegel, B., (1998) Running an Effective Helpdesk,. John Wiley, Chichester.

Greenwood, J. (2000) Critical thinking and nursing scripts: the case for the development of both. Journal of Advanced Nursing, 31, 428 - 436

Gremler, D.D; Bitner, M.J. and Evans, K.R. (1993) The internal service encounter. *International Journal of Service Industry Management* 5(2) 34 - 56.

Hahn, K. (1998), Qualitative investigation of an e-mail mediated help service. *Internet Research,* Vol. 8, No. 2, pp. 123 - 135.

Hubbert, A.R., Sehorn, A.G. and Brown, S.W. (1995) Service expectations: the consumer versus the provider. International Journal of Service Industry Management 6(1), 6- 21.

Leigh, T.W. and McGraw, P.F. (1989) Mapping procedural knowledge of industrial sales personnel: a script theoretic investigation. Journal of Marketing 53, 16-34

Marcella, R. and Middleton, I. (1996), The role of the help desk in the strategic management of information systems. *OCLC Systems and Services*, Vol. 12, No. 4, pp. 4 - 19.

Mohr, L.A and Bitner, M.J. (1991) Mutual understanding between customers and employees in service encounters' Advances in Consumer Research, 18, 611-617.

Pitt, L, Watson, R.T and Kavana, C.B. (1995) Service Quality: A measure of information systems effectiveness. MIS Quarterly 19,173 -

Pitt, L, Berthon, P and Lane, N. (1998) Gaps within the IS department: barriers to service quality. Journal of Information Technology 13, 191-200

Rands, T (1992) Information technology as a service operation. *Journal of Information Technology* 7, 189-201.

Reynoso, J and Moores, B. (1996) Towards the measurement of internal service quality. *International Journal of Service Industry Management* 6(3), 64 - 83.

Schank, R and Abelson, R. (1977) Scripts, Plans, Goals and Understanding. Lawrence Erlbaum, New Jersey.

Solomon, M.R., Surprenant, C, Czepiel, J.A. and Gutman, E.G. (1985) A role theory perspective on dyadic interactions: the service encounter. Journal of Marketing 49, 99-111

Watson, R.T., Pitt, L; Cunningham, C.J. and Nel, D. (1993) User satisfaction and service quality of the IT department: closing the gaps. Journal of Information Technology, 8, 257-265.

Computational Techniques for Pricing Options

Dr. Sanju Vaidya

Division of Math & Computer Information Science, Mercy College

555 Broadway, Dobbs Ferry, NY 10522, USA

Phone: (914) 674-7536, Fax: (914) 674-7518

Email: svaidya@mercy.edu

SECTION 1: INTRODUCTION

In 1973, Fischer Black and Myron Scholes [1] made a major breakthrough by developing a model for pricing stock options. In 1997, they were awarded the Nobel Prize in Economics for their outstanding work. The Black-Scholes model and its extensions are very popular for pricing many types of options. Individuals, corporations, and many financial institutions use derivatives like options and futures to reduce risk exposures.

The Black-Scholes model is based on the assumption that trading takes place continuously in time. In 1979, J. Cox, S. Ross, and M. Rubinstein [4] developed a binomial model that is based on discrete trading time. In applications such as American option valuation, the binomial model is widely used by many financial institutions.

Derivatives with more complicated payoffs than the standard European or American call options and put options are sometimes referred to as exotic options. Most exotic options trade in over-the counter market and are designed by financial institutions to meet the requirements of their clients.

In this paper we will discuss some computational techniques for pricing standard options and certain exotic options, American Lookback put options. The payoff from the Lookback options depend upon the maximum or minimum stock price reached during the life of the option. In 1992, S. Babbs [2] used the binomial tree approach for pricing American Lookback put options. Prof. E. Reiner proposed the same approach in a lecture at Berkeley.

The tree approach has many advantages. It could be used for both European and American style options. When exact formulas are not available (e.g. American put option), numerical procedures such as Monte Carlo simulation, binomial and trinomial trees are widely used in real life. Moreover, the analytic results assume that the stock price is observed continuously. But if the stock price is observed in a discrete manner, say once a day, to calculate the maximum or the minimum, the tree approach makes more sense.

Research Question

The main problem of the tree approach is the convergence of the values, which is slow. A large number of time steps are required to obtain a reasonably accurate result. So the question is as follows: How can we increase the speed of the algorithm? Can we reduce the computation time and get accurate results?

Research Method and Conclusion

In this paper, we will show that if we use Hull's Control Variate technique as described in [6], then the convergence of the values is much faster and the tree approach for the American Lookback put options is more efficient. By using Hull's Control Variate technique, we could reduce the number of arithmetical calculations performed by the algorithm. So the computation time is reduced and we get accurate results. As we know, saving in computation time is very important in a trading room where thousands of derivative prices need to be updated regularly.

SECTION 2: NOTATION AND TERMINOLOGY

In this section we will introduce the notation and terminology, which will be used throughout the paper. First let us define some standard concepts in option pricing.

There are two basic types of options. A **call option** gives the holder the right to buy the underlying asset by a certain date for a certain price. **A put option** gives the holder the right to sell the underlying asset by a certain date for a certain price. The price in the contract is known as the **exercise price or strike price**; the date in the contract is known as the **expiration date, exercise date, or maturity. American options** can be exercised at any time up to the expiration date. **European options** can be exercised only on the expiration date itself.

Derivatives with more complicated payoffs than the standard European or American calls or puts are referred to as **exotic options**. The payoff from a **European-style lookback put** is the amount by which the maximum stock price achieved during the life of the option exceeds the final stock price. When the **American-style lookback put** is exercised, it provides a payoff equal to the excess of the maximum stock price over the current stock price. We will use the following notation:

S: current stock price

X: Strike price of option

T: time of expiration of option

t: current time

r: risk-free rate of interest for maturity T (continuously compounded)

σ : volatility of stock price

SECTION 3. REVIEW OF PRICING OPTIONS

In this section, we will review some models for pricing options.

Black-Scholes Model: In 1973, Fisher Black and Myron Scholes [1] developed a model for pricing European call and put options. The exact formulas are as follows.

$$c = SN(d_1) - Xe^{-r(T-t)}N(d_2) \text{ and}$$

$$p = Xe^{-r(T-t)}N(-d_2) - SN(-d_1)$$

where

$$d_1 = \frac{\ln(S/X) + (r + \sigma^2/2)(T-t)}{\sigma\sqrt{T-t}}$$

$$d_2 = d_1 - \sigma\sqrt{T-t}$$

c = value of the European call option

p = value of the European put option

There is no exact formula for the value of an American put option on a non-dividend paying stock. When exact formulas are not available, numerical procedures such as Monte Carlo Simulation, Finite Difference Methods, Binomial and Trinomial trees are used to value derivatives.

Binomial Model of Cox, Ross, and Rubinstein: In 1979 C.Cox, S Ross, and M.Rubinstein [4] developed a binomial model for pricing options.

They used the binomial tree approach. This is a tree that represents possible paths that might be followed by the underlying stock price over the life of the option. The price of an option is calculated by discounting the expected payoff from the option.

The idea is as follows: - First divide the life of the option into small time intervals of length Δt. Assume that in each time interval the stock price moves from its initial value of S to one of two new values, Su and Sd; u is an up factor (u > 1), and d = 1/u which is the down factor. So at time Δt there are two possible stock prices, Su and Sd; at time 2 Δt there are three possible stock prices Su^2, S, and Sd^2 and so on. Continuing in this manner, we will get a binomial tree. The value of the option is known at the end of the tree (time T). For example, a put option is worth max $(X - S_T, 0)$, where S_T is the stock price at time T and X is the strike price. Then the value at each node at time T- Δt can be calculated as the expected value at time T discounted at rate r for a time period Δt. Similarly, the value at each node at time T – 2 Δt can be calculated, and so on. Finally, working backward, the value of the option at time zero (current time) is obtained.

SECTION 4: VALUATION OF AMERICAN LOOKBACK PUT OPTIONS

The payoff from the Lookback options depend upon the maximum or minimum stock price reached during the life of the option. In 1992, S. Babbs [2] used the binomial tree approach for pricing American Lookback put options. The idea is as follows: - Let F(t) be the maximum stock price achieved up to time t and S(t) be the stock price at time t. Let Y = F(t)/S(t). Then we have to construct a binomial tree for Y. Initially, Y is 1 since F = S at time zero. If there is an up movement in S during the first time step, then Y = 1. If there is a down movement in S during the first time step, then Y = 1/d = u. Continuing in this way we have a binomial tree for Y. Then we have to roll back through the tree to find the value of the option. The approach calculates the option price as the discounted value of the expected option pay-off.

Research Question

The main problem of the tree approach is the convergence of the values, which is slow. A large number of time steps are required to obtain a reasonably accurate result. So the question is as follows: How can we increase the speed of the algorithm? Can we reduce the number of time steps and get accurate results?

SECTION 5: RESEARCH METHOD AND CONCLUSION:

In this section, we will show that if we use the Control Variate technique as described in the paper [6] by Hull and White, then the convergence of the values is much faster and the tree approach for the American Lookback put options is more efficient.

Control Variate technique

The control variate technique can be used to improve the efficiency of numerical valuation procedures. It is applicable when we wish to value an option A, and we have an accurate solution for a similar option, B. Boyle suggested the use of control variate technique in conjunction with Monte Carlo simulation. Hull and White used it for lattice approach. The key element in the technique is that the same numerical procedure is used to value both option A, and option B even the accurate value for option B is known. To explain the technique, let V(A) = value of the option A to be determined, V(B) = accurate value of option B, V*(A) = estimated value of option A from the numerical procedure, and V*(B) = estimated value of option B from the numerical procedure. Then V(A) = V(B) + (V*(A) – V*(B)) gives a better estimate for the value of option A.

How to use the Control Variate technique to reduce the computation time for American lookback put option?

Let A be the American lookback put option on a non-dividend paying stock S and B be the European lookback put option on the same stock, with the same strike price and the maturity date. Goldman, Sosin, and Gatto [5] found valuation formulas for European lookback call and put options. So using their formula for put option we have the accurate value of option B. The formula is as follows.

$$S_{max} e^{-rT} (N(b_1) - \tfrac{\sigma^2}{2r} e^Y N(-b_3)) + S \tfrac{\sigma^2}{2r} N(-b_2) - SN(b_2)$$
$$where$$

$$b_1 = \frac{\ln(S_{max}/S) + (-r + \frac{\sigma^2}{2})T}{\sigma \sqrt{T}}$$

$$b_2 = b_1 - \sigma \sqrt{T}$$

$$b_3 = \frac{\ln(S_{max}/S) + (r - \frac{\sigma^2}{2})T}{\sigma \sqrt{T}}$$

$$Y = \frac{2(r - \frac{\sigma^2}{2})\ln(S_{max}/S)}{\sigma^2}$$

S_{max} is the maximum stock price achieved to date.

As described in Section 4, we could use the binomial tree for both the option A and B and find their estimated values. So by the Control Variate technique as described earlier, we have V(A) = V(B) + (V*(A) – V*(B)).

It turns out that the Control Variate technique improves the efficiency of the binomial tree approach suggested by S. Babbs for American lookback put options.

BIBLIOGRAPHY

1. F. Black and M. Scholes, "The Pricing of Options and Corporate Liabilities", *Journal of Political Economy*, 81 (May-June 1973), 637-659.
2. S. Babbs, "Binomial Valuation of Lookback Options", Working paper, *Midland Global Markets*, 1992.
3. P. Boyle, "Options; a Monte Carlo Approach," Journal of Financial Economics, 4 (May 1977), 323- 338.
4. J. Cox, S. Ross, and M. Rubinstein, "Option Pricing: A Simplified Approach", *Journal of Financial Economics*, 7 (October 1979), 229-264.
5. B. Goldman, H. Sosin, and M. A. Gatto, "Path-dependent Options: Buy at the Low, Sell at the High," Journal of Finance, 34 (December 1979), 1111-27.
6. J. Hull and A. White, "The Use of Control Variate Technique in Option Pricing", *Journal of Financial and Quantitative Analysis*, 23 (September 1988), 237–251.
7. J. Hull, Options, Futures, and Other Derivatives, third edition, Prentice Hall, 1997.

Teledensity, Privatization, and the Andean Community of Nations: The Peruvian Case

Heberto J. Ochoa-Morales
University of New Mexico
ochoah@unm.edu

ABSTRACT

The Andean Community of Nations' (CAN) country members among other less developed countries (LDCs) are located on the wrong side of the "digital gap" and confront an enormous challenge from the network revolution which is unfolding. To take advantage of this revolution, these countries must attract foreign direct investments (FDIs) to develop the necessary infrastructure in the telecommunication-computer realm and acquire the technological know-how embedded in the FDIs. Privatization plays a preponderant role to attract the FDIs. Teledensity is a relevant parameter regarding the telecommunication infrastructure, an important factor inserted in the productivity equation and therefore in the stimulus for economic growth.

INTRODUCTION

The majority population of the earth, about five billion people, live in Less Developed Countries (LDCs) and confront an enormous challenge from the networking revolution that is unfolding. These countries located on the wrong side of the "digital gap" could become victims or beneficiaries of the new changes as a sequel to the technological exigencies stimulated by the change itself (15). The location within the latter is based on the implementation of domestic and supranational policies and programs that allow them to develop the necessary infrastructure in the telecommunication-computing realm to attract the necessary foreign direct investments (FDIs) and technological "know-how" that is embedded. This allows them to establish competitive advantage. The FDIs within Asociacion Latino Americana De Integracion (ALADI) country members for the year 1998 were about $64.5 billion. Approximately 50% of the FDIs total $32 billion had converged in Brazil. This is the outcome of new policies and political reforms concerning deregulation, an aperture to foraneus investment, and the privatization of state owned enterprise in the sectors of telecommunications, and electrical power generation and distribution (12).

One of the circumstances causing great impact in the realm of computing is convergence taking place with computing and telecommunications. Firms perceive the capabilities of combining the hegemony of computer based information and telecommunications networks (3) and the rapid evolution of the Internet and Intranet extant play a preponderant role in this new array. It is emphasized that the drivers of the information revolution are cost, computing power, and convergence (2). These parameters are inter-related to computing infrastructure, new communication technology and governmental policies that will make the old telecommunication model, a monopoly, obsolete, and therefore, a new paradigm will evolve that makes this technology accessible to everyone, specially to the inhabitants of LDCs through a new system that promotes and encourages competition within the private sector.

Within this technological revolution, changes among the telecommunication sectors, the economy and society are present. Deregulation and privatization are contributors in this endeavor. Telecommunication has developed from state monopolized, technical obsolescence, low performance firms to the incumbent, privatized high performance state-of-the-art one's. Within this scheme competition is an important factor. The literature concurs regarding the elements that contribute to generate competition: interconnection, equal access, unbundling, and industry structure are, among others, the most important factors to reach the goals (10). Interconnection is the right of the network

operators to insure the users' compatibility between networks. Equal access is the right of the consumers to select the carrier that will be used to delivery the calls to the final destination. Unbundling requires the incumbent to provide basic network elements such as lines, switching, and transport. The structure of the industry, integration, structural separation, market share restrictions conform the other factor (10). Regarding the economy, the flow of information has been present as an integral part of activities related to production, trade, and investments. Therefore, historically a strong correlation does exist among economic and networking development. Also, the latter plays a very important part in the development of modern social and institutional structures. The report concurs with the research literature concerning the development of the telecommunication sector that has evolved very rapidly from a well defined state-sanctioned monopoly in the 1980s to a great majority acceptance of the benefits of liberalization and competition in the 1990s (15).

The literature defines teledensity as the number of main telephone lines for every 100 inhabitants, excluding wireless access. Teledensity is a term also used as a parameter to measure the level of telecommunication infrastructure of any country. A review of the literature shows the existence of a high correlation between teledensity and the Gross Domestic Product (GDP) of the country. Also, a positive correlation between teledensity and economic development, and a negative one between teledensity and population size has been found. Studies performed by the World Bank demonstrated the presence of teledensity as an input factor embedded in the production process. At the same time they emphasized the fact that telecommunications services do not have the same relevance to all sectors of the economy. These services are more prevalent within manufacturing and tourism than the primary sector such as agriculture (6).

Premise of the Paper

The purpose of this paper is to demonstrate the effect of privatization in the telecommunication sector and its impact on teledensity in country members of the CAN. The Peruvian case within this realm helps to prove the premise.

BACKGROUND

The decade of the 90s represents crucial changes in the structure of the telecommunication sector in Latin America and the Caribbean. Privatization and liberalization schemes dramatically change the patterns of ownership, the number of service providers, the source of financing, and primarily the regulatory environment. The telecommunications companies all over the world started as private enterprises, but by the 70s few still remained under those ownerships schemes. Within them could be mentioned the United States, Spain and the Philippines. In most of the other countries telecommunication services were provided by monopolistic government-owned entities. This concurs with the research literature stating that the rapid change of the technology, the mismanagement of state-owned enterprise among other factors erode the monopolies and clear the way to a privatization trend all over the world (8).

In Latin America the decade of the 80s was characterized by the lack of hard currency and hard economic times. Therefore, several governments look at privatization as a process to raise money on hard currency and also a way to acquire new technologies, know-how and/or upgrade and expand the existing networks. The latter has more to do with the presence of an economic opportunity than the political move departing from the socialist-prone system embedded in most of Latin America countries that has generated State-owned, ill run monopolies (5). All over the region the primary role of the government changed from owner of the monopoly to regulator. Venezuela was among the first to start restructuring their telecommunication realm and today the list of countries that have adopted and implemented reforms includes but is not limited to Bolivia, Colombia, Ecuador, and Peru (8).

Privatized telecommunications operators enjoy the status of quasi-monopoly entities in the basic service sector that includes the long-distance segment. After privatization the new enterprise searched for new business opportunities. Almost all Latin American Countries have participated in the World Trade Organization (WTO) Negotiations on Basic Telecommunications and most of them have made commitments to further liberalize their telecommunications service industry to include voice telephone, mobile services, and satellite services among others (8).

In Latin America, regional as well as multilateral integration schemes have a predominant role within integration agreements, the Andean Community of Nations (CAN) among them is composed of Bolivia, Ecuador, Colombia, Peru, and Venezuela. These organizations have the intent to institute the required infrastructure that, in the future, may evolve into a political union (9).

Currently businesses that transact on the Internet have had relevant cost reduction and an increase in revenues. A high correlation does exist between the growth of benefit and the increase of businesses performing such transactions within the network (14). E-commerce has shown a rapid development in Latin America. Brazil reached 4 million users in 1999. This represents 50% of the interconnected population - Mexico with 18%, Argentina 12% and Chile 4% (13). In March 2000, the number of users on the Internet was approximately 304 million. The United States of America and Canada have 45%, Europe 27%, The Asia-Pacific region 23%, and Africa and the Middle East 1.5%. Latin America and the Caribbean hold 8% of the world population, but only 3.5% of Internet users and less than 1% of the global e-commerce. Although in the year 1999, a noticeable increase in Internet host computers was extant. The growth rate has been the highest in the world, and the number of users is 14 fold within the 1995 to 1999 period (11). The literature concurs that computer information systems are a function of various parameters and among them the ones related to communication and diffusion could be identified as follows: cost of telephone service, and the structure and behavior of the market that compose the Internet services (13). Pertaining to the technology realm, a component that will exert large influence is the volatility of the communication sector due to the availability of new technology and changes thereof (7).

The impact of Peru's telecommunications reforms deserves special attention due to the fact that it depicts the trend of privatization of this sector in Latin America. In 1993, the Peruvian government started a major reform in this sector. The program was supported by two bank loans: the Privatization Adjustment Loan and the Privatization Technical Assistance. Both loans were approved in 1993. Two laws enacted in 1993 and 1994 provided the legal avenue for the privatization of Compania Peruana de Telefonos (CPT) and Empresa Nacional de Telefonos (ENTEL), both state-owned entities with the establishment of an independent regulator OSIPTEL. The Peruvian government agreed to grant the new foreign operator, Telephones of Spain, temporary exclusivity of four years for local, long-distance, and international telephony. The foreign company agrees to expand services in rural areas and to minimize tariffs under a price cap regime. Within this new framework the mobile telephone market was partially liberalized right away and now is fully competitive (with three current licensees, which included Bell South of the United States). When the exclusivity period ended in 1998, new operators entered the telephony market, and 172 companies are currently active. Private investment in rural areas is now promoted and partially subsidized by a one percent tax on phone bills (16). (See Table 1, Figure 1).

The governments of the region have accomplished basic strides so the mass population will have access to the Internet. Peru has created The Peruvian Scientific Network, known by its Spanish abbreviation, RCP. The network is composed of 1000 public centers that provide service to 40% of the network. In Argentina, the program argentina@internet.todos has approxi-

mately 1000 tele-centers located in low income and remote areas. Brazilian commercial banks are offering free access to the Internet, and Costa Rica is one the first country in the world that provides free e-mail to its citizens through state agencies. In the last decade, the telecommunication sector in Latin America has grown enormously. Privatization and the development of new technologies have performed a critical role in this process. During the decade of the 90s, 2/3 of the countries of the region totally or partially privatized the telecommunication domain. Also the arrival of new technologies such as cellular telephones, and cable television has generated substantial changes in the sector. During 1990, 100,000 cellular telephones were in use; 3.5 million during 1995, increasing to 38 million in 1999. The case of Venezuela and Paraguay deserves special attention due to the fact that there are more cell phones than conventional ones (11). In general Latin America still suffer from low teledensity rates, 26 lines per 100 inhabitants (1). The literature concurs that Internet host density is another indicator of network penetration and in conjunction with teledensity will provide a more accurate measurement to determine the presence of computer convergence.

In Latin America only 1/3 of all homes have telephone service. The growth and coverture of the telecommunication sector are functions of the regulatory framework in which they are developed, as well as the influence of the responsible regulatory agency. In many cases, monopolies have been created. During the '80s, seven telephone lines in the region - Argentina 12, Chile 10, served 100 people and repairs took 15 days. The last decade Argentina and Chile users ratio was increased to 22%. Other good indicators of improvement in the sector are the digitalization of the telephone systems, an increase in the number of public telephones, and the improvement of repair time (11). Social factors have to be taken in consideration regarding the infrastructure of telecommunications in Latin America. Twenty-five percent of the region's population lives on an income of $1 per day (13).

DISCUSSION

The privatization and deregulation of the communication sector act as an incentive to bring to the LDCs foreign direct investments that not only provide the financing required to develop the industry, but also provide the know-how embedded. It is critical to accentuate the fact that to attract these investments a well-defined legal and political framework must be in place. The only way that these countries located on the wrong side of the 'digital gap'

Figure 1.

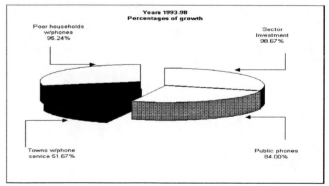

Table 1

The Impacts of Peru's Privatization in the Telecom realm

	1993	1998	%
SECTOR INVESTMENT (Million $)	28	2099	98.67%
FIXED LINES/PENETRATION (PER 100)	660000/2.9	1850000/7.6	
MOBILE PHONES LINES/PENETRATION (PER 100)	50000/0.2	600000/2.4	
PUBLIC PHONES	8000	50000	84.00%
TOWNS WITH PHONE SERVICE	1450	3000	51.67%
POOR HOUSEHOLDS WITH PHONE (%)	1	21	95.24%
AVERAGE WAITING TIME FOR CONNECTION	118 months	45 days	
CONNECTION FEE	$1,500	$150	90.00%

Source: World Bank Group (WBG) 2001

could be evolved within the technology environment rests on foreign sources of funding. At the same time, the developed countries (DCs) could augment their markets investing their financial resources and technology in Latin America. The Peruvian example depicts the importance of privatization versus a state monopoly in the telecommunication industry. Figure1 is self-explanatory regarding the higher growth within the most important parameters in the telecommunication industry. Connection fees in 1993 were $1500-after privatization in 1998, $150, a savings of 90%. The average waiting time for connection has been reduced from 118 months to 45 days. These statistics indicate that privatization not only increased the amount of investments and the growth of many parameters within the telecommunications realm, but also allows the mass population to have access to the technology. Convergence taking place with computing and telecommunication demonstrates the importance of the development of this sector and the socioeconomic impact on the economic perspective, and to the stimulus of economic growth. In Latin America different treaties, covenants, and multilateral agreements taking place as part of regional integration schemes have as a goal to evolve trading partners into a political union and therefore, generate competitive advantage. Information technology plays an integral role in enabling this to happen. Today the Latin America marketplace is in the most enviable position to define its telecommunication future; globalization, regionalization, privatization, and liberalization have been the driving forces (4).

REFERENCES

1.   Blazquez, J. & A. Morri. (2000). Universally slow in Latin America. *Tele Com*, 5, (1), 55.

2.   Bond, J. (1997). *Public Policy for the Private Sector*. The World Bank Group, Note No. 118, July.

3.   Carr, H. H. & C. A. Snyder. (1997). *The Management of Telecommunications: Business Solutions to Business Problems*. New York: Irwin McGraw Hill, 680-682.

4.   Hunt, D. (1997). The potential of telecommunications. *Vital Speeches of the Day*, 64, (3), November 15.

5.   Lecuona, R. A. & N. Momayezi. (2001). Privatization in Costa Rica: Political and economic impact. *International Journal on World Peace*, 18, (2).

6.   Mbarika, V. W., T. A. Byrd, & J. Raymond (2002). Growth of teledensity in Least Developed Countries: Need for a mitigated euphoria. *Journal of Global Management*, Apr-Jun, 10, (2), 16-17

7.   Ochoa-Morales, H. (2001). The digital gap between the industrialized countries and the less developed (LDC) ones: The transition toward a knowledgeable society in Latin America. *Journal of Issues in Information Systems*, 2, 337-342.

8.   Primo Braga, C, & V. Ziegler. (1998). Telecommunications in Latin America and the Caribbean: The role of foreign capital. *The Quarterly Review of Economics and Finance*, 38, (3), Fall, 409-419.

9.   Secretaria de la Comunidad Andina (S.C.A.). (1998). Cooperacion Francesa y CEPAL. *Multilaterismo y Regionalismo*. Seminario efectuado en Santa Fe de Bogota, 26 de Mayo, 1-2.

10.   Spiller, P. T. & C. G. Cardilli (1997). The frontier of telecommunications deregulation: Small countries leading the pack. *Journal of Economic Perspectives, Fall 97*, 11, (4).

11.   Union International de Telecomunicaciones: UIT. (2000). *Indicadores de Telecomunicaciones de las Americas 2000*. Resumen Ejecutivo, Abril, 1-22.

12.   UN-CEPAL (UN-ECLAC). (2000). *La Inversion Extranjera en America Latina y el Caribe*. Informe LC/G.2061-PE, Enero.

13.   _____. (2000b). *Latin America and The Caribbean in the Transition to a Knowledge-Based Society: An Agenda for Public Policy*. LC/L.1383, June, 5-25.

14.   U.S. Department of Commerce (1998). *The Emerging Digital Economy*.   (http://www.ecommerce.gov), 2, 4, 21, 23, 35.

15.   World Bank (2000). *The Network Revolution and the Developing World*. Analysis Report, Number 00-216, August 17.

16.   World Bank Group (2001). *Bridging the Digital Divide in The Americas*. Summit of the   Americas, April 20-22, 1-6.

Organisational Model and Organisational Information Systems: The Case of a Public Portuguese University

Professor Carlos Zorrinho and Paulo Resende da Silva
Center for Studies and Training in Management (CEFAG) and
Business Department, Évora University
Largo dos Colegiais, 2, 7000-803 Évora, Portugal
phone: 351-266-740892, fax: 351-266-742494
czorrinho@uevora.pt, pfs@uevora.pt

ABSTRACT

The actual context of educational sector, induced by the end of some boundaries and the information and communication technology, demand new approach on university management. Think the university in terms of organisational theory and understand the different organisational models that guide each university and try to identify the information architecture that support the organisational model is one of the key to adapt the university to answers to the new tendencies. So, this paper try to analyse the Portuguese public university in this subject area and the innovation of management systems on university, with the support of adequate information systems, to each particular institution, that answers to the higher education institution organisational model.

1 INTRODUCTION

Universities in all countries are face to serious changes in their positions in society and face a totally new competition, not only others universities, but also new competitors. The new demands from the knowledge market induce great changes on the organisational and management model, in one side, and on information model that supports the organisation, an the other side.

These changes, without any clear end positions, have different inputs, and are induced by three forces: political, social, and informational/technological.

Some work in the higher education field identified tendencies that university needs understand to capitalise [1, 2, 3, 4]. These tendencies can be reduced to five categories: the *restructuring of the economy* for new kinds of competitiveness, *changing role of the state* and the role of public services, *shifting demographics* and the new migrations process, new information communication *technologies*, and *increasing globalisation* and open the boundaries and the markets.

Our object study is the Universities and the analysis units are the organisational theory (how they modulate through the mission, the role and competency delegation from society), and the information systems (how they modulate or building her architectural).

This papers describes research in progress and analyses how the Portuguese public university should build the organisational model and how this model drives information architecture.

2 RESEARCH DESIGN

The new challenges put on the education sector and the *revolution* on information and communication technology created some particular needs in organisational and management contexts.

Universities will need innovative management systems, with the education sector, is the problem that the Portuguese Universities need to answer to the actual context and previous evolution to Education Sector in coming years.

How to built the correct information systems to support the higher education institution organisational mode is their big problem.

We need to understand the organisational and the management systems which will drive the change and/or adapt to internal needs of the university. Then we can build the adequate (in a general case) informational model to support the organisational model.

In order to build the models we need to visualise the university in two different dimensions. The first reality beginning on particular university knowledge logic with yours distinct decision freedom liberty and action – the curriculum, the learning process, and the research; and, secondly, they should need organise and building your particular structure in management and administrative units.

This work use the following methodology option:

1st   Begin with documents analysis, and with information from the organisations members (rector board team, senior managers, deans and other important actors). This is an intentional sample, which represents the University. Semi-directed interviews will be used as well questionnaires and work maps.

2nd   This is not experimental methodological approach, with a particular qualitative orientation, across triangular technical resources.

3 EMPIRICAL APPROACHES

We can look at the higher institution in a different manner, and study the organisational model by analyzing the leadership practises, the strategic options, the internal vision of the environment and the roles of the university in society, the internal structures, and others specials issues of analysis.

Universities are "knowledge management" organisations and they should define their business process to consolidate the information store. They should also manage the way they receive, store, generate and disseminate the knowledge.

The university organisational model should place the knowledge management, the learning and pedagogical management, and the innovation and research management as the central emphasis of their first approaches. The second approach should place a central emphasis on the academic community, the professors/teachers, the students and the staff support and other auxiliary members. The third approach should look at the university government, the internal services and the administration. The fourth approach should analyse the profissionalisation, democratisation and individualisation.

To find answers to our research design we start with the conception of two frameworks the support the methodological choices. This means, we assume some analytical perspectives that answer in easier way to our methodological option and orientation.

So, the two analytical perspectives can should answer to the two analysis units – Organisational Theory and the Information Systems.

One of the frameworks is the result of individual research with the support of four theoretical conceptions – university role, information systems impacts, systemic and behavioural approach, and resources theory [5, 6, 7, 8, 9, 10, 11, 12, 13, 14, 15, 16, 17, 18, 19, 20, 21, 22] (see figure 1) .

The second framework is the Zachman Framework [23], building from the IBM BSP, and very disseminate framework on information modelling of the company information systems.

Using these two frameworks , we should be able to understand the university including its environment, the Information Systems needed in the university, and the Management structure of the university. We should also be to identify the macro-processes and associated activities, and to assess the organisational variables with structural impacts on Economics Units – the strategy, the organisational culture, the power/leadership, and the formal structure [5, 15, 18, 20, 22, 23].

This kind of analysis answers to the major works and studies on the field of higher education when different authors make your personal analysis on basis on strategic planning, restructuring, resources allocation, innovation and entrepreneurial universities [4].

4 PRELIMINARY FINDINGS

The higher education institutions and the university in particular, should know that they are facing new challenges, social, political, economics and technological.

To respond to this, the university should find the references that make some guarantees of resource management, the higher quality level, demanded by society in general, and creating the incentives to the job.

This means that university should understand two realities. First, is that existing some knowledge logic that structure in three ways, in three processes - learning, research and knowledge. Second, the university should be organising in management and administrative division or units.

The two realities are built on different cultures; this means that each group have your cultures and subcultures that create some conflicting. The academic and professional need some freedom to works and without pressures and constraints versus administrative values when rules and regulations are the basis of their jobs [4][5][6][7][8][9].

The information model of university is intrinsic with the university model and has a very important (and are determinant by) the information technology.

The information technologies give the opportunity and enable the higher education institutions to learn and study internal processes, market and customer [4, 16, 22].

To study the Portuguese university we select three different data and information inputs.

With the three kinds of inputs we try to build the two frameworks and the major model, the organisational and the informational framework.

First, we interviewed the social actors that have the power and the leadership in the organisation, management and the information technologies on university - the chief executive office, the chief information office, the vice-rector or the pro-rector, the scientific board president, the pedagogical board president, and professors who work or research on this subject.

The second methodological strategy is a questionnaire that all the actors that I interviewed. Completed with this instrument we can find answers to the same question identified in last paragraph, but using international modelling.

Third, we shall analyse internal documents, such as the strategic plan, the Rector discourse in the university day, the student, professors and staff dates, the university policies, the computer strategy, internal studies on management and information systems, etc.

The reality of the information systems in the university are more dire. In general, with some exceptions, the university does not have any informational strategy, and has not t analysed the key processes. They have taken a reactive position to technology . The development of information technology is casual and not integrated, and the impacts of the information system is not evaluated.

The reason for this is that the university does not have a clear development strategy, the information systems are not considered critical factors to the university and hence there is less staff available to develop the systems.

5 CONCLUSION AND FURTHER WORK

The goal of this research is to understand the organisational and informational model of the university, including the new challenges to the university and the perceptions that the university administrators have about the university and it environment. We have some important previous conclusion.

The university have a large work on the field of strategy, of management change, of staff adaptation, of clear informational needs, and understanding what is organisational strategy, what is the information system and information technology, what are the key-role of this and what are the critical success factors.

This situations give to us some important direction and issues to furthers works, not only in this specific subject matter, but in others fields of university works.

This is a progress research project that have special aim, this is a doctoral project. So, the big further work is give a answer to the problem that I have, trying consolidate and validate the hypothesis, and give some perspective to the context of Portuguese public university on this field of work.

Acknowledgments

My work has two financial supporters: the Prodep Funding and my University.

My acknowledgment to Professors Carlos Zorrinho (Évora University) and José Tribolet (Technical Superior Institute of Lisbon Technical University) - my tutors of the work, and to Professors Susan Athey (Colorado State University) and Murray Young (Colorado Christian University) to help me on the text (correction my English), in discussion about my work, and on question that I need think and give some answers.

REFERENCES

[1]   M. Gibbon [et al.]. *The new production of knowledge – the dynamics of science and research in contemporary societies.* London: Sage Publications, (1994).

[2]   Peter Coaldrake. "Some challenges confronting higher education" in *Strategic asset management for tertiary institutions.* OECD. PEB Papers. Paris, pp. 23-26. (1999).

[3]   Unesco. "Tomo I - Informe final". World Conference on Higher Education - Higher Education in the Twenty-first Century: vision and action. Paris: 5-9 October 1998. http://unesdoc.unesco.org/image.pdf em 13-07-01.

[4]   Barbara Sporn. *Adaptive University Structures: an analysis of adaptation to socioeconomic environments of US and European universities.* Higher Education Policy Series 54. London: Jessica Kingsley Publishers, (1999).

[5]   Kenneth C. Laudon and Jane P. Laudon. *Management Information Systems: organization and technology in the networked enterprise.* Sixth Edition. Upper Saddle River: Prentice-Hall, (2000).

[6]   Burton Clark. *Creating Entrepreneurial Universities: organizational pathways of transformation.* Oxford: IAU Press/Pergamon, (1998).

[7]   M. D. Cohen, J. G. March and J. P. Olsen. "The garbage can model of organizational choice". *Administrative Science Quarterly*, 17 March, pp. 1-25, (1972).

[8]   Richard Hall. *Organizations: structures, processes, & outcomes.* 5th Edition. Englewood Cliffs, NJ: Prentice-Hall, (1991).

[9]   J. Pfeffer and G. R. Salancik. The external control of organizations: a resource dependence perspective. New York: Harper & Row, (1978).

[10]   Fremont E. Kast and James E. Rosenzweig. *Organization and management - a systems and contingency approach.* New York: McGraw-Hill, (1982).

[11]   Garreth Morgan. *The images of organizations.* London: Sage Publications, (1986).

[12]   G. M. Bull [et al.]. *Information technology - issues for higher education management.* Higher Education Policy Series 26. London: Jessica Kingsley Publishers, (1994).

[13]   William H. Bergquist. *The four cultures of the academy.* San Francisco: Jossey-Bass Publishers, (1992).

[14]   Henry Mintzberg. *Estrutura e dinâmica das organizações.* Ciências de Gestão - Gestão & Inovação - nº 4, Lisboa: Publicações dom Quixote, (1995).

[15]   Joseph Morabito, Ira Sack and Anilkumar Bhate. *Organization Modeling: innovative architecture for the 21st century.* Upper Saddle River: Prentice-Hall, (1999).

[16] Clark L. Bernard, Sandra L. Johnson and Jillinda J. Kidwell. *Reinventing the University: managing and financing institutions of higher education*. New York: John Wiley & Sons, (1998).

[17] Robert Birnbaum. *How Colleges Work: the cybernetics of academic organization and leadership*. San Francisco: Jossey-Bass, (1988).

[18] Melissa A. Cook. *Building Enterprise Information Architecture: reengineering information systems*. Upper Saddle River: Prentice-Hall, (1996).

[19] James Dunderstadt. *A University for the 21ˢᵗ Century*. Ann Arbor: University of Michigan Press, (2000).

[20] Lars Groth. *Future Organizational Design: the scope for the IT-based enterprise*. Chichester: John Wiley & Sons, (1999).

[21] Diana G. Oblinger and Richard N. Katz. *Renewing administration: preparing colleges and universities for the 21ˢᵗ century*. Bolton: Anker Publishing, (1999).

[22] OCDE. *Gérer les Stratégies de l'Information dans l'Enseignement Supérieur*. Documents OCDE. Paris : OCDE, (1996).

[23] Stevens H. Spewak. *Enterprise Architecture Planning: developing a blueprint for data, applications and technology*. New York: John Wiley & Sons, (1992).

[24] Mary Jo Hatch. *Organization theory: modern, symbolic and postmodern perspectives*. New York: Oxford University Press, (1997).

Automating Web Personalization with a Self-Organizing Neural Network

Victor Perotti, Ph.d.
Management Information Systems
Rochester Institute of Technology College of Business

The Internet's continuing transformation of business has created new and unique demands for information management. While these demands are multifaceted, perhaps none are more important than pursuing an understanding of website users, and leveraging this information to create site structure and content that is appropriate for users. Indeed, personalization and customization of web services are now commonplace features on many e-Business sites. Certainly, many sites use "cookies" or other technologies to track each individual as they come to the site. Consumers, however, are increasingly wary when their personal information is requested. A less invasive approach is to look at the aggregate behavior of all users, and to try to identify trends therein. Once these trends are identified, a user can be classified as a member of a particular group, and customized web content can be delivered.

Recommendation engines that identify user trends, and deliver user-appropriate content are an active field of research today. For example, Perkowitz & Etzioni (1997) challenged the Artificial Intelligence community to develop truly adaptive web sites that respond to the behavior of their users. Their more recent work (1998) introduces conceptual analysis as part of a "cluster mining" process which identifies groups of users that have common usage profiles. Similarly, Mobasher, Cooley and Srivastava. (2000) have developed an entire process for clustering web users, and have shown its performance relative to other algorithms. While the recovery of usage profiles by these two groups is fairly advanced, the degree of adaptation offered is fairly small.

A Complex Systems Approach to Web Personalization

The recommendation systems from the aforementioned research create "index pages" or recommended links so that users can access content that will be especially relevant to them. To accomplish this, they use data mining and statistical techniques to identify web usage clusters. An alternative and potentially superior approach is to utilize a complex system that continuously adapts to the user patterns at the web site. Perotti and Kiran (2002) employed this idea to visualize the usage patterns at a web site. In this work, a neural network called a Self-Organizing Map (SOM) was trained with website usage logs, and all subsequent user accesses could then be mapped to a particular cluster of web pages. The authors demonstrated a scatter plot that succinctly summarized the usage patterns at the studied web site.

The present research seeks to build on the work of Perotti and Kiran (2002) by automating personalized website content based on the up-to-the-minute adaptations in a Self-Organizing Map. Figure 1 shows a data flow diagram for the proposed personalization system. As users visit the site their usage patterns are continuously fed to the SOM as training information. In addition, when a user requests a web page, a CGI (common gateway interface) program is used to invoke and interpret the adapted SOM to identify structure and content that is appropriate user. A brief explanation of the Self-Organizing Map neural network will help to explain the recommendation system.

Kohonen Self Organizing Map

Kohonen's Self Organizing Map (SOM) is a well-known neural network technique to do data dimensionality reduction and clustering. In this technique, a neural network is created in the desired low dimensionality, say two dimensions for the sake of explanation. The network is then trained with a set of input patterns represented as a set of input vectors that correspond to the high dimensional data to be reduced. Each node in the network includes a model vector, which is that node's representation of the input vectors. The process of training involves comparing each input pattern with the model vec-

tor at every node. When a node's model vector is the closest to a given input vector, that node and all of its neighboring nodes are altered to be more like that input vector. Thus, through repeated training, one of the network nodes becomes highly associated with each input pattern, so that when the correct input pattern is presented, it will be the most highly active node in the network. After training, the neural network represents a simple (two dimensional) map with nearby nodes representing similar input patterns in the multidimensional input data.

Self organizing maps have been already used for a great variety of problems, including browsing a picture database, data exploration, representing large text collections and classifying web documents based on their textual content (Kohonen et al, 2000).

Self Organizing Maps as part of a recommendation engine

The advantages to using a complex system like a Self organizing map for website recommendations are many. For one, the neural network generalizes from its training items to any new items. Thus, any new data can be analyzed and compared to earlier items without having to go through training. Thus, a fully trained neural network can make almost instantaneous "decisions" about which cluster a given web site visit belongs in. This is not the case for other recommendation systems, which may have to go through the very large web log in order to include the latest information.

Furthermore, the training of the neural network can happen in parallel with making recommendations, and may in fact go on continually. Continuous training means that if desired, a website can make recommendations based on short term fluctuations in website usage. For example, if a web page deep within the website's structure suddenly becomes popular, the web site can recommend that page from the home page to simplify access for subsequent users.

Another advantage to the self organizing map approach is the generality of the training process. In its most generic form, training is a distance comparison between input vectors and model vectors. What is represented in the input vectors, and how it is represented as a vector are not constrained. In addition, the distance function itself is configurable, allowing certain elements in the vectors to have more weight than others. For the recommendation system, this means that web users can be clustered based not only on the specific web pages they visit, but also on any information available about them in the website log. This flexibility could allow a self organizing map system to recognize when, for example, different geographic regions are using the web site in unique ways. Thus a user from the Southwest United States accessing a page could be given recommendations that are popular in that location, while visitors from Thailand are given a different set of recommended pages. Similarly, website visitors could be differentiated based on their time of access. If the recommendation engine is supporting an electronic commerce site, early morning visitors could thus be directed toward products such as coffee or alarm clocks that are associated with the morning. Late night visitors, conversely, could see after dinner mints, or sleep enhancing medication as their recommendations.

Directions for future research

While the manipulation of the distance function allows the clustering of website visitors to happen in many different ways, it also raises some challenging issues. How can the weights be assigned to the different sources of user information to best serve the users? Given information about which web pages are being visited, when the visit is happening and where the visit is arriving from, many different clusters can be derived based on the relative weights of these factors. A suitable way to balance these factors to derive the best possible clusters has yet to be developed.

Another challenge for future research is the opportunity to tie in website content data to the process of making recommendations. In the basic form presented here, each webpage is distinguished based only on its name, and location in the site. Recent research on "Information Scent" (Pirolli and Pitkow, 2000; Pirolli, Chen & Pitkow, 2001) has shown the promise of including content information as part of the analysis of website usage.

References

Mobasher, B. Cooley, R. Srivastava, J. (1999) *Automatic Personalization Through Web Usage Mining*, Technical Report TR99-010, Department of Computer Science, Depaul University, 1999.

Mobasher, B. Cooley, R. Srivastava, J. (2000) *Automatic Personalization Based on Web Usage Mining*, Communications of the ACM, 43-8.

Perkowitz, M. and Etzioni, O. (1998). *Adaptive Web Sites: Automatically Synthesizing Web pages*, Presented at the American Association of Artificial Intelligence conference.

Perkowitz, M. and Etzioni, O. (1997). *Adaptive Web Sites: An AI Challenge*, Presented at International Joint Conferences on Artificial Intelligence.

Perotti, V. and Kiran, R., (2002) The Visualization of Usage Patterns for Web Customization, presented at the IRMA conference, Seattle, WA

Chi, E. Pirolli, P., Chen, K. And Pitkow, J. (2001). *Using Information Scent to Model User Information Needs and Actions on the Web* In Proceedings of the Conference on Human Factors in Computing Systems, CHI '2001 Seattle, WA. 490-497.

Chi, E. Pirolli, P., And Pitkow, J. (2000). *The Scent of a Site: A System for Analyzing and Predicting Information Scent, Usage, and Usability of a Web Site*. In Proceedings of the Conference on Human Factors in Computing Systems, CHI '2000 The Hague, Amsterdam. 161-168.

Business Transaction Standards for Electronic Commerce

Boriana Rukanova
University of Twente
School of Business, Public Administration and Technology
Department of Business Information Systems
P.O.Box 217, 7500AE Enschede, The Netherlands
Telephone: +31 53 489 40 64, Fax: +31 53 489 21 59
E-mail: b.d.rukanova@utwente.nl

1. STAGE OF THE RESEARCH

The research project "Business Transaction Standards for EC" started in June 2001. Currently we are at the meta model construction phase. We have first results of elements of business transactions based on theory, standards and practice and we are in a process of constructing the first version of the meta model based on these findings. As the meta model construction is an iterative process, in the following year we will add new elements and improve the meta model.

2. MOTIVATION AND OBJECTIVES

Our motivation is on one hand to facilitate practitioners when choosing standards to support the electronic execution of parts of their business transaction, and on the other hand to contribute to the scientific efforts in that direction. The goal of this research is to try to elicit problems that might occur due to mismatch between the distributed business transaction standards (DBTS) used for a particular business transaction and the requirements of that specific business transaction (BT).

To identify mismatch between the standard and the requirements of the situation means that we need to be able to compare the two. As we consider direct comparison to be very difficult, we propose to use a meta model for this purpose. Our objective is to *construct a meta model* to be used to 1) elicit requirements of a distributed business transaction (DBT) situation and 2) to elicit characteristics of a DBTS and by doing so, identify mismatches and elicit potential problems.

To do so, we need to answer the following questions:
o   How to construct a Meta model that can be used to (1) elicit requirements of a DBT and (2) elicit characteristics of a DBTS?
o   Can we identify mismatch and elicit some potential problems using the Meta Model?

The rest of the proposal is structured as follows. In part 3 we make a review of relevant literature, in Part 4 we outline the research approach, and further steps in the research are briefly described in part 5.

3. LITERATURE REVIEW

The idea to automate parts of a business transaction is not new. EDI standards promised significant advantages in facilitating the exchange between business partners, reducing errors, increasing speed, cutting cost, and building in competitive advantage (Kerke & Mukhopadyay, 1992; Mackay, 1993; Wrigly et al., 1994; Jelassi & Figon, 1994, Sokol, 1995; Damsgaardn, 2000). However, the EDI standards failed to capture the communication context, in order to support the complex business communication. They were more like languages for depositing character strings into a particular place of a remote computer, than languages for exchange of knowledge. EDI standards were lacking clear and complete lexicon; did not have fully specified grammar, and had nearly no semantics. Furthermore, the focus of many IS professionals on EDI was how to provide technical tools, rather than to support the way people do business (Huang, 1998; Covington, 1997; Kimbrough, 1999).

A lot of initiatives are going on now, trying to solve some of the problems that the EDI standards could not. A lot of efforts are devoted towards the development of new standards (ebXML, RosettaNet, BizTalk, HL7), new languages (FLBC (Moore 1997), BCL (McCarthy 1993)), classification of standards (Guarino 2000).

However, in order to have value for a particular business process, a standard needs to be linked to a particular situation, which might be different from what the standard developers had in mind. Thus, the standard needs to be evaluated (for a specific business process) whether it can cover the communication context (of the particular business transaction). The question is how to make sure that the chosen standards can cover the communication context of the specific business transaction?

4. RESEARCH APPROACH

To make sure that the chosen standards can cover the communication context of the specific business transaction, we will try to compare the characteristics of the standard chosen with the requirements of the business transaction.

How can we make such comparison? On one hand we have the requirements of the business transaction (or the context of communication), which could be described in documents, models or could as well be implicit. On the other hand we have the standard, which could be expressed in the form of a standard specification, and which might be developed according to a certain methodology. Direct comparison will be difficult to make. It might be possible, however to go a level higher and make a comparison at a meta level. Thus our main concern is:

Could a meta model help us to compare the characteristics of a standard with the requirements of the context, and to elicit some potential problems at operational level?

To solve this problem we need to answer the following questions:
o   How to construct a Meta model that can be used to (1) elicit requirements of a DBT and (2) elicit characteristics of a DBTS?
o   Can we identify mismatch and elicit some potential problems using the Meta Model?

The first research question refers to the meta model construction, while the second one refers to the meta model testing.

Figure 1 below illustrates the proposed approach. Our aim is to elicit problems with the use of standards at an operational level. The operational DBT is a combination between the DBT situation (communication context) and the DBT standard (DBTS). As we said above it is difficult to compare the context and the standard directly. We propose to go a level higher and to make the comparison at a meta level. Our objective is to create a meta model to be used to on one hand express the requirements of the DBT situation and on the other hand the characteristics of the DBTS. Once both are expressed in terms of the meta model we will be able to compare them. The expectation is that a possible mismatch on a meta level would signal some potential problems on an operational level.

Below we go further in detail in illustrating the meta model construction and the meta model testing.

Figure 1: Illustration of the research approach

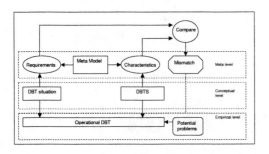

4.1. Meta Model Construction

The first research question, "How to construct a Meta model that can be used to (1) elicit requirements of a DBT and (2) elicit characteristics of a DBTS?", refers to the meta model construction.

As the meta model needs to be able check whether a set of standards could capture the communication context, the meta model needs to describe the elements of the context. We consider, that by describing the elements of a business transaction we can try to capture the context of communication. The meta model that we will construct will try to capture the context of communication by describing the elements of a BT.

In order to define the elements of BT and their relationships we will look at theory, practice and standards. Thus, to answer the first research question we need to find an answer to three other questions.

1. What relevant elements of DBT and their relationships (on a Meta level) are described in theory?
2. What relevant elements of DBT and their relationships (on a Meta level) are covered by the existing DBTS?
3. What additional relevant elements of DBT and relationships (on a Meta level) are encountered in practice?

By relevant we mean elements that describe the shared meaning and intentions within a business transaction.

4.2. Meta Model Testing

The second research question was: "Can we identify mismatch and elicit some potential problems using the Meta Model?" refers to the meta model testing.

We would like to do case studies to perform this evaluation. By conducting case studies we will get an in-depth insights about the usability of the meta model. The strategy that we'll follow to test the meta model is presented in Figure 2. For each case we will look at one transaction. We will analyze a practical situation, where standards have been used to automate parts of that business transaction. We will use different techniques to identify problems that occur while implementing and using standards. In that way we will arrive to a description of actual problems that occur in practice (See the lower part of figure 2).

Figure 2: Meta Model Testing

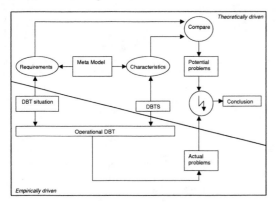

On the other hand, for the same case, looking at the same situation, we will try to theoretically identify potential problems, using the meta model. By walking the meta model and reasoning about the specific situation we can define which elements of the meta model are relevant for the specific situation. In that way, looking at the DBT situation and using the meta model we will be able to define the requirements of the situation in terms of the meta model. We can follow the same logic for the DBTS. Looking at the DBTS that were used and using the meta model we can identify the characteristics of the standards, again in terms of the meta model.

Once we have done that we can compare the requirements of the situation and the characteristics of the standards and identify mismatch between the two. A mismatch would signal that there are requirements of the DBT which are not met by characteristics of the DBTS. This means that theoretically there might be potential problems.

The next step is to confront the problems that actually occurred in practice to those that we identified using the meta model. A mismatch might signal potential problems. We are aware of the fact that by doing case studies we are not able to generalize our findings. However, by testing the meta model in two different industries we can get more and deeper insights about the findings and outline directions for further research.

5. FURTHER RESEARCH

The remaining time of the research project will be devoted to completing the construction and the testing of the meta model and writing the PhD thesis.

REFERENCES

Damsgaard J., Truex, D. (2000), Binary Trading Relationships and the Limits of EDI Standards: The Procrustean Bed of Standards. *European Journal of Information Systems*, 9(3) pp. 173-188

Guarino, N., Welty, C., Partridge, C. (2000), Web Content Standards, In Liddle, S.W., Mayr, H.C., and Thalheim, B. (Eds.): *ER 2000 Workshop*, LNCS 1921, pp. 1-6, Springer- Verlag Berlin Heidelberg 2000

Huang K. (1998), *Organizational Aspects of EDI: a Norm-oriented Approach*, PhD thesis, ISBN 90-3651095-3

Jelassi, T. and Figon, O. (1994), Competing through EDI at Brun Passot: Achievements in France and Ambitions for the Single European Market, *MIS Quarterly*, 18(4), pp. 337-352.

McCarthy, J. (1982), Common Business Communication Language. In Albert Endres and Jürgen Reetz, editors, *Textverarbeitung und Bürosysteme*. R. Oldenbourg Verlag, Munich and Vienna.

Moore, S.A. (1997), On Automated Message Processing in Electronic Commerce and Work Support Systems: Speech Act Theory and Expressive Felicity, *ACM Transactions on Information Systems*, Vol. 15, No 4, October 1997.

Kekre, S. and Mukhopadyay, T. (1992), Impact of Electronic Data Interchange Technology on Quality Improvement and Inventory Reduction Programs: A Field Study, *International Journal of Production Economics*, 28(3), pp. 265-282.

Kimbrough S., EDI, XML, and the Transperancy Problem in Electronic Commerce

Mackay, D.R. (1993), The Impact of EDI on the Components Sector of the Australian Automotive Industry, *Journal of Strategic Information Systems*, 2(3), pp. 243-263.

Sokol, P. K. (1995), *From EDI to Electronic Comemrce- a Business Initiative*, McGraw-Hill, Inc., New York, ISBN 0-07-059512-7.

Stegwee R.A., Lagendijk P.J.B. (2001), Healthcare Information and Communication Standards Framework, in: R.A. Stegwee & T.A.M. Spil, *Strategies for Healthcare Information Systems*, Idea Group Publishing Vermeer, B., How Important is Data Quality for Evaluating the Impact of EDI on Global Supply Chain? *Proceedings of the 33 Hawaii International Conference on System Science*.

Williams H., Li F., Whalley J. (2000), Interoperability and Electronic Commerce: A New Policy Framework for Evaluating Strategic Options, *JCMC 5 (3)*

Wrighly, C.D., Wagenaar, R.W., and Clarke, R. (1994), Electronic Data Interchange in National Trade: Frameworks for the Strategic Analysis of Ocean Port Communities, *Journal of Strategic Information Systems*, 3(3), pp. 211-234.

Techno-Economic Modeling of Basic Telecommunication Services in India: A System Dynamics Approach

Piyush Jain

Student of 'Fellow Programme in Management' at Indian Institute of Management, Lucknow. INDIA
FPM OfficeIndian Institute of ManagementOff Sitapur RoadLucknow – 226 013, UP; INDIA
Telephone: 91-522-2361889 to 97 Ext – 595; 919415006051(Mobile)
Fax: 91-522-2361840/2361843
piyushjain@iiml.ac.in

1. INTRODUCTION

Traditionally, voice communication has been characterized as three distinct types of services: local, national long distance and international long distance. Local telecommunication service (also referred to as Basic Telecom Service) is used to describe the provision of local access networks ("last mile" connection) over relatively short distances. Historically, basic telecom services were considered as "natural monopoly" because of the following reasons: there is huge fixed and sunk cost associated with the investment on the local loop; duplication of local loop is not possible and economically justifiable. In the U.S. basic services were opened up for competition after the landmark Tele-communications Act of 1996 was passed.

In India, basic services were provided by the government owned/controlled monopoly operators. The service areas are designated as circles. The government invited private participation in 1995 for the provision of local and intra-circle long distance calling and envisaged a duopoly structure. During 2001, the government decided to further open up basic services without any restrictions on the number of operators. Currently the new license holders are deploying infrastructure and have already started rolling out services in certain circles. India's tele-density is a little over 3.8 per 100 currently. The New Telecom Policy drafted in 1999 envisages a tele-density of 7 by 2005 and 15 by 2010 (NTP, 1999).

A thorough understanding of the mechanics of growth of the basic telecom services is of interest to policy makers, regulators and the service providers. Especially in developing countries such as India where the basic telecom services is still in its infancy, an understanding of the structure of the erstwhile monopoly market is the first step in this direction. This study can pave way for analyzing the more complicated oligopoly market, which countries such as India will face in the near future.

In this research work, we have used "systems dynamics" methodology to initially model the monopoly basic telecom services. Calibration of the model using data from Indian telecommunications industry indicates that the model indeed validates to the reality. This model will be extended to address 'oligopoly' market structure. Model will be used to predict the growth of basic services – the subscriber base of incumbent and new entrant(s). Rest of the paper has been organized into the following sections: literature survey, modeling, simulation & validation, sensitivity analysis and future research directions.

2. THE TECHNO-ECONOMIC SIMULATION MODELING – A BRIEF LITERATURE SURVEY

Techno-economic simulations can be used to replicate the conditions of the telecommunications technology and its environment so that growth of the services can be investigated and monitored by researchers, planners and managers. Technical parameters such as network bandwidth, quality of service and economic parameters such as sales, subscriber forecasts and revenue projection can be simulated using techno-economic models.

A techno-economic model encapsulates technical, economic, social, political, competition and infrastructural aspects, which are relevant in providing service. Song (2001) highlights the supply side cost parameters of telecom service provisioning such as facility investment, area/non area specific investment and quality related investments etc. Chatterjee (1998) stresses that the demand for services will vary based upon certain socio-economic (household income, profession) and demographic factors (educational level, age, family size, population density, location). Other economic forces that could influence the demand are the price of service (Cocchi, 1992), quality of service (Dutta, 2001A) and competition (Sice, 2000).

The relationship between the demand and supply components of the integrated techno-economic model is illustrated in Figure 1.

3. MODELING MONOPOLY BASIC TELECOM SERVICES USING SYSTEM DYNAMICS METHODOLOGY

The concept of system dynamics was first introduced by Jay W. Forrester at MIT in the 1960s. Basic approach of system dynamics is to identify and to study the influence of the forces operating in a feedback mode in a business, social, managerial or a scientific system. A feedback loop consists of four distinct types of entities- the *levels*, the *rates*, the *constants* and the *auxiliary* variables. Where the level (or state) variables describe the condition of the system at any particular time. The level variables accumulate the flows described by the rate (action) variables.. Auxiliary variables help in defining the rate variables. Constant equations are used to define parameters/decision variables.

The system dynamics approach begins with the identification of the forces that constitute and affect the system under study. This structural hypothesis of the system dynamic study is usually recorded and communicated to others in a "visual-model" called a causal loop diagram and is represented in Figure 2. It shows the existence of all major cause-and-effect links, indicates the "direction" of each linkage relationship, and denotes major feedback loops and their "polarities". A link is positive (or negative) if a change in the causal element produces a change in the same (or opposite) direction for the effect element. A closed sequence of causal links represents a causal loop. An even/odd number of negative polarity links in a loop results in a positive/negative feedback.

System dynamics has been used successfully to study the dynamics and forces in a wide variety of application areas of the telecommunication services. Kim (1997) explores a series of system dynamics models for explaining the fluctuating market shares of on-line services by combining externality effect and congestion effect. Dutta (2001B) emphasizes that contagion effects along with technical development, social factors such as literacy and economic development levels, social norms and regulatory climate have significant effect on the growth of on-line services. Dutta (2001A) integrates customer behavior, network performance and financial consequences in a system dynamics model in order to gain insight in to the business process under lying the network service provisioning.

The causal loop diagram for our techno-economic model is shown in Figure 2. To get an integrated view of the model, we start with the main variable- SUBSCRIBERS which represents the subscribers of the basic telecommunication services in a circle/area. Households subscribe to telecom services. An increase in the number of households in any circle/area leads to increase in the number of subscribers and depletes the potential subscribers. This bi-directional relationship forms a loop with –ive polarity i.e. negative feedback loop. An increase in economic development of an area/circle increases the income level of the people and hence the subscriber base for telecommunication services. As the number of subscribers of a telecommunication services increases, the amount of information traffic and frequency of request for connection establishment increase. This causes congestion, which deteriorates network performance. However, if the service provider synchronizes the infrastructural buildup i.e. setting up of switches, access loops and trunks, with the pace of building up of subscriber base, congestion reduces.

Quality of the access loop decides the type of services, a service provider can provide and subscriber can subscribe for. Economically, the access loop cost is one of the major components of total infrastructure cost of telecommunication services. Hence, as the quality of access loop improves, the variety of services being provided increases as well as the cost of services. Increase in cost of providing service enhances the price of subscription of the service, which in turn shows its negative effect on subscriber level based on their price elasticity of demand for services. The price for services gets lowered with increase in industry experience, service providers experience and economy of scale. Variety of services is not only governed by the quality of access loop but by the threat of competition also. If there is no expected competition in the market place, then monopolist does not feel motivated to provide higher quality services even though the access loop is capable of supporting such services. Similarly, even with high threat of competition, the service provider may not be able to provide multiple services immediately because of the low quality of the access loop. Similarly, threat level of competition and variety of services both dictate the time for deployment of services.

4. SIMULATION AND VALIDATION OF THE MODEL

A stock-and-flow simulation model was constructed based on the causal loop diagram shown in Figure 2, using VENSIM (www.vensim.com), a system dynamic simulation package (Educational edition). Data from different sources were collected to build and test the model (Natrajan, 1998; Economic survey, 2001; Thukral 1998; BSNL annual reports).

The basic telecom services monopoly feedback model was simulated for 200 months since Mar'96 for one circle. First 74 months (up to May 2002) details have been used for the validation and calibration of the model with the available data from erstwhile monopoly operator Bharat Sanchar Nigam Limited (BSNL). The results of the simulation are presented in Figure 3. As can be seen, the simulated subscriber base closely follows the actual subscriber base.

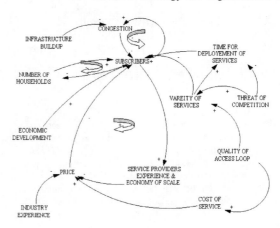

Figure 2: Causal Loop Diagram: Basic Monopoly Model

Literature identifies different ways of assessing prediction quality of these simulation results, all of which involve some averaging of individual error terms. One such measure is the Mean Absolute Deviation Percent Error (Dutta, 2001B) and is defined as follows:

$$\frac{\Sigma [|\text{Predicted} - \text{Actual}| / \text{Actual}]}{\text{No of Observations}}$$

The MAPE of this model is 6.61% indicating a high predictive quality. Further, regression of both simulated and actual values was carried out and the results are presented in Table 1. The high significance of regression equation indicates that simulated subscribers are close to actual subscribers.

After the calibration using past data, the model was also run to simulate the subscriber base forecast for the next 58 months. It is expected that the subscriber base in the circle under study will be double the present strength (3.36 million against the present subscriber base of 1.74 million), with in a span of five years under prevailing conditions.

5. SENSITIVITY ANALYSIS

The model can be used not only to predict the subscriber base in future, but also study the effect of changes in various variables in the model on the subscriber base. For example, we did sensitivity analysis by increasing infrastructure build-up by the service provider in tune with the boost in the economic development. Figure 4 shows the existing and experimented projections of subscriber base. Under this scenario, the number of subscribers will cross the 5 Million mark with in a span of five years. This can be explained by the dominance of the negative effect on congestion by the infrastructure buildup element and the positive effect on subscriber base by the economic development variable.

6. WORKS UNDER PROGRESS AND FUTURE RESEARCH DIRECTIONS

Indian Telecom industry is witnessing shift from an era of total monopoly to duopoly and even oligopoly. Researchers, academicians, regulators and telecom managers need to understand the complex dynamics of this transition

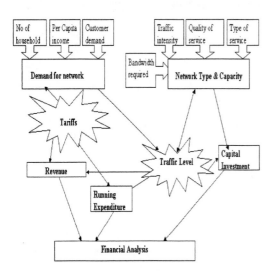

Figure 1: Components of Techno-Economic Model

Figure 3: Growth of subscribers (Simulated Vs Actual)

Table 1: Regression Results

Slope	R²	F	Significance
1.0173	.994	13143.967	0.000

phase of the Indian telecom industry to make future investment and/or extension of this policy decision. The system dynamics model proposed in this research encapsulates all the relevant techno-economic variables affecting the basic telecommunication industry. The model validates to reality and can be used as a decision support tool to analyze the effect of different variables on the subscriber growth. Further, calibration of the model for more service areas will be done to make it more robust. A model is under development to capture the duopoly structure and competition to decide the relative market share/ leadership.

REFERENCES

1. Chatterjee, S., C.S. Thachenkary, & J. L. Katz. (1998). Modeling the Economic Impacts of Broadband Residential Services. Computer Networks & ISDN Systems.

2. Cocchi, R., D. Estrin, S. Shenker, L. Zhang. (1992). A study of priority pricing in multiclass networks. Proceedings of SIGCOMM'91. Revised version.

3. Dutta, A. (2001A). Business Planning for Network Services: A Systems Thinking Approach. Information Systems Research, Vol.12, No.3, 260-283.

4. Dutta, A., & R. Roy. (2001B). The Mechanism of Internet diffusion in India: Lessons for developing countries, Proceedings of International Conference on Information Systems, 2001. New Orleans, LA.

5. Economic Survey. (2001). Govt. of India publication.

6. Kim, D.H., Jae-Ho Juhn, & Won-Gyu Ha. (1997). Dynamic Modeling of Competitive On-line Services in Korea. System Dynamics: an International Journal of Policy Modeling. Vol.IX, No.2.

7. Natrajan, I. (1998). Indian Market Demographics Report 1998. NCAER.

8. NTP. (1999). National Telecom Policy. Govt. of India. Retrieved on Sept 20, 2002 from http://www.trai.gov.in/npt1999.htm.

9. Sice, P, Erik Mosekilde, Alfredo Moscardini, Kevin Lawler, & Ian French. (2000). Using System Dynamics to analyze interactions in duopoly competition. System Dynamics Review Vol.16, No.2.113-133.

10. Song, J.D., & Jae-Cheol Kim. (2001). Is five too many? Simulation analysis of profitability and cost structure in the Korean mobile telephone industry. Telecommunications Policy 25. 101-123.

11. Thukral, R.K. (1998). India at a Glance. Jagran, India.

12. Vonstackelberg, H. (1952). The theory of market economy. Hodge: London.

Dimensional Modeling: Initial Approach for Identifying and Classifying Patterns

Mary Elizabeth Jones
Drexel University
College of Information Science & Technology

RESEARCH PROBLEM

It is recognized that software design is a difficult and time-consuming process that requires skill and experience. Software engineers continually seek methods for improving the efficiency and effectiveness of the software design process. For example, software engineers have used structured and object-oriented design techniques to improve the software design process. These techniques were developed to enhance the software design process by using a consistent standard approach. Yet, concentration on software design techniques alone has not guaranteed successful software design solutions [Brooks, 1995]. Ward Cunningham concurs:

A growing number of us in the object-oriented community feel we have misplaced our collective attention for some time. We no longer need to focus on tools, techniques, notations, or even code. We already have in our hand the machinery to build great programs. When we fail, we fail because we lack experience. [Fowler, 1997]

The dilemma remains – how do software engineers obtain experience in order to create effective solutions?

As software engineers implemented more and more systems and as the concept of a software pattern was recognized, software engineers became more aware of the similarities within systems. The software engineering community realized they could benefit from capturing and understanding software design similarities within and across various systems. Those similarities formed the basis for software patterns that can be reapplied when designing future systems. With each subsequent system, patterns are used, enhanced, and adapted to improve their usefulness for future systems. Thus patterns capture and combine successful design techniques as well as the experience of software engineers.

In the area of data warehousing, practitioners are trying to help software engineers obtain the experience necessary to create effective solutions. Several books provide data warehouse design solutions that are organized by domain [Kimball, 2002], [Kimball, 1998], [Adamson and Venerable, 1998], [Silverston, 2001]. The purpose of these books is to demonstrate data warehouse design techniques by example. These books are intended to assist the software engineer in understanding data warehouse design by studying and learning from the examples of those more experienced in data warehouse design and implementation. But the examples represent specific approaches to specific situations and therefore the examples may not address the software engineer's particular design problem. The data warehousing community has not used these existing design solutions to identify and classify patterns. Currently, the data warehousing community lacks patterns - a formal organized representation of recurring strategies worthy of following, applying, and repeating when designing data warehousing applications.

RESEARCH OBJECTIVES

The published design solutions are valuable. However, they are usually example solutions to a specific data warehousing problem. The next step is to analyze those solutions with the intent of seeking and extracting design techniques that commonly occur within and across application domain areas. Those repeating occurrences – which will be referred to and documented as data warehouse design patterns - can be reused on future design efforts.

The objective of this research project is to identify data warehousing design patterns, classify those patterns in a way that communicates their usefulness in a usable way, and determine if those patterns will help in designing a data warehouse. This research project will evaluate if the identified patterns help the data warehousing design process by testing the following null hypotheses:

- H0: Data warehousing patterns have no impact on the time to design a data warehouse schema.
- H0: Data warehousing patterns have no impact on the correctness of data warehouse schema design.

LITERATURE OUTLINE

The literature review
- Presents the historical and evolutionary perspectives of databases and software design patterns
- Defines dimensional modeling and software design patterns
- Presents the lessons learned from software design pattern experts in terms of the benefits and difficulties with software design patterns
- Provides an overview of the varieties of existing software design patterns

METHODOLOGY

The objectives of this research project are to identify and classify data warehousing schema patterns and then evaluate their impact on the design process. A classical pretest post-test experiment will be used to evaluate the impact of patterns on the software design process.

Two attributes will be used to evaluate the impact of patterns on data warehousing design solutions. They are the: 1) time it takes to create a solution and 2) correctness of the solution. Once the data warehousing patterns are identified and classified, a pretest post-test experiment will be conducted to evaluate the time it takes to solve a data warehouse design problem and the correctness of the data warehouse design solution. Therefore, the independent variable will be defined as "exposure to patterns" and the dependent variables will be: 1) time and 2) correctness. In other words, this pretest post-test experiment will be evaluating how exposure to patterns impacts the time it takes to solve a data warehouse design problem and the correctness of the solution.

For this experiment, the experimental units are graduate students. They will be selected from the population of graduate students enrolled in Drexel University's College of Information Science and Technology (IST). IST graduate students can pursue a Master of Science in Library and Information Science, Master of Science in Information Systems, a dual Master's of Science degree in Library and Information Science and Information Systems, Master of Science in Software Engineering, and a Doctor of Philosophy in Information Science and Technology.

The graduate students for this experiment must have an understanding of database concepts and system analysis as well as a rudimentary understanding of data warehousing design. Graduate students enrolled in the Applied Information and Database Technology course (INFO 607) are taught dimensional modeling and design techniques, which is used for the design of data warehousing databases. The prerequisites for this course are Database Management II (INFO 606) and Information System Analysis (INFO 620). Thereby making the graduate students taking INFO 607 well suited to participate in this experiment. Therefore, IST graduate students enrolled in INFO 607 will provide the data for this research project. This course typically has 25 to 30 students per class.

This pretest post-test experiment will use two groups – 1) a control group that will receive no exposure to the data warehousing patterns and 2) an experimental group that will receive exposure to the data warehousing patterns. The control group will be taught dimensional modeling and specific design examples will be reviewed and discussed. The experimental group will be taught dimensional modeling and will also be taught data warehousing design patterns. The subjects will be randomly assigned to either the control group or the experimental group using the simple random sampling technique. Students will be serially numbered. A random number table will be used to assign the students to either the control group or the experimental group.

EXPECTED OUTCOME

It is expected that this research project will add to the body of data warehouse design and software engineering knowledge by:
- Identifying and classifying data warehousing schema patterns
- Evaluating the efficiency and efficacy of data warehousing design schema patterns when used by graduate students of data warehousing

In terms of evaluating the efficiency and efficacy of data warehousing design schema patterns it is expected that the time to design a data warehouse schema is less for software engineers that have learned and applied data warehousing design patterns than those who have not learned and applied data warehousing design patterns. Also, it is expected that the correctness of the data warehouse schema design is more correct for those who have learned and applied data warehousing design patterns than those who have not learned and applied data warehousing design patterns.

BIBLIOGRAPHY

Adamson, Christopher and Venerable, Michael. Data Warehouse Design Solutions. New York: John Wiley & Sons, Inc., 1998.

Brooks, Frederick P. The Mythical Man-Month. Reading: Addison Wesley Longman, Inc., 1995.

Fowler, Martin. Analysis Patterns: Reusable Object Models. Menlo Park: Addison-Wesley, 1997.

Kimball, Ralph; Reeves, Laura; Ross, Margy; and Thornthwaite, Warren. The Data Warehouse Lifecycle Toolkit. New York: John Wiley & Sons, Inc., 1998.

Kimball, Ralph; and Ross, Margy. The Data Warehouse Toolkit, 2nd ed. New York: John Wiley & Sons, Inc., 2002.

Silverston, Len. The Data Model Resource Book, Vol. 1, revised ed. New York: John Wiley & Sons, Inc., 2001.

Tracing Variability in Software Product Families

Kannan Mohan
Georgia State University
Department of Computer Information Systems
9th Floor, 35 Broad Street, Atlanta GA, 30303
Phone: (404) 651 3869, Fax: (404) 651 3842
kmohan@cis.gsu.edu

ABSTRACT

Significant economic benefits can be achieved by software development organizations involved in customized software product development by adopting a product family approach. Managing variability, which refers to how members of a product family differ from each other, demands extensive process knowledge. Traceability, the capability to link various conceptual and physical artifacts, from requirements to other outputs of the development process, has been recognized as one of the prominent approaches that can be used to support knowledge intensive processes. A common problem in establishing traceability is identifying and capturing the relevant knowledge elements that will be useful in later phases of the development life cycle. Here, I investigate the use of traceability in managing variability in software product family development. This research focuses on the development of a traceability model for managing variability in product families. This model will identify the various knowledge elements that can be captured and that will be useful in managing variability. I adopt a three-phased approach in this dissertation. In the first phase, I use grounded theory method to develop a traceability model. In the second phase, I develop a prototype software system that is used to capture and use the knowledge represented by the traceability model. In the third phase, a laboratory experiment will be conducted to evaluate the usefulness of this traceability knowledge.

1. INTRODUCTION

Significant economic benefits can be achieved by software development organizations involved in customized software product development by adopting a software product family approach. Product family development is considered to be a knowledge intensive process (Bronsword and Clements 1996). The development process involves managing variations among different members of the product family by identifying common and variable aspects in the domain under consideration. Variability refers to how members of a product family differ from each other.

Prior research (Conklin and Begeman 1988) has suggested a variety of approaches to manage process knowledge for software development. Traceability, the capability to link various conceptual and physical artifacts, from requirements to other outputs of the development process, has been identified as one of the most prominent approaches that can used to support knowledge intensive processes (Gotel and Finkelstein 1994).

Motivated by the effectiveness of traceability in addressing the problems in knowledge intensive processes and the need for process knowledge management in handling variations in product families, **I use traceability to manage variability in software product family development.**

2. RESEARCH OBJECTIVES

The primary objectives of this dissertation are to:

- Develop a traceability model for variability management in the development of product families
- Build a prototype software system that will facilitate the capture and use of traceability knowledge
- Validate the usefulness of the knowledge represented by the traceability model, in managing variability in software product families

These objectives lead to the following research questions:

4. How do we trace requirements that demand variations to the variability points in the system? What knowledge about variability do we need to capture?
5. What are the capabilities that should be provided in a prototype software system for managing variability using traceability knowledge?
6. How do we assess the usefulness of the traceability knowledge in variability management in software product family development? Does this traceability knowledge represented by the model enhance maintenance performance for software product families?

3. RESEARCH METHODOLOGY

3.1 Phase 1: Traceability Model Development using Grounded Theory Method

To get an insight into the various pieces of process knowledge that are to be captured and related to each other, we need to understand how developers of a product family handle variability and various problems associated with it. I use Grounded Theory Method (Strauss and Corbin 1990) to develop a traceability model comprising of concepts representing knowledge elements related to variability. It includes appropriate relationships among the various concepts identified. Data collection and analysis were done iteratively, and analysis was progressively directing collection. Data collected using multiple methods were used for triangulation.

Grounded theory approach is an inductive theory development methodology. Since there has not been extensive research done on identifying the knowledge elements to be captured and linked with each other to facilitate effective variability management in software product families, a generative approach like grounded theory method is suitable. Also, grounded theory ap-

Figure 1: Research Phases

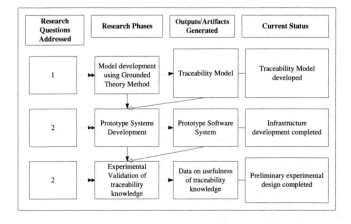

Research Questions Addressed	Research Phases	Outputs/Artifacts Generated	Current Status
1	Model development using Grounded Theory Method	Traceability Model	Traceability Model developed
2	Prototype Systems Development	Prototype Software System	Infrastructure development completed
2	Experimental Validation of traceability knowledge	Data on usefulness of traceability knowledge	Preliminary experimental design completed

proach is an appropriate method to generate theory rooted in practice. Here, I develop a traceability model that is grounded in practice, and that is reflective of what is done and needed by product family developers for variability management. Data collection was done from two sites, which facilitated comparison and elaboration of concepts that emerged from one to those from the other.

3.1.1 Description of the sites

One of the data collection sites is a software development firm (WMSCo) involved in the development of a warehouse management system (WMS) that is used to handle inventory sent to and from warehouses depending on orders from customers. WMSCo has developed a 'base' version of the product, which encompasses most of the functionality required by its entire customer base.

The second site is an organization (ECTCo) that develops software for electronically controlled diesel engines. They develop a core software build that can be used in different types of engines with customizations.

Six developers were interviewed from WMSCo. Two developers and a project manager were interviewed from ECTCo. The interviews were semi-structured and focused on how developers manage variability and the various issues faced by them. The total duration of all the interviews is about 34 hours. Project-related documents were also used as data sources. The purpose of these interviews was to get insights into the critical aspects of variability management and the specific needs faced by product family developers to manage knowledge about variability. Subjects were questioned about variability scenarios that they had handled in the past, and the needs for variability-related knowledge. The interviews were selectively transcribed and coded. Data analysis was done using open coding, axial coding and selective coding (Strauss and Corbin 1990) in an iterative and overlapped fashion. This process of iterative coding led to the generation of the traceability model discussed below.

The nodes in Figure 2 represent physical or conceptual objects involved in product family development. The links between them represent traceability between them. Variability demanded by variable requirements is made explicit by variation points incorporated in various design objects. These variation points are implemented using appropriate techniques or mechanisms. Variation points are bound to specific variant end products.

3.2 Phase 2: Prototype Systems Development

A prototype software system has been developed to demonstrate the feasibility of establishing traceability to support variability management using the traceability model. Functionalities in the system that addresses these requirements are described in Table 1.

Figure 3 shows the architecture of the prototype system. The arrows in the figure represent information and request flows.

3.3 Phase 3: Experimental Validation

Past research has investigated the effect of documentation on design and maintenance quality. Maintenance performance has been used in several studies as a dependent variable (Banker et al. 1998). I argue that the use of traceability knowledge as specified by the model in Figure 2, will significantly reduce the maintenance effort and enhance the maintenance quality. Also, I argue that maintenance task complexity will partially moderate the effect of traceability knowledge on maintainability of the design.

Figure 2: Traceability Model for Variability Management

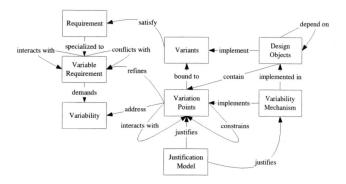

Table 1: Requirements and Capabilities of the Prototype System

Requirement	Capability
Structuring traceability knowledge	Diagrammatic interface to represent traceability knowledge and a knowledge schema that controls the trace data types and link types
Linking to design artifacts	Integration with work productivity and development tools
Identifying artifacts that are impacted by changes	Truth maintenance system: Propagation of status changes to related elements
Linking to knowledge elements of other projects	Facility to link elements from multiple models and sub-models
Tool-independent use of knowledge	HTML publisher that generates a HTML page with embedded pictures of the traceability knowledge captured with descriptions

Figure 3: Prototype System Architecture

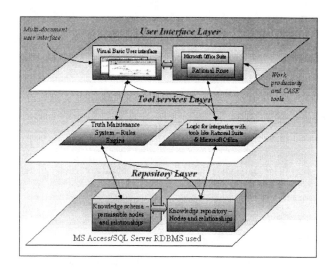

A 2x2 factorial design is appropriate as there is one independent variable and one moderator variable with 2 levels (Figure 5). Each subject will be provided a product family design model. Half of the subjects will receive designs that are supported by traceability knowledge documented using our traceability model and the other half will receive designs with standard documentation. UML has been used to create the product family design model. The subjects will be asked to perform maintenance tasks on each of the design model. The independent and moderator variables are operationalized by the treatment. Expert ratings on objective complexity of the tasks would be used as a measure for task complexity. The subjects will be asked to keep track of the time taken to solve each task. Expert ratings of the quality of the subjects' performance will be used as a measure for maintenance quality. We will test for differences due to demographic variables like experience to systems design using Unified Modeling Language and experience in performing maintenance tasks. Multiple Analysis of Variance (MANOVA) will be used to analyze the data.

4. EXPECTED CONTRIBUTIONS

The traceability model developed in this dissertation will provide a reference framework that can be tailored to project-specific needs. The capture and use of traceability knowledge is expected to enhance maintainability of the system. The key contributions of this dissertation are as follows:

- Traceability Model - Identification of useful knowledge elements related to variability.
- The prototype software system that provides tool support for traceability.

Figure 4: Conceptual Model to be tested

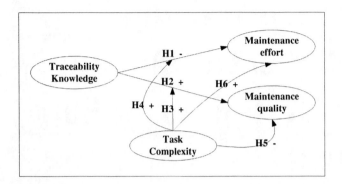

This research is expected to contribute to both theory and practice. Research can focus on tailoring the model produced to suit to different types of product families by identifying specific attributes of these families. Practitioners can use the models developed here as a reference to identify specific elements of knowledge that are to be captured to facilitate effective variability management.

5. LIMITATIONS AND FUTURE RESEARCH

The system that has been developed and used to demonstrate the usefulness of the traceability knowledge is just a research prototype. An industry standard implementation with user-friendly interfaces is beyond the scope of this work. Use of students as subjects for the experimental validation might pose a threat to external validity.

Figure 5: Factorial Design with Repeated Measures

	Complexity	
	Simple	Complex
With standard documentation	Group G11	Group G12
With traceability knowledge structured using our model	Group G21	Group G22

In this dissertation, the focus is on managing variability than on managing commonality. Future research will identify various issued related to commonality in product families and focus on traceability for product platforms. Development of appropriate sub-models that are related to specific elements in the traceability model developed in this dissertation, will be a potential research direction. Identification and retrieval of patterns of process knowledge capture is another area of research we are currently investigating.

6. FEEDBACK SOUGHT

In this dissertation, three different methodological paradigms have been used, viz., grounded theory approach (to develop the traceability model), design research methodology (to demonstrate the feasibility of the traceability approach by building a prototype system), and experimental approach (to evaluate the usefulness of the traceability knowledge in managing variability). I would like to have feedback on the appropriateness of such a combination of approaches to developing and validating a solution. As part of this dissertation, an experimental approach is used to evaluate the usefulness of the traceability knowledge in managing variability, but the various capabilities of the prototype system are yet to be evaluated. Several knowledge management based approaches have been proposed in the past to solve different problems in managing knowledge intensive processes. I would like to have suggestions on various validation techniques and the theoretical background that can be used to evaluate the effectiveness of knowledge management based approaches and the capabilities of the associated prototype systems.

7. REFERENCES

Banker, R., G. Davis and S. Slaughter (1998). "Software development practices, software complexity and software maintenance performance: A field study." *Management Science* 44(4): 433-450.

Bronsword, L. and P. Clements (1996). A Case Study in Successful Product Line Development. *Pittsburgh, PA*, Software Engineering Institute, Carnegie Mellon University.

Conklin, E. J. and M. Begeman (1988). GIBIS: A hypertext tool for exploratory policy discussion. *Proceedings of CSCW'88*.

Gotel, O. C. Z. and A. C. W. Finkelstein (1994). An Analysis of Requirements Traceability Problem. *IEEE International Conference on Requirements Engineering*, Colorado Springs, IEEE Computer Society Press.

Strauss, A. and J. Corbin (1990). Basics of Qualitative Research: Grounded Theory Procedures and Techniques. Newbury Park, CA, Sage Publications.

APPENDIX

Detailed Dissertation Plan

Developing and Optimizing Distribution Model of Electronic Supply Chain Management System in Indian Context

Satyendra Kumar
Doctoral Student, Indian Institute of Management, Ahmedabad, India
FPM House - 14, IIMA Campus, Vastrapur, Ahmedabad, India - 380015
+91-79-6324121 (O), 6327914(R), 6306896 (Fax)
satya@iimahd.ernet.in

ABSTRACT

The proposed study will develop a framework to assess the electronic supply chain management model based on the existing literature and the impact of information technology (IT) and electronic commerce (EC) on supply chain management (SCM). The framework will result in recognizing the structure, operations, and performance indicators of electronic supply chain in Indian context and optimizing the various variables considered. It will provide an interdisciplinary view of electronic commerce and supply chain modeling.

1. INTRODUCTION

Firms are facing intense competition in today's global business environment. They have to produce quality products at competitive prices with uncertain demand. To be competitive, a firm has to quickly respond to demand fluctuations, competition, and new market opportunities. Lagging the competition even slightly can be a threat to the viability of the business. In addition, businesses need to be increasingly customer-driven and more efficient both in the operations and in interaction with suppliers and partners. All these require a very efficient supply chain management.

1.1 Impact of IT and EC on SCM

Information technology is a critical enabler of effective supply chain management. Indeed, much of the current interest in supply chain management is motivated by the opportunities that appeared due to abundance of data and the savings that can be achieved by sophisticated analysis. Moreover, Internet is emerging as the most efficient way of sharing information between the globally dispersed partners and allowing them to address international markets. This has changed the nature of competition and firms' are forced to adopt electronic commerce.

Electronic Commerce is transforming the marketplace by changing firms' business model, by transforming relations among market actors, and by contributing to changes in market structure. It provides the opportunities for economic growth created by organizational change. It also creates the possibility of new models for organizing production and transacting business, by offering complementary products / services in business models.

One of the major effects of electronic commerce on supply chain management system is the emergence of Internet enabled distribution channel. The two of the most prominent sales channel on the Internet are *direct sales via Company Web sites* and *sales via Electronic Marketplaces* [Keskinocak and Tayur, 2001]. These distribution channels may require a different supply chain structure (number of echelon levels, location of warehouses, etc.) and policy (inventory and transportation policy).

1.2 Context

Firms are investing in electronic supply chain systems as it can create value at two levels: *increased visibility across the supply chain, and online sharing of information and collaboration between supply chain partners.* The online information sharing between the supply partners includes information related to orders, stock position, transportation details, etc. Theoretically, the electronic supply chain will lead to operate the functions of supply chain in more efficient and cost effective manner. The broader issue the firms are facing is how they can extract the benefits of electronic supply chain, what should be their supply chain structure, which operations they should automate, etc.

2. LITERATURE REVIEW

The theoretical foundation of the proposed study will be based on supply chain optimization, impact of information technology and information sharing on supply chain management, and Internet enabled distribution channel.

2.1 Supply Chain Optimization

The two major elements of supply chain optimization i.e. inventory and distribution models have attracted much attention from academics and practitioners.

At the discrete level, inventory model is designed to address two fundamental issues: when to replenish and how much be the order quantity, whereas a distribution model is designed to minimize the cost of distributing products located at a central facility to geographically dispersed facilities with different objectives to meet such as, minimization of variable distribution cost, optimization of fleet size, and minimization of delivery time. Much of the interest now lies in integrated distribution-inventory models.

One of the first papers that consider an integrated distribution-inventory has been done by Burns et al. (1985). They derived formulas for transportation and inventory costs, and determined the trade-off between these costs. Further, they analyzed and compared the two distribution strategies; direct shipping and peddling. Anily and Federgruen (1990) discussed a similar problem with a depot and many dispersed retailers to determine feasible replenishment strategies to minimize long run average transportation and inventory costs.

2.2 Information flow in Supply Chain

One of the important components of SCM is to manage the information flow between the partners in multi-stage production-distribution networks. Identifying and managing information requirements in the supply chain for decision-making process are becoming critical. Many authors have even argued that information flow within the chain can be a substitute to the inventory. Chen (1999) have shown that the information lead-time plays the similar role as the production / transportation lead-time in the determination of the optimal replenishment strategies; information lead-time being less costly.

Lee and Whang (2000) have discussed various types of information to be shared as inventory, sales, demand forecast, order status, and production schedule. Cachon and Fisher (2000) studied the value of sharing demand and inventory data. Chen et al. (2000) quantified the bullwhip effect and Lee et al. (2000) quantified the information sharing in a supply chain.

2.3 Information Technology and Supply Chain

Geoffrion and Krishnan (2001) discussed the prospects of Operations Research (OR) in the Electronic Commerce era. In a similar context, Sodhi (2001) provides a detailed example showing the use of Electronic Resource Planning (ERP) and Advanced Planning and Scheduling (APS) in a Web-enabled supply-chain environment for an electronics company.

2.4 Internet enabled distribution channel

Firms can have multiple benefits using the Internet as a distribution channel. The benefits include lower transactional cost, improved service level, ability to cater customer's preferences, etc. [Keskinocak and Tayur, 2001]. The Internet can provide value from increased visibility and collaboration among the supply chain partners, which refers to the ability to use the common information base. Because of its characteristics and foreseen benefits, Internet can be considered as a global virtual market distribution channel [Rahman and Raisinghani, 2000].

3. RESEARCH QUESTIONS

The research objective is *"to develop and optimize the distribution model of electronic supply chain in Indian context"*. The proposed study will be addressing following research questions:

*   *How the distribution model of electronic supply chain is different from the traditional supply chain in terms of structure, lead-time, inventory policy, cost elements, pricing structure, etc.?*
*   *How the distribution model of electronic supply chain can be optimized?*

4. RESEARCH METHODOLOGY

The proposed research will be an exploratory study to develop and optimize the distribution model of electronic supply chain in Indian context. The research will be using multiple methodologies to answer the research questions.

4.1 Conceptual Model

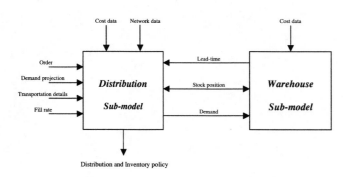

Distribution and Inventory policy

4.2 Research Approach

The broad approach of this research is appended in the following steps:

*   We have first assessed the supply chain theories and models in the context of electronic commerce era. One of the comprehensive supply chain models was discussed by Cohen and Lee (1988). Since, our study is limited to distribution model; we focused only on *Warehouse & Distribution Sub-models* from the above-mentioned comprehensive model. We further introduced the relevant variables based on *Electronic Supply Chain* context and thus formulated the conceptual model (Refer-Figure 1)
*   The conceptual model, formulated from theoretical inputs, requires a thorough verification for completeness of all the variables in the conceptual model. For this we adopted the case methodology approach. We have done comprehensive case studies with the three manufacturing organizations, which has implemented Web application for doing business, and studied their supply chain operations related to distribution. The profile of the studied organizations varies from *Industrial Product* to *Fast Moving Consumer Goods* with varied supply chain structure and operations. This has captured the issues involved in the distribution of electronic supply chain in Indian context.

*   The case studies with the organizations verified the variables considered in the conceptual model and provided the cost elements. We are in a process to formulate and optimize the generic model of the electronic supply chain for the specific industry taking the issues and cost elements from the case-studies. The model will address the worthiness of performing different operations through online computer applications. For example: the FMCG firm is dealing with a single inventory product. The majority of the plant production is consumed in a nearby metropolitan city. Now, through modeling approach (Refer-Appendix A) we will try to find out whether the online stock information at these retail outlets will be beneficial for the company. The approach will be to find out the total expected contribution with and without perfect stock information. The difference between the two cases and the total cost for the online information sharing and processing will allow deciding whether the online information sharing will help the firm.

5. SIGNIFICANCE OF THE STUDY

The aim of the study is to address the issues involved in the distribution model of electronic supply chain in Indian context, where currently limited knowledge exists. This study will address some current questions facing the Indian organizations to efficiently manage their logistics in electronic commerce era. It will result in recognizing the structure and operations of electronic supply chain and a framework for optimizing the various variables considered. It will provide an interdisciplinary view of electronic commerce and supply chain modeling.

REFERENCES

Anily, S., and Federgruen A. "One warehouse multiple retailer systems with vehicle routing costs", *Management Science,* Vol. 36, No. 1, January 1990, pp. 92-114.

Burns, L. D., Hall R. W., Blumenfeld, D. E., and Daganzo C. F. "Distribution strategies that minimizes transportation and inventory costs", *Operations Research,* Vol. 33, 1985, pp. 469-490.

Cachon, G. P., and Fisher M. "Supply Chain Inventory Management and the Value of Shared Information", *Management Science,* Vol. 46, No. 8, August 2000, pp. 1032-1048.

Chen, F. "Decentralized Supply Chains Subject to Information Delays", *Management Science,* Vol. 45, No. 8, Aug. 1999, pp. 1076-1090.

Chen, F., Drezner Z., Ryan J. K., and Simchi-Levi D. "Quantifying the Bullwhip Effect in a Simple Supply Chain: The Impact of Forecasting, Lead-times, and Information", *Management Science,* Vol. 46, No. 3, March 2000, pp. 436-443.

Cohen, M. A., and Lee H. L. "Strategic analysis of integrated production-distribution systems: Models and methods", *Operations Research,* Vol. 36, No. 2, Mar-Apr 1988, pp. 216-228.

Geoffrion, A. M., and Krishnan R. "Prospects for Operations Research in the E-Business Era", *Interfaces,* Vol. 31, No. 2, Mar-Apr 2001, pp. 6-36.

Keskinocak, P., and Tayur S. "Quantitative Analysis for Internet-Enabled Supply Chains", *Interfaces,* Vol. 31, No. 2, Mar-Apr 2001, pp. 70-89.

Lee, H. L., So K. C., and Tang C. S. "The value of Information sharing in a two-level supply chain", *Management Science,* Vol. 46, No. 5, May 2000, pp. 626-643.

Lee, H. L., and Whang S. "Information sharing in a supply chain", *International Journal of Technology Management,* Vol. 20, Nos. 3/4, 2000, pp. 373-387.

Rahman, S. M., and Raisinghani M. S. "Electronic commerce: Opportunity and Challenges", *Idea Group Publishing,* 2000.

Sodhi, M. S. "Applications and Opportunities for Operations Research in Internet-Enabled Supply Chains and Electronic Marketplaces", *Interfaces,* Vol. 31, No. 2, Mar-Apr 2001, pp. 56-69.

APPENDIX - A

Model Formulation

Sets

➤   r: Retailer
➤   p: Product

➢ v: Vehicle

Parameters

➢ X_{rp}: Quantity of product 'p' demanded at retail outlet 'r' (litres)
➢ $F_{rp}(X)$: The probability density-function of demand at retail outlet 'r' for product 'p'.
➢ US_p: Understocking cost of product 'p' (Rs. per litre)
➢ OS_p: Overstocking cost of product 'p' (Rs. per litre)
➢ N: Number of vehicles in the transportation system (number)
➢ VL: Vehicle capacity load (crates)
➢ Cap_r: Storage capacity at retail outlet 'r' (crates)
➢ Sup_p: Available supply of product 'p' (crates)
➢ Stk_{rp}: Stock of product 'p' available at retail outlet 'r' (litres)
➢ Qty_{rp}:Total quantity of product 'p' available at retail outlet 'r' for meeting the demand (litres)

Variables

➢ Q_{vrp}: Quantity of product 'p' to be delivered at retail outlet 'r' by vehicle 'v' (crates)
➢ Y_v: Is 1 if the vehicle 'v' is used for delivery purposes, otherwise 0 (binary decision variable)
➢ D_{rv}: Is 1 if the vehicle 'v' is used to deliver at retail outlet 'r', otherwise 0 (binary decision variable)

Note:

➢ A crate is a plastic container, which can hold 10 litres of milk.

➢ $Qty_{rp} = 10 * (\sum\limits_{v} Q_{vrp} + Stk_{rp})$

Objective function

The objective is to minimize the total expected understocking and overstocking cost at each retail outlet for each product.

$$E(z) = \sum_{p}(\sum_{r}(\int_{0}^{Qtyrp}(Qtyrp - Xrp).frp(X).dx)*OSp) + \sum_{p}(\sum_{r}(\int_{Qtyrp}^{\infty}(Xrp - Qtyrp).frp(X).dx)*USp)$$

Constraints set

➢ $$\sum_{v}\sum_{p}Qvrp \leq Capr$$

➢ $$\sum_{r}\sum_{p}Qvrp \leq Yv * VL$$

➢ $$\sum_{v}\sum_{r}Qvrp \leq Supp$$

➢ $$\sum_{v}Yv \leq N$$

➢ $$\sum_{p}Qvrp \leq Dvr * VL$$

➢ Non-negativity constraint.

Research on the Technology for Systems Design of E-Business

Masaru Makino
Associate Prof., Fukui University of Technology
3-6-1 Gakuen, Fukui City, 910-8505, Japan
E-mail: m-makino@ccmails.fukui-ut.ac.jp

ABSTRACT

The objectives of this paper are to study and investigate recent technologies concerning systems-design for virtual enterprise.

Recently we have global E-XX systems utilizing internet and server/client computers, such as E-Business, E-Commerce, E-Community, E-Learning, E-Government, and so on. Moreover we hear so often Mobile Computing and Ubiquitous Computing.

In this paper, the author pays considerable attention to E-Business, especially systems-design technology of E-Business. Generally we have four steps in systems design those are process of Plan, Do, Check, Action. P/D/C/A steps of this paper are as follows. First step P: We describe systems-design layer that is triple technological layer of application/middle/base. Second step D: The author introduces virtual enterprise that is composed of significant software and an instance of E-Business (B to B). Third step C: The author makes an original proposal that is tradeoff-valuation approach (TVA) between systems and security. Tradeoff means an exchange in which benefit is given up for another considered more desirable. Final step A: We have conclusion and estimated issues. These are to be activated works between in systems-design activity and in a bit future activity.

1. SYSTEMS-DESIGN LAYER

As shown in Table 1, the author asserts that the systems-design of E-Business has three points of view in its technological layer as follows.
1) Application layer such as Design Policy & Planning, Purchase Sys., Inventory Sys., Production Sys., Sales Sys., Receipts & Payment Sys., and Security Sys.
2) Middle layer such as Web Service, XML-Database, and Security Sys.
3) Base layer including the platform of E-Business, Server Operating Sys., and Security Sys.

The author presents submission that we would be able to make concept of systems design of E-Business by utilizing this triple layers. In case of consider systems-design, which direction do you select from top-down or bottom-up in this triple layer?

The answer of this issue depends on as the case may be that application oriented or base layer oriented is selected by needs of various situations of virtual enterprise. We design the systems not that usually from zero-based system but that often as revised-based system.

The author asserts that the most important technology for development of information systems is "Systems Design", and again asserts that the systems design of information application systems has double side of view which is main object-activity and keeping "SECURITY". Therefore in table 1 SECURITY SYS is bold typed on each three layers.

2. SIGNIFICANT SOFTWARE IN VIRTUAL ENTERPRISE

As shown in table 1, systems-design layer is in virtual enterprise. The author says that virtual enterprise isn't equal to real company. One of the greatest difference between virtual enterprise and real company is that virtual enterprise does not necessarily compose from single company but also often is composed from plural and omplex companies. Each layer has various sort of software-packages related with E-Business. To take a few examples, Layer'!has CRM (Customer Relationship Management), ERP (Enterprise Resource Planning), SCM (Supply Chain Management), and DWH(Data Warehouse). Layer a‡has Web Service software those are SOAP (Simple Object Access Protocol), WSDL (Web Service Description Language), UDDI (Universal Description Discovery Integration), XML-Database, and SQL Database. Layer b‡has server OS, and server-side significant software.

As for security systems in three layers, we have much security software such as Firewall-soft, PKI-soft, VPN-soft, Cipher-soft, Busting Virus-soft, Digital Money soft, and so on. We utilize these software as for encrypting business-document, digital certificates, detecting privacy, tracing hacking-route, seeking business-scam, access control and restriction, securing electronic money, packet filtering, discovering spoof etc.

3. AN INSTANCE OF E-BUSINESS (B TO B)

E-Business (B to B) has business-transaction data from business companies to business companies thorough internet communication.

3.1 Security System in Payment Activity

As shown in Fig.1, E-Business server-computer supervises business transaction-data with seller and buyer. Real seller and buyer in this system generally do not meet face to face mutually. The company or enterprise is often virtual, therefore security information for seller and buyer is exceedingly important in these systems.

Figure 1: E-Business (B to B) (Note: E-Business Server has condition with credit, insurance, etc.

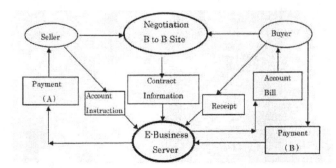

Table 1: Systems Design/Layer

			Virtual Enterprise
I	Application Layer	I	Design Planning/ Purchase Sys./ Inventory Sys./ Production Sys. / Sales Sys./ Receipts & Payment Sys./ **SECURITY SYS.**
II	Middle Layer	II	Web Service/ XML-Database/ **SECURITY SYS.**
III	Base Layer	III.	Platform/ Server Operating Sys./ **SECURITY SYS.**

Especially payment(B) and receipt are most important in Fig1. We must be exceedingly careful in selecting any sort of electronic and digital moneys those are E-credit, E-check, E-transfer, and any E-money (IC-card, Cyber cash, etc.). These electronic and digital money are recently called high-tech money which involves cellular phone & electronic wallet and other mobile & ubiquitous unit.

We utilize certification system for the purpose of certifying seller and buyer whether he is real being or false being. False being is called as spoof. It is not easy to perceive the truth in business transaction. However we must approach nearly risky situation for the purpose of getting profit. Generally we often hear that business management is challenge to the risk. Risk on the business activity often occurs as the criminal act of money trouble.

Therefore the author suggests that we should prepare the payment systems as much as various sorts of cases. Then we must select the payment system according to the significance of business relationship. Moreover the author says that E-Business has relationship with E-Banks (Finance), E-Commerce (General, Auction, Mail order Sys.), E-Government (Certification Sys.), E-Insurance, E-Community, and so on.

3.2 Dynamic and fresh Contents in E-Business Site-System

The contents of business-transaction site are most important for the success of business negotiations in E-Business system. Popularity of contents in web-site depends on break-through of technology. Technological popularity in present time is as follows. The author says that contents will be realized by combination of these technologies.
a) XML-Database
b) Video-Streaming
c) IP-Multicast
d) Web-3DCG
e) Interactive Communication
f) Mobile & Ubiquitous Computing

Java program, XML-multimedia source data and special program concerned with technologies ((a) ~ (f)) will be able to make dynamic contents of E-Business site systems.

3.3 The age of XML revolution in E-Business

The author asserts that we should meet the age of XML revolution in E-Business which is the next generation E-Business as follows.
1) E-Business systems would change in its style by XML systems.
2) E-Business systems would separate from one system to two or more subsystems.
3) E-Business systems would consist of inner system, middle system and outer system those are backend system, middle system and front-stage system.
4) E-Business systems would have connectivity between web-site and transaction systems those have continuity from portal site to transaction processing systems
5) The general aspect of XML revolution has new generation workflow systems in the next generation IT society.

4. TRADEOFF-VALUATION APPROACH (TVA) IN SYSTEMS DESIGN OF E-BUSINESS

4.1 Conceptual thinking of Tradeoff-Valuation Approach (TVA)

The author guesses that you know relationship between prices and employment in the economical society. If prices would be going up, then employment opportunities have more and more expanded. This relationship is approved in opposite situation. That is to say, if prices would be falling then employment opportunities have less and less become narrow, and as a logical consequence unemployment increases more and more. This relationship is defined as that A and B are in the tradeoff-relationship with each other.

In systems design, we expect much profit that is brought by the result of object-activity which is business transaction or systems model. However profit doesn't come true without security systems.

In this paper, the author suggests the next hypothetical formula in systems design.

Profitability = Feasibility + Security
Feasibility is expecting result of object-activity in systems design. Object-activity is brought from each system/subsystem in each layer of the table

1 which is exclusive of security systems. That is to say, feasibility is active technology on the other hand security is passive technology.

The author says that we would be able to see tradeoff-relationship between active technology and passive technology. So if we might reject passive technology then we could not realize expecting better result of active technology.

In this paper, the author asserts that we would be able to estimate necessary valuation of each system/subsystem by utilizing tradeoff-relationship as shown in the table2.

Information-systems security is in connection with C/I/A-A/A/R in the table 2. C/I/A-A/A/R are regulated in JIS X 5080, ISO/IEC 17799, BS 7799, ISO/IEC 15408. In this paper, the author would like to discuss relationship between C/I/A-A/A/R and tradeoff-valuation. Then we should be aware of the fact that the Table 2 is in connection with each layer of the Table 1.

Table 2: Tradeoff-Valuation Approach (TVA)

Sys Security	Sys/Sub A	Sys/Sub B	Sys/Sub C	Valuation
C/I/A	a	b	c	
A/A/R	m	n	o	
Others				
P				

Notes 1 : C/I/A is regulated as Security Policy.
C (Confidentiality),I(Integrity),A(Availability)
Notes 2 : A/A/R is regulated as Security Design.
A(Accountability),A(Authenticity),R(Reliability), P(Profitability)
Notes 3 : Estimated numerical value (earnings and costs) is written in each box.
a,b,c,~ = Earning (in Feasibility), m,n,o,~ = Loss (in Security)
Each row has similar meaning in each box.
Notes 4 : Tradeoff-Valuation Approach(TVA) / Masaru Makino, All rights reserved.

4.2 Procedure of Tradeoff-Valuation Approach (TVA)

For the purpose of filling Table 2 by value of sys/sub and cost of development for security system, the author asserts that we must have forward procedure as follows.

We have 4 steps of these procedures as shown in Fig 2.

Procedure I: This is the procedure concerned with management control. This procedure has sub-procedures, those are sales profit, sales amount, shared cost, cost of advertisement, and so on.

Procedure II: This is the procedure of software development. This procedure has sub-procedures, those are the cost of web application software, security concerned software, and so on.

Procedure III: This is the procedure of system operation control. This procedure has sub-procedures, those are outsourcing cost, organization measures cost, security measures cost, and so on.

Procedure IV: This is the procedure of web concerned technology analysis. This procedure has sub-procedures, those are portal site analysis, top-page hit number, search engine analysis, access log analysis (keyword and access person analysis), web-site analysis (link situation, site

Fig. 2 Procedure of TVA

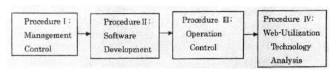

design etc.).

The author asserts that we must use these procedure ('!^ÿc!) for feasibility estimation of system/subsystems, and for security estimation of C/I/A or A/A/R in the Table 2. And moreover we must estimate other items for profit and loss situation.

We should always be aware of balancing for management and technologies those are great importance of trade-off valuation approach (TVA).

5. CONCLUSION

In this paper the author asserts the following conclusion on the technology for systems-design of E-Business. (1) Triple systems-design layer : We have triple layer for systems design of E-Business as shown in Table 1 those are Application, Middle, Base. (2) Virtual-enterprise software : We have significant software in virtual enterprise on each of the triple layer. (3) An instance of E-Business : The author gives typical model those are security system in payment activity and dynamic & fresh contents in E-Business site-system. (4) Tradeoff-valuation Approach : The author presents original Tradeoff-Valuation Approach (TVA) in systems design of E-Business by using the Table 1, Table 2 and the procedure of TVA (Proc.'!^ÿc!).

6. ESTIMATED ISSUES

In this paper, the author has issues that we should take measures to meet the new situation in the short distant future. Information-systems and computer-environment change year by year. Computer and network technology makes progress with tremendous speed. Therefore the author should always have preparation for the next step. For example of issues are (1) Connection and Balancing between E-Business and E-Government especially digital certificates or detecting privacy, (2) Social Security for Business scam, (3) Revolution on Virtual Enterprise, and so on.

REFERENCES

(1) Masaru Makino, " Security Systems Design for MIS/OA related with Computer Network ", Proceedings of 2000 MIS/OA International Conference, KMIS(Korea MIS Society), June 2000, pp.205-208.

(2) Yuusei Ishida, Masaru Makino, " Study on Cyber Information Security ", Memories of Fukui University of Technology (No.32), March 2002, pp.327-334.

(3) Masaru Makino, " Research for the SECURITY systems-design of information application-systems", Memories of Fukui University of Technology (No.31), March 2001, pp.313-319.

(4) Japan IBM Corp., " Developers guide of WebSphere-Application Server ", Pierson Education Corp., May 2001.

(5) Japan IBM Corp., "Approaches to the Next Generation of e-business", ProVISION (No.32), Winter 2002.

(6) IEEE Computer society, " Computer (September 2002) ", IEEE, September 2002.

(7) IEEE Computer society, " Computer (August 2002) ", IEEE, August 2002.

(8) IPSJ, "Revolution of Network Technologies to Support the Ubiquitous Computing Environment ", IPSJ Information Processing Magazine, Vol.43 No.6, June 2002.

(9) IPSJ, "Multi-Cast Technology", IPSJ Information Processing Magazine, Vol.42 No.8, August 2001.

(10) Kureha Odera, Others, "Intelligible ISMS (Information Security Mgt. Sys.)", NikkeiBP, August 2002.

(11) Bill Brogden, " Perfect guide of SOAP Programming by Java (Japanese Edition)", Technologies Criticism Corporation, November 2002.

(12) Web site concerned with IT (Information Technology): www.xmlconsortium.org/, www.unisys.co.jp, www.honda.co.jp/ACCESS/, www.sony.co.jp/index.html, www.verisign.co.jp, www.isms.jipdec.or.jp/, www.microsoft.com/japan/msdn, www.ibm/jp/services/ www.ebiz-ex.com/

State Certification of PK-12 Computer Teachers

Lawrence Tomei
Duquesne University, tomei@duq.edu

INTRODUCTION

Nearly all 50 states acknowledge severe shortages of teachers in most academic content areas. The need for teachers is particularly great in math, science, special education, foreign languages, bilingual education, and technology (Kronholz, 1997). Perhaps the hardest content area to secure qualified classroom teachers is technology (Volk, 1997). Professional education preparation programs are taking on renewed vigor as state departments of education clamor to certify their PK-12 (Preschool/Kindergarten to Grade 12) classroom computer teachers.

Educator proficiencies and standards are typically adopted by a board of education that has been given responsibility for educator preparation programs and specific certification areas meant to address a relevant knowledge base and skills set. Preparation programs provide relevant field-based experiences in a variety of educational settings with diverse student populations, including observation, modeling, and demonstration of promising practices to improve student learning.

The certification process promotes professional development and guarantees a certain level of performance with respect to classroom computer instruction. Certification also strengthens technical skills by: (a) providing for the sharing and exchanging of ideas, instructional techniques, lesson materials, and classroom procedures for use in educational computing; (b) promoting general recognition of the vital professional role played by computer technology professionals and high level of competence required for this role; and, (c) promoting and encouraging appropriate use of technology for the improvement of instruction and educational technology management.

CLASSIFICATIONS OF TECHNOLOGY CERTIFICATION

At issue, the 50 states do not agree on how to certify classroom computer teachers. In fact, there are at least seven different certification areas approved for classroom instruction in technology. Some states require only an elementary or secondary instructional certificate to teach computers. Others certify their teachers in:

- Computer Science
- Management Information Systems
- Instructional Technology
- Computer Literacy
- Business Technology
- Business Education

STATEMENT OF THE PROBLEM AND METHODOLOGY

The purpose of this study was to determine current certification procedures for classroom computer teachers as approved and administered by the 50 state departments of education. Specifically, the study sought to answer the following question. What is the predominant certification area for the PK-12 classroom computer teacher in the United States?

A short survey (Figure 1) was sent via electronic mail to each of the 50 state departments of education in an attempt to contact a representative from the credentialing, licensing, certification division. Email addresses were cho-

sen from the Council of Chief State School Officers web site seeking a state official responsible for teacher certification. Addressees were requested to complete the survey by replying to the email. If they were unable to complete the survey or if they were not the appropriate office for the response, they were requested to forward the survey to the proper certification office.

Dear State Teacher Certification Officer,

Below you will find 3 questions. We are in the data gathering phase of our research. All respondents will remain anonymous; replies with be identified only by state in the report. Copies of the final research paper will be available to all respondents upon request.

At this time, we are not interested in any other technology professionals category; only classroom computer teachers.

Initial Preparation Programs for K-12 Classroom Computer Teachers

1. The State of _____ certifies its K-12 (elementary and secondary) classroom computer teachers in …

____ a. Elementary or Secondary Education
____ b. Business Education
____ c. Computer/Information Technology
____ d. Instructional/Educational Technology
____ e. Other (please specify) _____

2. What skills/competencies/standards serve as the basis for developing the certification criteria for K-12 classroom computer teachers? If possible, please identify a link or attach a document file containing these criteria. You may select more than one alternative.

____ State standards   (URL: ___ or File Attached Y N)
____ National standards (NCATE)(URL: _____ or File Attached Y N)

____ International standards (ISTE) (URL: ____ or File Attached Y N)
____ Nat'l Bus Education Assc (NBEA)(URL: ___ or File Attached Y N)

____ Other:_____ (URL: _____ or File Attached Y N)

3. If you would like a copy of the final research paper, please provide your email address here: _____ .

Thank you for your participation in this research study.

Of the 50 states contacted, 49 responded with a completed survey. Additional research was conducted for the remaining state using their department of education web sites to determine certification requirements. The results of the survey are presented in Figure 2.

FINDINGS

Certification Areas for Classroom Computer Teachers in the US (Figure 2). By far, most states rely on traditional teacher preparation programs to groom their classroom computer teachers. Others recognize multiple certification areas as suitable for classroom computers teachers. Some states certify teachers in one or more content areas. As a result, the numbers shown in Figure 1 do not necessarily total 50 states.

Well over half of the states (38 elementary and 33 secondary) do not recognize computer technology as a discrete area of concentration. For them, any certified elementary or secondary teacher in the majority of states can teach computers.

In other states, distinct certifications are required before entering the PK-12 computer classroom. Several states call for preparation in Computer Science, Management Information Systems, Instructional Technology, Computer Literacy, or Business Technology. Three states insist exclusively on a Business Education experience for both elementary and secondary computer teachers.

CONCLUSIONS

This study determined that the predominant certification area for the classroom computer teacher in the United States remains the traditional elementary or secondary certification. For well over half of the states, computer technology is not its own area of certification. It was also later determined that there exists at this time no accepted teacher examination in technology (at least not from the Educational Testing Service, publishers of the widely accepted Praxis examinations). In 38 of the 50 states, elementary-certified teachers teach computers; in 33 states, secondary teachers take on this responsibility. In other states, Computer Science, Management Information Systems, Instructional Technology, Computer Literacy, or Business Technology certifications prepare the classroom computer teacher.

FINAL REMARKS

The classroom computer teacher has taken on a host of new responsibilities since the advent of the multimedia computer, integrated productivity tools, and the World Wide Web. Many states address the increased skills set required of the successful computer teacher. While certification offers the most consistent and professional means of ensuring adequate teacher preparation, much effort lies ahead in the search for an acceptable and mutual set of skills and competencies. This study recommends future research, especially with respect to certification, standards, teacher preparation programs, and teacher and student assessment.

Figure 2. Results of Certification Areas By Elementary and Secondary Classification

Certification Areas Applicable to Computer Teachers	Elementary Education	Secondary Education
Elementary Certificate Only	38	
Secondary Certificate Only		33
Computer Science	10	16
Management Information Systems	8	12
Instructional Technology	6	6
Computer Literacy	7	7
Business Technology	6	11
Business Education	3	3

Note: Some states recognize multiple certification areas as suitable for classroom computers teachers. As a result, the numbers shown in the figure exceed 50 states.

REFERENCES

International Society for Technology in Education (ISTE), Curriculum Guidelines for Accreditation of Educational Computing and Technology Programs, 2000-2002.

Kronholz, June. "Teacher Retirements Portend Acute Shortage," Wall Street Journal, July 24, 1997.

Volk, K. S., (1997). Going, going, gone? Recent trends in technology teacher education programs. Journal of Technology Education, 8(z), 6771.

Gathering User Needs: A Case Study on the Process Used to Gather User Needs for for the Adaptive Management Area's Forestry Portal

Balbinder Banga, Graduate Research Assistant, Oregon Health and Sciences University (OHSU), 14725 NW Glacier Way, Beaverton, Oregon, 97006, Phone: 503-671-0871, email: bangab@admin.ogi.edu

Lois Delcambre, Forestry Project Co-Director, CSE Department, OHSU; Eric Landis, Forestry Consultant; Fred Phillips, Department Head, MST Department, OHSU; Tim Tolle, Forestry Project Co-Director, US Department of Forestry

ABSTRACT

This paper will introduce the reader to the processes a cross-functional team of individuals from management, forestry, and computer science backgrounds employed to gather User Needs for a forestry Portal. Gathering User Needs prior to development is critical for the practical success of a technology project. However, more often than not, User Need surveys are forgotten and overlooked in the fast paced world of technology development. This paper will introduce the reader to some general research that has been done on the value of User Needs studies, provide some background on the Adaptive Management Area's Portal Project and then discuss in-depth the methodology and the results of the User Needs study conducted for the AMA Portal project. We will conclude the paper by presenting our findings, discussing the lessons learned and future steps in the project.

INTRODUCTION

User Needs Research:

If you build it and they will come," said Shoeless Joe Jackson's ghost in the movie, "*Field of Dreams*." Without asking for anyone's advice or opinion, Ray Kinsella built his baseball diamond and prayed that people would use it. Ray hoped for the best, but without knowing who the users were, what their needs were, and how they would use the (field of his dreams) baseball diamond., Ray was setting himself up for potential disaster.

Ray is not alone in his strategy of overlooking user needs and requirements. Although *usability* has become a buzzword for websites in the last few years, many projects still dismiss the need to conduct usability studies. Project directors assume usability studies are simply too time consuming, futile and take up too many resources. Project directors are not interested in slowing things down in the fast paced, need it yesterday world of Internet development.

Research has shown however, that spending a little more time upfront on conducting usability studies can prove to be good business. Studies show that if fixing a usability problem is $1 in the discovery phase of the project, the cost of fixing the same problem post-implementation will be between $100-$160 (McLaughlin, Intranet Journal 06/2001).

Barry W Boehm, in his book entitled *Software Engineering Economics* (Boehm 1981) analyzed sixty-three software development projects in Fortune 500 companies such as IBM, GTE and TRW. Boehm determined the ranges in cost for errors created by false assumptions in the requirements phase but not detected until later phases. The table below describes Boehm's finding that cost goes up based on the phase of the project. In his example, Boehm illustrates the cost benefit of including users in the initial requirements phase of the project as opposed to the operations phase, which can be very costly if changes have to be made based on user's input.

Relative Cost to Fix an Error

Phase in Which Found	Cost Ratio
Requirements	1
Design	3-6
Coding	10
Development testing	14-40
Acceptance testing	30-70
Operation	40-1000

Unclear user requirements continue to be the leading cause for software project failures. The Standish Group Report published in 1995 surveyed 365 IT executive managers representing over 8000 applications. One of the objectives of the study was to find out which factors cause projects to fail and be challenged. Lack of user input was the number one cause for project challenges followed by incomplete requirements and specifications and changing requirements and specifications. (The Standish Report, 1995)

Projects that fail to collect user needs may make incorrect assumptions as to what users are looking for. Catastrophic results can occur based on design decisions based on false assumptions. For example, the Johns-Manville Corporation decided to develop, manufacture and market asbestos building products. The company made the assumption that asbestos was safe to the human population. Their momentous, erroneous assumption cost the company $2 billion dollars and 52,000 law suits as residents in the area started encountering severe health problems as a result of asbestos in the air. The company eventually went bankrupt and reorganized as the Manville Company. (Gause and Weinberg, 1989)

The examples above have shown the importance and benefits that can be realized by including users in the initial design of projects. Users are central to the success or failure of a web-based project, for what use is there in *building something if they will not come.*

Background

Supported by a National Science Foundation grant, personnel from the Forest Service, Bureau of Land Management and Fish and Wildlife Service of the Pacific Northwest have joined forces with faculty and graduate students from the Oregon Health and Science University to develop a web-based portal for Pacific Northwest forestry information. The content of this portal will focus on forest ecosystem research and management. The agencies are faced with information management challenges similar to other organizations. Namely,

- increasingly diverse user base in interests, disciplines, and points of view,
- growing numbers of data and information users,
- very large amounts of information being generated and archived at multiple locations, and
- complexity in content and structure of information.

Initial activities of this three-year project focused on determining the needs and desires of the Portal's future users. For the Portal, probable users include researchers, educators, resource managers, policymakers, non-governmental organizations and the public.

Our Process

The following is a list of the tasks performed as part of our User Needs study:

- Identify the Target Audience
- Conduct Usability Interviews with Representatives of Target Audience
- Compile User Needs Statements

- Conduct User Needs Requirements Review with Interdisciplinary Team
- Write User Needs Statements Document highlighting which needs were accepted and rejected
- Conduct Retrospectives Study

Identify Target Audience

The usability team began the study by identifying the Portal's target audience. Prior to starting any user oriented study, it is critical to know exactly who the target user will be and what problem the user is trying to solve by using the product. A user is an individual who is affected by or affects the product that is being designed and, in some cases, will make or break the success of the product. For example, a study of software tools conducted at a major corporation indicated that seventy percent of tools purchased were never used. Of those tools that were used, just one person or a small group used ninety percent, even when the goal was to purchase the software for a large organization. (Gause and Weinberg, 1989)

In order to narrow down and define the target audience, representatives of the forest project interviewed people interested in agency work, natural resource scientists and agency people themselves. Through interviews and analysis, it was determined that the target audience was defined as:

Local forest communities of the Pacific Northwest, specifically those individuals on the management and research side of the public and private sectors.

With our target audience clearly defined, we could then focus on a distinct segment of the population for conducting our user interviews.

Conduct Usability Interviews with Representatives of the Target Audience

Beginning in the Spring of 2000, interviews were conducted with representatives of the targeted user population. Our goal was to gather requirements for the Adaptive Management Portal's system design. The majority of these interviews were conducted with potential information providers of the AM Portal. Many of these interviewees can be considered both providers and users of forest information and were interviewed in this light, e.g. queried from both aspects. Notes from these interviews can be reviewed at http://www.cse.ogi.edu/forest/team/phase1.html.

Interviews were conducted with PNW Research Station personnel (as information providers) to help determine what the station can do to make their information most useful and accessible to their customers. These interviews focused on information content, format, delivery, and customer profiles.

The interviewer was given a guiding questionnaire to work with so we could ensure that certain aspects of the information acquisition process were not overlooked. The following questions were available to the interviewer as a guide, but were not available to the interviewee. Certainly, not all the questions were addressed in every interview and scenario, but it was intended that the compilation of scenarios would enable the formulation of responses to all the questions with a significant degree of confidence. Below is a list of the questions that were available to the interviewers:

1. Briefly describe your current position/responsibilities.
2. What was your initial question?
3. What information, specifically, were you looking for? Did you know that it existed?
4. What information source (broker) did you use to search for the needed information? (library, WWW, backroom, personal contact, etc.) What did you like/dislike about the source you used?
5. Was there a particular information source(s) that you initially contacted? If so, why that source?
6. What tools did you use to assist with your information search? For instance, telephone, computer (if computer, pc? modem rate? OS? on a LAN?, etc.). Is this process pretty much standard for all your information searches?
7. What fields did you use to search for your information (e.g. title, creator, location, forest type, keywords, timeframe, etc.)? Do you generally use the same fields for information searching, e.g. location or author?
8. What terms did you use within these fields? Did the terms come from a standard vocabulary e.g. ITIS, HUC?
9. What formats and related software tools did you use to access, view, manipulate and use the information you located (e.g. excel, PDF, arc info, Word)? Why these formats?
10. How much time do you estimate was spent on this information inquiry? What percent of time was spent searching for it, retrieving it, reviewing it, evaluating its quality, or reformatting it for your own use?
11. Did you save the retrieved information to be used later if needed? If so, how did you organize this retrieved information (file folder, bookmark, manila folder, etc.)?
12. Was there information that you could not locate even though you were certain it existed?
13. Within your organization, did anyone besides you participate in the information acquisition process?
14. Outside of your organization, did anyone else participate in the acquisition process?
15. What was the intended purpose of the information you were seeking? Did it fulfill its purpose? If not, why?
16. Were you locating it for yourself or someone else?
17. What level of detail did you need the information to be (raw data, analysis, peer reviewed publication, newsletter, abstract, scribbled notes)?
18. How did you determine the level of quality of the information you accessed?
19. Next time you require information what will you do differently?
20. How do you feel your information searching and acquisition process could be made more efficient? (what features are missing or would be helpful (technical, organizational, etc.

Interviewees were asked to provide either responses to general inquiry regarding their information seeking and gathering behavior, or were asked to articulate an actual case of a recent information inquiry they conducted (scenario).

In all, approximately 45 interviews were conducted in person and by phone. All members of the Portal development team participated in the process, e.g., by attending interviews, reviewing the results from the interviews and suggesting follow-up questions. This full-team involvement is particularly important to assist with interdisciplinary (computer science, business management and biological science) collaboration and communication.

Compile User Needs Statements:

As a result of conducting user interviews, a list of desires and needs were identified (listed in the summary table section of this paper). Team members took the statements and used them to identify activities and attributes that were required to develop and operate the Portal. These activities and attributes were prioritized based on their importance to the overall success of the project, the level of effort and associated costs required, their feasibility and the risk involved in implementing them. Any attributes and activities not addressed were documented for later consideration.

The user community expressed a great amount of interest and excitement for the Portal. Most users rely on the Web to some degree for their information requests although the majority of the interviewees still rely on their personal contacts as their first step for information retrieval. Users generally employ various quality measurements to judge the credibility of a site principally, author's background, citations used, institution of origin.

Generally speaking, users were looking for an easy-to-use Portal which would provide them with verifiable, credible information for their research and management needs. The Pacific Northwest region is quite large and extensive, therefore the Portal development managers will have to employ great care in making the content applicable to a wide variety of subjects and information should always remain current and thorough . Users were looking for both raw data and analytical results and wanted to search for information using a variety of keyword options. Most users were Internet-savvy but still wanted some form of human interaction when it comes to assisting them if any questions arise. Users would like the Portal to be available and accessible "24x7."

A Portal that would gather and collaborate disparate islands of information into one site is highly desirable and required. For example, a forest entomologist for the Division of Forestry said that very little information on the

Web pertains to the maritime forests of Southeast Alaska. From the perspective of this user, there is a great void in information pertaining to the Alaska region.

We learned that often no records for the specific place of interest exist, so people would like to be able to search for documents about conditions that are similar to the ones of direct interest. The definition of similar may vary depending upon the question. For example, one may want to know similar with regard to climate and terrain or similar with regard to size of community. Most frequently, field biologists, foresters and other subject matter experts prepare reports, often synthesizing literature with spot observations or inventories and model results. Usually, these are for specific projects or watersheds, but always about a specific place. Their work then is usually to find out what is already known about a specific place, either in general or about a specific topic, such as the fish or the vegetation or the recreation setting. We identified 28 topics or domains that are frequently the source of information searches.

We learned that most of the agency personnel use a variety of location identifiers, some of which are used in common and some of which vary by agency, or even within an agency. On the other hand, four land classification systems are used, with as many as three different kinds used within one agency. Each federal agency seems to have its own road and trail classification and naming conventions.

Summary Table:
User comments and needs were summarized, divided into high-level categories and listed below. It is interesting to note that quite a few of these user needs are general enough to potentially be applicable to the development of Portals from other disciplines.

As we progressed along in the interview process, we noticed many of the user needs were repeated amongst several interviewees. This repetition is good news for Portal developers as it displays that users are generally interested in similar features.

Conduct User Needs Review with Interdisciplinary Team
From the list of user needs statements, team members identified activities that were required to build or develop the features. These activities were then prioritized based on their importance to the overall success of the project, the level of effort and associated costs required and the risk involved. All team members were invited to be involved in the analysis process, as together they have knowledge regarding the level of effort and time required.

The user needs review was conducted on August 28, 2002 with the technical team. Each user need was discussed and categorized:
- Category A: Need is taken care of
- Category B: More information about the need is required
- Category C1: Provide description of how or by whom it will be taken care of
- Category C2: Out of scope of the project

The meeting lasted approximately 2 hours and the end results were very positive. It was discovered that many of the user needs statements were being fulfilled in the design of the portal and those that were not were going to be discussed in the deployment plan. A good number of user needs were in fact policy related statements which the technical team could not answer. The next step in this process will be for the Forestry Department representative to discuss the policy related needs with his team.

Retrospectives Study
Reaction to the user needs study was generally positive. In the retrospectives study, (also commonly known as a post mortem review) we set out to find what worked, what didn't work, what we would do differently and any next steps that need to be taken. Some general observations are listed below:

What worked: Participants found the user needs study to be helpful as it was successful in obtaining direct feedback from end users. Technical members of the team particularly found the scenario type of user needs statements to be useful as they were able to picture how the users would utilize the system. The user needs study was also an important way of maintaining communications with the team as a whole as each member of the interdisciplinary team was involved at some level of the analysis.

What didn't work: The user needs study was spread over a one year time span. Participants felt this duration of time was too long as user's attention to the study would be unfocussed after a long duration of time. Participants also felt it would have been more beneficial to meet on a regular basis to uncover project progress and to keep team members fully engaged in the process.

What we will do differently: Although there were clear deliverables with the user needs project, it would have worked better in terms of timeline if a schedule and key milestone dates were maintained. The task list for the team was quite fluid as a result of a lack of schedule for the project. In the future, the user needs team feels there needs to be a master schedule that would maintain milestones, key deliverables, work breakdown structure and communications plan for the project.

CONCLUSIONS
The interviews that have been conducted thus far are one step in a longer user needs process. Work that preceded this interview process was centered on:
- identifying the primary activities to be supported by the portal, namely providing and seeking forest information in the form of documents and reports; and
- beginning the process of identifying the domains of interest for keywords that will be used to describe and to search for documents.

Ongoing work includes trial use of the prototype technology by field personnel and continued selection and evaluation of controlled vocabularies for the domains of interest.

The intent of the user interview method was to further incorporate user needs directly into the system design so that main decisions concerning architectural and functional requirements could be made based on user input.

Interviews of individuals and small groups of individuals continue as we move the Portal from being a "good idea" to demonstrations to prototypes, and finally to implementation. The target for full implementation on several of the sites is June, 2003.

REFERENCES
Bird, Drew. 2002 "Encouraging End User Self Sufficiency." http://www.intranetjournal.com/articles/200210/ij_10_03_02a.html

Donahue, George M. 1999. "Usability is Good Business." http://www.weinschenk.com/knowledge/usability.pdf

Donald C. Gause & Gerald Weinberg. 1989. "Exploring Requirement: Quality Before Design." Dorset House

Ivy Hooks and Kristin Farry, 2001. "Customer-Centered Products, Creating Successful Products through Smart Requirements Management." Amazon

Joseph S Dumas and Janice C Redish. 1993 "A Practical Guide to Usability Testing." Ablex PublishingCorporation

Standish Report "The Standish Group Report: Chaos." http://www.scs.carleton.ca/~beau/PM/Standish-Report.html

USER NEED DESCRIPTION

Ease of Use
- Users are looking for a well organized, fast, efficient, intuitive, free and easy to access Portal.
- Users are looking for a web-based filing system that permits reuse of retrieved documents.
- Novice portal users would like to be able to use the Portal with relative ease and minimal training. Users would like 'how to' documentation to be provided.
- Users look at document references to broaden their search and determine content and quality.
- Users would like to be able to browse for documents about related topics but do not want their mailboxes to be automatically flooded with those documents; instead they would like to be prompted about their further interest.

Credible
- Proven credibility is important to users.
- At the present time, many users rely on personal contacts for information.
- Users determine quality by researcher and institution. A few determine quality by looking at the science behind the document through research protocols and peer reviews.
- Bibliographies/ references within archived documents are important for helping users to determine quality.
- Users suggest a short background of the author and his or her affiliated organization be made available to assist in determining quality.
- Users do not want to have discussion rooms associated with the Portal, they want it to provide an easy way to store and access reliable "gray literature."

Applicable
- Users want to search for documents about a place.
- Often no records exist for the place of interest so users would like to ask about similar conditions.
- Users would like to be able to access incomplete, ongoing research activities.
- Researchers seek raw data.
- Decision makers seek assessment.
- The users of the AMA portal come from a wide variety of backgrounds and regions. Accordingly, a wide range of subjects should be covered in depth and effectively.

Personal Contact
- Site needs to employ multifaceted communication strategy (i.e. addresses, contact names, phone numbers and titles should be made available).
- Users would like a list of discipline experts to be provided.
- Users would like to be able to search by people. Questions they would like to be able to answer include: "who is working on this and how do I contact him?" "What is Lynn working on? What hypotheses is she studying?"

Searches
- Using place name as a keyword is important and using spatial location information is generally not used.
- Most contributors and users (and providers) don't use controlled vocabularies to search or archive. Some stated that they would like to use cv's if it was an accepted standard and readily available. Most users employ their personal knowledge to develop keywords for cataloguing and searching.
- Users would like to be able to search in a variety of ways, including: keywords, creator, location, timeframes, author and forest type, by bibliographies, institution specialists etc. Large categories should be broken down into smaller subtitles and more defined searches.
- Users commonly search by activity. Examples here include tree planting, thinning, burning invasive species, stream restoration, research and campground maintenance.
- Users search for documents by specific people.
- Users look for information in many formats including: reports, maps, decision records, photographs and data summaries.
- Users would like the ability to choose between the browse and search functions.

Available
- Users would like good customer service. If the information is not available on the Portal and a user calls an Information Agent, a deadline needs to be set as to when the user can expect a reply.
- Users would like the Portal to be available 24x7.

Format
- Users need to print, view and copy detailed maps, documents, PDF files, presentations, photographs and analytical results.
- Users would like to access full text documents.
- Users would like the ability to re-archive documents locally and some use bibliographic cataloguing systems.
- Users prefer the level of detail to be a white paper.
- Users would like a bulleted summary of page content to be provided
- Users would like to be able to choose whether they want to view large graphic files.

Current Information
- Users would like information to be date stamped and email updates of new or altered content should be sent if user requests it.

Thorough
- Users would like hypertext links to be made available if the user requires more in-depth information on a topic.

Bridging Knowledge Diversity in Distributed Multidisciplinary Teams

Violina Ratcheva, Lecturer in Entrepreneurship, Institute for Enterprise and Innovation, The University of Nottingham Business School, The University of Nottingham, Wollaton Road, Nottingham , NG8 1BB, United Kingdom, Tel: +44 115 8466192, E-mail:Violina.Ratcheva@nottingham.ac.uk

ABSTRACT

One way to achieve long-term competitiveness is through geographically distributed multidisciplinary teams as those can encompass diverse knowledge sources. However, previous empirical studies have shown that member heterogeneity and geographic separation hinder effective sharing and use of team knowledge. The paper explores how such teams interact to overcome the barriers and take advantage of their "built in" knowledge diversity. The findings indicate that teams lacking common background knowledge at the beginning of the project rely on their external intellectual and social communities in order to resolve team members' differences. The reported research establishes a positive correlation between team members' participation in multiple professional and social networks and teams' abilities to successfully build on their knowledge diversity.

INTRODUCTION

The key to obtaining long-term competitiveness is no longer related to the administration of existing knowledge but in the ability constantly to generate new knowledge about products and services by encouraging behaviour of continuous knowledge seeking, creation and sharing. In order to be able to do that many firms shift their organisational structures from hierarchical into flat, team-based and network-like structure in which the team, rather than the individual, has become the basic unit of production.

Geographically dispersed, multidisciplinary teams are increasingly espoused for enhancing learning and innovation (Boutellier et al, 1998; Gorton & Motwani, 1996; Madhavan & Grover, 1998; Kraut, 1999). Such teams that successfully draw on the diverse funds of knowledge of members from different intellectual and occupational backgrounds are expected to be more creative (Leonard, 1995; Madhavan & Grover, 1998) and effective (Brown & Eisenhardt, 1995).

While the potential advantages of multidisciplinary teams are theoretically attainable, empirical evidences suggest that knowledge diversity constrains effective sharing. These constraints have both occupational and contextual origins. Differences in perspectives, priorities, typical approach to problem solving and professional language can hinder understanding and team cohesion (Dougherty, 1992).

The literature on multidisciplinary teams is very limited and fragmented at this point. Providing a rational-structural definition for this type of teams, recent studies focused mainly on the team's composition aspects (Nonaka & Takeuchi, 1995; Duarte & Snyder, 1999). For example Nonaka and Takeuchi do not attend to the question of how and why would knowledge conversions take place and what processes will enhance or interfere with this task's performance. Spender (1998) argues that you cannot talk about knowing (and thus knowledge conversations) without probing the concept of the knower. Looking, therefore, only at the composition of the team is a very limited approach towards understanding the dynamics of multidisciplinary teams where knowledge conversations are taking place.

The paper explores how geographically distributed multidisciplinary teams interact to overcome the communication barriers and take advantage of their 'built in' knowledge diversity. The empirical data for this study was gathered through multi-method field research of five dispersed multidisciplinary teams. The findings indicate that often teams lack common background knowledge at the beginning of the projects and in order to resolve differences members rely on their external intellectual and social communities. The reported research establishes a positive correlation between team members' participation in multiple professional and social networks and teams' abilities to successfully build on their knowledge diversity. The findings also suggest a need to reconceptualise the boundaries of multidisciplinary teams and to consider the processes of sharing diverse knowledge in a wider social context.

SOURCES OF KNOWLEDGE DIVERSITY IN MULTIDISCIPLINARY TEAMS

The emerging literature on virtual teams (Alavi & Yoo, 1997; Cramton, 1999; Cramton & Webber, 1999; Leonard et al, 1998; Schultze & Orlikowski, 2001) provides limited insights into the effects of team dispersion. Much of this research stream focuses on the role of technology in supporting remote communication according to which team members are often selected on the basis of physical location rather than because of specialized expertise.

In the context of product and process development, researches have shown that the knowledge of individual contributors varies according to both what one does (occupation) and where one is (context). Individuals trained in a particular discipline, function or occupations have substantial conceptual and practical knowledge in common with others from that discipline or occupation (Fleck, 1997). They share terminology and mental frameworks (Vicenti, 1990) which facilitate the efficiency of communication among them. Different occupations, therefore, act as distinct 'thought worlds' (Douglas, 1986), have different funds of knowledge (what members know) and systems of meaning (how members know). Dougherty (1992) applied these concepts to organisational functions undertaking product development, and noted that, even though different functional communities were exposed to the same product development circumstances, team members from different functions understood those circumstances differently, selectively perceiving certain aspects as salient and drawing different implications. Recent research (Bechky, 1999) has focused on occupational knowledge particular to different communities such as engineers, technicians, and operators. Bechky (1999) suggested that even within the development function, occupational knowledge is sufficiently diverse as to require 'translation' in order for adequate understanding to emerge.

Contextual knowledge also pertains to the broader milieu of the working environment (Fleck, 1997; Tyre & Hippel, 1997). Many authors have noted the existence of knowledge that resides in systemic routines or ways of interacting, describing such knowledge variously as 'organising principles' (Kogut & Zander, 1992), 'embedded knowledge' (Badaracco, 1991; Granovetter, 1985) and 'organising routines' (Levitt & March, 1988; Nelson & Winter, 1982). Contextual knowledge is developed through repetitive collective actions and is "expressed in regularities by which members cooperate in a social community" (Kogut et al, 1992). It comprises knowledge of appropriate methods and resources, contributing to communication and task efficiencies and task effectiveness by leveraging taken for granted meaning associated with particular behavior within a specific setting. These associations and behaviors are learned over time from working in a specific setting, and so they are unlikely to be common knowledge among people who are not co-located. In addition, because contextual knowledge tends to be taken for granted by members of a community, it is not easily articulated to members of other communities.

MULTIDISCIPLINARY TEAMS AS INTEGRATORS OF DIVERSE KNOWLEDGE

In spite of the apparent advantages of designing teams for knowledge diversity, it is by no means clear how team members make effective use of this knowledge. Grant's (1996) observation is that knowledge integration, not knowledge itself is what generates an advantage for organisations and respectively teams. This is perhaps the most compelling explanation for why some teams comprised from the 'smartest' and 'brightest' experts still fail to perform well. Although the aggregate level of knowledge in such teams might be high, their lack of ability to integrate that knowledge can keep them from gaining any benefits from that resource pool. Knowledge integration, therefore, facilitates pollination, combination, and synthesis of diverse knowledge bases (Garud & Nayyar, 1994).

Knowledge integration is defined as the project team's ability to continually bring its members' and new external knowledge to collectively bear on the project's execution. Individually held specialist knowledge is synthesized into a new project-specific architectural knowledge. Grant (1996) describes this act as integration; others have referred to it as combination (Kogut & Zander, 1992), configuration (Henderson & Clark, 1990), and recombination (Galunic & Radan, 1998).

Penrose (1959) cautioned that the search for knowledge is so voluntary and deliberate, yet so much part of normal operations that it cannot be left outside our system of explanation. Although, organisational form and structure provide the 'bones', it is the group-level knowledge integration that provides the 'flesh and blood' (Van den Bosch et al, 1999) because that is the essence of organisational capabilities (Grant, 1996). As new product features are added, new types of specialized knowledge may be required (Penrose, 1959). As new knowledge is brought in on an as-needed basis, it must be integrated with the existing base of knowledge held by the team members. The knowledge integration therefore must be considered as a dynamic and evolving process involving collective actions (Crossan et al, 1999).

Previous studies concluded that team knowledge could be integrated through four key mechanisms: (1) directions, (2) routines, (3) transfer, and (4) sequencing (Grant, 1996). Integration through transfer is inefficient when tacit knowledge is involved. Sequential application of diverse knowledge is inefficient when multiple team members are involved in parallel execution of interdependent project tasks; it also prevents steady incorporation of new knowledge. Therefore, direction and routines provide two relatively efficient mechanisms that retain scope and flexibility.

Direction is provided by rules, directives, policies and procedures that allow specialists in different areas of expertise to integrate their knowledge without having to fully transfer it (Grant, 1996). When project tasks are relatively stable, routines help individuals to integrate their specialized knowledge without having to explicitly communicate it. Routines, therefore, support complex simultaneity and overcome the substantial knowledge losses that occur when tacit knowledge is converted to explicit knowledge in the form of rules, directives, expert systems, and heuristics.

In summary, in knowledge intensive projects executed in a dynamic technological environment, it is expected that team's ability to integrate knowledge across a diverse base of project participants will pronouncedly influence project execution success.

THEORETICAL FRAMEWORK

The ability of a project team to integrate its members' component knowledge into architectural knowledge influences its ability to execute a project successfully (Kogut & Zander, 1992). Such integration, however, is difficult to achieve because component knowledge is held tacitly at an individual level in the form of know-how, specialized skills, and individual expertise which are difficult to articulate in a team context. As previously mentioned, the knowledge creation processes are socially constructed and therefore the articulation of the tacitly held individual knowledge into a higher level collectively developed concepts, requires an appropriate context which can enable such processes to take place. However, recent studies predominantly focus on enabling context which resides inside specific companies organisational boundaries and therefore the new knowledge creation processes are well embedded in the organisational culture, routines, and established procedures developed over

period of time (Nonaka & Konno, 1998).

In contrast, the project-based teams are temporally in nature with limited lifespan, which requires to recreate the embedded, tacit practices and routines of working together every time because of the non-persistent social structure. The structural context must compensate for the loss of those social threads (Jarvenpaa & Tiller, 1999). Distributed teams, therefore, require design structure and relationships that are as agile as their markets are dynamic (Gilliers, 1999). Furthermore, unlike collocated teams operating in stable organisational environment, that largely depend on learning-before-doing (knowledge stocks), virtually operating teams must also integrate new and emergent knowledge in real time (learning-while-doing). Quick adaptation to market, technological and environment changes is therefore vital (Keil & Montealegre, 2000).

Based on the argument that knowledge can be integrated only by teams or groups (Grant, 1996), the ability of a multidisciplinary team to execute project successfully will be positively associated with the team's ability to integrate relevant knowledge, expertise and skills that might be distributed amongst team's members. Successful knowledge integration processes will be therefore largely determined by three complementary team attributes that together constitute teams' interaction context (see Figure 1): (1) interpersonal interactions and relational capital developed amongst members, (2) work organisational practices and procedures and team's ability to recognise, interpret, and value information from across its web of participant business units and the external environment, (3) cross-cultural communication behaviour.

RESEARCH METHODOLOGY

A case study methodology was adopted to investigate the factors which enable or hinder the integration of diverse knowledge in five geographically dispersed multidisciplinary teams. The study looked for establishing common patterns across the investigated teams' projects. Initially five companies were approached, operating in high-tech, knowledge intensive industries including multimedia design, software manufacturing and biotechnology. A common characteristic of the sample companies is that they went through major strategic and structural change processes in order to maintain their competitive positions. These change processes revolved around increased reliance on multidisciplinary virtual teams to handle a variety of business initiatives across organisational and country boundaries. The approached companies were asked to identify projects which involve key participants/companies from at least three physical locations.

Data was collected in two stages, through interviews, company documentation, and participant observation in project and team activities. In the first phase of the research, fifteen semi-structured interviews were conducted with potential key team players from the participant companies. Interview questions were designed to elicit information about the objectives of the projects, different understandings about team working, cultural and working practice differences amongst the participating companies. The final selection of the projects was based on the opportunities they provide to observe cross-functional and knowledge-intensive interactions.

Figure 1. Theoretical Framework

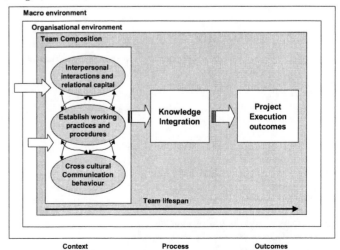

The second phase of data collection involved an intensive study of five projects identified in the first phase. All the projects were significant in terms of investment, risk and complexity and were studied during equivalent stages of the development projects. Opportunities for collecting data about each team and project were determined by the teams' current activities, and so the sources of data were quite different, although the total exposure time to each was approximately equal.

The data were analysed using content analysis and a coding scheme procedure (Weber, 1985) in order to illuminate the underlying differences between the partnerships and identify the key factors/processes affecting the teams' abilities to integrate diverse knowledge.

RESEARCH FINDINGS

The initially approached five companies showed a trend towards breaking with an old tradition of developing business. A common characteristic is that they currently develop their products or perform their operations relying entirely on partnerships which required implementation of profound changes in the organisational strategy, structure and everyday routines. Two distinctive paths in their developments were identified.

In three of the cases, the businesses were formed around an exciting idea and realised potential of working jointly across business boundaries. The team members which were former university colleagues and computer scientists in one of the cases and in another case professionals with a long standing experience from working for large corporations which felt that they do not really belong there, came together as teams because of their similar educational and professional backgrounds with clear understandings how to exploit the potential of information technologies. As one of the respondents stated: *"our futures depends on opportunities spotters rather than marketers"*.

In contrast, the other two businesses went through a long period of organisational and cultural adjustments to find a new way of radical thinking (complete changes of the product/service offered, sharing information / resources, learning to work and trust people which never met before, etc.), either forced by changing trends in the particular industry or by a new generation of the family taking over the business who was no longer excited with the founders' legacy. In both companies there was an understanding among the management team that the changing directions contradicted with some of the traditional working values. In one of the cases the changes have been accomplished by appointment of a new management team and in the other by training and development of the key staff over several years.

However, no significant differences were observed related to the factors triggering the initial formation of the investigated teams in which the above companies had key involvement. A common trend is that an opportunity is spotted or idea arises before the team is formed. The teams were formed in order to accomplish a particular project and, therefore, the team selection in all of the cases reflected on personal skills and knowledge. A similarity amongst teams was that both occupational and contextual knowledge sources were acknowledged and sought out at the teams' formation stage. Initially, when staffing the project teams, the focus was on occupational knowledge. Consistent with past research in product development, these teams were expected to leverage expertise of diverse functions and scientific fields to accomplish challenging development needs.

Clear occupational belonging of team members proved to be an influential factor during teams' initiation and formation. Because of the temporary nature of the projects, team members import to the partnerships their perception and understanding about each other's potential to contribute in terms of having an appropriate occupational knowledge. For example, *"He's electrical engineer"* or *"I'm an experimental scientist"* acted as shorthand for conveying information about distinct skills, expertise and conceptual insights that someone might bring to bear on a problem. The relationships building at that stage were based on the potential to contribute unique personal knowledge and are highly de-personalised. Team members interviewed stated that *"what others can bring to the project rather than how we feel about working with each other"* are the most important initial selection criteria. Positive expectations of members' valuable occupational knowledge, therefore, motivate participants to take a proactive part in the team, which resulted in strengthening the trustworthy relationships amongst team members and contributed to establishing more active knowledge sharing practices.

At the same time, a clear tendency to access help particular to a specific

site, led to considering the locally based or contextual knowledge as a new and distinct source of value for the development teams. In some cases understanding the context in which the product was targeted for use was critical for making appropriate social and cultural decisions regarding its design and implementation. Whenever possible, potential users of the product were intentionally sought to represent that unique viewpoint within the team. On number of occasions contextual knowledge simply entailed knowing who's to contact for further advice or resources in order to accomplish certain objectives.

An interesting relationships were observed between team members with clear occupational and others with contextual knowledge. Although acknowledged, that understanding the context in which the product/consultancy advise was targeted for use was critical for making appropriate social and cultural decisions, the occupational specialists were considered as the *"knowledgeable"* hard core of the teams and to rest was referred as *"social agents"* brought in on ad-hoc basis.

Teams which realised early in the formation stage the importance of continuously combining contextual and occupational knowledge throughout the lifespan of the partnership were more flexible in redirecting the project by recombining knowledge according to external, environmental changes such as changing customer requirements, new competitive offerings, new technological advances, etc. These external changes led to redefinition of roles and responsibilities in the team and introduction of complementary external expertise as required. This caused further changes in the team's patterns of interaction and knowledge base. Therefore, ensuring appropriate mix of expertise throughout the lifespan of the project contributed to the progress of the projects which increased members' confidence in the ability of the team.

The results of the study also confirm that social and personal relationships within a given local (physical) or virtual community were extremely effective in gaining team members 'just-in-time' access to specialist knowledge and practical skills as and when the team needed it. Through such boundary spanning activities, project teams gained access to broader and deeper skills and expertise which helped in addressing specific project issues. Teams' members, for example, regularly pulled in their collocated colleagues for assistance with practical advise or input on decisions, all of which enabled the projects to proceed to the next stage. Seeking assistance from a wider community, however, was more than just seeking additional feedback and task related assistance but also looking for moral support when faced with difficult decisions. Therefore, the intellectual, virtual or co-located communities of which members are part, became an integral part of the thinking and discovery processes and filled knowledge gaps by contributing timely and efficient access to broad expertise, practical assistance and emotional support which were not internally available.

The findings also raise number of questions such as: What is the impact of cross-cultural differences on developing collective knowledge?, What novel theoretical approaches can capture the complexity of such relationships?, How can we and should we separate in our analyses the team members from the organisations they represent and the wider community in order to gain an in-depth insight?, How to transfer the successful experience from one partnership to another?, etc.

A limitation of the reported results is that initially the participating companies rather than the partnerships were approached. The partnerships were identified based on the companies' preferences, which may have affected the validity of the results. Another limitation of this study is that because of the geographical distance of the partners involved not everybody associated with a particular project was approached during the data collection. In that respect the results presented here should be treated as preliminary.

REFERENCES

Alavi, M., & Yoo, Y. 1997. *Is Learning in Virtual Teams Real?* Boston, MA: Harvard Business School.

Badaracco, J. 1991. *The Knowledge Link.* Boston: Harvard Business School Press.

Barney, J. 1991. Firm resources and sustained competitive advantage. *Journal of Management*, 15: 175-190.

Bechky, B. 1999. Creating shared meaning across occupational communities: An ethnographic study of a production floor. *Academy of Management Conference*, Chicago, IL

Boutellier, R., Gassmann, O., Macho, H., Roux, M. 1998. Management of dispersed product development teams: The role of information technologies. *R&D Management*, 28(1): 13-26.

Brawn, J. S., & Duguid, P. 1998. Organising knowledge. *California Management Review*, 40(3): 90-111.

Brown, S., & Eisenhardt, K. 1995. Product development: Past research, present findings, and future directions. *Academy of Management Review*, 20(2): 343-378.

Cramton, C. D. 1999. *The Mutual Problem and its Consequences in Geographically Dispersed Teams*. Fairfax, VA: George Mason University.

Cramton, C. D., & Webber, S. S. 1999. *A Model of The Effects of Geographical Dispersion on Work Teams*. Fairfax, VA: George Mason University.

Dougherty, D. 1992. Interpretative barriers to successful product innovation in large firms. *Organization Science*, 3(2): 179-202.

Douglass, M. 1986. *How Institutions Think*. Syracuse, NY: Syracuse University Press.

Duarte, D. L., & Snyder, N. T. 1999. *Mastering Virtual Teams*. San Francisco. Jossey-Bass Publishers.

Fleck, J. 1997. Contingent knowledge and technology development. *Technology Analysis and Strategic Management*, 9(4): 383-398.

Garud, R., & Nayyar, P. 1994. Transformative capacity: Continual Structuring by intertemporal technology transfer. *Strategic Management Journal*, 15: 365-385.

Granovetter, M. 1985. Economic action and social structure: The problem of embeddedness. *American Journal of Sociology*, 91(3): 481-510.

Grant, R. 1996. Toward a knowledge-based theory of the firm. *Strategic Management Journal*, 17 (Winter Special Issue): 109-122.

Jarvenpaa, S., & Tiller, E. 1999. Integrating market, technology, and policy opportunities in e- business strategy. *Strategic Information Systems*, 8(3): 235-249.

Kogut, B., & Zander, U. 1992. Knowledge of the firm, combinative capabilities, and the replication of technology. *Organization Science*, 3 (3): 383-397.

Kraut, R., Steinfield, C., Chan, A. P., Butler, B. & Hoag, A. 1999. Coordination and virtualization: The role of electronic networks and personal relationships. *Organization Science*, 10(6): 722-740.

Leonard, D. A., Brands, P. A., Edmondson, A., & Fenwick, J. 1998. Virtual teams: Using communications technology to manage geographically dispersed development groups. In S. P. Bradley & R. L. Nolan (Eds.), *Sense and Respond: Capturing Value in the Network Era*: 285-198. Boston: Harvard Business School Press.

Levitt, B., & March, J. G. 1988. Organizational Learning. Stanford University Annual Review of Sociology, 14: 319-340.

Madhavan, R. & Grover, R. 1998. From embedded knowledge to embodied knowledge: New product development as knowledge management. *Journal of Marketing*, 62(4): 1-12.

Nelson, R., & Winter, S. 1982. *An Evolutionary Theory of Economic Change*. Cambridge, MA: The Belknap Press of Harvard Business School.

Nonaka, I., & Konno, N. 1998. The concept of 'Ba': Building a foundation for knowledge creation. *California Management Review*, 40 (3): 40-54.

Nonaka, I., & Takeuchi, I. 1995. *The Knowledge Creating Company. How Japanese Companies Create the Dynamics of Innovation*. Oxford University Press, New York, NY/Oxford.

Penrose, E.T. 1959. The Theory of the Growth of the Firm. New. York: Wiley & Sons.

Spender, J. 1998. *Pluralist Epistemology and the Knowledge Based Theory of the Firm*. Working Manuscript, New York Institute of Technology, New York, NY.

Schultze, U. & Orlikowski, W. A. 2001. Metaphors of virtuality: shaping an emergent reality. *Information and Organization*, 11(1): 45-77.

Tyre, M. J. & Hippel, E. V. 1997. The situated nature of adaptive learning in organisations. *Organization Science*, 8(1): 71-83.

Van den Bosch, F., Volberdsa, H., & Boer, M. 1999. Convolution of firm absorptive capacity and knowledge environment: Organisational forms and combinative capabilities. Organisation Science, 10(5): 551-568.

Vicenti, W. G. 1990. *What Engineers Know and How They Know It: Analytical Studies from Aeronautical History*. Baltimore & London: John Hopkins University Press.

Weber, R. 1985. *Basic Content Analysis*, CA: Sage.

Diversity and Needs in Web-Based Learning: What Do Students in Online Learning Contexts Need?

Arif Dagli
School of Information Studies, Florida State University, E-mail add5394@garnet.acns.fsu.edu; Tel: 850/877-3263

Technological changes and advancements have produced and fashioned wealthier and more affluence, consumption, and communication in the late 20th and early 21st century than ever before by changing society in fundamental ways. Also, it started bringing about the need for educational settings and requiring us to (re)evaluate the way traditional education is distributed so that more people can be reached.

Distance education is a fast growing method of delivery in higher education. People of all ages and characteristics take course at a distance for many different reasons. They may need the convenience that distance education can offer. The typical distance learning student is not easy to define or classify. Distance learners at colleges and universities are aged 18 and older, a much more diverse group than the traditional 18-24 year old found on many residential campuses. They work part or full time, and should balance all roles in their own lives, such as parent, spouse, employee, volunteer, and caregiver, to others. This particular group of learners are often times bounded by competing roles that they play in their jobs, families, or communities.

Web-based distance learning has become as a viable alternative to traditional campus based face-to face education and proven to be promising to the information professionals in today's digital world. It occurs when an instructor or teacher and student(s) are separated by physical distance and when the World Wide Web (WWW) is used to bridge the instructional gap. Instruction can be delivered either synchronously or asynchronously or combination of both. Regardless of the technology and the instruction format used (such as, text-based, HTML-based, and multimedia-based), throughout this paper, web-based distance learning refers to any instructional deliveries offered through the WWW at a distance as part of a graduate degree program and/or course. One should note that any instructional delivery over the web supplementing face-to-face education is beyond the scope of this paper.

It is also pushing programs and schools of information studies (IS) to redefine their curricula to include activities, resources, and participation beyond campus borders and routine hours. The number of IS schools in different countries increasingly started offering a various levels of degree programs through web-based learning. Furthermore, this delivery medium requires IS educators and information professionals to reexamine the understanding of students needs as the number of students lives away from their host institution and therefore may not have the same opportunities as those on campus in fulfilling their needs and getting what they need.

STATEMENT OF THE PROBLEM

Available technologies such as web-based distance learning opportunities for higher education provide institutions with new possibilities and horizons to increase enrollment. Additionally, asynchronous environments or distance learning programs offer their students convenient, affordable, and flexible schedules. Nevertheless, because of skyrocketing advancement and popularity, some universities and colleges have been caught unprepared to offer some distance education courses over the Internet. Thus, there are still some unanswered questions about the quality of the course offerings as well as meeting students' needs. Can web-based distance learning programs provide quality instruction that includes not only appropriate course content but also meeting students' academic and non-academic needs at a distance? Furthermore, since distance crosses geographic boundaries in today's world, with students from around the world registered together in courses, how higher educations institutions as well as academic support services, including information services and systems, should position themselves? As a result, the research reported here explores the needs of graduate students taking web-based distance education courses and thus providing what and how they need

The Research Questions

This study aims to answer the following research questions:
• What are the needs of graduate students the context of web-based distance learning in higher education?
• How and in what ways do students think their background affect their needs; and
• What are the factors that students encounter (or have encountered) in fulfilling their needs in web-based learning contexts?

Review of The Pertinent Literature

An early application of distance learning was the Open University (OU) in Britain, offering a model for universities to observe and pattern their own programs. Over two million students have taken courses since 1971 through OU's virtual education model that uses various multimedia methods. The university has offered personal tutoring and in some cases a weekend or weeklong class at a central location. It is noted that the institution tends to rank high in national assessment. (Blumenstyk, 1999)

While there are proponents of distance learning, some educators are not so sure that technology makes a significant difference. The book, *The No Significant Difference Phenomenon,* is comprised of numerous articles that suggest there is little difference in methods of learning, but the studies do provide substantial evidence that technology does not denigrate instruction. This opens doors to use technologies to increase efficiency, bridge distances or circumvent other obstacles, yet assure the outcomes will be comparable to conventional classrooms or those employing the use of expensive, sophisticated technology (Russell, 1999). Clearly research needs to move beyond comparative media studies to an examination of the key elements that may contribute to success or failure.

Learning and teaching over the Web is a fast growing method of delivery in higher education nationally and internationally. Web-based learning is enjoying popularity unprecedented by earlier distance learning delivery modalities. As reported in the March 30, 2001 *Chronicle of Higher Education,* the enrollments in Internet courses at the University of North Texas alone increased by nearly 300% between Fall 1999 and Spring 2001 (Young, 2001), and other institutions are reporting similar enrollment growth.

The literature about web-based learning instructional course design is rich. However, research about the academic and non-academic support services, including library and information services, which universities can and should provide their web-based distance learners is very limited.

For example, Abate (1998) is certainly one of a few researchers specifically interested in information needs of online learners at a doctoral research level. She surveyed students and faculty in the School of Computer and Information Sciences, the Center for Psychological Studies, and the School of Social and Systemic Studies, the Fischler Center for the Advancement of Education and the School of Business and Entrepreneurship at Nova Southeastern University. She evaluated the information needs of a selected segment of the distance learning graduate student population served by the Einstein Library at Nova Southeastern University, in Fort Lauderdale, Florida, and proposed a new model of library service based on the implementation of current and emerging technologies. Based upon her Quality Function Deployment Methodology analysis, a model for library services at Nova Southeastern University was proposed, integrating electronic and print resources into a unified system of information delivery. The researcher then compared various methods of presenting information resources compared and used as examples of potential solutions for delivery problems of online learners.

Flowers (2000) in her multi-method case study research, employing email interviews, in-depth interviews, focus groups, questionnaires, secondary data analyses, and descriptive and disaggregate quantitative statistical data, studied "the demands posed by web technologies and the subsequent online services, learning opportunities, flexibility, and challenges for adult learners and educators as adult programs prepare to go online" (p. xiii). Main research question asked what questions stakeholders should ask about web-based distance programs. The researcher measured on-campus and stop-out adult students' technical readiness, skills, and equitable access to technology needed for Internet-based courses. Also she asked adult educators, *FIPSE*, instructional designers, vendors of web courses, and evaluators (web experts) to generate questions needed for quality design and development. By using *Utilization-Focused Evaluation* approach developed by Michael Patton's (1997) to design an internal needs assessment for web-based distance education and a 360-degree approach to include all stakeholders, the study generated over 1000 questions and coded using qualitative software. This study found 110 topics needed for quality web-based distance education fifteen essential themes that were extracted from the holistic matrix. Finally, this study has provided some evidence that all stakeholders' data are necessary for developing quality programs in web-based distance education; that "the change agency needed to facilitate the diffusion and adoption of web technologies"(p. xiii); and that the criticality of learner analysis, support systems, pedagogical shift, and contextual environmental needs for adult learners in the virtual university.

Bayless (2001) in her dissertation also complains about lack of "little information" about the non-academic needs of distance learners at universities. This study underlines the need in the literature by exploring the non-academic needs of distance learners. Then, students and faculty members involved with distance learning at four-year institutions in the Fall of 2000 were surveyed to identify what needs distance learners may have outside of their classroom environment. Results of a web-based survey identified 34 possible non-academic needs with respondents' rankings. Findings of her research indicated that the non-academic needs of distance learners are very similar to those of campus-based students. The students' top four needs are the following:

- information about the institution and program,
- a way to purchase books,
- a contact person at the institution, and
- academic advising.

Additionally, for the students pursuing their bachelors degrees listed "more traditional developmental needs" such as leadership skills, experience with diversity, and career services than graduate students. The then researcher argues that some if not all services to meet these needs are currently not easily accessible or available to students. Therefore, she believes that most needs presents themselves throughout one's academic career and recommends that institutions involved with distance learning programs should consider addressing basic needs first and then "more traditional developmental needs". As for libraries and library resources available to online learners, students participating in this study addressed concerns relating specifically to academic courses and the resources. The issues that students complained focused on the access to the library resources, however.

Only three studies could have been identified so far that are related to some needs of distance learners in higher education. Certainly, more research is needed to explore and provide clearer picture about the new learning medium for the needs of special and diverse populations, such as bilingual or multilingual distance students, the handicapped, the adults and older adults, students with special needs, and foreign students and thus provide what and how they need. Therefore, this study aims at addressing this gap in the body of knowledge and attempting to explore academic and non-academic needs of web-based distance learners in graduate degree programs.

In turn, as review of the pertinent literature shows, knowing what online learners need is of interest to various stakeholders of web-based distance learning programs. First, as in the case of Information Science and Studies Schools and Departments, the trend of increasing use of the Internet by higher education institutions to deliver educational programs is likely to continue and grow. Therefore, researchers in several disciplines should be concerned about this research problem in order for higher education institutions and programs offering web-based courses as part of their curricula to understand the needs of their student populations well and provide better services to them in return.

Secondly, this study have both theoretical and practical implications. From the theoretical viewpoint, it is intended to contribute to understanding of the needs of a specific group of distance learners. On the practical side, it would be of interest and valuable to various stakeholders, including, but not limited to, instructors and faculty members, administrators of students support services, educational policymakers and instructional designers.

Thirdly, it is unclear how students in web-based distance learning programs fulfill their needs. It is almost unknown how these students use academic library resources and information services available through their universities and colleges. Additionally, research about whether some reported barriers related to language, cultural differences, and technology skills for on-campus students are still problems to the students in web-based distance degree programs is not in existence. As a result of this research, detailed information about academic and non-academic needs of students in web-based distance learning contexts will enable information professionals and service designers to provide appropriate services for their users.

METHODOLOGY

Research on web-based distance learning is in its infancy, and as is appropriate, even the most self-evident results are subject to questioning and controversy. Most of the research to date is limited in its generalizability because it is either too system specific, too course specific, or the population size is too small for statistical significance.

This study employs three data collection techniques: Focus groups, a survey questionnaire and in-dept interviews. For the purposes of data analyses, quantitatively, descriptive statistics on all questionnaire demographics and variables will be calculated for data using the statistical computer software package, Statistical Package for Social Science (SPSS). Qualitative data will be analyzed by data examination, categorization, sorting, collapsing, coding and synthesis. NU*DIST qualitative analytical software will be used to code phrases and concepts grounded in web-based distance learning research and literature.

The target population for this study is graduate degree seeking students who have partaken graduate level web-based distance learning degree programs and/or course. Study participants will be selected from a university in the US that offers a variety of types of degrees earned at a distance and serves varying students populations, including an increasing number of diverse student body. The participants are being chosen according to the following criteria: one is at least to have taken a distance course taught over the web. The course taken by students are to have or been taught at a distance. In other words, it should not have a face-to-face component.

This study assumes that all members of the targeted study population have similar needs. Also, students who have not taken any web-based course will not be studied in this study. In other words, only graduate web-based distance students will be studied although it will limit the generalizability of the study. Finally, due to the rapid evolution of technology, the accuracy of the data may not hold true as new technologies and new curricula for online courses are developed. Therefore, the data gathered during the study will represent the opinions and perceptions of the study participants during the time of data collection.

PILOT STUDY AND CONCLUSION

A pilot study was recently completed for this study. During the pilot study, students in a web-based graduate class at FSU School of Information Studies were asked to answer two semi-structured questionnaires. Initial survey was given at the beginning of the semester and students were asked to answer semi-structured survey questions about their perceived needs in web-based learning contexts. Similarly, the second survey was distributed at the end of the semester for the same students in the same course. This time they were to answer questions related to their experiences with respect to their needs in the web-based course that that they were about to complete or had just completed. The results of pilot study are being analyzed and prepared for the presentation of this paper at the IRMA 2003 Conference in May 2003 in Philadelphia, PA.

In conclusion, understanding of needs of these students in higher education is an important step for planning all services, improving existing services, and creating necessary and better teaching and leaning environments. Upon completion, this study will provide empirical findings that will assist in the design and development of web-based distributed learning courses and degree programs. Also, results of this ongoing research will be off interest to higher education administrators as well as faculty and/or instructors to provide informed decision-making regarding:

• Preparation and evaluation of proposals for web-based delivery of degree programs, including understanding student needs;
• The resources required to support well-designed web-based distance learning programs, particularly as relates to meeting student needs;
• The selection of course development products to assist faculty in designing online courses over the Web that have proper support services to help students fulfill their needs; and
• The selection of course delivery products and technologies particularly as they relates to provide support services.

ACKNOWLEDGMENT:

The writer would like to express his appreciation to Dr. Kathleen Burnett for her support of this paper and presentation and her contribution to this presentation. *He is a Ph.D. Candidate in Information Studies at Florida State University, Tallahassee, FL, USA and can be contacted via email at add5394@fsu.edu. His current research and teaching interests include online instructional delivery methods, research methods in information studies, global and international issues pertaining to information studies, information policy issues and information use and behavior research.*

REFERENCES

Abate, A. K. (1998). *The role of the Einstein Library of Nova Southeastern University in meeting the needs of distance learning students.* Unpublished doctoral dissertation, Nova Southeastern University.

Bayless, L. A. (2001). *What are the non-academic needs of distance learners.* Unpublished doctoral dissertation, Virginia Polytechnic Institute and State University.

Blumenstyk, G. (1999). Distance learning at the Open University. *The Chronicle of Higher Education, 45*(46), A35-A38.

Flowers, D. J. (2000). *Utilization-focused needs assessment: A case study of adult learners' web-based distance education needs.* Unpublished doctoral dissertation, University of South Alabama.

Pao, M. L. (1989). *Concepts of information retrieval.* Englewood, CO: Libraries Unlimited, Inc.

Russell, T. L., (compiler) (1999). *The no significant difference phenomenon: as reported in 355 research reports, summaries, and papers.* (pp. vii-viii). Raleigh, NC: North Carolina State University.

Faculty and Student Perceptions and Experiences on Interaction in Web-Based Learning

Arif Dagli

School of Information Studies, Florida State University, E-mail add5394@garnet.acns.fsu.edu; Tel: 850/877-3263

Much has changed since postmen served as the vehicle by which distance education reached the student in the nineteenth century when commercial correspondence colleges provided distance education via the mail to students across the country. The last century continued the trend of distance education with the inventions of radio, television and other media. Thanks to advanced communication technologies, students today experience education at a distance through significantly different formats of delivery. There is no need to wait any longer for the mailman to bring assignments and correspondence from an instructor, or gather around a television in a central location. Instead, one may simply turn on a computer, check their e-mail, an electronic bulletin board, or spend a few minutes on online chat software.

Under the guidance of Dr. Kathleen Burnett at the Florida State University (FSU) School of Information Studies, research reported here aims to explore some concerns related to web-based learning opportunities, and particularly, to answer the question: *Is high interaction positively correlated with student and program success in graduate web-based distributed learning degree programs?*

The utilization of new technology in providing education has raised concerns regarding interaction of learners and instructors. Must students and teachers be face-to-face to interact? What does interaction involve? How does online interaction compare with face-to-face interaction? Does more frequent interaction contribute to success? What roles do intensity and topicality of interaction play? Therefore, this research seeks to determine the importance of interaction to the success of web-based learning graduate degree programs. The understanding then can be used to guide decision making in a variety of areas related to the delivery of individual distance courses and entire degree programs.

REVIEW OF THE PERTINENT LITERATURE

There are generally three types of interaction that are considered aspects of a learning environment. They are:

· *Learner-content interaction* – the interaction of the student with the subject matter and the constructing of knowledge through new understanding.

• *Learner-instructor interaction* – the instruction, assisting, stimulation and support provided by the instructor to the learner. The learner can test the viability of new understanding with the instructor who serves as a representation of expert knowledge.

• *Learner-learner interaction* – the interaction between one learner and other learners whether alone or in a group. It may or may not be in the presence of an instructor (Soo & Bonk, 1998)

With today's evolving technology, distance learning is vastly different from the days of gathering students around a television in a central location. Learning at a distance includes activities or instruction where the learner is at a different location from the originator and a combination of media may be employed—such as computers, software, e-mail, telephone, fax, Internet, television, or videoconferencing—to facilitate learning (Phipps & Merisotis, 1999, p. 40). It generally includes synchronous and/or asynchronous communication. Synchronous communication occurs when the student and instructor are present at the same time during instruction, although they may be in different locations. Asynchronous communication occurs when the student and instructor

do not participate in direct person-to-person interaction at the same time or place.

Today's students expect and demand instruction with high levels of interaction between students and instructor and immediate access to information from around the globe. The demand for interactivity has placed a new focus on instructional design as well as the technologies that provide two-way delivery. With current technologies, students are encouraged to be self-reflective as the flow of instruction may no longer be sequential and interactive (Parker, 1999, p. 60).

Use of network technologies, known as third generation distance education systems, have provided models that add to the social component of the learning process while constructing new knowledge. The systems create learning communities where individuals can overcome isolation and benefit from group interaction. This approach also encourages learners to take an active part in setting objectives, defining the contents and capitalizing on life experiences, requiring that the learning process hinge on strong interaction between all participants (Trenton, 2000, p. 70)

Current technology changes the social dynamics of education by placing everyone (learners and teachers) on equal footing. All learners have equal opportunity to post and read messages, thereby allowing for ideas from everyone rather than just the instructor (Kearsley, 1997, p. 80).

Faculty whose experience is limited to lecturing in a classroom may find themselves in an electronic learning environment using technologies they did not grow up with but their students did and are very comfortable with using the technology. They will be faced with learning new ways of interacting, facilitating student-centered learning and becoming a resource for information (McClure, [undated], p. 90).

Rather than continuing to lecture online, instructors will be more successful by adopting the role of facilitator or moderator who encourages participation and keeps discussions focused (Kearsley, 1997, p. 80)

Interactive learning or collaborative learning is a natural outcome of distance education with technology and it provides many avenues for interactions between students, instructors and information. Collaborative learning is replacing an atmosphere of working alone and presenting one's "own" work. Group work is encouraged as it more closely emulates the way people work most often in the real world. Teamwork is encouraged as it provides different perspectives on issues, skills and ways to solve problems. Learning is becoming student-centered as opposed to the professor, library and other sources of information being at the center with students clustered around them for access or interaction. This allows the student to become self-directing in planning the acquisition of education. Therefore, key changes for education in the information age stress collaborative learning, interaction, and problem solving or reasoning rather than memorization (Oblinger, 1996).

Students are encouraged to be involved in learning activities and participate in group projects since modern business is generally built on teamwork. Collaborative learning in online classes means students work together without knowing each other, benefiting them is a variety of ways:

• Everyone on the team is equal
• Barriers related to gender, ethnicity, age or shyness are eliminated
• Face-to-face time may become more efficient
• Online lecture notes and readings allow students time to reflect

- Utilization of time is more flexible at the convenience of the student
- Instructors can stay in touch with students when off campus (Oblinger & Maruyama, 1996, p. 50)

While the benefits of collaborative learning seem positive and easily accomplished with distance learning, every student may not be an expert user of the technology that implements the online class. Therefore, it is necessary for students to become acquainted with the technology before beginning the class. Also, some students may be slow in opening up to the group and participating, choosing to be a lurker in the background instead, while other students may exhibit a greater degree of boldness online. Establishing group sizes of no more than four may enhance interactivity, encourage more interaction, and facilitate efficient teamwork (Carnevale, 2000, p. 120).

METHODOLOGY

This study consists of two parts: I. A detailed examination of the graduate web-based distributed learning degree program of the FSU School of Information Studies; and II. A comparative survey of comparable Information Studies web-based distributed learning degree programs in North America. Data collection for Part I is projected to come to conclusion by May 1, 2003. Preliminary findings of the collected data for Part 1 through faculty interviews and student focus groups are presented the presentation of this paper at the IRMA 2003 Conference in May 2003 in Philadelphia, PA.

Graduate professional education in Information Studies is chosen for this study in order to ensure specific applicability to the information technology area where the projected demand for education will far outstrip our universities' traditional classroom resources. There are three reasons to choose IS education. First, IS programs are meeting Library & IT workforce demands. Secondly, they are growing in terms of the number of students enrolled and changing traditional focus of LIS programs. Finally, they are using web-based delivery modalities to manage enrollment growth. For example, The School of Information Studies at FSU experienced 500% enrollment growth from 1994 to 2002. It has successfully managed this increase through adoption of web-based delivery modalities, with approximately half of its current students at all levels receiving their education at a distance. Finally, over 35% of all ALA accredited schools in North America offer a master's degree with no residency requirement. An additional 11% require limited residency (3-15 credit hours). This is a field that has considerable experience with distance delivery. Several institutions have offered full professional master's degree programs at a distance for more than ten years. Therefore, the artifacts of recent change (such as change in pedagogical style) that have been criticized in the literature on media effects are less likely to be present in this field than in many others (Clark, 1983).

The degree program at the FSU School of Information Studies was selected for Part I of this study because its web-based distributed learning program is relatively mature (6 years at the initiation of the study). It offers a sufficient number and range of courses (20 courses in two majors), and enrolls a sufficiently large number of students (approximately 400-450 students participate in web-based courses during an academic year).

In Part I of this study, web-based course offerings at the FSU School of Information Studies are examined using content analysis to determine type and degree of interaction. Upon examination of the logs, the researchers developed 9 open-ended questions to be asked faculty members during interviews and similar 9 questions for students during focus groups. In-depth interviews with faculty teaching the courses and focus-group interviews with students enrolled in the courses are being conducted to further probe these designations, and in-depth interviews and observations will be conducted at two other universities to ensure that the interaction types are transferable to other contexts.

FINDINGS AND CONCLUSION

Since the data collection process for the Part I is nearing completion as of May 1, 2003 and the data are being analyzed as they become available, the presentation of this paper will share the complete results of the Part 1 with the IRMA 2003 attendees. Nonetheless, some of the preliminary findings of the Phase I include the following: Faculty members

- didn't set any rules or communication guidelines but felt that there was an unwritten policy in effect during the semester;
- played usually moderator and facilitator role in synchronous discussions;

- required students to listen to prerecorded lectures and discussed the topic of day;
- encouraged students to interact with each other; and
- expressed the importance of time management in synchronous web-based classes.

The researchers also conducted focus group interviews both face-to-face and synchronous/online with students to probe their reactions to web-based interaction in general and to specific interaction modalities (synchronous vs. asynchronous).

The focus group participants were asked to discuss the role of the instructor in managing interaction and asked them to rate their satisfaction with the interaction in the course they took. The preliminary findings of both student focus groups revealed that students

- set high expectations if a student had prior experience;
- felt that interaction in a web-based course was more different than that in a face-to-face course;
- agree that instructors' effectiveness highly depend on their teaching styles and their prior experiences;
- expressed that their preferred delivery formats in a web based class varied; and
- didn't interact with their classmates unless they were required to participate in a group assignment.

In conclusion, this study will provide empirical findings that will assist in the design and development of web-based distributed learning courses and degree programs. For example, higher education administrators and instructors/faculty will be able to use these results to support informed decision-making regarding evaluation and preparation of proposals for web-based delivery of degree programs, including understanding interaction indicators for success; the selection of course development products to assist faculty in designing courses that have appropriate frequency, intensity and topicality of interaction; and the selection of course delivery products, resources to support distance programs and technologies that provide appropriate and well-designed interaction tools.

ACKNOWLEDGEMENT

The writer would like to express his appreciation to Dr. Kathleen Burnett for her support of this paper and presentation and acknowledge her contribution to preparation of this presentation. *He is a Ph.D. Candidate in Information Studies at Florida State University, Tallahassee, FL, USA and can be contacted via email at add5394@fsu.edu. His current interests include online instructional delivery methods, research methods in information studies, global and international issues pertaining to information studies, information policy issues and information use and behavior research.*

REFERENCES

Carnevale, D. (2000, May 31). Study groups let online students interact as they would in a classroom. *The Chronicle of Higher Education.* http://proquest.umi.com.pqdweb?TS=...&Sid=1&Idx=10&Deli=1&RQT=309&Dtp=1

Clark, R. E. (1983). Reconsidering research on learning from media. *Review of Educational Research, 53*(4), 445-459.

Kearsley, G. (1997). *A guide to online education.* http://gwis.circ.gwu.edu/~etl/online.html

McClure, P. (undated). Technology in university teaching and learning: Benefits and barriers from a technology viewpoint. file:///A|/mcclure.htm

Oblinger, D. G. & Maruyama, M. K. (1996). Distributed learning. Boulder, CO: CAUSE; 1996;CAUSE Professional Paper Series #14.

Parker, A. (1999). Interaction in distance education: The critical conversation. *Educational Technology Review.* 12, 13-17.

Phipps, R. & Merisotis, J. (1999). *What's the difference? A review of contemporary research on the effectiveness of distance learning in higher education.* Washington, DC: The Institute for Higher Education Policy.

Soo, K-S. & Bonk, C. J. (1998). *Interaction: What does it mean in online distance education?* ED428724. 8 pp. [Microfiche].

Trenton, G. (2000, Feb 28). The quality-interactivity relationship in distance education. *Educational Technology, 40*(1), 17-27.

Modelling Data Warehouse Structures

Michel Schneider
LIMOS, Blaise Pascal University
Complexe des Cézeaux
63173 Aubière, France
tel : 33 04 73 40 50 09, fax : 33 04 73 40 50 01
schneider@isima.fr

ABSTRACT

Two main problems arise in modelling of data warehouse structures. The first one consists in finding an adequate representation of dimensions in order to facilitate and to control the analysis operations. Second one relates to the modelling of various types of architectures. Research works were especially dedicated to the first problem and adequate solutions were proposed. The second problem have not received so much attention. However, there is a need to apprehend complex structures interconnecting dimensions and facts in various ways. We propose in this paper a model which permits to share dimensions at different levels between different facts and to describe various relationships between facts. We then define the notion of well forms for warehouse structures

1. INTRODUCTION

The tasks of design and implementation of a data warehouse cannot be achieved without an adequate modelling of dimensions and facts.

Concerning the modelling of dimensions, the objective is to find an organization which is in correspondence with the analysis operations and which permit to control strictly how the aggregations can be made. In particular it is important to avoid double-counting or summation of non-additive data. Many works were dedicated to this problem. Most recommend to organize the members of a dimension into hierarchies permitting to define explicitly the aggregation paths. In [7], hierarchies are defined by the means of a containment function. In [3] and [4], the organization of a dimension results from the functional dependences which exist between its members. In [1], relationships between levels in a hierarchy are apprehended through the Part-Whole semantics. In [10], dimensions are organized around the notion of dimension path which is a set of drilling relationships. In [6] and [9], a dimension is viewed as a lattice.

Modelling of facts and their relationships have not received so much attention. Facts are generally considered in a simple way which consists to relate a fact with the roots of the dimensions. However, there is a need for considering more sophisticated structures where a same set of dimensions are connected to different fact types and where several fact types are inter-connected. The model of [6] is one of rare to make it possible to connect the facts and dimensions in different ways.

Outside these works it is important to note various propositions (see for example [2]) for cubic models where the primary objective is the definition of an algebra for multidimensional analysis. It is interesting also to mention the work of [5] which takes place at the relational level and which proposes a normalized relational model for data warehouses.

Our objective in this paper is to present a model which permits to apprehend the sharing of dimensions in various ways and to describe different relationships between fact types. This model can thus be used to represent the different data warehouse structures encountered in the real word. We suggest also a graph representation for such structures which can help the users for designing and requesting a data warehouse. We illustrate how a typical case, the constellation structure, can be modelled and represented.

2. MODELLING FACTS

A fact allows to record measures or states concerning an event or a situation. Measures and states can be analysed through different criteria organized in dimensions. We model facts through fact types and fact instances.

A fact type is a structure:
    fact_name[(fact_key),
    (list_of_reference_attributes), (list_of_fact_attributes)]
where
- fact_name is the name of the type;
- fact_key is a list of attribute names; the concatenation of these attributes identifies each instance of the type;
- list_of_reference_attributes is a list of attribute names; each attribute references a member in a dimension or another fact instance;
- list_of_fact_attributes is a list of attribute names; each attribute is a measure for the fact.

The set RD of referenced dimensions comprises the dimensions which are directly referenced through the list_of_reference_attributes, but also the dimensions which are indirectly referenced through other facts.

Each fact attribute can be analysed along each of the dimensions of RD. Analysis is made through the computing of aggregate functions on the values of this attribute. As in [3], we distinguish three levels of summarizability for a fact attribute relatively to a dimension : S which means that SUM and all the other aggregate functions are possible; O (others) which means that all the aggregate functions are possible except SUM; C which means that only the COUNT function is possible. Indicators of summarizability are placed in parentheses after the name of each fact attribute.

3. MODELLING DIMENSIONS

The different criteria which are needed to conduct analysis along a dimension are introduced through member attributes (or shortly members). For example, the dimension TIME can include members such that DAY, MONTH, YEAR, … . Analysing a fact attribute A along a member M means that we are interested to compute aggregate functions on the values of A for any grouping defined by the values of M. We will also use the notation Mij for the j-th member of i-th dimension.

Member attributes of a dimension are generally organized in a hierarchy which is a conceptual representation of the hierarchies of their occurrences. Hierarchy in dimensions is a very useful concept permitting to impose constraints on member values and to guide the analysis. Hierarchies of occurrences result from various relationships which can exist in the real world : categorization, membership of a subset, mereology. We will model the hierarchy in a dimension via a hierarchical relationship (HR) which links a child member Mij (i.e. town) to a parent member Mik (region) and we will use the notation Mij->Mik. For the following we consider only situations where a child occurrence is linked to a unique parent occurrence in a type. However, a child occurrence can have several parent occurrences but each of different types.

We will also suppose that HR is reflexive, antisymmetric and transitive. This kind of relationship covers a great majority of real situations [1]. Existence of this HR is very important since it permits to organize the members of a dimension into levels and to guaranty correct aggregation of measure attributes along levels.

We propose the notion of member type, which incorporates the different elements presented above.

A member type is a structure:
member_name[(member_key),
dimension_name, (list_of_reference_attributes),
(list_of_property_attributes)]
where
- member_name is the name of the type;
- member_key is a list of attribute names; the concatenation of these attributes identifies each instance of the type;
- dimension_name is the name of the dimension to which the type belongs;
- list_of_reference_attributes is a list of attribute names where each attribute is a reference to the successors of the member instance in the cover graph of the dimension;
- list_of_property_attributes is a list of attribute names where each attribute is a property for the member.
Only the member_key and the dimension_name are mandatory.

4. MODELLING DIFFERENT WAREHOUSE STRUCTURES

Our model is able to represent the typical warehouse structures which are encountered in the real world : star and snowflake structures, constellation structure (sharing of dimensions), facts of facts and so on. To represent such structures, we suggest to use a graph representation called DWG (data warehouse graph). It consist to represent each type (fact type or member type) by a node containing the main information about this type, and to represent each reference by a directed edge. Due to the limited space, we illustrated here only the constellation structure. Representations of other structures can be found in [8].

The constellation structure appears when:
- there are at most two different fact types;
- two different fact types share a same dimension;
- a fact type does not reference another fact type.

Using the notion of DWG graph, figure 1 shows an example with the fact type *sales* and a second one *demography* memorizing demographic facts for a given category in a demographic zone. *Sales* has references to the roots of the dimension *time, product, customer*. *Demography* has a reference to the member *demozone* of the dimen-

sion *customer*. So, the dimension *customer* is shared partly between the two fact types.

The DWG shows clearly how the two fact types can be exploited separately or simultaneously. We can explore the graph from one of its two roots and use it as a single rooted graph. We can also exploit simultaneously the two fact types. For example, to the node *demozone*, one can associate different aggregates coming from the *demography* occurrences and use it for the analysis of the *sales* facts or vice-versa.

6. CONCLUSION

In this paper we propose a model able to describe various data warehouse structures. It extends existing models for sharing dimensions and for representing relationships between facts. It permits different entries in a dimension corresponding to different granularities. A dimension can also have several roots corresponding to different views and uses. It is possible to apprehend the concept of facts of fact which is very frequently encountered in the real world.

We have also proposed the concept of Data Warehouse Graph (DWG) to represent data warehouse structures. The DWG gathers main information on the schema of the warehouse. It can be very useful to the users for formulating requests. We think that the DWG graph can constitute a good support for a graphical interface to manipulate multidimensional structures through a graphical language.

Data warehouse structures must satisfy desirable properties in order to guaranty correct uses of the warehouse (acyclicity in a dimension or in the relationships between facts, independence of dimensions, roots must be facts, ...). We show in [8] how our model is able model to support such constraints. This permits us to define the notion of well formed warehouse structures. In [8], we show also how well formed structures can be efficiently mapped to the relational model.

It appears that this model has a natural place between the conceptual schema of the application and a relational implementation of the warehouse. It can thus serve as a helping support for the design of data warehouses.

REFERENCES

1. Abello A., Samos J., Saltor F. : Understanding Analysis Dimensions in a Multidimensional Object-Oriented Model. Proc. of Intl Workshop on Design and Management of Data Warehouses (DMDW'2001), Interlaken, Switzerland, June 4, 2001.
2. Datta A., Thomas H. : The Cube Data Model : A Conceptual Model and Algebra for on-line Analytical Processing in Data Warehouses. Decision Support Systems, pp. 289-301, 27(3), December 1999.
3. Hùsemann B., Lechtenbörger J., Vossen G.: Conceptual Data Warehouse Design. Proc. of Intl Workshop on Design and Management of Data Warehouses (DMDW'2000), Stockholm, Sweden, June 5-6, 2000.
4. Lehner W., Albrecht J., Wedekind H.: Multidimensional Normal Forms. 10th Intl Conference on Scientific and Statistical Data Management (SSDBM'98), Capri, Italy, July 1-3, 1998.
5. Levene M., Loizou G.: Why is the Star Schema a Good Data Warehouse Design. http://citeseer.ni.nec.com/457156.html, April 1999.
6. Pedersen T.B., Jensen C.S.: Multidimensional Data Modelling for Complex Data. In Proc. ICDE' 99, Intl Conference on Data Engineering, March, 1999.
7. Pourabbas E., Rafanelli M.: Characterization of Hierarchies and some Operators in OLAP Environment. DOLAP'99, Kansas City, USA, November, 1999.
8. Schneider M. : Well Formed Data Warehouse Structures. Internal Report, LIMOS, Blaise Pascal University, Clermont-Ferrand, France, November, 2002.
9. Vassiliadis P., Skiadopoulos S.: Modelling and Optimisation Issues for Multidimensional Databases. 12th Intl Conference CAISE, pp. 482-497, Stockholm, Sweden, June 5-9 2000.
10. Tsois A., Karayannidis N., Sellis T.: MAC: Conceptual Data Modeling for OLAP. Proc. of the Intl Workshop on Design and Management of Data Warehouses (DMDW'2001), Interlaken, Switzerland, June 4, 2001.

Fig. 1. *A constellation structure*

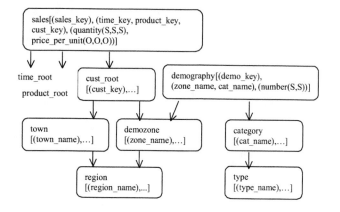

WORKSHOPS

In Class and Online Student Centered Discussion: Taking the Responsibility of Learning Away from the Instructor and Placing it into the Hands of the Student

Loreen Marie Butcher-Powell Ph.D. (A.B.D.)
Pennsylvania State University, CWC—Hazleton
Information Science and Technology, 76 University Drive
Hazleton, PA 18502; Lmb20@psu.edu, 570-450-3571

Believing the philosophy that learning is not a spectator sport, the instructor encourages the students to get involved in their educational experience. The probability of student learning improving by getting involved, talking and writing about what they have learned, relating it to past experiences, and most importantly applying it to their daily lives, is much greater then by students sitting in class listening to teachers, memorizing prepackaged assignments, and spitting out answers. The goal of each course is to provide the students with a challenging, critical thinking, novel, technology-focused, and learner-centered educational experience where they learn by pursuing knowledge, improving basic communication skills and most importantly taking responsibility for their own learning (Brown, Collins and Dugid, 1989). This workshop describes pedagogical strategy for undergraduate courses in the third year of the Information Science and Technology (IST) degree program at Pennsylvania State University, Hazleton. Courses have been transformed from a traditional lecture based model to a dynamic and situated learning environment by modifying a successful approach called "Student Centered Discussion (SCD).

Student Centered Discussion (SCD) is a delivery system for educational goals in the classroom via the integration of basic discussion skills. This technique is designed to allow a full implementation of all competency levels of Blooms Taxonomy model in hopes of promoting the active engagement of the students with their own education. (Shoop, Wright, unknown).

SCD has been proved to be an interactive model that encourages students to develop effective communication and interpersonal skills as well as strengthening critical thinking skills (Powell, Brazon, 2002). Moreover, this model is effective regardless of discipline or knowledge base (Shoop et al., unknown).

A modification of the SCD process in-class by forming small groups and gradually working towards one large group and extending the process online by writing down the lessons learned to have others elaborate upon them, has transpired into a cohesive 360° pedagogical strategy that extends beyond the classroom. This 360° pedagogical is aiding in the development of an inquiry based learning environment for teaching IST courses in which students can explore, analyze, and resolve issues in a cool way; the students way. Hence, this strategy takes the responsibility of learning away from the instructor and places it into the hands of the student.

While utilization of both in-class and on-line SCD involves reorganization of course content, and a reworking of the class assignments, it manages to provide a challenging and learner centered approach for the students to learn. Hence, the focus of the educational learning experience. This workshop will illustrate how a cohesive 360° pedagogical strategy was achieved by modifying SCD for in-class and online usage.

REFERENCES

Brown, J.S., Collins, A., & Dugid, P. (1989). "Situated cognition and the Culture of Learning." *Educational Researcher*, 18:32-42.

Powell, L. & Brazon, B. (2002). "Developing Interactive Competence through Student Centered Discussion." Journal of Computing Science in Colleges 18 (3) 235-240.

Shoop, L. & Wright, D. (unknown) "Developing Interactive Competence through Student Centered Discussions." Available [online] http://home.kiski.net/~dwright/scd/pres.html Accessed January 1, 2003.

Speeding Data Integration with Ontology Models

Joram Borenstein
Product Manager, Unicorn Solutions, Inc. (www.unicorn.com)
841 Broadway Ave., Suite 502, New York, NY 10003
1-646-367-1111 (phone), 1-646-367-1112 (fax), joram@unicorn.com

The generation of transformation scripts in SQL, XSLT, or other languages requires significant effort and is among the most crucial tasks currently existing in data management. The usual procedure for generating such scripts requires analysis of both the semantics and the structures of the source and target data files, followed by manual coding. However, by applying an ontology model to this task, data management can be greatly improved and accelerated.

An ontology is a formal model representing data semantics through Object-Oriented concepts such as classes, instances, properties, and inheritance. By describing a given domain of knowledge through its concepts and the relationships among these concepts, ontologies harmonize conflicting definitions; no single specific data representation needs to therefore be relied upon.

In data transformation and integration projects, ontologies are highly relevant. For example, for each new data source (e.g. application, file, database, etc.) that is added to a given data environment, each existing source must be manually mapped, thus requiring $O(n^2)$ (quadratic) effort. In contrast, a hub-and-spoke star integration with an ontology only requires $O(n)$ (linear) effort, significantly reducing the complexity inherent in extending and changing an ordinary point-to-point development effort. Additional benefits of using an ontology are reductions in ongoing mapping and maintenance needs.

As the first step of using an ontology in the data environment, the data integration analyst evaluates the business domain and defines a rich semantic model using the ontology. The next step is to express the semantics of each data schema by mapping it to the ontology. This mapping process involves relating the semantic meaning of a given data schema to a specific concept in the ontology model. Once this mapping is accomplished, the integration team now has a single expressive model describing all data resources, each of which can be accessed, compared, and viewed in a unified manner. As the final step in this process, the data expert selects which data source serves as a "source schema" and which as a "target schema." Ontological software then generates the SQL and XSLT transformation scripts automatically.

Transformation code generated through ontological software is scalable and reusable. Code maintenance also becomes simplified and made available to business users. SQL and XSLT code no longer requires deciphering by skilled database professionals. Moreover, automatic change detection ensures that modifications made on collaborative projects are immediately identified. Once automated code is generated, these scripts can then be deployed for routine database, data warehouse, ETL, or EAI tasks.

This workshop is aimed at database management specialists and others interested in ontologies, data semantics, and data modeling. It is also relevant to researchers and industry professionals looking for innovative ways to improve database management techniques.

Participants in this workshop will learn to create ontologies, apply ontologies to data schemas, map data sources to ontologies, and generate data transformations. Through the application of these techniques, data professionals handling fragmented data sources will learn of a more efficient way for producing transformation scripts and accessing corporate data.

Overcoming Organizational Communication Gaps with an Enterprise Data Thesaurus

Joram Borenstein
Product Manager, Unicorn Solutions, Inc. (www.unicorn.com)
841 Broadway Ave., Suite 502, New York, NY 10003; 1-646-367-1111
(phone), 1-646-367-1112 (fax); joram@unicorn.com

Knowledge Management systems built on overlapping and conflicting data vocabularies frequently break down as a result of data confusion. Without a single organizational Data Thesaurus that includes an agreed-upon vocabulary for all departments and employees, confusion reigns and knowledge cannot be managed effectively. Daily communications are the most visible expression of this problem; overcoming these misunderstandings should be a high priority for both researchers and managers.

Bridging the many communication gaps between employees, teams, and departments remains a significant problem in most medium and large-sized organizations. Teams tend to work with data vocabularies and terminology that are both convenient for their work and built on inherited standards. These vocabularies are often different in each team and confusing or incomprehensible to outsiders. To make matters worse, other departments and teams within the same organization frequently use alternative terms for the same concept, thereby increasing the risk of duplication and errors.

The absence of a unified corporate-wide understanding prevents coordination and causes personnel to rely on faulty information. Moreover, data translation mistakes affect planning, disrupt relationships with outside parties, and increase inter-departmental conflict.

Improving this situation is organizationally challenging. Departments prefer to use vocabularies with which they are comfortable and on which they rely. Individuals also tend to be territorial about their data and terminology, particularly where mission-critical information is concerned. The origins of this problem typically lie in mergers and acquisitions, unchecked historical growth, and international/vendor differences. Ignoring these communication gaps dooms large projects to enormous difficulties and even failure.

A common vocabulary providing semantic meaning to each groups' vocabularies is one of the most attractive solutions for this problem, enabling users to harmonize conflicting data terminologies. This organizational-wide understanding is most easily achieved by relating each vocabulary to a central Data Thesaurus.

A Data Thesaurus describes an enterprise's functions and entities by recognizing the acceptable synonyms for each item. Using a Data Thesaurus allows terminology owners to continue to use the terms and vocabularies they prefer, to be responsible for their own data, and to keep their existing tools and workflow.

This workshop will: (a) examine the benefits and challenges inherent in creating and maintaining a Data Thesaurus, (b) explain how organizations can choose to implement a Data Thesaurus in either a phased approach or as part of an overall strategy, (c) highlight a number of "Best Practice" scenarios through descriptive case studies, and (d) provide a complete project implementation template.

Attendees interested in overcoming barriers to full adoption of Knowledge Management systems and in leveraging Knowledge Management as a strategic issue for organizational growth will benefit most from this workshop. Participants will learn to assess current Knowledge Management needs for a Data Thesaurus and to prepare a comprehensive plan for implementing a Thesaurus within their own organizations.

Universal Information Presentation & Access: From Enterprise Portals to the Semantic Web

Dedric Carter
Nova Southeastern University; Graduate School of Computer and
Information Sciences; PO Box 2489 Fairfax, Virginia, USA
Tel: +1 703.267.8710 Fax: +1 703.267.2222; dedric@nova.edu

Information is exploding at an unprecedented rate. A 1999 University of California at Berkeley study described the glut of information in terms of millions of gigabytes (1-2 exabytes) being produced per year. As the world is inundated with data, the task of transitioning data into useful information becomes more challenging. Couple the challenges of data volumes with requirements on presentation such as the United States Americans with Disabilities Act Section 508 (which could threaten to spill over into the private sector) and concerns for secure access to information, and a confusing information interface domain emerges. This talk seeks to address the emerging methods of interfacing information from a universal presentation layer in enterprise portals through the Representational State Transfer (REST) architectural paradigm and culminates in the intriguing semantic web. The survey discussion will provide a background into the emerging area of information presentation and access. Detailed specifics of usability and interface design will not be covered; rather, the focus will be on emerging technologies and techniques for furthering information presentation and access.

In this session, a detailed explanation of enterprise information portals and the subsequent migration to enterprise application portals is presented with a discussion of the migration from intranets in the mid 1990s to a more ubiquitous web paradigm. A framework for understanding portal software functionality is presented with significant attention focused on the emerging portal initiatives in the standards bodies. As the portal migrates to the uniform presentation layer in the enterprise, a transformation similar to the convergence of the web server and application server is likely to occur resulting into new functions for key components of the current web architecture. The REST architectural style methodology is addressed and compared with the Resource Distribution Framework Site Summary (RDSS) method that has been widely implemented in the popular Web Log wave which has become prominent on the World Wide Web. Finally, a positioning of XML, Webservices, and supporting standards leads to an explanation of the potential role of the semantic web in the next generation enterprise architecture.

Developing Web Services: A Tutorial Using Visual Studio.NET

Mirza B. Murtaza and Timothy H. Greer
Computer Information Systems, Jennings A. Jones College of Business
Middle Tennessee State University, Murfreesboro, TN 37132

The development of E-commerce applications is one of the major trends that have emerged during the past few years. Several major E-commerce development projects failed to meet their objectives and some were scratched altogether in the past. Integration, interoperability, scalability, and portability have emerged as key issues in the development of E-commerce applications. One subject that is commonly mentioned as a major force in the future of E-commerce applications development is Web Services. A Web Service is an application that is exposed to the Internet. Based on XML, Web Services offer interoperability and flexibility when designing an E-commerce application.

This tutorial will explore the issues surrounding the emergence of Web Services, the advantages and disadvantages of using Web Services, the future of Web Services, and a simple example using Visual Studio .NET to create a Web Service.

Web Services have origins in distributed computing, component technology, and web development technologies. A Web Service can be requested by client applications through an exposed web interface. Web Services are based on XML, and require three other components. Those components are simple object access protocol (SOAP), the Web Service description language (WSDL), and the universal description, discovery, and integration (UDDI). SOAP is the protocol that allows a Web Service easier access through corporate firewalls than those applications relying solely on HTTP. WSDL incorporates the parameters and values needed to use and implemented the Web Service. UDDI acts as a directory of Web Services, analogous to the yellow pages.

Web Services are supported by most of the large vendors, including Microsoft, IBM, Sun Microsystems, and Oracle. Given this support and benefits such as being standards based, offering enterprise application integration, enhanced access to business functions, and location independence would indicate that Web Services will be a force in the development of E-commerce applications. Disadvantages have emerged such as the lack of a concise definition of Web Services, and the future and diffusion of Web Services. These benefits and disadvantages will be discussed along with any other issues that emerge pertaining to Web Services during the presentation.

The range of uses for a Web Service is limitless. Web Services are available to check everything from the weather to flight status. Organizations are able to build Web Services and expose them to other offices dispersed geographical. This allows an organization to take advantage of "the best" available code or application for a specific task. As stated earlier Web Services are supported by all of the major vendors, therefore the language and platform can be chosen based on the skill sets available to the organization.

The tutorial on Web Services development will utilize Visual Studio .NET integrated development environment (IDE) and Visual C# programming language. In the tutorial, development of a business-to-business e-commerce Web Service will be followed from both the server and client side perspective.

PANELS

Issues in Web-Based Education: Revisited

A.K. Aggarwal, University of Baltimore, USA, aaggarwal@ubmail.ubalt.edu
Apiwan Born, University of Illinois at Springfield, USA, born.apiwan@uis.edu
Minnie Yen, University of Alaska, USA, afmyy@uaa.alaska.edu
Daniel Gerlowski, University of Baltimore, USA, dgerlowski@ubmail.ubalt.edu
Pekka Makkonen, University of Jyväskylä, Finland -40014 , pmakkone@jyu.fi

Web-based education (WBE) is emerging by leaps and bound and it is expected over 200 universities will be offering web courses in one form or the other. Advances in technology have created many hardware and software solutions for WBE for "time", "place", "delivery" and "language". Virtual universities are emerging from all corners of the world, including many third world countries like India and China. WBE is moving from introductory to expansion phase and emphasis is shifting from introduction to pedagogy and many success and failures cases are emerging.

As WBE moves to the second phase some old issues are being settled but new ones are emerging. Several issues dominated the first phase and were discussed in previous IRMA panels on WBE (1999-2002). Issues like, What needs to be done to simulate face-to-face environment on the web? Is it sufficient to simulate face-to-face environment to the web? Are some courses like political science, management, human resource management more suitable on

the web than analytical courses? What are universities doing with "parallel" education systems? How are other (especially third world) countries responding to the challenges of web education? As universities and faculty get more experience with WBE, many questions related to faculty workload, delivery platforms and students assessments are being answered. However, new questions about the content quality, ownership, institutionalizing WBE and universities viability and survival are arising. This panel will discuss above issues as they relate to the "Next" phase of WBE. Panelists will share their thoughts and experiments in this area.

IRMA/DAMA Model Curriculum Explained: Executive Summary

Eli B. Cohen (chair)
Informing Science Institute (US) & , KoŸmiñski School of Entrepreneurship and Management (Warsaw), 131 Brookhill Court, Santa Rosa, California 95409-2764 USA, Phone: +1 707 537 2211 Fax: +1 815 352 9100; eli_cohen@acm.org

Panel Participants:
Linda Knight, DePaul University, School of Computer Science Telecommunications & Information Systems 243 S, Wabash Avenue Chicago, Illinois 60604-2301 USA, Phone: :+1 (312) 362-5165 / 8381, Fax: +1 (312) 362-5185, lknight@cti.depaul.edu

John G Gammack, Griffith University, School of Management, Nathan QLD 4111 Australia, Phone: (+61 7) 3875 7577, Fax: (+61 7) 3875 3887, j.gammack@mailbox.gu.edu.au

John Mendonca, Purdue University, School of Technology, West Lafayette, IN USA, Phone:+1 (765) 496-6015, Fax: :+1 (765) 496-1212, JaMendonca@tech.purdue.edu

Anthony Scime, State University of New York College at Brockport, Computer Science Department, 350 New Campus Drive Brockport, New York 14420-2933, Phone: +1 585-395-2323, Fax: +1 585-395-2304, ascime@brockport.edu

Theresa M. Vitolo, Gannon University, Department of Computer and Information Science, 109 University Square, PMB 3163, Erie, Pennsylvania 16541, Phone: :+1 814.871.7126, vitolo@gannon.edu

Ronald Vyhmeister, Adventist International Institute of Advanced Studies, Business Department, P.O. Box 038, Silang, Cavite 4118, Philippines, Phone +63-46-414-4380, Fax: +63-46-414-4361, rvyhmeister@aiias.edu

The Information Resource Management Association has provided a great service to the IRM community through its IRMA/DAMA model curriculum. Since its inception, the model curriculum has undergone continuing revisions. The roundtable is composed of selected members of the IRMA IT Education Committee, which has once again brought the model curriculum up to date..

The primary purpose of the roundtable is to explain the concept of the IRMA/DAMA model curriculum and how and why it has been revised and 2) promote feedback to the committee on where to go from here.

The members of the IT Education Committee taking part in this roundtable demonstrate the wide range of views and needs of our constituency, from academia to industry, and from educational institutions around the world. This is why "One size does not fit all". Below is a small number of the issues the committee dealt with:

- The changing curriculum, from IT to OB/OD specialists, combined programs in IS, CS, IT
- Industry-university collaboration through course partnerships
- Potential for continuing education (particularly part-time programs) in

IS/IT education.
- Issues in programming Language Selection
- Helping students achieve Real-world experiences
- What do we teach now as introduction to our field?
- Challenges being faced by developing countries
- Future of Business education in times of "just in time learning"
- How Web based education affects the delivery and teaching of IT
- Influence of the local culture on IT education
- IT Beyond the B-school
- Transitions into Tomorrow's workforce of Knowledge Workers
- Educating (future) general managers for IT
- IT Enabled constructivist and collaborative learning
- Teaching IT Management online
- Teaching research methods to MS in IS students.
- "On-line education - it's psychology, not technology"
- Teaching Case teaching, at a distance
- The role of on-line learning in a formal educational program
- The Importance of Faculty Development in the Updating of IS Courses

A secondary purpose of this session is to draw together individuals (from the roundtable and the audience) who have similar interests with an eye toward working together on IT Education research projects.

Reviewing Manuscripts: Considerations for Authors and Reviewers

Panel Co-Coordinators

Susan K. Lippert, Drexel University
Department of Management, 101 N 33rd Street, Room 331, Philadelphia, PA 19104, T: 215.895.1939 F: 215.895.2891, lippert@drexel.edu

Gordon Hunter, University of Lethbridge
Department of Management, Lethbridge AB T1K 3M4 CANADA, T: 403.329.2672 F: 403.329.2038, Email: ghunter@uleth.ca

Panelists

Steve Clarke, Luton Business School, Park Square, Luton LU1 3JU
United Kingdom, Email: saclarke@lineone.net

Karen D. Loch
Georgia State University
Director, Institute of International Business, Institute of International Business, Atlanta, GA 30303
T: 404.651.4095 F: 404.651.2606, Email: kloch@gsu.edu

Thomas F. Stafford, University of Memphis
Fogelman College of Business , Memphis, TN 38152
T: 901.678.4628 F: 901.678.2685
Email: tstaffor@memphis.edu

Heikki Topi, Bentley College
Computer Information Systems Department, Waltham, MA 02452-4705
T: 781.891.2799 F: 630.604.3126, Email: htopi@bentley.edu

Eileen M. Trauth, The Pennsylvania State University
Department of Information Sciences and Technology, University Park, PA 16802 , T: 814.865.6457 F: 814.865.6426, Email: etrauth@ist.psu.edu

ABSTRACT

Conducting effective journal reviews in a timely manner (Gray, 1999; Weber, 1999; Denning, 1979) is important to the MIS academic discipline (Moores, Chin, Compeau, Venkatesh & Benbasat, 2001). Scholars suggest that reviews tend to lack quality and rigor (Weber, 1999; Zmud, 1998; Ives, 1992) which may lead to ineffective evaluations. Suggestions for conducting effective reviews (Lee, 1995; Daft, 1985; Straub, Ang, & Evaristo, 1994) may offer strategies and techniques for improving the process. Some top journals describe the review process (Jackson, 1996) and offer the fate of manuscripts submitted for publication (Beyer, 1995). Still, other editors describe the impact of technology on publishing manuscripts in top IS journals (Lee, 1999) or establishing a digital publishing environment (Sumner & Shum, 1998). Yet, there is still a lack of consistency in what content and process should be used to conduct a quality assessment.

This panel will offer strategies for conducting effective and thorough academic journal reviews. Panelists were selected based on feedback from selected Idea Group journal editors regarding the individual's ability and contributions as exemplar reviewers. Panelists were asked to prepare a five-page summary describing how he/she reviews manuscripts in relation to the selected journal's mission. The summaries were segmented between issues related to content and process. Panelists were asked to identify what content they deemed to be important along with suggestions and guidelines for reviewers and potential authors. With respect to process, panelists were asked to share particular formats, which they felt offered a sound structure when conducting a review. An outline of what constitutes an effective segmentation of critical analysis will be offered along with a discussion pertaining to these issues will be undertaken.

The co-coordinators will prepare an overall analysis and identify emerging themes from the five summaries. The five summaries will serve as a catalyst for summarizing the presenter's key points. This panel will not discuss the contention of an open review process (Straub, 2000; Webber, 1999) but rather focus on strategies for conducting effective academic reviews.

The panel will include two moderators (Susan K. Lippert, Drexel University and Gordon Hunter, University of Lethbridge) and five panel participants identified by Idea Group Editors as their top reviewers (Steve Clarke, Luton Business School; Karen Loch, Georgia State University; Thomas F. Stafford, University of Memphis; Dr. Heikki Topi, Bentley College; Eileen M. Trauth, The Pennsylvania State University). Intellectual exchange stimulated through an environment of open discussion is proposed for this panel presentation.

REFERENCES
Beyer, J.M., Chanove, R.G., & Fox, W.B. (1995) The Review Process and the Fates of Manuscripts Submitted to AMJ. *Academy of Management Journal*, 38(5), 1219-1260.
Daft, R.L. (1985) Why I Recommended That Your Manuscript Be Rejected and What You Can Do About It. In L.L. Cummings & P.J. Frost (Eds.), *Publishing in the Organizational Sciences*, 193-209, Homewood, IL: Richard D. Irwin.
Denning, P.J. (1979) Publication Delays. *Communications of the ACM*, 22(9), 495-496.
Gray, P. (1999) CAIS – The First Year: A Report From the Editor. *Communications of the AIS*, 2, Article 4, 1-10.
Ives, B. (1992) Editorial Comments: Total Quality Management of Journal Reviews. *MIS Quarterly*, (June), 16(2). Available: http://www.misq.org/archivist/vol/no16/issue2/edstat.html.
Jackson, S.E. (1996) Editorial Comments. *Academy of Management Review*, 21(4), 907-911.
Lee, A. (1995) Reviewing a Manuscript for Publication. *Journal of Operations Management*, 13(1), 87-92.
Lee, A.S. The Role of Information Technology in Reviewing and Publishing Manuscripts at MIS Quarterly, *MIS Quarterly*, December 1999, (23:4), pg. iv-ix.
Moores, T., Chin, W., Compeau, D., Venkatesh, V., & Benbasat, Z. (2001) What I Think About Reviewing: Confessions of a Panel of Expert Reviewers. *Proceedings of the Twenty-Second International Conference on Information Systems*, New Orleans, LA, 649-650.
Straub, D., Robey, D. & Zmud, R. (2000) A Debate on the Blindness of IS Journal Reviews. *Proceedings of the Twenty-First International Confer-*

ence on Information Systems, Brisbane, Australia, 705-706.

Straub, D., Ang, S., & Evaristo, E. (1994) Normative Standards for MIS Research. *DATABASE*, 25(1), 21-34.

Sumner, T. & Shum, S.B. (1998) From Documents to Discourse: Shifting Conceptions of Scholarly Publishing. *Proceedings of the Conference on Human Factors and Computing Systems*, Los Angeles, CA, 95-102.

Weber, R. (1999) The Journal Review Process: A Manifesto For Change. *Communications of the AIS*, 2, Article 12, 1-26.

Zmud, R. (1998) Editorial Comments: A Personal Perspective on the State of Journal Refereeing. *MIS Quarterly*, (September), 22(3). Available: http://www.misq.org/archivist/vol/no22/issue3/edstat.html.

Beyond Enterprise Systems Curricula: Perspectives on the Integration of Next Generation ERP Technologies into Various Curricula

Chair: Yvonne Lederer Antonucci, Ph.D.
Widener University, Chester, PA 19013
610-499-4310; 610-499-4614 (fax), Yvonne.L.Antonucci@Widener.edu

Panelists: Michael zur Muehlen, Ph.D., Stevens Institute of Technology, Hoboken, NJ
Mary E. Shoemaker, Ph.D., Widener University, Chester, PA
Glenn Stewart, Ph.D., Queensland University of Technology, Brisbane, Australia
Bill Wagner, Ph.D., Villanova University, PA
Mathias Kirchmer, Pres. & CEO of IDS Scheer, Inc.

ABSTRACT

There has been tremendous growth and change in the integration of ERP software into curricula among various Colleges and Universities in recent years. Businesses have expanded their ERP implementations to a web-centric, business-to-business process orientation in an effort to remain competitive. In response Universities need to expand their curricula to prepare students for this new process oriented e-business world. This panel provides academic experiences and perspectives on current ERP curricula, and presents various experiences with the integration of extended enterprise system components such as CRM, SCM, EAI and BI. Both panelists and audience members will be encouraged to respond to and discuss the potential integration of next generation ERP technologies into curricula and their potential to address new e-centric business practices.

INTRODUCTION

For the past several decades, organizations on a worldwide scale have focused on improving business processes. As a result we saw the emergence and growth of Enterprise Systems in companies of all sizes (Greenbaum, 1999). In response the academic community began to integrate the concepts and use of enterprise systems into their curricula. Yet the industrial world has grown beyond the traditional enterprise systems to an e-centric level concentrating on communication and web-based business between organizations (Earthweb, 1999).

Gartner Inc. coined the term "ERPII" to describe the next generation of ERP technology, which focuses on value chain collaboration. According to Kalakota (2001), the next generation ERP technologies use the ERP system as a backbone to extend the organization beyond its four walls to customers, suppliers, and trading partners, creating a business-to-business marketplace. The integration of business processes within the enterprise has moved from an inward focus to various extensions such as; (1) upward integration with Data Warehouse (DW), Business Intelligence (BI), and Knowledge Management

(KM); (2) backward integration with Supply Chain Management (SCM); and (3) forward integration with Customer Relationship Management (CRM). As a result Enterprise Application Integration (EAI) has also emerged as a solution to linking these various extensions (Linthicum, 2002). Many ERP software vendors have responded by shifting their focus to web-based strategies and emerging into the e-commerce arena (Steadman, 1999). They have also extended their ERP software by releasing analytical software with data warehousing support and integrating the back-office to front-office with wider Customer Relationship Management (CRM) capabilities.

Once again the academic community is beginning to integrate these next generation ERP technologies into their curricula. As educators, we need to not only teach graduate and undergraduate students the concepts and use of these extended ERP technologies but also introduce them to the technical and organizational issues of new e-centric business practices.

There appears to be a clear shift of ERP software focus, yet the question remains how to integrate the next generation ERP technologies into the curriculum. This panel will provide various academic experiences with current ERP curricula, and present experiences and perspectives on the integration of extended enterprise system components such as CRM, SCM, EAI and BI. Both panelists and audience members will be encouraged to respond to and discuss the potential integration of next generation ERP technologies into curricula and their potential to address new e-centric business practices.

REFERENCES

EarthWeb. (1999). "ERP, componentization, and e-commerce", October 1999, EarthWeb, http://erphub.earthweb.com/scalability_991005.html.

Greenbaum, Joshua. (1999). "The Origin and Future of ERP Outsourcing", http://www.erpoutsourcing.com/main.htm.

Kalakota, Ravi and Marcia Robinson. (2001). *E-Business 2.0*, Addison-Wesley.

Linthicum, David. (2002). *Enterprise Application Integration*, Addison-Wesley.

Stedman, C. (July 19, 1999) "ERP Guide: Vendor Strategies, Future Plans", *Computerworld*, 33 (29), 22.

Information Security in the Era of Terrorist Attacks

Lech J. Janczewski
The University of Auckland
Department of Management Science and Information Systems, Private Bag 92019, Auckland, New Zealand, Phone: 64 9 3737599, Fax: 64 9 373 7430, Email: lech@auckland.ac.nz

ABSTRACT

September 11, 2001 changed dramatically attitude of the society towards safety of their home and offices. Both ordinary people as businessmen and women realised that there is a lot of things to do to attain relatively safety of their environment. These elements come from many aspect of life including technical as well as behavioural components. One of them is safety of computers or more generally, information technology.

Interest in the information security issues is growing steadily. The best measure of it that in many bookstores the Computer/Information system security occupies a separate shelve next to such topics like Operating Systems or Databases.

Somehow, security specialists predicted by-products of 9/11 events. Many publications clearly indicated that terrorist attacks could be launched against a country or businesses and stopping such attacks could be very difficult. For example: "Strategic Information Warfare, a New Face of War" ISBN 0-8330-2352-7 or "Cybercrime, Cyberterrorism, Cyberwarfare, Averting an Electronic Waterloo" ISBN 0-89206-295-9. On basis of that several books has been written concentrating of the issue, how to handle the cyberwarfare, for instance "Information Warfare and Security", ISBN 0-201-43303-6.

Information Warfare is a hot topic. Google.com search on "Information warfare" counted over 108,000 hits.

The situation is changing almost every day. There is a need to present a update outlook on the problem in view of all the events that happen around the world after the attack on the World Trade twin towers and Pentagon.

Therefore, the panel will discuss how the terrorist attacks changed the perspective of both IT and security managers. Also, we would examine the issue of the necessary tertiary sector curriculum changes.

Panel chair
Dr Lech J. Janczewski, The University of Auckland, Auckland, New Zealand, , lech@auckland.ac.nz

Panelists
Dr. James E. Goldman, Purdue University, West Lafayette, Indiana, USA
jegoldman@tech.purdue.edu

Dr. Omar Khalil, University of Massachusetts Dartmouth, Dartmouth, Massachusetts, USA, okhalil@UMassD.Edu

Dr. Murray E. Jennex, San Diego State University, San Diego, California, USA, MurphJen@aol.com

Dr. Merrill Warkentin, Mississippi State University, Mississippi, USA
mwarkentin@cobilan.msstate.edu

Dr. Nanda Kumar, University of British Columbia, Vancouver, British Columbia, Canada, nanda.kumar@commerce.ubc.ca

E-Commerce for Business Majors: A Panel

Professor Shirley Fedorovich and Dr. Michael Williams
Embry-Riddle Aeronautical University, 600 S. Clyde Morris Boulevard
Daytona Beach, Florida 32114, 386-226-6685 (Phone), 386-226-6696 (Fax), fedorovi@erau.edu, williamsm@erau.edu

There are divergent opinions on how an e-commerce/e-business course should be taught in a School of Business, for non-information systems majors. At first glance there appears to be two divergent paths: A technically-oriented approach that focuses on network infrastructure, intranets, extranets, the internet and telecommunications systems, with a discussion on how the enterprise can benefit. The other focus tends to be in a more esoteric direction, centering on e-commerce and how it affects and can be affected by major business functions. While many textbooks are starting to combine these two approaches, many faculty members have a tendency to emphasize either the technical or managerial side, based upon their background and experience.

The panel members will discuss the different approaches of teaching this course and their advantages and disadvantages, and solicit and input from the audience on their experiences. Various textbook "formats" will be offered, as well as a discussion as to the order of presentation of course topics. The recent trend of offering e-commerce within the discipline courses, marketing, finance, and management information system's course will also be discussed.

IS/IT Professional Organizations' Membership: Making the Choice

Omar Khalil, University of Massachusetts
N. Dartmouth MA 02748, (508)999-8443, okhalil@umassd.edu
Panelists:
Mehdi Khosrow-Pour, President, Information Resources Management association (IRMA)

Fahri Karakaya, Professor of Marketing, University of Massachusetts Dartmouth.
Nejdet Delener, Professor of Marketing and International Business, St. John's University

There is a recent trend of membership decline in almost all non-for-profit professional organizations, including IS/IT professional organizations. The growing number of competing professional organizations, volatile economic conditions, lifestyle changes, and the ever increasing pace of living and working are affecting the ability of professional organizations in recruiting and retaining members. This problem may negatively impact such organizations' capabilities to survive and grow. Most often, they have to find and relay on alternative financial resources in order to continue serving their clienteles and accomplishing their missions.

Membership management has become a major source of headache for professional organizations, and, consequently, it must be taken seriously. Professional organizations must know why members purchase memberships. When members decide to join a professional organization, they expect to purchase an entitlement with a host of 'add ons'. Professionals have their own individual reasons for purchasing the product/service (i.e., ensure maximization of earning powers and mobility in the members' work place, ensure that self-interest is catered for, and acquire tools, which they as individuals or organizations could not acquire, to enable them to be effective in their work). These reasons may vary with age, organizational occupation and seniority in the organizations from which the members come.

Like other professional organizations, IS/IT professional organizations should identify the reasons for the purchase and produce strategies to satisfy members' needs. Professional organizations that have been the most successful in recruiting and retaining members are those with sound membership management strategy and have established fully staffed and professional membership offices. Also, database systems for membership management and online members contact information are crucial to easily track membership information, including membership numbers from different membership groups, retention rates, average membership length, membership expirations, and reasons for dropping membership (e.g., fees, services, benefits, quality, competition, etc.).

This panel will address membership management in not-for-profit professional organizations in general and in IS/IT in particular. Membership strategies, benefits, activities, and promotion techniques will be discussed. More specifically, the panelists will raise and attempt to answer questions such as:

- What are the effective professional organizations' membership strategies?
- Do IS/IT have well defined membership strategies?
- Does membership development (growth) occupy a high priority in the IS/IT professional organizations' strategic plans?
- What are their market niches?
- How they justify their existence to the membership, to the IS/IT profession and to society at large?
- What are the reasons for purchasing IT/IS professional organizations memberships?
- Whom should IS/IT professional organizations target and serve (i.e., academicians, organizations, professionals in organizations, students etc)? Why?
- Should IS/IT professional organizations maintain and promote membership as a "cash cow" or as a symbol of existence and well-being?
- Should IS/IT consider establishing strategic alliances and partnerships and joint memberships with compatible peer organizations?

Additional panelists will be added as needed

The Academia – Industry Relationships Best Cases Panel

Andrew Targowski (WMU)USA-Moderator
targowski@wmich.edu

INDUSTRY

Tom Bennett (DoD) USA
Bennettt@NCR.DISA.MIL
Mehdi Ghods (Boeing) USA
mehdi.ghod@boeing.com

ACADEMIA

Cano Jeimy J., Colombia
jcano@hotmail.com
Karen Church, South Africa
kchurch@petech.ac.za
Steve Clark United Kingdom
steve.clark@luton.ac.uk
Liliane Esnault, France
esnault@em-lyon.com
Lech Janczewski, New Zealand
lech@auckland.ac.nz
Margherita Pagani, Italy
margherita.pagani@sdabocconi.it
Cecil Schmidt USA
zzschmid@washburn.edu
Sunil Samanta, US
ssamanta@mercynet.edu

The purpose of this panel is to share the experience on the Academia – Industry Relations best cases to:
1. Proof that the IT collaborations between Academia and Industry can be beneficial for both sides?
2. Know how to pursue this collaboration based on the successful examples?

The best cases will presented and discussed.

Author's Index